Weapons of Mass Destruction

Volume II: Nuclear Weapons

Weapons of Mass Destruction

An Encyclopedia of Worldwide Policy,
Technology, and History

Eric A. Croddy and James J. Wirtz, Editors

Jeffrey A. Larsen, Managing Editor

Foreword by David Kay

Volume II: Nuclear Weapons

James J. Wirtz, Editor

A B C CLIO

Santa Barbara, California   Denver, Colorado   Oxford, England

Library of Congress Cataloging-in-Publication Data
Weapons of mass destruction : an encyclopedia of worldwide policy, technology, and history / Eric A. Croddy and James J. Wirtz, editors.
   p. cm.
  Includes bibliographical references and index.
  ISBN 1-85109-490-3 (hardback : alk. paper)—ISBN 1-85109-495-4 (e-book)
  1. Weapons of mass destruction—Encyclopedias. I. Croddy, Eric, 1966– II. Wirtz, James J., 1958–
U793.W427 2005
358'.3'03—dc22 2004024651

08 07 06 05 10 9 8 7 6 5 4 3 2 1

This book is also available on the World Wide Web as an eBook. Visit abc-clio.com for details.

ABC-CLIO, Inc.
130 Cremona Drive, P.O. Box 1911
Santa Barbara, California 93116–1911

This book is printed on acid-free paper.

Manufactured in the United States of America

Contents

Weapons of Mass Destruction
An Encyclopedia of Worldwide Policy, Technology, and History
Volume II: Nuclear Weapons

Foreword

David Kay

*Senior Research Analyst, Potomac Institute,
Washington, D.C., and former Director,
Iraq Survey Group (2003–2004)*

The importance of this encyclopedia was underscored by the fact that virtually the only area of agreement in the 2004 U.S. presidential campaign between the two major candidates, President George W. Bush and Senator John F. Kerry, was that the proliferation of weapons of mass destruction poses the most serious national security threat with which the next president would have to deal.

While the prospect of chemical, biological, radiological, or nuclear weapons falling into the hands of terrorists or regimes hostile to the United States and its friends is indeed a frightening prospect, how many of us understand exactly what this means? When were such weapons first developed? Which states and scientists are leading these developments? Have these weapons actually been used in the past? How often and with what consequence—not only for the populations they were used against, but for those that used them, as well? Do these weapons really give states a decisive edge over their adversaries? How easy are they to develop and use? Does the ease of development or use of such weapons by states, like North Korea, differ from the obstacles faced by terrorist groups, like al-Qaeda? What are the tools available to the United States to halt the spread of such weapons? Have we had any success in limiting the spread of these weapons? Are there any protective measures that individuals can take to lessen their vulnerability if such weapons are used?

These are but a few of the questions that the authors of this authoritative two-volume study attempt to answer. This encyclopedia will have enduring importance as states and societies attempt to come to terms with the consequence of the collision of scientific progress with the failure to develop a reliable global security structure. The initial development of chemical, biological, and nuclear weapons, as this study makes clear, often involved scientific and engineering breakthroughs of the highest order. The paths to enriching uranium and genetically modifying pathogens are but two examples of such successes, scientific breakthroughs that have made new classes of weapons possible. But scientific progress marches at a very fast rate, leaving behind old, but still dangerous, knowledge. For example, the secrets regarding methods for enriching uranium were simply bought by the Iraqis from the U.S. Government Printing Office. That office could not imagine that there was anything important in a 40-year-old project from the dawn of the U.S. nuclear program.

In another remarkable case, uranium enrichment technology was stolen from a commercial company in Holland by A. Q. Khan—a rather ordinary Pakistani who went to Germany to earn an engineering degree. Khan subsequently used this technology to develop Pakistan's nuclear weapons and then sold the same technology to North Korea, Iran, and Libya. The techniques of gene modification, which less than 20 years ago were the stuff of Nobel prizes, are now routinely taught in American high schools and community colleges and have opened up whole new classes of biological weapons. As this study also makes clear, even the safe disposal of weapons of mass destruction following a state's decision to abandon or limit their programs presents serious challenges of preventing the weapons and associated technology from falling into the hands of terrorists. The thousands of Soviet-era nuclear weapons and the engineering talent that created them represent a clear and present danger with which the world has not yet completely dealt. The readers of this work will find numerous examples of the lowering of the barriers to the acquisition by states and terrorists of these most terrible of weapons.

But this study does not simply present the horrors of a world filled with weapons of mass destruction. It also catalogs and illuminates the various methods of

attempting to control and constrain these weapons—
including treaties and agreements such as the Nuclear
Non-Proliferation Treaty and the Chemical Weapons
Convention, as well as intrusive inspections, such as
the efforts of the United Nations to hunt such
weapons in Iraq after the first Gulf War. As will be
clear to the reader, such endeavors have had both successes and failures. Much remains to be done to ensure that their effectiveness matches the problems
posed by the proliferation of such weapons. The
largest gap in effective mechanisms of control and response to the acquisition of such weapons is with regard to the efforts of terrorists groups to acquire the
means of mass murder. While these volumes identify

the few efforts made in this regard, it is hard not to
come away with a sense of dread for the future. Most
control efforts have been aimed at states, not at terrorists operating outside of the control of states.
Hopefully students and policy makers using this
book a few years hence will be able to record more
progress toward meeting this new challenge.

The authors and editors have done an important
service by pulling together such an illuminating
study at exactly the point when there is a broad political consensus of the importance of the problem.
One can only hope that our citizens and our political leaders take the time to explore the depth of information presented here.

Preface: Weapons of Mass Destruction

Eric A. Croddy and James J. Wirtz

The term "weapon of mass destruction" (WMD) is a relatively modern expression. It was probably first used in print media following the international uproar over Germany's aerial bombardment of the Basque city of Guernica in April 1937. (The latter event was famously depicted in Picasso's painting *Guernica y Luno.*) Only a year before, another Axis power, Italy, had begun using mustard and other chemical warfare (CW) agents in Abyssinia (modern-day Ethiopia).[1] During the anxious years leading up World War II, WMD referred to the indiscriminate killing of civilians by modern weaponry, especially aircraft. It also echoed the fear of chemical weapons that was unleashed by World War I, which had come to a conclusion just a few years earlier.

Following the development of the atomic bomb in 1945, the term "WMD" came to include nuclear and eventually biological weapons. WMD was apparently first used to describe nuclear warfare by Soviet strategists. In 1956, during the 20th Communist Party Congress in Moscow, the Soviet Minister of Defense—and "Hero of Stalingrad"—Marshal Georgy Konstantinovich Zhukov prophesied that modern warfare "will be characterized by the massive use of air forces, various rocket weapons and various means of mass destruction such as atomic, thermonuclear, chemical and bacteriological weapons."[2] In that same year, the Hungarian Minister of Defense echoed Marshal Zhukov, stating that "Under modern conditions, the decisive aspect of operational planning is the use of nuclear and other weapons of mass destruction."[3]

When the West learned of Zhukov's speech, national security strategists in the United States and elsewhere became quite concerned. By inference, they concluded that WMD—nuclear, biological, and chemical weapons—were an integral part of Soviet military doctrine. Partly in response to Zhukov's ministrations on WMD, the United States reviewed its offensive chemical and biological weapons program in 1958. The U.S. military was never particularly enamored by chemical or biological weapons and treated them as a deterrent to be used in retaliation for the use of chemical or biological weapons used by the opponent. By the early 1990s, the U.S. military had abandoned offensive use of these weapons, although it maintained a research and development program designed to produce effective equipment, procedures, medications, and inoculations to defend against chemical and biological attack.

Over the last decade, much has been written about WMD. The meaning of the term itself is somewhat controversial, although there is a formal, legalistic definition. According to U.S. Code Title 50, "War and National Defense," per the U.S. Congress, the term "weapon of mass destruction" means "any weapon or device that is intended, or has the capability, to cause death or serious bodily injury to a significant number of people through the release, dissemination, or impact of toxic or poisonous chemicals or their precursors; a disease organism; radiation or radioactivity."[4] For its part, the U.S. Department of Defense has a similar characterization of WMD, although in addition it includes " . . . the means to deliver [WMD]."[5] So, what makes a weapon massively destructive? Is it the type of injurious agents involved, namely radioactive, chemical, or biological, or is it that the attack itself produces significant casualties or destruction? Also what would "significant" mean in this context: ten, a hundred, or a thousand casualties? What if very few people are actually killed or hurt by at attack? In the latter respect, the U.S. Federal Bureau of Investigation has a rather unique and somewhat satisfying interpretation of the term "WMD," invoked when the U.S. government indicted Timothy McVeigh with using a WMD in his 1995 terrorist attack in Oklahoma City. In this case, although the device used was a conventional bomb (employing ammonium nitrate-fuel oil explosive), "A weapon crosses the WMD threshold when the consequences of its release overwhelm local responders."[6]

Some analysts, however, have suggested that various technical hurdles prevent chemical and even biological weapons from causing casualties on a truly massive scale. Some point to the Aum Shinrikyo sarin attack on the Tokyo subway system on March 20, 1995, which resulted in eleven deaths, as an example of the *limits* of WMD. They note that high-explosives have been used with far greater lethal effects than sarin in the annals of modern terrorism. Others are increasingly concerned about the destructive potential of even rudimentary weapons. Analysts today are worried, for instance, that terrorists might try to employ radiological dispersal devices or "dirty bombs." These weapons do not detonate with a fission reaction, but rather utilize conventional explosives to distribute radiological materials and contaminate a given area. Few deaths are likely to result from the effects of a dirty bomb, but the consequences—in terms of anxiety, clean-up, and the recognized ability of a terrorist to conduct the very act itself— would likely be far reaching.

About the Encyclopedia

The very presence of chemical, biological and nuclear weapons in international arsenals and the potential that they might fall into the hands of terrorist organizations guarantees that weapons of mass destruction will be of great policy, public, and scholarly interest for years to come. We cannot resolve the debates prompted by WMD, but we hope that we and our contributors can provide facts to help the reader sort through the controversies that are likely to emerge in the years ahead. Much that is contained in these volumes is disturbing and even frightening; it is impossible to write a cheery encyclopedia about weapons whose primary purpose is to conduct postindustrial-scale mass murder. The sad truth of the matter is that chemical, biological, radiological, and nuclear weapons reflect the willingness of humans to go to great lengths to find increasingly lethal and destructive instruments of war and violence. We are pleased to note, however, that much of what is reported in these volumes is historical in nature and that civilized people everywhere reject the use of chemical and biological weapons. International law is replete with treaties, agreements, and regimes whose purpose is to proscribe the use of these weapons, or mitigate the consequences of any such use. In particular, the world has successfully kept nuclear weapons in reserve for almost sixty years as truly deterrent weapons of last resort.

Our encyclopedia covers a wide range of topics, some historical, some drawn from today's headlines. We describe many of the pathogens, diseases, substances, and machines that can serve as weapons of mass destruction, as well as their associated delivery systems. We also describe important events and individuals that have been influential in the development of weapons of mass destruction and doctrines for their use (or control). We have encouraged our contributors to highlight ongoing controversies and contemporary concerns about WMD and current international arms control and nonproliferation efforts intended to reduce the threat they pose to world peace and security. Even a work of this length, however, cannot completely cover the history, science, and personal stories associated with a topic of this magnitude, so we have included abundant references to help readers take those initial steps for further study of the topics we survey.

Acknowledgments

Our deepest debt is to the contributors who made this volume a reality. Many of them joined the project at its inauguration several years ago and have waited a long time to see their work in print. It is impossible for just three people to be experts on all of the subjects covered in this volume, and without the hard work of our contributors, this encyclopedia would never have been completed. Thanks to our research assistants, Abraham Denmark and Laura Fontaine, who uncovered most of the key documents in both volumes and wrote a few entries for us, as well. We also want to express our appreciation to a senior government official who reviewed Volume II for accuracy and sensitive material. We owe a special debt to Jeff Larsen, our managing editor, whose help was instrumental in the success of this project. Not only did he provide editorial support to both volumes, but he displayed a keen ability to deal with the publisher and our 95 contributors, keep track of timelines, requirements, and progress, and gently push the two of us when we needed encouragement during this multiyear project that involved over 500 separate parts. Finally, we also want to express our appreciation to Alicia Merritt, Martha Whitt, Giulia Rossi, and the behind-the-scenes copyeditors at ABC-CLIO who worked tirelessly to help get this manuscript into print. We discovered that nothing is a trivial matter when it comes to a manuscript of this size. The commitment of our publisher to this topic, and the dedication of the production staff at ABC-CLIO, greatly facilitated the completion of these volumes.

We hope that this encyclopedia will help inform the public debate about weapons of mass destruction and international security policy, with the goal of never again seeing such weapons used in anger.

Notes

1. Stanley D. Fair, "Mussolini's Chemical War," *Army,* January 1985, p. 52.
2. Jeffery K. Smart, "History of Chemical and Biological Warfare: An American Perspective," in Frederick R. Sidell, Ernest T. Takafuji, and David R. Franz, eds., *Textbook of Military Medicine, Part I: Warfare, Weaponry, and the Casualty: Medical Aspects of Chemical and Biological Warfare* (Washington, DC: Borden Institute, Walter Reed Army Medical Center, 1997), p. 54.
3. Quoted in the archives, "Report of Colonel-General István Bata, Hungarian Minister of Defense, to Members of the HWP Central Committee on the Conduct of the Staff-Command Exercise Held, 17 July 1956," found at the International Relations and Security Network (Switzerland), documents collection, *http://www.isn.ethz.ch/*
4. Title 50, Chapter 40, Sec. 2302.
5. Office of the Secretary of Defense, *Proliferation: Threat and Response* (Washington, DC: U.S. Government Printing Office, 2001), p. 4.
6. U.S. Federal Bureau of Investigation (FBI), "The FBI and Weapons of Mass Destruction," 4 August 1999, *http://norfolk.fbi.gov.wmd.htm*

Editors and Contributors

Editors

ERIC A. CRODDY (EDITOR, VOLUME I,
CHEMICAL AND BIOLOGICAL WEAPONS)
 Analyst with U.S. Pacific Command, Pearl
 Harbor, HI

JAMES J. WIRTZ (EDITOR, VOLUME II,
NUCLEAR WEAPONS)
 Professor and Chair, Department of National
 Security Affairs, U.S. Naval Postgraduate
 School, Monterey, CA, and Senior Fellow,
 Center for International Security and
 Cooperation, Stanford University, Palo Alto, CA

JEFFREY A. LARSEN (MANAGING EDITOR,
VOLUMES I AND II)
 Senior Policy Analyst, Science Applications
 International Corporation and President,
 Larsen Consulting Group, Colorado Springs,
 CO

Contributors

GARY ACKERMAN
 Deputy Director, Chemical and Biological
 Weapons Nonproliferation Program, Monterey
 Institute of International Studies, Monterey, CA

JEFFREY A. ADAMS
 Senior Analyst, Analytic Services, Inc. (ANSER),
 Arlington, VA

PETER ALMQUIST
 Bureau of Arms Control, U.S. Department of
 State, Washington, DC

ELIZABETH AYLOTT
 Plans and Policy Analyst, Science Applications
 International Corporation, Ramstein Air Base,
 Germany

JEFFREY M. BALE
 Senior Research Associate, Monterey Institute
 of International Studies, Monterey, CA

ZACH BECKER
 Science Applications International Corporation,
 Arlington, VA

ANJALI BHATTACHARJEE
 Research Associate, WMD Terrorism Project,
 Center for Nonproliferation Studies, Monterey
 Institute of International Studies, Monterey, CA

JENNIFER BROWER
 Science and Technology Policy Analyst, The
 RAND Corporation, Arlington, VA

WILLIAM D. CASEBEER
 Associate Professor, Department of Philosophy,
 U.S. Air Force Academy, CO

KALPANA CHITTARANJAN
 Research Fellow, Observer Research
 Foundation, Chennai Chapter, Chennai, India

CLAY CHUN
 Chairman, Department of Distance Education,
 U.S. Army War College, Carlisle Barracks, PA

WILLIAM S. CLARK
 Defense Policy Analyst, Science Applications
 International Corporation, Arlington, VA

CHRIS CRAIGE
 Graduate Student, U.S. Naval Postgraduate
 School, Monterey, CA

MALCOLM DAVIS
Lecturer, Defence Studies Department, King's College London, London, UK

ABE DENMARK
Graduate Student, Graduate School of International Studies, University of Denver, Denver, CO

JOHN W. DIETRICH
Assistant Professor, Bryant University, Smithfield, RI

ANDREW M. DORMAN
Lecturer in Defence Studies, King's College London, London, UK

FRANNIE EDWARDS
Office of Emergency Services, San Jose, CA

LAWRENCE R. FINK
Corporate Export Administration, International Legal Department, Science Applications International Corporation, Arlington, VA

STEPHANIE FITZPATRICK
Arms Control/Policy Analyst, Independent Consultant, Arlington, VA

SCHUYLER FOERSTER
President, World Affairs Council of Pittsburgh, Pittsburgh, PA

LAURA FONTAINE
Graduate Student, Graduate School of International Studies, University of Denver, Denver, CO

J. RUSS FORNEY
Associate Professor, Department of Chemistry and Life Science, U.S. Military Academy, West Point, NY

MARTIN FURMANSKI
Scientists Working Group on Biological and Chemical Weapons, Center for Arms Control and Nonproliferation, Ventura, CA

ANDREA GABBITAS
Graduate Student, Department of Political Science, Massachusetts Institute of Technology, Cambridge, MA

SCOTT SIGMUND GARTNER
Associate Professor, Department of Political Science, University of California–Davis, Davis, CA

MICHAEL GEORGE
Policy Analyst, Science Applications International Corporation, Arlington, VA

DON GILLICH
Nuclear Research and Operations Officer, U.S. Army, Colorado Springs, CO

DAN GOODRICH
Public Health Department, Santa Clara, CA

PHIL GRIMLEY
Professor of Pathology and Molecular Cell Biology, F. Edward Herbert Medical School, Uniformed Services University of Health Sciences, Bethesda, MD

EUGENIA K. GUILMARTIN
Assistant Professor, Department of Social Sciences, U.S. Military Academy, West Point, NY

JOHN HART
Researcher, Stockholm International Peace Research Institute, Solna, Sweden

PETER HAYS
Executive Editor, Joint Force Quarterly, National Defense University, Washington, DC

JAMES JOYNER
Managing Editor, Strategic Insights, Washington, DC

AARON KARP
Professor, Old Dominion University, and Assistant Professor, U.S. Joint Forces Staff College, Norfolk, VA

KERRY KARTCHNER
Senior Advisor for Missile Defense Policy, U.S. State Department, Washington, DC

MIKE KAUFHOLD
Senior National Security Policy Analyst, Science Applications International Corporation, San Antonio, TX

BRET KINMAN
Graduate Student, Department of National Security Affairs, U.S. Naval Postgraduate School, Monterey, CA

KIMBERLY L. KOSTEFF
Policy Analyst, Science Applications International Corporation, Arlington, VA

AMY E. KRAFFT
Research Biologist, Department of Molecular Genetic Pathology, Armed Forces Institute of Pathology, Rockville, MD

JENNIFER LASECKI
Computer Sciences Corporation, Alexandria, VA

PETER LAVOY
Director, Center for Contemporary Conflict, U.S. Naval Postgraduate School, Monterey, CA

SEAN LAWSON
Graduate Student, Department of Science and Technology Studies, Rensselaer Polytechnic Institute, Troy, NY

MICHAEL LIPSON
Assistant Professor, Department of Political Science, Concordia University, Montreal, Canada

BRIAN L'ITALIEN
Defense Intelligence Agency, Washington, DC

MORTEN BREMER MAERLI
Researcher, Norwegian Institute of International Affairs, Oslo, Norway

TOM MAHNKEN
Professor of Strategy, Naval War College, Newport, RI

ROBERT MATHEWS
Asia-Pacific Centre for Military Law, University of Melbourne, Victoria, Australia

CLAUDINE MCCARTHY
National Association of County and City Health Officials, Washington, DC

JEFFREY D. MCCAUSLAND
Director, Leadership in Conflict Initiative, Dickinson College, Carlisle, PA

PATRICIA MCFATE
Science Applications International Corporation, Santa Fe, NM

ROB MELTON
Assistant Professor of Military Strategic Studies, 34th Education Group, U.S. Air Force Academy, CO

BRIAN MORETTI
Assistant Professor, Department of Physics, U.S. Military Academy, West Point, NY

JENNIFER HUNT MORSTEIN
Senior Analyst, Science Applications International Corporation, McLean, VA

EDWARD P. NAESSENS, JR.
Associate Professor, Nuclear Engineering Program Director, Department of Physics, U.S. Military Academy, West Point, NY

T. V. PAUL
James McGill Professor of International Relations, McGill University, Montreal, Canada

ROY PETTIS
Science Advisor to the Office of Strategic and Theater Defenses, Bureau of Arms Control, U.S. State Department, Washington, DC

RICH PILCH
Scientist in Residence, Chemical and Biological Nonproliferation Program, Center for Nonproliferation Studies, Monterey Institute of International Studies, Monterey, CA

ELIZABETH PRESCOTT
International Institute for Strategic Studies, Washington, DC

BEVERLEY RIDER
Senior Scientist, Genencor International, Inc., Palo Alto, CA

GUY ROBERTS
Principal Director, Negotiations Policy, Office of the Secretary of Defense, Washington DC

J. SIMON ROFE
Lecturer, Defence Studies Department, King's College London, London, UK

KEN ROGERS
Professor of Political Science, Department of Social Sciences and Philosophy, Arkansas Tech University, Russellville, AR

STEVEN ROSENKRANTZ
Foreign Affairs Officer, Office of Strategic and Theater Defenses, Bureau of Arms Control, U.S. State Department, Washington, DC

C. ROSS SCHMIDTLEIN
Research Fellow, Department of Medical Physics, Memorial Sloan-Kettering Cancer Center, New York, NY

GLEN M. SEGELL
Director, Institute of Security Policy, London, UK

D. SHANNON SENTELL, JR.
Assistant Professor, Department of Physics, U.S. Military Academy, West Point, NY

JACQUELINE SIMON
Independent Consultant, Ottawa, Canada

JOSHUA SINAI
Analytic Services, Inc. (ANSER), Alexandria, VA

STANLEY R. SLOAN
Visiting Scholar, Middlebury College, and Director, Atlantic Community Initiative, Richmond, VT

JAMES M. SMITH
Director, USAF Institute for National Security Studies, U.S. Air Force Academy, Colorado Springs, CO

ROBERT SOBESKI
Assistant Professor, Department of Physics, U.S. Military Academy, West Point, NY

JOHN SPYKERMAN
Foreign Affairs Officer, U.S. State Department, Washington, DC

TROY S. THOMAS
Fellow, Center for Strategic Intelligence Research, Defense Intelligence Agency, Washington, DC

CHARLES L. THORNTON
Research Fellow, Center for International and Security Studies, School of Public Policy, University of Maryland, College Park, MD

ROD THORNTON
Lecturer, Defence Studies Department, King's College London, London, UK

ANTHONY TU
Department of Biochemistry and Molecular Biology, Colorado State University, Ft Collins, CO

PETER VALE
Nelson Mandela Professor of Politics, Rhodes University, Grahamstown, South Africa

GILLES VAN NEDERVEEN
Independent Consultant, Fairfax, VA

MICHAEL WHEELER
Senior Defense Analyst, Science Applications International Corporation, McLean, VA

JOLIE WOOD
Graduate Student, Department of Government, University of Texas, Austin, TX

JACK WOODALL
Visiting Professor, Department of Medical Biochemistry, Federal University of Rio de Janeiro, Brazil

ROBERT WYMAN
Arms Control Operations Specialist, Science Applications International Corporation, Arlington, VA

A to Z List of Entries, Volumes I and II

Syria: Chemical and Biological Weapons Programs

Tabun
Terrorism with CBRN Weapons
Thickeners
TNT
Tobacco Mosaic Virus
Tooele, Utah
Toxins (Natural)
Toxoids and Antitoxins
Tularemia
Tuberculosis (TB, Mycobacterium Tuberculosis)
Typhus (Rickettsia Prowazekii)

Unit 731
United Kingdom: Chemical and Biological
    Weapons Programs
United Nations Monitoring, Verification, and
    Inspection Commission (UNMOVIC)
United Nations Special Commission on Iraq
    (UNSCOM)
United States: Chemical and Biological Weapons
    Programs
Unmanned Aerial Vehicle (UAV)

Vaccines
V-Agents
Vector
VECTOR: State Research Center of Virology and
    Biotechnology
Vesicants
Vietnam War
Vincennite (Hydrogen Cyanide)

Weteye Bomb
World Trade Center Attack (1993)
World War I
World War II: Biological Weapons
World War II: Chemical Weapons
Wushe Incident

Xylyl Bromide

Yellow Rain
Yemen
Ypres

Volume II: Nuclear Weapons
Accidental Nuclear War
Accuracy

Acheson-Lililenthal Report
Actinides
Airborne Alert
Anti-Ballistic Missile (ABM) Treaty
Antinuclear Movement
Anti-Satellite (ASAT) Weapons
Arms Control
Arms Control and Disarmament Agency (ACDA)
Arms Race
Assured Destruction
Atomic Energy Act
Atomic Energy Commission
Atomic Mass/Number/Weight
Atoms for Peace

Backpack Nuclear Weapons
Balance of Terror
Ballistic Missile Defense Organization (BMDO)
Ballistic Missile Early Warning System (BMEWS)
Ballistic Missiles
Baruch Plan
Bikini Island
Bombers, Russian and Chinese Nuclear-Capable
Bombers, U.S. Nuclear-Capable
Boost-Phase Intercept
Bottom-Up Review
Brilliant Eyes
Brinkmanship
British Nuclear Forces and Doctrine
Broken Arrow, Bent Spear

Canada Deuterium Uranium (CANDU) Reactor
The Catholic Church and Nuclear War
Chelyabinsk-40
Chernobyl
Cheyenne Mountain, Colorado
Chicken, Game of
Chinese Nuclear Forces and Doctrine
City Avoidance
Civil Defense
Cold Launch
Cold War
Collateral Damage
Command and Control
Committee on the Present Danger
Compellence
Comprehensive Test Ban Treaty (CTBT)
Conference on Disarmament
Conference on Security and Cooperation in
    Europe (CSCE)

Survivability

Tactical Nuclear Weapons
Telemetry
Terminal Phase
Theater High Altitude Air Defense (THAAD)
Theater Missile Defense
Thermonuclear Bomb
Three Mile Island
Three-Plus-Three Program
Threshold States
Threshold Test Ban Treaty (TTBT)
Tinian
Titan ICBMs
Tous Asimuts
Transporter-Erector-Launcher
Triad
Trident
Trinity Site, New Mexico
Tritium
Two-Man Rule

U-2
Underground Testing

Unilateral Initiative
United Nations Special Commission on Iraq
   (UNSCOM)
United States Air Force
United States Army
United States Navy
United States Nuclear Forces and Doctrine
Uranium

Verification

Warfighting Strategy
Warhead
Warsaw Pact
Wassenaar Arrangement
Weapons-Grade Material
Weapons of Mass Destruction (WMD)

X-Ray Laser

Yield

Zangger Committee
Zone of Peace

Introduction: Nuclear Weapons

James J. Wirtz

On July 16, 1945, the world changed forever when British and American scientists and engineers tested an implosion-type atomic device in the desert near Alamogordo, New Mexico, producing the first nuclear explosion. Developed under the code name "Manhattan Project," this first-generation fission device was quickly weaponized, and when the U.S. Army Air Corps dropped atomic bombs on the Japanese cities of Hiroshima and Nagasaki in August 1945, World War II in the Pacific came to an end. The United States did not retain a nuclear monopoly for long. The Soviet Union detonated a nuclear device in 1949. By the early 1950s, a second generation of fusion weapons, with explosive power measuring in millions of tons of trinitrotoluene (TNT), was entering Soviet and U.S. nuclear arsenals. As the Cold War unfolded, the Soviet and U.S. militaries deployed tens of thousands of tactical, theater, and strategic nuclear weapons to deter both conventional and nuclear attacks. Soviet-American strategic relations reflected a situation of mutual assured destruction (MAD), which moderated superpower behavior but risked catastrophic destruction if some military or diplomatic insult upset the delicate "balance of terror." People everywhere breathed a collective sigh of relief as the risk of nuclear Armageddon became increasingly remote at the end of the Cold War. Since the early 1990s, Russia and the United States have cut the number of their deployed nuclear forces and ended nuclear force modernization and testing. At the turn of the century, it appeared that the threat posed by nuclear weapons was diminishing.

Just as the superpowers pulled back from the nuclear abyss, however, new nuclear threats appeared on the horizon. India and Pakistan tested nuclear weapons in the late 1990s, joining Great Britain, France, and China as overt nuclear powers. It also is widely believed that Israel and North Korea possess a nuclear arsenal. For a time, South Africa possessed a few nuclear weapons, but it renounced its nuclear ambitions and joined the Nuclear Nonproliferation

Treaty (NPT) as a non–nuclear weapons state in 1991. Ukraine, Belarus, and Kazakhstan inherited large nuclear arsenals for a short period following the collapse of the Soviet Union in the early 1990s, but all three states were persuaded to give up those weapons and join the NPT by the mid-1990s. Other states have made modest efforts toward acquiring their own arsenals but for various reasons have not yet reached that objective. Nonetheless, some thirty states remain technologically capable of creating atomic weapons fairly quickly should they decide to do so.

The September 11, 2001, terrorist attacks on the World Trade Center and the Pentagon highlighted the fact that terrorists and nonstate actors were interested in creating mass casualty attacks, and many believe that terrorists might be attracted to nuclear or radiological devices as weapons of terror. The risk that any state would employ its nuclear arsenal in a massive nuclear attack is diminishing, but the threat of a small-scale use by some state or nonstate actor is on the rise, especially as nonproliferation efforts fail to prevent the "hard cases" from acquiring nuclear weapons. Officials also worry about the emergence of an international black market in nuclear weapons technology, radiological materials, and even complete weapons. As world history enters the so-called "second nuclear age," nuclear weapons remain a force to be reckoned with, both on the battlefield and in international politics.

Is There a Nuclear Revolution?

Debate about the importance and impact of nuclear weapons on world politics is as fierce now as it was at the dawn of the nuclear era sixty years ago. Nuclear weapons, the advent of long-range delivery systems, and the establishment of a new organization, the U.S. Air Force, produced a revolution in military affairs (RMA) that fundamentally transformed warfare. Bernard Brodie, writing in 1946, was quick to recognize the nature of this RMA when he observed that national objectives for military efforts had changed: Whereas militaries traditionally strove to win wars, with the advent of nuclear weapons their purpose became deterring wars. Nuclear weapons would make major war a calamity, demanding that all military and diplomatic efforts be directed at deterring, by threat of retaliation in kind, nuclear war. Decades later, Robert Jervis (1989) noted that this RMA had produced a nuclear revolution: Stability (the absence of great-power war) now characterized relations between great powers because none dare risk direct military confrontation given the dark shadow of nuclear escalation. There were warnings that this nuclear stability might actually increase the likelihood of smaller wars, however, especially along the "periphery." Glenn Snyder (1961), for instance, identified a "stability-instability" paradox: Stability at the nuclear level of conflict actually made great powers more tolerant of instability (war) in peripheral areas or among clients. But at the end of the Cold War, it did appear that peace, or at least the absence of great-power conflict, was the by-product of the threat of massive nuclear destruction.

Nuclear weapons introduced stability in great-power relations because they produced a modicum of restraint in both diplomatic and military adventures undertaken by Soviets and Americans during the Cold War. Nuclear weapons effects also are predictable, and nuclear powers tend to share a similar knowledge base about the destructiveness of nuclear weapons. Both U.S. and Soviet officials recognized the destructiveness of a full-scale nuclear exchange. Moreover, as Thomas Schelling (1966) noted, the absence of an effective defense against massive nuclear attack allowed nuclear-armed states to engage in the "diplomacy of violence." States armed with large nuclear arsenals could destroy each other's societies while virtually bypassing direct engagement of the opponent's military forces. To a lesser extent than conventional warfare, which is influenced by strategy, tactics, leadership, equipment, training, and morale, the outcome of nuclear combat is driven by the enormous explosive yield of nuclear weapons themselves, not by superior strategy. In other words, once nuclear arsenals became very large and deployed in relatively survivable ways, there was little either the United States or the Soviet Union might do to prevent their opponent from undertaking a nuclear retaliatory strike. MAD was defense dominant because both sides had the ability to deny victory in a nuclear war to the opponent. No nation with a leader in his right mind would start a nuclear war that it would be sure to lose—at least that was the argument advanced by those who championed the nuclear revolution.

Critics of the nuclear revolution have generally come in two varieties: those who believe that it is mistaken to treat deterrence as the dominant nuclear doctrine, and those who believe that nuclear revolutionaries underestimate the risks involved in nuclear deterrence. Those who champion nuclear warfighting strategies believe that others might think nuclear war is winnable or that deterrence itself is unreliable and can fail because of misunderstandings, irrationality, or simple human frailty. Under these circumstances, they believe that for deterrence to be effective, it is imperative to develop credible nuclear warfighting options. Missile defenses that deny opponents the ability to hold U.S. or allied targets at risk thus become an important way to strengthen U.S. deterrent threats. They also believe that nuclear weapons should be integrated into forces and war plans to give national authorities limited nuclear options that could influence battlefield events in positive ways. The 2002 U.S. Nuclear Posture Review, for example, called for the development of highly selective and limited nuclear options to increase the credibility of U.S. deterrent threats and to hold opponents' small nuclear, chemical, and biological weapons arsenals at risk while reducing the prospect of collateral damage.

Other critics worry, however, that the circumstances that make nuclear deterrence "stable" are rare and unlikely to be found in emerging weapons states and regional rivalries. New nuclear weapons states might adopt nuclear doctrines or forces that are shaped by domestic political turmoil, by political dreams of regional domination, or by a specific leader's megalomania. Maintaining negative control over nuclear arsenals (preventing weapons from being used without proper authorization) is daunting in states that face ethnic, fundamentalist, or political unrest. Countries in immediate proximity to each other—here India and Pakistan come to mind—can expect virtually no tactical warning of nuclear attack, increasing the likelihood that they might adopt preventive or preemptive nuclear warfighting strategies. These critics also suggest that building "safe" nuclear weapons is technically challenging and financially demanding and might be beyond the resources of new nuclear powers. No matter what rich or poor states do, "normal accidents," the tendency of complex systems to interact with humans in unanticipated ways, are likely to defeat safety systems.

Those who champion disarmament as the best way to deal with nuclear weapons believe that nuclear deterrence is fundamentally immoral and misguided. Disarmament advocates suggest that those who believe in deterrence or warfighting strategies simply perpetuate a war system that is destined to fail catastrophically. They dismiss ideas about a so-called nuclear revolution as window dressing to justify using a nuclear arms race and threats of nuclear warfare as a means of achieving political objectives. In their view, nuclear weapons are so destructive that they are irrational instruments of war that place at risk far more people and infrastructure than their users can hope to protect. They point out that a full-scale nuclear exchange during the Cold War could have eliminated human beings from planet Earth. Disarmament advocates believe that efforts to develop forces for deterrence create arms races, fear, and hostility and that the only way to break this negative trend is to eliminate nuclear weapons as quickly as possible. Other disarmament advocates believe that nuclear deterrence was epiphenomenal when it came to maintaining stability during the Cold War. They believe that fear of conventional hostilities generally deters war, that most leaders are risk adverse, and often that the spread of democracy throughout the world will soon render nuclear weapons and deterrent strategies obsolete. Others believe that a nuclear taboo—a tradition of nonuse of nuclear weapons—governs the behavior of nuclear weapons states, and that nothing should be done to increase the likelihood that nuclear weapons could or would be used in battle. In general, disarmament advocates see nuclear weapons as simply a highly destructive and dangerous development in humanity's tendency to moderate behavior using threats and violence. They offer diplomacy, mediation, or accommodation as an alternative to nuclear threats to maintain the peace.

Nuclear Weapons Effects: A Primer

Unlike the debate about the political and strategic impact of nuclear weapons, the topic of basic nuclear physics holds few unknowns. The effects that nuclear weapons produce once they are detonated are well documented. A nuclear weapon is the general name given to any device that creates an explosion from energy involving atomic nuclei, either through a fission or a fusion reaction. A gun-type fission weapon is relatively simple to construct; the greatest barrier to obtaining this type of nuclear weapon is the difficulty in manufacturing or obtaining weapons-grade fissile material. By contrast, high-yield, low-weight fusion weapons are some of the most complex machines ever developed by human beings. They combine exquisite mechanical and electrical engineering design and manufacturing with innovative applications of nuclear physics and engineering. The details of specific weapons designs and operating principles are considered top secret by governments around the world.

When a nuclear weapon is detonated, it produces a series of weapons effects that occur in a predictable sequence: electromagnetic pulse (EMP), direct nuclear radiation, thermal radiation (which mostly takes the form of light), blast, and fallout. Bomb designers can vary the way the energy of a nuclear explosion is distributed across these effects. The so-called "neutron bomb," for instance, shifts more energy toward EMP and direct radiation in an effort to reduce collateral damage when used against targets on the ground (such as enemy armored formations) or to maximize damage to the electronic systems of targets in space (such as an opponent's incoming nuclear warheads). Weapons effects vary depending on a variety of influences, including the height of burst (for example, air burst, ground burst, underwater detonation, or underground detonation), weather, and local geography.

EMP and direct radiation are produced immediately upon detonation of a nuclear weapon. EMP is produced by the interaction of gamma radiation and matter that destroys all electronic systems that are not deliberately hardened against its effects. Although EMP effects fall off relatively quickly and are not harmful to humans, high-altitude air bursts can produce a very strong EMP wave that can affect systems thousands of miles away. It is easy to imagine ways that EMP can create indirect casualties as electronic systems necessary to sustain human life or prevent lethal accidents are destroyed by this burst of electronic energy. Although small nuclear weapons are capable of producing direct radiation that is lethal at greater ranges than are reached by other weapons effects, the lethal range of direct radiation for more powerful nuclear weapons is well within the lethal range of blast or thermal radiation produced by the explosion.

About 35 percent of the energy generated by a nuclear explosion takes the form of thermal radiation (in the form of a light pulse). The thermal radiation produced by a relatively large, 1-megaton air burst (a weapon that would have to be detonated at an altitude of about 8,000 feet to prevent the nuclear fireball from touching the ground) can produce first-degree burns on exposed skin at about a distance of 7 miles from the point of detonation, second-degree burns at a distance of about 6 miles, and third-degree burns within a radius of about 5 miles. Third-degree burns over 30 percent of the body will produce shock, a condition that requires immediate medical treatment. This weapon would also produce temporary flash blindness in anyone caught out in the open within about 13 miles on a clear day and within 53 miles on a clear night. The thermal light pulse also can produce retinal burn, causing permanent blindness, but this injury is relatively rare, suggesting those who suffer it probably would be killed by other weapons effects.

Blast, which arrives a few seconds after the light pulse, takes the form of overpressure (a quick rise in atmospheric pressure) and dynamic overpressure (wind). At about 1 mile away from a 1-megaton air burst, overpressure increases to about 20 pounds per square inch (psi) and wind velocities reach a peak of about 470 miles per hour. This is enough to level steel-reinforced concrete structures. At about 5 miles away from the blast, overpressure reaches about 5 psi and wind velocities reach about 160 miles an hour, which is sufficient to destroy lightly constructed commercial buildings and most residences. This "5-psi ring" is an important dividing line in terms of nuclear weapons effects: Planners assume that 50 percent of the people within this ring would be killed promptly by the blast effects of a nuclear weapon. At about 12 miles away from a 1-megaton air burst, overpressure drops to less than 1 psi and wind velocities drop to less than 35 miles per hour, making flying glass and debris the greatest hazard. When planners calculate damage expectan-

cies from nuclear weapons, they generally rely on blast effects, not thermal effects, to predict the damage and casualties that will occur.

Irradiated earth and debris that is carried aloft in a nuclear detonation and then returns to the ground is known as fallout. A nuclear ground-burst intended to destroy hardened targets such as missile silos or underground command facilities would produce the greatest amount of fallout; air bursts intended to destroy area targets such as cities or to barrage-attack the operating areas of land-based mobile missiles would produce the least. How fallout is deposited is highly variable and depends on wind speed and direction, the height to which the fallout is initially lofted by the fireball, weather (rain can wash fallout out of the sky, creating local "hot spots"), and geography (weapons effects can be shaped by local geographic features, such as hills). The amount of radiation produced by fallout will diminish over time as the irradiated materials "decay." Most radioactive materials have short half-lives; in other words, they decay relatively quickly. Highly radioactive materials will decay by a factor of 1,000 in about two weeks. Some radioactive materials, however, have extremely long half-lives: Strontium 90 and cesium 137 remain radioactive for years and can contaminate the food chain, for example.

Exposure to radiation kills at the cellular level. An exposure of 600 rem (Roentgen equivalent man) over about a week has a 90 percent chance of killing an individual; an exposure of 300 rem is probably the minimal dose necessary to create a lethal illness quickly. Individuals who suffer from preexisting medical conditions probably would succumb to radiation sickness or secondary infections at relatively low levels of radiation exposure. Exposure to between 50 and 200 rem interferes with the body's ability to heal itself, increasing the probability that people exposed to nonlethal levels of radiation will die from thermal or kinetic injuries produced by other weapons effects. Exposure to radiation also can have a long-term effect on a population. Exposure to 50 rem would probably increase the occurrence of fatal cancers at a rate of between 0.4 and 2.5 percent among an exposed population (*The Effects of Nuclear War*).

Living with the Bomb

Three methods of dealing with the presence of nuclear weapons have emerged in international relations: deterrence, arms control, and disarmament. Deterrence remains the dominant strategy of nations to prevent the use of nuclear weapons by other states. It creates a state of mind in an adversary that makes an act of aggression on the part of the opponent less likely. States using this strategy must have the capability to retaliate in kind if the opponent uses nuclear weapons and must make credible threats that nuclear retaliation will occur. There is much debate about the effectiveness of deterrence, when it has failed in the past, and under what circumstances it is likely to fail again in the future. During the Cold War, both the Soviet and U.S. militaries went to great lengths to construct secure second-strike forces and command and control facilities that could survive a nuclear attack and strike a retaliatory blow. But as political motivations for war have diminished among nuclear powers over the past couple of decades, many observers believe that a little nuclear deterrence goes a long way toward reducing the likelihood of war.

Negotiations among enemies to take actions of mutual interest—a process that came to be known as arms control—was a revolutionary idea when it reemerged in the 1950s as a way to moderate the nuclear arms race. With the goals of making war less likely, reducing death and destruction if war should break out, and reducing the resources devoted to armament, arms control negotiations achieved some successes during the Cold War. Arms control probably made its greatest contribution by allowing the superpowers to clarify their strategic intentions and expectations and by demonstrating to all concerned that negotiation offered an alternative to violent confrontation as a means of managing the nuclear standoff. Because the "Russian" or "American" threat no longer drives defense planning in Washington or Moscow, traditional approaches to arms control are starting to produce diminishing returns in Russian-American relations. But arms control, especially new types of confidence-building measures, might help to moderate other regional rivalries that have been exacerbated by nuclear proliferation and an accelerating race to develop more advanced nuclear delivery systems.

Disarmament efforts have made modest progress over the past half-century. The Nuclear Nonproliferation Treaty (NPT) serves as the basis of the international nonproliferation regime. The NPT is a means by which states not interested in developing nuclear weapons can register formally their nonnuclear status. It also pressures nuclear powers to take action to reduce not only the size of their nuclear arsenals but also their reliance on nuclear weapons in their military and foreign policies. The nonproliferation regime provides a method for regulating legitimate commerce in nuclear materials, and it provides an inspection and monitoring mechanism run by the International Atomic Energy Agency to guarantee that nuclear materials are not diverted into nuclear weapons production. Revelations of a black market in nuclear materials, technologies, and associated delivery systems, however, have cast doubts on current international efforts to prevent nuclear materials from falling into the wrong hands, especially nonstate actors and terrorist groups.

About Volume II: Nuclear Weapons

Nuclear weapons create a set of ethical, political, and military challenges that are difficult to understand. There are no easy solutions to the problems created by nuclear weapons. Indeed, the nuclear question has concentrated some of the best minds on the planet over the past sixty years. The output of this effort is enough to fill an average municipal library. It is impossible to capture this entire body of knowledge in a single volume, but our contributors have provided matter-of-fact explanations of key concepts and accessible descriptions of events to provide a ready reference for those interested in learning more about nuclear weapons. The more societies know about the true effects and dangers of nuclear weapons, the less likely it will be that nuclear weapons will ever be used in war again.

References

Brodie, Bernard, *The Absolute Weapon* (New York: Harcourt Brace, 1946).

Cochran, Thomas, William M. Arkin, and Milton M. Hoenig, *Nuclear Weapons Databook,* 5 vols. (Cambridge, MA: Ballinger, 1984–1987, and Boulder: Westview, 1994).

The Effects of Nuclear War (Washington, DC: Office of Technology Assessment, 1979).

Jervis, Robert, *The Meaning of the Nuclear Revolution: Statecraft and the Prospect of Armageddon* (Ithaca, NY: Cornell University Press, 1989).

Larsen, Jeffrey A., ed., *Arms Control: Cooperative Security in a Changing Environment* (Boulder: Lynne Rienner, 2002).

Lavoy, Peter, Scott Sagan, and James J. Wirtz, eds., *Planning the Unthinkable: How New Powers Will Use Nuclear, Chemical and Biological Weapons* (Ithaca, NY: Cornell University Press, 2000).

Mueller, John, *Retreat from Doomsday: The Obsolescence of Major War* (New York: Basic, 1989).

Rhodes, Richard, *The Making of the Atomic Bomb* (London: Touchstone, 1995).

Sagan, Scott, *The Limits of Safety* (Princeton, NJ: Princeton University Press, 1993).

Schell, Jonathan, *The Unfinished Twentieth Century* (New York: Verso, 2001).

Schelling, Thomas, *Arms and Influence* (New Haven, CT: Yale University Press, 1966).

Snyder, Glenn, *Deterrence and Defense* (Princeton, NJ: Princeton University Press, 1961).

The "nuclear age" began at five o'clock on the morning of 16 July 1945 with the detonation of the world's first atomic bomb—the Trinity test in the high desert of central New Mexico. This successful explosion marked the culmination of three years of frantic scientific and engineering research and development under the auspices of the U.S. Manhattan Project, which the United States had instituted in 1942 to ensure that the Allies achieved atomic weapons before Germany. There had been scientific discoveries and research in the field of radiology prior to World War II (primarily in the 1930s), but the threat of an adversary achieving the "ultimate weapon" before the Allies had one was a strong motivating factor in the efforts of the Manhattan scientists.

Following the war the world entered a long twilight period known as the Cold War. The United States and its allies faced off against a seemingly implacable foe, the Soviet Union. Both sides rapidly built up their nuclear arsenals until there were some 60,000 atomic warheads pointed at one another. After years of "standing toe to toe," threatening nuclear war and "looking into the abyss," reason slowly began to enter into the equation. Concepts like arms control and nuclear disarmament began to determine international relations. Stockpile levels were already coming down dramatically by the time the Soviet Union dissolved in 1991, following which the world shifted from a bilateral standoff to a less well-defined era. Despite the fact that there are fewer nuclear weapons today, whether the post–Cold War era will be one our children look back on as "safer" than the Cold War is a question still out for consideration.

The history of the Cold War is replete with events falling into two alternative categories: new developments in weapons design and capabilities as the arms race between the two superpowers accelerated, on the one hand, while on the other, we see attempts to improve relations between the two primary actors on the international scene, involving

Chronology: Nuclear Weapons

summit meetings, arms control negotiations and agreements, and force reductions.

In this short chronology we have listed merely some of the highlights of this two-pronged effort over the past seventy years.

1933	Hungarian physicist Leo Szilard theorizes atomic structure.
1938	Otto Hahan and Fritz Strassmann's discovery of fission steers Germany toward developing an atomic weapon.
July 1939	Szilard and Edward Teller meet with Albert Einstein in New York to describe Germany's efforts. Einstein writes letter to President Franklin Roosevelt warning him of the possibility of building an atomic weapon.
Fall 1939	United States grants small funding for research into nuclear fission. Key scientists involved include Szilard, Teller, and Enrico Fermi. Early work is carried out primarily at Columbia University and the Universities of California and Chicago.

1941	By 1941, Germany leads the race for the atomic bomb. They have a heavy-water plant (in Norway), high-grade uranium compounds, a nearly complete cyclotron, capable scientists and engineers, and the greatest chemical engineering industry in the world.	6 August 1945	A United States B-29 bomber drops atomic bomb on Hiroshima, Japan (another bomber drops a second bomb on Nagasaki, Japan three days later).
June 1942	The United States begins major research program to develop and build a usable atomic weapon. The effort is called the Manhattan Project, and is directed by Major General Leslie Groves and Robert Oppenheimer.	4 April 1946	United States passes Atomic Energy Act (also known as the McMahon Act), creating the U.S. Atomic Energy Commission (which was absorbed into the United Nations Disarmament Commission in 1952).
1942–1943	Three entirely new towns are created for the sole purpose of developing the components of an atomic bomb: Los Alamos, New Mexico (center of scientific and engineering efforts), Oak Ridge, Tennessee (where uranium enrichment is centered), and Hanford, Washington (where plutonium is reprocessed from spent reactor fuel). This is the beginning of what will become a massive American atomic infrastructure.	14 June 1946	Baruch Plan presented by the United States to the United Nations, an early disarmament effort to place all nuclear material and weapons under UN control. (Proposal is rejected by the USSR in December 1946.)
		29 August 1949	Soviet Union tests its first atomic bomb.
		1 November 1951	United States tests the world's first hydrogen bomb.
		3 October 1952	Great Britain tests its first atomic bomb.
		August 1953	Soviet Union tests its first hydrogen bomb.
2 December 1942	At the University of Chicago Fermi oversees the first controlled energy release from the nucleus of the atom using a uranium graphite reactor.	8 December 1953	United States makes an "Atoms for Peace" proposal to the UN General Assembly.
		January 1954	United States launches its first nuclear powered submarine.
16 July 1945	The United States tests the world's first atomic bomb at the Trinity Site in central New Mexico.	23 October 1954	In a protocol to the Brussels Treaty (which created the

West European Union) and in return for permission to rearm itself with conventional weapons, West Germany pledges not to produce, procure, or possess weapons of mass destruction.

December 1954 The North Atlantic Treaty Organization deploys atomic weapons in Europe.

26 October 1956 International Atomic Energy Agency created.

4 October 1957 USSR launches Sputnik, the world's first orbiting satellite.

15 October 1957 USSR and China sign a defense agreement whereby the Soviets agree to provide China with technical help in developing their own atomic bomb.

10 January 1958 United States tests the world's first intercontinental ballistic missile (ICBM).

31 October 1958 United States, United Kingdom, and USSR begin negotiations on a comprehensive test ban treaty (CTBT).

June 1959 United States launches the first nuclear powered submarine equipped with submarine-launched ballistic missiles (SLBM).

1 December 1959 Twelve nations sign the Antarctic Treaty, demilitarizing the continent, and leading the way to future geographic nuclear weapon free zones.

13 February 1960 France tests its first atomic bomb.

15–28 October 1962 The United States and the Soviet Union come close to nuclear war during the Cuban Missile Crisis.

20 June 1963 United States and Soviet Union establish a crisis communications link by signing the Hot Line Agreement.

5 August 1963 United States, United Kingdom, and USSR sign the Limited Test Ban Treaty, banning nuclear weapon tests in the atmosphere, outer space, and underwater.

1964 United States ceases production of highly enriched uranium.

16 October 1964 China tests its first atomic bomb.

27 January 1967 Outer Space Treaty signed by 67 nations; demilitarizes space and celestial bodies.

14 February 1967 Treaty of Tlatelcolco signed, creating the Latin American Nuclear Weapon Free Zone.

13 December 1967 United States announces that it has successfully tested ICBM warheads with multiple independently targetable reentry vehicles (MIRVs).

1 July 1968 Nuclear Non-Proliferation Treaty (NPT) signed by 73 countries (currently there are 187 states parties to the treaty).

3 September 1971	The Zangger Committee created by 33 nations to voluntarily restrict nuclear-related exports.	28 May 1976	Peaceful Nuclear Explosions Treaty signed by the United States and USSR.
30 September 1971	Nuclear War Risk Reduction Agreement signed by the United States and Soviet Union (also called the Accidents Measures Agreement).	March 1979	Three Mile Island nuclear power reactor accident in Pennsylvania.
26 May 1972	Strategic Arms Limitation Treaty (SALT I) signed in Moscow by the United States and Soviet Union. The first major strategic arms control treaty, it consists of an Interim Agreement on Strategic Offensive Arms (freezing the number of missile launch sites) and an Anti-Ballistic Missile Treaty (ABM) (which restricts the development of missile defenses).	18 June 1979	SALT II Treaty signed by the United States and Soviet Union (limiting the number and types of strategic delivery vehicles allowed); treaty is never ratified.
		June 1981	Israeli jets strike Iraqi nuclear reactor in preemptive attack.
		23 March 1983	United States announces its strategic defense initiative.
		6 August 1985	Treaty of Rarotonga signed, creating the South Pacific Nuclear Free Zone.
18 May 1974	India tests its first atomic "device."	April 1986	Soviet nuclear reactors explode and melt down at Chernobyl, Ukraine.
3 July 1974	United States and Soviet Union sign the Threshold Test Ban Treaty, limiting the size of allowable underground nuclear weapons test explosions.	7 April 1987	Missile Technology Control Regime established to reduce proliferation risks through controls on technology transfers.
23 April 1975	The Nuclear Suppliers Group is created to restrict the export of sensitive technology.	8 December 1987	Intermediate-Range Nuclear Forces Treaty (INF) signed by the United States and Soviet Union, eliminating an entire category of missiles with a range of 500 to 5,500 kilometers.
1 August 1975	The Helsinki Accords are signed by 35 states, creating the Conference on Security and Cooperation in Europe and emphasizing the value of confidence- and security building measures.	1988	United States closes its plutonium production facilities.

9 November 1989 — Berlin Wall falls in peaceful revolution; within two years NATO has declared the Cold War over (July 1990) and the Soviet Union disappears (December 1991).

3 April 1991 — Following the victory by the U.S.-led international military coalition that defeated Iraq in the Gulf War, the United Nations creates a Special Commission on Iraq (UNSCOM) to find and destroy Iraqi capabilities to make weapons of mass destruction.

9 July 1991 — Strategic Arms Reduction Treaty (START I) signed by United States and Soviet Union; limits strategic delivery vehicles on each side.

27 September 1991 — United States initiates series of reciprocated Presidential Nuclear Initiatives that eliminate or remove most tactical nuclear weapons systems from deployment and lead to the de-alerting or de-targeting of strategic systems.

27 November 1991 — U.S. Congress passes Nuclear Threat Reduction Act (also called the Nunn-Lugar Program) to help the Soviet Union transport, store, safeguard, and destroy its residual nuclear arsenal; leads to creation of the Cooperative Threat Reduction Program.

20 January 1992 — North and South Korea sign the Joint Declaration on the Denuclearization of the Korean Peninsula.

24 March 1992 — Treaty on Open Skies signed by 25 nations to allow intrusive aerial reconnaissance for arms control monitoring and compliance verification.

23 September 1992 — Last U.S. underground nuclear test.

3 January 1993 — START II Treaty signed by the United States and Russia; further limits number of strategic delivery systems and eliminates warheads with multiple independently targetable reentry vehicles (MIRV) and heavy ICBMs.

14 January 1994 — United States, Russia, and Ukraine sign Trilateral Agreement, whereby Ukraine agrees to return to Russia nuclear weapons left on its territory upon the demise of the Soviet Union.

24 March 1994 — South Africa admits it had a secret nuclear weapons program that since 1974 had produced six weapons, now destroyed.

30 May 1994 — United States and Russia agree to detarget their ICBMs and SLBMs away from each other's territory. Russia concludes similar agreements with Great Britain and China.

23 June 1994 — United States and Russia sign agreement on shutting down Russia's plutonium production facilities (also

	called the Gore-Chernomyrdin Agreement).
22 September 1994	United States releases its Nuclear Posture Review, calling for a smaller version of the Cold War nuclear triad.
23 October 1994	United States and North Korea sign Agreed Framework to stop North Korea's attempts to develop nuclear weapons in return for food and energy assistance.
23 March 1995	Fissile Material Cutoff Talks begin in the UN Conference on Disarmament.
12 May 1995	States parties to the NPT Extension Review conference agree to extend the treaty indefinitely
15 December 1995	Treaty of Bangkok signed, creating the Southeast Asian Nuclear Weapons Free Zone.
11 April 1996	Pelindaba Treaty signed, creating the African Nuclear Weapons Free Zone.
10 September 1996	UN adopts the Comprehensive Test Ban Treaty (the United States is the first country to sign it, but the U.S. Congress refuses to ratify it on 13 October 1999).
21 March 1997	United States and Russia agree on parameters for START III negotiations (which never occur).
11 May 1998	India tests atomic weapons.
28 May 1998	Pakistan tests its first atomic weapon.
22 September 1998	United States and Russia begin Nuclear Cities Initiative to provide nonmilitary work for Russian scientists and engineers formerly involved in the nuclear weapons complex
December 2001	United States releases Nuclear Posture Review, calling for a new triad consisting of strategic strike forces, missile defenses, and an enhanced infrastructure.
24 May 2002	United States and Russia sign Strategic Offensive Reductions Treaty (SORT, also known as the Moscow Treaty), calling for reductions in deployed strategic warheads to approximately 2,000 by 2012.
13 June 2002	United States withdraws from the ABM Treaty, citing a need to develop and deploy a working antiballistic missile system.
27 June 2002	G-8 countries agree to a Global Partnership against the Spread of Weapons and Materials of Mass Destruction.
5 October 2002	North Korea admits it has an ongoing nuclear weapons program in defiance of its responsibilities under the NPT.
September 2003	Proliferation Security Initiative signed by 11 countries.

ACCIDENTAL LAUNCH PROTECTION SYSTEM
See Strategic Defense Initiative

ACCIDENTAL NUCLEAR WAR

An accidental nuclear war would be one resulting from the use of nuclear weapons without the approval of legitimate political or military authorities in decision-making processes evaluating the need for a nuclear attack or retaliation in light of national security concerns. Several potential causes of accidental nuclear war have emerged in the literature.

An accidental war could be caused by the malfunction of some weapon system or from human error involved in the operation of a weapon. In terms of operator error or equipment malfunction, weapons literally would begin to launch or detonate "accidentally," a scenario that could lead to a nuclear exchange, especially in time of crisis. Although many procedures are followed to maintain negative control of nuclear weapons (that is, to guarantee that they will not be used without orders), highly complex systems can interact in unexpected ways, defying the best efforts of operators to maintain or regain control. During the Cold War, for example, observers worried that the Soviet and U.S. early warning networks and command and control systems actually formed a single and tightly linked mechanism that might produce a "ratcheting effect" in time of crisis, generating a feedback loop that would force both sides to take steps greatly increasing the prospect of war. Another concern was that early warning data could be mislabeled or misinterpreted, leading to a mistaken decision to retaliate.

"Inadvertent war" is sometimes used interchangeably with the term "accidental war," but it identifies a different phenomenon. Inadvertent war is caused by the close interaction of opposing military forces in peacetime or during a crisis. Fighting erupts as a result of locally rational decisions or mistakes made by local commanders, decisions that

effectively disconnect the use of force from political control. Inadvertent war is not accidental in the sense that it is caused by mechanical failure or operator error; rather, it is caused by the tendency of military interactions to unfold according to their own logic.

Since the dawn of the nuclear era, substantial thought and effort have gone into preventing accidental and inadvertent nuclear war. Nuclear powers have attempted to construct the most reliable technology and procedures for command and control of nuclear weapons, including robust, fail-safe early warning systems for verifying attacks. The United States and the Soviet Union also maintained secure second-strike capabilities to reduce their own incentives to launch a preemptive strike against each other during crisis situations or out of fear of a surprise attack. The two nuclear superpowers worked bilaterally to foster strategic stability by means of arms control and confidence-building measures and agreements. Several confidence-building agreements were negotiated between the two superpowers to reduce the risk of an accidental nuclear war: the 1971 Agreement on Measures to Reduce the Risk of Outbreak of Nuclear War, the 1972 Agreement on the Prevention of Incidents on and over the High Seas, and the 1973 Agreement on the Prevention of Nuclear War. Following the end of the Cold War, the United States and the Russian Federation have continued to offer unilateral initiatives and to negotiate bilateral agreements on dealerting and detargeting some of their nuclear forces to further reduce the likelihood of a catastrophic nuclear accident. They have concluded agreements on providing each other with notifications in the event of ballistic missile launches or other types of military

1

activities that could possibly be misunderstood or misconstrued by the other party.

The likelihood of accidental nuclear war has always been viewed as low, but the consequences of such a war or incident were, and remain, viewed as so potentially catastrophic as to require serious diplomatic and scholarly attention and analysis. Today, many analysts consider the risk of accidental nuclear war greater than the possibility of a premeditated nuclear exchange between nations. As additional nuclear powers have emerged, so have concerns about the technology and procedures for command and control of nuclear weapons. The proliferation of nuclear weapons has been thought to increase the probability of accidental or inadvertent nuclear war, especially since stability criteria are less obvious in a multiplayer game. In addition, the risks of dramatic political changes in states possessing nuclear weapons, highlighted by the breakup of the Soviet Union and the political fragility of a nuclear-armed Pakistan, leave many observers uneasy about the safety and security of nuclear arsenals amid politically or militarily chaotic situations.

—*Steven Rosenkrantz*

See also: Reciprocal Fear of Surprise Attack; Surety
Reference
Sagan, Scott, *The Limits of Safety* (Princeton, NJ: Princeton University Press, 1993).

ACCURACY

A weapon's accuracy is usually measured in terms of "circular error probable" (CEP), that is, the radius within which a warhead or bomb will land 50 percent of the time. The lower the CEP, the more accurate the weapon. As technology and delivery systems have improved, CEP for most weapons has shrunk. Early bombs had CEPs only as accurate as the bombardiers or pilots who dropped them. The "precision-bombing" of World War II had CEPs of hundreds or even thousands of feet. Similarly, early cruise missiles and intercontinental ballistic missiles (ICBMs) also had CEPs in the thousands of feet. Because of this, nuclear warhead yield was very large to ensure destruction of a target. Today, accuracy is in the hundreds of feet for modern nuclear weaponry. Precision-guided technology is allowing CEPs as small as a few feet, allowing the use of very low-yield nuclear or conventional warheads to destroy even hard or deeply buried targets.

—*Zach Becker*

See also: Inertial Navigation and Missile Guidance; Safeguards
References
Lennon, Alexander, *Contemporary Nuclear Debates: Missile Defenses, Arms Control, and Arms Races in the Twenty-First Century* (Cambridge, MA: MIT Press, 2002).
MacKenzie, Donald, *Inventing Accuracy: A Historical Sociology of Nuclear Missile Guidance* (Cambridge, MA: MIT Press, 1993).
Volkman, Ernest, *Science Goes to War: The Search for the Ultimate Weapon—From Greek Fire to Star Wars* (Indianapolis: John Wiley & Sons, 2002).

ACHESON-LILIENTHAL REPORT

The Acheson-Lilienthal Report, formally entitled *Report on the International Control of Atomic Energy*, was the first major nuclear proliferation-control document of the post–World War II era. It proposed the establishment of a safeguarding regime for nuclear materials.

The report, released in 1946 by Assistant Secretary of State Dean Acheson and the chairman of the Tennessee Valley Authority, David Lilienthal, was a result of a major effort to understand the global strategic environment following the use of atomic weapons against Japan. The devastation at Hiroshima and Nagasaki sparked immediate fear in the United States about the spread of atomic weapons.

The Acheson-Lilienthal Report also recognized the inherent interrelationship between peaceful and military uses of atomic energy and foresaw that no ban on atomic activities could be enacted without adversely affecting the development of peaceful uses that could benefit humankind. This need to constrain the military use of nuclear technology, on the one hand, while sharing its commercial applications, on the other, is reflected in subsequent nuclear nonproliferation efforts, such as the Nuclear Nonproliferation Treaty of 1968.

The report outlined the critical components of a safeguards regime and distinguished between safe and dangerous nuclear activities in terms of their relationship to the development of nuclear weapons. It also proposed establishing an international authority to monitor the nuclear fuel cycle. This report is an important foundational document for understanding current nonproliferation strategies.

—*Jennifer Hunt Morstein*

Reference
Scheinman, Lawrence, *The International Atomic Energy*

Agency and World Nuclear Order (Washington, DC: Resources for the Future, 1987).

ACTINIDES

Actinides are a series of heavy elements that are chemically similar to actinium, including uranium and plutonium, the two major elements used in nuclear power and weapons. Actinides include fifteen different elements, ranging from actinium (atomic number 89) to lawrencium (atomic number 103) on the periodic table. Many of these elements are manmade and have half-lives of thousands of years. All of these elements are radioactive, generally emitting alpha and gamma radiation. Other actinides, referred to as minor actinides, include neptunium, americium, and curium. These are produced in nuclear power plants and are present in spent fuel.

Certain unique chemical properties of actinides facilitate the ability to reprocess spent fuel from nuclear power reactors. These chemical properties allow for the extraction of actinides, particularly uranium and plutonium, from spent fuel using a solvent-extraction method. A solvent-extraction method uses water or other solutions to extract elements based on their ability to dissolve in the solution.

The United States does not currently reprocess spent fuel to recover usable fissile material. However, reprocessing methods are being used in France and may be used in the United States in the future. Terrorist organizations and rogue nations may seek to acquire spent fuel with the purpose of extracting actinides.

—*Don Gillich*

See also: Enrichment; Plutonium; Reprocessing; Uranium

References

Glasstone, Samuel, and Alexander Sesonske, *Nuclear Reactor Engineering* (Princeton, NJ: D. Van Norstrand, 1967).

AIR-LAUNCHED CRUISE MISSILES

See Cruise Missiles

AIRBORNE ALERT

The U.S. alert operation, code-named Chrome Dome, was a realistic training mission designed by the Strategic Air Command (SAC) to deter enemy forces from a surprise attack on the United States. Chrome Dome was established in 1960 following a series of planning and training flights in the late 1950s, and a portion of the U.S. strategic nuclear bombing fleet remained on continuous airborne alert until 1968. In later years, these missions operated under the code names Head Start, Round Robin, and Hard Head. The alert ensured that up to a dozen nuclear-armed bombers were airborne twenty-four hours a day. It also demonstrated SAC's nearly immediate retaliatory capability in case of a Soviet surprise attack, thus strengthening America's nuclear deterrent. Fully combat-configured B-52s carrying nuclear weapons flew routes to points along the Soviet border. The southern route crossed the Atlantic, the Mediterranean, and then returned to the United States; the northern route went up the eastern coast of Canada, across Canada west toward Alaska, then down the west coast of North America. Other mission routes were substituted as required. The Hard Head missions were intended to ensure continuous visual surveillance of Thule Air Base, Greenland, and its vital Ballistic Missile Early Warning System (BMEWS) radar, a critical element for the U.S. response to a Soviet surprise attack on North America. SAC wings launched two combat-ready B-52s every twenty to twenty-three hours for thirty- to sixty-day operations (the duty rotated among SAC's B-52 wings). To keep the B-52s airborne for long periods, KC-135 tankers were launched to keep bombers air-refueled.

Airborne alert flights ended following two serious accidents involving nuclear bombs and B-52s. On January 17, 1966, a B-52 collided with its KC-135 during aerial refueling and crashed off the coast of Palomares, Spain, and on January 22, 1968, a B-52 crashed near Thule, Greenland. SAC thereafter placed 30 percent of its bomber force on ground alert with crews ready to take off within minutes if a warning was received from a BMEWS site or other radar.

—*Gilles Van Nederveen*

See also: Bombers, Broken Arrow, Bent Spear; U.S. Nuclear-Capable; Strategic Air Command and Strategic Command

References

Newhouse, John, *War and Peace in the Nuclear Age* (New York: Vintage, 1990).

Polmar, Norman, ed., *Strategic Air Command: People, Aircraft, and Missiles* (Annapolis, MD: Nautical and Aviation Publishing Company of America, 1979).

ALPHA PARTICLES
See Radiation

ANTI-BALLISTIC MISSILE (ABM) TREATY

Signed in 1972 between the United States and the Soviet Union, the Anti-Ballistic Missile (ABM) Treaty severely restricted their respective development and deployment of ballistic missile defenses and was considered a significant milestone in the history of arms control. It was the first formal treaty between the two nations limiting systems related to their central strategic deterrent capabilities. The U.S. government at the time portrayed it as a significant first step in a new era of mutual restraint and arms limitation between the Cold War superpowers that would provide for a more stable strategic balance and lead to a broader, more comprehensive series of arms control agreements. The treaty also set important precedents that were followed by later arms control treaties, including the legitimization of "national technical means" of verification and the establishment of a commission to oversee implementation and compliance. Over the course of its existence, from May 26, 1972, until June 13, 2002, the ABM Treaty was viewed by many as the basis of Soviet- and then Russian-American strategic relations. Promoted on the one hand as the cornerstone of strategic stability, and vilified on the other as a constraint on U.S. self-defense that shackled Washington to a strategic doctrine of perpetual vulnerability, the ABM Treaty represented both the best and the worst aspects of modern arms control (*see* Missile Defense).

Negotiation of the Treaty
Soviet leaders were at first opposed in principle to the very idea of negotiating limits on missile defenses—which, after all, were entirely defensive weapons. Within days of the U.S. Senate's June 24, 1968, approval of a major U.S. ABM deployment program (*see* Sentinel Anti-Ballistic Missile System) designed to match the Soviet Union's own ABM system then being deployed around Moscow, however, they did a complete about-face on the subject and agreed to accept the U.S. proposal to begin immediate discussions on limiting ballistic missile defenses. Although the United States was most interested in achieving a treaty on offensive force limitations, following two years of negotiations it accepted a treaty limiting ABM systems along with an interim agreement on offensive arms limitations, with the prospect of pursuing a more comprehensive formal treaty on offensive arms in the future (*see* Strategic Arms Limitation Talks [SALT I and SALT II]).

Terms of the Treaty
The ABM Treaty originally limited the United States and the Soviet Union to two sites of 100 antiballistic missile launchers each, separated by at least 1,300 kilometers. A protocol to the treaty, signed in 1974, reduced this limit to just one site for each side. The treaty banned the deployment of ABM systems for a defense of national territory and obligated the parties not to provide a base for such a defense or for the defense of an individual region, except as provided for in the treaty. ABM systems were defined, for the purposes of the treaty, as ABM interceptor missiles, ABM launchers, and ABM radars. ABM missiles and ABM radars were defined as those "constructed and deployed for an ABM role, or of a type tested in an ABM mode"—a formulation that later posed significant problems of interpretation. The application of the treaty terms to ABM systems that used mechanisms other than missiles to intercept strategic missiles, such as lasers or directed-energy weapons, also became the subject of an intense controversy in the years subsequent to the signing of the treaty.

The ABM Treaty further provided for a complete prohibition on developing, testing, or deploying ABM systems or components that were not fixed and land based, that is, sea-, air-, space-, or mobile land-based systems or components. To reduce the potential for circumventing the terms of the treaty, the treaty also prohibited upgrading theater-range antiballistic missiles (which were not otherwise limited by the treaty), testing them concurrently with strategic ABM systems or components, or transferring ABM systems or components to other nations. ABM radars were limited to those at ABM launcher bases or located on the periphery of the national territory and oriented outward (restrictions violated by the Soviet ABM radar at Krasnoyarsk).

Relationship of the Treaty to Other Treaties
Many ABM Treaty supporters considered it the basis of international arms control regimes, which were all predicated to one degree or another on the assumption that the ABM Treaty had forestalled a U.S.-Soviet arms race between offensive and defensive weapons.

Premier Leonid Brezhnev and President Richard Nixon shake hands in Moscow after signing the Anti-Ballistic Missile Treaty, May 1972. (National Archives)

The Soviets took steps to codify a linkage between their interest in further strategic offensive arms reductions and preservation of the ABM Treaty. For example, they insisted, prior to the conclusion of the Strategic Arms Reduction Treaty (START), that START would be "effective and viable only under conditions of compliance with" the ABM Treaty as signed on May 26, 1972. Soviet negotiators also made clear in a unilateral statement associated with START that "events related to withdrawal by one of the Parties" from the ABM Treaty could be grounds for exercising the right to withdraw from START. A similar condition was associated with the Russian Duma's consent to ratify START II. Russia eventually chose not to implement this threat with respect to START I, which continues in force, but did issue a statement, the day after the U.S. withdrawal from the ABM Treaty became effective, saying it considered itself free of the constraints of START II, which in any event had never entered into force (*see* Strategic Arms Reduction Treaty [START I]; Strategic Arms Reduction Treaty [START II]).

Problems Interpreting the ABM Treaty

Almost from the beginning, the necessarily vague diplomatic language of the ABM Treaty posed serious problems of interpretation. One controversy in particular arose in the mid-1980s, soon after President Ronald Reagan announced the intention of the United States to pursue robust missile defenses through a Strategic Defense Initiative (SDI). Some argued that although the treaty banned the deployment of sea-, air-, space-, and mobile land-based ABM systems, it did not prohibit research and development into ABM systems related to those areas. Advocates of this position, which came to be known as the "broad interpretation," further argued that the language of Agreed Statement D, referring to the potential creation in the future of ABM systems "based on other physical principles," allowed their development and testing but not their deployment. Others believed that the ABM Treaty prohibited the development and testing as well as the deployment of such exotic ABM systems. This position came to be known as the "narrow interpretation." The Reagan

6 ANTI-BALLISTIC MISSILE TREATY

administration officially adopted the broad interpretation in 1985, and this eventually led to a confrontation with the U.S. Congress over which interpretation had been associated with the treaty during its ratification process and whether the executive branch had a right to reinterpret treaties once ratified. In 1992, President William Clinton's administration officially renounced the "broad interpretation" and reinstated the "narrow interpretation" as the official policy of the United States. Thereafter, it substantially reduced funding for research into missile defenses and dismantled existing missile defense research and development programs.

The U.S. Decision to Withdraw
from the ABM Treaty

Upon assuming office in 2001, President George W. Bush announced that it was the policy of his administration to deploy effective missile defenses against the threat of limited attacks by a handful of missiles launched by rogue states, and to do so as soon as technically feasible. This set the United States on an inevitable collision course with the ABM Treaty. On December 13, 2001, President Bush gave formal notice to Russia that the United States was withdrawing from the ABM Treaty in accordance with the requirement contained in Article XV of the treaty to give six months advance notice. In making his announcement, the president noted that the world was vastly different from that which existed in 1972 when the treaty was signed, that one of the signatories, the Soviet Union, no longer existed, and neither did the hostilities that once characterized relations between the two countries. He cited the imperative of having the freedom and flexibility to develop effective defenses against ballistic missile attack by terrorists or hostile rogue states and the need to move beyond mutual assured destruction (MAD) as the basis of deterrence. This withdrawal became effective on June 13, 2002.

Although the Bush administration had held a series of intense discussions with Russia over the fate of the ABM Treaty, in which ideas for revising or modifying it were discussed as alternatives to withdrawing from the treaty, the Bush administration was increasingly convinced that a clean break with the past was in order. There were three principal reasons for this decision. First, the ABM Treaty was no longer an appropriate basis for the increasingly cooperative U.S.-Russian relationship. Second, deterrence based solely on mutual assured destruction, as institutionalized by the ABM Treaty, could no longer be considered necessary vis-à-vis Russia nor credible against likely adversaries. Deterrence needed to be reinforced by both offensive and defensive means. Third, the ABM Treaty presented an obstacle to those testing and development activities considered essential by the administration to finding the most effective and affordable means of defending against ballistic missiles of all ranges. Moreover, the ABM Treaty prohibited cooperation between the United States and its allies in developing missile defenses, an avenue the United States was determined to pursue through NATO as well as bilaterally with key friends and allies.

Russia reacted with moderation, given the dire warnings its leaders and diplomats had issued up to that time regarding the potentially negative effects that would surely accompany any U.S. effort to withdraw from or substantially modify the ABM Treaty. In a response given the same day as the U.S. withdrawal announcement, President Vladimir Putin said Russia believed the U.S. decision to be mistaken but asserted it would not pose a threat to the national security of Russia. He reaffirmed his commitment to improving U.S.-Russian relations and called on the United States to put into legally binding form the unilateral strategic offensive reductions that both he and President Bush had respectively announced a month earlier during a summit meeting in Washington and at President Bush's ranch in Crawford, Texas. In fact, the United States and Russia subsequently agreed to a legally binding treaty on further reductions in strategic offensive arms in May 2002, despite the U.S. announcement of its pending withdrawal from the ABM Treaty.

—*Kerry Kartchner*

See also: Arms Control; Standing Consultative Commission; Strategic Offensive Reductions Treaty

References

"ABM Treaty," in *Arms Control and Disarmament Agreements: Texts and Histories of the Negotiations* (Washington, DC: U.S. Arms Control and Disarmament Agency, 1990), pp. 155–166.

Chayes, Antonia H., and Paul Doty, eds., *Defending Deterrence: Managing the ABM Treaty Regime into the 21st Century* (Washington, DC: Pergamon-Brassey's International Defense Publishers, 1989).

Daily, Brian D., "Deception, Perceptions Management, and Self-Deception in Arms Control: An

Examination of the ABM Treaty," in Brian D. Daily and Patrick J. Paker, eds., *Soviet Strategic Deception* (Lexington, MA: Hoover Institution/Lexington Books, 1987), pp. 225–260.

Garthoff, Raymond L., *Policy Versus the Law: The Reinterpretation of the ABM Treaty* (Washington, DC: Brookings Institution, 1987).

Lin, Herbert, *New Weapon Technologies and the ABM Treaty* (Washington, DC: Pergamon-Brassey's, 1988).

Smith, Gerard C., *Doubletalk: The Story of SALT I* (Garden City, NY: Doubleday, 1980).

U.S. House of Representatives, Committee on Foreign Affairs, *ABM Treaty Interpretation Dispute,* Hearing before the Subcommittee on Arms Control, International Security and Science, 99th Congress, 1st Session, 22 October 1985.

Wirtz, James J., and Jeffrey A. Larsen, eds., *Rockets' Red Glare: Missile Defenses and the Future of World Politics* (Boulder: Westview, 2001).

ANTINUCLEAR MOVEMENT

Since the dawn of the nuclear age, the antinuclear movement has raised logistic, safety, environmental, moral, and other concerns about the use of nuclear technology for peaceful or military purposes. The movement's main policy goals, its size, and its perceived influence have varied over time, and its history can be divided into four main periods of activity. From 1944 to 1948, the movement consisted of elites who pushed for civilian control of nuclear technology and considered establishing international control of nuclear knowledge under the United Nations. From 1957 to 1963, the movement included the broader public and pushed for arms control, specifically focusing on limits on nuclear testing. From the late 1960s through 1980, the antinuclear movement worked with the emerging environmental movement to oppose the widespread use of nuclear power plants. And from 1979 through 1984, the movement was at its largest and most influential and was focused on the proposal for a U.S. and Soviet "nuclear freeze."

Distinct issues emerged in each of these four periods, but they all reflected changing views on two key questions: First, is it possible to get benefits from nuclear energy without encountering dangerous side effects such as the diversion of nuclear technology for military purposes or environmental damage? Second, is it possible to have arms control even when a nation fears its opponent's military strength? Across the four periods, the movement accumulated

strength, even though most of its membership changed, because leaders and organizations involved in one issue often reemerged to provide leadership in later periods.

History and Background

Even as the first research and testing of nuclear weapons went forward, some of the scientists involved began to question the long-term implications of their work. These questions moved to a broader setting with the use of nuclear weapons at Hiroshima and Nagasaki. Within elite academic, political, and scientific circles, many expressed a mix of fear of the new weapons' power and hope that peaceful uses of nuclear energy might aid future development. There also was a general view that decisive action to establish control of the new technology was necessary, but there was less agreement on what action should be taken. The majority of the public, however, more focused on recovering from the end of a long war and keeping the postwar economy growing, expressed few worries about these issues.

Several leading scientists formed the Federation of Atomic Scientists in hopes of influencing debate. Because of the technical nature of the issues involved, the scientists' views were accorded great weight, but some politicians and military officials believed that the scientists were naive in their political objectives. Many of the scientists were pleased, though, when the 1946 Atomic Energy Act gave the civilian-led Atomic Energy Commission a near monopoly on control of peaceful and military U.S. nuclear programs (*see* Federation of American Scientists).

Debate then shifted to the idea of international control. This idea brought other groups, such as existing peace groups and world federalist organizations, into the antinuclear movement. Their hopes for real action on the Baruch Plan, the U.S.-backed initiative to give control of all nuclear weapons to the United Nations, were dashed by mounting Cold War tensions (*see* Baruch Plan). As fear of an emerging Soviet threat spread, support for any type of arms control or international action declined rapidly. Soon, those who continued to question U.S. government policies faced scrutiny by the Federal Bureau of Investigation and supporters of Senator Joseph McCarthy.

Although Cold War tensions played a major role in ending the first phase of antinuclear activity, they also contributed to activists staying focused on the issue and to the emergence of a second major phase of activity in the mid-1950s. By then, nuclear weapons technology had moved forward with the development of the hydrogen bomb and missile delivery systems, the defense budgets of both superpowers were increasing rapidly, and there was mounting global tension. Several new groups, notably Pugwash and the Committee for a Sane Nuclear Policy (SANE), were established to inform policymakers and the public on the dangers of nuclear escalation and possible flaws in deterrence strategies.

These new groups generated significant media and policymaker attention, but the mass public became more focused on issues related to nuclear testing. In 1954, radioactive fallout from a U.S. test on Bikini Island covered a Japanese fishing boat. There also were mounting reports that radioactive fallout would cause genetic defects and cancer. Quickly, polls showed widespread public support for a test ban, and existing antinuclear organizations began to push it as an important first step in arms control. Support for the test ban also came from religious figures, including Pope Pius XII, leaders in the nonaligned movement, such as Jawaharlal Nehru, and political parties from Japan to England. A small number of activists also used direct action, such as sailing boats close to test sites. It is difficult to say precisely how much influence these polls and various groups had, but it certainly was clear to both U.S. and Soviet leaders that they could win public opinion points by adopting moratoriums on testing and negotiating a test ban. In 1963, the Limited Test Ban Treaty, which banned testing in the atmosphere, under water, or in outer space, was signed. The treaty was a victory for the antinuclear movement, but now lacking a main issue around which to rally support, the movement again receded.

During the 1960s and 1970s, smaller groups of people continued to criticize the overall development of nuclear strategy, specific weapons systems, and missile defense systems. Many peace groups and other foreign policy–oriented groups shifted their focus to the Vietnam War. Another branch of the antinuclear movement began to work with environmental and local citizens groups to protest nuclear power plants. At first, these protests were small, but in time, four factors emerged that strengthened the movement. First, rising oil prices made nuclear energy a more attractive alternative. Second, the U.S. government radically reorganized its energy bureaucracy. Plans for the reorganization gave the movement an issue to focus on and, later, it had new entry points for lobbying. Third, both government and private research showed that the dangers of nuclear power had been understated. Fourth, several small accidents and near-accidents highlighted potential problems.

In their attempts to limit the spread of nuclear power, movement strategists first used legal action and demands for full environmental impact reports. By 1976, they had moved to an electoral strategy, placing several antinuclear referenda on ballots and supporting the Democratic Party's platform, which called for developing nonnuclear sources of energy. They then added tactics of direct action. For example, members of the Clamshell Alliance occupied the construction site of the Seabrook nuclear power plant in New Hampshire. These actions revitalized the old debate over whether the benefits of nuclear energy would outweigh the dangers. The movement was gradually gaining public support, although it lost a key referendum battle in California in 1976. Then, the debate was radically changed, settling in favor of opponents of nuclear power because of accidents at Three Mile Island, Pennsylvania, and Chernobyl, Ukraine (*see* Chernogyl; Three Mile Island).

Nuclear Freeze

By the late-1970s, many people in both the public and policymaking circles saw Cold War tensions, the dangers of nuclear war, and arms races that were only partially limited by arms control agreements as unpleasant but unavoidable facts of modern life. Randall Forsberg, a researcher trained at the Massachusetts Institute of Technology, disagreed. Forsberg argued that, as the first step toward international security, the United States and the Soviet Union needed to end the arms race by freezing the testing, production, and deployment of nuclear weapons. Forsberg took the idea to existing peace, religious, and antinuclear groups. By early 1980, an Ad Hoc Task Force for a Nuclear Freeze had been created. The idea captured the attention of peace activist Randy Kehler, who then led efforts to put a freeze referendum on the ballot in three western Massachusetts districts. The freeze referendum passed in all three districts and did well even in areas that supported Ronald Reagan for president.

The freeze's early popularity was striking. Ironically, the movement's later success and expansion into a national movement were due to the actions of one of its greatest opponents. Reagan and many of his top advisers, fearing a rising Soviet threat, spoke repeatedly of increasing U.S. defense spending, purging arms control supporters from the bureaucracy, negotiating only from a position of strength, and fighting and winning a nuclear war. These statements led many to conclude that Reagan was determined to confront the Soviet Union at all costs and that he was not serious about arms control. These people supported the freeze both as a bold policy alternative and as a symbolic sign of disapproval of Reagan's ideas. As the movement gained strength, Reagan and his supporters speculated that it was inspired by Communist forces. They also argued that a freeze would lock any Soviet superiority in place, potentially worsen the U.S. position if the Soviets cheated on the agreement, and weaken the position of U.S. arms control negotiators. Ironically, these administration arguments only served to further convince many that Reagan was exaggerating the Soviet threat and was unwilling to negotiate seriously.

The spread of the freeze movement was dramatic and reflected a combination of opposition to Reagan's policies, a general antinuclear mood in the country following the accident at Three Mile Island, and a widespread desire to achieve arms control objectives without increasing the Soviet threat. Freeze proposals were passed by dozens of town and city governments, by legislatures from Massachusetts to Oregon, and in eight statewide referenda votes in 1982. Polls consistently showed that over 70 percent of the public supported a freeze, although the numbers declined significantly if the question was worded to suggest that the freeze could lead to Soviet military superiority. In November 1982, a march in New York drew 750,000 people and an initiative signed by more than 2 million people was delivered to the United Nations.

The freeze idea also developed support in Congress. Congressional activity was ultimately a mixed blessing for the movement. Although the movement's concerns got attention in the halls of power and drew increased press attention, the movement's original organizers lost some authority. More important, once the freeze entered the legislative process, it became subject to political negotiation and compromises that were not supported by everyone in the grassroots movement. In 1982, the House of Representatives considered a freeze resolution, but it lost 204–202 in the key vote. The resolution was defeated largely by Republicans and southern Democrats who supported the administration's view that a freeze should come only after significant arms reductions were achieved. In 1983, following an election that brought many freeze supporters to office, debate began anew. The House passed a freeze resolution 278–149 following a complicated debate that stretched some forty hours. Dozens of amendments were proposed, and the final resolution included one that would terminate the freeze if no mutual arms control agreements were reached. Both supporters and detractors of the freeze claimed the wording as a victory. The final vote likely overstated actual support for a freeze, since many saw the vote as a way of prodding the administration to support arms control. The Republican-controlled Senate never formally voted on the freeze.

Proponents of the freeze remained active through the 1984 election, but the movement had begun to wane. Disputes over whether to use legislative or grassroots tactics, what final language would be acceptable, and whether the freeze would really lead to peace or only distract attention from other initiatives began to split the movement. Voters in 1984 seemed more interested in Reagan's economic policies than Walter Mondale's support for the freeze. Reagan also greatly affected the movement by restarting arms control negotiations and calling for a missile defense system that would arguably remove the need for a freeze and bring new security. Supporters of the freeze argued that these Reagan initiatives were spurred by public support for the freeze, claiming that they won the war even if they lost the battle.

—*John W. Dietrich*

See also: Nuclear Weapons Free Zones
References
Kojm, Christopher A., ed., *The Nuclear Freeze Debate* (New York: H. W. Wilson, 1983).
Meyer, David S., "Protest Cycles and Political Process: American Peace Movements in the Nuclear Age," *Political Research Quarterly,* vol. 46, 1993, pp. 451–479.
Muravchik, Joshua, "The Perils of a Nuclear Freeze," *World Affairs,* vol. 145, 1982, pp. 203–207.

Price, Jerome, *The Antinuclear Movement* (Boston: Twayne, 1982).

Waller, Douglas C., *Congress and the Nuclear Freeze: An Inside Look at the Politics of a Mass Movement* (Amherst: University of Massachusetts Press, 1987).

ANTI-SATELLITE (ASAT) WEAPONS

Anti-satellite (ASAT) weapons are designed to attack satellites in orbit. Potential destruction and disruption mechanisms for ASAT weapons include nuclear warheads, high explosives, directed energy, kinetic energy, and electronic warfare.

The United States became concerned about countering the potential for nuclear weapons delivery systems in orbit soon after the beginning of the space age. It first tested an air-launched ASAT weapon from a B-47 bomber under the U.S. Air Force's Bold Orion program in 1959, and in the early 1960s the U.S. Navy tested systems launched by F-4 fighters. All of these earliest ASAT systems would have used nuclear warheads as the kill mechanism, but none of them became operational. In the early 1960s, Secretary of Defense Robert S. McNamara authorized development and deployment of limited numbers of two ground-based, nuclear-tipped ASAT systems. The army's Program 505 system used a Nike-Zeus launcher to conduct seven tests from Kwajalein Island in the Pacific between 1964 and 1966. Program 437, the U.S. Air Force system, used a Thor booster from Johnson Island and was tested sixteen times from 1964 to 1970. The indiscriminate nuclear kill mechanism on these systems could have destroyed or disabled all satellites in low-Earth orbit by pumping up radiation belts.

Both the Soviet Union and the United States began work on more discriminating ASAT systems during the 1960s. The Soviets developed a radar and optical guided co-orbital system with a high-explosive warhead that was launched from a Tsyklon-2 (SL-11) booster and tested it at least twenty times between 1968 and 1982. U.S. efforts during this period culminated in the successful September 13, 1985, test of the Miniature Homing Vehicle (MHV), a direct-ascent kinetic kill ASAT launched from an F-15 fighter.

Some analysts argued that these systems undermined strategic stability, and they were quite controversial in the United States. Congressional restrictions on testing led the administration of President Ronald Reagan to cancel the MHV system in 1988. The superpowers also attempted to address ASAT issues through formal arms control efforts, holding three rounds of dedicated ASAT negotiations in 1978–1979 and discussing the issue in the Defense and Space Talks from 1985 to 1991. None of these negotiations produced an agreement, an illustration of the considerable challenges surrounding efforts to control ASAT capabilities.

There has been no testing of dedicated ASAT systems by any nation since the 1980s, and there are no operational systems deployed today. There is, however, a large amount of residual ASAT capability worldwide, including nuclear-tipped ballistic missiles and ballistic missile defense systems, ground- and air-based lasers, and a wide range of electronic capabilities to spoof, disrupt, degrade, or destroy satellites.

—*Peter Hays*

References

Carter, Ashton B., "Satellites and Anti-Satellites: The Limits of the Possible," *International Security,* vol. 10, Spring 1986, pp. 46–98.

Cooper, Henry F., "Anti-Satellite Systems and Arms Control: Lessons from the Past," *Strategic Review,* vol. 17, Spring 1989, pp. 40–48.

Stares, Paul B., *The Weaponization of Space: U.S. Policy, 1945–1984* (Ithaca, NY: Cornell University Press, 1985).

U.S. Department of Defense, "Report to the Congress on U.S. Policy on ASAT Arms Control," 31 March 1984, available at http://www.security-policy.org/papers/other/ASAT-0384.html.

Wilson, Tom, "Threats to United States Space Capabilities," Space Commission Staff Background Paper, 11 January 2001, available at http://armedservices.house.gov/Publications/107thCongress/article05.pdf.

ARMS CONTROL

Arms control is any tacit or explicit agreement among states aimed at reducing the likelihood of war, the costs of preparing for war, or the damage should war occur. Arms control agreements seek to achieve these goals by restricting or reducing the numbers of military weapons or by placing limits on their operation. They may include a variety of verification and transparency measures such as on-site inspections, reciprocal exhibitions of military hardware, notifications, joint exercises, and data exchanges. Arms control encompasses both formal and informal means of agreement. As the focus of

Arms control in practice: negotiators from the United States, Japan, China, North Korea, South Korea, and Russia begin talks on the North Korean nuclear crisis in Beijing, February 2004. (Greg Baker/Pool/Corbis)

arms control efforts increasingly shifts to combating the proliferation of weapons of mass destruction and other types of weapons, recent arms control arrangements have come to include agreements among supplier states to limit the export of certain categories of weapons or materials that have military application, such as missiles, conventional arms, land mines, and chemical weapon precursor ingredients. For this reason, a recent textbook offered a very broad definition of arms control as "any agreement among states to regulate some aspect of their military capability or potential" (Larsen, p. 1). Unilateral measures, undertaken with a view to influencing the military force policies of another state, also may be considered a form of arms control.

Arms control is a relatively modern concept and must be distinguished from "disarmament," which refers specifically to a reduction in weapons. Arms control may include a mutual freeze in levels of armaments, an agreed-upon reduction, or even a controlled increase in certain areas of weapons (such as those considered more "stabilizing" or "verifiable" than others). It may also include provisions for controlling how subject weapon systems are operated, or even where they are based.

The modern concept of arms control arose in the late 1950s and early 1960s as a response to the onset of an increasingly intense and strictly bipolar nuclear competition between the United States and the Soviet Union. Its basic tenets were originally formulated by mathematicians and game theorists seeking to resolve the instabilities inherent in the dynamic interplay between the fear of nuclear surprise attack and the buildup of nuclear weapons stockpiles. The arms race then emerging between the two superpowers, which many feared would spiral out of control without some concerted effort to check it, provided the incentive and urgency for exploring diplomatic and political means of slowing, stopping, or eventually reversing the U.S.-Soviet competition in nuclear weapons. Arms control theory arose out of these concerns. It postulated that given the means to independently verify military capabilities through newly developed satellite technology, the two nations should be able to surmount the distrust that had given rise to the Cold War through the implementation and mutual verification of incremental arms control arrangements. In theory, these incremental arrangements, initially very modest, would in turn engender sufficient trust to proceed toward more complete arms control agreements, and eventually toward a process of actual disarmament.

The "build-down" concept developed in the 1980s was a variation of this theory. This concept was conceived near the height of the U.S.-Soviet arms race when both sides were building scores of new nuclear warheads each year. The idea would have involved a series of reciprocal reductions in U.S. and Soviet strategic nuclear warheads whereby three or more older warheads would have been withdrawn and dismantled for every new warhead introduced into the respective arsenals of the two nations, thereby gradually enforcing a drawdown. Eventually, the two sides simply agreed to radical cuts in strategic nuclear missiles and warheads.

Arms Control Objectives

These early theoretical explorations of the possibilities for arms control identified three fundamental objectives: to reduce the likelihood of war by creating and reinforcing a stable structure of international arms control agreements; to reduce the costs of preparing for war by providing for equivalent levels of security at lower quantities of armaments; and, by laying the basis for smaller armed forces, to limit the damage should war nevertheless occur.

With these ends in mind, the early theorists of modern arms control developed a coherent series of principles to guide negotiators and policymakers in approaching arms control as a process. These principles may be summarized as follows:

- Arms control "was not an end in itself but a means to an end and that end was first and foremost the enhancement of security, especially security against nuclear war" (Bull, p. xx).
- The superpowers shared a common interest in avoiding nuclear war, and that common interest could and should be the basis for effective arms control agreements.
- Arms control was an adjunct of national security, and not the other way around. Arms control and a nation's national security strategy should work together to promote national objectives. Were they to work at cross-purposes, the legitimacy of one or the other would necessarily suffer.
- Arms control encompassed more than the conclusion of formally negotiated

agreements. It could include informal arrangements and unilateral confidence-building measures.

Originally, the concept of arms control, while designed to promote stability, was neutral with regard to the form of that stability. However, as the interaction of offensive and defensive strategic nuclear technology gave way in the mid- to late 1960s to the rise of offensive-dominant approaches to deterrence, and deterrence itself came to be defined narrowly as threatening a massive retaliation, eventually it became assumed that the main objective of arms control was to stabilize the situation of mutual assured destruction between the superpowers (*see* Massive Retaliation; Mutual Assured Destruction). Thus the operational objectives of arms control came to focus on stabilizing and perpetuating a condition of mutual deterrence by prohibiting new technology that threatened to increase the vulnerability of either side's offensive retaliatory forces. This thinking eventually led to the conclusion of the Anti-Ballistic Missile Treaty of 1972, which severely restricted the deployment of ballistic missile defenses (*see* Anti-Ballistic Missile [ABM] Treaty).

Determining Success or Failure

Ever since the rise of classical arms control theory and its application in national security policy, there has been an intense debate over the prospects and necessary conditions for the success or failure of arms control measures. On the one hand, the pro–arms control community has largely focused on the intangible benefits allegedly accruing from the process of negotiation, which include greater mutual understanding, a deliberate shift to more stable avenues of competition, a lessening of political tension, and improvements in the "learning curve" each nation experiences with regard to its security policies and structures. This school of thought has generally assumed that arms control could transcend political tensions among prospective arms control partners and could be used as an instrument to ameliorate those tensions. The successful negotiation of increasingly ambitious arms control arrangements by more and more states on both a bilateral and multilateral basis is taken as evidence of the benefits of this approach.

On the other hand, those skeptical of arms control have focused on the allegedly poor track record of tangible arms control results, the modest negotiated outcomes of arms control processes, and their impact on other national security objectives. They have also taken issue with the very assumptions of arms control theory, arguing that arms control has emphasized the inherently futile task of finding technical solutions to essentially political problems. For example, many skeptics have held that arms control theory and practice pay too little attention to problems of verification and compliance. The essential verification problem has been the limited ability of surveillance technology to fully and adequately monitor the activities of a treaty party determined to find ways to cheat. The compliance problem consists of the reluctance of some states to act on unavoidably ambiguous evidence of cheating, where standards of evidence are set unrealistically high, out of concern that raising such issues would itself complicate the prospects for further progress in the arms control process. These two problems are, according to the critics of arms control, compounded by the asymmetries between an open and basically law-abiding Western culture and those closed, controlled, and distrusting governments bent on exploiting advantages to be gained by cheating on assumed international obligations.

Skeptics of arms control during the Cold War further held that arms control theory exaggerated the extent to which a mutual interest in avoiding nuclear war could serve as a sound basis for effective arms control, overestimated the extent to which arms control agreements could curb allegedly destabilizing technologies, and underestimated the extent to which the arms control process itself could be insulated from the overall politics of the U.S.-Soviet relationship. Critics also alleged that, too often, arms control became an end in itself, divorced from or out of synch with larger national security objectives, in contradiction to the original tenets of classical arms control theory.

Nevertheless, arms control evolved into a legitimate instrument of national security and an important forum for international conflict management. Early bilateral U.S.-Soviet efforts were soon complemented by a series of multilateral arms control efforts, many under the auspices of the United Nations, others as ad hoc arrangements among groups of nations. Beginning with the 1968 multilateral Nuclear Nonproliferation Treaty, several international arms control agreements emerged in the 1970s, 1980s, and early 1990s. These arms control efforts involved, for example, arrangements for nuclear weapons free zones, constraints on specific weapon systems, agreements on measures designed to promote transparency and confidence-building among states, and nuclear testing constraints. Another series of multilateral arms control agreements have been directed at limiting and reducing the proliferation of conventional weapons and ballistic missile technology. See Table A-1 for a more comprehensive list of existing international arms control regimes.

The Process of Arms Control Negotiations

With regard to the mechanics of negotiating an arms control agreement, it has been traditional for delegations from the prospective parties to meet on neutral ground. For this reason, Geneva, Switzerland, has been a favored location. Once draft treaty text has been agreed to, a "summit" meeting is held between the heads of state of the various parties (so called because this is the highest possible level of meeting between representatives of states) and copies of the actual text in all relevant languages are signed. It also is common for modern arms control agreements to incorporate annual reviews of compliance as one of their obligations. Most review conferences take place in Geneva, but Vienna, Austria, also has become home to several key arms control implementation bodies, such as the International Atomic Energy Agency, which has responsibility for overseeing compliance with the Nuclear Nonproliferation Treaty.

Arms Control after the Cold War

Arms control, like many other aspects of national security, has been subject to considerable rethinking in the aftermath of the collapse of the Soviet empire. For some, the end of the bilateral U.S.-Soviet competition has meant that arms control has lost its primary relevance, that the new era of American preeminence requires that the United States free itself from as many arms control "constraints" as possible, and that legally binding treaties incorporating complex verification measures have outlived their usefulness. For others, the end of the Cold War has meant a realignment of the arms control agenda but not diminishment of arms control as an instrument of national strategy. Most agree that the new focus of arms control must be on combating the proliferation of

Table A-1: Examples of Arms Control Regimes

Nuclear Weapons Free Zones	Weapons Systems Constraints	Confidence-Building Measures	Nuclear Testing Constraints	Suppliers Club & Export Controls
• Outer Space Treaty	• ABM Treaty	• Hot Line	ˆ Limited Test Ban Treaty	• Non-Proliferation Treaty (NPT) & Zangger Committee
• Seabed Treaty	• INF Treaty	• Accidents Measures Agreement	• Threshold Test Ban Treaty (TTBT)	
• Africa NWFZ	• START I Treaty	• Confidence- and Security-Building Measures (CSBMs)		• Australia Group
• Treaty of Tlatelolco [Latin America & Caribbean NWFZ]	• START II Treaty • Biological and Chemical Wpns Conventions	• Open Skies	• Peaceful Nuclear Explosions Agreement	• Missile Technology Control Regime (MTCR)
• South Pacific NWFZ	• SORT Treaty	• ICBM & SLBM Launch Notifications	• Comprehensive Test Ban Treaty (CTBT)	• Fissile Material Cut-Off Treaty (FMCT)
		• De-targeting Agreement		

weapons of mass destruction through a new focus on multilateral mechanisms. Securing residual nuclear stockpiles in Russia and the United States, as well as in other countries, also has loomed large on the post–Cold War security agenda, and several new policy initiatives address these concerns. These initiatives, such as the Nunn-Lugar Program and the Cooperative Threat Reduction Program, fall outside the traditional definition of arms control. Yet their objectives correspond with the fundamental objectives of classic arms control theory—that is, they consist of cooperative efforts to reduce the threat of war; to promote stability, transparency, and predictability; and to limit the damage should war occur. Other multilateral nonproliferation efforts also enlarge the definition of arms control because they are not based on legally binding or formal treaties but instead involve nonbinding "supplier groups," or groups of nations that have formed voluntary associations to restrict international trade in weapon systems deemed destabilizing. Such is the case, for example, with the Missile Technology Control Regime, which includes more than thirty countries agreeing to restrict the international transfer of missiles and missile technology.

Arms control, then, in its broadest sense, is likely to remain a critical component of international stability and national strategy, even as the forms it takes

may evolve to meet the changing and dynamic requirements of the international system.

—*Kerry Kartchner*

See also: Détente; Disarmament; Entry into Force; Implementation; Verification

References

Adler, Emanuel, ed., *The International Practice of Arms Control* (Baltimore: Johns Hopkins University Press, 1992).

Bull, Hedley, *The Control of the Arms Race,* second edition (New York: Praeger, 1965).

Burns, Richard Dean, ed., *Encyclopedia of Arms Control and Disarmament,* 3 vols. (New York: Scribner's Sons, 1993).

Goldblat, Jozef, *Arms Control: A Guide to Negotiations and Agreements* (London: Sage, 1994).

Larsen, Jeffrey A., *Arms Control: Cooperative Security in a Changing Environment* (Boulder: Lynne Rienner, 2002).

U.S. Arms Control and Disarmament Agency, *Arms Control and Disarmament Agreements: Texts and Histories of the Negotiations* (Washington, DC: U.S. State Department, 1996).

ARMS CONTROL AND DISARMAMENT AGENCY (ACDA)

The Arms Control and Disarmament Agency (ACDA) served as the lead U.S. government agency for dealing with arms control issues for nearly forty years. It was legally established by President John F. Kennedy on September 26, 1961, in response to congressional and presidential views that a strong institutional advocate for arms control was needed to integrate arms control considerations into U.S. defense and foreign policy. ACDA was juxtaposed between the weapons-centric mandate of the U.S. Department of Defense and the "desk officer" mentality of the U.S. Department of State.

Until its merger into the Department of State in April 1999, ACDA was responsible for formulating and implementing arms control and disarmament policies that promoted the national security of the United States and its relations with other countries. In carrying out these responsibilities, ACDA prepared and participated in discussions and negotiations with foreign countries on such issues as strategic arms limitations, conventional force reductions in Europe, protocols for preventing the spread of nuclear weapons to countries that did not possess them, chemical weapons prohibitions, and international arms trade regulations. The main functions of the agency were to prepare for and manage U.S. participation in negotiations on arms control and disarmament, to conduct and coordinate arms control research, to ensure that the United States could verify compliance with existing agreements, and to disseminate information on arms control and disarmament to the public.

The agency took the lead in framing U.S. options and providing staff support for the Chemical Weapons Convention (CWC) negotiations, performed an important watchdog role in the nuclear nonproliferation field, and took a policy lead in designing improved safeguards to strengthen nuclear nonproliferation. ACDA promoted the utilization of confidence-building measures in regions of tension, particularly on the Korean peninsula, to address the demand side of proliferation problems.

In 1993, support for maintaining the agency began to wane. In 1996, Senator Jesse Helms, chairman of the Senate Foreign Relations Committee, demanded the William Clinton administration's acquiescence in his goal to merge the independent foreign affairs agencies into the State Department as the price for ratifying the Chemical Weapons Convention. Pursuant to the Foreign Affairs Reform and Restructuring Act of 1998, an undersecretary of state for arms control and international security was created within the State Department. This under-

secretary took on duties previously handled by personnel of the former State Department Bureau of Political-Military Affairs and ACDA, effective April 1, 1999. In many ways, ACDA was a victim of its own success, having effectively integrated arms control considerations into the fabric of U.S. foreign and defense policymaking.

—*Kerry Kartchner*

References

Clarke, Duncan L., *Politics of Arms Control: The Role and Effectiveness of the U.S. Arms Control and Disarmament Agency* (New York: Free Press, 1979).

Graham, Thomas, Jr., *Disarmament Sketches: Three Decades of Arms Control and International Law* (Seattle: University of Washington Press, 2002).

The U.S. Arms Control and Disarmament Agency: The First Twenty-Five Years (Washington, DC: Arms Control and Disarmament Agency, 1986).

The U.S. Arms Control and Disarmament Agency: Thirty Years Promoting a Secure Peace (Washington, DC: U.S. Arms Control and Disarmament Agency, 1991).

ARMS RACE

The concept of a nuclear arms race was the subject of considerable debate during the Cold War era. Many observers expressed concern about whether the rivalry between the superpowers would inevitably result in a global nuclear war, with its accompanying devastation, or lead to a stable strategic relationship where the necessary conditions to avoid such a calamity could be maintained. More recently, concern about nascent arms races have spread to regional rivalries. India and Pakistan, which have both undertaken a series of nuclear tests and remain at loggerheads over Kashmir, appear to be locked in an arms race, for example, and many analysts predict that the problem will worsen as other countries develop new weapons of their own.

The term "arms race" is highly debated. Some thinkers choose to dismiss the concept, while others identify it as one of the principal causes of war. The term itself suggests a degree of folly or mutual hysteria between two or more states whereby they find themselves "trapped" in a competition to build larger or more destructive arsenals. True arms races, which are animated by an action-reaction dynamic, are relatively rare. Notable examples, however, include the Anglo-German naval race before World War I and the race between the United States and the Soviet Union to develop intercontinental ballistic missiles (ICBMs) during the 1950s. Nuclear weapons have highlighted the potential costs such races can have if they lead to catastrophic war.

The acquisition of arms is a normal part of state behavior. States acquire arms as part of their duty to help preserve the state and protect their citizens. Individual states do not exist in a vacuum, however. A national decision to increase the size or capability of an arsenal prompts other states to counter any increase in capability. The "security dilemma" (that is, actions taken to increase one's security tend to decrease the security of others) precludes leaders from taking at face value reassurances that their competitors' military programs are only being undertaken for defensive purposes. The security dilemma sometimes produces an action-reaction cycle that may lead to competitive arms races as states seek to gain advantages over their neighbors. After China tested a nuclear weapon in the 1960s, for example, Indian officials felt compelled to develop and test their own nuclear capability, which eventually led to a decision by Pakistani officials to also field a nuclear arsenal.

The term also implies a deviation from the norm of military modernization. Colin Gray has identified four criteria that must be present to produce an arms race (an action-reaction competition): (1) there must be two or more parties that are deliberate rivals; (2) the parties must structure their armed forces to improve the probable effectiveness of the forces in combat with, or as a deterrent to, the other arms-race participants; (3) they must compete in terms of the quantity or quality of their arsenals; and (4) there must be rapid increases in either the quantity or quality of competing arsenals beyond normal evolutionary improvements in force structure (Gray, p. 40).

Real danger from such arms races arises when one state gains a temporary advantage and sees its opponent's armaments program as a threat to this advantage, which leads to pressures to take preventive or preemptive action (for example, the Israel strike on Iraq's Osirak nuclear reactor in 1981). States also may act when an arms race is seen as threatening a general military equilibrium. These dangers are exacerbated by the secrecy that surrounds all types of military activities, especially the procurement and testing of new military hardware. Decisions are invariably based on incomplete information and often rely on worst-case assumptions about a potential opponent's intentions and capabilities.

A balanced strategic relationship may develop when neither side has an advantage and sees no way of gaining one. Here, nuclear weapons may be the ultimate guarantee of arms-race stability: Both parties ensure the devastation of the other—in a phenomenon known as "mutual assured destruction"—even if their conventional capabilities are unbalanced.

Since arms races are about relative military power, they can be volatile. Developments in military technology, such as the advent of nuclear weapons or long-range delivery systems, can alter the relative balance between offensive and defensive capabilities. For example, World War I often is cited as an instance when defensive technologies had the advantage, leaving millions to die in the trenches for relatively little gain.

The term "arms race" also is used in a less technical sense simply to describe the nuclear arms race that ensued following the first use of an atomic weapon against Hiroshima on August 6, 1945. Successive military development, such as Soviet acquisition of nuclear weapons, the development of the hydrogen bomb, the development of ballistic missiles, the deployment of multiple independently targetable reentry vehicles, and the advent of missile defenses, thus constitutes an "arms race." Although scholars suggest that Soviet and U.S. planners and scientists often marched to their own drum—weapons developments did not always follow an action-reaction pattern—popular discourse uses the term "arms race" to describe the balance of terror at the heart of superpower relations during the Cold War.

In the aftermath of the Cold War, a new international dynamic is producing a new type of arms race. As so-called "rogue states" seek nuclear, chemical, or biological weapons, an arms race is emerging between those who want to develop such a capability and those who wish to prevent them from doing so—either by restricting access to the relevant technology or by developing appropriate defenses (for example, ballistic missile defenses). The latter represents the classic competition between offense and defense, an action-reaction dynamic that lies at the heart of the notion of an arms race.

—*Andrew M. Dorman and James J. Wirtz*

See also: Cold War; Russian Nuclear Forces and Doctrine

References

Buzan, Barry, *An Introduction to Strategic Studies: Military Technology and International Relations* (Basingstoke, UK: Macmillan, 1987).

Gray, Colin S., "The Arms Race Phenomenon," *World Politics,* vol. 24, 1971, pp. 39–79.

Sheehan, Michael, *The Arms Race* (Oxford, UK: Martin Robertson, 1983).

ARMS RACE STABILITY
See Arms Race

ASSURED DESTRUCTION

The term "assured destruction" is often used interchangeably with the term "unacceptable damage." Secretary of State Robert S. McNamara in 1967 defined assured destruction as "an ability to inflict at all times and under all foreseeable conditions an unacceptable degree of damage upon any single aggressor or combination of aggressors—even after absorbing a surprise attack." During the Cold War era, U.S. strategic nuclear forces were assessed, in part, in terms of their assured-destruction capabilities, that is, the amount and type of damage they could inflict on an enemy in a retaliatory strike. The other measure of military readiness—damage limitation—described the degree to which U.S. forces were capable of reducing the damage that an enemy could inflict on U.S. forces, territory, and population.

In the mid-1960s, McNamara dropped the damage-limitation criterion, and assured destruction became the principal measure of the adequacy of the posture, size, and composition of U.S. strategic nuclear forces. Eventually, assured destruction came to describe the dominant theory of deterrence underlying U.S. declaratory strategic doctrine and arms control policy. According to this theory, it was necessary for the sake of deterrence that U.S. and Soviet societies remain vulnerable to nuclear destruction by the other side. It therefore was necessary to avoid endangering the enemy's own strategic forces and assured-destruction capability, which meant avoiding counterforce, first strike–type forces, or even giving one's own forces sufficient accuracy to threaten the other side's forces. Also according to this theory, the notion of strategic superiority was dismissed because once one or both sides achieved sufficient nuclear power to assure the total societal destruction of the other, any additional amount of nuclear force would be irrelevant.

U.S. nuclear strategy has incorporated some form of assured-destruction targeting since McNamara's era, but the designated targets covered by this concept have evolved considerably. McNamara originally defined assured destruction as the ability to destroy one-third of the Soviet population and two-thirds of its industry. These figures were derived not from any assessment of what actually deterred the Soviet Union but from the physics of nuclear strikes against a widely dispersed population. Pentagon analysts in the 1960s believed that it would take nuclear weapons representing the equivalent of approximately 400 megatons to destroy 30 percent of the Soviet population and about 50 percent of its industrial capacity, and that this level represented the point of diminishing returns. That is, using more and more weapons did not produce appreciably more damage. The figure of 400 equivalent megatons (EMTs) then became the canonical measurement of an adequate "assured destruction" capability, symbolizing the minimum amount of nuclear force needed for the United States to be able to unleash "unacceptable" damage on the aggressor after surviving a first strike.

Over the following years, the Pentagon successively reduced the percentage of Soviet population and industry they believed should be held at risk for assured-destruction purposes. Nevertheless, later administrations retained the assured-destruction targeting mission but moved away from defining it in terms of population and industry. Under President Richard Nixon, for example, the operational definition of assured destruction was revised to focus on Soviet economic recovery capabilities rather than pure urban industrial targets. Military planning under this approach consisted of more limited, flexible targeting options. Under President Jimmy Carter, the assured-destruction mission was further revised to include strikes limited to Soviet leadership and the war-supporting industry. By the end of the first Ronald Reagan administration, assured destruction had come to describe the mission assigned only to those nuclear forces that would be held in reserve from the initial phases of a conflict. In other words, the assured-destruction mission represented the types of attacks that would be initiated only if all else had failed, as a last resort. Even then, the actual targeting strategy no longer focused on deliberate strikes against urban industrial and population targets but on targets more relevant to the actual military objectives of the overall war plans. Thus, the concept of what represented "unacceptable damage" or having an "assured-destruction capability" has been a more or less subjective assessment that has evolved considerably over the years in keeping with the evolution of U.S.-Russian relations.

—*Kerry Kartchner*

See also: Deterrence; First Strike; Mutual Assured Destruction

References

Enthoven, Alain C., and K. Wayne Smith, *How Much Is Enough? Shaping the Defense Program, 1961–1969* (New York: Harper & Row, 1971).

McNamara, Robert S., "Address before the United Press International Editors," San Francisco, California, 18 September 1967, reprinted in Philip Bobbit, Lawrence Freedman, and Gregory F. Treverton, eds., *U.S. Nuclear Strategy: A Reader* (New York: New York University Press, 1989), pp. 267–282.

Sagan, Scott D., *Moving Targets: Nuclear Strategy and National Security* (Princeton, NJ: Princeton University Press, 1989).

Speed, Roger D., *Strategic Deterrence in the 1980s* (Stanford, CA: Hoover Institution, 1979).

ATOMIC BOMB

See Fission Weapons

ATOMIC ENERGY ACT

The Atomic Energy Act, which was originally enacted in 1946 and significantly modified in 1954, lays out the government structure for control of atomic energy in the United States and the core legal framework governing the spread of information on atomic energy. The 1946 act was submitted by Senator Brien McMahon (D–CT) and is thus sometimes referred to as the McMahon Act. It sought to keep a U.S. monopoly on atomic technology by banning most kinds of international cooperation. Within the United States, the government was given complete ownership of all fissile materials, of the facilities for producing them, and of restricted patents for research funded by the government. The act resolved the crucial question of military versus civilian governmental control by establishing the Atomic Energy Commission (AEC), led by five civilians, and giving the AEC oversight of all weapons work as well as civilian usage. To balance this new executive-branch commission, the act also created the congressional Joint Committee on Atomic Energy

(JCAE) and gave it jurisdiction over all bills related to atomic energy and oversight of AEC activities (*see* Atomic Energy Commission).

In 1954, three significant changes were made. Restrictions on sharing weapons information with other countries were reduced in response to the need for an allied Cold War defense. Limits on the international exchange of other types of information were lowered in line with President Dwight D. Eisenhower's Atoms for Peace initiative (*see* Atoms for Peace). Crucially, the government monopoly of ownership was broken to allow for the development of a private atomic-power industry.

To regulate atomic information, the 1946 act also created the category of "restricted data," defined to include any information on the manufacture or utilization of fissile material. It then greatly limited the dissemination of such information. In essence, all atomic energy information was controlled, or "born secret," unless the government released the information. In time, critics argued that this policy was slowing research, costing the government millions of dollars in security precautions, and fueling popular distrust of a government that refused to release data on events such as atomic tests conducted on civilians.

—*John W. Dietrich*

See also: Nuclear Regulatory Commission

References

Allardice, Corbin, and Edward R. Trapnell, *The Atomic Energy Commission* (New York: Praeger, 1974).

Green, Harold P., and Alan Rosenthal, *Government of the Atom: The Integration of Powers* (New York: Atherton, 1963).

ATOMIC ENERGY COMMISSION

The Atomic Energy Commission (AEC), created in 1946 by the Atomic Energy Act, oversaw all development and uses of atomic energy and controlled the flow of information about atomic energy under the act's restrictive terms (*see* Atomic Energy Act). Its responsibilities were modified over time, and the AEC was dissolved in 1974. Its creation was shaped by post-Hiroshima debates over whether control of atomic energy should rest in military or civilian hands and on how to develop the peaceful uses of atomic energy. The AEC was led by a commission of five civilians appointed by the president. It had four operating divisions, including one for military applications, and had a Military Liaison Committee of six senior officers. Beyond weapons work, the AEC controlled all fissile materials, all facilities used in their production, and much of the research conducted in the field. In Congress, because jurisdiction over these issues was given to the special Joint Committee on Atomic Energy (JCAE), an unusually tight relationship developed between the executive agency and congressional officials influential in AEC oversight and appropriations.

In 1954, the Atomic Energy Act was revised to allow for the development of a private atomic-power industry. This gave the AEC a new regulatory role. Critics charged, though, that this new role created conflicts of interest because the AEC was subsidizing research and facilities in the same industry that it was overseeing. AEC officials also had an institutional interest in promoting the development of the atomic industry and often relied on information supplied by that industry. These problems were heightened by the tight secrecy that enveloped all atomic policy and by the degree of technical knowledge necessary to understand it. Few people outside of the AEC and JCAE were able to challenge regulatory decisions. Rising concerns that the AEC was overly restricting and suppressing potentially damaging information on atomic safety and other issues, along with a view that it had oversold the usefulness of its product, led to the AEC's dissolution. Its responsibilities were transferred to the Energy Research and Development Administration, which later shifted control to the U.S. Department of Energy and the Nuclear Regulatory Commission.

—*John W. Dietrich*

See also: Nuclear Regulatory Commission

References

Allardice, Corbin, and Edward R. Trapnell, *The Atomic Energy Commission* (New York: Praeger, 1974).

Ford, Daniel F., *The Cult of the Atom: The Secrets of the Atomic Energy Commission* (New York: Simon & Schuster, 1982).

Lilienthal, David E., *Change, Hope and the Bomb* (Princeton, NJ: Princeton University Press, 1963).

ATOMIC MASS/NUMBER/WEIGHT

Atomic number is the number of protons present in the nucleus of an atom and is usually indicated by the symbol Z. The atomic mass number is the sum of the number of protons and neutrons in the nucleus of an atom and is usually denoted by the symbol A.

Atomic weight is the mass of an atom compared to the mass of the carbon 12 atom, which is defined, by international agreement, as having a mass of exactly 12.00000. Atomic weight usually refers to the average atomic weight of a given element with all its naturally occurring isotopes.

Atomic weight is sometimes referred to as atomic mass. Where atomic weight refers to the average atomic weight of an element, atomic mass is the term typically used to describe the weight of an individual isotope.

J. L. Proust in 1797 and John Dalton in the early 1800s both performed initial work with atomic weights. Proust theorized the law of definite proportions that states that the ratio of the weights of elements that make up a compound is constant. Dalton hypothesized that atoms of the same elements have the same atomic weight and that atoms of different elements have different atomic weights. He also created a scale of atomic weight based on hydrogen, which he set equal to 1. This early work with atomic weight eventually led to more accurate methods of measuring the atomic weight of elements and ultimately to D. I. Mendeleyev's 1869 table of elements arranged according to atomic weight.

The atomic mass number of an atom is equal to the atomic number (that is, the number of protons) plus the number of neutrons, usually denoted by the symbol N. Therefore, the equation for atomic mass is:

$$A = Z + N$$

As an example, the isotope uranium 235 has 92 protons and 143 neutrons. In this example, the atomic number is 92 and the atomic mass number is 235. Uranium 238 has 92 protons and 146 neutrons. In this example, the atomic number is 92 and the atomic mass number is 238. Therefore, different isotopes of the same element have the same atomic number but different atomic mass numbers based on the number of neutrons present in the nucleus.

Because atomic weight is defined as the mass of an atom relative to the mass of another atom, it is essentially the ratio of two masses and therefore unitless. However, the atomic mass unit, abbreviated "amu," has been defined as exactly one-twelfth of the mass of the carbon 12 atom. With this definition of the atomic mass unit, carbon 12 is equal to 12 amu, and all other atoms may be expressed in terms of atomic mass units relative to the carbon 12 standard.

Following the example above, the atomic mass for uranium 235 is approximately 235.0439 amu and the atomic mass for uranium 238 is approximately 238.0508 amu. The average atomic weight of uranium is 238.03 amu, because natural uranium is approximately 99.3 percent uranium 238 and 0.7 percent uranium 235.

—*Don Gillich*

References

Krane, Kenneth S., *Introductory Nuclear Physics* (New York: John Wiley and Sons, 1988).

Lamarsh, John R., and Anthony J. Baratta, *Introduction to Nuclear Engineering,* third edition (Upper Saddle River, NJ: Prentice-Hall, 2001).

ATOMS FOR PEACE

In 1953, President Dwight D. Eisenhower addressed the General Assembly of the United Nations proposing an "Atoms for Peace" program that would establish an international agency to promote the peaceful uses of atomic energy. To achieve this objective, the agency would allow some sharing of nuclear materials while instituting safeguards to ensure that the materials would not be diverted to military applications. The new policy represented a compromise between promising access to nuclear technology and restricting access to it. It led to the founding of the International Atomic Energy Agency (IAEA) in 1957, which remains the most visible organ of nuclear nonproliferation. The IAEA is an autonomous agency representing 128 member states and is operated by an international staff (*see* International Atomic Energy Agency).

Prior to 1953, U.S. policy under the Atomic Energy Act was to maintain nuclear secrecy to preserve a nuclear monopoly. As more nations acquired nuclear weapons capabilities, however (the Soviet Union and the United Kingdom, in particular, had tested nuclear explosives, and others were pursuing civil nuclear programs), the policy was revised so that the United States could participate in the global market for emerging commercial applications of nuclear technology.

Originally, the Atoms for Peace program was envisioned to have an international agency that would serve as a depository for excess nuclear materials that, in turn, could be shared with nonnuclear nations for peaceful purposes. This would serve to

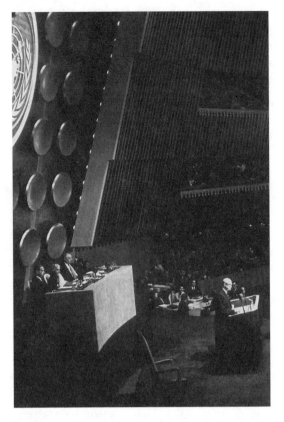

President Dwight D. Eisenhower delivers his "Atoms for Peace" speech to the United Nations, 1953. (Corel Corp.)

limit the stockpiles of nuclear countries while allowing nonnuclear nations the peaceful benefits of nuclear technology and materials, which would ideally encourage them to not seek a nuclear program of their own. Meanwhile, the application of safeguards on all shared materials would control the spread of materials to military programs.

The IAEA was assigned two specific tasks. First, it was intended to make technical and safety advancements available to member states and to join with organizations in identifying and promoting innovative applications. Second, the IAEA was supposed to administer an international safeguards system to control nuclear bilateral and multilateral exports.

By 1962, the Atoms for Peace program had supplied twenty-six nations with training, research reactors, and fissile materials. Critics, however, claimed that the program was responsible for actually spreading rather than restricting nuclear weapons technology, charging that its members took a casual approach toward safeguards. However, the establishment of the IAEA allowed for the implementation of the Nuclear Nonproliferation Treaty (NPT) following its signing in 1968. The tension between protecting national interests by restricting access to nuclear technology and materials and promoting their use for peaceful purposes could be difficult to navigate. This was a problem that had to be recognized before the NPT could be finalized. For states without a nuclear weapons program, the novel technology was desirable because of its purported economic and social advantages. Compromise was essential, however, if nuclear materials were to be controlled while the technology spread. This tension remains an essential piece of the structure of the nuclear nonproliferation regime in place today.

—*Jennifer Hunt Morstein*

See also: Nuclear Nonproliferation Treaty; Nuclear Weapons States

References

Gardner, Gary T., *Nuclear Nonproliferation: A Primer* (Boulder: Lynne Rienner, 1994).

Scheinman, Lawrence, *The International Atomic Energy Agency and World Nuclear Order* (Washington, DC: Resources for the Future, 1987).

Sokolski, Henry, "Atoms for Peace: A Non-Proliferation Primer?" *Arms Control,* vol. 10, no. 8, September 1980, pp. 199–230.

———, "Nonproliferation: The Last 50 Years." Presented at the American Political Science Association Annual Meeting, Chicago, 1995. Washington, DC: The Non-Proliferation Policy Education Center.

B

BACKFIRE BOMBER
See Bombers, Russian and Chinese Nuclear-Capable

BACKPACK NUCLEAR WEAPONS
Small, backpack nuclear weapons, also known as "man-portable nuclear weapons" or "special atomic demolition munitions," were developed during the Cold War and have become a matter of concern in recent years because of the danger of their use in a terrorist attack. With the miniaturization of nuclear devices in the late 1960s, the United States and the Soviet Union developed atomic mines that were man-portable. Some were so small (0.1 kiloton) that they fit into a backpack weighing only about 60 pounds. Others were designed for demolition work by combat engineers. The latter were carried in pieces by teams and could weigh in the hundreds of pounds, with an explosive yield of about 100 kilotons.

Although knowledge of Soviet weapons is limited, the man-portable devices were probably scheduled for use by Spetsnaz commando teams and KGB sabotage units against command and control installations, headquarters, and other high-value targets. They had a small nuclear core with a yield of about 10 kilotons. U.S. weapons were deployed with Special Forces units and engineer companies focusing on demolition work. Atomic mines or special demolition munitions were designed to create barriers to Soviet conventional force advances into Western Europe.

Suitcase nuclear devices became a matter of public concern after the Cold War when in 1997 Alexander Lebed, a retired Russian general and presidential hopeful, claimed that Russia could not account for 100 man-portable weapons. If they fell into terrorist hands, these weapons could be used to cause catastrophic damage. Other Russian and U.S. stockpiles of man-portable devices were eliminated in the early1990s.

—*Gilles Van Nederveen*

See also: Russian Nuclear Weapons and Doctrine; Tactical Nuclear Weapons

References

Gibson, James N., *Nuclear Weapons of the United States* (Arlington, TX: Schiffer, 1996).
Yablokov, Alexei, "Comments on Russia's Atomic Suitcase Bombs," *Frontline*, February 1999, available at http://www.pbs.org/wgbh/pages/frontline/shows/russia/suitcase/comments.html.

BALANCE OF TERROR
The concept of the "balance of terror" was predicated during the Cold War upon the idea that a stable deterrent relationship would result if both superpowers could inflict unsustainable destruction upon the other. In other words, the threat of mutually assured destruction would cause both sides to be cautious in their interaction, and thus a stable strategic relationship would emerge.

It was originally thought that deterrence depended upon the West's monopoly of the control of nuclear weapons. Even after the Soviet Union conducted its first test of a nuclear weapon in 1949, many political and military leaders in the West thought that the preponderance of U.S. nuclear forces, along with the geographical advantages of the United States and U.S. technological leadership, would keep any Soviet expansionist tendencies in check. Peace would not, therefore, benefit from a "balance of terror," because the West did not need to be deterred. However, developments in Soviet nuclear forces ultimately resulted in both sides achieving an assured-destruction capability, leading to a situation of "mutually assured destruction" (*see* Mutual Assured Destruction), or the "balance of terror."

Two alternative theories emerged to challenge the notion of a balance of terror. First, the idea of a *preventive* war was suggested at various points during the Cold War. This idea sought either to take advantage of the U.S. nuclear monopoly, or, later on, its overwhelming superiority, to preserve the West's strategic advantage. Once the Soviets developed an assured-destruction capability, these ideas fell into abeyance. Since the end of the Cold War, similar ideas have been espoused at times in discussions about the development of a nuclear capability by states such as Iraq, Iran, and North Korea.

The other alternative theory focused on the idea of a *preemptive* war. Although preventive war and preemptive war are similar concepts, preemption implies an attack launched against the opponent because it is thought that a strike by the other side is imminent.

—*Andrew M. Dorman*

See also: Cold War; Mutual Assured Destruction; Parity; Preemptive Attack

References

Freedman, Lawrence, *The Evolution of Nuclear Strategy,* third edition (New York: Palgrave Macmillan, 2003).

BALLISTIC MISSILE DEFENSE ORGANIZATION (BMDO)

The Ballistic Missile Defense Organization (BMDO) was an agency within the U.S. Department of Defense charged with providing a missile defense system to protect the United States, its forces deployed abroad, and its friends and allies from ballistic missile strikes. The agency's primary missions were to provide theater missile defense (TMD) in order to address the dangers associated with short- to medium-range missile systems in regional conflicts. It was also charged with creating a national missile defense (NMD), to defend against ballistic missile attacks against the United States, as well as advanced technology developments to enhance the performance of all TMD and NMD systems.

The predecessor to BMDO, the Strategic Defense Initiative Organization (SDIO), was created by President Ronald Reagan in March 1983. The original mission of the SDIO was to explore the technical feasibility of deploying missile defense systems in the hope that such defenses might be able to defend the United States from a large-scale attack by the Soviet Union's Strategic Rocket Forces. Following the end of the Cold War, President George H. W. Bush shifted the focus of SDIO from defending the United States against a major Soviet attack to protecting

A payload launch vehicle carrying a prototype interceptor is launched from the Kwajalein Missile Range on January 18, 2001, for a planned intercept of a ballistic missile target over the Pacific Ocean. (Department of Defense)

against a small-scale missile attack from terrorists or rogue states. In May 1993, President William Clinton changed the name of SDIO to BMDO to reflect the changing mission of the organization.

In January 2002, President George W. Bush again changed the name of the organization to the Missile Defense Agency (MDA). The National Missile Defense Act of 1999 called upon the United States to deploy a missile defense of the country as soon as technically possible, a responsibility that was inherited by the MDA. The MDA combines all aspects of the different missile defense systems programs (theater and national missile defenses) into a single program without regard for the recently abrogated Anti-Ballistic Missile Treaty. The new agency's director reports to the undersecretary of defense for acquisition, technology, and logistics.

—*Abe Denmark*

References

Duston, Dwight, *Ballistic Missile Defense Organization (BMDO): Technology Applications Report* (Collingdale, PA: Diane Publishing, October 1999).

Matthews, Ron, and John Treddenick, eds., *Managing the Revolution in Military Affairs* (New York: Palgrave Macmillan, September 2001).

Woolf, Amy F., "U.S. Nuclear Weapons: Changes in Policy and Force Structure," Report for Congress, Congressional Research Service, 28 October 2002.

BALLISTIC MISSILE DEFENSE
See Missile Defense

BALLISTIC MISSILE EARLY WARNING SYSTEM (BMEWS)

After the Soviets launched Sputnik in 1957, U.S. government authorities worried about a surprise missile attack on the continental United States. Thus, a more powerful set of radars, designed to warn U.S. and British strategic forces of transpolar missile attack, was added to the Distant Early Warning (DEW) Line. The program started with a prototype on Trinidad, and between 1960 and 1963 three sites were built. They were located at Thule AB, Greenland; Clear AFS, Alaska; and RAF Fylingdales Moor, Great Britain.

These radars provided the capability to detect an incoming intercontinental ballistic missile (ICBM) attack from the Russian heartland as well as submarine-launched ballistic missiles (SLBMs) fired from the Arctic and North Atlantic oceans 15 minutes before the strike was due to reach its target. Warning time to the United Kingdom from European-launched intermediate-range missiles was about 4 minutes.

The Ballistic Missile Early Warning System (BMEWS) also provided tracking data on most orbiting satellites. With the advent of warning satellites, the U.S. Air Force ensured that both space and terrestrial warning networks provided overlapping coverage and warning of foreign missile attack. The old mechanical radars were upgraded to solid-state, phased-array systems in 1987 to make the operation more effective and efficient, and they continue in operation for North American Aerospace Defense Command today.

—*Gilles Van Nederveen*

See also: Cheyenne Mountain; Distant Early Warning Line; Early Warning; Phased-Array Antenna

References

Bracken, Paul, *The Command and Control of Nuclear Forces* (New Haven, CT: Yale University Press, 1983).

Schaffel, Kenneth, *The Emerging Shield: The Air Force and the Evolution of Continental Air Defense, 1945–1960* (Washington, DC: Office of Air Force History, 1991).

BALLISTIC MISSILES

A ballistic missile is a weapon that relies on a power source to guide it into flight and then uses unguided free flight, its trajectory subject only to the forces of gravity and atmospheric drag, to reach its target. Ballistic missiles have provided a relatively fast, long-range delivery device for a number of weapons of mass destruction. There are several types of ballistic missiles. These may be characterized by range and source of launch. The main classifications are: short-range ballistic missiles (SRBMs), medium-range ballistic missiles (MRBMs), intermediate-range ballistic missiles (IRBMs), and intercontinental ballistic missile (ICBMs). An SRBM has a range of up to 1,000 kilometers (621 miles), MRBMs can reach from 1,000 to 3,000 kilometers (621 to 1,864 miles), IRBMs can threaten targets from 3,000 to 5,500 kilometers (1,864 to 3,418 miles), and ICBMs have ranges in excess of 5,500 kilometers. Ballistic missiles have various types of launch platforms, including fixed land sites such as silos, submarines (which fire submarine-launched ballistic missiles, or SLBMs), or mobile launchers such as trucks or rail cars. Ballistic missiles can carry a host of weapons, including both nuclear and conventional warheads.

A ballistic missile has several components. The missile is comprised of a propulsion system, a guidance system, a warhead (and a warhead bus, if it carries multiple warheads), and, in some cases, penetration aids. Engineers design ballistic missiles to use either liquid- or solid-fuel motors. Generally, solid-fuel systems have fewer support requirements and a higher rate of readiness than liquid-fuel systems. Most ballistic missiles also have an inertial guidance system to put the warhead close enough to destroy its target. A ballistic missile may have a single warhead or reentry vehicle (RV), or it may carry several RVs, either to hit several targets or to deploy more than one RV against a single target. Finally, a ballistic missile may possess penetration aids to ensure it defeats a ballistic missile defense system.

Today, several nations possess active missile systems or have the technical capability to develop ballistic missiles. The rationale for maintaining such weapons often includes national pride as well as a

Distant Early Warning Line station on Barter Island in the Beaufort Sea, off Alaska. (Scott T. Smith/Corbis)

military requirement for the means to deliver a significant strategic attack in a cost-effective manner. Missile proliferation, in terms of systems and technology, has increased in recent years as nations seek means to expand their security and countries use missile exports for financial gain.

History and Background

Development of the first modern ballistic missiles began before World War II. German Army engineers and scientists in 1930, under then Captain (later General) Walter Dornberger, started research to develop a liquid-fueled, long-range rocket to replace heavy artillery. By 1932, Dornberger had convinced Wernher von Braun, later a key contributor to America's space program, to join his development team. Through the 1930s, the German military designed, developed, and tested a host of missile components. These efforts led to the introduction of the Vergeltungswaffe 2 ("vengeance weapon" 2 or V-2; the German designation was A-4). The V-2 was first launched successfully on June 6, 1942. Full-scale production soon began on the 47-foot-tall missile. These missiles carried a 1,620-pound high-explosive warhead composed of cast amatol and were powered by a liquid oxygen and methyl alcohol

motor that sped the rocket to a maximum range of 205 miles. The German Army eventually launched 3,255 V-2s against targets in Western Europe.

The V-2's ability to conduct strategic bombardment and defy Allied countermeasures was not lost on American and Soviet political and military leaders. The introduction of the nuclear age also played a significant role in the search for ways to deliver this new weapon. During the Cold War, the United States and the Soviet Union started an extensive program to develop operational ballistic missiles. Immediately after World War II, available technology did not exist to launch missile attacks from the continental United States against the Soviet Union or vice versa. Likewise, early missiles could not carry a sufficiently large payload to handle first-generation nuclear weapons that weighed several tons.

The United States initially focused on strategic bombers, cruise missiles, and shorter-range missiles requiring overseas basing to deliver nuclear weapons. The U.S. Air Force funded the Consolidated Vultee MX-774 project in 1946, which concluded with three test launches in 1948. This program's success sparked interest in building an ICBM. The first American ICBM was named the Atlas. In the meantime, the country focused its attention on fielding SRBM and

IRBM systems. The first SRBMs were the army's Corporal and Honest John rockets. These weapons were tactical delivery weapons that had very limited ranges. The liquid-fueled Corporal, first available for field training in 1954, had limited operational capability owing to its significant logistical requirements and the tendency of its radar/radio guidance control system to jam. The Honest John was a nuclear-armed, solid-fuel system designed to support battlefield operations.

Technological advancements and strategic demands pushed U.S. efforts to develop ICBMs. The country still required an interim capability to deliver nuclear weapons. IRBM and MRBM systems gave the nation a means to launch an attack directly on the Soviet Union or its allies. These relatively inaccurate weapon systems were primarily aimed at enemy cities and large concentrations of military forces. The army's Redstone and Jupiter systems and the air force's Thor ballistic missiles were deployed to offer a limited means to deliver nuclear weapons, but research to develop these systems also proved helpful in supporting the nascent U.S. space program. The army's Pershing I, a battlefield-deployable MRBM system, was first fielded in 1962 and served until 1985, when it was replaced by the Pershing II. The Pershing II was withdrawn from service in 1989 following the 1987 signing of the Intermediate-Range Nuclear Forces (INF) Treaty.

U.S. Intercontinental Ballistic Missiles
The United States developed four ICBM models. The first, Atlas, was a one-and-a-half-stage missile that had a maximum range of about 9,000 miles. It carried an RV with a yield of 4 megatons. Atlas D first went on alert on October 21, 1959, and the last Atlas F was retired on June 22, 1964. The two-stage, liquid-fueled Titan I ICBM started development in 1955 and began operations on September 28, 1963. An updated version, Titan II, carried the largest nuclear weapon ever deployed by the United States, with a yield of 9 megatons. The last Titan II was retired from active duty in 1987. The first solid-fueled ICBM, Minuteman, was a great advancement in reliability and logistical support. Minuteman IA was introduced into service on July 23, 1962, and the series has been improved several times in the intervening years. The Minuteman was the most successful ICBM developed by the United States. At its zenith, crews monitored 1,000 active Minuteman

missile sites, with some models carrying three RVs. A single-warhead Minuteman (limited by various arms control treaties and agreements) still serves today. The most recent ICBM deployed in the United States was the Peacekeeper, a three-stage, solid-fuel system with a fourth that utilizes a storable liquid fuel. The Peacekeeper was capable of carrying up to ten RVs. It had its first test flight in 1983, was deployed in 1986, and began a three-year retirement program in 2002.

Soviet/Russian Ballistic Missiles
The Soviet Union's ballistic missile program first concentrated on copying and improving on the German V-2. This effort led to the SS-1 Scud, which has survived, in slightly more advanced versions, to this day. This SRBM has been the most widely exported ballistic missile in the world and has the capability of carrying either conventional warheads or payloads containing weapons of mass destruction. These weapons were originally designed as tactical battlefield weapons, but some countries now use them as strategic weapons. With the SS-1's success, the Soviet Union conducted an intensive program to improve its ballistic missile program in order to develop a strategic counter to America's ballistic missile and strategic bomber forces. The Soviet military thus designed, produced, and operated a series of tactical ballistic missiles mounted on various types of mobile launchers. The SS-1 entered service in 1955 with a small-yield nuclear device, and Soviet development of several IRBM and MRBM systems continued through the 1960s. Although the Soviets built these systems, they had a difficult time developing their first ICBM, the SS-6 Sapwood, and were forced to rely on their IRBM and MRBM force. Some argue that the Soviet deployment of these relatively shorter-ranged missiles on Cuba in October 1962 represented a move to improve the Soviet Union's strategic position vis-à-vis the United States and provide a counterbalance to the development of the Atlas and Titan ICBMs.

Eventually, Soviet engineers developed many ICBM models. As in the United States, Soviet programs evolved from liquid-fueled to solid-fueled systems. The Soviets' first successful ICBM was the SS-7 Saddler, which was deployed in 1961 and served until 1979. The Soviets then developed a series of systems, from the SS-8 up to the SS-25. The SS-18 Satan was the largest Cold War ICBM deployed by either side. The missile was designed to carry a single 20-megaton yield nuclear weapon or ten 500-kiloton RVs. The last Soviet ICBM was the road-mobile, single-warhead SS-25 Sickle, deployed in 1982. Since the dissolution of the Soviet Union, Russia has introduced the SS-27 Topol, a solid-fueled silo or road-mobile missile that possesses countermeasures to ballistic missile defenses.

Submarine-Launched Ballistic Missiles

SLBM development progressed in both nations as well. The United States first used submarine-launched cruise missiles but produced Polaris ballistic missiles in 1960. The first Polaris SLBM had a range of about 1,600 miles. These missiles originally had a single warhead, but later versions had three. The U.S. Navy later improved the Polaris with the longer-range Poseidon, which carried ten RVs. Poseidon began service in 1971. The current U.S. SLBM is the Trident, which entered service in 1979 as C-4. The Trident II D5 has improved range, yield, and accuracy that approach the parameters of land-based ICBMs. The Soviet Navy started deployment of SLBMs in 1955 with an SS-1 converted for naval use. The Soviets went to sea with a number of SLBMs. The first to have ICBM range was its SS-N-8 in 1971. Today, the Russian Navy operates the SS-N-18, the SS-N-20, and the SS-N-23, all containing multiple RVs. The SS-N-23 is the only solid-fueled SLBM and has ten RVs.

Other Countries

During the Cold War, other nations also acquired ballistic missiles. The United Kingdom acquired Thor IRBMs and the Polaris and Trident SLBMs from the United States. It eliminated its Thor force in 1964. France developed its own nuclear ballistic missile force, which included land-based IRBMs and SLBMs. It still maintains its SLBM force today, although it retired its IRBMs in the 1990s. The Soviet Union sold Scud technology to a number of countries throughout Eastern Europe and to North Korea. North Korea, in turn, has sold this technology to other nations. North Korea is one of world's largest proliferators of missile technology. India, Pakistan, and Iran have sought to acquire MRBMs or IRBMs to deliver weapons of mass destruction. China has developed a range of ballistic missiles, from SRBMs to ICBMs, and is attempting to deploy an SLBM force.

Accuracy

Missile characteristics such as payload, range, and reliability are important. However, accuracy may be the most important consideration in determining the military value of a ballistic missile. Missileers use "circular error probable (CEP)" as a means to measure performance. CEP is the radius of a circle within which half of all weapons targeted for the center are expected to fall. Many developing nations have ballistic missiles that might have a CEP of several miles, even if fired from only 100 miles away. U.S. missiles, however, have sophisticated guidance systems allowing them to strike targets across continents with a CEP of only a few yards.

Current Status

More than two dozen nations possess ballistic missiles. The United States and Russia have the largest arsenals of ICBMs and SLBMs. Since the introduction of the Scud, some twenty-nine nations have purchased or used its technology to develop their own Scud versions. The vast majority of these are SRBMs. However, a number of nations seek longer-range ballistic missiles that can strike targets within their region and potentially attack global targets. Several nations seeking the capability of launching satellites may hope to use satellite boosters as ballistic missiles to carry weapons payloads.

North Korea, Iran, and Pakistan are the leading nations seeking to improve their ballistic missile technologies. North Korea, in particular, has made the greatest advances toward developing ICBMs. China and Russia also have active ICBM and SLBM programs.

—*Clay Chun*

See also: British Nuclear Forces and Doctrine; Chinese Nuclear Weapons; Depressed Trajectory; Downloading; Indian Nuclear Weapons Program; Iranian Nuclear Weapons Program; Missile Defense; North Korean Nuclear Weapons Program; Pakistani Nuclear Forces; Reentry Vehicle; Russian Nuclear Forces and Doctrine; United States Nuclear Forces and Doctrine; Warhead

References

Gibson, James Norris, *The History of the US Nuclear Arsenal* (Greenwich, CT: Brompton, 1989).

Lee, R. G., T. K. Garland-Collins, D. E. Johnson, E. Archer, C. Sparkes, G. M. Moss, and A. W. Mowat, *Guided Weapons*, third edition (London: Brassey's, 1998).

Lennox, Duncan, ed., *Jane's Strategic Weapon Systems* (London: Jane's Information Group, 1969).
Neufeld, Jacob, *Ballistic Missiles* (Washington, DC: Office of Air Force History, 1990).

BARUCH PLAN
On June 14, 1946, the U.S. representative to the recently created United Nations Atomic Energy Commission, Bernard M. Baruch, presented a U.S. proposal for controlling nuclear weapons. This was the first nuclear arms control proposal in history and drew on the work of a team led by then Undersecretary of State Dean Acheson and David Lilienthal, soon to become the first chairman of the U.S. Atomic Energy Commission. The major technical contributions to the plan were made by J. Robert Oppenheimer, the physicist who had been the science leader of the World War II project to develop the atomic bomb (*see* Manhattan Project).

Aside from the technical details of the Baruch Plan, the event was significant in several important respects. It represented a difficult decision by the United States to give up its sole possession of the atomic bomb if an acceptable political regime to control the new weapon could be established. It sought to pursue arms control through the multilateral channels of the newly created United Nations instead of first negotiating details bilaterally with the Soviet Union. It recognized the uniquely threatening character of nuclear weapons by proposing to set aside the Security Council veto for nuclear matters. And when the plan was debated, the question of the legitimacy of anticipatory defense was raised at the United Nations for the first time.

Recognizing that the key to nuclear weapons production was obtaining fissile materials, the plan called for creation of an International Atomic Energy Development Authority, to which would be entrusted all phases of the development and use of atomic energy, starting with the raw material. When an adequate system for control of atomic energy, including the renunciation of the bomb as a weapon, had been agreed to and put into operation, and when sanctions had been set up for violations of the rules of control (violations that would be stigmatized as international crimes), then national manufacture of atomic bombs would stop, existing bombs would be disposed of pursuant to terms of the treaty, and the Authority would possess full information on how to produce atomic energy.

The Soviet Union objected to the phased approach, insisting that stockpiles first should be destroyed and possession or use of nuclear weapons characterized as an international crime, prior to establishing a technical control regime. Talks quickly stalemated as the Cold War set in. Although some critics have argued that with a different approach to the negotiations the United States might have secured a compromise, most scholars of the Baruch Plan today recognize that Soviet leader Joseph Stalin was set on acquiring nuclear weapons, negotiations notwithstanding.

Nuclear arms control progressed in later years through bilateral and multilateral channels and remains one of the main issues on the international agenda.

—*Michael Wheeler*

See also: Atomic Energy Commission
References
Acheson, Dean, *Present at the Creation* (W. W. Norton, 1969).
U.S. Department of State, *The International Control of Atomic Energy: Growth of a Policy* (Washington, DC: U.S. Government Printing Office, 31 March 1947).

BASELINE INSPECTION
See Verification

BETA PARTICLE
See Radiation; Radiation Absorbed Dose (RAD)

BIKINI ISLAND
Bikini Island is an atoll in the Ralik chain of the Marshall Islands in the Western Pacific Ocean that was used for early atomic testing by the United States. North of the equator and 225 miles northwest of Kwajalein, the atoll consists of islands only 7 feet above sea level forming a ring around a 15- by 25-mile lagoon, comprising 2 square miles of dry land. Before World War II, the atoll was known as Escholtz Atoll. It was occupied by Japan until 1944 and administered by the United States from 1947 to 1979 as part of the Trust Territory of the Pacific Islands under a United Nations trusteeship. In 1979, it became a part of the Republic of the Marshall Islands.

In 1946, Bikini became the site of Operation Crossroads, a joint military and scientific project to determine the impact of nuclear bombs on naval vessels. The 166 native Micronesians living on the atoll had to be relocated to Kili Island, about 500

Underwater atomic blast in Bikini Lagoon, Marshall Islands, July 1946. (Library of Congress)

miles southeast. On July 1, 1946, Bikini became the site of the world's first peacetime atomic weapon explosion. With eighty retired battleships and aircraft carriers as targets, a 20-kiloton atomic bomb was dropped from an airplane. On July 25, 1946, the world's first underwater atomic explosion took place nearby, raising a column of radioactive water that sank nine ships.

From 1954 through 1958, Bikini and Enewetak Atoll, which is located about 150 miles southwest of Bikini, became the Pacific Proving Ground for the U.S. Atomic Energy Commission. Tests included thermonuclear devices, and in 1956, the first hydrogen bomb was dropped near Bikini by a U.S. airplane. The tests resulted in severe radioactive contamination of the atoll.

In the 1960s, some of the original islanders tried to return to Bikini, but the radiation levels proved unsafe. In 1969, the United States began work on a long-term project to reclaim the islands. The islanders filed a suit against the government in 1985, and as a result of this action, the U.S. government funded a cleanup that started in 1991. The first radiation cleanup project was completed in 1998. Although radiation levels were too high for residence, in 1996 the Bikini Lagoon was reopened for scuba diving, and in 1998 sport fishing was again permitted.

—*Frannie Edwards*

See also: Kwajalein Atoll

Reference

Bauer, E., *The History of World War II: The Full Story of the World's Greatest Conflict* (New York: Military Press, 1984).

BOMBERS, RUSSIAN AND CHINESE NUCLEAR-CAPABLE

During the Cold War, both the Soviet Union and the United States developed a "Triad" of nuclear delivery systems consisting of intercontinental ballistic missiles (ICBMs), submarine-launched ballistic missiles (SLBMs), and manned bombers. Although in Soviet doctrine the ICBM became the primary means of nuclear deterrence, for many years the Soviet Union's only means of delivering nuclear weapons was the manned bomber. Even as aircraft fell out of favor as the main delivery system, the Soviet Air Force continued to maintain a heavy bomber fleet, and Russia, as the successor state to the Soviet nuclear arsenal, still maintains a bomber fleet, though it is only a fraction of the size of the Soviet force at its height.

Chinese nuclear doctrine, which calls for minimal deterrence, relies heavily on ballistic missiles as delivery vehicles. Chinese officials have announced that in the future they do not intend to rely on bombers as nuclear delivery vehicles. Nevertheless, China maintains a small force of theater bombers that could be used to deliver nuclear-capable gravity weapons.

Soviet Union/Russian Bombers

Following the detonation of its first atomic bomb on August 29, 1949, the Soviet Union possessed nuclear weapons but lacked the means to deliver them. Until the development of a useful ICBM, the Soviets relied on a series of manned bombers to supply a nuclear deterrent capability.

Tupolev Tu-4 (NATO Designation: Bull)

As early as September 1943, the aviation design bureau headed by A. N. Tupolev was authorized to start work on a new strategic bomber based on the American B-29 Superfortress. The result was the Tupolev Tu-4 (NATO designation: Bull). The Tu-4 entered series production in 1947 and entered active service in 1949. With a range of only 6,200 kilometers (km) (3,348 nautical miles [nm]), it could not reach the continental United States from interior Soviet bases. While aerial refueling technology, and some efforts at intermediate basing on the Arctic icecap, provided some marginal enhancement of the Tu-4's capabilities, a completely new aircraft was needed to perform the strategic nuclear strike mission

Myasishchev M-4 (NATO Designation: Bison)

Production of V. I. Myasishchev's M-4 turbojet bomber (NATO Designation: Bison) began in 1954. In 1956, the M-4 underwent a major redesign that provided the aircraft with improved engines that extended its range to 12,000 km (6,480 nm). Only 116 Bison bombers of all versions were produced through 1960, and there were never more than 60 aircraft in the operational inventory at any one time.

Tupolev Tu-95 (NATO Designation: Bear)

While Myasishchev was working on his turbojet design, Tupolev was working on a fundamentally different aircraft. Tupolev's research had shown that the same performance as a turbojet could be achieved with a turboprop engine. Entering service in 1956, the Tu-95 (NATO Designation: Bear) was the Soviet Union's first intercontinental bomber; its turboprop engines gave it greater range than the jet engines of the day. Spawning nine different variants, the Tu-95 continues in service today.

Tupolev Tu-160 (NATO Designation: Blackjack)

By the late 1970s, the bomber leg of the Soviet Triad was clearly the least important, behind the ICBM force and the SLBM fleet, and in many respects it was approaching obsolescence. Responding to the Kremlin's call for a new supersonic bomber, Tupolev developed plans for a variable geometry wing aircraft called Aircraft 70 (NATO Designation: Blackjack). Very similar in appearance to the U.S. B-1A, though larger and heavier, the new design first flew in 1981. Eventually designated as the Tu-160, the Blackjack entered series production in 1984. Although original plans called for 100 aircraft, production halted in 1992 following the collapse of the Soviet Union after only 36 aircraft had been built. Production resumed in 1998, and the first new aircraft entered service in May 2000.

Bomber Development Lags

The primacy of Long Range Aviation in the strategic nuclear force began to decline in the late 1950s. U.S. B-29 losses during the Korean War suggested that bombers could not survive modern air defenses. The Soviets also were concerned about command and control once the bombers left Soviet airspace and the pilots controlled the release of nuclear weapons. These issues, coupled with the successful launch of intercontinental-capable ballistic missiles, spelled the end of the primacy of the Soviet bomber force.

At the same time that new bomber designs were being developed, advances in cruise missile technology promised to give the bomber new life as a strategic nuclear delivery vehicle. In 1968, the Soviets conducted a study to examine future trends in strategic weapons. It focused on the use of a small, subsonic weapon on the premise that a smaller weapon would allow a delivery system to carry more. The result was the Kh-55 air-launched cruise missile (ALCM) (NATO designation: AS-15 Kent). The Soviets, however, now needed to develop an aircraft capable of delivering the cruise missile system. The Tu-160 was the aircraft most likely to carry the new missile, but in the late 1970s and early 1980s that aircraft was still undergoing flight tests. Considering it infeasible to upgrade the existing Tu-95M to carry the Kh-55, the Soviets opted to build a new aircraft, the Tu-95MS (NATO designation: Bear H), based on the Tu-142 currently in service as an antisubmarine warfare and maritime reconnaissance aircraft. Although only a low-cost, stopgap measure until the Tu-160 was brought on line, the Tu-95MS has shouldered the cruise missile carrier burden since the Soviet collapse and the end of Tu-160 production.

Theater Bombers

While developing its intercontinental bomber force, the Soviet Union also built a theater bomber force capable of threatening targets close to home. Tupolev began designing a replacement for the Tu-4 while work continued on the Tu-95 intercontinental bomber. Serial production for the design, which became the Tu-16 (NATO Designation: Badger), began in 1953 and ended in 1963 after 1,509 aircraft had been built. Soon after its delivery to line units in 1954, the Tu-16 became the primary Soviet theater bomber, serving with Soviet Air Force and Soviet Naval Aviation units until its retirement in 1993. The Tu-16 was a very successful design and underwent seven modifications that adapted the aircraft to carry improved weapons, particularly missiles. The Tu-16A was designed to carry free-fall nuclear bombs. In addition, the Soviets developed a unique wingtip-to-wingtip refueling system for the aircraft, modifying some Tu-16s, known as Tu-16Zs, to serve in the tanker role.

After Tu-16 serial production began in 1953, Tupolev began work on a new supersonic bomber design. Billed as the replacement for the Tu-16, the Tu-22 (NATO designation: Blinder) was, in fact, capable of carrying a similar payload to the Tu-16, but only to a slightly greater range. Before production ended in 1969, 300 Tu-22s were built. Ukraine is believed to be the only country currently operating the aircraft.

Despite his lack of success improving the Tu-22's performance, Tupolev continued to work on a new medium-range bomber. The result was an aircraft with variable sweep wings and a subsonic range claimed to be 6,000–7,000 km (3,254–3,780 nm). First flown in 1969, the Tu-22M (NATO designation: Backfire) was adopted by both the Soviet Air Force and Naval Aviation in 1976. The aircraft was a subject of controversy during early Strategic Arms Limitation Talks (SALT I). The Soviets agreed to remove the aircraft's air refueling probes and to limit production to thirty aircraft per year as part of the SALT I agreement.

Russia currently maintains a bomber inventory including 74 Tu-95MSs, 15 Tu-160s, and 117 Tu-22Ms, a mere shadow of the old Soviet bomber force. Plagued by shortages of spare parts and fuel, the bomber force finds it difficult to keep its aircraft flyable. These shortages have contributed to a training crisis among bomber crews. In 1998, Russian bomber crews averaged only about twenty-one hours of flying time per year, compared to twenty-five hours per *month* in the U.S. Air Force. Still, the bomber force remains a key portion of Russia's nuclear deterrent capability. Russia also acknowledged the importance of airpower in rapid reaction operations. To this end, Russia reorganized Long Range Aviation into the 37th Air Army in 1998. This organization is tasked with the delivery of both nuclear and conventional ALCMs (*see* Russian Nuclear Forces and Doctrine; Strategic Forces).

Chinese Bombers

Founded in 1949, the People's Liberation Army Air Force (PLAAF) received significant Soviet aid prior to the 1960 Sino-Soviet split. Having only 100 aircraft at its birth, the PLAAF began to receive this aid as a result of its large losses (2,000 aircraft) during the Korean War. The Soviets rebuilt World War II Chinese aircraft production facilities in Shenyang and Harbin, equipping them with the latest in Soviet production technology. These facilities had produced combat aircraft in the 1930s and 1940s but had been stripped by the Soviets in 1945. At the same time, the Soviets provided production licenses, drawings, and tools: everything the Chinese needed to build aircraft. As part of this exchange, China received licenses to produce its two main bomber aircraft, the Hong-5 and the Hong-6.

China's decision to develop an independent strategic nuclear force was probably made by early 1956. In 1964, China detonated its first nuclear weapon, and within months it established the Second Artillery, the organization responsible for controlling China's ballistic missile forces. In 1966, China launched its first medium-range ballistic missile (MRBM). It was capable of carrying a 20-kiloton nuclear warhead. Meanwhile, the Hong-6, based on the Soviet Tu-16 medium-range bomber, entered service in 1968 and reached an inventory of 100 aircraft by 1972. Capable of carrying a single 1-megaton bomb, the Hong-6 force grew only slowly, with developers emphasizing qualitative improvements over quantity, while China continued to improve its ballistic missile force. The decision to focus on ballistic missile forces over bomber forces may have reflected concerns over bomber survivability. Improvements in air defense capabilities likely suggested to the Chinese that the manned bomber would not make it to the target.

Table B-1: Russian Nuclear Bombers

Aircraft Models	Tu-22M (NATO: Backfire) Tu-22MO Tu-22M-1 Tu-22M-2 Tu-22M-3	Tu-95MS (NATO: Bear H) Tu-95MS6 Tu-95MS16	Tu-160 (NATO: Blackjack) Tu-160
Crew	4	7	4
Speed	Cruise: 485 kts Max Level: Mach 1.88 (1,080 kts) at high altitude	Cruise: 384 kts Max Level: 447 kts at 38,000 ft	Cruise: 518 kts at 45,000 ft Max Level: Mach 2.05 (1,200 kts) at 48,000 ft
Combat Radius	1,300 nm (subsonic high-low-high mission profile)	3,455 nm (unrefuelled) 4,480 nm (with one refueling)	1,080 nm at Mach 1.5
Defensive Armament	2 X tail mounted twin Gsh-23 23mm cannon	1 or 2 X tail mounted 23mm cannon	None
Weapons Load	3 X Kh-22 missiles or 52,910 lbs conventional bombs or mines internally and on wings or 6 X Kh-15P SRAMs	Tu-95MS16:16 X Kh-55 or RVK-500B ALCMs Tu-95MS6: 6 X Kh-55 or RVK-500B	12 X Kh-55 ALCMs OR 12-24 Kh-15P SRAMs
Air Refueling Capable	No	Yes	Yes

China now maintains a small bomber fleet while emphasizing the other elements of the Triad. It has a bomber force of 40 Hong-5s and 110 Hong-6s; only about 100 Hong-6s, however, are part of China's nuclear force, and some sources indicate that all Hong-5 aircraft are now dedicated to training. Some A-5 Fantan short-range attack aircraft are also used in the nuclear delivery role.

Technical Details

Emerging Technologies

Russia currently operates the Tu-95MS, Tu-160, and Tu-22M, as shown in Table B-1. China currently operates only two medium bomber aircraft: the Hong-5 and Hong-6. Technical details of these aircraft are shown in Table B-2.

There have been rumors of a new Russian bomber since the early 1980s. Little is known about this aircraft, although it is believed to incorporate low observable technology and have two thrust-vectoring turbofans. Russia's lack of hard currency, however, has led some observers to believe that military aircraft are increasingly designed for export. Security concerns make it unlikely that Russia would offer a nuclear-capable bomber for export, thus pushing further bomber development into the

more distant future. It is more likely Russia will upgrade existing aircraft, improve weapons delivery capabilities, and develop new cruise missiles to improve strategic bombers' standoff capability.

Table B-2: Chinese Nuclear Bombers

Aircraft	Hongzhaji-5/ Hong-5/B-5 "Beagle"	Hongzhaji-6/ Hong-6/B-6 "Badger"
Soviet Equivalent	Il-28 (NATO: Beagle)	Tu-16 (NATO: Badger)
Models	H-5	H-6A B-6D
Crew	3	6
Speed	Cruise: 415 kts Max Level: 487 kts at 14,760 ft	Cruise: 424 kts
Range	1,176 nm at 32,800 feet	2,320 nm
Defensive Armament	2 X forward firing 23mm NR-23 cannon 2 X tail mounted 23mm NR-23 cannon	6 or 7 guns mounted in dorsal, ventral, and tail positions

At one time strategic bombers made up 45 percent of the Chinese nuclear delivery capability, but changes in Chinese nuclear doctrine in the late 1960s and early 1970s shifted the emphasis on nuclear delivery toward intercontinental and short-range ballistic missiles. By the late 1990s, further doctrinal evolution suggested the Chinese intended to rely increasingly on submarine-launched ballistic missiles. In addition, the economic importance of China's space program may also have influenced the Chinese decision to base strategic nuclear modernization efforts on improved missile technology. Although the Chinese expressed an interest in acquiring the Tu-22M from Russia, as of 2004 there were no indications that the Soviets will sell the bomber. Instead, China is concentrating on developing newer fighter and fighter-bomber aircraft.

—*Rob Melton*

See also: Chinese Nuclear Weapons; Russian Nuclear
  Forces and Doctrine; Strategic Forces

References

Federation of American Scientists website,
  http://www.fas.org.
Gurtov, Mel, and Byong-Moo Hwang, *China's Security:
  The New Role of the Military* (Boulder: Lynne
  Rienner, 1998).
International Institute for Strategic Studies, *The Military
  Balance, 2001–2002* (London: Oxford University
  Press, 2001).
Jane's All the World's Aircraft, 2002–2003 (Alexandria,
  VA: Jane's Information Group, 2003).
Lin, Cong-Pin, *China's Nuclear Weapons Strategy:
  Tradition with Evolution* (Lexington, MA: Lexington
  Books, 1988).
Podvig, Pavel, ed., *Russian Strategic Nuclear Forces*
  (Cambridge, MA: MIT Press, 2001).
Zaloga, Steven J., *The Kremlin's Nuclear Sword: The Rise
  and Fall of Russia's Strategic Nuclear Forces,
  1945–2000* (Washington, DC: Smithsonian
  Institution Press, 2002).

BOMBERS, U.S. NUCLEAR-CAPABLE

Bombers are long-range aircraft that can carry large amounts of nuclear or conventional ordnance. The United States has designed, developed, produced, and operated several types of bomber aircraft for the primary mission of delivering nuclear weapons. During the Cold War, bombers, along with intercontinental ballistic missiles (ICBMs) and submarine-launched ballistic missiles (SLBMs), were a key element of America's strategic "Triad," serving as the U.S. nuclear deterrent against Soviet aggression. National leaders created specialized organizations, infrastructure, support aircraft, and systems devoted solely toward ensuring that these aircraft could reach an adversary's homeland and drop a nuclear device or launch a nuclear-armed missile against a foe. The strategic bomber was the first weapons platform to shoulder the burden of carrying nuclear weapons, and it did so for years even as ballistic missiles were deployed. Advances such as stealth technology, jet engines, and the advent of aerial refueling continue to make long-range bombers an important nuclear delivery system.

History and Background

The evolution of nuclear-armed bombers began with the use of the Boeing B-29 Superfortress, an aircraft designed in World War II to carry conventional weapons. Crews flew this aircraft to drop the 13-kiloton Little Boy atomic bomb that destroyed Hiroshima on August 6, 1945, and the 23-kiloton-yield Fat Man that shattered Nagasaki eight days later. The B-29 and a variant, the B-50, then served as the U.S. Air Force's only nuclear-capable bombers, under the Strategic Air Command, well into the early 1950s. Despite improvements to the propeller engine aircraft and the refinement of operations such as aerial refueling, they were too slow to avoid jet interceptors and lacked the range to hit targets from bases in the continental United States (*see* Fat Man; Little Boy).

The air force developed several aircraft to replace the B-29 and B-50 during the 1950s. The massive Consolidated B-36 Peacemaker was a six-engine propeller aircraft that was the first truly intercontinental bomber, and it was the largest bomber ever to enter operational service. Later versions had four auxiliary jets for a total of ten engines. The aircraft had a 10,000-mile range. The U.S. Air Force, which had to penetrate increasingly sophisticated Soviet air defense systems, needed a more responsive bomber fleet, however, and started work on a jet bomber. The Boeing B-47 Stratojet was a swept-winged craft that first flew operational missions in 1951. Using aerial refueling, this aircraft had intercontinental range. More B-47s have been produced in the years since World War II than any other bomber. The air force also designed, produced, and deployed the longest-serving bomber, the Boeing B-52 Stratofortress. It accepted the first production B-52 in

B-52G Stratofortress carrying air-launched cruise missiles. (Department of Defense)

1954. The B-52 has eight turbofan engines and is capable of dropping nuclear and conventional gravity weapons and guided missiles. This aircraft stood nuclear alert for decades and served as a conventional bomber in conflicts from Vietnam to Afghanistan. Its latest variant, the B-52H, remains on duty today.

Throughout the 1950s and 1960s, the U.S. Air Force and U.S. Navy also designed or deployed nuclear-capable jet aircraft with relatively limited operational ranges and payloads. Development of smaller nuclear bombs allowed tactical aircraft to carry such weapons to strike a host of potential targets. The U.S. Air Force purchased the North American B-45 Tornado, a British-designed Martin Marietta B-57 Intruder, and the Douglas B-66 Destroyer. The U.S. Navy deployed the Douglas A-3 Skywarrior (the U.S. Air Force B-66 was a variant of this aircraft) and the supersonic North American A-5 Vigilante. The A-3 and A-5 were carrier-based aircraft and provided the U.S. Navy with a strategic bomber force.

As Soviet air defenses improved, the U.S. Air Force demanded bombers that flew at higher speeds and altitudes. These requirements led to the introduction of the supersonic Convair B-58 Hustler in 1960. Rapid advances in Soviet surface-to-air missiles, radar, and improved jet interceptors soon negated the plane's ability to outfly air defenses. In addition, the plane's continuing operational problems forced the service to retire the jet within ten years. Advancements in ballistic missiles, cost, technical problems, and the change in Soviet defense capabilities also forced the John F. Kennedy administration to cancel the ambitious North American B-70 supersonic bomber about the same time.

In the 1970s, the sole supersonic operational bomber deployed by the United States was a version of the controversial General Dynamics F-111 fighter. The FB-111 Aardvark could reach speeds of Mach 2.5 but had a much smaller payload than the B-58. The U.S. Air Force purchased FB-111s to replace older B-52s and the retiring B-58. They served as an interim bomber force until the service's advanced B-1 was made operational.

The Rockwell International B-1 Lancer was controversial from its program start. Technical concerns, cost, and political debate forced its cancellation by President Jimmy Carter on June 30, 1977. President Ronald Reagan reversed this decision in 1981. The aircraft was redesigned to become a penetrating bomber with some stealth capability. Only 100 were built as a short-term replacement for a more advanced radar-evading aircraft, the Northrop B-2 Spirit. The B-2 was designed to defeat enemy air defenses and deploy conventional or nuclear weapons. Post–Cold War demobilization forced severe program cuts, and the U.S. Air Force purchased only 21 operational aircraft—at a cost of approximately $2 billion each.

U.S. Bombers Today

U.S. Air Force bombers today can deploy a range of nuclear weapons, including the AGM-86 air-launched cruise missile, the AGM-129 advanced cruise missile, and a number of gravity-delivered nuclear bombs. Serving B-2 and B-52 aircraft possess a nuclear capability. Owing to arms control restrictions, the B-1 can only carry conventional weapons. As of January 2003, the U.S. Air Force maintains 85 B-1s (plus one in the Air National Guard), 21 B-2s, and 85 B-52s (plus 9 in the U.S. Air Force Reserve) in its inventory.

Currently, the Air Force does not have a bomber replacement in development for the B-1, B-2, or B-52. Continual improvements in avionics, standoff weapons, service life, and other modifications have extended the operational service of all three bomber types.

—*Clay Chun*

See also: Airborne Alert; Stealth Bomber (B-2 Spirit); Strategic Air Command and Strategic Command; United States Nuclear Forces and Doctrine

References

Brown, Michael E., *Flying Blind* (Ithaca, NY: Cornell University Press, 1992).

Knaack, Marcelle Size, *Post–World War II Bombers* (Washington, DC: Office of Air Force History, 1988).

BOOST-PHASE INTERCEPT

The term "boost-phase intercept" (BPI) refers to programs, strategies, and systems designed to intercept ballistic missiles during the course of their initial phase of flight, beginning with ignition and lasting through that period of time during which the missile's stages are firing and providing thrust. The boost phase can last anywhere from 20 to 240 seconds, depending on the type and range of the missile. From the point of view of developing an effective missile defense system, there are distinct advantages to attempting to intercept a missile during this phase, but there also are daunting technical challenges involved. The advantages include the fact that a ballistic missile is traveling at its slowest speed while accelerating, the missile's exhaust plume is bright and hot against the atmosphere and the surface of the Earth and thus more easily detected and tracked, and any countermeasures the missile might be carrying will not yet have been deployed. In many respects, a ballistic missile is at its most vulnerable during its boost phase. Having the capability to intercept missiles during this phase can contribute to a layered defense; if a missile fails to be intercepted during this phase, there remain the midcourse and terminal phases during which additional attempts can be made to intercept it.

Achieving an intercept during the boost phase is technologically very challenging. Since this phase of the missile's flight is so short, there is very little time available for the process, which includes detecting its launch, tracking its flight, determining whether it is hostile, deciding whether to launch an interceptor missile or initiate some other interception method (such as using an airborne laser), and actually reaching the ascending and accelerating missile with another missile or kill mechanism. This approach thus places maximum stress on command and control systems and on the acceleration capacities of interceptor missiles, since their acceleration often must be many times that of the missiles they are intended to intercept. To be effective, a BPI system probably needs to be located very close to the bases from which the targeted missiles are launched.

Sea-based BPI systems have the advantage of mobility; they can be deployed off the shores of a hostile nation and relocated as circumstances require. They can also be deployed closer to the launch point, making early interception during the boost phase more likely. The United States is currently developing a very fast acceleration missile for deployment on navy ships intended as a boost-phase interceptor. Sea-based systems, however, would be ineffective against missiles launched from deep within a hostile nation's territory.

Space-based BPI systems, if developed, could orbit over any part of the Earth's surface, providing global reach. The United States is pursuing long-range research and development into both a kinetic kill space-based intercept capability (designed to physically ram hostile missiles) and a directed-energy space-based system (which would employ laser beams or focused X-rays to destroy a missile). But the first tests of prototypes for such systems are ten to twelve years off, and their effectiveness has yet to be validated.

—John Spykerman

See also: Ballistic Missiles; Missile Defense
References
Garwin, Richard L., "Boost-Phase Intercept: A Better Alternative," *Arms Control Today,* September 2000, available at http://www.armscontrol.org/act/2000_09/bpisept00.asp.
Lamb, Frederick K., and Daniel Kleppner et al., "Boost-Phase Intercept Systems for National Missile Defense," American Physical Society Report, July 2003, available at http://www.aps.org/public_affairs/popa/reports/nmdexec.pdf.
"Missile Defense Systems and Boost-Phase Intercept," Raytheon Corporation, available at http://raytheonmissiledefense.com/boost/.

BOTTOM-UP REVIEW

U.S. Secretary of Defense Les Aspin initiated the Bottom-Up Review (BUR) in March 1993 in response to the dramatic changes that occurred in the international security environment following the collapse of the Soviet Union and the end of the Cold War. It was a comprehensive review of U.S. defense strategy, force structure, infrastructure, and modernization plans.

Issued in September 1993, the review was supposed to offer a way to reduce defense spending while gradually transforming and modernizing the U.S. military for the "long peace" that was expected to follow the end of the Cold War. Although it called for reducing the size of the U.S. military, it failed to break with many traditional planning assumptions. It maintained current military capability against familiar, if vanishing, threats but did not preserve long-term U.S. military capability or focus on new dangers. It kept the requirement to wage two nearly simultaneous major regional conflicts and concentrated on improving U.S. capabilities to re-fight the Gulf War (capabilities that ironically came in handy nearly a decade later). It failed to increase U.S. peacekeeping forces and unconventional operations, however, capabilities that many analysts believed were needed to deal with the instability that emerged following the collapse of Soviet power. Advocates of the so-called revolution in military affairs (RMA) also believed that the BUR failed to exploit the information revolution.

Ultimately, the BUR created an unaffordable force. Given a defense budget that remained flat throughout the 1990s, the existing force structure and modernization plans contained in the BUR exceeded the amount the U.S. Congress was willing to spend on defense. Yet the Bottom-Up Review process was deemed valuable enough to warrant major reviews of America's defenses at regular intervals over the next decade through the Quadrennial Defense Reviews.

—James J. Wirtz

See also: Quadrennial Defense Review
Reference
Freedman, Lawrence, *The Evolution of Nuclear Strategy,* third edition (New York: Palgrave Macmillan, 2003).

BREAKOUT
See Arms Control

BRILLIANT EYES

Brilliant Eyes, a spacecraft research and development program pursued by the United States from 1990 to 1994, was an element of the layered ballistic missile defense system envisioned by the Strategic Defense Initiative Organization (SDIO). It was intended to be deployed as a constellation of satellites designed to track reentry vehicles (RVs) during exoatmospheric flight and to help discriminate RVs from penetration aids using infrared and visible-light sensors.

Tracking RVs during exoatmospheric flight (rather than using only tracks from the missile plume) enables early intercept attempts and impact prediction, verifies an actual missile attack by tracking the warheads, and provides long-term tracking of the motions and characteristics of the set objects resulting from a launch. The resulting "birth-to-death tracking" enhances the ability to discriminate RVs from the rocket bodies, debris, and penetration aids that may accompany a ballistic missile launch.

The whimsical name Brilliant Eyes was derived from the space-based interceptor program Brilliant Pebbles, under way at the same time. Brilliant Eyes was one in a series of programs, starting in the late 1970s and continuing to the present, intended to develop systems capable of tracking relatively cold RVs and spacecraft as they move through space. These programs include the Space-Based Surveillance System, the Space Surveillance and Tracking System, Brilliant Eyes, the "SBIRS-Low" component of the

Space-Based Infrared System, and, as of 2004, the Space Tracking and Surveillance System (STSS).

—*Roy Pettis*

See also: Missile Defenses; Reentry Vehicles; Strategic Defenses

References

Friedman, George, and Meredith Friedman, *The Future of War: Power, Technology, and American World Dominance in the Twenty-First Century* (New York: St. Martin's Press, 1998).

Graham, Bradley, *Hit to Kill: The New Battle over Shielding America from Missile Attack* (New York: Public Affairs, 2001).

Isaacson, Jeffrey A., and David R. Vaughn, *Estimation and Prediction of Ballistic Missile Trajectories* (Santa Monica, CA: RAND Corporation, 1996).

BRILLIANT PEBBLES

See Strategic Defense Initiative

BRINKMANSHIP

Brinkmanship is a policy of creating a crisis so that one party knowingly challenges another in the expectation that the adversary will back down in the face of this challenge. The purpose of such a policy is to achieve specific political objectives by means of coercion or the possibility of escalation to war. Although the escalatory cycle is employed in inducing a crisis, the policy is a success when war is avoided and the opponent complies without a fight.

Brinkmanship has sometimes been undertaken without good evidence that the adversary would back down, forcing the party generating a crisis to back down, which adversely affects its own credibility and deterrence posture. Factors inducing states to consider employing brinkmanship, and therefore increase the risk of war, can come from either foreign or domestic sources. In terms of external threats, an important motive that can prompt leaders to embark on a brinkmanship policy is the expectation of a considerable shift in the balance of power that would leave them worse off. This probably was a primary motive behind Soviet Premier Nikita Khrushchev's decision to install missiles on Cuba as a response to the first-strike capability of the United States.

An alternate explanation for adopting a brinkmanship policy springs from the need of leaders and states to divert attention from domestic problems by securing achievements in foreign affairs. North Korea's policy of nuclear brinkmanship that began in the 1990s might be an effort to divert domestic attention away from a myriad of problems while seeking to extract tangible benefits from the international community by threatening to develop weapons of mass destruction.

—*J. Simon Rofe*

See also: Cold War

Reference

Lebow, Richard Ned, *Between Peace and War: The Nature of International Crisis* (Baltimore: Johns Hopkins University Press, 1981).

BRITISH NUCLEAR FORCES AND DOCTRINE

The United Kingdom of Great Britain and Northern Ireland maintains a declared independent nuclear deterrent, relying solely on Trident submarines with ballistic missiles, in conjunction with the U.S. Navy. The United Kingdom is one of only two European Union countries to possess and deploy nuclear weapons, the other being France.

History and Background

Until 1945, Britain collaborated with the United States in the research and development of atomic technology. It was actively involved in civilian research prior to World War II through individuals such as Ernest Rutherford and in experiments with heavy water and nuclear accelerators, and during World War II as part of the Manhattan Project—a joint U.S.-UK endeavor (*see* Heavy Water; Manhattan Project). In 1945, British officials, presiding over a shrinking empire and anxious to arrest the nation's decline in world politics, realized the significance of the nuclear bombs dropped on Hiroshima and Nagasaki and decided to proceed with atomic research, with the aim of producing atomic bombs, using plutonium as the fissile material. When the United States passed the McMahon Atomic Energy Act (1946) forbidding the transfer of nuclear weapons technology to other nations, Britain boosted its efforts at the Atomic Weapons Establishment (Aldermaston, Berkshire) for an independent nuclear weapons program. It made the decision in 1947 to build and test an atomic weapon. Through agreement reached with Australia, Britain successfully tested its first 25-kiloton nuclear device aboard a ship moored off the northwest coast of Australia, near Monte Bello Islands, on October 3, 1952. This was followed by Britain's first hydrogen bomb test in 1957 in the Pacific Ocean. Renewed collaboration with the United

Britian's V-Bomber trio—the "Vulcan," "Valiant," and "Victor"—flying in formation over southern England, 1957. (Hulton-Deutsch Collection/Corbis)

States led to the transfer of nuclear propulsion technology. Subsequent joint U.S.-UK nuclear warhead tests continued between 1962 and 1991.

Initially it was envisaged that the British independent nuclear deterrent would be airborne, with free-fall gravity bombs delivered by the V-force bombers (Valiant, Victor, Vulcan). The introduction of the Tornado aircraft into Royal Air Force service in 1978 saw a continuation of this doctrine, with eight operational squadrons of multirole, dual-capable Tornado GR.1/1A aircraft, until the withdrawal of the last remaining WE177 bombs from operational service in March 1998. This terminated the Tornados' nuclear role, bringing to an end a four-decade history of RAF aircraft carrying nuclear weapons. By the end of August 1998, all remaining WE177 bombs had been dismantled.

Britain acquired a seaborne independent nuclear deterrent at the same time that its RAF program was in operation. Following the cancellation of the U.S. Skybolt program as an air-launched nuclear ballistic missile for the Vulcan aircraft, President John F. Kennedy and Prime Minister Harold MacMillan

signed the Nassau Agreement in December 1962. Under this treaty, Britain acquired a Polaris nuclear submarine fleet for the Royal Navy. The doctrine since the purchase of Polaris has remained unchanged: "Britain's strategic nuclear force has been committed to NATO [North Atlantic Treaty Organization] and targeted in accordance with Alliance policy and strategic concepts under plans made by the Supreme Allied Command Europe (SACEUR)" (*Strategic Defence Review*, para. 4). NATO's concept of nuclear deterrence is in turn based predominantly on U.S. nuclear doctrine. The Polaris fleet has been replaced by a Trident submarine fleet, the first of which entered into service in 1994. (The last Polaris was retired in 1996.) The British Army during the Cold War also manufactured artillery shells and land mines that could have had nuclear components for tactical use in compliance with NATO's doctrine of the "Triad of Forces," but these were never independently tested or deployed.

The United States deploys tactical nuclear weapons in seven NATO European countries, including Britain, and has agreements with these countries allowing them to take control of the weapons and use them in a state of war. At no stage has Britain ever used nuclear weapons in combat, and it is a party to the Nuclear Nonproliferation Treaty (1968), the Limited Test Ban Treaty (1963), the Outer Space Treaty (1967), the Seabed Arms Control Treaty (1971), and the International Code of Conduct for Ballistic Missiles (2002).

Britain's Nuclear Deterrent Force Today

Britain today maintains a nuclear deterrent posture based solely on nuclear-powered ballistic missile submarines (SSBNs). The first submarine of the Vanguard class began its first patrol in December 1994. The second submarine, *Victorious*, entered service a year later. The third, *Vigilant*, was launched in October 1995 and entered service in fall 1998. The fourth and final submarine of the class, *Vengeance*, was launched September 19, 1998, at the Marconi-Marine Shipyard in Barrow-in-Furness and commissioned on November 27, 1999. It entered operational service with the First Submarine Squadron, beginning patrols in February 2001. The estimated cost of the production program was $19.8 billion. Each Vanguard-class SSBN has a complement of 205 men, which includes a ship's company of 130 men while on patrol, and carries 16 U.S.-made Trident II (D5) submarine-launched ballistic missiles (SLBMs). The D5s are three-stage, rocket-propelled inertial guidance missiles; they are 44 feet long, 130,000 pounds, and have a range of 4,000 nautical miles. Each missile has a possible maximum of three warheads, for a total of 48 multiple independently targetable reentry vehicles (MIRVs) per submarine. These warheads are a variation of the USN W76 warhead designed for Trident I C4 and Trident II D5 missiles, enclosed in a USN Mk-4 reentry vehicle (RV).

One of the four subs is normally on patrol, and its operations are normally coordinated with those of France's SSBNs. Two others would, in rotation, be in training, in port, or in local waters and could be deployed to patrol positions on relatively short notice. The fourth submarine would be undergoing repair and maintenance and would require significantly longer preparation for deployment. Each SSBN is protected by one or two hunter-killer submarines (SSNs) while en route to and from its patrol area.

The United States and Britain share a pool of

SLBMs kept at the Strategic Weapons Facility Atlantic, Kings Bay Submarine Base, Georgia. Although Britain has title to 58 SLBMs, technically it does not own them. A missile deployed on a U.S. Navy SSBN may at a later date be deployed on a British sub, or vice versa. British submarines conduct their missile flight tests at the U.S. Eastern Test Range off the coast of Florida. The *Vanguard* conducted two successful Demonstration and Shakedown Operations (DASO) in May and June 1994, launching two missiles. The *Victorious* fired two missiles during its DASOs in July and August 1995. In October 1997, the *Vigilant* also launched two missiles during two DASOs. On September 21, 2000, the *Vengeance* launched a Trident II D5 during a DASO exercise.

The independent part of Britain's nuclear deterrent is its warhead research and production capability. Warheads are designed at the Atomic Weapons Establishment (AWE) at Aldermaston, a 670-acre site in Berkshire, a county west of London. AWE employs 3,600 people and is managed by an industrial consortium consisting of Lockheed Martin, Serco Limited, and British Nuclear Fuels, which took over in April 2000 under a ten-year, $3.6 billion contract. The component manufacturing facility at Cardiff closed after thirty-six years in February 1997, when its functions were transferred to Aldermaston and Burghfield (a 270-acre site 7 miles to the east). Here, weapons also undergo final assembly, warhead maintenance, and disassembly. Special fissile materials (plutonium and highly enriched uranium) are acquired through the European Atomic Energy Community (EURATOM) Supply Agency (ESA), which maintains safeguards and conducts inspections. (The International Atomic Energy Agency is not responsible for safeguarding European Union (EU) nuclear weapon states other than inspecting selected facilities on a voluntary basis.) On April 1, 1999, the chief of defence logistics, UK, assumed overall responsibility for the routine movement of nuclear weapons within Britain. Day-to-day duties are carried out by the Ministry of Defence Police, with support from AWE civilians and the Royal Marines.

Current Status

In July 1998, the New Labour Party government under Prime Minister Tony Blair announced changes to its nuclear doctrine resulting from the Strategic Defence Review conducted that year. The doctrine states that the ultimate aim of Britain's nuclear forces is to continue to make a unique contribution to ensuring stability and preventing crisis escalation. They also would help guard against any possible reemergence of a strategic scale threat to British security (that is, a threat similar to that presented by the Cold War). In a constantly changing and uncertain world, Britain continues to require a credible and effective minimum nuclear deterrent based on the Trident submarine force in both a strategic and substrategic role. The Royal Navy's Trident force provides an operationally independent strategic and substrategic nuclear capability in support of NATO's strategy of war prevention and serves as the ultimate guarantee of British national security.

Only one Royal Navy SSBN is to patrol at any given time, carrying a maximum load of 48 warheads and assigned to a range of secondary tasks. This submarine patrols at a reduced state of alert, and its missiles are detargeted. It is capable of firing its missiles within several days, not minutes as during the Cold War. Given 4 Trident submarines, if all were fully loaded (MIRVed with three warheads), that would total 192 warheads, with 8 additional warheads for maintenance rotation. This creates a nuclear doctrine that needs to maintain no more than 200 operationally available nuclear warheads. Of these, 100 would be classified as strategic and 100 as tactical. With implementation of these decisions, the total explosive power of Britain's operationally available weapons has been reduced by more than 70 percent since the end of the Cold War. The explosive power of each Trident submarine will be one-third less than that of the Chevaline-armed Polaris submarines, the last of which was retired in 1996.

The Future

A consideration for Britain's future stockpile of operationally deployable nuclear warheads is the "substrategic mission" of the Trident submarine. The substrategic strike mission would be the limited and highly selective use of nuclear weapons in a manner that falls demonstrably short of a strategic strike, but with a sufficient level of violence to convince an aggressor that it would have to halt its aggression and withdraw or face the prospect of taking a dev-astating strategic strike. This substrategic mission began with *Victorious* and became fully robust when *Vigilant* achieved operational availability on February 1, 1998. This policy means that some Trident II SLBMs have a single warhead instead of the standard three and are assigned targets once covered by Royal Air Force WE177 gravity bombs on Tornado aircraft. Thus, when an SSBN is on patrol, ten, twelve, or fourteen of its missiles may carry as many as three warheads, while the other two, four, or six missiles may be armed with only one. There is thus some flexibility in the choice of yield. For instance, choosing to detonate only the unboosted primary could produce a yield of 1 kiloton or less, choosing to detonate the boosted primary could produce a yield of a few kilotons, and full explosive power would be available through use of both the primary and secondary. Reducing the number of RVs also could extend the range of a missile. In its "substrategic" configuration, a missile carrying a single warhead would have a range of more than 6,000 miles. With dual missions, an SSBN would have approximately 36–44 warheads on board during patrol instead of the maximum complement of 48. Notwithstanding the debate on the number of warheads, the Trident submarine fleet will have a potential in-service operational life until 2026, which could be extended with refits.

—*Glen M. Segell*

See also: Strategic Forces; Submarine-Launched Ballistic Missiles; Submarines, Nuclear-Powered Ballistic Missile

References
Atomic Weapons Establishment website, http://www.awe.co.uk.
Gaddis, John Lewis, *Cold War Statesmen Confront the Bomb: Nuclear Diplomacy since 1945* (Oxford: Oxford University Press, 1999).
Gowing, Margaret, *Independence and Deterrence: Britain and Atomic Energy, 1945–1952* (London: Macmillan, 1974).
Segell, Glen, *Weapons Procurement in Phase Considerations* (London: GS Press, 1998).
Strategic Defence Review, Cm 3999 (London: The Stationery Office, July 1998).
UK Defence Council, Ministry of Defence, *The United Kingdom Trident Programme*, Defence Open Government Document 82/1 (London: The Stationery Office, March 1982).
UK Ministry of Defence website, http://www.mod.uk.

Crewmen on board the submarine USS Petrol *lash down a U.S. hydrogen bomb recovered from a depth of 2,500 feet in the Mediterranean Sea 81 days after a B-52 collided with a KC-135 during refueling over Palomares, Spain, in January 1966. (Bettmann/Corbis)*

BROKEN ARROW, BENT SPEAR

Broken Arrow and Bent Spear are U.S. Department of Defense terms used to report accidents involving nuclear weapons or components. Broken Arrow is the flag word for the most serious of these accidents, including: (1) accidental or unauthorized launching, firing, or use of a nuclear-capable weapons system by the United States or a U.S. ally; (2) accidental, unexplained, or unauthorized nuclear detonation; (3) nonnuclear detonation or burning of nuclear weapons or components; (4) radioactive release and contamination; (5) actual or perceived public hazard; and (6) jettisoning of a nuclear weapon or its components.

A Bent Spear is a mishap falling into the following categories: (1) radioactive contamination from the burning, theft, seizure, or destruction of a radioactive limited-life component; (2) evident damage to a nuclear weapon or nuclear component that requires major rework, replacement, examination, or recertification by the U.S. Department of Energy; (3) events requiring immediate action in the inter-

ests of nuclear surety or which could result in adverse national and international public reaction or the premature release of information; (4) events indicating that a nuclear weapon or warhead has been armed; and (5) events that could lead to a nuclear weapon system accident and thus warrant the informational interest of, or action by, any of the following agencies in the United States: an appropriate military department or service, the Office of the Assistant to the Secretary of Defense (Nuclear and Chemical and Biological Defense Programs), the Office of the Assistant of Defense (Strategy and Threat Reduction), the Office of the Secretary of Defense (Public Affairs), the Federal Emergency Management Agency.

An example of a Broken Arrow occurred in Goldsboro, North Carolina, in 1961 when two Mk39 nuclear bombs were jettisoned from a B-52. The plane had disintegrated owing to structural failure. Three of the eight crew members were killed in the accident. One bomb parachuted to the ground and was found intact. The other struck the soggy ground of a farm at terminal velocity. The mechanisms designed to prevent detonation worked, and no nuclear blast occurred.

—*Zach Becker*

References

"Air Force Instruction 91-204: Safety Investigations and Reports," available at http://afpubs.hq.af.mil.

Gregory, Shaun, *The Hidden Cost of Deterrence: Nuclear Weapons Accidents* (Dulles, VA: Brassey's, 1990).

May, John, *The Greenpeace Book of the Nuclear Age: The Hidden History of the Human Cost* (London: Victor Gollancz, 1989).

Sagan, Scott D., *The Limits of Safety: Organization, Accidents, and Nuclear Weapons* (Princeton, NJ: Princeton University Press, 1993).

BUILDDOWN

See Arms Control

CANADA DEUTERIUM URANIUM (CANDU) REACTOR

C

The Canada Deuterium Uranium (CANDU) reactor is a pressurized, heavy-water moderated and cooled reactor that uses natural uranium as fuel. All nuclear power reactors in Canada are of the CANDU type. Canada's worldwide marketing has enticed several other countries to produce or coproduce CANDU reactors since the 1970s (*see* Deuterium; Uranium).

An organization of private Canadian industry and government representatives designed the CANDU reactor in the late 1950s. The first CANDU reactor, the Pickering A, Unit 1, began operation in 1971. By 1973, Canada's Pickering A Nuclear Generating Station had four CANDU reactors and led the world in the production of nuclear power.

From the late 1970s to the mid-1980s, Canada built and put into operation nine more CANDU reactors. By the early 1990s, all of the CANDU reactors operational in Canada today were already in commission.

In 1973, India put its first CANDU reactor into service. In the early 1980s, South Korea began operating a CANDU reactor, and it put three more reactors into operation by the end of the 1990s. Argentina began running its CANDU reactor in 1984, and in 1996, Romania began commercial operation of a CANDU reactor. By the summer of 2003, China had two CANDU reactors operational.

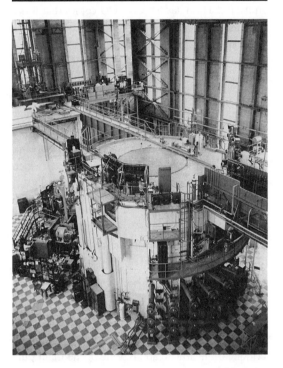

The interior for one of the CANDU reactor buildings at the Chalk River project of Atomic Energy of Canada Limited, 1955. (Bettmann/Corbis)

Technical Details

A CANDU reactor uses deuterium to moderate, or slow down, neutrons to thermal energies. Heavy water has a very low absorption cross section for thermal neutrons so there are more neutrons available at the proper energy range to cause fission in the natural uranium fuel (*see* Heavy Water).

Moderating neutrons in heavy water is not as efficient as in regular water because neutrons generally lose less energy per collision with deuterium compared to hydrogen. As a result, the CANDU reactor uses a horizontal cylindrical tank called a "calandria," which contains the moderator at normal pressure. The calandria has a series of pressure tubes that contain the heavy-water coolant at high pressure so that it will not boil away (approximately 10 million Pascal) and it has fuel elements running through it. Because the coolant is pressurized, an extremely large pressure vessel to contain the entire core is not needed.

One important aspect of a CANDU reactor is that it can be refueled at full power. The refueling process involves two machines: one to push the "new" fuel bundle in and the other to receive the "old" bundle as it is being forced out of the assembly. This practice allows for about a 90 percent reactor availability. The movable fuel bundles also allow for increased use of the fissile material.

Current Status

There are currently fifteen CANDU reactors operating in Canada, four in South Korea, two in China, two in Romania, and one each in Argentina and India. India also has ten CANDU copies that it has manufactured based on the original design sold by Canada.

The Advanced CANDU Reactor (ACR) is being developed by Atomic Energy of Canada Limited (AECL) to provide for a smaller reactor core while maintaining a comparable power output. The new design entails the use of higher-pressure steam turbines, light-water instead of heavy-water coolant, and slightly enriched uranium (1.65 percent), which will reduce the amount of fuel needed annually.

—*Don Gillich*

See also: Reactor Operations
Reference
Nero, Anthony V., *A Guidebook to Nuclear Reactors* (Berkeley: University of California Press, 1979).

THE CATHOLIC CHURCH AND NUCLEAR WAR

Officials and scholars working within the Catholic tradition have developed a comprehensive moral critique of nuclear weapons. One of the main purposes of the critique is to nurture a continuing, serious, mutually respectful dialogue on acceptable nuclear policies and practices, not only for the church but for the wider communities in democratic countries. Not surprisingly, there is a great deal of disagreement even within Catholic circles on specific questions, such as first use of nuclear weapons.

The Second Vatican Council declared in December 1965 that any act of war aimed indiscriminately at the destruction of entire cities or extensive areas along with their population is a crime against God and man himself and merits unequivocal and unhesitating condemnation (*Gaudium et spes*). This was the only condemnation issued by the council, which convened in October 1962, the same month that the Cuban missile crisis began.

In the face of the bombing experiences of World War II and the possibility of civilization-threatening nuclear war, Catholic leaders have reaffirmed an absolute prohibition against deliberately targeting civilians while walking a fine line on recognizing the realities of the nuclear age, especially the importance of nuclear deterrence in helping secure a just peace. Some Catholic thinkers have reverted to nuclear pacifism, arguing that the inherent threat to human survival from large-scale nuclear war calls for an absolute moral prohibition on any use of nuclear weapons. Others find nuclear deterrence to be compatible with the just war tradition, when combined with a call for active diplomacy and arms control to reduce, and eventually eliminate, the nuclear threat. Still other Catholic thinkers have championed missile defenses in the hopes that policies of deterrence could be transcended. There are various shades and combinations of the above themes that appear periodically in the literature.

The tension between contrasting views carried over into the three-year effort that, in May 1983, resulted in the American Catholic bishops issuing a much-cited pastoral letter, "The Challenge of Peace." The American bishops again condemned any policy that deliberately targeted noncombatants. They judged nuclear deterrence morally acceptable not as an end in itself but as a stage toward progressive disarmament—a position articulated by Pope John Paul II in his message to the United Nations Special Session on Disarmament in 1982. They also opposed any policy of first use of nuclear weapons. The bishops affirmed this position in 1993 in a new letter, also entitled "The Challenge of Peace."

Catholic thought and debate continues to evolve on these issues as governments adapt nuclear doctrines to the changing conditions of the post–Cold War world.

—*Michael Wheeler*

References
American Catholic Bishops, "The Challenge of Peace," 1983 pastoral letter, available at www.americancatholic.org/Newsletters/CU/ac0883.asp.
———, "The Challenge of Peace," 1993 pastoral letter, available at www.usccb.org/sdwp/harvestexr.htm.
Murnion, Philip J., ed., *Catholics and Nuclear War* (New York: Crossroad, 1983).
O'Brien, William V., and John Langan, S.J., eds., *The Nuclear Dilemma and the Just War Tradition* (New York: Lexington, 1986).

CHALLENGE INSPECTIONS
See Verification

CHELYABINSK-40
Chelyabinsk-40 is also known by its geographic name of Kyshtym or as the Mayak chemical complex. Located near the Chelyabinsk-65 plutonium production facility on the east side of the southern Urals, this site handled waste product storage from five channel-type plutonium production reactors. Construction began in November 1945 and the facility became operational in June 1948. To expedite development of the first Soviet atomic weapons, waste was dumped in Lake Kyzyltash and the Techa River. The radioactive contamination forced twenty-four villages along the Techa River banks to be evacuated, and the river was fenced off to prevent people and livestock from using the water. When radioactivity was discovered downriver in the Arctic Ocean, a waste-processing facility was built.

The separation process used by the Soviets on irradiated fuel elements was an acetate-settling process incorporating nitric acid. The highly radioactive waste solutions produced heat that required the waste holding tanks to be cooled. Following a further extraction process of uranium and plutonium, the remainder of the waste was discharged into lakes and canals in the area.

On September 29, 1957, an explosion occurred in one of the waste tanks, with a force equivalent to between 70 and 100 tons of TNT. The accident was caused by a failure of a cooling pipe in one of the tanks. Cooling fluids began to evaporate, at 350 degrees Celsius, and some 80 metric tons of waste containing 20 million curies of radioactivity were released—about one-third of the amount released in the 1986 Chernobyl accident. In 1967, another calamity struck the area when drought reduced the water level of the lake and gale-force winds spread the radioactive dust throughout 25,000 square kilometers, further irradiating half a million people.

After the 1957 accident, villages were resettled from the surrounding area, but the CIA noticed that on subsequent Soviet maps a large area around Kyshtym was devoid of human settlement. Not until 1989 did the West learn the true extent of pollution and accidents in the area. Kyshtym is now considered one of the most polluted parts of the world,

and the radioactive fallout there is considered to have been worse than at Chernobyl.

—Gilles Van Nederveen

See also: Chernobyl; Plutonium; Radiation; Uranium
References
Cochran, Thomas B., and Robert S. Norris, "A First Look at the Soviet Bomb Complex," *Bulletin of the Atomic Scientists*, vol. 47, no. 4, May 1991, available at http://www.thebulletin.org/issues/1991/may91/may91chochran.html.
Medvedev, Zhores A., *Nuclear Disaster in the Urals* (New York: W. W. Norton, 1979).
"The Most Contaminated Spot on the Planet," available at http://www.thescreamonline.com/strange/strange08-01/cheyabinsk40.html.
Peterson, D. J., *Troubled Lands: The Legacy of Soviet Environmental Destruction* (Boulder: Westview, 1993).
Zalloga, Steven J., *Target America: The Soviet Union and the Strategic Arms Race, 1945–1964* (Novato, CA: Presidio, 1993).

CHERNOBYL
Chernobyl is a nuclear power generating station located in Pryp'yat, Ukraine, 10 miles southwest of the city of Chernobyl and 65 miles north of Kiev. The plant contains four reactors, each capable of producing 1,000 megawatts of electric power. The reactors were activated between 1977 and 1983. In 1986, Chernobyl became the site of the worst nuclear power generation disaster in history.

On April 25–26, 1986, a poorly designed experiment led to a chain reaction in the core of Unit 4, causing the reaction to go out of control. Several explosions triggered a huge fireball that blew off the steel and concrete lid of the reactor. The fire in the graphite reactor core led to a partial meltdown of the core and the release of radioactive material into the atmosphere, On April 27, 30,000 residents of Pryp'yat were evacuated. A Swedish monitoring station initially discovered the release. The accident triggered international criticism of Soviet power plant designs and their unsafe operating procedures.

Between 50 and 185 million curies of radionuclides escaped into the atmosphere, several times more than were generated by the Hiroshima and Nagasaki bombs. Windborne radioactive contamination was carried as far away as France and Italy. Reindeer herds in Finland were affected, and millions of acres of forest and farmland were contaminated.

Deformed livestock were born for several years after the accident.

A rapid cleanup led to radioactive material being buried at 800 temporary sites, and the core was encapsulated, but the container was later found to be unsound. Thirty-two people died initially, and dozens of others contracted radiation sickness. It is expected that several thousand radiation-induced illnesses and cancers will develop over time as a result of the worst nuclear accident in history.

Unit 2 remained operating after the accident, but it, too, was shut down following a fire in 1991. Units 1 and 3 remain on line.

The accident sparked renewed interest in the Soviet Union's use of nuclear generating facilities to create weapons-grade nuclear materials. Some commentators blamed the magnitude of the accident on the design's focus on weapon production. The accident led to a reemergence of a strong international antinuclear lobby in a campaign that almost stopped the construction of new nuclear power plants worldwide.

—*Frannie Edwards*

See also: Graphite; Isotopes; Radiation; Reactor Operations

Reference

Read, Piers Paul, *Ablaze: The Story of the Heroes and Victims of Chernobyl* (London: Secker and Warburg, 1993).

CHEYENNE MOUNTAIN, COLORADO

Opened in 1966, Cheyenne Mountain was designed to provide an operations center in the event of a Soviet nuclear attack on North America. Excavation began on May 18, 1961, at a site southwest of Colorado Springs, Colorado. Located under 2,000 feet of the Rocky Mountains, the Cheyenne Mountain Operations Center (CMOC) was ultimately designed to withstand a multimegaton weapon at a range of less than 2 miles. Behind 25-ton blast doors a third of a mile inside the mountain, a steel building complex is mounted on huge steel springs, covering 4.5 acres. Incoming air can pass through a series of chemical/biological/radiological (CBR) filters to remove harmful material, and six backup diesel generators and four water reservoirs allow the

A military shuttle bus exits the entrance to the Cheyenne Mountain Complex, headquarters for North American Aerospace Defense Command, May 11, 2004, in Colorado Springs, Colorado. (Robert Nickelsberg/Getty Images)

CMOC to carry out its mission while cut off from the outside world.

At present, Cheyenne Mountain, known as Cheyenne Mountain Air Force Station (CMAFS), is host to four commands: the North American Aerospace Defense Command (NORAD), the United States Northern Command (USNORTHCOM), the United States Strategic Command (USSTRATCOM), and the Air Force Space Command (AFSPC). The CMOC furnishes both NORAD and USNORTHCOM with a command center for monitoring the internal airspace of Canada and the United States to provide early warning of missile, air, or space threats to North America. Approximately 15 percent of the 210 people who work inside the operations center are Canadian; the remainder are members of the U.S. military. The mission of Cheyenne Mountain has evolved in the face of changing threats. Whereas in the past its focus was on manned bomber attack and intercontinental ballistic missile strikes, it now places greater emphasis on theater ballistic missile warning and support of homeland defense.

—*J. Simon Rofe*

See also: Early Warning; North American Aerospace Defense Command; Surveillance

References

Cheyenne Mountain website, http://www. cheyennemountain.af.mil.

Tudor, Jason, "Cheyenne Mountain Air Force Station: A Look inside NORAD," available at http:// usmilitary.about.com/library/milinfo/milarticles/ blnorad.html.

CHICKEN, GAME OF

The Game of Chicken, also called a game of right-of-way, has frequently served as a metaphor in studies of escalation scenarios resulting in possible nuclear war. In Chicken, two rational players, A and B, drive toward each other head-on. Each player chooses at the same time whether to swerve (change policy, or "chicken out") or to continue driving straight ahead (maintain the status quo). There are four possible outcomes, A swerves and B continues straight, B swerves and A stays the course, both turn, or finally, neither swerves and there is a collision. Each player does best if he goes straight and his opponent swerves. When solved, this game suggests three likely observed behaviors (equilibria). A swerves and B does not, B swerves and A does not,

or both players randomly swerve half the time (resulting in each of the four possible outcomes occurring 25 percent of the time).

In addition to motivating nuclear deterrence literature, the game has three additional implications. First, besides convincing one's adversary that he should swerve, one can "win" by appearing to eliminate one's own ability to swerve. Thus, states in Chicken-like deterrence situations might have incentives to create rigid standard operating procedures for the use of nuclear weapons or take steps to detach their nuclear arsenals from rational control by political authorities, forcing the decision to swerve onto their opponents. Second, if the moves are not simultaneous, but are sequential, the predicted outcomes are quite different, which demonstrates the importance of timing. Third, given the information in the game, one cannot select between the two equilibrium outcomes where one player swerves and the other goes straight. This suggests that the third, more symmetrical outcome, "the mixed strategy," where each side swerves half the time, may be the most likely result, which would mean that 25 percent of the time the players would "collide" in a nuclear war.

—*Scott Sigmund Gartner*

See also: Game Theory

References

Axelrod, Robert, *The Evolution of Cooperation* (New York: Basic, 1984).

Morrow, James D., *Game Theory for Political Scientists* (Princeton, NJ: Princeton University Press, 1994).

CHINA SYNDROME

See Reactor Operations

CHINESE NUCLEAR FORCES AND DOCTRINE

China tested its first nuclear device—and became the world's fifth nuclear power—in October 1964. Since that time, China's nuclear stockpile has grown to about 400 weapons—the world's third largest nuclear arsenal. China's nuclear capabilities are concentrated in its roughly 120 land-based missiles under the command of the Second Artillery. Although China's efforts to deploy a submarine-launched ballistic missile (SLBM) have been largely unsuccessful, Western analysts expect China to deploy a new SLBM on a new submarine by about 2010. China's bomber fleet is obsolete, and its air force may no longer have a nuclear role.

Origins of China's Nuclear Weapons Program

China's nuclear program had its origins in a confluence of events that occurred in late 1954 and early 1955. The United States signaled an increasing willingness to rely on nuclear weapons at the close of the Korean War and a desire to incorporate them into its force planning under President Dwight Eisenhower's "New Look" policy. In the fall of 1954, Soviet Premier Nikita Khrushchev rejected Mao Tse-tung's request for Soviet assistance in developing nuclear weapons. On December 2, 1954, in the midst of China's bombardment of the Nationalist-held islands of Quemoy and Matsu in the First Taiwan Straits Crisis, the United States and Taiwan signed a Mutual Defense Treaty—a significant U.S. commitment to the island's defense. That month, U.S. nuclear weapons also were deployed to Okinawa and on the USS *Midway* in the waters around Taiwan. In early January 1955, the chairman of the U.S. Joint Chiefs of Staff publicly suggested that preparations had been made to use nuclear weapons in Asia.

On January 15, 1955, Mao and an enlarged meeting of the Politburo's Central Secretariat decided to proceed with a nuclear weapons program, designated "02." Two days later, the Soviet Union announced it would assist China with peaceful nuclear energy research. The following year, Mao told a meeting of the Chinese Communist Party Central Committee that "now it is time for us to pay attention" to acquiring nuclear weapons (Lewis and Xue Litai 1988, p. 39). By 1958, day-to-day direction of the nuclear weapons program was under the leadership of Vice Premier Nie Rongzhen, who would oversee China's nuclear weapons program for the next thirty years.

The Soviet Union, apparently more willing to cooperate with Beijing in the wake of the 1956 Hungarian uprising, played a key role in China's nuclear weapons program. On October 15, 1957, the countries agreed to the New Defense Technical Accord, in which the Soviet Union promised to supply nuclear weapons design information and even a prototype atomic weapon. The accord collapsed in 1959 and 1960 as the Soviet leadership came to view China as an untrustworthy ally and potentially dangerous adversary and sought to improve relations with the United States. China, however, had already acquired the basis for its own nuclear weapons program.

China's Nuclear Weapons Infrastructure

China's nuclear weapons design and production infrastructure benefited from Soviet guidance until nuclear cooperation was curtailed in June 1959. With the help of Soviet advisers, the Beijing Nuclear Weapons Research Institute, or "Ninth Academy," was established in 1958. Soviet nuclear weapons designers traveled to Beijing in mid-1958 and provided detailed information about nuclear weapon design (based on a 1951 Soviet model) and testing, as well as on organizing a design institute. According to chief designer Yevgeniy Negin, a teaching model and full documentation of the 1951 bomb were ready to be shipped to China—and had been for several months—when they were ordered destroyed by Moscow.

With Soviet help, the Chinese also began construction of several nuclear weapons–related production facilities. The key enterprises were:

- The Baotou Nuclear Fuel Component Plant (Plant 202), which began operation in 1962 and produces uranium tetrafluoride (UF_4), uranium fuel rods for the Jiuquan facility, and lithium-6 and tritium for thermonuclear weapons;
- The Lanzhou Gaseous Diffusion Plant (Plant 504), which was started in 1958 and produced its first highly enriched uranium (HEU) on January 14, 1964;
- The Jiuquan Atomic Energy Complex (Plant 404), including a plutonium production plant that became operational in 1966 and a plutonium reprocessing plant that became operational in 1970.

While the Chinese pursued both an HEU and plutonium program, the former was significantly more advanced when Soviet aid was cut off.

In 1962, the Beijing Nuclear Weapons Research Institute was closed and its design work shifted to the newly established Northwest Nuclear Weapons Research Institute, also known as Plant 221, in Haiyan, Qinghai province. According to one Chinese report, "sixteen nuclear weapons were invented" at Plant 221 before it closed in 1987.

As part of Mao's "Third Line" program that emerged in the late 1960s, duplicates of these enterprises were built in China's interior, where they were believed to be less vulnerable to Soviet or

American attack. China's nuclear design work shifted from Haiyan to the China Academy of Engineering Physics (CAEP), located in Mianyang, by the early 1970s. The plutonium production and processing facilities at the Baotou Nuclear Fuel Component Plant were mirrored in the Yibin Nuclear Fuel Component Plant, and the gaseous diffusion uranium enrichment facilities at Lanzhou Gaseous Diffusion Plant were replicated at the Heping Nuclear Fuel Complex. Plutonium production and separation facilities at the Jiuquan Atomic Energy Complex (Gansu) were duplicated at Guangyuan (Plant 821).

China reportedly halted uranium enrichment for military purposes in 1987, and production of plutonium for weapons in 1991, although it has not officially announced either change in policy. Although nuclear weapons–related work continues at CAEP, China's signing of the Comprehensive Test Ban Treaty in 1996 and its moratorium on nuclear testing severely limit the development of new nuclear weapons.

Production and presumably maintenance of the existing stockpile reportedly takes place at the China National Nuclear Corporation's Special Parts Factory (or Factory 903) in Sichuan.

Nuclear Weapons Design and Testing

Ninth Academy Director Li Jue had overall responsibility for the research, development, and design of China's fission and fusion warheads in the 1950s and 1960s and led the design of China's first nuclear weapon. His team designed and assembled China's first atomic weapons at Plant 221. China's first nuclear test, an HEU implosion device, took place on October 16, 1964, with a yield of about 22 kilotons.

Even before the first nuclear explosive test, China's leaders directed the Ninth Academy's design team to begin work on a thermonuclear weapon. In February 1967, the design was completed. The device was tested on June 17, 1967, and had a yield estimated at 3 megatons.

Between its first test in 1964 and its announcement of a moratorium on nuclear testing in July 1996, China completed forty-five nuclear explosive tests. These included a test of a "neutron" warhead in 1988, based on a breakthrough made in 1984, and reportedly a test of a "miniaturized" warhead in 1992. The latter capability led to charges—vehemently denied by Chinese scientists—that Beijing

had gained access to U.S. nuclear secrets through espionage.

China does not reveal information about its nuclear weapons stockpile. The Natural Resources Defense Council (NRDC) estimates that China has produced about 750 nuclear weapons over the life of the program and that China's nuclear weapon stockpile reached 75 nuclear weapons by 1970; 185 by 1975; 280 in 1980; 425 in 1985; and 430 in 1990. NRDC further estimates that China has maintained a force of about 400 weapons, including 150 tactical nuclear warheads, since 1994, but cautions that these estimates "are probably not accurate to better than 50 percent, due to the uncertainty in the number of tactical warheads." China clearly has the ability to produce tactical nuclear weapons, but there is no confirmation that it has produced or deployed them.

Ballistic Missiles

In early 1956, Qian Xuesen, an American-trained jet propulsion expert who had returned to China the year before, was appointed director of the country's new "Fifth Academy," the entity charged with developing China's missile and rocket capability. Chinese engineers were able to work with two R-1 (the SS-1, a Soviet version of the German V-2) and two R-2 (SS-2) missiles, provided by the Soviet Union in 1956 and 1957. When the U.S.S.R. withdrew its assistance, Chinese scientists continued their work and successfully tested a Chinese version of the R-2, the DF-1 (Dongfeng-1, or East Wind–1) in November 1960.

By 1965, the Fifth Academy was able to formally propose a program to design and build four different missiles over the next eight years. These would become the DF-2 (for which research and development [R&D] actually began in 1960), the DF-3 (R&D initiated in 1964), the DF-4 (R&D initiated in 1965), and the DF-5 (R&D also began in 1965).

The DF-2 (Western designation: CSS-1) and its longer-range variant, the DF-2A, were deployed from the late 1960s until 1978. With a range of 1,050 km (1250 km for the 2A), the DF-2 "medium-short-range missile" was reportedly designed to reach Japan carrying a relatively low-yield (12- to 20-kiloton) warhead.

The DF-3/CSS-2, deployed since 1970 or 1971, is a road-transportable medium-range ballistic missile capable of being launched from permanent pads or portable stands. Designed originally to reach U.S. bases in the Philippines, the DF-3 has a range of up to 2,650 km (up to 2,800 km for the longer-range version, the DF-3A) and carries a single 3.3-megaton warhead. It has reportedly been deployed at Tonghua, Jianshui, Kunming, Yidu, Dengshahe, and Lianxiwang and is being phased out in favor of the DF-21/CSS-5.

The DF-4/CSS-3 intercontinental ballistic missile (ICBM), deployed since 1980, also carries a single 3.3-megaton warhead but has a range of up to 7,000 km. The missile is deployed in two launch configurations: a roll-out-to-launch site and an elevate-to-launch silo. Reportedly intended originally to reach U.S. bases in Guam, its range was extended to reach Moscow in the wake of Sino-Soviet border clashes in 1969. The dozen DF-4s that are currently deployed are "almost certainly intended as a retaliatory deterrent against targets in Russian and Asia" (National Intelligence Council, p. 8). The DF-4 has reportedly been deployed at Da Qaidam, Delingha, Sundian, Tongdao, and Xiao Qaidam.

The DF-5/CSS-4 ICBM, designed to reach the continental United States, also was first deployed as early as 1980. The silo-based missile has a range of up to 12,000 km and carries a single 4- to 5-megaton warhead; the DF-5A, replacing the DF-5, is reported to have a 13,000-km range. Between eighteen and twenty DF-5s are deployed with the Second Artillery, and most (one press report, citing a "leaked" document, indicated thirteen) are believed to target major U.S. cities. DF-5s are reportedly deployed at Luoning, Xuanhua, and Jiuquan.

The DF-21/CSS-5, a land-mobile solid-fueled medium-range ballistic missile (MRBM), was based on the JL-1 SLBM. It has been deployed since about 1985, replacing the liquid-fueled DF-3. The DF-21, with a range of 1,800 km, carries a single 200- to 300-kiloton warhead. Forty-eight DF-21s and DF-21As (its longer-range variant) are reportedly deployed at Tonghua, Chuxiong, Datong, Lianxiwang, and Jianshui. Like the DF-3, these are presumably intended for targets in Russia and Asia. A model with a conventional warhead variant is reportedly under development.

China probably maintains its land-based missiles in an unfueled status and without their nuclear warheads. It would likely take several hours to prepare them for launch. Chinese designers long ago recognized that such land-based, fixed-site missiles would

be increasingly vulnerable to enemy preemption. In 1975, they experimented with rail-mobile basing for the DF-4. Three years later, Deng Xiaoping emphasized that he was most interested in mobility on land; that is, the use of modern weapons to fight guerrilla war, and soon after, the state committee overseeing missile development indicated that "to fight a modern guerilla war, the second generation strategic ballistic missiles must be mobile, rapid [in preparation time], and concealable, with mobility as the focus" (Lewis and Xue Litai 1988, p. 26).

This focus on increasing mobility and reaction time led the Chinese designers to develop the DF-21/CSS-5 from the JL-1/CSS-N-3, a submarine-launched ballistic missile (SLBM) with a range of 1,700 km that had been under development since 1967. The Chinese Navy had little success integrating the SLBM, which carries a 200- to 300-kiloton warhead, into the Type 092 (Xia) submarine, based at the North Sea Fleet's Jianggezhuang submarine base. The Xia, launched in 1981, has had a spotty record, spending years in overhaul, and was considered "nonoperational" for many years. Its current status is unclear.

Since 1986, the Chinese also have been developing the land-mobile DF-31 intermediate-range ballistic missile (IRBM) and its seagoing sibling, the JL-2 SLBM. The DF-31, which received priority over the JL-2 in development, is expected to begin deployment by 2005. The JL-2 is expected to be deployed by 2010 on a new submarine, the type 094, currently under development. The Chinese also have been developing a 12,000-km-range variant of the DF-31, the DF-31A, capable of reaching the entire continental United States.

In addition to these strategic missiles, China deploys two conventionally armed short-range ballistic missiles (SRBMs), the DF-15/CSS-6 and DF-11/CSS-7, opposite Taiwan. As of 2004, China reportedly had about 500 of these SRBMs and their variants deployed, and it is adding about 75 per year.

China's ballistic missiles, like its nuclear weapons, were developed by teams of specialists. The first generation of ballistic missile designers responsible for the DF-2 and DF-3 included chief designer Xie Guangxuan, The chief-designer system collapsed during the Cultural Revolution but was reinstated in the late 1970s.

Although dozens of factories are involved in producing key components for China's ballistic missiles, Nanyuan's Factory 211 (also known as the Capital Aerospace Machinery Company) is generally responsible for assembling liquid-fueled ballistic missiles. The Nanjing Factory 307 (the Nanjing Chenguang Machine Factory) is generally responsible for solid-fueled strategic missile production. China's CSS-6 SRBM was reportedly designed and produced by the China Aerospace Corporation's Academy of Launch Technology (CALT—the current name of the original Fifth Academy). The CSS-7 SRBM was reportedly designed at the 066 Base (the Sanjiang Space Group) and is produced at a Sanjiang factory in Yuan'an.

In 1966, China established the Second Artillery to control its new land-based missile forces. It is reportedly organized into six "bases" (at Shenyang, Huangshan, Kunming, Luoyang, Huaihua, and Xining. Each base oversees a number of launch brigades with one missile type, consisting of up to four launch battalions. As of 2003, the Second Artillery's force structure reportedly comprised fewer than 50 DF-3/CSS-2s; about a dozen DF-4/CSS-3s; about 20 DF-5/CSS-4s; about 48 DF-21/CSS-5s; and about 450 CSS-6s and CSS-7s.

Bombers
China's first bombers were the Hong-5, a 1950s copy of the Soviet Il-28 Beagle, and the Hong-6, a licensed copy of the Soviet Tu-16 Badger produced in Xi'an. Some of the Nanchang Q-5 attack aircraft, based on the MiG-19, also may have had a nuclear role. However, China's commitment to a nuclear bomber capability is increasingly uncertain: Its 2002 White Paper on National Defense notes a nuclear mission for the Second Artillery and the navy but none for the air force. The air force's new bomber, the Xi'an JH-7 (or FB-7), is not believed to have a nuclear mission. The U.S. Department of Defense Annual Reports on the military power of the People's Republic of China do not mention a nuclear bomber capability (see Bombers, Russian and Chinese Nuclear-Capable).

Chinese Strategic Thought
Since the beginning of nuclear weapons development in China, two main ideas have influenced Chinese nuclear policy: first, dedication to building a small, high-quality force, and second, commitment to a no-first-use policy. Mao laid the groundwork for the first principle in the early days of the program when he indicated that China should build a few high-quality nuclear weapons. China's no-first-use pledge was made the day of its first nuclear test, when Beijing stated, "At any time and under any situation, China will not use nuclear weapons first" (http://www.nit.org/db/china/engdocs/zhu0297.htm). These two pillars of Chinese nuclear planning continue to have a profound influence on Chinese strategy. If the key components of nuclear strategy are timing and targeting, a commitment to a small force and a no-first-use posture severely constrains China's strategic options—and helps control spending.

As a result, China has apparently adopted a strategy—and force structure—based on riding out an attack and retaliating by targeting large, soft targets, including cities and industrial and military targets. Western and Chinese authors have characterized this strategy as one of "minimum deterrence." Such a posture, however, cannot be sustained if China's small force becomes vulnerable, either to preemption on the ground or to missile defenses. China is clearly shifting to more survivable mobile forces and away from its fixed site forces. But there also continues to be an extensive internal discussion—and advocacy—of a shift to a "limited deterrent." While the logic underpinning a minimal deterrent is an emphasis on inflicting unacceptable pain on an attacker, a limited deterrent is intended to undermine the enemy's military capabilities by striking militarily significant targets.

For the foreseeable future, a minimum deterrent may be the only realistic—and desirable—option for China vis-à-vis the continental United States. But a limited deterrent may be more realistic against regional adversaries or U.S. forces based in Asia. Western experts increasingly distinguish between China's minimum strategic deterrent, directed at the United States and Russia, a limited deterrent for regional adversaries, and a warfighting strategy for its conventional SRBM force.

—Peter Almquist

See also: Negative Security Assurances; Strategic Forces; Submarine-Launched Ballistic Missiles; Submarines, Nuclear-Powered Ballistic Missile

References
Lewis, John Wilson, and Xue Litai, China Builds the Bomb (Stanford, CA: Stanford University Press, 1988).

————, *China's Strategic Seapower: The Politics of Force Modernization in the Nuclear Age* (Stanford, CA: Stanford University Press, 1994).

Li, Xiaobing, "PLA Attacks and Amphibious Operations during the Taiwan Strait Crises of 1954–55 and 1958," in Mark A. Ryan, David M. Finkelstein, and Michael A. McDevitt, eds., *Chinese Warfighting: The PLA Experience since 1949* (Armonk, NY: M. E. Sharpe, 2003).

Manning, Robert, Brad Roberts, and Ron Montaperto, *China, Nuclear Weapons, and Arms Control* (New York: Council on Foreign Relations Press, 2000).

Mulvenon, James C., and Andrew N.D. Yang, eds., *The People's Liberation Army as Organization: Reference Volume 1.0* (Santa Monica, CA: RAND Corporation, 2002).

National Intelligence Council, *Foreign Missile Developments and the Ballistic Missile Threat Through 2015* (Washington, DC: National Intelligence Council, 2001).

Norris, Robert S., Andrew S. Burrows, and Richard W. Fieldhouse, *Nuclear Weapons Databook*, vol. 2: *British, French, and Chinese Nuclear Weapons* (Boulder: Westview, 1994).

Stokes, Mark A., *China's Strategic Modernization: Implications for the United States* (Carlisle, PA: U.S. Army War College Strategic Studies Institute, 1999).

U.S. Department of Defense, *Annual Report on the Military Power of the People's Republic of China* (Washington, DC: U.S. Department of Defense, 1997–2003).

CIRCULAR ERROR PROBABLE
See Accuracy

CITY AVOIDANCE

The term "city avoidance" refers to a nuclear policy decision to target another state's military forces or industry rather than its population centers. Targeting policy has always been a contentious issue in warfare. With the advent of nuclear weapons, the potential damage that could be inflicted upon a city became very real, and throughout the Cold War there were debates about whether population centers or solely military targets should be emphasized in defense planning.

The issue of city avoidance came to prominence in the early 1960s. The John F. Kennedy administration inherited a single plan that called for launching many nuclear weapons at once without regard for the increasing Sino-Soviet split. Under U.S. Secretary of Defense Robert McNamara, the United States developed a series of nuclear options that sought to establish and maintain a ladder of escalation. These became known as Single Integrated Operational Plan 62 (SIOP-62). McNamara articulated this new policy in 1962 in a speech at Ann Arbor, Michigan, in which he sought to encourage the avoidance of city targeting.

If population centers were to be avoided, however, the obvious alternate target became an opponent's strategic nuclear forces. Since there was little point targeting an opponent's strategic forces after they had been launched, city avoidance strategies became associated with counterforce strategies. Thus, from the 1960s until the end of the Cold war, debate raged over targeting options, especially over which strategies would best preserve deterrence and maintain the peace.

—*Andrew M. Dorman*

See also: Counterforce Targeting; Countervalue Targeting

References

Freedman, Lawrence, *Evolution of Nuclear Strategy*, second edition (New York: St. Martin's Press, 1989), pp. 234–244.

Halperin, Morton, "The 'No Cities Doctrine,'" *New Republic*, 8 October 1962.

CIVIL DEFENSE

Civil defense is the passive protection of a population against damage or casualties resulting from a strategic attack. Debate over the requirement for some form of defense has surrounded nuclear weapons almost from their inception. The debate about civil defense has focused on two issues. First, there has been the question of balance between offensive and defensive measures. In other words, given finite resources, what share of expenditure should civil defense have compared to a nuclear weapons program? What is the most appropriate balance for the state, given the potential scale of physical and societal damage that a nuclear attack could inflict? Second, what is the minimum requirement for civil defense capability? In other words, what is the minimum requirement for the preservation of some form of civilian administration for the survivors of a nuclear attack?

Although this debate was largely a Cold War phenomenon, recent events have led to new assessments of the proper balance between offensive forces and civil defense measures. The attacks of

September 11, 2001, on the United States, the earlier use of chemical weapons on the Tokyo underground, and the increasing proliferation of knowledge about weapons of mass destruction and weapons of mass effect have led a revival of the civil defense debate. This has now been couched in the terms of societal resilience and the protection of critical infrastructure.

Defining civil defense today thus creates an interesting challenge. At its broadest, it refers to all elements that are designed to protect the state from the effects of attack rather than merely its armed forces. In the Cold War, this would have included elements such as shelters for all or part of the civilian population. It incorporated the stockpiling of material and equipment that would help preserve society. It also might have included more active elements of defense, such as an air defense system and ballistic missile defenses. Since the end of the Cold War, the debate has shifted toward the protection of critical infrastructure and large-scale disaster management. Such a definition now incorporates counterterrorism forces and the ability to maintain the continuity of supply for critical elements such as food, water, and fuel supplies to civil society.

History and Background

Throughout the evolution of warfare, technological breakthroughs have been rapidly countered as advantage swung between the offense and defense. The images many Americans have of World War I are about the success of the defense, with trenches and machine guns inflicting mass casualties on the attacking side. It was the advent of the airplane and its ability to carry bombs beyond the battlefield, however, that led to interest in civil defense. Although World War I witnessed the bombing of some cities, these air attacks were limited. Between the wars, advocates of airpower, such as military theorists Guilio Douhet, Billy Mitchell, and Hugh Trenchard, advocated the bombing of strategic targets, including cities, as a means of avoiding trench warfare. Concern was expressed by many that cities might be targeted with gas bombs and conventional munitions, leading to hundreds of thousands of casualties and the breakdown of society. By the outbreak of World War II, a number of states had quite significant civil defense programs as a means of limiting the impact of potential air raids. In the United Kingdom, for example, there was a wide-scale dis-tribution of gas masks, a major program to provide underground shelters in towns and cities, and the mass evacuation of significant numbers of children and their teachers to the countryside for much of the war.

It was hardly surprising, then, that as soon as the first atomic bomb was dropped on Hiroshima, the issue of potential defenses against atomic attack was discussed. Initially, debate centered on whether a radiation antidote could be developed. While studies continued in this area, other active and passive measures were examined, such as the dispersion of key assets and increased protection. These ideas were reviewed and adopted in varying levels by different cities and states. Because early atomic bombs were large and carried by bomber aircraft, both sides of the superpower standoff developed air defenses to protect themselves. With the advent of the hydrogen bomb and ballistic missiles capable of carrying thermonuclear warheads, active defenses in general were increasingly reduced in scale in the West, although the Soviet Union maintained a considerable defensive capability. This difference in approach reflected differences in the strategic nuclear forces of the two nations. The Soviets, for example, had only a relatively small bomber force and relied almost entirely upon submarine and land-based ballistic missiles. It also reflected differences in outlook about the utility of defenses that existed between Soviet and U.S. officials.

The advent of ballistic missiles saw the offense-defense cycle come full circle. As both sides developed intercontinental ballistic missiles (ICBMs), the Soviet Union and United States each sought to develop an antiballistic missile system. Developments in their respective programs were limited by the Anti-Ballistic Missile Treaty (1972). Until recently, only the Soviet Union (and now Russia) had deployed an active defense with an antiballistic missile system. The Gerald Ford administration decided to scrap the Sentinel/Safeguard system in the mid-1970s. In 1983, however, President Ronald Reagan launched the Strategic Defense Initiative (SDI), which sought to create an active defensive screen. This would have been undertaken in conjunction with an air defense initiative to provide complete protection for the United States from air and missile attack. This program has been modified over the decades since Reagan's term in office but in a more modest form is scheduled for deployment beginning in 2004 (*see* Anti-Ballistic Missile [ABM] Treaty; Safeguard Antiballistic Missile (ABM) System; Sentinel Anti-Ballistic Missile System; Strategic Defense Initiative [SDI]).

Several different approaches to passive defense were also undertaken. Passive measures included the dispersion of key targets and encasing them, where possible, in reinforced concrete to protect them from the effects of nuclear blast. Protection against nuclear fallout required carefully constructed filtration systems and the ability to be self-sustaining for some time (estimates varied between a few days and several months), which necessitated the accumulation and preservation of considerable stockpiles of foodstuffs and other materials. Many commentators believed that such measures were impracticable in Europe and the United States, where population densities were too great and societies too vulnerable. To survive in such an apocalyptic future, a society would have to become cellular, consisting of independent, self-sustaining units. It would require a significant program of shelter construction and a devolved, autocratic system of government in wartime. This seemed to run counter to many Western values, and critics suggested that such a program was merely delusionary and very expensive. Nevertheless, in the United States the question of civil defense ebbed and flowed as a subject of debate with no all-encompassing program ever being fully enacted. Instead, more active forms of defense tended to receive investment, such as the Sentinel program, the Strategic Defense Initiative, and the National Missile Defense program.

Other Western governments adopted a policy of universal provision of civil defense, seeking to protect their societies through active civil defense programs, with a focus on passive measures. In Sweden and Switzerland, the goal was to provide sufficient shelters for the entire population. In the Swiss case, this included the preservation of a significant infrastructure to support Swiss society. Similarly, Israel undertook a significant civil defense program, which it was able to utilize during the 1991 Gulf War when concerns were expressed about the potential use of weapons of mass destruction by Iraq. The Soviet Union also engaged in a significant civil defense program, but this could not match the capabilities of the Swiss program. A number of analysts argued that this program, when matched to a first-strike capability, was destabilizing because it ran counter to the principle of assured destruction. At issue was the amount of damage that a state could sustain and still survive. As a comparative measure, the damage wreaked on Germany by the Allied strategic bomber offensive of World War II was equivalent to more than 400 Hiroshima-size atomic bombs. The costs associated with such defenses and concern about their relative value meant that for most states, few defenses were adopted. Deterrence, rather than defense, was seen as the more affordable option, especially if that deterrent was provided by another state.

The Future of Civil Defense

With the end of the Cold War, civil defense has shifted in focus away from preparations to counter a devastating attack by one state upon another. Now, planners focus their attention on managing the effects of catastrophic terrorism from a weapon of mass destruction or from a conventional bomb attached to some nuclear material in some form in a so-called "dirty bomb." During the Cold War, analysts were greatly concerned about the physical damage nuclear weapons could wreak on society. The "dirty bomb" raises the question about radioactive contamination of key industrial, commercial, or cultural sites. For example, the use of such a device in London or New York could have a devastating impact upon the economy of not just the target states but also the wider world. Western economic systems are based on a small number of centralized stock markets, so a disturbance in one of them could potentially be quite catastrophic. Nevertheless, globalization and the shift to the information age has enabled increased resilience as companies and governments can create back-up facilities quite quickly.

—Andrew M. Dorman

See also: Radiological Dispersal Device; Peacekeeper Missile; Submarine Launched Ballistic Missile

References

Royal United Services Institute (RUSI), *Nuclear Attack: Civil Defence: Aspects of Civil Defence in the Nuclear Age* (London: Brassey's, 1982).

Vale, Lawrence J., *The Limits of Civil Defence in the USA, Switzerland, Britain and the Soviet Union: The Evolution of Policy since 1945* (Basingstoke, UK: Macmillan, 1987).

COLD LAUNCH

Cold launch is a technical innovation that allows a missile to be ejected from its silo or missile tube by a gas generator or mortar charge. The first-stage missile motor ignites after the missile has cleared the silo or launch tube. The Soviet intercontinental ballistic missiles (ICBMs) SS-11, SS-17, and SS-18 were all cold-launched, and throughout the Cold War U.S. officials believed that these silos could be quickly reloaded with ICBMs in a nuclear conflict. But it now appears that the Soviets had to adopt the cold-launch technique to limit the heat and acoustical stresses on their third-generation ICBMs. This allowed Soviet missile designers to use reconditioned silos for the new ICBM designs without having to expand them.

The Soviet Union initially used gas generators to eject the ICBMs, but mobile fourth-generation ICBMs such as the SS-25 and SS-27 are ejected by means of a mortar charge in the launch tube within the transporter-erector-launcher.

Submarine-launched missiles also must be cold-launched because they have to be ejected from a submarine-based tube and pushed to the surface of the ocean before the first-stage motor can ignite. The cold launch method increases the payload capability by approximately10 percent and prevents costly rebuilding to the launch silo.

The MX Peacekeeper was the first U.S. ICBM to use cold-launch technology. The missile was placed inside a canister and loaded into the launch facility. When launched, high-pressure steam ejected the canister from the launch silo to an altitude of 150 to 300 feet, and once the missile cleared the silo, the first stage ignited and sent the missile on its course. This technique allowed Strategic Air Command to launch the Peacekeeper from Minuteman silos despite the fact that the Peacekeeper was three times larger than the Minuteman III.

—*Gilles Van Nederveen*

See also: Launchers

References

Gunston, Bill, *The Illustrated Encyclopedia of the World's Rockets and Missiles* (London: Salamander, 1979).

Menaul, Air Vice Marshal Stewart, *The Illustrated Encyclopedia of the Strategy, Tactics and Weapons of the Soviet War Machine* (London: Salamander, 1980).

COLD WAR

"Cold War" refers to the political, ideological, and strategic standoff between the United States and the Soviet Union that emerged from the destruction of World War II, and which ostensibly ended with the disappearance of the Soviet Union in 1991. It was a "cold" war because it never took the form of direct military confrontation between the two superpowers, although many Soviets and Americans died at each others' hands in the proxy wars and clandestine operations that characterized the second half of the twentieth century. It was "war," rather than "competition," because it involved mutually irreconcilable strategic objectives. Each side prepared to engage in "hot" war if its own strategic position or vital national interests were threatened by its opponent.

In the view of most observers, what kept the Cold War "cold" was the terrifying prospect of a full-scale nuclear exchange. Throughout the Cold War, both U.S. and Soviet officials and military planners presumed that direct military hostilities between the superpowers could lead to nuclear escalation that might culminate in Armageddon. Given the crises that punctuated some forty-five years of Cold War, it is easy to imagine, in the absence of nuclear weapons, both superpowers resorting to military force, generally on someone else's territory. The undeniable fact of nuclear weapons, however, virtually guaranteed unacceptable destruction on the territory of the superpowers, once direct warfare began. There was never a point when the political objectives to be gained justified the self-destruction that would likely result from escalation to nuclear weapons.

There are those who argue that the *real* political objectives of the superpowers—rather than the objectives presumed by the opposing superpower—were never so irreconcilable as they seemed, and that, as a result, the Cold War was unnecessary—a conflict produced by miscalculation, mistrust, and the security dilemma. Once started, the Cold War took on a life of its own as both parties created institutions; policy communities that had a vested interest in fulfilling their part of the superpower standoff.

There is no agreement about either the exact beginning or the end of the Cold War. There was no military attack or declaration of war to mark its beginning, yet most scholars note that the Soviet-American wartime alliance had deteriorated beyond repair by 1947. There was no clear demarcation between the "prelude to war" and war itself, although many point to speeches and policies—generally in 1946 or 1947, sometimes earlier—that seem to be the moral equivalent of a declaration of Cold War.

A U.S. P-3 Orion overflies a Soviet guided missile cruiser during the Cold War. (Corbis)

Likewise, there was no "peace treaty" to signify the end of the war. Victory for the West came as a result of the Soviet Union's disappearance or transformation as a political entity, which occurred on Christmas Day, 1991. Yet, even the selection of this date is somewhat arbitrary; the political transformation of the Soviet Union had already been under way for some time, and some believe that the political competition between the United States and Russia has survived the end of the Cold War.

The nature of the Cold War changed often during the nearly half century that it lasted. The level of hostility and cooperation between the superpowers varied. There was a certain rhythm as successive Soviet and American political leaders consolidated their own positions, probed for weaknesses in the other side, discovered their own vulnerabilities, and occasionally sought to escape from the intractable dynamics of the conflict. Even during the most hostile periods of the Cold War, the United States and the Soviet Union shared a fairly common understanding of the logic and character of nuclear weapons and their effect on their relationship.

The Origins of the Cold War

There was never a time during the seventy-four-year existence of the Soviet Union in which it enjoyed "good" relations with the United States. Even in its early years, when the Soviet Union could not directly threaten the United States, American policymakers were suspicious of Bolshevism, which was viewed as dangerous. Although the Soviet Union had conspired with Nazi Germany to attack Poland in September 1939, the Nazi surprise attack on the Soviet Union in June 1941—almost six months prior to Japan's attack on Pearl Harbor—made the Soviets a de facto ally of the United States. U.S. officials had little sympathy for Joseph Stalin's regime, but Nazi conquest of the Soviet Union was unacceptable. U.S. material assistance in the form of food and war materiel helped keep the Soviet Union in the war. The Soviets tied down the bulk of the German military while the Allies prepared a "second front" in Europe and liberated Western Europe.

From the Soviet perspective, Allied delays opening a second front in Europe reinforced Stalin's distrust of the West, which he feared might make common cause with the Nazis to destroy Soviet communism. With their backs against the wall in 1942, the Soviets demanded an Allied counteroffensive, but they were disappointed when it materialized only in North Africa and, in 1943, in Italy. By the summer of 1943, however, Soviet victory over the Nazis seemed assured as the Red Army began to push west. To Stalin, the Allies' delay in opening a second front only proved that they were quite content to let the Russians bear the brunt of fighting the Nazis. Moreover, to Stalin, the urgency with which the Allies finally did mobilize to attack Normandy in June 1944 simply reflected their realization that the Red Army was poised to march alone through Eastern Europe and into Berlin.

As wartime allies, the United States and the Soviet Union were wary of each other's strategic intentions. By the end of the war, Soviet military and political domination of Eastern Europe was a fait accompli, and Stalin was determined to ensure that an attack from the capitalist West would have to fight its way through a significant buffer zone before reaching Soviet territory. Within the U.S. political leadership, the end of the war witnessed a debate about whether inducements could mobilize the Soviet Union to play a cooperative role in ensuring postwar security, rebuilding destroyed economies, and reconstructing former adversaries. By 1946, it was increasingly clear to U.S. policymakers that the prospect of political and economic aid would not alter these Soviet strategic interests, and that it would be counterproductive to accommodate Soviet concerns. As early as February 1946, U.S. Secretary of State James F. Byrnes spoke of a "get tough with Russia" policy, which was soon followed by Winston Churchill's "Iron Curtain" speech. In 1947, this perspective became a policy—"containment"—which became U.S. strategy for the rest of the Cold War.

The Cold War Hardens, 1947–1957

Cause and effect are intertwined in the immediate postwar period, but a series of moves and countermoves inexorably hardened the division in both Europe and Asia. The Truman Doctrine (1947) and the Marshall Plan (1948) were designed to counter Communist advances; successive Eastern European states became Communist; and the Soviets tried to blockade West Berlin (1948) to force the Western powers to reach a political settlement on the future of Germany. The Western European Union's Brussels Treaty (1948) preceded—by design—formation of the North Atlantic Treaty Organization (NATO, 1949). The front lines of the Cold War became represented by divided states in Korea (1948), Germany (1949), China (1949), and Vietnam (1954).

The U.S. response to the Chinese Communist victory, and especially to the Soviet Union's development of a nuclear capability, both of which occurred in 1949, was a comprehensive reappraisal of America's strategic position. The document summarizing this reappraisal, National Security Council Document 68 (NSC-68), concluded that the Soviet Union sought world domination and redefined containment in military terms, calling for U.S. development of thermonuclear weapons and a greater capability to fight conventional wars wherever Communist aggression would occur. The Korean War, which began in June 1950, confirmed many of the dire predictions offered by NSC-68, leading Congress and President Harry S. Truman to endorse its political and programmatic recommendations.

The Korean armistice in July 1953 ended a "hot battle" in the Cold War, but without offering a solution to the problem of a divided Korea, a problem that has endured well beyond the demise of the Soviet Union. The new Dwight D. Eisenhower administration, however, had campaigned on the platform that "hot wars"—especially in Asia—played into the hands of the Communists. With Stalin dead and a new leadership jockeying for position in Moscow, Eisenhower decided that reliance on nuclear deterrence—which was governed by a "New Look" in procurement policy and the declaratory policy of "massive retaliation"—was a more affordable and therefore more sustainable strategy for what was clearly going to be a protracted strategic standoff (*see* Massive Retaliation; New Look). Under U.S. Secretary of State John Foster Dulles, the United States proceeded to expand or establish alliances around the periphery of the Soviet Union. These efforts resulted in NATO (with the Federal Republic of Germany as an armed partner, and later Greece and Turkey), the Southeast Asia Treaty Organization (SEATO), the Baghdad Pact (with the UK, Iran, Iraq, and Turkey), the ANZUS (with Australia and New Zealand) Pact, and bilateral agreements with numerous other states, including Japan, the Republic of Korea, and Taiwan.

Alliances bring their own complications. As NATO's military capabilities in Western Europe grew, including deployment of tactical nuclear weapons to stop any Soviet military advances, some of America's NATO allies began to question the desirability of reliance on nuclear deterrence. In a much-publicized war game conducted in June 1955 called Carte Blanche, NATO simulated the "limited" use of tactical nuclear weapons, most of which necessarily were targeted on German territory. According to game results, more than 1.5 million Germans would have been killed and some 3.5 million incapacitated in a real event of this type. This poignant reminder of the dilemmas of the nuclear age left many wondering whether the defense of Europe might mean its destruction. In subsequent years, however, attempts to reduce reliance on nuclear weapons in the defense of Europe brought opposite protests. Any reduction was thought to signal Washington's reluctance to fulfill its deterrent threats and its understandable preference for keeping the destruction of war confined to a European battlefield. As the nuclear age unfolded and the United States became increasingly vulnerable to direct attack, sustaining the credibility of its nuclear deterrent guarantee to NATO became problematic (*see* Missile Gap).

Brinkmanship, 1957–1962

On November 17, 1956, Soviet leader Nikita Khrushchev threatened to "bury" the West. In 1957, there were growing concerns that he just might succeed. In August, Moscow announced its first test of an intercontinental ballistic missile, and six weeks later it launched Sputnik, the first satellite to orbit the earth. Following Sputnik, U.S. officials began to worry that the United States no longer led the Soviet Union in the nuclear arms race and that it was becoming vulnerable to massive nuclear attack by ballistic missiles. Eisenhower's memoirs speak of trying to calm "mass hysteria" in American public opinion as the 1957 Gaither Committee and the 1957 and 1958 Rockefeller reports warned of a significant American strategic vulnerability.

Within a year of Sputnik, Khrushchev declared the first of three ultimatums in an attempt to get the West out of Berlin. Although none of these challenges succeeded, each brought an additional increment of military and political tension, with U.S. and Soviet tanks eventually facing each other across checkpoints in Berlin. During this same period, relations alternated between threat-induced crises and periods of thaw. During the latter, Khrushchev visited the United States and the first U.S.-Soviet arms control treaty was signed (Antarctic Treaty). There were moratoriums on nuclear testing, but there were also boasts of Soviet tests in excess of 50 megatons. The so-called "Spirit of Camp David," however, reached an abrupt end when an American U-2 was shot down during a reconnaissance flight over Soviet territory in May 1960.

By the time John F. Kennedy was elected president in November 1960, U.S.-Soviet relations were growing highly unstable and unpredictable. In their first summit meeting in Vienna in June 1961, Khrushchev badgered Kennedy in an attempt to test the young president's resolve following the U.S. disaster at Cuba's Bay of Pigs. Two months later, the Berlin Wall went up. Fourteen months after that, Khrushchev tested the United States again by placing nuclear-armed intermediate- and medium-range ballistic missiles in Cuba.

The Cuban missile crisis was the closest that the United States and the Soviet Union ever came to nuclear war. Both Kennedy and Khrushchev realized after the crisis that they had come dangerously close to war and undertook a series of initiatives to reduce some of the precarious aspects of the Cold War. Within a year of the crisis, a "Hot Line," a direct teletype link to facilitate communication in a crisis, was in place between Washington and Moscow. The United States and the Soviet Union also concluded a Limited Test Ban Treaty in 1963 to bar nuclear tests except those conducted underground (*see* Cuban Missile Crisis; Limited Test Ban Treaty [LTBT]).

Prelude to Détente, 1964–1968

During the mid-1960s, both the United States and the Soviet Union discovered several common interests, leading them to explore additional means of managing their conflict and controlling the nuclear technology that formed the unavoidable backdrop to their relationship. First, the brinkmanship of the Cuban missile crisis mobilized both sides to explore mechanisms to inject greater stability into the relationship. Maturation of the missile age—by this time, both intercontinental ballistic missiles (ICBMs) and submarine-launched ballistic missiles (SLBMs) were entering respective inventories—enabled both superpowers to begin protecting their own forces in hardened underground silos and command centers and to move away from vulnera-

President Kennedy meets with U.S. Army officials in Florida during the Cuban Missile Crisis, October 1962. (Corbis)

ble above-ground missile launch platforms. These developments helped to make the deterrence relationship between the United States and the Soviet Union more crisis stable by eliminating the incentives of all concerned to use nuclear weapons first in a crisis.

Second, both superpowers shared concerns about the proliferation of nuclear weapons technology to other countries, even their respective allies. China and France joined the nuclear club in the 1960s. China had benefited from the assistance of the Soviet Union in the 1950s but wanted to gain nuclear independence from Moscow. French nuclear capabilities derived from the determination of French President Charles de Gaulle to develop an *independent* nuclear capability outside the NATO alliance, thereby reducing France's reliance on the United States. The West Germans, for their part, also began agitating for some kind of participation in NATO's nuclear deterrent so they would not be totally dependent on decisions made in Washington, London, or Paris.

Concerns about nuclear proliferation led to a surge in diplomatic activity. Superpower interest in slowing the proliferation of nuclear weapons was motivated not only by the desire to impose some control and predictability on strategic competition, but also by a desire to control allies who seemed determined to establish their own independent nuclear capabilities. Indeed, the greatest negotiating challenge of the Nuclear Nonproliferation Treaty related more to how the United States would manage its own allies' nuclear aspirations than to its own nuclear capabilities. When the treaty was signed by the United States in July 1968, both France and China refused to sign (although both qualified as "nuclear weapons states" in the treaty). West Germany did not sign the treaty until after a change of government in 1969, thus clearing the way for U.S. and Soviet ratification.

Third, both superpowers found themselves distracted in the mid-1960s and therefore inclined to keep their mutual competition on a safer plane. Within the Soviet Union, Leonid Brezhnev and Alexei Kosygin replaced Khrushchev in 1964, but it would be at least another four years before Brezhnev had consolidated his political position and power. China was a competitor with the Soviet Union for influence in the Communist world, a competition that made the Third World not only a Cold War "battleground" but also one in which the two Communist giants would compete for influence. Sino-Soviet ideological and political competition and acrimony actually erupted in open hostilities along their border in 1969. For the United States in the mid-1960s, Vietnam was the inexorable policy focus, consuming both attention and resources and diverting military forces from NATO's front line.

By the mid-1960s, the European allies of each superpower started exploring relationships across the East-West divide and contemplating ways in which their destinies might be improved, even though they seemed forever frozen in the immutable blocs of the Cold War. West Germany, in particular, began to probe for improved relations with East Germany, and—when East Berlin proved implacable—to circumvent both East Berlin and Moscow in developing linkages with other Eastern European capitals. For Bonn, it was necessary to overcome the stagnation in European politics that followed erection of the Berlin Wall and to push for progress on German reunification. Similarly, in capitals such as Prague, and, to a lesser degree, Warsaw and Budapest, there was a growing desire for both political and economic liberalization, to which Moscow seemed amenable—at least for a time. Neither set of allies was content with the status quo; both launched policies designed to stimulate political movement.

For the Soviet Union, such political movement was intolerable, and tanks rolled into Prague to suppress the "velvet revolution" in August 1968. The United States—in a year filled with its own political and military crises in Southeast Asia—tolerated the move as a tacit recognition of the Soviets' sphere of influence. Ironically, however, the Soviet move asserted a "rule of the game": The road for the West to Prague or Warsaw went through Moscow. A comparable rule was adopted by the incoming Nixon-Kissinger regime, leading the way to a period of far-reaching arms control treaties and political agreements called "détente."

Détente, 1969–1975

In 1969, the United States and the Soviet Union began the Strategic Arms Limitation Talks (SALT), culminating in the 1972 Interim Agreement on Offensive Arms and the Anti-Ballistic Missile (ABM) Treaty. They followed these negotiations with additional arms control agreements limiting the deployment of both offensive and defensive missiles,

strengthening crisis communications (through "Hot Line" Agreements), and beginning negotiations on further strategic arms limitations (*see* Anti-Ballistic Missile [ABM] Treaty; Strategic Arms Limitation Talks [SALT I and SALT II]).

By the early 1970s, a new government in Bonn also had embarked on "Ostpolitik," or an "Eastern policy," that led to a series of agreements with East Berlin, Moscow, Warsaw, and others, as well as a Four Power Agreement on Berlin. Washington was an active participant in this process with Moscow, not so much to record agreements with a Cold War adversary, but to preserve the cohesion of the alliance on which U.S. strength depended.

A new rapprochement in Europe and a stabilization of the bilateral nuclear relationship created further pressures to continue the arms control process within Europe itself, especially since Soviet conventional superiority was viewed as a destabilizing factor in itself. Negotiations within the Conference on Security and Cooperation in Europe (CSCE) began in parallel with negotiations toward a Mutual and Balanced Force Reductions (MBFR) agreement, although neither superpower was especially keen on achieving tangible results. In the end, CSCE produced the Helsinki Final Act in 1975. MBFR persisted without agreement until it was replaced, in 1989, by negotiations toward a Conventional Forces in Europe (CFE) Treaty.

Return to Confrontation, 1976–1985

Despite the appearances of a potential reconciliation of strategic interests that might point the way to the end of the Cold War, détente proved to be a tactical move for both superpowers that masked a deeper political and ideological hostility. Advances in nuclear weapons delivery technology—notably multiple independently targetable reentry vehicles (MIRV) and increasingly accurate guidance systems—created new forms of strategic instability. Instead of being protected in hardened silos, nuclear forces were becoming more valuable as targets (because they housed multiple warheads) and more vulnerable to preemption. The advent of "hard target kill" capabilities increased the incentive of one side to attack first in a crisis, rather than waiting to retaliate. Combined with continuing Warsaw Pact conventional superiority in Europe—which theoretically gave the Soviets a usable war-fighting option as it deterred the United States from escalating to a suicidal nuclear response—the strategic landscape appeared to many analysts in the United States as worse than at any other time in the Cold War.

Part of the solution to these problems was supposed to be a SALT II Treaty that limited Soviet heavy land-based missiles, while parallel efforts within NATO promised deployment of missiles on European soil capable of holding Soviet territory at risk. To many, however, the 1979 SALT II Treaty failed to address the U.S. strategic conundrum, and ratification was doubtful. NATO's "two-track" decision to deploy intermediate-range nuclear forces created its own political friction, since each "track"—deployment and arms control—drew its own share of critics.

At the same time, Soviet behavior in other parts of the world suggested to Washington that Moscow's ultimate political objectives had not changed. Six weeks after U.S. diplomats in Tehran were taken hostage in 1979, the Soviet Union invaded Afghanistan. The United States responded by encouraging, through aid and weapons, a form of "holy war" by Islamic militants and guerrillas against Soviet occupation.

Domestic political change in both countries in the early 1980s further polarized U.S. and Soviet policies, leading to a heightened confrontation reminiscent of the late 1950s. The election of President Ronald Reagan produced a surge in rhetoric about the "evil empire," substantial increases in U.S. defense spending, and a determination to build a national missile defense system that would overturn over a quarter century of theory about what constituted strategic stability. Within the Soviet Union, three leaders—Brezhnev, Yuri Andropov, and Konstantin Chernenko—died in almost as many years. Meanwhile, the occupation of Afghanistan deteriorated into a costly quagmire, Poland's Solidarity movement endured despite martial law, and the Soviet economy continued to decline under the burden of defense spending. The shoot-down of Korean Airlines flight 007 in September 1983 also highlighted the fact that the Soviet military command and control system was becoming increasingly unreliable.

In such circumstances, a new round of arms control negotiations in Geneva to address strategic force reductions, ballistic missile defense, and intermediate nuclear forces was bound to fail. The Soviet walkout from the talks on intermediate nuclear forces in late 1983 spelled stalemate until new Soviet leadership emerged in the person of Mikhail Gorbachev in 1985.

Beginning of the End, 1985–1991
Gorbachev had a radical impact on both the Soviet Union and the dynamics of the Cold War. Domestically, he advocated *perestroika* (restructuring) and *glasnost* (openness) to reform both a declining Soviet economy and a stifling political system. He also announced plans to withdraw Soviet troops from Afghanistan. A protégé of Andropov, who had been head of the Soviet KGB before he succeeded Brezhnev as head of the Communist Party, Gorbachev understood that the Soviet Union could not possibly compete with the United States unless radical reforms were undertaken. Ultimately, Gorbachev could not control the process of perestroika and glasnost, and the entire edifice of the Soviet state unraveled.

Some of Gorbachev's strategic proposals were equally revolutionary, including a 1985 proposal to eliminate nuclear weapons entirely, provided that nuclear disarmament be accompanied by a ban on strategic defenses. The next year, Gorbachev again surprised Reagan at their Reykjavik meeting by proposing elimination of strategic ballistic missiles, again conditioned on elimination of strategic defenses. Reagan would not accept the condition, so there was no agreement—a disappointment to some, but a source of considerable relief within NATO as allies contemplated the future of a U.S. deterrent guarantee without nuclear weapons. The two leaders did agree on total elimination of intermediate nuclear forces and a 50 percent reduction in deployed strategic weapons, culminating in the 1987 Intermediate-Range Nuclear Forces (INF) Treaty and the 1991 Strategic Arms Reduction Treaty (START I), respectively, as well as further improvements to crisis communications through Nuclear Risk Reduction Centers (*see* Intermediate-Range Nuclear Forces [INF] Treaty; Strategic Arms Reduction Treaty [START I]).

For many U.S. observers, Gorbachev's reforms seemed incredible—perhaps too good to be true. Some saw deception. They claimed that Soviet troops were not really leaving Afghanistan, or that unilateral concessions made by Moscow were simply a ploy to get the West to let down its guard. Others saw the call for arms control and nuclear disarmament as a ruse: Doing away with nuclear weapons would increase the importance of the Warsaw Pact's conventional force superiority in Europe. Even skeptics were converted, however, when Soviet negotiators agreed to reduce Warsaw Pact conventional forces to a level 5 percent below existing NATO force levels. Although Gorbachev agreed to such unilateral reductions to reduce defense spending and avert Soviet collapse, his direct intervention trumped the objections of the Soviet military leadership and led to the signing of the CFE Treaty in November 1990.

In 1989, the division of Europe into two hostile camps was nearly over. Gorbachev told East European Communist leaders that they needed to accommodate change on their own. "Roundtable talks" in Poland led to the election of a non-Communist government. The Berlin Wall was brought down. Communist leaders resigned, were expelled, or were executed. In 1990, the Warsaw Pact officially disappeared, and the two Germanys reunified. Remarkably, Gorbachev also acceded to the West's demand that the newly unified Germany remain a NATO member, recognizing that the Soviet Union's World War II foe was less likely to be a threat within NATO, with military restrictions, than as a strategically isolated power in Central Europe.

Within months of signing START I, Gorbachev resigned as Soviet president and the Soviet Union as a political entity ceased to exist. In its place, fifteen "newly independent states" emerged, with the Russian Federation serving as the successor state to the Soviet Union's obligations as well as privileges, including taking its seat in the United Nations Security Council and becoming sole inheritor of the former Soviet Union's nuclear weapons. Belarus, Kazakhstan, and Ukraine yielded control of former Soviet weapons that were deployed on their territory.

After 1990, rhetoric from virtually every political capital spoke of the end of the Cold War, but there were times in which behavior did not match that rhetoric. Strategically, the United States and Russia pursued additional arms control agreements—including START II and the 2002 Moscow Treaty—but Russian concerns about strategic disadvantage vis-à-vis the United States—a distinctly Cold War concern—blocked ratification in the Russian Duma. Arguments for enlarging NATO's membership to include former members of the Warsaw Pact

and even Russia sometimes sounded like an extension of a half-century-old strategic competition. By the same token, there has been substantial cooperation in dismantling the legacy of the Soviet Union that would not be possible if Cold War mentalities persisted.

The Cold War in Retrospect

For decades, the Cold War provided a clear and often one-dimensional lens through which policymakers were able to gauge foreign policy actions. As U.S. officials defined their global role following World War II, the choice of whether to intervene in a particular crisis often resolved to a single question—What side are the Communists on? In the chaotic and globalized world of the twenty-first century, with amorphous and unprecedented strategic threats facing the United States, the relative simplicity of the Cold War sometimes looks appealing.

For U.S. policy, the Cold War also reflected a remarkable bipartisan consensus in American foreign policy priorities. America had become a global power for reasons largely shared across the domestic political spectrum and among America's allies, notwithstanding often-difficult debates about tactics, methods, and policy priorities. That consensus, too, has dissipated as new debates have emerged about the ends and means by which America's power in the world is to be exercised.

American policy in the Cold War—beginning with containment—was essentially a status quo policy. The United States sought to protect the status quo from a revolutionary ideology antithetical to U.S. interests. The policy required more than "patience" and "vigilance," as George Kennan had suggested when he introduced the policy of containment in his famous 1946 "long telegram." It demanded that the United States manage a strategic relationship in which it was increasingly vulnerable by virtue of the dynamics of the nuclear age. Likewise, it also demanded that the United States manage a set of alliance relationships, lest the West appear divided and invite aggression. Ironically, in both these endeavors, the United States found a remarkable degree of shared interests with its Cold War adversary, notwithstanding the ideological incompatibility of the two countries. Perhaps more than anything else, that is what helped keep the Cold War "cold."

—*Schuyler Foerster*

See also: Arms Control; Containment; Cuban Missile Crisis; Deterrence; Game Theory; North Atlantic Treaty Organization; Russian Nuclear Forces and Doctrine; United States Nuclear Forces and Doctrine

References

Beschloss, Michael R., and Strobe Talbott, *At the Highest Levels: The Inside Story of the End of the Cold War* (Boston: Little, Brown, 1993).

Brown, Seyom, *The Faces of Power: Constancy and Change in United States Foreign Policy from Truman to Reagan* (New York: Columbia University Press, 1983).

Foerster, Schuyler, and Edward N. Wright, eds., *American Defense Policy,* sixth edition (Baltimore: Johns Hopkins University Press, 1990).

Gaddis, John Lewis, *The United States and the Origins of the Cold War, 1941–1947* (New York: Columbia University Press, 1972).

———, *Now We Know* (New York: Oxford University Press, 1997).

Garthoff, Raymond L., *Détente and Confrontation: American-Soviet Relations from Nixon to Reagan* (Washington, DC: Brookings Institution, 1985).

Kennan, George, "The Chargé in the Soviet Union (Kennan) to the Secretary of State" (also known as "The Long Telegram"), 22 February 1946, available at www.gwu.edu/~nsarchiv/coldwar/documents/episode-1/kennan.htm.

Kissinger, Henry, *Diplomacy* (New York: Simon and Schuster, 1994).

Nitze, Paul H., with Ann M. Smith and Steven L. Reardon, *From Hiroshima to Glasnost: At the Center of Decision—A Memoir* (New York: Grove Weidenfeld, 1989).

Zubok, Vladislov, and Constantine Pleshakov, *Inside the Kremlin's Cold War: From Stalin to Khruschchev* (Cambridge: Harvard University Press, 1996).

COLLATERAL DAMAGE

Collateral damage is unintentional or incidental damage affecting facilities, equipment, or personnel that occurs as a result of deliberate military action against targeted enemy forces or facilities. According to the U.S. Defense Intelligence Agency's Battle Damage Assessment (BDA) Quick Guide, collateral damage is assessed and reported during the BDA process.

Determining how much care must be taken to minimize collateral damage constraints is a commander's responsibility. If national command or theater authorities do not predetermine constraint levels for collateral damage, a corps or higher commander will normally be responsible for doing so. When a commander is planning strikes near his or her own forces, there is always some element of risk. Usually, conservative calculations will be used (except under emergency conditions) to minimize risks to friendly forces. Planning also may lead to maximizing collateral damage to enemy facilities near planned targets.

Conventional weapons have relatively small effective radii against personnel, but their use in close support of tactical operations still involves some risk to friendly forces. Nuclear weapons increase this risk considerably because of their larger effective radii. Therefore, in the analysis of a potential nuclear target close to friendly troops or to a friendly civilian population, safety risk is carefully evaluated by planners and commanders. When weapons are considered for employment against targets close to friendly forces or civilians, troop safety considerations may determine whether nuclear weapons will be used. If they are used, troop safety may influence the selection of yield, delivery means, location of the desired ground zero, height of burst, and time of burst, as well as the ground commander's scheme of maneuver. Because of delivery errors and prevailing weather and terrain conditions, calculating the risk to friendly troops involves the use of probabilities and good judgment. It would be desirable to have a 100 percent assurance that no friendly casualties would result from the use of nuclear weapons, but as long as the possibility of delivery error exists, such an assurance is unlikely. As a rule, the commander will want a very high assurance (0.99 probability) that his troops will not be exposed to weapon effects higher than those considered acceptable given the military situation on the ground.

The high risk of great collateral damage is partly behind the call in the 2001 Nuclear Posture Review to develop low-yield nuclear weapons and earth-penetrating delivery systems. Critics charge, however, that by reducing the potential for collateral damage, these weapons lower the nuclear threshold, making it more likely that U.S. officials will decide to use nuclear weapons in dire military circumstances.

—*Mike Kaufhold and James J. Wirtz*

References

U.S. Air Force, "Targeting Guide," Air Force Pamphlet 14-210, 1 February 1998.

U.S. Defense Intelligence Agency, DIA Pamphlet PC-8060-1-96, February 1996.

COMMAND AND CONTROL

Command and control generally refers to a set of protocols and communication links and procedures that ensure that weapons of mass destruction, especially nuclear weapons, are launched only upon the orders of authorized individuals. This includes positive control—ensuring that weapons are released in a timely manner upon the order of civil authorities—and negative control—preventing accidental, irrational, and unauthorized release. There is a trade-off between these two objectives. Safeguards that can always guarantee negative control might be too difficult to release if the time ever came to launch weapons, especially if the launch crews were given short notice.

Command and control functions are performed through an arrangement of personnel, equipment, communications, facilities, and procedures employed by a commander in planning, coordinating, and controlling forces and operations in the accomplishment of the mission.

Perhaps the most essential component of precluding accidental or unauthorized launch of a delivery vehicle carrying a nuclear weapon is to ensure that procedures are in place before a crisis occurs, obviating the need to make critical decisions during times of highest stress. Breakdowns in command and control have occurred in the past and will likely occur again. In the 1950s, a flock of Canadian geese was interpreted as a Soviet bomber attack by the U.S. early warning radar system. A similar event occurred in 1960 when meteor showers and lunar reflections spooked early warning systems. In 1980, the failure of a 46-cent computer chip led to mistaken indications that a Soviet submarine had just launched its missiles against the United States. In each case, there were sufficient backup systems and safeguards in place to prevent a panicked retaliatory attack.

Ultimate nuclear command authority in the United States is exercised by the president, vice president, and secretary of defense, collectively referred to during the Cold War as the National Command Authority (NCA). Although this process is still in place today, the NCA designation has been eliminated.

By the 1960s, the United States set up a decentralized system consisting of primary and secondary (including airborne) command centers to provide redundancy in case of a Soviet strike, ensuring the ability to launch retaliatory strikes against Moscow. This was deemed crucial as a means of preventing Soviet strikes in the first place as part of the larger doctrine of mutual assured destruction. Although authorization to release nuclear weapons theoretically can come only from the president, most sources believe that the authority to fire the U.S. strategic arsenal might devolve to senior military officers in the event of a catastrophic attack that disabled presidential communication or decision-making ability. Details about the command and control procedures maintained by nuclear states are highly guarded secrets.

—*James Joyner*

References
Bracken, Paul, *The Command and Control of Nuclear Forces* (New Haven, CT: Yale University Press, 1983).
Sagan, Scott, *The Limits of Safety* (Princeton, NJ: Princeton University Press, 1993).
Stein, Peter, and Peter Feaver, *Assuring Control of Nuclear Weapons* (Lanham, MD: University Press of America, 1987).

COMMITTEE ON THE PRESENT DANGER

In the early 1950s and again in the mid-1970s, former top policymakers, leading academics, and industrial leaders formed citizens' groups called the Committee on the Present Danger to warn of rising Soviet capabilities and to support tough U.S. policy responses. The two groups were distinct, although there was a small overlap of membership and the second group consciously chose to revive the name.

The first committee was formed in 1950 soon after the completion of National Security Council Document 68 (NSC-68) and the start of the Korean War. Its founders were Harvard University President James Conant, former Undersecretary of the Army Tracy Voorhees, and atomic scientist Vannevar Bush. Soon other leading university presidents, including Dwight D. Eisenhower (then at Columbia University), and other former government officials became involved. The group repeatedly warned of the aggressive designs of the Soviet Union and argued for a response in the form of European rearmament, a U.S. military buildup, and universal military service. The goal of its members was to rally public opinion behind the internationalist and more militarist containment policies of the Harry Truman administration and NSC-68, in particular (*see* Cold War).

The second committee was formed in 1976 in response to what some saw as a revived Soviet threat, the softness of détente and arms control, and the emergence of the Trilateral Commission as a voice of the elite establishment. Its founders included former Undersecretary of State Eugene Rostow, former author of NSC-68 and Secretary of the Navy Paul Nitze, former Secretary of the Treasury Henry Fowler, and roughly 150 other government, academic, and business elites. Like the first committee, the group warned of rising Soviet military capabilities and goals and argued that the only appropriate response was U.S. military strength. The group became a leading opponent of the treaty resulting from the Strategic Arms Limitation Talks (SALT II) and took some credit for its failure.

Technically, the committee was a nonprofit research organization, not a lobbying group, but the members used their extensive governmental contacts to try to shape government decisions. The committee also produced research reports, worked closely with newspaper editorial boards, and conducted polls attempting to show that although public sentiment in general favored arms control, few citizens understood or supported the terms of SALT II. With the 1980 election, committee members moved back into positions of power. Ronald Reagan himself had been a member of the committee, and thirty-two other members joined his administration, becoming leading designers of his policies.

—*John W. Dietrich*

References

Sanders, Jerry W., *Peddlers of Crisis: The Committee on the Present Danger and the Politics of Containment* (Boston: South End Press, 1983).

Tyroler, Charles, II, ed., *Alerting America: The Papers of the Committee on the Present Danger* (Washington, DC: Pergamon-Brassey's International Defense Publishers, 1984).

COMPELLENCE

Compellence is an attempt to get an adversary to perform a requested action by threatening the use of force if the adversary does not comply with the request. It includes convincing the target to do something, to reverse an action already taken, or to otherwise change the status quo. An attempt to convince a state to give up or roll back its nuclear weapons program is compellence, for example, when marked by threat of force.

The term "compellence" was created by Thomas Schelling to illustrate the difference between two different types of coercion: "deterrence," by which the coercer tries to convince the adversary not to carry out a specific action that he intends to perform, and "compellence," by which the coercer is attempting to get the adversary to carry out a specific action. Both tasks require the threat of force (or some adverse action) to make noncompliance with the demands more costly for the adversary than compliance.

Compellence is generally regarded as a difficult task, given that it is harder to get people to do something than to get them to refrain from doing something. When a state is compelled, it appears weak. If the adversary performs the requested task in response to a threat, its submission to following threats will often be obvious to onlookers. Thus, there can be reputational costs associated with bowing to the coercer's will. Complying with the compeller's demands may cause the target to "lose face" at home or abroad and may cause domestic instability or even encourage the coercer or other states to make further demands. By contrast, if a state is deterred, it is difficult to tell whether it did not perform the action because it was coerced or because the action was not in its interests for another reason. Proving that deterrence actually succeeded (that is, demonstrating conclusively why something did not happen) is very difficult.

There are two ways to increase the likelihood that compellence will succeed. First, the party attempting to compel an adversary can increase the cost of the threat. Second, the party practicing compellence can increase the credibility of its intention to carry out the threat. Threats usually must be both significant and credible to succeed. If the adversary expects to suffer greater costs from complying with the demand than he expects if the threat is carried out, then compellence is likely to fail. If the adversary is certain that the coercer will follow through with a strong threat, compellence is likely to succeed.

The United States often tries to compel nuclear proliferators to give up their nuclear programs. Cases of successful compellence include Ukraine, Belarus, Kazakhstan, and South Korea, while compellence has failed in North Korea, India, and Pakistan.

—*Andrea Gabbitas*

See also: Deterrence
References
Byman, Daniel L., Matthew C. Waxman, and Eric
    Larsen, *Air Power as a Coercive Instrument* (Santa
    Monica, CA: RAND Corporation, 1999).
Schelling, Thomas D., *Arms and Influence* (New Haven,
    CT: Yale University Press, 1966).

COMPREHENSIVE TEST
BAN TREATY (CTBT)

The Comprehensive Test Ban Treaty (CTBT) is an international agreement to ban nuclear testing in any environment. The treaty is an extension of efforts begun in the mid-twentieth century to limit nuclear weapons proliferation. It is not yet in force. The CTBT requires that all member states enact a moratorium on detonating nuclear weapons, in effect preventing new states from acquiring them and current nuclear powers from developing newer and more advanced nuclear weapons (*see* Moratorium). Originally proposed in the 1950s, but not opened for signature until 1996, the treaty will enter into force following ratification by the 44 states that own nuclear power or research reactors. As of September 2004, 32 of the 44 nuclear-capable states had ratified the treaty, 116 total states had ratified, and 172 states had signed. Under President Bill Clinton, the United States signed the treaty in 1996, but the Senate failed to ratify it in a vote taken in October 1999.

With international concerns over Cold War tensions and radiological fallout rising, Prime Minister Jawaharlal Nehru of India first suggested a treaty to ban nuclear explosions in 1954. U.S. presidents Dwight D. Eisenhower and John F. Kennedy backed the idea of such an agreement, and the international community eventually came to support a Limited Test Ban Treaty (*see* Limited Test Ban Treaty [LTBT]). Such a treaty was signed in 1963, outlawing nuclear tests underwater, in space, and in the atmosphere. The 1968 Nuclear Nonproliferation Treaty prohibited non–nuclear weapons states from acquiring such weapons and committed the declared nuclear powers (the United States, the Soviet Union, the United Kingdom, France, and China) to eventual, although nonbinding, nuclear disarmament (*see* Nuclear Nonproliferation Treaty [NPT]). A comprehensive ban, however, would prove to be illusive. Given the state of verification technologies during this period, many critics doubted that underground explosions could be accurately detected or differentiated from normal seismic activity, and little progress was made on CTBT negotiations.

The end of the Cold War and improvements in monitoring technologies led to a renewed interest in a zero-yield ban on nuclear testing, with the United Nations Conference on Disarmament beginning a three-year negotiation on the CTBT in 1993 (*see* Conference on Disarmament). In addition to a prohibition on nuclear weapons explosions, the treaty establishes organizations to implement verification measures, resolve international disputes, and periodically review the status of or amend the treaty. President George H. W. Bush did not explicitly endorse the treaty, but he did initiate a moratorium on U.S. testing in 1992 that is still in effect. The Clinton administration signed the treaty but waited three years to submit it to the Senate for ratification because of foreign policy disagreements with some Republican senators. Even then, political hostility and lingering doubts on the effectiveness of verification regimes led the Senate to reject the treaty 48–51, mostly along party lines and well short of the two-thirds majority needed for ratification. President George W. Bush did not pursue another vote on ratification.

The CTBT consists of 17 articles and various annexes and protocols detailing the scope of the agreement and will enter into force 180 days after the last of the 44 nuclear-capable states ratifies it. The formal organization of the regime includes a Conference of States Parties, an executive council consisting of 51 members that serves as the executive organ of the Comprehensive Test Ban Treaty Organization (CTBTO), and a Technical Secretariat that assists member states with implementation measures.

Following implementation of the treaty, states parties will be able to activate various noncompliance measures, and a verification regime will begin monitoring compliance with the test ban. Verification measures in the CTBT include an International Monitoring System (IMS) of more than 300 seismic, radiological, hydroacoustic, and infrasound detectors around the world set up to detect seismic and other activities that could indicate a nuclear detonation; they will transmit data to the CTBTO headquarters in Vienna. The headquarters will analyze suspected events and distribute the information to member states. The treaty text details the locations of IMS facilities, which were designed to ensure global coverage. In addition to detecting possible nuclear explosions, the monitoring stations can supply member states with information on volcanic, seismic, and nonnuclear radiological activities. IMS facilities are owned by the state in which they are located. In some cases, these facilities are preexisting installations; in others, the CTBTO and relevant states parties must yet fund and initiate their construction. In the event that member states suspect an illegal nuclear explosion, the CTBT allows for a series of options for on-site inspections, including overflight observation and photography, environmental sampling, and drilling to obtain radioactive samples. The CTBT does not explicitly provide for noncompliance measures other than the suspension or restriction of rights outlined in the framework of the treaty. However, the treaty does recommend that states found to be in violation of its obligations be subject to actions by the United Nations, including sanctions (*see* Underground Testing; Verification).

During negotiations, the United States ensured that the treaty banned only nuclear explosions, and not all activities resulting in nuclear energy release. Given this wording, the CTBT would allow the United States (and other signatories) to conduct a range of nuclear weapons tests, such as subcritical explosions involving fissile material, which could result in a release of nuclear energy, to guarantee the reliability of its nuclear weapons stockpile.

Without ratification from the United States and several other countries, the treaty cannot enter into force (*see* Entry into Force). Among the other declared nuclear powers, Russia, France, and the United Kingdom have ratified the treaty, and China has signed it. India, Pakistan, North Korea, and Iraq would also need to ratify the CTBT in order for it to enter into force because they all possess or are suspected of developing nuclear weapons. However, none of these states has yet signed the treaty.

—*John Spykerman*

See also: Arms Control; Limited Test Ban Treaty; Nuclear Test Ban; Peaceful Nuclear Explosions Treaty (PNET); Ratification

References

Holdren, John P., et al., "Technical Issues Related to the Comprehensive Nuclear Test Ban Treaty," National Academies of Science, 2002.

Shalikashvili, John, "Findings and Recommendations concerning the Comprehensive Nuclear Test Ban Treaty," U.S. Department of State report, January 2001, available at http://www.state.gov/www/global/arms/ctbtpage/ctbt_report.html.

CONFERENCE ON DISARMAMENT

The Conference on Disarmament (CD) is an autonomous negotiating body that serves as the principal forum established by the international community to negotiate multilateral arms control and disarmament agreements. Although it is not considered a United Nations (UN) body, the UN does provide administrative support and negotiating subjects. Informal CD-UN linkages occur because most nations are represented by the same diplomats in the CD, the UN Disarmament Committee (UNDC), and the First Committee (disarmament and international security) of the UN during formal sessions. The CD submits a purely informational annual report to the UN.

The CD had its genesis in the late 1950s when the UN General Assembly (UNGA) began to pay more attention to disarmament matters, primarily because of the increasing concern over growing nuclear arsenals. Consequently, the UN First Committee was established in 1957 but quickly collapsed when the Soviet Union refused to participate. Various attempts to resurrect multilateral disarmament talks floundered because of Cold War animosities until 1962, when both the Soviet Union and the United States agreed to establish the Eighteen Nation Disarmament Committee (ENDC). Membership was based on five members from each alliance (the North Atlantic Treaty Organization [NATO] and the Warsaw Pact) and eight countries from different geographical areas. Membership expanded to thirty in 1969 when the group became the Conference of the Committee on Disarmament (CCD). The name was changed again in 1978 to the Conference on Disarmament, and membership increased to forty. The CD predecessor bodies successfully negotiated a number of important arms control agreements, notably the Nuclear Nonproliferation Treaty, the Biological and Toxin Weapons Convention, the Seabed Arms Control Treaty, and the Environmental Modification Convention. The CD has negotiated two treaties: the Chemical Weapons Convention (signed in 1993 and entered into force in 1997) and the Comprehensive Test Ban Treaty (signed in 1996, not yet in force).

Currently the CD has sixty-six members (including all five nuclear weapon states) and more than forty other states have observer status. These members are ostensibly divided into three political groups: the Western Group, consisting primarily of NATO state members of the CD, Australia, and Japan; the Eastern Group, consisting of many of the former Warsaw Pact states; and the Neutral/Nonaligned Group. The People's Republic of China has refused to join any group (referring to itself as the Group of One), and since the end of the Cold War the dynamics of these groups have changed significantly, with a number of states breaking out of these traditional groupings to form other politically "like-minded" blocs. The composition of these blocs depends on the particular issue to be addressed.

The CD meets at the UN's Palais des Nations in Geneva for three sessions each year, each lasting approximately two months. (Until 2000 it met for two three-month sessions each year.) It conducts its business through plenary sessions in which representatives make basic policy statements, through informal meetings, and through ad-hoc committees established to address specific issues. Plenary sessions are open to the public and have verbatim records. The ad-hoc committees submit reports to the conference, which are incorporated into the CD's annual report to the UNGA. Although many delegations submit and circulate proposals and working papers, there are formal records only of the plenary sessions. Member states agreed that the work of the CD would be undertaken by consensus and under its own rules of procedure. Members also adopt their own agendas based on input from the UNGA and proposals made by CD members. The UN secretary general appoints the secretary of the CD, who acts as his personal representative, and assists the CD in organizing the business and timetables for scheduling sessions. The presidency of the CD rotates on a monthly basis in alphabetical order. Consensus by the member states is a prerequisite for any measure to clear the CD.

The CD's current multilateral arms control initiatives include the cessation of the nuclear arms race and nuclear disarmament; prevention of nuclear war; prevention of an arms race in outer space; the establishment of effective international arrangements to assure non–nuclear weapon states against the use or threat of use of nuclear weapons (see Negative Security Assurances [NSAs]); the identification and limitation of new types of weapons of mass destruction (such as radiological weapons); and the

creation of a comprehensive program of disarmament and transparency in armaments. Discussions of a Fissile Material Cut-off Treaty also have been undertaken, but as with all the other issues up for discussion, there has been little or no progress on the matter. Nevertheless, the CD is the only multilateral forum for disarmament and arms control negotiations, and many states believe that the continued dialogue that it facilitates is important as a transparency- and confidence-building measure that enables states to continue to strive toward disarmament in all its forms.

—Guy Roberts

References

Conference on Disarmament website, http://www. unog.ch/disarm/dconf.htm or http://disarmament2. UN.org/cd/.

"Conference on Disarmament," Monterey Institute of International Studies, Center for Nonproliferation studies, available at http://cns.miis.edu/pubs/ inven/pdfs/cd.pdf.

CONFERENCE ON SECURITY AND COOPERATION IN EUROPE (CSCE)

The Conference on Security and Cooperation in Europe (CSCE) was the precursor to what is now the Organization of Security and Cooperation in Europe (OSCE), with headquarters in Vienna, Austria. It currently includes fifty-five participating states, including all European countries, all of the former Soviet Union, and the United States and Canada.

Originally opened in July 1973 among the members of the North Atlantic Treaty Organization (NATO), the Warsaw Treaty Organization (WTO), and several neutral states, the CSCE produced the Helsinki Final Act on August 1, 1975. That document included provisions relating to security ("Basket I"), economic cooperation ("Basket II"), and humanitarian and other fields ("Basket III").

The Helsinki Final Act also provided for a series of follow-up meetings during which states would discuss progress in each of these areas. These were held in Belgrade (1978), Madrid (1983), and Vienna (1989). Each of these meetings represented stand-alone negotiations; no CSCE institutions continued to work on this extensive agenda in the interim between the formal meetings. The 1990 Charter of Paris for a New Europe occurred alongside signature of the Conventional Forces in Europe (CFE)

Treaty and the Vienna Document on Confidence and Security Building Measures (CSBMs), marking the end of the Cold War in Europe (*see* Confidence- and Security-Building Measures [CSBMs]). At the 1992 Helsinki Follow-Up Meeting, the CSCE began to formalize its structures, seeking to adapt to the needs of the post–Cold War world. In 1994, the CSCE changed its name to the Organization of Security and Cooperation in Europe.

The CSCE had begun as a creature of the Cold War. Since the 1950s, the Soviet Union had repeatedly called for a "European Security Conference" so that Europeans—excluding the United States and Canada—might discuss their security landscape. In the early 1970s, the Soviets agreed to the CSCE—including the United States and Canada as well as thirteen neutral European states—as a parallel to launching the Mutual and Balanced Force Reduction (MBFR) negotiations to limit NATO and Warsaw Pact conventional forces.

Within the security "basket," the CSCE gave birth to confidence- and security-building measures designed "to contribute to reducing the dangers of armed conflict and of misunderstanding or miscalculation of military activities which could give rise to apprehension, particularly in a situation where the participating States lack clear and timely information" (Helsinki Final Act, Sec. 2, para. 4). Observers also credit the human rights focus of Basket III for giving a certain political cover to "Helsinki human rights" dissidents within the Soviet Union and Eastern Europe.

The end of the Cold War brought new challenges. Newly independent states faced the need to restructure their political and economic systems. Ethnic conflict stimulated internecine violence. Over the past decade, the OSCE has expanded its reach beyond CSBMs to encompass peacekeeping and political observer missions as a means of conflict prevention and management. Additional OSCE offices focus on democratic institutions, freedom of the media, and national minorities. Economic forums address the challenges of privatization and conversion to new civilian industries. More recently, the OSCE has added control of light weapons, terrorism, and trafficking in human beings to its agenda.

—*Schuyler Foerster*

References

"Conference on Security and Cooperation in Europe, Helsinki Final Act," 1 August 1975, available at http://www.osce.org/docs/english/1990-1999/summits/helfa75e.htm.

Fry, John, *The Helsinki Process: Negotiating Security and Cooperation in Europe* (Washington, DC: National Defense University Press, 1993).

Organization for Security and Co-operation in Europe website, http://www.osce.org.

CONFIDENCE- AND SECURITY-BUILDING MEASURES (CSBMS)

The concept for confidence- and security-building measures (CSBMs) emerged in the early 1970s as a complement to arms control and disarmament. Within the 1975 Helsinki Final Act of the Conference on Security and Cooperation in Europe (CSCE), "Basket I" focused on security issues, whereby participating states agreed to undertake measures designed to reduce the dangers of armed conflict and of misunderstanding or miscalculation of military activities that could give rise to apprehension, particularly in situations where participating states lacked clear and timely information (*see* Conference on Security and Cooperation in Europe [CSCE]).

The CSCE represented a multilateral process involving neutral states as well as members of the North Atlantic Treaty Organization (NATO) and the Warsaw Pact. Participants believed that development of CSBMs were complementary to other ongoing nuclear and conventional arms control negotiations that were essentially bilateral between the two blocs or their superpowers.

Initial CSBMs in the Helsinki Final Act included a requirement to issue prior notification of military maneuvers and movements and exchange of observers. In 1986, CSCE participating states agreed in the Stockholm Document to lower notification thresholds and provide for mandatory on-site inspections to verify notified military maneuvers. Subsequent Vienna Documents (1990, 1992, 1994, and 1999) added detailed requirements to agreements calling for the exchange of military information, further lowered thresholds for notifying military maneuvers, and introduced new measures relating to reporting of hazardous incidents and improved crisis communications.

The initial emergence of CSBMs in Europe reflected fears about instability in the military standoff between NATO and the Warsaw Pact. For many, the concentration of substantial opposing military forces in a high state of readiness in such close proximity recalled the specter of 1914, in which miscalculation and fear prompted actions that were seen as threatening by others, causing a crisis to escalate into war. Likewise, the lack of transparency between NATO and Warsaw Pact military formations and operations was viewed as a source of miscalculation. CSBMs were viewed largely as a mechanism to begin creating transparency, reducing the likelihood of inadvertent escalation or accidental war.

There is a strong political component to CSBMs. Although the initial provisions in the Helsinki Final Act were quite general, supporters believed that it was important to establish the precedent of reporting to the opposing alliance the details about large military maneuvers. Subsequent agreements offered specific guidelines about the conduct of required notifications, set more detailed parameters for exchange of military information, and established the important precedent of on-site inspection to verify exchanged information. These precedents also spilled over into the worlds of nuclear and conventional arms control, where information exchange and on-site inspection are crucial to maintaining confidence in the regimes.

Since the end of the Cold War, the relevance of the Vienna Documents for NATO members and states from the former Warsaw Pact has declined significantly. Yet the principles and experience represented by this effort have potential application in other contexts. Nuclear CSBMs between the United States and Russia—including crisis communications, information exchange, on-site inspection, and exchange of officers in respective command centers—are being discussed. India and Pakistan also might benefit from CSBMs to reduce the risk of escalation in their enduring rivalry. In the Balkans, a regime of CSBMs is considered essential to ensuring some transparency in military relationships and improving crisis stability.

—*Schuyler Foerster*

See also: Crisis Stability; Implementation; Verification
References
Larsen, Jeffrey A., *Arms Control: Cooperative Security in a Changing Environment* (Boulder: Lynne Rienner, 2002).
Organization for Co-operation and Security in Europe website, http://www.osce.org.

CONTAINMENT

"Containment" is virtually synonymous with the Cold War—it is the grand strategy that the United States pursued for some forty-five years vis-à-vis the Soviet Union. Essentially a defensive strategy, it was a policy designed to manage an antagonistic relationship in which it was not possible to quickly defeat the adversary. The strategy required the United States to confront Soviet power and influence wherever and whenever necessary, even at the risk of war. Containment reflected the traditions of classic balance-of-power thinking (*see* Cold War).

The term was first coined by George F. Kennan, writing under the pseudonym "X," in an article entitled "The Sources of Soviet Conduct" published in the July 1947 edition of *Foreign Affairs*. Kennan—then director of the U.S. State Department's new Policy Planning Staff—called for a "long term, patient but firm and vigilant containment of Russian expansionist tendencies" (X, p. 575). Kennan's anonymity did not survive for long, as the article drew substantial publicity, and the concept of containment became elevated to doctrine.

As Kennan noted in his memoirs, he had not intended the article to be a formal policy pronouncement. The article prompted Walter Lippman to pose his own critique of containment in the pages of the *New York Times* and published in the same year in his *The Cold War: A Study in U.S. Foreign Policy*. Kennan also recounted how his arguments had been misunderstood and acknowledged his agreement with much of Lippman's critique, noting "My only consolation is that I succeeded in provoking from him so excellent and penetrating a treatise" (Kennan, p. 360).

However unofficial its intentions, Kennan's thesis sparked a public debate about America's role in the immediate postwar world and found resonance in policy responses from the Truman administration through the end of the Cold War and beyond.

Kennan's Thesis
Containment represented a critique of the prevailing notion in Washington that the United States could somehow work with the Soviet Union—its wartime ally—in restoring peace in Europe. President Franklin D. Roosevelt had hoped to integrate the Soviet Union into the postwar international system through the United Nations, thereby giving it both status and the security it so desperately needed.

Washington's ambassador to Moscow, W. Averill Harriman, similarly advocated the use of economic enticements to an impoverished nation to induce the Soviet government to be a responsible player in world affairs.

In Moscow in February 1946, Kennan responded to a request from Washington for an analysis of increasingly uncooperative and even hostile Soviet behavior. The result was the famous "Long Telegram." Its central thesis was, "We have here a political force committed fanatically to the belief that with [the] U.S. there can be no permanent *modus vivendi*" (quoted in Kennan, p. 557). The Soviet government *presumed* a hostile international system, a conviction deriving from a combination of Soviet ideology's belief in the antipathy of capitalist states, a traditional Russian fear of foreign influences, and the expediency of using foreign enemies to justify totalitarian rule. Any policy based on the expectation that it would influence the Soviet government to cooperate with Western aims was therefore depicted as being bound to fail. U.S. "dealings with Russia must be placed on [a] realistic and matter of fact basis" (quoted in Kennan, p. 559).

Kennan's "X" article brought this same argument about the nature of Soviet society into the public view. More important than the policy prescriptions, Kennan was concerned with explaining "the sources of Soviet conduct." It also coincided with growing concerns that Moscow actually favored a dismembered Germany riddled with debt and reparations, dragging down Europe's recovery and fostering the conditions for greater Communist influence—a scenario that would simply repeat with greater ferocity the mistakes following World War I and place an enormous burden on the United States both militarily and financially. Already, the Truman Doctrine and the Marshall Plan had committed the United States to the support of freedom and the economic recovery of Europe. Western governments concluded that they should consolidate and strengthen what they had so as to stem further political and economic deterioration and to block Communist expansion.

The more controversial elements of Kennan's thesis stemmed from the article's sweeping policy prescriptions: "Soviet pressure against the free institutions of the Western world is something that can be contained by the adroit and vigilant application of counterforce at a series of constantly shifting geographical and political points, corresponding to the shifts and maneuvers of Soviet policy, but which cannot be charmed or talked out of existence." Out of context, this prescription suggested a U.S. policy that was essentially reactive, responding to Soviet challenges wherever they occurred. To many, containment suggested that the United States should rely on force to stem the spread of Soviet military and diplomatic influence.

The Critique of Containment

Kennan argued that containment was a long-term strategy but that the fragile crust of Soviet power would eventually give way to its own internal political, economic, and social weaknesses: "The United States has it in its power to increase enormously the strains under which Soviet policy must operate, to force upon the Kremlin a far greater degree of moderation and circumspection than it has had to observe in recent years, and in this way to promote tendencies which must eventually find their outlet in either the break-up or the gradual mellowing of Soviet power" (X, p. 582).

Nonetheless, critics such as Lippman argued that the United States would be condemned to maintaining an indefinite defensive posture against Soviet expansionism for several reasons. The projections of inevitable Soviet self-destruction were optimistic and risky; the strategy required a mobilization of American resources incompatible with the nature of American politics; the United States would have to create and maintain subordinate alliances with nations along the Soviet periphery and become excessively involved in those nations' internal affairs; and the prospect of eventual war between the United States and the Soviet Union on a European battlefield would ultimately undermine the "natural" alliance between the United States and Western Europe.

Ironically, virtually all of these criticisms reflected Kennan's later critique of how containment was applied over the ensuing years. Kennan consistently argued that his concept of containment was neither universal nor militaristic. Throughout the subsequent four decades, however, successive U.S. administrations struggled with both issues—how universal the doctrine of containment should be, and how much should be invested in the military dimension of policy, especially as nuclear weapons played an increasingly dominant role in the standoff between the superpowers.

Issues in Implementing Containment

Kennan himself argued in 1948 at the National War College, "We are great and strong; but we are not great enough or strong enough to conquer or to change or to hold in subjugation by ourselves all . . . hostile or irresponsible forces. . . . To attempt to do so would mean to call upon our own people for sacrifices which would in themselves completely alter our way of life and our political institutions, and we would lose the real objectives of our policy in trying to defend them" (quoted in Gaddis, p. 28).

Such logic reflected an essentially "particularist" view of American strategy, which one would expect from a traditional "realist" who differentiated between vital and less-than-vital national interests. Kennan, for example, dissented from the Truman Doctrine's aid to Greece and Turkey on two counts. First, he objected to Truman's sweeping statement in support of "free peoples who are resisting subjugation by armed minorities or outside pressures," arguing that it would not necessarily be in U.S. interests to come to others' aid in every instance and that the United States could not fulfill such an expectation (Kennan, pp. 319–324). Second, he was skeptical of the need to give much aid to Turkey, since he doubted communism would ever be able to make substantial gains in the Islamic world.

Over time, U.S. administrations often took a more universalist view of containment, leading them into conflicts in which they had few interests other than to oppose a political force influenced by communism. In 1950, Paul Nitze—occupying Kennan's former position as director of the State Department's Policy Planning Staff—argued in National Security Council Document 68 (NSC-68): "It is not an adequate objective merely to check the Kremlin design, for the absence of order among nations is becoming less and less tolerable. This fact imposes on us, in our own interests, the responsibility of world leadership" (NSC-68, Sec. IV[B]). Under President Dwight D. Eisenhower, Secretary of State John Foster Dulles likewise presided over the establishment of a system of alliances around the periphery of the Soviet Union reminiscent of Lippman's earlier critique. And President John F. Kennedy promised "to pay any price, bear any burden" as the 1960s ushered in a series of "proxy" conflicts in virtually every Third World region, and, most tragically, in Vietnam.

By the end of the 1940s, Kennan's call for subtlety in the application of containment seemed increasingly out of place. Nitze began drafting NSC-68 in response to communism's victory in China and Soviet detonation of an atomic bomb. Even here, the debate is instructive. Kennan, for example, argued that these developments were not really cause for alarm: First, any alliance between the Soviet Union and the new Communist China would ultimately break down because of Russo-Chinese antipathy; second, Soviet membership in the nuclear club was inevitable, even if it came earlier than expected, and the United States had no intentions of using its nuclear monopoly to eliminate the Soviet Union anyway. By this time, however, Kennan's views were no longer mainstream.

The "misunderstanding" that Kennan lamented most was that he had not meant "the containment by military means of a military threat, but the political containment of a political threat" (Kennan, p. 358). Kennan, for example, also dissented from early plans to incorporate all of Western Europe—including West Germany—into the North Atlantic Treaty Organization (NATO). In a memo to Secretary of State George Catlett Marshall in 1948, Kennan argued that "this would amount to the final militarization of the present line through Europe . . . [creating] a situation in which no alteration or obliteration of that line could take place without an accentuated military significance" (quoted in Gaddis, pp. 72–73).

For Nitze, like others after him, the West needed "superior aggregate military strength . . . without which containment is no more than a policy of bluff" (NSC-68, Sec. VI). As the United States implemented containment through the years, military force—particularly NATO in Europe—played a major role in U.S. efforts to contain the Soviets. Nitze argued in NSC-68 for a major increase both in nuclear capability and in conventional military forces. Later, Dulles, like Lippman, argued that the United States could not sustain such large outlays for defense, but relied on new nuclear weapons technologies to fill the gap. Kennedy and his successors tried to reduce reliance on nuclear weapons but found that increased conventional military power was expensive, provoked concerns from allies about the credibility of the nuclear guarantee, and was still inadequate in dealing with conflicts such as Vietnam. President Richard M. Nixon tried to manage the military threat through arms control. President Ronald Reagan reverted to a military buildup even as he tried to advance substantial arms reductions.

Contemporary Strategy: Is Containment Relevant?

In the end, Kennan's prediction came true—the Soviet Union disintegrated through its own weaknesses. As Kennan suggested, it ultimately could not compete in the realm of ideas and economics, critical failings that slowly eroded the basis of Soviet military power. Yet, containment continued as a dominant force in U.S. policy thinking, applied to North Korea, Iran, Iraq, and, for many, to China. For those who authored President George W. Bush's 2002 National Security Strategy, the issue has been whether containment is too passive: "We seek instead to create a balance of power that favors human freedom: conditions in which all nations and all societies can choose for themselves the rewards and challenges of political and economic liberty" (*National Security Strategy*). In June 2003, applauding Operation Iraqi Freedom, Thomas Donnelly of the American Enterprise Institute declared, "In [the Bush Doctrine's] rejection of containment and deterrence, it has likewise restored to prominence the historic characteristics of American policy: a proactive defense and the aggressive expansion of freedom."

Containment worked in the Cold War. It required patience—ultimately the Soviet Union fell—but the threat was clear and understandable, and there were few alternatives. Today, threats are more amorphous, and arguably more lethal, than in the Cold War. The ends of policy are more universal than particular, and military force is a more usable instrument of national policy. The dilemmas of containment remain—but how long can these policies be sustained and what are the risks between trying to change strategic realities on the ground versus trying to contain their effects?

—*Schuyler Foerster*

References

Donnelly, Thomas, *The Meaning of Operation Iraqi Freedom*, National Security Outlook, American Enterprise Institute, June 2003, available at http://www.aei.org/publications/pubID.17229/pub_detail.asp.

Gaddis, John Lewis, *Strategies of Containment: A Critical Appraisal of Postwar American Security Policy* (New York: Oxford University Press, 1992).

Kennan, George F., *Memoirs: 1925–1950* (Boston: Little, Brown, 1967).

Lippman, Walter, *The Cold War: A Study in U.S. Foreign Policy* (New York: Harper and Row, 1947).

The National Security Strategy of the United States of America (Washington, DC: The White House, September 12, 2002), available at http://www.whitehouse.gov/nsc/nssintro.html.

NSC-68: United States Objectives and Programs for National Security, available at http://www.fas.org/irp/offdocs/nsc-hst/nsc-68-6.htm.

X, "The Sources of Soviet Conduct," *Foreign Affairs,* July 1947, pp. 566–582.

CONTROL RODS
See Reactor Operations

COOPERATIVE THREAT REDUCTION (THE NUNN-LUGAR PROGRAM)

Since 1991, the United States has sponsored the Nunn-Lugar Cooperative Threat Reduction Program to assist the states of the former Soviet Union dismantle their weapons of mass destruction, secure their nuclear weapons and associated materials, technology, and expertise, and convert their nuclear facilities to other purposes. U.S. Senators Sam Nunn (D–GA) and Richard Lugar (R–IN) cosponsored the 1991 legislation that created this program. The term "Nunn-Lugar" thus has come to refer to the full range of threat reduction and nonproliferation programs undertaken by the U.S. government in cooperation with the states of the former Soviet Union, including those managed by the U.S. Departments of Commerce, Energy, and State. "Cooperative Threat Reduction (CTR)" is more accurately applied to the U.S. Department of Defense element of Nunn-Lugar.

At the time of its collapse, the Soviet Union possessed approximately 30,000 strategic and tactical nuclear weapons in its arsenal, in addition to some 1,000 tons of highly enriched uranium, 200 tons of plutonium, 40,000 tons of chemical weapons agents, and a massive biological weapons program. Perhaps more significantly, the Soviet collapse created three new nuclear weapons states in Belarus, Kazakhstan, and Ukraine. In the immediate aftermath of the Cold War, the denuclearization of these three new nuclear powers was not a foregone conclusion. Most analysts believe that the eventual denuclearization of all three states by the mid-1990s—leaving Russia as the sole former Soviet nuclear

Russian soldiers wearing protective suits check chemical agents at a military base for troops specializing in chemical warfare, east of Moscow, in 1993, as part of an initiative under the Cooperative Threat Reduction program. (Reuters/Corbis)

legacy state—would not have occurred, or would have taken a much longer time, without the assistance of the Nunn-Lugar Program.

Although Nunn-Lugar is a unique program that was fraught with growing pains, bureaucratic battles, and international misunderstandings, the program has matured into a complex and comprehensive foreign policy and national security mechanism. Nunn-Lugar has generated considerable domestic momentum throughout the legislative, executive, industrial, and nongovernmental communities, which has carried it through the ebbs and flows of U.S.-Russian bilateral relations.

Organizational Elements of CTR

The various U.S. government agencies that manage elements of the Nunn-Lugar Program provide specific objectives for their individual programs. For the U.S. Department of Defense, CTR program objectives reflect the fact that Ukraine, Kazakhstan, and Belarus are non–nuclear weapons states. Nunn-Lugar is intended to: (1) assist Russia in accelerating strategic arms reductions to the second Strategic

Arms Reduction Treaty (START II) levels; (2) enhance safety, security, control, accounting, and centralization of nuclear weapons and fissile material in the former Soviet Union to prevent their proliferation and encourage their reduction; (3) assist Ukraine and Kazakhstan to eliminate START II limited systems and weapons of mass destruction infrastructure; (4) assist the former Soviet Union to eliminate and prevent proliferation of biological and chemical weapons and associated capabilities; and (5) encourage military reductions and reform while reducing proliferation threats in the former Soviet Union.

The primary Department of Energy initiative dedicated to Nunn-Lugar work in Russia is the Material Protection, Control, and Accounting (MPC&A) Program. Its mission is to support U.S. national security objectives by enhancing the protection of international nuclear weapons and weapons-usable nuclear material at high risk of theft or diversion. The MPC&A Program's goals include assisting Russia and other nations in this endeavor, helping Russia to enhance its capabilities and commitment to operating and maintaining improved nuclear security, and establishing and maintaining a collaborative environment with MPC&A Program customers and stakeholders.

Whether coordinated by the U.S. Departments of Defense, Energy, or State, or by other U.S. government agencies, aspects of the Nunn-Lugar Program are negotiated, implemented, managed, and monitored through overarching "umbrella" agreements maintained between the United States and recipient governments that specify the rights and scope of the country-specific program. These agreements are set for a specific duration and include audit procedures. Separate implementing agreements are negotiated and maintained for each specific initiative. Congress authorizes each element of the program annually. The president annually certifies the eligibility of each recipient state for assistance against specified criteria required by Congress. U.S. agencies must notify Congress of their intent to commit funds to a specific country, and they must provide a full range of periodic reports about the program. The United States executes the program by providing goods and services, not aid. Audits of assistance provided ensure that goods and services are used in the manner specified by Congress.

Since the mid-1990s, the U.S. Congress has funded Nunn-Lugar at approximately $1 billion per year. Of that amount, the U.S. Departments of Defense and Energy are allocated about $400 million to $500 million each year, with the balance going to programs managed by other U.S. government agencies.

CTR Expansion Possibilities

Expansion of the Nunn-Lugar cooperative security model beyond the former Soviet Union holds tremendous promise for dealing with not only global chemical, biological, and nuclear threats such as fissile material stocks and infrastructure conversion but also for addressing a broad range of security issues. To do so, however, would require changes in the Nunn-Lugar legislation based on the lessons learned in the former Soviet Union as well as acceptance of the program by potential recipient states. Even if Congress passed legislation authorizing global application of Nunn-Lugar projects, it is unclear whether states with material at risk would be willing to participate. Furthermore, there are existing domestic and international legal constraints, including the 1946 Atomic Energy Act as modified in 1954 and Article 1 of the 1968 Nuclear Nonproliferation Treaty, on providing assistance to non–nuclear weapon states. Security and nonproliferation objectives, coupled with the unique benefits of the Nunn-Lugar process, however, might overcome these obstacles. Moreover, other important U.S. military and economic allies appear interested in providing international assistance to states seeking to rid themselves of dangerous chemical, biological, and nuclear weapons and infrastructure.

—*Charles L. Thornton*

See also: Arms Control; Russian Nuclear Weapons and Doctrine

References

Allison, Graham T., Owen R. Cote, Richard R. Falkenrath, and Steven E. Miller, *Avoiding Nuclear Anarchy: Containing the Threat of Loose Russian Nuclear Weapons and Fissile Material* (Cambridge, MA: MIT Press, 1996).

Bunn, Matthew, Anthony Wier, and John Holdren, "Controlling Nuclear Warheads and Materials: A Report Card and Action Plan," Project on Managing the Atom, Belfer Center for Science and International Affairs, John F. Kennedy School of Government, Harvard University (Commissioned by the Nuclear Threat Initiative), March 2003, available at http://www.nti.org/cnwm.

Shields, John M., and William C. Potter, eds., *Dismantling the Cold War: U.S. and NIS Perspectives on the Nunn-Lugar Cooperative Threat Reduction Program* (Cambridge, MA: MIT Press, 1997).

COORDINATING COMMITTEE FOR MULTILATERAL EXPORT CONTROLS (COCOM)

The Coordinating Committee for Multilateral Export Controls, or COCOM, was an international committee chartered to establish and coordinate restrictions for exporting technology to the Soviet Union and its allies. Established in 1949, members included Australia, Belgium, Canada, Denmark, France, Germany, Greece, Italy, Japan, Luxembourg, Netherlands, Norway, Portugal, Spain, Turkey, the United Kingdom, and the United States. Austria, Switzerland, and the Netherlands undertook varying degrees of participation in COCOM, although none of these states were official members. Headquartered in Paris, COCOM was not codified by treaty or international law. Rather, it made recommendations to member states by informal arrangement with no explicit enforcement mechanism to punish noncompliance.

COCOM established three separate lists of controlled items: the International Atomic Energy List, which restricted nuclear weapons technology; the International Munitions List, which restricted hardware and technology with direct military application; and the Industrial List, which restricted technologies with both a civilian and military use. Changes to these lists required unanimous consent from COCOM member states.

With the fall of the Eastern bloc and the collapse of the Soviet Union in the early 1990s, COCOM's original mission lost much of its relevance. In November 1993, members agreed to dismantle COCOM and replace it with an organization focused on nonproliferation strategies more suitable to the post–Cold War era. As a result, members began negotiating a successor to COCOM. The committee was officially disbanded on March 31, 1994, and replaced by the Wassenaar Arrangement in July 1996. During the interim period between COCOM and Wassenaar, many states continued to observe COCOM restrictions.

—*Lawrence R. Fink*

See also: Wassenaar Arrangement

References

Bolkcom, Christopher, and Sharon Squassoni, *Cruise Missile Proliferation* (Washington, DC: Congressional Research Service, July 2002).

History of the Department of State during the Clinton Presidency (1992–2001) (Washington, DC: Office of the Historian, Bureau of Public Affairs), available at http://www.state.gov/r/pa/ho/pubs/8535.htm.

Mastanduno, Michael, *Economic Containment: CoCom and the Politics of East-West Trade* (Ithaca, NY: Cornell University Press, 1992).

CORRELATION OF FORCES

During the Cold War, both Soviet and U.S. analysts and planners developed ways to measure the balance of strategic forces. U.S. planners tended to focus on quantitative measures of the strategic balance. For example, they counted the number of nuclear warheads and delivery systems deployed by both sides, estimated missile throw weight (the amount of payload that could be carried by either side's ballistic missiles), or determined the number of megatons and equivalent megatons that could be delivered by Soviet and U.S. nuclear forces. Various types of quantitative measures were then combined to develop politically and strategically meaningful estimates of each side's prompt hard-target kill capability or second-strike capability. U.S. concepts of arms race and crisis stability often emphasized quantitative measures of the strategic balance, even though politics and threat perception greatly influenced arms race and crisis stability (*see* Crisis Stability).

Soviet planners tended to take a broader view of the strategic nuclear balance than their American counterparts. In addition to these quantitative measures of the balance of strategic nuclear forces available to both sides, they incorporated many other kinds of qualitative and quantitative measures of the strategic situation in an effort to estimate the likelihood of war at any given moment. Their term for this measure—"correlation of forces"—incorporated estimates of political, social, moral, and economic trends. The correlation-of-forces method also took into account conventional military capabilities.

Many U.S. observers believed that Soviet efforts to measure the correlation of forces were superior to U.S. efforts to measure the strategic balance because it could yield not just a static snapshot but a comprehensive analysis of international trends. Because they were so comprehensive, however, correlation-of-forces estimates tended to be highly conservative. Thus, correlation-of-forces estimates never indicated to the Soviets that nuclear war was likely.

—*James J. Wirtz*

Reference

Freedman, Lawrence, *The Evolution of Nuclear Strategy*, third edition (New York: Palgrave Macmillan, 2003).

COUNTERFORCE TARGETING

"Counterforce targeting" describes an attack against an opponent's military forces rather than against its civilian population. Such attacks would, in theory, allow nuclear war to be fought as limited war rather than as total war leading to the mutual annihilation of the parties involved in a conflict. By emphasizing counterforce rather than countervalue (urban-industrial) targeting, an incentive is given to the opponent not to conduct a countervalue attack in response to a counterforce strike. In reality, the proximity of military facilities to cities means that even a counterforce nuclear strategy would inevitably result in wide-scale devastation of urban areas. It may not be possible to fight such a limited nuclear war, and escalation to countervalue exchanges may be unavoidable.

Counterforce targeting was devised as a response to the problems associated with the decreasing credibility of the doctrine of "massive retaliation" in the face of growing Soviet nuclear capability, and increasing interest in the concept of limited war, that emerged in the 1950s. The shortcomings of massive retaliation were highlighted to the Dwight D. Eisenhower administration during the 1958 crisis with China over Quemoy and Matsu in the Taiwan Straits, when U.S. nuclear threats against China were deemed not to be credible. Four years later, the John F. Kennedy administration faced similar choices during the 1962 Cuban missile crisis, when an "all or nothing" nuclear strategy was seen to offer the National Command Authority (NCA) little flexibility for effective crisis management. Because a counterforce strategy could be undertaken more readily than a countervalue attack on cities, it might be more credible as a deterrent in the eyes of the opponent, and, failing that, offer the possibility that a nuclear war could be fought in a manner leading to some form of victory. Because nuclear war would be a "come as you are" conflict—the forces at hand being the only ones that would be used—if the opponent's forces could be eliminated by attacking first, then "victory" might be possible. Counterforce offered the prospect of damage limitation, while attacks on urban areas virtually guaranteed that the opponent would respond in kind. Counterforce attacks also were made possible by an increase in the number of nuclear warheads available for use. By 1966, the U.S. nuclear arsenal had peaked at 32,200 strategic and tactical warheads—clearly an arsenal far in excess of the one demanded by a countervalue strategy, since there were only some 200 Soviet cities large enough to warrant being targeted. The large number of warheads available opened up a wide array of targeting options beyond "city busting."

As Soviet nuclear capabilities improved and parity with the United States was established in the 1970s, it became clear that a counterforce nuclear strategy offered the United States the most credible deterrent in the face of a Soviet nuclear threat. Counterforce-orientated nuclear strategy has dominated U.S. nuclear thinking ever since and was reflected in the different versions of the Single Integrated Operational Plan (SIOP) that were developed during the latter half of the Cold War.

With the fall of the Soviet Union in December 1991, U.S. nuclear strategy continued to emphasize counterforce rather than countervalue targeting. Although U.S. and Russian strategic nuclear forces are officially "detargeted," reducing the danger posed by an accidental missile launch, both sides can quickly reenter targets into the guidance systems of their weapons. The Nuclear Posture Review (NPR), which was submitted to Congress on December 31, 2001, embraces the notion of limited nuclear war and counterforce targeting and includes nonnuclear strikes and strategic information warfare (SIW) as part of U.S. strategic deterrent capabilities. This means that the United States would be less dependent on large-scale use of nuclear weapons in a crisis, even against a nuclear-armed state such as Russia or China.

The United States no longer plans its nuclear arsenal purely on the basis of targeting the Russian Federation. Targeting of nuclear weapons will be based on the nature of the threat or the nature of the target being destroyed using adaptive, capabilities-based planning, which will replace the deliberate planning process used to create the SIOP. Although the components of the old "Triad" of nuclear delivery systems (intercontinental ballistic missiles [ICBMs], submarine-launched ballistic missiles [SLBMs], and manned bombers) will remain (though at significantly reduced numbers, and in some cases at reduced alert levels), new nuclear capabilities more suited to dealing with twenty-first-century security challenges may be developed, including very low-yield "mini-nukes" to attack hard and deeply buried targets (HDBTs) such as command and control bunkers and chemical and biological weapons laboratories.

Although there is no longer an emphasis on preparing to fight a major nuclear war, U.S. planners have identified a need to maintain credible warfighting options as the basis of deterrence. Counterforce targeting, as a guiding principle of nuclear war planning, continues to remain attractive today.

—*Malcolm Davis*

See also: City Avoidance; Cold War; Countervalue
    Targeting

References

Freedman, Lawrence, *The Evolution of Nuclear Strategy*, second edition (New York: St. Martin's Press, 1989).
Gray, Colin S., *The Second Nuclear Age* (Boulder: Lynne Rienner, 1999).

COUNTERMEASURES

To counter antiballistic missile (ABM) systems and confuse radars and telemetry sensors, intercontinental ballistic missile (ICBM) warhead buses are equipped with devices called "penetration aids" to help warheads evade detection by radar and blast from ABM systems. These measures are meant to counter an adversary's ability to stop a missile from reaching its target. The concept is to overwhelm both the ground-based radars guiding the antiballistic missile systems and the seekers in the individual antiballistic missiles. To overcome the initial Soviet ABM system deployed around Moscow in the 1970s, for example, the United States MIRVed (that is, incorporated multiple independently targetable reentry vehicles as a weapons payload) its ICBMs and submarine-launched ballistic missiles (SLBMs). The number of warheads exceeded the number of interceptor missiles available to the Soviet ABM system.

Using radar-absorbing materials on the reentry vehicles (RV), booster fragmentation, jammers, metallic chaff, or aluminum balloons prevents the enemy from detecting or destroying RVs. Other techniques are spin stabilizing the RV, reorienting the RV, and separating the RV from the bus and providing it with its own aerodynamic or rocket-propulsion system. The last technique can become too expensive if an exact replica of the RV has to be built. By using atmospheric screening, all decoys and false RVs will burn up on reentry, allowing antiballistic missiles to recognize and strike the remaining warheads inside the Earth's atmosphere. A two-tiered approach to defense to defeat most of these penetration aids in space requires the design of weapons with a seeker that can discriminate between the false and real RV.

The ultimate way to overcome ABM systems came with the development of RVs that could fly different flight profiles. The Soviet Union attempted to give its warheads aerodynamic features that allowed them to maneuver while in terminal reentry phase. Rocket thrusters, or motors fitted to individual warheads, also would constitute a countermeasure. New materials technology has led to the development of other countermeasures. The debate about countermeasures has reemerged with the planned U.S. deployment of an antiballistic missile system.

—*Gilles Van Nederveen*

See also: Missile Defense; Moscow Antiballistic Missile System; Penetration Aids

References

McMahon, K. Scott, *Pursuit of the Shield: The U.S. Quest for Limited Ballistic Missile Defense* (Lanham, MD: University Press of America, 1997).

Sessler, Andrew M., et al., *Countermeasures: A Technical Evaluation of the Operational Effectiveness of the Planned US National Missile Defense System* (Boston: Union of Concerned Scientists, MIT Security Studies Program, April 2000).

COUNTERPROLIFERATION

"Counterproliferation" refers to the full range of military preparations and activities conducted to reduce and protect against the threat posed by nuclear, biological, and chemical (NBC) weapons and their associated delivery systems. Counterproliferation (CP) is a multitiered effort and enables U.S. forces to survive, fight, and win in an NBC environment. It is enhanced by proliferation prevention and military support to nonproliferation efforts. In CP operations, a sequence of mutually supporting, offensive and defensive measures form a continuum of interrelated activities built on six core capabilities or principles: prevention, deterrence, counterforce, active defense, passive defense, and consequence management. The success or failure of efforts in one area impacts other functions throughout the operational cycle.

Proliferation prevention includes those actions taken to deny attempts by would-be proliferants to acquire or expand their NBC capabilities by providing inspection, monitoring, verification, and enforcement support for nonproliferation treaties and NBC arms control regimes; supporting export-control activities; assisting in the identification of potential proliferants before they can acquire or expand their NBC capabilities; and, if so directed by the National Command Authority, planning and conducting denial operations.

Deterrence involves a state of mind in the opponent brought about by the existence of a credible threat of unacceptable counteraction; that is, it is the prevention of military action through fear of the consequences (*see* Deterrence).

The objective of counterforce is to eliminate an adversary's NBC capability. Counterforce operations can be conducted as joint strategic attack, special operations, nuclear operations, and offensive counter air. Key operational considerations for counterforce operations include joint intelligence preparation of the battlespace; battle management; targeting; and battle damage assessment.

The objective of active defense is to eliminate an incoming NBC threat. Active defense operations can be conducted against aircraft, ballistic and cruise missiles, rockets, long-range artillery, submarines, surface vessels, special operations forces, and terrorists. Key operational considerations for active defense operations include detection; warning, identification, and reporting; tracking; engagement; and assessment. Counterforce operations and active defense probably would be employed together to lessen the number of attacks friendly forces have to absorb and to reduce the burden on passive defense measures.

Passive defense is the protection of personnel and facilities from the effects of NBC attack to sustain operations. The objective is to minimize the loss of operational capability caused by an enemy use of NBC weapons. Passive defense focuses on mission continuation while providing for force survivability. Key operational considerations include vulnerability analysis; attack warning and threat assessment; detection and identification; contamination avoidance; individual and collective protection; and contamination control.

The objective of consequence management is to mitigate the long-term effects of an attack and enable a return to operational capability. It can be performed in a military context whereby decontamination and cleanup allows a return to full, normal operations. It can also be performed as military support to foreign or domestic civil authorities.

—*Jeffrey A. Adams*

See also: Nonproliferation; Proliferation

References

Bush, George W., *The National Security Strategy of the United States of America* (Washington, DC: The White House, September 2002).

U.S. Department of Defense, Joint Publication (JP) 3-40, *Joint Doctrine for Counterproliferation Operations* (Washington, DC: U.S. Department of Defense, November 2002).

COUNTERVAILING STRATEGY

Upon taking office in 1976, President Jimmy Carter ordered a review of U.S. nuclear weapons policy under Presidential Directive 18 (PD-18). The review resulted in a new concept known as "countervailance," which was designed to ensure that "no plausible outcome of a Soviet nuclear attack would represent a success or any rational definition of a success." What would eventually result would be a wider range of nuclear options that the president and the National Command Authority (NCA) could choose from under Presidential Directive 59. PD-59 and countervailance took the notion of "flexible response" to perhaps its ultimate level during the Cold War. The Ronald Reagan administration then reaffirmed the concept of countervailance in National Security Decision Memorandum 13, issued in October 1981, which emphasized the importance of command and control, survivable postattack forces, and greater coordination between strategic and theater nuclear forces.

The emergence of a countervailing strategy really began with a desire by U.S. decision makers to find a way out of the situation of mutual assured destruction (MAD) brought about by nuclear parity in warheads and delivery systems achieved by the Soviet Union in the late 1960s. Henry Kissinger, U.S. secretary of state under Richard Nixon, asked, in a report to Congress in February 1970, "Should a President, in the event of a nuclear attack, be left with the single option of ordering the mass destruction of enemy civilians, in the face of the certainty that it would be followed by the mass slaughter of Americans?" Kissinger's question highlighted the need for nuclear forces and capabilities that offered credible deterrent options proportionate to the level of provocation. Even with the move away from reliance on countervalue in the mid-1960s, the options open to the president still emphasized large-scale counterforce attacks, many of which would also be directed at counterforce targets located within or near urban areas. There was little in the way of thinking about selective or limited nuclear strikes on specific targets, small-scale nuclear exchanges, or demonstration attacks. There was also growing concern over the potential ability for the Soviet Union to remove or significantly reduce the U.S. counterforce capability, which rested primarily with the Minuteman intercontinental ballistic missile (ICBM) force.

The Schlesinger Doctrine emerged in 1974 from a desire expressed by Kissinger in 1970 to offer the president a wider range of options than that offered under MAD. James Schlesinger's belief in a wide range of options for the employment of nuclear weapons, with an emphasis on developing capabilities for smaller, selective strikes, would lay the groundwork for President Carter's defense secretary, Harold Brown, to argue for a posture of countervailance in 1979. Central to both the Schlesinger Doctrine and countervailance theory was a belief that nuclear war could be fought at a lower level than what was envisaged under MAD. In effect, the war could be limited and controlled by both sides.

The key challenge to both concepts was ensuring Soviet compliance with the same doctrine. Documentary evidence of the period indicated that rather than embracing limited options, Soviet thinking about nuclear war still emphasized large-scale nuclear offensives against both counterforce and countervalue targets. This was particularly the case within the European theater of operations, in which the first use of nuclear forces by either side would see an order of magnitude shift in the conflict, with nuclear weapons employed fully and comprehensively to destroy enemy forces.

Given the challenge of uncertainty about Soviet thinking on nuclear war, the 1979 countervailing doctrine sought to emphasize escalation dominance, ensuring that the Soviet Union realized that no matter what level of nuclear force was used, the United States would prevail through effective command and control, survivable delivery systems, and an ability to maintain operational flexibility under any circumstances. Most significantly, countervailance sought to ensure the ability to wage a protracted, limited nuclear war, possibly lasting up to two months, rather than the short spasm exchange considered by earlier countervalue and counterforce concepts. A range of new target options would emerge with countervailance, including the Soviet command structure and political leadership, its nonnuclear forces, and its economic and industrial base. Furthermore, the importance of countervalue strikes was considered, and a survivable second- or third-strike strategic reserve was seen as vital.

—*Malcolm Davis*

See also: Cold War; Flexible Response; United States Nuclear Forces and Doctrine

References

Arkin, William M., and Richard W. Fieldhouse, *Nuclear Battlefields: Global Links in the Arms Race* (Cambridge, MA: Ballinger, 1985).

Freedman, Lawrence, *The Evolution of Nuclear Strategy,* second edition (New York: St. Martin's Press, 1989).

COUNTERVALUE TARGETING

Countervalue targeting is the use of nuclear weapons against targets of high value to the adversary, in particular urban areas, key industrial sites, leadership, or government facilities. Countervalue targeting is thus differentiated from counterforce targeting, which is directed against an adversary's military capabilities, especially its strategic nuclear forces and associated command and control systems.

During the early Cold War, U.S. nuclear policy emphasized countervalue rather than counterforce targeting, and it was not until the 1960s that counterforce targeting assumed predominance. The limited number of nuclear weapons available for use until the mid-1950s, and the challenges in delivering those weapons onto a target via manned bombers in the face of Soviet air defenses, made it difficult to target anything but large urban areas.

Doubts about the credibility of deterrent threats drove debate about the desirability of countervalue targeting. With Soviet advances in nuclear delivery systems and the gradual expansion of the destructive power of the Soviet nuclear arsenal, there was less confidence that the United States would be safe from Soviet nuclear retaliation if nuclear war occurred. A nuclear strategy that emphasized attacks on urban areas might lead to a Soviet retaliation against urban-industrial targets, leaving the United States devastated in the aftermath of a countervalue nuclear exchange. The impact of the Cuban missile crisis, the growing popularity of notions of limited war, and improvements in the accuracy and responsiveness of intercontinental ballistic missiles (ICBMs) and nuclear-armed long-range bombers meant that countervalue targeting would soon give way to a more flexible deterrent posture based around limited nuclear options and counterforce targeting.

Countervalue targeting did not completely disappear from U.S. nuclear strategy in the second half of the Cold War. Until the deployment of the Trident D5 submarine-launched ballistic missile (SLBM) in the late 1970s, the submarine-based leg of the U.S. nuclear "Triad" (ICBMs, SLBMs, and manned bombers) lacked the hard-target kill capability (a combination of accuracy and yield) of land-based ICBMs, and thus SLBMs were aimed either at soft targets (airbases and ports) or countervalue targets (cities). Furthermore, many command and control targets existed within Soviet cities, meaning that even a counterforce attack would inevitably see such cities devastated and would almost certainly result in a Soviet countervalue response against U.S. cities.

It is extremely unlikely that the United States or the Russian Federation would return to countervalue targeting today. Although both sides maintain substantial nuclear arsenals as an insurance against an unforeseen crisis, the United States no longer bases its nuclear war planning on responding to a signal Russian threat. With new strategic nonnuclear strike options, U.S. officials now concentrate on ways to disarm opponents that possess small nuclear, chemical, and biological weapons arsenals.

The same cannot be said necessarily for other emerging nuclear weapons states, which still perceive utility in targeting cities to coerce or deter opponents. A second-strike deterrent capability, such as that being pursued by India, is most effective if it is aimed at cities, especially given that Indian military doctrine suggests that nonnuclear forces would preemptively launch counterforce attacks on an adversary's nuclear forces. Pakistan's nuclear strategy seems to be designed as a deterrent against an Indian conventional attack. India's reliance on a nonnuclear counterforce attack at the outset of any conflict with Pakistan increases the risk of nuclear escalation in a full-scale conventional war with Pakistan, especially if Pakistani officials face a "use it or lose it" predicament.

It is difficult to predict or even determine the employment doctrine of most states. The smaller the number of deliverable warheads available, the greater the likelihood that the state will adopt countervalue targeting. Thus, states such as Iran and North Korea, both of which are pursuing nuclear weapons capabilities, may rely heavily on threatening a few key urban areas within range of their limited number of missiles rather than seeking to develop complex and costly counterforce capabilities.

—*Malcolm Davis*

See also: Counterforce Targeting; Deterrence; Massive Retaliation

References
Lavoy, Peter R., Scott D. Sagan, and James J. Wirtz, eds., *Planning the Unthinkable: How New Powers Will Use Nuclear, Biological, and Chemical Weapons* (Ithaca, NY: Cornell University Press, 2000).
Kahn, Herman, *On Thermonuclear War* (Princeton, NJ: Princeton University Press, 1961).

COUPLING

The term "coupling" often refers to a mechanical device that unites two things. In nuclear strategy, it refers to the linking of issues, and during the Cold War it was used to describe the United States' nuclear guarantee to Western Europe and other U.S. strategic partners.

Article 5 of the Charter of the North Atlantic Treaty refers to the idea that an attack on any North Atlantic Treaty Organization (NATO) state would be considered an attack on all the members of NATO. This charter committed the United States and Canada to the defense of Europe, especially against the perceived threat posed by the Soviet Union. For much of NATO's history, the alliance relied on the deterrent provided by U.S. nuclear forces to offset the conventional superiority of the Soviet Union. It was this "coupling" of the U.S. strategic nuclear deterrent to the defense of Western Europe that became a principal focus of concern for policymakers, especially once the situation of mutual assured destruction (MAD) emerged between the United States and the Soviet Union. Analysts debated whether the U.S. nuclear guarantee was credible, given the likely Soviet response if the United States chose to use nuclear weapons against Russia in the defense of Western Europe. Concerns about decoupling the U.S. strategic nuclear force from the defense of NATO was often used as a justification for the U.S. decision to launch the Strategic Defense Initiative (SDI) in 1983, and for the 1979 decision to modernize NATO's theater nuclear forces in the 1970s. Earlier debates about the credibility of NATO's policy of massive retaliation and the shift to flexible response in 1967 also were in part a response to the credibility of U.S. extended deterrence and the coupling of U.S. nuclear forces to the defense of NATO.

—*Andrew M. Dorman*

See also: North Atlantic Treaty Organization (NATO)

References
Cordesman, Anthony H., "Deterrence in the 1980s, Part 1: American Strategic Forces and Extended Deterrence," *Adelphi Paper* (London: International Institute for Strategic Studies, 1982).

Representatives from twelve nations convene in Washington, D.C., on April 4, 1949, to sign the North Atlantic Treaty, which coupled the defense of Western Europe and North America. (NATO Photos)

Haftendorn, Helga, *NATO and the Nuclear Revolution: A Crisis of Credibility, 1966–67* (Oxford, UK: Clarendon, 1996).

CREDIBILITY

The issue of credibility has long been associated with nuclear weapons. For strategists and policy-makers, doubts always existed about whether a rational decision could ever be made to use nuclear weapons. Thus, nuclear threats, especially against similarly armed opponents, appeared to lack credibility; nuclear use could be tantamount to national suicide. To many it seemed that only when the very survival of the state itself was threatened did nuclear threats become credible. This was one of the main criticisms of the concept of massive retaliation, a U.S. declaratory policy early in the Cold War that suggested that minor Soviet military operations might be met with a massive U.S. nuclear response.

Many observers also believed that policies of extended deterrence—in which the United States threatened to employ its strategic nuclear arsenal in defense of Western Europe—were not credible. Once the Soviet Union had achieved an assured second-strike capability, the U.S. threat to initiate nuclear hostilities in the event of a Soviet invasion of Europe appeared to many to lack credibility. Frequently the argument was put in terms of whether the United States would be prepared to sacrifice New York and Washington for London and Paris.

Today, many observers believe that nuclear threats lack credibility because most military threats are minor and the destructive power of existing nuclear forces is extraordinarily large. Because the use of nuclear weapons would be viewed as a disproportionate response to all but the most devastating attacks, threats to use nuclear weapons are viewed by friend and foe alike as lacking credibility.

—*Andrew M. Dorman*

See also: Deterrence; Massive Retaliation

References

Freedman, Lawrence, *The Evolution of Nuclear Strategy,*
    third edition (New York: Palgrave Macmillan, 2003).
Rush, Kenneth, Brent Scowcroft, and Joseph P Wolf,
    "The Credibility of the NATO Deterrent: Bringing
    the Deterrent Up to Date," *NATO Review,* October
    1981, pp. 7–13, and December 1981, pp. 23–27.

CRISIS STABILITY

The first half of the twentieth century saw two dev-astating world wars, the onset of the nuclear age, and the emergence of weapons of mass destruction, leading the political scientist Raymond Aron to call it "the century of total war" (Aron). Bernard Brodie, in his 1946 classic *The Absolute Weapon,* described what became axiomatic for how much of the world looked at war and peace: "Thus far the chief purpose of our military establishment has been to *win* wars. From now on its chief purpose must be to *avert* them. It can have almost no other useful purpose" (Brodie, p. 77). This so-called "nuclear revolution" changed the very purpose of military forces from winning to preventing the outbreak of wars in the first place.

This focus on deterring rather than fighting major wars spawned a whole body of literature deal-ing with the requirements of deterrence, especially the prospective use of nuclear weapons. These theo-rists suggested that the strategic antagonists—no-tably the United States and the Soviet Union—would be locked in a long-term competition. Conflict was not likely to be *resolved;* therefore, it had to be *managed*—the relationship had to be *sta-ble* in the sense that neither side had an incentive to use nuclear weapons first in a crisis.

A stable strategic relationship is one that is not easily disturbed by new or changing circumstances. It is a relative concept—a more stable relationship is more resilient in the face of new pressures; a less sta-ble relationship is one in which the perception of changing risks or opportunities is more likely to lead to changed behavior that alters the character of the relationship. Assessing whether deterrence is likely to succeed requires an assessment not only of one's capability and will to make good on one's de-terrent threats, but also of how the other *perceives* whether it is in its interests *not* to provoke a war—not only during normal circumstances, but also in a crisis, when it might calculate its interests, risks, and opportunities differently.

For a strategic relationship to possess crisis sta-bility, it should not promote incentives during a cri-sis for either side to initiate conflict or challenge the position of the other in a way that would provoke conflict. For example, there might not be any incen-tive for a state to go to war during normal circum-stances—peace, even with the tensions of the Cold War, would be preferable to war. However, rising political tensions might cause a state to conclude that war is likely, that it faces a higher risk of being attacked itself, and that there are advantages to at-tacking first if war were to occur. In such circum-stances, a normally stable relationship would be un-stable in a crisis.

The circumstances that would jeopardize crisis stability typically involve some combination of *vul-nerability* and *opportunity*—that is, situations where the state sees an opportunity to reduce its own vul-nerability by taking advantage of an opponent's weakness. During the Cold War and beyond, im-proving crisis stability encouraged policy choices that sometimes involved not only increasing the survivability of one's nuclear forces, but taking steps to increase the survivability of a potential adver-sary's nuclear forces. If both sides in a dispute pos-sessed a secure second-strike capability, then neither would feel much incentive to use nuclear forces first in a crisis.

For example, the dominant characteristic of the missile age has been the lack of adequate defense against attack. Such vulnerability means that the only way to avoid unacceptable destruction in a war is to destroy the opponent's attack capability. Dur-ing the late 1950s and early 1960s, both the United States and the Soviet Union possessed ballistic mis-siles that were themselves vulnerable to attack; thus each had an opportunity to destroy that threat be-fore being attacked by launching a nuclear attack first in the hope of catching the opponent's nuclear arsenal on the ground. In a crisis, each would have had an incentive to strike first, in the hopes of elim-inating a substantial portion of the missiles against which it could not defend, rather than waiting to be attacked.

By contrast, if the missiles in question were pro-tected, then the opportunity to defeat the threat posed by those missiles disappears. In the early 1960s, the United States not only began to put its intercon-tinental ballistic missiles in underground silos but also encouraged the Soviet Union to do the same. By placing their missiles in silos, both sides increased the survivability of their retaliatory capability.

Preserving crisis stability was likewise the rationale for urging—as the United States did in the late 1960s and early 1970s—that both superpowers forgo building national ballistic missile defenses. With no ability to reduce society's vulnerability to destruction, and no guarantee that a first strike would succeed (that is, result in total destruction of the opponent's nuclear arsenal), crisis stability was enhanced, at least in theory. In short, vulnerable societies and invulnerable retaliatory capabilities—the elements of mutual assured destruction (MAD)—constituted the formula for a stable deterrent relationship.

Improvements in military technology did not allow such a simple formula to endure. By the 1970s, larger nuclear arsenals, plus the ability to destroy even hardened military targets, meant that retaliatory capabilities were increasingly vulnerable and therefore lucrative targets for preemption. This new reality, in turn, prompted renewed interest in national missile defense as a way of removing the vulnerability of both strike forces and society at large.

Even after the Cold War ended, this debate continued. Critics of national missile defense—including the Russian government—argued that a one-sided development of such defenses would create first-strike incentives in a crisis. The only way to improve crisis stability would be to develop missile defenses jointly.

Because crisis stability largely depends on how states perceive threats, risks, opportunities, and incentives, mechanisms to improve communication in a crisis also have been important—beginning with the Hot Line Agreements from the early 1960s and continuing with the more recent exchange of military personnel in strategic command and warning centers. Beyond the bilateral nuclear relationship, provisions to improve communication and avoid miscalculation in a crisis have become standard elements in managing conflict situations around the world.

Crisis stability is ultimately about keeping all parties in an antagonistic relationship believing that they are secure even if the threat of war increases. This involves efforts to reduce the incentives of all parties to use nuclear weapons first in a crisis. Paradoxically, this means that a larger military capability may be more stabilizing than a smaller one, if the smaller one is more vulnerable to being destroyed in a surprise attack. Hence, the pursuit of crisis stability in a deterrent relationship may be at odds with the purposes of disarmament.

—Schuyler Foerster

See also: Deterrence; Disarmament; Downloading; Escalation; Firebreaks; Mutual Assured Destruction; Survivability

References

Aron, Raymond, *The Century of Total War* (Boston: Beacon Press, 1955).

Brodie, Bernard, ed., *The Absolute Weapon* (New York: Harcourt Brace, 1946).

Foerster, Schuyler, William A. Barry, III, William R. Cloutz, Harold F. Lynch et al., *Defining Stability: Conventional Arms Control in a Changing Europe* (Boulder: Westview, 1989).

Freedman, Lawrence, *The Evolution of Nuclear Strategy* (New York: St. Martin's Press, 1981).

Schelling, Thomas C., and Morton H. Halperin, *Strategy and Arms Control* (Washington, DC: Pergamon-Brassey's, 1985).

CRITICAL NUCLEAR WEAPONS DESIGN INFORMATION (CNWDI)

Critical Nuclear Weapons Design Information (CNWDI) is information classified as "top secret" or "secret" relating to the theory of operation, design, and function of nuclear weapons. This information covers overall weapon design, weapon component, and subassembly data. Other information may relate to fusing and arming nuclear weapons or to the material composition of the weapons and the quantities of special materials incorporated into them. Security functions such as a permissive action link (PAL), a lock that prevents unauthorized use of a nuclear weapon, may also have a CNWDI restriction.

This level of security clearance is required for persons with access to weapons, plans, weapons labs, or forums discussing this information. Security managers at specific locations can verify current clearance levels and clear individuals for CNWDI as needed.

—Bret Kinman

Reference

U.S. Department of Defense website, http://www.defenselink.mil.

CRITICALITY AND CRITICAL MASS

The key requirement for making a nuclear weapon or a practical nuclear reactor is to create a self-sustaining chain reaction. In such a chain reaction, neutrons released by fission in one atom are likely, on average, to induce the fission of one or more subsequent atoms. An assembly of fissile and other materials that can support a self-sustaining chain reaction is said to be a "critical" assembly or to have achieved "criticality."

Criticality depends on the type and amount of fissile material as well as on assembly details such as mass, surface area, geometry, and the composition of nonfissionable materials used in construction. The primary criterion for criticality is that the multiplication factor (k)—the ratio of neutrons in one generation of fissions to the number produced in the final generation—be greater than unity. The $k > 1$ criterion is a primary design consideration for any practical use of nuclear energy and is achieved by creating designs that balance the production and loss rate of neutrons. The criticality condition can be met with a variety of assembly structures, sizes, and time scales; can be exceeded significantly or barely met; and can be met with different fissionable materials that produce combinations of fast and slow neutrons. The most significant differences in design of nuclear assemblies are between nuclear weapons and nuclear reactors.

Criticality in Nuclear Weapons

A nuclear weapon explodes because the assembly is designed to release energy from a fission chain reaction so quickly that the fissile material vaporizes. If two subcritical assemblies ($k < 1$) are brought together too slowly, they will release heat and melt rather than produce an explosion. A nuclear weapon requires an explosive assembly that goes quickly from a subcritical state to a supercritical state ($k \sim 2$: On average, neutrons from any single fission event are likely to produce two subsequent fissions).

Once assembled into the supercritical state, the chain reaction can only occur for a brief moment because criticality causes the fissile material to blow itself apart. But the time scale between fissions in a critical assembly is about ten nanoseconds; for $k \sim 2$, all the atoms in a kilogram of uranium would completely fission in less than a microsecond. The nuclear energy released from the complete fission of one kilogram of uranium would be equivalent to the energy released from about 17,000 kilograms of chemical explosives.

Shape has a major impact on the size and mass required for a critical assembly. A long, thin rod, with a large surface area, would lose many neutrons through the surface before they could participate in a chain reaction. The optimum shape for achieving a critical assembly with the smallest possible mass is a sphere; the number of fissionable atoms increases with the cube of the radius, but the surface area for escaping neutrons increases only with the square of the radius. Not all nuclear weapons use spherical assemblies, but early nuclear weapons depended on this optimum shape.

For nuclear weapons, the timing of achieving criticality is very important. The weapon works best if the assembly goes from subcritical to supercritical instantaneously. If subcritical assemblies come together very slowly, fission energy will be dissipated in heating the materials, possibly moving them out of an appropriate shape to sustain criticality. The spontaneous fissions from uranium or plutonium also can initiate a chain reaction before supercriticality is achieved. Such a premature chain reaction would not use up much of the fissile material, would dramatically reduce the nuclear yield, and would be referred to as a "fizzle."

The term "critical mass" is something of a misnomer. Achieving criticality depends upon the density, configuration, and timing of a nuclear weapon assembly, and only partly on the total mass of fissile material available to participate in the chain reaction; there is no single "critical mass" used to construct a nuclear weapon. The amount of fissile material used in a nuclear weapon depends on the yield sought, the assembly design and configuration, and the predicted fraction of the nuclear material that will generate the explosion before being explosively disassembled.

Nonetheless, it is common to speak of the critical mass for the primary fissile materials in a particular assembly. In many unclassified books and articles, it is common to see a single number quoted as "the critical mass" for uranium 235 (usually quoted as a number between about 9 and 25 kg) or plutonium 239 (usually between 4 and 20 kg). These different numbers reflect different assumptions about the assembly requirements needed to construct explosive devices. Efficient designs, involving spheres of pure material and surrounding the nuclear assembly with materials that reflect neutrons and delay the dispersion of explosive products, require less fissile material. Conservative designs use extra material to ensure that supercritical conditions are met and to make up for uncertainty in the fraction of nuclear material that might be involved in the explosive chain reaction.

There are significant differences when it comes to using fissile uranium and plutonium in designing a nuclear weapon. Plutonium is a denser material, and a smaller amount of plutonium will usually be required to produce a given yield from a particular design. Variations in isotopic content and metallurgic mixture, however, can overwhelm this difference in density. The spontaneous fission rate for plutonium (and especially of the isotope Pu-240) also is much higher than the spontaneous fission rate of uranium. Because of this higher rate of spontaneous neutron generation, plutonium weapons need to be assembled rapidly to avoid premature fizzle yields.

Weapon designers consider a design to have fizzled when only a small amount of the fissile material is consumed in a chain reaction. It is important that weapon designs make efficient use of fissile plutonium or uranium because the cost and effort involved in producing these materials is high. Given the resources put into creating a nuclear weapon, it is not cost-effective unless it is much more powerful than a conventional high-explosive device. This was a major concern on the part of scientists working on the Manhattan Project during World War II. The mass of the hardware needed to make a nuclear weapon dwarfs that of the fissile material itself; for example, the nuclear weapon dropped on Nagasaki weighed about 10,000 pounds but used only 10 to 20 pounds of plutonium (*see* Manhattan Project).

A nuclear "dud" can be caused by a variety of miscalculations or malfunctions. Similarly, it is difficult to predict the exact yield of a nuclear weapon. In the extreme case, assembly time might be so slow that plutonium might begin to melt into a new shape and never achieve a significant nuclear yield. But a fizzle—an extremely inefficient nuclear weapon—may still produce a large explosion and many deaths. The uranium bomb dropped on Hiroshima was inefficient and is believed to have created a chain reaction in only about 1 or 2 percent of the 140 pounds of highly enriched uranium in its nuclear assembly. But the yield of this weapon was equivalent to between 10,000 and 15,000 tons of TNT—2,000 times greater than the blast effect that would have been produced by 10,000 pounds of

TNT. It instantly killed between 70,000 and 130,000 people. New nuclear powers and terrorists may be satisfied with very inefficient nuclear weapons if the yield is large enough, and they may tolerate great uncertainties in the percentage of fuel contributing to the explosion (*see* Fission Weapons; Gun-Type Devices; Implosion Devices; Plutonium; Uranium).

Criticality in Nuclear Power Production

A nuclear reactor also depends on the property of criticality. A practical reactor, used to generate electric power, must maintain a chain reaction to take more energy out than is being used to operate the reactor. Nuclear reactors are usually designed to operate with k near unity. Reactor design balances the loss of neutrons through the surface and by absorption in nonfissile materials (including the coolant that captures the energy for electricity generation) with the generation of many neutrons from a chain reaction in a large amount of fissile material. The fuel rods of nuclear reactors tend to have large surface areas, and the total amount of nuclear fuel used in a single critical assembly is typically measured in tons. The reactor consists of an assembly of fissile material, moderators to slow the neutrons and increase the likelihood of fission, control elements that can absorb neutrons and decrease the likelihood of fission, coolant to take away the heat generated by absorption of neutrons, and other elements as required. Varying the position of control elements and the rate of coolant flow allows the reactor to be operated in a self-sustaining chain reaction or maintained at a subcritical level.

The relatively low multiplication factor in a reactor design means that nuclear energy is released at a much lower rate than in a nuclear explosion. The nuclear energy generated by fission is released over a much larger period of time than in a nuclear weapon. At $k = 1$, a kilogram of uranium atoms takes decades to completely fission. The same factors that determine criticality in a nuclear weapon—total amount of fissionable material, density, configuration, and timing—are managed in a nuclear reactor design. But the reactor design creates a barely sustained chain reaction, with the percentage of fissile material participating in the chain reaction during each second very low (approximately 10^{-14} percent). A high total power level is achieved by arranging large amounts of fissionable materials into a nuclear assembly participating in the chain reaction.

The level of criticality and the kind of chain reaction that occurs is determined by the design of a nuclear assembly. A fast assembly cannot be used to produce a sustained power generation over a long period of time, and a distributed nuclear reactor cannot be made to explode. Even an uncontrolled chain reaction allowed to operate well outside design parameters in a nuclear reactor would lead only to the melting of the fissile materials and a drop below criticality (*see* Reactor Operations).

—*Roy Pettis*

See also: Fission Weapons; Thermonuclear Bomb
References

"Critical Mass," http://encyclopedia.thefreedictionary. com/Critical%20Mass.

"Decide the Nuclear Issue for Yourself: Nuclear Need Not Be Unclear," http://www.magma.ca/~jalrober/Decide.htm.

Hanlen, D. F., and W. J. Morse, *Nuclear Physics Made Very, Very Easy,* United States Atomic Energy Commission and National Aeronautics and Space Administration, Space Nuclear Propulsion Office Report NTO-T-0026, July 1968.

"How Things Work: Explaining the Physics of Everyday Life—Nuclear Weapons," available at http:// howthingswork.virginia.edu/nuclear_weapons.html.

Serber, Robert, and Richard Rhodes, eds., *The Los Alamos Primer: The First Lectures on How to Build an Atomic Bomb* (Berkeley: University of California Press, 1992).

Smyth, Henry De Wolf, and Philip Morrison, *Atomic Energy for Military Purposes: The Official Report on the Development of the Atomic Bomb under the Auspices of the United States Government* (Berkeley: University of California Press, 1992).

Weisman, Joel, ed., *Elements of Nuclear Reactor Design,* second ed. (Melbourne, FL: Krieger, 1983).

CRUISE MISSILES

The cruise missile has been defined as "an unmanned self-propelled guided vehicle that sustains flight through aerodynamic lift for most of its flight path and whose primary mission is to place an ordnance or special payload on a target" (Werrell, p. 223). Cruise missiles can be divided into two main categories: unmanned air vehicles (UAVs) and unmanned combat air vehicles (UCAVs), which are essentially UAVs that carry ordnance. The United States introduced a fleet of air-launched cruise missiles (ALCMs), submarine-launched (or surface

ship–launched) cruise missiles (SLCMs), and ground-launched cruise missiles (GLCMs) in 1974, all of which are experiencing a contemporary resurgence in military operations. Cruise missiles were first used in combat during World War II. The most famous version of this type of weapon was Nazi Germany's V-1, or "buzz bomb." Inexpensive to produce, early postwar cruise missiles utilized aircraft fuselages and jet engine technology and carried nuclear warheads in the megaton range to compensate for their limited accuracy.

Two technical breakthroughs in the early 1970s transformed the cruise missile into a highly lethal weapon system. The first breakthrough was produced by the dramatic reduction in the size of computers coupled with equally dramatic increases in the computational capabilities of on-board computer guidance systems. These sophisticated guidance systems enabled cruise missiles to fly preprogrammed flight paths at very low altitudes, making them difficult to detect. The second breakthrough, advances in jet propulsion, allowed engineers to decrease the size of the missiles while increasing their range and payload. Equipped with a new navigation system called terrain contour matching (TERCOM), which allowed the missiles to follow preprogrammed terrain maps on the way to their targets, U.S. cruise missiles achieved extremely high accuracies. Newer generations of cruise missiles rely on global positioning system (GPS) signals to achieve high accuracy without the need for the TERCOM maps (which are expensive and time consuming to create).

Cruise missiles require several subsystems: airframe, propulsion, guidance, control and navigation, and weapons integration. None of these systems is extraordinarily expensive, and the decreasing price and increasing capability of modern guidance systems promises to reduce the price tag of cruise missiles in the future. The survivability and cost-effectiveness of cruise missiles influenced President Jimmy Carter's decision to cancel the B-1 bomber in 1977 and to use cruise missiles to extend the life of the B-52 force as part of the airborne leg of the U.S. nuclear "Triad" (intercontinental ballistic missiles [ICBMs], submarine-launched ballistic missiles [SLBMs], and manned bombers).

ALCMs improved the ability of manned bombers to strike multiple targets from a safe standoff range. Cruise missiles thus make a unique

Test flight of a Tomahawk cruise missile, used by U.S. and British naval forces. (Raytheon/Reuters/Corbis)

contribution to aircraft effectiveness and surviv-ability. Older bombers can become a first-class strategic threat—witness the USAF B-52 and the Russian Bear-H. The Soviets spent a good part of the Strategic Arms Limitation Talks (SALT II, 1979) attempting to limit the deployment and range of the new American cruise missiles. Bombers carry-ing the cruise missiles were actually counted against MIRVed weapon sublimits in these arms control agreements. The first Boeing AGM-86 ALCM was deployed on a B-52G at Griffiss AFB, New York, in January 1981; it was added to the B-52H in 1985. After Desert Storm in 1991, the U.S. Air Force re-quested money to begin reequipping the ALCM with conventional warheads. This became the con-ventional ALCM, or CALCM AGM-86C/D. It was used for the first time against Iraq in Desert Fox in

1996. At first the CALCMs were simply converted nuclear ALCMs. The U.S. Air Force has since re-opened the production line to produce more CAL-CMs outfitted with both a hard-target penetrator and a submunitions dispenser warhead.

The U.S. Navy also developed a cruise missile for its submarines and ships. The submarine-launched version was kept in a capsule and launched from one of the submarine's torpedo tubes. Later, Los Angeles–class attack submarines were fitted with vertical launch tubes outside of the pressure hull, saving valuable on-board space for torpedoes and other weapons. The U.S. Navy's Tomahawks (also known as Tomahawk land-attack missiles, or TLAMs) were fired extensively during Operation Desert Storm, and again during Allied Force (Kosovo, 1999), Enduring Freedom (Afghanistan,

2001), and Iraqi Freedom (2003), attacking a variety of targets. Their conventional warhead limited their utility against hardened targets, but upgrades are improving the lethality of the Tomahawk. The U.S. Navy has approximately 120 vessels from which it can be launched. The TLAM became the first cruise missile system sold to a foreign country when, in 1996, the Royal Navy added the weapon to its inventory, initially carrying the Tomahawk on attack submarines. The first combat employment of the TLAM by the Royal Navy occurred during Operation Allied Force against Serbia. The U.S. Navy was able to increase its deployment flexibility when the weapon was certified for use in vertical launch arrays emplaced on modern cruisers and destroyers.

As the Soviet Union reequipped and expanded its theater nuclear capabilities in the 1970s with the SS-20 intermediate-range ballistic missile, NATO decided to challenge the deployments with its own intermediate-range nuclear weapons, one of which was the ground-launched cruise missile. Using the Tomahawk cruise missile mounted on a flatbed trailer in four round armored box launchers, 464 cruise missiles were deployed to Western Europe in quick reaction alert. This class of cruise missile was eliminated by the Intermediate-Range Nuclear Forces (INF) Treaty of 1987 (see Intermediate-Range Nuclear Forces [INF] Treaty).

The Soviet Union had developed its own family of cruise missiles by 1986. The AS-15 Kent is an ALCM carried by both the Bear-H and Blackjack bombers. The SS-N-21 was the SLCM deployed on Victor-, Akuala-, and Sierra-class attack submarines. Other submarines, such as the Oscar guided-missile submarines, also carried these cruise missiles. A Soviet GLCM, the SSC-X-4, was banned under the INF Treaty.

As the first of the stockpile of about 1,600 ALCMs were converted to conventional explosive warheads, the U.S. Air Force developed a new stealth cruise missile for the nuclear strike mission. The AGM-129 Advanced Cruise Missile purchase was completed in 1999. Success in Desert Storm, and the availability of navigational satellite systems, led to the proliferation of cruise missiles, which now could be placed into two categories: land-attack cruise missiles and antishipping cruise missiles. Only France, Russia, Great Britain, and the United States possessed land-attack cruise missiles in 2004. Antishipping cruise missiles are manufactured and exported to a wider network of countries. Some can be modified to attack land targets, but most lack the range to carry out deep-strike missions. Among the best known is the French Exocet antishipping missile.

Cruise missiles are the weapon of choice to attack high-value, heavily defended targets. Combined cruise missile and tactical aircraft attacks now dominate the conduct of air warfare.

—*Gilles Van Nederveen*

See also: Ground-Launched Cruise Missiles; Missile Defense; Sea-Launched Cruise Missiles

References

Froggett, Steve, "Tomahawk in the Desert," *Proceedings*, January 1992.
Huisken, Ronald, *The Origins of the Strategic Cruise Missile* (New York: Praeger, 1992).
Rip, Michael Russell, and James M. Hasik, *The Precision Revolution: GPS and the Future of Aerial Warfare* (Annapolis, MD: Naval Institute Press, 2002).
Werrell, Kenneth, *The Evolution of the Cruise Missile* (Maxwell AFB, AL: Air University Press, 1985).

CUBAN MISSILE CRISIS

The Cuban missile crisis was a diplomatic and military standoff between the United States and the Soviet Union precipitated by the U.S. discovery of a Soviet installation of intermediate- and medium-range ballistic missiles (IRBMs and MRBMs) in Cuba on October 14, 1962. The ensuing crisis brought the two countries to the brink of nuclear confrontation, only ending when the Soviets agreed to remove their missiles and bombers from Cuba.

Fearing a U.S. invasion of Cuba (which had become Communist with the accession of Fidel Castro as president in 1959), and wishing to respond in kind to the U.S. placement of Jupiter IRBM missiles in Turkey, Soviet Secretary General Nikita Khrushchev had considered the deployment of IRBMs and MRBMs to Cuba as early as April 1962. By September 1962, parts and equipment for forty-two SS-4 MRBMs and thirty-two SS-5 IRBMs began arriving in Cuba. In addition to the missiles, the Soviets sent 42,000 troops, MiG-21 jets, IL-28 bombers, and coastal defense forces.

The Crisis

On October 14, 1962, an American U-2 reconnaissance aircraft photographed Soviet missile sites in San Cristobal, Cuba. Shortly thereafter, the

An aerial reconnaissance photograph showing a missile launch site in San Cristobal, Cuba. The discovery of such Soviet missile sites led to the Cuban Missile Crisis in October 1962. (Bettmann/Corbis)

administration of President John F. Kennedy decided that the United States could not allow the missiles to remain in Cuba. By October 21, Kennedy had decided to impose a naval blockade on Cuba. The next day, the president addressed the nation, announcing the presence of Soviet missiles in Cuba and the U.S. naval blockade of the island. Simultaneously, U.S. forces worldwide were put at Defense Condition (Defcon) 3 and U.S. nuclear forces were put at Defcon 2, only one level short of war.

On October 25, U.S. intelligence reported that at least some of the Soviet missiles were operational. At the same time, the Kennedy administration agreed to Operational Plan 316. The plan, involving a full-scale invasion of Cuba, was deemed the best option if military action became necessary to remove the missiles. It would have involved massive air strikes, an airborne assault, and an amphibious landing.

October 27 was the most pivotal day of the crisis. The day began with a message from Khrushchev suggesting that the U.S.S.R. would remove its missiles from Cuba if the United States removed its Jupiter missiles from Turkey. On that same day, however, an American U-2 was shot down over Cuba, an event that U.S. officials viewed as a deliberate act of escalation. That evening, Attorney General Robert Kennedy met with Soviet Ambassador Anatoly Dobrynin. In the meeting, the attorney general told Dobrynin that time was running out, that the United States was willing to use military force, and that the Kremlin had one day to agree to remove the missiles. He also indicated that the United States would consider removing its missiles from Turkey. The following morning, October 28, Khrushchev announced via Moscow radio that the missiles would be removed from Cuba (*see* Inadvertent Escalation).

Post-Crisis Relations

Though the immediate danger lessened significantly on October 28, there were still a number of important issues remaining between the two superpowers.

The United States also demanded that a number of Soviet IL-28 bombers be removed from Cuba, something that Khrushchev did not agree to do until November 20. On that same day, President Kennedy announced the lifting of the U.S. naval blockade of the island. However, Kennedy continued to resist Khrushchev's pressure to sign a formal noninvasion agreement regarding Cuba, citing Cuba's refusal to allow on-site inspection and verification of the Soviet missile removals. Consequently, there was never a formal, negotiated settlement to the crisis.

—*Sean Lawson*

References

Allison, Graham, *Essence of Decision* (New York: Harper-Collins, 1971).

Chang, Laurence, and Peter Kornbluh, eds. *The Cuban Missile Crisis, 1962* (New York: New Press, 1992).

D

DAMAGE LIMITATION

Damage limitation is the ability to reduce, contain, preempt, intercept, or prevent harm inflicted on one's own forces or other assets by an enemy attack. Efforts to limit damage may be applied to military forces, troops, and equipment as well as to cities, industry, population, leadership, critical communication nodes, transportation systems, national infrastructure networks, or whatever else a nation values and believes is subject to outside threats. From an operational point of view, the strategies are divided into active and passive damage limitation. Air defense, antisubmarine warfare, and missile defense are examples of active damage limitation, as is preemptive attack against the enemy's offensive forces (in order to destroy them before they can inflict casualties on one's own forces). Passive forms of damage limitation include hardening the assets to be protected, proliferating their numbers (to increase the chances that more survive and to increase the costs of attacking them), making the assets mobile so they can move around to avoid being targeted, camouflaging them, burying them, or hiding them. Civil defense measures designed to protect urban populations in the event of an attack are also a prominent example of passive damage limitation (*see* Civil Defense; Preemptive Attack).

Recently, there has been a revival of interest in damage limitation as a form of deterrence as a response to new threats that may be less amenable to traditional forms of deterrence. Therefore, the United States is increasingly pursuing forms of damage limitation such as missile defenses to back up and reinforce deterrence and to provide some insurance in case traditional deterrence fails (*see* Deterrence; Missile Defense).

—*Kerry Kartchner*

Reference

Enthoven, Alain C., and K. Wayne Smith, *How Much Is Enough? Shaping the Defense Program, 1961–1969* (New York: Harper and Row, 1971).

DATA EXCHANGES

Verifying compliance with arms control agreements is a function of intelligence collection and analysis of all the information available concerning a particular activity. It is accomplished by national technical means (NTM) supplemented by cooperative measures, that is, negotiated or volunteered measures requiring the cooperation of another party or parties to the agreement. One type of cooperative measure is the exchange of data. Data exchanges involve the exchange of comprehensive sets of information, frequently including the numbers and locations of treaty-limited equipment or other items, technical characteristics of specific weapons and their associated launchers, site diagrams, information regarding force structure, and the like.

From the mid-1950s until the 1987 Intermediate-Range Nuclear Forces (INF) Treaty, verification of arms control proposals and agreements relied primarily on NTM. However, the Ronald Reagan administration pressed for very extensive and intrusive bilateral provisions, including cooperative measures, in the INF Treaty. The verification regime of the INF Treaty contained the most stringent provision in any arms control agreement negotiated to that date. It included an unprecedented exchange of data on the systems limited by the treaty, including numbers, locations, and technical characteristics of all INF missiles and launchers.

There are significant synergistic effects between NTM and data exchanges. While NTM provides useful information on the nature and scope of information expected to be included in data exchanges, the exchanges themselves provide useful information for enhancing present and future

NTM capabilities. For example, information on technical characteristics, numbers, locations of treaty-limited equipment, and site diagrams provides "sanity checks" on data based on NTM and guidance for revising and upgrading the overall conclusions and capabilities of NTM.

—Patricia McFate

See also: National Technical Means; Telemetry; Verification

References

Graybeal, Sidney, George Lindsay, James Macintosh, and Patricia McFate, *Verification to the Year 2000,* Arms Control Verification Studies No. 4 (Ottawa, Canada: Ministry of External Affairs and International Trade, February 1991).

McFate, Patricia, and Sidney Graybeal, "Synergies among Verification Modes and Techniques," SAIC report prepared for the U.S. Department of Energy, Washington, DC, 10 January 1992.

THE DAY AFTER

The Day After was a controversial made-for-television movie aired by the American Broadcasting Corporation (ABC) in 1983. It dramatized the prelude to a nuclear strike on Kansas City, Missouri, and the after-effects felt in nearby Lawrence, Kansas, following a fictional limited nuclear exchange between the United States and the Soviet Union. The story followed characters coping with radiation sickness, the injuries and deaths of family and friends, and massive physical destruction.

The movie was the subject of criticism even prior to its airing and received much public and media interest. It was shown at a time of worsening relations between the United States and the Soviet Union in the early 1980s following the Soviet invasion of Afghanistan, tougher rhetoric between the two countries following the period of détente, an increase in planned nuclear arms procurement, and stalled arms control talks. In this atmosphere, concerns about the outbreak of nuclear war were widespread among the American public.

Critics of the film believed that the graphic scenes depicting a nuclear attack and its effects were gratuitously shocking and would breed antinuclear and pacifist sentiment among the American public. They also charged that the movie was overtly political and that it aimed to erode public support for the nuclear policies of the Ronald Reagan administration and the U.S. nuclear deterrent. Those opposing the deployment of new nuclear systems sought to

use the movie to highlight the dangers of nuclear war and to advocate nuclear disarmament, hosting public gatherings to view the movie followed by discussions on nuclear policy.

—Michael George

References

"The Day After," Internet Movie Database, 1983, available at http://www.imdb.com/title/tt0085404/.

Getler, Michael, "Schultz Says Movie Is Not the Future," *Washington Post,* 21 November 1983.

Hoffman, David, and Lou Cannon, "ABC's 'The Day After': White House to Counterattack Movie," *Washington Post,* 18 November 1983.

Weisman, Steven R., "Administration Mounts Drive to Counter Atom War Film," *New York Times,* 19 November 1983.

DEALERTING

Dealerting is a reduction in the day-to-day alert status of strategic nuclear forces that diminishes their readiness for launch or introduces deliberate delays into the process of preparing them for launch. Substantial dealerting of U.S. heavy bombers, tactical and theater nuclear weapons, and North Atlantic Treaty Organization (NATO) dual-capable aircraft took place under a series of 1991 presidential nuclear initiatives.

In the mid- to late 1990s, additional proposals were introduced calling for dealerting U.S. and Russian strategic nuclear forces, ostensibly as a means of making them more secure from theft, loss, unauthorized access, or accidental launch and as a way to accelerate the dismantling and disarmament process already taking place under the Strategic Arms Reduction Treaties (START I and START II). These proposals were, in part, responses to the perceived deterioration in the Russian command and control of its nuclear forces. Measures proposed included removing nuclear warheads from operationally deployed intercontinental ballistic missiles (ICBMs), submarine-launched ballistic missiles (SLBMs), and bombers and storing them at a small number of centralized locations; removing or deactivating navigational equipment needed to guide strategic nuclear delivery vehicles; piling gravel on top of missile silos; reducing at-sea deployment rates of U.S. Trident submarines; and removing the launch keys or launch codes from command and control facilities and placing them in centralized containers monitored by officials from the United

States and Russia. These proposals sometimes had much in common with other, similar proposals relating to "detargeting," "decommissioning," "deactivation," "demating," and "deposturing."

Dealerting proposals were not received enthusiastically by either U.S. or Russian officials, who feared such measures would make their respective forces less secure and more vulnerable and undermine rather than promote stability and deterrence. Also, many dealerting proposals would have been difficult to verify or implement. Ultimately, proposals for dealerting strategic nuclear forces were overtaken by other, less-problematic initiatives. For example, the United States and Russia began pursuing a Joint Data Exchange Center to improve awareness of missile threats to both countries and to share early warning data. And the security of the Russian nuclear stockpile continued to be addressed in the context of aid provided to Russia through the U.S. Cooperative Threat Reduction Program.

—*Kerry Kartchner*

See also: Cooperative Threat Reduction (The Nunn-Lugar Program); Presidential Nuclear Initiatives

References
Blair, Bruce G., Harold A. Feiveson, and Frank N. von Hippel, "Taking Nuclear Weapons off Hair-Trigger Alert," *Scientific American,* 1 November 1997.
Karas, Thomas H. *De-alerting and De-activating Strategic Nuclear Weapons,* Sandia National Laboratories, Report SAND2001-0835, April 2001, available at http://www.prod.sandia.gov/cgi-bin/techlib/access-control.pl/2001/010835.pdf.

DECAPITATION

"Decapitation" refers to an attack intended to destroy a country's political and military leadership to eliminate the decision-making authority necessary to authorize and execute a nuclear counterstrike. It is an extraordinarily risky strategy because it communicates the message that one side no longer believes that a negotiated settlement of the conflict is possible and that a final nuclear showdown is now preferable to other possible solutions to a crisis or ongoing conflict. It also is dangerous because an opponent's nuclear command and control infrastructure could be constructed so that it "fails deadly." Local commanders, for instance, might be preauthorized to fire their nuclear weapons in the event they lose contact with higher authorities or if national command assets are attacked with nuclear

weapons. Leaders who believe they are vulnerable to decapitation attacks also might be willing to adopt launch-on-warning or launch-under-attack strategies.

Fear of decapitation strikes thus raises the risk of accidental or inadvertent nuclear war in two ways. Pre-delegation of launch authority can reduce the negative control national authorities can exercise over their nuclear forces, increasing the threat that local commanders might use nuclear weapons on their own initiative. Launch-on-warning strategies might also be activated by false indications of attack, a threat that greatly increases during crises when militaries are on high alert.

—*Andrea Gabbitas and James J. Wirtz*

Reference
Carranza, Mario E., "An Impossible Game: Stable Nuclear Deterrence after the Indian and Pakistani Tests," *Nonproliferation Review,* Spring–Summer 1999, pp. 11–24.

DECLARED FACILITY

The term "declared facility" is a technical term often associated with arms control and disarmament treaties. A declared facility is a site, manufacturing plant, or military base that is subject to inspection and compliance review by other parties to a treaty or by an international governing body created to verify compliance with an international agreement (*see* Verification).

Signatories of the 1993 Chemical Weapons Convention (CWC), for example, are subject to a stringent inspection regime in which they must provide a list of "declared facilities" that are, or once were, involved in the manufacture or storage of chemical weapons. A declared facility that has been identified by a state party as a former chemical weapons facility is subject to systematic verification or on-site inspection based on declared chemical weapons–related activities or functions. Under the CWC, declared and undeclared facilities are subject to challenge inspections. Other states parties may request that the site in question be visited by a team of international inspectors to verify that the host nation has abandoned its chemical arsenal. The Organization for the Prohibition of Chemical Weapons (OPCW), created by the CWC, provides an international team of professional inspectors to undertake challenge inspections.

The 1968 Nuclear Nonproliferation Treaty (NPT) also includes a method of monitoring "declared facilities" to verify that nuclear materials are not being diverted to produce weapons. The International Atomic Energy Agency (IAEA) implements an NPT Safeguards agreement by using a system of material accountancy to make sure that nuclear materials are not being removed from declared facilities (in this context, facilities involved in peaceful nuclear activity).

—*James J. Wirtz*

Reference
Freedman, Lawrence, *The Evolution of Nuclear Strategy*, third edition (New York: Palgrave Macmillan, 2003).

DECOYS

Anything designed to draw fire away from a military target by providing alternative or additional targets is called a "decoy." Decoys are used most often to confuse defensive systems (such as missile defense, air defense, or antisubmarine warfare) during an engagement. Decoys also can be targets for offensive systems. Cardboard airplanes and rubber submarines, for example, may serve as decoys.

Decoys are expected to be less expensive and less massive than the systems they are designed to mimic. If the cost of a decoy is comparable to the weapon system, it is usually more effective to buy real weapons and overwhelm the adversary. Concepts for operation of the MX missile used decoys that were otherwise identical launch sites without missiles in them, but these were eventually judged too costly.

Decoys fool the sensors, the information processing, or the battle management logic of the enemy. They are usually divided into three categories: high-fidelity decoys (which attempt to mimic the target in several respects), low-fidelity decoys (which usually mimic one critical characteristic), and traffic decoys (which attempt to overwhelm the information processing despite low fidelity). Examples of low-fidelity decoys are flares (against infrared sensors), noise-makers (against acoustics), and metallic balloons (against radar). For countering missile defense, high-fidelity decoys are proposed to mimic the shape, infrared signature, and motion of a reentry vehicle.

Decoys work best when they can meet three criteria: (1) they work for a sufficient amount of time;

(2) decoy assembly or release can be accomplished out of the adversary's view; and (3) decoy operations can minimize the viewing angles and sensor bands available to the adversary.

—*Roy Pettis*

See also: Missile Defense; Penetration Aids

References
Greenwood, Ted, *Making the MIRV: A Study of Defense Decision Making* (New York: Ballinger, 1975).
Hartunian, Richard A., "Ballistic Missile and Reentry Systems: The Critical Years," *Crosslink: The Aerospace Corporation Magazine of Advances in Aerospace Technology*, vol. 4, no. 1, Winter 2003.
Nebabin, Victor G., *Methods and Techniques of Radar Recognition* (Norwood, MA: Artech House Radar Library, 1994).

DEFENSE THREAT REDUCTION AGENCY (DTRA)

The Defense Threat Reduction Agency (DTRA) is the U.S. Department of Defense (DOD) agency tasked with stewarding the U.S. nuclear stockpile and reducing the threat posed to the United States by weapons of mass destruction (WMD).

In 1997, U.S. Secretary of Defense William Cohen announced that among other agencies and departments affected by the DOD Defense Reform Initiative, three DOD agencies—the Defense Special Weapons Agency (DSWA), the On-Site Inspection Agency (OSIA), and the Defense Technology Security Administration (DTSA)—and elements of the Cooperative Threat Reduction (CTR) and Chemical-Biological Defense programs—would be consolidated into a threat reduction and treaty compliance agency. On October 1, 1998, the ceremony establishing the Defense Threat Reduction Agency and placing its director, Dr. Jay C. Davis, at its helm was held at Washington Dulles International Airport, the site of DTRA headquarters.

DTRA's mission, while diverse, is tied to the threat posed by weapons of mass destruction, and its directorates are appropriately mission-focused. DTRA began with eight mission-support directorates (Technology Security, Cooperative Threat Reduction, On-Site Inspection, Counterproliferation, Chemical-Biological Defense, Force Protection, Nuclear Support, and Special Weapons Technology Development) and has since reduced the number of its mission directorates to six:

- The Technology Development Directorate is focused on the development of technologies that improve force-application and protection-modeling capabilities, providing enhanced weapons and sensors for defeat of WMD-related facilities and optimizing capabilities for use by U.S. forces to enhance the survivability and operability of U.S. military equities.
- The Cooperative Threat Reduction Directorate consolidates and streamlines all aspects of management and implementation of the CTR program.
- The On-Site Inspection Directorate acts as the U.S. government lead for implementing U.S. arms control inspection, escort, and monitoring activities.
- The Combat Support Directorate provides operational and analytical support to DOD and other organizations for critical nuclear and other WMD defense matters. It is mainly responsible for DOD's nuclear stockpile stewardship and technical support duties for all DOD nuclear weapons.
- The Chemical-Biological Defense Directorate acts as the central point for all DOD chem-bio defense efforts.
- The Weapons Elimination Directorate is DTRA's newest directorate. Classified until late March 2003 when a media leak exposed its existence, the Weapons Elimination Directorate is charged with finding, cataloging, and destroying weapons of mass destruction found in Iraq.

In addition to implementing arms control agreements, DTRA has been in the forefront of many controversial technological developments, including the thermobaric warhead used in Afghanistan in 2002 and Iraq in 2003 and the Biodefense Initiative, which is intended to bolster the ability to defend the U.S. homeland and infrastructure against attack from biological weapons. DTRA also coordinates with other U.S. government agencies and departments to improve WMD counterproliferation programs; lend support and technical advice to WMD planning exercises; and provide force protection assessments and improvements.

In 2002, DTRA relocated its headquarters to Fort Belvoir, Virginia. Following the end of the term of its second director, Dr. Stephen J. Younger, in February 2004, it has been placed under the guidance of Acting Director Major General Trudy H. Clark, USAF.

—*Jennifer Lasecki*

See also: Cooperative Threat Reduction; Department of Defense

References
Defense Threat Reduction Agency website, http://www.dtra.mil/.
Harahan, Joseph P., and Robert J. Bennett, *Creating the Defense Threat Reduction Agency,* Defense Threat Reduction Agency History Series (Washington, DC: Defense Threat Reduction Agency, 2002).

DENSE PACK

"Dense pack" refers to a proposal made by the Ronald Reagan administration during its first term to develop a survivable basing mode for the new MX (for Missile Experimental) intercontinental ballistic missile (ICBM). It was an alternative to the Jimmy Carter administration's proposal to deploy the MX missile on a transporter-erector-launcher so that the missile could be shuttled along a race-track system of twenty-three shelters for each missile. It was hoped that this "shell-game" would increase the survivability of the MX, but eventually the race-track system was abandoned.

The question of missile basing was a major defense issue for the Carter and Reagan administrations. Congress, in particular, wanted to ensure that the land-based ICBM force would retain a second-strike capability. A variety of earlier proposals had been rejected as too expensive or too vulnerable to Soviet countermeasures. The Dense Pack proposal, put forward by the Reagan administration in November 1982, was one alternative that appeared to increase the survivability of the U.S. ICBM force at modest cost. Dense Pack was based on the "fratricide effect." Instead of dispersing missile silos, it would group silos closely together so that if successive enemy warheads were aimed at these silos, the effects of earlier explosions would disable the ones following. As a result, a number of the silos would be more likely to survive. In order to destroy all the silos, a nuclear strike would have to "walk" across the Dense Pack field from south to north, and if detonations occurred too quickly, they would destroy additional incoming warheads, allowing some MX missiles to survive.

Dense Pack ran into political trouble because it would have abrogated the unsigned treaty resulting from the Strategic Arms Limitation Talks (SALT II), which banned the construction of new missile silos. The idea was abandoned in favor of deploying MX missiles in existing Minuteman ICBM silos, which would receive additional protection (hardening).

—*Andrew M. Dorman*

See also: Silo Basing

References

Dunn, David H., *The Politics of Threat: Minuteman Vulnerability in American National Security Policy* (Basingstoke, UK: Macmillan, 1997), pp. 153–160.

Garfinkle, Adam M., "Dense Pack: A Critique and an Alternative," *Parameters*, December 1982, pp. 14–23.

DENUCLEARIZATION

See Disarmament

DEPARTMENT OF DEFENSE (DOD)

The U.S. Department of Defense (DOD) is the bureaucratic agency responsible for housing and deploying all nuclear, biological, and chemical weapons in the U.S. arsenal. Since 1972, the United States has formally renounced the use of biological weapons even in response to an attack with biological weapons. In 1997, it committed to eliminating its chemical stockpile by 2007.

History and Background

In terms of both budget and personnel, the DOD is by far the largest bureaucracy in the U.S. government.. The defense budget routinely takes up nearly half of all discretionary spending ($336 billion in fiscal year 2002 versus $382 billion for all other categories) and employs 1,370,000 active-duty, uniformed personnel; 669,000 civilians; and another 1,280,000 uniformed military reservists (all figures as of June 2003).

The department was created with a 1949 amendment to the National Security Act of 1947 that consolidated the Departments of the Army, Navy, and Air Force under the secretary of defense, removing cabinet status from the individual services. Despite this move, early secretaries of defense found that they had little power because the individual services still controlled most aspects of budgeting, planning, and coordination within the military. A 1958 amendment to the National Security Act helped change this by removing the service chiefs from the operational chain of command and having the four-star unified commanders-in-chief, or CINCs (pronounced "sinks"), report directly to the secretary of defense.

Because most long-term planning and budgeting takes place outside of the operational commands, the services continue to wield enormous power. This has been exacerbated by the designation of the chairman of the Joint Chiefs of Staff, a subordinate of the secretary of defense, as the principal military adviser to the president by the Goldwater-Nichols Department of Defense Reorganization Act of 1986. The independent power of the chairman, the continued influence of the individual services, and congressional wrangling over the distribution of the largest pool of discretionary money have all hindered secretaries of defense in their efforts to centralize the control of military planning and spending.

Organization

The DOD's nuclear and chemical weapons arsenals are under the operational control of the services and specifically the combatant commanders.

The department's role in treaty verification is administered by the Office of Arms Control Implementation and Compliance, which is under the deputy undersecretary of defense for acquisition and technology. Two DOD agencies, the Defense Threat Reduction Agency (DTRA) and the Missile Defense Agency (MDA), also have significant roles in helping to equip and manage U.S. offensive and defensive strategic programs (*see* Defense Threat Reduction Agency [DTRA]).

The forerunner of DTRA was founded in 1991 as an outgrowth of the Intermediate-Range Nuclear Forces (INF) Treaty and the Strategic Arms Reduction Treaties (START I and START II) with the Soviet Union. Since 1993, it has been the principal DOD coordinating agency for countering the WMD threat, focusing on four functions: combat support, technology development, threat control, and threat reduction. The director of DTRA reports to the undersecretary of defense for acquisition, technology, and logistics. The director receives information from an adviser for science and technology and from senior officials from the Department of State, the Department of Energy, and the Federal Bureau of Investigation, as well as from a Threat Reduction Advisory Committee composed of distin-

The Pentagon in Arlington, Virginia, houses the Department of Defense. (Library of Congress)

guished policy, scientific, and defense experts. DTRA also has an Advanced Systems and Concepts Office charged with analyzing emerging weapons of mass destruction threats and the future technologies and concepts needed to counter them.

The predecessor of the Missile Defense Agency was created in 1984 as part of the Strategic Defense Initiative. Its role has evolved, but the agency is still responsible for developing and fielding a ballistic missile defense system, including research, development, testing, and evaluation (*see* Strategic Defense Initiative [SDI]).

As of April 2003, the United States had 10,729 intact nuclear warheads, with 274 awaiting dismantlement under the 2002 Treaty of Moscow. Of these, approximately 7,000 are strategic and 1,700 tactical. Pursuant to START II, the United States has pledged to have only 3,500 warheads active, with 500 of these on intercontinental ballistic missiles; approximately 1,650 on submarine-launched ballistic missiles; and approximately 1,350 deployed via bombers. Another 6,500 warheads, however, are authorized to be placed in an "inactive reserve," with verification protocols in place (*see* Hedge).

On April 24, 1997, the U.S. Senate ratified the Chemical Weapons Convention, which entered into force five days later. This treaty commits signatories to destroy all existing chemical weapon stockpiles, production, and other related facilities within ten years of the convention's entry into force. DOD's role in implementing this requirement is divided among several agencies. The DOD Compliance Review Group will be responsible for coordination, and the army for destruction of stockpiles, closure of storage facilities, and preparation of facilities for inspection. The navy and air force, which lack organic chemical arsenals, are responsible for preparedness for challenge inspections that could occur.

—*James Joyner*

References

Blechman, Barry M., William J. Durch, and David R. Graham, *The American Military in the Twenty-First Century* (New York: St. Martin's Press, 1993).

Cimbala, Stephen J., *Nuclear Weapons after the Cold War: From Deterrence to Denuclearization* (Washington, DC: Georgetown University Press, 1995).

Paulsen, Richard A., *The Role of U.S. Nuclear Weapons in the Post–Cold War Era* (Montgomery, AL: Air University Press, 1994).

U.S. Department of Defense website, http://www.defenselink.mil/.

DEPARTMENT OF ENERGY (DOE)

The U.S. Department of Energy (DOE) is a cabinet-level department that focuses federal efforts and funding on energy and national security issues. The mission of DOE is to advance energy security, to promote energy advances through research and development, and to ensure that the environment remains free from nuclear weapons facility pollution. The department's overarching goal is one of national security, and it is responsible for the Stockpile Stewardship Program that maintains the long-term viability of the U.S. nuclear weapons stockpile.

The lineage of DOE started in the aftermath of World War II. The Atomic Energy Act of 1946 established the Atomic Energy Commission, a government agency responsible for U.S. nuclear weapons and the military reactor program. The civilian government had control of nuclear energy until the Atomic Energy Act of 1954 gave impetus to the commercial nuclear power industry.

The Energy Reorganization Act of 1974 established the Energy Research and Development Administration (ERDA) and the Nuclear Regulatory Commission (NRC). The ERDA was given the responsibility of developing and producing nuclear weapons and promoting nuclear energy. The NRC is responsible for regulating nuclear facilities in the United States (*see* Nuclear Regulatory Commission [NRC]).

In the mid-1970s, when the United States was faced with an energy crisis produced by high oil prices, President Jimmy Carter created the Department of Energy through the Department of Energy Organization Act of 1977. On October 1 of that year, the Department of Energy was established and given the responsibility of promoting programs in energy, environmental integrity, national security, energy conservation, and general science. DOE assumed the responsibilities of the ERDA, the Federal Energy Administration, and other federal energy-related programs and agencies.

Since the early 1990s and the moratorium on testing nuclear weapons, DOE has focused on national security, nuclear weapons stockpile stewardship, conservation of energy initiatives, and environmental cleanup of nuclear weapons facilities. The department employs approximately 16,000 federal workers and 100,000 contractors. It has twenty-six laboratories, four power marketing-administration offices, and twenty-four other facilities. The annual budget for DOE is approximately $22 billion.

DOE funds a plethora of research initiatives. To surmount technical and scientific concerns over the use of nuclear energy, it has established the Nuclear Energy Research Initiative (NERI), which focuses on next-generation (Generation IV) nuclear energy technology.

As part of the NERI program, DOE has sought international collaboration with the International Nuclear Energy Research Initiative (I-NERI) to research and develop nuclear energy technology to be used worldwide. One design funded by the NERI program is the International Reactor Innovative and Secure (IRIS), a collaborative effort between the United States, the United Kingdom, Italy, Spain, Brazil, Russia, Mexico, Japan, and Croatia.

Current Stockpile Stewardship programs include Advanced Simulation and Computing, which is intended to advance computational modeling, and the National Ignition facility, which provides a new basic research tool for nuclear physics. The Department of Energy, in partnership with the auto industry, is developing hydrogen fuel cells and hydrogen delivery systems to power automobiles. The Office of Science is examining new energy sources and is focused on advanced technologies to combat the terrorist threat.

—*Don Gillich*

See also: Nuclear Emergency Search Teams; Stockpile Stewardship Program

References

Tuggle, Catherine, and Gary E. Weir, *The Department of Energy* (New York: Chelsea House, 1989).

U.S. Department of Energy website, http://www.energy.gov/engine/content.do.

DEPARTMENT OF HOMELAND SECURITY (DHS)

In the aftermath of the September 11, 2001, terrorist attacks on the Pentagon and the World Trade

Center, President George W. Bush and the U.S. Congress formed a commission (Public Law 107-306, November 27, 2002) to investigate why the government and military were caught by surprise and to study the way existing local, state, and federal organizations responded to the attack. One of the findings of the National Commission on Terrorist Attacks upon the United States was that U.S. intelligence and law enforcement activities were divided literally at the water's edge. Coordination and cooperation between foreign intelligence, military, police, and civil defense entities and a variety of federal agencies were at best ad hoc and at worst nonexistent.

Unwilling to wait until the public debate and congressional fact finding had ended, the Bush administration requested that Congress take immediate steps to bolster the ability of a myriad of federal, state, and local agencies to defend the U.S. homeland from terrorist attack. The administration suggested that the country would be better served if a single organization was responsible for domestic border and transportation security; emergency preparedness and response; chemical, biological, radiological, and nuclear countermeasures; and information analysis and infrastructure protection. This organizational scheme is reflected in the Department of Homeland Security (DHS), which was created by the Homeland Security Act of 2002.

DHS is intended to unify the vast national network of organizations, agencies, and institutions involved in efforts to secure the nation. DHS created a strategic plan to guide the 180,000 employees who work at the various agencies that are included in the department. DHS now includes several government agencies that once existed as independent agencies; for example, the U.S. Coast Guard, the Immigration and Naturalization Service (INS), and the U.S. Customs Service. It also works with the Department of Defense and U.S. Northern Command to pool all available resources to defend North America. The ultimate goal of DHS is to prevent terrorist attacks within the United States, reduce domestic vulnerability to terrorism, and minimize the damage and speed recovery if all efforts to prevent terrorism fail.

—*Jeffrey A. Larsen and James J. Wirtz*

See also: U.S. Northern Command

References

Department of Homeland Defense website, http://www.dhs.gov/dhspublic/.

The 9/11 Commission Report (New York: W. W. Norton, 2004), available at http://www.whitehouse.gov/deptofhomeland/book.pdf.

DEPLETED URANIUM (U-238)

Depleted Uranium (DU), or U-238, is a very hard, dense substance that is slightly radioactive. It is a by-product of the production of enriched fuel for nuclear reactors and weapons. In this process, many of the U-235 isotopes that are normally present in uranium are removed—thus "depleting" it—leaving behind a preponderance of U-238 isotopes (*see* Actinides; Highly Enriched Uranium [HEU]; Mixed Oxide Fuel; Uranium).

In the process of manufacturing fuel for most nuclear reactors or the pits for nuclear weapons, the isotopic content of the uranium must be enriched in U-235 in order for these systems to function. At the end of the enrichment process, there are two products. One is the uranium enriched in U-235, ready for its intended nuclear applications. The other, referred to as "tails," is also known as depleted uranium.

Depleted uranium was originally viewed as simply a waste product from the enrichment process, but in the 1970s uses for depleted uranium began to emerge. The primary use of depleted uranium is in armor and penetrating weapons for U.S. tanks. Recently this application has generated considerable controversy owing to popular speculation that depleted uranium is responsible for illnesses in people exposed to the residue. Although depleted uranium is considered chemically toxic, it is not considered a radiation hazard. Depleted uranium is about 40 percent less radioactive than natural uranium.

Depleted uranium's density makes it ideal for use in tank armor and antiarmor projectiles because its mass- to-size ratio means it carries great penetrating power. Depleted uranium is extremely dense, with a density of approximately 19.1 g/cm^3 (1.7 times the density of lead). On impact, depleted uranium shears normal to the impact surface, creating a self-sharpening effect that greatly aids its penetration. This combination of high density and shearing makes it an ideal material to use in making antiarmor ammunition that uses kinetic energy as its primary mechanism of destruction. It appears mostly in tank shells and in the 30 mm rounds fired by the

U.S. A-10 ground-attack aircraft. DU munitions have been employed in recent wars in Iraq and Kosovo.

After passing through a target, DU rounds tend to burn up, creating tiny airborne particles of U-238. These particles can be inhaled and ingested and are not only chemically toxic but, since they can lodge in the body for many years and emit small quantities of both alpha and gamma radiation, can be radiologically toxic as well. U-238 dust has been suggested as one source of "Gulf War Syndrome," a series of mysterious illnesses that afflicted U.S. veterans of the first Gulf War. There is some debate, however, over the actual danger that DU represents. The U.S. military denies that it is especially hazardous and continues to use DU because it is an inexpensive and highly effective weapon. In fact, the Department of Energy, which maintains a stockpile of some 320,000 metric tons of depleted uranium, gives DU away free to U.S. arms manufacturers. Alternatives, such as tungsten, are expensive and not as effective.

In addition to its use as an antitank weapon and tank armor, depleted uranium is used in numerous commercial applications requiring a very dense material. Products using it include stabilizers in planes and boats, counterweights, radiation shielding, and breeding blankets in fast breeder reactors for the creation of plutonium.

Another application of depleted uranium is in nuclear weapons. It is used as a tamping device in nuclear weapons because of its high density and neutron-scattering properties. When used in this manner the depleted uranium's inertia holds the weapon together longer, allowing it to more thoroughly fission its fuel, thus increasing the yield of the weapon. Also, depleted uranium can undergo fission by fast neutrons. As a result, depleted uranium can be added to the exterior of a thermonuclear weapon to enhance its total yield. Such a weapon is referred to as a fission-fusion-fission weapon. This process greatly increases both the amount of yield and the fallout from the weapon. The largest nuclear weapons ever built or tested are of this type.

—*Rod Thornton and C. Ross Schmidtlein*

References

Bailey, M. R., A. W. Phipps, and Katie Davis, *The Hazards of Depleted Uranium Munitions, Parts 1 and 2* (London: The Royal Society, May 2001 and March 2002).

Flounders, Sara, *Metal of Dishonor: Depleted Uranium* (New York: International Action Center, 1997).

Harley, N. H., E. C. Foulkes, L. H. Hilborne, A. Hudson, and C. R. Anthony, *Depleted Uranium*, National Defense Research Institute, vol. 7 (Santa Monica, CA: RAND Corporation, 1999).

DEPLOYMENT

"Deployment," or the associated term, "deployment doctrine," can have three meanings when used to describe chemical, biological, or nuclear weapons: (1) the movement of military units and equipment to combat positions, perhaps overseas; (2) the distribution of chemical, biological, or nuclear munitions to military units; or (3) the final stage in the weapons acquisition process, after production, in which delivery systems and the weapons themselves are turned over to military units.

Deployment decisions thus signal the readiness of a state or a nonstate actor to use chemical, biological, or nuclear weapons. Deploying nuclear weapons to operational units on a day-to-day basis would thus generate a willingness to use nuclear weapons quickly on the battlefield. Deploying forces in a "dealerted" status, for instance separating warheads from delivery systems that are not deployed with operational units, would demonstrate that war plans are unlikely to call for the immediate use of chemical, biological, or nuclear weapons in the event of war. A decision to deploy an unconventional weapon also provides conclusive evidence that a state or nonstate actor has weaponized an experimental "device" and is ready to incorporate nuclear, chemical, or biological weapons into its war plans and operational forces.

Deployment decisions also are important because they can greatly influence the survivability of military units, a key measure of deterrence effectiveness. Traditional ways of deploying weapons to increase their survivability include making them mobile (rail-mobile or land-mobile missiles), placing them in structures hardened to resist blast effects (missile silos), hiding them (submarine-launched ballistic missiles, airborne alert for bombers), or relying on speed to escape attack (maintaining bombers on ground alert). Deployment decisions that seek to increase the survivability of forces tend to be taken as evidence that a state has adopted a deterrence policy. Countries that intend to use nuclear,

chemical, or biological weapons first in a crisis probably would not be willing to spend resources on creating a secure second-strike capability.

—*Roy Pettis and James J. Wirtz*

References

Carter, Ashton B., John D. Steinbruner, and Charles A. Zraket, eds., *Managing Nuclear Operations* (Washington, DC: Brookings Institution, 1987).

Freedman, Lawrence, *The Evolution of Nuclear Strategy*, third edition (New York: Palgrave Macmillan, 2003).

DEPRESSED TRAJECTORY

Ballistic missiles fly in an elliptically shaped trajectory. They are launched vertically, then orient themselves in the direction of the target while their rocket engines are still burning (the boost phase). To maximize range, they are launched on a minimum-energy trajectory, which involves a missile apogee (the highest point of flight) of about 20 percent of the distance the missile travels down range. To fly below missile defense systems or to reduce the warning time provided by ground-based radars, missiles can be launched along a "depressed trajectory." In such cases, the apogee is achieved at low altitudes, causing warheads to streak toward their targets at relatively flat reentry angels and relatively high reentry speeds.

Depressed trajectory missile shots can complicate the task faced by missile defense; they also reduce the time of flight needed to strike targets that are well within the maximum range of the missile. During the Cold War, it was feared that Soviet ballistic missile submarines lurking off the United States could strike coastal cities in as little as five minutes after launch, and targets further inland in as little as fifteen. A demonstrated ability to fly ballistic missiles along a depressed trajectory would be considered highly threatening because this capability could be used to strike an opponent's urban areas or military forces with virtually no warning. Because they provide the capability to strike opponents within minutes, depressed-trajectory capabilities are likely to produce crisis instability.

—*James J. Wirtz*

See also: Ballistic Missiles; Missile Defense

Reference

Freedman, Lawrence, *The Evolution of Nuclear Strategy*, third edition (New York: Palgrave Macmillan, 2003).

DÉTENTE

"Détente" means a lessening of tensions and improvement of relations between antagonistic states.

Although President John F. Kennedy used the term as early as 1963 to describe a relaxation of tensions between the United States and the Soviet Union, it has become synonymous with the Richard M. Nixon administration's approach to international affairs. The Nixon administration's philosophy of détente was based on an acceptance of the realities of the international system and was an attempt to manage the interests of the two superpowers in a manner unconstrained by ideology. The Nixon administration believed that U.S. foreign policy toward a particular country should be based upon U.S. national interests and that country's conduct within the international system. Although such an approach may currently sound unremarkable, at the time it represented a significant philosophical reorientation of U.S. foreign policy. Although many legitimate criticisms of détente have been raised, the Nixon administration's adherence to the principle of détente led to the end of U.S. involvement in the Vietnam War; the establishment of formal relations with China; and the conclusion of two significant strategic arms control agreements with the U.S.S.R. during an uncertain period of the Cold War.

Given the economic strain that the Soviet strategic arms buildup had placed on its economy, Soviet leaders were anxious to reach an agreement on strategic arms limitations with the Nixon administration. On the day that President Nixon was inaugurated, the Soviet Foreign Ministry issued a formal announcement of Soviet willingness to enter into discussions with the United States concerning strategic arms limits. Eleven months later, on November 17, 1969, the first round of the Strategic Arms Limitation Talks (SALT) began in Helsinki. Over the course of the next two years, representatives from the United States and the U.S.S.R. met regularly to hammer out the terms of the agreement. The issue of compliance verification became a particularly contentious problem for both sides to agree upon. Despite such difficulties, on May 26, 1972, the first round of SALT ended with the signing of the Anti-Ballistic Missile (ABM) Treaty and the Interim Agreement on Strategic Offensive Arms at a formal ceremony in Moscow. This marked the beginning of a twenty-year period of improving relations that eventually led to the end of the Cold War.

—*William S. Clark*

See also: Anti-Ballistic Missile (ABM) Treaty; Arms
    Control; Cold War; Disarmament; Strategic Arms
    Limitation Talks (SALT I and SALT II); Verification
References
Dobrynin, Anatoly, *In Confidence: Moscow's Ambassador
    to America's Six Cold War Presidents (1962–1986)*
    (New York: Random House, 1995).
Federation of American Scientists website,
    http://www.fas.org.
Gaddis, John Lewis, *Strategies of Containment: A Critical
    Appraisal of Postwar American National Security
    Policy* (Oxford, UK: Oxford University Press, 1982).
Kissinger, Henry, *Diplomacy* (New York: Simon and
    Schuster, 1994).

DETERRENCE

Deterrence is the act of dissuading another state or party from undertaking a politically or militarily undesirable action, such as an arms race or an attack, that it might otherwise carry out, and can be achieved in any of three ways: by implicitly or explicitly threatening to retaliate if the undesirable action is undertaken; by providing a defense to deny an attacker's objectives; or by offering a reward for not carrying out the undesired action.

Popular notions of deterrence revolve mainly around deterrence by threat of retaliation and often ignore or discount the other two means of deterring, primarily because the threat of an overwhelming offensive nuclear retaliation became the principal, if not the exclusive, means by which the United States underwrote its policy of deterrence during the Cold War. Deterrence by threat of retaliation seeks to convince a potential adversary that the benefits of his actions will be outweighed by the costs incurred in the course of a retaliatory strike. Deterrence by denial seeks to dissuade a potential adversary by convincing him that he will not be able to achieve his objectives and is a function of some combination of passive and active defenses. Examples include civil defense, air defense, antisubmarine warfare, and missile defense. Deterrence by reward relies on inducing a potential adversary not to undertake an action by offering him a greater benefit for restraining his behavior. The policy of détente, or seeking to integrate the Soviet Union more fully into world politics through trade and security enticements, can properly be considered a reward form of deterrence.

Deterrence is at times confused with the notion of compellence. Compellence differs from deterrence in that it involves forcing or coercing another person or state to do something they would not otherwise do, rather than persuading or dissuading them not to do something they would otherwise be inclined to do (*see* Compellence).

With the dawning of the nuclear age, deterrence assumed the status of a preeminent national security objective and strategy, supplanting traditional military objectives such as seizing and holding territory or militarily defeating the enemy. As military historian and strategic analyst Bernard Brodie noted in a seminal collection of essays published in 1946, "Thus far the chief purpose of our military establishment has been to win wars. From now on its chief military purpose must be to avert them. It can have almost no other useful purpose" (Brodie, p. 76). With the advent of large nuclear arsenals in the service of competing Cold War ideologies, deterrence became the centerpiece of U.S. national security strategy and foreign policy as well as the principal objective of strategic arms control.

How Deterrence Works

Each of the three approaches to deterrence relies heavily on a rational decision-making process of evaluating costs versus benefits. Each assumes that the potential opponent will rationally choose not to undertake the forbidden action in exchange for avoiding the retaliation or the costs of surmounting a defense or accepting the proffered reward. But for this rational choice to be made, several conditions must obtain.

The deterrent threat (or reward) must be understood. Deterrence is fundamentally a process of communication. The nation making the deterrent threat must know what actions it wants to deter, who it wants to deter from undertaking those actions, and how to communicate that threat. The target of the deterrence strategy, or the "deterree," must recognize the deterrent threat and understand the costs and consequences of failing to be deterred. Obviously, lack of clear communication channels, differences in the interpretation of deterrent threats, misperceptions, miscommunications, and misunderstandings can all undermine an effective deterrence policy.

The deterrent threat must also be credible (*see* Credibility). The credibility of a deterrent threat is a function of the deterring state's collective political will to carry out the deterrent threat (or provide the promised reward) and its perceived ability or capability to carry it out (or provide the reward). If a state threatens to retaliate with means that are not at its disposal, or to carry out retaliatory threats that it may itself not believe to be credible, the chances of deterrence failure will be increased.

The issue of credibility has posed a dilemma in two key respects for U.S. nuclear weapons policy. The first dilemma is the so-called "usability" paradox. On the one hand, there are pressures to refrain from nuclear weapons development and testing (*see* Comprehensive Test Ban Treaty [CTBT], for example), which will inevitably lead to the eventual obsolescence and degradation of a nation's nuclear weapons, thus undermining their deterrent value. On the other hand, many believe that efforts to make nuclear weapons more "usable" (by developing earth-penetrating warheads or enhanced radiation warheads, for example) undercut U.S. efforts to convince other countries not to develop their own nuclear weapons by promulgating the perceived political utility of having a nuclear arsenal, thus undermining U.S. nonproliferation objectives. Others believe such development efforts are essential to enhance and strengthen deterrence.

The second dilemma involves making threats that one is unable or unwilling to carry out. Many analysts believed, at least early on in the nuclear age, that the horror of nuclear war would reduce the likelihood of war. By contrast, it is difficult to reconcile the certain consequences of all-out nuclear war with any of the key principles of just war doctrine, meaning that the United States seems at times to have placed itself in a position, for the sake of deterrence, of threatening to do that which it is morally prohibited from doing (the mass slaughter of noncombatants). Any prospective opponent, then, has to consider whether the United States could overcome its own moral inhibitions to actually carry out a deterrent threat.

Deterrence Today

Deterrence is no less important in the post–Cold War era (sometimes referred to as the "second nuclear age") than it was during the Cold War, and it remains a key pillar of national security. It is generally recognized that the implementation of an effective deterrent strategy is now immensely more complicated because the number of players (including so-called "rogue states") who have to be taken into

consideration has increased. Many of these players are less well understood than enemies of past eras, and their concepts of rationality may not correspond with our own.

New threat assessments have given rise to concerns about the adequacy of traditional approaches to deterrence. U.S. officials have publicly expressed reservations about whether the traditional sole reliance on purely offensive retaliatory threats would be sufficient in all cases to dissuade leaders of rogue states from attacking the United States or its forces and allies overseas. Among the reasons for these reservations are the following:

- Leaders of rogue states may feel less constrained in their use of force, and may be more prone to take risks, than were America's adversaries during the Cold War.
- The foundation of past deterrent success— vested interest in preserving a stable environment for economic development, a mutually understood diplomatic vocabulary, and established communication channels—may not exist or may be difficult to establish.
- The United States and its allies may not understand the fundamental political and military values within potential aggressor governments well enough to implement deterrence by offensive threats alone.
- There may be significant asymmetries in the stakes involved in a regional crisis that could work to undermine deterrence. For example, some potential adversaries may believe that while their own survival is at stake in a regional conflict, the survival of the United States is not. As a consequence, these adversaries may calculate that the United States, possibly acting with its allies, with less to lose, may decline to intervene, or may back down if the stakes are escalated.
- Leaders of rogue states may believe that they have more to lose from *not acting* than from taking a particular course of action. Failure to act may cause a leader to lose face within his ruling party or power base.
- Potential adversaries may hope that the acquisition of WMD and their delivery systems, such as long-range ballistic

missiles, would deter the United States from intervening in, or leading coalitions against, their efforts at regional aggression, or these states may believe that such capabilities would give them the ability to threaten allied countries in order to dissuade them from joining such coalitions.

Some believe that the leaders of such states may see nuclear, biological, and chemical weapons and ballistic missile capabilities as tools of coercion, terror, blackmail, and aggression. Nuclear weapons and other weapons of mass destruction, as well as ballistic missiles, also may be regarded as symbols of power and prestige by rogue states. These weapons may even be considered weapons of choice, rather than weapons of last resort. Thus, nuclear weapons use may not have the same stigma associated with it as among established nuclear powers.

Some American and European commentators claim that America's overwhelming military supremacy alone constitutes an adequate deterrence against any attack by a rogue state. But in a study of deterrence failures throughout history, RAND analyst Barry Wolf identified three types of circumstances under which weaker states actually attacked stronger states, that is, instances where deterrence failed: (1) The weaker state was highly motivated by a strong commitment to particular values, by an agenda set by a psychopathological leader, or by a cost-benefit calculus that differed from the international norm or expectation and was thus "irrational" by definition; (2) the weaker state misperceived some aspect of the situation—for example, the weaker state perceived a vulnerability that did not exist, expected no retaliation from the strong state, or believed that allies would come to its aid; (3) the stronger state was vulnerable in some respect, and the weaker state exploited this asymmetry.

Some contemporary threats may be "undeterrable" by their very nature. This includes the accidental or unauthorized launch of a long-range ballistic missile—an eventuality many believe is increasingly likely. The threat of offensive retaliation would have little bearing on preventing such incidents, thus falling outside the range of threats addressed by deterrence alone.

Today, the concept of deterrence is being expanded to include efforts to deter nonstate actors as well, and this has further complicated the formulation of effective deterrence strategies. The increasing prevalence and lethality of terrorism has spurred efforts to further explore the psychology of terrorist groups and leaders with the objective of establishing more effective deterrence policies. Some observers believe that given their bloodlust and commitment to using violence to achieve their objectives, terrorists are ultimately undeterrable and have to be stopped from carrying out their nefarious schemes.

In some respects, however, there is nothing new about focusing on individuals as the ultimate target of deterrence strategies. Scholars have long recognized that a state of deterrence exists only in the minds of the leaders of the states on both sides of the deterrence equation. In the immediate aftermath of the Cold War, some scholars briefly entertained the idea that certain rogue leaders may be literally "undeterrable," and while history suggests that there were cases where leaders were motivated by decidedly irrational factors (for example, Adolf Hitler's determination to respond to "voices" in his mind) that virtually placed them beyond the effects of any deterrent strategy, for the most part, all leaders are in some way "rational" and responsive to certain threats and enticements. Analysts increasingly recognize that what one leader considers "rational," however, may differ considerably from what other leaders would consider "rational." This recognition has, in turn, spawned increasing academic efforts to explore cultural differences in decision-making and political and military motivation.

Criticism of Deterrence

Deterrence as a theory, a strategy, and a policy has been the subject of considerable criticism in academic studies of decision-making and defense policy. Much of this criticism is focused on retaliatory deterrence, however, rather than on deterrence that takes the form of denial or rewards. Critics focus on several points:

- Deterrence relies too heavily on assumptions of rationality, on the assumption that the prospective opponent is a rational, unitary decision-maker.
- Effective deterrence assumes perfect, unimpeded communications, both in terms of the sender of the deterrence threat knowing what his objectives are, and the

receiver understanding the deterrence threat and its implications, which are difficult conditions to achieve in practice.

- It is difficult, if not impossible, to design deterrence strategies that correspond to all options open to a potential adversary.
- Since deterrence is defined as ensuring that an opponent does not do something he might otherwise do, it is difficult to prove that any given deterrence strategy has been successful.
- Alternatively, deterrence strategies can fail incrementally, and governments historically have had difficulty recognizing when a deterrent strategy is in the process of failing until it is too late to deter a direct attack.
- Deterrence has been interpreted as primarily a function of military force, with a lack of attention to the political, cultural, and perceptual aspects of communicating threats to potential adversaries.
- Deterrence is most necessary in crisis situations, but it is precisely under intense crisis situations that rationality breaks down, communication becomes difficult, and perceptions become distorted (*see* Crisis Stability).

Recent policy initiatives by the U.S. government have sought to restore balance and diversity to the notion of deterrence, long thought of exclusively in terms of offensive retaliation. These initiatives acknowledge the potential contributions of damage limitation and active defenses to deterrence. In any case, deterrence remains a central objective of national and international security and stability.

—*Kerry Kartchner*

See also: Cold War; Damage Limitation; Extended Deterrence; Firebreaks; Game Theory; Minimum Deterrence; Superiority

References

Brodie, Bernard, ed., *The Absolute Weapon* (New York: Harcourt Brace, 1946).

George, Alexander L., and Richard Smoke, *Deterrence in American Foreign Policy: Theory and Practice* (New York: Columbia University Press, 1974).

Green, Philip. *Deadly Logic: The Theory of Nuclear Deterrence* (Columbus: Ohio State University Press, 1966).

Lavoy, Peter, Scott Sagan, and James Wirtz, *Planning the Unthinkable: How New Powers Will Use Nuclear, Biological, and Chemical Weapons* (Ithaca, NY: Cornell University Press, 2000).

Morgan, Patrick M., *Deterrence: A Conceptual Analysis,* second edition (Beverly Hills, CA: Sage, 1983).

Payne, Keith B., *Deterrence in the Second Nuclear Age* (Lexington: University of Kentucky Press, 1997).

Snyder, Glenn H., *Deterrence and Defense: Toward a Theory of National Security* (Princeton, NJ: Princeton University Press, 1961).

Wolf, Barry, *When the Weak Attack the Strong: Failures of Deterrence,* Document No. N3261-A (Santa Monica, CA: RAND Corporation, 1991).

DEUTERIUM

Deuterium, also known as heavy hydrogen, is the name given to one of two stable isotopes of the element hydrogen. Deuterium makes up 0.015 percent of all hydrogen. Deuterium's additional mass results from its nucleus containing a neutron in addition to the single proton held by normal hydrogen. Deuterium has nuclear properties that are very useful in both fission and fusion reactions. It is used extensively in the commercial nuclear industry, where it is combined with oxygen to form heavy water (D_2O) (*see* Heavy Water). In thermonuclear weapons, deuterium is used in both the primary and secondary stages of the weapon.

Speculation on the existence of a heavy isotope of hydrogen was first made in 1919 by O. Stern and M. Volmer in Germany. This speculation attempted to explain hydrogen's departure from an atomic weight of 1. In 1920, both W. D. Harkins and E. Rutherford began to suspect that a new particle, the neutron, might exist that would help account for hydrogen's anomalous mass. In 1931, H. C. Urey, F. G. Brickwedde, and G. M. Murphy of the U.S. National Bureau of Standards conducted a thorough search for a heavy hydrogen isotope through an evaporation experiment. In this experiment, a large mass of liquid hydrogen was evaporated to concentrate the heavy hydrogen in the remaining liquid. Subsequent analysis of the optical spectra showed spectral lines that indicated an isotope with a mass very near two, indicating the presence of heavy hydrogen. The discoverers named this heavy isotope deuterium from the Greek word *deuteros* (second) (*see* Isotopes).

Deuterium is useful in both fission and fusion reactions (*see* Fission Weapons; Fusion). In fission reactions, deuterium, in heavy water, is used to moderate (slow) neutrons for enhanced absorption of the neutrons in the fuel. This occurs because of deuterium's large scattering-to-absorption cross-section ratio. In fusion reactions, deuterium and tritium collisions have the highest probability of undergoing fusion at the temperatures that exist in most fusion systems and are thus the reaction of choice for most fusion applications (see Tritium). This is true for both commercial and military applications of fusion reactions. In a nuclear weapon, deuterium is used in two systems within the weapon. In a nuclear weapon's primary stage, a small quantity of deuterium and tritium gas is used to boost the yield through these fusion reactions. In the second stage of a thermonuclear weapon, deuterium with lithium in the form lithium-deuteride (LiD) is used to produce a compact fusion energy source, adding greatly to the weapon's total yield (see Thermonuclear Bomb).

Deuterium will remain important for both fission and fusion nuclear systems. In particular, it is used in Canada's Deuterium Uranium (CANDU) and Advanced CANDU reactors (see Canada Deuterium Uranium [CANDU] Reactor). Both magnetic and inertial confinement fusion systems will continue to extensively use deuterium as a fuel. Additionally, deuterium will remain a primary component in the primary and secondary stage of thermonuclear weapons.

—C. Ross Schmidtlein

References

Glasstone, S., Source Book on Atomic Energy (New York: Van Nostrand, 1950).

Lamarsh, J. R., and A. J. Baratta, Introduction to Nuclear Engineering, third edition (Upper Saddle River, NJ: Prentice-Hall, 2001).

Parrington, Josef R., Harold D. Knox, Susan L. Breneman, Edward M. Baum, and Frank Feiner, Nuclides and Isotopes: Chart of the Nuclides, fifteenth edition (New York: General Electric and KAPL, 1996).

DIRTY BOMB

See Radiological Dispersal Device

DISARMAMENT

Disarmament refers to the reduction or abolition of a nation's military forces and armaments. Although it is often thought of as a process resulting from mutual agreement, historically it has most often been something imposed on the vanquished by the victors. For example, the ancient Romans imposed disarmament restrictions on their rivals and on those lands conquered by the Roman legions. Napoleon dictated limits on the military strength of Prussia and Austria after defeating them. The Rush-Bagot Agreement of 1817, which followed the War of 1812, demilitarized the Great Lakes between the United States and Canada.

The term "disarmament" is often used interchangeably with "arms control," but the two terms should be considered distinct concepts. "Arms control" can refer to an agreed reduction in the level of a nation's armaments, to a mutual freeze in producing new weapons, or even to a controlled increase in certain areas of weapons, whereas "disarmament" refers strictly to a reduction or abolition of arms. "Disarmament" has been a recognized entry in the lexicon on international politics and diplomacy throughout history, but "arms control" per se is a relatively recent conceptual and diplomatic development, specifically elaborated as a more modest and practical alternative to the long-standing post–World War II impasse on disarmament proposals.

Contemporary notions of disarmament by mutual agreement have their origins in the nineteenth century, when it was believed that major wars were the result of arms competitions among the major powers. If the unchecked buildup of arms were a primary cause of war, it was reasoned, then negotiated controls on this process, accompanied by substantial reductions in the quantity of arms accumulated by the great powers, would reduce the tensions and mutual suspicions that resulted from unconstrained arms competition, and thus reduce the likelihood of war.

The events leading up to World War I seemed to confirm the hypothesis that unfettered arms competitions lead to war, and disarmament became a major feature of the postwar settlement. The Treaty of Versailles disarmed Germany, imposed limits on the size and composition of its army and navy, and was intended to prevent Germany from posing a military threat thereafter to the region. The Washington and London Naval Agreements were negotiated after World War I, but they were not strictly disarmament agreements. Rather, they imposed limitations on the buildup of naval battleships and the locations of naval facilities. Lengthy disarmament conferences under the auspices of the League of Nations during the 1920s and 1930s failed to achieve any effective disarmament or to stop the onset of World War II. After World War II, both Germany and Japan were once again disarmed. More than fifty years later, both nations still observe important limitations on their military forces and how those forces may be used.

Disarmament negotiations again dominated the post–World War II agenda, with a new focus on nuclear weapons rather than battleships. From 1946 through 1948, diplomats argued the merits of competing U.S. and Soviet plans for international control of atomic weapons, but American insistence on the internationalization of atomic energy (a stance it later dropped), and Soviet reluctance to accept intrusive verification, led to a prolonged stalemate in these negotiations. Plans for "general and complete disarmament" were repeatedly proposed in the United Nations but yielded no results. It was not until after the shock of the first testing of a Soviet intercontinental ballistic missile and the orbiting of Sputnik in the fall of 1957 that the superpowers began taking the need for nuclear disarmament seriously. A series of conferences was convened beginning in 1958 to discuss ways to reduce mutual fears of a nuclear surprise attack. These led in turn to small incremental steps, such as the 1958 moratorium on nuclear testing, the 1959 agreement to demilitarize the Antarctic, and measures to demilitarize outer space and establish a "Hot Line" communication link between the superpowers. The development of surveillance satellites would eventually usher in an era of increasingly ambitious arms control agreements, but anything resembling actual disarmament would have to await the winding down of the Cold War that began in the 1980s. The Intermediate-Range Nuclear Forces (INF) Treaty of 1987 and the Strategic Arms Reduction Treaties (START I and II) of 1991 and 1993 must be considered the first superpower agreements to actually call for partial nuclear disarmament (see Cold War; Intermediate-Range Nuclear Forces [INF] Treaty; Moratorium; Strategic Arms Reduction Treaty [START I]; Strategic Arms Reduction Treaty [START II]).

Article VI of the 1968 Nuclear Nonproliferation Treaty, one of the most important modern international arms control agreements, contains an obligation "to pursue negotiations in good faith on effective measures relating to cessation of the nuclear arms race at an early date and to nuclear disarmament, and on a treaty on general and complete disarmament under strict and effective international control." But it does not impose a timeline for achieving these objectives. These obligations are assumed by all parties to the NPT (see Nuclear Nonproliferation Treaty [NPT]). Nevertheless, the United States and the other nuclear weapon states are frequently called on to justify their compliance with the nuclear disarmament obligations. U.S. officials note, in reply, the series of strategic arms limitation agreements signed with the Soviet Union and its successor states, which have led to a substantial reduction in medium- and intermediate-range nuclear forces (such as the 1987 INF Treaty) and in strategic nuclear weapons (START I and the 2002 Moscow Treaty), as well as those unilateral disarmament measures and initiatives undertaken shortly after the end of the Cold War.

Denuclearization, or the complete elimination of nuclear weapons, is a form of disarmament advocated by contemporary peace groups. Applied universally, this has proven to be a utopian aspiration. However, agreements have been concluded regarding the denuclearization of specific geographic regions, such as the Antarctic, outer space, Latin America, and the seabed (see Nuclear Weapons Free Zones [NWFZs]).

The prolonged deadlock in international disarmament negotiations has led some to advocate a strategy of unilateral disarmament by undertaking one-sided initiatives. Such schemes are predicated on the assumption that fear, tension, and mistrust on both sides interfere with natural preferences to disarm, and that by demonstrating peaceful intentions through undertaking unilateral disarmament measures, one side or the other could evoke reciprocation from the other side, thus leading to a reverse arms race cycle of incremental reduction in armaments and tensions.

—Kerry Kartchner

See also: Arms Control; Détente; Downloading; Fissile Material Cutoff Treaty; Presidential Nuclear Initiatives; Verification

References

Arms Control and Disarmament Agreements: Texts and Histories of Negotiations (Washington, DC: U.S. Arms Control and Disarmament Agency, 1990).

Brennan, Donald G., ed., *Arms Control, Disarmament, and National Security* (New York: Braziller, 1961).

Burns, Richard Dean, ed., *Encyclopedia of Arms Control and Disarmament*, 3 vols. (New York: Charles Scribner's Sons, 1993).

Larsen, Jeffrey A., ed. *Arms Control: Cooperative Security in a Changing Environment* (Boulder, CO: Lynne Rienner, 2002).

DISTANT EARLY WARNING (DEW) LINE

Construction of the Distant Early Warning (DEW) Line began in February 1954 when President Dwight D. Eisenhower signed the bill approving construction. Located north of the Arctic Circle, the integrated chain of sixty-three radar and communications sites stretched 3,000 miles from Point Barrow on Alaska's northwest coast to the Eastern Shore of Baffin Island opposite Greenland. Construction took place between 1955 and 1957.

The DEW Line was an extension of two previous radar picket lines installed in Canada to provide warning of a Soviet transpolar airborne attack: the Mid-Canada, or McGill, Line, and the Pine Tree Line. The Pine Tree Line was sited along the U.S.-Canadian border and provided warning and control functions for the North American Aerospace Defense Command (NORAD). The Mid-Canada Line was not a radar line but a microwave fence that signaled when anything (including geese) flew through it.

The purpose of these warning networks was to prevent strategic surprise by manned Soviet bombers and allow American nuclear forces warning time to retaliate. The system thus had defense in depth and backups in case of failure. The DEW Line was upgraded in 1985 and renamed the North Warning System. It still forms part of the NORAD warning system.

—*Gilles Van Nederveen*

See also: Ballistic Missile Early Warning System; Early Warning; North American Aerospace Defense Command

Reference

Schaffel, Kenneth, *The Emerging Shield: The Air Force and the Evolution of Continental Air Defense, 1945–1960* (Washington, DC: Office of Air Force History, 1991).

DOWNLOADING

Downloading of nuclear warheads is the process whereby nuclear warheads are removed from the reentry vehicle (RV) or "bus" that sits atop intercontinental ballistic missiles (ICBMs) or submarine-launched ballistic missiles (SLBMs). Downloading RVs is the preferred way to reduce the number of nuclear warheads contained in an arsenal for arms control purposes because it allows the parties involved to retain expensive delivery vehicles while reducing the overall number of deployed nuclear weapons. Downloading also is reversible. If the strategic situation deteriorates, RVs can be replaced on the bus over a period of months to once again increase the overall size of a nuclear arsenal. Disarmament advocates often criticize RV downloading because it is a reversible step in the reduction of a nuclear arsenal.

If done in a reciprocal fashion, RV downloading also increases the survivability of land-based ICBMs. Because it is generally believed necessary to attack a single hardened missile silo with at least two nuclear warheads to guarantee its destruction, an opponent armed with single-warhead missiles would exhaust its nuclear arsenal in an effort to destroy a land-based missile force of equal size. It is unlikely that an opponent would launch this type of "self-disarming" attack knowing that the opponent would be left with about half of its nuclear force intact. Downloading thus increases crisis stability by decreasing both the incentive and capability of either side in a nuclear balance to be first to use nuclear weapons in a crisis.

—*James J. Wirtz*

See also: Crisis Stability; Intercontinental Ballistic Missiles; Reentry Vehicles

Reference

Freedman, Lawrence, *The Evolution of Nuclear Strategy*, third edition (New York: Palgrave Macmillan, 2003).

DUAL-TRACK DECISION

The "dual-track decision" was a policy of the North Atlantic Treaty Organization (NATO) adopted in 1979 to pursue arms control negotiations and missile deployments in Europe simultaneously.

In the mid-1970s, the Soviet Union had achieved rough strategic parity in strategic nuclear arms with the United States, and the Soviet Union turned its attention to confronting European and Asian forward-based systems. The aging Soviet intermediate-range SS-4 and SS-5 missiles at fixed bases were replaced with a new SS-20 missile. In early 1977, the Soviet Union began deployment of the SS-20 missile, a modern, mobile, nuclear-armed, intermediate-range ballistic missile with three independently targetable warheads and the range to target all of Western Europe.

West German Chancellor Helmut Schmidt feared a decoupling of the American strategic nuclear deterrent from the defense of Western Europe. In a 1975 London speech, he warned that the United States needed to counter the growing Soviet threat. These theater nuclear forces were referred to as "gray area weapons" by Schmidt and other Western leaders because they had not been included in the treaties resulting from the Strategic Arms Limitation Talks (SALT I and SALT II). Some also referred to the weapons as "Euro-Strategic" forces. During a 1979 meeting on the island of Guadeloupe, U.S. President Jimmy Carter, President Giscard d'Estaing of France, Prime Minister James Callaghan of Great Britain, and Chancellor Schmidt agreed to develop a political and military response to the SS-20 deployments. The problem for Western European leaders was that after the debacle surrounding the Carter administration's decision not to deploy the enhanced radiation warhead in Europe, they needed to show some consensus about the Western strategic policy.

In 1977, the NATO Nuclear Planning Group started a study, and in 1979 it proposed a dual-track approach to the Soviet Union regarding the SS-20 deployment that encompassed both NATO force modernization and arms control initiatives. The NATO alliance planned to deploy 464 ground-launched cruise missiles to Italy, Belgium, the Netherlands, Britain, and West Germany. It would also deploy 108 Pershing II intermediate-range ballistic missiles with earth-penetrating warheads and a longer range to replace the Pershing I in West Germany. These missiles were particularly well suited to destroying Soviet command and control bunkers. The alliance also proposed negotiations in Geneva that, if successful, would preclude the need for this proposed modernization of NATO theater nuclear force modernization. On December 12, 1979, NATO unanimously adopted the dual-track decision.

NATO had no equivalent missile to the SS-20 and the Soviet deployment was widely perceived as upsetting the balance of nuclear forces in Europe. One track of the dual-track decision called for arms control negotiations with the Soviet Union to restore the balance in intermediate-range nuclear forces (INF) at the lowest possible level. NATO's second track was to modernize its INF arsenal. Both tracks would be pursued simultaneously, with the goal of reaching an arms control treaty that would limit INF modernization or even eliminate the need for the deployment of new NATO theater nuclear forces. Deployment of these systems in Western Europe was scheduled to begin in December 1983. NATO, as a sign of good faith, also decided to withdraw 1,000 of its approximately 7,400 tactical nuclear warheads deployed in Europe and to retire an existing nuclear weapon for every new nuclear weapon deployed.

In October 1980, preliminary INF talks between the United States and the Soviet Union began in Geneva. The talks continued through November 1983. The Soviet delegation walked out of the talks following the West German Bundestag's approval of Pershing II deployments on November 22, 1983. Unable to block further NATO deployments through political pressure, and facing increasing criticism for obstructing the arms control track, the Soviet Union agreed in early 1985 to resume INF talks as a subset of the new U.S.-Soviet Nuclear and Space Talks (NST). Both the arms control and deployment tracks were brought to a close on December 8, 1987, with the signing of the Treaty on the Elimination of Intermediate-Range and Shorter-Range Missiles (INF Treaty).

—*Steven Rosenkrantz and*
Gilles Van Nederveen

See also: Arms Control; Intermediate-Range Nuclear Forces (INF) Treaty; North Atlantic Treaty Organization (NATO)

References
Beschloss, Michael, and Strobe Talbott, *At the Highest Levels: The Inside Story of the Cold War* (Boston: Little, Brown, 1993).
Matlock, Jack F., Jr., *Reagan and Gorbachev: How the Cold War Ended* (New York: Random House, 2004).
Newhouse, John, *War and Peace in the Nuclear Age* (New York: Vintage, 1990).
Talbott, Strobe, *Endgame: The Inside Story of SALT II* (New York: Knopf, 1979).
———, *The Master of the Game: Paul Nitze and the Nuclear Peace* (New York: Knopf, 1988).

EARLY WARNING

"Early warning" refers to the prompt detection of the launch or approach of incoming reentry vehicles or bombers, thus enabling the targeted country to retaliate, take cover, or possibly shoot down the opponent's attacking forces. Early warning is usually accomplished by a network of surveillance satellites and long-range radar.

The United States maintains several surveillance satellite systems to provide early warning of attack. The Defense Support Program (DSP) uses heat-sensing devices to detect missile launches and nuclear explosions anywhere on the planet and then instantaneously relays that information to the U.S. command and control networks. The DSP satellites are placed in geosynchronous-equatorial orbit. Their infrared telescopes provide intermittent coverage of events on the Earth because the satellites rotate at about six revolutions per minute to maintain stability while in orbit. There are three primary and two backup satellites in orbit at 60°E, 70°W, and 134∞W. Because of the importance of the mission, a new satellite will normally be launched as the oldest one on-orbit nears the end of its operational life. The newly launched satellite will then assume frontline duty, the eldest of the three front-line satellites will assume backup status, and the oldest satellite will be retired.

The 1960s technology employed in DSP is becoming obsolete. In response, the U.S. Air Force is developing and deploying two different types of satellites: the Space-Based Infrared Radar System (SBIRS)-High and the SBIRS-Low. SBIRS-High satellites will replace the DSP satellites by about 2010. Because it is three-axis stabilized, the sensors on SBIRS-High can "stare" at the ground continuously rather than sweeping over a specific point every ten seconds, thereby providing a continuous data flow of events on the ground. SBIRS-Low satellites will operate in low Earth orbit and track missiles as they fly above the horizon, offering much more accurate information on their trajectories.

Such information is necessary for an effective antiballistic missile defense. In 2001, the George W. Bush administration changed the name of SBIRS-High to simply SBIRS, and SBIRS-Low became the Space Tracking and Surveillance System.

—Abe Denmark

See also: Ballistic Missile Early Warning System; Distant Early Warning Line; North American Aerospace Defense Command; Phased-Array Antenna; Reconnaissance Satellites; Space-Based Infrared Radar System; Surveillance

References

Day, Dwayne, "Missile Early Warning Satellites," U.S. Century of Flight Commission, available at http://www.centennialofflight.gov/essay/SPACEFLIGHT/warning/SP37.htm.

Richelson, Jeffrey, *America's Space Sentinels: DSP Satellites and National Security* (Lawrence: University Press of Kansas, 1999).

"Space Based Infrared Systems (SBIRS)," available at http://www.globalsecurity.org/space/library/report/1998/sbirs-brochure, 1998.

ELECTROMAGNETIC PULSE

See Nuclear Weapons Effects

EMERGENCY ACTION MESSAGE (EAM)

An Emergency Action Message (EAM) is a data communication from the U.S. Joint Chiefs of Staff that contains preplanned, time-sensitive instructions from high-level authorities to carry out nuclear attacks . EAMs also may contain information (coded authorization materials) needed to carry out the attack itself. They are in predetermined formats and transmitted through a variety of communication systems. Teams tasked with processing EAMs practice decoding EAMs so that they can implement their orders as quickly as possible when a real message arrives. The EAM processes, responses, and handling procedures are closely guarded secrets.

—*Zach Becker*

References

Bracken, Paul, *The Command and Control of Nuclear Forces* (New Haven, CT: Yale University Press, 1985).

Ford, Daniel F., *The Button: The Pentagon's Strategic Command and Control System* (New York: Simon and Schuster, 1985).

ENOLA GAY

The *Enola Gay* was the B-29 Superfortress that dropped the first atomic bomb on Japan. It was manufactured by the Boeing Aircraft Company and assembled by the Glenn L. Martin Company, Omaha, Nebraska. The *Enola Gay* was flown from the United States to the South Pacific, arriving at North Field on the Island of Tinian on July 2, 1945. The crew spent approximately one month training for the mission.

Colonel Paul W. Tibbets, Jr., pilot of the Enola Gay, *waves from his cockpit before takeoff to bomb Hiroshima, August 6, 1945. (National Archives)*

On the morning of August 6, 1945, the *Enola Gay,* commanded by Colonel Paul W. Tibbets, left Tinian for its target, the city of Hiroshima, Japan, carrying one atomic bomb named "Little Boy." The *Enola Gay* dropped its bomb on the city of Hiroshima at 8:16 A.M. Three days later, another B-29 (*Bockscar*) dropped an atomic bomb ("Fat Man") on Nagasaki, Japan. Japan surrendered on September 2, 1945.

The Smithsonian Institution's decision to place the *Enola Gay* on display in the new Air and Space Museum located near Washington's Dulles Airport in commemoration of the fiftieth anniversary of World War II stirred much controversy in the 1990s.

—*Sean Lawson*

See also: Fat Man; Hiroshima; Little Boy; Nagasaki

References

Thomas, Gordon, *Enola Gay: Mission to Hiroshima* (Osceola, WI: Motorbooks International, 1995).

Tibbets, Paul W., website, http://www.theenolagay.com.

ENRICHMENT

Enrichment is a process that turns natural uranium into a fissionable material. Naturally occurring uranium contains only 0.72 percent of U-235, the highly fissionable isotope, and the rest of the material consists of less fissionable isotopes. The fissile material must be separated from the rest of the uranium through enrichment. Uranium enriched to 20 percent or more U-235 is called "highly enriched uranium" (HEU). Uranium enriched to less than 20 percent is called "low enriched uranium" (LEU) (*see* Highly Enriched Uranium [HEU]; Low Enriched Uranium [LEU]; Uranium).

The earliest successful enrichment methods were electromagnetic isotope separation (EMIS), a process that utilizes large magnets to separate ions of the two isotopes; and gaseous diffusion, where the gas uranium hexafluoride (UF_6) is passed through a porous barrier material to separate the lighter molecules containing U-235. The first large-scale uranium-enrichment facility, the Y-12 plant at Oak Ridge, Tennessee, used EMIS in devices designated "calutrons." The process was developed by Edward Lawrence. EMIS was abandoned in the United States because of its high consumption of electricity but was adopted by the Iraqis prior to the first Gulf War.

More efficient enrichment methods were developed after World War II. Gas centrifuges, in which UF_6 gas is whirled inside a complex rotor assembly and centrifugal forces push the molecules containing the heavier isotope to the outside, are the most common. Many stages are required to produce the highly enriched uranium needed for a weapon, but the gas centrifuge enrichment technique requires substantially less electricity than either of the older technologies. Atomic or molecular laser isotope separation is still under development in the most technologically advanced countries. This process uses lasers to selectively excite atoms or molecules containing one isotope of uranium so that it can be preferentially extracted. The South African nuclear program used an aerodynamic separation technique in an indigenously designed and built device called a "vortex tube." In the vortex, a mixture of UF_6 gas and hydrogen is injected tangentially into a tube that tapers into a small exit aperture at one or both ends, and centrifugal force causes the separation. The Becker Nozzle Process, another aerodynamic separation technique, was developed in West Germany. Aerodynamic enrichment processes require large amounts of electrical power and are not currently considered economically competitive.

Yellowcake

UF_6 is used as the feedstock in the gas-centrifuge and gaseous-diffusion processes, and uranium tetrachloride (UCl_4) is used as feed in the EMIS process. Uranium ore concentrates, known as yellowcake, typically contain 60 to 80 percent uranium and up to 20 percent impurities. There are two commercial processes used to produce purified UF_6 from yellowcake: the solvent extraction/fluorination ("wet") process and the fluorination/fractionation ("dry") process. In each case, chemical reactions are used to convert the yellowcake to a metal or powder for use in the gaseous-diffusion and gas-centrifuge processes.

Manhattan Project scientists and engineers explored several uranium-enrichment technologies. Production plants employing three uranium-enrichment processes—EMIS, liquid thermal diffusion, and gaseous diffusion—were constructed at Oak Ridge, Tennessee. The term "oralloy" was used during World War II as a contraction of "Oak Ridge alloy" and denoted U-235 enriched to 93.5 percent.

Electromagnetic Isotope Separation

The EMIS process is based on the principle that a charged particle will follow a circular trajectory when passing through a uniform magnetic field. Two ions with the same kinetic energy and electrical charge, but different masses (such as U-235 and U-238), will have different trajectories, with the heavier U-238 ion having the larger diameter trajectory. This allows for the development of means to separate the two isotopes. EMIS is a batch process that can produce weapons-grade material from natural uranium in two stages.

In the EMIS program of 1945 in the United States, production of weapons-grade uranium took place in two enrichment stages, referred to as the "a" and "b" stages. The first stage used natural or slightly enriched uranium as feed and enriched it to 12 to 20 percent U-235. The second stage used the product of the first stage as feed and further enriched it to weapons-grade uranium. To allow more efficient use of magnets and floor space, the individual stages were arranged in continuous oval or rectangular arrays (called "racetracks" or simply "tracks") with separator tanks alternated with electromagnetic units. The EMIS separators are referred to as "calutrons" because the development work was carried out at the University of California at Berkeley during the early 1940s using cyclotrons.

Thermal Diffusion

Thermal diffusion utilizes the transfer of heat across a thin liquid or gas to accomplish isotope separation. By cooling a vertical film on one side and heating it on the other side, the resultant convection currents will produce an upward flow along the hot surface and a downward flow along the cold surface. Under these conditions, the lighter U-235 gas molecules will diffuse toward the hot surface and the heavier U-238 molecules will diffuse toward the cold surface. These two diffusive motions, combined with the convection currents, will cause the lighter U-235 molecules to concentrate at the top of the film and the heavier U-238 molecules to concentrate at the bottom of the film.

The thermal-diffusion process is characterized by its simplicity, low capital cost, and high heat consumption. A production plant containing 2,100 columns (each approximately 15 meters long) was operated in Oak Ridge for less than a year. Each of these columns consisted of three tubes. Cooling water was circulated between the outer and middle tubes, and the inner tube carried steam.

Gaseous Diffusion

The gaseous-diffusion process depends on the separation effect arising from the molecular flow of gas through small holes. Gas is forced through a series of porous membranes with microscopic openings. Lighter molecules are more likely to enter the barrier pores than are heavier molecules. For UF_6 the difference in velocities between molecules containing U-235 and U-238 is small (0.4 percent), and, consequently, the amount of separation achieved by a single stage of gaseous diffusion is small.

UF_6 is a solid at room temperature but becomes a gas when heated above 135 degrees Fahrenheit. The solid UF_6 is heated to form a gas, and the gaseous-diffusion enrichment process begins. Because the U-235 is lighter, it moves through the barriers more easily.

The main components of a single gaseous-diffusion stage are a large cylindrical vessel, called a diffuser or converter, that contains the barrier; a compressor to compress the gas to the pressures needed for flow through the barrier; an electric motor to drive the compressor; a heat exchanger to remove the heat of compression; and piping and valves for stage and inter-stage connections and process control. The entire system must be essentially leak free, and the compressors require special seals to prevent both out-leakage of UF_6 and in-leakage of air. The chemical corrosiveness of UF_6 requires use of metals such as nickel or aluminum for surfaces exposed to the gas (for example, piping and compressors).

Gas Centrifuge

In the gas-centrifuge uranium-enrichment process, gaseous UF_6 is fed into a cylindrical rotor that spins at high speed inside a casing. When the flowing gas is rotated, enriched gas gathers at one end and depleted gas at the other end, facilitating separation of enriched from depleted atoms.

One of the key components of a gas centrifuge enrichment plant is the power supply (frequency converter) for the gas-centrifuge machines. Enriching uranium to weapons grade typically requires several thousand stages and thus is usually done in large facilities. Large transformers are required to take commercially supplied power and

convert it into higher frequencies to supply gas-centrifuge motors. This power plant signature can give away a facility's purpose and can be used by U.S. intelligence to detect nuclear activities in other nations.

Aerodynamic Processes

Aerodynamic uranium-enrichment processes include the separation-nozzle process and the vortex tube–separation process. These aerodynamic separation processes depend upon separation produced by pressure gradients, as does the gas-centrifuge method. In effect, aerodynamic processes can be considered nonrotating centrifuges. Since pure UF_6 gas cannot give these processes the velocity rate needed for separation, a carrier gas (for example, hydrogen and helium) is used.

The separation-nozzle process was developed by E. W. Becker and associates at the Karlsruhe Nuclear Research Center in Germany. In this process, a mixture of gaseous UF_6 is compressed and then directed along a curved wall at high velocity. The heavier U-238 bearing molecules move preferentially out to the wall relative to those containing U-235. At the end of the deflection, the gas jet is split by a knife edge into a light fraction and a heavy fraction, which are withdrawn separately.

The Uranium Enrichment Corporation of South Africa developed and deployed its own aerodynamic process, characterized as an "advanced vortex tube" or "stationary-walled centrifuge," at the so-called "Y" plant at Valindaba, South Africa. In this process, a mixture of UF_6 is compressed and enters a vortex tube tangentially at one end through nozzles or holes at velocities close to the speed of sound. This tangential injection of gas results in a spiral or vortex motion within the tube, and two gas streams are withdrawn at opposite ends of the vortex tube.

Owing to the very small cut of the vortex tube stages and the extremely difficult piping requirements that would be necessary based on traditional methods of piping stages together, the South Africans developed a cascade design technique called "Helikon." In essence, the Helikon technique permits twenty separation stages to be combined into one large module, and all twenty stages share a common pair of axial-flow compressors. None of these processes are currently used in commercial applications.

Atomic Vapor Laser Isotope Separation

The atomic vapor laser isotope separation (AVLIS) process is based on the fact that U-235 and U-238 atoms absorb light at different frequencies (or colors). Although the absorption frequencies of these two isotopes differ only by a very small amount, the dye lasers used in AVLIS can be tuned so that only the U-235 atoms absorb the laser light. In the vaporizer, metallic uranium is melted and vaporized to form an atomic vapor stream. The vapor stream flows through the collector, where it is illuminated by the precisely tuned laser light. The AVLIS laser system is a pumped laser system comprised of one laser used to optically pump a separate dye laser, which produces the light used in the separation process. A total of three colors are used to ionize the U-235 atoms.

Many countries are pursuing some level of AVLIS research and/or development, and major programs exist in the United States, France, Japan, and probably Russia. Principal advantages of the AVLIS process include a high separation factor, low energy consumption (approximately the same as in the centrifuge process), and a small volume of generated waste. However, no country has yet deployed an AVLIS process, although several have demonstrated the capability to enrich uranium with the process.

Molecular Laser Isotope Separation

The idea for the molecular laser isotope separation (MLIS) process was conceived by a group of scientists at the Los Alamos National Laboratory in 1971. There are two basic steps involved in the MLIS process. In the first step, UF_6 is irradiated by an infrared laser system operating near the 16 mm wavelength, which selectively excites the U-235 atom, leaving the U-238 atoms relatively unexcited. In the second step, a laser system (infrared or ultraviolet) is required for conversion and separation.

There is currently no known MLIS optical system designed to handle both infrared and ultraviolet bands. Consequently, most MLIS concepts use an all infrared optical system, which has not proven to be effective.

There are many complexities associated with the process, and the United States, United Kingdom, France, and Germany have stated that their MLIS programs have been terminated. Japan also has had a small MLIS program.

Chemical and Ion Exchange

Chemical-exchange isotope separation requires segregation of two forms of an element into separate but contacting streams. For heavy elements such as uranium, achieving a suitable separation factor involves contact between two valence (oxidation state) forms. The U-235 isotope exhibits a slight preference for the higher valence in the laboratory. At present, no country has built or operated a full-scale uranium-enrichment plant based on an exchange process, but research continues in technologically advanced countries.

Plasma Separation

The plasma separation process (PSP) has been studied as a potentially more efficient uranium-enrichment technique that makes use of the advancing technologies in superconducting magnets and plasma physics. The only countries known to have had serious PSP experimental programs are the United States and France.

Proliferation Issues

Enrichment technology is not widely available, but electromagnetic separation methods have been declassified. Europe's URENCO, a British, German, and Dutch consortium established in the 1970s to enrich uranium primarily at a plant in Almelo, Netherlands, found that its centrifuge technology was compromised when a Pakistani scientist working there returned to Pakistan with in-depth knowledge of the process. URENCO makes some information available on its website, as it sells its services as a light-water reactor fuel producer.

Any country pursuing nuclear weapons has to use one of the technologies listed above to enrich uranium. Although most of these processes can be detected on the basis of building size or cooling towers for heat dissipation, some programs have surprised the West. An increasing large "gray market" allows nations to purchase only technologies and then acquire scientists and engineers to improve or refine the process. Iraq's work with EMIS, only discovered at the conclusion of the 1991 war at Tarmiya, shocked the world. The Iraqis were still a few years away from full-scale production, but the scope of their program and their successful acquisition of technology had gone undetected. South African, Argentinian, and Brazilian efforts were more conventional. Pakistan, too, managed some technological shortcuts via acquisition of material and know-how to enrich uranium to bomb fuel, and Iran also has managed to acquire technology and know-how from the gray market.

—*Gilles Van Nederveen*

See also: Manhatten Project; Nuclear Fuel Cycle; Reactor Operations

References

Albright, David, "A Proliferation Primer," *Bulletin of Atomic Scientists,* 1993, available at http://www.thebulletin.org/issues/1993/j93/j93Albright.html.

Bichel, Lennard, *The Deadly Element: The Story of Uranium* (New York: Stein and Day, 1979).

Cochran, Thomas H., William M. Arkin, Robert S. Norris, and Milton M. Hoenig, *Nuclear Weapons Databook,* vol. 2: *U.S. Nuclear Warhead Production* (Washington, DC: Ballinger, 1987).

Gardner, Gary T., *Nuclear Nonproliferation: A Primer* (Boulder, CO: Lynne Rienner, 1994).

Nuclear Regulatory Commission website, http://www.nrc.gov/materials/fuel-cycle-fac/ur-enrichment.html.

Pigford, T. H., and H. W. Levi, *Nuclear Chemical Engineering,* second edition (New York: McGraw-Hill, 1981).

Settle, Frank, "Nuclear Chemistry Uranium Enrichment," General Chemistry Case Studies, available at http://www.chemcases.com/nuclear/nc-07.htm.

"Uranium Enrichment," Nuclear Issues Briefing Paper 33, Uranium Information Centre, Melbourne, Australia, June 2003, available at http://www.uic.com.au/nip33.htm.

Wilson, P. D., ed., *The Nuclear Fuel Cycle: From Ore to Wastes* (Oxford: Oxford University Press, 1996).

World Nuclear Association, Information and Issue Briefs, "Uranium Enrichment," June 2003, available at http://www.world-nuclear.org/info/inf28.htm.

ENTRY INTO FORCE

The term "entry into force" refers to the point in time when the provisions of a treaty become legally binding on the parties. It is rare for an arms control agreement to come into force immediately upon signing the document. It more often occurs at a later point in time. Usually, after signature a treaty becomes subject to approval by the respective legislatures or other domestic approval processes of the countries signing the agreement. In the United States, this function is reserved to the Senate. The terms of a given treaty will often specify that the treaty will enter into force "upon the exchange of instruments of ratification."

Instruments of ratification are documents, usually signed by the head of government or head of state, attesting to the approval of ratification by the given country's government. Once all the parties to a given treaty have ratified it through whatever process is dictated by their own constitutions—a process which may take several years—the parties to a given treaty will meet at an agreed place and time and exchange these instruments of ratification, thus bringing the terms of the treaty into force. In the meantime, customary international law obligates the signatories not to do anything that might undermine the "object and purpose" of the agreement, pending its ratification and entry into force.

In the case of most multilateral arms control agreements, it is usually necessary for some number of signatories, or certain specified signatories, to ratify the agreement before it is allowed to enter into force. For example, the Comprehensive Test Ban Treaty, opened for signature on September 24, 1996, must be ratified by forty-four specified countries before it can come into force. By 2003, only thirty-one had ratified the treaty.

—*Kerry Kartchner*

See also: Arms Control; Comprehensive Test Ban Treaty

Reference

Blix, Hans, and Jirina H. Emerson, eds., *The Treaty Maker's Handbook* (Dobbs Ferry, NY: Oceana, 1973).

EQUIVALENT MEGATON

The destructive power of nuclear weapons often is represented by a measure known as "equivalent megatons" (EMTs). EMT is obtained by multiplying the raw blast yield (megatons) by 0.66. EMT is a useful measure of the ability of nuclear weapons to destroy soft targets like cities and can help planners determine whether to launch barrage-attacks against large areas (such as operating areas for mobile missiles).

For intermediate blast overpressures needed to destroy soft targets such as mobile missiles, the lethal radius of a nuclear weapon increases by approximately one-third the power of the yield. The lethal area of blast overpressure thus changes by about two-thirds the power of the yield. The area that can be barrage-attacked by nuclear weapons is about equal to the number of warheads times two-thirds the power of the yield. When measured in EMT, larger numbers of small nuclear warheads actually are more destructive than a few large nuclear weapons. Because it takes roughly eight times the raw yield to double the destructive blast damage from a nuclear device, EMT better reflects the "equivalent lethality" that can be achieved by substituting several small nuclear weapons for one large one when used against all but the hardest targets. Four 1-megaton nuclear warheads, for instance, have the same EMT as one 8-megaton nuclear warhead.

—*James J. Wirtz*

See also: Megaton

References

Freedman, Lawrence, *The Evolution of Nuclear Strategy*, third edition (New York: Palgrave Macmillan, 2003).

ESCALATION

Escalation is the intensification of conflict along one or more of three axes: the level of violence or the means employed, the geographic scope of combat operations, or the tempo of operations. These factors are sometimes referred to, respectively, as vertical escalation, or the transition from conventional to nuclear war; horizontal escalation, or the spreading of conflict to a greater number of theaters of operation; and temporal escalation, or an increase in the speed or tempo of combat operations. "Horizontal escalation" also can refer to the proliferation of nuclear, chemical, biological, or ballistic missile weapons to a greater number of countries. The term "escalation" also refers to the process by which previous limits in a war (involving any of the three criteria noted above) are crossed and new ones established.

During the Cold War, considerable academic and policymaking attention was devoted to understanding the dynamics of nuclear escalation; that is, the decision to begin employing nuclear weapons, or to "cross the nuclear threshold," in a conflict that has otherwise been limited to combat with conventional military weapons. This process was most fully elaborated by Herman Kahn, a prominent defense analyst in the 1960s. He developed a notional "ladder of escalation" and identified a series of rungs on that ladder to help identify potential limits, or "firebreaks." See Figure E-1 for a summary of Kahn's escalation ladder. According to Kahn and other theorists, "firebreaks" are those theoretical points in an escalation process at which either or both sides have built-in opportunities to reassess the escalation dynamic and to either restrain further escalation or increase the level, scope, or tempo of the conflict.

Figure E-1: A Summary of Herman Kahn's Escalation Ladder with Six Key Thresholds

| Nuclear strikes against population centers |
| *City Targeting Threshold* |
| Nuclear strikes against military targets |
| *Central War Threshold* |
| Limited strikes intended to deter further escalation |
| *Central Sanctuary Threshold* |
| Limited local nuclear attacks and countermeasures |
| *Nuclear Use Threshold* |
| Breaking off diplomatic relations, conventional war |
| *Nuclear War Is Unthinkable Threshold* |
| Shows of force, mobilization, confrontation |
| *Don t Rock the Boat Threshold* |
| Subcrisis maneuvering |

Source: Herman Kahn, *On Escalation: Metaphors and Scenarios* (New York: Praeger, 1965)

A number of other terms are associated with the process of escalation. "Escalation control" refers to efforts to stop or slow the escalation of a crisis or conflict from increasing further in terms of the level, scope, or tempo of violence. According to the theory of escalation control, demonstrating flexibility and restraint by withholding strikes from certain targets, introducing pauses into the escalation process, or otherwise exploiting opportunities to show an opponent that one is stopping short of an all-out response will maximize the chances that the opponent will reciprocate this restraint, thus bringing the process of escalation under control. The success of such efforts derives from the ability to control one's own forces throughout the escalation process through effective and redundant command and control. It depends, as well, on having forces that are capable of selective, limited, and restrained strikes.

"Escalation dominance" refers to the ability of a side to dominate its opponent at any given rung on the escalation ladder, or at any point along either the vertical, horizontal, or temporal axis of escalation. In theory, if an opponent is aware of the other side's ability to win a conflict at successively higher rungs on the escalation ladder, it will be deterred from taking actions that would escalate the conflict. Deterrence would therefore come into play. Escalation dominance differs from escalation control in that it does not rely on reciprocal restraint on the part of one's opponent.

"Inadvertent escalation" refers to a dynamic escalation process that is precipitated by accident, misperception, or miscalculation, where neither side intended to escalate a conflict nor crisis but feels compelled to respond to an event by increasing the level, scope, or tempo of conflict. Others describe inadvertent escalation as incidents in which military forces begin to operate out of, or beyond the control of, higher political authorities. For example, one or both sides in a conflict or intense crisis might respond to an incident, such as the accidental detonation of a nuclear device or inadvertent launch of a ballistic missile, by launching a retaliatory strike that leads to escalation, or may act on the basis of a misperception or miscalculation, such as mistaking the launch of a peaceful space booster or weather sounding rocket for an offensive military strike. The United States and Russia have established a number of communication links and protocols designed specifically to prevent such incidents from leading to inadvertent escalation, such as the 1963 Hot Line Agreement and the 1972 Incidents at Sea Agreement.

—*Kerry Kartchner*

See also: Crisis Stability; Firebreaks; Horizontal Escalation; Inadvertent Escalation

References

Brodie, Bernard, *Escalation and the Nuclear Option* (Princeton, NJ: Princeton University Press, 1966).

Holsti, Ole R., *Crisis, Escalation, War* (Montreal: McGill-Queen's University Press, 1972).

Kahn, Herman, *On Escalation: Metaphors and Scenarios* (New York: Praeger, 1965).

Posen, Barry R., *Inadvertent Escalation: Conventional War and Nuclear Risks* (Ithaca, NY: Cornell University Press, 1991).

Smoke, Richard, *War: Controlling Escalation* (Cambridge, MA: Harvard University Press, 1977).

ESCALATION DOMINANCE

See Escalation

ESSENTIAL EQUIVALENCE

The term "essential equivalence" emerged within U.S. political debates during the Strategic Arms Limitation Talks (SALT I) of the late 1960s to describe the key U.S. objective: maintaining strategic nuclear parity (defined as an absence of unilateral advantage for either side). Essential equivalence was based on the notion that the United States and the Soviet Union had developed nuclear weapons along broadly similar lines. Because of technological, political, and geographic differences, however, Soviet and U.S. strategic forces also exhibited important differences. Thus, given the disparity in the quantity and quality of both states' forces, any successful arms control agreement designed to stabilize the strategic situation could not settle on equal numbers but would have to be based on roughly equivalent forces.

According to U.S. Secretary of Defense James Schlesinger, such equivalence was important for two reasons. First, essential equivalence would preserve the situation of mutual assured destruction (*see* Mutual Assured Destruction) without either side gaining a distinct military advantage. Second, strategic nuclear weapons were a symbol of superpower status. Therefore, an absence of equivalence might lead to serious diplomatic or military miscalculation that could lead to war if one side believed that it had somehow obtained a decisive advantage over its nuclear-armed adversary.

SALT negotiators confronted a significant problem, however, when it came to establishing standards for essential equivalence. Measuring equivalence is a highly subjective matter. Criteria by one group of observers to assess equivalence might suggest that strategic parity exists, while equally reasonable criteria adopted by other observers might lead them to believe that a dangerous imbalance in strategic forces exists. Some observers might focus on the accuracy, yield, or throw weight of an arsenal to assess its capability, whereas others might be more interested in assessing survivability. Debate over essential equivalence became so heated in the United States that the U.S. Congress demanded that the Strategic Arms Reduction Treaties (START I and II) be based not on essential equivalence, but on numerical parity.

—*Andrew M. Dorman*

Reference

Freedman, Lawrence, *The Evolution of Nuclear Strategy*, third edition (New York: Palgrave Macmillan, 2003).

EUROPEAN ATOMIC ENERGY COMMUNITY (EURATOM)

The European Atomic Energy Community (EURATOM) was founded to support the development of the nuclear power industry across the entire European Economic Community (EEC), now the European Union (EU), by procuring nuclear material and by using inspections to enforce safeguards at civilian nuclear facilities. All European Union states are automatically members of EURATOM.

EURATOM was established by the Treaty of Rome in 1957. It was created to foster a civil nuclear fuel cycle industry in response to the fear that the demands of the Cold War might cause uranium to be in short supply. The EURATOM Supply Agency (ESA) has operated since 1960 to ensure the supply of ores by means of a common supply policy based on the principle of equal access to sources with the right of option to acquire ores, source materials, and special fissile materials produced in the EU.

EURATOM is the official owner of all nuclear materials in all EU countries. The exception to this rule, however, occurs when producers retain responsibility for the storage or disposal of special fissile materials (plutonium and highly enriched uranium). It also has the exclusive right to validate contracts dealing with nuclear materials made by utilities located in the EU. The export of special fissile materials outside of the EU can only be undertaken by the ESA with the approval of the EU Commission. EURATOM maintains safeguards and inspections to ensure that no diversion of nuclear materials takes place "for other than intended uses." EURATOM thus permits use of nuclear materials in military applications. In this way it contrasts with the International Atomic Energy Agency (IAEA), which regulates peaceful uses of atomic energy. The IAEA has no right to engage in any monitoring activities or to conduct inspections in EU nuclear weapon states other than at selected facilities on a voluntary basis (*see* International Atomic Energy Agency).

There are no reactors under construction in the European Union. Only Britain and France are declared nuclear weapon states, and they are in the process of reducing their nuclear arsenals. Furthermore, no other EU state is seeking to develop nuclear weapons. Seven EU states do not have nuclear power, and four that currently possess a nuclear power industry have embraced the political objective of phasing out their nuclear power programs. Fourteen of the fifteen EU states have rejected any growth in civil nuclear capacity, which stands in stark contrast to EURATOM's original objective of promoting the development of nuclear power for peaceful purposes.

EURATOM offers loans for the construction of nuclear power plants in EU accession countries and states that were once part of the Soviet Union. Safeguard agreements with the IAEA will be changed in the EU accession states. In the future, the IAEA will only verify EURATOM inspections.

—*Glen M. Segell*

See also: Reactor Operations; Safeguards
References
Howlett, Darryl A., *Euratom and Nuclear Safeguards* (New York: Macmillan, 1990).
Polach, Jaroslav G., *Euratom: Its Background, Issues and Economic Implications* (New York: Oceana, 1964).

EXTENDED DETERRENCE

Extended deterrence is the act of providing security for another state through the threat of punishment against a third party. For the North Atlantic Treaty Organization (NATO), the American guarantee of extended deterrence has provided the basis for security against aggressors, particularly the Soviet Union. During the Cold War, deterrence was often equated with nuclear weapons. Today, NATO and other U.S. allies around the world rely on continuing promises of deterrence based on America's nuclear arsenal as the ultimate guarantor of their security.

Deterrence (the prevention of action through fear of the consequences) involves a state of mind brought about by the existence of a credible threat of unacceptable counteraction. Extended deterrence is exercised by threatening action or reaction against a third party in an attempt to convince that party not to take some action. This reaction includes, in extreme circumstances, the actual use of military power. The aim of deterrence is to pose the prospect of failure or destruction to a potential attacker. Extended deterrence is simply a geographical extension of this concept.

The U.S. nuclear arsenal was designed and deployed in a manner that would provide credible security guarantees to allies. The United States extended deterrence by making it clear that it would, if necessary, use nuclear weapons in response to a Soviet nuclear or conventional attack on allies, especially in Europe and Japan. Although the United States, together with its NATO allies, sought to deploy a conventional force posture that could avoid an early resort to nuclear weapons, the alliance did not forgo the option of first use of nuclear weapons if needed. The extended deterrence concept (sometimes called "active deterrence" because it involves a clear decision and willful act on the part of the nation that owns the weapons and extends its deterrence) underscored the coupling between the United States and its allies (see Coupling). It existed in a strategic setting in which the United States extended an explicit security guarantee to its allies, backed by vast nuclear and conventional military capabilities and the forward deployment of hundreds of thousands of U.S. troops and their families in Europe and Asia. In a crisis, deterrence involved signaling the U.S. commitment to a particular country or an alliance and expressing national interest by enhancing warfighting capabilities in the theater. In short, extended nuclear deterrence gave the United States and its allies the confidence to stand toe to toe with potential adversaries and not blink.

History and Background: Europe
Nuclear weapons became an integral part of NATO strategy in 1954 when the United States, facing superior Soviet conventional forces in Europe, first threatened "massive retaliation" against the Soviet Union in the case of a Soviet attack against Western Europe. By so doing, the United States "extended" deterrence to its European allies against a Soviet attack and created what also was referred to as a "nuclear umbrella" sheltering Western Europe. America's nuclear guarantee was backed up by the deployment of some 250,000 U.S. troops and their families to Europe. This substantial U.S. presence in Europe served as a "tripwire" ensuring American vulnerability to an attack against Western Europe, thereby providing the linkage to U.S. strategic nuclear forces.

By the early 1960s, the credibility of the massive retaliation threat was called into question when the Soviet Union achieved the ability to also hit U.S. cities with its nuclear weapons (see Credibility). Therefore, in 1967, the allies agreed to replace "massive retaliation" with "flexible response," a doctrine designed to give NATO a variety of nuclear and conventional force responses to a Soviet attack. The discussion over whether to adopt flexible response drove France out of NATO's military

arrangements in 1966 (see Flexible Response; Massive Retaliation).

According to early alliance documents, it was clear that both the United States and the European allies understood that the U.S. security commitment to Europe included nuclear protection against coercion or aggression. Much of NATO's history has been marked by debates over the meaning of this nuclear guarantee. During the Cold War, Europe's leaders reached consensus that a U.S. nuclear presence on the ground in their countries was a requirement for credible extended deterrence.

Nuclear weapons, particularly tactical or theater weapons, were the next logical step above conventional forces on the escalatory ladder of conflict and thereby provided a link—"coupling"—to the United States (see Escalation). To this purpose, nuclear weapons had to be flexible, survivable, have sufficient range, and have a doctrine for their use. Also, allied participation in planning and deterrence through threatened use helped assuage potential desires for independent nuclear capabilities and made Washington's NATO allies feel a part of the shared risk and responsibilities.

The deployment of U.S. short- and medium-range missiles that could hit Soviet territory from locations in Western Europe was meant to convince the Soviet Union that a war in Europe could not be kept at the conventional level. Escalation would put Soviet territory at risk, too, thus raising the stakes for Russia. Unlike strategic forces, intermediate-range missiles would become vulnerable to preemptive attack early in a European war, potentially forcing the destabilizing decision to use these weapons early rather than risk losing them to capture or destruction.

A question arose regarding the ultimate political purpose of nuclear weapons in Europe: Were they there to provide deterrence, or to reassure America's allies? Obviously they served both purposes. Coupling the United States to Europe created a condition where the integrity of the chain of escalation was complete, from conventional forces in Europe, to theater nuclear forces in theater, to the U.S. strategic nuclear force. This symbolized the social, political, and historical links between the two sides of the Atlantic. A challenge, however, resulted from the geographical separation of Europe and the United States and the uncertainty that separation engendered in the minds of European allies. This was one aspect of "NATO's nuclear dilemma."

Europeans suspected and feared that the United States *could*, in the event of crisis or war, decouple itself from Europe's problems. Every move made by the alliance since the 1960s, as U.S. nuclear superiority ended, that involved nuclear forces or strategy reinvigorated this worry about "the specter of decoupling."

This question revolved around the deliberately ambiguous strategy of flexible response. This strategy marginally satisfied both parties, but only because of its doctrinal ambiguity. Europeans focused on the response side of the equation (deterrence by punishment) and the "seamless web" of deterrence; the United States, in contrast, focused on flexibility and deterrence by denial (a warfighting approach).

If conflict were to break out in Europe, it was reasoned, the United States and Europe would have different responses. The United States would favor a limited war confined to the Continent, would want to prevent its spread to North America, and would want to keep it conventional as long as possible. This approach reflected its warfighting preference. Tactical nuclear weapons stationed (and, if necessary, used) in Europe would serve these warfighting strategies. Europeans, who did not want to see any type of war break out on their soil, preferred a policy of immediate, catastrophic, automatic escalation to nuclear war at the highest possible level, thereby increasing the level of deterrence effect. They feared that if war broke out, it could be fought "over their heads" and that the American preference for smaller tactical weapons could be destabilizing.

Both points of view therefore called for European-based nuclear weapons in NATO's arsenal, though for different reasons. These weapons supported both types of deterrence—one directly, one indirectly. Neither perspective justified nuclear weapons in terms of reassurance, but they were reassuring nonetheless, especially in light of the transatlantic linkage argument, which Europeans stressed. Thus a constituency arose on both sides of the Atlantic that wanted nuclear weapons in Europe. There has been little change in the underlying rationale for nearly fifty years. It is a sensitive topic, however, and the issues relating to it are normally kept out of the public eye.

Deterrence in Other Regions

Nuclear weapons did not ensure the end of war, but they did appear to limit the size of the conflicts that occurred "underneath the nuclear umbrella." It is hard to say whether nuclear deterrence succeeded, since deterrence can only be assessed if it fails. But the lessons of Europe appeared compelling and were thought to be transferable elsewhere in the world.

America's extended nuclear deterrence to Japan was implied; in South Korea the guarantee was blatant (with nuclear weapons deployed in Korea until 1992). The United States also implied that it would defend Israel with nuclear weapons (until Israel developed its own nuclear forces). These guarantees were backed up by multiple regional alliances, including NATO, ANZUS (the Australia-New Zealand-U.S. alliance), SEATO (the Southeast Asia Treaty Organization), and CENTO (the Central Asian Treaty Organization).

The Future

American extended deterrence rests on a combination of conventional and nuclear retaliatory capabilities, active and passive defenses, and counterforce policies. Notwithstanding consistent allied declarations concerning NATO strategy and the continued importance of U.S. substrategic weapons deployed in Europe, a number of questions may be posed. The most basic issue is whether a U.S. nuclear guarantee for European security is still essential and, if so, how to implement that guarantee.

The region that may most need America's extended deterrent is East Asia. American allies in the region feel and fear the ripple effects of multiple simultaneous strategic changes: North Korea's nuclear aspirations; China's growth into a regional hegemon with the potential for strategic military capabilities that match its economic strength; instability in states such as Indonesia; and the ongoing competition between India and Pakistan. All of this points to greater uncertainty and raises the specter of new threats to traditional allies such as Japan, South Korea, and Taiwan. The strategic defense leg of the new U.S. strategic "Triad" (*see* Triad), rather than the offensive nuclear approach that NATO took in Europe, may be appropriate for these states.

A recent RAND Corporation study listed a number of ways in which the United States could increase the credibility of its regional deterrent:

- Increase the perception of U.S. resolve through traditional diplomatic and military activities
- Extend security commitments to regional allies
- Station troops overseas in a crisis
- Emphasize U.S. military capabilities to impress adversaries
- Deploy theater defenses to make the U.S. homeland less vulnerable to WMD attack. (Wilkening and Watman)

These points suggest several conclusions about the future of American nuclear strategies to ensure viable extended deterrence. Such strategies should strive not only to maintain traditional nuclear deterrence for U.S. allies but also to protect U.S. forces overseas from weapons of mass destruction (WMD). Nuclear weapons assume a less central but still important role. Conventional weapons also have a role to play, as do overseas basing decisions and access capabilities.

All of these measures are based on one key assumption: that the United States retains its role as the leading great power in the world, with commensurate global responsibilities.

—*Jeffrey A. Larsen*

See also: Cold War; Deterrence; Minimum Deterrence; North Atlantic Treaty Organization

References

Larsen, Jeffrey A., "Extended Deterrence: The Continuing Role of the U.S. Nuclear Guarantee in Europe," in James J. Smith, ed., *Deterrence and Defense in a Dangerous World* (Colorado Springs: USAF Institute for National Security Studies, forthcoming).

Sloan, Stanley R., "NATO Nuclear Strategy beyond the Cold War," in Jeffrey A. Larsen and Kurt J. Klingenberger, eds., *Controlling Non-Strategic Nuclear Weapons: Obstacles and Opportunities* (Colorado Springs: USAF Institute for National Security Studies, July 2001).

U.S. Nuclear Policy in the 21st Century: A Fresh Look at National Strategy and Requirements, Final Report (Washington, DC, and Lawrence, CA: National Defense University and Lawrence Livermore National Laboratory, July 1998).

Wilkening, Dean, and Kenneth Watman, *Nuclear Deterrence in a Regional Context* (Santa Monica, CA: RAND Corporation, 1995). Highlights from the book can be found in "Regional Deterrence: The Nuclear Dimension," available at http://www.rand.org/publications/RB/RB24/rb24.html.

Yost, David S., *The U.S. and Nuclear Deterrence in Europe,* Adelphi Paper 326, International Institute for Strategic Studies (New York: Oxford University Press, March 1999).

FAILSAFE

During the Cold War, the term "failsafe" referred to the turnaround point for nuclear-armed strategic bombers flying airborne alert; that is, the decision point en route to the target at which the crew members would have to decide whether to proceed forward with their mission and bomb their targets in Eastern Europe and the Soviet Union, or turn around and head for home. In the absence of positive orders to the contrary, they would turn around—in other words, in the absence of a positive order to proceed with their mission, negative control of nuclear release authority would prevail, and the bombers would return to base. "Failsafe" entered the popular lexicon as a word symbolizing the concern during the Cold War that strategic nuclear war would erupt owing to mechanical or human error or inadvertent escalation during a crisis.

A book with the title *Failsafe* was released in 1962 and made into a best-selling movie the following year. Written by Eugene Burdick and Harvey Wheeler, it was based on the 1958 book *Red Alert* by Peter Bryant. The premise in *Failsafe* was that a rogue commander of a U.S. bomber wing uses a false message to send his fleet of B-52s past their failsafe points. His hope is to force the president, once he realizes that there is no calling the bombers back, to follow through with the full might of the U.S. arsenal while it has strategic superiority, thus ending the Cold War standoff once and for all. As things turn out in the story, one bomber gets through and destroys Moscow, and the president decides to destroy New York, using an American bomber, to show the Soviets that the United States is sincerely sorry about the incident, thereby preventing a massive nuclear exchange between the superpowers. Its message was distinctly antiwar and reflected the apocalyptic attitudes prevalent during this era.

A 1964 spoof on this serious subject was made into another motion picture. *Dr. Strangelove: Or How I Learned to Stop Worrying and Love the Bomb* followed much of the script from *Failsafe*, but with a dark comedic approach that satirized Strategic Air Command and the logic of deterrence theory, mutual assured destruction, and the quasi-religious approach to nuclear weapons.

—*Jeffrey A. Larsen*

References

Bryant, Peter, *Red Alert* (New York: Ace Books, 1958).
Burdick, Eugene, and Harvey Wheeler, *Failsafe* (Hopewell, NJ: Ecco, 1964).

FALLOUT

The term "fallout" refers to radioactive particles created from the tons of soil and debris irradiated by a nuclear detonation. This material is scooped up and carried into the mushroom cloud of the explosion, and the particles return to the Earth's surface as fallout.

When the fireball from a nuclear detonation touches the Earth's surface, it forms a crater. The earth from this crater is pulverized into microscopic, radioactive particles by the force of the explosion. These particles, along with surface structures pulverized by the explosion, are carried up into the distinctive mushroom-shaped cloud created by the detonation and eventually fall out of the cloud and return to the Earth's surface. Each contaminated particle continuously emits radiation while in the mushroom cloud, while descending, and on the ground. There are two categories of fallout: early and delayed. Early fallout descends to Earth within twenty-four hours after the explosion. Delayed fallout arrives after this twenty-four-hour period.

The largest, heaviest fallout particles reach the ground first, landing in locations close to the explosion. The smaller particles could be carried by the wind for hundreds of miles before falling to Earth. Additionally, they fall so slowly that most could remain airborne for weeks to years before reaching the ground. By that time, their dispersal and radioactive decay would make them much less dangerous. The radioactive particles that rise only a short distance (those in the "stem" of the mushroom cloud) will fall back to earth within a matter of minutes and land close to ground zero (the focal point of the detonation). Such particles are unlikely to cause many deaths because they will fall into areas where most people have already been killed by other nuclear weapons effects. The radioactivity contained in this fallout, however, will complicate rescue and recovery operations. The particles that rise higher in the cloud will be carried some distance by the wind before returning to earth.

The area and intensity of the fallout is strongly influenced by local weather conditions. Much of the material is simply blown downwind, forming a plume-shaped pattern on the ground. Rainfall also can influence the way fallout is deposited, since rain will carry contaminated particles to the ground. The areas receiving such contaminated rainfall become "hot spots," with greater radiation intensity than their surroundings.

A nuclear explosion creates four kinds of radiation: alpha, beta, gamma, and neutron. Gamma radiation is by far the most dangerous because its rays are more penetrating and harmful. The roentgen (R) is the unit most commonly used to measure gamma radiation. Most American civil defense instruments give readings in roentgens or roentgens per hour (R/hr). Until 1980, the U.S. military used the rad (radiation absorbed dose) as its unit of measurement. It now uses gray (Gy), for interoperability with the North Atlantic Treaty Organization (NATO). The danger from fallout radiation lessens with time. The radioactive decay, as this lessening is called, is rapid at first, and then becomes slower. The dose rate (the amount of radiation received per hour) decreases accordingly.

—*Jeffrey A. Adams*

See also: Airborne Alert; Cold War; Half-Life; Nuclear Weapons Effects; Radiation

References

Adams, Jeffrey A., and Stephen Marquette, *First Responders Guide to Weapons of Mass Destruction (WMD)* (Alexandria, VA: American Society for Industrial Security (ASIS), February 2002).

Glossary of Terms: Nuclear Power and Radiation (Washington, DC: U.S. Nuclear Regulatory Commission, June 1981).

U.S. Army Field Manual (FM) 4-02.283, *Treatment of Nuclear and Radiological Casualties* (Washington, DC: Headquarters, Department of the Army, n.d.).

FAST BREEDER REACTORS

The fast breeder reactor (FBR) is a type of nuclear reactor that uses fast, or high-energy, neutrons to cause fissions. It can produce more fuel nuclei than are consumed in the fission process and can thus substantially extend the supply of nuclear fuel.

The first breeder reactor, designed by the Argonne National Laboratory in Illinois, became the first reactor of any type to generate electricity when it went on line in 1951. The development of FBRs gave impetus to the prospect of using nuclear fuel as a long-term energy source. In April 1977, President Jimmy Carter decided that the United States would not reprocess and recycle plutonium from commercial reactors; this decision effectively curtailed the development of commercial breeder reactor technology by the United States.

Fissile isotopes, including uranium 235 (U-235) and plutonium 239 (Pu-239), fission readily when struck by low-energy neutrons (*see* Isotopes). Other isotopes, including the much more naturally abundant U-238, readily fission only when struck by fast neutrons. The development of the fast reactor is an attempt to exploit the potential of the most abundant uranium isotope, U-238. The U-238 in the fast reactor can capture a neutron and convert it into Pu-239, a fissile isotope. This plutonium can then be reprocessed and used as fuel in another reactor. A breeder reactor breeds fuel by producing more fissile nuclei, through neutron capture, than are consumed in fission.

FBRs are not currently operating in the United States, although other nations, such as Japan and France, operate research FBRs. The fear that the Pu-239 produced in the reactor would somehow manage to find its way into clandestine nuclear weapons programs, plus the difficulty of working with liquid sodium, often used as the reactor coolant, has caused many countries to discontinue their plans to build commercial FBRs.

—*Brian Moretti*

See also: Reactor Operations

Reference
Lamarsh, J. R., and A. J. Baratta, *Introduction to Nuclear Engineering,* third edition (Upper Saddle River, NJ: Prentice-Hall, 2001).

FAT MAN

On August 9, 1945, the United States targeted Nagasaki, Japan, with the second atomic bomb to be used against an adversary in wartime. Dropped by a B-29 bomber, *Bockscar,* the weapon was nicknamed "Fat Man" by its designers because of its large size, which was necessary to accommodate the early implosion design. Fat Man was detonated three days after the first atomic bomb, "Little Boy," was dropped on Hiroshima, and Japan had not yet responded to President Harry S. Truman's call for unconditional surrender. The combined devastation of these two weapons is credited with hastening the end of the war with Japan and ushering in an atomic age.

In Fat Man, a sphere of plutonium 239 (Pu-239) was compressed by many timed, simultaneous chemical explosive charges. The implosion of the subcritical sphere increased the density of the plutonium to a supercritical state. Additionally, an initiator that produced an initial burst of neutrons was centered in the sphere to increase the rapidity of the fissile chain-reaction. To lengthen the time of the reaction, a "tamper" of uranium 238 (U-238), a very strong material, held the components together long enough to ensure that a sufficient amount of Pu-239 could fission and release enough energy to create a blast. Neutron reflectors surrounded the device to further feed the nuclear reaction, thus maximizing the explosive power. The sophistication of the implosion device was greater than that of Little Boy's gun-type device, and so testing before use was considered necessary. The first atomic explosion in history, at the Trinity Site in New Mexico three weeks before Little Boy was dropped on Hiroshima, had used an implosion device similar to the one in Fat Man.

—*Jennifer Hunt Morstein*

See also: Fission Weapons; Implosion Devices; Little Boy; Nagasaki; Nuclear Weapons Effects; Trinity Site

References
Gardner, Gary T., *Nuclear Nonproliferation: A Primer* (Boulder: Lynne Rienner, 1994).
Rhodes, Richard, *Making of the Atomic Bomb* (New York: Simon and Schuster, 1986).
Walker, P. M. B., ed., *Chambers Nuclear Energy and Radiation Dictionary* (New York: Chambers, 1992).

FEDERAL EMERGENCY MANAGEMENT AGENCY (FEMA)

The U.S. Federal Emergency Management Agency (FEMA) was once an independent agency tasked with responding to, planning for, aiding recovery from, and mitigating disasters. FEMA became part of the newly created U.S. Department of Homeland Security in March 2003.

FEMA can trace its beginnings to a congressional act of 1803. An early piece of disaster legislation, it provided assistance to a New Hampshire town following an extensive fire. Over the next century, ad-hoc legislation was passed by Congress scores of times in response to natural disasters.

By the 1970s, federal emergency and disaster response duties were shared by many agencies. When the full range of hazards associated with nuclear power plants, transportation of hazardous substances, and natural disasters were combined, more than 100 federal agencies were involved in responding to emergencies. The National Governor's Association, seeking to decrease the many agencies with which state and local governments were forced to work, asked President Jimmy Carter to centralize federal emergency functions.

President Carter's response was a 1979 executive order merging many of the separate disaster-related responsibilities into a new Federal Emergency Management Agency. FEMA incorporated the Federal Insurance Administration, the National Fire Prevention and Control Administration, the National Weather Service Community Preparedness Program, the Federal Preparedness Agency of the General Services Administration, and the Federal Disaster Assistance Administration activities from the Department of Housing and Urban Development. The Defense Department's Defense Civil Preparedness Agency also transferred responsibility for civil defense in the event of nuclear war to FEMA. FEMA developed an Integrated Emergency Management System to respond to the challenges created by a range of natural and manmade disasters. With the end of the Cold War in the early 1990s, FEMA redirected resources from civil defense into disaster relief, recovery, and mitigation programs.

The terrorist attacks of September 11, 2001, focused FEMA on issues of national disaster preparedness and homeland security. The agency coordinated its activities with the newly created White House Office of Homeland Security, and FEMA's Office of National Preparedness was given responsibility to ensure that the nation's first responders could cope with incidents involving weapons of mass destruction. FEMA also moved funding directly to local communities to help them face the threat of terrorism. A few years past its twentieth anniversary, FEMA was directing its "all-hazards" approach to disasters toward homeland security issues.

In March 2003, FEMA joined twenty-two other federal agencies, programs, and offices in forming the Department of Homeland Security. FEMA is one of five major branches of the department. About 2,500 full-time employees in the Emergency Preparedness and Response Directorate are supplemented by more than 5,000 stand-by disaster reservists (*see* Department of Homeland Security).

—*Steven Rosenkrantz*

Reference
Federal Emergency Management Agency, http://www. fema.gov.

FEDERATION OF AMERICAN SCIENTISTS (FAS)

The Federation of American Scientists (FAS) is the oldest organization dedicated to what its members believe is an ongoing, worldwide arms race that could result in the use of nuclear weapons. It was founded in 1945 as the Federation of Atomic Scientists by alumni of the Manhattan Project who were deeply concerned about how nuclear weapons threatened the future of humankind.

FAS, known in its early years as the "scientists' lobby," is a nonprofit, nongovernmental organization (NGO) that offers analysis and opinion about a range of science, technology, and public policy issues. During the FAS presidency of Jeremy J. Stone (1970–2000), the NGO expanded its membership and staff by addressing new issues such as energy conservation and the environment, areas previously outside of its traditional focus on international security. Stone gave FAS a higher profile internationally by working to encourage scientific exchange with the People's Republic of China after President Richard M. Nixon's 1972 visit to China and by devising solutions to technical obstacles during the U.S.-Soviet Strategic Arms Reduction Treaty

(START I and II) of the late 1980s and early 1990s. In the human rights arena, Stone and FAS supported Soviet dissident Andrei Sakharov in the 1970s and 1980s, and it lobbied in the late 1980s and early 1990s to help prevent the Khmer Rouge's return to power in Cambodia.

FAS offers a scientific perspective on contemporary public policy issues through lobbying and advocacy, expert testimony, briefings with policymakers and the press, and public education and outreach. It often collaborates with civil rights, human rights, and arms control groups.

—*Steven Rosenkrantz*

References
Federation of American Scientists website, http://www. fas.org.
Stone, Jeremy J., *"Every Man Should Try": Adventures of a Public Interest Activist* (New York: Public Affairs, 1999).

FIREBALL
See Nuclear Weapons Effects

FIREBREAKS

"Firebreaks" were theoretical rungs on the Cold War escalatory ladder that provided opportunities to demonstrate to all concerned the seriousness of a situation. As the concept of mutual assured destruction (MAD) began to emerge between the United States and the Soviet Union in the early 1960s, analysts attempted to devise both political and warfighting strategies to make nuclear weapons militarily relevant on the battlefield and politically relevant in superpower relations. Drawing on game theory, several analysts, led by the Harvard economist Thomas Schelling, came to believe that nuclear threats, or the actual detonation of a nuclear weapon, could be used for purposes of intrawar deterrence, bargaining, and signaling. Schelling conceived of deterrence, and the nuclear infrastructure and arsenal that supported it, as creating a "threat that leaves something to chance" (Schelling 1960, p. 188); that is, nuclear threats and limited nuclear use created a distinct path to nuclear Armageddon that no one wanted. The side willing to run the greater risk of a full-scale nuclear exchange, however, would have a distinct advantage during a crisis or in wartime, which in theory would force the less committed party to back down.

Theory and practice suggested that it was possible to communicate with other parties without verbal or written communication, even during wartime. In other words, certain types of events had clearly implied messages, and these messages were plain for all to see regardless of culture, history, or ideology. In the literature on nuclear war, these "firebreaks," or key rungs on the escalation ladder, demonstrated to all concerned the seriousness of the situation. Opponents theoretically recognized when an adversary was holding violence below a firebreak or crossing a threshold and would respond accordingly. The most important firebreak was the outbreak of war itself. Another key firebreak was the first use of a nuclear weapon by either side. A distinction also could be made between attacks on the home territory of either superpower or attacks against allies or client states. Herman Kahn, a leading nuclear theorist in the 1960s who developed several schemes to classify the process of escalation, identified six crucial firebreaks: (1) don't rock the boat; (2) nuclear war is unthinkable; (3) no nuclear use; (4) central sanctuary; (5) central war; and (6) city targeting. Kahn's escalation ladders often ended with a full-scale nuclear exchange, which he described as "spasm war," and once even as "war-gasm."

Theorists who believed in nuclear warfighting suggested that it was wrong to treat war, escalation, and nuclear attacks as an exercise in bargaining and a competition in risk taking. They recognized the existence of firebreaks, but they believed that nuclear war should be prosecuted like a conventional conflict by attempting to find ways to fight and win, or at least to emerge from the conflict better off than the opponent. They believed their view was vindicated by the U.S. experience during the Vietnam War. Many believe that the Lyndon B. Johnson administration undertook limited military attacks early in that conflict to signal its resolve and superior military capability to the North Vietnamese, an effort that had little impact on Hanoi's willingness to use military force to achieve its objectives. More recently, the North Atlantic Treaty Organization's 1999 air campaign against Serbia suggested that the threat of additional destruction—the crossing of firebreaks—could be used to coerce opponents to comply with one's political demands.

—*James J. Wirtz*

See also: Crisis Stability; Escalation; Game Theory; Mutual Assured Destruction

References

Freedman, Lawrence, *The Evolution of Nuclear Strategy*, third edition (New York: Palgrave Macmillan, 2003).
Kahn, Herman, *On Escalation* (New York: Praeger, 1965).
Schelling, Thomas, *The Strategy of Conflict* (New York: Oxford University Press, 1960).
———, *Arms and Influence* (New Haven, CT: Yale University Press, 1966).

FIRST STRIKE

A first-strike strategy is a policy and a capability whereby nuclear (or precision-guided conventional) weapons are used to strike first, destroying an opponent's nuclear arsenal before it can be launched in retaliation. A first strike also might involve attacks against an opponent's military and political leadership and command and control infrastructure, thereby decapitating its command leadership and further reducing the likelihood of an effective retaliatory strike.

One of the key U.S. proponents of the first strike was nuclear strategist Herman Kahn. In his seminal 1961 work *On Thermonuclear War*, Kahn argued that the United States should develop such a capability—not to conduct an unprovoked surprise attack against the Soviet Union, but to reinforce deterrence by avoiding a mutual "balance of terror." Kahn suggested that a balance of terror was dangerous because the Soviet Union could exploit the stability-instability paradox by undertaking a conventional thrust across Europe, knowing that any U.S. retaliation raised the prospect of mutual assured destruction (MAD). The U.S. president, faced with the prospect of escalation to a full-scale nuclear exchange, probably would choose not to use nuclear weapons to respond to a Soviet conventional attack on the North Atlantic Treaty Organization (NATO). Kahn suggested that deterrence would be better served if the United States possessed the means to launch a first strike against Soviet nuclear forces in the event that nuclear deterrence had failed or was failing to stop a conventional attack against Western Europe.

The difficulty of actually creating the first-strike capability called for by Kahn in 1961 became obvious as the Soviet and U.S. nuclear arsenals continued to grow in size and quality throughout the

1960s, 1970s, and 1980s. First, the emergence of both a Soviet and U.S. "Triad" of nuclear forces—consisting of land-based intercontinental ballistic missiles (ICBMs), submarine-launched ballistic missiles (SLBMs), and long-range heavy bombers—greatly increased the survivability of both sides' retaliatory capability, placing a first-strike capability beyond the reach of both Soviet and American strategists. Placing nuclear forces on high day-to-day alert levels—for example, U.S. Strategic Air Command bombers and command and control aircraft on airborne alert—increased the likelihood that both Soviet and U.S. strategic arsenals possessed a launch-on-warning, or launch-under-attack, capability, greatly reducing the prospects that they would fall victim to a first strike.

The development of effective early-warning and command-and-control systems also reduced the prospects that either side would launch a first strike. The deployment of U.S. and Soviet early-warning satellites enabled both sides to detect the heat from the rockets of ICBMs and SLBMs within 90 seconds of their launch, giving each side up to 30 minutes of warning in an attack. A series of ground-based radar networks would then progressively characterize the attack under way. Emergency evacuation procedures ensured that at least some political and military leaders would survive to authorize retaliation from surviving nuclear forces (*see* Early Warning).

But toward the end of the Cold War, U.S. planners worried increasingly about the vulnerability of command and control to a decapitation attack (*see* Decapitation). Very-high-altitude nuclear detonations could create an electromagnetic pulse (EMP) that would burn out electronic and telecommunications systems, blocking the transmission of orders to nuclear forces. Many also feared that Soviet SLBMs fired at short range on depressed trajectories might kill U.S. political leaders before they could be dispersed or give nuclear release orders. It also was feared that bomber forces could be targeted by depressed-trajectory SLBM attacks, reducing warning time to a few minutes at most and making it less likely that pilots would be able to get bombers off the ground and out to safe escape distances (*see* Depressed Trajectory). Although these potential capabilities did not guarantee that a Soviet first strike would be successful, planners were concerned that the Soviets might think they would have a significant edge in a nuclear war, and that this trend could

produce incentives for them to use nuclear weapons first in a crisis.

Since the end of the Cold War, the likelihood of a deliberate Russian attack on the United States has been extremely low. But today, the proliferation of long-range delivery systems and weapons of mass destruction creates incentives for U.S. policymakers to contemplate nuclear and conventional first-strike policies and capabilities to prevent nascent chemical, biological, or even nuclear arsenals from being used first in a crisis or war.

—*Malcolm Davis and James J. Wirtz*

See also: Second Strike

References

Kahn, Herman, *On Thermonuclear War* (Princeton, NJ: Princeton University Press, 1961).

Lavoy, Peter R., Scott D. Sagan, and James J. Wirtz, eds., *Planning the Unthinkable: How New Powers Will Use Nuclear, Biological, and Chemical Weapons* (Ithaca, NY: Cornell University Press, 2000).

FISSILE MATERIAL CUTOFF TREATY (FMCT)

The purpose of a fissile material cutoff treaty (FMCT) is to curb the amount of fissile material available for nuclear weapons by banning production of fissile material for nuclear weapons or other explosive devices. Proposals for an FMCT have been part of international arms control talks since the end of World War II. Almost all variations of FMCT proposals target the activities of the five nuclear weapons states (the United States, the United Kingdom, Russia, China, and France) and the three "threshold states" (Israel, Pakistan, and India). Fissile materials are the fundamental ingredient of all nuclear weapons. They also are the most difficult and expensive part of a nuclear warhead to produce. Consequently, there would be obvious benefits to stopping, or "cutting off," the production of fissile materials. An FMCT would limit the size of potential nuclear arsenals, making reductions irreversible if fissile materials were transferred from dismantled weapons and other unsafeguarded stocks to non-weapons use or disposal under international standards. It would also strengthen the nonproliferation regime by opening nuclear facilities in all nations to some form of international inspection.

An FMCT is generally considered a disarmament initiative because it would eliminate all stockpiles of fissile materials for nuclear weapons or nuclear explosives. Any proposal for an FMCT would include at least three elements: a ban on the production of fissile material; an agreement not to assist other states in such activities; and a verification mechanism or process in which the International Atomic Energy Agency (IAEA) would play a prominent role. An FMCT would not address previously produced stockpiles of fissile materials, nor would it apply to fissile materials not used for weapons systems, such as naval nuclear-propulsion systems. Although there exists no internationally agreed-upon definition of "fissile material," in the context of proposed negotiations on an FMCT the term usually refers to any fissionable material that could be used for a nuclear explosion, that is, "weapons-grade" or "weapons-usable" material. This would include any isotope of plutonium, uranium 233, or uranium enriched to that point that it contains 20 percent or more of the isotope U-235. FMCT proponents generally agree that the proposed "fissile material" ban would not apply to other radioactive materials, nor would it apply to exotic materials such as tritium or americium (*see* Enrichment; Highly Enriched Uranium [HEU]; Isotopes).

There have been several proposals for an FMCT, but there is currently no negotiating text. Although the United Nations Conference on Disarmament (CD) established a mandate to negotiate an FMCT in March 1995, formal negotiations remain stalled. In 1998, the mandate for negotiations expired, and the CD must now agree on a new mandate before any negotiations can begin. A standoff in the CD has developed over the FMCT in a number of significant areas. First, the nonaligned group in the CD has complained that the nuclear weapons states (NWS) have followed an incremental approach to nuclear disarmament through stand-alone treaties and have, in effect, abandoned any effort at a comprehensive approach to disarmament. Many in the nonaligned group, including India and Pakistan, have characterized the Nuclear Nonproliferation Treaty (NPT) of 1968 and a future FMCT as unequal and discriminatory. In their view, such treaties create two classes: the nuclear "have" and "have-not" states. India has argued that these types of treaty-based regimes encourage the monopolization of nuclear weapons by the nuclear weapons states and perpetuate inequality because they fail to address a timetable for disarmament. Intrinsic to this argument is the belief that the FMCT would not repre-

sent a significant constraint upon the NWS. Another contentious issue is the scope of a future FMCT. Several in the nonaligned group object to an FMCT focused solely on halting future production, arguing that an FMCT that does not consider past production would translate into a freeze of the status quo.

Negotiations have been further complicated by attempts by several participating states, including Russia and China, to "link" progress on FMCT negotiations to other arms control initiatives. China, for example, linked FMCT to the continuation of the Anti-Ballistic Missile (ABM) Treaty. Then, when the United States terminated the treaty, China continued to insist that no FMCT negotiations could begin until there was a negotiating mandate for talks on the prevention of an arms race in outer space. China and other states also insist on linkage of an FMCT with a timetable for nuclear disarmament. These "linkage" proposals were unacceptable to the United States. Although the United States' first priority in the CD is the negotiation of a comprehensive, effectively verifiable FMCT, it has stated that it will not do so at the expense of agreeing to negotiations on outer space or a timetable for nuclear disarmament, which it has called "not ripe" for multilateral negotiations. Russia agreed that it would not discuss nuclear disarmament but expressed a willingness to negotiate on outer space issues. The UK and France generally have agreed with the U.S. view opposing linkage on these two issues, although on various occasions they have been more amenable to agreeing to "talks" or discussions without a negotiating mandate. Possible alternatives to negotiating an FMCT outside the CD have been proposed, such as having only the nuclear weapons states and threshold states meet to negotiate an agreement, but such proposals have been unable to muster political support.

It is generally assumed that the IAEA would be called upon to conduct verification activities to support an FMCT (*see* Verification). Another key issue, when and if negotiations begin on an FMCT, will be how to verify the absence of clandestine enrichment and reprocessing facilities. In addition to verifying whether fissile material is being sequestered or stockpiled, the IAEA would be called upon to search for and inspect undeclared facilities, which would be subject to either "special" or "challenge" inspections. A special inspection is an inspection that the

IAEA may perform at any site in the territory of a state party, regardless of whether it is declared, on the sole initiative of the IAEA. A challenge inspection is one conducted at the request of another state party. The original mandate for negotiating an FMCT required that any agreement be "effectively verifiable." Given the nature of the materials to be subjected to an FMCT, this point would require intrusive challenge and special inspections anywhere, anyplace, and anytime. For the United States and other nuclear weapons states, this requirement would be difficult to meet, given the need to protect nuclear weapons information, weapon delivery system technologies, commercial proprietary information, information related to highly sensitive naval nuclear-propulsion technology, and other classified information or technology unrelated to nuclear weapons or nuclear technology.

—*Guy Roberts*

Reference

Roberts, Guy, *This Arms Control Dog Won't Hunt: The Proposed Fissile Material Cut-Off Treaty at the Conference on Disarmament,* INSS Occasional Paper 36 (Colorado Springs: USAF Institute for National Security Studies, January 2001).

FISSION WEAPONS

A fission weapon is a highly explosive device utilizing uranium or plutonium that is brought to a critical mass under pressure from a chemical explosive detonation. It produces significant blast, thermal radiation, and nuclear radiation through fission.

History and Background

In the late 1930s, many scientists around the world were working to achieve a theoretical understanding of a sustained fission reaction, with the idea that it might be possible to build a bomb of tremendous power utilizing the process of fission. Physicists repeatedly brought the idea of an atomic bomb to the attention of the military and other government offices in the United States and Great Britain with no real success.

It was not until December 6, 1941, the day before the Japanese bombed Pearl Harbor, that the decision was taken to begin substantial financial and technical support of a program to produce the bomb. The project became known as the Manhattan Project (*see* Manhattan Project). The primary purpose of the Manhattan Project was not only to pro-

The "Grable" atomic bomb test, May 25, 1953, Nevada Test Site. (Corbis)

duce a workable atomic weapon but to do so before the Germans could develop a nuclear weapon. The physicists and engineers working on the project succeeded in their undertaking at 5:30 A.M. on July 15, 1945, at a spot in the New Mexican desert codenamed Trinity. The fission weapons produced by the Manhattan Project were used twice in war, against Hiroshima, Japan, on August 6, 1945, and on Nagasaki, Japan, on August 9, 1945 (*see* Hiroshima; Nagasaki). Bomb production did not end at the conclusion of World War II. Weapons production continued with new, larger designs. The 500-kiloton Ivy King nuclear test by the United States on November 15, 1952, was probably the largest fission-based nuclear weapon ever detonated. The device exploded in this test was the Mk-18 Super Oralloy Bomb.

Technical Details

The two basic types of fission weapons are the gun and implosion designs. Both types use fissile material, and several designs make use of the fusion of lighter elements to improve weapon efficiency and "boost" the energy release (*see* Fusion). Similar components are present in each design: chemical explosives (or in the case of the gun-type, propellants) to compress the fissile material into a supercritical mass that will sustain an explosive chain reaction; nonfissile materials to reflect neutrons and tamp the explosion; electronics to trigger the explosion; a neutron generator to start the nuclear detonation at the appropriate time; and associated electronic and mechanical safety, arming, and firing mechanisms.

The gun-type weapon is the simplest method for creating a fission weapon. Gun-type designs use uranium 235 or U-233 as the fissile material. The fissile material is kept in the form of two hemispheres, each of which is subcritical, but which when brought together form a supercritical mass. "Tampers," constructed of a heavy material around the fissile material to contain it for the amount of time needed to produce the desired yield and act as a neutron reflector, are located around both hemispheres. The nuclear explosion is initiated by detonating a high-explosive propellant behind one of the hemispheres, which accelerates rapidly down the barrel toward the other. At the instant the two hemispheres meet, a burst of neutrons is injected to initiate a chain reaction.

The primary advantage of the gun-type design is its simplicity. It is as close to a foolproof design as technology allows. The drawbacks to the gun-type design are the lack of compression, which results in a need for large amounts of fissionable material and leads to low efficiency; inefficiency in its use of fissile material, as only about 3 percent of the material is fissioned, on average; a slow insertion speed, which means that only U-235 and U-233 can be used; and the weight and length of the gun barrel, which make the weapon heavy and fairly long. The gun-type design is highly predictable, as was evident by its use in the bomb dropped on Hiroshima without prior testing. The gun-type weapon used at Hiroshima contained about 42 kilograms of 80 percent enriched U-235 and yielded 12.5 kilotons of explosive power.

The implosion-type design makes use of the fact that increasing the density of the fissile material decreases the critical mass required for a supercritical state. This is the principle employed in most modern nuclear weapons designs of the five declared nuclear states. In an implosion design, the fissile material is in the form of a small subcritical sphere surrounded by a tamper. Outside this is a high explosive, which is detonated simultaneously at a number of points on the exterior to produce a symmetrical, inward-traveling shock wave. This "implosion" compresses the fissile material to two to three times its normal density. At the moment of maximum compression, a burst of neutrons is injected to initiate a chain reaction. The primary advantages of the implosion-type design include a high insertion speed, which allows materials with high spontaneous fission rates (that is, plutonium) to be used; a high density, leading to a very efficient weapon and a need for relatively small amounts of material; and the potential for lightweight designs—in the best designs, only several kilograms of high explosive are needed to compress the core.

The principal drawback to the implosion-type design is its complexity and the precision required to make it work. Implosion designs take extensive research and testing and require high-precision machining and electronics. The crucial timing and simultaneous detonation of the high explosives leads to increased concern over the predictability of the yield or even a complete malfunction of the weapon. This is the type of weapon dropped on Nagasaki, but not before it was tested in the New Mexico desert. The implosion-type weapon used at Nagasaki yielded 20 kilotons of blast energy.

—*D. Shannon Sentell, Jr.*

See also: Criticality and Critical Mass; Deuterium; Gun-Type Devices; Hiroshima; Implosion Devices; Nagasaki; Neutron Bomb (Enhanced Radiation Weapon); Neutrons; Nuclear Weapons Effects; Plutonium; Radiation; Uranium; Yield

References
Nuclear Weapons Archive, http://nuclearweaponarchive. org/.
Rhodes, Richard, *The Making of the Atomic Bomb* (New York: Simon and Schuster, 1995).

FIZZLE
See Criticality and Critical Mass; Nuclear Weapons Effects

FLEXIBLE RESPONSE
The flexible response doctrine stipulates that a state or alliance will meet any level of aggression with equivalent conventional or nuclear force and will increase the level of force, if necessary, to end the conflict. The doctrine originally emerged as a North Atlantic Treaty Organization (NATO) response to the Soviet Union's development of nuclear weapons

capabilities, which called into question NATO's "massive-retaliation" strategy. Flexible response was adopted as the military strategy of NATO in 1967. Since the end of the Cold War, the doctrine has been modified by two new NATO "strategic concepts," but not formally replaced.

History and Background

NATO's first nuclear strategy, approved as Military Committee (MC) 48 in December 1954, threatened massive retaliation against the Soviet Union should it attack a member of the alliance (*see* Massive Retaliation). This heavy reliance on the nuclear threat was driven by the U.S. attempt to save money on defense and the failure of European allies to meet their non–nuclear force goals. It did not sufficiently anticipate the implications of future Soviet nuclear force deployments. The Soviet Union had successfully tested an atomic device in 1949 and a hydrogen bomb in 1953. But when MC 48 was approved, the Soviet Union had only limited means for delivering its few weapons on Western targets and virtually no means for threatening American territory. The launch of the Sputnik satellite in 1957 demonstrated the progress the Soviet Union had made in a very few years toward developing its own strategic nuclear weapons delivery systems and suggested that it would soon be capable of holding European *and* American cities hostage to a nuclear threat. This called into question the credibility of massive retaliation as the basis of NATO strategy.

The NATO allies struggled from the mid-1950s with attempts to adjust NATO's strategy and force posture to the evolving strategic environment. From the U.S. perspective, the steady growth of Soviet nuclear capabilities clearly necessitated a more flexible set of guidelines for the use of nuclear weapons. It was no longer credible simply to threaten attacks on the Soviet heartland with nuclear weapons in response to an attack on Western Europe. The American heartland had become vulnerable to a response in kind. The need for change was signaled by U.S. Secretary of Defense Robert McNamara in 1962. Such a momentous change in nuclear strategy, however, met with skepticism in Western Europe, largely from fear that the credibility of the nuclear guarantee would be destroyed by a strategy that foresaw the possibility of limited or controlled nuclear exchanges.

NATO's adoption of the doctrine of flexible response in 1967 followed several wrenching years of discussion and debate among the allies. The doctrine attempted to accommodate the American desire for more flexible nuclear options and European concerns about the credibility of the U.S. nuclear deterrent for Western Europe. Under the doctrine, Chicago might not be put at risk in the early stages of a conflict, but the possibility of escalation supposedly "coupled" the fate of Chicago to that of Paris, Hamburg, or London. The new nuclear doctrine did not reconcile American and European differences on nuclear strategy, but it did provide a formula that was sufficiently ambiguous to achieve political credibility on both sides of the Atlantic (*see* Coupling; Credibility; Deterrence; Escalation).

With the advent of flexible response and the development of limited nuclear options, the certainty implied by massive retaliation was replaced by the elusive goal of "escalation control." That NATO advantage was countered in the 1970s by Soviet nuclear force improvements, including deployment of the SS-20, a mobile, accurate missile system capable of carrying three independently targetable warheads on each missile.

In December 1979, led by U.S. President Jimmy Carter, the NATO allies decided on a dual-track approach: to modernize their theater nuclear forces to ensure the continued viability of the flexible-response doctrine while seeking to negotiate limits on such forces with the Soviet Union. The decision came in spite of growing public opposition to new missile deployments in several West European countries.

After defeating President Carter for the presidency, Ronald Reagan on November 18, 1981, called for the total elimination of all Soviet intermediate-range nuclear weapons in return for cancellation of NATO deployment plans. The initial Soviet response was negative. Tough negotiations stretched out over several years, until Soviet President Mikhail Gorbachev, judging that the Soviet Union could not afford to engage in an open-ended arms competition with the United States, decided to cut a deal.

On December 8, 1987, the United States and the Soviet Union signed the Intermediate-Range Nuclear Forces (INF) Treaty, which was designed to eliminate two categories of intermediate-range nuclear missiles: long-range and short-range INF. The treaty's terms were being implemented when the

Cold War came to an abrupt end with the breakup of the Warsaw Pact and the collapse of the Soviet Union. At the end of the Cold War, the United States initiated sweeping unilateral reductions in U.S. tactical nuclear weapons in Europe and elsewhere (*see* Cold War; Intermediate-Range Nuclear Forces [INF] Treaty).

Current Status

NATO twice revised its strategic plan in the 1990s, on both occasions passing up the opportunity to replace flexible response with a new strategy but substantially diminishing the role of nuclear weapons. In 1999, the allies stated that nuclear weapons continued to play an "indispensable" but largely political role in NATO strategy "to preserve peace and prevent coercion and any kind of war."

NATO has not directly linked its flexible-response doctrine, its nuclear weapons capabilities, or the concept of deterrence to the new problems of terrorism and the potential use of weapons of mass destruction by rogue states.

—Stanley R. Sloan

See also: Deterrence; North Atlantic Treaty
    Organization; Second Strike
References
"The Alliance's Strategic Concept," 1999, NATO
    Handbook, available at http://www.nato.int/docu/
    handbook/2001/.
Lodal, Jan, *The Price of Dominance: The New Weapons of
    Mass Destruction and Their Challenge to American
    Leadership* (New York: Council on Foreign Relations
    Press, 2001).
Sloan, Stanley R., *NATO, the European Union and the
    Atlantic Community: The Transatlantic Bargain
    Reconsidered* (Lanham, MD: Rowman and Littlefield,
    2002).

THE FOOTBALL

The "football," also known as the Presidential Emergency Satchel, contains the President's Nuclear Decision Handbook. It also includes the Single Integrated Operational Plan (SIOP), a list of classified bunkers for the president to go to in case of an emergency, and a communications packet that includes the authentication codes for the president to authorize the use of nuclear weapons through a secure satellite communications (SATCOM) radio. The football is carried by a military officer from one of the armed services who is always in the general vicinity of the president.

The official name of the football is classified. The nickname stems from the first SIOP, known by the code name "Dropkick" and initiated during the Dwight D. Eisenhower administration. The John F. Kennedy administration established the use of a briefcase to carry the SIOP and associated communications equipment in response to the Cuban missile crisis. The football established a direct command and control link from the president to the U.S. Nuclear Command.

The football is a black leather Zero-Halliburton brand briefcase with approximate dimensions of 18 by 15 by 10 inches. An inner titanium lining protects the contents from damage. The requirement for the football to be in close proximity to the president may change in the future; in fact, one proposal for downgrading the U.S. nuclear weapons posture is to distance the football from the president.

—Don Gillich

See also: Single Integrated Operational Plan
Reference
Patterson, Robert, *Dereliction of Duty: The Eyewitness
    Account of How Bill Clinton Endangered America's
    Long-Term National Security* (Washington, DC:
    Regnery, March 2003).

FORWARD-BASED SYSTEMS

Forward-based systems (FBS) are nuclear delivery vehicles located outside one's own country but close to the adversary's territory, thus shortening the distance a weapon has to travel to strike an adversary. The Soviet Union was always concerned about the short warning time it would get from weapons launched at it from Western Europe. It was this very concern that presented one of the chief obstacles during the Strategic Arms Limitation Talks (SALT I) in 1969 and during SALT II in 1977. In an attempt to delineate what the SALT I Treaty would cover, the Soviets argued that any system that was capable of reaching the territory of the other side was strategic and hence subject to the treaty limits being negotiated. This language would have meant that U.S. fighter bombers and carrier-based attack aircraft would have been included, but Soviet intermediate-range ballistic missiles aimed at Western Europe would have been excluded. U.S. negotiators disagreed with the Soviet position, and the issue was put aside for a future arms control treaty. West European governments closely watched the U.S. position, fearing that the United States might bargain away its European-based nuclear assets, leaving Europe vulnerable to Soviet nuclear blackmail, given Soviet superiority in intermediate-range missiles. This issue would reemerge during the Soviet SS-20 and NATO dual-track decisions in 1979 (*see* Strategic Arms Limitation Talks [SALT I and SALT II]).

Washington believed that the Soviet position on forward-based systems was unacceptable and countered that its nuclear-capable aircraft and battlefield systems in Europe were there primarily for the defense of Europe and not for strategic missions against Soviet territory. In the SALT II negotiations, forward-based systems were dropped from consideration again when the Soviets refused to cut back on their heavy SS-18 intercontinental ballistic missile (ICBM) force. Since the early 1950s, the Soviets had maintained a potent offensive posture through the deployment of long-range theater nuclear forces (LRTNFs) in the western half of the Soviet Union. Made up chiefly of medium-range and intermediate-range ballistic missiles (MRBMs and IRBMs) and medium bombers, this Soviet force provided the capability to obliterate within a few minutes the entire fixed North Atlantic Treaty Organization (NATO) nuclear infrastructure. Likely targets included airfields, fixed defense and missile sites, nuclear storage depots, and all nonmobile support facilities.

The United States never attempted to match the Soviet effort in LRTNFs, preferring to rely on strategic nuclear systems, especially the U.S. submarine-launched ballistic missile (SLBM) force, which had a proportion of its targeting dictated by NATO requirements. U.S. land-based systems in Europe (chiefly tactical aircraft such as the F-4 and F-111) had both the nuclear weapons and the potential range needed to attack the U.S.S.R. Whether U.S. weapon systems had or did not have such a role in U.S. nuclear attack plans would not make any difference to a Soviet planner. The Soviets would have had to base their defense preparations on the assumption that U.S. FBS did have such a role and would respond accordingly. Based on this sort of logic, it is easy to understand why the Soviet Union maintained very large numbers of LRTNF systems—some 500 S-4 MRBMs, 100 SS-5 IRBMs, and several hundred medium bombers—for more than two decades. The flight times of those Soviet missiles from their silos to NATO airfields was about ten minutes, so even tactical warning of Soviet missile

launch would not greatly increase the survivability of U.S. nuclear-equipped tactical aircraft.

With NATO-based systems and Soviet LRTNFs not subject to any superpower arms control treaty, a wave of modernization of these forces began in the 1970s. The Soviet Union retired its SS-4/5 missiles and replaced them with mobile SS-20s armed with multiple independently targetable reentry vehicles (MIRVs). In addition, Backfire TU-22M bombers were deployed that were capable of reaching most targets in Western Europe. Because Europe, and especially West Germany, feared decoupling from the U.S. strategic nuclear arsenal, NATO's theater nuclear forces were modernized with ground-launched cruise missiles (GLCMs) and the Pershing II mobile missile. Prior to deployment, superpower talks on intermediate-range nuclear forces (INF)—part of the so-called "dual-track" approach to NATO INF force modernization—began in Geneva. Both short-range and medium-range systems were included in the INF talks, which reached an impasse until 1987, when the Soviets accepted the opening U.S. proposal in the negotiations and agreed to a treaty banning intermediate nuclear forces.

—*Gilles Van Nederveen*

See also: Coupling; Intermediate-Range Nuclear Forces Treaty; North Atlantic Treaty Organization

References
Talbott, Strobe, *Endgame: The Inside Story of SALT II* (New York: Knopf, 1979).
Thornton, Richard C., *Nixon Kissinger Years: The Reshaping of American Foreign Policy* (New York: Paragon House, 1989).

FRACTIONAL ORBITAL BOMBARDMENT SYSTEM (FOBS)

A fractional orbital bombardment system (FOBS) is an orbital nuclear weapons delivery system that inserts a payload into an orbital trajectory from which a reentry vehicle (RV) is deorbited. The Soviet Union attempted twenty-four FOBS test launches between 1965 and 1971 and deployed the system operationally from 1969 to 1983. FOBS are now prohibited under the Strategic Arms Reduction Treaty (START I) of 1991.

The earliest concrete proposal for this type of system originated from Soviet Chief Designer Sergey P. Korolev, who began preliminary work on the so-called Global Missile 1 (GR-1) in 1960. For Korolev, the GR-1 was part of the plan to develop a booster for the Soviet manned lunar effort. By 1962–1963, the U.S.S.R. had at least three major orbital weapons projects: the GR-1, a second FOBS project headed by General Designer Vladimir N. Chelomey, and a third by Mikhail K. Yangel's design bureau. In early 1965, prior to full testing of any system, the Strategic Rocket Forces conducted a comparative analysis and selected the Yangel option. After the twentieth test launch attempt, in August 1969 the first battalion of FOBS (R-36-O missiles) was put on combat duty at Tyuratam, located in Kazakhstan. In 1982, the U.S.S.R. began to dismantle the R-36-O, and the last missile was removed from duty in February 1983. Estimates on the yield of the FOBS warhead vary from between 2 and 20 megatons, and it was assessed to be able to hit within 3 to 5 kilometers of its intended target.

The apparent purpose of the FOBS was to provide the U.S.S.R. with more attack planning flexibility and options. The system could, for example, be used to strike the United States from the south, the direction with the fewest strategic early warning sensors. Secretary of Defense Robert S. McNamara publicly announced the existence of the system in November 1967 but attempted to downplay its significance, denying that it posed a major new strategic threat to the United States or violated the 1967 Outer Space Treaty, since the nuclear payloads were not in sustained orbit.

—*Peter Hays*

References

Siddiqi, Asif A., "The Soviet Fractional Orbital Bombardment System: A Short History," available at http://home.earthlink.net/~cliched/spacecraft/fobs.html.

Stares, Paul B., *The Militarization of Space: U.S. Policy, 1945–1984* (Ithaca, NY: Cornell University Press, 1985).

FRATRICIDE

The term "fratricide" often refers to "friendly fire" incidents in which troops accidentally kill or wound their comrades instead of the enemy. In nuclear war planning, it is used to refer to the inadvertent destruction of nuclear warheads or delivery systems by other warheads and delivery systems that are part of the same attack.

When a nuclear weapon detonates, it creates blast, extreme atmospheric disturbance, electro-magnetic pulse, and possibly enormous debris in the atmosphere (*see* Nuclear Weapons Effects). Incoming delivery systems or reentry vehicles that encounter these weapons effects can be destroyed, damaged, or knocked off course, leading to fratricide. Estimating fratricidal effects is extraordinarily difficult because it depends on the nature and severity of the effects encountered and the ability of the incoming weapon or delivery system to withstand these effects. To be safe, however, U.S. and Soviet nuclear war planners literally spent years "deconflicting" nuclear war plans to prevent fratricide while developing complex "walking barrages" to make sure that incoming warheads and delivery systems avoided the effects created by nearby detonations (in space and time).

Fratricide effects conspired to reduce confidence in any effort to launch a first strike to disarm an opponent. Since a massive and complex counterforce attack had never been undertaken, planners could never be sure of the extent or the true nature of the fratricide effects that would be produced by the detonation of thousands of nuclear weapons in relatively confined areas over a short period of time. The "dense pack" deployment scheme for land-based missiles developed in the late 1970s actually capitalized on the fratricide effect (*see* Dense Pack). Many believed that it would be difficult to destroy all missiles deployed in dense pack simultaneously because multiple nearby detonations would result in warhead fratricide.

—*James J. Wirtz*

Reference

Freedman, Lawrence, *The Evolution of Nuclear Strategy*, third edition (New York: Palgrave Macmillan, 2003).

FREEZE

See Disarmament

FRENCH NUCLEAR FORCES AND DOCTRINE

France has pursued its own nuclear weapons programs and policies since the early days of the nuclear age. The instability of the Fourth Republic after World War II and a shortage of financial resources slowed French nuclear research, which lagged behind Soviet and American weapons programs. Gradually, however, France developed its nuclear weapons infrastructure and delivery systems.

History and Background

In October 1945, only two months after a nuclear weapon destroyed Hiroshima (*see* Hiroshima; Nagasaki), General Charles de Gaulle, as president of the Provisional Government, set up the Commissariat à l'Energie Atomique (French Atomic Energy Commission) to undertake research related to the use of atomic energy in the fields of science, industry, and national defense. In late 1954, the French government launched a secret program to develop a nuclear weapon. In April 1958, a ministerial top-secret order was given to prepare for the first series of atomic tests, which were to take place in early 1960.

The French decision to acquire nuclear weapons was influenced by several factors. A nuclear arsenal was seen as a way to promote France's position as a great power and to reduce its reliance on the U.S. nuclear deterrent, thereby bolstering its diplomatic and military leverage with its allies and adversaries. Dismissing the North Atlantic Treaty Organization (NATO) concept of integrated forces, de Gaulle established an arsenal capable of acting on behalf of French interests. His aims for the *Force de Frappe* (or "Strike Force") were the restoration of French grandeur, the reunification of Europe under French leadership, and the subordination of West Germany to French leadership in Europe. Ultimately, a credible French nuclear arsenal would make possible an independent role for Europe in world affairs.

General de Gaulle continued to support the construction of an independent French nuclear arsenal throughout the 1960s. The *Force de Frappe* became a military priority for France, and several initiatives were launched simultaneously to make the French nuclear program a reality. An industrial complex was constructed that would enable France to manufacture highly enriched uranium (the only fissile material available to France had been plutonium) (*see* Highly Enriched Uranium [HEU]; Plutonium; Uranium). Mirage IV strategic bombers entered production and would eventually provide one arm of the nascent French nuclear Triad. A land-based prototype of a nuclear submarine power plant was put into operation as the initial step in building a new generation of French nuclear-powered submarines to be equipped with nuclear-armed ballistic missiles. The French also began work on an intermediate-range ballistic missile intended to hold at risk targets well within the borders of the Soviet Union.

In February 1960, the French program produced its first French nuclear device. A plutonium fission device, when tested at Reggane in the Algerian Sahara Desert it had a yield of about 65 kilotons and was three times more powerful than the Trinity device tested by the United States in 1945 (*see* Fission Weapons; Trinity Site). De Gaulle had rejected the moratorium on atmospheric testing proposed by the United States and the United Kingdom, and in a stand that outraged environmentalists worldwide, France refused in 1963 to sign the Limited Test Ban Treaty banning atmospheric tests. Testing continued as weapons and test devices were mounted on barges or suspended from balloons at France's Pacific Testing Center in Polynesia. In August 1968, following delays in the uranium isotope-separation process under way at a nuclear complex in Pierrelatte, the French detonated their first fusion device (*see* Fusion; Limited Test Ban Treaty; Thermonuclear Bomb).

General de Gaulle closely monitored the construction of France's emerging nuclear arsenal. In July 1960, the minister for the armed forces presented to Parliament a four-year plan to construct Mirage IV bombers and a nuclear-powered ballistic missile submarine (SSBN) and called for more research into thermonuclear weapons. The first Mirage IV squadron became operational in October 1964 as part of the new nuclear bomber force that now included Boeing C-135F air-to-air refueling aircraft sold to France by the U.S. government. The tankers greatly increased the range of the Mirage IV, thereby increasing the ability of the Mirage to penetrate Soviet airspace by adopting low level or circuitous flight profiles that increased the survivability of the Mirages. Initially, the French military chose the Mirage IV bomber as its primary nuclear delivery system for the *Force de Frappe*. In 1967, the *Force de Frappe* became operational with sixty-two aircraft, each capable of delivering a 60-kiloton nuclear bomb.

To save time and money, de Gaulle incorporated U.S.-supplied enriched uranium in the development of the nuclear power plant for France's new submarine fleet. A second military budget act covering the period 1966–1970 financed the construction of two nuclear submarines and strategic ballistic surface-to-surface missiles buried in silos on the Plateau d'Albion in Provence. Both forces became operational in 1971. De Gaulle also decided, in

President Charles de Gaulle observes a French nuclear test in Polynesia, 1966. (Corbis Sygma)

1963, that France, like the United States, should procure tactical nuclear weapons to be deployed on Mirage III and Jaguar aircraft and Pluton tactical nuclear missile launchers forward-deployed in West Germany.

Political Rationale for the Force de Frappe

By 1967, expenditures on the nuclear arsenal peaked at about 50 percent of France's defense capital expenditures. This proportion decreased steadily during the following years. De Gaulle's nuclear objectives were essentially political: to restore France's "greatness" by making the French directly and fully responsible for their own defense. The same considerations prompted him to refuse all proposals to cooperate with NATO in its nuclear war plans: He refused to have medium-range missiles installed on French soil, and he rejected French participation in a NATO multilateral nuclear force. In 1958, he also breached a secret protocol negotiated under the Fourth Republic to begin nuclear cooperation with the Germans and Italians.

The general's overriding focus on political ends did not mean, however, that he took no interest in the strategy of deterrence as it applied to France: deterrence of the strong by the weak. What really counted for him was the determination of the "deciding party." He vested sole power to decide the use of France's nuclear arsenal in the Office of the President of the Republic. French doctrine reflects a concept of "nonemployment," that is, there is no question of using nuclear weapons in conflicts that do not threaten vital interests. Contrary to the NATO doctrine of flexible response, French doctrine did not incorporate the threat of gradual nuclear escalation to back up conventional deterrence. French nuclear doctrine is instead motivated by the effort to guarantee that France can deter an adversary by inflicting damage that is out of proportion to any benefits that could be achieved by attacking France. The French posture was one of immediate and massive retaliation once French territory was threatened.

The credibility of the French nuclear deterrent was of course in the mind of the beholder, but after about 1969 doubts emerged about the ability to make good on these deterrent threats. The ability of the fixed-site ballistic missiles to escape destruction if the Soviets struck first was suspect, and the ability of the Mirage IV to penetrate Soviet air defenses was questionable. French planners recognized these shortcomings and worked diligently to deploy a submarine-based deterrent force. Financial constraints and difficulties in development resulted in delays. In 1971, the first nuclear-armed submarine, *Le Redoutable,* became operational (*see* Credibility; Deterrence; Escalation; Flexible Response; Massive Retaliation).

French Forces and Doctrine after de Gaulle

A defense doctrine review ordered by President Giscard d'Estaing deemphasized the role of nuclear weapons in French defense strategy, although French scientists continued work on the next generation of nuclear weapons. Neutron warheads were developed, but never deployed, for the Hades short-range surface-to-surface missile system. Work also progressed on penetration aids for French ballistic missiles.

During the Euro-missile debate of the early 1980s, which was prompted by NATO's decision to upgrade its intermediate-range nuclear forces (INF), French and British officials refused to include their nuclear forces in the superpower INF talks in Geneva. The French government supported NATO's dual-track (negotiating while deploying) decision and its upgrades to its intermediate-range nuclear delivery systems. President François Mitterrand, who was wary of neutralist trends that had emerged in West Germany, all but endorsed the West German government's center-liberal proposals in the 1983 election to deploy both Pershing and ground-launched cruise missiles.

In the aftermath of the Cold War, French nuclear doctrine began to adjust to new strategic realities. The Mirage IV was retired, the missile field in the Plateau d'Albion was dismantled, and France settled on a dyad of systems: SSBNs and the Mirage 2000 and Super Entendard equipped with standoff cruise missiles. The Rafale will take their place as it enters service in the French Air Force and French Navy. Along with downsizing their nuclear forces, French officials have placed greater emphasis on developing improved space-based reconnaissance and communications capabilities. French nuclear weapons policy and doctrine have remained remarkably stable and consistent over the past thirty years through periods of government under right-wing, centrist, and socialist parties.

—*Gilles Van Nederveen*

See also: Strategic Forces; Submarine-Launched Ballistic Missiles; Submarines, Nuclear-Powered Ballistic Missile; Tous Asimuts

References

Fieldhouse, Richard W., Robert Norris, and Andrew S. Burrows, *Nuclear Weapons Databook, vol. 5: British, French, and Chinese Nuclear Weapons* (Boulder: Westview, 1994).

"France's Nuclear Weapons, from High Energy Weapons Archive," available at http://www.fas.org/nuke/hew/France/index.html.

"French Nuclear Weapons Policy after the Cold War," available at http://www.iris-france.org/francais/rdpresse/french%20nuclear.html.

Gordon, Philip, "France and Virtual Nuclear Deterrence," in Michael J. Mazarr, ed., *Nuclear Weapons in a Transformed World* (New York: St. Martin's Press, 1997), pp. 219–228.

Hopkins, John C., and Weixing Hu, *Strategic Views from the Second Tier: The Nuclear Weapons Policies of France, Britain, and China* (San Diego: Institute on Global Conflict and Cooperation, University of California, San Diego, 1994).

Norris, Robert S., and William M. Arkin, "NRDC Nuclear Notebook: French and British Nuclear Forces," *Bulletin of the Atomic Scientists,* September/October 2000, pp. 69–71.

Sabrosky, Alan Ned, "France," in Douglas J. Murray and Paul R. Viotti, eds., *The Defense Policies of Nations: A Comparative Study* (Baltimore: Johns Hopkins University Press, 1989), pp. 206–260.

Sublette, Carey, "Declared Nuclear States: Britain," from "Nuclear Weapons: Frequently Asked Questions," available at http://www.fas.org/nuke/hew/Nwfaq/Nfaq7-2.html#france.

Yost, David, "Nuclear Debates in France," *Survival,* Winter 1994–1995.

FUEL FABRICATION

Fuel fabrication is part of the nuclear fuel cycle, the process of converting uranium ore into the fissile isotope uranium 235 (U-235), which is used to generate electricity. Uranium ore is mined, milled, and converted into the gas uranium hexafluoride (UF_6) so that it can be enriched and fabricated into fuel. Different types of reactors require different types of nuclear fuel.

Light-water reactors can use two types of fuel. Some require low enriched uranium (LEU). To fabricate LEU, UF_6 is chemically processed to uranium dioxide powder, pressed into pellets, and loaded into

Zircaloy tubes. These fuel rods form the fuel assemblies that power the reactor. Plutonium and uranium, recovered by reprocessing spent fuel from light-water reactors, may be reused as fuel. Light-water reactors also may be fueled with mixed oxide, a combination of uranium dioxide and plutonium oxide. This second fuel-fabrication process offers an important way to render highly enriched uranium (HEU) contained in retired nuclear weapons less dangerous. The U.S. Department of Energy "down-blends" HEU taken from retired Russian and U.S. nuclear weapons with other uranium to create LEU reactor fuel.

Small reactors used for research, testing, and training that do not generate electrical power sometimes use specialized "plate" fuels. Plate-type fuel consists of several layers of various uranium mixtures that are packed into aluminum plates. Although HEU can be used to fuel these small reactors, proliferation concerns have discouraged the use of HEU in specialized reactor applications.

—*James J. Wirtz*

See also: Highly Enriched Uranium; Isotopes; Low
  Enriched Uranium; Nuclear Fuel Cycle; Plutonium;
  Reactor Operations; Uranium

Reference

Weaver, Lynne, and David Elliot, *Education and Research in the Nuclear Fuel Cycle* (Norman: University of Oklahoma Press, 1972).

FUSION

Fusion is the process by which one heavier nucleus is produced from two lighter nuclei. According to Albert Einstein's special theory of relativity, mass and energy are equivalent. In fusion, some of the mass of the two lighter nuclei is converted to energy. Fusion reactions power the sun and stars and are responsible for the enormous release of energy from a hydrogen bomb. The use of nuclear fusion reactions as a controlled source of energy is feasible, but there are significant engineering problems still to overcome.

The search for a safe, efficient, and plentiful source of energy has been ongoing since the very dawn of mankind. Our current energy of choice, obtained from fossil fuels, is finite. The promise of fission power as an energy source has faded somewhat owing to public concerns over nuclear waste disposal and the dangers of accidental radiation release. Fusion energy holds the promise of providing an inexhaustible energy supply that is safe, reliable,

efficient, economical, and environmentally friendly. This technology, however, is not yet mature. Significant problems still must be overcome.

The nucleus of an atom is held together by the strong force. This short-range attractive force acts as a sort of nuclear glue, counteracting the repulsive electrical force between positively charged protons. For fusion to occur, the two light nuclei must be brought into very close proximity. Since each nucleus has a net positive charge, the nuclei must overcome a very strong repulsive force, the "Coulomb barrier," before they can be brought close enough together to fuse. One way to overcome the Coulomb barrier is to raise the kinetic energy of the particles by increasing their temperature. A high density of light nuclei, along with a long confinement time, will ensure a high probability of collisions and the fusion rate necessary to produce useful amounts of energy. In stars these conditions exist naturally. To harness fusion power in a reactor, scientists and engineers must, in essence, re-create the conditions that exist in a star.

Owing to their availability and their interaction probability, the light elements of choice for producing usable energy in a fusion reactor are deuterium and tritium (D-T) in combination (*see* Deuterium; Tritium). Deuterium can be extracted from sea water, where 1 in 6,500 hydrogen atoms is deuterium. D_2O is known as "heavy water" (*see* Heavy Water). Tritium can be bred from lithium, which is abundant in the Earth's crust. Thus, the fuel for the fusion reaction is considered inexhaustible and accessible.

As the temperature of the D-T mix is raised, a gas-like mixture of electrons and ions, called a "plasma," is established. The plasma must be heated to nearly 100 million degrees Celsius to give the D-T particles sufficient kinetic energy to overcome the Coulomb barrier. Since the electrons and ions have electric charge, the plasma can, in principle, be confined by a magnetic field. The challenge is to confine the plasma in sufficient density for a long enough time for the reactions to take place, and for the energy to be extracted. One method for containing the high-temperature plasma is through use of a magnetic field that is toroidal, or doughnut-shaped. In the toroid, the plasma forms a continuous circuit and the particles are forced to follow a path along the magnetic field lines. The Russian-designed *tokamak* (a toroidal confinement machine) has been the most successful confinement approach. No material can withstand the high temperatures of a fusion plasma. Fusion plasmas cool quickly if they touch the wall of the vacuum chamber, however. The tokamak uses strong externally applied magnetic fields to contain the plasma and maintain separation from the chamber walls. Among many engineering challenges to be solved before controlled fusion reactions become commonplace is the development of materials that are resistant to high-energy particle bombardment, thermal stresses, and magnetic forces.

As a cost-effective way to further worldwide fusion research, and to demonstrate the essential technologies necessary for the eventual commercial production of fusion power, the international community is scheduled, in 2006, to begin building the International Thermonuclear Experimental Reactor (ITER). The ITER is a power reactor–scale fusion research project and is to be completed in 2014. The United States was a member of the original planning team (with Canada, the European Union, Japan, and Russia) but withdrew from the project in 1999 because of the ITER's high projected cost. Both the United States and China have recently rejoined the negotiations for the construction and operation of the ITER. In the United States, the National Ignition Facility at Lawrence Livermore National Laboratory is working to attain fusion ignition in the laboratory. This will provide the basis for future decisions about fusion's potential as a long-term energy source.

—*Brian Moretti*

See also: Deuterium; Reactor Operations

Reference

Tipler, P. A., and R. A. Llewellyn, *Modern Physics,* third edition (New York: W. H. Freeman, 1999).

FUSION WEAPONS

See Hydrogen Bomb; Implosion Devices; Thermonuclear Bomb

G

G8 GLOBAL PARTNERSHIP PROGRAM

The Global Partnership Against the Spread of Weapons and Materials of Mass Destruction is an initiative of the Group of Eight, a forum for eight industrialized countries (the G8, which includes the United States, the United Kingdom, Canada, France, Germany, Italy, Japan, and Russia). The Global Partnership Program is aimed at preventing terrorists from obtaining weapons of mass destruction by denying them access to material and personnel, in Russia, that could be used for that purpose.

At the 2002 G8 Summit in Kananaskis, Canada, the G8 countries committed to raise up to $20 billion over ten years to fund nonproliferation projects, primarily in Russia. Under the "10 plus 10 over 10" plan, the United States is to provide $10 billion, with the other half to come from the remaining G8 members over a ten-year period. The European Union, Norway, Sweden, Switzerland, Finland, the Netherlands, and Poland agreed to support the plan as donors in 2003, as did Australia, Belgium, the Czech Republic, Denmark, Ireland, the Republic of Korea, and New Zealand in 2004. The program focuses on four priority areas: destroying chemical weapons stockpiles, dismantling decommissioned nuclear submarines, securing nuclear and radiological materials, and finding civilian employment for former weapons scientists. As part of the initiative, G8 leaders established nonproliferation principles, guidelines for projects, and a Senior Officials Group to coordinate partnership programs. The partnership incorporates preexisting programs as well as new initiatives. At the June 2004 Sea Island, Georgia, summit, G8 leaders considered and supported in principle expanding the program to recipient countries other than Russia, including Ukraine and other former Soviet states, Iraq, Libya, and Albania.

Results to date have been mixed, with destruction of chemical stockpiles proceeding slowly and pledges, as of early 2004, just short of $20 billion. Disputes over liability protection, tax exemptions, and access to sensitive sites have hindered projects. The partnership, however, establishes a framework for increased cooperation to deal with the threat of terrorist acquisition of weapons of mass destruction.

—*Michael Lipson*

References

Canada, Department of Foreign Affairs and International Trade, "Global Partnership Program," available at http://www.dfait-maeci.gc.ca/foreign_policy/global_partnership/menu-en.asp.

Center for Strategic and International Studies, "Strengthening the Global Partnership Program," available at http://www.sgpproject.org.

Monterey Institute for International Studies, Center for Nonproliferation Studies, "Global Partnership Resource Page," available at http://cns.miis.edu/research/globpart/index.htm.

GAITHER COMMISSION REPORT

In November 1957, a committee of security experts and consultants chaired by H. Rowan Gaither, Jr., an attorney and RAND Corporation board member, submitted a secret report to President Dwight D. Eisenhower recommending a sharp increase in U.S. offensive and defensive capabilities to combat Soviet military and diplomatic initiatives. Eisenhower had organized the committee in response to growing debate on the need for civil defense measures. During its deliberations, the committee vastly expanded the scope of the study to include an overview of strategic policy. The committee consisted of twenty scientific, industrial, and military leaders as well as about seventy consultants. The final report, however, probably best reflected the views of two members of the group: Colonel

George A. Lincoln, who had coordinated strategic planning during World War II, and Paul H. Nitze, who had served on the Policy Planning Staff in the State Department under President Harry S. Truman and was a sharp critic of Eisenhower's New Look strategy of massive retaliation.

The Gaither Commission Report stressed an emerging Soviet threat, including an operational Soviet intercontinental ballistic missile. It called for increasing the U.S. missile arsenal, reducing bomber vulnerability, enhancing the ability to fight limited wars, implementing a nationwide system of civil-defense shelters, and reorganizing the military to address emerging threats. The report estimated these goals would require a $44 billion increase in defense spending over four years.

The report's impact has been debated. Eisenhower and others rejected some of its assumptions on Soviet capabilities. The president also was opposed to massive budget increases. The United States did, however, launch a major buildup of its strategic nuclear forces in the late 1950s and 1960s. Other factors, such as a gradual loss of faith in massive retaliation and the Soviet launch of Sputnik just prior to the report's completion, make it difficult to assess whether the report changed views or only reinforced perceptions that would have led to a U.S. nuclear buildup in any case. Some scholars argue that the report was central to shifts in planning under Eisenhower and even more influential in the incoming John F. Kennedy administration. President Kennedy read the report and brought some of its authors into his administration. The report's critical assessment of the efficacy of basing U.S. defense policy on a deterrence strategy helped lend weight to early arms control efforts.

—*James J. Dietrich*

See also: Cold War; Deterrence; Massive Retaliation

References

Rearden, Steven L., "Reassessing the Gaither Report's Role," *Diplomatic History,* vol. 25, 2001, pp. 153–157.

Snead, David L., *The Gaither Committee, Eisenhower, and the Cold War* (Columbus: Ohio State University Press, 1999).

GAME THEORY

Game theory is useful in conducting systematic analyses of the interdependent effects of actors' decisions in strategic planning and wartime responses.

It can help theorists to understand the potential for use of weapons of mass destruction (WMD) and related topics such as mutual assured destruction, deterrence, extended deterrence, and credible threats. In game theory, two (or more) rational players simultaneously choose actions that maximize their expected payoffs. The particular payoffs players receive depend on their own choices as well as those of the other players. Recognizing this interdependence, players anticipate the behavior of the other players when choosing their actions. Game theorists predict behavior by determining the game's equilibrium outcomes, that is, the joint outcomes where players cannot unilaterally improve their payoffs. Analyzed through mathematical deduction, game theory models identify the implications of a particular set of assumptions. Games are theoretical, not empirical, but some can be tested using statistical, qualitative, or computer-simulation analyses. Game theoretic arguments are precise, necessarily logical (that is, the arguments flow from the assumptions), and sometimes result in counterintuitive or surprising implications.

Games used to motivate WMD topics commonly involve two players choosing between two choices, such as whether or not to increase funding for nuclear weapons development (Schelling; for problems with this type of theorizing, see Wagner). The most famous game is the Prisoner's Dilemma, where two players are taken prisoner and given the choice of implicating their partner or remaining silent. This game is unusual in that regardless of the prisoners' anticipation of what their partner will do (talk or remain silent), they each have an incentive to talk. This situation represents a "dominant strategy," where a choice is superior regardless of one's expectations of the other players' actions (Morrow). When applied to nuclear deterrence during the Cold War, the Prisoner's Dilemma, for many theorists, represented the pressures that led to the race between the superpowers to arm themselves with larger and more sophisticated nuclear arsenals.

Game theory has a number of implications for studies of weapons of mass destruction. First, the value of an action is not intrinsic to that choice but also depends on what one expects others to do, since the payoff received is the result of the decisions of all the players. Conversely, in situations represented by games such as the Prisoner's Dilemma, there may be "dominant" strategies that represent superior choices regardless of an adversary's actions. However, efforts such as reputation building and repeat interaction may moderate these dominant-strategy situations and facilitate cooperation (Axelrod). Recent game theoretic treatments of deterrence focus on the information necessary for actors to *signal credible threats* (Powell). These models are sometimes known as "signaling games" and "games of limited or incomplete information," and although they can be quite complex mathematically they reflect a more realistic and interesting decision-making environment. Some studies show that players can gain a signaling advantage by appearing to eliminate their own ability to act. Thus, states in some deterrence situations might have incentives to create automatic processes for the use of their nuclear weapons (*see* Chicken, Game of). Finally, game theory illustrates the importance of thinking about the choices that players do not make—a concept called "off-the-equilibrium-path behavior." Analyses suggest that expectations about the consequences of unobserved choices influence the behavior that we do observe. Off-the-equilibrium-path behavior theories are especially effective at capturing the important difference in studies of deterrence between threatening to use weapons of mass destruction and actually using them, and the concept can also help to link arguments about selection effects (having weapons of mass destruction) and behavior (employing them).

—*Scott Sigmund Gartner*

See also: Credibility; Deterrence; Extended Deterrence; Mutual Assured Destruction

References

Axelrod, Robert, *The Evolution of Cooperation* (New York: Basic, 1984).

Morrow, James D., *Game Theory for Political Scientists* (Princeton, NJ: Princeton University Press, 1994).

Powell, Robert, *Nuclear Deterrence Theory: The Search for Credibility* (New York: Cambridge University Press, 1990).

Schelling, Thomas C., *The Strategy of Conflict* (New York: Oxford University Press, 1960).

Wagner, Harrison R., "The Theory of Games and the Problem of International Cooperation," *American Political Science Review*, vol. 77, 1983, pp. 330–346.

GAMMA RAYS
See Radiation

GAS-GRAPHITE REACTORS

A gas-graphite reactor is a graphite-moderated, gas-cooled atomic reactor used for developing electrical power. Compared to other types of reactors, gas-graphite reactors enjoy greater thermal efficiency (generally between 40 and 50 percent).

The first commercial nuclear power reactor to provide electricity was a Magnox-type gas-graphite reactor at Calder Hall in Cumbria, England, in 1956. The cladding material, which contains the natural uranium fuel, is a magnesium alloy called Magnox.

In the 1950s and 1960s, gas-graphite reactors were built in the United Kingdom, France, Italy, and Japan. The advanced gas reactor (AGR) was developed by the United Kingdom in 1964. The British built five AGR nuclear power plants in England and two in Scotland.

In 1967, the United States developed the high-temperature gas-cooled reactor (HTGR). Germany developed and built HTGRs in the 1980s. North Korea built three Magnox-type gas-graphite reactors in the mid-1980s to mid-1990s. South Africa developed the pebble-bed modular reactor (PBMR) design in the 1990s.

The coolant used in gas-graphite reactors is usually carbon dioxide (CO_2). CO_2 is used because it has a low absorption cross-section for thermal neutrons and does not react with the moderator or the fuel at temperatures below 540 degrees Celsius. The AGR is graphite moderated and CO_2-gas cooled. The fuel is slightly enriched uranium in stainless steel cladding.

HTGRs are helium-cooled reactors fueled with a mixture of thorium and highly enriched uranium. PBMRs are helium-cooled reactors that use graphite-coated, enriched-uranium fuel spheres.

South Africa is constructing a PBMR-type reactor that is scheduled to begin operation in 2007. The United States and Japan are conducting research into PBMR technology.

—*Don Gillich*

See also: Enrichment; Graphite; Highly Enriched Uranium; Reactor Operations; Uranium

References

Lamarsh, John R., and Anthony J. Baratta, *Introduction to Nuclear Engineering,* third edition (New York: Prentice-Hall, 2001).

Nero, Anthony V., *A Guidebook to Nuclear Reactors* (Berkeley: University of California Press, 1979).

GEIGER COUNTER

The Geiger counter, also known as a Geiger-Mueller counter, is an instrument used to detect and measure all three types of radioactivity (alpha, beta, and gamma radiation). It was invented by Hans Geiger and Ernest Rutherford in Manchester, England, in 1911 and later improved by Geiger and Walther Mueller in 1928.

Radioactive materials emit particles called "fast electrons" (electrons that have been accelerated to about a third of the speed of light) and "ions" (atoms that have gained or lost an electron). A Geiger counter usually consists of a gas-filled metal tube with a thin metal wire running through it. Each of these metal pieces serves as an electrode. The electrons and ions emitted by the radioactive material penetrate the tube and are attracted to electrons from the atoms of gas, thus "ionizing" the gas. Ionized gas conducts electricity, completing an electrical circuit between the two electrodes. The current created is amplified electronically to produce a series of clicks that alert the user to the presence of radiation. The amount of radiation present can be counted because every particle passing through the tube produces a separate pulse.

Geiger counters could quickly and easily be used to detect radiation emitted through the detonation of a radiological weapon, thus allowing the identification of harmful materials that otherwise could not be seen and warning of the presence and the level of danger to people in the area. Using a Geiger counter would be a quick way to determine the difference between a conventional explosion and a dirty bomb.

—*Andrea Gabbitas*

See also: Radiation
Reference
Lawrence Livermore National Laboratory website, http://www.lbl.gov/abc/.

GENEVA, SWITZERLAND

See Arms Control

GLOBAL PROTECTION AGAINST LIMITED STRIKES (GPALS)

Global Protection Against Limited Strikes (GPALS) was the George H. W. Bush administration's effort to reorient its ballistic missile defense program away from the threat of a massive Soviet attack and toward the threat posed by accidental and unauthorized missile launches and small attacks by Third World countries.

The end of the Cold War and the collapse of the Soviet Union reduced the likelihood of the United States suffering a massive nuclear attack. The 1991 Gulf War demonstrated that shorter-range missiles posed a threat to U.S. friends, allies, and forces abroad. In his 1991 State of the Union Address, President Bush announced that he had directed the Strategic Defense Initiative (SDI) program to focus on providing protection against limited ballistic missile strikes, whatever their source (*see* Strategic Defense Initiative [SDI]). Henceforth, ballistic missile defense would deal with future threats "to the United States, our forces overseas and to our friends and allies."

The ensuing concept, dubbed GPALS, was intended to defend against an accidental or unauthorized missile launch from Russia or a small volley of missiles launched from another country. The system's goal was to protect the United States against a strike of up to 200 warheads launched from anywhere in the world. It also put a greater emphasis on theater missile defense (TMD) (*see* Theater Missile Defense).

Three main components were to be included in GPALS: a ground-based TMD, a ground-based national missile defense (NMD), and a space-based global missile defense (GMD). NMD would include 750 ground-based interceptors (GBIs) deployed at six sites in the United States to defend against accidental and unauthorized strikes from any source. GMD would be composed of 1,000 space-based "Brilliant Pebbles" satellites to destroy missiles with ranges greater than a few hundred miles. TMD systems would be deployed to protect U.S. forces overseas, friends, and allies.

Spearheaded by Senators Sam Nunn (D–GA) and John Warner (R–VA), Congress passed the Missile Defense Act of 1991, which called for the deployment by 1996 of a 100-interceptor antiballistic missile site "as the initial step" toward the fielding of a nationwide defense. The Bush administration also pursued the possibility of using GPALS as the nucleus of a joint U.S.-Russian missile defense system (*see* Missile Defense).

After the William Clinton administration took office in 1993, it replaced GPALS with a ballistic missile defense architecture that emphasized NMD and TMD and deemphasized space-based defenses such as Brilliant Pebbles.

—*Tom Mahnken*

Reference

Cooper, Amb Henry F., "Limited Ballistic Missile Strikes: GPALS Comes Up with an Answer," *NATO Review*, vol. 40, no. 3, June 1992, pp. 27–30.

GRAPHITE

Graphite is used as a moderator and reflector of neutrons in some nuclear reactors because of its low mass number, low absorption, and high scattering cross-sections. Even though it is not a metal, graphite is a good conductor of heat. It also is abundant in nature and inexpensive.

Enrico Fermi achieved the first nuclear chain reaction at Stagg Field Stadium, Chicago, on December 2, 1942, using a "pile" of natural uranium and approximately 400 tons of graphite as the moderator. Graphite also was used as the moderator for the Hanford "B" reactor in Hanford, Washington. Hanford "B" provided the plutonium for the implosion devices tested at the Trinity Site and dropped on Nagasaki, Japan, in 1945.

The RBMK-1000 type nuclear reactor at Chernobyl in the former Soviet Union was a graphite-moderated reactor. During the accident at Chernobyl on April 25–26, 1986, a rapid energy release from the fuel caused the graphite to ignite. The subsequent graphite fire destroyed the containment facility and spread radioactive contamination into the atmosphere and surrounding area (*see* Chernobyl).

Natural graphite is not pure enough to be used in nuclear reactors. Reactor-grade graphite is manufactured from a mixture of petroleum coke and coal tar pitch through a baking process. Reactor-grade graphite has a density of approximately 1.6 grams per cubic centimeter.

—*Don Gillich*

See also: Gas-Graphite Reactors; Hanford, Washington; Reactor Operations; Uranium

References

Glasstone, Samuel, and Alexander Sesonske, *Nuclear Reactor Engineering* (Princeton, NJ: D. Van Nostrand, 1967).

GRAVITY BOMBS

A "gravity bomb," also known as a "dumb bomb," is an aircraft-delivered bomb that does not contain a guidance system but free-falls to its target. The United States carries a wide variety of gravity bombs in its arsenal (*see* Tactical Nuclear Weapons).

MK-80 series bombs are typically armed with the M904 nose and M905 tail fuses or the radar-proximity FMU-113 air-burst fuse. The MK-80s also can be fitted with a "ballute" parachute to retard the fall of the bomb. MK-80s can been used against a wide variety of targets, including artillery, vehicles, bunkers, missile sites, antiaircraft artillery sites, radars, and supply depots. There are many different sizes in the MK-80 series of bombs, which differ in terms of their weight and the size of the blast they produce. The MK-82 is a 500-pound bomb, the MK-83 is a 1,000-pound bomb, and the MK-84 is a 2,000-pound bomb.

Most cluster bombs used by the United States are gravity bombs. Cluster bombs open at a fixed height above a target area and then disperse dozens of small "bomblets," which are occasionally retarded by parachutes. These bomblets drop in a preplanned pattern into the target zone. Filled with explosives, they are usually scattered over hundreds of square meters and detonate individually. Typically, cluster bombs are used against "softer targets," namely personnel and equipment that lacks armor protection.

—*Abe Denmark*

Reference

"Weapon Systems in Use by U.S.," available at http://www.fas.org/terrorism/str.

GROUND-LAUNCHED CRUISE MISSILES (GLCMs)

The ground-launched cruise missile (GLCM) is a mobile, highly accurate, land-attack, precision-guided combination of airframe and munition that flies to its target along a preprogrammed flight path. It can be armed with either nuclear or conventional weapons. A 1979 North Atlantic Treaty Organization (NATO) decision to deploy a new generation of theater nuclear forces, including GLCMs, exacerbated tension with the Warsaw Pact and led to a revival of the peace movement and a series of mass protests throughout Europe. By 1987, before the full deployment was carried out, the Intermediate-Range Nuclear Forces (INF) Treaty was signed by the United States and the Soviet Union, halting NATO INF modernization (*see* Intermediate-Range Nuclear Forces [INF] Treaty).

A ground-launched cruise missile being test fired from its camouflaged transporter-erector-launcher, 1985. (Tech. Sgt. Bill Thompson/Corbis)

With its 1979 decision to deploy 108 Pershing II ballistic missiles and 464 GLCMs to five NATO members, NATO aimed to replace the existing force of obsolete strike aircraft and Pershing I missiles with longer-range, more accurate weapons to restore the credibility of the long-range theater nuclear force and counter the deployment of Soviet SS-20 missiles.

GLCMs, like the sea-launched cruise missiles (SLCMs) and air-launched cruise missiles (ALCMs) initially deployed by the United States in the late 1970s, were subsonic, terrain-following aircraft designed to fly a preset course up to a range of 2,500 kilometers. They were deployed in groups of four on transporters with an ability to maneuver off-roads. Four transporters formed a flight of missiles. The planned deployment was to Italy, the United Kingdom, the Netherlands, and Belgium.

The system was eliminated under the INF Treaty. GLCM bases in Europe remain subject to inspection.

—*Andrew M. Dorman*

References

Garthoff, Raymond, *Détente and Confrontation* (Washington, DC: Brookings Institution, 1985).

Schwartz, David N., *NATO's Nuclear Dilemmas* (Washington, DC: Brookings Institution, 1983).

GROUND ZERO

Ground zero is the epicenter of a nuclear explosion and the area of maximum damage produced by the heat and blast of a nuclear detonation. The areas referred to as "ground zero" at Hiroshima, Nagasaki, and the test areas at the Nevada Test Site designate exactly where nuclear explosions occurred. As a reference to the total destruction of the World Trade Center on September 11, 2001, rescue workers quickly dubbed the area where the Twin Towers stood as "ground zero," suggesting that the level of devastation resembled the aftermath of a nuclear attack (*see* Hiroshima; Nagasaki; Nevada Test Site).

In the aftermath of a nuclear detonation, destruction will radiate outward from ground zero as the surrounding area is struck by an initial blast wave and a secondary reflected wave. Objects that are in the path of the blast waves are susceptible to sharp and severe increases in atmospheric pressure and severe winds. Residual effects following a nuclear blast at ground zero include high levels of radiation (*see* Nuclear Weapons Effects; Radiation; Underground Testing).

Ground zero, or Designated Ground Zero (DGZ), is a term used by nuclear war planners to identify the exact aim point where a nuclear weapon is targeted. DGZs are selected to maximize damage to targets within the destructive range of the weapon. A key variable in varying the nuclear weapons effects surrounding the DGZ is the weapon's "height of burst," or the altitude at which the weapon detonates.

In an example of black humor, the central courtyard of the Pentagon in Washington, D.C., has a small snack bar in the middle sometimes referred to as the "Ground Zero Café."

—*Laura Fontaine and James J. Wirtz*

Reference

"Nuclear Weapon Blast Effects," 21 October 1998, available at http://www.fas.org/nuke/intro/nuke/blast.htm.

GUN-TYPE DEVICES

A gun-type device creates a supercritical mass of fissionable material, uranium 235 (U-235), to produce a nuclear explosion. This technique involves the use of conventional propellants or explosives to drive a subcritical, fissionable projectile into a second subcritical, fissionable target to achieve a supercritical mass. The technique also can entail using more than two subcritical masses that are brought together rapidly to achieve a nuclear explosion.

The first nuclear weapon ever used in combat was the gun-type device "Little Boy," the bomb dropped by the United States on Hiroshima, Japan, on August 6, 1945 (*see* Hiroshima; Little Boy). Its explosive yield was approximately 15,000 tons of TNT. The gun-assembly method of attaining a supercritical mass was considered to be so infallible, and highly enriched uranium so valuable, that the Little Boy designers chose not to test the bomb prior to its use. In fact, the Little Boy weapon used the entire stockpile of highly enriched uranium in the United States at the time of its construction (*see* Highly Enriched Uranium [HEU]; Uranium).

Unlike the implosion technique for attaining a supercritical mass, the gun-assembly method is inefficient because it does not compress the fissionable material to achieve greater density (*see* Criticality and Critical Mass). Although it was an inefficient way to achieve nuclear fission, the United States

used the gun-assembly method to develop special-purpose weapons, such as penetration weapons for subsurface detonations and early tactical nuclear weapons, including artillery-fired atomic projectiles (AFAPs). Because of the simplicity of the design, the gun-type device has been used by other countries and is the weapon of choice for emerging nuclear weapons states.

History and Background

After the discovery of fission in late 1938, there was much debate about the possibility of harnessing the energy of fission to make a nuclear weapon. Otto Frisch and Rudolf Peierls authored a memorandum in February 1940 that served as the impetus for the development of the gun-type device. In the Frisch-Peierls Memorandum, the authors discuss the possibility of constructing a "super bomb" using a "critical size" of pure U-235. They describe how to keep two (or more) subcritical pieces of uranium apart to avoid the possibility of premature detonation due to stray neutrons. They also discuss providing a mechanism to bring the two parts together rapidly to achieve a nuclear explosion. Frisch and Peierls were living in the United Kingdom at the time, and they submitted their manuscript through Mark Oliphant, the director of the physics department at the University of Birmingham, to Henry Tizard, the chairman of a scientific committee devoted to the defense of the UK.

In April 1940, Tizard formed a separate group, known as the MAUD Committee, to discuss the possibility of building a nuclear weapon. The MAUD Committee's final report, composed before the group disbanded in July 1941, concluded that nuclear weapons were feasible and that the development of this type of weapon could result in decisive victory in World War II. It also provided technical details about the amount of uranium necessary and the expected yield as well as cost estimates to build a nuclear weapon.

Based on the findings of the MAUD Report, President Franklin D. Roosevelt decided to expand support for a U.S. program to develop nuclear weapons. After a slow start, the U.S. nuclear bomb project was consolidated in September 1942 into the Manhattan Project, which was led by Major General Leslie Groves and Professor J. Robert Oppenheimer (*see* Manhattan Project). Groves and Oppenheimer created a laboratory at Los Alamos, New Mexico. As scientists arrived at Los Alamos, theoretical physicist Robert Serber gave a series of lectures designed to sum up the current knowledge of nuclear weapons design. As part of these lectures, Serber outlined the gun-assembly method of creating a supercritical mass of fissionable material through the use of a cylindrical projectile fired into a spherical target. These lectures were later published as the *Los Alamos Primer* (1992).

The original plan was to use the gun-assembly method to attain a supercritical mass for both uranium 235 and plutonium 239. The Los Alamos Ordnance Division under Navy Captain William Parsons was in charge of directing gun-type weapons research. Early research focused on developing a gun with a very high velocity, greater than 3,000 feet per second, to assemble a critical mass of plutonium. Plutonium has a high spontaneous fission rate, which means that a high muzzle velocity would be required to assemble a supercritical mass before the plutonium could predetonate, resulting in low or no nuclear yield.

In April 1944, Italian physicist and emigrant Emilio Segrè, who was working on the Manhattan Project, measured the spontaneous fission rate of plutonium and found that it was much higher than previously thought owing to the existence of trace amounts plutonium 140, which contaminated the plutonium. As a result, the plutonium gun-type weapon was abandoned, and the implosion technique would be used to achieve a supercritical mass for a plutonium-based weapon. A crash program to develop the implosion device required a complete reorganization of effort in the Manhattan Project.

In August 1944, Navy Commander A. Francis Birch was given the responsibility of completing the uranium gun-type weapon dubbed Little Boy. Birch completed testing of the Little Boy gun tube using natural uranium. By May 1945, the design and testing of the weapon were complete; the only component missing was the highly enriched uranium core. In July 1945, approximately 60 kilograms of highly enriched uranium was fabricated into both target and projectile and the first gun-type weapon was ready for use.

After World War II, several designs of gun-type weapons were developed. The gun-type weapons Mark 8, 10, and 11 were developed as penetrating weapons to be used against armored, reinforced, or underground targets. Early gun-type AFAPs also were developed. The first AFAPs were the Mark 9 and Mark 19, which were 11-inch-diameter artillery shells. An 11-inch howitzer had to be designed and built to accommodate these new nuclear weapons, since the largest howitzer in the army at the time was only 8 inches in diameter. Another AFAP was the Mark 23, a 16-inch-diameter projectile designed for naval guns. By the mid-1950s, the Mark 33, a gun-type, 8-inch AFAP, had been designed and tested for the army's 8-inch howitzer.

Technical Details

Timing in a gun-type weapon, as with any nuclear weapon, is critical because it largely determines the amount of energy yield that can be achieved given a specific quantity of fissile material. Each generation of neutrons takes approximately 10 nanoseconds to generate once the supercritical chain reaction is started. The challenge is to create as many generations of neutrons as possible before the device explodes due to the heat and pressures produced by fission. To produce an appreciable yield, it is desirable to hold the supercritical chain reaction together for 50 to 100 generations, that is, 0.5 to 1 microseconds. Consequently, there are several basic components to a gun-type device that are necessary for its proper function in addition to the subcritical, fissionable target and projectile.

One basic component is a neutron initiator that must be present to provide a large number of initial neutrons to generate the explosive chain reaction at the precise time that the mass becomes supercritical. In the case of Little Boy, this initiator consisted of polonium and beryllium. When crushed together, polonium emits large numbers of alpha particles that are energetic enough to separate neutrons from the beryllium. This provides the first generation of neutrons as the supercritical mass begins the explosive chain reaction.

The supercritical mass is usually a sphere. A sphere is used because compared to all other solid shapes from which neutrons can escape, it has the smallest surface area. The more neutrons that are available to the supercritical mass, the more fissions will occur, and thereby, more energy will result. Another basic component of a gun-type device is the use of a reflector. A reflector is a metal shield that surrounds the spherical supercritical mass with the purpose of reflecting neutrons back into the core.

The material for a reflector should have a high probability of scattering neutrons back into the core, that is, it requires a high scattering cross-section and a low absorption cross-section.

A "tamper" is a layer of heavy metal that surrounds the reflector and fissionable core in order to contain the core long enough to obtain an appreciable yield of energy. As the explosive chain reaction takes places, the heat and pressure of fission forces the fissionable material apart, thereby stopping the chain reaction. The tamper holds the supercritical mass together long enough to achieve the desired yield.

An example of early gun-type devices, the Little Boy bomb weighed 8,900 pounds and was 126 inches long and 28 inches in diameter. The main sections of this bomb included the nose section, which contained the fissionable target, a 3-inch-diameter cannon barrel, and the breechblock of the cannon. A 6-inch-thick steel and tungsten carbide tamper weighing 5,000 pounds was in the nose section surrounding the fissionable target. The smooth-bore cannon barrel was 6 feet long, made of steel, and weighed about 1,000 pounds. A hole in the breechblock allowed for the projectile and propellant to be inserted. Later gun-type weapons were improvements to this first weapon in terms of efficiency, yield, size, and weight.

The low efficiency of the gun-type weapon was expected from the Little Boy explosion and illustrates one of the disadvantages of using this method to assemble a supercritical mass: It wastes highly enriched fissionable material. The amount of fissionable material necessary to make a gun-type weapon is two to three times the amount needed to make an implosion weapon. Another disadvantage to using the gun-assembly method is that it is based on a "single point detonation" device that is not safe in terms of accidental detonation. Implosion devices can be "two or more points safe" (that is, they can withstand explosive shocks in more than one direction without going supercritical). The timing of the initiator is another drawback to gun devices because the time at which the initiator functions cannot be controlled as precisely as in the implosion technique.

There are distinct advantages to the gun-type devices. The most important advantage is that the simplicity of the device increases its reliability. Early gun-type devices also were smaller and lighter than the implosion devices, making their delivery easier. Finally, since gun-type devices generally have a smaller diameter than implosion devices of the same yield, the gun-assembly method has been used to develop all U.S. weapons designed specifically for subsurface bursts.

Developing Technologies

Although there is a moratorium on developing new U.S. nuclear weapons, strategists and military officers in the United States often speak about the need to develop a precision-guided, "bunker buster" nuclear weapon that could hold at risk deeply buried and hardened targets. The gun-assembly method of creating a supercritical mass may be the preferred method for this application.

Emerging nuclear states are more likely to develop nuclear weapons utilizing a gun-type device to create a supercritical mass than they are to develop implosion weapons because the design is simpler and they can be developed without testing. Nonstate actors such as terrorist organizations also may strive to develop gun-type devices for the same reasons. Technology is not a stumbling block in creating a gun-type device. What slows and complicates the construction of this type of weapon is the need for large quantities of highly enriched uranium to create a supercritical mass.

—Don Gillich

See also: Fission Weapons; Implosion Devices; Proliferation

References

Cochran, Thomas B., William M. Arkin, and Milton M. Hoenig, "Chapter Two: Nuclear Weapons Primer," in *Nuclear Weapons Databook*, vol. 1: *U.S. Nuclear Forces and Capabilities* (Cambridge, MA: Ballinger, 1984), pp. 22–36.

Hansen, Chuck, *Swords of Armageddon* (Sunnyvale, CA: Chukelea, 1996).

Rhodes, Richard, *The Making of the Atomic Bomb* (New York: Simon and Schuster, 1986).

Serber, Robert, *The Los Alamos Primer* (Berkeley: University of California Press, 1992).

HALF-LIFE

"Half-life" is defined as the time in which half of the radioactive nuclei in a radioactive substance will disintegrate or decay. A specific rate of radioactive decay is characteristic of each radionuclide. It is the time required for the disintegration of one-half of the radioactive atoms present when measurement starts. It does not represent a fixed number of atoms that disintegrate, but a fraction of the total number of atoms that were present at the measurement.

Radioactive elements are unstable and can decay spontaneously, causing them to produce radiation. Half of the residue present in a radioactive substance will disintegrate in another equal period of time and decay into another form. When several half-lives of a radioactive substance occur, only a fraction of the original radionuclides remains. Half-lives can range from a few seconds to hundreds of years depending on the type of radionuclide. Another term for half-life is "decay constant."

—*Laura Fontaine*

See also: Depleted Uranium (U-238); Isotopes; Plutonium; Radiation; Uranium

References

Brodine, Virginia, *Radioactive Contamination* (New York: Harcourt Brace Janovich, 1975).

"Radioactive Waste Primer," available at http://www.emnrd.state.nm.us/wipp/radprimer.htm

U.S. Nuclear Regulatory Commission, "Fact Sheet: Plutonium," October 2003.

HANFORD, WASHINGTON

Facilities at Hanford, Washington, were originally constructed in 1943 to produce plutonium for the first of America's atomic weapons. The facility is located on about 560 square miles of land astride the Columbia River in south central Washington state, near the city of Richland. The site's remoteness helped maintain the secrecy necessary for its work, and the river provided the water for cooling its reactors. By the 1960s there were nine reactors

in operation at Hanford, only one of which supplied electricity to the civilian grid. The rest of the reactors were devoted to producing plutonium for weapons.

Hanford has proven to be environmentally problematic because it was built in haste and at a time when the problems associated with handling radioactive materials were little understood and production techniques related to weapons-grade plutonium were in their infancy. Mistakes were made. Radioactive waste was not disposed of properly. It was initially poured into water basins and storage tanks located at the Hanford site that eventually allowed radioactive and other toxic substances to leak into the surrounding soil and aquifers. Radioactive gases also were accidentally vented into the atmosphere.

Over the years, Hanford is reputed to have released more radioactivity than did the Soviet reactor accident at Chernobyl in 1986. The reactors at Hanford were finally shut down in 1980 because of concerns about their effect on the local environment. Ever since its closure, thousands of people have been employed at Hanford to clean up the facility.

—*Rod Thornton*

See also: Chernobyl; Manhattan Project; Plutonium; Radiation; Reactor Operations

References

Lanier-Graham, Susan, *The Ecology of War* (New York: Walker and Company, 1993).

Makhijani, Arjun, Howard Hu, and Katherine Yih, eds., *Nuclear Wastelands: A Global Guide to Nuclear Weapons Production and Its Health and Environmental Effects* (Cambridge, MA: MIT Press, 1995).

Steel drums full of class-A low-level radioactive waste buried in a large trench at the Hanford Nuclear Reservation. (Roger Ressmeyer/Corbis)

HARD AND DEEPLY BURIED TARGETS

Hard and deeply buried targets (HDBTs) are facilities that have been designed and constructed to make them difficult to identify, target, and defeat using currently available conventional weapons. Potential adversaries increasingly use such facilities to produce and store nuclear, biological, and chemical (NBC) weapons and to house military command and control centers. There are two categories of HDBTs. One is hardened by placing soil, concrete, and rock boulders atop a structure once it has been built. These "cut-and-cover" facilities are often built into an excavation and then covered. The other category includes tunnels and deep shafts, where protection is provided by existing rock and soil. There is a depth threshold at which it becomes more economical to tunnel rather than to excavate and cover. Below this threshold, costs generally are constant regardless of the depth of the tunnel, so tunneled facilities can exist hundreds of meters below the surface.

Tunneling has become the method of choice for NBC weapons producers because of the limitations of Western weapons capabilities to destroy deeply buried targets with conventional weapons and the increasing availability of advanced tunneling technologies. Hardened surface and cut-and-cover facilities may be vulnerable to existing air-to-surface penetrating weapons, but facilities housed in tunnels are nearly invulnerable to direct attack by conventional means. For this reason, the United States has explored numerous weapons options and damage or functional-kill mechanisms. One is to attack the tunnel portals with weapons that penetrate into the thinner cover rock above the portal or through the exterior doors, resulting in an internal detonation that can damage NBC weapons housed within deep tunnels.

—*Peter Lavoy*

Reference

Office of the Secretary of Defense, *Proliferation: Threat and Response* (Washington, DC: U.S. Government Printing Office, January 2001).

HARDENING

See Silo Basing

HARMEL REPORT

In the mid-1960s, the warming of East-West relations raised questions about the relevance of the North Atlantic Treaty Organization (NATO). Following the proposal of Belgian Foreign Minister Pierre Harmel, the December 1966 meeting of NATO foreign ministers commissioned a year-long study on "The Future Tasks of the Alliance." NATO allies adopted the Harmel Report in December 1967. It declared that NATO's mission was to seek détente with the Soviet Union and the Warsaw Pact as well as mounting deterrence against the Soviet threat and defense against a potential Warsaw Pact attack. Cold War negotiations for the Conference on Security and Cooperation in Europe (CSCE) and Mutual and Balanced Force Reduction (MBFR) grew out of NATO's Harmel initiative.

The Harmel Report stated that the alliance had "two main functions." The first was "to maintain adequate military strength and political solidarity to deter aggression and other forms of pressure and to defend the territory of member countries if aggression should occur." The second, and newly assigned, function of the alliance was "to pursue the search for progress towards a more stable relationship [with the East] in which the underlying political issues can be solved" (Sloan, p. 48).

NATO has continued the Harmel Report's mission by promoting post–Cold War arms control initiatives, particularly concerning weapons of mass destruction, establishing partnerships with all interested European states, and inviting qualified countries to join the alliance.

—*Stanley R. Sloan*

See also: Détente; Deterrence; Dual-Track Decision
References
Harmel Report, available at the North Atlantic Treaty Organization (NATO) website, http://www.nato.int/docu/basictxt/b671213a.htm.
Sloan, Stanley R., *NATO, the European Union and the Atlantic Community: The Transatlantic Bargain Reconsidered* (Lanham, MD: Rowman and Littlefield, 2002).

HEAVY BOMBERS

Rising to prominence during World War II, heavy bombers are aircraft with multiple engines, long range, and the ability to carry large quantities of munitions. They played a major role early in the Cold War, when their intercontinental ranges and enhanced payload capacities made them a key element in U.S. and Soviet nuclear deterrent forces.

Although their prominence diminished with the development of intercontinental ballistic missiles and submarine-launched ballistic missiles, heavy bombers possessed two important characteristics those systems did not: flexibility during missions and the ability to be recalled once launched. They were vulnerable to attack, while on the ground, however, because of the time required from the decision to launch to the moment of "escape" from their bases, and vulnerable in the air because of steadily improving air defenses. Heavy bombers also were slower to reach their targets than ballistic missiles, with flight times between U.S. bomber bases and Moscow measured in hours instead of minutes.

To overcome these weaknesses, the U.S. bomber force was placed on constant alert to avoid being surprised, and improvements were made to their survivability. For example, to evade Soviet air defenses, the B-52 was given a standoff mission, allowing it to fire long-range nuclear-armed cruise missiles at its targets outside the range of Soviet air defenses. Additionally, the B-1 was designed to fly fast and low to avoid air defenses, and the B-2 "stealth bomber" was designed to make it difficult to detect by radar.

With the end of the Cold War, heavy bombers began to play a greater role in conventional military operations. Their long range and high payloads again made them the weapon of choice when it came to delivering large amounts of ordnance against weakly defended targets. Although some bombers are still dedicated to the nuclear mission, they have played important roles as conventional bombers and cruise missile carriers in both Gulf Wars, Kosovo, and Afghanistan.

—*Michael George*

References
Barefield, James L., "The Heavy Bomber Industrial Base: A Study of Present and Future Capabilities," Air Command and Staff College, Maxwell AFB, AL, March 1997, available at http://www.fas.org/nuke/guide/usa/bomber/97-0070.pdf.
Herbert, Adam J., "The Long Reach of the Heavy Bombers," *Air Force Magazine*, November 2003, pp. 24–29.

Kotz, Nick, *Wild Blue Yonder* (Princeton, NJ: Princeton University Press, 1988).

Smoke, Richard, *National Security and the Nuclear Dilemma* (New York: Random House, 1987).

"U.S. Air Force White Paper on Long Range Bombers," March 1999, available at http://www.fas.org/nuke/guide/usa/bomber/bmap00.pdf.

HEAVY ICBMS

The first intercontinental ballistic missiles (ICBMs), such as the Soviet SS-6, the American Atlas, and the U.S. Titan I and II, were large, liquid-fueled rockets with payloads of 5 to 8 tons, the weight of thermonuclear warheads in the late 1950s. With a single warhead to destroy cities and large military installations, these missiles reaffirmed prevailing strategic assumptions. As smaller replacements, such as the Soviet SS-7, -9, and -11 and the U.S. Minuteman, appeared, the original heavy missiles were retired or reassigned to secondary missions.

The second generation of heavy ICBMs carried large numbers of much smaller reentry vehicles called MIRVs (multiple independently targetable reentry vehicles). The Soviet SS-18 was tested in 1973 with ten MIRVs and had an intercontinental throw weight (payload) of nearly 9 metric tons. This aroused concern in the United States that the Soviet Union would soon be able to destroy American ICBM fields in a disarming first strike using only a small portion of its total missile force. This superiority would make American threats of retaliation less credible.

Controlling heavy ICBMs became a major goal of American arms control efforts in the mid-1970s. The SS-18 was specifically defined as a heavy ICBM under the 1979 treaty resulting from the Strategic Arms Limitation Talks (SALT II). This limited the Soviet Union to no more than 308 heavy ICBMs and forbade testing an ICBM with more than ten warheads. Under the 1993 Strategic Arms Reduction Treaty (START II), destruction of SS-18 silos in Russia and Kazakhstan began in 1993–1994. The last silos were destroyed or converted, with the aid of U.S. funding, by the end of 2003. Decommissioned SS-18 missiles are being converted to service as Dnepr space launch vehicles.

The United States responded to the SS-18 with the MX Peacekeeper (LGM-118A). Although its throw weight was less than 3 tons—which in a technical sense did not make it a "heavy" missile—design innovations enabled the MX to carry ten warheads. Following the recommendations of the 1983 Scowcroft Commission Report, which was chaired by Lieutenant General Brent Scowcroft, USAF (ret.), fifty MX missiles were deployed in existing Minuteman silos. The first became operational in 1986. Under START II, all fifty MX ICBMs must be retired by 2004.

—*Aaron Karp*

HEAVY WATER

Heavy water, or deuterium oxide (D_2O), can moderate a reactor in which plutonium is bred from natural uranium. Although it looks like ordinary water, both hydrogen atoms have been replaced with deuterium, the isotope of hydrogen containing one proton and one neutron. It is present naturally in water, but in only small amounts, less than one part in 5,000. In the process of producing heavy water, deuterium molecules are separated from the vast quantity of water consisting of H_2O.

The importance of heavy water to a nuclear proliferator is that it provides a way to bypass uranium enrichment and produce plutonium for use in weapons. The world's first source of commercial heavy water came from the Vemork plant, Norway, as a by-product of the Norsk Hydro-Elektrisk station, which could produce 12 metric tons of heavy water per year. This facility, built in 1934, became the subject of German efforts to moderate a reactor, especially after the German occupation of Norway in 1940. Allied forces and the Norwegian resistance engaged in persistent and somewhat successful efforts to sabotage production. German interest in heavy water was one intelligence indicator that seemed to justify the decision to launch the Manhattan Project in the United States to obtain an atomic bomb before it could be acquired by German science (*see* Manhattan Project).

Besides the five declared nuclear weapons states, countries able to produce heavy water now include Argentina, Canada, India, and Norway. The Bruce Heavy Water Plant in Ontario, Canada, built in 1979, is the world's largest producer, capable of generating 700 metric tons of heavy water per year.

—*J. Simon Rofe*

See also: Deuterium; Isotopes; Plutonium; Uranium

Reference

Dahl, Per F., *Heavy Water and the Wartime Race for Nuclear Energy* (Philadelphia: Institute of Physics Publishers, 1999).

HEDGE

Although the 2002 Moscow Treaty (officially the Strategic Offensive Reductions Treaty, or SORT) limits Russia and the United States to 1,700–2,200 nuclear weapons deployed on strategic delivery systems, it does not specify how many nuclear weapons can be kept in reserve by both parties. To supplement its deployed warheads, the United States has maintained a ready reserve of nuclear warheads (referred to as the "hedge" force) in storage. These warheads are capable of being returned to military service on relatively short notice.

President Bill Clinton's administration planned to establish a hedge capability in its September 1994 Nuclear Posture Review. Not all warheads taken out of service in compliance with the Strategic Arms Reduction Treaty (START II) were going to be sent to the Pantex Plant near Amarillo, Texas, to be dismantled. Instead, about 2,500 to 2,700 weapons—the W62 and W78 warheads from the Minuteman III intercontinental ballistic missile, W76s from downloaded Trident submarine-launched ballistic missiles, and B61 and B83 bombs and W80 air-launched cruise missile warheads—were to be placed in the hedge force. The hedge was never officially created, however, since START II never entered into force (*see* Strategic Arms Reduction Treaty [START II]).

In its 2002 Nuclear Posture Review, the George W. Bush administration announced that it also would continue to maintain a "responsive force" of surplus nuclear weapons held in ready reserve as a hedge against emerging threats and as a way to address technical or safety issues that may emerge in the deployed force. The Bush administration also stated that it believes that the responsive force will serve to dissuade potential challengers from attempting to win a future nuclear arms race. The responsive force would allow the United States to field a large nuclear force faster than opponents could build nuclear weapons.

Critics charge that the responsive force, or any other stockpile scheme for nondeployed nuclear weapons, violates the goal of irreversibility in arms control and disarmament measures. They would prefer policies that completely dismantled nuclear warheads in such a way that they could never be re-deployed.

—*James J. Wirtz*

Reference

"2002 Nuclear Posture Review," available at http://globalsecurity.org/wmd/librarv/policy/dod/npr.htm.

HIGHLY ENRICHED URANIUM (HEU)

Highly enriched uranium is a man-made substance that increases the level of fissile material in natural uranium to the point where it can be used for atomic reactor fuel or nuclear weapons. In nature, uranium consists largely of two isotopes, U-235 and U-238. The production of energy in nuclear reactors results from the fission, or splitting, of the U-235 atoms, a process that releases energy in the form of heat. U-235 is the main fissile isotope of uranium. U-235 and U-238 are chemically identical but differ in their physical properties, particularly their mass. The difference in mass between U-235 and U-238 allows the isotopes to be separated and makes it possible to increase, or "enrich," the percentage of U-235. All currently used enrichment processes directly or indirectly make use of this small mass difference. Naturally mined uranium has 0.7 percent U-235. Most power reactors use 3 to 5 percent enriched uranium, and weapons require 90 percent enriched uranium. During the Manhattan Project, enriched uranium was given the code name "oralloy," a shortened version of the name "Oak Ridge alloy," after the plant where the uranium was enriched in Tennessee. The term is still occasionally used to refer to enriched uranium. U-238 with extremely low U-235 content is known as depleted uranium and is considerably less radioactive than even natural uranium (*see* Actinides; Depleted Uranium [U-238]; Enrichment; Isotopes; Low Enriched Uranium [LEU]; Oak Ridge National Laboratory; Reactor Operations; Uranium).

Enrichment Processes

A number of enrichment processes have been demonstrated in the laboratory, but only two, the gaseous-diffusion process and the centrifuge process, are operating commercially. In both of these processes, uranium hexafluoride (UF_6) is used as the feed material. Molecules of UF_6 with U-235 atoms are about 1 percent lighter than the rest of the feed material, and this difference in mass is the basis of both processes. The gaseous-diffusion process involves forcing uranium hexafluoride gas under pressure through a series of porous membranes, or diaphragms. Since U-235 molecules are lighter than the U-238 molecules, they move faster and have a slightly better chance of passing through the pores in the membrane. The UF_6 that diffuses through the membrane is thus slightly enriched, and the gas that did not pass through is depleted in U-235 atoms. The process is repeated many times in a series of diffusion stages called a "cascade." Each stage uses a compressor, a diffuser, and a heat exchanger to remove the heat caused by compression of the gas. The enriched product is withdrawn from one end of the cascade and the depleted gas is removed at the other end. The gas must be processed through some 1,400 stages to obtain a product with a concentration of 3 to 4 percent U-235. At present, the gaseous-diffusion process accounts for about 40 percent of world enrichment capacity. Although they have proved durable and reliable, most gaseous-diffusion plants are now nearing the end of their design life. In the future, they are likely to be replaced by processes based on centrifuge enrichment technology.

Like the diffusion process, the centrifuge process uses UF_6 gas as its feed and makes use of the slight difference in mass between U-235 and U-238. The gas is fed into a series of vacuum tubes, each containing a rotor 1–2 meters long and 15–20 centimeters in diameter. When the rotors are spun rapidly, at 50,000 to 70,000 revolutions per minute (rpm), the heavier molecules with U-238 increase in concentration toward the cylinder's outer edge. There is a corresponding increase in the concentration of U-235 molecules near the center. The enriched gas forms part of the feed for the next stages, while the depleted UF_6 gas goes back to the previous stage. Eventually, enriched and depleted uranium are drawn from the cascade at the desired levels of purity. Although the capacity of a single centrifuge is much smaller than that of a single gas-diffusion stage, its capability to separate isotopes is much greater. Centrifuge stages normally consist of a large number of centrifuges in parallel. Such stages are then arranged in cascade similarly to those for diffusion. In the centrifuge process, however, the number of stages may only be ten to twenty, compared to a thousand or more for diffusion.

Laser enrichment processes, a possible third-generation technology, could bestow significant economic advantages because of the potential for lower energy inputs and capital costs. Atomic vapor laser isotope separation uses a laser to excite and ionize uranium atoms of a specific uranium isotope so they can be selectively removed. Molecular laser isotope separation also uses a laser, but to excite and ionize uranium hexafluoride molecules for selective removal. Another process is the Becker nozzle aerodynamic process, in which a mixture of gaseous UF_6 and helium is compressed and then directed along a curved wall at high velocity. The heavier U-238-bearing molecules move preferentially out to the wall relative to those containing U-235. At the end of the deflection, the gas jet is split by a knife edge into a light and heavy fraction, which are then separately withdrawn. Laser enrichment technology, however, is not yet ready for commercial use.

Use of HEU in Weapons

Uranium gun-assembly weapons are the easiest of all nuclear devices to design and build. It is generally considered impossible to prevent any nation that has the requisite amount of HEU from building one or more gun-assembled weapons. Electromagnetic separation was used to produce HEU for the first U.S. atomic weapon, and it was the technique used by Iraq in its efforts to develop nuclear weapons in the late 1980s. In the process, uranium atoms are ionized, given an electrical charge, then sent in a stream past powerful magnets. The heavier U-238 atoms are deflected less in their trajectory than the lighter U-235 atoms by the magnetic field, so the isotopes separate and can be captured by collectors. The process is repeated until a high concentration of U-235 is achieved. The American version of this process featured "calutrons" and was used in the Manhattan Project (*see* Manhattan Project).

The Little Boy bomb dropped on Hiroshima on August 6, 1945, was a uranium bomb. HEU is no longer being produced in the United States because all HEU is drawn from current stocks and commercial (non–weapons grade) sources.

—*Gilles Van Nederveen*

See also: Portsmouth Enrichment Facility

References
Cochran, Thomas, William Arkin, and Milton Honig, *Nuclear Weapons Databook*, vol. 1: *U.S. Nuclear*

Forces and Capabilities (Cambridge, MA: Ballinger, 1984).

Edwards, Gordon, "Uranium: The Deadliest Metal," *Perception,* vol. 10, no. 2, 1992, available at http://www.ccnr.org/uranium_deadliest.html#bombs.

Energy Information Administration website, http://www.eia.doe.gov/fuelnuclear.html.

Wikipedia, "Uranium," at http://en.wikipedia.org/wiki/Uranium.

Winter, Mark, "The Periodic Table on the World Wide Web," available at http://www.webelements.com.

HIROSHIMA

Hiroshima is a major port city in western Honshu, Japan, on the Inland Sea that was destroyed at the end of World War II by an atomic bomb. Historically a military center, it was the site of a major castle from the shoganate and later of the headquarters for several army elements, including the Second General Army, which was responsible for the de-

fense of the home islands. During World War II it had a population of about 380,000, which was reduced by evacuations to 255,000. Manufacturing and storage facilities for military materiel were located in Hiroshima, and it was a point of embarkation for troops moving to the South Pacific.

By the summer of 1945, Japan was clearly defeated. The only remaining question was how the emperor's household was going to allow the war to end. The U.S. conquest of Okinawa had cost 49,151 American casualties. In addition, 763 U.S. aircraft were shot down and 36 U.S. ships were sunk, with another 368 damaged. The Japanese lost 110,000 men, 7,800 aircraft (1,465 in kamikaze attacks), and 16 ships. The Japanese civilians had been taught to defend the home islands to the death, so based on the costs of Okinawa, American military planners estimated that a ground invasion to secure surrender could cost 1 million American lives as well as millions of lives of Japanese civilians. The fire bombing of Tokyo had already resulted in 125,000

The center of Hiroshima, Japan, shortly after the first atomic bomb was dropped on August 6, 1945. (Bettmann/Corbis)

civilian deaths in one night, with no offer of surrender forthcoming from the Japanese.

During the war, U.S. scientists and engineers working on the Manhattan Project had developed and produced three atomic bombs. One was used in the first test at the Trinity Site, and the other two were ready for use in July 1945. Desiring to bring the war to an end without additional American casualties, President Harry S. Truman authorized the use of an atomic bomb against Hiroshima.

The bomb dropped on Hiroshima was "Little Boy," a gun-assembly weapon designed at Los Alamos, New Mexico, with an explosive uranium 235 core using material extracted at the Oak Ridge National Laboratory, Tennessee. A B-29 bomber, the *Enola Gay*, piloted by Colonel Paul W. Tibbets, carried the bomb. It was dropped at 8:15 A.M. on August 6, 1945, on a bridge in central Hiroshima. The bomb detonated at 2,000 feet, with a force calculated at about 17,000 tons of TNT. Four and three-quarter square miles of the city were completely destroyed by the blast and resulting firestorm. Two-thirds of the buildings within 10 square miles surrounding the detonation were destroyed, including 26 percent of the production facilities in the city. The memorial cenotaph in the city's museum acknowledges that 61,443 people were victims of the bomb, but the United States estimated 71,379 known dead, with almost 70,000 additional people injured. Radiation sickness among the civilian population overwhelmed the surviving medical personnel and facilities. International medical aid did not arrive until September 1945, too late for many of the severe burn victims who needed hydration and supportive therapy.

Ground Zero in Hiroshima is a memorial park that includes the "Atomic Dome," a building preserved in its post-bomb state, a fountain, and other memorials as well as a large museum that describes the bombing from the Japanese perspective. The museum does not include documentation of the events leading to the bombing, information about atrocities committed by the Japanese military during the war, or any acknowledgment of Japan's role in the instigation of the Pacific War. The city of Hiroshima has been rebuilt as a thriving commercial area with a major port.

—*Frannie Edwards*

See also: *Enola Gay;* Fission Weapons; Gun-Type Devices; Little Boy; Manhattan Project; Radiation; Tinian

References
Bauer, E., *The History of World War II* (New York: Military Press, 1984).
Sherwin, Martin J., *A World Destroyed: Hiroshima and Its Legacies,* third edition (Palo Alto, CA: Stanford University Press, 2003).

HORIZONTAL ESCALATION

Horizontal escalation is the expansion of conflict to new geographic areas or to new actors in the international community. Advocates of the strategy suggest that key military or diplomatic advantages can be gained by expanding, or threatening to expand, hostilities to geographic areas not of the opponent's choosing. Critics of the concept believe that it squanders resources on secondary operations and creates new opponents gratuitously. During the Cold War, the Ronald Reagan administration, for example, adopted the military strategy of horizontal escalation. In the so-called maritime strategy, Reagan officials argued that in the event of war along the inner German border, U.S. forces would launch attacks against the Soviet Far East to tie down Soviet forces that might be used in the European theater. Strategies based on horizontal escalation require increases in force structure and defense spending in order to maintain the military forces needed to fight the war along the "central front" while deploying additional forces to launch secondary attacks against the enemy.

Vertical escalation, by contrast, refers to an increase in the level of violence in a given conflict rather than the expansion of the conflict to new regions. The decision to employ nuclear weapons to stop a conventional attack by armored units, for instance, would be considered a vertical escalation of a given conflict.

—*Laura Fontaine*

See also: Escalation; Inadvertent Escalation
Reference
Korb, Lawrence J., "The Myth of the Two-Front War," *Washington Monthly*, vol. 29, no. 3, 1997, pp. 23–26.

HOT LINE AGREEMENTS

The "Hot Line" between Washington and Moscow is a series of dedicated transmission lines to ensure immediate communication between the two superpower leaders in time of crisis. While the 1958 Surprise Attack Conference recessed without achieving conclusive results, proposals from the conference stimulated U.S. and Soviet technological research on reducing the danger of an accidental nuclear war. The Cuban missile crisis of October 1962 underlined the importance of prompt, direct communications between the heads of state of the United States and the Soviet Union. In December 1962, a U.S. working paper submitted to the Eighteen Nation Disarmament Committee (ENDC) in Geneva proposed a number of cooperative measures, including establishment of dedicated transmission lines between major capitals to ensure reliable and rapid communication in times of crisis (see Accidental Nuclear War; Cuban Missile Crisis).

On June 20, 1963, American and Soviet representatives to the ENDC completed negotiations and signed a "Memorandum of Understanding Between the United States and the Union of Soviet Socialist Republics Regarding the Establishment of a Direct Communications Link." The link consisted of two terminal points with teletype equipment, a full-time duplex wire telegraph circuit, and a full-time duplex radiotelegraph circuit.

The Hot Line Agreement was the first bilateral agreement that sought to reduce the risk of a nuclear war stemming from accident, miscalculation, or surprise attack. Advances in technology in the 1960s offered the possibility of greater reliability for the communications link. During the Strategic Arms Limitation Talks (SALT I and II), a special working group was established to improve Washington-Moscow direct communications. On September 30, 1971, the Hot Line Modification Agreement was signed in Washington, D.C. The improved system included twin U.S.-Soviet satellite communications circuits, along with multiple terminals, in each country. The system continues to be upgraded and operated on a daily basis.

—Patricia McFate

References

"Arms Control Agreements," available at http://www.fas .org/nuke/control.
Arms Control and Disarmament Agreements (Washington, DC: U.S. Arms Control and Disarmament Agency, 1990).

HYDROGEN BOMB

The hydrogen bomb, also known as the H-bomb, the fusion bomb, and the thermonuclear bomb, is based on nuclear fusion, where light nuclei of hydrogen or helium atoms combine together into heavier elements and release large amounts of energy. The effects of a hydrogen bomb vary depending on the size of the weapon, but it is easily capable of devastating 150 square miles by blast and generating searing heat effects and radioactive fallout for more than 800 square miles.

The U.S. decision to develop hydrogen bombs began on September 23, 1949, when President Harry S. Truman announced that the Soviet Union had tested its first atomic bomb. The announcement caused panic in the country and created a flurry of activity in scientific and political circles. On January 31, 1950, President Truman announced the United States' reaction to the Soviet nuclear test, a crash program to develop a hydrogen bomb.

Physicist Edward Teller, mathematician Stanislaw Ulam, and other scientists spent more than a year of research in Los Alamos, New Mexico, solving the technical problems involved in producing a hydrogen bomb. On November 1, 1952, the first hydrogen bomb was detonated at the Enewetok Atoll with an explosive power of 10.4 million tons (megatons) of TNT. It caused an island to disappear and created in its place a crater a mile wide and 175 feet deep. A deliverable bomb was developed and successfully tested in 1954.

The Soviet Union tested its first true fusion bomb on November 22, 1955, using a 1.6-megaton device designed by Andrei Sakharov. On October 31, 1961, the Soviet Union detonated a device at their range on the Arctic Ocean island of Novaya Zemyla; it turned out to be history's largest nuclear explosion, the Tsar Bomba, with a yield of 58 megatons.

On May 15, 1957, the United Kingdom successfully detonated a fusion device at Christmas Island with a yield of between 200 and 300 kilotons—surprisingly low. In September of that year, the United Kingdom detonated a hydrogen bomb with a yield of 1.8 megatons.

China next entered the hydrogen bomb club on June 17, 1967, when it tested a bomb with a yield of 3.3 megatons that was designed and manufactured with little assistance from the Soviet Union.

France tested its first hydrogen bomb at the Fangataufa Atoll on August 24, 1968. It had a yield of 2.6 megatons. Other nations, such as India, Israel, and Pakistan, have either tested fusion devices or claim to have the capability to produce them.

The hydrogen bomb is based on the tremendous power of nuclear fusion—the collision of neutrons

American's first hydrogen bomb test, the 10-megaton Mike shot in the Marshall Islands of the Pacific, November 1952. (Bettmann/Corbis)

with the nucleus of an unstable isotope of hydrogen, either deuterium or tritium, under high temperatures. The reason for the power of fusion is originally found in Albert Einstein's famous equation, $e = mc^2$, in which mass and energy are directly related and, during the right conditions, interchangeable. By combining two atoms into one, when the product weighs less than its original components, the excess weight can be translated into a tremendous amount of energy (*see* Deuterium; Fusion; Isotopes; Tritium).

The hydrogen bomb explosion is actually a chain reaction triggered by a normal fission bomb that produces temperatures and pressure within the thermonuclear device that allow for nuclear fusion. A modern hydrogen bomb has at its center an atomic bomb surrounded by a layer of lithium deuteride (the isotope of hydrogen with a mass number of two). This is surrounded by a thick outer layer known as the "tamper," which is often com-

posed of fissionable material and functions to hold the contents together to contain the pressure and heat long enough to obtain a larger explosion. Neutrons from the atomic explosion cause the lithium to fission into helium, tritium (the isotope of hydrogen with mass number three), and a tremendous amount of energy. The initial atomic explosion also supplies the heat required for fusion, raising temperatures within the thermonuclear device to as high as 400 million degrees Celsius. Enough neutrons are produced in the fusion reactions to produce further fission in the core and to initiate fission in the tamper.

Like other large nuclear explosions, the hydrogen bomb creates an extremely hot zone near the blast site. Because of the high temperature, nearly all of the matter near the blast site is vaporized. The high pressure generated by such a large blast progresses away from the center of the explosion as a shock wave. It is this wave, containing most of the energy released, which is responsible for most of the destructive mechanical effects of a nuclear explosion. The details of shock-wave propagation and its effects vary depending on whether the burst is in the air, under water, or underground.

Like other large nuclear blasts, hydrogen bomb blasts scatter a large amount of radioactive material. Even low concentrations of radiation can be lethal, causing death and illness for years after the blast.

—*Abe Denmark*

See also: Fusion; Implosion Devices; Nuclear Weapons Effects; Radiation; Thermonuclear Bomb

References

Rhodes, Richard, *Dark Sun: The Making of the Hydrogen Bomb* (New York: Simon and Schuster, 1996).

Rosenberg, David Alan, "The Origins of Overkill: Nuclear Weapons and American Strategy, 1945–1960," *International Security,* vol. 7, no. 4, Spring 1983, pp. 3–71.

IMPLEMENTATION

The process of complying with treaty provisions and verifying such compliance is called "arms control implementation." Arms control treaties and agreements are intended to enhance international security and to preserve peace by allowing states to take measures to eliminate military weapons, control weapons technology, or promote understanding between those who sign the agreement. Most treaties or agreements contain confidence-building and verification provisions. Confidence-building measures may include data declarations, formal visits, challenge inspections, systematic inspections, continuous monitoring of key facilities, and aircraft overflights geared toward ensuring compliance with the provisions of a specific treaty. Some treaties, such as the Biological (and Toxin) Weapons Convention (1975), have no verification provisions at all; others, such as the Chemical Weapons Convention (1997), call for short-notice, detailed, intrusive inspection verification measures by an international inspection team. Challenge inspections, probably the most intrusive type of verification measure, are usually governed by complex and comprehensive rules and procedures authorizing an international team of investigators to explore concerns about possible noncompliance with arms control agreements by visiting sites where prohibited activities may be occurring.

In the United States, responsibility for arms control implementation and compliance is largely the responsibility of the Department of Defense (DOD) and the individual services. Within the U.S. Navy, for example, DOD Directive 2060.1 gives responsibility for arms control implementation to the director of the Naval Treaty Implementation Program (NTIP), who supports the assistant secretary of the Navy for research, development, and acquisition (ASN [RDA]) in the planning and implementation of all arms control agreements that affect the Department of the Navy. ASN (RDA) has designated NTIP as the executive agent to carry out the daily work of treaty implementation and compliance.

—*James J. Wirtz*

See also: Arms Control; Confidence- and Security-Building Measures; Ratification; Verification

Reference

Larsen, Jeffrey A., ed., *Arms Control: Cooperative Security in a Changing Environment* (Boulder: Lynne Rienner, 2002).

IMPLOSION DEVICES

An implosion device is a nuclear weapon that relies on a spherical compression of fissile material to achieve critical mass. It is more sophisticated and efficient than the gun-type compression system. It was first designed, built, and tested by the Manhattan Project, the World War II Anglo-American program that constructed the first nuclear weapons.

History and Background

During the initial phase of the Manhattan Project two designs were proposed. One was the gun-type device, which was attractive because of its simplicity, ease of construction and operation, and high reliability (*see* Gun-Type Devices). The second design, the implosion device, was also attractive because it offered a more elegant solution to producing nuclear fission and did not require highly enriched uranium, which was very difficult to produce (*see* Highly Enriched Uranium [HEU]; Uranium). Using a similar amount of fissile material, an implosion device will produce a far greater explosive yield than a gun device. Serious material and engineering hurdles had to be overcome, however, before an implosion device became a reality.

The implosion device required extensive testing using explosives, detonators, triggering mechanisms, and timers to arrive at a design that would work. Therefore, both gun and implosion designs were developed by the Manhattan project: The gun-type device would be immediately available for wartime use, and the implosion device would be developed to create the next generation of more sophisticated and powerful nuclear weapons.

In the summer of 1944, a new impetus emerged for the development of the implosion device with the discovery that nuclear reactors created an isotopic impurity, plutonium 240, which could not be used in gun-type assemblies. All of the plutonium for atomic bombs would have to be made in reactors, so the only way to make use of the plutonium coming from the Hanford, Washington, production reactors built by DuPont was to find a way to perfect implosion (see Hanford, Washington; Isotopes; Plutonium).

Los Alamos National Laboratory organized Division GX (for "gadget explosive") to develop the nuclear and high-explosive components of the implosion device. Dr. Robert Oppenheimer, head of the Manhattan Engineering Project, created the Trinity Project in September 1944. A design team at Los Alamos National Laboratory, New Mexico, arrived at a functional design far ahead of schedule. As a result, the implosion device was constructed simultaneously with the gun-type device. On July 16, 1945, the Trinity nuclear device was detonated at the Alamogordo Bombing Range in New Mexico (see Manhattan Project; Trinity Site).

The theoretical expectations about the greater efficiency of the implosion device were confirmed by use of both types of weapon in combat. "Little Boy," the gun-type device dropped on Hiroshima, had an estimate yield of approximately 12.5 to 20 kilotons. "Fat Man," the implosion device dropped on Nagasaki, had a yield of approximately 21–23 kilotons.

Technical Details

The fission implosion device consists of arming and power mechanisms and the physics package (known as the "pit"; see Pit). The core is usually plutonium 239 with a beryllium casing wrapped with an explosive material. The high-explosive shell is lined by detonators at a predetermined spacing to produce uniform compression of the fissile material and ensure complete, instantaneous detonation.

When the explosive is detonated, an inwardly directed implosion wave is produced, uniformly crushing and tamping the fissionable material. The decreased surface volume, plus the increased density, makes the mass supercritical. This is what is often referred to as "splitting the atom." From this chain reaction, energy is released in an uncontrolled fashion. This energy takes the form of intense heat, pressure from the shock wave created by the blast, electromagnetic pulse, and radiation. The size of the blast is determined by the amount of fissile material and the efficiency with which it was compressed. Early designs were not efficient—that is, they were "dirtier" than current weapons, producing great amounts of radioactive material (see Fallout; Radiation).

In a hydrogen (or fusion) implosion device, the process of creating a nuclear explosion contains several additional steps. The pit must include a neutron source, usually tritium gas. This is surrounded by plutonium 239 (Pu-239), then uranium 235 (U-235), a vacuum, uranium 238 (U-238), a beryllium casing, and an explosive casing. The nuclear explosion depends on fission to release the binding energy in certain nuclei, which is rapid and violent. The fissile materials, such as plutonium and uranium, can be split into two roughly equal-mass fragments when a neutron is forced into them. A self-sustaining chain reaction occurs.

The minimum mass of fissile material for a nuclear chain reaction is called a critical mass (see Criticality and Critical Mass). The amount of material needed to create a critical mass depends on the material used as well as on the surrounding material, known as a reflector or tamper. This surrounding material reflects the escaping neutrons back into the critical mass. For example, a bare sphere requires 56 kilograms (kg) of U-235 and 11 kg of Pu-239. A thick tamper requires only 15 kg of U-235 and 5 kg of Pu-239. Critical mass decreases rapidly as density increases, so an implosion device requires substantially less nuclear material then a gun-type device. For example, Fat Man used 6.2 kg of plutonium and produced a yield of 23 kilotons. Until 1994, the Department of Energy stated that 8 kg would be needed to make a small nuclear weapon, but later experiments proved that 4 kg would be sufficient. Some scientists believe that 1 kg of plutonium would be adequate in modern designs to create a critical mass.

A second type of hydrogen implosion device, the Teller-Ulam fusion bomb, uses thermal radiation. This type of bomb was created in 1953 at a time when tritium gas was difficult to obtain and store (*see* Tritium). A fission implosion device is used as the triggering mechanism to release thermal radiation in the form of soft X-rays. The X-rays are directed into the pit, setting off a secondary stage that leads to fusion reaction. The bomb casing included an implosion fission bomb and a cylinder casing (tamper) of U-238. Within the tamper are lithium deuteride (fuel) and a hollow rod of Pu-239. A shield of U-238 and plastic foam fills the spaces in the bomb casing. The fission bomb explodes, giving off X-rays, exerting pressure against the lithium deuterate, causing it to compress thirty-fold, and initiating fission in the plutonium rod. The neutrons released in this process go into the lithium deuterate to make tritium, yielding fusion reactions that result in a fusion explosion.

Current Status

Since the deployment of the Fat Man device, radical improvements and refinements have occurred in the design and execution of implosion devices. Less fissile material is required, and improved explosives and casings have led to smaller and lighter weapons that can produce enormous explosive yields. These devices are currently used in intercontinental ballistic missiles, theater tactical weapons, cruise missiles, torpedoes, and man-portable devices.

The largest implosion device ever detonated (estimated at 56 megatons of yield) was produced by the Soviet Union. Today, high-yield devices are gradually being retired from nuclear arsenals because low-yield weapons designed for battlefield use are believed to offer a more credible deterrent threat. The increased accuracy of modern delivery systems also now allows smaller nuclear weapons to destroy very hard or deeply buried targets (*see* Accuracy; Credibility; Deterrence).

The B61 series of bombs is the largest family of implosion devices used by U.S. forces. Production was first begun in 1966, and they have been produced for more than thirty years at Los Alamos National Laboratory. This bomb can be delivered as a free-fall air burst, a retarded air burst, a free-fall surface burst, or in "laydown" mode from an aircraft flying as low as 50 feet and using a parachute to slow the bomb's descent and control its trajectory. This type

of bomb has been carried by the B-52, FB-111, B-1, and B-2 bombers. Tactical versions with lower yield have been carried by the United States and other members of the North Atlantic Treaty Organization (NATO) aboard a variety of tactical aircraft (for example, F-100, F-104, F-15E, F-16, F-111, F-117, and Tornado). The U.S. Navy and Marines have used the B61 in their A-6, A-7, and F/A-18 aircraft.

Two strategic versions of the B61 are currently in use. The B61-7 is a variable yield gravity bomb for the B-52 and B-2. The B61-11 is an earth-penetrating weapon for the B-2. The tactical weapons are the B61 Mods 3, 4, and 10. These are stored within the United States at Nellis Air Force Base, Nevada, and Kirtland Air Force Base, New Mexico, and probably with additional fighter wings in North Carolina and New Mexico. The B61s also have been stored with U.S. Air Force units in Britain, Germany, Greece, and Turkey and have been held in U.S. custody for NATO air forces in Belgium, Germany, Italy, and the Netherlands.

Although implosive devices are fairly simple to design in theory, building one is quite difficult, making them an unlikely initial path for emerging nuclear weapons states. The machining tolerances necessary for the casing, the layering of explosive material, the positions of the detonators, and the design of the triggering mechanism for the detonators are extremely complex. Manufacturing and assembly of a nuclear bomb would require a large organization's financial backing to develop the tools and expertise required. Although basic implosion designs are now the stuff of high-school physics, individuals or small terrorist cells continue to lack the ability to manufacture a nuclear weapon that utilizes implosion to create a fission reaction.

Some nations that have developed nuclear weapons, such as South Africa and Pakistan, have only developed gun-type devices. North Korea could easily possess a gun-type device. The United States, Russia, Britain, France, India, and China possess implosion devices.

Developing or Future Technologies

Further improvements in the design and performance of nuclear weapons will likely be based on implosion-type devices. Variations in design, though theoretically possible, appear to be less practical. A biconical mini–nuclear weapon design, for instance, has been created to provide a low-yield battlefield weapon with a 1- to 2-kiloton yield. The biconical design uses two shaped charges facing each other with the fissile material between them. Upon detonation, the shock wave of each charge is directed into the fissile material. This method was apparently an attempt to combine the simplicity and reliability of a gun-type device with the efficiency of a implosion device.

—*Dan Goodrich*

See also: Fission Weapons; Proliferation
References
Brown, Richard K., "Nuclear Weapons Diagrams," available at http://nuketesting.enviroweb.org/hew/Library/Brown.
Freudenrich, Craig C., "How Nuclear Bombs Work," available at http://science.howstuffworks.com/nuclear.bomb.htm.
Leventhal, Paul, "Present Assessments Understated Iraq's Nuclear Weapons Potential" (Washington, DC: Nuclear Control Institute, 1990).
Mello, Greg, "New Bomb No Mission," *Bulletin of the Atomic Scientists*, vol. 53, no. 3, May/June 1997, pp. 28–32.
Norris, Robert S., "Nuclear Notebook," *Bulletin of the Atomic Scientists*, vol. 59, no. 1, January/February 2003, pp. 74–76.
"Special Weapons Primer: Nuclear Weapons Design," http://www.fas.org/nuke/intro/nuke/.

IMPROVISED NUCLEAR DEVICES

Improvised nuclear devices—sometimes referred to as "crude nuclear weapons"—are simple, unsophisticated atomic bombs. They would probably utilize a gun-type device to create a critical mass and explosive yield. Although these weapons will probably not be based on complicated designs that use a combination of nuclear fission and fusion to boost the nuclear explosive yield of a weapon to extremely high levels, they could have an explosive yield of up to a few tens of kilotons.

Essential for any nuclear fissile weapon design is a swift compression of the fissile material to create a supercritical mass and to avoid preignitions that would cause the device to fizzle (that is, no yield or minimal explosive yield) (*see* Criticality and Critical Mass). The requirements for creating an improvised weapon depend on the type of fissile material used and the mass, density, and geometry of the fissile material. The probability of creating a critical mass increases with the quantity and density of the fissile material available.

To create a critical mass in a gun-type design, one subcritical mass is fired using conventional explosives into another subcritical mass of fissile material. Highly enriched uranium is the preferred fissile material for gun-type weapons. Depending on the design and sophistication of the device, 15 to 25 kilograms of highly enriched uranium could be sufficient to produce a functional improvised nuclear device (*see* Gun-Type Devices; Highly Enriched Uranium [HEU]).

If terrorists were to construct their own nuclear weapons, they would probably select a gun-type device. This type of weapon is easy to construct, and terrorists would probably not be attracted to more efficient ways of creating a critical mass to generate high yields. Gun-type devices are relatively unsafe in the sense that they are more likely to detonate accidentally than other nuclear designs, but terrorists might not be concerned about the safety of their nuclear arsenal. Gaining access to enough high-quality fissile material to construct a nuclear weapon is probably the greatest obstacle faced by state and nonstate actors when it comes to creating an improvised nuclear device.

—*Morten Bremer Maerli and James J. Wirtz*

References
Levi, Michael A., and Henry C. Kelly, "Weapons of Mass Disruption," *Scientific American,* November 2002.
Maerli, Morten Bremer, "The Real Weapon of Mass Destruction: Nuclear, Biological, and Chemical Warfare in the Era of Terrorism and 'Rogue' States," *Security Policy Library,* no. 1, Altanterhavskomiteen, January 2003, available at http://www.atlanterhavskomiteen.no/publikasjoner/sp/2003/1.htm.
Richelson, Jeffrey T., "Defusing Nuclear Terror," *The Bulletin of the Atomic Scientists,* March/April 2002, available at http://www.thebulletin.org/issues/2002/ma02/ma02richelson.html.
Von Hippel, Frank, "Recommendations for Preventing Nuclear Terrorism," *FAS Public Interest Report,* vol. 4, no. 6, November/December 2001, available at http://www.fas.org/faspir/2001/v54n6/prevent.htm.

INADVERTENT ESCALATION

Inadvertent escalation occurs when a state unintentionally or unexpectedly crosses the nuclear threshold in response to a conventional attack. In military escalation, adversaries increase the intensity of violence or widen the geographical scope of a war in the attempt to gain victory. During the Cold War, the concept of escalation generally referred to the leap from conventional military warfare to the use of nuclear weapons.

The decision to escalate can be viewed as a cost-benefit calculation of the possibility of gaining important objectives and the likelihood of counter-escalation by the enemy. This contrasts with the concept of inadvertent escalation, where crossing the nuclear threshold is not intended by legitimate political or military authorities and arises from the unexpected results of conventional attacks. These escalation-producing conventional attacks could take several forms: For example, conventional forces could come into direct contact with the adversary's nuclear forces, possibly threatening their survivability and hastening their use; conventional attacks could degrade the command and control of the adversary's nuclear forces; or conventional attacks could be mistaken for a preemptive first strike, starting a nuclear alert cycle that leads to launch on warning by an opponent who believes that an attack on its forces is imminent.

The difference between deliberate and inadvertent escalation was illustrated during the 1962 Cuban missile crisis. When the United States announced a quarantine of Cuba, U.S. armed forces, including nuclear forces, were put on full alert. This deliberate escalation on the part of the United States was meant to warn Moscow to remove its missiles from Cuba.

While these deliberate actions were taking place, unintended events transpired. For example, a U-2 reconnaissance plane overflew the Soviet Union (the overflight was caused by a navigational error), and a squadron of U.S. fighter aircraft was scrambled to escort the errant U-2 out of Soviet airspace. The Soviets could have mistaken these incidents as a nuclear attack and launched a retaliatory nuclear strike against the United States. How close the world came to inadvertent nuclear escalation during the Cuban missile crisis was not fully appreciated until classified documents were released many years later.

—Peter Lavoy

See also: Cuban Missile Crisis; Escalation; Horizontal Escalation

Reference

Posen, Barry R., *Inadvertent Escalation* (Ithaca, NY: Cornell University Press, 1989).

INDIAN NUCLEAR WEAPONS PROGRAM

In 1964, Indian Prime Minister Lal Bahadur Shastri promoted research and development into what was called a "Subterranean Nuclear Explosion for Peaceful Purposes." India detonated its first atomic device ten years later, on May 18, 1974, using fissile material derived from a Canada Deuterium Uranium (CANDU) reactor. Although India had previously claimed its atomic forays were solely for peaceful nuclear purposes, in May 1998—after testing five nuclear devices—India formally declared itself a nuclear weapons state. India is not a member of the Nuclear Nonproliferation Treaty (NPT) of 1968, however, and refuses to join, claiming that the NPT is a discriminatory regime. According to the Wisconsin Project's *Risk Report* (2003), India may possess sufficient fissile material to produce up to 100 nuclear warheads.

In establishing its nuclear command and control organization, India promulgated its own nuclear doctrine in 1999, claiming its policy was "no first use" and that its nuclear forces were intended to provide only a "credible minimum deterrent." The Indian government also claims that it has nuclear devices possessing the capability of low yields to 200 kilotons involving fission, boosted-fission, and two-stage thermonuclear designs (*see* Fission Weapons; Thermonuclear Bomb). India is reportedly pursuing a triad of nuclear forces to include air-, land-, and sea-based delivery platforms (for example, submarines). As of 2004, India's primary means of delivering nuclear warheads included ballistic missiles such as the Privthi I short-range ballistic missile (SRBM) and the medium-range Agni II. For aircraft delivery, India would most likely use modified versions of the MiG-27 Flogger and the Jaguar IS/IB. Intense enmity and occasional wars with Pakistan—as well as ongoing conflict in the disputed Kashmir region—have led to even more heightened tensions in the twenty-first century because the two South Asian nations both possess nuclear weapons.

Estimates of how many warheads India possesses range from 30 to 150. At the end of 1999, India was believed to possess 240–395 kilograms of weapons-grade plutonium, which could be used to build 45–95 nuclear warheads. The amount of plutonium that could be extracted from India's six heavy-water nuclear power plants could be used to build as many as 200 nuclear devices (*see* Heavy Water; Plutonium).

Indian troops and short-range ballistic missiles near the Pakistani border, May 2002. (Arko Datta/Reuters/Corbis)

In August 1999, the Indian government released a draft nuclear doctrine prepared by the nonofficial National Security Advisory Board. The Indian government continues to develop its nuclear doctrine and has stated that no-first-use of nuclear weapons and civilian control over nuclear weapons are key to their effort to develop a credible minimal deterrent based only on retaliation. Indian officials also assert that global, verifiable, and nondiscriminatory nuclear disarmament remains as a "national security objective."

The Indian government announced the establishment of the Nuclear Command Authority (NCA), which will manage and administer all of India's nuclear and strategic forces, in January 2003. The NCA includes the civilian Political Council, headed by the prime minister, which will have sole authority over the release of nuclear weapons.

In May 1998, India announced a voluntary moratorium on further nuclear testing, excluding computer simulation and subcritical tests. India is developing several ballistic missile systems, particularly the Agni I with a tested range of 800 kilometers, Agni II with a demonstrated range of more than 2,000 kilometers, and the Agni III with a planned range of up to 3,500 kilometers. India and Russia are jointly developing a supersonic cruise missile, the Brahmos, with a range of 280 kilometers. The Brahmos entered production in 2004. India also is working on at least two naval systems that may be equipped to carry nuclear warheads.

—*Claudine McCarthy*
and Jolie Wood

See also: Negative Security Assurances; Nonproliferation; Nuclear Nonproliferation Treaty; Pakistani Nuclear Forces; Strategic Forces

References

"India Nuclear Weapon Update 2003," *The Risk Report*, vol. 9, no. 5, September-October 2003.

"India Profile," Nuclear Threat Initiative, 2003, available at http://www.nti.org.

National Security Council (India), National Security Advisory Board, "Draft Report of National Security Advisory Board on Indian Nuclear Doctrine," 17 August 1999, available at http://www. indianembassy.org/policy/CTBT/nuclear_doctrine_ aug_17_1999.html.

"WMD around the World: India Special Weapons Guide," available at http://www.fas.org/nuke/guide/ india/index.html.

INERTIAL NAVIGATION AND MISSILE GUIDANCE

Although large rocket engines are the sine qua non of long-range missile capabilities, engine capability alone is useless without an effective guidance system. The basic problem of missile development is achieving accurate flight over a specific trajectory. As missile ranges increase, accuracy tends to decrease proportionately. Through most of the Cold War, missile accuracy was an essential consideration in nuclear strategy. Since the end of the Cold War, guidance has offered one of the most important bottlenecks for restraining emerging missile programs through export controls. Technical innovation in the 1990s, however, made it much easier and cheaper to achieve extremely high accuracy at long ranges. This has the potential to eliminate one of the most important levers on the international control of missile proliferation.

Range and Accuracy Tradeoffs

At short ranges, sufficient accuracy to assure damage with conventional high-explosive warheads usually can be achieved with "passive guidance" alone. The small size of the rockets permits very rapid acceleration, which when combined with clean aerodynamic design compensates for atmospheric disturbances such as wind. Short-range systems, such as multiple-launched artillery rockets, are fired in large volleys, relying on numbers to compensate for lack of accuracy. The effectiveness of these weapons was demonstrated by the destruction of large swaths of Kabul, Afghanistan, in 1994, inflicted entirely with thousands of unguided artillery rockets.

Beyond ranges of about 70 kilometers (km), however, "active guidance" becomes essential to ensure accurate flight. At greater ranges, accuracy declines, creating an incentive to turn from conventional high-explosive armaments to weapons of mass destruction, especially nuclear warheads. Less costly guidance methods, such as radio-command guidance or strap-down gyros, which are constructed by suspending a rotor on at least three rings to reduce the effect of outside torque on the rotor's own spinning motion, may be sufficient to ensure adequate capability to ranges of about 300 km. Even at these ranges, the greater financial cost of the rockets makes it progressively harder to rely on sheer numbers to compensate for weakness of design. This explains why long-range missiles—especially those capable of traveling beyond 1,000 to 1,200 km—tend to be designed to carry nuclear payloads.

Guidance Alternatives

The least costly and technically demanding guidance approach is to mount the gyros and accelerometers in a rigid package attached directly to the airframe of the missile or rocket. Known as "strap-down guidance," this type of system is not especially accurate, a problem that was apparent in its first major application in the V-2. Strap-downs remain widespread in technically less demanding roles. It is the technique used in Scud ballistic missiles and Silkworm cruise missiles, for example. The approach also has been improved by adding another guidance system to provide correction. In an air-to-air missile such as the AMRAAM or AIM-9, for example, strap-down guidance maintains the missile in stable flight, while infrared or radar guidance directs it to the target.

Early intercontinental ballistic missiles (ICBMs), such as the American Atlas-D and the Soviet SS-7, relied on strap-down gyros augmented by radar tracking and radio control. Radio or command guidance was highly effective, but it worked only so long as the missile was above the horizon, beyond which the curve of the Earth degraded signals. It also suffered from the risk of jamming and interference. Although it was abandoned by the superpowers as quickly as they could replace it with more advanced systems, it appears to have found new applications among emerging missile powers. As radio signal–processing abilities improved in the 1970s and 1980s, command guidance became more reliable and appealing again, especially for short- and medium-range applications.

Because control of the vehicle relies on engines and aerodynamics for directional control, active guidance is possible only so long as the engines are burning or the vehicle is inside the Earth's atmosphere. Following engine burnout, which typically happens well into outer space (3 to 5 minutes into the flight depending on the size and range of the rocket), the vehicle begins to coast along its ballistic trajectory. In long-range missiles, coasting is no problem. Inaccuracies will build up again, however, as the reentry vehicle begins descent upon return to the atmosphere.

The inevitable deterioration in accuracy at the end of a warhead's trajectory can be offset through the use of small vernier engines in space or through aerodynamic surfaces mounted on the reentry vehicle. As the reentry vehicle approaches its target, guidance can be switched to "terminal guidance" mechanisms, usually relying on optical or radar sensors. These techniques were first deployed in the U.S. cruise missiles and Pershing II intermediate-range systems developed in the 1970s. Relying on a photographic or radar image of the target, these systems greatly improved accuracy. But there is a tradeoff involved in using improved guidance systems. Because terminal guidance requires that the guidance package and maneuvering systems be carried the full length of the trajectory, the weight and drag associated with this additional payload can severely reduce the maximum range of the missile itself.

The Dominance of Inertial Navigation

The need for a completely autonomous guidance system capable of sufficient accuracy to ensure effective attack with nuclear weapons created enormous pressure on designers in the 1950s and early 1960s. The preferred solution was the inertial navigation system (INS).

INS technology relies on gyros mounted on independent gimbals that allow them to move freely, unaffected by the motion of the rocket carrying them. Sensors mounted around the gyro detect changes in angular motion. Each gimbal also carries an accelerometer to measure changes in velocity. Normally three gyros and three accelerometers, one for each axis of motion (roll, pitch, and yaw), their associated sensors, and their gimbaled mountings are combined in a single package. In addition, an INS must have motors to power the gyros and lubrication systems to minimize friction on the moving elements. The result is a stable platform able to detect even very small changes in direction and velocity. The complete platform looks like a metal sphere, 6 to 18 inches in diameter, covered with access panels and adjustment points. External elements convert its signals into guidance commands that direct the engine and aerodynamic surfaces of the vehicle.

The first stable platform INS was designed for improved versions of the Nazi German V-2, but it could not be flown until after the war. Subsequently perfected at the U.S. Army's Redstone Arsenal by General Electric in the 1950s, this design equipped the first generations of American ballistic missiles, including the Redstone, Jupiter, Atlas-E/F, and Pershing I missiles. The early sets were heavy, prone to break down, and suffered from significant drift (or inaccuracy), but they were good enough to ensure that a nuclear-armed missile would reach its target. At the longest ranges, though, the extensive lethal radius produced by large thermonuclear weapons was the only way to compensate for the limited accuracy of early INS technology.

A major source of friction and drift were the bearings where the gyros and accelerometers were attached to the guidance platform. In the German design, these were made from jewels (usually ruby or sapphire) identical to those used in watches of the day. An alternative design pioneered in the 1950s by Charles Stark Draper of the Massachusetts Institute of Technology (MIT) replaced the mechanical bearings with floated-ball systems that suspended the gyros in an oil film. This was followed with air bearings, which eliminated the need to physically link the gyro to its suspending gimbals. This last innovation created systems capable of even greater accuracies.

The Draper approach culminated in the Northrop AIRS (Advanced Inertial Reference Sphere) guidance system for the MX missile. The AIRS houses gyros and accelerometers within a beryllium sphere that floats in a fluorocarbon fluid. The whole system is floated within an outer shell and can thus rotate in any direction. Although details have not been declassified, AIRS is said to have achieved unmatched accuracy. Its faults reportedly contributed less than 1 percent of the inaccuracy in the MX ICBM's 100-meter circular error probable (or CEP, the radius within which a warhead or bomb will land 50 percent of the time). Such precision came at great cost and production difficulty. The package reportedly has 19,000 parts. In 1989, a single accelerometer used in the AIRS (there are three) cost $300,000 and took six months to manufacture.

In the best INS, gyro drift can be as low as about 0.001 degrees per hour, which is roughly the theoretical minimum of the system. Even this translates to a positional error of about 0.1 nautical miles per hour of operation, a major consideration, especially when the navigation system must operate at high alert for extended periods and cannot necessarily be aligned immediately before flight. In an ICBM with a flight time of about 30 minutes, such inaccuracies still can become serious enough to compromise a mission. A more typical INS suffers from gyro drift of 0.01 degrees per hour, or 1 nautical mile per hour.

The high cost and limited reliability of the best INS technology did not undermine its enormous advantages. Improvements in accuracy made it possible for the United States to switch from targeting cities to targeting opponents' missile fields. The accuracy of the best air-bearing INS also made it possible for both the United States and Russia to reduce missile armament from megaton to kiloton warheads because they could still be assured of destroying the intended target.

Beyond Inertial Navigation

The great cost, high-maintenance requirements, and limited reliability of INS weapons showed the limits of the INS approach to missile guidance. Alternatives were invented in the 1960s and 1970s and began to be used in the 1980s. Initially, these innovations focused on cheaper ways to construct gyros, such as using laser gyros, which rely on a beam of light instead of mechanical methods. Although these were cheaper and more robust than the older systems, they suffered from poor accuracy, making them unsuitable for long-range missile applications. This appears to be changing as accuracies of 0.01 degrees per hour are now achieved using these systems. Even more reliable are fiber-optic gyros, which have achieved drift performance up to 1 degree per hour. The latter are used by commercial airliners but have yet to reach any confirmed missile applications. Both approaches cost less than traditional INS technology.

In the late 1980s, developments in gyros based on micro-circuitry began to show greater promise. Based on micro-electromechanical systems (MEMS), these use microscopic components carved in silicon chips. The technology is most familiar in the accelerometers used to ignite car airbags in collisions. MEMS makes possible low-cost, strap-down gyros and accelerometers with drift rates of as much as 20 degrees per hour. A newer approach using tuning-fork technology is expected to achieve drift rates of 1 to 10 degrees per hour in a package the size of a lemon. Although these do not compare to the drift rates of 0.01degrees per hour achieved by the best INS weapons, such systems cost as little as a few thousand dollars. Such systems currently cannot guide a long-range ballistic missile by themselves, but they have enormous potential as components in an augmented guidance system.

GPS-INS and Kalman Filtering

The developmental philosophy of INS was to create the best possible components. As these operated together, however, their individual weaknesses were exposed, and the level of accuracy achieved amounted to less than the capability of the component parts. A newer approach works synergistically to achieve capabilities significantly better than any of its components could alone. Low-cost, low-accuracy MEMS gyro sets can serve as the core element in a total guidance package that provides continuous updates to correct for their inaccuracies. The result is a low-cost, rugged, and highly accurate system.

Augmented guidance systems rely on a combination of gyro platforms and signals from the satellite-based Global Positioning System (GPS). The resulting GPS-INS can achieve capabilities surpassing the very best INS alone. This method of guidance relies not on any one sensor or set of sensors, but on Kalman filtering. This exploits the powerful synergism between GPS and INS technology, a synergism based on their highly complementary strengths and weaknesses. INS weapons are extremely accurate in the short-term, but errors accumulate over time and rapidly become a serious problem. A GPS is not as inherently accurate, but because its positional readings are continuously recalculated, its errors do not compound with time. Using a Kalman filter, new readings from the GPS essentially are used to correct the drift in the INS. Combining the two systems reduces navigational uncertainties to centimeters or a few meters.

Kalman filtering is an algorithmic process developed in the early 1960s for the systematic elimination of signal errors and integration of multiple guidance signals. It relies on a Covariance Matrix to compare its own estimate of uncertainty against the relative uncertainty of sensor outputs. These are corrected to achieve optimal outputs. The key function of Kalman filtering is to use GPS readings to correct the inherent drift of INS sensors.

Although developments in INS, such as the use of MEMS gyros, have received the most attention, GPS technology has benefited from breakthroughs as well. From its inception in the late 1970s, the GPS was used to aid prelaunch alignment of missile gyros, but the system was too slow for in-flight use.

A new generation of GPS satellites permits much faster signal transmission, while improvements in micro-circuitry have accelerated interpretation of GPS data.

The most famous application of the GPS-INS is the Joint Direct Attack Munition (JDAM), an air-dropped bomb used for the first time in the 1999 Kosovo war. GPS-INS guidance is also increasingly accepted in spacecraft. It is used in the space shuttle and in most civilian and military satellites in low-Earth orbits. The system appears to be used in the U.S. Minuteman ICBM through the Guidance Replacement Program, finalized in 1998 to replace the Minuteman's aging 1970s-vintage Autonetics NS-20 guidance set. It also is available as an option in the newly introduced Russian Iskander (SS-26) ballistic missiles, which have a range of 300 km. RAND Corporation analyses show that the same approach can be used to significantly improve the accuracy of a 1950s-vintage Scud missile with minimal change in equipment. The approach is even easier to apply in cruise missiles.

A major issue for non-American GPS users is the accuracy of the signal. Under the old policy of selective availability, publicly available signals were degraded to 100-meter accuracy. On May 1, 2000, the U.S. Department of Defense (DOD), which controls the GPS network, ceased degrading the quality of the signals available to non-DOD users. With ordinary transceivers, accuracies of 5–10 meters are freely available. In theory, the Defense Department can return to selective availability in time of national emergency. In practice, though, the reliance of commercial users on the undegraded version would make this difficult. Availability will be further guaranteed when the European Galileo, a satellite network virtually identical to the GPS, becomes available around 2010.

What do these changes auger for the future of deterrence and arms control? The increasing availability of GPS-INS technology will make it easier for emerging missile powers to shift from countervalue to counterforce targeting (see Counterforce Targeting; Countervalue Targeting). The implications of these developments for the Missile Technology Control Regime have not been fully debated. But it appears likely that the effectiveness of missile technology export controls will significantly decline as a result.

—*Aaron Karp*

References

Fiszur, M., and J. Grusczynski, "Bolt from the Blue: Russian Precision-Strike Missiles," *Journal of Defense Electronics*, March 2003, pp. 42–50.

Lawrence, A., *Modern Inertial Technology: Navigation, Guidance and Control*, second edition (New York: Springer Verlag, 1993).

MacKenzie, D., *Inventing Accuracy: A Historical Sociology of Nuclear Missile Guidance* (Cambridge, MA: MIT Press, 1993).

May, M. B., "Inertial Navigation and GPS," *GPS World*, September 1993, pp. 56–66.

Mohinder, S. G., L. R. Weill, and A. P. Andrews, *Global Positioning Systems, Inertial Navigation and Integration* (New York: John Wiley, 2001).

Rip, M. R., and J. P. Hasik, *The Precision Revolution: GPS and the Future of Aerial Warfare* (Annapolis, MD: Naval Institute Press, 2002).

Williams, J. E. D., *From Sails to Satellites: The Origin and Development of Navigational Science* (Oxford: Oxford University Press, 1992).

INSTITUTE FOR ADVANCED STUDY

The Institute for Advanced Study (IAS), located in Princeton, New Jersey, is an institution of higher learning and research dedicated to exploring the fundamental mysteries of pure science. It does not offer formal courses, labs, or degrees. Rather, faculty members and fellowship recipients conduct scholarly work without the burden of giving lectures or administering coursework and exams. IAS has no formal ties with any academic institution but does collaborate with other universities, particularly with Princeton University.

IAS was founded in 1930 by an endowment from Louis Bamberger and his sister, Caroline Bamberger Fuld. Abraham Flexner was the first director of the institute. Robert Oppenheimer, also known as the "father of the atomic bomb," was the director of IAS from 1947 until 1966. Albert Einstein became a lifetime member of IAS in 1933 and lived a mile and a half from the institute for the rest of his life.

IAS offers fellowships to 190 people annually. The scholars come from approximately 100 universities from across the United States, and about a third are from about twenty-five countries worldwide. A fifteen-member board of trustees administers the endowment funds for IAS.

IAS consists of four schools: the School of Mathematics, the School of Natural Sciences, the

School of Historical Studies, and the School of Social Science.

—Don Gillich

Reference

Institute for Advanced Study website, http://www.ias.
edu.

INTERCONTINENTAL BALLISTIC MISSILES (ICBMS)

The intercontinental ballistic missile (ICBM) provides nations with the ability to destroy targets thousands of miles away. These land-based missiles have ranges in excess of 5,500 kilometers and usually are nuclear armed. Three nations have developed ICBMs: the United States, Russia, and China. The United States maintains two types of silo-based ICBMs. The Russian Strategic Rocket Forces have been in decline since the end of the Cold War. Arms control, aged weapons, and budgetary pressures have forced Russia to reduce its ICBM force, although it still maintains thousands of nuclear-armed warheads to equip hundreds of silo-based, rail-mobile, and road-mobile ICBMs. China's small fleet of ICBMs carries single, high-yield nuclear reentry vehicles (RVs), and China also has a program to develop ICBMs that can carry multiple independently targetable reentry vehicles (MIRVs). Other nations (such as North Korea) have attempted to develop ICBMs.

Defenses against ICBMs and other ballistic missiles are difficult to construct, making them an ideal deterrent weapon because they are a reliable means to deliver nuclear weapons against a variety of targets. Compared to modern long-range bombers or aircraft carriers that might be used in a deterrent role, ICBMs are relatively easy to maintain and operate. For states seeking to develop a credible delivery system for weapons of mass destruction, ICBMs offer a cost-effective way to penetrate an opponent's defenses and strike targets at long ranges.

History and Background

ICBM development began in Germany during World War II. The first operational ballistic missile, the V-2, was a prototype of a longer-range missile that would be capable of striking the United States. This long-range variant of the V-2, called the A-9/A-10, was designed to carry a high-explosive warhead to a target 3,500 miles away. U.S. Navy engineers and scientists believed that the A-10's intended targets were New York and Washington. The Germans

Soviet ICBMs paraded in Red Square on the anniversary of the Bolshevik revolution, 1969. (Jerry Cooke/Corbis)

might have been able to launch these attacks as early as 1946. Knowledge gained about the V-2 program and the development of the atomic bomb focused national leadership in the Soviet Union and the United States on the development of ICBMs.

The U.S. Army Air Corps started a series of research programs to investigate the use of ICBMs in 1946. One project, the Consolidated Vultee MX-774, began as a comparison of subsonic cruise missiles and long-range ballistic missiles. The study indicated that ballistic missiles offered a superior delivery system because there were no defenses against ballistic missiles at the time. Subsonic cruise missiles, such as the German V-1, could be defeated by a combination of conventional radar detection, antiaircraft artillery, and relatively slow propeller-driven aircraft. Convair (the renamed Consolidated Vultee firm) continued research on long-range ballistic missiles. Unfortunately, the weight of first-generation atomic bombs in the 1940s was measured in tons, well beyond the payload of the V-2. When the Soviets detonated an atomic bomb on August 19, 1949, however, renewed emphasis was placed on the effort to develop nuclear delivery systems that could reach the Soviet Union. Convair won a contract to develop the first U.S. ICBM, the Atlas. Meanwhile, development of nuclear weapons continued. The first thermonuclear device (the hydrogen bomb) was detonated by the United States on November 1, 1952. Because they produced a relatively high yield for a relatively low weight, thermonuclear weapons were the ideal warhead to mount on the ICBMs under development (*see* Hydrogen Bomb; Thermonuclear Bomb).

After several years of design, development, and testing, the United States deployed the liquid-fueled Atlas ICBM in 1959. The system evolved from a vertical aboveground launch system (gentry tower) to a horizontal aboveground system (coffin launch) and finally to a below ground silo system. Atlas served until 1965. The U.S. Air Force operated Atlas squadrons from California to New York. At one point, the service deployed 72 Atlas F missiles. The Atlas F carried a 4-megaton warhead, and its range was between 6,400 and 9,000 miles. Crews required about 30 minutes to prepare and launch an Atlas.

The U.S. Air Force also developed and deployed the Titan series of ICBMs. Titan development started in 1955. The system was designed as a backup to Atlas and provided the air force with a two-stage, liquid-fueled ICBM that eventually would have a longer range and larger payload than the Atlas. Titan I, which served from 1962 until 1965, had a range of 6,300 miles and could carry a multimegaton nuclear warhead, and its crews needed only 15 minutes to launch their weapon. Titan II had much better performance: With a 9,000-mile range, it could carry a 9-megaton warhead, the largest single warhead ever carried by a U.S. ICBM. Titan II was also more responsive than the Atlas. Crews required only a single minute to launch the missile. Fifty-four Titan IIs defended the nation from 1963 to 1987. Both Titan I and Titan II were silo-based systems.

U.S. Air Force officials, impressed with propellant developments in the 1960s, moved to build a solid-fueled ICBM. Ultimately, the air force would design and deploy three versions of the Minuteman, the first such missile to be built in the United States. Minuteman used a three-stage, solid-fueled rocket motor system and was deployed in underground silos. Minuteman I had a range of 6,300 miles and carried a single reentry vehicle with a 1-megaton yield. This model first went on alert in 1962, and 800 missiles eventually served the country. Minuteman II started to replace the earlier model in 1967. It carried a warhead with a 1.2-megaton yield and had longer range, improved guidance, and penetration aids. Minuteman II served until 1991. A Minuteman III design began in 1964. It had a range of 8,000 miles and carried two to three RVs with a yield of 170 to 375 kilotons. The U.S. Air Force built 500 Minuteman III ICBMs, which continue to serve today.

The Peacekeeper is the latest U.S. ICBM (the single-warhead Midgetman was under development when it was canceled at the end of the Cold War). The Peacekeeper was designed to carry ten RVs, each having a yield of 300 kilotons. Initial air force design efforts concentrated on developing an air- or ground-mobile ICBM to replace the silo-based, and increasingly vulnerable, Minuteman system. Many concepts were tested, and in 1977, air force officials selected a four-stage missile that could be deployed in existing Minuteman silos. The Peacekeeper's range is more than 6,780 miles. The first three stages are solid-fuel systems, and the fourth stage has a liquid-fueled motor. The Peacekeeper was acquired to replace the Minuteman system, but the treaty resulting from the Strategic Arms Limitations Talks

(SALT II) limited the number of ICBMs with multiple RVs. These arms control provisions led to an agreement stipulating that the United States would deploy only fifty Peacekeeper missiles. Peacekeeper is scheduled to be withdrawn from service by 2007.

The Soviet Union also experimented with ICBMs throughout the 1950s. The Soviets introduced their first ICBM, the SS-6 Sapwood (its NATO designation), in 1959. The first truly successful ICBM was the SS-7 Saddler that saw service in 1961. The Soviet Strategic Rocket Forces operated 186 missiles until 1979 when SALT I restrictions forced the Soviets to scrap their SS-7s. This two-stage, liquid-fueled missile had a range of more than 7,100 miles. Soviet missile engineers also employed a similar, less technically sophisticated variant of the SS-7, the SS-8 Sasin. A small number of Sasins served from 1965 to 1977.

Soviet ICBM forces received a boost when they received the SS-9 Scarp, a heavy, two-stage, liquid-fueled system, in 1966. The SS-9 carried the largest nuclear yield of any ballistic missile, a 25-megaton warhead. The missile was also powerful enough to test launch a fractional orbiting bombardment system that would attack the United States from a launch profile that came from the southern hemisphere instead of the shorter northern polar route. This tactic would achieve strategic surprise by avoiding radar and satellite detection.

The Soviet Strategic Rocket Forces continued ICBM development throughout the Cold War. The SS-11 Sego was a liquid-fueled missile that could carry three RVs like the United States' Minuteman III. Soviet solid-fueled ICBMs began being fielded with the two-stage SS-13 Savage, which entered service in 1972. The system stayed on active duty until the end of the Cold War. The Soviets developed and deployed several other ICBMs during the 1970s: the SS-16, SS-17, SS-18, SS-19, and SS-20. These missile developments evolved from silos that were only used once to a design that included a missile in a canister that would limit the damage to the silo, thus allowing multiple uses. Other devices included a "cold launch" that would use a gas generator to push the missile out of the silo before ignition of the missile to allow the silo to escape major damage (*see* Cold Launch). Soviet weapons development also focused on road-mobile missiles that would limit Soviet vulnerability to U.S. missile or aerial strikes. The SS-18 Satan was the largest ICBM fielded by either

the United States or the Soviet Union. It could carry a 20-megaton warhead or up to ten smaller RVs.

The SS-24 Scalpel was another Soviet advance. It was a rail-mobile system that began service in 1987. A second version was a silo-based system that carried ten warheads. The last Soviet ICBM was the road-mobile SS-25 Sickle, thought to be designed to survive a nuclear attack and retaliate against American targets. The Russian government has also recently deployed the SS-27. This missile has silo and road-mobile versions that carry countermeasures to defeat a ballistic missile defense system.

The People's Republic of China has fielded two ICBMs, the CSS-3 and CSS-4 liquid-fueled missiles. The CSS-3 is a two-stage weapon that carries a single warhead with a range in excess of 3,400 miles. The CSS-4 has similar characteristics to the CSS-3, but with a range of 8,000 miles.

Technical Details

One of the unique characteristics of the ICBM is its ability to carry a large payload. This capability enables new nuclear weapons states to compensate for relatively inaccurate missiles by means of mounting a warhead with a large nuclear yield atop the missile. However, as technology improves and guidance systems allow for reductions in yield, nations may still opt for the ICBM because it can also carry many light warheads. The missile can carry penetration aids, such as decoys, to help confuse ballistic missile defenses, or a post-boost vehicle to launch several warheads over different trajectories to strike many targets (multiple independently targetable reentry vehicles, or MIRVs). ICBMs that carry more than two RVs are called multiple reentry vehicles.

Current Status and Developing Technologies

The United States possessed 500 Minuteman III and 50 Peacekeeper missiles as of September 20, 2001. Russia, however, still has the largest ICBM force in the world, with about 700 missiles, including SS-18, SS-19, SS-24, SS-25, and SS-27 systems. About half of the force is composed of SS-25 missiles. China has fewer than 45 single-warhead ICBMs but is developing solid-fueled DF-31 road-mobile weapons with an estimated range of 4,500 miles. China has also tested the DF-31A, a mobile missile with a greater range, 7,000 miles. The North Koreans have tested a potential ICBM, in the guise of a space launch vehicle, the Taepo Dong 2, a liquid-fueled, single-warhead delivery vehicle with a range of about 3,400 miles.

Russia, China, North Korea, and Iran are engaged in active programs to improve their ICBM forces. Two emerging threats, China and North Korea, are very focused toward this effort. The Chinese want solid-fueled ICBMs that provide better reliability, quicker reaction, and lower operational costs. The North Koreans have flight-tested many components of the Taepo Dong, which has the range to hit Hawaii and Alaska. Unfortunately, North Korea's past willingness to sell technology and systems may enable many nations to purchase an ICBM capability. Although Iran has not tested an ICBM, it seeks such capability through foreign assistance.

—*Clay Chun*

See also: Heavy ICBMs; Midgetman ICBMs; Minuteman ICBMs; Missile Defense; Mobile ICBMs; Titan ICBMs

References
Gibson, James N., *The History of the US Nuclear Arsenal* (Greenwich, CT: Brompton, 1989).
Miller, David, *The Cold War* (New York: St. Martin's Press, 1998).
Neufeld, Jacob, *Ballistic Missiles* (Washington, DC: Office of Air Force History, 1990).
Spencer, Jack, *The Ballistic Missile Threat* (Washington, DC: Heritage Foundation, 2000).
———, *The Ballistic Missile Threat Handbook* (Washington, DC: Heritage Foundation, 2000).
Stumpf, David K., *Titan II: A History of a Cold War Missile Program* (Fayetteville: University of Arkansas Press, 2000).
Zarchan, Paul, *Tactical and Strategic Missile Guidance* (Reston, VA: American Institute of Aeronautics and Astronautics, 2002).

INTERMEDIATE-RANGE NUCLEAR FORCES (INF) TREATY

The Treaty Between the United States of America and the Union of Soviet Socialist Republics on the Elimination of Their Intermediate-Range and Shorter-Range Missiles—better known as the Intermediate-Range Nuclear Forces (INF) Treaty—was the first arms control agreement to eliminate an entire class of weapon systems (that is, all U.S. and Soviet intermediate-range and shorter-range ballistic and cruise missiles with a range of 500–5,500 kilometers). It was signed in Washington, D.C., on December 8, 1987, by U.S. President Ronald Reagan and Soviet General Secretary Mikhail Gorbachev.

The treaty entered into force the following year and called for all treaty-related items to be eliminated within three years. It also provided for an on-site inspection regime that not only promoted confidence on compliance with the treaty provisions but also served as the model for on-site inspections for subsequent arms control agreements. Additionally, the INF Treaty incorporated asymmetric reductions (for example, the Soviet Union was forced to eliminate a significantly larger number of weapon systems than the United States). The INF Treaty comprises the basic treaty, a memorandum of understanding, two protocols, and an annex.

The basic treaty included seventeen articles that defined terms, the types of missiles and support systems covered by the treaty, and verification procedures. Intermediate-range missiles were defined as ground-launched ballistic missiles or ground-launched cruise missiles having a range in excess of 1,000 kilometers but not in excess of 5,500 kilometers. Shorter-range missiles were defined as ground-launched ballistic missiles or ground-launched cruise missiles having a range capability to or in excess of 500 kilometers but not in excess of 1,000 kilometers.

The memorandum, entitled "The Memorandum of Understanding Regarding the Establishment of the Data Base for the Treaty Between the Union of Soviet Socialist Republics and the United States of America on the Elimination of Their Intermediate-Range and Shorter-Range Missiles," contained seven articles. It established the database for the number and location of missiles, launchers, transporters, missile bases, and other support equipment covered by the treaty.

The protocol governing the elimination of weapons included five articles that outlined the missiles and missile-related systems subject to the treaty. The INF Treaty resulted in asymmetric reductions in Soviet and U.S. weapon systems. The United States had an aggregate total number of 859 deployed and nondeployed missiles and 283 deployed and nondeployed launchers included under the treaty. The Soviets had an aggregate total number of 1,752 deployed and nondeployed missiles and 845 deployed and nondeployed launchers included under the treaty.

Several U.S. missile systems were affected by the INF Treaty. The intermediate-range Pershing II ballistic missile, the BGM-109G cruise missile, and the

Mikhail Gorbachev and Ronald Reagan signing the Intermediate-Range Nuclear Forces Treaty, December 8, 1987. (Tim Clary/Bettmann/Corbis)

shorter-range Pershing IA (which was not deployed) all had to be eliminated. In addition, the tested (but nondeployed) Pershing IB missile was included. The treaty also included the Pershing II launcher and launch pad shelter, the BGM-109G cruise missile launch canister and launcher, and the Pershing IA launcher. The Soviet systems covered by the treaty included the intermediate-range SS-20, the SS-4, the SS-5 (which was not deployed), the shorter-range SS-12, and the SS-23. An advanced cruise missile being developed by the U.S.S.R., the SSC-X-4, also was included in the treaty. The SS-20 launch canister, launcher, missile transporter vehicle, and fixed structure for a launcher; the SS-4 missile transporter vehicle, missile erector, launch stand, and propellant tanks; the SS-12 missile launcher and missile transporter vehicle; the SS-23 missile launcher and missile transporter vehicle; and the SSC-X-4 launch canister and launcher were additional Soviet systems that had to be eliminated according to the provisions of the INF Treaty. The INF protocol outlined the specific guidelines and procedures for eliminating each of these treaty-related items.

The protocol on inspections contained eleven articles that outlined inspector responsibilities and guidelines as well as on-site inspection rules and procedures. The protocol limited both parties to 200 inspectors. The inspection regime was more difficult to implement for the United States than for the Soviet Union because U.S. inspectors had more than 130 sites in the Soviet Union, East Germany, and Czechoslovakia to inspect. In contrast, Soviet inspectors had a total of about 30 sites to inspect in the United States, the United Kingdom, West Germany, the Netherlands, Belgium, and Italy. The protocol provided for a number of different types of inspections: base-line inspections (to verify the total number of treaty-related items within the first 90 days of the treaty entering into force); close-out inspections (to verify that a missile facility or base was no longer operational); elimination inspections (to verify that the treaty items were eliminated in accordance with the treaty provisions); and quota inspections (a limited number of short-notice inspections for verifying compliance).

An additional annex on privileges and immunities to be accorded to inspectors and aircrew members granted diplomatic privileges to INF inspectors and flight crews involved in transporting inspection teams in accordance with Articles 29, 30, 31, and 34 of the Vienna Convention on Diplomatic Relations.

The INF Treaty was an important arms control agreement between the United States and the Soviet Union that signaled the beginning of an expanded dialogue between U.S. President Reagan and Soviet leader Gorbachev. The success of the INF Treaty served to bolster confidence in the arms control process and encourage further negotiations to reduce strategic nuclear arms. Thus, the INF Treaty is considered to be a watershed arms control agreement.

—*Ken Rogers*

See also: Arms Control; Entry into Force; Implementation; North Atlantic Treaty Organization; Verification

References
Frederking, Brian, *Resolving Security Dilemmas: A Constructivist Explanation of the INF Treaty* (Aldershot: Ashgate, 2000).
Gallagher, Nancy W., *The Politics of Verification* (Baltimore, MD: Johns Hopkins University Press, 1999).
INF Treaty text, available at http://www.state.gov/www/global/arms/treaties/inf1.html.
Matlock, Jack F., Jr., *Reagan and Gorbachev: How the Cold War Ended* (New York: Random House, 2004).
Rueckert, George L., *Global Double Zero: The INF Treaty from Its Origins to Implementation* (Westport, CT: Greenwood, 1993).

INTERNATIONAL ATOMIC ENERGY AGENCY (IAEA)

The International Atomic Energy Agency (IAEA) is an autonomous organization under the United Nations. Founded in 1957, it promotes and monitors the peaceful uses of atomic energy. Following its statute, the agency seeks "to accelerate and enlarge the contribution of atomic energy to peace, health and prosperity throughout the world" and to "ensure, so far as it is able, that assistance provided by it or at its request or under its supervision or control is not used in such a way as to further any military purpose." The IAEA was given an enhanced role in promoting worldwide nuclear safety following accidents at Three Mile Island in Pennsylvania and Chernobyl in the Soviet Union. Over time, the agency's emphasis has shifted away from promoting peaceful uses of nuclear power and toward security concerns such as diversion of atomic material for

nuclear proliferation. It has therefore become associated with inspections tied to the 1968 Nuclear Nonproliferation Treaty (NPT) and efforts to prevent proliferation in Iraq and North Korea. The IAEA's mandate to lead global efforts in three areas of atomic energy—peaceful usage, safety, and limitation of proliferation—has proven challenging. IAEA resources are limited, and these three objectives at times conflict. The IAEA has come under increasing criticism in recent years.

President Dwight D. Eisenhower's Atoms for Peace initiative of 1953 was the genesis of the IAEA (*see* Atoms for Peace). Eisenhower joined many scientists and others in suggesting that peaceful uses of atomic energy could play a major role in future human development. The IAEA has a General Conference composed of representatives from all member states. As of 2004, there were 134 member states. The organization also has a thirty-five-member Board of Governors. Some seats on the board are reserved for the ten states most advanced in nuclear technology, and others are elected by the General Conference. The IAEA is financed by a regular budget, dependent on assessments from member states and voluntary contributions to the Technical Cooperation Fund. In 2001, the regular budget was $230 million and voluntary contributions equaled $73 million. The agency's staff consists of just over 2,000 people, and its inspections and monitoring activities are based on more than 225 safeguard agreements in force with 141 states.

One key area of IAEA activity has been oversight of the use of atomic energy in electricity production. Particularly when oil prices rose in the 1960s and 1970s, many saw nuclear energy as a cheap and environmentally friendly alternative to fossil fuels. When the IAEA was founded, there were fewer than twenty nuclear power plants worldwide. In 2000, the IAEA was monitoring 440 reactors that produced 17 percent of the world's electricity. The agency also promotes nuclear power through the international exchange of information, leads many training programs, and publishes manuals that are used globally.

The IAEA has been a leader in other peaceful uses of nuclear technology. In several countries, the agency has led efforts to raise and sterilize male insects such as the tsetse fly using radiation. Upon release these flies cannot mate and therefore gradually reduce insect populations. Elsewhere, trace amounts of isotopes have been added to water supplies so that water management specialists can study water movement and reservoir resupply (see Isotopes). Nuclear materials also have been widely used in medical applications. The IAEA maintains its own research laboratories and often works in conjunction with other UN agencies, such as the Food and Agriculture Organization and the World Health Organization.

Since the late 1980s, the IAEA has played a growing role in nuclear safety. The agency has promoted several international conventions on nuclear safety, physical protection of nuclear material, and waste management. It has established international standards for power plants, research reactors, radioactive waste management, and industrial uses of radioactive material. When states need help reaching the standards, the IAEA provides safety reviews and technical assistance.

One of the IAEA's original goals, preventing the diversion of nuclear material to military projects, became much more significant after the 1968 NPT was signed. Non–nuclear weapons states sign "comprehensive safeguard agreements," which cover all declared nuclear material and activities. Nuclear weapons states sign "voluntary offer agreements," which cover only facilities voluntarily submitted by the states, which effectively prohibits monitoring of existing military programs. The IAEA monitors activities by carrying out material accounting and inventory duties, by enforcing containment and surveillance measures at nuclear sites, and by conducting on-site inspections. The agency currently monitors more than 1,000 installations in more than 70 countries.

Some observers have questioned the effectiveness of IAEA monitoring in cases of noncompliant states. These concerns were highlighted and grew more widespread with the IAEA's interactions with both Iraq and North Korea. IAEA inspectors monitored Iraq before the 1991 Gulf War. After the war, however, it became clear that Iraq had a much more extensive nuclear program than was realized, that it had been actively concealing information from the inspectors, and that inspectors at times had checked on and certified parts of complexes that later turned out to contain extensive other facilities. With these problems in mind, new IAEA safeguard agreements were developed that allowed access to all sites, not just those declared by the state, and that focused less

on nuclear material accountancy and more on complete assessments of a state's facilities and intentions. The new safeguards and the weight of UN Security Council resolutions on inspections did not end questions of Iraq's compliance, however. Instead, there were twelve post–Gulf War years of disputes between the IAEA and Iraq. At times, the IAEA and the United States also had conflicts over Iraq, such when they disagreed on intelligence assessments and proper tactics for encouraging compliance. This simmering dispute between Iraq and the international community eventually led to the U.S. invasion of Iraq in 2003 as the George W. Bush administration decided to eliminate the Iraqi threat through military action. Ironically, evidence uncovered in the aftermath of the second Gulf War suggested that Iraq had maintained only a rudimentary chemical, biological, and nuclear weapons program (see Iraqi Nuclear Forces and Doctrine).

The IAEA has also played a central role in disputes with North Korea. Some analysts see North Korea's removal of IAEA inspectors and monitoring equipment, along with reports that North Korea has built a nuclear weapon, as further proof that the IAEA system only works with countries that already intend to comply. Other observers argue that the strong international reaction in response to these cases of noncompliance show that IAEA goals and inspections have become institutionalized, global norms (see North Korean Nuclear Weapons Program).

Iraq, North Korea, and other cases of covert nuclear proliferation also have led some to argue that the IAEA is too cautious and slow. Several former IAEA inspectors became well-known critics of the inspection regime. These criticisms flow from three main institutional limitations. First, as the IAEA depends on states for some intelligence information and for enforcement, it can be greatly affected by states' political calculations and efforts at denial and deception. Second, the IAEA's budget and staffing are small compared to its expanded goals and responsibilities—a problem that may worsen as the IAEA takes on new roles and responsibilities in the war on terrorism. Third, the IAEA's main goals of promoting the spread of nuclear energy, while maintaining tight restrictions to prevent diversion, inherently conflict to some degree.

—*John W. Dietrich*

See also: Proliferation; Safeguards

References

Fischer, David, *History of the International Atomic Energy Agency: The First Forty Years* (Vienna: International Atomic Energy Agency, 1997).

McGeary, Johanna, "The Trouble with Inspections," *Time,* 16 December 2002, pp. 36–42.

Scheinman, Lawrence, *International Atomic Energy Agency and World Nuclear Order* (New York: Resources for the Future, 1987).

U.S. Department of State, "International Atomic Energy Agency Fact Sheet," 2003, available at http://usinfo.state.gov/topical/pol/arms/stories/iaesfact.htm.

INTRUSIVE VERIFICATION
See Verification

IRANIAN NUCLEAR WEAPONS PROGRAM

The Iranian nuclear program was initiated by Shah Reza Pahlavi in 1957 with the assistance of the United States. Under the auspices of President Dwight D. Eisenhower's Atoms for Peace program, in that year the United States signed a civil nuclear cooperation agreement with Iran (*see* Atoms for Peace). The agreement provided Iran with a 5-megawatt reactor, which came on line in 1967 and has been in continuous operation since that time. The shah established the Atomic Energy Organization of Iran in 1974 and concluded nuclear fuel agreements with the United States, Germany, and France. All U.S. assistance came to an end in 1979, however, when the U.S.-backed shah was ousted from power in a coup that brought the fundamentalist cleric Ayatollah Khomeini to power.

After the revolution, Iran's nuclear program lay dormant until it was revitalized in 1987 by the Ayatollah Khomeini. Since the United States and European governments had halted cooperation in nuclear matters with Iran after the takeover, China became the primary supplier of Iran's nuclear technology and equipment. There also have been reports of assistance provided by Pakistan, India, Argentina, Brazil, and North Korea.

China signed a ten-year scientific nuclear cooperation agreement with Iran in 1990. It supplied Iran with three subcritical and zero-power reactors and a 30-kilowatt thermal research reactor. Assistance from Russia also has played a pivotal role in Iran's nuclear program. Russia and Iran are engaged in a joint project to complete the 1,000-megawatt Bushehr reactor, a project left unfinished by Germany in 1979 and bombed repeatedly during the Iran-Iraq War.

Russia is to receive $800 million in exchange for completion of the reactor and instruction in reactor operations, development of uranium mines, and the construction of a gas-centrifuge plant. Russia has attempted to assuage U.S. concerns about the reactor by ensuring that all spent fuel from the plant would be returned to Russia. In addition, the type of commercial nuclear power plant being constructed at Bushehr is poorly suited to plutonium production (*see* Plutonium; Reactor Operations).

Iran does not have a known unsafeguarded reactor capable of producing plutonium. It has purportedly attempted to obtain fissile material on the black market to compensate for its lack of an indigenous capability to produce fissile materials. Iranian scientists, however, may have utilized hot cells obtained from the United States in the 1960s and Argentina in the 1990s to separate significant quantities of plutonium. It is also plausible that Iran may have attempted gas-centrifuge development and laser enrichment using four lasers shipped to Iran in 1978 by the United States.

In February 2003, Iran announced that it had discovered uranium reserves near Yazd, exacerbating concerns about an Iranian nuclear program. Indigenous production of uranium could make the return of spent fuel from Bushehr to Russia largely irrelevant. For its part, Iran stated that it plans to use the uranium extracted from Yazd to fuel its civilian nuclear power program. Iranian officials have insisted that the material will be used only for peaceful purposes and invited the International Atomic Energy Agency (IAEA) to inspect their nuclear facilities. The IAEA has not found any evidence in the past to support accusations of nuclear proliferation in Iran, a member of the Nuclear Nonproliferation Treaty (NPT) since 1970. Iranian officials, however, have resisted pressure to sign enhanced safeguards agreements with the IAEA, known as "93+2 provisions," on the grounds that Iran is being denied civilian nuclear technology for the Bushehr reactor (*see* International Atomic Energy Agency).

Iran is known to have one of the largest ballistic missile programs in the Middle East. Experts have expressed concern that Iran may become a secondary proliferator of missiles and missile technology, in addition to developing longer-range missiles for its own arsenal.

The Iranian missile program has benefited from assistance offered by Russia, China, and North

Korea. Iranian officials have actively backed North Korea's ballistic missile program and reportedly agreed to purchase 150 Nodong-1 missiles from the North Koreans. Iran now possesses approximately 150 Scud-C missiles, up to 200 Scud-B missiles, and an unknown number of indigenous Mushak missiles. It has conducted three tests of the Shahab-3 and deployed the Shahab-4 missile. The Shahab-3 has an 800- to 900-mile range and a payload of 1,650 pounds, while the Shahab-4 has a 1,200-mile range and a 2,200-pound payload. Iran also reportedly is developing the Shahab-5, which would presumably have even greater range and payload capacity than earlier modes. It has stated publicly that the Shahab-4 and Shahab-5 are intended to be space-launch vehicles with no military applications.

—*Jacqueline Simon*

See also: Iraqi Nuclear Forces and Doctrine; Nonproliferation; Nuclear Nonproliferation Treaty; Rumsfeld Commission

References

Cordesman, Anthony H., *Weapons of Mass Destruction in the Middle East* (Washington, DC: Center for Strategic and International Studies, 2002).

Katzman, Kenneth, *Iran: Arms and Technology Acquisitions*, CRS Report RL30551 (Washington, DC: Congressional Research Service, 2001).

Kemp, Geoffrey, ed., *Iran's Nuclear Weapons Options: Issues and Analysis* (Washington, DC: Nixon Center, 2001).

Nelson, Richard, and David H. Saltiel. *Managing Proliferation Issues with Iran* (Washington, DC: Atlantic Council of the United States, 2002).

IRAQI NUCLEAR WEAPONS PROGRAM

Iraq's nuclear weapons program was established in 1988 with the objective of producing a small nuclear arsenal. The program was intended to produce its first weapon by 1991. The destruction of its research and production facilities during the Gulf War virtually eliminated the program. Iraq had a well-funded nuclear program under Saddam Hussein that was intended to develop an indigenous capability to produce fissile nuclear material (highly enriched uranium [HEU] derived from domestic sources), nuclear technology, and nuclear weapons designs. Iraqi scientists and engineers also were hard at work developing various nuclear delivery systems (such as ballistic missiles).

The Iraqi nuclear materials program was divided into seven production and engineering initiatives:

- Research and development of a full range of enrichment technologies to exploit gas enrichment technology;
- Indigenous production and illegal procurement of natural uranium compounds;
- Research and development of irradiated fuel;
- The formation of industrial-scale facilities to produce uranium compounds for fuel fabrication or isotopic enrichment;
- The creation of design and feasibility studies for a local plutonium production reactor;
- Research and development of weapon capabilities for implosion-based nuclear weapons;
- A crash program aimed at safeguarding reactor fuel and recovering HEU for use in nuclear weapons.

In the aftermath of the second Gulf War, the UN Special Commission on Iraq (UNSCOM) was created to verify Iraqi declarations concerning nuclear, chemical, and biological forces by undertaking a series of inspections of declared and undeclared Iraqi weapons facilities and suspected storage sties. Iraqi officials failed to give their complete cooperation to UNSCOM, which resulted in nearly a decade of acrimony that culminated in the second Gulf War that began in 2003. In the aftermath of the second Gulf War, Iraq's nuclear program has been terminated, but the extent of the threat posed by the Iraqi nuclear, chemical, and biological weapons programs remains a source of controversy.

Although as of late 2004 it is impossible to say exactly what Iraqi scientists and engineers were working on, the U.S. and allied intelligence communities apparently began to overestimate the scope and capability of Iraq's programs to develop weapons of mass destruction (WMD) in the aftermath of Operation Desert Fox (1998). This overestimate was in part caused by Iraqi efforts at denial and deception. A consensus formed within intelligence and policymaking communities that Iraqi officials were doing everything in their power to preserve their WMD capabilities and remaining stocks of weapons and to set the stage for a return to production as soon as they could escape UN scrutiny. Saddam Hussein and many of his senior officers apparently believed that they possessed a significant chemical weapons capability, but they never managed to use it in defense of their regime. In the aftermath of the September 11, 2001, terrorist attacks on the United States, the Bush administration was no longer willing to live in a world in which the prospect of Iraq's WMD capability might find its way into the hands of Islamic militants, no matter how farfetched that prospect appeared to critics of the administration. History still must judge whether the Bush administration was correct in ending the Hussein regime, but the war was fought to end the potential threat posed by Iraq's chemical, biological, and nuclear weapons programs.

—Laura Fontaine and James J. Wirtz

See also: Highly Enriched Uranium; International Atomic Energy Agency; Nonproliferation; Nuclear Nonproliferation Treaty; Nuclear Suppliers Group; Payload; Plutonium; Rumsfeld Commission; United Nations Special Commission on Iraq; Uranium

References

"Iraqi Nuclear Weapons," 3 November 1998, available at http://www.fas.org/nuke/guide/iraq/nuke/program.htm.

"Iraq's Weapons of Mass Destruction Programs," October 2002, available at http://www.fas.org/irp/cia/product/Irq_Oct_2002.htm.

ISOTOPES

Isotopes are atoms of the same element that have the same number of protons (atomic number) but different numbers of neutrons in the nucleus. Since different isotopes of the same element have different numbers of neutrons, the atomic mass (the sum of the protons and neutrons) is different. Isotopes are denoted by the element name or symbol and the atomic mass number. As an example, uranium has 92 protons in the nucleus. Uranium 238, which has 146 neutrons in the nucleus, and uranium 235, which has 143 neutrons in the nucleus, are examples of uranium isotopes.

An alternative term for isotope is "nuclide." This general term is used to identify any atom that is described by the number of protons and neutrons present in the nucleus.

English chemist Frederick Soddy first hypothesized the existence of atoms of the same element with different atomic masses in 1912, and on February 18, 1913, he coined the term "isotope." The word comes from the Greek term for "at the same place," referring to the fact that the isotopes of a given element are located at the same place on the periodic table (Wikipedia).

British physicist J. J. Thompson discovered the first evidence that isotopes exist in stable elements while experimenting with neon in 1913. He concluded that two different stable forms of neon existed in nature, thereby supporting the existence of isotopes.

Thompson's assistant was chemist Francis W. Aston, who later, in 1918, invented the mass spectrograph. A mass spectrograph is a device that separates electrically charged atoms according to mass and can accurately measure the mass of the atom. From his work with the mass spectrograph between 1918 and 1930, Aston discovered 212 naturally occurring isotopes. He also was able to formulate "the whole-number rule which states that all atomic masses are close to integers and that fractional atomic weights of elements are due to the presence of two or more isotopes, each of which has an approximately integral value" (Parrington et al., p. 3).

Most naturally occurring elements have two or more isotopes; just 20 of the 90 elements that occur in nature have only one isotope. Some isotopes are stable and others are unstable (or radioactive), that is, they may decay into other isotopes or elements. There are 266 stable and 65 unstable naturally occurring isotopes. The latter are also called "radionuclides."

Bombarding certain elements with other particles, for example neutrons, alpha particles, and protons, can create so-called "manmade" isotopes. More than 2,500 isotopes have been produced through such processes. Many of these nuclides are artificially produced radioactive isotopes.

Because two isotopes of the same element are chemically similar, they are difficult to separate. Due to differences in atomic mass, stability, and other physical characteristics, however, isotopes may be separated by several methods. Examples of separation techniques that are used for uranium enrichment, for example, build on this knowledge and include gaseous diffusion, gas centrifuge, electromagnetic separation, and laser isotope separation.

—Don Gillich

See also: Enrichment; Highly Enriched Uranium; Neutrons; Uranium

References

Parrington, Josef R., Harold D. Knox, Susan L. Breneman,

Edward M. Baum, and Frank Feiner, *Nuclides and Isotopes: Chart of the Nuclides,* fifteenth edition (New York: General Electric and KAPL, 1996).

Wikipedia, "Isotope," available at http://en.wikipedia.org/wiki/Isotope.

ISRAELI NUCLEAR FORCES AND DOCTRINE

After the horrors of the Holocaust, the creation of the State of Israel on May 14, 1948, brought with it existential fears about the survival of the new Jewish state. These fears brought forth the consideration of a nuclear weapons option. With help from the French, the Israelis constructed their own nuclear reactor at Dimona in the Negev desert as a source of fissile material and as a means to establish a nuclear industry. Estimates of how many nuclear weapons Israel has assembled range from 75 up to 400. The nuclear weapons stance that Israel takes is one of ambiguity. It neither confirms nor denies the existence of an Israeli nuclear arsenal.

History and Background

In 1949, the Israel Defense Forces (IDF) Science Corps (known in Hebrew by its acronym, HEMED GIMMEL) conducted a geological survey in the Negev desert to study the potential extraction of uranium reserves. No main source of uranium was found, but researchers discovered that it could be extracted from phosphate deposits. The Israel Atomic Energy Commission (IAEC) was formed in 1952. By 1953, the Science Corps, by then renamed Machon 4, found a way to extract the uranium from the Negev and developed a way to produce heavy water. Possessing these two capabilities provided Israel with the ability to make the nuclear materials most important in creating a nuclear weapon (*see* Heavy Water; Uranium).

Israel had collaborated with France in the construction of a reactor in Marcoule, France, in the early 1950s. When Israel was ready to build its own reactor, it turned to France for help. In 1956, France agreed to give Israel an 18-megawatt research reactor. Due to the Suez Canal crisis, this agreement was never carried out. Instead, on October 3, 1957, France and Israel signed an agreement that committed France to construct a 24-megawatt reactor, in conjunction with an unwritten agreement that France also would build a chemical reprocessing plant. The arrangement was supposed to be carried out in secret and outside the confines of the International Atomic Energy Agency (IAEA) inspections regime. The French went along with Israel's secrecy and provided the materials until May 1960, when France threatened not to supply reactor fuel unless Israel publicized the plant project and agreed to submit to IAEA site inspections. The Israelis soothed French fears, and French contractors finished building the reactor and reprocessing plant. The uranium fuel was also delivered, and the reactor was finished and went critical in 1964.

The United States did not become aware of the Dimona facility until 1958. By December 1960, U.S. intelligence officials realized that Israel was constructing a nuclear facility. Prime Minister David Ben-Gurion had stated that the Dimona facility was a nuclear research center for peaceful purposes. By the mid-1960s, the CIA station in Tel Aviv, Israel, concluded that the Israeli nuclear weapons program was an "irreversible fact."

Current Status

Israeli officials often state that Israel will not be the first state to introduce nuclear weapons into the Middle East. If Israel were to openly declare a nuclear weapons capability, however, the announcement could cause other nuclear powers to grant nuclear guarantees to the Arab states, force the United States to reduce its support of Israel, or force Israel's neighbors to redouble their own efforts to obtain weapons of mass destruction. Since these would all be extraordinarily dangerous developments, Israeli officials will continue to shroud their nuclear programs in ambiguity while quietly maintaining the most capable nuclear arsenal in the Middle East.

In the late 1990s, U.S. intelligence estimated that Israel had 75–130 nuclear weapons, including warheads for its Jericho missiles and bombs for Israeli aircraft. Israel has never tested a nuclear weapon, although many suspect that a 1979 explosion in the southern Indian Ocean was a South African–Israeli joint nuclear test.

—Kimberly L. Kosteff

See also: Nonproliferation; Nuclear Nonproliferation Treaty; Payload; Strategic Forces

Reference

Cohen, Avner, *Israel and the Bomb* (New York: Columbia University Press, 1998).

JOINT CHIEFS OF STAFF (JCS)

The purpose of the U.S. Joint Chiefs of Staff (JCS) is to advise the president and secretary of defense on military affairs. It includes a chairman, a vice chairman, the chief of staff of the Army, the chief of naval operations, the chief of staff of the Air Force, and the commandant of the Marine Corps. The JCS is assisted in its duties by the Joint Staff, which has no authority in planning or operational matters. The chairman of the Joint Chiefs of Staff is the senior military officer within the U.S. Department of Defense, followed in order by the vice chairman and

J

the other chiefs of staff based on their dates of rank as general.

The JCS is headed by the chairman (or the vice chairman in the chairman's absence), who sets the agenda for the JCS and presides over its meetings. When acting in their capacity as members of the

The Joint Chiefs of Staff includes the heads of the U.S. armed services. Here, the Joint Chiefs meet on November 29, 1949. Left to right: Gen. J. Lawton Collins, U.S. Army; Gen. Hoyt S. Vanderberg, U.S. Air Force; Gen. Omar N. Bradley, Chairman of the Joint Chiefs, and Adm. Forrest P. Sherman, Chief of Naval Operations. (National Archives)

Joint Chiefs of Staff, they are supposed to serve primarily as military advisers to senior elected officials, not just as the chiefs of their respective military services. The chairman of the Joint Chiefs of Staff is the principal military adviser to the president, the secretary of defense, and the National Security Council (NSC). All JCS members are by law military advisers, however, and they may respond to any request for information or advice they receive or voluntarily submit, through the chairman, advice to the president, the secretary of defense, or the NSC.

Over time, the executive authority of the Joint Chiefs of Staff has evolved. In World War II, the joint chiefs acted as executive agents in dealing with theater and area commanders. With the passage of the National Security Act of 1947, their role shifted and they became planners and advisers to the president and secretary of defense rather than commanders of combatant commands. Nevertheless, under the 1948 Key West Agreement, the joint chiefs served as executive agents for unified commands, a responsibility that allowed the service component executive agent (who provided logistical and administrative support to the combatant commands) to originate direct communication with the combatant command. Congress abolished this authority in a 1953 amendment to the National Security Act. Today, as a result of the Goldwater-Nichols DOD Reorganizations Act of 1986, the JCS has no authority to command combatant forces. Their role now is to serve as military advisers to the highest levels of the U.S. government.

—Guy Roberts

References
"The Joint Chiefs of Staff," DefenseLink, available at
   http://www.dtic.mil/jcs/.
Perry, Mark, Four Stars: The Inside Story of the Forty Year
   Battle between the Joint Chiefs of Staff and America's
   Civilian Leaders (New York: Houghton Mifflin,
   1989).

JOINT DECLARATION ON DENUCLEARIZATION OF THE KOREAN PENINSULA

Signed on January 20, 1992, by the prime minister of the Republic of Korea (ROK, or South Korea) and representatives of the Democratic People's Republic of Korea (DPRK, or North Korea), the Joint Declaration on the Denuclearization of the Korean Peninsula sought to limit the danger of nuclear conflict in the region by eliminating nuclear weapons from the Korean peninsula. The six-point agreement came into force on February 19, 1992.

In the agreement, both countries pledged not to test, produce, receive, possess, store, deploy, or use nuclear weapons. The agreement sought to regulate the use of nuclear energy to ensure that it was used for peaceful purposes and not for reprocessing or uranium enrichment. It also created a South-North Joint Nuclear Control Commission to implement an inspection regime in order to monitor compliance with the agreement.

The commission's activities, however, have been placed on hold since 1993 because the parties have been unable to agree on the terms of a reciprocal inspection regime. No inspections have been conducted under the terms of the agreement. This failure was overshadowed by the 1994 Agreed Framework, in which North Korea pledged to implement the terms of the Joint Declaration and engage in North-South dialogue.

The Joint Declaration has subsequently become part of a wider diplomatic dispute between the DPRK and the United States. At almost regular intervals, tensions peak on the Korean peninsula as the regime in Pyongyang makes veiled and not so veiled threats about the DPRK's nuclear capabilities and intentions, much to the consternation of the international community. In December 2003, for example, North Korea openly claimed to have several operational nuclear warheads.

—J. Simon Rofe

See also: North Korean Nuclear Weapons Program; South Korean Nuclear Weapons Program

References
Cummings, Bruce, Korea's Place in the Sun (New York:
   W. W. Norton, 1998).
——, North Korea: Another Country (New York: New
   Press, November 2003).
"Joint Declaration of the Denuclearization of the
   Korean Peninsula," Carnegie Non-Proliferation
   Project, available at http://www.ceip.org/files/
   projects/npp/resources/koreadenuclearization.htm.
Oberdorfer, Don, The Two Koreas: A Contemporary
   History (New York: Basic, 2002).
United States Institute of Peace Library website,
   http://www.usip.org/library/pa/n_skorea/
   n_skorea06152000.html.

K

KILOTON

A kiloton is a measure of the energy released during a nuclear detonation. A 1-kiloton blast is equal to an explosion of 1,000 tons of trinitrotoluene (TNT), a high explosive. This definition refers to all of the energy released by a weapon, regardless of the form. When a nuclear explosion occurs, only a small part of the released energy is in the form of explosive energy—other types of energy released include heat, pressure, thermal energy, and radiation. A chemical explosion, in contrast, mostly takes the form of blast. The Hiroshima explosion was estimated to be 12–18 kilotons, for example.

—*Zach Becker*

See also: Fission Weapons; Megaton
References
Pringle, Laurence, *Nuclear War: From Hiroshima to Nuclear Winter* (Hillside, NJ: Enslow, 1985).

KWAJALEIN ATOLL

Kwajalein Atoll is part of the Marshall Islands, which were wrested from the Japanese in February 1944, during World War II. The world's largest coral atoll, it lies east of the Philippines and northeast of New Guinea in the South Pacific Ocean.

Kwajalein consists of 97 islands, comprising 6.5 square miles that surround a 1,100 square mile lagoon. At the end of the war, it served as a refueling stop for the B-29s en route to the atomic bombing missions in Japan. During the Korean and Vietnam wars, Kwajalein served as a refueling stop for cargo and personnel transports.

Between 1958 and 1963, Vandenberg Air Force Base, California, and a Kwajalein test facility were built to allow Atlas, Minuteman, and Titan rockets to be launched from the United States, and Nike-Zeus rockets, and later Spartan missiles, to intercept them over the Pacific. The first successful interception occurred in 1962. In the 1970s, the Homing Overlay Experiment (HOE) demonstrated that incoming missiles could be destroyed while they were outside the Earth's atmosphere without using nuclear warheads. The successful HOE system was the cornerstone of the Ronald Reagan administration's Strategic Defense Initiative (*see* Strategic Defense Initiative [SDI]). By the 1990s, facilities on Kwajalein were participating in space tracking missions and other space operations.

Kwajalein lagoon serves as the splashdown point for intercontinental ballistic missiles fired from Vandenberg AFB some 4,200 miles away. About 3,000 Americans connected with the test site live on the islands.

—*Frannie Edwards*

See also: Bikini Island Missile Defense; Strategic Defense Initiative
References
Manhattan Project Heritage Preservation Association website, http://www.childrenofthemanhattanproject.org.
"Kwajalein Atoll: Republic of the Marshall Islands," available at http://www.angelfire.com/hi2/kwa/.

L

LAUNCH ON WARNING/
LAUNCH UNDER ATTACK

An increase in prompt hard-target kill capability in the 1980s appeared to enable the Soviet Union to destroy much of the U.S. land-based strategic capability as well as its command and control centers. This development forced U.S. nuclear planners to consider adopting a launch-on-warning or launch-under-attack posture for U.S. strategic deterrent forces. A launch-on-warning policy would stipulate that strategic nuclear forces would be launched upon detection of an enemy attack, before the ultimate confirmation of a nuclear attack—explosions on U.S. territory—occurred. A launch-under-attack policy would set in place the ability to launch nuclear forces only after nuclear weapons had begun detonating over their targets.

To make a launch-on-warning posture a reality, effective early warning systems and a responsive national command authority must be available in peacetime and in crisis. Following deployment of Defense Support Program satellites in 1971, U.S. policymakers could expect about 30 minutes of warning from the moment of a Soviet intercontinental ballistic missile (ICBM) launch to its impact on U.S. territory. Soviet submarines equipped with submarine-launched ballistic missiles (SLBMs) posed the threat of reducing potential reaction times. If deployed near the coastline of the United States, submarines could launch their SLBMs on depressed trajectories, thereby reducing missile flight times to U.S. cities and strategic bases to a matter of minutes. Under these circumstances, a launch-on-warning policy was highly demanding: When on day-to-day alert, early warning, presidential launch authority, and launch orders would have to be generated in a matter of minutes to avoid a decapitating attack. Furthermore, the president would have to make the decision to use nuclear weapons while being evacuated by helicopter to the E-4B National Airborne Operations Center (NAOC), hopefully located somewhere outside the lethal blast radius of weapons targeted against Washington, D.C. Because of the significant challenges involved in alerting the appropriate parties, making crucial decisions, and releasing launch authority under compressed time periods, launch authority would likely be predelegated further down the chain of command. The risk of inadvertent or accidental nuclear war would be high.

The launch-under-attack posture clearly minimizes the risks of inadvertent or accidental nuclear war. However, it demands highly survivable retaliatory forces, such as road- or rail-mobile ICBMs as well as mobile, hardened command and control systems able to function effectively throughout a nuclear attack. Predelegation of launch authority is still a key component of a launch-under-attack strategy because of the assumption that the national command authority would be one of the first targets struck by an opponent.

—*Malcolm Davis*

See also: Cheyenne Mountain, Colorado; Command and Control; Ride Out

References

Blair, Bruce G., *The Logic of Accidental Nuclear War* (Washington, DC: Brookings Institution, 1993).
Carter, Ashton B., John D. Steinbruner, and Charles A. Zraket, eds., *Managing Nuclear Operations* (Washington, DC: Brookings Institution, 1987).

LAUNCHERS

A missile launcher is a vehicle or fixed structure that serves as a firing position for a ballistic missile. Launchers must be capable of storing a missile in a ready launch status for extended periods of time, protecting it from the elements and keeping it secure from unauthorized destruction and direct attack by an opponent (*see* Intercontinental Ballistic Missiles).

Land-mobile missiles are often carried on vehicles called transporter-erector-launchers (TELs). TELs can be sophisticated, tracked vehicles that carry missiles in a horizontal cradle over rough terrain or roads, or they can be simple conversions of commercially available trucks that have little cross-country capability. Once a TEL leaves its garrison, it generally hides in the countryside, under culverts, bridges, or in rugged terrain that provides some overhead cover, and then moves into a pre-surveyed firing position to launch its missile. The missile is then raised into a vertical firing position. Simple TELs can be destroyed once they give away their position as a result of firing the missile, but more sophisticated TELs and other support vehicles associated with the missile launch generally "scoot" to another predetermined hiding position to avoid counter battery fire. Missiles also can be deployed on railroad cars. These rail-based launch cars work like TELs in that they carry the missile in a horizontal position and then move to pre-surveyed launch sites to erect and fire the missiles. Because of the great weight of intercontinental ballistic missiles, rail-mobile systems offer advantages over land-mobile systems. The cars, camouflaged to appear as much as possible like a normal train, can be shuttled across large areas, making it difficult to detect and attack them.

Fixed-site launchers initially were simple steel and concrete structures that provided a level and stable platform to raise, fuel, and fire a missile. These surface structures, however, were easily detectable from the air and were relatively fragile, making the missiles an easy target. These launch tables also exposed the missiles to the elements, increasing maintenance problems and reducing the amount of time a missile could be placed on alert. To solve these problems, most later missiles were placed in underground missile "silos," steel-reinforced concrete structures that created a controlled environment for the missiles. These silos also could be hardened to withstand extraordinarily high amounts of blast overpressure, which forced opponents to develop accurate delivery systems to attack them with relatively large nuclear warheads. Silos were connected to launch control officers located at remote underground command "capsules."

Most missile silos were designed for "hot launch," that is, the missile silo door would be blown off by explosive charges, and the missile would ignite in the silo and then fly to its target. Hot launch would destroy the silo, however. The Soviet Strategic Rocket Forces experimented with "cold launch" systems in which the missiles would be ejected from the silo by a compressed gas, for example, and ignite only after clearing the launcher. This raised the possibility that Soviet missile silos might have been capable of reloading, although many believed that it was unlikely that personnel could regain access to missile fields that had been subjected to nuclear attack or that missile silos that had been attacked would remain functional (*see* Cold Launch; Silo Basing).

Submarines that carry ballistic missiles are generally equipped with launch tubes that allow the submarine to fire its missiles under water. The missile is expelled from the launch tube using pressurized gas and ignites after clearing the surface. If ignited inside the submarine, missiles would quickly burn a hole through the hull. Submarines must be equipped with sophisticated navigation and buoyancy systems to launch missiles while submerged. Knowledge of the exact launch position is a key requirement for missile accuracy. The submarine also must remain at a constant depth and angle during the launch process, a challenge given the tons of seawater that rushes into the missile tube after the missile is shot to the surface (*see* Submarines, Nuclear-Powered Ballistic Missile [SSBNs]).

—*James J. Wirtz*

References

Evangelista, Matthew, *Innovation and the Arms Race* (Ithaca, NY: Cornell University Press, 1988).

Wirtz, James J., *Counterforce and Theater Missile Defense: An ASW Approach to the SCUD Hunt* (Carlisle, PA: Strategic Studies Institute, U.S. Army War College, March 1995).

LAWRENCE LIVERMORE NATIONAL LABORATORY

Operated under a contract with the University of California Board of Regents, Lawrence Livermore National Laboratory (LLNL), a 12-square-mile U.S. Department of Energy facility, conducts research and development activities associated with all phases of the nuclear weapons life-cycle as well as research on nonproliferation, arms control, and treaty verification technology. Facilities include the High Explosive Application Facility (HEAF); a tritium facility; the NOVA laser used for Inertial Confinement Fusion (ICF) research; and the Atomic Vapor Laser Isotope Separation (AVLIS) plant. The National Ignition Facility (NIF), a new ICF laser facility, is under construction at the laboratory. Lawrence Livermore employs about 7,800 people.

Following the Soviet Union's first atomic explosion in August 1949, Ernest O. Lawrence, the director of what was then called the University of California Radiation Laboratory (UCRL), voiced his grave concerns about the possibility that the Soviets would quickly proceed with the development of the hydrogen (fusion) bomb. Sharing this worry was Edward Teller, who had worked at the Los Alamos Laboratory during the war, and who had, in 1949, headed the project there that was exploring the possibility of producing a thermonuclear device. Lawrence and Teller, sharing a passion for science and a dedication to the United States, wanted to respond to those uncertain times in a direct and useful way that would ensure America's supremacy in the field of nuclear weapons. They met in October 1949 to discuss their concerns about the Soviet atomic program. Teller believed that friendly competition for Los Alamos—the only weapons laboratory in the United States at the time—would accelerate the development of thermonuclear weapons and fuel scientific accomplishments. In June 1952, at an abandoned Naval Air Station in Livermore, California, a branch of the UCRL was created.

Most nuclear warheads that have entered the stockpile since 1960 have benefited from the scientific competition between Los Alamos and Lawrence Livermore. Several are still in the arsenal. The B83, designed by LLNL, is an Air Force gravity bomb intended to be delivered in low-level flight against "hardened" targets (concrete missile silos and command and control centers). First deployed in 1983, it has a high yield (somewhere between 1 and 2 megatons). As many as 950 of these weapons may be in the U.S. arsenal. The W87 warhead was designed by LLNL for the Air Force's Peacekeeper intercontinental ballistic missile. It was first deployed in 1986, and 500 W87s remain in the arsenal.

Its proximity to Silicon Valley also helped Lawrence Livermore to become the center of computer-simulated nuclear explosion modeling. After the completion of Comprehensive Test Ban Treaty negotiations in 1996, the laboratory instituted an accelerated strategic computing initiative designed to ensure that verification requirements could be met by the time the treaty entered into force. (The U.S. Senate considered the treaty in 1999 but has not yet ratified it.) The shift relied on computer simulation to obtain more accurate modeling data and valid computer code predictions of fission and fusion reactions to compensate for prohibitions on testing actual devices. Massive parallel processing utilizing the world's premier supercomputers allow for complex modeling and data collection. For example, in the field of computational fluid dynamics, the turbulent fluid flow of high ionization states of radioactive elements may be modeled and three-dimensional flow modeling and spatial dimensional calculations are possible. Weapon design effects and fusion energy production can also be modeled. Today, Lawrence Livermore, along with the other national laboratories, runs a nuclear stockpile stewardship program to guarantee the reliability and safety of the U.S. nuclear weapons stockpile.

—*Gilles Van Nederveen*

See also: Los Alamos National Laboratory; Sandia National Laboratories; Stockpile Stewardship Program

References

Cochran, Thomas B., William M. Arkin, Robert S. Norris, and Milton M. Hoenig, *Nuclear Weapons Databook*, vol. 2: *U.S. Nuclear Warhead Production* (Cambridge, MA: Ballinger, 1987).

Cochran, Thomas B., William M. Arkin, Robert S. Norris, and Milton M. Hoenig, *Nuclear Weapons Databook*, vol. 3: *U.S. Nuclear Warhead Facility Profiles* (Cambridge, MA: Ballinger, 1987).

Lawrence Livermore websites, http://www.llnl.gov and http://www.education.llnl.gov.

LAYERED DEFENSE
See Missile Defense

LEAKAGE
See Missile Defense

LIGHT-WATER REACTORS
The most widely used nuclear reactor in the world today is the light-water reactor. In these reactors, water acts as both moderator and coolant; that is, fission neutrons are moderated (slowed down) and

heat is transferred to the water. The two principal designs for light-water reactors are the boiling-water reactor (BWR) and the pressurized-water reactor (PWR). In BWRs, the water is allowed to boil in the reactor core, and the steam is used to drive a turbine generator to create electricity. In PWRs, the water is under higher pressure and does not boil; however, this water goes to a steam generator where heat is transferred from the primary loop to another water loop (or secondary loop) at a lower pressure, producing steam, which drives a turbine generator to create electricity (see Pressurized-Water Reactors [PWRs]; Reactor Operations).

History and Background

Over sixty years ago, on December 2, 1942, the world's first self-sustaining nuclear chain reaction took place on a squash court beneath Stagg Field on the campus of the University of Chicago in an experiment led by Manhattan Project scientist Enrico Fermi (see Manhattan Project). The age of nuclear power had begun. By the end of World War II, the U.S. Navy believed it was possible to develop a nuclear propulsion program for its ships. The first light-water reactor designed for nuclear propulsion followed on the work of Admiral Hyram Rickover in the 1940s and 1950s. After spending some time at the Oak Ridge National Laboratory in 1946, Rickover was convinced that a sufficient technological base was available, and Westinghouse received a contract to build a light-water prototype reactor for submarines. This prototype, known as the Mark I, was tested in early 1953, and its successor, the Mark II, was installed in the submarine *Nautilus*. The *Nautilus* was launched in early 1954 and had no major problems in its sea trials. The performance of the first two nuclear reactors signified that light-water reactors were a viable power source.

At the 1955 Peaceful Uses of the Atom Conference in Geneva, the light-water reactor was selected as the type of reactor that could best fill the energy needs of the future. Although the first commercial reactor to be connected to a power grid was the gas-graphite reactor at Calder Hall in the United Kingdom in August 1956, the second one to be connected to a power grid was a light-water reactor at Shippingport, Pennsylvania, in December 1957 (see Gas-Graphite Reactors). Under the 1958 Euratom Accord and the 1954 Atoms for Peace Program, light-water reactors were introduced to Europe and

were quickly accepted by those countries not having indigenous reactor programs (see Atoms for Peace; Three Mile Island).

In the 1950s and 1960s, the U.S. Atomic Energy Commission investigated a variety of commercial power-reactor designs, carrying several to the prototype stage. Westinghouse and General Electric were at the forefront of developing light-water reactors for domestic commercial use and export. Westinghouse, which developed the light-water reactor for U.S. Navy propulsion systems, continued to market the PWR. General Electric, which had developed an unsuccessful liquid metal–cooled type of reactor for the navy, marketed BWR reactors. In the early 1960s, light-water reactors began to enter commercial service. About 80 percent of all the nuclear power plants built or under construction in the world today are light-water reactors.

Technical Details

The prompt fission neutrons (that is, those neutrons emitted immediately from the fission process) created in fission reactions are high-energy (fast) neutrons. Fissile isotopes such as uranium 235 (U-235) and plutonium 239 (Pu-239) have a very low probability of undergoing fission with the absorption of fast neutrons; consequently, these fast neutrons must be moderated (slowed down) to sustain fission reactions. The fissile isotopes have a much higher probability of undergoing fission with low-energy (thermal) neutrons. The parameter used to describe this probability of fission interaction is called the "microscopic fission cross-section." For example, the microscopic fission cross-section of U-235 for thermal neutrons is approximately 420 times greater than for fast neutrons.

The primary mechanism by which fast neutrons are slowed down is through elastic scattering. Consider the collision between two identical billiard balls where one ball is stationary and is hit head-on by a moving billiard ball. After the collision, the moving ball will become stationary and the stationary ball will then move off with the same speed as the incident ball before the collision. In this example of an ideal elastic collision, the moving ball gives all of its energy to the stationary ball. Now assume the same moving billiard ball has a collision with a stationary bowling ball. Upon colliding, the billiard ball will bounce off with very little change in speed (and energy). The relative mass of the particles in the collision are important in determining how much energy the colliding particle will lose during each collision. These examples are analogous to what is happening in light-water reactors. The fission neutrons undergo elastic collisions with light water, or regular H_2O, which is made primarily of hydrogen. The hydrogen nucleus is approximately the same mass as the neutron; consequently, the neutron loses relatively large amounts of energy during every collision. If the moderator were a material with a much more massive nucleus, the fission neutrons would require many more collisions in order to slow down, since they would not lose nearly as much energy per collision.

In a light-water reactor, the water serves a dual purpose as both the moderator and the coolant. The heat from fission comes from approximately 200 mega electronvolts (MeVs) of recoverable energy from each fission event. This heat energy comes primarily from the kinetic energy (the energy of motion) of the fission products emitted by each fission event. The heat transferred from the fuel to the water heats the water to high temperatures. If the reactor is a PWR, the high pressure will ensure that the water remains in liquid form. The hot water in the PWR goes through a steam generator that uses conduction to heat the water in a secondary loop to high temperatures. The water in this secondary loop is at a much lower pressure, which allows the water to become steam. BWRs operate at a lower pressure in the reactor; consequently, the water boils in the upper portion of the reactor. It is the steam from these reactors that drives the turbine blades (*see* Isotopes; Plutonium; Uranium).

Development of Future Technologies
The design and implementation of nuclear reactors has progressed from very simple "proof of concept" designs to the complex machines of today. One way that scientists and engineers describe the evolution of these reactors is by categorizing them in groups. Each group of reactors is characterized by the performance standards it meets and the technological advances it utilizes, referred to in terms of "technological generations," or "Gen." The first demonstration reactors were classified as Gen-I reactors. The Gen-II reactors are mostly of the BWR and PWR type and are used today throughout the world. In 1996, Japan and a few other nations began producing power with Gen-III reactors, also called "advanced reactors." These reactors are evolutionary rather than revolutionary and are based upon safer, more robust, proliferation-resistant designs and proven concepts. In all likelihood, the next group of reactors built in the United States will be Gen-III+ reactors that will utilize the experience gained in building the Gen-III reactors to produce a more refined version of the light-water reactor. The future of reactor technology is wide open. Some concepts will be evolutionary designs based upon existing technology; others may be radical departures from current designs. This class of future reactors, which may be under construction as early as approximately 2025, is collectively known as Gen-IV.

—*Edward P. Naessens, Jr.*

References
Cowan, Robin, "Nuclear Power Reactors: A Study of Technological Lock-In," *Journal of Economic History*, vol. 50, September 1990, pp. 541–566.

Glasstone, S., and A. Sesonske, *Nuclear Reactor Engineering,* third edition (New York: Van Nostrand Reinhold, 1981).

Lamarsh, J. R., and A. J. Baratta, *Introduction to Nuclear Engineering* (Upper Saddle River, NJ: Prentice-Hall, 2001).

Parrington, Josef R., Harold D. Knox, Susan L. Breneman, Edward M. Baum, and Frank Feiner, *Nuclides and Isotopes: Chart of the Nuclides,* fifteenth edition (New York: General Electric and KAPL, 1996).

LIMITED NUCLEAR WAR
Limited nuclear war is a situation in which two or more states use nuclear weapons in an armed conflict but do not attempt to annihilate their enemies by striking massively at the other side's urban-industrial targets. In a limited nuclear war, nuclear weapons would be used on one or more elements of a nation's land-based nuclear infrastructure or other critical military, industrial, logistical, or command and control centers. The purpose of a limited nuclear attack could be to create military paralysis, to destroy a single sector of the adversary's economy, or to simply demonstrate the attacker's resolve and willingness to employ nuclear weapons in the conflict.

The state that attempts to fight a limited nuclear war presupposes that a limited nuclear attack would seriously damage its opponent's military infrastructure while causing a relatively low level of civilian deaths. This is to ensure that, while a state's ability to fully retaliate is paralyzed, its population will not immediately demand a full-scale nuclear response. The attacking state anticipates that the civilian population will hope to end hostilities and assent to the demands of the attacker to avoid a large-scale attack.

The ultimate purpose of limited nuclear war is both political and military. In a military sense, the goal is to affect the course of the war in one's favor. The political objective is to raise the prospect of a full-scale nuclear exchange in the mind of the opponent, thereby bringing about a rapid termination of hostilities. The limited nuclear war doctrine was put forward in the 1960s by security analysts such as Robert Osgood in response to the Soviet Union's acquisition of a credible nuclear capability. To make the threat of nuclear weapons use more credible while devising options for something less than a full-scale nuclear attack that would make mutual nuclear annihilation likely, policymakers sought a flexible nuclear doctrine that would not necessarily result in escalation to all-out nuclear war. Technological advances that produced small, relatively low-yield, accurate nuclear weapons led some strategists to believe that it might be possible to fine-tune nuclear strikes and limit the scope and destructiveness of nuclear war.

Secretary of Defense James Schlesinger announced in 1974 that the United States had adopted the concept of limited nuclear war as part of U.S. strategic doctrine. This decision was in part due to the overwhelming destructive power of both sides' nuclear arsenals. As the destructive capability of the superpowers' nuclear arsenals increased, it became clear that an all-out nuclear confrontation between the United States and the Soviet Union would lead to unprecedented devastation and the death of hundreds of millions of people. A lack of options in doctrine and capabilities increased the possibility that a conflict over peripheral issues could escalate into an all-out nuclear war. By adopting a limited nuclear warfighting doctrine, the United States was able to tailor its response to the requirements of the situation. Although some saw limited nuclear options as a way to reestablish deterrence after it had failed to prevent the outbreak of conventional war, others saw limited nuclear options as a way to actually fight and win a nuclear war between the United States and the Soviet Union.

The controversy surrounding the adoption of the limited nuclear war doctrine was centered on the attacking state's ability to control the situation. Counting on one's ability to destroy the enemy's will to fight, if not its retaliatory capability, is a significant gamble. Since nuclear war is a zero-sum game, and all states want to retain control and legitimacy, many analysts believe that limited nuclear war doctrine is insanely risky and places too much faith on the attacker's ability to predict and control its enemy's response.

Following the end of the Cold War, smaller nuclear powers have also adopted limited nuclear war doctrines because of their limited nuclear capabilities and the limited threats they face. India has publicly announced its adoption of the doctrine, for example, not only to prepare the public for the demands, albeit limited, that such a war would entail, but also to send a message to Pakistan that India would not rely on nuclear weapons alone in a conflict but would also bring its conventional military superiority to bear.

—*Abe Denmark*

References

Clark, Ian, *Limited Nuclear War: Political Theory and War Conventions* (Princeton, NJ: Princeton University Press, 1982).

Halperin, Morton H., "Nuclear Weapons and Limited War," *The Journal of Conflict Resolution*, vol. 5, no. 2, June 1961, pp. 146–166.

LIMITED TEST BAN TREATY (LTBT)

The Limited Test Ban Treaty (LTBT), signed originally by the United States, England, and the Soviet Union in August 1963, prohibits nuclear explosions in the atmosphere, under water, in outer space, or in any other environment if the explosion would cause radioactive debris to be present outside the border of the state conducting the explosion. The LTBT's signing followed years of negotiations on a comprehensive nuclear test ban that had been slowed primarily by disputes over verification of underground tests (*see* Verification). Once the countries agreed to set aside the underground testing issue, the treaty was negotiated in a matter of weeks. It also was quickly ratified by a vote of 80–19 in the U.S. Senate and came into force in October 1963. The treaty later was opened to other signatories, and more than 100 countries have now signed. France and China remain formally outside of the treaty but have pledged to adhere to its restrictions. The treaty has helped to protect the global environment from further contamination from radioactive fallout.

Attempts to negotiate an international nuclear test ban began in 1955. In addition to disputes over underground testing, the attempts were complicated by both U.S. and Soviet efforts to link the test ban to broader arms control measures unacceptable to the other side. Support for a ban grew in both public and government circles as surveys showed increasing global radioactive fallout levels. Scientists warned of possible genetic defects and higher cancer rates, and several accidents exposed civilians to high levels of fallout (*see* Fallout; Radiation). The Cuban missile crisis then gave new impetus to arms control efforts and increased the personal efforts of President John F. Kennedy and Soviet Premier Nikita Khrushchev to find ways to reduce tensions and the risk of nuclear war between the superpowers (*see* Cuban Missile Crisis).

The 1963 negotiations centered on atmospheric, water, and space tests. These tests could be verified with existing capabilities and therefore required neither the creation of a new international monitoring agency nor onsite inspections. Additionally, these types of tests were presumed to be causing the worst fallout, so banning them would produce the greatest benefit for the environment. The treaty's terms prohibit all nuclear explosions, not just tests, to prevent any disputes over peaceful explosions versus weapons testing. The treaty is of unlimited duration, although parties can withdraw with three months' notice if they decide that extraordinary events related to the subject matter of the treaty have jeopardized the supreme interests of their country. Also, amendments can be added if they are approved by a majority of the parties and the three original parties.

In arguing for ratification of the LTBT, President Kennedy suggested it could affect the world in four ways. First, he claimed that it could reduce world tension and encourage further agreements. The LTBT was the first major international nuclear arms control agreement, and it set a precedent that helped lead to later arms control agreements and détente. Second, the president argued it could reduce radioactive fallout globally. Despite some atmospheric testing by nonsignatories, fallout levels returned to the level of natural background radiation within ten years after LTBT went into effect. Third, Kennedy suggested the LTBT could help limit the prolifera-

tion of nuclear weapons. The treaty's impact here is questionable, and certainly it did not prevent proliferation. Fourth, Kennedy argued that the treaty would have a major "braking effect" on the arms race. Instead, both superpowers continued to develop more weapons with greater yields and technical sophistication by simply relying on underground testing. The LTBT itself called for a comprehensive test ban in the future to stop underground tests. A Comprehensive Test Ban Treaty (CTBT) was signed in 1996, but the United States has so far refused to ratify such a treaty. Thus, the LTBT has had mixed results in achieving Kennedy's vision.

—John W. Dietrich

See also: Arms Control; Détente; Nuclear Test Ban; Underground Testing

References

Kennedy, John F., "Radio and Television Address to the American People on the Nuclear Test Ban Treaty," July 26, 1963, available at http://www.cs.umb.edu/jfklibrary/j072663.htm.

"Limited Test Ban Treaty," available at http://www.state/gov/t/ac/trt/4797pf.htm.

Loeb, Benjamin S., "The Limited Test Ban Treaty," in Michael Krepon and Dan Caldwell, eds., *The Politics of Arms Control Treaty Ratification* (New York: St. Martin's Press, 1991), pp. 167–228.

LITHIUM

Lithium (Li) is a low-density metal. It has three protons in its nucleus. With a density only about half that of water, it is the lightest of all metals. It does not occur freely in nature; in compounds, it is found in small units in nearly all igneous rocks and in the waters of mineral springs. The metal has the highest specific heat of any solid element. Lithium is currently recovered in Searles Lake, California, and in Nevada and North Carolina. Since World War II, the production of lithium metal and its compounds has increased. Lithium is often used in heat transfer applications. It is highly corrosive, however, and requires special handling.

Lithium 6 (Li-6), an isotope, has two nuclear weapons applications: as a reactor target and control rod material for the production of tritium, and as a thermonuclear weapons material. In both cases, tritium is produced by means of a neutron absorption process. Li-6 is a critical material for the manufacture of dry thermonuclear devices that do not require the use of liquid deuterium and tritium as boosters. Li-6 has the special property of being readily transformed into helium 4 and tritium when its nucleus is struck by a neutron. To produce a thermonuclear device, lithium is combined with deuterium to form the compound lithium-6 deuteride. Neutrons from a fission (primary) device bombard the lithium in the compound, liberating tritium that fuses with the deuterium. The alpha particles are electrically charged and at a higher temperature contribute directly to forming the nuclear fireball (see Deuterium; Isotopes; Hydrogen Bomb; Tritium).

Lithium enriched in the isotope Li-6 is most often separated from natural lithium by the column-exchange electrochemical process, which exploits the fact that Li-6 has a greater affinity for mercury than does Li-7. A lithium-mercury amalgam is first prepared using the natural material. The amalgam is then agitated with a lithium hydroxide solution, which also is prepared from natural lithium. The desired Li-6 concentrates in the amalgam, and the more common Li-7 migrates to the hydroxide. A counterflow of amalgam and hydroxide passes through a cascade of stages until the desired enrichment in Li-6 is achieved.

The containment vessel of a thermonuclear device is cylindrical, but it is rounded at the end where the plutonium (Pu) implosion device (called the "primary") sits. This design helps to scatter the X-ray flash down the tube. The containment vessel is made of some thick, dense metal, such as uranium 238 (U-238). The fusion fuel capsules are also cylindrical and are mounted in polystyrene foam (better known by its Dow Chemical Company trade name, Styrofoam). The fuel capsules are surrounded by a blanket of U-238 (or U-235). This blanket acts as a radiation shield on the side of the capsules facing the primary. Fusion fuels often consist of lithium-6 deuteride and possibly some lithium-6 tritide. These are chemically stable solid compounds of lithium with deuterium and tritium, respectively. This reaction provides additional tritium for the fusion reaction.

As the implosion process begins, the X-rays from the primary rapidly burn down through the polystyrene foam, creating a high-pressure plasma, which compresses the first fuel capsule in a cylindrical implosion. However, the fuel is still not hot enough to undergo fusion. This is where the second major design innovation comes in. A cylindrical rod of either U-235 or Pu-239 is located on the axis of the fuel capsule and arranged so that the cylindrical implosion will cause it to become supercritical. A small aperture in the radiation shield allows neutrons from the primary to initiate a chain reaction in the rod, which then supplies neutrons to transmute the lithium into helium and tritium and supply the extra energy required to spark off the fusion reaction. Using an analogy drawn from the way fuel is ignited in a car engine, this rod is called the "spark plug" by nuclear weapon designers. The very high-energy neutrons released by the fusion reaction are capable of inducing additional fissions in the U-238 blanket and the confinement casing. Each individual fission produces more than ten times the energy of the previous fusion; thus these tertiary fissions can significantly augment the yield of the weapon. It is possible to extend the yield of the device to virtually any desired value by adding additional fusion capsules (see Plutonium; Thermonuclear Bomb; Uranium).

Like the U.S. program, the Soviet thermonuclear program initially focused on igniting nonequilibrium detonation in liquid deuterium (a scheme eventually shown to be impractical, if not impossible). And like American scientists, the Soviets had tried to amplify the yield of a fission bomb by igniting a limited fusion reaction in a lithium-6 deuteride blanket. Unlike the Americans, however, the Soviets turned this idea into a deliverable weapon. The detonation of the RDS-6s device in the fifth Soviet nuclear test (dubbed "Joe 4" in the West) used fusion in a practical weapons design. Not a "true" hydrogen bomb, this device obtained nearly its entire yield from fission and was limited for practical purposes to yields of less than 1 megaton. It was never widely deployed.

The RDS-6s used a U-235 fissile core surrounded by alternating layers of fusion fuel ((lithium-6 deuteride spiked with tritium) and fusion tamper (natural uranium) inside a high-explosive implosion system. The small U-235 fission bomb (about 40 kilotons) acted as the trigger. The total yield was 400 kilotons. Fifteen to 20 percent of the energy was released by fusion, and 90 percent was produced by the fusion reaction.

—*Gilles Van Nederveen*

References

Cochran, Thomas B., William M. Arkin, Robert S. Norris, and Milton M. Hoenig, *Nuclear Weapons*

Databook, vol. 2: *U.S. Nuclear Warhead Production* (Cambridge, MA: Ballinger, 1987).

Lide, D. R., ed., *CRC Handbook of Chemistry and Physics, 1999–2000: A Ready-Reference Book of Chemical and Physical Data*, CRC Handbook of Chemistry and Physics (Boca Raton, FL: CRC Press, 1998).

"Lithium: Key Information," *Chemistry: WebElements Periodic Table: Professional Edition*, available at http://www.webelements.com/webelements/elements/text/Li/key.html.

Muller, Richard A., "Nuclear Weapons Basics," available at http://muller.lbl.gov/teaching/Physics10/chapters/6-NuclearWeapons.html.

LITTLE BOY

On August 6, 1945, the first atomic weapon, named "Little Boy," was released from the U.S. bomber *Enola Gay* over the Japanese city of Hiroshima. The resulting devastation, as well as the devastation of Nagasaki by a second bomb named "Fat Man" three days later, has been credited with hastening the end of the war with Japan. Little Boy's uranium-fueled, gun-type design was a simple first-generation weapon that is likely to be duplicated by nations or nonstate actors that want to acquire a nuclear device.

The casing of the gun-type design resembles a cannon. Rings of uranium 235 (U-235) were placed at the muzzle, and a cylindrical-shaped mass of U-235 was placed at the other end in front of a conventional explosive. The simplicity of Little Boy's gun-type design meant that designers had high confidence that it would work without being tested. Because uranium was in short supply, the design was not tested prior to the destruction of Hiroshima.

Little Boy was dropped from the *Enola Gay* with the fuse set to explode at a specific altitude above the ground to maximize its destructive force. When the barometric sensors recorded a specific air pressure (that is, altitude), the conventional explosive was ignited and propelled the cylindrical-shaped mass into the center of the rings. The contact of the subcritical masses of U-235 created a critical mass to cause a fission reaction that exploded with the force of approximately 20,000 tons of TNT.

Later gun-type designs created a greater yield by encasing the components with uranium 238 (U-238), a very strong material, to serve as a "tamper" to hold the weapon together longer, allow the fissioning process to continue, and to reflect stray neu-

trons back into the fission reaction. Both measures led to larger yields.

—Jennifer Hunt Morstein

See also: *Enola Gay*; Fat Man; Fission Weapons; Gun-Type Devices; Hiroshima; Nuclear Weapons Effects

References

Gardner, Gary T., *Nuclear Nonproliferation: A Primer* (Boulder: Lynne Rienner, 1994).

Rhodes, Richard, *Making of the Atomic Bomb* (New York: Simon and Schuster, 1986).

Walker, P. M. B., ed., *Chambers Nuclear Energy and Radiation Dictionary* (New York: Chambers, 1992).

LONDON NUCLEAR SUPPLIERS CLUB

See Nuclear Suppliers Group

LONG-RANGE THEATER NUCLEAR FORCES

Long-range theater nuclear forces (LRTNFs) are nuclear weapons on delivery systems that can reach deep within an adversary's rear areas, including possibly his home territory. There is no firm distance at which short- or intermediate-range forces are considered long-range TNF, but the upper end of the range spectrum is a bit clearer—LRTNF weapons are shorter range than strategic intercontinental systems.

Debate about long-range theater nuclear weapons rose to prominence in the late 1970s following a decision by the North Atlantic Treaty Organization (NATO) to upgrade its capabilities by deploying Pershing II ballistic missiles and ground-launched cruise missiles (GLCMs) in response to the Soviet military buildup, which included the deployment of the SS-20 intermediate-range ballistic missile (IRBM). Alliance acrimony over the modernization of NATO's LRTNFs added impetus to the rebirth of the peace movement within Western Europe and led to significant protests as individual NATO countries allowed these weapons to be deployed on their territory. Ultimately, all three systems, together with the Soviet SS-4s and SS-5s, were eliminated as part of the Intermediate-Range Nuclear Forces (INF) Treaty of 1987.

Once strategic parity was reached between the Soviet Union and the United States, concern grew within Europe over the nuclear balance within the European theater and the U.S. nuclear guarantee. Because of the close proximity of a number of U.S.

theater nuclear systems to the Soviet Union, the Soviet officials were alarmed about any adverse change in the theater nuclear balance in Europe.

By the mid-1970s, increasing concerns were voiced within NATO about the relative lack of success of détente and the continuing Soviet conventional, tactical nuclear, and long-range theater nuclear weapons buildup within Europe. In May 1977, the NATO heads of state agreed to increase defense expenditures, and in the following year they approved the Long-Term Defence Program (LTDP). This identified nine conventional areas for improvement in addition to the modernization of NATO's long-range theater nuclear forces. In the 1970s, NATO's LRTNFs consisted of five U.S. Poseidon missile submarines with 400 warheads, four British Polaris missile submarines, U.S. F-111 fighter-bombers based in the United Kingdom, and British Vulcan bombers. Some NATO strategists and officials were worried that NATO aircraft were vulnerable to Soviet conventional or nuclear attack and wondered if nuclear-armed missiles launched from the submarines dedicated to NATO missions would be seen as strategic rather than theater nuclear forces by the Soviets. In late spring 1979, NATO's High Level Group put forward a plan to modernize NATO's LRTNFs by deploying a mix of 106 Pershing II missiles and 464 ground-launched cruise missiles (GLCMs) while withdrawing obsolete nuclear weapons deployed as part of NATO's theater nuclear force. The group also agreed on a "dual-track" deployment: NATO LRTNF modernization would be accompanied by negotiations with the Soviet Union to cap, if not eliminate, LRTNFs in Europe.

Soviet leaders immediately attempted to derail NATO's LRTNF plans, arguing that it would upset the delicate military balance in Europe. The Soviets made a series of counterproposals, which NATO found equally unacceptable. Negotiations continued over the years as NATO began deployment of its new weapons and the Soviet Union continued to deploy the SS-20. Wide-scale civilian protests in Western Europe against NATO's LRTNF modernization continued.

Ultimately, LRTNFs were eliminated from the arsenals of the Soviet Union and United States under the INF Treaty. Ironically, as NATO applauded the treaty, the Cold War ended, eliminating the need for LRTNFs in Europe.

—Andrew M. Dorman

References

Garthoff, Raymond, *Détente and Confrontation* (Washington, DC: Brookings Institution, 1985).

Matlock, Jack F., Jr., *Reagan and Gorbachev: How the Cold War Ended* (New York: Random House, 2004).

Park, William, *Defending the West: A History of NATO* (London: Wheatsheaf, 1987).

Schwartz, David N., *NATO's Nuclear Dilemmas* (Washington, DC: Brookings Institution, 1983).

LOS ALAMOS NATIONAL LABORATORY

The U.S. Army established the Los Alamos National Laboratory (LANL) in Los Alamos, New Mexico, in January 1943 to design, assemble, and test the first atomic bombs. During 1942, the War Department had established a site at Oak Ridge, Tennessee, for uranium and plutonium refinement and enrichment, and another site at Richland (Hanford), Washington, for plutonium metal production (*see* Hanford, Washington; Oak Ridge National Laboratory). An expenditure of $1.7 billion and the efforts of thousands of scientists, engineers, and technicians resulted in the development of the first atomic bomb, which was detonated at the Trinity Site near Alamogordo, New Mexico, in July 1945 (*see* Trinity Site). As the sole purpose of the Los Alamos Laboratory was to develop the atomic bomb, the War Department planned to dismantle it upon completion of the project. At the end of World War II, however, distrust of the Soviet Union led to the perception that America needed to further develop its nuclear arsenal, and U.S. officials decided to establish a permanent nuclear weapons research and design operation at Los Alamos. Los Alamos, a 43-square-mile facility, has always operated under a contract with the University of California Board of Regents, and it now employs about 8,000 people.

LANL originally manufactured plutonium pits in small numbers for weapons tests at its TA-55 (Technical Area-55) plant. This 4-acre facility is currently the only full-function plutonium-handling facility in the United States. In 1952, Los Alamos tested the first fusion device at Enewetak Atoll in the Pacific. Until 1958, Los Alamos designed all the nuclear weapons that entered the stockpile. Since then, both Los Alamos and Lawrence Livermore National Laboratory (LLNL) have produced nuclear weapons (*see* Hydrogen Bomb).

Several weapons with Los Alamos–designed warheads are currently in the U.S. nuclear arsenal. The

B-61, designed by LANL for the air force, for example, is equipped with "dial-a-yield," allowing the operator to select the yield of the weapon. There are many versions and modifications of the B-61, the latest being the earth-penetrating B-61-11. Current versions were introduced to the stockpile in 1979.

The W-76 was designed by LANL for the U.S. Navy's Trident I submarine-launched ballistic missile. Each Trident submarine can carry up to 24 missiles with eight warheads each. The W-76 was first deployed in 1979. It was replaced on the Trident II missile by the LANL-designed W-88 beginning in 1986. The W-88 was first deployed in 1990 and is considered the most advanced U.S. nuclear weapon. Its plutonium pit is the first scheduled for refurbishment if and when U.S. stockpile pit production resumes.

The W-78 warhead was designed by LANL as a replacement for the Lawrence Livermore–designed W-62 on the Air Force's Minuteman III ICBMs. It was first deployed in 1979.

The W-80, produced by LANL, is a cruise missile warhead that was first deployed in 1984. W-80s are still in the arsenal for potential use by air- or sea-launched cruise missiles.

The B-53 bomb was a variant of the W-53 Titan II ICBM warhead. Some of these weapons were kept in service following the end of the Cold War, but all have now been retired. The B-53 had the distinction of having the largest yield of any warhead ever produced by the United States, at some 9 megatons. It was originally designed for countervalue targeting against cities, but it probably remains in the arsenal as a tool for digging out underground bunkers or buried facilities for producing weapons of mass destruction.

—*Gilles Van Nederveen and Jeffrey A. Larsen*

See also: Fission Weapons; Lawrence Livermore National Laboratory; Manhattan Project; Pit; Sandia National Laboratories; Thermonuclear Bomb

References
Cochran, Thomas B., William M. Arkin, Robert S. Norris, and Milton M. Hoenig, *Nuclear Weapons Databook,* vol. 2: *U.S. Nuclear Warhead Production* (Cambridge, MA: Ballinger, 1987).

Cochran, Thomas B., William M. Arkin, Robert S. Norris, and Milton M. Hoenig, *Nuclear Weapons Databook,* vol. 3: *U.S. Nuclear Warhead Facility Profiles* (Cambridge, MA: Ballinger, 1987).

Los Alamos National Laboratory website, http://www.lanl.gov/worldview/.

Shroyer, Jo Ann, *Secret Mesa: Inside Lost Alamos National Laboratory* (New York: John Wiley and Sons, 1998).

LOW ENRICHED URANIUM (LEU)

Low enriched uranium, or LEU, is uranium that is enriched to less than 20 percent by its fissile isotope, uranium 235 (U-235). Most commercial power reactors require low enriched uranium to function. Typical enrichments for these power plants are between 2 and 5 percent. Some fuels in research reactors, however, are enriched to nearly 20 percent to allow for more compact cores.

Low enriched uranium is mainly produced by processing natural uranium at an enrichment plant. Mixing natural uranium with highly enriched uranium is another way to produce LEU (*see* Enrichment; Highly Enriched Uranium [HEU]; Isotopes; Uranium).

History and Background

Early in the development of nuclear reactors, it was recognized that U-235 is the only naturally available isotope that is fissile. In its natural form, uranium contains only 0.72 percent U-235, severely limiting the availability of this fuel source. To create a critical mass using natural uranium, moderators with special properties were necessary to slow the neutrons down. Owing to the limited amount of fissile uranium available, moderators had to slow these neutrons down without absorbing them, leaving as many neutrons as possible available for fission. This requirement forced scientists and engineers to use graphite and heavy-water moderators in their attempts to build a sustained chain reaction. As the supply of enriched uranium slowly increased, it eventually became feasible to build reactors that used LEU as the fuel source. These reactors could now use light water as the coolant/moderator, which greatly reduced reactor construction and operating costs. Most reactors in the world today use LEU as their fuel source (*see* Light-Water Reactors).

The enrichment processes that are used to create low enriched uranium are similar to the processes used to create highly enriched uranium. Because the different isotopes of uranium are chemically identical, all enrichment schemes rely upon the small mass differences that exist between the isotopes. Gaseous diffusion, gas centrifuge, Becker nozzle, electromagnetic separation, and laser isotope separation are some of the different methods that exploit this mass difference. All of these techniques, except laser separation, require a very large multistage cascade system to achieve significant enrichment. These large cascade systems require large amounts of space and electrical power.

Another method for creating low enriched uranium is through the process of diluting highly enriched uranium with natural uranium. This is often referred to as "downblending." The United States and some former Soviet states use this relatively new method to create low enriched uranium because it allows them to dispose of their inventories of highly enriched (weapons-grade) uranium. Low enriched uranium is unsuitable for use in nuclear weapons.

Technical Details

The primary reason that low enriched uranium is the most prevalent fuel in modern reactors is that fuel enriched in U-235 can use light water as a moderator/coolant. In nuclear reactors, neutrons are more easily absorbed after they have slowed down. Slowing neutrons is called "moderation." To reduce the velocity of neutrons three tasks must be accomplished. First, nuclei should have low mass numbers so that each scattering event causes the neutrons to lose a large fraction of their energy. Second, the nuclei need to have large probabilities that scattering, and hence energy loss, will occur over short distances. Third, moderating nuclei should have low probabilities for absorption so that when scattering interactions take place few neutrons are removed from the system. Light water meets these requirements but sill has a much smaller scattering-to-absorption ratio than either graphite or heavy water. As result, a graphite or heavy-water reactor can use natural uranium as a fuel, but a light-water reactor requires slightly enriched uranium to function (see Gas-Graphite Reactors; Heavy Water).

All current enrichment methods only slightly enrich the uranium as it passes through one of the many stages in the enrichment facility. This process of feeding the material repeatedly through many enrichment stages is referred to as a "cascade system," and the measure of separation that takes place in each stage is called a "stage separation factor." For U-235, the stage separation factor is theoretically limited to 1.0043, but it is typically much closer to 1.003. Using the ideal stage separation factor at a gaseous-diffusion plant, at least 1,100 stages are required to enrich uranium to 3 percent by weight. For a gaseous-centrifuge, the separation factor is higher, and as few as 90 stages may be required for the same enrichment.

—*C. Ross Schmidtlein*

References

Glasstone, S., and A. Sesonske, *Nuclear Reactor Engineering*, third edition (New York: Van Nostrand Reinhold, 1981).

Lamarsh, J. R., and A. J. Baratta, *Introduction to Nuclear Engineering*, third edition (Upper Saddle River, NJ: Prentice-Hall, 2001).

Parrington, Josef R., Harold D. Knox, Susan L. Breneman, Edward M. Baum, and Frank Feiner, *Nuclides and Isotopes: Chart of the Nuclides*, fifteenth edition (New York: General Electric and KAPL, 1996).

MANEUVERING REENTRY VEHICLE (MARV)

A maneuvering reentry vehicle (MARV) is a reentry vehicle (RV) capable of performing preplanned flight maneuvers during the reentry phase of its flight trajectory while en route to its target. A MARV deploys fins or other aerodynamic surfaces when it reenters the atmosphere, which allows it to turn and dodge rather than following a standard ballistic course.

MARV technology delivers a wide variety of improvements over a standard RV. The ability to maneuver while dropping to earth allows for higher degrees of accuracy. More accurate and precise modes of delivery of nuclear warheads can help avoid high levels of collateral damage and provides a higher degree of certainty that the warhead will directly hit a target that may be reinforced against indirect nuclear blasts.

Additionally, MARVed warheads can better avoid any antiballistic missile interceptors they encounter in transit to their target. The maneuvering capability could be used to complicate hit-to-kill or conventional warhead ballistic missile defense systems. MARVed warheads may be able to avoid kinetic-kill missile defenses by flying a nonstatic post-boost trajectory that foils attempts to destroy the RV based upon an assumption that it will fly a ballistic reentry course predetermined by its launch trajectory.

—*Abe Denmark*

See also: Reentry Vehicles

References

Ball, Desmond J., "The Counterforce Potential of American SLBM Systems," *Journal of Peace Research,* vol. 14, no. 1, 1977, pp. 23–40.

Delaney, William P., "Air Defense of the United States: Strategic Missions and Modern Technology," *International Security,* vol. 15, no. 1, Summer 1990, pp. 181–211.

Snow, Donald M., "Current Nuclear Deterrence Thinking," *International Studies Quarterly,* vol. 23, no. 3, September 1979, pp. 445–486.

M

MANHATTAN PROJECT

The United States initiated the top secret Manhattan Project in September 1942 to build an atomic bomb before Germany could develop its own nuclear weapon. The undertaking, named for the fact that it was managed out of the Army Corps of Engineers' Manhattan District, was a massive and costly project engaging many top U.S., Canadian, and British scientists. It benefited from contributions by numerous U.S. corporations and universities. After overcoming substantial scientific, technical, and practical obstacles, the project produced the weapons that were used on Hiroshima and Nagasaki, leading to Japan's surrender in August 1945. (Germany had surrendered in May 1945, before the bombs were ready.) The use of atomic weapons against these two Japanese cities brought a rapid conclusion to hostilities in the Pacific. However, the development and use of atomic weapons, ushering in the nuclear age and a four-decade nuclear standoff between the United States and the Soviet Union, has remained the object of political, policy, and moral debate.

History and Background

The origins of the Manhattan Project were shaped in the crucible of the tumultuous 1930s. By 1934, the idea of using nuclear chain reactions to produce an atomic bomb had received a patent in the United Kingdom. Many European scientists who had been working to understand the dynamics and potential of atomic energy sought to escape from the reach of Adolf Hitler's Nazi regime, which targeted the field of physics itself because it was populated by many Jewish scientists. Many of these refugees ended up

Dr. J. Robert Oppenheimer, director of the Manhattan Project and Los Alamos National Laboratory during World War II. (Library of Congress)

making critical contributions to the Manhattan Project.

German scientists had split the first uranium atom in 1938, which provided experimental evidence that it was possible to use nuclear fission to produce a very destructive weapon. The next year, Albert Einstein, who in 1933 had left Germany and settled in the United States, was urged by three Hungarian refugee physicists (Leo Szilard, Edward Teller, and Eugene Wigner) to alert U.S. political authorities to the dangers posed by Germany's nuclear research. Einstein signed a letter to U.S. President Franklin D. Roosevelt describing German atomic research and the possibility that Hitler could produce an atomic bomb based on that research. Roosevelt responded by creating a special Advisory Committee on Uranium, referred to as "S-1." In June 1940, the committee was placed under the auspices of the National Defense Research Committee (NDRC), led by the Carnegie Institution's director, Dr. Vannevar Bush. It immediately launched a major research program through contracts with universities and other institutions. In November 1941, the S-1 committee was placed under the jurisdiction of the U.S. Office of Scientific Research and Development (OSRD), the parent organization of the NDRC.

Much of the research contracted by the Uranium Committee had been oriented toward using uranium 235 (U-235), a rare isotope constituting less than 1 percent of uranium metal in its natural state, to produce a controlled chain reaction. It was not known at that time whether sufficient quantities of highly refined U-235 could be produced to manufacture an atomic bomb. Some experts believed it could not be done, certainly not in the near future. A second broad approach to the problem suggested that U-238, more abundant than U-235, could be converted into plutonium, which then could be used as the foundation for the atomic chain reaction (*see* Enrichment; Highly Enriched Uranium [HEU]; Plutonium; Uranium).

World War II had begun in Europe in September 1939 when Germany invaded Poland and Britain and France declared war on Germany and its allies. The United States remained technically neutral for the next two years even though it provided both material and moral support to Great Britain. Formal U.S. neutrality came to an end when Germany's ally Japan mounted a surprise attack on U.S. naval facilities in Pearl Harbor, Hawaii, on December 7, 1941, bringing the United States into the war against the Axis Powers.

The Project

On June 17, 1942, Vannevar Bush reported to President Roosevelt that the Uranium Committee's research program had demonstrated that production of fissionable uranium and plutonium could produce an atomic weapon. Roosevelt decided to move the atomic program from the research and development stage to large-scale production. That same month, Roosevelt directed the army to manage this transition, and the task was given over to the Army Corps of Engineers, which created a new organization known as the "Manhattan Engineer District (MED)," located in New York City. The Manhattan Project got under way in September. West Point graduate and army engineer Leslie R. Groves was chosen as its director and promoted from colonel to brigadier general so that he would have the status and authority required for the important job.

General Groves was known for his ability to deliver results irrespective of whose toes he had to step on or whose feelings he might hurt. He took on the task somewhat reluctantly, having preferred an assignment in an active theater of operations to another Washington posting. He later wrote that his initial reaction was one of "extreme disappointment." However, the disappointment was mitigated when he was told that his appointment had been made by the secretary of war and approved by the president. One official told him, "If you do the job right, it will win the war" (Groves, pp. 3–4).

Groves's initial assignment was to organize production of the atomic bomb. It soon became clear that the production effort could not succeed unless ongoing research efforts were focused more effectively on the practical task of producing enough fissionable material to yield several bombs. The Uranium Committee's research programs had focused on five basic ways of producing fissionable material: U-235 could be separated from the parent uranium by using a centrifuge, gaseous-diffusion, or electromagnetic process; or plutonium could be produced by organizing uranium and graphite blocks in a "pile," or reactor, or in a reactor using heavy water instead of graphite to control the chain reaction during the production process. The Uranium Committee decided to move all five approaches from the research to the production stage. General Groves, after examining research into the centrifuge separation method at the University of Virginia and the Westinghouse Research Laboratories in Pittsburgh, Pennsylvania, decided to drop further work on this method and concentrate on the other four.

Atomic research was being conducted in a number of locations across the country, but three became critical centers for the transition from research to production. Scientists at Columbia University in New York, under the direction of Professor Harold Urey, concentrated on issues related to using gaseous diffusion to separate out U-235. Scientists at the University of California at Berkeley, led by Professor Ernest O. Lawrence, worked on the process of electromagnetic separation. And at the University of Chicago, a team of scientists led by Arthur Compton and including Italian Nobel Prize winner Enrico Fermi as well as Hungarian expatriate physicists Leo Szilard and Eugene Wigner concentrated on the process of producing fissionable plutonium with the uranium/graphite pile. A critical breakthrough in the research process came in December 1942 when Fermi demonstrated the first

self-sustaining nuclear chain reaction at a pile built under a squash court at the University of Chicago.

The scientific challenges posed by the project were considerable, including the seemingly mundane but extremely difficult tasks of developing filters, valves, pipes, and other processing equipment to stand up to demanding production requirements. Equally challenging was the task of building facilities for production processes that were still being developed. In November 1942, a remote and undeveloped site in Los Alamos, New Mexico, was selected as the location for a laboratory in which the actual production of atomic bombs would take place (see Los Alamos National Laboratory). Dr. Robert J. Oppenheimer, from the University of California–Berkeley, was chosen to head the lab. Also late in 1942, a large site in Oak Ridge, Tennessee, was selected for construction of what was then called the "Clinton Engineer Works," renamed after the war as the Oak Ridge National Laboratory (see Oak Ridge National Laboratory). The site became the factory for the production of plutonium in "the Clinton Pile," and for separation of U-235 in gaseous-diffusion and electromagnetic plants. The main production facilities for weapons material were the K-25 gaseous-diffusion plant, the Y-12 electromagnetic plant, and the S-50 thermal-diffusion plant.

A third major facility, the Hanford site, was constructed in Richland, Washington, to produce plutonium. At the peak of the construction effort, some 45,000 construction workers were employed at the Hanford site, with 11,000 pieces of major construction equipment on hand (see Hanford, Washington).

All three facilities had to be built quickly and without knowing exactly how all the production methods would work. The projects included housing for the construction workers, engineers, and scientists who would construct and operate the facilities. The purpose of the facilities was closely held, and most of the thousands of engineers, construction workers, and technicians had no idea exactly what the facilities were intended to produce. The project relied on contributions from many of America's major companies, including Allis-Chalmers, Celotex, Chrysler, Dupont, Eastman Kodak, Goodyear, IBM, Ingersoll-Rand, International Nickel, Stone and Webster, Union Carbide, and Westinghouse,

As the Manhattan Project approached the point where enough fissionable material would be available to produce a few weapons, the war in Europe moved toward a successful conclusion. The end of the Third Reich and Germany's surrender in May 1945 removed the threat of a German-produced atomic bomb being used against the United States or its allies. In fact, Germany's nuclear weapons program had been severely disrupted by Norwegian resistance fighters, who had bombed the German heavy-water facility in occupied Norway; when it was repaired, it was bombed again by Allied forces.

Japan remained a stubborn combatant, and President Harry S. Truman, who had succeeded Roosevelt after his death early in 1945, decided to use nuclear weapons against Japanese cities to force a Japanese surrender (the deaths of over 100,000 Japanese civilians in firebombing attacks against Tokyo had not accomplished that goal).

The development of U-235 weapons and those made from plutonium, in spite of various setbacks along the way, came to fruition at roughly the same time in 1945. The first U-235 bomb produced was detonated on July 16, 1945, at a test range in Alamogordo, New Mexico, with Robert Oppenheimer in charge. The test site was code-named "Trinity" (*see* Trinity Site). With the test's success, two other weapons, nicknamed "Little Boy" and "Fat Man," were rushed to an air base in the Pacific. On August 6, 1945, Little Boy, a U-235 weapon, was flown from a U.S. air base on Tinian in the Marianas Islands on a B-29 named *Enola Gay* and dropped on the city of Hiroshima, Japan. Fat Man, a plutonium bomb, was dropped by another B-29, *Bockscar*, on Nagasaki, Japan, on August 9. Japan surrendered three weeks later, bringing World War II to an end.

Consequences

The Manhattan Project produced atomic weapons that were used to expedite the end of the war against Japan. The overall cost of the effort has been estimated at $20 billion (in 1996 dollars), for a cost of approximately $5 billion per bomb (the one that was tested at Alamogordo, one each delivered on Hiroshima and Nagasaki, Japan, and one that remained unused). In spite of the extraordinary security that surrounded the Manhattan Project, the Soviet Union managed to obtain critical nuclear secrets from spies inside the project. The acquisition of this information greatly facilitated the development of the Soviet nuclear weapons program, lead-

ing to the Cold War nuclear standoff that ended only when the Soviet Union and the Warsaw Pact began disintegrating in 1989. The reality of widespread nuclear proliferation today ensures that nuclear weapons technology, first brought to use in war through the Manhattan Project, will remain a source of debate and division in global affairs.

—*Stanley R. Sloan*

References

Groueff, Stephane, *Manhattan Project: The Untold Story of the Making of the Atomic Bomb* (Boston: Little, Brown, 1967).

Groves, Leslie M., *Now It Can Be Told: The Story of the Manhattan Project* (New York: Da Capo, 1983).

Rhodes, Richard, *The Making of the Atomic Bomb* (New York: Simon and Schuster, 1986).

U.S. Department of Energy, *The Manhattan Project: Science in the Second World War* (Washington, DC, 1990).

MASSIVE RETALIATION

Massive retaliation is a theory of deterrence that holds that conventional wars and nuclear attacks can be deterred by the threat of responding with massive nuclear retaliation endangering the very survival of the targeted state or society. As a national security doctrine or policy, it was used by the Dwight D. Eisenhower administration to justify the expansion of U.S. nuclear forces in the 1950s and to limit the need for standing conventional forces, which were considered more expensive to acquire and maintain. Furthermore, it was assumed that nuclear forces could substitute, in a deterrence strategy, for extensive conventional forces. Under this doctrine, U.S. nuclear forces expanded from approximately 250 nuclear devices in 1949 to more than 18,000 tactical, theater, and strategic nuclear weapons by 1960.

The declared public doctrine of massive retaliation also was used to cope with the threat of limited, peripheral wars threatened by the Communist Soviet bloc as well as the threat of a Soviet invasion of Western Europe. By threatening a massive nuclear retaliation, the United States hoped to offset perceived Soviet superiority in conventional military forces in Central Europe. Shortly after World War II, it became clear that a doctrine of "anywhere, anytime" defense would become an enormous fiscal burden, and the Eisenhower administration soon adopted the "New Look" doctrine, which placed emphasis on responding to aggression by threatening a massive retaliation "at places and times of our own choosing," in the words of John Foster Dulles, secretary of state under President Eisenhower (Dulles, p. 143).

There was a mismatch between the "declaratory" and "operational" policies of massive retaliation. Publicly, U.S. officials declared that the United States would respond to limited Soviet or Chinese aggression with massive nuclear strikes against the aggressor's homeland. The U.S. military, however, planned to respond in a flexible manner at times and places of its own choosing, selecting options from the full spectrum of U.S. military capability, from conventional forces up to limited nuclear strikes or massive nuclear retaliation. Despite the popular image of nuclear weapons as "city busters" and of nuclear strategy as a "countervalue targeting" option, the actual targeting policies were decidedly "counterforce," that is, directed at military targets (see Conterterforce Targeting; Countervalue Targeting). Nevertheless, in execution, this targeting strategy included both military bases and the Soviet military-industrial complex, including facilities in or near 118 of the 134 largest cities in the Soviet bloc, and would have resulted in millions of casualties. In this sense, it would have been indistinguishable from a true "countervalue" strike deliberately aimed at cities.

Massive retaliation was a declaratory policy well-suited to an era of American nuclear monopoly and superiority. Nevertheless, the doctrine of massive retaliation was short-lived. Its credibility was eventually undermined by the Soviet acquisition—in the late 1950s and early 1960s—of an ability to use nuclear weapons to hold U.S. cities at risk, thus matching America's threat of massive retaliation. Once the United States itself was subject to such an attack, it became less credible to threaten massive retaliation (see Credibility). The John F. Kennedy administration moved to adopt a new doctrine of "flexible response" that was reflected in the emergence of a new "balance of terror" in Soviet-American relations.

—*Kerry Kartchner*

See also: Balance of Terror; Cold War; Flexible Response; New Look; Second Strike

References

Dulles, John Foster, "Massive Retaliation," in Robert J. Art and Kenneth N. Waltz, eds., *The Use of Force*, second edition (Lanham, MD: University Press of America, 1983), pp. 142–145.

Peeters, Paul, *Massive Retaliation: The Policy and Its Critics* (Chicago: Regnery, 1959).

Rosenberg, David Alan, "The Origins of Overkill: Nuclear Weapons and American Strategy, 1945–1960," *International Security*, vol. 7, no. 4 (Spring 1983), pp. 3–71.

MEDIUM-RANGE BALLISTIC MISSILES

Medium-range ballistic missiles (MRBMs) are offensive strike systems capable of carrying conventional or nuclear warheads over a range of hundreds of miles. Like a few other delivery systems, especially cruise missiles, MRBMs have come and gone repeatedly since their initial appearance in the late 1950s. Originally developed by the Soviet Union and the United States to attack each other, they were long viewed as the most destabilizing nuclear weapons delivery systems. Today they are deployed exclusively by other powers to reach targets in their own vicinity.

Definitions of MRBMs vary depending on the motives involved. Most countries never developed a formal definition because they had no such weapons or no ballistic missiles larger than MRBMs. The U.S. Department of Defense distinguished short-range weapons placed under the control of corps or regional theater commanders and intercontinental ballistic missiles (ICBMs) under Strategic Air Command (now Strategic Command). Under this approach, an MRBM is a ballistic missile with a range of between 1,100 and 2,750 kilometers (600 to 1,500 nautical miles). In practice, this is often rounded to 1,000 to 3,000 km.

The problem of defining MRBMs was complicated by a shift in language in the mid-1970s that came with the appearance of the new generation of missiles led by the Soviet SS-20. The term "intermediate nuclear forces" (INF) took the place of "medium-range ballistic missiles" in strategic discussions, although the two terms often referred to exactly the same weapons.

First-Generation MRBMs

First-generation MRBMs were not developed because of intrinsic interest in their specific capabilities. They emerged, rather, as a way of coping with the limits of early rocket technology. By 1954, both superpowers were committed to developing long-range ICBMs, but this technology was complex and slow to be perfected. Medium-range systems offered a seemingly elegant shortcut, a way to use some of the simpler components of ICBMs in more rapidly developed weapons. Although these could not fly all the way from one superpower to another, they could be based in other countries or targeted at an enemy's allies.

The first generation of MRBMs, weapons such as the U.S. 2,400-kilometer-range Jupiter and Thor and the Soviet SS-3, SS-4, and SS–5, used engine designs originally developed for the still emerging ICBMs. Instead of multiple staging, storable fuels, inertial guidance, and high-beta reentry vehicles, none of which had been perfected by the late 1950s, these systems were designed to use proven, albeit less desirable, technologies. As a result, they were single-stage designs burning cryogenically cooled liquid oxygen, mostly using strap-down inertial and radio-command guidance and heat-sink reentry vehicles. Like all MRBMs deployed by the superpowers, they were armed exclusively with nuclear warheads.

Because of their limited range, they had to be based close to their targets. Since they could not be fueled until just before launch, a process taking an hour or more, they required a lengthy countdown. They were not highly accurate and thus could only target cities. All of this made them tempting targets vulnerable to preemptive attack. Not surprisingly, they usually were decommissioned or upgraded as quickly as possible.

The United Kingdom canceled its Blue Streak MRBM program in 1960. The United States, which had deployed Thor missiles in the United Kingdom and Jupiters in Italy and Turkey, eliminated all its first-generation MRBMs after the 1962 Cuban missile crisis. The Soviet Union got rid of its SS-3 inventory but retained its SS-4s and SS-5s, slowly upgrading their capabilities as better technologies appeared. China deployed its first aboveground DF-2, a 1,200 km MRBM using cryogenic liquid oxygen, in 1966. This was replaced by the DF-3, a 2,800 km MRBM, deployed initially in 1971. China also sold DF-3 missiles to Saudi Arabia in the late 1980s. France deployed a silo-launched MRBM of its own, the S2, with a range of 3,500 km, in 1971. Both the DF-3 and the S2 used storable liquid propellant.

Second-Generation MRBMs

A second generation of MRBMs appeared in the mid-1960s. Weapons such as the American Pershing I and the Soviet SS-12 had less range, but in ex-

change for this decrease in performance and the switch to storable propellants, they could be readily transported. This mobility greatly reduced their vulnerability to preemptive attack. An even more important role for missiles in this category was as submarine-launched ballistic missiles, such as the American Polaris A1 (operational in 1962), the French M1 (1972), and the Chinese JL-2 (1982). All of the latter were MRBMs in term of range, but they had multiple stages and used fully inertial guidance.

Third-Generation MRBMs and INF

Largely forgotten in strategic discussions, land-based MRBMs drifted to the background of superpower force postures until their importance revived in the mid-1970s following initial deployment of the Soviet SS-20. This road-mobile system, using solid fuels and multiple warheads, was not vulnerable to preemptive attack. By giving the Soviet Union the ability to attack Western Europe separately from the United States, it represented a major challenge to the strategy of flexible response adopted by the North Atlantic Treaty Organization (NATO). The United States developed the Pershing II in response to the SS-20. Both weapons, along with all other Soviet (Russian) and U.S. MRBMs, were banned under the 1987 Intermediate Nuclear Forces (INF) Treaty.

Current Status

Just as MRBMs were being eliminated from superpower forces, they found a new role as the weapon of choice for many regional ballistic missile forces. This had been presaged by weapons such as the Israeli Jericho, reportedly a 500 km system based on French technology, first deployed in the early 1970s. In 1988, Iraq attacked Iran with several hundred Scud missiles modified to reach distances of 600 km, the same missiles it fired at Israel and allied targets in 1991. In 1989, India began testing developmental models of its Agni, a solid-fuel intermediate-range ballistic missile (IRBM) with a range of approximately 1,500 km (see Indian Nuclear Weapons Program; Iraqi Nuclear Forces and Doctrine; Israeli Nuclear Weapons Capabilities and Doctrine.)

The greatest source of MRBM technology and complete systems is North Korea, which developed the Nodong, a single-stage weapon with a range of 1,300 km that appears to be based on Scud technologies. Since its first flight in 1993, versions of the Nodong have appeared in Pakistan and Iran. Pakistan also has developed a family of solid-fuel MRBMs, known as the Shaheen-1 and -2, and the Haft-5 and -6. These appear to be single-stage missiles with a range of 800 km and two-stage missiles with a range of 2,500 km, respectively, versions of the same basic motor. The Pakistani solid-fuel MRBMs bear a clear similarity to Chinese missiles such as the M-9, on which they are widely thought to be based.

—*Aaron Karp*

See also: Iranian Nuclear Weapons Program; North Korean Nuclear Weapons Program; Pakistani Nuclear Weapons Program

References

Dean, Jonathon, "The INF Treaty Negotiations," *SIPRI Yearbook, 1988* (Oxford: Oxford University Press, 1988), pp. 375–394.

Emme, Eugene M., ed., *The History of Rocket Technology* (Detroit: Wayne State University Press, 1964).

Lavoy, Peter R., Scott D. Sagan, and James J. Wirtz, eds., *Planning the Unthinkable: How New Powers Will Use Nuclear, Biological and Chemical Weapons* (Ithaca, NY: Cornell University Press, 2000).

Nash, Philip, *The Other Missiles of October: Eisenhower, Kennedy, and the Jupiters, 1957–1963* (Chapel Hill: University of North Carolina Press, 1997).

Norris, Robert S., Andrew S. Burrows, and Richard W. Fieldhouse, *Nuclear Weapons Databook*, vol. 5: *British, French and Chinese Nuclear Weapons* (Boulder: Westview, 1994).

Report of the Commission to Assess the Ballistic Missile Threat to the United States (Rumsfeld Commission Report): Appendix III (Washington, DC: U.S. Government Printing Office, 15 July 1998).

MEGATON

A megaton is a measure of the energy released during a nuclear explosion. One megaton is equal to 1 million tons of trinitrotoluene (TNT), a high explosive. This definition refers to all of the energy released by the weapons, regardless of the form. When a nuclear explosion occurs, only a small part of the released energy is in the form of explosive energy, whereas the energy of a chemical explosion is mostly released as blast. The Hiroshima explosion was estimated to be 12–18 kilotons (or 0.18 megaton). The largest U.S. detonation was the Castle/Bravo test in 1954, which had a yield of 15 megatons. The Soviet Union reportedly tested a hydrogen bomb in 1961 that measured 58 megatons.

—*Zach Becker*

See also: Equivalent Megaton; Hydrogen Bomb; Kiloton; Thermonuclear Bomb

Reference

Pringle, Laurance, *Nuclear War: From Hiroshima to Nuclear Winter* (Hillside, NJ: Enslow, 1985).

MEGAWATT

A megawatt is a unit of power equal to 1 million watts. Commercial nuclear power plants normally produce thousands of megawatts of power.

The first nuclear reactor, built at Hanford, Washington, in 1943, generated 250 megawatts of thermal power, that is, 100 million times more power than the 2 watts produced by Enrico Fermi's experimental pile at the University of Chicago in 1942 (*see* Hanford, Washington; Manhattan Project).

A megawatt (electric), abbreviated MWe, is equal to 1 megawatt of electric power, and a megawatt (thermal), abbreviated MWt, is equal to 1 megawatt of thermal power. Nuclear reactors are approximately 30 percent efficient at converting thermal power generated by the fission process to electric power. In terms of converting megatons to megawatts, a megaton of explosive energy is approximately equivalent to the heat generated by a 1,000 MW nuclear power plant operating for about 20 days.

Approximately 440 nuclear power plants worldwide produce about 350,000 MWe. There are 103 nuclear power plants in the United States producing about 86,000 MWe of power.

In the 1990s, the United States began to purchase highly enriched uranium (about 90 percent enriched with uranium 235) from the Russian nuclear weapons industry to convert it to reactor-grade uranium (3 to 5 percent enriched). The United States Enrichment Corporation manages this program to convert potential megatons of explosive energy into megawatts of power.

—*Don Gillich*

See also: Ballistic Missiles; Highly Enriched Uranium; Intermediate-Range Nuclear Forces; Low Enriched Uranium

Reference

Garvin, Richard L., and Georges Charpak, *Megawatts and Megatons: A Turning Point in the Nuclear Age* (New York: Knopf, 2001).

MIDGETMAN ICBMS

The Midgetman program was a plan to deploy a new series of single-warhead intercontinental ballistic missiles (ICBMs) on mobile launchers. It was the direct result of the 1983 Scowcroft Commission Report, the findings of a Commission on Strategic Forces led by Lieutenant General Brent Scowcroft, USAF (ret.), on the increasing vulnerability of U.S. ICBMs to destruction by a Soviet nuclear strike.

ICBM vulnerability had been the subject of considerable debate within the United States as the Soviet Union began to equip heavy ICBMs with multiple independently targetable reentry vehicles (MIRVs). In the early 1980s, the U.S. Air Force had hoped to deploy the large MX ICBM with its highly accurate MIRV warheads to increase the prompt hard-target kill capability of the U.S. "Triad" of nuclear forces (ICBMs, submarine-launched ballistic missiles [SLBMs], and manned bombers). The U.S. Congress, however, had expressed its reservations about the various basing models proposed for the MX because they did little to protect the new missile from a Soviet first strike. President Reagan appointed the Scowcroft Commission to recommend ways to improve the survivability of the land-based leg of the U.S. strategic deterrent. The commission recommended limiting the size of the MX missile deployment and proposed the deployment of 600 mobile, single-warhead ICBMs, dubbed Midgetman. The Midgetman transporter would have been capable of off-road movement, reducing its vulnerability to a Soviet nuclear attack.

The Reagan administration was never supportive of the Midgetman program. Instead, it believed that the Strategic Defense Initiative (SDI) offered the best long-term solution to the problem of ICBM survivability. The Midgetman ICBM program was terminated following the end of the Cold War

—*Andrew M. Dorman*

See also: Intercontinental Ballistic Missile; Strategic
Defense Initiative

Reference

Freedman, Lawrence, *The Evolution of Nuclear Strategy*,
third edition (New York: Palgrave Macmillan, 2003).

MILITARY TECHNICAL REVOLUTION (REVOLUTION IN MILITARY AFFAIRS)

A "military technical revolution" (MTR) occurs gradually when new systems and technology are applied to existing concepts of warfare. The development and use of aircraft carriers, which extended the striking range of naval forces and replaced battleships as the dominant warship on the high seas, for example, constituted an MTR. A "revolution in military affairs" (RMA) encompasses profound changes in military technology that affect the conduct of warfare. In an RMA, the innovative application of new technologies causes dramatic changes in military doctrine and operational and organizational concepts, fundamentally altering the character and conduct of military operations. An RMA thus involves a paradigm shift in the nature and conduct of military operations that renders one or more core competencies of a dominant player obsolete or irrelevant. Alternatively, this shift creates one or more new core competencies in some new dimension of warfare.

An MTR is an evolutionary, not a revolutionary, process: It develops as new technology is incorporated into existing doctrine and organizations. Today, an MTR is under way as advances in computers, telecommunications, and robotics—to name a few obvious technological candidates—are being integrated into military forces.

By contrast, an RMA has a revolutionary effect on warfare. It occurs when technological advances stimulate radical changes in military affairs. The nuclear revolution, for example, had the effect of changing the fundamental nature of warfare. Before nuclear weapons, military forces were intended to achieve victory in war. After the advent of nuclear weapons, the primary purpose of military forces was to deter war.

—*Bret Kinman*

References

Hundley, Richard O., *Past Revolutions, Future
Transformations: What Can the History of Revolutions
in Military Affairs Tell Us about Transforming the U.S.
Military?* (Santa Monica, CA: RAND Corporation,
1999), available at http://www.rand.org/publications/
MR/MR1029.

Krepinovich, Andrew F., Jr., *The Military Technical
Revolution: A Preliminary Assessment* (Washington,
DC: Center for Strategic and Budgetary Assessments,
September 2002), available at http://www.csbaonline.
org.

Williamson, Murray, "Thinking about Revolutions in
Military Affairs," *Joint Forces Quarterly*, vol. 16,
Summer 1997, pp. 69–76.

MINIMUM DETERRENCE

Minimum deterrence is predicated on the ability of a state to absorb a nuclear strike and maintain the ability to inflict enough of a damaging nuclear strike on the enemy's population centers to deter the initial nuclear strike. It encompasses the idea that only a limited retaliatory capability of a few score nuclear weapons is sufficient for a credible nuclear threat, regardless of the size of the opponent's arsenal. Although at first the size and then the capability of both Soviet and U.S. nuclear arsenals increased during the Cold War, advocates of minimum deterrence believed that the arms race had produced a situation of unnecessary "nuclear overkill" and that a small, secure second-strike capability was sufficient to deter nuclear attack. Critics of the concept stated that small nuclear forces lacked redundancy and in the end would offer a tempting target to an opponent wishing to obtain a first-strike capability.

In the aftermath of the Cold War, states with small nuclear arsenals—France, the People's Republic of China, India, and Pakistan—seem to have adopted minimal deterrent postures out of necessity, if not strategic choice. At the heart of this doctrine is the idea that the major nuclear powers will not be willing to lose a population center during a conflict with a foreign nuclear power and therefore will be deterred by the threat of even minimal retaliation.

—*Abe Denmark and James J. Wirtz*

See also: Deterrence; Extended Deterrence
References
Johnston, Alastair Iain, "China's New 'Old Thinking': The Concept of Limited Deterrence," *International Security*, vol. 20, no. 3, Winter 1995–1996, pp. 5–42.
Sagan, Scott D., "The Perils of Proliferation," *International Security*, vol. 18, no. 4, Spring 1994, pp. 66–107.

MINISTRY OF ATOMIC ENERGY (MINATOM)

In January 1992, following the dissolution of the Soviet Union, the Russian Federation Ministry of Atomic Energy (MINATOM) was established by presidential decree. MINATOM, which replaced the Soviet Ministry of Atomic Power and Industry, controls 151 production and research facilities. At the time it was established, it employed approximately 1 million people. The ministry has its own education and training institutes, export organization, and banks.

MINATOM is responsible for the production of all Russian nuclear materials and the development, testing, and production of its nuclear weapons. It is also responsible for the elimination of nuclear warheads and nuclear munitions as stipulated by various treaties. Responsibility for decommissioned nuclear-powered submarines was transferred from the Ministry of Defense to MINATOM in late 1998. The ministry controls most of the weapons-usable highly enriched uranium and plutonium not contained in nuclear weapons. It also has responsibility for Russia's commercial nuclear power program, nuclear safety oversight, basic and applied research, and the conversion of military facilities to civilian uses.

MINATOM was restructured at the end of 1998. It consists of fourteen departments: Nuclear Fuel Cycle; Nuclear Munitions Development and Testing; Nuclear Munitions Production; Nuclear Power Engineering; Industry Economics and Planning; Social Policy, Industrial Relations, and Cadres; Security and Emergency Situations; International and Foreign Economic Cooperation; Nuclear Science and Engineering; Finances, Analysis, and Calculations; Protection of Information, Nuclear Materials, and Facilities; Construction of Nuclear Facilities; Regulatory-Legal Support and Regulation of Forms of Ownership; and Nuclear Industry Conversion.

—*Steven Rosenkrantz*

Reference
"Russia: Ministry of Atomic Energy—Minatom," in Pavel Podvig, ed., *Russian Strategic Nuclear Forces* (Cambridge, MA: MIT Press, 2001), pp. 74–78, 106, 111, 578.

MINUTEMAN ICBM

The U.S. LGM-30 Minuteman is a three-stage, solid-fuel intercontinental ballistic missile (ICBM) with a range of approximately 5,500 nautical miles. It possesses an inertial guidance system and is deployed in hardened underground launch silos.

History and Background

Minuteman grew out a series of design studies initiated in the mid-1950s to develop a simple, efficient three-stage solid-fuel ICBM that could be produced and deployed in large numbers. Development of the missile began in the summer of 1957. A consortium of five contractors produced four distinct Minuteman models: Minuteman I (models "A" and "B"), Minuteman II (model "F"), and Minuteman III (model "G").

During the early development of the missile, the Strategic Air Command (SAC) favored deploying at least a portion of the force on railroad cars. The air force, by contrast, emphasized a silo-based missile. In March 1961, President John F. Kennedy deferred the development of a mobile missile in favor of the silo-based model, and in December of that year Secretary of Defense Robert McNamara canceled the mobile Minuteman program.

Minuteman IA achieved initial operational capability (IOC) in December 1962 with twenty missiles. A full squadron was on alert by the end of February 1963. The Minuteman I was based in hardened, widely dispersed underground silos. An underground launch control center monitored each flight of ten launch facilities, with five flights per squadron. The first Minuteman IB entered service on September 30, 1963.

In 1966, the U.S. Air Force initiated the Minuteman Force Modernization Program to replace all Minuteman Is with either the Minuteman II or III. The program continued through the late 1960s and into the mid-1970s. The Minuteman I was deactivated in 1972 when the air force began fielding the Minuteman III.

Minuteman II had an improved second stage and a dramatically improved guidance system and was equipped with microelectronic circuitry. It achieved IOC on October 31, 1965. In all, 1,000 Minuteman IIs were deployed.

The Minuteman III was the world's first ICBM to carry multiple independently targetable reentry vehicles (MIRVs). It featured an enlarged third stage as well as a new warhead section, or "bus," that housed the guidance system, its own liquid-fueled rocket motor, and three warheads with reentry vehicles. The missile went into regular development in 1966 and was first deployed in April 1970. A total of 500 Minuteman IIIs were fielded. Each missile was deployed with three warheads; there were 200 missiles with W-62 warheads and Mk-12 reentry vehicles, and 300 missiles with larger-yield W-78 warheads and Mk-12A reentry vehicles.

Current Status

All 500 Minuteman IIIs—located at F. E. Warren Air Force Base, Wyoming; Malmstrom Air Force Base, Montana; and Minot Air Force Base, North Dakota—are expected to stay in the U.S. inventory until 2020. When the Peacekeeper ICBM is retired, the Minuteman III will become the only U.S. ICBM. Under the Safety Enhanced Reentry Vehicle

program, some Minuteman IIIs will be downloaded to a single W-87 warhead and Mk-21 reentry vehicle. The missile also is to be fitted with the Peacekeeper's Advanced Inertial Reference Sphere. To increase its service life, its aging solid-fuel first and second stages will be refilled with new propellant and bonding materials and its third stage will be remanufactured.

—Tom Mahnken

References

Cochran, Thomas B., William A. Arkin, and Milton M. Hoenig, *Nuclear Weapons Databook,* vol. 1: *U.S. Nuclear Forces and Capabilities* (Cambridge, MA: Ballinger, 1984).

Mackenzie, Donald, *Inventing Accuracy: An Historical Sociology of Nuclear Missile Guidance* (Cambridge, MA: MIT Press, 1990).

Neufeld, Jacob, *The Development of Ballistic Missiles in the United States Air Force, 1945–1960* (Washington, DC: Office of Air Force History, United States Air Force, 1990).

MISSILE DEFENSE

The term "missile defense" refers to a system or systems designed to defend against ballistic missile attack, including both active and passive measures to detect, identify, assess, track, and defeat offensive ballistic missiles during any portion of their flight trajectory. It most often refers to the use of ballistic missiles to shoot down other ballistic missiles but may include other means of interception such as directed-energy or laser weapons. The term "antiballistic missile" refers strictly to a ballistic missile that intercepts another ballistic missile. The term "ballistic missile defense" is sometimes used interchangeably with the term "missile defense" and can refer either to defense against ballistic missiles (such as silo-based intercontinental ballistic missiles, or ICBMs) by any means, or defense of any potential target by means of antiballistic missiles (*see* Ballistic Missiles).

History and Background

Throughout most of the Cold War, missile defenses were divided into two categories. "Theater missile defense" referred to defense against short-, medium-, or intermediate-range ballistic missiles and was associated with defense of forces deployed to a given theater of combat against ballistic missile attack. "National missile defense" referred to broader defense of the national territory against long-range or intercontinental ballistic missiles. This distinction was institutionalized by the 1972 Anti-Ballistic Missile (ABM) Treaty, which strictly limited the development and deployment of missile defenses against intercontinental missiles but did not limit theater missile defenses (*see* Anti-Ballistic Missile Treaty). Following U.S. withdrawal from the ABM Treaty in June 2002, and the blurring of technological distinctions between systems designed to detect and counter intercontinental ballistic missiles and those designed to detect and counter shorter-range ballistic missiles, however, the distinction between theater missile defense and national missile defense has nearly faded away. Those systems devoted to missile defense are now grouped into three categories, depending on that phase in the trajectory of an incoming missile during which interception is intended to occur. These are the boost phase, the mid-course phase, and the terminal phase. Attempting to intercept a missile during each phase poses its own advantages and challenges from the defender's perspective.

During its "boost phase," an offensive missile's booster rockets continue to fire, lifting it into a ballistic trajectory. This phase is very short, lasting anywhere from 3 to 10 minutes. The missile may attain an altitude of up to 200 kilometers, and the heat generated by the firing rocket plumes during this phase presents a brighter, more easily detected thermal signature, facilitating detection, tracking, and identification, especially from space-based infrared sensors. Since the missile is traveling relatively slowly in the early stages of this phase, it may be more easily intercepted by high-acceleration ground- or sea-based interceptors located within range, or by air- or space-based directed-energy or kinetic-kill mechanisms. Decoys or other devices intended to distract or confuse the interceptor missile will not have been released during this phase, thus easing the problem of discriminating between the warhead and other items traveling through space

An exoatmospheric kill vehicle interceptor is launched from the Kwajalein Atoll in the Marshall Islands during a test in March 2002. (Reuters/Missile Defense Agency/Corbis)

with it. In many hypothetical scenarios, space-based missile defense systems would be ideally suited to attempting boost-phase intercepts, since they would be based in orbit high above the launching territory, although the practical development and deployment of such systems are many years off. Missiles launched from deep inside an attacking nation's territory, however, may be difficult to reach by land- or sea-based interceptors. Since this phase is very short, warning and response timelines must be extremely compressed, making it challenging to detect and assess a hostile launch and then cue and direct interceptors in time to destroy the attacking missile while it is still in the boost phase of its flight. Also, it is difficult to determine a missile's ultimate trajectory or intended impact point during the first moments of its flight while it is striving to escape gravity, so unless the missile's basing or other characteristics allow a predetermination of its hostile intent, or the launch occurs in the midst of a crisis or conflict, it may not be possible to ascertain in a timely manner whether it is a peaceful space launch or an attack (*see* Boost-Phase Intercept).

During the "mid-course phase," the missile's boosters cease firing and the warheads, and in many cases decoys, separate from the third stage. This phase may last up to 20 minutes, constituting the longest portion of the trajectory, and thus offers the best opportunity for an adversary to track the missile, assess its intended target, and attempt one or more intercepts. Most concepts for a national missile defense are designed to achieve interception during this phase. The land-based, long-range missile defense system that the United States is currently beginning to deploy in Alaska and California is a mid-course interception system. Nevertheless, interception during this phase poses its own set of challenges. Offensive missiles may release multiple warheads and/or penetration aids, such as decoys or chaff, during this phase or incorporate other ways of complicating the task of discriminating between warheads and other items and avoiding interception (*see* Decoys; Penetration Aids).

The "terminal phase" begins upon a missile warhead's final approach to its intended target. For intercontinental ballistic missiles and long-range theater missiles, this phase begins with the warhead reentering the atmosphere and may last for only a minute or less. At this point, the warhead is traveling at its fastest speed, leaving only a slight window

for attempting an intercept. The atmosphere, however, tends to strip away decoys and chaff upon reentry, simplifying the discrimination task. Terminal defense systems can only provide protection to individual targets or to discrete assets such as troop concentrations, ports, airfields, staging areas, or command and control posts (*see* Terminal Phase).

Kill Mechanisms

A variety of kill mechanisms have been devised to achieve the destruction of an incoming missile or warhead, though not all have been fully developed or even tested. Blast fragmentation devices are designed to explode in proximity to an incoming warhead or missile and to destroy or damage it through collisions with fragments of the interceptor warhead. This is the mechanism employed by most theater missile defenses, and its shortcomings were highlighted by the partial successes of the Patriot missile defense efforts to shoot down Iraqi Scud missiles during the 1991 Persian Gulf War. Early U.S. and Soviet antiballistic missile systems employed nuclear warheads as their primary kill mechanism. The Russian ABM system around Moscow still carries interceptor warheads that rely on nuclear blasts to destroy incoming warheads. Sometime in the late 1980s, the United States made a decision to forgo using nuclear weapons as a missile defense kill mechanism for political and technical reasons, including the fratricide problem (that is, the chance that the nuclear blast would do as much or more damage to U.S. space assets as it did to incoming enemy warheads), a political commitment to cease further nuclear tests, which would have been necessary to develop a missile defense warhead, and an emerging confidence in kinetic kill mechanisms. Kinetic kill mechanisms, or hit-to-kill devices, use the tremendous energy released by direct collisions between interceptors and attacking warheads, both traveling thousands of miles per hour. Such collisions obliterate both the interceptor and the offensive warhead so thoroughly that any nuclear, biological, or chemical weapon carried by the offensive warhead is incinerated. The long-range missile defense system the United States is deploying beginning in 2004 will use a kinetic kill vehicle. Another kill mechanism that is under study employs focused or directed high-energy beams, such as laser or X-ray beams, to destroy missiles. The Israeli government has developed a ground-based antimissile laser device that has been effective in tests against short-range battlefield rockets, and the United States is developing an airborne antimissile laser based on a Boeing 747 aircraft frame that is expected to be tested in 2004–2005.

Political Considerations

Few issues in the field of foreign and defense policy have been of such enduring controversy and debate as missile defense. This debate, which has raged since the mid-1960s, has revolved around two basic questions: (1) *Could* a truly effective and affordable missile defense system be developed and deployed? And, (2) *Should* such a system be developed and deployed, even it if is possible to build one? The first question involves issues of technology, the reliability of complex command and control networks, the pros and cons of automated decision-making, resilience in the face of countermeasures, and the rigors and "realism" of the testing regime. The second question concerns the implications of deploying a missile defense system for international and regional stability in general, for its potential to provoke action-reaction arms races, for whether it would help or hinder efforts to combat the proliferation of weapons of mass destruction and offensive ballistic missile threats, and for whether it would undermine or buttress chances for achieving further strategic arms reduction agreements. These same issues were revisited during the course of three successive debates on missile defense. The first occurred during the mid- to late-1960s and into the early 1970s, culminating in the conclusion of the ABM Treaty in 1972, which settled the debate in favor of those opposed to missile defense. The debate was revived again in the early 1980s when President Ronald Reagan called for the development of a Strategic Defense Initiative (SDI) to provide a hemispheric shield against a potential attack by thousands of Soviet ballistic missiles. This debate was rendered moot by the dissolution of the Soviet Union, after which subsequent administrations dramatically reduced and dismantled the SDI program (*see* Strategic Defense Initiative).

The administration of Bill Clinton (1992–2000) responded to the fall of the Soviet Union by reconfirming the status of the ABM Treaty as the "cornerstone of strategic stability" and discontinuing negotiations with Russia for a cooperative evolution toward a "Global Protection Against Limited Strikes," or GPALS, system. The GPALS system was aimed at loosening or amending ABM Treaty restrictions on missile defense and would have led to the joint development of a modest capability to intercept missile launches by rogue states in certain regions (*see* Global Protection Against Limited Strikes). During the first Clinton administration, funding for SDI was reduced by nearly 80 percent, for theater missile defenses by nearly 25 percent, and for advanced science and technology research by over 95 percent. Nevertheless, the debate over missile defense flared up again for the third time in the late 1990s in the face of increasing proliferation of ballistic missiles among rogue states, and in particular by North Korea's test launch of a three-stage missile of apparent intercontinental range in August 1998. The Clinton administration formulated four criteria for evaluating whether to deploy some form of missile defense as a response to the proliferation threat: the degree to which the threat of ballistic missile attack justified such a response; whether a technically feasible system could be developed; the affordability of such a system; and the likely impact of a U.S. decision to deploy missile defenses on the ABM Treaty and other U.S. arms control and nonproliferation objectives. Eventually, in a speech given on September 1, 2000, President Clinton chose to defer a decision on deploying a missile defense system, largely out of concern about its anticipated impact on U.S.-Russian relations and arms control.

Shortly after assuming office in January 2001, President George W. Bush declared that it was the policy of his administration to deploy a limited missile defense capability as soon as technically feasible. The Bush administration believed that the ABM Treaty had blocked fully exploring all technological avenues of achieving an effective missile defense, that an effective system was affordable, that it was justified by the prospective threat, and that the arms control and international stability ramifications could be managed. In December 2001, President Bush exercised the U.S. right to withdraw from the ABM Treaty on six months' notice, and shortly afterward he announced a decision to begin deploying a limited missile defense system in 2004. This system was to consist initially of twenty silo-based midcourse interceptors deployed in Alaska and California, up to twenty sea-based interceptors on existing Aegis ships, deployment of air-transportable Patriot

Advanced Capability-3 (PAC-3) missiles, and a variety of land-, sea-, and space-based sensors, including upgrades to three existing early warning radars located in Clear, Alaska; Thule, Greenland; and Fylingdales, Great Britain (see Early Warning).

Initial reports regarding the performance of the Patriot missile defense system in the war with Iraq in March and April 2003 indicated a high degree of success in intercepting shorter-range (and slower) Iraqi missiles, although serious questions have arisen related to several friendly-fire incidents wherein Patriot missiles downed allied aircraft. Thus, the debate over missile defense is far from over.

—Kerry Kartchner

See also: Early Warning; Moscow Antiballistic Missile
   System; Sentinel; Space-Based Infrared Radar
   System; Surveillance; Theater High Altitude Air
   Defense; Theater Missile Defense

References

Butler, Richard, Fatal Choice: Nuclear Weapons and the
   Illusion of Missile Defense (Boulder: Westview, 2001).
Payne, Keith B., Missile Defense in the 21st Century:
   Protection against Limited Threats, Including Lessons
   from the Gulf War (Boulder: Westview, 1991).
Wirtz, James J., and Jeffrey A. Larsen, eds., Rockets' Red
   Glare: Missile Defenses and the Future of World
   Politics (Boulder: Westview, 2001).

MISSILE DEFENSE AGENCY (MDA)
See Ballistic Missile Defense Organization

MISSILE GAP

Estimates that the Soviet Union would create a missile gap and gain strategic advantage by surpassing the United States in the production of intercontinental ballistic missiles (ICBMs) sparked considerable public and official concern during the late 1950s and early 1960s. The Soviet launch of Sputnik on October 4, 1957, was the proximate cause for missile-gap fears that did not subside until well into the John F. Kennedy administration's term in office. In reality, a reverse missile gap developed during the early years of the missile age because the United States deployed many more ICBMs than the Soviet Union until the late 1960s.

Americans were concerned about their potential vulnerability to rapid or surprise nuclear attack during the 1950s because of their memories of Pearl Harbor, developments in nuclear weapons and missile delivery systems, lack of hard strategic intelligence, the Dwight D. Eisenhower administration's defense policies, and domestic politics. Fears of a bomber gap developed after Western military attachés observed a greater than expected number of intercontinental M-4 Bison bombers during a Moscow air show in July 1995. After Sputnik, bomber gap fears were replaced by greater fears about the apparent failure of American science and the terrifying threat of nearly instantaneous attack from ICBMs. Congressional Democrats, in particular, used the missile gap to attack Eisenhower's "New Look" and massive retaliation defense policies and were aided by the sober assessments in the Gaither Report, which was completed for the National Security Council in November 1957. The missile gap and American defense preparedness in general were significant issues in the 1960 presidential campaign. The missile gap issue dissipated, however, after analysis of photos of the U.S.S.R. produced by U-2 aircraft and, especially, CORONA reconnaissance satellites in the early 1960s revealed far fewer ICBMs than had been estimated.

—Peter Hays

See also: Cold War

References

Bottome, Edgar M., The Missile Gap: A Study in the
   Formulation of Military and Political Policy
   (Rutherford, NJ: Fairleigh Dickinson University
   Press, 1971).
Prados, John, The Soviet Estimate: U.S. Intelligence
   Analysis & Russian Military Strength (New York:
   Dial, 1982).
Wohlstetter, Albert, "The Delicate Balance of Terror,"
   RAND Report P-1472 (Santa Monica, CA: RAND
   Corporation, December 1958), available at http://
   www.rand.org/publications/classics/wohlstetter/
   P1472/P1472.html.

MISSILE TECHNOLOGY
CONTROL REGIME (MTCR)

The Missile Technology Control Regime (MTCR) is a set of guidelines regulating the export of ballistic and cruise missiles, unmanned aerial vehicles (UAVs), and related technology for those systems capable of carrying a 500-kilogram payload at least 300 kilometers.

On April 16, 1987, Canada, France, Germany, Italy, Japan, the United Kingdom, and the United States established the MTCR to govern the export of missiles and related technology. The regime is an informal, voluntary arrangement rather than a treaty or international agreement. It consists of a set of common export policies applied to a list of controlled items. Each member implements its commitments in the context of its own national export laws. In addition to the states that have formally joined the MTCR, a number of countries unilaterally observe or adhere to the guidelines.

The MTCR guidelines cover ballistic missiles, space launch vehicles, sounding rockets, cruise missiles, drones, and remotely piloted vehicles. The guidelines explicitly state that the regime is "not designed to impede national space programs or international cooperation in such programs as long as such programs could not contribute to delivery systems for weapons of mass destruction." When announced in 1987, the regime was concerned only with nuclear-capable delivery systems. In January 1993, however, the adherents extended the guidelines to cover systems capable of delivering all nuclear, biological, and chemical weapons.

The MTCR's annex of controlled equipment and technology includes equipment and technology, both military and dual-use, relevant to missile development, production, and operation. It is divided into Category I and Category II items. Export of Category I items—including complete rocket systems, cruise missiles, and unmanned aerial vehicles, specially designed production facilities for these systems, and certain complete subsystems—is subject to a presumption of export denial. Category II items—such as propellants, structural materials, test equipment, and flight instruments—may be exported at the discretion of the MTCR partner government on a case-by-case basis for acceptable end uses. They also may be exported after the exchange of government-to-government assurances, which provide that they not be used on a missile system capable of delivering a 500-kilogram payload to a range of at least 300 kilometers.

MTCR partners hold an annual plenary meeting chaired on a rotational basis. Inter-sessional consultations take place monthly though Point of Contact meetings in Paris. The MTCR also undertakes outreach activities to nonpartners.

The current members of the MTCR are Argentina, Australia, Austria, Belgium, Brazil, Canada, Denmark, Finland, France, Germany, Greece, Hungary, Iceland, Ireland, Italy, Japan, Luxembourg, the Netherlands, New Zealand, Norway, Portugal, Russia, South Africa, Spain, Sweden, Switzerland,

Turkey, the United Kingdom, and the United States. Several others, including China, Israel, and Ukraine, have pledged to adhere to the export control regime but have not been invited or do not seek to become members.

—Tom Mahnken

See also: Nonproliferation

References
Bowen, Wyn Q., *The Politics of Ballistic Missile Nonproliferation* (New York: Palgrave Macmillan, 2000).
Nolan, Janne E., *Trappings of Power: Ballistic Missiles in the Third World* (Washington, DC: Brookings Institution, 1991).
U.S. Department of State website, http://www.state.gov/www/global/arms/np/mtcr/mtcr.html.

MIXED OXIDE FUEL (MOX)

Mixed oxide fuels are mixtures of uranium and plutonium oxides used in reactor operations. These mixtures are often referred to as MOX. The plutonium that makes up MOX comes from two main sources: fuel reprocessing and weapon disassembly. The uranium content of MOX is depleted uranium. The primary use of MOX fuel is to burn excess plutonium generated from spent fuel and disassembled weapons in conventional reactors to generate energy.

Technical Details

The limited use of mixed oxide fuels does not appreciably change the operating characteristics of a reactor. If the core of a reactor is more than 50 percent MOX, however, significant changes must be made to the core layout and to control-rod positioning within the reactor. MOX fuels enjoy an advantage over low enriched uranium (LEU) fuels in this application because concentrations of plutonium within MOX fuel rods can be very cheaply increased, whereas uranium enrichment is expensive. This issue becomes important when designing cores that require a larger initial loading of fissile material (*see* Enrichment; Low Enriched Uranium).

The plutonium that is mixed with uranium to form MOX comes from two sources. One source is spent nuclear fuel. The plutonium from spent nuclear fuel is generated in the fuel during the irradiation process. Nonirradiated LEU fuel does not contain plutonium; however, approximately one-third of the energy it produces is generated by the fissioning of plutonium. Plutonium is formed in the reactor through neutron capture by the uranium. By the end of the life of a typical fuel bundle in a thermal reactor, the fuel contains about 1 percent plutonium. This form of plutonium is commonly referred to as "reactor-grade" plutonium, where the plutonium contains more than 19 percent Plutonium 240 (Pu-240) and less than 60 percent Pu-239. Mixed oxide fuel using reactor-grade plutonium is typically 7 percent plutonium, which is roughly equivalent to 4.5 percent Uranium 235 (U-235) owing to the presence of other plutonium isotopes. About 50 metric tons of reactor-grade plutonium are produced each year in the spent fuel from the many operating reactors around the world. This rate of production adds yearly to the 1,000 metric tons that have already been produced. The vast majority of this plutonium remains held within the spent fuel.

Plutonium from disassembled nuclear weapons is typically referred to as "weapons grade" when the plutonium is at least 92 percent Pu-239. Mixed oxide fuels using weapons-grade plutonium are typically 5 percent plutonium. Spent MOX fuel that has been burned in a reactor with weapons-grade plutonium contains an isotopic distribution similar to that of spent LEU fuel. The current world inventory of weapons-grade plutonium is estimated to be approximately 200 to 270 metric tons, with the United States holding 85 metric tons and Russia holding between 100 to 165 metric tons.

All plutonium except that containing more than 80 percent Pu-238 is considered, by the International Atomic Energy Agency (IAEA), to be "direct-use" plutonium. The IAEA's position is that it is theoretically possible to build a nuclear explosive from direct-use plutonium. There are many technical challenges that must be overcome to build an explosive from anything other than weapons-grade plutonium. Among these challenges are issues of weapon reliability, useful yield, deliverable size, and storage life. An issue that further clouds this picture is that in 1962 the United States successfully tested a device that used what was referred to as reactor-grade plutonium, but what U.S. officials referred to as reactor-grade plutonium in this test contained a much higher proportion of Pu-239 than what is produced in the spent fuel of power reactors today. It is estimated that the device contained between 70 and 75 percent Pu-239, compared to about 55 percent Pu-239 produced by power reactors. The actual content of plutonium used in the test is classified and has not been released.

Current Status

Mixed oxide fuel was originally developed to run in fast reactors, but in 1963 it saw its first use in a thermal reactor. Since that time, MOX has been seen more and more in terms of the opportunities it offers, both to recover energy from spent nuclear fuel and from surplus weapons plutonium and to reduce the volume of waste produced by nuclear power plants as well as the stockpiles of weapons material.

All modern light-water reactors can use a 30 percent MOX fuel load without significant modification to their core assembly. At least thirty-two European reactors are licensed to use 30 percent MOX in their cores. The United States and Russia have recently signed agreements to each convert 34 metric tons of weapons-grade plutonium into MOX fuel. Both countries are in the process of licensing reactors to burn this fuel. Japan is planning to use MOX in as many as one-third of its reactors in the near future. In addition to using MOX in thermal reactors, France and Russia are using it as a primary fuel source for their fast reactors. About 8 to 10 metric tons of plutonium are converted to MOX and used each year. Currently, MOX is produced in two facilities in France, one in Belgium, and one in the United Kingdom. European MOX production generates about 300 metric tons of MOX per year using approximately 20 metric tons of plutonium.

The use of MOX fuel is expected to increase in the near future until the production of MOX and the use of MOX are in balance. The United States and Russia are expected to build MOX fabrication facilities by 2005. These will most likely be located at the Savanna River Facility in the United States and at the Mayak facility in Russia. These plants are expected to produce together 40 metric tons of MOX per year using 2 metric tons of weapons-grade plutonium. In the short term worldwide, processed plutonium stockpiles are expected to increase before this balance is reached. In the future, the production and use of MOX should increase as the use of reprocessing becomes the standard practice within the nuclear fuel cycle.

—*C. Ross Schmidtlein*

See also: Depleted Uranium (U-238); Fast Breeder
   Reactors; Light-Water Reactors; Plutonium;
   Uranium

References
"Fact Sheet on Mixed Oxide Fuel," U.S. Nuclear
   Regulatory Commission, March 2003.
"Mixed Oxide Fuel (MOX)," World Nuclear Association,
   February 2002.
"Mixed Oxide Fuel (MOX)," Uranium Information
   Center, Nuclear Issues Briefing Paper 42, February
   2002.
"Plutonium Recycling: The Use of 'MOX' Fuel,"
   Australian Safeguards and Non-Proliferation Office,
   DFAT, 1999 Annual Report.

MOBILE ICBMS

To increase the survivability of land-based intercontinental ballistic missiles (ICBMs), military planners have always turned to mobility in order to complicate the calculations of an attacker. For the Soviet Union, development of mobile ICBMs was slow until the late 1960s owing to concerns about command and control and the ability to maintain positive control of Soviet missiles under all circumstances. Lack of communications links were an additional Soviet concern. In the United States, high operating costs and the need to operate systems over enormous expanses of land limited interest in mobile missiles. The U.S. Air Force pursued the rail-mobile Minuteman option in 1960, which would have been deployed at Hill Air Force Base, Utah, but for budgetary reasons Secretary of Defense Robert McNamara canceled the planned procurement of additional Minuteman ICBMs, which eliminated the need for the deployment scheme. As the accuracy of ICBMs improved, creating concerns about the survivability of ICBMs deployed in fixed silos, both superpowers revisited the issue of deploying mobile ICBMs.

The Soviets first attempted to use a tank chassis as a transporter for the SS-15 in 1968. After discovering that vibration of the chassis caused missile component failures, they canceled the system after ten test flights. After reviewing its options, the Soviet Strategic Forces decided that a truck chassis was a better vehicle than a tank chassis as a missile transporter, offered better road speeds, was relatively easy to maintain, and created fewer vibration problems. The SS-16 system that emerged in 1972 was concealable, highly mobile, and successful. It also became one of the major stumbling blocks in superpower arms control talks. The United States could not detect the missile launchers using reconnaissance satellites and tried to have mobile missiles banned. The SS-16 was specifically banned in the treaty resulting from the Strategic Arms Limitation Talks (SALT I), although the Soviets kept the missile in their inventory in violation of the treaty. It was eventually withdrawn from service when better systems were ready for deployment.

After the SS-16 was decommissioned, the designs were used in the highly successful SS-20 intermediate-range ballistic missile (IRBM) that entered the Soviet arsenal in the 1970s. Soviet planners also decided that they required a secure second-strike capability and eventually deployed the road-mobile SS-25 and the rail-mobile SS-24 ICBMs. The SS-25 carried a single warhead, while the SS-24 carried ten multiple independently targetable reentry vehicles (MIRVs). The SS-24 was deployed on missile trains that carried three missiles, their launchers, support equipment, and security railcars. These missile trains usually patrolled for about five days out of garrisons that were situated along the Trans-Siberian Railroad. In order to keep its defense posture as other strategic arms treaties entered into force, Russia replaced the SS-25 with the SS-27, another road-mobile missile.

During the Jimmy Carter administration and the early Ronald Reagan years, a debate raged in U.S. policy circles about how to deploy the new U.S. ICBM that was under development. It made little sense to deploy the new missile in fixed silos because these could easily be destroyed by Soviet nuclear forces. Shuttling the missile among multiple shelters was suggested, but creating this giant "shell game" would have been enormously expensive and required enormous amounts of land. A "dense pack" scheme was suggested that relied upon fratricide among incoming warheads to prevent the new land-based missiles from being destroyed quickly in a Soviet nuclear attack (see Dense Pack). Eventually, two mobile systems were developed to reduce the vulnerability of U.S. land-based ICBMs. The MX Peacekeeper would be deployed in rail garrison in times of crisis, and U.S. missile trains would move on to U.S. civilian railroads to complicate Soviet efforts to destroy them. The Midgetman, a road-mobile single-warhead missile, also was under development. Both deployment schemes were canceled at the end of the Cold War.

—*Gilles Van Nederveen*

See also: Midgetman ICBM; Peacekeeper Missile
References
A History of Strategic Arms Competition, 1945–1972, vol. 3, *A Handbook of Selected Soviet Weapon and Space Systems* (Washington, DC: United States Air Force, June 1976), pp. 204, 205, 209, 216.
Jane's Weapon Systems 1987–88 (London: Jane's Publishing Company, 1988).
Podvig, Pavel, ed., *Russian Strategic Nuclear Forces* (Cambridge, MA: MIT Press, 2001).

MORATORIUM

A moratorium is a legal or legislative action for the temporary suspension or prohibition of an ongoing or planned activity. In the world of nuclear weapons, the term usually refers specifically to the suspension of nuclear weapons testing.

On October 31, 1958, U.S. President Dwight D. Eisenhower declared a unilateral moratorium on nuclear testing. The United Kingdom and the Soviet Union also voluntarily observed this informal nuclear test moratorium until September 1, 1961, when the Soviet Union conducted a series of nuclear tests. On September 15, 1961, the United States resumed testing of nuclear weapons at the Nevada Test Site.

For political purposes, the Soviet Union observed unilateral nuclear testing moratoriums during three separate time periods: December 1962 to March 1964; August 1985 to October 1987; and November 1989 to October 1990.

In October 1991, Soviet President Mikhail Gorbachev declared a unilateral nuclear testing moratorium. On October 2, 1992, U.S. President George H. W. Bush signed the Hatfield-Exon-Mitchell Amendment, which imposed a nine-month nuclear test moratorium. U.S. President Bill Clinton extended the moratorium several times before signing the Comprehensive Test Ban Treaty (CTBT) on September 24, 1996. This treaty precludes the necessity for further nuclear testing moratoriums. However, the U.S. Senate has not ratified the treaty and it has therefore not entered into force.

A nuclear test moratorium is an instrument of disarmament because over time it reduces confidence in the reliability of one's nuclear arsenal and diminishes a state's ability to build nuclear weapons

or update an existing arsenal to meet new requirements. Newly designed weapons may require testing. The George W. Bush administration, while agreeing to adhere to the specifications of the nonratified CTBT, also refused to permanently surrender the option of eventually testing new U.S. weapons.

—*Don Gillich*

See also: Comprehensive Test Ban Treaty; Disarmament; Nuclear Test Ban
References
"Nuclear Testing Moratorium Act, S.2064 (and other nuclear testing issues)," Hearing before the Committee on Foreign Relations, United States Senate, 102d Cong., 2d sess., 23 July 1992.
Weinberg, Alvin M., ed., *Economic and Environmental Impacts of a U.S. Nuclear Moratorium, 1985–2010*, second edition (Boston: MIT Press, 1979).

MOSCOW ANTIBALLISTIC MISSILE SYSTEM

The Russian antiballistic missile (ABM) system surrounding the capital of Moscow was the only active ABM system in the world until the United States commissioned its missile defense system in Alaska in October 2004. Soviet research into antimissile defense started in 1948 but did not begin in earnest until 1955, when a special antimissile test site was established near Sary Shagan on Lake Balkash in Central Asia. In tests conducted at the site, rockets, usually SS-3 or SS-4 medium-range ballistic missiles, were launched toward Sary Shagan from Kapustin Yar near Volgograd. These rockets served as targets for the antiballistic missile systems being tested at Sary Shagan. To demonstrate that antiballistic missile components could withstand a nuclear blast environment and operate in that environment, nuclear tests also were conducted at the site (*see* Missile Defense).

Construction of the first Soviet ABM system, called ABM-1 (or "Galosh") by the West, began in October 1962. Eight separate complexes were constructed in a ring about 45 nautical miles from the center of Moscow, but only four eventually became operational as part of the ABM-1 system. The interceptor missiles were kept in aboveground, reloadable launchers. Sixty-four exoatmospheric missiles became operational in 1967. They had a 200-mile range and carried a relatively large nuclear warhead intended to detonate in the path of incoming U.S. nuclear-armed reentry vehicles. By 1976, these first

The Moscow ABM system's missile detection center, the "Don 2N" site, January 2000. (Caw/Str Reuters/Corbis)

missiles had been replaced by variants that could start and stop their rocket motor so that the system radars could discriminate between warhead, chaff, and decoys. ABM-1 relied on four battle management radars at each of the four missile sites (named "Try Add" by the West) and two large phased-array radars for battle management near Moscow ("Dog House" and "Cat House"). Six early-warning radars located on the intercontinental ballistic missile (ICBM) and submarine-launched ballistic missile (SLBM) approach corridors to the Soviet heartland provided early warning to the Moscow system.

Soviet ABM deployments continued throughout the Cold War. The ABM-2 was a road-mobile system that never reached operational status. The current system is designated ABM-3. It is similar to the old U.S. Safeguard system, which employed one type of interceptor to attack incoming warheads outside the atmosphere and a shorter-range missile to engage incoming warheads in their terminal phase. The Soviets also developed a high-acceleration missile similar to the U.S. Sprint. Deployed in 1984, it was modified to improve its intercept capabilities against the U.S. Army's Pershing II missile

stationed in West Germany. The SH-08 Gazelle was designed for endoatmospheric interception with a range of 80 miles and a 1-kiloton warhead. The SH-11 Gorgon is an exoatmospheric interceptor with a 200-mile range. Currently there are thirty-six SH-11 Gorgons, and sixty-four Gazelles are deployed around Moscow in underground silos at eight sites.

The most visible part of the system is the Pill Box phased-array radar at Balabanovo that serves dual roles as a surveillance and engagement radar. A new family of phased radars, Pechora, also was deployed in the mid-1980s to improve early warning for the ABM-3 system. Some of these radars were located outside of Russia in the newly independent republics, so following the collapse of the Soviet Union, Russia was forced to build radars at new sites or pay those governments for access.

One system that caused much controversy during Ronald Reagan's term as president in the United States was the Soviet SA-12B surface-to-air missile system. This system was primarily designed to intercept aircraft but probably also had some capability against tactical and intermediate-range missile warheads. It has a 100-mile range and is equipped with a high-explosive warhead. The Russian Army currently deploys mixed SA-12 battalions that contain both the shorter-range SA-12A and the longer-range SA-12B, plus radars and support equipment. The exact ABM abilities of the SA-12B are unknown but are probably similar to those of the U.S. Patriot system.

—*Gilles Van Nederveen*

See also: Safeguard Anti-Ballistic Missile System

References

"Moscow ABM Facilities," available at http://www.fas. org/spp/starwars/program/soviet/moscow.htm.

Podvig, Pavel, ed., *Russian Strategic Nuclear Forces* (Cambridge, MA: MIT Press, 2001).

Zaloga, Steven J., *The Kremlin's Nuclear Sword: The Rise and Fall of Russia's Strategic Nuclear Forces, 1945–2000* (Washington, DC: Smithsonian Institution Press, 2002).

MOSCOW TREATY

See Strategic Offensive Reductions Treaty

MULTILATERAL NUCLEAR FORCE

The idea for a European Multilateral Force (MLF) emerged in the early 1960s at about the same time that the North Atlantic Treaty Organization (NATO) was considering the introduction of a new flexible-response strategy. The concept was seen as a way for NATO members to share nuclear responsibility by deploying nuclear weapons on naval vessels that would be manned by crews drawn from all member nations (*see* North Atlantic Treaty Organization).

The thought of equipping NATO allies with nuclear weapons was initially considered by U.S. strategists during the 1950s. By the early 1960s, in an effort to slow nuclear proliferation and to increase the credibility of the U.S. nuclear guarantee to NATO, the John F. Kennedy administration offered to create an MLF, a surface or submarine fleet manned by NATO crews equipped with nuclear-armed Polaris missiles. Some observers, including U.S. Secretary of Defense Robert McNamara, however, were concerned that the MLF might not fit into the new NATO strategy of flexible response, which demanded centralized decision-making to fine-tune escalation from conventional to nuclear war.

The West German government supported the U.S. proposal, but most NATO members were ambivalent about the MLF. British officials were concerned about the potential cost of the concept. In 1965, the British proposed an Atlantic Nuclear Force

(ANF), which would be made up of submarine-based Polaris ballistic missiles maintained by the United States and the United Kingdom. The British ANF proposal reduced the momentum behind the MLF, much to the annoyance of the West German government. The MLF was abandoned by the Lyndon B. Johnson administration in favor of something amounting to the British ANF proposal. Throughout most of the Cold War, the U.S. and British navies dedicated part of their ballistic missile submarines to NATO contingencies.

—*Andrew M. Dorman and James J. Wirtz*

References

Freedman, Lawrence, *The Evolution of Nuclear Strategy*, second edition (New York: St. Martin's Press, 1989), pp. 327–329.

Schrafstetter, Susanna, and Stephen Twigge, "Trick or Truth? The British ANF Proposal, West Germany and U.S. Nonproliferation Policy," *Diplomacy and Statecraft*, vol. 11, no. 2, June 2000.

MULTIPLE INDEPENDENTLY TARGETABLE REENTRY VEHICLE (MIRV)

First deployed in the 1970s, the multiple independently targetable reentry vehicle (MIRV) revolutionized the capabilities of nuclear-armed ballistic missiles by enabling a single missile to destroy several targets. As accuracies improved, this prompt hard-target kill capability threatened the crisis stability of superpower nuclear deterrence. Widely remembered as the most dangerous technological innovation after the introduction of the intercontinental ballistic missile (ICBM), MIRVing undermined the achievements of the first arms control treaties and contributed to new superpower tensions. Although restricted in 1991 by the Strategic Arms Reduction Treaty (START I), smaller numbers of MIRVed missiles continue to be deployed by Russia and the United States. They also have been deployed by Britain and France.

Progressive increases in launcher control mechanisms, as well as refinement of missile accuracy, reentry-vehicle design, and warhead size enables individual launchers to carry three to ten or even more nuclear warheads and to target these warheads against multiple targets within the "MIRV footprint" (that is, the geographic area within the range of warheads on one missile). Although individual warheads deployed in this way are smaller in size and destructive power than the large unitary warheads they replaced, their greater accuracy and numbers actually increased the ability of the superpowers to guarantee the destruction of more targets.

Individually too small to insure the destruction of geographically large targets such as major cities, MIRVs are more suitable for attacks on specific targets, especially ballistic missile silos and command and control facilities. With their capability to engage such counterforce targets, MIRVs introduced unprecedented potential for preemptive nuclear war, enabling an attacker to use a small proportion of their missiles to eliminate a large share of their adversary's nuclear missiles (see Counterforce Targeting). By threatening the survivability of much of the victim's retaliatory capability, it was argued, MIRVs could weaken the victim's ability to retaliate through a disarming first strike, potentially reducing the surviving force below the threshold at which retaliation was credible. By threatening to undermine the stability of superpower deterrence, MIRVs raised the possibility of new vulnerabilities and instability in times of crisis (see Crisis Stability; Deterrence).

MIRV technology originated with development of a special stage, or "bus," to launch several orbital satellites with a single launcher. The United States started full-scale development of the three-stage Minuteman III ICBM with three warheads in 1966. Initial operational capability with 170-kiloton warheads was achieved in 1970. The Soviet Union began full-scale development of its SS-18 ICBM in 1969. Although this initially was fielded with a unitary warhead, in 1976 the Mod-4 version was tested with ten warheads.

Whereas the Minuteman III was justified by the U.S. Air Force as an incremental improvement in warhead and reentry technology, the Soviet SS-18 was seen by conservative American analysts as proof of Soviet planning for a disarming first strike. Anxieties about a "window of vulnerability," provoked by Soviet SS-18 deployments, were an important ingredient in Ronald Reagan's successful 1980 presidential campaign.

MIRV deployment was tightly regulated by START I in 1991 and banned completely by START II, signed in 1993. The failure to ratify START II and its replacement by the subsequent Moscow Treaty of 2002 effectively permits MIRVing within overall warhead ceilings. The United States continues to deploy MIRVed Trident II submarine-launched ballistic missiles, and Russia emphasizes MIRVed SS-19

ICBMs as the dominant element of its nuclear forces. China was believed to have perfected the basic capability for MIRVing by the mid-1990s, although there is no evidence that the Chinese military has conducted operational testing of MIRVs.

—*Aaron Karp*

See also: Ballistic Missiles; Reentry Vehicles; Strategic Arms Reduction Treaty

References

Buchonnet, Daniel, *MIRV: A Brief History of Minuteman and Multiple Reentry Vehicles* (Livermore, CA: Lawrence Livermore Laboratory, February 1976).

Greenwood, Ted, *Making of the MIRV: A Study of Defense Decision Making* (Cambridge, MA: Ballinger, 1975).

MULTIPLE LAUNCH ROCKET SYSTEM (MLRS)

The multiple launch rocket system (MLRS) fires salvos or single rounds of artillery rockets. The simplest form of contemporary missile weapon, the artillery rocket is a direct descendent of thirteenth-century Chinese rockets, Indian rockets of the Anglo-Mysore wars of 1780–1799, and William Congreve's rockets of the Napoleonic wars. Better propellants and aerodynamics allowed the major powers to develop more powerful versions beginning in the 1930s. An early success was the Soviet BM-13 Katyusha, a truck-mounted MLRS battery used widely in World War II, also called "Stalin's Organ."

Since then, the range of artillery rockets has increased from 6 kilometers to 70 or more in current models such as the American MLRS, the Chinese WS-1, and the Russian Smerch. As unguided weapons, they lack accuracy, but their low cost and their ability to be fired in large volleys compensate for this drawback. Guided versions with longer range also have been developed to serve more specialized missions, such as artillery suppression. Smaller models, especially the Chinese-made Type-63, have become popular as long-range weapons for guerrilla forces and terrorists.

Combining small payloads with adequate range and low cost, artillery rockets are well suited for delivery of chemical and biological warheads. Even when conventionally armed, they offer an asymmetric mass destruction capability. In Lebanon, Hezbollah, an anti-Israeli terrorist group, had reportedly accumulated 8,000 to 9,000 rockets as of late 2002, enough to cause massive damage. In

1994, thousands of artillery rockets were used by several warring factions to destroy much of Kabul. Hamas, the main Islamic group in the Palestinian territories, improvised designs of its own in 2002–2003 that were subsequently used for attacks on Israel from Gaza.

The Israeli Defense Forces and the U.S. Army are developing active defenses to shoot down artillery rockets. The technical ability of lasers to perform this mission was proven by tests in 2002–2003, although design of a rugged, affordable, and easily transportable interceptor system remains to be achieved.

—*Aaron Karp*

References

Bellamy, Chris, *Red God of War: Soviet Artillery and Rocket Forces* (Herndon, VA: Brassey's, 1986).

O'Malley, T. J., *Artillery: Guns and Rocket Systems* (London: Greenhill, 1994).

Spasskiy, Nikolai, *Rocket and Artillery Armament of the Ground Forces* (Moscow: Oruzhie I Tekhnologi, 2001).

MUTUAL ASSURED DESTRUCTION (MAD)

Mutual assured destruction (MAD) is a situation in which two or more states possess a secure second-strike capability allowing them to destroy their adversaries even after absorbing a major nuclear attack. During the Cold War, MAD was depicted as a stable deterrence relationship by many theorists who believed that the threat of massive retaliation could prevent each side from initiating a surprise nuclear first strike. They therefore recommended having enough survivable nuclear weapons to assure the adversary's destruction as a modern society in a retaliatory response. These theorists often assumed that such a second strike would target cities in a strictly punitive retaliation with no specific military objective other than the complete annihilation of the attacker's nation. Many believed that the possession of a secure second-strike capability was the only sure means of deterring a surprise nuclear attack and that MAD was thus the inescapable basis of crisis stability in a Cold War environment dominated by two heavily armed superpowers. The acronym became an ironic metaphor for the belief that the destructiveness of war has reduced the danger of war.

In the mid-1960s, as Soviet nuclear power grew to rival that of the United States, U.S. Secretary of Defense Robert S. McNamara came to believe that a mutual ability to assure the destruction of the opponent's society in a second strike provided the United States and the Soviet Union with the strongest possible motive to avoid nuclear war. This belief that the Soviet Union shared an assured destruction strategy gave rise to the term "mutual assured destruction" and was used to justify opposing the deployment of antiballistic missile (ABM) systems that would undermine either side's ability to hold the other's society at risk.

MAD did not describe the actual targeting strategy followed by either the United States or the Soviet Union, both of which pursued more operationally oriented counterforce targeting strategies, although U.S. war plans called for withholding a "strategic reserve," and the strike plans for these reserves came close to resembling a MAD targeting doctrine (*see* Counterforce Targeting; Countervalue Targeting). Nevertheless, many believed that MAD described an existential reality that neither superpower could really transcend no matter what its actually targeting strategy was, as long as the nuclear arsenals of the two sides far exceeded what was needed for strictly military targeting objectives, and that as a last resort, one or both sides would ultimately respond to a nuclear escalation with an all-out attack on the other's cities (*see* Escalation).

Most criticisms of MAD revolved around its credibility, or lack thereof. Some asserted that no one would actually believe that either side was politically capable of unleashing an all-out attack against urban-industrial centers, especially if it came in the aftermath of a series of nuclear exchanges that had already left most of both sides in ruins. Moreover, religious authorities noted that it was not morally sustainable to threaten to do what one was morally forbidden to do, and that a strategy of assured destruction violated the most fundamental precepts of the just war tradition.

Despite these criticisms and the end of the Cold War, many continue to believe that as long as the United States and Russia maintain large residual nuclear arsenals, a condition of MAD will exist between them, and that such a condition could come to include China in the near future.

—*Kerry Kartchner*

See also: Assured Destruction; Cold War; Deterrence; Second Strikes; Superiority

References

Enthoven, Alain C., and K. Wayne Smith, *How Much Is Enough? Shaping the Defense Program, 1961–1969* (New York: Harper and Row, 1971).

Martel, William C., and Paul L. Savage, *Strategic Nuclear War: What the Superpowers Target and Why* (New York: Greenwood, 1986).

McNamara, Robert S., "Hearings on Military Posture before the U.S. Congress," excerpted in P. Edward Haley and Jack Merritt, eds., *Nuclear Strategy, Arms Control, and the Future,* second edition (Boulder: Westview, 1988), pp. 86–96.

McNamara, Robert S., "Address before the United Press International Editors, San Francisco, California, September 18, 1967," reprinted in Philip Bobbitt, Lawrence Freedman, and Gregory Treverton, eds., *U.S. Nuclear Strategy: A Reader* (New York: New York University Press, 1989), pp. 267–282.

MX ICBMS

See Peacekeeper Missile

NAGASAKI

Nagasaki is a commercial port city on the southern Japanese island of Kyushu that was the site of the second U.S. atomic attack against Japan. The attack occurred on August 9, 1945, three days after the first nuclear bomb ever to be used in warfare was dropped on Hiroshima on August 6. On September 2, 1945, Japan surrendered and World War II came to an end.

Nagasaki was the site of the first European influence in Japan. Portuguese traders and missionaries established a community there in the late 1500s, followed by the Dutch. Even during the shogunate period of "enclosure," Nagasaki remained open to foreigners for trade, although all Western religious activity was banned. Because of its clay deposits, the

N

area has long been a center for ceramics, including pottery and fine china, and its commercial port made Nagasaki a more cosmopolitan area than many other parts of Japan. The Giacomo Puccini opera *Madama Butterfly* is set in Nagasaki.

During World War II, the U.S Manhattan Project developed atomic bombs for use by U.S. forces. Two types of bombs were developed: a gun-type device that used uranium to create a critical mass, and an implosion device that used plutonium as its fissile

The remains of a Catholic cathedral, Nagasaki, August 1945. (National Archives)

material. By the summer of 1945, one bomb of each type was available for use against Japan (*see* Criticality and Critical Mass; Fission Weapons; Gun-Type Devices; Implosion Devices; Manhattan Project; Plutonium; Uranium).

U.S. war plans had included an invasion of the Japanese home islands as a means to force the surrender of the Japanese government. The successful, though costly invasion of Okinawa (which resulted in 49,151 U.S. fatalities) was to be followed by the invasion of Kyushu by 190,000 U.S. troops. It was estimated that the invasion of Kyushu would result in 69,000 U.S. fatalities. President Harry S. Truman determined to delay a home island invasion and use aerial atomic bombing to save U.S. troops and Japanese civilian lives.

Nagasaki was not among the original target cities selected for nuclear destruction as a means to force a Japanese surrender. It was substituted for Kyoto when Secretary of War Henry L. Stimson moved to protect Kyoto's antiquities. Nagasaki was selected because of its large commercial harbor and four large Mitsubishi war production plants.

The bomb dropped on Nagasaki was "Fat Man," an implosion weapon that used plutonium 239 (Pu-239) produced in nuclear reactors at Hanford, Washington (*see* Fat Man; Hanford, Washington). It was dropped from a B-29 named *Bockscar*. Due to weather problems, the original commercial target site was missed and the bomb was dropped over Nagasaki's industrial center. The plutonium bomb created a blast equivalent to 20,000 tons of TNT. Fat Man was more powerful than the gun-type device dropped on Hiroshima, "Little Boy" (*see* Hiroshima; Little Boy), and the hills surrounding Nagasaki concentrated the blast produced by the bomb. The hills also served to protect some of Nagasaki's population from radiant heat and ionizing radiation, leaving about 25 percent of the population dead or injured. The area of destruction was one and a half square miles. About 23,753 people were killed and a similar number were injured. The topography prevented a firestorm from developing and localized the direct effects of the blast, resulting in less public panic than in Hiroshima. The industrial damage was high, partly owing to the inadvertent targeting of the industrial zone, leaving 68 percent of the non-dockyard industrial production destroyed.

The area of the explosion has been rebuilt as a modern city center. There is a museum and park memorializing the lives lost in the attack. The museum is less politicized than the larger and more famous one in Hiroshima, with descriptive materials confined to the events in Nagasaki.

—*Frannie Edwards*

See also: Tinian
Reference
Bauer, E., *The History of World War II* (New York: Military Press, 1984).

NATIONAL COMMAND AUTHORITY

The individuals within the U.S. government possessing the ultimate responsibility for decisions to use nuclear weapons and the constitutional authority to direct the U.S. Armed Forces are collectively called the National Command Authority (NCA). The term is drawn from the Unified Command Plan, a classified document that regulates military procedures and lines of authority. The individuals traditionally designated as the NCA are the president and the secretary of defense, and upon their death or incapacitation their successors as set forth in the Constitution and the Presidential Succession Act of 1947. The process by which the NCA might order the use of nuclear weapons has not been discussed publicly and is classified. In 1974, the House Foreign Affairs Committee stated that no military officer may initiate the use of nuclear weapons unless authorized by the president or his successor. Additionally, by law no one else in the chain of command has the authority to order the use of nuclear weapons simply on their own initiative. The president, on the basis of personal preference, decides procedures for NCA operations. Overall authority to use U.S. nuclear weapons rests with the NCA.

In 2002, U.S. Secretary of Defense Donald Rumsfeld stated that the term "National Command Authority" would be discontinued. Currently, on Department of Defense documents, the term "National Command Authorities" has been replaced with the words "President" and/or "Secretary of Defense."

—*Laura Fontaine*

References
"Memorandum for Joint Staff Directors," Joint Chiefs of Staff, Washington, DC, 11 January 2002.
"Military Abbreviations, Acronyms and Terms," available at http://www.periscope.ucg.com/terms/.

NATIONAL EMERGENCY AIRBORNE COMMAND POST (NEACP)

The growth of the Soviet nuclear threat and the resulting fear that the U.S. president and secretary of defense could be killed in Washington, D.C., before ordering a retaliatory strike led the U.S. Air Force in 1962 to establish the National Emergency Airborne Command Post (NEACP, pronounced "kneecap"). For this purpose, the Air Force converted four KC-135A tankers, equipping them with extensive communication suites. Designated EC-135J Nightwatch, these aircraft were designed to give the president, the secretary of defense, and other members of the National Command Authority (NCA) the ability to command nuclear forces in the event that ground command posts were destroyed. From the aircraft, a member of the NCA had access to the digital codes required to unlock the U.S. nuclear arsenal and launch a nuclear strike (see National Command Authority).

In 1974, the original EC-135s were replaced with four Boeing 747-200s converted to the NEACP role and given the military designation E-4B. Modified to carry thirty different communications systems (VLF to SHF) and up to 114 crew members, the E-4Bs also were hardened to withstand the electromagnetic pulse created by a nuclear blast. Originally based at Andrews Air Force Base (AFB) outside of Washington, D.C., the aircraft were moved to Offutt AFB in Nebraska in the 1980s to keep them safe from submarine-launched ballistic missile strikes. The aircraft now have alternate bases throughout the United States and frequently deploy with the president overseas to ensure reliable and secure communications. In August 1994, the E-4Bs flying the NEACP mission were renamed National Airborne Operations Center (NAOC) to reflect the fact that the Federal Emergency Management Agency (FEMA) could now also use the airborne command post to respond to national disasters.

—*Gilles Van Nederveen*

See also: Strategic Air Command/Strategic Command

References
Blair, Bruce, *The Logic of Accidental Nuclear War* (Washington, DC: Brookings Institution, 1993).
———, *Strategic Command and Control* (Washington, DC: Brookings Institution, 1993).
Bracken, Paul, *The Command and Control of Nuclear Forces* (New Haven, CT: Yale University Press, 1983).
Newhouse, John, *War and Peace in the Nuclear Age* (New York: Vintage, 1990).

NATIONAL STRATEGIC TARGET LIST

The National Strategic Target List (NSTL) is one of the most closely guarded U.S. military secrets. A prioritized list of identified targeting points and planning functions, it is used in conjunction with the National Strategic Targeting and Attack Policy (NSTAP) and the Nuclear Weapons Employment Policy (NUWEP). During the Cold War, the Joint Strategic Target Planning Staff (JSTPS) of the Strategic Air Command developed and maintained the NSTL. The Joint Planning Staff uses the list to assign weapons to various functions according to availability and effectiveness for particular tasks. The NSTL was developed to provide for the integration of committed forces for the attack of a minimum list of targets, the destruction of which would accomplish given objectives. Additionally, military planners use the NSTL in their task of processing and analyzing target data. President Dwight D. Eisenhower approved the Strategic Air Command's request to prepare the National Strategic Target List on August 11, 1960.

Since the 1940s, target lists have been kept classified because they provide information concerning current target selection criteria, strategy, intelligence sources and methods, and nuclear weapons effects. U.S. nuclear war plans have included a wide range of target types: military forces, bases, installations, and stockpiles; economic and industrial centers; political and administrative centers; and, after 1950, Soviet nuclear forces. In 1961, the Single Integrated Operational Plan (SIOP) introduced greater flexibility into the U.S. strategic nuclear war plans. The NSTL has been divided into various target sets to provide the National Command Authority (NCA) with a range of options, such as withholding attacks against urban-industrial areas (see National Command Authority).

Due to the classified nature of the NSTL, target sets are not known or shared publicly. The Joint Strategic Capabilities Plan from 2000 (an unclassified document) offers broad guidance to combatant commanders planning nuclear operations. The Joint Strategic Plan does not identify the NSTL, however it does explain a few points concerning tactical planning. For example, combatant commanders must comply with several operational constraints when preparing plans for nuclear weapons employment options: (1) Nuclear weapons use is not authorized except in response to an enemy nuclear attack, although the United States reserves the right to use nuclear weapons first; (2) every effort will be made to limit attacks against populated areas; (3) weapon yields will be limited to those only essential in accomplishing the mission; and (4) the allocation of nuclear weapons and handling and storage of these weapons will follow approved plans.

Although the U.S. Strategic Command, the successor to SAC, has increasingly turned to adaptive planning, rather than the deliberate planning that lay behind creation of the SIOP, the United States continues to use the National Strategic Target List in determining nuclear weapons objectives.

—*Laura Fontaine*

References

Ball, Desmond, "U.S. Strategic Target Forces: How Will They Be Used?" *International Security,* vol. 7, no. 3, Winter 1982–1983, pp. 31–60.

Ball, Desmond, and Robert C. Toth, "Revising the SIOP," *International Security,* vol. 14, no. 4, Spring 1990, pp. 65–92.

Rosenberg, David Allen, "A Smoking Radiating Ruin at the End of Two Hours: Documents on American Plans for Nuclear War with the Soviet Union, 1954–1955," *International Security,* vol. 6, no. 3, Winter 1981–1982, pp. 3–38.

NATIONAL TECHNICAL MEANS

The term "national technical means" (NTM) was chosen by the United States and the Soviet Union during the Cold War to avoid the term "espionage" when describing efforts to monitor arms control compliance. To verify compliance with strategic arms limitation agreements, the United States and Soviet Union agreed to employ nonintrusive methods of treaty verification. The NTM verification network included satellite observation as well as terrestrial sites located outside each superpower's national boundaries. On-site arms inspections were not considered a viable alternative to NTM because Soviet officials believed that as a closed society, they had more to lose than did an open society like the United States in allowing inspectors free access to their territory. Soviet officials also refused to allow aerial overflights (often referred to as Open Skies proposals) as a confidence-building and arms control verification measure during the 1950s and 1960s, leaving satellites and electronic eavesdrop-

ping sites located outside national boundaries as the preferred method of arms control verification.

NTM can include photoreconnaissance satellites, radar, and signal-collection facilities located on aircraft, ships, satellites, and ground stations. These monitoring systems and the information-processing capabilities that support them are sophisticated and deployed across the globe. National technical means provide generally high confidence that significant cheating on Cold War arms control agreements will be detected and helped shift the political balance in the United States in support of arms control.

At times during the Cold War, NTM became a significant domestic political issue in the United States. In 1980 during the Carter administration, for example, verification of the treaty resulting from the second round of Strategic Arms Limitation Talks (SALT II) became a stumbling block for treaty ratification in the U.S. Senate. Critics of the SALT II Treaty believed that the loss of monitoring stations in Iran following the fall of the shah in 1979 hampered America's ability to verify Soviet compliance with the treaty. These stations were critical to intercepting the telemetry generated by Soviet intercontinental ballistic missiles (ICBMs) as they flew across their test ranges in Central Asia to their impact points in the Soviet Far East. President Jimmy Carter tried various methods of convincing the Senate that the U.S. intelligence community could verify the new SALT II Treaty. Ultimately, other nations provided U.S. intelligence access to their territory to replace lost listening stations needed to monitor Soviet telemetry data. SALT II was never ratified by the U.S. Senate, but for the most part Soviet and U.S. policymakers abided by its terms.

Although noninterference with national technical means of verification was addressed in the SALT treaties, Soviet officials sometimes failed to adhere to the spirit, if not the letter, of those agreements. Members of the Ronald Reagan administration probably had the greatest doubts about the ability of the U.S. intelligence community to verify compliance in light of the spotty Soviet track record on such matters. The Reagan administration charged that the Soviets encrypted telemetry, which was a serious impediment to verification and a violation of arms control specifications. There also were charges that the Soviets were camouflaging and concealing launchers. Soviet officials countered these charges by claiming that U.S. environmental shelters over Minuteman silos were concealment measures and that the United States had exceeded its authorized launcher limits when Minuteman silos were modernized. The angry exchange led the United States to demand that any future arms control agreements would have to include more extensive verification measures: on-site inspections, data-exchange challenge inspections, and cooperation with NTM observation.

No other state has matched U.S. and Russian investment in national technical means, which remains important today. Verification of several treaties, especially those concerning threshold and nuclear test bans, still relies on seismic stations and satellites.

—*Gilles Van Nederveen*

See also: Arms Control; Open Skies Treaty; Reconnaissance Satellites; Strategic Arms Limitation Talks; Strategic Arms Reduction Treaty; Strategic Arms Reduction Treaty; Verification

References

Burrows, William, *Deep Black: Space Espionage and National Security* (New York: Random House, 1986).

Federation of American Scientists website, http://www.fas.org/nuke/control/start1/abatext.htm.

Frank Barnaby, ed., *A Handbook of Verification Procedures* (New York: St. Martin's Press, 1990).

Kolodziej, Edward, and Patrick Morgan, eds., *Security and Arms Control,* vol. 2: *A Guide to International Policymaking* (Westport, CT: Greenwood, 1989).

Peebles, Curtis, *Guardians: Strategic Reconnaissance Satellites* (Novato, CA: Presidio, 1987).

NEGATIVE SECURITY ASSURANCES (NSAs)

Negative security assurances (NSAs) are statements made by declared nuclear weapons states not to use nuclear weapons against non–nuclear weapons states subject to certain conditions. The best description of NSAs is contained in the 1995 statement of U.S. Secretary of State Warren Christopher: "The United States reaffirms that it will not use nuclear weapons against non-nuclear-weapon States Parties to the Treaty on the Non-Proliferation of Nuclear Weapons except in the case of an invasion or any other attack on the United States, its territories, its armed forces or other troops, its allies, or on a State toward which it has a security commitment, carried out or sustained by such a non-nuclear-

weapon state in association or alliance with a nuclear-weapon State."

All the other nuclear weapons states have made similar statements except for China, which offered an unconditional guarantee not to use nuclear weapons against a non–nuclear weapons state. By contrast, the NSAs of the other nuclear weapons states are void if a non–nuclear weapons state is acting in concert with or allied with a nuclear weapons state. It is not clear whether China's NSA still applies to India and Pakistan, given their status as de facto nuclear weapons states. Prior to May 1998, when India and Pakistan conducted their nuclear weapon tests, Chinese officials specifically stated that China's NSA applied to both India and Pakistan even though these countries were not NPT signatories. China's NSA currently applies to Israel, another non-NPT signatory. Also, in 1996 and 1999, China issued NSAs guaranteeing that it would not use nuclear weapons against Taiwan (*see* Chinese Nuclear Weapons).

NSAs should be contrasted with "positive security assurances" (PSAs), in which nuclear weapons states pledge that they will come to the aid of a non–nuclear weapons state if that state is the victim of a nuclear attack. There is no formal treaty on NSAs, although the five nuclear weapons states have harmonized their PSAs through the adoption, in April 1995, of UN Security Council Resolution 984. China and other states in the nonaligned group at the Conference on Disarmament have pressed for a legally binding agreement on NSAs (*see* Conference on Disarmament). This has been resisted by the United States and other nuclear weapons states, which continue to believe that agreeing to such a treaty would diminish the deterrent value of nuclear weapons.

—*Guy Roberts*

References

Bunn, George, "The Legal Status of U.S. Negative Security Assurances to Non-Nuclear Weapon States," *Nonproliferation Review,* vol. 4, no. 3, Spring-Summer 1997, p. 1, available at http://cns.miis.edu/pubs/npr/vol04/43/bunn43.pdf.

Christopher, Warren, "Statement on Negative Security Assurances," 5 April 1995, available at http://www.armscontrol.org/pdf/negsec.pdf.

"U.S. Nuclear Policy: Negative Security Assurances," Arms Control Association Fact Sheet, available at http://www.armscontrol.org/factsheets/negsec.asp.

NEUTRON BOMB
(ENHANCED RADIATION WEAPON)

The enhanced radiation weapon is a specialized type of small thermonuclear weapon that produces minimal blast and heat but releases a large amount of lethal radiation. Often referred to as the "neutron bomb," an enhanced radiation weapon is a nuclear warhead designed to be launched by artillery or a battlefield missile or rocket. It can be defined as a third-generation nuclear device (after fission and fusion bombs). Third-generation nuclear weapons are fusion devices that transform, select, or direct their energy in some unique way. The definition includes inertial confinement fusion, X-ray lasers, nuclear explosion–powered directed-energy weapons, nuclear kinetic-energy weapons, and enhanced microwave devices.

Based on work conducted by U.S. weapons laboratories in the 1950s, weapons designers discovered that by removing the uranium casing on a hydrogen bomb, neutrons could travel farther, and that the lethal effects of high-energy neutrons produced by the fusion of deuterium and tritium could be maximized. A 1962 test demonstrated the viability of the concept (see Deuterium; Tritium).

The destructive power of nuclear weapons depends on the combination of different effects. Typically, the energy released by a fission-type explosion is made up of 50 percent blast, 35 percent thermal radiation, 5 percent prompt radiation, and 10 percent residual radiation. If a pure fusion weapon were possible, then the proportions might be 20 percent blast and thermal energy, with the majority (80 percent) of a weapon's energy being released as prompt radiation. Such a pure fusion weapon would produce very little residual radiation. Research aimed at altering the balance between the fission trigger and the fusion element of the bomb, however, has only managed to increase the percentage of a weapon's yield that takes the form of radiation by a small margin.

Although many believed that the enhanced radiation artillery shell only produced radiation, it just tipped the balance between blast and radiation produced by a nuclear detonation. It was hoped, however, that this change in weapons effects would make its use appear more credible to potential Warsaw Pact opponents. This was seen as particularly necessary in the case of short-range weapons, where minimizing the effects on friendly forces was critical. Used over a battlefield, a 1-kiloton neutron bomb would kill or incapacitate people over an area twice as large as the lethal zone of a 10-kiloton standard nuclear weapon, but with a fifth of the blast (see Nuclear Weapons Effects; Radiation).

This third generation of nuclear weapon also prompted a surge in nuclear protest movements because many believed that the enhanced radiation weapon lowered the nuclear threshold, making nuclear weapons use more likely. Others pointed to the relative absence of long-term weapons effects (fallout) that would make the weapons appear to be more usable on battlefields adjacent to urban areas. The debate became quite shrill, with German socialist politicians referring to enhanced radiation weapons as immoral and the "perversion of humanity."

Supporters believed that the enhanced radiation weapon offered a significant improvement in the credibility of the nuclear deterrent posed by the North Atlantic Treaty Organization (NATO). The prompt radiation produced by the neutron bomb could disable troops even in tanks while reducing the risk of collateral damage and long-term radiation. By the late 1970s, NATO was preparing to deploy the neutron bomb in the form of artillery shells and Lance warheads in West Germany.

The weapon that killed humans but spared buildings unleashed a political firestorm of protest throughout Western Europe in 1977, shaking NATO to its core. What followed was one of the worst defense debacles suffered by the Jimmy Carter administration. The West German government of Chancellor Helmut Schmidt told U.S. officials that Germany could not be the only recipient of the enhanced warhead weapons. Unable to get another NATO country to take the weapons, and after a long, acrimonious debate accompanied by noisy antinuclear demonstrations, President Carter reversed his deployment and production decisions in April 1978.

Although the Soviets tested an enhanced radiation weapon, there is little evidence of the weapon's deployment by the Soviet Union. The French revealed on June 26, 1980, that they had tested a neutron device and that their enhanced radiation warhead would have been deployed on the Hades short-range ballistic missile system, which was canceled at the end of the Cold War. The Chinese also tested an enhanced radiation weapon, according to the 1999 Cox Report on U.S. national security and exports of sensitive materials and equipment to the People's Republic of China. The design details were obtained through espionage at U.S. nuclear weapons labs. Deployment data on the Chinese enhanced radiation warhead is not available.

After President Carter deferred production, President Ronald Reagan, in August 1981, ordered production of both the enhanced radiation artillery shell and the Lance warhead. These weapons were never deployed to Europe but were stockpiled in the United States. These weapons were dismantled by the late 1990s.

—*Gilles Van Nederveen*

References

Cochran, Thomas B., William M. Arkin, Robert S. Norris, and Milton M. Hoenig, *Nuclear Weapons Databook*, vol. 2: *U.S. Nuclear Warhead Production* (New York: Ballinger, 1987).

Herf, Jeffrey, *War by Other Means: Soviet Power, West German Resistance and the Battle of the Euromissiles* (New York: Free Press, 1991).

Newhouse, John, *War and Peace in the Nuclear Age* (New York: Vintage, 1990).

Wasserman, Sherri, *The Neutron Bomb Controversy: A Study in Alliance Politics* (Westport, CT: Praeger, 1984).

NEUTRONS

Atoms consist of a massive, positively charged nucleus surrounded by a cloud of negatively charged electrons. Neutrons and protons are the constituent particles of the nucleus. Neutrons are slightly more massive than protons but have no electrical charge. The neutron is of central importance in the fission process, since it is the absorption of a neutron by, for example, a uranium or plutonium nucleus that causes that nucleus to fission. A free neutron, as a neutral particle, is not affected by the positive charge of the nucleus, and so it can easily approach the nucleus.

James Chadwick received the Nobel Prize for his 1932 discovery of the neutron. This discovery completed the basic description of the atom and the nucleus and led, in 1938, to the discovery of the ability of the neutron to cause nuclear fission.

In heavier nuclei, stability requires that there be more neutrons than protons to counteract the repulsive electrical force between protons. Uranium and plutonium have many more neutrons than protons. In fission, a free neutron strikes the heavy target nucleus, bringing its rest mass energy and kinetic energy into the nucleus. This energy splits the nucleus, releasing some of the binding energy that holds the nucleus together and releasing more neutrons. These neutrons can then strike other uranium or plutonium nuclei, continuing the fission chain reaction. The chain reaction effect of neutrons causing fissions, and producing more neutrons to cause more fissions, is the fundamental process that releases energy in a controlled manner in a nuclear reactor—or in an uncontrolled manner in a nuclear bomb.

Neutrons are sometimes emitted in the radioactive decay of unstable isotopes. Neutrons, like gamma rays, alpha particles, and beta particles, can cause damage to the human body. Due to its ability to deposit great amounts of energy in the body, the neutron is a particularly damaging form of radiation (*see* Isotopes; Radiation).

Neutrons are not fundamental particles of nature but rather belong to a class of particles called "baryons." Baryons are composed of three quarks. The neutron is composed of one "up" quark and two "down" quarks.

—*Brian Moretti*

Reference

Lamarsh, J. R., and A. J. Baratta, *Introduction to Nuclear Engineering*, third edition (Upper Saddle River, NJ: Prentice-Hall, 2001).

NEVADA TEST SITE

Established in December 1950, the Nevada Test Site (NTS) has served as the nation's nuclear test site within the United States. Today, NTS personnel continue to support the nation's security requirements by maintaining a capability to test nuclear weapons. The site also has test facilities used by scientists and technicians to undertake nonfissile tests of nuclear weapons to assure the safety and security of the remaining nuclear stockpile. The test site now includes several training facilities involving counterterrorism and response to incidents involving weapons of mass destruction. Other government agencies, including the U.S. Department of Defense

Monitoring station and subsidence crater formed by an underground nuclear test at the Nevada Test Site (Huron King test, June 1980) (DTRA)

and the Defense Threat Reduction Agency, use the Nevada Test Site to support their efforts.

Scientists from the nation's nuclear weapons laboratories use the test site for experiments. At the U1a facility, scientists conduct explosive experiments on special nuclear material some 1,000 feet underground. At the Jasper facility, a 90-foot-long, two-stage gas gun targets special nuclear material at speeds up to five times the speed of sound.

The Nevada Test Site receives and disposes of low-level solid waste from the cleanup of the nation's nuclear weapons complex. In fiscal year 2003, more than 3.2 million cubic feet of material was disposed of at the Nevada Test Site's radioactive low-level waste facilities.

The NTS is large, covering 1,375 square miles. Its size, remoteness, security controls, and embedded safety culture make it well suited to support hazardous and unique scientific and military work.

—*Bret Kinman*

References

Cochran, Thomas, William B. Arkin, Robert S. Norris, and Milton M. Hoenig, *Nuclear Weapons Databook,* vol. 3: *U.S. Nuclear Warhead Facility Profiles* (Cambridge, MA: Ballinger, 1987), pp. 62–64.

Defense Nuclear Weapons School website, http://www.dnws.mil.

Defense Threat Reduction Agency website, http://www.dtra.mil.

NEW LOOK

"New Look" was the name used to describe the Dwight D. Eisenhower administration's defense procurement policy and military strategy. President Eisenhower was a fiscal conservative who desired a balanced federal budget and a defense strategy able to meet the demands of a long Cold War. His administration rejected the notion, embodied in the Truman Doctrine and National Security Council Document 68 (NSC-68), that defense spending needed to be targeted to meet an impending "year of maximum danger." To maintain deterrence while limiting defense spending, Eisenhower greatly increased the size of the U.S. nuclear arsenal and air force while reducing the overall size of the U.S. military, especially the army.

Eisenhower's principal defense policy document was NSC-162/2, published in October 1953. This paper defined the security problem facing the United States as "meeting the Soviet Threat" while avoiding "seriously weakening the U.S. economy or undermining our fundamental values and institutions." Eisenhower did not believe that a general war with the Soviet Union was likely; however, the possibility of "satellite conflicts" was high. Eisenhower also believed that the United States could not maintain strong enough conventional military forces to match the Soviet Union and its clients everywhere in the world. Instead, it turned to bolstering the South Koreans and the North Atlantic Treaty Organization (NATO) to contain the Soviet menace.

NSC 162/2 also articulated the concept of "massive retaliation." This concept threatened a massive nuclear attack in response to Communist military aggression, not a symmetrical conventional response in the region where the attack occurred. In an attempt to bolster the credibility of this policy, President Eisenhower himself sometimes mentioned that he considered nuclear weapons no different than conventional weapons when used on the battlefield. The intended effect of this policy was to deter the Soviets from taking any aggressive action beyond what had already occurred in Korea. By the late 1950s, the New Look and massive retaliation were the subject of much criticism. Critics, especially U.S. Army officers, believed that the New Look had led to a hollow military. They charged that the United States lacked the ground forces needed to conduct even minor operations. Massive retaliation was considered by many to be an incredible threat, especially as the Soviet nuclear arsenal grew. It was unlikely that the United States would initiate nuclear war in response to conventional military attack, especially in areas deemed peripheral (that is, anywhere other than the inter-German border). Although the New Look integrated nuclear weapons into virtually every service and weapons system available to the United States, it did have the effect of restraining U.S. defense spending.

—*Bret Kinman and James J. Wirtz*

See also: Cold War; Deterrence; Massive Retaliation
References
Freedman, Lawrence, *The Evolution of Nuclear Strategy,* third edition (New York: Palgrave Macmillan, 2003).
"The New Look" (NSC-68), available at http://www.eisenhower.utexas.edu/listofholdingshtml/listofholdingsw/whoosansa/nscseriespolicypapers.pdf.

NIKE ZEUS

In 1955, the U.S. Army began studying the possibility of developing a derivative of the Nike Hercules surface-to-air missile as an interceptor against hypersonic aircraft and ballistic missiles. The first version was a straightforward modification of Nike Hercules. It used the same ground command guidance as the original system and was armed with a 20-kiloton nuclear warhead. The two-stage rocket flew at a speed of Mach 4 and had a range of 200 miles. After the Russians launched Sputnik in 1957, the United States developed a completely new missile sharing only the guidance method and first-stage booster with the previous variant. Since it was designed to intercept its targets in space, it did not need large maneuvering fins. Instead, the missile featured a special third stage with small control jets to maneuver in space. The first three-stage flight of a Nike Zeus B occurred in September 1961. In July 1962, a Nike Zeus B succeeded in intercepting an Atlas intercontinental ballistic missile (ICBM) nose cone over the South Pacific Ocean.

The U.S. Army developed a sophisticated antiballistic missile (ABM) test range over the South Pacific in the late 1950s. Its primary operating base was on Kwajalein Atoll, located southeast of Hawaii (see Kwajalein Atoll). By the end of 1963, more than a dozen reentry vehicles had been successfully intercepted there.

From June 1963 until May 1966, a Nike Zeus B with a 50-kiloton nuclear warhead stood alert at the Kwajalein complex to intercept Soviet satellites. The U.S. Air Force also deployed the Thor intermediate-range ballistic missile in an anti-satellite interception role. The Thor was based at Johnston Island. Despite performing the same mission, the two missiles complemented each other. The Nike Zeus had a faster reaction time but a smaller range. The Thor had a slower reaction time, since it used liquid propellants, but a greater range. Because the Nike Zeus system was to use mechanical radars, however, it was deemed too slow to be effective as a missile defense weapon. Additionally, the radar system utilized by Nike Zeus could handle only a few targets at a time and was inefficient at filtering out decoys deployed by incoming reentry vehicles. As antiballistic missile research and development continued in the 1960s, the whole ABM system was redesigned and renamed Nike-X. In 1967, it was replaced by Sentinel, which used the Spartan missile to carry out ballistic missile intercepts.

—*Gilles Van Nederveen*

See also: Missile Defense; Sentinel; Strategic Defenses
References
Chun, Clayton K. S., *Shooting Down a "STAR": Program 437, the U.S. Nuclear ASAT System and Present-Day Copycat Killer,* CADRE Paper No. 6 (Maxwell AFB, AL: Air University Press, 2000).
Gibson, James N., *Nuclear Weapons of the United States* (Arlington, TX: Schiffer, 1996).
Gunston, Bill, *The Illustrated Encyclopedia of Rockets and Missiles* (London: Salamander, 1979).

NO FIRST USE

A no-first-use policy is a pledge by a government not to be the first to use nuclear weapons in a conflict. For much of the Cold War, the issue for North Atlantic Treaty Organization (NATO) allies was preserving the credibility of the U.S. nuclear guarantee to the European members of NATO through its policy of extended deterrence. When the Ronald Reagan administration entered office in 1981, it took this commitment seriously and concluded that in certain circumstances the United States would have to initiate the use of nuclear weapons, as had been NATO policy since the early 1950s. To make this threat credible it would need to find some means of using such weapons without leading to mutual destruction.

In response, in 1982 four former policymakers advocated a policy of no-first-use of nuclear weapons, arguing that NATO's willingness to use weapons of mass destruction was wrong. This criticism raised fundamental questions about the credibility of NATO's policy of extended deterrence, which was predicated on the willingness of the United States to use nuclear weapons to offset Soviet conventional capabilities and raise the intensity of conflict to a level at which the Soviets could not win. In effect, these former policymakers sought to

put a veto on the ladder of escalation and thus raise serious questions about NATO's strategy of flexible response, which was predicated on managing escalation. This issue was not fully resolved until the end of the Cold War, when it effectively became redundant. NATO adopted a nuclear policy of "weapons of last resort," although it never endorsed a no-first-use policy. However, the tragic events of September 11, 2001, undermined this movement toward making nuclear weapons less integrated in alliance military planning and politics. Advances in deep-earth hardened shelters for weapons of mass destruction development and storage have once again raised the question of the value of preemption as a mechanism of defense and as a means of preventing proliferation.

—*Andrew M. Dorman*

See also: Credibility; Deterrence; Escalation; Extended Deterrence; Flexible Response; Mutual Assured Destruction
References
Bundy, McGeorge, George F. Kennan, Robert S. McNamara, and Gerard Smith, "Nuclear Weapons and the Atlantic Alliance," *Foreign Affairs,* vol. 61, no. 1, Fall 1982.
Freedman, Lawrence, *The Evolution of Nuclear Strategy,* third edition (New York: Palgrave Macmillan, 2003).
McNamara, Robert S., "The Military Role of Nuclear Weapons: Perceptions and Misperceptions," *Foreign Affairs,* vol. 61, no. 1, Fall 1982.

NON–NUCLEAR WEAPONS STATES

A non–nuclear weapons state (NNWS) is a legal distinction rather than simply a state with no nuclear weapons. Non–nuclear weapons states are defined in international law and their obligations are set forth in several documents, specifically the Nuclear Nonproliferation Treaty (NPT) of 1968.

The NPT defines non–nuclear weapons states as those that had not manufactured or detonated a nuclear weapon or other nuclear explosion device by January 1, 1967. It also stipulates that signatory NNWS agreed not to receive nuclear weapons from any source or accept control over them, not to manufacture or acquire nuclear weapons, not to seek or receive assistance in the manufacturing of nuclear weapons, and to accept international safeguard systems for all peaceful nuclear programs with the International Atomic Energy Agency (IAEA). As of

2001, IAEA safeguards agreements were in force with 142 states (*see* International Atomic Energy Agency).

Some NNWSs are signatories to regional nuclear weapons free zone (NWFZ) treaties, which obligate signing parties not to acquire or possess nuclear weapons or to permit the storage or deployment of nuclear weapons on their territories by other countries. NWFZ treaties are currently in force in Latin America, through the Treaty of Tlatelolco (1967); the South Pacific, through the Treaty of Rarotonga (1985); Southeast Asia, through the Treaty of Bangkok (1995); and Africa, through the Treaty of Pelindaba (1996).

Additionally, most nuclear weapons states have made no-first-use declarations or negative security assurances, meaning that they have agreed not to use nuclear weapons against non–nuclear weapons states that have signed the NPT except when invaded or otherwise attacked.

—*Abe Denmark*

See also: Negative Security Assurances; Nuclear Nonproliferation Treaty

References

Arms Control Association, "Nuclear-Weapon-Free Zones (NWFZ) at a Glance," July 2003, available at http://www.armscontrol.org/factsheets/nwfz.asp.

Stein, Eric, "Legal Restraints in Modern Arms Control Agreements," *American Journal of International Law,* vol. 66, no. 2, April 1972, pp. 255–289.

U.S. Department of State, "The Treaty on the Non-Proliferation of Nuclear Weapons: A Global Success," 20 January 2001, available at http://www.state.gov/t/np/rls/fs/2001/3055.htm.

NONPROLIFERATION

The term "nonproliferation" refers to a worldwide effort to prevent the spread of nuclear weapons and their delivery systems as well as to keep nations that do not have nuclear weapons from acquiring them. Another focus of nonproliferation activities is disposing of plutonium and highly enriched uranium from dismantled Russian nuclear weapons, as well as preventing any form of nuclear materials from falling into the hands of terrorists or ending up on the black market. Nonproliferation also involves efforts to compel nuclear weapons states, including the United States, to pursue complete nuclear disarmament under the terms of the 1968 Nuclear Nonproliferation Treaty (NPT). In the aftermath of the

terrorist attacks of September 11, 2001, the focus of nonproliferation efforts has shifted from nation states to terrorist groups in the goal of keeping them from acquiring nuclear weapons. There are many U.S. agencies that have programs focusing on nuclear nonproliferation, but the three main departments where nonproliferation activities occur are the Department of State, the Department of Defense, and the Department of Energy.

Nonproliferation Efforts

Since the 1950s, the United States has been a leader in nonproliferation efforts, creating a broad international structure including treaties, inspection mechanisms, and agreements backstopped by a wide range of domestic legislation. The Nuclear Nonproliferation Treaty is the centerpiece of the international structure. Under the NPT, there are five declared nuclear states: the United States, the United Kingdom, Russia, China, and France. These nuclear weapons states have agreed not to assist non–nuclear weapons states to acquire nuclear weapons. Under the NPT, the declared nuclear states have agreed to reduce and eventually eliminate their nuclear stockpiles. The signatory non-weapon states agreed not to develop nuclear weapons and to allow for inspections of their nuclear facilities and materials by the International Atomic Energy Agency to ensure that peaceful nuclear technology will not be used for military purposes. The NPT also guarantees non-weapon states access to peaceful nuclear technology. Participation in the NPT has been almost universal since the end of the Cold War. Within the world community, only Israel, India, and Pakistan have refused to sign the NPT. (Cuba joined in November 2002.) (*See* Non–Nuclear Weapons States; Nuclear Nonproliferation Treaty; Nuclear Weapons States.)

The international community relies on a variety of positive and negative incentives to discourage states from acquiring nuclear weapons. If a nation is facing security threats, the United States might provide security guarantees in the form of "extended deterrence," making it possible for allies to avoid developing nuclear weapons of their own (*see* Extended Deterrence). An additional nonproliferation tool has been technology denial and export controls. Nations that are suppliers of nuclear technology try to prevent the countries that are trying to develop nuclear weapons from buying the necessary equipment, particularly the fissile material, to build a nuclear device. The focus of these technology and material denial efforts has been on Russia and the former Soviet republics. Lost or stolen nuclear material and technology in these regions could easily find its way to a nuclear materials black market. Sanctions are another way to deter and punish proliferators. These sanctions cut off U.S. and international aid, military cooperation, economic assistance, and technology if a nation violates nonproliferation agreements. By maintaining a strong military force, the U.S. Department of Defense tries to deter the acquisition and use of nuclear weapons. Counterproliferation is the military component of a nonproliferation policy, using military force to destroy or preempt the development of weapons of mass destruction.

Nonproliferation experts have identified three major issues facing the international community. The first is a regional focus on a number of potential flash points: the Middle East (specifically Iraq, Iran, and Israel), North Korea, and the India-Pakistan arms race. The second problem is the disposal of plutonium and highly enriched uranium from dismantled Russian nuclear weapons. Another major issue is the international effort to convince nations that have signed the NPT to fulfill their pledge and abandon their nuclear arsenals (see Highly Enriched Uranium; Indian Nuclear Weapons Program; Iran's Nuclear Weapons Program; Iraqi Nuclear Forces and Doctrine; Israeli Nuclear Weapons Capabilities and Doctrine; North Korean Nuclear Weapons Program; Pakistani Nuclear Forces; Plutonium; Uranium).

Structure and Organization of the International Nonproliferation Regime

The goal of the international nonproliferation regime is to prevent the spread of nuclear weapons. The regime consists of treaties, international organizations, and agreements. There are four major components of the regime. First is the Nuclear Nonproliferation Treaty, which entered into force in 1968. Second is the International Atomic Energy Agency (IAEA). The IAEA is an international organization with close ties to the United Nations. It helps to verify NPT compliance and polices a safeguards regime. It also negotiates inspection agree-

ments with NPT members to help demonstrate that the use of nuclear materials is for peaceful uses (see International Atomic Energy Agency).

Third, informal international groups play an important part in the international effort to slow the proliferation of nuclear weapons. The Nuclear Suppliers Group, for instance, is a committee of nuclear supplier nations that upholds the multilateral guidelines for nuclear exports. The Zangger Committee is an NPT affiliate that maintains a trigger list of nuclear items requiring safeguards. In 1992 the Nuclear Suppliers Group and Zangger guidelines were strengthened following the end of the Gulf War and the crisis with Iraq's nuclear weapon program. Another component of the nonproliferation structure is the Missile Technology Control Regime (MTCR), which restricts exports of nuclear-capable missiles (see Missile Technology Control Regime; Nuclear Suppliers Group; Zangger Committee).

The fourth component of the nonproliferation regime is the Convention on Physical Security for Nuclear Materials, which began in 1987. The convention set the stage for international security standards for using, transporting, and storing nuclear materials.

Current Concerns and Issues

The five permanent members of the UN Security Council are also the five NPT-designated nuclear weapons states. Nevertheless, there are few states that view nuclear weapons as the best way to ensure their security. Two major powers, Germany and Japan, are non-weapons states. In 1991, South Africa dismantled its nuclear program and renounced nuclear weapons. Under civilian rule, Brazil and Argentina abandoned their secret nuclear programs and joined the NPT. Countries of the former Soviet republic, such as Ukraine, Belarus, and Kazakhstan viewed nuclear weapons as creating more problems then security benefits, returned the Soviet weapons and joined the NPT.

The interest in gaining nuclear weapons has not disappeared, however. The ultimate goal of nonproliferation advocates—complete nuclear disarmament—is still a distant dream. India and Pakistan continue to test nuclear devices. Iran's pursuit of nuclear technology remains a threat. North Korea may have recently become the world's newest unofficial nuclear state. Overall, the international community needs to continue its nonproliferation efforts to ensure that rogue states and nonstate actors do not acquire radioactive materials or nuclear weapons.

—*Laura Fontaine*

See also: Disarmament; Proliferation

References

Behrens, Carl E., "Nuclear Nonproliferation Issues," *CRS Issue Brief for Congress,* 7 October 2003.

Bush, George W., policy statements, available at http://www.ceip.org/files/projects/npp/resources/bushadminnukepolicy.htm.

"Fact Sheet: Nonproliferation and Export Control Policy," 27 September 1993, available at http://www.fas.org/spp/starwars/offdocs/w930927.htm.

NORTH AMERICAN AEROSPACE DEFENSE COMMAND (NORAD)

On August 18, 1940, President Franklin D. Roosevelt and Canadian Prime Minister Mackenzie King issued the "Ogdensburg Declaration," a document based on the concept of joint defense of "the northern half of the western hemisphere." During World War II, a Joint Board of Defense created at Ogdensburg made recommendations on mutual defense activities to the two governments. After the war, Canada and the United States issued a joint statement that set forth the main principles that would underlie their continued collaborative relationship, including exchange of selected service personnel, cooperation in defense exercises, testing of defense materials, encouragement of common designs and standards in arms, equipment, and training, and mutual and reciprocal availability of military, naval, and air facilities in each country.

The vulnerability of Canada and the United States to air attack, possibly involving the use of Soviet atomic weapons, led to the creation of a continental early warning system in the years 1951–1955. In the "Pinetree" agreement of August 1951 (officially the "Exchange of Notes [August 1, 1951] between Canada and the United States of America Constituting an Agreement Regarding the Extension and Co-ordination of the Continental Radar Defence System"), the two governments approved the extension of the continental radar defense system. In 1953, they authorized an experimental pro-

gram known as "Project Counterchange," an initiative that was to grow into the Distant Early Warning Line established under an exchange of notes in May 1955. Three years later, the idea of a hardened command and control center was identified as an important defensive measure against Soviet bombers. After the Soviet launch of Sputnik in 1957, the U.S. government focused more on early warning and the ballistic missile threat.

An integrated North American Air Defense Command (NORAD) became operational on September 12, 1957. The binational command was based in Colorado Springs, Colorado, first at Ent Air Force Base and then, since the early 1980s, at Peterson Air Force Base, with its various warning centers located inside Cheyenne Mountain, also near Colorado Springs (*see* Cheyenne Mountain). Cheyenne Mountain was selected based on three key criteria: It was geographically centered in North America; it was an area of low seismic activity; and there was already an established military presence in Colorado Springs. Excavation and construction for the complex began in June 1961, and the complex was operational on April 20, 1966.

On May 12, 1958, the North American Air Defense agreement between the United States and Canada officially establishing NORAD was formalized. This document included principles governing the organization and operation of NORAD and called for a renewal of the agreement every ten years. It has been reviewed, revised, renewed, or extended several times in the years since NORAD's founding.

The original objectives of NORAD were to assist Canada and the United States in safeguarding the sovereignty of their airspace; to contribute to the deterrence of an attack on North America by providing a capability for aerospace surveillance, threat evaluation, and attack warning and for defense against attack by air or space; and, should deterrence fail, to ensure an appropriate response against attack by providing for the effective use of the two countries' air defenses. In 1975, responsibility for warning and assessment of an aerospace attack was added to the NORAD mission. In 1981, the name of the command was changed to the North American Aerospace Defense Command, reflecting a changed threat to North America in the form of Soviet intercontinental ballistic missiles.

The commander in chief of NORAD (CINCNORAD) is a U.S. general officer, and the deputy commander in chief is a Canadian. Until October 2002, CINCNORAD was "double-hatted" as commander in chief of the U.S. Space Command (CINCSPACE). On October 1, 2002, USSPACECOM disestablished and moved under the U.S. Strategic Command (USSTRATCOM) at Offutt Air Force Base, Nebraska. U.S. Northern Command (USNORTHCOM) was established on October 1, 2003, and CINCNORAD is now dual-hatted as the commander of USNORTHCOM. USNORTHCOM plans, organizes, and executes homeland defense and civil support. Its area of responsibility for this command includes air, land, and sea approaches to the continental United States, Alaska, Canada, Mexico, and surrounding waters out to 500 miles.

—*Patricia McFate*

See also: Early Warning

References

North American Aerospace Defense Command website, http://www.norad.mil.

U.S.-Canadian agreements and treaties, available at http://www.lexum.umontreal.ca/ca_us/s_15_en.html.

NORTH ATLANTIC TREATY ORGANIZATION (NATO)

The North Atlantic Treaty Organization (NATO) was founded by the North Atlantic Treaty, signed in Washington, D.C., on April 4, 1949. The treaty's original purpose was to help the United States, Canada, and European allies deal with the military and ideological threat posed by the Soviet Union. At the end of the Cold War following the collapse of the Soviet Union, NATO members decided to preserve the alliance to help emerging democracies become integrated into the European community and to deal with new risks and uncertainties, including threats from rogue states and weapons of mass destruction. In the early years of the twenty-first century, the allies decided to allow NATO to take on tasks beyond Europe to deal with more distant threats to the security of the member states.

The North Atlantic Treaty was designed to counter Soviet expansion and military power, but it was based on common values, specified no enemy, protected the sovereign decision-making rights of all members, and was written in sufficiently flexible

language to accommodate changing international circumstances.

The first major adjustment made by NATO came early. In the aftermath of the North Korean attack on South Korea, NATO members launched a military buildup in Europe. They also began to construct an integrated command structure in the early 1950s. Neither of these developments had been anticipated when NATO was first formed but were judged necessary after the outbreak of war in Korea. The alliance was adapted again following the 1954 failure of the European Defense Community (EDC), which was intended to coordinate a common European military policy. In the mid-1960s, NATO had to adapt to France's departure from the Integrated Command Structure. In 1967, the allies revamped NATO's strategy by adopting the doctrine of "flexible response" to a possible Warsaw Pact attack (*see* Flexible Response). In the same year, NATO approved the Harmel Report, taking on the mission of promoting détente in addition to the more traditional mission of sustaining deterrence and defense (*see* Détente; Deterrence). In the 1990s, the allies reoriented NATO's goals and activities to take into account the peaceful democratic revolutions in Eastern and Central Europe and the dissolution of the Warsaw Pact and the Soviet Union. NATO became a way to integrate the democracies that emerged out of the former Warsaw Pact into an expanding Euro-Atlantic security structure that helped to prevent the emergence of balance-of-power politics on the continent.

At its founding, the most prominent aspect of NATO was its requirement for individual and collective action for defense against armed attack. Article 5, the North Atlantic Treaty's collective defense provision, provided that "an armed attack against one or more of them in Europe or North America shall be considered an attack against them all."

At the end of the Cold War, the allies began adapting NATO strategy and force deployments to the new circumstances. The changes gave more prominence to Article 4, which stated, "The Parties will consult together whenever, in the opinion of any of them, the territorial integrity, political independence or security of any of the Parties is threatened." The allies also placed additional emphasis on problems posed by the proliferation and potential use of nuclear, biological, and chemical weapons of mass destruction. At the NATO summit meeting in

Headquarters of the North Atlantic Treaty Organization on the outskirts of Brussels, Belgium. (NATO Photos)

Washington in 1999, the allies established a NATO Weapons of Mass Destruction Center designed to improve intelligence and information-sharing about proliferation, to assist allies in enhancing the military capabilities to work in a nuclear, chemical, or biological environment, and to support nonproliferation efforts.

Meeting in Prague, Czech Republic, in November 2002, the NATO allies agreed to establish a NATO Response Force that could respond to security challenges in or beyond Europe. This marked acceptance by all the allies that NATO's security responsibilities are not limited by geography. In the 1990s, the allies had already taken the first step in expanding NATO's roles and missions by undertaking important peace enforcement and peacekeeping missions in the Balkans. NATO took a further step beyond Europe in 2003 when the allies agreed to take responsibility for the International Security Assistance Force in Afghanistan and play a role in post–Gulf War Iraq.

NATO also has adapted by enlarging its membership. The Czech Republic, Hungary, and Poland joined NATO in the 1990s. At the November 2002

Prague summit, the allies invited seven additional countries (Bulgaria, Estonia, Latvia, Lithuania, Romania, Slovakia, and Slovenia) to join, bringing membership to a total of twenty-six Euro-Atlantic nations. NATO has also established special cooperative relationships with both Russia and Ukraine.

In recent years, NATO and the European Union have worked out ways of ensuring that defense cooperation in the EU remains consistent with NATO cooperation.

The North Atlantic Council is NATO's main decision-making body. The "permanent representatives" of the member states meet regularly at its headquarters in Brussels, Belgium; foreign ministers meet twice a year; and member heads of state and government attend occasional summits. NATO's defense policy decision-making organization, the Defense Planning Committee, is composed of NATO ministers of defense or their representatives (excluding France, which left the NATO Integrated Command Structure in 1967). Nuclear matters, including policy, force structure, and basing locations, are decided in the Nuclear Planning Group (NPG). All members are invited to participate, although only seven NATO states have nuclear missions. (The United States, Great Britain, and France are the only member states possessing their own nuclear weapons; the other four use U.S. nuclear warheads under "dual key" arrangements whereby the United States retains release authority even when the weapon is deployed on another nation's delivery system.) Beginning in the 1970s, the NPG was supported by a new committee, the High Level Group, which conducted outside studies and analyses for the Nuclear Planning Group.

The Military Committee includes the chiefs of staff of NATO militaries. The Integrated Command Structure, following substantial reform and consolidation in the 1990s, includes the Supreme Allied Command Europe, headed traditionally by an American four-star general (the supreme allied commander Europe, or SACEUR), with a European deputy commander. The new NATO Transformation Command is led by a U.S. flag officer with a European deputy. NATO's civilian organization is run by an International Staff headed by a secretary general from one of the European member states, NATO's top civilian official.

NATO continues to serve as an important bridge between the United States and Europe. This "indispensable link" allows the allies to coordinate their security policies, including responses to challenges posed by terrorism and weapons of mass destruction. The absence of a unifying threat such as that posed by the Soviet Union during the Cold War, the emergence of new challenges well beyond NATO's borders, and differences between the United States and some allies over how best to deal with those threats have fed speculation that NATO is dead or dying. NATO's demise, however, has been predicted by observers since its inception, and the alliance has withstood several severe tests in the past. Whether it will continue in the future will depend on the extent to which the United States and the allies adapt the alliance to meet changing security demands and use it as a means for promoting U.S.-European security cooperation and for dealing with future threats to their security.

—*Stanley R. Sloan*

References

Sloan, Stanley R., *NATO, the European Union and the Atlantic Community: The Transatlantic Bargain Reconsidered* (Lanham, MD: Rowman and Littlefield, 2002).

Yost, David S., *NATO Transformed: The Alliance's New Roles in International Security* (Washington, DC: United States Institute of Peace Press, 1998).

NORTH KOREAN NUCLEAR WEAPONS PROGRAM

Suspicions of ongoing weapons of mass destruction programs in the Democratic People's Republic of Korea (DPRK, or North Korea) have been a focal point of international security concerns since the 1990s. The Korean peninsula remains a volatile region decades after the Korean War, which ended in a ceasefire in 1953. Movement toward unification of North and South Korea has been very slow and fraught with tension. The parties to the conflict never signed a peace agreement and remain technically at war. As a result, one of the DPRK's longstanding aspirations has been to sign a peace treaty with the United States, distinct from any peace treaty involving the Republic of Korea (ROK, or South Korea), a goal consistently rejected by South Korea and the United States. This history has exacerbated the security threat posed by weapons of mass destruction in North Korea.

The genesis of a North Korean nuclear arms program likely dates back to Premier Kim Il Sung's decision to obtain a nuclear capability following the Korean War, and to North Korea's acquisition in 1965 of its first nuclear research reactor. The North Korean nuclear program has focused on the acquisition of fissionable material. The country possesses vast natural uranium deposits, which have been developed and mined since the mid-1970s.

In the early 1980s, it became known that North Korea was constructing a small graphite reactor at Yongbyon. This revelation led the international community to pressure North Korea to accede to the Nuclear Nonproliferation Treaty (NPT) of 1968. The North Koreans signed the NPT in 1985. North Korea's Yongbyon nuclear reactor came online in 1986. It was reported to have startup problems but could have produced 4 to 7 kilograms of plutonium—roughly enough for one nuclear weapon— per year. The production of plutonium at Yongbyon is the basis of frequent public assertions that Pyongyang may possess one to three nuclear weapons (*see* Nuclear Nonproliferation Treaty).

Although it joined the NPT in 1985, North Korea asserted that it would not sign a nuclear safeguards agreement with the International

Workers pour concrete at a construction site to build nuclear reactors in the North Korean village of Kumho, August 2002, under the auspices of the Korean Peninsula Energy Development Organization. (Lee Jae-won N/Reuters/Corbis)

Atomic Energy Agency (IAEA), a requirement of its NPT membership, until the United States removed its tactical nuclear weapons from South Korea. President George H. W. Bush agreed to do this in 1991, and in 1992 North Korea signed the safeguards agreement. Many believed that the threat posed by the Yongbyon reactor had been contained. In 1991, North Korea also signed the North-South Joint Declaration on Denuclearization of the Korean Peninsula, under which the signatories agreed not to develop, receive, test, or use nuclear weapons (*see* International Atomic Energy Agency; Joint Declaration on Denuclearization of the Korean Peninsula).

In May 1992, the IAEA began inspections to verify the initial declaration of nuclear materials provided by the DPRK. The North Koreans asserted that they had separated approximately 100 grams of plutonium when they removed a few damaged fuel rods from their reactor in 1990. IAEA inspections revealed discrepancies in this report and indicated that plutonium had been separated in 1989, 1990, and 1991. North Korea denied separating plutonium on these occasions.

Adding to suspicions aroused by this discrepancy were intelligence reports that indicated the existence of two hidden nuclear waste sites at Yongbyon. Requests by the IAEA to perform special inspections on these sites were rejected, and in February 1992, the IAEA announced that it could not verify North Korea's declaration of its plutonium inventory.

It was in response to ultimatums presented to North Korea requiring it to submit to special inspections of the two hidden nuclear waste sites that the DPRK announced, on March 12, 1993, its intention to withdraw from the NPT. The DPRK ultimately agreed to postpone this withdrawal following assurances provided by the United States. In these assurances, the United States said it would refrain from the use or threat of use of force, pledged nonintervention in North Korean affairs, and promised to hold bilateral talks with North Korea. Negotiations between the United States, North Korea, and the IAEA, however, yielded little progress on resolving North Korean noncompliance with its NPT obligations.

In April 1994, North Korea announced its intention to unload a small nuclear core from a reactor. It proceeded to do so at a pace that undermined the IAEA's ability to ascertain if it had diverted spent fuel in the past. In addition, the IAEA was unable to test any of the fuel rods that were moved during the unloading process. In addition to its reactors, North Korea had begun to build a plutonium separation plant to handle reprocessing of reactor fuel. It is believed that Russia and China provided North Korea with the basic knowledge necessary to reprocess plutonium, although investigations have indicated that North Korea did not receive significant foreign assistance for its nuclear program.

IAEA director Hans Blix expressed his reservations about the North Korean nuclear program to the UN Security Council in June 1994. This news was met with calls for decisive action against the DPRK and increased the pressure on the United Nations to impose sanctions. North Korea indicated that it would consider the imposition of sanctions an act of war. A crisis was temporarily averted by a diplomatic visit to North Korea by former U.S. President Jimmy Carter, who offered high-level bilateral talks in exchange for a freeze on North Korea's nuclear program, including a pledge not to reload a small reactor with fresh fuel or to reprocess discharged fuel. North Korea also agreed to allow two IAEA inspectors to remain at the reactor site to monitor activities there.

After a brief period of uncertainty following the death of North Korean leader Kim Il Sung, the promised high-level talks took place. They resulted in an "Agreed Statement" in August 1994, which laid the foundation for the "Agreed Framework" reached on October 16 of the same year. The stated objective of the agreement was to reach an overall resolution of the nuclear issue on the Korean peninsula.

The implementation of the Agreed Framework was to occur gradually. North Korea froze activity at its 5-megawatt experimental reactors and reprocessing facilities. This freeze was monitored by the IAEA, which also resumed its routine and ad hoc inspections of facilities not subject to the freeze. North Korea agreed not to build any other reactors or reprocessing facilities and to remain party to the NPT.

Integral to the Agreed Framework was the signatories' promise to provide North Korea with two light-water reactors in exchange for its concessions to restrict its nuclear ambitions and to dismantle its graphite-moderated reactors (see Gas-Graphite Reactors; Light-Water Reactors). An international consortium, the Korean Energy Development Organization (KEDO), was to fund and undertake construction. The United States also agreed to make up North Korea's energy deficiency in the interim period by supplying it with 500,000 tons of heavy fuel oil annually. U.S. officials provided formal assurances against the threat or use of nuclear weapons against North Korea.

Concerns about a possible North Korean nuclear program were reignited by intelligence reports in 1998 of an underground nuclear facility at Kumchang-ni. North Korea eventually agreed to accept an inspection of Kumchang-ni in 1999 in exchange for food assistance, and no evidence of nuclear activities was found at the site at that time or in follow-up visits in 2000.

Progress was made in U.S.–North Korea relations in the final months of President Bill Clinton's administration. A joint communiqué issued in 2000 stated that the parties had "no hostile intention" toward each other. This trend reversed during the George W. Bush administration, and bilateral relations deteriorated rapidly following President Bush's description of North Korea as a member of an "axis of evil" and the reported consideration of the use of nuclear weapons against North Korea in the 2002 U.S. Nuclear Posture Review. In March 2002, the United States decided not to certify North Korea as compliant with the Agreed Framework for the first time since 1994, and the DPRK threatened to walk away from the deal in response to U.S. pressure.

Implementation of the agreement was delayed by various factors, and initial projections of completing the first light-water reactor by 2003 were pushed forward as far as 2008. These delays, in addition to the perceived failure of the United States to implement fully the security assurances provided in the Agreed Framework, purportedly led to the decision of North Korea to revitalize its nuclear weapon program. Others believed that the North Korean decision to abandon the Agreed Framework was motivated by nuclear extortion, an effort to extract additional economic and political concessions in exchange for a commitment to abandon its nuclear ambitions.

On October 16, 2002, North Korea admitted to U.S. delegates that despite its obligations under the NPT and the 1994 Agreed Framework, it had an ongoing nuclear weapons program based on uranium enrichment. It stated its belief that this admission nullified the 1994 Agreed Framework. This situation constituted a major violation of the NPT and called the future of the Korean Energy Development Organization, created to implement the Agreed Framework, into question, precipitating yet another crisis situation on the Korean peninsula.

After North Korea's admission, the United States, Japan, and South Korea halted oil deliveries. In response, North Korea expelled IAEA inspectors and removed surveillance cameras at its nuclear facilities. It then announced its withdrawal from the NPT and demanded direct negotiations with the United States, to which the United States agreed in February 2003 despite previous assertions that North Korea's abandonment of its nuclear program was a prerequisite to discussions.

North Korea has undertaken four and possibly five missile development and production programs. These programs have produced missiles that were reverse engineered, such as the Scud-B, improvements of existing designs, such as the Scud-C, and weapons primarily of North Korean origin, such as the Nodong. North Korea began its first missile reverse-engineering program utilizing a small number of samples, possibly from Egypt. Since then, it has received modest foreign assistance with its missile programs, which has produced missiles of ever-increasing range and reliability. Extensive exports of its missiles and missile technology have provided a much-needed influx of hard currency for the North Korean regime.

North Korea's missile exports have been a major source of tension in its relations with the United States. In 1996, the United States and North Korea met for their first round of bilateral missile talks. Relations were strained in 1999 by North Korea's test of the multistage Taepo Dong-1 missile over Japan. The missile traveled more than 850 miles, landing between northern Japan and Russia. Bilateral missile talks yielded little substantial results until September 1999, when North Korea agreed to a moratorium on testing any long-range missiles for the duration of talks with the United States. North Korea continued to adhere to this self-imposed testing moratorium, and periodic negotiations aimed at resolving the issue of North Korea's missile programs and exports continued up until its revelation of a secret nuclear program in 2002.

—*Jacqueline Simon*

See also: International Atomic Energy Agency; Joint Declaration on Denuclearization of the Korean Peninsula; Missile Defense; Payload; Rumsfeld Commission; South Korean Nuclear Weapons Program; Strategic Forces

References

Abramowitz, Morton I., and James T. Laney, *Meeting the North Korean Nuclear Challenge* (Washington, DC: Korean Task Force, Council on Foreign Relations, 2003).

Bermudez, Joseph S., Jr., *The Armed Forces of North Korea* (New York: I. B. Tauris, 2001).

Cirincione, Joseph, with Jon B. Wolfsthal and Miriuam Rajkumar, *Deadly Arsenals: Tracking Weapons of Mass Destruction* (Washington, DC: Carnegie Endowment for International Peace, 2002).

Cordesman, Anthony H., *Proliferation in the "Axis of Evil": North Korea, Iran and Iraq* (Washington, DC: Center for Strategic and International Studies, 2002).

Federation of American Scientists website, http://www.fas.org/nuke/guide/dprk.

Niksch, Larry, *North Korea's Nuclear Weapons Program,* Issue Brief for Congress (Washington, DC: Congressional Research Service, 2002).

Oh, Kongdan, and Ralph C. Hassig, *North Korea through the Looking Glass* (Washington, DC: Brookings Institution, 2000).

NSC 20/4; NSC 30; NSC 68; NSC 162/2; NSDD 13; NSDM 242

See United States Nuclear Forces and Doctrine

NUCLEAR BINDING ENERGY

Nuclear binding energy is the amount of energy necessary to separate protons or neutrons from a nucleus during the fission process. It is also the energy released when separate protons and neutrons are combined to form a single nucleus in the fusion process. In essence, it can be thought of as the energy that holds the nucleus together. Binding energy is important to nuclear power and weapons because it is the energy that is released in nuclear processes.

Nuclear binding energy comes from the strong nuclear force, that is, the force that holds the nucleus together. The strong nuclear force, which is sometimes called the "strong interaction," is a fundamental force in nature. The nucleus is made up of positively charged protons, and neutrons, which have no charge association. Even though the strong nuclear force is not completely understood, the force must be strong enough to overcome the repelling force of positively charged protons.

Figure N-1: Binding Energy per Nucleon

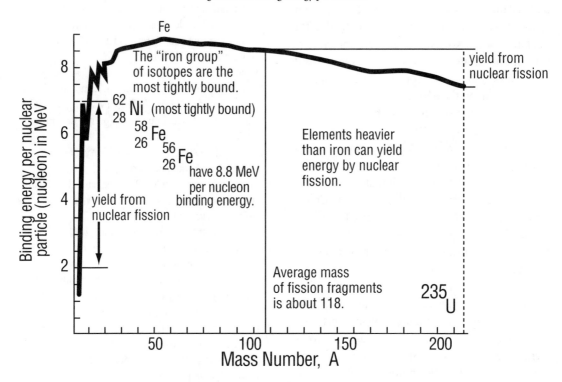

Protons and neutrons are sometimes called "nucleons." A nucleus always has less mass than the sum of its constituent nucleons. This difference in mass is called the "mass defect" of the nucleus. Since mass can be equated to energy by Einstein's equation, it follows that the mass deficit also can be expressed in terms of energy.

The binding energy of an atom can be calculated using Einstein's equation: $E = \Delta mc^2$, where E is rest energy, Δm is the difference between the mass of constituent nucleons and the mass of the nucleus, and c is the speed of light.

Binding energy may be conveniently represented as the amount of energy per nucleon. Figure N-1 shows the binding energy per nucleon by atomic mass number. It illustrates which elements release energy by the fusion and fission processes. This curve also shows that, in general, lighter elements have a relatively smaller amount of binding energy (that is, fewer nucleons with less binding energy per nucleon) and heavier elements have a higher amount of binding energy.

—*Don Gillich*

See also: Fission Weapons; Fusion; Neutrons

References

Krane, Kenneth S., *Introductory Nuclear Physics* (New York: John Wiley and Sons, 1988).

Lamarsh, John R., and Anthony J. Baratta, *Introduction to Nuclear Engineering*, third edition (Upper Saddle River, NJ: Prentice-Hall, 2001).

Nuclear Binding Energy website, http://hyperphysics.phy-astr.gsu.edu/hbase/nucene/nucbin.html.

NUCLEAR EMERGENCY SEARCH TEAMS (NESTS)

Nuclear Emergency Search Teams (NESTs) are national response teams that react to nuclear threat incidents. NEST capabilities include searching for, identifying, and disarming stolen or manufactured nuclear weapons, nuclear materials, or radiological dispersal devices. These teams are staffed with nuclear weapons experts from the national labs and the Department of Energy (DOE).

In 1974, the Federal Bureau of Investigation (FBI) received a threat that unless a large sum of cash was delivered, a nuclear device would be detonated in Boston, Massachusetts. Even though the threat was later determined to be a hoax, the federal government viewed it as a threat that could materialize for real in the future. In response to this new threat assessment, Nuclear Emergency Search Teams were established by the end of 1975 to assist the FBI in responding to nuclear and radiological incidents.

The Department of Energy's Nevada Operations Office determines which assets will be sent in response to a given situation. NESTs are usually tailored to a particular situation or threat, and operations officers can draw on a pool of more than 600 individuals who are experts in nuclear weapons design, radiation, and other nuclear weapons effects. NEST personnel include experts in more than twenty disciplines, including chemistry, physics, mathematics, and communications.

The teams also have specialized equipment, including helicopters, airplanes, and a fleet of vehicles specially modified with advanced radiological sensing devices. Other specialized equipment includes hand-held and remote radiation detection systems. Because NESTs are usually secretly deployed, most of the equipment at their disposal is concealed from public attention by using briefcases or backpacks for the smaller detection devices, and vans and trucks that appear to be commercial vehicles for the larger sensors.

There are two branches of NEST: the Accident Response Group, which responds to accidents and incidents pertaining to U.S. nuclear weapons, and the Joint Technical Operations Team, which responds to the threat of nuclear and radiological weapons by terrorist organizations.

Since the events of September 11, 2001, greater emphasis is being placed on NEST training and readiness to respond to events involving nuclear or radiological materials and weapons. NESTs are now periodically deployed to conduct searches in major U.S. cities. The Department of Homeland Security and the Department of Energy are establishing new command and control relationships for NEST.

—*Don Gillich*

Reference

Richelson, Jeffrey T., "Defusing Nuclear Terror," *Bulletin of Atomic Scientists*, vol. 58, no. 2, March/April 2002.

NUCLEAR FREEZE MOVEMENT
See Antinuclear Movement

NUCLEAR FUEL CYCLE

The nuclear fuel cycle describes the transformation of uranium (U) from its raw material into either enriched uranium or plutonium (Pu) fuel for use in nuclear energy production or in a nuclear weapon. The cycle is dual-use in nature, and materials can be diverted for use in nuclear weapons development at any stage of the cycle.

Uranium is a naturally occurring element, but plutonium must be created through a nuclear reaction. Uranium can either be enriched to concentrate its fissionable isotopes into enriched uranium, or it can be transformed into plutonium in a reactor. Both materials are usable in power-generating nuclear reactors as well as in the manufacture of nuclear weapons.

Depending on the type of fuel and the purpose of the reactor, there are two main routes uranium can thus follow through the nuclear fuel cycle: natural uranium reactors and enriched uranium reactors. Both routes have consequences for nuclear weapons proliferation.

The Cycle

The nuclear fuel cycle is a complex process. The first stage of the fuel cycle involves the geological exploration of uranium reserves followed by the mining of the raw material, uranium ore. Because percentages of uranium in ore are very low, large amounts must be mined to obtain material for use in a reactor. Mining can be accomplished in two ways: in situ leaching, and traditional mining. Traditional mining involves blasting and digging the uranium ore rock from the earth. The ore is separated from the rock, then purified and refined into a powdery yellow substance called "yellowcake." Yellowcake is also referred to as "natural uranium." In situ leaching involves the pumping of a leaching liquid such as ammonium-carbonate or sulfuric acid into the ground and extracting the fluid. A processing plant separates the leaching liquid from the uranium. The extracted uranium is then purified and refined into yellowcake.

Before being usable in a reactor, yellowcake must be further refined, converted, and fabricated into fuel. It is converted through a multistep chemical process into uranium metal or into the gas uranium hexafluoride (UF_6) to be used as feedstock for enrichment. Fuel fabrication produces fuel assemblies that are composed of tubes of fuel pellets called fuel

Figure N-2: The Nuclear Fuel Cycle

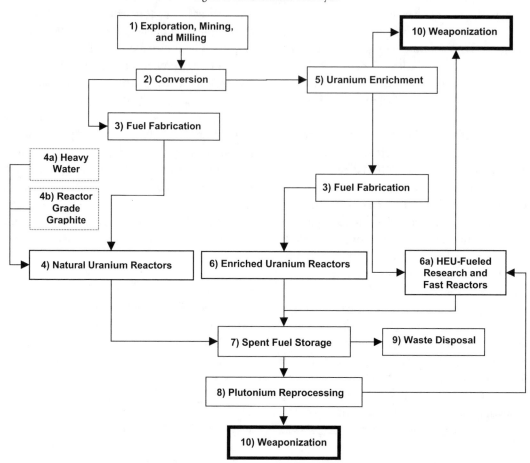

rods. In a nuclear reactor, the fuel rods are bombarded with neutrons to cause a nuclear reaction that releases energy that can be converted into electricity. A certain percentage of the rods are also transformed into materials usable in the nuclear weapons production process.

Natural uranium–fueled reactors, such as heavy-water reactors, graphite-moderated reactors, and some research reactors, use uranium that has not had its isotope level enriched. Moderators are used to slow the bombardment of neutrons at the fuel long enough to allow the nucleus of the uranium 235 (U-235) to split. These reactors are particularly dangerous in terms of weapons proliferation. These types of reactors produce material that does not require an enrichment capability to produce plutonium, a by-product of the nuclear reaction and a fuel for nuclear weapons. As part of the energy production process, the fuel rods in these natural ura-

nium–fueled reactors are irradiated, and as the uranium absorbs neutrons, it becomes plutonium. This plutonium requires reprocessing before it can be used as fuel for a nuclear weapon (see Fuel Fabrication; Gas-Graphite Reactors; Heavy Water; Isotopes; Neutrons; Plutonium; Reactor Operations; Research Reactors; Uranium).

Natural Uranium Reactors
Several types of reactors are used to produce electricity. Heavy water (deuterium oxide), a moderator, allows for the fission of natural uranium, making uranium enrichment unnecessary, and thus bypassing a difficult step of the fuel process. This feature makes heavy-water production highly desirable to nations seeking an indigenous nuclear infrastructure. Tritium, used as a neutron source to boost the explosive power of a nuclear weapon, can be produced from heavy water. Some reactors use graphite

as a moderator. Reactor-grade graphite also allows for the fission of natural uranium, making uranium enrichment unnecessary and thus also bypassing a difficult step of the fuel process.

Uranium Enrichment

The enrichment of uranium involves the separation of the uranium into U-238 and U-235 atoms. U-235 atoms are fissionable. By concentrating U-235 atoms it is possible to produce a nuclear reaction. Uranium can be enriched to different concentrations. An enrichment level less than 20 percent U-235 is considered low enriched uranium (LEU); greater than 20 percent U-235 is considered highly enriched uranium (HEU), and weapons-grade uranium is enriched to greater than 90 percent. To produce 25 kilograms of weapons-grade uranium, it would require approximately 5,000 kg of natural uranium.

There are several methods of uranium enrichment. For determined proliferators with the ability for high technical precision, the gas-centrifuge method is likely to have appeal, as it can produce large amounts of weapons-grade uranium quickly. In this method, uranium hexafluoride is spun in cylinders so that centrifugal force moves the heavier U-238 atoms to the outer edges of the cylinder. The concentrations of U-238 are then removed, and repeated iterations continue to increase the ratio of U-235 atoms to U-238 atoms until the desired concentration of U-235 is reached. A nation seeking weapons-grade uranium could acquire enough for several nuclear weapons per year with a large facility of centrifuges.

Gaseous diffusion is the most common enrichment method and is attractive to nations seeking an indigenous nuclear weapons capability because it can produce substantial quantities of weapons-grade uranium relatively quickly. It requires large amounts of electricity, however, which makes it difficult to undertake clandestinely. At one time, gaseous diffusion cascades in the United States consumed 4 percent of the electricity produced in the country.

Gaseous diffusion involves the transfer of uranium hexafluoride through a series of membranes. The membranes create a separation between a high- and low-pressure environment. The change in pressure causes the atoms to move from the high-pressure side through the membrane to the low-pressure side. The lighter U-235 atoms are collected as they move through the membranes faster than the U-238 atoms. As in the gas-centrifuge method, in gaseous diffusion multiple iterations are required to reach higher and higher concentrations of U-235 atoms. Approximately 4,000 iterations are required to enrich uranium to weapons grade.

Laser separation remains an experimental enrichment method. This method has great appeal because it is extremely efficient. Unlike gas centrifuge and gaseous diffusion, which require many reiterations, laser separation is efficient enough to separate all U-235 atoms in one pass. When perfected, it would provide a means of exploiting nuclear waste for usable uranium.

Another form of enrichment uses laser light to ionize the vapor of U-235 but not U-238. The desired U-235 atoms can then be collected by attracting them with a negatively charged plate. Examples of this method include the atomic vapor laser isotope separation (AVLIS) and molecular laser isotope separation (MLIS) processes.

Aerodynamic separation also uses an enormous amount of energy. In this enrichment method, a gas that includes some uranium hexafluoride is projected across an aerodynamically curved surface into a swirling chamber (much like a centrifuge). As the gas passes over the curved surface, the lighter U-235 atoms separate from the heavier U-238 atoms. It requires hundreds of iterations to reach a desired concentration level in this method. The Becker Nozzle Process, for example, is inefficient and an unlikely choice for nations seeking an indigenous enrichment capability (see Enrichment; Highly Enriched Uranium; Low Enriched Uranium).

Enriched Uranium Reactors

Light-water reactors (LWR) fueled with LEU are less of a proliferation threat than heavy-water reactors (HWR) fueled with natural uranium. The spent fuel rods from light-water reactors contain plutonium that requires reprocessing to be usable in a nuclear weapon. By contrast, the spent fuel rods from HEU-fueled research and fast reactors contain weapons-grade plutonium, which makes them highly desirable to nations seeking nuclear weapons. Breeder reactors are designed to produce more fuel than then they are fed. U-235 and Pu-239 release neutrons, which creates a chain reaction and transforms the U-238 into plutonium. The plutonium fissions and helps to keep the reactor critical; alternatively, it can be used in another reactor or reprocessed for a nuclear weapon.

Spent Fuel Storage, Use, and Waste

It is necessary to store fuel leaving a reactor in pools of water to reduce its radioactivity and heat before it is reprocessed for plutonium retrieval. It also has to cool before being sent to a permanent waste disposal facility. Despite the presence of plutonium in spent fuel, the risk of diversion of material at this stage is very low because of the dangers of handling it.

After fuel rods are kept for several months in storage ponds, they can be reprocessed to extract the plutonium from the uranium. The plutonium is then ready to be converted for use as reactor fuel or as fissile material in a nuclear weapon.

In contrast, uranium requires enrichment in order to be used as fissile material. Although the extraction method is fundamentally a chemical one—involving chopping the material, stripping the cladding, and using chemical solvents such as nitric acid to extract radioactive isotopes, facilities must be very carefully constructed to handle nuclear materials. Reprocessing is done with remote manipulators behind heavy shielding (called "hot cells") for safety reasons.

Waste from the nuclear fuel cycle is considered high-level waste and must be stored in a way that protects the environment against radioactivity and toxicity of the substances for an extremely long time. Advanced waste storage includes sealing waste in an insoluble, glass-like material and deep-mine disposal.

Weapons-grade uranium or plutonium must be fabricated into a fissile core for a nuclear weapon, which involves casting and high-precision milling of the metal. The fissile core must be paired with a device capable of causing a fissile reaction in the core. The development of the nonnuclear portion of the weapon is an extremely complex process requiring high-precision arming, fuzing, firing, and safing.

—*Jennifer Hunt Morstein*

References

Gardner, Gary T., *Nuclear Nonproliferation: A Primer* (Boulder: Lynne Rienner, 1994).

Walker, P. M. B., ed., *Chambers Nuclear Energy and Radiation Dictionary* (New York: Chambers, 1992).

NUCLEAR NONPROLIFERATION TREATY (NPT)

The Nuclear Nonproliferation Treaty (NPT) came into force on March 5, 1970, after being opened for signature on July 1, 1968. The treaty was the result of several years of negotiations involving nuclear weapons states (NWS) and non–nuclear weapons states (NNWS). It has several major objectives: to prevent the spread of nuclear weapons, weapons materials, and technology to additional countries; to promote cooperation among nations in the peaceful uses of nuclear energy; and to achieve global nuclear disarmament.

The NPT is the pivotal component of the nuclear nonproliferation regime, which comprises a set of norms, principles, treaties, and procedures through which countries pledge not to obtain nuclear weapons or help other states acquire a nuclear arsenal. International and bilateral safeguards verify national commitments and thereby prevent defection and cheating. The International Atomic Energy Agency (IAEA), which administers the NPT's safeguards system, is the chief institutional component of the regime. The main principle of the regime is that the spread of nuclear arms is a threat to international security, and its underlying norm is that nonnuclear members of the regime should not develop nuclear weapons and no member should help another nation to build such weapons (*see* International Atomic Energy Agency; Nonproliferation; Safeguards; Zangger Committee).

The NPT is governed by two principles: that the spread of nuclear weapons undermines international peace and security, and that the peaceful application of nuclear energy should be made available to all parties of the treaty. The treaty contains eleven articles. Article I calls upon all NWS parties to the treaty not to transfer nuclear weapons or nuclear explosive devices directly or indirectly, or encourage NNWS to manufacture such devices. Article II stipulates that NNWS will not undertake weapons programs or receive transfers of nuclear weapons or assistance in their manufacture. Under Article III, each NNWS party to the treaty undertakes to accept IAEA safeguards, as negotiated with the IAEA, on their nuclear facilities. It also requires NNWS not to provide fissionable materials to other states without safeguards. Article IV reassures all NNWS of their inalienable right to peaceful nuclear energy research and development, and Article V offers the potential benefits of peaceful nuclear explosions, made available through appropriate international procedures. Article VI requires NWS to pursue negotiations in good faith on effective measures relating to the cessation of the nuclear arms race at an early date and the conclusion of a treaty on general and complete disarmament under strict and effective international control. Article VII states that nothing in the treaty shall prevent any group of states from concluding regional treaties. Article VIII discusses the amending procedure, and Article IX identifies the signature and ratification procedures. Article X guarantees the sovereign right of each party to withdraw from the treaty if it decides that extraordinary events have jeopardized its supreme national interests. Article XI discusses the depository procedures.

Article VI was crucial for many NNWS to agree to sign the treaty. This article remains the only binding commitment to nuclear disarmament in a multilateral treaty on the part of the NWS. The treaty defines a NWS as one that had manufactured and exploded a nuclear weapon or other nuclear explosive device prior to January 1, 1967. All other states are considered NNWS. Under this criterion, only the United States, the Soviet Union (Russia), the United Kingdom, China, and France are legally allowed to keep nuclear weapons. To a great extent, this cap on the so-called "nuclear club" makes the treaty unamendable because there is no room for a future nuclear weapons state to emerge with international legitimacy. Unless the treaty is modified, India and Pakistan, which detonated nuclear weapons in 1998, will remain outside the treaty.

History and Background

Nuclear proliferation has been a concern of the international community ever since the first atomic weapon was used on Hiroshima on August 6, 1945. The United States took the initiative to prevent the spread of nuclear weapons—largely for reasons of preserving its nuclear monopoly—through the Baruch Plan and the Atoms for Peace proposal in the 1950s (see Atoms for Peace; Baruch Plan). The Soviet Union opposed these proposals, but by the 1960s Moscow came to the realization that atomic weapons should not spread to other states, especially Germany and Japan. In 1961, an Irish resolution titled the "Prevention of the Wider Dissemination of Nuclear Weapons" was unanimously adopted by the UN General Assembly. In 1965, the General Assembly adopted resolution 2028 setting out five principles on which the nonproliferation treaty was to be based. In early 1968, the Eighteen-Nation Committee on Disarmament submitted a draft treaty to the UN General Assembly, which the assembly subsequently adopted as Resolution 2373 (XXII), by which it approved the NPT.

The NPT was one of the few instances of U.S.-Soviet security cooperation during the Cold War era that also received the support of other key states. The treaty emerged from a U.S.-Soviet consensus that the spread of nuclear weapons to additional states was not in the interest of international security, especially in the management of the superpower competition. The United Kingdom strongly supported this initiative. France and China initially opposed the treaty on political grounds but changed their positions in the early 1990s. France joined the treaty in 1991 and China in 1992, although the latter has continued its supply of nuclear materials to Pakistan, thereby violating its commitment under Article I of the treaty. Despite the superpower initiative, in the end, the treaty came into being as a result of a grand bargain between the NWS and NNWS. Under this bargain, a large number of the NNWS agreed to forgo their nuclear weapons options on two conditions: that the nuclear states commit themselves to supplying technology and materials necessary for civilian applications, and that they pursue nuclear disarmament in good faith.

The superpowers anticipated that the NPT would help put a lid on the nuclear aspirations of potential nuclear states while not upsetting their nuclear arms buildup. Middle powers with major power aspirations (most prominently India and Brazil) and others wishing to maintain a high level of foreign policy autonomy (such as Argentina, Israel, and South Africa) opposed the treaty and initially refused to sign it. These states were not under the security umbrella of a major power and felt that they needed to keep their military options open. The French and Chinese criticism of the treaty was mostly based on symbolic political opposition to superpower politics rather than a frontal assault on the treaty. The two major economic powers, Germany and Japan, were under the security umbrella of the United States and had been pursuing low-profile foreign policies. Despite initial hesitation, these states joined the treaty and ratified it in a few years. Thus a key systemic condition, that is, the dearth of dissatisfied major power challengers, was a necessary condition for the treaty to come into existence. Second-tier nuclear states—China, the United Kingdom, and France—were treated equally and their nuclear weapons status bestowed with legitimacy.

At the time the treaty entered into force, no new state, except the five major powers, had acquired the necessary capabilities for building a nuclear weapons force. Reluctant smaller states were offered side-payments to obtain their adherence to the nonproliferation regime. Many minor powers joined the regime willingly because the NPT was better than nothing at all. With the end of the Cold War in 1991, remaining opposition to the treaty waned. Several previous opponents to the treaty signed the NPT, including Argentina (1995), Brazil (1996), and South Africa (1991, after dismantling the seven nuclear devices it had built). The three successor states of the Soviet Union that had inherited Soviet nuclear weapons based on their soil, Ukraine, Kazakhstan, and Belarus, also joined the treaty in the mid-1990s.

Technical Details

The treaty was initially intended to be in force for a twenty-five-year period. In 1995, however, the members agreed to extend it in perpetuity. Since 1975, the parties have held review conferences every five years. In addition, PrepCom (Preparatory Committee) meetings are held periodically to review the global efforts at nuclear nonproliferation. The IAEA is the chief organization verifying NPT compliance by member states. It conducts periodic safeguard inspections of the member states' nuclear facilities to make sure no violation takes place (that is, it verifies that nuclear materials or technology are not being diverted to military purposes). It also acts as the organization responsible for helping to transfer nuclear materials and technology for peaceful purposes. These IAEA safeguards are technical means of verifying a state's fulfillment of its commitments to the peaceful uses of nuclear energy. In the event of violation by the signatory, the IAEA will refer the matter to the UN Security Council, which has the ultimate authority to determine what sanctions are to be authorized to force compliance (see Verification).

Current Status

As of February 2003, there were 188 members to the treaty. With the Cuban government's announcement on September 14, 2002, of its decision to join the treaty, the NPT has become nearly universal. The only states outside the treaty are India, Israel, and Pakistan. North Korea officially withdrew from the treaty in March 2003. This was the first withdrawal by a signatory state, thereby effectively reducing membership to 187. Two NPT signatories—Iraq and Iran—have reportedly been pursuing nuclear acquisition even though they have committed not to do so under the treaty. The forceful regime change in Iraq by the U.S. military intervention in March 2003 would suggest that the future government in Baghdad will adhere to the treaty (see Indian Nuclear Weapons Program; Iranian Nuclear Weapons Program; Iraqi Nuclear Forces and Doctrine; Israeli Nuclear Weapons Capabilities and Doctrine; North Korean Nuclear Weapons Program; Pakistani Nuclear Forces).

In April 1995, delegates from 174 of the 178 member states existing at that time met at the UN in New York to discuss the extension of the treaty. Most states parties did not want to bury the treaty, but the deliberations showed the bargaining positions of different states. They were presented with three main options: a proposal by Mexico to extend the treaty in perpetuity with the condition of time-bound progress in nuclear disarmament; rolling extensions of twenty-five years each tied to specific progress in nuclear disarmament, introduced by Indonesia on behalf of six nonaligned movement states; and a proposal for indefinite extension, introduced by Canada, on behalf of the Western countries. More than 100 countries, including the major powers, their allies, and several smaller states, favored the Canadian draft, and 14 nonaligned states opted for the Indonesian option. After a month of negotiations, which initially were deadlocked, the delegates from 174 countries adopted a motion without a vote to extend the treaty in perpetuity. This extension document included "declarations on principles and objectives for nuclear nonproliferation and disarmament" and a resolution on a strengthened review process that met with the support of a majority of states. The review process would include conferences at five-year intervals and preparatory committee meetings three years prior to the conferences to consider ways to promote full implementation of the treaty. In addition, the member states adopted a resolution calling on all countries in the Middle East to accede to the treaty, place their nuclear facilities under IAEA safeguards, and conclude a zone free of weapons of mass destruction and delivery systems.

The NPT is likely to be helped by future verification technologies. The biggest threat to the treaty, however, comes from political changes. The most persistent criticism of the treaty is that it creates two categories of states, haves and have-nots, and assigns them different obligations and responsibilities. The commitment by the five declared nuclear weapons states to achieve nuclear disarmament has not been met and is unlikely to be fulfilled any time soon. The continued proliferation of chemical, biological, and nuclear weapons, and the threat that these weapons might fall into the hands of terrorists, slowly undermines the long-term viability of the regime. The nonratification of the Comprehensive Test Ban Treaty of 1996 by the United States is another challenge to the regime. Another potential challenge is the new U.S. nuclear and counterproliferation policy, which relies heavily on preemption, prevention, and first use. The United States also may develop new earth-penetrating mini-nukes, making the possibility of nuclear use more likely in future conflicts. This would break the taboo against their use in existence for over fifty years. The George W. Bush administration has been more focused on unilateral policies, and thus its support for multilateralist instruments such as the NPT is coming under strain. The demand by NNWS for effective security assurances, including a no-first-use pledge, is not being met by the NWS. The treaty is likely to survive as a somewhat weakened instrument as long as there are no other options in sight in the near future.

—*T. V. Paul*

See also: Arms Control; Disarmament; Threshold States
References
British American Security Information Council website, http://www.basicint.org/nuclear/NPT/main.htm.
Nuclear Nonproliferation Treaty (NPT), available at http://disarmament.un.org/wmd/npt/npttext.html.
Paul, T. V., *Power versus Prudence: Why Nations Forgo Nuclear Weapons* (Montreal: McGill-Queen's University Press, 2000).
———, "Systemic Conditions and Security Cooperation: Explaining the Persistence of the Nuclear Non-Proliferation Regime," *Cambridge Review of International Affairs,* vol. 16, no. 1, April 2003, pp. 135–155.
Rauf, Tariq, and Rebecca Johnson, "After the NPT's Indefinite Extension: The Future of the Global Non-Proliferation Regime," *Nonproliferation Review,* vol. 3, 1995.

NUCLEAR PLANNING GROUP

The origins of the Nuclear Planning Group (NPG) can be traced to U.S. Secretary of Defense Robert McNamara's Athens speech of 1962. In the aftermath of this speech, and following the demise of the European Multilateral Force idea and the adoption by the North Atlantic Treaty Organization (NATO) of the strategy of flexible response, the NPG was formed as a NATO forum for discussion of nuclear matters among the allies.

From the start there were disagreements within NATO over nuclear issues, and the French chose not to be a member of the NPG. At its first meeting, McNamara outlined the tasks he envisaged for the NPG. These included analyzing the threat from the Warsaw Pact and the research and development programs needed to develop weapons to meet emerging threats. McNamara also charged the NPG with sizing NATO's nuclear force structure and developing strategic and operational plans for the actual use of NATO's nuclear forces. The NPG did not offer European members of NATO control over nuclear weapons, nor did it provide a vehicle for other NATO states to have a veto over U.S. nuclear strategy. The United States retained control of NATO's plans for the employment of nuclear weapons in war. Instead, the NPG planned for the use of tactical and theater-level nuclear weapons. Decisions about the strategic use of nuclear weapons remained with the United States, and to a lesser degree, France and the United Kingdom.

Initially, membership in the NPG included four permanent members (the United States, the United Kingdom, West Germany, and Italy) and three rotating members. Nuclear-armed France was the obvious absentee from the NPG. Membership in the NPG was eventually opened to all NATO members, but today not all choose to participate in the NPG sessions. Sensitive issues involving NATO intermediate-force modernization in the late 1970s and 1980s also were limited to a NATO High-Level Group, which conducted studies for the NPG.

Since the end of the Cold War, the NPG has broadened its remit to encompass nonproliferation and the safeguarding of nuclear weapons, especially those found in the former Soviet Union. It has retained its mandate to update NATO's nuclear strategy, but its influence and importance have declined. Nevertheless, it still meets regularly and issues communiqués twice a year.

—Andrew M. Dorman

References

Buteux, Paul, *The Politics of Nuclear Consultation in NATO, 1965–80* (Cambridge: Cambridge University Press, 1983).

Larsen, Jeffrey A., *NATO Counterproliferation Policy: A Case Study in Alliance Politics,* INSS Occasional Paper 17 (Colorado Spring, CO: USAF Institute for National Security Studies, November 1997).

North Atlantic Treaty Organization (NATO) website, http://www.nato.int.

Park, William, *Defending the West: A History of NATO* (London: Wheatsheaf, 1987).

Schmidt, Gustav, ed., *A History of NATO: The First Fifty Years,* vol. 3 (Basingstoke, UK: Palgrave, 2001).

NUCLEAR POSTURE REVIEW

In 1994 and again in 2001, the U.S. Congress directed the Defense Department to undertake a comprehensive Nuclear Posture Review (NPR) as a way to map out the future of American nuclear forces. Although it remains classified, the 2001 Nuclear Posture Review proposed profound changes in the composition and strategy governing U.S. nuclear forces. Linked to the new National Security Strategy and the latest Quadrennial Defense Review, the NPR offers a blueprint for transforming America's strategic posture.

The NPR calls for a new strategic "Triad" made up of conventional and nuclear offensive forces, missile defenses, and a robust nuclear infrastructure (*see* Triad). It downplays the role of Russia in U.S. strategic deterrence and highlights the need to deter and preempt emerging state and nonstate actors armed with weapons of mass destruction. Unlike the U.S. Cold War nuclear deterrent posture, which was intended to inflict massive damage against the Soviet Union under all conceivable circumstances, the NPR calls for a range of conventional and nuclear deterrence options to provide a credible deterrent across a wide range of scenarios.

The NPR is a complex and controversial document. On the one hand, it downplays the role of nuclear weapons and deterrence in the Russian-American strategic relationship, highlighting the need to make cooperation the cornerstone of Russian-American relations. The George W. Bush administration's decision to withdraw from the Anti-Ballistic Missile (ABM) Treaty is thus portrayed by the administration as an important step in eliminating the last vestiges of the Soviet-American Cold War relationship that was based on mutual assured destruction. On the other hand, the NPR calls for the integration of conventional and nuclear strike assets and missile defenses to generate credible deterrent and counterforce options against emerging threats posed by chemical, biological, and nuclear weapons. Critics charge that by calling for a new generation of low-yield earth-penetrating warheads to hold deeply buried targets at risk, the NPR will lower the nuclear threshold by making the battlefield use of nuclear weapons an increasingly attractive option to U.S. policymakers.

—Andrew M. Dorman

See also: Quadrennial Defense Review; United States Nuclear Forces and Doctrine

References

"National Security Strategy of the United States of America," 2002, available at http://www.whitehouse.gov/nsc/nss.pdf.

"Nuclear Posture Review Report," 2002, available at http://www.defenselink.mil/news/Jan2002/d20020109npr.pdf.

"Quadrennial Defense Review," 2001, available at http://www.defenselink.mil/pubs/qdr2001.pdf.

NUCLEAR REGULATORY COMMISSION (NRC)

The Nuclear Regulatory Commission (NRC) is an independent U.S. government commission created by the Energy Reorganization Act of 1974. It is responsible for licensing and regulating the civilian use of nuclear energy to protect the public and the environment. The NRC also conducts public hearings on nuclear and radiological safety and on environmental and antitrust issues relevant to nuclear energy.

A five-member commission heads the NRC. The president of the United States designates one member to serve as official spokesperson and chairman. The commission formulates policies and regulations governing nuclear reactor and materials safety, issues orders to licensees, and adjudicates legal matters brought before it. As part of the regulatory process, the NRC's four regional offices conduct inspection, enforcement, and emergency response programs for licensees within their borders and investigate nuclear incidents.

Before the NRC was created, nuclear regulation was the responsibility of the Atomic Energy Commission (AEC), which Congress first established in the Atomic Energy Act of 1946. Congress replaced that law with the Atomic Energy Act of 1954. This act assigned the AEC the functions of both encouraging the use of nuclear power and regulating its safety (*see* Atomic Energy Act; Atomic Energy Commission).

During the 1960s, an increasing number of critics charged that the AEC's regulations were weak in terms of radiation protection standards, reactor safety, plant siting, and environmental protection. By 1974, Congress decided to abolish the AEC. Supporters and critics of nuclear power agreed that the promotional and regulatory duties of the AEC should be assigned to different agencies. In passing the Energy Reorganization Act of 1974, Congress created the NRC and transferred all of the licensing and regulatory powers of the AEC to the new agency. The NRC began operations on January 19, 1975.

—*Steven Rosenkrantz*

References

"Nuclear Regulatory Commission," *Columbia Encyclopedia,* sixth edition, 2003, available at http://www.encyclopedia.com.

Nuclear Regulatory Commission (NRC) website, http://www.nrc.gov/.

NUCLEAR RISK REDUCTION CENTERS (NRRCs)

Nuclear Risk Reduction Centers (NRRCs) were established to reduce the risk of nuclear war between the United States and the Soviet Union resulting from accidents, miscalculations, or misinterpretations of world events. In September 1987, U.S. Secretary of State George P. Shultz and Soviet Foreign Minister Eduard Shevardnadze signed the agreement to establish the centers in Washington, D.C., and Moscow. The U.S. and Soviet centers opened on April 1, 1988, and their operations were authorized for an unlimited duration. The U.S. NRRC now operates seven communications systems that can establish communications with more than 100 countries, including the Russian Federation, Ukraine, Belarus, Kazakhstan, and most of the other member states of the Organization for Security and Cooperation in Europe.

The NRRCs' purpose is to exchange notifications required under existing and future security and arms control agreements and to undertake other security and confidence-building measures. The centers were not designed to duplicate the existing U.S.-Soviet "Hot Line," which was established in 1963 through a bilateral agreement. The Hot Line is reserved for communication between heads of state in times of emergency or crisis. The NRRCs have no crisis management role but were intended to help prevent crises by providing a way to exchange accurate information on a day-to-day basis. They are charged with the exchange, translation, and dissemination of the many government-to-government notifications required in the implementation of more than twenty different arms control treaties and security agreements.

Located in the two national capitals, the NRRCs are connected by dedicated, high-speed communications links. The centers are equipped with modern computers and are staffed with trained communication technicians. The U.S. Department of State's Bureau of Verification and Compliance is assigned responsibility for operating the U.S. NRRC.

—*Steven Rosenkrantz*

Reference

"Nuclear Risk Reduction Centers," Federation of American Scientists website, http://www.fas.org/nuke/control/nrrc/.

NUCLEAR SUPPLIERS GROUP

The Nuclear Suppliers Group (NSG) is an organization of nuclear supplier nations voluntarily united in an effort to control the exports of certain materials and technologies that are dual-use—that is, items that could be used for either peaceful or weapons purposes. The goal of the group was to prevent the contribution of nuclear suppliers to the proliferation of nuclear weapons while not impeding legitimate international nuclear trade and technological cooperation.

The NSG, also known as the "London Club," was created in 1975 in response to a growing concern that tighter export controls of nuclear weapons–related materials were necessary. The environment was marked by concern that the first Indian nuclear detonation in 1974 would prompt an increase in global activities to obtain nuclear technology.

The NSG was conceived to limit the trade of dual-use materials and technologies to further the nonproliferation goals of the Nuclear Nonproliferation Treaty (NPT) of 1968. NSG guidelines serve to inhibit the progress of aspiring nuclear nations' programs by closing down reliable channels for supply and forcing them to seek alternative routes. This increases costs to these nations in their effort to pursue nuclear weapons development and also causes time delays (see Nuclear Nonproliferation Treaty [NPT]).

The 1971 Zangger Committee laid the groundwork for the Nuclear Suppliers Group (see Zangger Committee). The Zangger Committee's mission was to interpret the vague safeguard requirements of Article III.2 of the NPT, which addressed the export of nuclear equipment and material. Zangger Committee members entered into an ad hoc, voluntary agreement, which was not legally binding or formally connected to the NPT, in which they agreed not to export certain items without first ensuring that they would be safeguarded. Their "Trigger List" contained the items subject to safeguards. In 1978, the NSG prepared a set of guidelines, taking into consideration the Zangger Committee's Trigger List, and published it in International Atomic Energy Agency (IAEA) document INFCIRC/254. The NSG labeled its expanded list the "Critical Technologies List" (CTL). It has become a significant contribution to the current nuclear nonproliferation regime.

The membership of the NSG is larger than that of the Zangger Committee and further extended the latter's restrictions on nuclear trade. A strong tool of the NSG is the exchange of information amongst the thirty-four members to increase awareness of potential weapons proliferation.

Restrictions on trade include:

- Strict security arrangements for nuclear exports;
- A consent requirement from the original supplier in case of reexport;
- Withholding of critical materials and technologies used for uranium enrichment, plutonium reprocessing, fuel fabrication, and heavy-water production equipment and plants from export to countries of concern; and
- Full-scope safeguards for supply to any non–nuclear weapons state.

The NSG also controls a second tier of transfers regarding technology and materials that are not exclusively used for nuclear purposes but could make critical contributions to a nation's nuclear fuel cycle. These technologies are prevalent in nonnuclear industries.

In 1992, in response to lessons learned from revelations of the extent of the Iraqi nuclear program, the NSG extended its CTL to encompass an even broader definition of dual-use items related to the nonnuclear elements of nuclear weapons development. Evidence mounted that Iraq's progress toward the building of a nuclear weapons infrastructure was being achieved through purchases of dual-use technologies and materials from unwitting suppliers (see Iraqi Nuclear Weapons Program).

The CTL is an extensive list but it has limitations. It does not cover all potentially nuclear-relevant technologies useful for the construction of a nuclear weapons infrastructure. It includes all key categories of nuclear-related dual-use technologies, but some of the foundational technologies that are components of these key categories are simply too ubiquitous to be easily controlled. Although common in many industries and considered to be too unimportant in the past to merit much scrutiny, the trade of these items has aided some nations with nuclear aspirations.

The NSG suffers from other limitations. For one thing, its membership is not comprehensive. Nations such as India, Israel, and Pakistan are notable nonmembers. The group itself does not have implementation provisions, so member nations individually incorporate the NSG guidelines into their national export controls in a manner of their choosing. Responsibility for implementing the NSG is left to the member nation and requires self-policing.

—*Jennifer Hunt Morstein*

See also: Dual Use; International Atomic Energy Agency; Nonproliferation; Proliferation

References

Gardner, Gary T., *Nuclear Nonproliferation: A Primer* (Boulder: Lynne Rienner, 1994).

Schmidt, Fritz W., "The Zangger Committee: Its History and Future Role," *Nonproliferation Review*, vol. 2, no. 3, Fall 1994, pp. 38–44.

Strulak, Tadeusz, "The Nuclear Suppliers Group," *Nonproliferation Review*, vol. 1, no. 1, Fall 1993, pp. 2–10.

NUCLEAR TABOO

The nuclear taboo is a norm that makes the leaders of nuclear-armed states almost unthinkingly rule out the employment of nuclear weapons. Perhaps the most notable characteristic of nuclear weapons is that they have not been used in conflict since the United States dropped two atomic bombs on Japan to end World War II. Why no nuclear weapons have been used in combat since 1945 is a matter of controversy. Several conditions could explain the nonuse of nuclear forces: deterrence; lack of suitable targets; availability of other military options; or constraints created by public opinion, luck, or a normative inhibition against inflicting nuclear devastation. The last factor is called the "nuclear taboo."

The armed forces of all nuclear weapons states plan and train to use nuclear forces under certain contingencies, but the use of these weapons has been most seriously considered only a few times, such as during the Korean and Vietnam wars and the Cuban missile crisis. After considerable debate, U.S. officials ruled out nuclear use during these crises mainly out of fear of provoking direct military conflict with the Soviet Union, although moral and political considerations also mattered. In the aftermath of these episodes, U.S. policymakers made it a priority to avoid circumstances in which the president would have to contemplate nuclear use.

It is difficult to know just how strong and universal the nuclear taboo has become. The normative constraint against nuclear use probably grows stronger with the passage of time since the last nuclear detonation. The next use of nuclear weapons, particularly if that use is deemed effective, however, could seriously erode the taboo and make the possession of nuclear weapons more desirable and their use more thinkable.

—*Peter Lavoy*

Reference
Tannenwald, Nina, *The Nuclear Taboo: The United States and the Non-Use of Nuclear Weapons since 1945* (Cambridge: Cambridge University Press, 2004).

NUCLEAR TEST BAN

The first nuclear test took place in July 1945 when the United States tested an atomic bomb at the Trinity Test Site in New Mexico. Since then, almost 2,000 nuclear tests have been conducted around the globe. When Indian Prime Minister Jawaharlal Nehru first called for a "standstill" agreement on nuclear testing in April 1954, many governments and much of world opinion backed this sentiment. The United States, the Soviet Union, and the United Kingdom began discussions about the scope and nature of a nuclear test ban in Geneva in October 1958. The process became bogged down over verification procedures, however, and was soon placed on the diplomatic back burner as East-West tension rose in the early 1960s (*see* Underground Testing).

Nevertheless, tripartite negotiations in Moscow in the summer of 1963 produced the Limited Test Ban Treaty (LTBT), which came into force on October 11, 1963. The LTBT banned nuclear tests in the atmosphere, under water, or in space and contained a clear commitment to work toward prohibiting underground tests, as did the preamble to the 1968 Nuclear Nonproliferation Treaty (NPT). Further partial bans followed. The 1974 Threshold Test Ban Treaty (TTBT) limited underground tests to yields of less than 150 kilotons, and the Peaceful Nuclear Explosions Treaty of 1976 imposed a similar ban on nonmilitary tests. Both the LTBT and the TTBT anticipated a complete test ban, but negotiations on such a ban between 1977 and 1980 failed (*see* Limited Test Ban Treaty; Nuclear Nonproliferation Treaty; Peaceful Nuclear Explosions Treaty; Threshold Test Ban Treaty).

It was not until 1993, with strong support from the United Nations General Assembly, that negotiations for a comprehensive treaty began. These would ultimately produce the Comprehensive Test Ban Treaty (CTBT), which prohibits all nuclear test explosions in all environments. The CTBT was opened for signature in September 1996, when it was signed by seventy-one states, including the five nuclear weapons states. Although President William Clinton signed the CTBT, the U.S. Senate has failed to ratify the agreement.

—*J. Simon Rofe*

See also: Comprehensive Test Ban Treaty
References
Edmonds, John, "A Complete Nuclear Test Ban—Why Has It Taken So Long?" *Security Dialogue*, vol. 25, no. 4, December 1994, pp. 375–388.
Mutimer, David, "Testing Times: Of Nuclear Tests, Test Bans and the Framing of Proliferation,"

President John F. Kennedy signing the Limited Test Ban Treaty, October 7, 1963. (National Archives)

Contemporary Security Policy, vol. 23, no. 1, April 2000, pp. 1–22.

NUCLEAR WARHEAD STORAGE AND TRANSPORTATION SECURITY (RUSSIA)

Despite occasional claims since 1989 that nuclear warheads inherited by the Russian Federation from the Soviet Union are missing, that Russian officers have sold warheads on the black market, or that warheads have been stolen from storage depots, no credible evidence exists to support these allegations. Nonetheless, the Russian Ministry of Defense has not been sheltered from Russia's general economic and social problems. Historically, Russia has relied heavily on guard forces, and its transition to techno-logical solutions to defense and security problems has been slow. With persistent personnel reliability issues, security concerns remain, and international efforts to provide Russia with nuclear security en-hancements assistance have met with limited progress.

Russia currently possesses an arsenal of 18,000 to 20,000 nuclear warheads. Within the Ministry of Defense, the Twelfth Main Directorate (or 12th GUMO, for Glavnoye Upravleniye Ministerstvo Oborony) of the General Staff is in charge of ensur-ing the safety, security, accountability, and function-ality of the military's nuclear munitions. The 12th GUMO issues regulations governing the security and accountability of all Russian warheads and manages those functions for all nondeployed war-heads. For deployed warheads, 6th Directorates within each military service—Navy, Air Force, and Strategic Rocket Forces—are in charge of security functions and coordination with the 12th GUMO.

Few of Russia's nuclear warheads are mated to delivery systems (intercontinental ballistic missiles, submarine-launched ballistic missiles, air-launched cruise missiles, and gravity bombs). From a prolifer-ation perspective, operationally deployed warheads are the most secure. Deployed weapons are subject to constant physical and electronic scrutiny, are kept within militarily secured perimeters, and are the most difficult to remove clandestinely and without substantial equipment and personnel.

The majority of Russia's nuclear warheads are not deployed. These warheads are either in long-term central storage facilities, in short-term storage facilities at or near deployment bases, at assembly or disassembly plants, or in transit between these sites. Perhaps the most significant security enhancement Russia has undertaken recently was to reduce the number of storage depots from more than 500 in the late 1980s to fewer than 100 by the late 1990s. Each facility may contain one or several bunkers of various sizes and store from a few spares to several hundred warheads. All facilities are secured through physical protection, electronic measures, and guard forces. An outer perimeter provides the first physical barrier to a facility. Each bunker is then individually secured with several layers of sensored and nonsensored fencing plus a comprehensive suite of equipment that may include command and control systems; closed-circuit television; interior and exterior intrusion detection systems; rapidly deployable sensor systems; fire and safety systems; access control; vehicle and personnel barriers and access delay systems; and hazardous or prohibited material detection systems. The Ministry of Defense assigns the responsibility of each warhead to one officer, and warheads may only be accessed by a minimum of three officers (enlisted personnel are not permitted to access the warheads). On-site guard forces are supplemented by proximate response teams.

Russia does not transport its nuclear warheads by air. Rather, it uses special trucks for local movements and the railways for long-distance transports. In special cases, for example in 2000 when Russia transferred warheads to Kaliningrad, Russia may use surface ships to move warheads over sea routes. Prior to transport, warheads are wrapped in armored blankets and placed in special containers. These supercontainers provide thermal and ballistic protection as well as an additional measure of security owing to their size and weight. Transportation routes are classified and managed by the Ministry of Railways, and each train is accompanied by a guard force contingent.

—*Charles L. Thornton*

See also: Russian Nuclear Forces and Doctrine

Reference

Sergeev, Igor, ed., *Entsiklopediia XXI vek. Tom 1: Strategicheskie iadernye sily. / Russia's Arms and Technologies: The XXI Century Encyclopaedia*, vol. 1: *Strategic Nuclear Forces* (Moscow: Oruzhie i tekhnologii, 2000).

NUCLEAR WEAPONS EFFECTS

The principal effects of nuclear weapons are thermal radiation, blast, nuclear radiation, and electromagnetic pulse (EMP). The severity of these effects depends on the yield (size) of the weapon (expressed in kilotons or megatons), the design of the weapon, and the way it is employed. Fifty percent of the energy from a low-altitude atmospheric detonation of a moderate-sized nuclear weapon is in the form of blast, and 35 percent is in the form of thermal radiation. Radiation accounts for 15 percent of the destructive force from this type of explosion. Five percent of this radiation takes the form of initial radiation (neutrons and gamma rays), which is emitted within the first minute after detonation, and 10 percent is in the form of residual nuclear radiation, which is primarily fallout. EMP does not come directly from the detonation itself but is a secondary effect created by the interaction of nuclear radiation with the Earth's atmosphere.

Technical Details

Two ounces of uranium 235 (U-235), fully fissioned, will yield the equivalent explosive power of 2 million pounds of trinitrotoluene (TNT) high explosive. Because of these large equivalent values, nuclear weapon yields are expressed in terms of kilotons and megatons. One kiloton is the energy equivalent of 1,000 tons of TNT, and 1 megaton is the energy equivalent of 1 million tons of TNT (*see* Kiloton; Megaton).

The altitude at which the nuclear weapon is detonated influences the relative effects of blast, thermal radiation, nuclear radiation, and EMP. Altitude refers not only to the height of the burst, but also to whether the fireball from the burst comes in contact with the Earth's surface. The term "fireball" refers to the luminous sphere of hot gases that forms a few millionths of a second after the detonation of a nuclear weapon and immediately starts expanding and cooling. Nuclear explosions are thus classified as high-altitude bursts, airbursts, surface bursts, and subsurface bursts. See Table N-1.

A high-altitude burst occurs when a weapon is detonated at an altitude greater than 30 kilometers.

Table N-1: Summary of Nuclear Weapon Effects

Effect	Percentage of Nuclear Burst Energy	Products
Thermal radiation	35%	Heat, fire, burns
Blast	50%	Shock wave
Residual radiation	10%	Fallout, neutron-induced gamma activity
Initial radiation	5%	Casualties
Electromagnetic pulse (EMP)	0%	No known biological effects; extensive damage to electronics

Source: Joint Chiefs of Staff WMD Handbook.

This type of detonation produces a very large fireball that expands rapidly. At this altitude, EMP will be the dominant nuclear weapons effect.

An airburst occurs when a nuclear weapon is exploded in the atmosphere at an altitude of less than 30 kilometers. The fireball produced by the detonation does not contact the surface of the Earth. Although initial radiation will be significant, the residual radiation (fallout) hazard is minimal. Burns to exposed skin and eye injuries can occur. Fission products will be dispersed over a large area, and neutron-induced radiation will concentrate around ground zero (see Ground Zero; Neutrons). EMP will cause major damage to electronic systems.

A surface burst occurs when the weapon is detonated on or slightly above the surface so that the fireball actually contacts the Earth. The area affected by the blast, thermal radiation, and initial nuclear radiation will be less extensive than for an airburst. Destruction is concentrated at ground zero. In contrast to an airburst, a ground burst produces an extreme amount of fallout that extends well beyond the area affected by blast and thermal radiation.

A subsurface burst occurs beneath land or water. This type of detonation might occur in a subway, in the basement of a building, or under water in a harbor or port. This type of detonation generally produces a large crater. If the burst does not penetrate the surface, the only hazard will be from ground or water shock. If the blast penetrates the surface, effects will be present, but less than for a surface burst of similar yield. Local fallout will be heavy.

A low-order nuclear reaction that creates only a minor explosion but releases a burst of radiation is called a fizzle. A weapon designed improperly or physically damaged may, when triggered, begin producing a chain reaction. But as the nuclear events begin to occur to sustain that chain reaction, improper physical positioning introduces inappropriate elements into the fission process. For instance, a moderator used to reflect neutrons back into the core may itself have been forcefully injected into the core by a physical event (such as the bomb hitting the ground). This stops the reaction before it ever develops into a sustained chain reaction. Misshaped cores, misdirected compression explosions, and many other events cause the reaction to fizzle out. When this occurs, many of the effects usually associated with a nuclear detonation fail to materialize.

Thermal Radiation
Thermal radiation is the heat and light produced by the nuclear explosion. Thermal radiation travels in a straight line at the speed of light, can be easily absorbed or attenuated, and can be scattered or reflected. When a nuclear weapon is detonated, burns from the thermal radiation are the most common injury among casualties from the blast. The thermal radiation emitted by a nuclear detonation causes burns in two ways: by the direct effect on exposed body surfaces (flash burns), and from the fires started by the flash (flame burns). The relative importance of these two processes will depend on the environment. If a nuclear detonation occurs in inflammable surroundings, indirect flame burns could outnumber all other types of injury. Because of the complexity of burn treatment and the increased logistical requirements associated with the management of burns, they constitute a difficult problem for medical personnel.

Since the thermal pulse is direct infrared energy, flash burn patterns on the body will be determined by spatial relationships and clothing pattern absorption. Exposed skin will be burned on the side facing the explosion. Persons shaded from the direct light of the blast are protected. Light colors will reflect the infrared, while dark portions of clothing will absorb it and cause pattern burns. Records from the Hiroshima and Nagasaki bombings indicate that, in some cases, dark-colored clothing actually bursts into flames. At temperatures below those required to ignite clothing, it is still possible to transfer sufficient thermal energy through clothing to the skin to produce flash burns; however, clothing significantly reduces the risk of flash burns.

Flame burns result from exposure to fires caused by thermal radiation igniting surrounding structures, vehicles, and a person's clothing. Firestorm and secondary fires will cause flame burns, but they will be aggravated by closed-space fire injuries. Patients with toxic gas injury from burning plastics and other material, superheated air inhalation burns, steam burns from ruptured pipes, and all other similar injuries will require treatment. Complications arise in the treatment of skin burns created, in part, from the melting of synthetic fibers.

Since the majority of people caught in a nuclear environment will not be wearing protective goggles, eye injuries will occur. Factors that determine the extent of eye injury include pupil dilation, spectral transmission through the ocular media; spectral absorption by the retina and choroid; and length of time of exposure. Optical equipment such as binoculars will increase the likelihood of damage. Other eye injuries include flash blindness and retinal burns.

Blast

The majority of material damage caused by a nuclear explosion is due to the blast wave that accompanies the explosion. The blast wave is a brief and rapid movement of air vapor away from the fireball. It is characterized by sharp pressure increases and winds. At a fraction of a second after a nuclear explosion, a high-pressure wave develops and moves outward from the fireball. This is the blast wave. The front of the blast wave, called the shock wave, travels rapidly away from the fireball and behaves much like a moving wall of highly compressed air. When the blast wave strikes the surface of the ground, it is reflected back, similar to a sound wave producing an echo. This reflected blast wave, like the original (or direct) wave, is also capable of causing material damage. The reflected wave eventually catches up with and reinforces the direct wave.

A phenomenon called the "mach stem" may accompany an airburst. The mach stem is formed as a result of the reflected wave traveling more rapidly within the heated medium of the incident wave. Pressures and wind velocity from the mach stem are considerably higher than from the primary shock wave alone. The blast wave initially travels at

speeds seven to eight times that of sound, but its strength diminishes rapidly until the wave approaches the speed of sound. The maximum pressure will occur the moment the blast wave arrives at a given location.

Pressure will begin to drop off immediately after the initial blast pulse passes. If the reflected wave has not caught the incident wave at a particular location, two pressure increases will be experienced— the first from the incident wave, and the second from the reflected wave. At a certain distance from ground zero, a negative phase of the blast wave will develop. Winds in the negative phase are lower than in the positive phase. The negative phase is caused by air rushing in to replace the rising fireball and the cooling of the heated air around ground zero. As this gas cools, the pressure decreases and can drop up to 4 pounds per square inch below normal atmospheric pressure. The negative phase is not considered a significant damaging effect. The pressure resulting from winds (mass airflow) directly behind the shock front is called "dynamic pressure." These winds affect damage to drag targets, that is, targets dragged along, set into a rolling motion, or torn apart by wind.

The direct blast wave overpressure force is measured in terms of atmospheres of overpressure. When this blast wave acts directly upon the human body, rapid compression and decompression result in transmission of pressure waves through the tissues. These waves can be quite severe and will result in damage primarily at junctions between tissues of different densities (bone and muscle) or at the interface between tissue and air spaces (lung tissue and the gastrointestinal system). Perforation of the eardrums will be a common blast injury. The range of overpressures causing deaths can vary greatly. It is important to note that the human body is remarkably resistant to direct blast overpressure, particularly when compared to rigid structures such as buildings.

The indirect blast wind drag force is measured in the velocities of the winds created by the detonation. These winds vary with distance from the point of detonation, yield of the weapon, and altitude of the burst. The winds are of relatively short duration but are extremely severe and may reach speeds of several hundred miles per hour. Indirect blast injuries will result when individuals are thrown against immobile objects and impaled by flying debris. Broken bones and head injuries will be commonplace. The distance from the point of detonation at which severe indirect injury will occur is considerably greater than that for serious direct blast injuries (see Yield).

Nuclear Radiation

All nuclear detonations will create neutron, gamma, beta, and alpha radiation. This radiation is categorized as either initial radiation or residual radiation. Neutron and gamma radiation are present in the initial burst, while alpha, beta, and gamma rays make up the residual radiation.

Approximately 5 percent of the energy released in a nuclear airburst is transmitted in the form of initial neutron and gamma radiation. The neutrons result almost exclusively from the energy produced by fission and fusion reactions. Initial gamma radiation is produced by these reactions as well as from the decay of short-lived fission products. The intensity of the initial nuclear radiation decreases rapidly with distance from the point of burst. The character of the radiation received at a given location also varies with distance from the explosion. Near the point of the explosion, the neutron intensity is greater than the gamma intensity, but it reduces quickly with distance. The range for significant levels of initial radiation does not increase markedly with weapon yield. Therefore, the initial radiation becomes less of a hazard with increasing yield, as individuals close enough to be significantly irradiated are killed by the blast and thermal effects.

Residual radiation from a nuclear explosion is primarily radioactive fallout. In a surface burst, large amounts of earth or water will be vaporized by the heat of the fireball and drawn up into the radioactive cloud, especially if the explosive yield exceeds 10 kilotons. This material becomes radioactive and is dispersed by the wind. It will eventually settle to Earth as fallout. The larger particles will settle as local fallout within twenty-four hours. Severe local fallout contamination can extend far beyond the blast and thermal effects, particularly in the case of high-yield surface detonations (see Fallout; Radiation).

Electromagnetic Pulse

EMP does not result directly from the detonation itself but is a secondary effect created by the interaction of specific nuclear radiation with the Earth's atmosphere. It is essentially a very strong radio signal of short duration. If the burst point of the nuclear explosion is greater than 30 kilometers in altitude, the EMP will cover a very large area (thousands of square kilometers). The effects of EMP from a surface or low-altitude nuclear burst will extend about as far as the other weapon effects. EMP can produce a current in any electrical conductor and temporarily disrupt or damage all electrical components not properly protected. EMP must be taken into consideration in any scenario involving the threat of nuclear weapons. There are no known biological effects of EMP; however, indirect effects may result from the failure of critical medical or transportation equipment.

Radioactive Contamination Hazards

Radioactive material released into an area can pose both internal and external contamination hazards to people living there. External hazards are generally associated with skin contamination and increased probabilities of internal contamination. Internal contamination hazards are associated with the exposure of internal organs to radioactive material that has been taken into the body via inhalation, ingestion, or absorption through the skin or a wound.

Significant amounts of radioactive material will be deposited on ground surfaces as well as on people by nuclear weapons and radiological dispersal devices (RDDs). Destruction of nuclear reactors, nuclear accidents, or the improper disposal of radiological waste also can contaminate the environment. Lethal doses of external radiation can occur if protective measures are not taken.

Fallout may be deposited onto clothing and/or skin and may enter the body. In a nuclear reactor accident, radionuclides may enter the body through wounds or by the inhalation of radioactive gases or particulate matter. Radioactive material that falls onto food or into the water supply could be ingested. A source of exposure is radioactive material that has entered the food chain, such as occurred in Europe following the Chernobyl accident (see Chernobyl). Other sources of internal contamination are by medical mistake or the ingestion of radioactive materials from an RDD.

Shielding

Shielding is any material or obstruction that absorbs or attenuates radiation, thereby reducing radiation

Figure N-3: Shielding for Various Types of Radiation

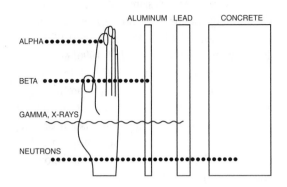

Joint Chiefs of Staff (JCS) J-3 Weapons of Mass
    Destruction (WMD) Handbook (Washington, DC:
    Government Printing Office, 2001).
Levi, Michael, Federation of American Scientists (FAS)
    Strategic Security Project, 2002.
U.S. Army, The Effects of Nuclear Weapons, Pamphlet 50-
    3 (Washington, DC: Headquarters, Department of
    the Army, March 1977).
U.S. Army, Treatment of Nuclear and Radiological
    Casualties, Field Manual 4-02.283 (Washington, DC:
    Headquarters, Department of the Army, 23 January
    1989).

exposure. Alpha radiation has heavily charged particles with a very low airborne range. Unbroken skin
stops these particles. Light clothing and gloves will
also provide protection. Problems arise when the
particles enter the body through a break in the skin,
via contaminated food, or through breathing.

Although airborne beta particles can travel significant distances, solid materials stop them. A sheet
of aluminum will stop beta emissions. Beta emitters
present two potential external radiation hazards: the
beta particles themselves, and the X-rays they can
produce when they strike certain materials, such as
lead. Although beta particles can travel significant
distances in air, materials such as aluminum, plastic,
or glass can provide appropriate shielding. Because
the lens of the eye is radiosensitive, eye protection
such as goggles or a protective mask is recommended if exposure to beta particles is likely.

Gamma radiation is highly penetrable and could
present a hazard. Protection from gamma radiation
depends on the type, density, and thickness of the
shielding. As the thickness of the shielding increases,
the gamma radiation will decrease. Lead, tungsten,
concrete, and steel can be used as shielding from
gamma emissions (see Figure N-3).

—Jeffrey A. Adams

See also: Fission Weapons; Hydrogen Bomb; Neutron
    Bomb (Enhanced Radiation Weapon); Nuclear
    Winter; Thermonuclear Bomb; Weapons of Mass
    Destruction

References
Adams, Jeffrey A., and Stephen Marquette, First
    Responders Guide to Weapons of Mass Destruction
    (Alexandria, VA: American Society for Industrial
    Security, 2002).

NUCLEAR WEAPONS
FREE ZONES (NWFZS)

Nuclear weapons free zones (NWFZs), which mandate the complete prohibition of nuclear weapons
within a distinct geographic area, are steps toward a
nuclear weapons–free world. NWFZs are an instrument of both nonproliferation and disarmament,
causing states to abandon their nuclear weapons
programs. In the case of Argentina and Brazil, this
occurred before nuclear weapons development had
progressed to the point of having a nuclear weapons
capability. In the case of South Africa, the emergence of an NWFZ helped a state dismantle the nuclear weapons it possessed.

There are six NWFZs in the world today, and two
more zones are in the process of forming. Most of
the NWFZs have been created by regional treaties.
Mongolia (2000) and Austria (1999), however, declared their nuclear weapons–free status through
domestic laws, thus creating single-state zones. New
Zealand, though a member of the South Pacific
NWFZ, still enacted strong domestic legislation creating its own NWFZ in 1987. The constitution of
the Philippines also forbids the placement of nuclear weapons on its territory.

The regional NWFZ treaties share several provisions. All of the treaties prohibit the member states
from manufacturing, producing, possessing, testing,
acquiring, receiving, and deploying nuclear
weapons. They also include provisions for security
assurances from nuclear weapons states to treaty
members.

History and Background

The first regional treaty banning nuclear weapons
from a region was the Antarctic Treaty, which
opened for signature on December 1, 1959, and en-

tered into force on June 23, 1961. The treaty forms the Antarctic Treaty Area, which covers everything south of the latitude 60°S. The treaty was meant to ensure that "Antarctica shall continue to be used exclusively for peaceful purposes and shall not become the scene or object of international discord." The Treaty for the Prohibition of Nuclear Weapons in Latin America (and the Caribbean) is also known as the Tlatelolco Treaty. Signed on February 14, 1967, and entered into force on April 22, 1968, it calls for the creation of the Agency for the Prohibition of Nuclear Weapons in Latin America and the Caribbean (OPANAL) in Mexico City, Mexico. The words "and the Caribbean" were added to the title of the treaty in July 1990. Cuba became the final Latin American state to ratify the treaty on October 23, 2002.

The South Pacific Nuclear Free Zone Treaty, also is known as the Treaty of Rarotonga, was signed on August 6, 1985, and entered into force on December 11, 1986. Thirteen states are full members to this treaty: Australia, Cook Islands, Fiji, Kiribati, Nauru, New Zealand, Niue, Papua New Guinea, Samoa, Solomon Islands, Tonga, Tuvalu, and Vanuatu. The five nuclear weapons states (China, France, the Russian Federation, the United Kingdom, and the United States) are all adhering to the treaty's protocols.

Unlike the Tlatelolco Treaty, the Treaty of Rarotonga bans nuclear explosions and explosive devices for peaceful purposes from the territory covered by the treaty and bans the dumping of nuclear waste in the regional seas. Furthermore, the Treaty of Rarotonga established that the director of the South Pacific Bureau for Economic Co-operation would be responsible for the implementation of the treaty, monitoring compliance and issuing reports.

The Treaty on the Southeast Asia Nuclear Weapon Free Zone, also known as the Bangkok Treaty, was signed on December 15, 1995, and entered into force on March 28, 1997. This NWFZ covers Brunei, Darussalam, Cambodia, Indonesia, Laos, Malaysia, Myanmar, Philippines, Singapore, Thailand, and Vietnam. It also includes all of their continental shelves and maritime exclusive economic zones. The treaty calls for the organization of a commission for the Southeast Asia Nuclear Weapon Free Zone that may meet in conjunction with the Association of Southeast Asian Nations (ASEAN) Ministerial Meeting.

The Treaty for the Nuclear Weapons Free Zone in Africa is known as the Pelindaba Treaty. It covers the continent of Africa, island states members of the Organization of African Unity (OAU), and all islands considered by the OAU to be part of Africa. The treaty was signed on April 11, 1996. Along with the provisions similar to those set forth in other regional treaties, the Pelindaba Treaty prohibits any armed attack on nuclear installations. It calls for the Organization of the African Commission on Nuclear Energy as the mechanism for compliance. The members to the treaty report to the commission and engage in exchanges of information.

At the same time as the signing of the Pelindaba Treaty, Egypt authored the "Cairo Declaration" to state that the signing of the Pelindaba Treaty was a positive step for nonproliferation and that it was "a highly significant contribution to the enhancement of international peace and security." Furthermore, acting within the scope of Egypt's typical role at nonproliferation discussions, it was emphasized in the declaration that "the establishment of nuclear-weapons-free-zones, especially in regions of tension, such as the Middle East, on the basis of arrangements freely arrived at among the states of the regions concerned, enhances global and regional peace and security."

Current Status

Only one of the regional treaties has been ratified by every country within its zone, and a number of protocols to the treaties need to be joined by the nuclear weapons states. There is no Middle East Nuclear Weapons Free Zone (MENWFZ), although it was an initiative pushed by Egypt that has yet to come to fruition. The plans for a Central Asian Nuclear Weapons Free Zone (CANWFZ), which will include Kazakhstan, Kyrgyzstan, Tajikistan, Turkmenistan, and Uzbekistan, started with the Almaty Declaration of February 28, 1997. Many drafts of a CANWFZ accord have circulated within the United Nations, and on September 27, 2002, a UN-sponsored Expert Group, which had contributed to the formulation of a treaty text, concluded its negotiations on the text. On October 8, 2002, the UN Department for Disarmament Affairs had its first consultative meeting to gain the agreement of the permanent members on the Security Council to extend the negative security assurances that are part of the protocol that is annexed to the treaty.

—*Kimberly L. Kosteff*

See also: Antinuclear Movement; Arms Control;
    Negative Security Assurances; Proliferation; Rapacki
    Plan
References
"Nuclear Weapon Free Zones," available at http://www.
    nuclearfiles.org/redocuments/treaties-nwfz.html.
"Nuclear Weapon-Free Zones at a Glance," Arms
    Control Association, available at http://www.
    armscontrol.org/factsheets/nwfz.asp.
Treaty of Pelindaba text, available at http://www.
    nuclearfiles.org/redocuments/1996/
    960411-pelindaba2.html.

NUCLEAR WEAPONS STATES

The Nuclear Nonproliferation Treaty (NPT) of 1968
defined a nuclear weapons state (NWS) as one that
had manufactured and exploded a nuclear weapon
or other nuclear device by January 1, 1967. This limited the list of nuclear weapons states to five countries: the United States, the Soviet Union (now Russia), France, the United Kingdom, and China.

Although these five states are the only legally recognized nuclear weapons states, there are certainly
more states with nuclear weapons. In fact, India,
Pakistan, and Israel, the only three major countries
that remain outside of the NPT, are also de facto nuclear weapons states.

Nuclear weapons states have many obligations
that are defined by international law. The nuclear
weapons states that signed the NPT agree not to
transfer nuclear weapons or control over them to
any non–nuclear weapons state or to assist non–nuclear weapons states in the manufacturing of nuclear weapons. Additionally, nuclear weapons states
are obligated to accept international safeguard systems implemented and monitored by the International Atomic Energy Agency (IAEA) for all of their
peaceful nuclear programs. As of 2001, IAEA safeguard agreements are in place with 142 states. Finally, the five nuclear weapons states agreed to move
toward general nuclear disarmament.

—Abe Denmark

See also: Disarmament; International Atomic Energy
    Agency; Negative Security Assurances;
    Nonproliferation; Nuclear Nonproliferation Treaty;
    Proliferation; Strategic Forces; Threshold States
References
Bunn, George, "Nuclear Tests Violate International
    Norm," Arms Control Today, May 1998, available at
    http://www.armscontrol.org/act/1998_05/
    bnmy98.asp.
Stein, Eric, "Legal Restraints in Modern Arms Control
    Agreements," American Journal of International Law,
    vol. 66, no. 2, April 1972, pp. 255–289.
U.S. Department of State, "The Treaty on the Non-
    Proliferation of Nuclear Weapons: A Global Success,"
    20 January 2001, available at http://www.state.gov/
    t/np/rls/fs/2001/3055.htm.

NUCLEAR WINTER

"Nuclear winter" is a term referring to the environmental disaster that some scientists believe would
occur following a full-scale nuclear war. According
to the nuclear winter theory, the cumulative effects
of extreme heat, blast, radiation, and dust thrown
into the air in such an exchange would destroy the
ozone layer and block the sunlight needed to warm
the Earth. The effect would be global and perhaps
result in the extinction of most forms of life on
Earth.

Several studies on the possibility of nuclear winter were conducted in the 1970s, the most famous
being the 1983 TTAPS (Turco, Toon, Ackerman,
Pollack, and Sagan) study. This particular study
took into account various factors such as forest fires,
burning fossil fuels, and intense smoke covering the
Earth for periods lasting for weeks or months. The
authors of the study further postulated that a period
of darkness would exist that could plunge average
temperatures by as much as 40 degrees Fahrenheit
(thus, the term "nuclear winter"). Many scientists
disputed the idea of a nuclear winter, saying that it
did not follow normal meteorological processes and
that the smoke would not stay aloft for so great a
time. In 1990, a more detailed study (TTAPS 1990)
was conducted with extensive meteorological modeling. Although the new study revealed that between
10 and 25 percent of the ejected soil would fall to the
ground by immediate precipitation (black rain,
such as was seen at Hiroshima), it also showed that
the smoke would spread through different hemispheres, reducing temperatures within one to two
weeks. The long-term effects of a nuclear winter
could last from one to two years and kill an estimated 1 to 2 billion people.

Since the fall of the Soviet Union and the slashing of strategic arsenals, nuclear winter studies
have become passé. Almost all of them were based
upon a nuclear exchange in the 5,000-megaton

range, which now seems both politically implausible and beyond the deployed nuclear capability of Russia and the United States. It is now believed by many that nuclear exchanges in the twenty-first century would involve considerably less explosive power and relatively small nuclear weapons that would be targeted with great precision—perhaps fewer than ten weapons of 100 kilotons or smaller. Although these would have devastating local results, they would have no significant impact on global weather patterns. One area where the TTAP studies have made a lasting useful impact was in studying the effects of an asteroid impact on Earth. The impact of large asteroid on Earth would not generate residual radiation, but the widespread fires and dust ejected into the atmosphere could easily exceed the nuclear winter effect created by a large-scale nuclear exchange.

—*Zach Becker*

References

Harwell, Mark, *Nuclear Winter: The Human and Environmental Consequences of Nuclear War* (New York: Springer Verlag, 1986).

Sagan, Carl, and Richard Turco, *A Path Where No Man Thought: Nuclear Winter and the End of the Arms Race* (New York: Random House, 1990).

Sederberg, Peter, *Nuclear Winter, Deterrence, and the Prevention of Nuclear War* (Westport, CT: Praeger, 1986).

Turco, R. P., O. B. Toon, T. P. Ackerman, J. B. Pollack, and C. Sagan, "Climate and Smoke: An Appraisal of Nuclear Winter," *Science*, vol. 247, 1990, pp. 166–176.

———, "Global Atmospheric Consequences of Nuclear War," *Science*, vol. 222, 1983, pp.12–83.

NUNN-LUGAR COOPERATIVE THREAT REDUCTION ACT

See Cooperative Threat Reduction (The Nunn-Lugar Program)

OAK RIDGE NATIONAL LABORATORY

Oak Ridge National Laboratory was established in eastern Tennessee in 1942 to serve as one of the development sites for the Manhattan Project. The lab's primary wartime mission was the production of uranium 235 for use in atomic weapons. It was home to the first graphite reactor, which was used as a model for the larger production reactors built at Hanford, Washington, to create plutonium. Today, the Oak Ridge National Laboratory has developed into a multipurpose organization (*see* Hanford, Washington; Manhattan Project; Plutonium).

Originally a secured area with a wartime population of 75,000 people, by 1946 Oak Ridge had become the world's foremost source for radioisotopes for medicine, agriculture, and industry. After the war, the area was privatized, and a town was developed and incorporated in 1959.

Uranium fission was discovered by two German scientists in 1939. By 1942, the U.S. War Department had launched the Manhattan Project to create the nuclear bomb under the scientific leadership of Robert Oppenheimer and Enrico Fermi. To create a nuclear weapon, an adequate supply of fissile material had to be manufactured. Oak Ridge National Laboratory was created to pioneer methods of producing highly enriched uranium (HEU) and producing and separating plutonium, a product of uranium neutrons freed by the fission chain reaction and captured by uranium atoms. In addition to perfecting plutonium reprocessing, the Oak Ridge lab created enough highly enriched uranium to power the "Little Boy" atomic bomb that was dropped on Hiroshima on August 6, 1945. The HEU was produced at K-25, a gaseous-diffusion plant at Oak Ridge that was closed in 1985. Another plant, Y-12, continues to do weapons- and nonweapons-related work, including recycling of nonfissile components of decommissioned warheads (*see* Highly Enriched Uranium; Little Boy; Uranium).

The Oak Ridge National Laboratory currently covers 58 square miles and has a staff of 3,800, in-

cluding 1,500 scientists and engineers. One current research focus of the laboratory is the exploration of sources of clean energy. Radioactive pharmaceuticals, electronic instrumentation, and basic science are also current research areas, and the laboratory is a leading center for work on neutron science, energy, high-performance computing, complex biological systems, and advanced materials.

—*Frannie Edwards and Jeffrey A. Larsen*

References

Cochran, Thomas B., William M. Arkin, Robert S. Norris, and Milton M. Hoenig, *Nuclear Weapons Databook*, vol. 3: *U.S. Nuclear Warhead Facility Profiles* (Cambridge, MA: Ballinger, 1987), pp. 65–75.

Oak Ridge National Laboratory website, http://www.ornl.gov.

ON THE BEACH

On the Beach was an antiwar novel by Nevil Shute, published in 1957, which had a dark influence on the early nuclear age. It was later made into an acclaimed movie. It tells the story of the survivors of an accidental global nuclear war that has killed everyone in the Northern Hemisphere. Shute depicts a world in which even Third World countries possess nuclear weapons, and in the story it is a nuclear exchange between Third World countries that eventually draws the world's superpowers, the United States and the Soviet Union, into the conflict. The massive nuclear exchange between the superpowers, consisting mainly of fictional hydrogen "cobalt bombs" meant to create massive radioactive fallout, leaves the Northern Hemisphere, where the vast majority of nuclear detonations occurred, devoid of life.

The world's only survivors live in the Southern Hemisphere, and global weather patterns have yet to bring radioactive fallout to this part of the world. The four main characters of the novel are living out their last seven months of life in Falmouth, Australia. This is the length of time the fictional scientists expect that it will take for global winds to bring the fallout to Australia. The reader follows the characters as they live out their last days, coping with the knowledge that their time is limited. One couple, married with a new baby, plants a garden for the following spring even though they will have died by then. Another character has become an alcoholic. The last is a U.S. Navy submarine commander who ended up in Australia after the war and is in a state of denial, refusing to come to grips with the fact that his wife and children in Connecticut are dead. In the end, each must decide for him or herself whether to die a painful death from radiation poisoning or to commit suicide by taking the cyanide caplets that have been provided by authorities.

Shute provides an ironic and anticlimactic vision of the way the world might end in the event of global nuclear war. But his book provides insight into the existential fear of nuclear Armageddon that gripped much of the planet during the Cold War. It is a vision that takes its cue from the T. S. Eliot quote found on the title page of the book: "This is the way the world ends; Not with a bang but a whimper."

The 1959 movie *On the Beach* was directed by Stanley Kramer and starred Gregory Peck, Ava Gardner, Fred Astaire, and Anthony Perkins.

—*Sean Lawson*

Reference

Shute, Nevil, *On the Beach* (New York: Ballantine, 1957).

ONE-POINT DETONATION/
ONE-POINT SAFE

One-point detonation, common in early versions of nuclear weapons, was a design feature of high-explosive systems whereby the detonation was initiated at a single point. It has been replaced with much safer systems today that feature multiple-point initiation. Specifications for U.S. nuclear weapons now require that a one-point detonation of the high-explosive system will have less than a one in a million chance of producing 4 pounds equivalent yield of trinitrotoluene (TNT), and weapons meeting this requirement are said to be "one-point safe." A nuclear weapon also may be de-

signed to have an inherent one-point detonation self-destruct system. In other words, self-destruct systems have to be as safe as the primary detonators used to generate a full nuclear yield, making it unlikely that a self-destruct sequence will generate a nuclear yield. Friendly forces may use this self-destruct mechanism to deny the enemy use of a nuclear weapon or to prevent sabotage of the weapon.

The one-point safe design of U.S. nuclear weapons was tested in an accident on January 17, 1966, when a B-52 bomber collided with an air-refueling aircraft (a KC-135) over Palomares, Spain. The subsequent crash resulted in the one-point detonation of two nuclear weapons. Even though the one-point detonation of one of the weapons created a crater that was 20 feet in diameter, and approximately 1,400 tons of contaminated soil had to be removed from the area, there was no nuclear yield from either weapon.

By current Department of Energy standards, any newly designed nuclear weapon must be one-point safe. Given the moratorium on testing nuclear weapons, one-point detonation-related tests will have to be done using evolving three-dimensional computational capabilities.

—*Don Gillich*

See also: Broken Arrow; Surety

References

"Arms Control Today: The Technology of Nuclear Weapons," Arms Control Association, November/December 1997, http://www.armscontrol.org/act/1997_11-12/garwinbx.asp.

Cockburn, Andrew and Leslie Cockburn, *One Point Safe* (New York: Anchor, 1997).

Sagan, Scott D., *The Limits of Safety: Organizations, Accidents, and Nuclear Weapons* (Princeton, NJ: Princeton University Press, 1993).

"Special Weapons Primer: Introduction," Federation of American Scientists, available at http://www.fas.org/nuke/intro/nuke/intro.htm.

ON-SITE INSPECTION AGENCY (OSIA)

The On-Site Inspection Agency (OSIA) is a U.S. Department of Defense organization under the control of the Defense Threat Reduction Agency. This joint-service agency is responsible for the verification of international nuclear and conventional arms control treaties and confidence-building agreements. OSIA accomplishes its mission by conducting inspections abroad, escorting foreign officials as they inspect U.S. facilities, and monitoring the truthfulness of foreign treaty-related assertions. The agency is in constant contact with international organizations responsible for the enforcement of nuclear arms reduction and control. OSIA personnel also coordinate closely with foreign counterparts to achieve treaty objectives.

The origins of the On-Site Inspection Agency can be traced to the Intermediate-Range Nuclear Forces (INF) Treaty of 1987, in which the United States and the Soviet Union agreed to destroy all intermediate-range nuclear missiles. One of the provisions of the treaty was for both parties to be able to verify the destruction of these weapons by the other side. OSIA was established on January 26, 1988, to conduct INF Treaty inspections. On February 1, 1988, U.S. Army Brigadier General Roland Lajoie became the first director of OSIA, with a staff of forty military and civilian personnel (*see* Intermediate-Range Nuclear Forces Treaty).

In preparation for an expanded role for OSIA pertaining to the Conventional Forces in Europe (CFE) Treaty, OSIA hired additional personnel. There were more than 600 OSIA staff members by 1992. The CFE Treaty was provisionally entered into force on July 17, 1992, and two days later, OSIA conducted its first baseline inspection in Russia.

In addition to carrying out INF and CFE treaty verification and monitoring provisions, OSIA has participated in a myriad of other missions. It has conducted monitoring for the Threshold Test Ban Treaty (1963); supported inspections for the United Nations Special Commission on Iraq (1991); assisted Operation Provide Hope, a humanitarian mission, in distributing food and medicines to former Soviet Union states (1992); and monitored compliance with the 1992 Open Skies Treaty and the Strategic Arms Reduction Treaties (START I and START II, 1991 and 1993). OSIA also provided support for peace efforts in Bosnia (*see* Open Skies Treaty; Strategic Arms Reduction Treaty; Strategic Arms Reduction Treaty; Threshold Test Ban Treaty).

OSIA is headquartered at Fort Belvoir, Virginia. Approximately 850 men and women from all four services as well as the Federal Civil Service are assigned to it, including inspectors, escorts, and linguists. The agency also manages the Defense Treaty Inspection Readiness Program (DTIRP), an outreach and educational program to prepare Department of Defense and U.S. contractor facilities for foreign inspections. OSIA has been assigned new

duties in supporting operations in the global war on terrorism.

The On-Site Inspection Agency will continue to play an important role in the nation's security in the future. In addition to conducting managed access inspections of sensitive facilities in compliance with existing treaty verification regimes, it will likely be assigned new duties as new arms control treaties and agreements come into existence.

—Don Gillich

See also: Defense Threat Reduction Agency; Department of Defense; Verification

References

Defense Threat Reduction Agency website, http://www.dtra.mil/os/os_index.html.

OPEN SKIES TREATY

President Dwight D. Eisenhower first proposed a bilateral Open Skies initiative to the Soviet Union in 1955 but no formal agreement resulted for over thirty years. In 1989, President George H. W. Bush proposed a multilateral Open Skies agreement that was accepted by the nations of Europe. The treaty was designed to enhance military openness and transparency by providing each state party with the right to overfly the territory of any other signatories using an unarmed observation aircraft. The members of the North Atlantic Treaty Organization (NATO) and the former Warsaw Pact signed the treaty in Helsinki on March 24, 1992. The treaty was scheduled to enter into force sixty days after the last state deposited its instruments of ratification. It further allowed any state to accede to the agreement following entry into force of the treaty.

Following the demise of the Soviet Union, the governments of the Russian Federation, Belarus, Georgia, and Ukraine acknowledged their support for the agreement and submitted it for ratification by their respective parliaments. The United States ratified Open Skies in 1993, but the treaty languished in parliamentary committees in Belarus and Russia. These last two signatories finally ratified it in November 2001. The treaty entered into force on January 1, 2002. There are currently twenty-nine states parties to the treaty.

Open Skies is of unlimited duration, and all signatories must accept the overflights allowed under the treaty. The agreement covers the national territory of all signatories including territorial waters and islands. No portion may be excluded. The treaty has four primary objectives. First, it seeks to promote greater openness and transparency of military activities. Second, the treaty is designed to improve the monitoring of current and future arms control arrangements. Third, Open Skies is intended to strengthen the capacity of crisis prevention and crisis management. Finally, it provides aerial observation based on equity and effectiveness for all signatories.

Each participating state has the right to conduct, and the obligation to receive, flights over its territory based on an established quota. For example, the United States has a quota of forty-two overflights per year; however, during the initial four calendar years only thirty-one are permitted in any single year. Any signatory to the treaty may receive the results from an overflight. States are required to provide seventy-two hours' notice prior to commencing an overflight.

Open Skies observation aircraft are authorized to carry still and video cameras, infrared scanning devices, and side-looking radars. Since signing the agreement, many countries have developed Open Skies observation aircraft in accordance with treaty limitations. Numerous "practice flights" over the territory of participating states also have been conducted to insure all parties were fully prepared for implementation. By 2003, the United States had conducted more than ninety training flights over the territory of other nations and hosted thirty flights over U.S. territory.

—*Jeffrey D. McCausland*

Reference

Williams, Allen B., "Treaty on Open Skies," briefing prepared by Science Applications International Corporation, 10 September 1992.

ORGANIZATION FOR SECURITY AND COOPERATION IN EUROPE (OSCE)

See Conference on Security and Cooperation in Europe (CSCE)

OUTER SPACE TREATY

The Outer Space Treaty of 1967 is the most important space-related arms control agreement to date. It has been described as the Magna Carta for space. The treaty channels human space activity onto peaceful paths and prohibits some types of military deployments. It extends international law into space and establishes the principle that space is to be free for exploration by all and used solely for peaceful purposes. The treaty also bans nuclear weapons and weapons of mass destruction in space. It laid a foundation for every major subsequent international space agreement: the 1968 Rescue and Return Agreement, the 1972 Liability Convention, and the 1975 Registration Convention. The treaty's vision for cooperative, noncommercial exploration and use of space was rooted in the Antarctic Treaty of 1959 and culminated in the (unratified) 1979 Moon Treaty, which emphasized that space is the common heritage of mankind. More than 125 states have signed or acceded to the Outer Space Treaty.

Even before the Soviet launch of Sputnik in 1957, both superpowers and the United Nations had become involved in structuring the legal regime for outer space. In the setting of the Cold War and the space race, some of the earliest space treaty initiatives seemed to be designed more for propaganda purposes than as serious negotiating positions. But by the early 1960s, more serious efforts emerged in the United Nations General Assembly (UNGA) and the Committee on the Peaceful Uses of Outer Space (COPUOS) that led to the adoption of UNGA Resolution 1721 in December 1961. UNGA 1721 was the first significant piece of space arms control and it established several foundational principles. It extended international law to outer space and celestial bodies, established that the exploration and use of space was to be free and open to all states, called for registration of all space launches, and sought cooperative agreements on international communication and meteorological space systems.

The John F. Kennedy administration intensified U.S. space arms control efforts, in part by relaxing verification standards, which helped lead to UNGA 1884 in October 1963 and UNGA 1962 in December 1963. These were the last two major UN space resolutions prior to the Outer Space Treaty, and they contained many of the most important provisions later codified in the treaty. UNGA Resolution 1962 declared that outer space was free for exploration by all and out of bounds to national sovereignty, that space activities were to be carried on for the benefit and in the interest of all humankind in accordance with the UN Charter and international law, and that states had to bear responsibility for all their national space activities, whether carried out by government or nongovernmental agencies. The resolution also stated that nations had to be guided by principles of cooperation and mutual assistance, with "appropriate international consultations" to precede any activity potentially harmful to peaceful uses of space, and that spacecraft were to remain under the jurisdiction of the launching state, with the latter accepting liability for any damage caused to foreign property by accidents. Astronauts, according to the General Assembly, were to be regarded as "envoys of mankind" and rendered every assistance in case of peril.

The Outer Space Treaty was negotiated at the UN during most of 1966 and was open for signature in January 1967. Many provisions of the treaty echo UNGA Resolutions 1884 and 1962. Several sections of the treaty also have direct military relevance. Article II indicates that "outer space, including the moon and other celestial bodies, is not subject to national appropriation by claim of sovereignty, by means of use or occupation, or by any other means." The most specific military prohibitions are found in Article IV:

States Parties to the Treaty undertake not to place in orbit around the Earth any objects carrying nuclear weapons or any other kinds of weapons of mass destruction, install such weapons on celestial bodies, or station such weapons in outer space in any other manner. The moon and other celestial bodies shall be used by all States Parties to the Treaty exclusively for peaceful purposes. The establishment of military bases, installations and fortifications, the testing of any type of weapons and the conduct of military maneuvers on celestial bodies shall be forbidden. The use of military personnel for scientific research or for any other peaceful purpose shall not be prohibited. The use of any equipment or facility necessary for peaceful exploration of the moon and other celestial bodies shall also not be prohibited. (Outer Space Treaty)

Although some analysts emphasize that the treaty only bans activities in which the superpowers had little interest anyway, the treaty certainly marked an important constraint on the development of ambitious military space capabilities during the Cold War. Foreclosing military options reduced incentives to consider space as the high ground in war. Perhaps most important, U.S. support for the unenforceable and nonverifiable prohibitions in the treaty—especially the possibility that nuclear weapons might be placed in space—signaled that U.S. officials viewed the interrelationships between space and national security in broad and holistic ways rather than in strictly military or strategic terms.

—Peter Hays

See also: Arms Control; Weapons of Mass Destruction
References
Christol, Carl Q., Space Law: Past, Present, and Future (Dordrecht, Netherlands: Kluwer, 1991).
Goldman, Nathan C., American Space Law: International and Domestic (San Diego: Univelt, 1996).
Reynolds, Glenn H., and Robert P. Merges, Outer Space: Problems of Law and Policy (Boulder: Westview, 1988).

OVERHEAD SURVEILLANCE

"Overhead surveillance" is a term used to describe a variety of space and aircraft systems that rely on different types of sensors to monitor developments on the ground.

Forward air controllers and unmanned aeries vehicles—small manned and unmanned aircraft that use a variety of sensors to monitor events on the ground—fly at relatively low altitudes and monitor events in limited areas. J-STARS aircraft (Joint Surveillance Target Attack Radar Systems) can search hundreds of miles of terrain, looking for moving tanks and low-flying aircraft. Rivet Joint aircraft (converted Boeing 707s) can monitor the radio airwaves, eavesdropping on the frequencies used by opposing militaries. At even higher altitudes, U-2 or unmanned Global Hawk aircraft, which operate at altitudes in excess of 60,000 feet, can gather signals and other types of photographic and electronic intelligence across an entire theater of operations. This information can be provided in real time to data-fusion centers to provide local commanders with a "god's-eye view" of the battlefield.

Satellites in orbit also can provide a variety of electronic signals and photographic intelligence. These national systems can be used to provide strategic intelligence to senior officials and to "cue" battlefield systems so that they can target areas of interest.

During the Cold War, overhead surveillance helped make arms control a reality by providing a nonintrusive way to verify compliance with arms control treaties. But because it can also be used to improve targeting against an opponent's arsenal, overhead surveillance can produce crisis instability if parties in a conflict lack a secure second-strike capability. Overhead surveillance is a key component of the transformation of the U.S. military and the emergence of a global precision-strike complex.

—*James J. Wirtz*

Reference

Freedman, Lawrence, *The Evolution of Nuclear Strategy*, third edition (New York: Palgrave Macmillan, 2003).

PAKISTANI NUCLEAR WEAPONS PROGRAM

Pakistan tested a handful of nuclear weapons and declared itself a nuclear weapons state in May 1998. These tests brought to fruition a secret nuclear bomb production program that began soon after Indian troops defeated Pakistani forces in a 1971 war that saw Bangladesh (formerly East Pakistan) emerge as an independent state. Pakistan's initial motive for acquiring nuclear weapons was Prime Minister Zulfiqar Ali Bhutto's desire to have a way to ensure Pakistan's national security against an increasingly powerful adversary without having to rely on Western military assistance, which had proved to be unreliable. Especially after India tested its first nuclear explosive device in 1974, Bhutto and senior Pakistani military officials believed that nuclear weapons could help the Pakistan armed forces overcome the growing disparity in conventional military capabilities with India. Nuclear weapons also were attractive because they could be developed largely indigenously, with some financial support from Saudi Arabia and Libya and technical assistance from China and North Korea (the Koreans helped Pakistan build the Ghauri, Pakistan's first ballistic missile).

Pakistan initially attempted to acquire the facilities needed to produce weapons-grade plutonium. But when U.S. nonproliferation diplomacy blocked these efforts, Islamabad redirected its focus to produce gas-centrifuge machinery to en-

General Muhammad Aziz Khan, chairman of Pakistan's Joint Chiefs of Staff Committee, and other military personnel stand in front of Pakistan's short-range surface-to-surface ballistic missile HATF-III Ghaznavi before a test flight, October 2003. (ISPR/Handout/Reuters/Corbis)

rich uranium for nuclear weapons. In 1976, Abdul Qadeer Khan, a Pakistani metallurgist working for the European nuclear consortium Urenco, managed to flee Europe with stolen centrifuge designs and a list of 100 companies that supplied centrifuge parts and materials. He soon set up a uranium enrichment plant at Kahuta, and by the mid-1980s he had navigated his way through the international export controls of the nuclear nonproliferation regime to produce enough bomb-grade material for a few nuclear weapons (*see* Enrichment; Plutonium; Uranium).

Sometime in the 1980s, Khan turned from recipient to supplier of nuclear technology. He was still bringing in material and components for Pakistan's nuclear bomb–making program, but he ordered more material than Pakistan needed. At the same time, Khan Research Laboratories (KRL) was maturing. KRL scientists published papers starting in 1987 on the construction of more difficult centrifuges made of maraging steel, rather than the earlier aluminum-based designs. Both trends—over-ordering and technological evolution—left Khan with excess inventory. During the 1990s, Khan became the world's most notorious nonstate exporter of nuclear material, selling nuclear technology, materials, and in at least one case, even bomb designs, to Iran, Libya, and North Korea.

Today Pakistan possesses stockpiles of nuclear weapon components and could assemble and deploy nuclear weapons within a few days to a week. Although Islamabad refuses to reveal information about the size, composition, and operational status of its nuclear arsenal, a rough estimate can be calculated from publicly available information. Assuming that Pakistan's Kahuta enrichment plant is able to produce between 80 and 140 kilograms of weapons-grade uranium per year, Pakistan could have between 900 and 1,370 kilograms of highly enriched uranium (HEU) available for weapons production. (The amount of HEU required for a bomb is believed to range between 12 and 25 kilograms, depending on the weapon design.) In addition, in 1998 Pakistan commissioned an unsafeguarded heavy-water research reactor at Khushab capable of yielding enough plutonium to make a few nuclear weapons annually. Combining these possible plutonium and HEU inventories, Pakistan could possess enough fissile material to fabricate between 37 and 100 weapons, with

65 as the median estimate found in the open literature (*see* Highly Enriched Uranium).

The Pakistan Air Force flies two kinds of aircraft that are probably capable of nuclear weapons delivery: U.S.-supplied F-16s and French Mirage 5 jets. After the United States suspended F-16 sales to Pakistan in 1990, however, Islamabad placed a high priority on acquiring ballistic missiles to offset India's conventional military superiority and to ensure reliable delivery of nuclear weapons. Liquid-fueled Ghauri missiles, developed with North Korean assistance, and solid-fueled Shaheen 1 and 2 missiles, developed with Chinese assistance, probably would be employed to deliver Pakistan's nuclear weapons.

—*Peter Lavoy*

See also: Strategic Forces

References

Albright, David, "India and Pakistan's Fissile Material and Nuclear Weapons Inventory, End of 1999," 11 October 2000, available at http://www.isis-online.org.

Broad, William J., David E. Sanger, and Raymond Bonner, "A Tale of Nuclear Proliferation: How Pakistani Built His Network," *New York Times*, 12 February 2004.

Lavoy, Peter R., "Managing South Asia's Nuclear Rivalry: New Policy Challenges for the United States," *Nonproliferation Review*, vol. 10, no. 3, Fall-Winter 2003, pp. 84–94.

Lavoy, Peter R., "Pakistan's Nuclear Doctrine," in Rafiq Dossani, ed., *Prospects for Peace in South Asia* (Stanford, CA: Stanford University Press, forthcoming).

PANTEX FACILITY, TEXAS

Pantex is the primary facility in the United States for dismantling and storing excess nuclear warheads, including those designated as part of America's strategic hedge. The facility is located near Amarillo, Texas. During the Cold War, it also manufactured the high-explosive components of nuclear weapons. Pantex and its 3,200 employees have been managed since 2001 by BWXT Pantex, a consortium company created by BWX Technologies, Honeywell, and Bechtel for the Department of Energy.

Pantex was established in 1942 as a U.S. Army ordnance plant for conventional ammunition. Closed following World War II, it was reopened in 1950 by the Atomic Energy Commission to provide an additional site for the development of high-explosive components of nuclear weapons. By the

1970s, the activities of several such plants around the country were consolidated at Pantex.

Many of the manufacturing processes at Pantex take place in self-contained buildings known as "Gravel Gerties." These were designed to collapse upon themselves in the event of an accidental explosion, thus minimizing the spread of radioactivity.

Since the end of the Cold War, the Pantex plant has remained busy dismantling excess warheads. It serves as the primary facility for storage of nuclear weapons components, including fissile triggers, and, since the closure of the Rocky Flats facility, plutonium pits. The "hedge force" of nondeployed nuclear weapons called for in the Nuclear Posture Review is also stored at Pantex.

—*Jeffrey A. Larsen*

See also: Fission Weapons; Hedge; Nuclear Posture Review; Pit; Rocky Flats, Colorado; Thermonuclear Bomb

References

Cochran, Thomas B., William M. Arkin, Robert S. Norris, and Milton H. Hoenig, *Nuclear Weapons Databook*, vol. 3: *U.S. Nuclear Warhead Facility Profiles* (Cambridge, MA: Ballinger, 1987).
Pantex Facility website, http://www.pantex.com.

PARITY

No strategic issue generated greater controversy during the Cold War than the assessment of the balance of nuclear forces between the United States and the Soviet Union. After Washington lost its nuclear monopoly in 1949 and its overwhelming numerical superiority a decade later, Western strategists worried that the emergence of parity—the absence of a nuclear advantage on either side—might produce political and military gains for communism. These fears and the debates they generated produced two very different understandings of nuclear parity.

The minimalist concept of parity refers to a situation in which the weaker side has enough nuclear capability to inflict unacceptable damage on the stronger party. Moscow's deployment of long-range missiles in the late 1950s caused Americans to worry about their growing vulnerability to Soviet attack, but President Dwight D. Eisenhower calculated that an attack was unlikely because the Soviets were more vulnerable to U.S. nuclear strikes. Even when the disparity of vulnerability waned in the early 1970s, President Richard M. Nixon contended that the United States still could inflict a level of damage

on a potential aggressor sufficient to deter him from attacking.

Hawkish critics pointed out that parity referred not to the possible destruction of population centers inherent in each side's nuclear arsenal, but rather to the balance of forces as a whole, and specifically to counterforce capacity. By this measure, Moscow had pulled equal to Washington in the late 1970s and was on its way to fielding a superior nuclear capability, which caused some analysts to warn that the Kremlin might try to initiate a disarming first nuclear strike or use its superiority to coerce Western governments. These contrasting strategic visions and definitions of parity were never reconciled and still inform strategic debates in the United States and elsewhere.

—*Peter Lavoy*

See also: Balance of Terror; Counterforce Targeting; Deterrence; Mutual Assured Destruction

References

Betts, Richard K., *Nuclear Blackmail and Nuclear Balance* (Washington, DC: Brookings Institution, 1987).
Freedman, Lawrence, *The Evolution of Nuclear Strategy*, third edition (New York: Palgrave Macmillan, 2003).

PAYLOAD

"Payload" is the term used to describe the amount of weight that can be carried to a specific range by a weapons delivery system or the type of weapon carried by a delivery system. Although the term can be used to describe the number of bombs or overall weight of bombs carried by an aircraft, it is most often used as a synonym for missile "throw weight."

Within certain limits, the amount of payload that a missile can deliver varies by range. Range can be extended by reducing payload, or higher payloads can be carried over shorter ranges. Payloads can include single-warhead reentry vehicles; multiple independently targetable reentry vehicles (MIRVs) loaded onto a MIRV bus; satellites; or special communication equipment. Payload limitations place a premium on the construction of "light" thermonuclear warheads that are relatively difficult to design and manufacture.

The United States and the Soviet Union have deployed missiles with the longest ranges and highest payloads of any produced in the five nuclear weapons states. The U.S. Peacekeeper MX intercontinental ballistic missile (ICBM) can carry a 3,950-

kilogram payload to a range of about 11,000 kilometers. The Soviet S-18 could carry an 8,000 kg payload to a range of about 10,000 km. The Chinese DF 31 ICBM that is currently under development will have a range of about 8,000 km and have a throw weight of about 700 kg.

Theater delivery systems have much shorter ranges and payloads. The SCUD-Bs that were once deployed by Iraq had a range of 300 km when carrying a 1,000 kg payload. The North Korean Nodong-1 has a 1,300-km range and a 750 kg payload. The Israeli Jericho-2 has a 1,500-km range and a 100 kg payload.

—James J. Wirtz

References
"The Ordnance Shop: Missile Components, available at http://www.ordnance.org/missile_components.htm.
"Weapons of Mass Destruction in the Middle East: Range and Payload of Ballistic Missiles and Space Launch Vehicles (SLV) Deployed in the Middle East," Center for Nonproliferation Studies, available at http://cns.miis.edu/research/wmdme/ch_bldep.htm.

PD-59
See United States Nuclear Forces and Doctrine

PEACEFUL COEXISTENCE
Peaceful coexistence is the maintenance of cordial and peaceful relations based on mutual understanding between parties who may hold conflicting views. It entered the Cold War vernacular in George Kennan's "Long Telegram" (February 1946). In this document, which he sent from his post in Moscow following a State Department request for suggestions on how to deal with an increasingly recalcitrant Soviet leadership, Kennan claimed that in the long term the Soviet Union and the United States could not exist in a state of permanent peaceful coexistence. As some aspects of the Cold War thawed in the late 1950s, however, the term did come to describe relations between the Soviet Union and the United States. Soviet leader Nikita Khrushchev saw peaceful coexistence as a continued absence of direct superpower confrontation, the resolution of disputes by negotiation, noninterference in internal affairs, and an increased amount of cooperation in economics, trade, science, and technology. This approach was epitomized by his trip to the United States in 1959 (*see* Cold War; Containment).

In the aftermath of the Cuban missile crisis, with mutual assured destruction a possibility, peaceful coexistence was spoken of as a clear alternative to nuclear Armageddon. From the Soviet point of view, peaceful coexistence did not prescribe any letup in the ideological struggle with the West, only a removal of the "hot war" option between the two superpowers. By the time of détente, peaceful coexistence was viewed by some in the West, notably by Henry Kissinger, as a tactical maneuver to gain time and consolidate Soviet economic and military potential.

Peaceful coexistence has also been used to describe the relationship between China and Taiwan since 1949 and is sometimes used to characterize the primary objective of the Roadmap for Peace in the Middle East (2003) between Israel and the Palestinians.

—J. Simon Rofe

Reference
Kohler, Foy D., Mose L. Harvey, Leon Goure, and Richard Soll, *Soviet Strategy for the Seventies: From Cold War to Peaceful Coexistence* (Miami, FL: University of Miami Press, 1973).

PEACEFUL NUCLEAR EXPLOSIONS
Peaceful nuclear explosions (PNEs) have been viewed at various times by the United States, the Soviet Union, and the People's Republic of China as a promising method to use in certain types of civilian projects that require the excavation of large amounts of earth.

From the 1950s until 1973, the United States detonated twenty-seven nuclear devices in Nevada, Alaska, New Mexico, Colorado, and other states as part of its "Plowshare" program. The tests were intended to determine the usefulness of nuclear explosions for the stimulation of oil and gas production and for other excavation projects. In the late 1950s and 1960s, U.S. officials considered excavating a new canal through the isthmus of Central America with nuclear explosives.

The largest excavation test experiment was conducted in 1962 at the Department of Energy's Nevada Test Site. This test, known as Sedan, displaced 12 million tons of earth, creating the largest manmade crater in the world. It also generated a large amount of fallout material that drifted beyond Nevada and over Utah. Explosions in oil and gas fields did stimulate production, but in some cases

Inspecting the crater created by the Project Sedan nuclear test explosion, Nevada Test Site, 1962. (Corbis)

they also made the fuel so radioactive that it could not be used. The Plowshare program was discontinued in 1973, after U.S. officials concluded that the negative aspects of PNEs (including criticism from the growing environmental movement) far outweighed their benefits.

The Soviet Union pursued a more vigorous PNE program. It began investigating the use of PNEs in the early 1960s and carried out a total of 124 PNEs by the late 1980s. The Soviet goals for PNEs included stimulating fossil-fuel production, blowing out oil and gas fires, creating underground cavities for storing fossil fuels, and disposing of toxic waste. With a technique called "seismic sounding," the Russians also created images of buried geologic formations by observing how they reflected shock waves produced by PNEs.

The first Soviet PNE detonations were conducted on October 25 and November 16, 1964. In January 1965, on the Semipalatinsk range, the Soviets carried out their first nuclear blasting operation

for the purpose of excavation. They stopped their PNE program in 1988 as a result of Soviet leader Mikhail Gorbachev's disarmament initiatives.

In an effort to limit the yield of nuclear tests, the United States and the Soviet Union signed the Threshold Test Ban Treaty (TTBT) on July 3, 1974. The TTBT was negotiated under the assumption that it would be accompanied by a Peaceful Nuclear Explosions Treaty (PNET). The PNET was intended to allow a higher yield for PNEs conducted outside of weapons test sites specified under the TTBT. Because completing the PNET and negotiating its verification procedures turned out to be more challenging than concluding the TTBT, the Peaceful Nuclear Explosions Treaty was not signed until May 28, 1976. The PNET ended up setting the same upper yield limitation of 150 kilotons that had been agreed to in the TTBT. The PNET, however, allowed for several explosions to have an aggregate yield of up to 1.5 megatons (1,500 kilotons). The TTBT and the PNET did not enter into force until December

11, 1990, after the United States and the Soviet Union agreed on new verification protocols to the treaties (*see* Peaceful Nuclear Explosions Treaty; Threshold Test Ban Treaty).

Although China has never conducted a PNE, during the negotiations for the Comprehensive Test Ban Treaty (CTBT) China called for PNEs to be permitted under the CTBT regime. China's interest in PNEs may be the result of its interest in replicating the Soviet PNE program, or at least investigating the underlying reasons for Soviet interest in PNEs. A compromise was later reached, and the CTBT leaves open the possibility that PNEs could be allowed following a unanimous agreement to amend the treaty by signatories at a CTBT review conference to be held at regular intervals after the treaty's entry into force (*see* Comprehensive Test Ban Treaty).

—*Steven Rosenkrantz*

References

Nuclear Threat Initiative website, http://www.nti.org/db/china/pnetorg.htm.

"Peaceful Nuclear Explosions," *Scientific American*, June 1996, pp. 14–16.

Podvig, Pavel, *Russian Strategic Nuclear Forces* (Cambridge, MA: MIT Press, 2001), pp. 452–455, 469–481.

PEACEFUL NUCLEAR EXPLOSIONS TREATY (PNET)

In the July 1974 Threshold Test Ban Treaty (TTBT), the United States and the Soviet Union recognized the need to negotiate an agreement to regulate underground nuclear explosions for peaceful purposes (also known as peaceful nuclear explosions, or PNEs). There is no essential distinction between the technology of a nuclear explosive device that would be used as a weapon and that of one used for a peaceful purpose, such as excavation or mining (*see* Peaceful Nuclear Explosions; Threshold Test Ban Treaty).

Negotiations on the PNE agreement began in Moscow on October 7, 1974, and culminated in the Treaty on Underground Nuclear Explosions for Peaceful Purposes, or the Peaceful Nuclear Explosions Treaty (PNET), signed in Washington and Moscow on May 28, 1976. The Treaty entered into force on December 11, 1990. The PNE agreement

consists of the treaty, a detailed protocol to the treaty concluded in 1990, and an agreed statement describing activities that do not constitute a peaceful application as that term is used in the treaty.

The PNET governs all nuclear explosions carried out at locations outside the weapons test sites specified by the TTBT. Under the PNET, the United States and the Soviet Union agreed not to carry out any single nuclear explosions having a yield exceeding 150 kilotons, not to carry out any series of explosions (consisting of a number of individual explosions) having an aggregate yield exceeding 1,500 kilotons, and not to carry out any series of explosions having an aggregate yield exceeding 150 kilotons unless the individual explosions in the group could be identified and measured by agreed-upon verification procedures. The parties also reserved the right to carry out nuclear explosions for peaceful purposes in the territory of another country if requested to do so, but only in full compliance with the yield limitations and other provisions of the PNET and in accord with the Nuclear Nonproliferation Treaty (NPT).

Articles IV and V of the PNET set forth verification arrangements and authorize the use of national technical means. It states that information and access to sites of explosions will be provided by each side and includes a commitment not to interfere with verification means and procedures (*see* National Technical Means; Verification).

The protocol to the PNET identifies specific arrangements for ensuring that no weapons-related benefits precluded by the TTBT are derived by conducting a PNE. The statement that accompanies the treaty specifies that a "peaceful application" of an underground nuclear explosion would not include the developmental testing of a nuclear weapon. Such testing must be carried out at the nuclear weapons test sites specified by the terms of the TTBT and therefore is considered to be a nuclear weapon test.

The provisions of the PNET, together with those of the TTBT, established a comprehensive system of regulations to govern all underground nuclear explosions of the United States and the Soviet Union (and later, Russia). Both treaties have the same five-year duration, and neither party may withdraw from the PNET while the TTBT remains in force. Either party may withdraw from the PNET upon termination of the TTBT.

The PNET and the TTBT were both submitted to the U.S. Senate for its advice and consent on June 28, 1990. Following the Senate's approval of the treaties, the United States and the Soviet Union exchanged instruments of ratification. The treaties entered into force on December 11, 1990. A Joint Consultative Commission was created to discuss compliance questions, to develop further procedures for the on-site inspection process, and to facilitate cooperation in various areas.

If the Comprehensive Test Ban Treaty (CTBT) enters into force, both the TTBT and the PNET will be superseded, with all nuclear tests, including PNEs, prohibited. The CTBT does, however, leave open the possibility that PNEs could be allowed in the future. Article VIII provides that parties to a CTBT review conference, to be held ten years after the treaty's entry into force, could agree unanimously to amend the CTBT to permit PNEs (*see* Comprehensive Test Ban Treaty; Nuclear Test Ban).

—*Steven Rosenkrantz*

References

Defense Threat Reduction Agency website, http://www.dtra.mil/os/ops/nuclear/os_pnet.html.

Nuclear Threat Initiative website, http://www.nti.org/db/china/pnetorg.htm.

"Peaceful Nuclear Explosions," *Scientific American,* June 1996, pp. 14–16.

Union of Concerned Scientists website, http://www.uscusa.org/global_security/nuclear_weapons/page.cfm?pageID=1038.

U.S. State Department website, http://www.state.gov/t/ac/trt/5182pf.htm.

PEACEKEEPER MISSILE

In the early 1970s, U.S. policymakers became concerned about the emergence of "heavy" Soviet intercontinental ballistic missiles (ICBMs) that could potentially carry up to a score of nuclear weapons. The first step in countering this ballistic missile threat was the construction of a heavy U.S. ICBM that also could carry many warheads. Peacekeeper was the U.S. Air Force name for the U.S. "missile experimental" (MX) intercontinental ballistic missile that would be developed as a counter to the Soviet SS-18 heavy ICBM. Peacekeeper was named after the famous six-shot revolver preferred by lawmen in the American West, the "gun that tamed the West," because of its supposed ability to quell Soviet ambi-

tions once deployed (*see* Intercontinental Ballistic Missiles; Heavy ICBMs).

The MX was designed to carry up to fourteen multiple independently targetable reentry vehicles (MIRVs), but it was deployed with only ten warheads that gave the weapon a range of 8,100 miles. Research and development on the MX began in 1974, its first flight took place in June 1983, and it was deployed to F. E. Warren Air Force Base, Wyoming, in 1986. The Peacemaker has four stages. The first three stages use solid fuel and the last stage is liquid fueled. These four stages gave the MX greater range, payload, and accuracy than the Minuteman missile. As the end of the Cold War became apparent, production of the missile was capped at fifty missiles in 1990, curtailing the original plan to procure 100 Peacekeepers. In 2002, the United States began retiring Peacekeeper as part of its obligations under the Strategic Arms Reduction (START) treaties (*see* Accuracy; Minuteman ICBM; Strategic Arms Reduction Treaty; Strategic Arms Reduction Treaty).

MX is probably best remembered for the controversy it produced when it came to deciding how to base the missile. Because ICBMs were becoming increasingly vulnerable to attack as the number of accurate Soviet reentry vehicles increased, various plans were devised to create a "survivable" basing mode for the MX. The Jimmy Carter administration proposed a racetrack scheme in which the missile would be shuttled among many shelters in the American Southwest in a sort of shell game to frustrate Soviet efforts to target the missile. The Ronald Reagan administration initially developed a dense-pack plan whereby warhead fratricide would protect missiles in their shelters because the Soviets would not be able to destroy simultaneously all the missiles in densely clustered silos. Rail-garrison, a plan to deploy the MX on railroad cars that could be flushed onto the civilian railroad network in time of crisis, was the preferred deployment plan for MX as the Cold War came to an end, when further work on the Peacekeeper was more or less abandoned (*see* Dense Pack; Fratricide).

—*Jeffrey A. Larsen*

References

Gibson, James N., *Nuclear Weapons of the United States: An Illustrated History* (Atglen, PA: Schiffer, 1996).

"Strategic Missiles," *Air Force Magazine,* USAF Almanac, May 2004, p. 159.

PELINDABA, TREATY OF
See Nuclear Weapons Free Zones

PENETRATION AIDS
As work on missile defenses accelerated in the late 1950s, engineers developed a variety of deceptive techniques to fool defenses and ensure that offensive warheads could reach their targets. Based initially on technologies developed during World War II to spoof enemy radar, a variety of penetration aids have been developed. The most useful ones were perfected in the 1960s. These remain in widespread use on long-range missiles today and represent a fundamental challenge for successful missile defense.

Deployed on the same rocket stage as the actual warhead, most penetration aids (or "penaids") are released in space. They are intended to overwhelm defenses by reducing the ability of defensive radars to acquire or track actual attacking warheads. The most widely used types include inflatable decoys designed to resemble attacking warheads, dipole reflectors or chaff that reflect radar signals at the same wavelength as attacking warheads, active radar jamming systems, and radar signature-reducing (or stealth) coatings. Except for the last, all of these attempt to overcome defensive radars by making their operating frequencies useless or saturating defenses with the appearance of innumerable incoming warheads. They work exclusively during mid-course flight as warheads travel through space. Upon reentering the Earth's atmosphere, they burn up rapidly or otherwise begin to appear differently on tracking radar. Spoofing through reentry requires heavy decoys that mimic the flight characteristics of actual reentry vehicles. The latter require more missile payload, however, sharply reducing the number that can be carried, if any. Every full-size decoy that is carried means one less real warhead on that missile.

The first long-range missile capable of deploying penaids was the American Titan II intercontinental ballistic missile (ICBM), which became operational in 1963. The first Soviet missile to carry them reportedly was the R-36 (NATO designation: SS-9 Scarp), which became operational in 1966. Whether these weapons originally were equipped with penaids or acquired them in a subsequent modification is not clear in unclassified discussions. Most Soviet and American long-range missiles deployed since the mid-1960s are assumed to have been equipped with some sort of penaid. The United Kingdom created its own system in the 1970s, the Chevaline, an upgrade package for its U.S.-supplied Polaris submarine-launched ballistic missiles (SLBMs), which used both decoys and chaff. China also has penaid systems. Emerging missile powers should be expected to invest in penaids as well, including unintended varieties—such as rocket booster fragments—that confuse radar and guidance systems and complicate intercept solutions.

Overcoming penaids remains one of the most difficult problems of missile defense. The task depends largely on interpretive software to allocate radar resources, evaluate closely spaced objects, and discriminate the signature of actual warheads. As progress is made on this problem, states could adopt maneuvering reentry vehicles (MARVs) or even more exotic decoy systems to aid penetration by complicating interception fire control.

—*Aaron Karp*

See also: Countermeasures; Decoys; Missile Defense
References
Gertz, Bill, "China Develops Warhead Decoys to Defeat U.S. Defenses," *Washington Times,* 16 September 1999, p. 1.
Norris, Robert S., Andrew S. Burrows, and Richard W. Fieldhouse, *Nuclear Weapons Databook,* vol. 5: *British, French and Chinese Nuclear Weapons* (Boulder: Westview, 1994).
Podvig, Pavel, ed., *Russian Strategic Nuclear Forces* (Cambridge, MA: MIT Press, 2001).
Walpole, Robert D., "The Ballistic Missile Threat to the United States," Statement for the Record to the Senate Subcommittee on International Security, Proliferation, and Federal Services, 9 February 2000.

PERMISSIVE ACTION LINK (PAL)
A Permissive Action Link (PAL) is a device to prevent the unauthorized detonation of a nuclear weapon. The PAL system, originally designed by the United States, consists of a series of codes and mechanical devices that are either integrated into or attached to the nuclear weapon. Although utilized on some submarine-launched ballistic and cruise missiles, the PAL is most commonly linked to aircraft-delivered nuclear bombs, with the pilot or crew communicating with the PAL device from the cockpit. This differs from other delivery systems, such as land-based missile systems, which utilize elaborate

procedures involving codes, mechanical keys, and participation by a crew to authorize launch and to arm the warhead.

PALs evolved during the 1950s as decision makers sought greater control over the developing nuclear force. Although the PAL design guards against unauthorized action by rogue U.S. military officers, a main concern was allied and enemy access. In the early days of the North Atlantic Treaty Organization (NATO), some U.S. nuclear weapons were at least partially controlled by allied countries. The PAL locks allow operators more freedom to disperse weapons while retaining ultimate negative control over their use. Certain PAL codes also can disable the weapon if a pilot or crew believes that it is about to fall into enemy hands. The PAL's electronic and cryptographic mechanisms can also sense attempts to bypass or override the PAL and will render the weapon inoperable.

PALs are classified as category A–F, in ascending order of sophistication. Although specific details of PAL construction and operation remain classified, it is known that the basic design lock contains electromechanical or solid-state electronics with six or twelve digits for code entry. One set of codes enables the system, or "unlocks" the PAL, while another set "authorizes" the functioning of the weapon. Early PALs were attached to the existing weapon's circuitry, but more modern PALs are "buried" within the weapon, making access more difficult. Additionally, on some PALs a limited-try feature disables the weapon if too many incorrect keys are entered.

—Chris Craige

References
Bellovin, Steven M., "Permissive Action Links," from AT&T Labs Research, available at http://www.research.att.com/~smb/nsam-160/pal.html.

Feaver, Peter D., *Guarding the Guardians: Civilian Control of Nuclear Weapons in the United States* (Ithaca, NY: Cornell University Press, 1992).

PERSHING II MISSILE

The Pershing II was an evolutionary improvement of the Pershing IA missile system that was fielded by the U.S. Army. Its performance and capabilities led the Soviets to fear it more than cruise missiles because of its short time of flight to targets in the western Soviet Union, its maneuvering reentry vehicle (MARV, designed to evade missile defenses), and its earth-penetrating nuclear warhead designed to destroy deeply buried command bunkers. It was deployed as part of the 1979 North Atlantic Treaty Organization (NATO) dual-track decision that matched intermediate-range nuclear force (INF) modernization with negotiations to remove these forces from Europe (*see* Dual-Track Decision; North Atlantic Treaty Organization).

The Pershing II, deployed to counter the Soviet SS-20, was perhaps the most political weapon to emerge in the nuclear age. As Soviet deployments of the triple-warhead SS-20 increased during the 1970s, NATO searched for ways of countering this Soviet threat. The Pershing II and the nuclear-tipped ground-launched cruise missile were selected to reaffirm the U.S. nuclear guarantee to NATO.

Equipped with an earth-penetrator warhead and a terminal guidance package in the nosecone that improved accuracy to feet instead of miles, the missile could reach Soviet command bunkers in Moscow 12 minutes after launch. Each Pershing II carried a single nuclear warhead. The system was deployed in Baden-Wurttemberg in southern West Germany, eventually reaching a complement of 108 launchers. The Pershing II was carried on an all-terrain wheeled trailer to allow for faster dispersal if placed on heightened alert.

The opposition to the Pershing II in West Germany was fierce, especially when the Soviets walked out of INF negotiations in Geneva over its deployment. The turmoil in Bonn was unprecedented. In one demonstration, 560,000 people protested the deployment of Pershing II. On November 22, 1983, however, the Bundestag approved the deployment, and the first missiles arrived the same day. NATO and the United States had won a political victory against the Soviet Union.

Soon after Pershing II was deployed, the Soviets returned to the negotiating table and agreed to eliminate all INF systems. The U.S. government, following the terms of the Intermediate-Range Nuclear Forces (INF) Treaty, destroyed all of its Pershing II missiles.

—Gilles Van Nederveen

See also: Intermediate-Range Nuclear Forces Treaty
References
Gunston, Bill, *The Illustrated Encyclopedia of the World's Rockets and Missiles* (London: Salamander, 1980).

Hansen, Chuck, *U.S. Nuclear Weapons: The Secret History* (New York: Orion, 1988).

Herf, Jeffrey, *War by Other Means: Soviet Power, West German Resistance, and the Battle of the Euromissiles* (New York: Free Press, 1991).

PHASED-ARRAY ANTENNA

Mechanically steered radar beams cannot establish the position of an object moving at a high rate of speed, such as a warhead reentering the atmosphere from outer space, because they lack sufficient receiver sensitivity and transmitter power. In the 1950s, U.S. engineers at the Massachusetts Institute of Technology working on the first antiballistic missile systems developed the phased-array radar to track high-speed objects. Soviet scientists developed a similar system, housed in massive arrays, to detect incoming missile warheads.

To make a very narrow beam with microwaves, an antenna must be very large, often stretching hundreds of feet in diameter. A physical dish antenna of that size would be awkward and slow to steer from one direction to another as it searched the sky for targets. A phased array is a lens of hundreds or thousands of small radar sets that emit microwaves so that the microwave peaks all line up in a specific direction. By changing the relative spacing of the peaks electronically, operators can steer the resulting narrow beam in any direction in a fraction of a second without causing any mechanical motion. Advances in solid-state electronics, especially fast phase shifters and computer technology for phase-array control, allowed these systems to mature.

Beam steering is accomplished by electronically controlling the timing, or phase, of the incoming and outgoing signals. A phased-array system can track while scanning because it has a large number of antenna elements that can carry out different tasks electronically independent of each other. The most impressive examples of phased-array radars are the ten-story-tall U.S. PAVE PAWS radars for submarine missile launch detection at Beale Air Force Base, California, and Cape Cod Air Force Station, Massachusetts; and the Ballistic Missile Early Warning Radar System (BMEWS) for intercontinental ballistic missile detection at Clear Air Force Station, Alaska; Thule, Greenland; and Fylingdale Moor, Great Britain.

—*Gilles Van Nederveen*

See also: Ballistic Missile Early Warning System; Early Warning; Missile Defense

References
Browne, J. P. R., *Electronic Warfare* (London: Brassey's, 1998).
Fenn, Alan J., Donald H. Temme, William P. Delaney, and William E. Courtne, "The Development of Phased-Array Radar Technology," *Lincoln Laboratory Journal*, Massachusetts Institute of Technology, vol. 12, no. 2, 2000.

PIT

"Pit" is a slang term used to describe the "trigger" inside the physics package of a nuclear bomb. When scientists in the Manhattan Project developed an implosion device at Los Alamos, New Mexico, they used this term to describe the radioactive materials at the heart of the devices used in the Trinity device tested at White Sands and the "Fat Man" bomb dropped on Nagasaki, Japan. The term has since been used by the Department of Energy to identify the explosives and explosive material, from the detonators all the way into the core material that will be used for a fissile device, in both implosion devices and fusion-boosted fission devices. It is best to think of the "pit" of a nuclear device as being like a peach pit. It is the core of the device (*see* Fat Man; Implosion Devices; Manhattan Project; Nagasaki).

The term is used to differentiate the radioactive core of a nuclear weapon from the arming and power mechanisms that are part of the device. The specific composition of the pit varies from one type of device to another. In general terms, in an implosion device it is a ball-shaped piece of radioactive metal surrounded by conventional high explosives on the outer layer, with detonators spaced at specific intervals. This produces an even compression of the materials contained inside the pit and ensures simultaneous detonation of all explosive materials. A typical implosion-device pit consists of a core of radioactive material (such as uranium 235 [U-235] or plutonium 239 [Pu-239]) encased in a shell (beryllium, for example) surrounded by high explosives (such as composition 4). The conventional explosion compresses the pit and creates a fission reaction in which an atom is split into two smaller fragments with a neutron. This method usually involves isotopes of uranium (U-235, U-233) or Pu-239. Nuclear fusion occurs when two smaller atoms are brought together (usually hydrogen or hydrogen isotopes such as deuterium or tritium) to form a larger atom (helium or helium isotopes). (*See* Deuterium; Isotopes; Plutonium; Tritium; Uranium.)

In weapons such as Fat Man, the plutonium would be at the core of the pit, and its casing would be manufactured to such tolerances that the explosive shell would uniformly compress the casing along with the plutonium inward to achieve a nuclear chain reaction, called a "critical mass." This compression creates a tamper effect and reflects neutrons back into the fissioning mass, making this type of device more efficient than other designs, such as the "Little Boy" gun-type device used in Hiroshima, Japan (*see* Criticality and Critical Mass; Gun-Type Devices; Hiroshima; Little Boy).

The pit is subject to decomposition over time owing to breakdown of both the fissile and explosive materials. Routine inspection is therefore required to ensure that the physics package remains functional. The only way to conduct the inspection is through disassembly in a controlled environment. In the United States this inspection routine is supervised by the Department of Energy.

Although the design of implosive nuclear weapons is sixty years old, refinements in materials and design have resulted in weapons of increasing yield using fewer materials. Improved technology has resulted in a gradual reduction in size of nuclear weapons from the 5-ton Fat Man to man-portable weapons that have three times the yield. Future designs of the pit will be greatly dependent on supercomputer modeling and subcritical testing due to current restrictions on nuclear arms tests.

—*Dan Goodrich*

References

Brown, Richard K., "Nuclear Weapon Diagrams," available at http://nuketesting.environweb.org/hew/Library/Brown.

Freudenrich, Craig C., "How Nuclear Bombs Work," available at http://science/howstuffworks.com/nuclear.bomb.htm

PLUTONIUM

Plutonium (Pu) is a manmade radioactive element, the ninety-fourth in the periodic table. Its radioactivity, toxicity, and explosive yield have made it one of the most feared elements in history. Plutonium is a by-product of the fission process that takes place in nuclear reactors and results from neutron capture by uranium 238 (U-238), in particular. The separation and extraction process consumes large amounts of energy. All plutonium isotopes are radioactive. The most important is plutonium 239 (Pu-239) because it is fissionable, has a long half-life (24,360 years), and can be readily produced in large quantities in breeder reactors by neutron irradiation of plentiful but nonfissile U-238. The metal has a silvery appearance and takes on a yellow tarnish when exposed to air. It is chemically reactive. A relatively large piece of plutonium is warm to the touch because of the energy given off in alpha decay (*see* Half-Life; Isotopes; Neutrons; Nuclear Fuel Cycle; Reactor Operations; Uranium).

Critical mass (the amount that will spontaneously explode when brought together) becomes a safety consideration when handling quantities of plutonium in excess of 300 grams. The critical mass of Pu-239 is only about one-third that of U-235, hence its utility in weapons design. The element was first detected in 1940 as the isotope Pu-238 by Glenn Seaborg, Joseph Kennedy, and Arthur Wahl, who produced it by deuteron bombardment of U-238 at Berkeley, California (*see* Criticality and Critical Mass).

Pu-238, Pu-240, and Pu-242 emit neutrons as their nuclei spontaneously fission. They also decay, and the decay heat of Pu-238 enables it to be used as an electricity source in the radioisotope thermoelectric generators (RTG) of some cardiac pacemakers, space satellites, and navigation beacons. Plutonium is toxic in a chemical sense and its ionizing radiation also makes it a radiation hazard. The main threat to humans from plutonium comes from inhalation. Although it is very difficult to create airborne dispersion of a heavy metal, in the case of plutonium particles the size of 10 microns or less are a hazard because they can be taken into the lungs. The alpha particles have a high rate of emission, and the element is absorbed on bone surfaces and collected in the liver; thus, plutonium and other transuranium elements are radiological poisons and must be handled with very special equipment and precautions. Plutonium in liquid solution is more likely to become critical than solid plutonium.

Plutonium is also a fire hazard, especially finely divided material. Its chemical reaction with oxygen and water may result in an accumulation of plutonium hydride, a pyrophoric compound (that is, a material that will burn in air at room temperature). Plutonium expands considerably in size as it oxidizes and thus may break its shipping container if oxidation begins. Magnesium oxide sand is the most effective material for extinguishing a plutonium fire. It both cools the burning material, acting as a heat sink, and blocks oxygen flow to the fire.

The production of plutonium is carried out in two industrial stages. The first involves the irradiation of uranium fuel rods by neutrons in nuclear reactors. The second involves the chemical separation of plutonium from the uranium, transuranic elements, and from fission products contained in discharges or irradiated fuel. These techniques are usually referred to as "reprocessing" when applied commercially and "plutonium separation" when undertaken to recover material to be used in nuclear weapons. The nuclear weapons producers have obtained optimal isotopic content of plutonium mainly by controlling the extent to which uranium fuel elements are bombarded with neutrons in nuclear reactors.

It takes about 10 kilograms of nearly pure Pu-239 to make a bomb. Producing this amount would require 30 megawatt-years of reactor operation, with frequent fuel changes and reprocessing of hot fuel rods. Plutonium is a key component in nuclear weapons. Care has to be taken to avoid accumulation of amounts of plutonium that approach critical mass—the amount of plutonium that will self-generate a nuclear reaction. For weapons use, Pu-240 is considered a serious contaminant, and it is not feasible to separate Pu-240 from Pu-239.

The Trinity test on July 16, 1945, used about 6 kilograms of plutonium to achieve the world's first nuclear explosion. Fat Man, dropped on Nagasaki, Japan, on August 9, 1945, used 6.2 kilograms of plutonium. Plutonium for the weapons were made at Hanford, Washington, and Savannah River, South Carolina. The fuel rods for these reactors were produced in gaseous-diffusion plants. After the fuel was irradiated in the reactor, it was sent for reprocessing to the plutonium-uranium extraction plant (the PUREX Plant). (See Hanford, Washington; Oak Ridge National Laboratory; Savannah River Site; Trinity Site.)

During reprocessing, plutonium is separated from spent nuclear fuel rods. Reprocessing plants handle spent fuel mechanically and chemically to extract plutonium from uranium and other fission products in the burnt fuel rods. Plutonium separa-

tion occurs in three main stages. In the first, the spent fuel assemblies are dismantled and the fuel rods are chopped into short segments, after the cladding on the fuel rods has been removed mechanically. In the second stage, the extracted fuel is dissolved in hot nitric acid. In the third and most complex stage, the plutonium and uranium are separated from other products in the fuel rods, such as actinides and fission products, and then from each other, through a technique known as "solvent extraction." The plutonium and uranium are usually passed through several solvent-extraction cycles to remove other impurities and reach the required levels of purity.

During the Cold War, the Z plant, or plutonium finishing plant at the Hanford nuclear complex, converted liquid plutonium nitrate from the PUREX Plant into solid, disc-shaped metal buttons the size of hockey pucks. The machined plutonium was then shipped to the Rocky Flats Plant, Colorado, to be turned into nuclear weapon components. Since the end of the Cold War, the United States and Russia have been converting some of their excess plutonium stockpiles to mixed oxide fuel, where uranium and plutonium are blended so that they can be burned in commercial electrical power reactors. The Rocky Flats plant has been closed, and the only remaining plutonium manufacturing facility in the United States is located at Los Alamos National Laboratory, New Mexico (see Rocky Flats, Colorado).

—Gilles Van Nederveen

See also: Mixed Oxide Fuel; Reprocessing

References

"Plutonium and Reprocessing," Nuclear Control Institute, Washington, DC, available at http://www.nci.org/new/pu-repro.htm.

"Plutonium: Key Information," Chemistry: WebElements Periodic Table, Professional Edition, available at http://www.webelements.com/webelements/elements/text/Pu/key.html.

"Plutonium Recovery from Spent Fuel Reprocessing by Nuclear Fuel Services at West Valley, New York, from 1966 to 1972," U.S. Department of Energy, February 1996, available at http://www.osti.gov/html/osti/opennet/document/purecov/nfsrepo.html.

Von Hippel, Frank N., "Plutonium and Reprocessing of Spent Nuclear Fuel," Science, vol. 293, no. 5539, 28 September 2001, pp. 2297–2398, available at http://www.princeton.edu/~globsec/publications/pdf/Sciencev293n5539.pdf.

Wick, O. J., ed., *Plutonium Handbook: A Guide to the Technology,* vols. 1 and 2 (La Grange Park, IL: American Nuclear Society, 1980).

Winter, Mark, "WebElements™: The Periodic Table on the World Wide Web," available at http://www. webelements.com/.

POLARIS SLBMS/SSBNS

Polaris, named after the North Star, was a two-stage ballistic missile powered by solid-fuel rocket motors and controlled by a self-contained inertial guidance system. It was designed to be launched from a submerged submarine. On July 20, 1960, Polaris became the first ballistic missile to be launched from a submarine under water. (In 1942, Germany had successfully test-fired mortar rounds from partially submerged mortar tubes, but no missile had ever been launched from a submerged submarine.) A second A1 Polaris missile was fired three hours later, demonstrating that multiple wartime missile launches were feasible. The Polaris program was the culmination of an intensive four-year program by the Department of the Navy.

There were three versions of the Polaris, designated A1, A2, and A3. Each modification of the missile improved its range, accuracy, target flexibility, and throw weight. Polaris was launched from three classes of fleet ballistic missile nuclear-propelled submarines (SSBNs): the George Washington class, the Ethan Allen class, and the Lafayette class.

The first Polaris A2 launch occurred on October 23, 1961, and the first Polaris A3 launch took place on October 26, 1963. Polaris A1 had an initial range of 1,200 nautical miles, and the A2 missile had a range of 1,500 nautical miles. Polaris A1 and A2 carried a single nuclear warhead, and the Polaris A3 carried multiple but not independently targetable warheads. On May 6, 1962, a nuclear-armed Polaris A1 was launched from the USS *Ethan Allen* while submerged in the Pacific, and its nuclear warhead was detonated over the South Pacific on target. This 1962 launch and nuclear weapon detonation remains the only complete proof test of a U.S. strategic missile ever conducted. The A2 missile became operational in 1962 when it was first deployed on the USS *Ethan Allen*. The A1 missile was retired in 1965, and the A2 was retired from service in 1974.

The Polaris A3 represented a significantly greater technological advance over Polaris A2, and with an approximately 85 percent new design, it was practically an entirely new missile. With a range of 2,500 nautical miles, it had the ability to reach any land target on the Earth. It also was the only Polaris missile to be equipped with multiple (three) reentry bodies, which were initially intended to serve as a way to penetrate primitive Soviet missile defenses. The first flight test of the A3 was conducted in August 1962, and the A3 became operational in September 1964 when the USS *Daniel Webster* began its initial operational patrol with sixteen A3s aboard. All Polaris A3 missiles were retired by the U.S. Navy when the last U.S. Polaris SSBN offloaded in February 1982.

The term "Polaris" also is used to describe the submarine on which the Polaris ballistic missiles were deployed. The Polaris submarine was 380 feet long with a 33-foot beam and weighed 6,700 tons. It was designated the 598 class and later the 608 class. There were five submarines in each class. The last Polaris A3 SSBN was reclassified as a nonstrategic submarine and eventually retired from service in 1983.

—*Guy Roberts*

See also: Poseidon SLBMs/SSBNs; Submarines, Nuclear-Powered Ballistic Missiles

References

Dicerto, Joseph, *Missile Base beneath the Sea: The Story of Polaris* (New York: St. Martin's Press, 1967).

Spinardi, Graham, *From Polaris to Trident: The Development of U.S. Fleet Ballistic Missile Technology* (New York: Cambridge University Press, 1994).

"Submarine Launched Ballistic Missiles," from United States Nuclear Forces Guide, Federation of American Scientists, available at http://www.fas.org/nuke/guide/usa/slbm.

PORTSMOUTH ENRICHMENT FACILITY

The Portsmouth gaseous-diffusion facility located near Piketon, Ohio, was the United States' primary plant during the Cold War for the production of highly enriched uranium (HEU). It had a sister facility located in Paducah, Kentucky, which produced low enriched uranium that was fed to the Portsmouth facility for increased enrichment to HEU levels greater than 90 percent. Earlier gaseous-diffusion facilities were operated at Oak Ridge, Tennessee (*see* Highly Enriched Uranium; Low Enriched Uranium; Oak Ridge National Laboratory).

The Portsmouth facility housed 4,080 gaseous-diffusion cascades in three buildings constructed in the mid-1950s. This technique for producing HEU, while proven, was extremely expensive because it required a large amount of electricity. A new technology using gas centrifuges was chosen by the Department of Energy in the 1980s to replace gaseous diffusion, and a new plant was begun at Portsmouth to house this process. It was scheduled for completion in 1994 but canceled in 1985.

The Portsmouth facility was only running at 25 percent of its capacity in the 1990s. It was privatized in 1998 by the U.S. Enrichment Corporation (USEC). It was closed completely (put in a "cold standby" status) in June 2001 because of its high energy costs, a global glut of enriched uranium, and excess U.S. capacity to produce HEU (the Paducah plant was kept open by the USEC to produce reactor fuel). Environmental cleanup efforts at Portsmouth will last for decades.

In early 2004, USEC chose Piketon, Ohio, for a new facility to test the centrifuge method of uranium enrichment. It plans to start testing in 2005, using the mothballed gas centrifuges left on site after the aborted 1980s effort to shift to centrifuge enrichment. It will then use the facility (called the American Centrifuge Demonstration Facility) to help gain financing for a full-scale, commercial centrifuge plant, which it aims to bring on line in 2010.
—*Jeffrey A. Larsen*

References

Lenders, Maurice, "Uranium Enrichment by Gaseous Centrifuge," Presentation by Executive Director, Urenco Limited, to Deutsches Atomforum, Annual Meeting on Nuclear Technology, 16 May 2001, Dresden, Germany, available at http://www.urenco.com/pdf/atomforum_May_2001.pdf.

Nuclear Waste Cleanup: DOE's Paducah Plan Faces Uncertainties and Excludes Costly Cleanup Activities, U.S. General Accounting Office, GAO/RCED-00-96, 28 April 2000.

"Uranium Enrichment Enterprise," in Thomas B. Cochran, William M. Arkin, Robert S. Norris, and Milton M. Hoenig, eds., *Nuclear Weapons Databook,* vol. 3: *U.S. Nuclear Warhead Facility Profiles* (Cambridge, MA: Ballinger, 1987), pp. 126–131.

POSEIDON SLBMS/SSBNS

The Poseidon submarine-launched ballistic missile, the follow-on system to the Polaris program, was a two-stage, solid-propellant missile designed to be launched from a submerged fleet ballistic missile (FBM) submarine. It was 2 feet longer than the 32-foot Polaris A3 missile but had a much larger diameter (74 versus 54 inches) and was 30,000 pounds heavier. Despite the increase in size of the Poseidon missile, the growth potential of the FBM submarines allowed Poseidon missiles to fit into the same sixteen missile launch tubes that had earlier carried Polaris missiles. The Poseidon C3 missile was a substantial improvement over Polaris. It provided a greater payload capacity and was capable of delivering multiple warheads, widely spaced, on separate targets over a variety of target footprints. This capability of using multiple independently targetable reentry vehicles (MIRVs) enabled Poseidon to cover a wide range and hold at risk a greater number of targets with nuclear weapons.

The Poseidon C3 missile had a range of 2,500 nautical miles and was the first submarine ballistic missile to be capable of targeting a number of different targets located within the "footprint" of the missile (the area in which individual warheads can be delivered by a single missile). Each 64,000-pound Poseidon C3 could carry up to fourteen Mark 3 reentry bodies. These could be targeted to maximize damage against a single target or targeted against fourteen individual targets. It was also possible to extend the range of the Poseidon by offloading warheads or penetration aids (devices intended to complicate any efforts at missile defense from the payload. Apart from the much-increased size and weight, Poseidon's main advantage over the Polaris A3 missile was its ability to deliver a warhead to multiple targets. Poseidon C3 also incorporated substantial improvements over Polaris in accuracy and resistance to countermeasures.

The Poseidon missile was deployed initially on thirty-one of the U.S. Navy's forty-one FBM submarines. The first ten fleet ballistic missile submarines to be built, including five in the George Washington class and five in the Ethan Allen class, were not retrofitted to carry Poseidon. The first launching of a Poseidon missile from a submerged submarine occurred on August 3, 1970, from the USS *James Madison* (SSBN 627) off the coast of Florida near Cape Canaveral. The Poseidon C3 became operational on March 31, 1971, when the USS *James Madison* began its initial operational patrol carrying sixteen Poseidon C3 missiles.

In addition to being deployed on Polaris submarines, Poseidon C3 missiles were deployed on submarines, also named Poseidon, that were specially converted to accommodate the larger and heavier missile. In 1970, four SSBN-627 class submarines were converted to carry the Poseidon C3 missile. Although some Polaris submarines were later converted to carry Poseidon, the new Poseidon submarines, at 425 feet long, were much larger than the submarines designed to carry the Polaris missile. They had the same beam width (33 feet) and displaced 8,250 tons (versus 6,700 tons for Polaris). In the 1980s, of the thirty-one Poseidon FBM submarines, twelve were later backfitted to carry the Trident I (C4) missile. The last Poseidon SSBN offloaded its Poseidon C3 missiles and was retired from service in September 1992 (*see* Polaris SSBNs/SLBMs).

—Guy Roberts

See also: Submarines, Nuclear-Powered Ballistic Missiles

References

"Poseidon," available at http://www.warships1.com/ Weapons/WMUS_Poseidon.htm.

Spinardi, Graham, *From Polaris to Trident: The Development of U.S. Fleet Ballistic Missile Technology* (New York: Cambridge University Press, 1994).

"Submarine Launched Ballistic Missiles," from United States Nuclear Forces Guide, Federation of American Scientists, available at http://www.fas.org/nuke/ guide/usa/slbm.

POST-ATTACK COMMAND AND CONTROL SYSTEM (PACCS)

Fearing a Soviet nuclear surprise attack, the U.S. Strategic Air Command (SAC) began modifying KC-135A tankers to serve as airborne command posts in 1957. Pleased with initial tests, officials continued the program, and the fleet soon grew to fifteen EC-135 aircraft. These aircraft, code-named "Looking Glass," carried a general officer who could take command of nuclear forces in the event SAC's underground command post at Offutt Air Force Base (AFB), Nebraska, was destroyed. Between February 1961 and July 1990, a Looking Glass EC-135 was on continuous airborne alert over the United States. Other EC-135s were assigned to the numbered air forces at Westover AFB, Massachusetts; Barksdale AFB, Louisiana; and March AFB, California. In the 1960s, as fears grew about a submarine-launched surprise attack on U.S. coastal areas, additional bases acquired air command posts. The number of command posts grew as nuclear warfighting commanders were given their own EC-135s, which were deployed at

Langley AFB, Virginia (Atlantic Command); Hickam AFB, Hawaii (Pacific Command); and Mildenhall AFB, UK (European Command). Together, these posts formed the Post-Attack Command and Control System (PACCS).

To tie the National Emergency Airborne Command Post (NEACP) aircraft to Looking Glass and other airborne command posts, officials assigned special radio-relay aircraft to Ellsworth AFB, South Dakota, and Grissom AFB, Indiana. Soviet SS-9 intercontinental ballistic missile (ICBM) deployments, which gave the Soviet Union the ability to strike Minuteman launch control centers, prompted SAC planners to add airborne launch control center (ALCC) equipment to some EC-135s, giving them the capability to launch the land-based U.S. ICBM force. Based around an EC-135C Looking Glass operating from Offutt, auxiliary command posts stood 15-minute ground alert at Offutt and Minot AFB, North Dakota. Three ALCCs also stood alert at Minot, and two radio aircraft were located at Grissom and Rickenbacker AFB, Ohio.

In the event of an emergency, Looking Glass and the two auxiliary command posts would fly over the central United States, the three ALCCs would fly above the Minuteman missile fields in the north central and northwestern United States, and the two radio-relay aircraft would fly over the Midwest, establishing and maintaining communications links with the NEACP airborne over the East Coast of the United States.

Looking Glass aircraft carried out an airborne alert for decades, flying over the Midwest day and night to preserve positive nuclear command and control in the event of a surprise Soviet nuclear attack. Looking Glass personnel also would communicate with the U.S. Navy's EC-130 "take charge and move out" (TACMO) aircraft airborne over the Atlantic and Pacific oceans to guarantee that the U.S. Fleet Ballistic Missile Submarine force on their patrol stations could receive Emergency Action Messages ordering them to execute their missions in the event of nuclear war. In 1998, as strategic forces in the United States were realigned, the Air Force command posts were retired and the Looking Glass and ALCC missions were transferred to the U.S. Navy's E-6B TACMO aircraft based at Tinker AFB, Oklahoma, and forward deployed to Offutt and other U.S. locations.

—Gilles Van Nederveen

See also: Command and Control; National Emergency
Airborne Command Post

References

Hopkins, Robert S., *Boeing KC-135 Stratotanker: More
Than Just a Tanker* (North Bennet, MN: Specialty
Press, 1997).

Logan, Don, *The Boeing C-135 Series* (Atglen, PA:
Schiffer Military History, 1998).

POUNDS PER SQUARE INCH
See Silo Basing

PREEMPTIVE ATTACK
A preemptive attack is one undertaken based on
clear and convincing evidence that an opponent is
about to attack. It is often used interchangeably and
incorrectly with the term "preventive war," which
denotes a situation in which policymakers believe
war is inevitable, but not imminent. A preemptive
attack is premised on a right recognized under customary international law that a state has the legal
right and obligation to respond to an imminent
danger to its national security. National officials do
not and should not have to wait until physically attacked to respond, especially when that attack is self-
evidently imminent. The right to a preemptive attack is often couched in terms of anticipatory
self-defense, although states that launch a preemptive attack shoulder the moral and political burden
of convincing an international audience that an attack against their interests was about to be launched.

Secretary of State Daniel Webster in the famous
Caroline Case of 1842 articulated this right of preemptive response or anticipatory self-defense. He
stated that the right of preemptive attack was restricted to those cases where the necessity "is instant,
overwhelming, and leaving no choice of means, and
no moment for deliberation." He further argued
that the act should involve "nothing unreasonable
or excessive, since the act justified by the necessity of
self-defense must be limited by that necessity and
clearly within it" (D'Amato, p. 32). Webster's criteria
are internationally accepted as the basis for determining the legitimacy of a preemptive attack.

As with preventive attacks, necessity is the most
important precondition to the legitimate use of military force. The initial determination of necessity is
made by the target state based on a number of facts.
These include, but are not limited to, the nature of
the coercion being applied, the relative size and

power of the aggressor state, the nature of the aggressor's objectives, and the consequence if those
objectives are achieved. One example of a preemptive attack is the Israeli preemptive strike on Egypt-
ian, Jordanian, and Syrian forces as they massed
against Israel, which precipitated the 1967 war.

—*Guy Roberts*

See also: Preventive War; Reciprocal Fear of Surprise
Attack

References

Bush, George W., *The National Security Strategy of the
United States of America* (Washington, DC: The
White House, 17 September 2002), available at
http://usinfo.state.gov/topical/pol/arms/.

D'Amato, Anthony, *International Law: Process and Prospect* (Ardsley, NY: Transnational Publishers, 1995).

Roberts, Guy, "The Counterproliferation Self-Help
Paradigm: A Legal Regime for Enforcing the Norm
Prohibiting the Proliferation of Weapons of Mass
Destruction," *Denver Journal of International Law
and Policy*, vol. 37, no. 483, Summer 1999.

Sofaer, Abraham D., "On the Necessity of Preemption,"
European Journal of International Law, vol. 14, no. 2,
2003, pp. 209–227.

PRESIDENTIAL NUCLEAR INITIATIVES
The Presidential Nuclear Initiatives (PNIs) of 1991
and 1992 were a set of unilateral declarations by
U.S. president George H. W. Bush and Soviet
leader Mikhail Gorbachev (and later Russian President Boris Yeltsin). In these initiatives, they
pledged significant steps to lessen the dangers associated with large stockpiles of nuclear weapons.
The PNIs laid out plans to withdraw and eliminate
some of the most dangerous weapons—tactical
nuclear weapons (TNWs)—and to take measures
that would reduce the alert levels and increase the
physical security of the remaining nuclear
weapons, thus making nuclear war less likely and
reducing the danger of proliferation. The result of
these unilateral declarations was that, for the first
time in history, the United States and the Soviet
Union pledged to withdraw and destroy a significant portion of their large nuclear arsenals without
a treaty.

In 1991, the impending breakup of the Soviet
Union and a coup attempt against Gorbachev highlighted the risks that instability posed to the security of the massive Soviet nuclear arsenal, which
was spread across many of the Soviet republics. In
September, Bush gave an address to the nation on

the reduction of U.S. and Soviet nuclear stockpiles. He announced unilateral reductions in U.S. tactical nuclear weapons—a category that had been left out of earlier treaties—calling upon Gorbachev to reciprocate. The United States announced plans to eliminate its short-range nuclear missile warheads, nuclear artillery shells, and nuclear depth charges. It promised to withdraw other naval TNWs and place them in storage, leaving only tactical bombs—part of the U.S. commitment to NATO—unaffected. Bush also canceled the only U.S. TNW in development, showing the U.S. intent to maintain these reductions.

In addition, Bush called for the rapid ratification of the Strategic Arms Reduction Treaty (START I, 1991), which had been signed in July, to mandate nuclear weapons reductions and to implement a regime that would verify these moves. He announced that all U.S. bombers would stand down from their alert status immediately and that U.S. intercontinental ballistic missiles (ICBMs) would be removed from their alert posture as soon as START was ratified. Two new nuclear weapons programs were canceled, and an agreement to eliminate missiles with multiple independently targetable reentry vehicles (MIRVs) was encouraged (see Strategic Arms Reduction Treaty; Multiple Independently Targetable Reentry Vehicle).

President Bush claimed that the United States and the Soviet Union no longer needed such large nuclear arsenals and that these changes would increase the stability and security of the U.S. and Soviet arsenals. In addition, a reduction in the number of nuclear weapons—especially of smaller TNWs that could be more easily stolen or diverted—made nuclear proliferation, and therefore the chance that terrorists could acquire nuclear weapons, less likely. Thus, President Bush suggested cooperation on measures to increase the safety and stability of the remainder of the Cold War arsenals, to ensure that the weapons would be safely transported and stored as they awaited dismantlement, and to maintain sufficient command and control structures to prevent unauthorized or accidental launch.

Eight days after the U.S. initiative was announced, Gorbachev responded, stating that the Soviet Union would destroy its short-range nuclear missile warheads, nuclear artillery shells, and nuclear land mines. The Soviets would withdraw their naval and land-based nuclear air defense weapons

and either destroy them or put them in storage. Gorbachev also announced the withdrawal of TNWs from the four other former Soviet republics, a move that was completed in 1992.

Bush responded to Gorbachev's announcement by declaring that the United States would withdraw all of its nuclear weapons from South Korea and reduce the number of tactical bombs in Europe by half. By 1998, only seven years after the PNIs were first announced, the United States had reduced the number of its tactical bombs in Europe by some 90 percent. Russia pledged to eliminate nearly 14,000 of the more than 21,000 TNWs that the Soviet Union possessed at the time the initiatives were announced, although whether Russia has carried out these promised reductions is unclear.

After the dissolution of the Soviet Union at the end of 1991, Boris Yeltsin became the first president of the Russian Federation. Yeltsin reaffirmed Gorbachev's pledges and pressed for further reductions. He announced that half of the TNWs in the Russian Air Force, along with one-third of Russian naval TNWs and one-half of Russian air defense weapons, would be destroyed by the year 2000. He also stated that production of two types of heavy bombers would cease and that 1,250 nuclear warheads had been taken off of high-alert status, reducing the likelihood that they would be launched accidentally. He proposed deep cuts in the U.S. and Russian strategic arsenals. Although the United States did not respond to many of the measures Yeltsin proposed, the groundwork was laid for a more stable nuclear environment.

The Presidential Nuclear Initiatives reflected the changing nature of the nuclear threat after the end of the Cold War. As the Soviet Union collapsed, it became unlikely that a Soviet invasion of Europe—which U.S. tactical nuclear weapons were built to counter—would occur. The massive U.S. and Russian strategic nuclear arsenals were thought to be a strong enough deterrent against nuclear war. The largest threat perceived by analysts in the post–Cold War world was that "loose" nukes from the crumbling Soviet empire would make it into the hands of rogue states or terrorists. Because of the PNIs, the post–Cold War period started off with confidence-building measures that helped to reduce tensions and eliminate the threat posed by the smallest and most portable nuclear weapons.

—Andrea Gabbitas

References

Bush, George H. W., "Address to the Nation on Reducing United States and Soviet Nuclear Weapons," 27 September 1991, available at http://bushlibrary.tamu.edu/papers/1991/91092704.html.

Gorbachev, Mikhail, "Statement on Nuclear Weapons," 5 October 1991, in Jeffrey A. Larsen and Kurt J. Klingenberger, eds., *Controlling Non-Strategic Nuclear Weapons: Obstacles and Opportunities* (Colorado Springs: USAF Institute for National Security Studies, 2002), pp. 281–289.

Yeltsin, Boris, "On Russia's Policy in the Field of Limiting and Reducing Armaments," 29 January 1992, in Jeffrey A. Larsen and Kurt J. Klingenberger, eds., *Controlling Non-Strategic Nuclear Weapons: Obstacles and Opportunities* (Colorado Springs: USAF Institute for National Security Studies, 2002), pp. 281–289.

PRESSURIZED-WATER REACTORS (PWRs)

One of the most widely used nuclear reactor types in the world today (along with the boiling-water reactor, or BWR), the pressurized-water reactor (PWR) was one of the first types of power reactors developed in the United States for the commercial production of electricity. Both BWRs and PWRs are called "light-water reactors" because light water (H_2O) typically flows through the core to act as a coolant, reflector, and moderator. In a PWR, this water is pressurized to approximately 2,250 pounds per square inch to prevent the water from boiling.

PWRs were originally designed as the power plant for ships of the U.S. Navy, and then adapted for use in the commercial power industry. The first nuclear-powered submarine, the USS *Nautilus*, put to sea in 1955 equipped with a PWR.

Commercial PWRs generally operate with slightly enriched uranium as the fuel (that is, with a higher concentration of uranium 235 than found in nature—typically 2 to 5 percent, compared to 0.72 percent in nature.) The pressurized water flowing through the core is heated by the energy released in the fission of the fuel and then flows through a heat

The first useful electricity from atomic energy was produced by the Pressurized Water Reactor in the foreground, operating on heat from the Experimental Breeder Reactor at the Nuclear Reactor Testing Station, Arco, Idaho, 1951. (Bettmann/Corbis)

exchanger. The heat is exchanged to a secondary fluid, generally water, that is not pressurized and so turns to steam. The steam drives a turbine that powers a generator, producing electricity.

The next generation of nuclear reactors will seek to enhance the economic competitiveness of commercial nuclear power. New modular designs will utilize simple technology to improve resistance to proliferation and enhance safety.

—*Brian Moretti*

See also: Light-Water Reactors; Reactor Operations; Uranium

Reference

Lamarsh, J. R., and A. J. Baratta, *Introduction to Nuclear Engineering,* third edition (Upper Saddle River, NJ: Prentice-Hall, 2001).

PREVENTIVE WAR

A preventive war is one that occurs when national leaders believe that war is inevitable and that it is better to initiate hostilities rather than letting the opponent attack when the situation is favorable for them. It reflects the political judgment that diplomacy or other measures short of war would not be sufficient to eliminate an increasingly acute security threat. Preventive war is different from preemption because the threat is not imminent; that is, it occurs in the absence of clear indications that the opponent is about to strike. A preventive attack is premised on a state's fundamental right, recognized under the UN Charter (Article 51), to respond to threats to its national security, although the general thrust of the United Nations is to resolve international disputes without resorting to violence.

One recent type of threat, the development of weapons of mass destruction, has prompted some states to launch preventive attacks and war. The 1981 Israeli attack on the Iraqi nuclear reactor at Osirik, for example, was intended to cripple Saddam Hussein's quest to obtain nuclear weapons. The Israelis never claimed Iraq had a nuclear weapon, only that the reactor was a key part of Iraq's clandestine nuclear weapons program and that if Israel waited it would not be able to effectively interrupt the program's progress. Similarly, in the spring of 2003, the United States launched a preventive war against Iraq to eliminate the threat that Iraq would develop, use, or transfer weapons of mass destruction to terrorist organizations.

Given the emerging international norm against preventive war, those advocating preventive war as national policy, regardless of the perception of dire threat, shoulder an enormous political and moral burden to justify their policies. Some would argue, however, that no war should ever be considered inevitable and that preventive war is simply a euphemism for aggression.

—*Guy Roberts*

See also: Preemptive Attack

References

Brierly, J., *The Law of Nations* 426 (6th ed.) (New York: Oxford University Press, 1963).

Fenwick, Charles, *International Law,* 4th ed. (New York: Meredith Publishing, 1965).

Roberts, Guy, "The Counterproliferation Self-Help Paradigm: A Legal Regime for Enforcing the Norm Prohibiting the Proliferation of Weapons of Mass Destruction," 27, *Denver Journal of International Law and Policy* 483, 1999.

Sofaer, Abraham, "On the Necessity of Pre-Emption," 14, *European Journal of International Law* 209, 2003.

Westlake, John, *International Law* (Cambridge, UK: Cambridge University Press, 1904).

Wirtz, James and James Russell, "US Policy on Preventive War and Preemption," 113, *The Nonproliferation Review,* Spring 2003.

PRIMARY STAGE

The primary stage of a thermonuclear warhead is a fission device that creates the necessary conditions for a subsequent fusion reaction. Modern thermonuclear warheads use both fission and fusion reactions, traditionally referred to as the primary and secondary stages, to generate a desired explosive force.

When the warhead is detonated, chemical explosives compress the primary stage, which is often composed of plutonium 239. Because of the high temperatures and pressures generated by the chemical explosives, the plutonium begins to split into new types of atoms. These new atoms have a collective weight less than the weight of their original components; the remaining mass is released as a tremendous amount of energy and neutrons. The energy is what makes up the power of an atomic blast, and the additional neutrons perpetuate the fission chain reaction (*see* Neutrons).

In modern thermonuclear warheads, this primary mechanism is surrounded by a layer of lithium deuteride (the isotope of hydrogen with a mass number of two; see Isotopes), which is in turn encased in a thick outer layer known as the "tamper," which is often composed of fissionable material and functions to hold the contents together to contain the pressure and heat needed to generate a fusion explosion. Neutrons from the atomic explosion cause the lithium to fission into helium and tritium (the isotope of hydrogen with the mass number three), which yields a tremendous amount of energy.

The primary stage generates the conditions required for fusion, raising temperatures within the warhead to as high as 400 million degrees Celsius. The majority of the overall energy or yield released by a two-stage nuclear warhead is derived from the secondary (fusion) stage.

—Abe Denmark

See also: Fission Weapons; Fusion; Thermonuclear
    Bomb
Reference
Rhodes, Richard, *Dark Sun: The Making of the Hydrogen Bomb* (New York: Simon and Schuster, 1996).

PROLIFERATION

Proliferation is the spread of knowledge or materials related to a specific type of weapon system to additional states or nonstate actors. The term has been applied primarily to the field of nuclear weapons and the spread of nuclear knowledge and capabilities. "Nuclear nonproliferation" is the prevention or deterrence of the acquisition or increase in materials, technology, or expertise utilized for the production of nuclear weapons and their delivery systems by states or subnational organizations that did not previously possess them (*see* Nonproliferation).

History and Background
The need to prevent the spread of materials, technology, or expertise related to the production of nuclear weapons was evident from the first days of the nuclear era. What gave impetus to nonproliferation efforts was the emergence of the first five declared nuclear weapons states—the United States, the Soviet Union, the United Kingdom, France, and China—and the fear that many more states would develop nuclear weapons. In addition to the declared states, there are four "de facto" nuclear states: India, Pakistan, Israel, and North Korea. Both India and Pakistan tested nuclear devices in May 1998; Israel and North Korea are widely assumed to have nuclear weapons (*see* Nuclear Weapons States).

Although the desire to acquire nuclear weapons was prevalent in the early 1960s, the introduction of full-scale commercial nuclear power as an energy source was just as promising. Developing as well as developed countries were eager to benefit from this new energy source. Nuclear technology had application in power generation, desalination, and the production of special isotopes for science and medicine. So nuclear technology flowed out of countries such as the United States and the former Soviet Union, and foreign students and scientists flowed in, eager to master nuclear technology. Peaceful nuclear technologies and expertise, however, could also be used to produce nuclear weapons. Early attempts at safeguards could not prevent covert weapons programs or the diversion of materials or technology from declared programs. If the many peaceful uses of nuclear technology were to be developed, states needed credible assurances that nuclear programs would not be used to hide programs to develop nuclear weapons.

These assurances materialized with the development of a broad range of international nuclear nonproliferation agreements, the most significant of which is the Nuclear Nonproliferation Treaty (NPT). This agreement, opened for signature on July 1, 1968, was extended indefinitely in 1995. It currently has more than 180 member nations and commits both nuclear and non–nuclear weapons states to work to prevent the proliferation of materials, technology, and expertise used in the production of nuclear weapons. This agreement is widely considered to be the cornerstone of the nonproliferation regime. The NPT represents a bargain between the original five declared nuclear weapons states and non–nuclear weapons states. The non–nuclear weapons states agreed not to manufacture or otherwise acquire nuclear weapons or other nuclear explosives and to accept international safeguards on their peaceful nuclear activities to confirm that commitment. In return, the nuclear weapons states agreed to negotiate in good faith toward ending the nuclear arms race and pursuing eventual elimination of their nuclear arsenals, not to assist non–nuclear weapons states to acquire nuclear weapons, and to make available the peaceful benefits of nuclear energy. In 1995, the Review and Extension Conference of the NPT emphasized the need for excess fissile materials to be permanently removed from the stockpiles available for weapons, concluding that these materials "should, as soon as practicable, be placed under Agency safeguards" (*see* Nuclear Nonproliferation Treaty).

Many states have entered into additional binding nonproliferation commitments. Several nuclear weapons free zones have been created, and even more restrictive nuclear agreements have been negotiated in some regions. On the Korean peninsula, for example, the Republic of Korea (South Korea) and the Democratic People's Republic of Korea (North Korea) agreed not to have facilities for either plutonium reprocessing or uranium enrichment. North Korea has chosen to abandon the nonproliferation regime by withdrawing unilaterally from both the NPT and the ban on developing weapons-grade fissile material (*see* North Korean Nuclear Weapons Program; Nuclear Weapons Free Zones).

International Compliance

The NPT and many of these other nonproliferation commitments are verified by International Atomic Energy Agency (IAEA) safeguards. IAEA safeguards are designed to detect the diversion of significant quantities of nuclear materials to construct nuclear weapons, to provide assurance that such diversions have not occurred, and to verify that states are complying with their nonproliferation obligations. The effectiveness and credibility of IAEA safeguards are fundamental to the international nonproliferation regime. Traditionally, at the instruction of the member states, the IAEA focused primarily on inspecting declared nuclear material at declared sites. In recent years, however, and particularly after the revelation of Iraq's secret nuclear weapons program, new attention has been focused on measures to detect undeclared activities at secret locations sponsored by rogue states or terrorist organizations. Under the NPT, non–nuclear weapons states are obligated to accept IAEA "full-scope" safeguards on all their civilian nuclear activities. Since the IAEA does not monitor nuclear weapons or military materials, the nuclear weapons states do not have similar obligations. The declared nuclear weapons states, however, have entered into "voluntary offer" agreements with the IAEA, under which they make certain facilities on their territory eligible for IAEA safeguards. These voluntary agreements help build confidence in the commitment of the nuclear weapons states to support international safeguards, reduce the extent of discrimination between nuclear and non–nuclear weapons states, and give the IAEA experience in safeguarding complex nuclear facilities (*see* International Atomic Energy Agency).

Supplementing these international commitments and verification regimes is a system of internationally coordinated export controls of materials and technologies that could contribute to nuclear weapons programs. The Nuclear Suppliers Group (NSG), for example, represents the major nations that provide nuclear-related products and services to other countries and meets to coordinate agreed-upon export control policies. Like IAEA safeguards, the international export control system has been significantly strengthened in recent years, particularly after revelations of Iraq's covert effort to circumvent export controls and purchase the essential technologies for a nuclear weapons program. The NSG also works to prevent nuclear materials from falling into the hands of terrorist organizations. The NSG has now agreed not to undertake major new nuclear exports to countries other than the declared nuclear weapons states that do not accept full-scope IAEA safeguards and to control the export of dual-use items. A variety of nuclear supply agreements also forms part of the international nonproliferation structure: The United States, for example, has reached bilateral nuclear cooperation agreements with the European Union, Japan, and other countries that include a range of important nonproliferation commitments, as required under the Atomic Energy Act and the Nuclear Nonproliferation Act of 1978 (*see* Nuclear Suppliers Group).

Security for nuclear materials and other measures to prevent nuclear theft and smuggling also are key international efforts to prevent the spread of nuclear weapons. States handling nuclear materials bear the primary responsibility for ensuring their security. Given the dire threat posed by the possibility of terrorists or rogue states gaining access to plutonium or highly enriched uranium (HEU), the international community has a legitimate interest in ensuring the adequacy of states' protection of these materials. The international Convention on the Physical Protection of Nuclear Materials, which entered into force on February 8, 1997, specifies physical protection measures that should be applied, particularly in international shipments of nuclear materials. The NSG guidelines also specify measures to be taken by states receiving materials from NSG member states. In addition, the International Atomic Energy Agency has issued nonbinding recommendations on security measures to be taken to safeguard nuclear materials. All of these guidelines, however, are expressed in broad and general terms to allow for substantial differences in approach to achieve these common objectives. Some states, for example, rely primarily on armed guards to ensure security at nuclear facilities, while other states have no armed guards at all, even at facilities with substantial quantities of plutonium and HEU, and instead rely on high technology to alert authorities of potential instances of foul play. The economic, political, and social transformations recently experienced by states that were once part of the Soviet Union have significantly weakened security at many nuclear facilities, creating new nuclear proliferation concerns that represent part of the rationale for carrying out disposition of excess fissile materials.

Many factors influence national decisions to acquire or not acquire a nuclear arsenal. Preventing nuclear proliferation in the long run will require strenuous efforts to address both the "supply side" and the "demand side" of a nuclear weapons program. Thus, for example, efforts to resolve conflicts in the Middle East, South Asia, and elsewhere represent key parts of the global nonproliferation effort to combat the "demand side" of weapon acquisition. In many cases, nontechnical considerations, rather than technical ones, may dominate not only whether a country decides to pursue nuclear weapons but also its ability to acquire a nuclear arsenal. These factors, which are country dependent, include the ability of a government to organize, manage, and carry through complex, long-term projects involving a large scientific and technological infrastructure, and to keep state secrets. A country's foreign trade contacts, its supply of hard currency, and its political will to become a "member" of the nuclear club also shape the nature of its nuclear weapons program.

Technical Challenges to Proliferation

To acquire nuclear weapons, a state must overcome a number of technical hurdles. It must obtain enough fissile material to form a supercritical mass (thus permitting an explosive chain reaction) (see Criticality and Critical Mass). It must produce a weapon design that will bring that mass together in the time allotted, before the heat from early fissions

blows the material apart. It also must design a weapon small and light enough to be carried by available delivery vehicles. These hurdles represent threshold requirements for use of a weapon. Unless each one is adequately met, the proliferator ends up not with a less powerful weapon, but with a device that cannot produce any significant nuclear yield or that cannot be delivered to its intended target. Limited access to the principal weapon-usable materials has been for many years the primary technical barrier against the spread of nuclear weapons capabilities to additional nations and to subnational groups. The technologies for producing separated plutonium and HEU are demanding and costly. The plutonium and HEU that have been produced by weapons states generally have been well guarded or have resided in forms awkward to steal and difficult to use in weapons (for example, plutonium contained in spent nuclear reactor fuel that is not separated from accompanying uranium and fission products). In contrast, the basic knowledge and expertise needed to make at least crude nuclear weapons is available to virtually any country or subnational group or terrorist organization. Therefore, the ability to buy fissile materials on a nuclear black market could circumvent this important roadblock to the proliferation of nuclear weapons (see Highly Enriched Uranium; Plutonium; Uranium).

There are few radioactive isotopes capable of sustaining an explosive chain reaction: two isotopes of uranium (U-233 and U-235) and several isotopes of plutonium (especially Pu-239, Pu-240, Pu-241, and Pu-242) (see Isotopes).

Uranium 235 is the only potential nuclear explosive isotope that occurs naturally in significant quantities. It constitutes 0.7 percent of natural uranium, so its nuclear explosive properties emerge only if the proportion of U-235 atoms in the uranium is much higher than in the natural element. Nuclear explosives can in principle be made with material containing somewhat less than 20 percent U-235, but the amount of material required at that level of enrichment is very large. In international practice, all uranium with a U-235 concentration of 20 percent or more is referred to as highly enriched uranium (HEU). For fission explosives, nuclear weapon designers prefer a U-235 fraction of more than 90 percent, and HEU in this concentration range is called "weapons-grade." Increasing the U-235 concentration above its level in natural uranium—uranium enrichment—is a technologically demanding and costly enterprise. Enrichment techniques include gaseous diffusion, gas centrifuge, aerodynamic methods (Becker nozzle), chemical exchange (Chemex process), electromagnetic isotope separation, laser excitation, and plasma centrifuge (*see* Enrichment).

Plutonium is nonexistent in nature but can be produced by bombarding U-238 with neutrons in a nuclear reactor or an accelerator. (U-238 is the most abundant uranium isotope, constituting 99.3 percent of natural uranium.) Reactors have proven to be more practical than accelerators for producing plutonium in large quantities. To use the plutonium produced in a nuclear reactor in a nuclear weapon, it first must be chemically separated from the other fission products produced with it and from the residual U-238. This separation process, called "reprocessing," also is a technically demanding and costly operation. Because of the intense gamma radioactivity of fission products and the health risks posed by the alpha activity of plutonium if it is inhaled or otherwise taken into the body, reprocessing also requires stringent measures to mitigate its health and safety hazards. Although virtually all combinations of plutonium isotopes can be used to manufacture nuclear explosives, nuclear weapons designers prefer to work with plutonium containing more than 90 percent Pu-239 (weapons-grade plutonium). This high Pu-239 concentration is commonly achieved by removing the plutonium from the reactor before the higher isotopes, which result from successive neutron absorptions, have a chance to build up. The longer refueling intervals typical of civilian nuclear electricity generation result in plutonium that contains only 60–70 percent Pu-239 (reactor-grade plutonium).

Reactor-grade plutonium can nonetheless be used to produce nuclear weapons. Three characteristics of reactor-grade plutonium, however, pose difficulties for weapons design and manufacture: Its high neutron background increases the likelihood of "pre-initiation" of the nuclear chain reaction just before the weapon reaches the optimum configuration for maximum yield; its tendency to generate heat while in storage may affect the stability and performance of the weapon's components; and its high radioactivity creates great danger for those fabricating and handling weapons produced from reactor-grade plutonium. The more sophisticated the weapon design, the more likely these difficulties can be overcome. Unsophisticated designers could make crude but highly destructive nuclear bombs from reactor-grade plutonium, using technology no more sophisticated than that required for making similar bombs from weapons-grade plutonium, and sophisticated designers could use reactor-grade plutonium to make very effective nuclear bombs quite suitable for the arsenals of major nation-states.

A state or subnational group using designs and technologies no more sophisticated than those used in first-generation nuclear weapons could build a nuclear device from reactor-grade plutonium that would have a reliable explosive yield of between 1 and 20 kilotons. At the other end of the spectrum, advanced nuclear weapons states such as the United States and Russia, using modern designs, could produce weapons from reactor-grade plutonium having reliable explosive yields, weight, and other characteristics generally comparable to those of weapons made from weapons-grade plutonium.

The quantities of weapons-usable material needed to make a nuclear weapon are not large. Although the amounts used in specific nuclear weapon designs are classified, numbers in the range of 4 to 6 kilograms of plutonium metal are widely cited in the unclassified literature as typical (and the figure would not be very different if reactor-grade rather than weapons-grade plutonium were used). A comparison of critical masses suggests that obtaining a comparable explosive yield from weapons-grade HEU would require a mass of uranium metal approximately three times greater. The required amounts of material can be easily carried by one person and easily concealed. These materials themselves are not radioactive enough to deter theft and handling. Because of the very long half-lives of Pu-239 (24,000 years) and U-235 (700 million years), the radiological dose rates from these materials are orders of magnitude lower than those that arise, for example, from spent fuel when it is unloaded from a nuclear reactor, which contains intensely radioactive fission products such as cesium 137 and strontium 90.

Weapons Designs

With access to sufficient quantities of fissile materials, most nations and even some subnational groups would be capable of producing a nuclear weapon. Nuclear weapons are generally gun-type and implosion-type designs. Both types use fissile material, and several designs make use of the fusion of lighter elements to improve weapon efficiency and "boost" the energy release. Similar components are present in each design: chemical explosives to assemble the fissile material into a supercritical mass that will sustain an explosive chain reaction; nonfissile materials to reflect neutrons and tamp the explosion; electronics to trigger the explosion; a neutron generator to start the nuclear detonation at the appropriate time; and associated command, control, and, if needed, guidance systems (*see* Gun-Type Devices; Implosion Devices).

The gun-type design is the simplest nuclear weapon. Gun-type designs use U-235 or U-233 as the fissile material. The fissile material is kept in the form of two subcritical hemispheres that when brought together form a supercritical mass. Tampers, made of a heavy material placed around the fissile material in both hemispheres, contain the fissile material for the amount of time needed to produce the desired yield. The tampers also act as a neutron reflector. The nuclear explosion is initiated by detonating a high-explosive propellant behind one of the hemispheres, which accelerates rapidly down the barrel toward the other. At the instant the two hemispheres meet, a burst of neutrons is injected to initiate the chain reaction. The primary advantage of gun-type design is simplicity. It is as close to a foolproof design as technology allows. The drawback to the gun-type design is that low compression requires large amounts of fissionable material and leads to low efficiency. Only about 3 percent of the material is fissioned by a gun-type design, and only U-235 and U-233 can be used owing to the slow insertion speed of the device. The weight and length of the gun barrel makes the weapon heavy and long.

The implosion-type design makes use of the fact that increasing the density of the fissile material decreases the critical mass required for a supercritical state. This is the principle employed in most modern nuclear weapons designs. The fissile material is in the form of a small subcritical sphere surrounded by a tamper. Outside this is a high explosive, which is detonated simultaneously at a number of points on the exterior to produce a symmetrical, inward-traveling shock wave. This "implosion" compresses the fissile material two to three times its normal density. At the moment of maximum compression,

a burst of neutrons is injected to initiate the chain reaction. The implosion-type design creates a high insertion speed that allows materials with high spontaneous fission rates (such as plutonium) to be used. Implosion devices are lightweight and efficient weapons that use relatively small amounts of material. Advanced implosion-type designs are complex and require extensive research and testing and high-precision machining and electronics. Imprecise timing and lack of a simultaneous detonation will cause the weapon to malfunction.

Today, proliferation of all weapons of mass destruction is a pressing global security issue. As dual-use technologies spread across the globe, policy-makers are becoming increasingly concerned that existing arms control and nonproliferation regimes are failing to stop the spread of chemical, biological, nuclear, and radiological weapons and that it may be only a matter of time before these weapons are either stolen or manufactured by terrorists. Today, the greatest impediment to the proliferation of nuclear weapons into the hands of state and nonstate actors is the international regime to safeguard fissile materials.

—*D. Shannon Sentell, Jr.*

See also: Proliferation Security Initiative

References

Mark, J. C., "Explosive Properties of Reactor Grade Plutonium," *Science and Global Security,* vol. 4, 1993.

Nuclear Nonproliferation Treaty (NPT), INFCIRC/140, June 1968.

Office of Technology Assessment, *Technologies Underlying Weapons of Mass Destruction,* OTA-BP-ISC-115, December 1993.

Papazoglou, I. A., E. P. Gyftopolous, N. C. Rasmussen, M. M. Miller, and H. Raiffa, "A Methodology for the Assessment of the Proliferation Resistance of Nuclear Power Systems," MIT Energy Lab Report, MIT-EL-78-021, September 1978.

Sentell, D. Shannon, Jr., and M. W. Golay, "A Quantitative Assessment of Nuclear Weapons Proliferation Risk Utilizing Probabilistic Methods," The MIT Center for Advanced Nuclear Energy Systems (CANES), MIT-NFC-TR-042, June 2002.

PROLIFERATION SECURITY INITIATIVE

The Proliferation Security Initiative (PSI) is a cooperative effort initiated by the United States in 2003 to interdict shipments of weapons of mass destruction, their delivery systems, and related materials to and from states and nonstate actors of proliferation concern. In May 2003, the United States began working with ten like-minded countries (Australia, France, Germany, Italy, Japan, the Netherlands, Poland, Portugal, Spain, and the United Kingdom) to develop PSI. On September 4, 2003, PSI participants committed to a Statement of Interdiction Principles, vowing to take measures to interdict proliferation-related shipments; to streamline related information sharing; to enforce and strengthen relevant national and international law; and to take other specified steps to facilitate interdiction of proliferation-related cargoes. Canada, Norway, and Singapore have subsequently begun participating in PSI plenary meetings, and more than sixty states have endorsed the initiative's objectives. As President George W. Bush said in his May 2003 speech in Poland, "We will extend participation in PSI as broadly as possible to keep the world's most destructive weapons away from our shores and out of the hands of our common enemies."

In the PSI's first year, participants took several steps to improve their operational capacity to interdict shipments of concern. They conducted nine training exercises to practice interdicting proliferation-related shipments and held regular meetings, including five operational experts meetings. The United States is pursuing PSI boarding agreements with key flag states to facilitate interdictions of proliferation-related shipments on those states' vessels; the first such agreement was signed with Liberia on February 11, 2004. In October 2004, Japan hosted the first PSI exercise in Asia.

Although PSI participants at the June 2003 meeting in Brisbane, Australia, identified North Korea and Iran as states of particular concern, PSI is a global initiative and is aimed against proliferation-related shipments to and from all states and nonstate actors of proliferation concern. For example, in October 2003 German and Italian authorities, acting on information from U.S. and UK intelligence, stopped a shipment of advanced centrifuge parts bound for Libya.

—*Michael Lipson*

See also: Nonproliferation; Proliferation
References
Bush, George W., "The Proliferation Security Initiative Speech at Krakow, Poland, May 31, 2003," available at http://www.whitehouse.gov/news/releases/2003/05/20030531-2.html.

U.S. Department of State, "Proliferation Security Initiative," available at http://www.state.gov/t/np/c10390.htm.

White House, "Fact Sheet: Proliferation Security Initiative: Statement of Interdiction Principles," Washington, DC, 4 September 2003, available at http://www.whitehouse.gov/news/releases/2003/09/print/20030904-11.html.

PUGWASH CONFERENCES

Since 1957, the Pugwash Conferences on Science and World Affairs have brought together influential scientists, scholars, and public figures interested in reducing the danger of nuclear war and seeking cooperative solutions to world problems. After the events at Hiroshima and Nagasaki, Japan, in August 1945 and the subsequent expansion of nuclear forces by both the United States and the Soviet Union, many scientists began to discuss the moral implications of their work. The true driving force behind Pugwash, though, was philosopher Bertrand Russell. He obtained the support of key figures, such as Albert Einstein, and in 1955 they issued the Russell-Einstein Manifesto describing the potential horrors of a nuclear war and calling for a conference featuring top scientists from around the world to discuss ways to reduce the risk of nuclear war. The idea caught the attention of industrialist and philanthropist Cyrus Eaton, who offered to finance the conference and host it at his summer home in Pugwash, Nova Scotia. The 1957 conference was considered a huge success, so the meetings became regular events. Its founders argued that Pugwash could apply the scientific method of analyzing a problem to contentious scientific and political issues.

The first Pugwash Conference brought together twenty-two participants from ten countries, including the United States, England, the Soviet Union, and China. The hope was that the participants could bring ideas back to their own governments. Also, by building personal contacts, the scientists could increase confidence in their opponents' rationality, a concept central to deterrence. Physicist Joseph Rotblat, who had worked on the Manhattan Project, led the conference and became the leader of the group for the next forty years. Despite their diverse backgrounds, the participants agreed on certain technical issues and, even more important, on the idea that scientists had social responsibilities and should be part of future policy debates.

The original Russell-Einstein Manifesto and the first meeting generated significant press attention, and Pugwash quickly became well known in policy-making circles as well as among the general public. The group did its best to remain politically independent, and meeting participants always came as individuals, not representatives of their countries. The group also chose not to have a constitution or formal structure so that participants of different perspectives would remain equals. Some observers, however, portrayed the group as too soft, or even sympathetic to communism, because its calls for preventing war and pursuing disarmament overlapped somewhat with Soviet propaganda. Others noted the heavy percentage of the group who served as U.S. or British advisers and questioned whether it was a tool of those governments.

Over the years, Pugwash has chosen to remain a small group with attendance by invitation only rather than opening its meetings to the public. Although most participants are physical scientists, the number of social scientists has increased over time. By 2002, there had been more than 275 Pugwash conferences or workshops with over 3,500 partici-pants. Most of the group's early conferences were focused on nuclear policy and the Cold War. Now, its scope has expanded to include proliferation, chemical and biological weapons, land mines, regional disputes, and ethical problems tied to other scientific advances. The group has tried to encourage more women and more young scientists to become members, but there is some question whether Pugwash will survive after its leading figures retire or die.

Supporters credit the group with serving as an important link between East and West during the Cold War, with helping shape policy debates globally, and with encouraging arms control ideas. Pugwash has received numerous awards, including the 1995 Nobel Peace Prize.

—*John W. Dietrich*

References

Moore, Mike, "Forty Years of Pugwash," *Bulletin of the Atomic Scientists,* vol. 53, 1997, pp. 40–45.

Rotblat, Joseph, "The Early Days of Pugwash," *Physics Today,* vol. 54, 2001, pp. 50–55.

———, "The Pugwash Movement," *UNESCO Courier,* vol. 54, 2001, pp. 34–35.

Q

QUADRENNIAL DEFENSE REVIEW

The first Quadrennial Defense Review (QDR) of 1997 was the fourth comprehensive review of the U.S. military since the end of the Cold War. It built upon the experience of the 1991 Base Force Review, the 1993 Bottom-Up Review, and the 1995 Commission on Roles and Missions of the Armed Forces. It was mandated by the 1997 Military Force Structure Review Act and was designed by the U.S. Department of Defense to be a comprehensive examination of America's emerging defense needs between 1997 and 2015.

The QDR covers issues of potential threat, strategy, force structure, readiness levels, deployment patterns, infrastructure, and modernization. The review has served as a model for nations' efforts to realign their military force structures. The United Kingdom, for example, conducted a 1998 Strategic Defence Review.

The QDR is designed to be a collaborative effort between the U.S. secretary of defense and the Joint Chiefs of Staff and may be modified to reflect the changing world situation. The 1997 QDR followed the Bosnian War, and the 2001 QDR was finalized in the immediate aftermath of the terrorist attacks of September 11, 2001. The next one is scheduled for 2005.

—*Andrew M. Dorman*

See also: Bottom-Up Review; Joint Chiefs of Staff; Nuclear Posture Review; United States Nuclear Forces and Doctrine

References

Larson, Eric V., David T. Orletsky, and Kriston Leuschner, et al., *Defense Planning in a Decade of Change: Lessons from the Base Force, Bottom-Up Review and Quadrennial Defense Review* (Santa Monica, CA: RAND Corporation, 2001).

Quadrennial Defense Report, 1997, available at http://www.defenselink.mil/qdr.

Quadrennial Defense Report, 2001, available at http://www.defenselink.mil/qdr.

RADIATION

Ionizing radiation is one of the three principal effects produced by a nuclear explosion, along with blast and thermal radiation. It is composed of alpha particles, beta particles, gamma rays, X-rays, neutrons, high-speed electrons, high-speed protons, and other particles capable of producing ions. Radiation, as used in this context, does not include nonionizing radiation.

Technical Details

All material is composed of atoms. Atoms, in turn, are composed of a nucleus, which contains minute particles called protons and neutrons, and an outer shell made up of particles called electrons. The nucleus carries a positive electrical charge, and the electrons carry a negative charge. As electrons are bound to the nucleus of the atom, so are the particles within the nucleus. These forces work toward a strongly stable balance. The process by which the nuclei of atoms work toward becoming stable is to get rid of excess energy. Unstable nuclei may emit a quantity of energy, or they may emit a particle. This emitted atomic energy or particle is called "radiation." A nuclear explosion produces ionizing radiation. The process by which atoms gain or lose electrons is called "ionization." In ionizing radiation, the energy from the radiation is sufficient to remove electrons from atoms, leaving two positively charged particles (ions) behind. Some forms of radiation, such as visible light, microwaves, or radio waves, do not have sufficient energy to remove electrons from atoms. They are called "nonionizing radiation."

A nuclear explosion creates four kinds of radiation—alpha, beta, gamma, and neutron. Only three of these are significant to this discussion: alpha, beta, and gamma.

Alpha radiation has low penetrating power and a short range (a few centimeters in air). Because of this short range, the danger to the external surface of the human body is negligible. The most energetic alpha particle will generally fail to penetrate the dead layers of cells covering the body and can be easily stopped by a sheet of paper. Alpha particles are hazardous if allowed to enter the body through a break in the skin, ingestion, or the respiratory tract, however. Once inside the body, the alpha particles, with their high ionizing ability, will expend their energy into a single group of cells. This causes a very high degree of localized tissue damage. Alpha emitters present an internal hazard twenty times as great as beta or gamma emitters.

Even though airborne beta particles can travel significant distances, solid materials will stop them. Beta emitters present two potential external radiation hazards: the beta particles themselves and the X-rays they can produce when they strike certain materials, such as lead. Although beta particles can travel significant distances in air, materials such as aluminum, plastic, or glass provide appropriate shielding. However, these emitters should be handled with care. Because the lens of the eye is radiosensitive, eye protection such as goggles or a protective mask is recommended.

Gamma radiation does not consist of particles, it has no electrical charge, and science has demonstrated that it has no mass. Gamma radiation is far more dangerous than alpha or beta because its rays are more penetrating and harmful. How successfully one is protected depends on the type, density, and thickness of the shielding. Simply stated, as the thickness of the shielding increases, the penetration of the gamma radiation decreases. Higher density materials such as lead, tungsten, concrete, and steel can be effective shields against gamma emissions.

Although radiation is perhaps the best-known effect of nuclear weapons, it accounts for only 15 percent of the destructive force of the explosion. This includes initial radiation (neutrons and gamma rays), which is emitted within the first minute after detonation, and residual nuclear radiation, which is emitted after the first minute.

Approximately 5 percent of the energy released in a nuclear burst is transmitted in the form of initial neutron and gamma radiation. The neutrons result almost exclusively from the energy produced by the fission and fusion reactions. The initial gamma radiation arises from these reactions as well as from the decay of short-lived fission products. The intensity of the initial nuclear radiation decreases rapidly with distance from the point of burst. The character of the radiation received at a given location also varies with distance from the explosion. Near the point of the explosion, the neutron intensity is greater than the gamma intensity, but it diminishes quickly with distance. The range for significant levels of initial radiation does not increase markedly with weapon yield. Therefore, initial radiation actually becomes less of a hazard with increasing yield, as individuals close enough to be significantly irradiated are killed by the blast and thermal effects.

Residual Radiation (Fallout)

Residual radiation from a nuclear explosion accounts for 10 percent of the energy released and primarily takes the form of fallout. Fallout is created when a nuclear weapon surface burst vaporizes large amounts of earth or water because of the heat of the fireball. This debris is drawn up into the radioactive "mushroom" cloud, especially if the explosive yield exceeds 10 kilotons. This material becomes radioactive and will eventually settle to earth as fallout. The area and intensity of the fallout is strongly influenced by local weather conditions. Much of the material is simply blown downwind, forming a plume-shaped pattern on the ground. Rainfall can also have a significant influence on the ways in which fallout is deposited, since rain will carry contaminated particles to the ground. The areas receiving such contaminated rainfall become "hot spots" with greater radiation intensity than their surroundings.

Severe local contamination can extend far beyond the limits of the blast and thermal effects, particularly in the case of high-yield surface detonations. The danger from fallout lessens with time. This lessening is called "decay." In technical terms,

radioactive decay is the process by which large, unstable atoms become more stable by emitting radiation. The radiation can be in the form of a positively charged alpha particle, a negatively charged beta particle, or gamma rays.

—Jeffrey A. Adams

See also: Fallout; Neutrons; Nuclear Weapons Effects; Radiation Absorbed Dose (Rad); Roentgen Equivalent Man (Rem)

References

Adams, Jeffrey A., and Stephen Marquette, *First Responders Guide to Weapons of Mass Destruction (WMD)* (Alexandria, VA: American Society for Industrial Security [ASIS], February 2002).

U.S. Army Field Manual (FM) 4-02.283, *Treatment of Nuclear and Radiological Casualties*, Headquarters, Department of the Army, Washington, DC.

U.S. Nuclear Regulatory Commission, *Glossary of Terms: Nuclear Power and Radiation*, Washington, DC, June 1981.

RADIATION ABSORBED DOSE (RAD)

The radiation absorbed dose, or "rad," is a measurement of the energy absorbed by any material (for example, water, human tissue, or air) as it passes through a field of ionizing radiation. It is a unit of absorbed dose. "Absorbed dose" is that radiation which is actually absorbed into material (such as the human body). The term should not be confused with "exposure dose," which is radiation available to be absorbed. A rad of one type of radiation does not necessarily produce the same biological effect as a rad of another kind. The difference in biological effectiveness is given in terms of the relative biological effectiveness (RBE).

One rad is the absorption of 100 ergs of energy per gram of absorber. An erg is an extremely small amount of energy. To raise a 1-pound weight the distance of 1 foot, for example, would require about 13.6 million ergs.

Another unit of absorbed dose is the Roentgen equivalent man (rem). One rem is an absorbed dose of any ionizing radiation that will produce the same biological effect in man as the absorbed dose from exposure to 1 roentgen of X-ray or gamma radiation.

—Jeffrey A. Adams

See also: Radiation; Roentgen Equivalent Man (Rem)

References

U.S. Army Field Manual (FM) 4-02.283, *Treatment of Nuclear and Radiological Casualties*, Headquarters, Department of the Army, Washington, DC.

U.S. Department of Defense, *Weapons of Mass Destruction (WMD) Handbook,* JCS J-3 (Washington, DC, February 2001).

U.S. Nuclear Regulatory Commission, *Glossary of Terms: Nuclear Power and Radiation,* Washington, DC, June 1981.

RADIOLOGICAL DISPERSAL DEVICE

Radiological dispersal devices (RDDs) cause contamination and health risks by dispersing radioactive substances into a populated area. The most spectacular type of RDD is the so-called dirty bomb. In a dirty bomb, radioactive material is wrapped around a conventional explosive and detonated, contaminating the surroundings. Unlike nuclear weapons, dirty bombs do not involve a nuclear chain reaction but rely on the innate radioactivity of the materials released.

Radioactive substances are widely available in society because of their use in industry, medicine, and research. Substantial contamination would require highly radioactive materials that are difficult to procure and to handle. The amount of radioactive material used, dispersal effectiveness, exposure time, and exposure patterns would all influence the risk of acute death from a dirty bomb, but generally the risk of lethal exposure from an RDD is low. The danger to health and life is thus primarily due to long-term effects (for example, increased cancer risks). The use of RDDs could create a strong psychological impact and widespread panic.

Terrorists could spread radioactive substances simply by pouring out or dispersing the material in high-traffic areas. Decontamination could be very difficult, time consuming, and expensive. Food and drinking water also could be contaminated, again with huge societal and economic losses. More sophisticated perpetrators could use spreading devices to contaminate the air with radioactive dust.

A team from the Seattle Fire Department participated in this May 2003 simulation of a "dirty bomb" incident. (Reuters/Corbis)

In 1995, Chechnyan rebels threatened to blow up several assembled dirty bombs in Moscow, but the threats were never carried out. Although government officials across the globe are concerned that terrorists will employ a dirty bomb against a civilian target, their worst fears have not become a reality.

—Morten Bremer Maerli

References

Ferguson, Charles D., Tahseen Kazi, and Judith Perera, *Commercial Radioactive Sources: Surveying the Security Risks,* Occasional Paper 11 (Monterey, CA: Center for Nonproliferation Studies, Monterey Institute for International Studies, January 2003), available at http://www.cns.miis.edu/pubs/opapers/op11/index.htm.

Ford, James L., "Radiological Dispersal Devices: Assessing the Transnational Threat," *Strategic Forum,* no. 136, National Defense University, March 1998, available at http://www.ndu.edu/inss/strforum/SF136/forum136.html.

THE RAND CORPORATION

The RAND Corporation was the first and most influential of the "think tanks" that arose in the years following World War II to explore the impact of the advent of nuclear weapons on the character and conduct of war.

In 1946, the Air Materiel Command signed a $10 million, three-year contract with Douglas Aircraft Corporation to found Project RAND (its name based on the initials for "research and development"). In 1948, the group split from Douglas and became the independent RAND Corporation.

The RAND Corporation pioneered the development of nuclear strategy in the years following World War II. It was home to some of the most influential U.S. nuclear strategists, including Bernard Brodie, Thomas Schelling, and Albert Wohlstetter. Working in an environment that was largely devoid of bureaucratic constraints, RAND researchers developed many of the concepts that became fundamental to nuclear strategy and deterrence theory, such as first- and second-strike forces, escalation, and stability. A number of RAND alumni, including James Schlesinger and Andrew W. Marshall, later held influential positions within the U.S. Defense Department.

RAND also conducted a number of important studies of military technology. RAND analysts were among the first to argue, in December 1950, that an intercontinental ballistic missile was feasible and to explore the possibility of using an artificial satellite to conduct reconnaissance.

—Tom Mahnken

References

Collins, Martin J., *Cold War Laboratory: RAND, the Air Force, and the American State, 1945–1950* (Washington, DC: Smithsonian Institution Press, 2002).

Kaplan, Fred M., *The Wizards of Armageddon* (New York: Simon and Schuster, 1983).

RAPACKI PLAN

The Rapacki Plan of the early 1950s was the first nuclear weapons free zone (NWFZ) formally proposed in an international forum. Put before the twelfth session of the United Nations General Assembly by Polish foreign minister Adam Rapacki, the plan proposed banning the manufacture and deployment of nuclear weapons in Central Europe, including Poland, Czechoslovakia, the German Democratic Republic (GDR), and the Federal Republic of Germany. Nuclear-armed states would be expected to respect the nonnuclear status of the region and not use or deploy nuclear weapons anywhere in the NWFZ. The plan was to be ratified by all signatories, and verification and compliance with its provisions would be monitored by a commission made up of neutral states as well as members of the Warsaw Pact and the North Atlantic Treaty Organization (NATO).

NATO rejected the proposal on the grounds that it failed to limit conventional forces in the region and to address the issue of German reunification. Rapacki responded in 1958 with a new proposal for phased nuclear reductions in the region. Under the new plan, a nuclear freeze would be followed by negotiated reductions in existing stockpiles maintained in the proposed NWFZ.

Soviet and Polish officials advanced the Rapacki Plan as a way to prevent West Germany from obtaining access to NATO nuclear weapons and as a vehicle to gain Western recognition of the GDR. Polish officials also viewed it as a way for smaller members of the Warsaw Pact to open trade and cultural relations with NATO. The failure of Rapacki's initiative heralded the onset of Soviet-U.S. acrimony over a divided Germany that culminated in the second Berlin Crisis that began to heat up in 1958 and culminated in 1961.

—*James J. Wirtz*

See also: Cold War; Nuclear Weapons Free Zones
Reference
Freedman, Lawrence, *The Evolution of Nuclear Strategy,* third edition (New York: Palgrave Macmillan, 2003).

RAROTONGA, TREATY OF

See Nuclear Weapons Free Zones (NWFZs)

RATIFICATION

Ratification is a process whereby a treaty is formally approved by a sovereign governing entity (usually a state or group of states). Ratification follows treaty negotiation and is normally a prelude to implementation. Often, treaties negotiated by the executive branch of a government are ratified by the legislative branch; in the United States, for example, the Constitution (Article II, Section 2) explicitly states that the president "shall have the Power, by and with the Advice and Consent of the Senate, to make treaties, provided two thirds of the Senators present concur" (although the president can also make "congressional-executive agreements" that are "ratified" with only a majority from both the Senate and the House).

The Vienna Convention on the Law of Treaties, drafted in 1969, and which entered into force in 1980, codified international customary treaty law. Although the United States is not a party to the Vienna Convention, it nonetheless recognizes the convention's binding nature because it restates already accepted international laws. The Vienna Convention defines ratification as "the international act so named whereby a State establishes on the international plane its consent to be bound by a treaty."

Generally, individual treaties contain provisions specifying how many nations must actually ratify the treaty for it to enter into force. In terms of the Comprehensive Test Ban Treaty (CTBT), for example, forty-four states—those possessing nuclear power or research reactors at the time of the 1996 United Nations Conference on Disarmament, where the CTBT was negotiated—must sign and ratify the CTBT for it to enter into force. Only thirty-two of those states had done so as of mid-2004. (The United States is among those which have not ratified the treaty.) The ratification process

highlights the potential for domestic political concerns to influence international attempts to regulate weapons of mass destruction.

—*William D. Casebeer*

See also: Arms Control; Comprehensive Test Ban Treaty; Entry into Force; Implementation; Underground Testing; Verification
References
Krepon, Michael, and Dan Caldwell, eds., *The Politics of Arms Control Treaty Ratification* (New York: Palgrave MacMillan, 1991).
Lindsay, James M., *Congress and the Politics of U.S. Foreign Policy* (Baltimore: Johns Hopkins University Press, 1994).
Vienna Convention text, United Nations website, available at http://www.un.org/law/ilc/texts/treatfra.htm.

REACTOR OPERATIONS

"Reactor operations" is a broad term that can be interpreted to mean a number of different operations associated with nuclear power plants. A nuclear reactor is a device that controls and sustains the nuclear fission process for extended periods of time to harness the associated energy or to conduct research. "Reactor operations" refers to the nonnuclear and nuclear components of a nuclear power plant that are necessary to harness fission energy in the form of heat and convert that energy to electricity. The term may also refer to reactor core operations, the day-to-day operations of a nuclear power plant, or other procedures associated with nuclear power plants.

Background
The first reactor was designed and built by Enrico Fermi at Stagg Field Stadium, University of Chicago, on December 2, 1942. Fermi achieved this first self-sustaining nuclear chain reaction for research purposes. The first reactor that supplied power, designed, built, and operated in December 1951 by Argonne National Laboratory, was the Experimental Breeder Reactor (EBR-1) at the Nuclear Reactor Testing Station in Arco, Idaho. Argonne National Lab also built a prototype pressurized water reactor submarine in 1953 that produced electrical power and was an important predecessor to the first commercial power reactor built by the United States.

The first nuclear power plant built and operated in the Soviet Union was a 5-megawatt reactor that

Inside a functioning graphite reactor at Chernobyl, Ukraine, 1996. (Kleschuk Anatoly/Corbis Sygma)

began operation in 1954. England built a nuclear power plant for commercial purposes in 1956, a 50-megawatt gas-graphite reactor at Calder Hall in Cumbria, England. The first central-station nuclear power plant in service in the United States was the 60-megawatt Shippingport pressurized-water reactor (PWR), which went into operation on December 2, 1957, in Shippingport, Pennsylvania.

Technical Details

Nuclear power plants are much like any other power plant (for example, fossil fuel–burning power plants) because the objective is to burn fuel that will generate heat, which is used to produce steam. Steam is then used to turn turbines, which generate electrical power. The difference between nuclear and conventionally fired reactors is that nuclear power plants burn nuclear fuel in the fission process in the form of fissile material as opposed to burning coal or another fossil fuel.

Even though there are many different reactor designs, nuclear power plants have common components. All nuclear power plants have a reactor core with associated fuel, moderator, coolant, and shielding materials; a boiler, condenser, and turbines used to generate electrical power; and control and safety

features. Figure R-1 is a diagram of a pressurized-water reactor and illustrates the basic components of a nuclear power plant.

The core of a nuclear reactor is where the sustained nuclear chain reaction is accomplished and the energy from fission released. The heat generated by the reactor core is used to boil water, which turns turbines to generate electrical power. The reactor core is generally composed of the nuclear fuel or fissile material, coolant, reflector material, moderator (if the reactor uses thermal neutrons to sustain the chain reaction), and reactor control material.

The control of neutrons in the reactor core is essential to reactor operations. In order for a reactor to sustain a nuclear chain reaction, each generation of fissions must generate enough neutrons to cause another generation of fissions to occur. As neutrons escape from nuclei during the fission process, they may be absorbed or captured by the nuclei of materials in the reactor, they may escape or leak out of the reactor core entirely, or they may cause other nuclei to fission.

Fortunately, the most common fissile fuel used in nuclear reactors in the United States, uranium 235, releases an average of 2.4 neutrons for every fission event. Reflector material is used to scatter neu-

Figure R-1: Pressured Water Reactor

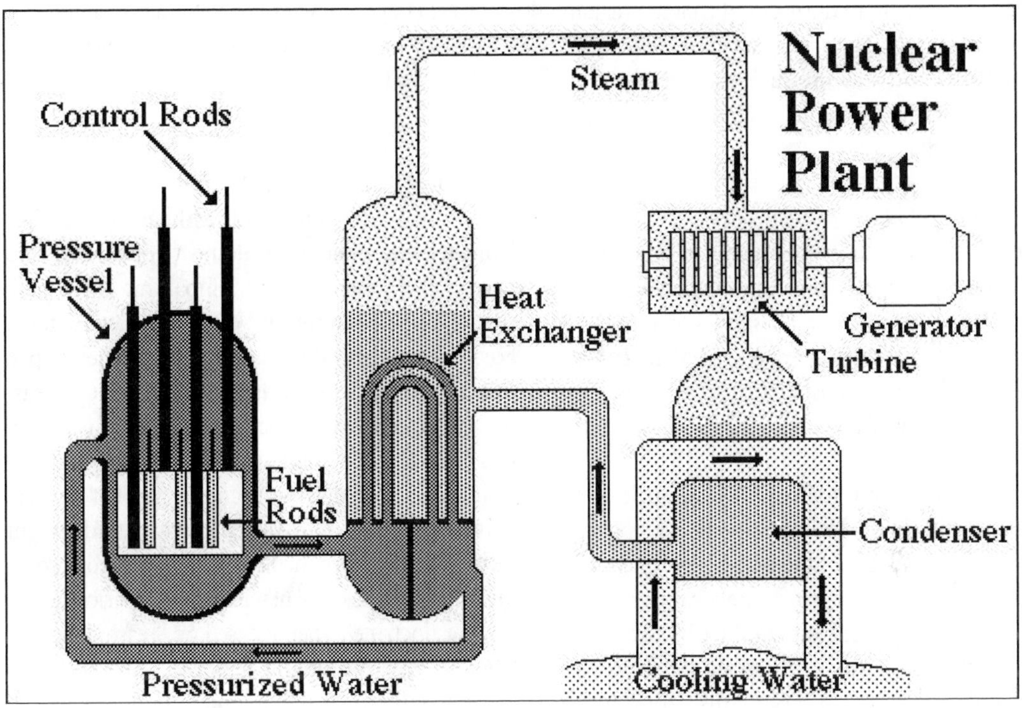

Source: http://www.hibbing.tec.mn.us/programs/dept/chem/V.11/page_id_70977.html.

trons back toward the fissile material, thereby precluding their escape from the reactor core. Moderator material is used to slow neutrons down to energy levels that are conducive to causing fission. Coolant in the core is used to ensure that the core materials do not "melt down" due to excessive heat caused by the fission process. Control rods also may be added to the core to control how many neutrons are present. Control rods generally absorb neutrons, which means that there would be fewer neutrons to cause fission events when they are inserted. The reactor core vessel is designed with the shielding materials necessary to shield workers and the environment from the harmful effects of the radiation associated with the fission process.

The boiler and condenser are two basic components of a nuclear power plant. The boiler is the device in which water is allowed to boil to generate steam. The steam is then used to turn turbines. These turbines generate electricity. After the steam is used to turn the turbines, it is diverted to a condenser, where the steam is cooled to become water.

Control and safety features for nuclear power plants became the focus of intense scrutiny by the nuclear regulatory commission and other governing bodies after the Three Mile Island accident in March 1979 near Harrisburg, Pennsylvania. The main purpose of these control and safety features is to control the environment within the reactor core. Control rods play an important role in controlling the number of neutrons, and thereby the number of fissions, that occur in the core.

Other than the number of fissions occurring in the core, another major concern is the temperature of the reactor core. Coolant is critical to maintaining the temperature of the core. Without coolant present, the fission process would generate enough heat to melt the material of the reactor core. Emergency safety features have been implemented to prevent a loss of coolant accident (LOCA). One of these safety features is the emergency core cooling system (ECCS), which is capable of introducing more coolant into the core using both passive and active systems. The passive system is essentially large accumulator tanks that hold water to be introduced to the core in the event of a large break in the coolant system. The active system includes a series of high- and low-pressure coolant injection systems, which are used to maintain the proper level of coolant.

Nuclear Power Today

Nuclear reactors are operating in countries throughout the world. Thirty-one countries use approximately 440 reactors to supply commercial power, and 56 countries operate more than 280 reactors for research purposes. Nuclear reactors supply approximately 17 percent of the world's electricity needs.

There are currently 104 commercial nuclear reactors operating in the United States that supply approximately 20 percent of the nation's power. Additionally, there are approximately 36 research reactors operating in 23 states in the United States.

With increasing concerns about the environment and emissions of pollutants from fossil fuel–burning power plants, reactor operations offer an alternative energy source. Operating a nuclear power plant is generally better for the environment than fossil fuel–burning plants in terms of the production of greenhouse gases. Nuclear power plants produce no nitrous oxides, sulfur dioxides, or carbon dioxides and emit only very small amounts of radioactive gases.

Reactor operating costs for a nuclear power plant also offer advantages to nuclear power. Even though there is a considerable front-loaded capital cost to build and license a nuclear reactor, the fuel and operating costs are relatively inexpensive compared to some types of electric plants that rely on fossil fuel.

—*Don Gillich*

See also: Canada Deuterium Uranium Reactor; Fast Breeder Reactors; Gas-Graphite Reactors; Light-Water Reactors; Mixed Oxide Fuel; Neutrons; Nuclear Fuel Cycle; Pressurized-Water Reactors; Research Reactors; Three Mile Island; Uranium

References

Glasstone, Samuel, and Alexander Sesonske, *Nuclear Reactor Engineering* (Princeton, NJ: D. Van Norstrand, 1967).

Lamarsh, John R., and Anthony J. Baratta, *Introduction to Nuclear Engineering*, third edition (Upper Saddle River, NJ: Prentice-Hall, 2001).

Gonyeau, Joseph P. E., *The Virtual Nuclear Tourist*, available at http://www.nucleartourist.com/.

Hibbing Community College Chemistry Department "Chem Card" website, Card 109, available at http://www.hibbing.tec.mn.us/programs/dept/chem/V.11/page_id_70977.html.

REASONABLE SUFFICIENCY

In 1985, Soviet President Mikhail Gorbachev launched the policies of glasnost (openness) and perestroika (restructuring), embarking on a path that culminated in the end of the Warsaw Pact, the Soviet Union, and the Cold War. Gorbachev hoped to revitalize Soviet communism to make it increasingly competitive with the capitalist West. As part of this program, he sought to reduce international tension and Soviet defense spending so that Russia's natural resources and Western aid and trade might be used to revitalize the Soviet economy. To accomplish this goal, Gorbachev began to describe Soviet nuclear doctrine as being based on "reasonable sufficiency." At a meeting in Berlin in May 1987, reasonable sufficiency was adopted as policy by the Warsaw Pact.

Reasonable sufficiency rejected traditional Soviet military doctrine, which had been based on the notion that offense was the best type of defense. Under that doctrine, if the threat of war loomed with the United States or the North Atlantic Treaty Organization (NATO), Warsaw Pact forces would launch an offensive thrust using both nuclear and conventional weapons to destroy NATO forces and occupy all of Europe to the Atlantic coast. Reasonable sufficiency abandoned the idea of preventive war or preemptive attack, reduced the capability of Soviet mechanized forces to attack Western Europe, eliminated theater nuclear forces, and cut conventional capabilities to a level equal to NATO forces. Warsaw Pact units would retain some offensive capability to counter a NATO attack or to intervene if revolution threatened Communist regimes that controlled Eastern Europe. Reasonable sufficiency slowly emerged as a truly "defensive" form of defense.

Reasonable sufficiency elicited much NATO interest in reciprocal force reductions, confidence-building measures, and other diplomatic initiatives that demonstrated to all concerned that it was possible to break the cycle of armament and mistrust that animated the Cold War in Europe.

—*James J. Wirtz*

See also: Cold War
Reference
Hines, John G., and Donald Mahoney, *Defense and Counteroffense under the New Soviet Military Doctrine* (Santa Monica, CA: RAND Corporation, 1991).

RECIPROCAL FEAR OF SURPRISE ATTACK

The concept of a reciprocal fear of surprise attack focuses on the circumstances that may allow for the possibility of an accidental war breaking out during a peaceful but tense situation. The theory rests on the fact that it is theoretically possible to seize a tremendous advantage by striking first in a nuclear conflict. A preemptive nuclear strike against an opponent's command structure, communications network, and nuclear capabilities may cripple or completely eradicate the opponent's ability to retaliate. Since both sides of a conflict are aware of this advantage, there is a necessary premium on mobilizing a swift and decisive assault. Because of the reciprocal fear of surprise attack, both sides would be tremendously sensitive to the actions of the other side, increasing their readiness to unleash a devastating preemptive strike before the other side was capable of doing the same.

The reciprocal fear of surprise attack is the primary motivating factor that some believe can accidentally lead to a large-scale nuclear war without a catalytic military or political event. A situation of this sort is inherently more unstable than a situation where retaliatory forces are secure and where there is thus no incentive to preempt. The delicacy of the balance of first- and second-strike capabilities is therefore the source of this instability. If one side of a conflict determines that its retaliatory capability is insecure, the fear of a surprise attack may encourage a preemptive attack.

These concerns led the United States and the Soviet Union to the negotiating table several times during the Cold War in an attempt to find a way to prevent a dangerous situation from escalating out of control. A surprise attack conference was convened in 1958 to discuss this possibility, and the first in a series of "Hot Line Agreements" was signed in 1963, establishing a direct communications link between Washington and Moscow to ensure the ability to talk about a situation before undertaking military action. Confidence- and security-building measures also attempt to reduce the possibility of surprise attack.

—*Abe Denmark and Jeffrey A. Larsen*

See also: Accidental Nuclear War; First Strike; Hot Line Agreements; Preemptive Attack; Surprise Attack Conference

References
Jervis, Robert, "Arms Control, Stability, and Causes of War," *Political Science Quarterly*, vol. 108, no. 2, Summer 1993, pp. 239–253.
Schelling, Thomas, *Strategy of Conflict* (New York: Oxford University Press, 1963), pp. 207–229.

RECONNAISSANCE SATELLITES

Intelligence-gathering or reconnaissance satellites (sometimes called spy satellites, or spysats) are an important means of collecting information about denied targets in another country, including weapons of mass destruction (WMD). There are two basic types of reconnaissance satellites: imaging systems that create "pictures" from sources such as infrared energy, visible light, ultraviolet light, or radar returns; and signals intelligence (SIGINT) systems that collect data from other portions of the electromagnetic spectrum such as voice communications, telemetry signals, or radar emissions. For most of the Cold War, spysats were a top-secret monopoly of the superpowers. They became increasingly important in later years as national technical means (NTM) of verification for arms control agreements (*see* National Technical Means). Today, spysats are becoming less expensive and more capable, and they are being used and operated by a growing number of states and commercial enterprises.

History and Background

Obtaining accurate intelligence data on the Soviet Union, especially on its nuclear weapons and ballistic missile programs, was a major challenge for the United States during the early Cold War period. This problem became particularly acute after the shock of the Soviet fission and fusion weapons tests, which began in 1949 and succeeded in producing a fusion device in 1955. In 1954, President Dwight D. Eisenhower commissioned a year-long study by influential scientists, the Technological Capabilities Panel (TCP), to address the evolving strategic environment and the threat of surprise attack. Following the July 1955 failure of its Open Skies proposal (a plan to allow the superpowers to overfly each other's territory with intelligence-gathering aircraft), the Eisenhower administration focused on space as a potential means of opening up the closed Soviet state. Creating a legal regime that would legitimize satellite overflight and intelligence gathering from space was the secret but overriding priority of America's first space policy, National Security Council (NSC) Memorandum 5520, promulgated in May 1955. This policy, some two and a half years before the Soviet Sputnik launch opened the space age, called for the United States to secretly develop spysats and openly develop scientific satellites to support the International Geophysical Year (IGY). The Eisenhower administration planned to orbit the IGY satellites first to establish a peaceful precedent for satellite overflight of sovereign space.

The TCP and NSC-5520 led directly to America's first high-tech spy programs: the high-flying U-2 spy plane and the WS-117L spysat system. The WS-117L program was begun in March 1955 and grew to encompass three types of intelligence gathering from space: photoreconnaissance via film return under the Corona program; photoreconnaissance via electro-optical signal return under the Samos program; and infrared early warning of ballistic missile launch under the Midas program. All of these programs were pushing the technology envelope and ran into significant delays and hurdles during the 1950s and 1960s. In August 1960, the first successful Corona photoreconnaissance mission returned film, which helped to dispel fears of a missile gap. But the first operational space-based infrared early-warning system was not established until the Defense Support Program (DSP) system was orbited in the late 1960s, and the electro-optical photoreconnaissance system was not deployed until the first launch of the KH-11 system in December 1976.

To maintain the veil of secrecy around the development and operation of spysats, the Eisenhower administration created the National Reconnaissance Office (NRO), an organization composed primarily of Central Intelligence Agency (CIA) and Department of Defense (air force and navy) personnel. The very existence of the NRO was an official state secret from its inception in August 1961 until its existence was declassified in September 1992. Under directives developed during the Kennedy administration, spysats and other types of military space activity were wrapped in deepest secrecy. The NRO quietly influenced U.S. space policy and programs during the Cold War. Examples of NRO influence included cancellation of the air force's Manned Orbiting Laboratory for intelligence gathering in favor of the NRO's KH-9 spysat; the evolution of the cross-range, payload, and cargo bay design for the space shuttle to accommodate future generation spysats; and NRO's success in the 1980s as the only organization allowed to build a backup launcher for the shuttle, the Complementary Expendable Launch Vehicle.

Satellites and Arms Control

Starting with the Vela Hotel nuclear detonation detection system, created to verify compliance with the 1963 Limited Test Ban Treaty, spysats became the linchpin in enabling strategic arms control between the superpowers—their most important role during the Cold War. Prior to the advent of increasingly capable space-based intelligence collection systems, U.S.-Soviet arms control negotiations had always broken down, often over the contentious issue of how compliance with agreements was to be verified. The United States had consistently called for on-site inspections (OSIs) to verify compliance, while the Soviet Union had rejected this approach as a violation of its national sovereignty. By the mid-1960s, however, U.S. negotiators had enough confidence in using spysats for verification that they were willing to forgo their previous insistence on OSIs. This change in policy was critical in bringing about the 1972 treaty resulting from the Strategic Arms Limitation Talks (SALT I), the first comprehensive arms control agreement between the superpowers. The Anti-Ballistic Missile (ABM) Treaty portion of SALT I contains the first euphemistic reference to highly secret spysats as "national technical means" of verification. There was also a subtle but critical link between what a spysat could "see" and arms control units of accounting. This linkage was an important factor in optimizing spysat improvements for the NTM mission during the latter half of the Cold War.

Satellites in the Post–Cold War Era

Following the end of the Cold War, the United States reordered its spysat priorities and policies. With recognition of the significant force-enhancement capabilities of space systems during Operation Desert Storm (the "first space war"), the United States moved to make the NRO's imagery more quickly and openly available to operational commanders and units on the battlefield. This shift has enabled the reconnaissance, precision-strike revolution in military affairs that has characterized the new American way of war.

Changes in the commercial remote sensing sector are perhaps even more significant. Under the Land Remote Sensing Policy Act of 1992 and Presidential Decision Directive (PDD) 23 of March 1994, the United States now seeks to create incentives for the development of a commercial high-resolution remote sensing industry that will be dominated by U.S. firms. The National Imagery and Mapping Agency (NIMA) was created in 1996, in part to support this new policy and to facilitate dissemination of high-resolution commercial remote-sensing data to users throughout the U.S. government. Reflecting the availability of high-quality commercial imagery, the director of Central Intelligence recently ordered that commercial systems rather than government spysats become the primary data source for all U.S. mapping efforts.

It is unclear how more and increasingly capable spysats used and operated by a growing number of state and nonstate actors will impact privacy, transparency, and the proliferation of weapons of mass destruction. It is likely, however, that these systems will continue to have a significant effect on global security and play a growing role in international security and commerce in the years ahead.

—Peter Hays

See also: Early Warning; Open Skies; Outer Space Treaty; Verification

References

Day, Dwayne A., John M. Logsdon, and Brian Latell, eds., *Eye in the Sky: The Story of the Corona Spy Satellites* (Washington, DC: Smithsonian Institution Press, 1998).

Dehqanzada, Yahya A., and Ann M. Florini, *Secrets for Sale: How Commercial Satellite Imagery Will Change the World* (Washington, DC: Carnegie Endowment for International Peace, 2000).

McDougall, Walter A., *The Heavens and the Earth: A Political History of the Space Age* (New York: Basic, 1985).

Richelson, Jeffrey T., *America's Secret Eyes in Space: The U.S. Keyhole Spy Satellite Program* (New York: Harper and Row, 1990).

Ruffner, Kevin C., ed., *Corona: America's First Satellite Program* (Washington, DC: Center for the Study of Intelligence, Central Intelligence Agency, 1995).

Taubman, Philip, *Secret Empire: Eisenhower, the CIA, and the Hidden Story of America's Space Espionage* (New York: Simon and Schuster, 2003).

RED MERCURY

The substance known as "red mercury," purportedly a mystery ingredient in Soviet pure fusion weapons, gained both U.S. congressional and worldwide media attention in the wake of the 1991 collapse of the Soviet Union when it began appearing on the nuclear materials black market. The red mercury furor began over reports that the Soviet Union had perfected a pure fusion nuclear warhead, which reportedly relied on heavy hydrogen—deuterium and lithium isotopes—as its fuel.

It is said that under the proper heat and pressure, the lithium and deuterium isotopes fuse, releasing high-energy neutrons that kill living matter in their path. Identified by traffickers with the composition $Hg_2SB_2O_7$ (that is, a combination of mercury, sulphur, boron, and oxygen), red mercury has since been surmised to be the Russian code name for lithium deuteride, Li_6D, a legitimate component in thermonuclear weapon production, or the heavy metal osmium.

Though there are some detractors who insist that red mercury is legitimate, much of the nuclear scientific community has stepped forward to discredit it as an important component in pure fusion weaponry. Instead, it is generally accepted that red mercury was touted by intelligence organizations or criminals as a weapons material to hoodwink terrorists and states with nuclear ambitions. Reports of it appearing on the nuclear black market have become less frequent in recent years.

—Jennifer Lasecki

References

Badolato, Edward V., and Dale Andrade, "Red Mercury: Hoax or the Ultimate Terrorist Weapon?" *Counter Terrorism and Security,* Spring 1996, pp. 18–20.

Edwards, Rob, "Cherry Red and Very Dangerous," *New Scientist,* 29 April 1995, pp. 4–5.

"Red Mercury: Is There a Pure-Fusion Bomb for Sale?" *International Defense Review,* vol. 27, June 1994, pp. 79–81.

REENTRY VEHICLES

A reentry vehicle (RV) is a casing that protects a missile payload during descent through the Earth's atmosphere. At intercontinental distances, reentry velocities can reach Mach 20 (that is, twenty times the speed of sound), creating enough atmospheric friction to destroy an unprotected object. Reentry vehicles are separate from the payloads they protect. Their design is complicated by the need to balance weight, drag, and thermal protection without compromising accuracy.

When long-range ballistic missiles were conceived in the 1940s, there was no way to deliver a payload safely back to Earth. The first solutions in the 1950s relied on blunt shapes to rapidly attenuate speed and heating. Soviet designers used spherical RVs coated with heavy metals. Chinese ballistic missiles appear to rely on a similar approach today. U.S. engineers pioneered radical shapes with low ballistic coefficients, or beta ratios. These "heat sink" designs—shaped like a backwards cone or an inverted bell—dissipate velocity through shock-wave propagation at high altitudes where heating is less extreme. High drag and low speed also had unwanted effects, reducing payload capabilities and degrading accuracy.

The optimal solution to the beta-dilemma of maximizing both reentry cooling and accuracy was perfected in the United States in the 1960s through development of ablative coatings. These plastic-based materials burn evenly from narrow cone-shapes during high-speed reentry. This enables the attenuation of heating without compromising accuracy. No less important was development of small nuclear warheads adapted to these shapes. The first fully successful ablative, high-beta design was the Mark-12 reentry vehicle for the Minuteman III intercontinental ballistic missile. The Mk-12, which became operational in 1970, was the basis for all subsequent American nuclear reentry vehicles. By the late 1970s, a similar approach to the reentry problem was perfected in the Soviet Union.

—*Aaron Karp*

See also: Ballistic Missiles; Downloading; Intercontinental Ballistic Missiles; Maneuvering Reentry Vehicle; Multiple Independently Targetable Reentry Vehicle

References

"Advanced Reentry Vehicles," U.S. Centennial of Flight Commission, 2003, available at http://www.centennialofflight.gov/essay/Evolution_of_Technology/advanced_reentry/Tech20.htm.

Buchonnet, Daniel, *MIRV: A Brief History of Minuteman and Multiple Reentry Vehicles* (Livermore, CA: Lawrence Livermore Laboratory, February 1976).

Hartunian, Richard A., "Ballistic Missiles and Reentry Systems: The Critical Years," *Crosslink (The Aerospace Corporation Magazine)*, vol. 5, no. 1, Winter 2004.

Stewart, J. D., and D. H. Greenshields, "Entry Vehicles for Space Programs," *Journal of Spacecraft and Rockets*, October 1969.

RELIABILITY

The term "reliability" is often used to describe the likelihood that nuclear weapons and associated delivery systems will function according to expectations and that personnel charged with maintaining and operating nuclear-equipped forces will carry out their duties according to instructions and accepted procedures.

Reliability is an important factor in nuclear war plans, and analysts have devised specific formulas for calculating the reliability of various weapon systems. For example, the probability of killing a mobile missile launcher can be calculated using the equation $PK = r(Ai/Aii)$, where PK equals the probability of destroying the mobile launcher ("probability of kill"); r equals the reliability of the attacking weapon (generally assumed to be about 0.9 for a U.S. intercontinental ballistic missile); Ai equals the area over which a warhead can generate lethal overpressure (generally assumed to be about 5 pounds per square inch); and Aii equals the area of uncertainty about the location of the mobile launcher (*see* Accuracy; Intercontinental Ballistic Missiles; Nuclear Weapons Effects; Yield).

The U.S. Personnel Readiness Program (PRP) is intended to guarantee that only emotionally stable, physically capable, dedicated professionals are responsible for the maintenance or delivery of nuclear weapons. Individuals who are part of the PRP program are subject to continuous evaluation in terms of their reliability, trustworthiness, conduct, and behavior. PRP also evaluates the medical condition of all individuals who come into contact with nuclear weapons, especially those who are charged with providing security to nuclear storage facilities. This evaluation includes random drug testing.

—*James J. Wirtz*

Reference

Pry, Peter Vincent, *Nuclear Wars: Exchanges and Outcomes* (New York: Taylor and Francis, 1990).

REPROCESSING

Reprocessing is the industrial process of removing plutonium from spent nuclear reactor fuel. When uranium fuel rods are put into a reactor and irradiated, they are described as spent fuel. Irradiated fuel has to be removed from a reactor's core when only about 3 percent of its uranium has been burned, if plutonium recovery is the goal. Weapons-grade plutonium is produced when special rods are used to convert uranium 238 (U-238) into plutonium in a so-called target. Irradiated fuel and special weapons targets from production or power reactors are chemically processed for the separation and recovery of fissile uranium and plutonium. Reprocessing plants consist of heavy reinforced-concrete structures to provide shielding against the intense gamma radiation produced by the decay of short-lived isotopes in the spent fuel rods. The most challenging technical component of a reprocessing plant is the separation system (consisting of mixers/settlers, extracted columns, or centrifugal contractors). Flow rates through the reprocessing plant must be monitored precisely, the chemistry must be exact, and any accumulation of radioactive products large enough to reach critical mass leading to massive radioactive release must be prevented (*see* Criticality and Critical Mass; Isotopes).

Radioactive isotopes also can be recovered that are used for special radio-chemistry purposes. These include plutonium 238, strontium 90, cesium 137, and krypton 85 as well as the by-product transuranic elements neptunium, americium, curium, and californium. Spent fuel from reactors is stored in water ponds from six months to four years to allow for a decrease in radioactivity. This permits short-lived, highly radioactive isotopes to decay. Reprocessing involves removing the metal casing from around the fuel (decladding) and dissolving the fuel in hot concentrated nitric acid. The most common method for chemically processing irradiated fuel is the PUREX (plutonium-uranium extraction) process. Two early methods for separating plutonium—the bismuth phosphate process and the Redox process—are important historically but no longer in use.

Early Methods

The bismuth phosphate process was developed during World War II at the Metallurgical Laboratory at the University of Chicago. It was used to separate the first plutonium in 1942 that had been produced in a cyclotron. The bismuth phosphate process was then developed on an engineering scale and demonstrated at the Oak Ridge, Tennessee, X-10 plant in 1944. It was put into full operation at Hanford, Washington, to separate plutonium from production fuel. The bismuth phosphate process recovered plutonium but was unable to separate and recover any uranium from the irradiated fuel. This was a serious disadvantage, since it meant that half of the reusable isotopes from the fuel rods were wasted. After the fuel elements were dissolved in nitric acid, bismuth nitrate and sodium phosphate were added to the solution, and plutonium was then removed. This method created a large amount of hot radioactive waste that is still stored at Hanford.

The Redox process was the first counter-current process used in the United States for large-scale extraction of plutonium and uranium from irradiated fuel. Unlike the bismuth phosphate process, it could operate continuously rather than in batches (when the reactor fuel was cool and ready for processing). In the Redox process, plutonium, uranium, and fission products were recovered and discharged in separate streams. After spent fuel was dissolved in nitric acid, an aqueous solution of uranyl nitrate, plutonyl nitrate, and fission product nitrates remained. This was followed by the introduction of an organic solvent, hexone, in which the uranyl and plutonyl nitrates concentrated. Fission product nitrates were left in the liquid phase. In three subsequent steps, the fission products were first removed and the plutonium was then chemically reduced and removed as plutonium nitrate. The bismuth phosphate process was in use from 1944 until 1956, the Redox process from 1956 until 1968. The Redox process recovered both plutonium and uranium and thus was a more efficient means of producing weapons fuel.

The PUREX Process

In the PUREX process, the irradiated fuel is dissolved in an aqueous solution of nitric acid, and the desired chemical elements are extracted in a series of steps with an organic solvent. Fuel rod elements are chopped into smaller pieces to expose the fuel material for subsequent acid leaching. Fuel cladding is frequently not soluble in nitric acid, so the fuel rod itself must be opened to allow chemicals to reach the fuel inside. Developed in 1954, the PUREX process was used at both Hanford and the Savannah River,

South Carolina, production sites. The aqueous solution contains uranyl nitrate, plutonium nitrate, and other fission product nitrates. The liquid solution is then fed into a solution extraction contractor.

The uranium and plutonium are separated from each other in further extraction steps. Plutonium is then converted to a solid oxide or metal form before it is shipped or stored. Uranium is generally converted to uranium trioxide.

All nuclear weapons states have reprocessing facilities. The ones in the United States are currently in a stand-by mode. Russian plants switched to the production of civilian reactor fuel after the end of the Cold War. In 2003, only the United Kingdom (Sellafield) and France (Cape La Hague) were reprocessing commercial reactor fuel. Japan ships its fuel to France for reprocessing. Russia had a large nuclear power and reprocessing infrastructure, but today little reprocessing goes on in Russia owing to lack of funding. Hopes in the 1970s of having plutonium, mixed oxide (uranium and plutonium mixed fuel rods), or fast-breeder (plutonium-producing) reactors on line to produce power have given way to environmental and proliferation fears. Civilian nuclear power reactors produce plutonium even if natural uranium is burned; thus, reprocessing and proliferation concerns go hand in hand.

Reprocessing has produced vast amounts of radioactive waste for fifty years. Everything that comes into contact with spent fuel is radioactive and must be disposed of in special storage sites. Some items will be radioactive for tens of thousands of years. The discharges by these plants into the atmosphere, water, and ground are frequently cited by Greenpeace in its reports about the most contaminated places on earth.

—*Gilles Van Nederveen*

See also: Plutonium; Uranium

References

Pigford, T. H., and H. W. Levi, *Nuclear Chemical Engineering*, second edition (New York: McGraw-Hill, 1981).

"Plutonium & Reprocessing," Nuclear Control Institute, available at http://www.nci.org/new/pu-repro.htm.

"Plutonium and Uranium Reprocessing," Nuclear Energy Institute, available at http://www.nei.org/index.asp?catnum=3&catid=583.

"Plutonium Recovery from Spent Fuel Reprocessing by Nuclear Fuel Services at West Valley, New York from 1966 to 1972," U.S. Department of Energy, February 1996, available at http://www.osti.gov/html/osti/opennet/document/purecov/nfsrepo.html.

Von Hippel, Frank N., "Plutonium and Reprocessing of Spent Nuclear Fuel," *Science*, vol. 293, no. 5539, 28 September 2001, pp. 2297–2398, available at http://www.princeton.edu/~globsec/publications/pdf/Sciencev293n5539.pdf.

RESEARCH REACTORS

Research reactors are nuclear reactors designed to generate neutrons for investigational and experimental purposes. These reactors often are not used to generate and supply power commercially. Research reactor designs vary widely and have a range of uses.

Many research reactors are used for educational purposes and are located at academic institutions throughout the world. Other research reactors are designed for the production of isotopes used in medical, industrial, scientific, and research applications. Research reactors also may be used for materials testing and general scientific experimentation

The first research reactor was designed and built by Enrico Fermi at Stagg Field Stadium, Chicago, on December 2, 1942. Fermi used this reactor to achieve the first nuclear chain reaction. The number of research reactors multiplied significantly in the 1960s and early 1970s. Many of these reactors are still in use today, with two-thirds of the research reactors in the world being more than thirty years old.

Research reactors are generally smaller than nuclear reactors designed to generate electricity, and they generate significantly less or essentially no electric power. The enrichment level of the fuel for research reactors is generally higher than for nuclear power reactors, about 20 to 95 percent uranium 235–enriched fuel compared to approximately 3 to 5 percent uranium 235–enriched fuel.

There are approximately 36 research reactors licensed in the United States, located in 23 states, and approximately 283 additional research reactors in 56 countries throughout the world.

—*Don Gillich*

See also: Low Enriched Uranium; Radiation; Reactor Operations

Reference

"Research Reactors," World Nuclear Association, available at http://www.world-nuclear.org/info/inf61.htm.

RESTRICTED DATA (RD)

"Restricted Data" (RD) is a classification level for all U.S. information related to the design, manufacture, or use of nuclear weapons and the fissionable material used in nuclear devices. Examples of RD include information about the design of thermonuclear weapons or their unique components, including specific information about the relative placement of weapons components and their role in initiating and sustaining a thermonuclear reaction. RD also covers information about the construction and operation of the nonnuclear portions of a nuclear weapon, consisting of the high-explosive system with its detonators and firing unit, "pit" system, and nuclear initiating system. Information about design features or vulnerabilities of nuclear weapons that might permit their unauthorized detonation also is considered to be Restricted Data (*see* Fission Weapons; Pit; Thermonuclear Bombs).

Under the 1954 Atomic Energy Act, the secretary of energy is responsible for issuing orders, guides, and manuals concerning the protection of RD. RD includes several subcategories, ranging from "Top Secret" to "Confidential." Information held at the level Confidential RD, for instance, includes the amount of high explosive used in a nuclear weapon.

The term "Formerly Restricted Data" (FRD) refers to information that is no longer considered to be RD but remains classified. Special restrictions apply to the release of FRD to foreign nationals. Individuals who are given clearances to view RD go through a lengthy screening process and background check to determine that they will be reliable custodians of this highly sensitive information.

—*James J. Wirtz*

Reference

Newman, Elizabeth L., *Security Clearance Law and Procedure* (Arlington, VA: Dewey, 1998).

REVIEW CONFERENCE

See Arms Control

REYKJAVIK SUMMIT

The Reykjavik Summit, held in Iceland October 11–12, 1986, was initially billed as a meeting to reinvigorate superpower arms control. President Ronald Reagan's Strategic Defense Initiative (SDI) had called into question the "offense dominance" concept that had served as the basis of arms control since the early 1970s. In addition, the Soviets sought

to keep this new SDI technology in the laboratory. An earlier summit in Geneva in 1985 made little progress in terms of reaching a compromise on how strategic defenses might be integrated into the existing arms control regime.

At the Icelandic capital of Reykjavik, face-to-face negotiations took place between Reagan and Soviet general secretary Mikhail Gorbachev. Gorbachev proposed a 50 percent reduction in all strategic weapons, the total elimination of Soviet and U.S. intermediate-range missiles in Europe, and strict compliance with the 1972 Anti-Ballistic Missile (ABM) Treaty, which would have prevented the SDI program from deploying a missile defense system for at least ten years. Gorbachev agreed to the U.S. demand for on-site inspections and dropped the demand to count British and French missiles as part of the U.S. arsenal. U.S. officials countered with specific proposals to reduce existing nuclear arsenals on both sides (6,000 nuclear warheads and 1,600 strategic nuclear delivery vehicles for each side). Although the original summit was focused on Europe, the Soviets also agreed to limit medium-range missile deployments in Asia to 100 warheads and to recognize human rights as a legitimate point of future superpower negotiations.

The final meeting started with a Soviet demand that the United States make concessions on SDI. Reagan offered only to keep SDI in the lab for ten years and made the fantastic offer to eliminate all intercontinental ballistic missiles within a decade. Although Gorbachev appeared willing to consider banning ballistic missiles, he could not allow the United States to develop space-based missile defenses. In the end, no agreement was reached, and the summit was considered by many to be a failure.

The Reykjavik Summit, however, demonstrated that both Soviet and U.S. officials were willing to address fundamental Cold War assumptions and explore innovative ways to reduce political tension and armaments. Several initiatives discussed at Reykjavik actually served as the basis for eventual treaties. In 1987, for example, Soviet and U.S. officials agreed to ban an entire class of nuclear delivery systems when they signed the Intermediate-Range Nuclear Forces (INF) Treaty. According to one State Department official, this was the turning point in the Cold War, the moment when the superpowers stopped building up nuclear weapons. And in 1991, both sides signed the Strategic Arms Reduction

Treaty (START I), which used the Reykjavik numbers as the goal for strategic reductions.

—Frannie Edwards and James J. Wirtz

See also: Anti-Ballistic Missile (ABM) Treaty; Arms Control; Cold War; Intermediate-Range Nuclear Forces (INF) Treaty; Strategic Arms Reduction Treaty (START I); Strategic Defense Initiative (SDI)

Reference
Fitzgerald, Frances, *Way Out There in the Blue: Reagan, Starwars and the End of the Cold War* (New York: Touchstone, 2000), available at http://eightiesclub.tripod.com/id258.htm.

RIDE OUT

A military force is said to have the capability to "ride out" an attack if it can survive the attack and continue to operate in its aftermath. Officials who make the ability to ride out a nuclear attack a matter of policy must procure and deploy nuclear forces accordingly. Forces that can ride out an attack increase crisis stability because they reduce the incentives for both sides in a deterrence relationship to use nuclear weapons first in a crisis.

The survivability of military forces and command and control operations is crucial to the success of deterrence because it is the threat of retaliation under all circumstances that reduces the likelihood of aggression. Survivable forces also are not dependent on strategic or tactical warning to ride out an attack; in the event of human or technical error, they can still undertake their retaliatory mission.

Launch-on-warning or launch-under-attack doctrines can be adopted if the survivability of retaliatory forces is in doubt. These doctrines are generally considered to be inferior to forces and doctrines that create conditions to ride out attack because they place a heavy burden on policymakers to make split-second decisions at moments of deep national crisis. Launch on warning also requires policymakers to use nuclear weapons before undisputable evidence is available that they are under attack, namely nuclear detonations on their own soil. Developing a ride-out capability, however, is both technically and financially challenging. New nuclear weapons states often lack the resources or even geography needed to create a survivable nuclear force.

—James J. Wirtz

See also: Crisis Stability; Deterrence; Launch on Warning/Launch under Attack

Reference
Wohlstetter, Albert, "The Delicate Balance of Terror," *Foreign Affairs,* vol. 37, no. 2, January 1959, pp. 211–234.

ROCKY FLATS, COLORADO

Rocky Flats is a 10-square-mile site just northwest of Denver, Colorado, where, for nearly forty years, the U.S. government manufactured nuclear weapons components, specializing in plutonium pits, or nuclear triggers (*see* Pit). Production has now ceased at the site and a cleanup is under way. Rocky Flats is one of the most contaminated tracts of land in the United States.

The plant was set up in 1952, originally to make plutonium spheres, which served as triggers for hydrogen bombs. Plutonium from old nuclear warheads and weapons parts machined from beryllium also were recycled at the Rocky Flats facility. Plutonium and beryllium are just some of the radiological and chemically toxic substances that were used at the plant. Several accidents took place at the facility, including serious fires in 1957 and 1969, which vented plutonium into the atmosphere. Additionally, poor storage techniques allowed radioactive and other toxic substances to leak into the soil and ultimately into drinking-water reservoirs.

The fact that incidents kept reoccurring and that safety standards seemed so lax at a plant only 16 miles from downtown Denver led to a raid by the Federal Bureau of Investigation (FBI) in 1989. The plant immediately ceased its production of plutonium. The fact that the plant was shut down suddenly, rather than gradually over many years, created problems when it came to disposing contaminated materials and equipment. Great efforts have been made since 1989 to clean up the facility, including further removal of topsoil and the transfer of waste plutonium to the Savannah River, South Carolina, site. Today, there are still some 10,250 people working to decontaminate Rocky Flats.

—Rod Thornton

See also: Savannah River Site

References
Makhijani, Arjun, Howard Hu, and Katherine Yih, eds., *Nuclear Wastelands: A Global Guide to Nuclear Weapons Production and Its Health and Environmental Effects* (Cambridge, MA: MIT Press, 1995).

"Rocky Flats Plant (DOE)," U.S. Environmental Protection Agency, available at http://www.epa.gov/region08/superfund/sites/co/rocky.html.

ROENTGEN EQUIVALENT MAN (REM)

Roentgen equivalent man (rem) is a unit of measurement of the absorbed dose of ionizing radiation deposited in body tissue. One rem is the dose from any type of radiation that corresponds to the exposure to 1 roentgen of radiation from X-ray or gamma radiation.

The "rad" (for "radiation absorbed dose") is a measure of absorbed dose from any kind of radiation in any medium in terms of fundamental energy units. "Roentgen" is also a unit of absorbed dose but is used only in relation to X-ray and gamma radiation (see Radiation).

Rem takes into account the biological effects of different kinds of radiation. The numerical value of an exposure or dose in roentgens is approximately the same as the value given in rems or rads. Simply stated, rem puts all kinds of radiation on an equal level. One rem of gamma radiation plus 1 rem of alpha radiation equals 2 rem of absorbed radiation.

"Absorbed dose" is radiation actually absorbed into some material, such as the human body. The term should not be confused with "exposure dose," which is radiation available to be absorbed.

—*Jeffrey A. Adams*

See also: Radiation Absorbed Dose (Rad)

References

U.S. Army Field Manual (FM) 4-02.283, *Treatment of Nuclear and Radiological Casualties,* Headquarters, Department of the Army, Washington, DC.

U.S. Department of Defense, *Weapons of Mass Destruction (WMD) Handbook,* JCS J-3 (Washington, DC, February 2001).

U.S. Nuclear Regulatory Commission, *Glossary of Terms: Nuclear Power and Radiation,* Washington, DC, June 1981.

RUMSFELD COMMISSION

On July 15, 1998, the Rumsfeld Commission released its conclusion that several countries hostile to the United States—particularly Iran, North Korea, and Iraq—would be able to attack the United States with ballistic missiles within five to ten years of a decision to acquire such technology. The commission predicted that the United States might have little or no warning before an enemy state acquired long-range ballistic missiles because it was difficult to gauge how outside financial or technical aid could accelerate indigenous weapons programs. Led by former (and future) secretary of defense Donald Rumsfeld, the commission was created by Republican members of Congress interested in challenging existing intelligence estimates of missile threats and reshaping the debate on pursuing a national missile defense (NMD) system. The group was not given a mandate to suggest a policy to address the threats it identified, but the report influenced congressional debates, helped reshape the timetable for national missile defense under President Bill Clinton, and influenced George W. Bush's administration in its drive to deploy an antiballistic missile system to defend the United States.

The commission's report directly challenged the conclusions of the Central Intelligence Agency (CIA) in its 1995 "National Intelligence Estimate" (NIE). According to CIA projections, no rising power would have ballistic missiles capable of threatening the United States for fifteen years. The NIE also argued that countries pursuing missiles would have to rely on domestic resources, since foreign assistance in the field remained relatively rare. Therefore, the intelligence community would have several years' warning of any successful missile development. These views helped support Clinton's plan to spend three years developing a defense that could be deployed within another three years if a threat emerged.

The Rumsfeld Commission, and supporters of NMD, disagreed with the NIE on each point. The shorter timetable suggested by the commission grabbed headlines. It was based on a new methodology in assessing threats that put more focus on possibilities for future development than on known past actions. Additionally, the commission argued, new states would be able to acquire weapons more quickly and more secretively than other states had done in the past because they would be less concerned with high standards of accuracy and safety. Furthermore, they argued that an international market of missile technology was emerging, creating possibilities to acquire technology from Russia, China, and Pakistan. Given the intense secrecy surrounding clandestine weapons programs and the possibility for rapid acquisition of materials and technology, the commission concluded that the United States might have little or no warning before an enemy acquired missiles.

Critics of the commission's report questioned its methodology, some of its statements, and the way the report was used in the overall NMD debate. The commission centered its methodology on possibilities, and usually worst-case scenarios for possibilities. Critics charged that this left out calculation of the probability of actual actions. For example, although Iran may be able to get weapons quickly, the threat is less immediate if political or other calculations discourage nuclear weapons or missile acquisition in the first place. The commission also focused exclusively on ballistic missile threats, which ignored the possibly more immediate threats from cruise missiles or terrorist attacks. Critics also believed that the Rumsfeld report overstated both the reliability of missiles, by assuming that all launches would be successful, and the extent of ongoing international technology sales. Finally, within the NMD debate there have always been three central questions: (1) Is a defense technically possible? (2) Does a threat exist to justify a defense? and (3) Would a defense bring too many negative ramifications? The Rumsfeld report focused only on the second question, but critics believed its dramatic language shifted focus away from the possible negative implications of missile defense by creating the impression that only technical questions remained to be solved.

—*John W. Dietrich*

References

Gronlund, Lisbeth, and David Wright, "What They Didn't Do," *Bulletin of the Atomic Scientists,* vol. 54, no 6, November/December 1998, pp. 46–51.

"Report of the Commission to Assess the Ballistic Missile Threat to the United States: Executive Summary, Pursuant to Public Law 201, 104th Congress, July 15, 1998," *Comparative Strategy,* vol. 18, no. 1, January–March 1999, pp. 87–100.

RUSSIAN NUCLEAR FORCES AND DOCTRINE

After the detonation of the first Soviet atomic device in 1949 and the Soviet hydrogen (fusion) device in 1953, the Soviet military went about acquiring the world's largest arsenal of nuclear weapons. In addition, the Soviet military introduced ballistic and cruise missiles, satellites, computers, and other automation devices into their arsenal. Soviet military writings since the late 1950s asserted that there had been a revolution created by the introduction of nuclear weapons and long-range, high-speed delivery systems. In Soviet defense publications, these inventions were referred to as a "revolution in military affairs." But of all these developments, nuclear weapons most affected Soviet strategy. Soviet writers believed that nuclear weapons altered the nature and methods of armed struggle on the strategic level because they could accomplish the military's strategic tasks without operational art or tactics. According to Soviet military theory, this revolution fundamentally altered the character of any future war by increasing the importance of the opening moments of a conflict. It changed the relationship between strategic and nonstrategic forces. It also created the requirements for a new force posture, geared to a new tempo, scope, and scale of nuclear operations at the continental and intercontinental ranges. The heart of this force posture and associated doctrine was developed in the 1960s and recorded in Marshal Vasily Sokolovsky's three editions of *Military Strategy* (published in 1962, 1963, and 1968) (*see* Military Technical Revolution [Revolution in Military Affairs]).

In the Soviet Union, where strategy is considered a science and the special province of the military, nuclear weapons were not held to be "absolute." The idea of mutual deterrence was never accepted. Soviet theorists rejected the idea that technology determines strategy and instead adapted nuclear weapons to their traditional Clausewitzian view of war as an extension of politics (based on the well-known military concepts of Karl von Clausewitz [1780–1831]). Transition to a nuclear strategy began in the mid-1950s, when Soviet military thinkers recognized the importance of surprise and the first stages of a war and sought to use nuclear strikes to determine the course and outcome of battle. This concept stressed the importance of preemption—striking before the enemy could strike the Soviet heartland or other socialist countries. The increased mobility of the Red Army, the traditional battlefield force, and the power of nuclear weapons allowed the Soviets to explore deep offensive operations. They concluded that their political objectives and their views on war dictated a force posture that would enable them to take the offensive from the outset of a war, thereby setting the conditions in the so-called initial period, which would determine the course and outcome of the conflict. Their strategy also held out the promise that some level of damage limitation to the Soviet Union could be achieved if hostile offensive forces could be destroyed before they could be employed. As a result, the Soviets required reliable forces able to destroy distant targets quickly. Their ballistic missiles possessed a unique combination of range, speed, accuracy, reliability, controllability, and in-flight invulnerability. This combination of attributes made intercontinental ballistic missiles (ICBMs) the ideal weapon to fulfill their military strategy (*see* Preemptive Attack).

The first formal Soviet doctrine for the nuclear age was that of Nikita Khrushchev's "one-variant war." According to this view, a future war would be extremely short and swift and would have an initial period of hostilities that would decide the course and outcome of the entire war. Consequently, Soviet nuclear strategy emphasized mass nuclear strikes and dismissed Western notions of escalation thresholds or limitations to the character and size of nuclear operations. These strikes were best characterized as countervalue, since counterforce targeting required accuracies in missile systems that did not exist until the early 1970s. Because an advantage would accrue to the side that struck first, and because Soviet strategic offensive forces in the 1960s were relatively unreliable, inflexible, and vulnerable, Soviet nuclear strategy focused on the rapid detection of enemy preparations for war (*see* Counterforce Targeting; Countervalue Targeting).

The drawbacks to the one-variant war concept soon became apparent to Soviet political and military leaders. The threat of massive retaliation served only to deter direct, massive attacks on the Soviet homeland; it was of doubtful utility in responding to less-than-all-out attacks. Furthermore, the Khrushchevian strategy offered no prospect for Soviet survival in the event of a general nuclear war. Soviet strategists realized that a more robust strategic force posture was required to meet Soviet political and military options. Although the means for preemptive counterforce operations were unavailable in the 1960s, the Soviets set about to create the desired force structure.

By the late 1970s, the Soviets began to acknowledge that even successful preemption was unlikely to determine the outcome of a nuclear war. Initial strikes by land-based ballistic missiles, it was said, would have a decisive impact on the initiation and course of hostilities but could not determine the

Russian nuclear missile silo opened for inspection by Strategic Rocket Forces at a site near Saratov, November 1994. (km/str/Reuters/Corbis)

outcome. This was the signal that the Soviets believed that more than a single massive nuclear salvo was required for victory. Such formulations also gave an increasing role to other Soviet nuclear forces, the submarine-launched missiles and bombers, in determining the course and outcome. The targeting objectives for the fleet ballistic submarine force suggest that although the use of submarine-launched ballistic missiles (SLBMs) in initial strikes was contemplated, the majority of the SLBMs at sea would be withheld to conduct follow-on strikes that could determine the overall course of the war.

Discussions of the prospects for victory in a strategic nuclear war appeared to turn on judgments regarding the ability of Soviet offensive and defensive forces to avoid suffering a preemptive attack and to destroy the opponent's nuclear forces in order to limit damage to the Soviet homeland. Despite the attainment of strategic parity in the mid seventies, the continued production of nuclear weapons by itself was seen as providing no enduring advantages to the Soviet Union. Chief of General Staff Marshal Nikolay Ogarkov made a number of provocative statements between 1982 and 1985 about the paradox existing between the continued acquisition of nuclear weapons and their inability to achieve decisive victories against opponents of the Soviet Union.

Stalin and Nuclear Inferiority

Joseph Stalin saw the turmoil at the end of World War II as an opportunity for expanding the Communist empire. At that time, however, he lacked a nuclear capability and therefore attempted to exploit low-risk situations. He was not prepared to risk a full-scale conflict with a United States that could use nuclear weapons with impunity. Nuclear weapons, strategy, and employment were taboo subjects while Stalin was in power.

Khrushchev and Strategic Capability

By 1955, Nikita Khrushchev had emerged as the major figure of the Soviet leadership. The U.S.S.R. was building a strategic nuclear arsenal, which Khrushchev was prepared to brandish in confronting Western powers. Khrushchev made it clear that he considered the nuclear-tipped strategic missile to be the basis of Soviet military power. In his statement to the Supreme Soviet in January 1960, he proposed reducing the armed forces by 1.2 million men and disposing of military aviation and surface ships. In its place, the Strategic Rocket Forces (SRF) were to become the premier Soviet armed service. Its missiles could strike at theater and intercontinental ranges and give the Soviets leverage in the Cold War. The lack of Western intelligence made it easy for Khrushchev to exaggerate the size and capability of the Soviet nuclear arsenal as a means of bullying, bluffing, and boasting his way through crises.

Although Khrushchev publicly stated that deterrence was the goal of Soviet defense policy, Soviet military planners tended to believe that preemption remained a viable strategy if nuclear war with the West appeared inevitable. By delivering a preemptive strike against the opponent's offensive systems and countervalue targets, Soviet planners believed they could blunt the capability and the will of the opponent to retaliate. Soviet planners also believed that the battlefield use of nuclear weapons would allow them to seize the initiative and win decisively.

During the Khrushchev era, the Soviet Strategic Rocket Forces deployed first-generation liquid-fu-

eled missile systems on aboveground launchers. These launch complexes could not withstand a nuclear strike. Between 1955 and 1961, the Soviets deployed the intermediate-range SS-4 and SS-5 along their western border. The SS-7 ICBM also was deployed at about the same time. The SS-8 ICBM, a silo-based system that entered service in the Strategic Rocket Forces in the early 1960s, increased the survivability of the Soviets' land-based missile force. These first-generation systems had low combat readiness. Because the liquid rocket fuels used at the time were so corrosive, the missiles could only be kept fueled for thirty days. Time to prepare missiles varied from a few minutes to hours, depending on the complexity of the missile being readied to fire (*see* Cold War; Intercontinental Ballistic Missiles).

Brezhnev and Nuclear Parity

During the Leonid Brezhnev era, the Soviet Union achieved strategic "parity"—a rough equivalence in strategic nuclear capability—with the United States (*see* Parity). Second-generation Soviet systems, created in the second half of the 1960s, included permanently fueled missiles with a very high level of readiness. This time period also saw the use of hardened single silo launchers and command centers in the Soviet Union. The use of single silo launchers in a wide crescent, stretching from the Ukraine into Kazakhstan along the trans-Siberian railroad, significantly improved the survivability of the missile force. Second-generation solid-fuel Soviet ballistic missiles could now be kept on a high state of alert, increasing the survivability of the Strategic Rocket Forces. The SS-11 became the main component of the land-based nuclear deterrent, with a force of 990 deployed missiles. The SS-9, a heavy ICBM capable of lofting a 10-megaton warhead against U.S. ICBM complexes, was also deployed. Eventually the U.S.S.R. deployed 308 of these heavy ICBMs.

U.S.-Soviet arms control negotiations during the Brezhnev era often highlighted the fact that Soviet planners failed to accept the situation of mutual assured destruction (MAD) as an unalterable fact. Soviet military writings, political statements, and force structure suggested to many Western observers that Soviet planners believed they could benefit from the early and massive use of nuclear weapons in any serious conflict with the West. In the 1970s, a Soviet conventional and theater nuclear force buildup was accompanied by redoubled civil defense measures and preemptive nuclear doctrines. Observers suggested that the Soviets had adopted a policy of "deterrence by denial," that is, their notion of deterrence was based on the ability to fight and win a nuclear war. Soviet officials, however, probably never believed that they could actually use nuclear war as an instrument of policy or that victory in an all-out nuclear war was really within their reach (*see* Deterrence; Mutual Assured Destruction).

By the early 1980s, the Soviets began deploying a third generation of strategic systems that bolstered their nuclear warfighting capabilities. The SS-18 emerged to replace the SS-9, and the SS-17 and SS-19 replaced the SS-11 force. Soviet ICBMs also were equipped with multiple independently targetable reentry vehicles (MIRVs), which increased the overall prompt hard-target kill capability of the Soviet nuclear arsenal. The SS-20, a MIRVed, road-mobile intermediate-range ballistic missile (IRBM), and the Tu-22M Backfire bomber also were deployed during this period and greatly increased the ability of Soviet forces to hold theater targets at risk with nuclear weapons.

Soviet Strategy at the End of the Cold War
Fourth-generation Soviet strategic forces were entering service by 1991, just as the Cold War was ending. Soviet planners had begun to increase the survivability of their land-based missile force by deploying rail-mobile (SS-24) and land-mobile (SS-25) ICBMs. As the range of Soviet submarine-launched ballistic missiles increased, they began to deploy their fleet ballistic missile submarines in "bastions" operating close to Soviet bases. These were heavily defended by the Soviet Navy and land-based aviation. The culmination of Soviet ballistic missile submarine development was the Typhoon class, which had a unique hull configuration and was equipped with a new MIRVed missile. Each Typhoon could carry up to 200 nuclear warheads. The Soviets also began to produce an intercontinental jet bomber, the Blackjack. But by 1989, only sixteen of these expensive bombers had been built.

Russian Nuclear Doctrine Today
As the Soviet empire slipped away, Russian nuclear force modernization slowed to a snail's pace as Russian officials, in conjunction with their U.S. counterparts, greatly reduced the size of their strategic nuclear arsenal. Although the Russians have stated that they still contemplate the first use of nuclear weapons in response to serious strategic threats, economic realities have forced them to make significant reductions in their nuclear arsenal.

In the fifty years from the Soviet acquisition of the atomic bomb (1949) to the beginning of the end of the Soviet empire (1989), Soviet nuclear doctrine was transformed from a quest to achieve victory in nuclear war to a gradual acceptance of the fact that a large-scale nuclear exchange between the United States and Russia would produce mutual assured destruction.

—*Gilles Van Nederveen and James J. Wirtz*

See also: Arms Race; Bombers, Russian and Chinese Nuclear-Capable; Détente; Nuclear Warhead Storage and Transportation Security (Russia); Strategic Forces; Submarines, Nuclear-Powered Ballistic Missile; Submarine-Launched Ballistic Missiles; United States Nuclear Forces and Doctrine

References
"The CIA's Analysis of the Soviet Union, 1947–1991," Center for the Study of Intelligence, Central Intelligence Agency, 2001, available at http://www.cia.gov/csi/books/princeton/.
Defense Intelligence Agency, annual publications of "Soviet Military Power," available at http://www.fas.org/irp/dia/product/smp_index.htm.
Federation of American Scientists website, http://www.fas.org/nuke/guide/russia/doctrine/intro.htm.
Garthoff, Raymond L., *Deterrence and Revolution in Soviet Military Doctrine* (Washington, DC: Brookings Institution, 1990).
Herspring, Dale, *The Soviet High Command, 1967–1989: Personalities and Politics* (Princeton, NJ: Princeton University Press, 1990).
Lynn-Jones, Sean, Steven Miller, and Stephen Van Evera, eds., *Soviet Military Policy* (Cambridge, MA: MIT Press, 1989).
Main, Steven J., "Soviet Strategic Rocket Forces 1991–2002," Conflict Studies Research Centre, August 2002, available at http://www.da.mod.uk/CSRC/documents/Russian/D66.
Parrott, Bruce, ed., *The Dynamics of Soviet Defense Policy* (Washington, DC: Wilson Center Press, 1990).
Pipes, Richard, "Why the Soviet Union Thinks It Could Fight and Win a Nuclear War," *Commentary*, vol. 64, July 1977, pp. 21–34, available at http://www.etpv.org/bills_page/nuclear.html.

Podvig, Pavel, ed., *Russian Strategic Nuclear Forces* (Cambridge, MA: MIT Press, 2001).

Scott, Harriet Fast, and William Scott, eds., *The Soviet Art of War: Doctrine, Strategy, and Tactics* (Boulder: Westview, 1982).

Scott, Harriet Fast, and William Scott, *Soviet Military Doctrine: Continuity, Formulation, and Dissemination* (Boulder: Westview, 1988).

Turbiville, Graham, ed., *The Voroshilov Lectures: Materials from the Soviet General Staff Academy*, 3 vols. (Washington, DC: National Defense University Press, 1989).

Zaloga, Steven J., *The Kremlin's Nuclear Sword: The Rise and Fall of Russia's Strategic Nuclear Forces, 1945–2000* (Washington, DC: Smithsonian Institution Press, 2002).

SAFEGUARD ANTIBALLISTIC MISSILE (ABM) SYSTEM

Safeguard was a U.S. ballistic missile defense (BMD) system deployed for a short time in 1975. In 1969, President Richard M. Nixon announced plans for the system, basing it on earlier U.S. BMD proposals such as the Sentinel and Nike-Zeus programs. Nixon changed the mission of U.S. missile defense, however, from national protection of the general public to providing cover for U.S. land-based strategic missiles at a few crucial military sites. Safeguard consisted of detection radar and long- and short-range antiballistic (ABM) missiles equipped with nuclear warheads designed to intercept incoming missiles or fractional orbital bombardment systems (FOBS).

Safeguard became operational on October 1, 1975, but on the next day the U.S. House of Representatives voted to shut down the program. Opponents of the system argued that the development of Soviet multiple independently targetable reentry vehicles (MIRVs) meant that Safeguard could not handle an overwhelming attack. In addition, several other technical problems reduced its effectiveness. For example, simulations showed that tracking radars would fail after the interceptor detonated its nuclear warhead.

Political issues, both domestic and international, played heavily in the Safeguard debate. The U.S. Senate approved Phase I of the program on a 50–50 vote, with Vice President Spiro T. Agnew casting the tie-breaking ballot. Supporters maintained that in addition to its defensive value Safeguard would create a bargaining chip in upcoming arms control talks with the Soviet Union. Safeguard designers originally intended the system to be deployed at twelve sites, but in negotiations with the Soviet Union over the Anti-Ballistic Missile Treaty, negotiators reduced the number of sites to two: Grand Forks Air Force Base, North Dakota, and Washington, D.C. Following an amendment to the ABM Treaty in 1974 limiting each side to just one ABM

site, Grand Forks, home to 150 Minuteman intercontinental ballistic missiles (ICBMs), emerged as the sole location of a U.S. BMD system.

With Safeguard's detection equipment working in conjunction with a nearby radar installation, the system could detect Soviet ICBMs as they passed over the North Pole, thereby giving operators just a few minutes to react to an incoming missile attack. The U.S. response consisted of two types of missiles: the long-range Spartan and the short-range Sprint, both armed with nuclear warheads. Designers created Safeguard to provide a layered defense. The Spartan ABMs would first attack incoming clusters of warheads, booster rockets, and decoys, and then Sprint ABMs would intercept surviving warheads as they penetrated the atmosphere.

Opponents of missile defenses, however, argued that with only 100 interceptors stationed in North Dakota, the Soviet Union could easily overpower the defense. Congressional faith in the project began to diminish. The Senate initially resisted efforts to terminate the program, but following revelations that the Pentagon had come to the same conclusions about Safeguard's lack of effectiveness a year earlier, senators agreed to end operational funding. The army then began dismantling Safeguard, finishing the task in February 1976. The entire program cost was $5 billion (some $25 billion in current dollars).

U.S. BMD programs have since rejected Safeguard's method of using nuclear weapons to destroy incoming missiles. For moral and technical reasons, the United States now pursues other BMD options, including hit-to-kill kinetic-energy devices and directed-energy lasers.

—*John Spykerman*

See also: Anti-Ballistic Missile (ABM) Treaty;
  Intercontinental Ballistic Missiles; Minuteman
  ICBM; Missile Defense; Nike Zeus; Sentinel; Spartan;
  Sprint
References
Morgan, Mark L., and Mark A. Berhow, *Rings of
  Supersonic Steel: Air Defenses of the United States
  Army, 1950–1974,* second edition (Bodega Bay, CA:
  Hole in the Head Press, 2002).
Wirtz, James J., and Jeffrey A. Larsen, *Rockets Red Glare:
  Missile Defense and the Future of World Politics*
  (Boulder: Westview, 2001).

SAFEGUARDS

Safeguards are methods of controlling and handling nuclear materials, equipment, and technology of potential use in nuclear weapons programs. They are usually established in international agreements and treaties, implemented through domestic legislation, and subject to domestic and international regulation, oversight, and inspections.

A statute of the International Atomic Energy Agency (IAEA) authorizes it "to establish and administer safeguards designed to ensure that special fissionable and other materials, services, equipment, facilities, and information made available by the Agency or at its request or under its supervision or control are not used in such a way as to further any military purpose; and to apply safeguards, at the request of the parties, to any bilateral or multilateral arrangement, or at the request of a State, to any of that State's activities in the field of atomic energy." It thus typically falls to the IAEA to administer the safeguards related to the international nonproliferation regime. In this role, it conducts inspections and other verification activities (*see* International Atomic Energy Agency; Verification).

Safeguards ensure that there has been no diversion of declared nuclear material or illicit production of undeclared material at declared facilities. There are three main ways of accomplishing this objective. First, all nuclear material must be accounted for. Personnel thus establish the quantities of nuclear material present within defined areas and then record changes in these quantities over time. Second, containment and surveillance measures must be put into place. The IAEA takes advantage of physical barriers to restrict, control, or monitor the movement of or access to nuclear material. Finally,

the credibility of the other two verification measures must be established. IAEA procedures dictate the use of on-site inspections. These activities are undertaken pursuant to negotiated agreements between the IAEA and nations with nuclear industries. Agreements in place prior to the Nuclear Nonproliferation Treaty (NPT) or with non-NPT members are called INFCIRC/66 (Information Circular Number 66) agreements. Agreements with NPT states parties are called INFCIRC/153 agreements. Both types of agreements have the primary objective of building confidence that states are complying with their nonproliferation commitments. IAEA safeguards were not designed to detect undeclared clandestine activities at undeclared nuclear facilities (*see* Nuclear Nonproliferation Treaty [NPT]).

In 1997, in response to its failure to detect Iraq's nuclear weapons program prior to the 1991 Gulf War, the IAEA developed a new "Model Protocol Additional" (INFCIRC/540) to append to the INFCIRC/153 agreements. This new protocol allows the IAEA to provide greater assurances concerning prohibited nuclear weapons activities under the NPT and to alert the international community to the possible production or diversion of nuclear materials for military purposes. The protocol requires states parties to provide extensive information, including data on the manufacture and export of sensitive nuclear-related technologies, to IAEA personnel. It mandates inspector access to all aspects of states parties' nuclear fuel cycle and gives inspectors the right to collect environmental samples. One important element of the new protocol is the affirmation of the right of the director general of the IAEA to conduct "special inspections" (both within and outside declared facilities and locations). This clause was already contained in INFCIRC/153 agreements but had rarely been applied in practice.

There are several complementary regional and bilateral nuclear inspection arrangements that do not directly involve the IAEA. Those in the European Union are performed by the European Atomic Energy Community (EURATOM) inspectorate of the European Commission, for example, and those between Brazil and Argentina are carried out by the Agency for Accounting and Control of Nuclear Material. There are also various bilateral agreements concerning safeguards and cooperation between other states (*see* European Atomic Energy Community).

During NPT negotiations, objections were raised regarding the perception that non–nuclear weapons states were put at a commercial disadvantage in competition with nuclear weapons states because IAEA safeguards were not required for the latter's nuclear activities, including the nuclear power industry. To achieve agreement on the NPT, the United States and all of the other nuclear weapons states put their civilian nuclear power industry under safeguards through the negotiation of a "voluntary offer" safeguards agreement with the IAEA (known as INFCIRC/288). Facilities used for nuclear weapons production were excluded from these inspections. Currently, the IAEA inspects four U.S. facilities. In addition, in 1993 the United States announced that it would place nuclear material deemed in excess of its defense needs under IAEA safeguards. In 1998, the United States also signed an Additional Protocol Agreement with the IAEA, which was ratified by the U.S. Senate in March 2004, and it has submitted a list of more than 200 facilities for possible safeguards arrangements under this protocol.

Under the Nuclear Nonproliferation Treaty, states parties pledge to negotiate and conclude agreements with the IAEA to accept and implement its safeguards system. The objective is to prevent "diversion of nuclear energy from peaceful uses to nuclear weapons or other nuclear explosive devices." Each state party agrees not to provide any nuclear materials, equipment, or technology to any other state unless these materials are subject to safeguards. States are allowed to share nuclear information, materials, and technology for peaceful purposes.

Exporting countries formed two nuclear export control groups, the Nuclear Suppliers Group and the Zangger Committee, to maintain lists of these controlled items. The Nuclear Suppliers Group, currently made up of representatives from thirty-four nuclear supplier countries, established two sets of guidelines to govern the export of items for nuclear use, including dual-use items. The Zangger Committee, or Nuclear Exporters Committee, is an informal group of representatives from nuclear supplier states who meet regularly to define what constitutes, under Article III of the NPT, "equipment or material especially designed or prepared for the processing, use or production of special fissile material" and to set forth the conditions and procedures governing the exports of such items. These

items are put on a "trigger list," that is, they are items that "trigger" IAEA safeguards and may be exported only if subject to safeguards.

—Guy Roberts

References
"IAEA Safeguards and Verification," available at http://www.iaea.org/worldatom/Programmes/Safeguards/.
International Atomic Energy Agency (IAEA) website, http://www.iaea.org.
U.S. Congress, Office of Technology Assessment, *Nuclear Safeguards and the International Atomic Energy Agency,* OTA-ISS-615 (Washington, DC: U.S. Government Printing Office, June 1995).

SAFETY RODS
See Reactor Operations

SANDIA NATIONAL LABORATORIES
The creation of Sandia National Laboratories dates to the World War II Manhattan Project. Originally part of the Los Alamos Scientific Laboratory, Sandia began as Z Division in July 1945 and was created to perform ordnance engineering for the first atomic bomb and to assemble the weapon based on the designs produced by Los Alamos. Los Alamos in 1945 was crowded and suffered periodic water and other utility shortages, and the Manhattan Engineering District wanted a new home for field testing and weapon-assembly operations. Transportation shortfalls in the area also necessitated the relocation of production activities. All material for Los Alamos had to be trucked from the airfield in Albuquerque or from the rail depot in Lamy, both two hours away. A site near Albuquerque, New Mexico, was transferred to the army to be used as an assembly site for nuclear weapons components. Personnel from the Los Alamos Ordnance Division were transferred here, and it was operated as a branch of Los Alamos by the University of California. It was renamed Sandia Laboratory in 1948.

With the establishment of the Atomic Energy Commission after World War II, President Harry S. Truman asked the Bell System to manage activities at the site. On November 1, 1949, a new entity called Sandia Corporation (a wholly owned subsidiary of Western Electric) assumed direction of Sandia Laboratory (*see* Los Alamos National Laboratory; Manhattan Project).

Sandia is still primarily an ordnance engineering laboratory. It designs the nonnuclear parts of nuclear weapons. These include the electronics, arming, fusing, and firing systems, neutron generators, command and control devices, security and safety features, and new delivery concepts. Tritium reservoirs, weapons structure cases, aerodynamic shapes, and parachutes are also produced by Sandia. Until late 1947, the main assembly job at Sandia was to collect, inspect, and assemble the various weapon parts that remained in the U.S. inventory at the end of World War II into bombs. At the time, assembling components into a bomb took about sixty days, which was far too slow for U.S. military planners, who were hoping to have 400 bombs in the arsenal by 1951.

The main facility at Sandia is located on what is now Kirtland Air Force Base in Albuquerque. In 1956, Sandia established a lab at Livermore, California, to support the programs at Lawrence Livermore National Laboratory. Sandia also operates the Tonopah Test Range northwest of the Nevada Test Site. Sandia engineers developed concepts that allowed atomic bombs to be assembled and stored with little maintenance. It developed parachute systems for the safe deployment of nuclear gravity bombs. It also devised and produced the permissive action link, a device that permits only authorized users with the proper code to operate a nuclear weapon, for the U.S. inventory (see Permissive Action).

In conjunction with the two design laboratories (Lawrence Livermore and Los Alamos), Sandia is responsible for the research and development associated with weapon engineering for all phases of the nuclear-warhead life cycle. Sandia's major functions are in weapons research and development. It also improves existing weapons designs and engineers new weapons based on objectives such as reaching deeply buried targets.

Sandia collaborated with the Pantex Plant in Amarillo, Texas, to develop test assemblies used in Nevada until that work ceased following the imposition of a moratorium on nuclear testing in the United States in 1992 (see Moratorium; Pantex Facility, Texas). Sandia's real expertise lies in testing the effects of nuclear weapons on U.S. warheads. Sandia is also responsible for security, weapons safety, inventory control, and inventory maintenance of U.S. nuclear weapons. It trains military personnel who assemble and maintain nuclear weapons. The shipment, transportation, and containers for nuclear weapons are designed and tested by Sandia, and the storage bunkers and surveillance systems that monitor U.S. nuclear weapons storage sites are all designed by Sandia. The actual installation of these systems is conducted by the military service that owns the weapons and bunker, but Sandia inspects and certifies these installations.

Sandia has assumed a central role in designing the technology required to monitor and verify compliance with international accords. This know-how is also useful in monitoring foreign nuclear developments (see Verification). During the Cold War, when underground nuclear testing was still in progress, Sandia designed seismic arrays to monitor foreign nuclear tests and the nuclear Threshold Test Ban Treaty. In 1963, Sandia designed optical sensors that were installed on VELA satellites to monitor the globe for foreign nuclear explosions. Sandia worked on many of the Strategic Defense Initiative projects of the late 1980s. It has also produced numerous civilian technology spin-offs, such as laminar flow clean rooms, has spearheaded improvements in computer coding and processing, and has helped to design synthetic aperture radar, which can be used to look through clouds and weather.

—*Gilles Van Nederveen and Jeffrey A. Larsen*

References

Allison, Graham T., Robert Blackwill, Albert Carnesale, Joseph S. Nye, and Robert P Beschel, eds., "A Primer for the Nuclear Age," available at http://bcsia.ksg.harvard.edu/BCSIA_content/documents/a_primer_for_the_nuclear_age.pdf.

Cochran, Thomas B., William M. Arkin, Robert S. Norris, and Milton M. Hoenig, *Nuclear Weapons Databook*, vol. 2: *U.S. Nuclear Warhead Production* (New York: Ballinger, 1987).

———, *Nuclear Weapons Databook*, vol. 3: *U.S. Nuclear Warhead Facility Profiles* (New York: Ballinger, 1987).

Hewlett, Richard G., and Francis Duncan, *A History of the United States Atomic Energy Commission*, vol. 2: *Atomic Shield, 1947/1952* (University Park: Pennsylvania State University Press, 1969).

Rosenthal, Debra, *At the Heart of the Bomb: The Dangerous Allure of Weapons Work* (Reading, MA: Addison-Wesley, 1990).

Sandia National Laboratories website, http://www.sandia.gov.

West, George T., *United States Nuclear Warhead Assembly Facilities, 1945–1990* (Amarillo, TX: Mason and Hanger, Silas Mason Company, Pantex Plant, March 1991).

SAVANNAH RIVER SITE, SOUTH CAROLINA

Called the Savannah River Plant when it first opened in 1950 as a military facility devoted to the production of nuclear weapons, the Savannah River Site (SRS) was one of the largest nuclear weapons facilities in the Department of Energy's infrastructure and is capable of handling highly irradiated and extremely dangerous materials. The facility, which sits on 310 square miles (250,000 acres) on the east side of the South Carolina–Georgia border, is also one of the most polluted locations in the world. The site includes several distinct areas dedicated to different missions: the production reactors, the Savannah River Laboratory, a heavy-water plant, fuel and target fabrication facilities, and chemical separation (reprocessing) facilities.

Built by DuPont for the U.S. government, Savannah River's purpose was to provide the tritium necessary to boost the yield of thermonuclear weapons. Its reactors and reprocessing facilities would also provide plutonium, supplementing the production of the Hanford, Washington, facility. The plant provided all the heavy water (deuterium) produced in the United States until 1982, when that facility was closed. During the Cold War, five heavy-water reactors were built at Savannah River. Over their lifetime, these reactors produced 36 metric tons of weapons-grade plutonium (40 percent of the total U.S. production) and 225 kilograms of tritium.

Savannah River also produced some 34 million gallons of highly radioactive waste, which it stored at the site in tanks. Other poisonous substances were stored in a vast array of pits and basins around the complex. Leaks into local aquifers from both tanks and pits have occurred over the years, creating contamination problems. By 1988, all of the site's reactors had been shut down, mostly for safety reasons. Over $2 billion was spent in a short-lived attempt to restart one of the reactors in the early 1990s. The project was canceled when a leak of radioactive liquid developed in the cooling system. The fuels stored at the SRS, given their level of radioactivity and immensely long half-lives (rate of decay), will require close maintenance for hundreds, if not thousands, of years.

—*Rod Thornton and Jeffrey A. Larsen*

See also: Deuterium; Half-Life; Hanford, Washington; Heavy Water; Plutonium; Reprocessing; Tritium

References

Cochran, Thomas B., William M. Arkin, Robert S.

Norris, and Milton M. Hoenig, *Nuclear Weapons Databook,* vol. 3: *U.S. Nuclear Warhead Facility Profiles* (Cambridge, MA: Ballinger, 1987).

Makhijani, Arjun, Howard Hu, and Katherine Yih, eds., *Nuclear Wastelands: A Global Guide to Nuclear Weapons Production and Its Health and Environmental Effects* (Cambridge, MA: MIT Press, 1995).

SCRAM
See Reactor Operations

SEA-LAUNCHED CRUISE MISSILES

Cruise missiles fired from surface ships and submarines are referred to as sea-launched cruise missiles (SLCMs). Cruise missiles are guided missiles with wings that fly primarily in a "cruise" mode, a state of flight that occurs when the engine's thrust is more or less equal to the air's resistance, aerodynamic lift is more or less equal to the weight of the aircraft, and the aircraft maintains an almost constant speed and altitude. Similar to other guided missiles, a cruise missile consists of four major components: an engine, a guidance system, a warhead, and a missile body. The cruise missile generally has an air-breathing jet engine and, from the moment it is launched until the moment it strikes its target, flies mainly in a "cruise" mode under the control of the engine's thrust and the guidance system (in contrast to the ballistic trajectory flown by most other missiles). Cruise missiles obtain their name from this flight profile.

Depending on the combat mission, a cruise missile can be classified as being either a strategic cruise missile or a tactical cruise missile. Missiles that are comparatively long range (generally considered to be a range greater than 500 kilometers) and are used to attack strategic targets are referred to as strategic cruise missiles. These cruise missiles have traditionally been equipped with a nuclear warhead and represent an important force in maintaining nuclear deterrence and providing an offensive nuclear-strike capability. As improvements have been made in their accuracy, it has become possible to use cruise missiles that carry a conventional warhead, and potentially a variety of more exotic nonnuclear warheads, to attack strategic targets. These innovations have reduced the significance of the distinction between strategic and tactical guided missiles, so that, as a rule, cruise missiles of this type are today referred to as conventional land-attack cruise missiles. Cruise missiles that have a shorter range and are used either to attack high-value ground targets or to attack ships are referred to as tactical cruise missiles.

Approximately nineteen countries currently produce cruise missiles, and several more have the capability to produce them. A least fifty-four other countries have cruise missiles of some type (air-launched, ground-launched, ship-launched, or submarine-launched) in their arsenals. Only a handful of countries currently possess submarine-launched cruise missiles, including the United States, France, the United Kingdom, and Russia. Modern cruise missiles are increasingly attractive because they can carry a warhead about the size of a ballistic missile over a similar range but can deliver it with far greater accuracy and at a fraction of a ballistic missile's cost. Moreover, the means to develop advanced cruise missiles can increasingly be obtained on the open market.

Under the first Strategic Arms Reduction Treaty (START I) signed in 1991, the United States and the former Soviet Union agreed to provide annual declarations regarding their deployment of strategic (nuclear) SLCMs. In a series of Presidential Nuclear Initiatives in 1991 and 1992, the United States and the Soviet Union also agreed to withdraw all tactical nuclear weapons from surface ships and submarines. Nearly all of the stocks of ground-launched cruise missiles that were developed by the United States and the Soviet Union have been eliminated in accordance with the provisions of the 1987 Intermediate-Range Nuclear Forces (INF) Treaty (*see* Intermediate-Range Nuclear Forces Treaty; Presidential Nuclear Initiatives; Strategic Arms Reduction Treaty).

The primary SLCM for the United States is the BGM-109 Tomahawk. The Tomahawk is an all-weather surface or underwater (submarine)-launched land-attack cruise missile. After launch, a solid propellant propels the missile until a small turbofan engine takes over for the cruise portion of flight. Tomahawk is a highly survivable weapon. Its small cross-section and low-altitude flight make it extremely difficult to detect on radar. The Tomahawk land-attack cruise missile has been used to attack a variety of fixed targets, including air defense and communications sites, often in high-threat environments.

The primary SLCM deployed by Russia will likely be the NE-08 and the SS-N-21, both of which have characteristics similar to the Tomahawk. The NE-08 will be deployed on surface ships and the SS-N-21 on submarines. An advanced model of the SS-N-21 (P version) is under development.

The focal point of advanced research on all types of cruise missiles is to improve the missiles' ability to penetrate enemy defenses. Countries are developing cruise missiles that have enhanced stealth characteristics or that fly low at subsonic speeds to evade detection and tracking by enemy radar. For example, the radar cross-section of the U.S. advanced cruise missile is less than 0.01 square meter, making it very hard for enemy radar to detect and track its flight. Another approach to increasing the ability to penetrate defenses is to emphasize research and development of supersonic and hypersonic cruise missiles, which would be very difficult to intercept. The United States, for example, is currently exploring the possibility of developing hypersonic cruise missiles that may travel at speeds as high as Mach 8. Russia, too, is engaged in research and development work on supersonic cruise missiles.

—*Guy Roberts*

See also: Cruise Missiles
Reference
Gormley, Dennis M., *Dealing with the Threat of Cruise Missiles*. Adelphi Papers 339. (London: International Institute of Strategic Studies, 2001).

SECOND STRIKE

The term "second strike" refers to the ability of a state to retaliate with its nuclear weapons after absorbing another country's initial attack. To have a second-strike capability, a state must have weapons that are hidden (that the enemy cannot hit because he does not know about them), that are impervious to attack (stored in such a way that a nuclear strike would not damage or destroy them), or that cannot be targeted (such as on deployed submarines). Even in the event of a surprise nuclear attack, a country that possessed a secure second-strike capability would retain some nuclear weapons that could be launched against the enemy.

During the Cold War, the United States and the Soviet Union built survivable nuclear forces to create a second-strike capability that took the form of a "Triad" of land-based intercontinental ballistic missiles (ICBMs), bombers, and deployed submarines.

Because submarines are difficult to locate, it would be hard for a state to determine that it had located and destroyed all of the adversary's submarines, thereby eliminating the opponent's ability to retaliate. Today any state with nuclear weapons deployed on submarines can be assumed to have a secure second-strike capability.

A secure second-strike capability is key to nuclear deterrence and crisis stability. The guarantee that a state will have nuclear weapons in reserve that can be used to retaliate against aggression can deter attack because the opponent can expect retaliation from surviving weapons. Crisis stability is enhanced because no state has any incentive to launch its nuclear weapons first in a crisis if its leaders expect that the attack will only invite a nuclear second strike (see Crisis Stability; Deterrence).

A second-strike capability also reduces the incentives for officials to adopt a launch-on-warning policy by firing a retaliatory strike upon detection of an incoming attack. Because decision makers with a secure second-strike capability know that they can absorb a nuclear strike—especially a small nuclear strike—they can wait to assess the unfolding situation before choosing an appropriate response. A secure second-strike capability eliminates the need to make snap judgments in crisis and wartime, judgments that could lead to nuclear accidents or inadvertent escalation.

—*Andrea Gabbitas*

See also: Escalation; First Strike; Flexible Response; Launch on Warning/Launch under Attack; Massive Retaliation; Selective Options; Survivability

References

Lodal, Jan, "Pledging 'No First Strike': A Step toward Real WMD Cooperation," *Arms Control Today*, vol. 31, no. 2, March 2001, pp. 3–8.

Sagan, Scott D., and Kenneth N. Waltz, *The Spread of Nuclear Weapons: A Debate* (New York: W. W. Norton, 1995).

SELECTIVE OPTIONS

As a situation of mutual assured destruction between the United States and the Soviet Union became a reality in the late 1960s, U.S. nuclear war plans began to contain ideas about limiting escalation and avoiding countervalue attacks when possible. By making nuclear attacks more selective, planners believed that they could increase the credibility

of nuclear deterrence despite the prospect that retaliation in kind was inevitable. National Security Decision Memorandum 242 (NSDM-242), issued by the Gerald Ford administration in 1974, reflected this new approach to nuclear targeting. It provided the president with a range of nuclear options, offered a prospect of controlling escalation, and devised a series of "nuclear withholds" (targeting options that excluded certain categories of targets). (*See* Counterforce Targeting; Countervalue Targeting; Escalation.)

The Jimmy Carter administration continued the effort to create "credible" nuclear targeting options. Presidential Directive 59 (PD-59) called for the development of selective counterforce options in the nuclear war plan, especially options to target centers of Soviet political and military control. The Carter administration also took steps to improve the survivability of U.S. nuclear command and control to be able to execute selective counterforce options even after suffering a Soviet nuclear attack. Ronald Reagan's administration focused on improving the ability of the United States to conduct prompt counterforce attacks by developing new delivery systems (including the MX–rail garrison intercontinental ballistic missile and the Trident II D5 submarine-launched ballistic missile) that provided a secure second-strike counterforce capability. These efforts to create secure nuclear second-strike capabilities and options were largely suspended with the end of the Cold War.

The rise of the U.S. precision global strike complex has added a new dimension to the prospect of devising selective options. The 2002 Nuclear Posture Review calls for the integration of nuclear and conventional strike options to hold critical targets at risk, especially small arsenals of nuclear, chemical, and biological weapons. Planners also have been instructed to abandon the deliberate planning method used during the Cold War to develop selective nuclear attack options. Instead, planners use adaptive, capabilities-based planning to devise options tailored to meet specific contingencies.

—*James J. Wirtz*

See also: Deterrence; Second Strike

Reference

Ball, Desmond, and Robert C. Toth, "Revising the SIOP: Taking War-Fighting to Dangerous Extremes," *International Security*, vol. 14, no. 4, Spring 1990, pp. 65–92.

SENTINEL ANTI-BALLISTIC MISSILE SYSTEM

The 1960s-era Sentinel antiballistic missile (ABM) system was intended to provide protection of the United States from a Soviet missile attack. The program was to consist of two different types of nuclear-tipped missiles, one designed to intercept incoming Soviet warheads in the exoatmosphere and a second, shorter-range missile to strike any remaining warheads once they reentered the Earth's atmosphere. From its inception, however, the program was contentious. For individuals such as U.S. Secretary of Defense Robert McNamara, the program represented a direct challenge to the concept of assured destruction. If either side developed a successful defensive system, then deterrence could no longer be based on the threat of holding the opponent's homeland at risk. For others, Sentinel was desirable because it held out the prospect of restoring America's ability to strike the Soviet Union with relative impunity. Within the scientific community there was considerable opposition even to limited deployment, and the pages of *Scientific American* were used as the main forum for the critique of the program. With the Vietnam War in the background, public opinion was against deploying interceptor missiles armed with nuclear warheads based near urban areas.

President Richard M. Nixon's administration sought to deflect criticism of the U.S. ABM program by announcing in March 1969 the reorientation of the program away from the defense of cities and toward the defense of U.S. intercontinental ballistic missile silos against a Soviet attack. Now called Safeguard, the system was intended to ensure that the United States retained an assured destruction capability against the Soviet Union. This change in the mission of the planned U.S. ABM system also was subjected to much criticism. The program remained a key negotiating chip for the United States during the Strategic Arms Limitation Talks (SALT I and II).

—*Andrew M. Dorman*

See also: Deterrence; Missile Defense

Reference

Newhouse, John, *The Nuclear Age: From Hiroshima to Star Wars* (London: Michael Joseph, 1989).

SHORT-RANGE ATTACK MISSILES (SRAMS)

After the cancellation of the Skybolt air-launched ballistic missile in December 1962, the U.S. Air Force had to devise another way to modernize the strike capabilities of its strategic bomber force. The Strategic Air Command (SAC) proposed the development of a short-range, air-to-ground attack missile (SRAM) in 1963 and accepted its first SRAM in 1972. SRAM was a small missile that could fly 100 miles with a W69 nuclear warhead. Designed to attack targets such as air defense sites from either high or low altitude in any direction from its carrier aircraft, the SRAM allowed a SAC bomber to strike multiple targets. The 2,240-pound SRAM was powered by a two-stage solid-fuel rocket motor. The first motor stage propelled the missile to Mach 3, and the second stage was ignited near the target for a powered terminal approach. Maximum range varied from 55 kilometers (35 miles) for low-altitude launches to 160 km (100 miles) for high-altitude firings. The SRAM was guided by an inertial navigation system, assisted by a terrain clearance sensor, and could achieve an accuracy (or circular error probable) of about 430 meters (1,400 feet). (*See* Accuracy.)

The weapon was originally proposed for the B-52G and H fleets, but the FB-111 and B-1 also carried the weapon. Each B-52 bomber could carry eight SRAM missiles on a rotary launch "revolver" cylinder carried in the aft bomb bay. Pylons under each B-52 wing, which were built to carry Hound Dog missiles, were modified to carry six SRAMs each, for a total load of twenty SRAMs per B-52. FB-111s could carry a maximum of six SRAMs, but a normal load was four, two in the weapons bay and two more on the inboard wing pivot points. The B-1 could be fitted with the B-52 rotary launcher in each of its three weapon bays. For both the B-52 and the B-1, one rotary launcher was usually installed in the aft weapons bay, while the other weapons bay held four thermonuclear gravity bombs. A total of 1,500 SRAMs were produced. The weapons were removed from the bombers on June 7, 1990, as part of President George H. W. Bush's nuclear force reductions at the end of the Cold War.

—*Gilles Van Nederveen*

References

Chant, Christopher, *World Encyclopedia of Modern Air Weapons* (London: Patrick Stephens, 1988).

Gibson, James N., *Nuclear Weapons of the United States* (Arlington, TX: Schiffer, 1996).

Gunston, Bill, *The Illustrated Encyclopedia of Rockets and Missiles* (London: Salamander, 1979).

SHROUDING

Shrouding is a managed access technique often used during arms control inspection procedures that involves either completely or partially covering an object from view. This technique is used to prevent visitors or international inspectors from being able to view proprietary or national security information. Shrouding conceals large objects, panels on objects, or the size and design of an object. If an entire machine or object needs to be protected, then a tarp or trash bag can be used to cover the object. If the size and shape need to be protected, a large box can be used to cover the object, or items can be placed under a tarp to conceal or alter the shape of the machine being shrouded. To shroud only part of an object, black tape and cardboard can be used to cover panels on a machine or words on a pipe that might give away a proprietary process.

Whenever shrouding or any managed access technique is used under an arms control agreement or treaty, the inspected party must make every attempt possible to demonstrate treaty compliance to the party carrying out the inspection. This could include partially removing a shroud or providing documentation about the compliance concern instead of granting full access to an area.

—*Robert Wyman*

References

Defense Threat Reduction Agency, DTIRP Outreach Program, "Guide to Managed Access under the Chemical Weapons Convention," April 2000, Order Number 122X.

Defense Threat Reduction Agency, DTIRP Outreach Program, "Arms Control Security Glossary," June 2001, Order Number 941X.

SILO BASING

Missile "silos" are heavily reinforced-steel and concrete underground structures that can be hardened to withstand thousands of pounds of blast overpressure generated by a nuclear detonation. Intercontinental ballistic missiles (ICBMs) are usually based in silos. Compared to road-mobile, air-launched, and sea-based missile launch platforms, silos enjoy higher alert rates and better communications and security, although in the past thirty years improvements in accuracy have made them increasingly vulnerable to both nuclear and conventional attack.

An intercontinental ballistic missile in its hardened underground silo. (Marvin Koner/Corbis)

Initially, silo-based missiles represented the most secure nuclear deterrent available to the United States and the Soviet Union. Since the silos were constructed deep within the territory of their respective states, and ICBMs often had a circular error probable (CEP) measured in miles (*see* Accuracy), silos offered a relatively inexpensive, effective, and survivable way to deploy ICBMs. As missile accuracies improved, however, missile silos (which could be located using satellite reconnaissance) and the weapons they sheltered became vulnerable to destruction.

However, the silo also has weaknesses in comparison with other warhead-delivery platforms. Most important, silos cannot move. Since they are in a fixed position, attacking forces know exactly where to target silos. To help improve survivability, most U.S. missile silos were hardened to withstand 2,500–4,000 pounds per square inch (psi) of pressure. Some were hardened to 7,000 psi. There was even research to create a "super-hard" silo capable of withstanding 50,000 psi. Some officials also suggested novel ways to incorporate silos in innovative basing schemes. The "racetrack" option involved moving ICBMs within a chain of connected silos so that Soviet intelligence would never know exactly where the missile was located at any given moment. The shelters would be dispersed and hardened, requiring the Soviets to expend dozens of warheads to destroy a single ICBM. Construction of this type of "warhead sink" was expensive and used vast tracks of land and raw materials, especially water. Another option, "dense pack," involved the construction of silos grouped closely together so that "fratricide" (the tendency of nearby nuclear explosions to damage other incoming warheads) would wreak havoc among a wave of attacking warheads, thus allowing a substantial portion of the defending force to survive the attack. Critics worried, however, that by continually subjecting the dense pack to a creeping missile barrage, Soviet forces could achieve a mission kill against the ICBM force by preventing missile launch.

—*Abe Denmark*

See also: Dense Pack

Reference

Davis, Lynn E., and Warner R. Schilling, "All You Ever Wanted to Know about MIRV and ICBM Calculations but Were Not Cleared to Ask," *The Journal of Conflict Resolution,* vol. 17, no. 2 (June 1973), pp. 207–242.

SINGLE INTEGRATED OPERATIONAL PLAN (SIOP)

As new weapon systems and new ways of fighting have emerged, the requirement to command and control such capabilities has remained, but the means by which this control is exercised has changed. The advent of nuclear weapons posed significant new challenges for command and control in wartime because failure of positive or negative control could have potentially devastating results. Since the Dwight D. Eisenhower administration, successive Single Integrated Operations Plans (SIOPs) have been developed to manage how U.S. nuclear forces would be used in war. Shrouded in secrecy, and with many attendant myths, successive plans have been developed over the years to encompass a variety of targeting options based on broad guidance received from successive presidents, secretaries of defense, and the Joint Chiefs of Staff. The

SIOP has been the employment plan for several declaratory nuclear doctrines, including assured destruction in the 1960s and sufficiency and controlled response in the 1970s.

History and Background

The SIOP was developed initially by Strategic Air Command (SAC, now U.S. Strategic Command, or STRATCOM) in its Joint Strategic Targeting and Planning Section (JSTPS) as a way to integrate a growing multiservice and multiplatform U.S. nuclear arsenal into a coherent war plan and to develop operational war plans that matched civilian guidance on nuclear deterrent policy. The SIOP was literally a *single* plan produced through a deliberate planning process that often took years to complete. Its goal was to use all available nuclear weapons under day-alert and fully generated scenarios to maximize damage against the Soviet Union and its allies. A secondary goal was to deconflict attack routes and time over target to minimize fratricide. The John F. Kennedy administration did not like the single option provided by the first SIOP, known as SIOP-62, and pushed for additional policy options. Administration officials argued that the single option failed to give the president flexibility in meeting unexpected contingencies. Successive SIOPs have since been developed that offered an increasing array of attack options to the president as a means of attempting to control nuclear escalation. A more flexible SIOP was supposed to increase the credibility of deterrent threats because it provided several limited options that might be used under dire circumstances to demonstrate resolve or to terminate a conflict quickly on U.S. terms (*see* Credibility; Deterrence).

With the end of the Cold War, the transformation of SAC to STRATCOM, and the need for even more flexibility when it came to planning for unexpected threats and conflicts, the deliberate and time-consuming SIOP planning process is being phased out in favor of an adaptive "capabilities-based" planning process. The 2001 Nuclear Posture Review produced by the George W. Bush administration marked a watershed in the history of U.S. nuclear policy. Planners may now be able to plan military operations on relatively short notice using a menu of nuclear and nonnuclear strike options. Instead of focusing on guaranteeing that a massive nuclear attack can be launched against the Soviet

Union under all circumstances, planners now focus on providing options and capabilities to match all conceivable future threats. New versions of the "SIOP" will create additional requirements for improved command and control (*see* Nuclear Posture Review).

Technical Details

The SIOP integrates all the nuclear weapons maintained by the various services and all the plans of the various commands to ensure civilian control over nuclear weapons and to ensure that nuclear weapons are used in a coherent manner to produce some tangible military effect. Planning for such an eventuality has rested with a joint targeting team, traditionally under the command of a navy flag officer stationed at Offutt Air Force Base, Omaha, Nebraska.

Presidents do not become fully familiar with the SIOP and their responsibilities until they receive their SIOP briefing, which is developed by military staffs at STRATCOM. The SIOP describes to the president the range of targeting options he would have available should he decide to employ them. It is framed in terms of launch procedures and the target sets against which the weapons will be launched. The executive version of the SIOP, including the code books and unlock authority for weapons, often is visible to the public. Known as the "football," it consists of a briefcase carried by an officer who accompanies the president wherever he goes. In the event that the president becomes incapacitated (such as after the attempted assassination of Ronald Reagan in 1982), access to the football can pass to others, for example, the vice president, along with authority to command the U.S. nuclear arsenal (*see* The Football).

Implementing and maintaining the SIOP requires the continual updating of the command and control system, a significant reconnaissance and interpretation capability, and the maintenance of alert based nuclear forces. These are regularly tested. The results of the various war games have been kept secret, although elements from them have leaked. The SIOP requires the preservation of a leadership to authorize nuclear release, and this means that the president and his successors need to remain invulnerable. As a result, forces are always on alert to move the president out of harm's way and get him aboard the special Boeing 747 command aircraft,

which is currently designated the National Emergency Airborne Command Post (NEACP). (*See* National Emergency Airborne Command Post [NEACP].)

Traditionally, the SIOP was based on an effort to match available weapons to various target sets. Targets have included Russian nuclear bases and other military targets, leadership headquarters, and urban industrial targets. Using sophisticated modeling techniques, planners calculate how hard each potential target would be to destroy, what type of nuclear weapon should be used, how many weapons would need to be allocated to destroy it, and how much damage such an attack would be likely to have in terms of both physical damage and human casualties.

—*Andrew M. Dorman and James J. Wirtz*

See also: Strategic Air Command and Strategic Command

References

Carter, Ashton B., John D. Steinbruner, and Charles A. Zraket, eds., *Managing Nuclear Operations* (Washington, DC: Brookings Institution, 1987).
National Resources Defense Council, "The US Nuclear War Plan: A Time for Change," 2001, available at http://www.nrdc.org/nuclear/nwarplan.asp.
Pringle, Peter, and William Arkin, *SIOP: Nuclear War from the Inside* (London: Sphere Books, 1983).

SKYBOLT

The Douglas AGM-48A Skybolt was an air-launched missile with a nuclear warhead that was to have been deployed on U.S. B-52 bombers in a plan that would have transformed the bombers into mobile ballistic missile launchers. It was a joint project with Great Britain, which intended to use Skybolt to modernize its independent nuclear force of Vulcan bombers. In return for codevelopment of the missile, the British agreed to grant the U.S. Navy access to the Holy Loch submarine base in Scotland.

Skybolt was a 39-foot, two-stage missile that weighed 11,000 pounds and had a range of 950 nautical miles. When dropped from a B-52 at 40,000 feet, the missile could reach its target in as little as 12 minutes. The government initially intended to build 1,000 Skybolt missiles to equip 22 bomber squadrons by mid-1967 for $2.5 billion ($600 million of this cost was tied up in equipping Skybolt with its 800-kiloton warhead). The missile's primary mission, defense suppression, would have been to destroy air defense batteries, thereby providing the bombers clear paths to Soviet targets.

Skybolt was canceled in December 1962 by the John F. Kennedy administration because of concerns about cost and effectiveness. This decision led to a major crisis in Anglo-American relations. To smooth over tensions with British allies, the Kennedy administration, following the Nassau Summit, promised to provide Great Britain with access to the Polaris submarine-launched ballistic missile. This offer, in turn, angered French officials, leading to their veto of British entry into the European Economic Community in January 1963.

—*Glen M. Segell*

Reference

Neustadt, Richard E., *The Skybolt Crisis in Perspective* (Ithaca, NY: Cornell University Press, 1999).

SOUTH AFRICAN NUCLEAR WEAPONS PROGRAM

South Africa was a secret nuclear weapons state in the 1980s and 1990s until unilaterally renouncing its program and destroying its six warheads in 1994. Readily available South African sources of yellowcake had helped to fuel the nuclear industry in the United States immediately after World War II. Reciprocally, South Africans were trained in the United States, which later provided South Africa with a nuclear research reactor. This arrangement operated under a safeguards agreement between the International Atomic Energy Agency (IAEA), the United States, and South Africa. In 1957, the United States signed a bilateral nuclear cooperation agreement with South Africa that committed Washington to supply enriched uranium to the regime in Johannesburg.

Although South Africa had signed the 1963 Limited Test Ban Treaty, it refused to sign the 1968 Nuclear Nonproliferation Treaty (NPT). In 1971, South Africa began investigations into building a nuclear device. This initiated deep suspicion over South Africa's long-term intentions, especially because the country faced growing international isolation over its policy of apartheid. Three years later, the South African government authorized a nuclear program and began secret work on a nuclear test site in the Kalahari Desert.

Notwithstanding efforts to use its strategic location to impress its importance to the West, pressure on South Africa both over apartheid and over its nuclear program increased by the mid-1970s. The Jimmy Carter administration was especially active in the quest to end apartheid. Although Washington opposed a complete ban on nuclear cooperation with South Africa, the 1978 U.S. Nuclear Non-Proliferation Act (NNPA) ended the possibility for the reexport of enriched uranium (even of South African origin) to South Africa to fuel a French-built nuclear power station. In response, South Africa set out to develop local alternatives by constructing a plant to produce highly enriched uranium (HEU) on an industrial scale (*see* Enrichment; Highly Enriched Uranium [HEU]).

In August 1977, the Soviets detected preparations for a "cold test" at the Kalahari facility. Setting aside ideological differences, the superpowers pressured South Africa not to go forward with its nuclear program. Two years later, however, the United States detected a low-yield, high-altitude nuclear explosion off South Africa's coast. What happened remains a mystery. The possibility of nuclear cooperation with Israel remains the most plausible explanation of the event. In 1977, South Africa was removed from its seat on the IAEA board of governors and replaced by Egypt; two years later it was denied participation in the IAEA General Conference. South Africa also might have sold enriched uranium to Iraq in the late 1980s.

The end of apartheid broke the impasse over South Africa's nuclear program. In early July 1991, South Africa acceded to the NPT, and it completed its IAEA safeguards agreement three months later. In March 1993, South Africa's last minority-elected president, F. W. de Klerk, announced the unilateral dismantling of its six nuclear weapons. Some believe that the decision was made to prevent technology from falling into the hands of a "black government" or to halt the possible transfer of weapons-grade uranium to Libya, Cuba, or the Palestine Liberation Organization. The country's majority-elected government also has followed a nonnuclear policy.

South Africa joined the Zangger Committee in 1994 and the Nuclear Suppliers Group in 1995. Its officials were instrumental in winning indefinite extension of the NPT in 1995 and played a leading role in the successful conclusion of the 2000 NPT Review Conference as a member of the "New Agenda Coalition."

—*Peter Vale*

See also: Nuclear Nonproliferation Treaty (NPT);
Nuclear Suppliers Group; Zangger Committee
References
Paul, T. V., *Power versus Prudence: Why Nations Forgo
Nuclear Weapons* (Montreal: McGill-Queen's
University Press, 2000).
Reiss, Mitchell, *Bridled Ambition: Why Countries
Constrain Their Nuclear Capabilities* (Washington,
DC: Woodrow Wilson Center, 1995).

SOUTH KOREAN NUCLEAR WEAPONS PROGRAM

Since the end of the Korean War in 1953, the Republic of Korea (ROK, or South Korea) has occasionally made limited attempts to pursue the development of weapons of mass destruction. However, it joined the nonproliferation regime in 1975 when it signed the Nuclear Nonproliferation Treaty (NPT) and has maintained its commitments under that treaty. The country, which came into existence in August 1948, has meanwhile had to contend with the threat of weapons of mass destruction in the Democratic People's Republic of Korea (DPRK, or North Korea). South Korea has maintained a close relationship with the United States and now finds itself precariously positioned between the brinkmanship of Pyongyang and Washington's identification of North Korea as a "rogue state."

Under the dictatorship of General Park Chung Hee, South Korea pursued a nuclear weapons program in the 1970s but backed down under U.S. pressure before producing any fissile material. In 1972, South Korea discussed the acquisition of a nuclear plant with Canada and France. A contract with France for the purchase of a reprocessing plant was signed early in 1975. The significance of these negotiations was apparent to U.S. officials, who placed pressure on the South Koreans to abandon any ambitions to build a nuclear weapon. South Korea yielded to U.S. pressure and canceled its order for nuclear reprocessing plants (*see* Reprocessing).

When South Korea signed the NPT in 1975, it accepted all International Atomic Energy Agency (IAEA) inspection and auditing procedures. In 1991, President Roh Tae Woo declared that South Korea would not "manufacture, possess, store, deploy, or use nuclear weapons" and added that Seoul would not possess nuclear fuel reprocessing and enrichment facilities. In 1992, North and South Korea signed the Joint Declaration on the Denucleariza-tion of the Korean Peninsula and the Basic Agreement, under which the two sides promised reconciliation, nonaggression, exchanges and cooperation, and the denuclearization of the Korean peninsula. Both sides, however, have failed to implement the bilateral inspection regime called for by these agreements (*see* International Atomic Energy Agency; Joint Declaration on Denuclearization of the Korean Peninsula; Nuclear Nonproliferation Treaty [NPT]).

North Korea's nuclear ambitions have continued to supply evidence in support of a hard-line minority in the South Korean legislature that wants to match North Korea's nuclear programs. Although South Korea initially renounced its right to reprocess and enrich nuclear fuel, the revelations regarding North Korea's clandestine nuclear program in the early 1990s caused a change in policy. South Korea set up a reprocessing plant at a nuclear research facility outside of Seoul to close its nuclear fuel cycle and give it nuclear independence.

All South Korean nuclear facilities and materials are under full-scope international inspections by the IAEA, in compliance with its NPT safeguards obligation, and there is no suspicion of a covert nuclear program. In 2002, following further declarations from North Korea that it is pursuing a nuclear program, South Korean president Kim Dae Jung issued a statement with U.S. president George W. Bush and Japanese prime minister Junichiro Koizumi condemning North Korea's pursuit of nuclear weapons, declaring it a violation of the Agreed Framework, the NPT, North Korea's IAEA safeguards agreement, and the Joint Declaration on Denuclearization of the Korean Peninsula. Today, South Korea is a "virtual" nuclear power, a country that has the technical capability needed to build a nuclear arsenal but has made the political decision not to acquire nuclear weapons.

—*J. Simon Rofe and Elizabeth Aylott*

See also: North Korean Nuclear Weapons Program
Reference
Cumings, Bruce, *Korea's Place in the Sun* (New York: W. W. Norton, 1997).

SOVIET UNION

See Bombers, Russian and Chinese Nuclear-Capable; Chelyabinsk-40; Chernobyl; Moscow Antiballistic Missile System; Nuclear Warhead Storage and

Transportation Security (Russia); Russian Nuclear Forces and Doctrine

SPACE-BASED INFRARED RADAR SYSTEM (SBIRS)

The Space-Based Infrared Radar System (SBIRS) is the planned follow-on surveillance system to the aging Defense Support Program (DSP) system. During the Cold War, the United States constructed a network of surveillance posts, radar sites, and satellite systems to provide early warning of a first strike attack by the Soviet Union. One of these systems was the DSP, a constellation of infrared satellites in geostationary orbit. First launched in November 1970, DSP's primary mission remains detection and warning of missile launches through recognition of their boost phase.

SBIRS is being developed to meet U.S. surveillance needs during the next two to three decades. Its four primary missions are missile warning, missile defense, technical intelligence, and battlespace characterization. SBIRS is a "system of systems" that will integrate space assets in several orbit configurations with a consolidated ground segment to provide effective integration of data and improved transmission of data to the battlefield.

The SBIRS architecture includes satellites located in Geostationary Earth Orbit (GEO), Highly Elliptical Orbits (HEO), and Low Earth Orbit (LEO) to provide global coverage in support of its four missions. The satellites in GEO and HEO, "SBIRS-High," provide improved missile warning and defense. Those in LEO, originally termed "SBIRS-Low," track ballistic missile targets through midcourse and terminal flight. In 2002, the SBIRS-Low program was restructured, incorporated into the Missile Defense Agency, and renamed the Space Tracking and Surveillance System (STSS). STSS will detect and track ballistic missiles; in addition, it will enhance the ability of ballistic missile defense system interceptors to differentiate the warhead of an incoming missile from other nearby objects, such as decoys.

—*Patricia McFate*

See also: Decoys; Early Warning; Missile Defense; Surveillance

References

Missile Defense Agency website, http://www.acq.osd. mil/bmdo/bmdolink/.

SPARTAN MISSILE

The Spartan air-defense missile was designed as the first line of defense in the U.S. Sentinel and Safeguard antiballistic missile programs of the 1960s and 1970s. The earlier Nike-X system had incorporated two missiles; one of them was exoatmospheric, that is, a long-range missile designed to intercept warheads outside of the Earth's atmosphere. Work on an extended-range Nike-Zeus B (or Nike-Zeus EX) was started in 1965. The name of this missile was changed to Spartan two years later, when the Nike-X system was renamed Sentinel (*see* Anti-Ballistic Missile System; Nike Zeus; Sentinel).

The first test of this missile occurred in March 1968. The Spartan carried a large, multimegaton warhead that was designed to kill an enemy reentry vehicle (RV) by X-ray radiation flux, rather than by blast. In this sense, its warhead was the first enhanced radiation weapon, or "neutron bomb." Spartan had a range of 460 miles. In August 1970, a Minuteman RV was successfully intercepted by a Spartan for the first time. In January 1971, Spartan intercepted a Polaris submarine-launched ballistic missile that had deployed decoys and penetration

Two Spartan missiles are launched seconds apart en route to a successful intercept of an ICBM reentry vehicle high over the Pacific as part of the Safeguard ABM system tests at the Kwajalein Range, January 1971. (Bettmann/ Corbis)

aids in an attempt to overwhelm the Spartan radar systems (*see* Neutron Bomb [Enhanced Radiation Weapon]; Penetration Aids).

The Sentinel system soon gave way to Safeguard, the antiballistic missile system the United States eventually deployed in 1975 at Grand Forks, North Dakota. Thirty Spartan interceptors were stored in underground silos along with seventy high-speed Sprint interceptors.

—*Gilles Van Nederveen*

See also: Safeguard Anti-Ballistic Missile System; Strategic Defenses

References

Gibson, James N., *Nuclear Weapons of the United States* (Arlington, TX: Schiffer, 1996).

Gunston, Bill, *The Illustrated Encyclopedia of Rockets and Missiles* (London: Salamander, 1979).

McMahon, K. Scott, *Pursuit of the Shield: The U.S. Quest for Limited Ballistic Missile Defense* (New York: University Press of America, 1997).

SPENT FUEL

See Reactor Operations

SPRINT MISSILE

The Sprint air-defense missile was designed to serve as the point defense missile in the U.S. Sentinel and Safeguard antiballistic missile (ABM) systems of the 1960s and 1970s. It was endoatmospheric, that is, designed to intercept missiles within the Earth's atmosphere. In November 1965, the first Sprint was tested after research showed that a very high speed interceptor was possible.

The cone-shaped Sprint was powered by a two-stage solid-propellant rocket motor. The motor ignited after the missile had been ejected from its underground silo by gas pressure and was capable of accelerating at more than 100 G's. The missile reached a speed greater than Mach 10, and the extreme thermodynamic heating demanded sophisticated ablative shielding. The nose of the Sprint actually glowed a second after launch. Special command links, hardened and protected against electromagnetic pulse, guided the missile. The Sprint was equipped with a low-yield enhanced radiation warhead that was intended to destroy the incoming reentry vehicle with a very high neutron flux. The flight time for an intercept was expected to be less than 15 seconds.

Testing continued until 1973, validating the design, and seventy Sprints were deployed in North Dakota as part of the Safeguard ABM system. That system was inactivated in 1975.

—*Gilles Van Nederveen*

See also: Missile Defense; Neutron Bomb (Enhanced Radiation Weapon); Safeguard Antiballistic Missile System; Sentinel; Strategic Defenses

References

Gibson, James N., *Nuclear Weapons of the United States* (Arlington, TX, Schiffer, 1996).

Gunston, Bill, *The Illustrated Encyclopedia of Rockets and Missiles* (London: Salamander, 1979).

McMahon, K. Scott, *Pursuit of the Shield: The U.S. Quest for Limited Ballistic Missile Defense* (New York: University Press of America, 1997).

SPUTNIK

Sputnik, launched by the Soviet Union on October 4, 1957, was the world's first artificial satellite. Two more Sputniks were launched on November 3, 1957, and May 15, 1958. In opening the space age, Sputnik caused an international sensation. In response, the United States established the National Aeronautics and Space Administration (NASA). Sputnik thus inspired the space race that culminated in the U.S. moon landings twelve years later.

Sergey P. Korolev, who would become Soviet chief missile designer, began preliminary work on a satellite program in the early 1950s. In May 1954, he requested permission to develop and launch a satellite on an RL-7 booster, but the government did not give full approval to the satellite project, called Object D, until January 1956. The approval was influenced by the U.S. announcement in July 1955 of plans to launch a satellite during the International Geophysical Year (IGY) scheduled to begin in 1957. News in September 1956 that the U.S. Army had launched a Jupiter C on a ballistic flight over a distance of 5,300 kilometers prompted Korolev to modify his efforts to avoid being beaten into space. In November 1956, he introduced a lighter and more modest satellite proposal. This version was approved in February 1957 and became *Sputnik I*.

It would be hard to overstate the dramatic effect of the Sputniks on world, and especially U.S., public opinion. The Soviet space triumphs accelerated the growing feelings of insecurity experienced by many Americans during the early years of the nuclear age. The U.S. response to the challenge was broad and deep, ranging from bolstering education to increased military spending and government re-organization.

—*Peter Hays*

References

Bulkeley, Rip, *The Sputniks Crisis and Early United States Space Policy: A Critique of the Historiography of Space* (Bloomington: Indiana University Press, 1991).

Divine, Robert A., *The Sputnik Challenge* (New York: Oxford University Press, 1993).

McDougall, Walter A., *The Heavens and the Earth: A Political History of the Space Age* (New York: Basic, 1985).

Siddiqi, Asif A., *Sputnik and the Soviet Space Challenge* (Gainesville: University Press of Florida, 2003).

STANDING CONSULTATIVE COMMISSION

The Standing Consultative Commission (SCC) was a forum established to help implement the objectives and provisions of the May 1972 Anti-Ballistic Missile (ABM) Treaty and to deal with ambiguities and compliance questions related to the treaty. Article XIII of the ABM Treaty provided for the establishment of the SCC, and a December 1972 Memorandum of Understanding (MOU) between the United States and the Soviet Union established the Commission. The MOU also gave the SCC jurisdiction over the Accidents Measures Agreement of 1971 and the 1972 Interim Agreement on Strategic Offensive Arms. The SCC was thus charged with dealing with the three associated agreements that emerged during the first Strategic Arms Limitation Talks and Treaty (SALT I). The SCC also helped to implement the signed but never ratified 1979 SALT II Treaty. From the late 1980s, the SCC exclusively concerned itself with ABM Treaty–related issues. The SCC served as a model for later arms control treaty implementation commissions, such as the Special Verification Commission of the 1987 Intermediate-Range Nuclear Forces (INF) Treaty and the Joint Compliance and Inspection Commission of the 1991 Strategic Arms Reduction Treaty (START I).

The SCC MOU established basic organizational matters but left much discretion to U.S. and Soviet officials as to how the SCC should actually operate. Each side was to be represented by a commissioner and a deputy commissioner, assisted by such staff as it deemed necessary. Commission sessions were to be held not less than two times per year and could be convened as soon as possible, following reasonable notice, at the request of either commissioner. The sessions were to be held in Geneva, Switzerland, unless another location was selected by mutual consent. The SCC was charged with making its own regulations and could revise, repeal, or replace the regulations as it deemed necessary. The United States and the Soviet Union agreed upon regulations in May 1973 at the opening of the first SCC session.

After the dissolution of the Soviet Union in December 1991, an issue arose about which of the Soviet successor states were or should be parties to the ABM Treaty, and by extension, the SCC. In September 1997, a Memorandum of Understanding on ABM Treaty succession was signed by the United States, Russia, Belarus, Kazakhstan, and Ukraine. An associated document provided revised regulations to govern the multilateral operation of the SCC. These ABM Treaty succession documents, however, were overtaken by events and never entered into force.

Although Russia, Belarus, Kazakhstan, and Ukraine attended SCC sessions from 1992 until 2001, in the absence of entry into force of the ABM Treaty Succession MOU, the status of the Soviet successor states with respect to the ABM Treaty and the SCC was never resolved. The United States gave a six-month notice of its intention to withdraw from the ABM Treaty on December 13, 2001. This withdrawal notice was given pursuant to the withdrawal requirements of Article XV of the ABM Treaty. U.S. withdrawal took effect on June 13, 2002. The SCC ceased to function after its sixty-third session in December 2001.

—*Steven Rosenkrantz*

See also: Anti-Ballistic Missile Treaty; Intermediate-Range Nuclear Forces Treaty; Strategic Arms Limitation Talks; Strategic Arms Reduction Treaty

References

U.S. State Department websites, http://www.state.gov/t/ac/tr/ and http://www.state.gov/www/global/arms/treaties/abmpage.html.

STEALTH BOMBER (B-2 SPIRIT)

The U.S. Air Force B-2 stealth bomber is America's premier long-range nuclear and conventional strategic bomber. The stealth bomber project was first announced by the Carter administration in the

A B-2 Spirit bomber from Whiteman Air Force Base in Missouri drops a B-61/11 "bunker buster" bomb in a March 1998 test. (Reuters/Corbis)

heat of the 1980 presidential campaign, in response to Republican criticism of the decision to cancel the B-1A bomber. Since its unveiling on November 22, 1988, the bomber has been highly controversial for its high development and production costs—$45 billion—and high ongoing maintenance costs.

When the Rockwell B-1A was canceled in 1977, design work on a new bomber with stealth technology was already under way. The program, code-named Advanced Technology Bomber (ATB), was officially launched in 1978. In 1981, Northrop's design was chosen over a Lockheed/Rockwell concept. Boeing would play a large role as a Northrop subcontractor. The U.S. Air Force originally planned to acquire 133 B-2s, which were designed to penetrate Soviet airspace and attack mobile intercontinental ballistic missile (ICBM) launchers such as the SS-24 and the SS-25.

The B-2 was to take over the penetration mission from the 100 B-1Bs that had been procured by the air force in the mid- to late 1990s. The B-1s, in turn, were to take over the stand-off attack mission from the B-52s. The B-2 needed to survive the penetration of Soviet airspace and be undetectable as it

attacked strategic targets inside the Soviet Union. The B-52 and B-1 fleets relied on low-altitude mission profiles with extensive countermeasures, which have the drawback of giving away their position and making them vulnerable to detection. The B-2 thus had to incorporate new low-observable technology that already had been developed for a fighter-sized aircraft, the F-117. Since the stealth low-observable technology had worked, a bomber was quickly proposed.

Although work on the ATB was clouded in secrecy, it was soon rumored among aviation enthusiasts that Northrop's design was a variation of its flying-wing work from the 1940s. Northrop had built the XB-35 and XB-49 flying wings, but neither was ultimately accepted into service. Both were advanced for their time. A flying-wing bomber has no fuselage or tail, so there is less drag-producing area, and loads within the airframe can be distributed over the entire wing to produce a lighter structure. Advances in computing capabilities allowed radar engineers to work out solutions for curved aircraft surfaces. The F-117 was very straight lined to deflect radar beams, but the ATB had to be designed with rounded airframe surfaces. Northrop was able to design the B-2 using radar-beam prediction programs. When designing a stealth aircraft, radar engineers try to make sure the aircraft will either absorb radar energy or deflect it away from the adversary's radar receiver.

New and improved radar-absorbing material allowed the external shape to be very smooth. The B-2's flying-wing configuration also made it possible to build an airframe without any protrusions, bury the engines in the wings, and eliminate the vertical stabilizer and control surfaces that normally add to an airframe's radar signature. By placing the engines into the wings and shielding the engine's turbine blades and engine air intakes from direct radar observation, more stealth is incorporated into the B-2. Since radar is not the only means by which a flying aircraft can be detected, the engine exhaust is mixed with cooler outside air to reduce the heat signature of the B-2. This makes it harder for an infrared guided weapon to target the bomber. Since all of the stealth design and engineering concepts used to reduce an aircraft's signature require tradeoffs, the secrecy surrounding a stealth aircraft is meant to not only protect the stealth technologies but also the choices and mixes made within the program design.

With the end of the Cold War and the corresponding cuts in defense spending, the B-2 program was also reduced. Only twenty-one aircraft, including a development model, were built for the United States. They are assigned to the 509th Bomb Wing at Whiteman Air Force Base in Missouri. They flew their first combat mission against Serbia in 1999 and since then have conducted sorties lasting up to forty-five hours to deliver precision-guided conventional munitions against Afghanistan and Iraq. Advanced avionics allow the B-2 to attack up to sixteen separate targets nearly simultaneously—that being the number of Joint Direct Attack Munitions (JDAM) or B-61 nuclear bombs the B-2's bomb bay can hold. New advanced munitions are constantly being fitted to the B-2's bomb bay: For example, the B-2 will carry up to 162 small-diameter bombs, each capable of hitting a separate target. The B-2 avionics also have been updated and communications systems improved to allow the bomb crew to reprogram its target coordinates while in flight to the target. The B-2 remains the most technologically advanced bomber in the world.

—*Gilles Van Nederveen*

References
Brown, Michael, *Flying Blind: The Politics of the U.S. Strategic Bomber Program* (Ithaca, NY: Cornell University Press, 1992).

Donald, David, ed., *Black Jets: The Development and Operation of America's Most Secret Warplanes* (Norwalk, CT: AIRTime, 2003).

"Striking from the Heartland: B-2 'Spirit' Stealth Bombers Fly Record Sorties to Afghanistan," available at http://www.spear.navy.mil/profile/profile/dec01/pages/page18.html.

Sweetman, Bill, *Stealth Bomber* (Osceola, WI: Motorbooks International, 1989).

STOCKPILE STEWARDSHIP PROGRAM

The cessation of underground nuclear testing in the early 1990s created a major challenge for the U.S. Department of Energy (DOE): how to continue to certify the safety and readiness of its nuclear weapons without this key aspect of the annual certification program. Nuclear testing was the core activity that allowed DOE to certify to the president on an annual basis that the stockpile remained safe and capable. The replacement for the underground nuclear test program is the Stockpile Stewardship Program (SSP). (*See* Underground Testing.)

History and Background
Between July 1945 and September 1992, the United States conducted 1,054 nuclear weapons tests. In the early years of the program, testing allowed the United States to present its president with a nuclear option to end World War II. The arms race with the Soviet Union drove the need for future tests as the United States worked to stay ahead of Soviet scientists and the Soviet nuclear arsenal.

The collapse and breakup of the Soviet Union brought an end to this nuclear arms race. However, the Department of Energy was tasked to retain a nuclear deterrent capability, increase its efforts in nonproliferation of nuclear weapon technology, and ensure the United States was not surprised by nuclear arms developments elsewhere in the world.

The future of the nation's nuclear weapons program was changed in 1995 when President William Clinton announced that the United States would pursue a comprehensive nuclear test ban. The president also directed that necessary programmatic activities to ensure stockpile safety and reliability in the absence of nuclear testing be developed. The DOE Stockpile Stewardship Program was developed in response to this directive. In 1996, the president signed the Comprehensive Test Ban Treaty to end all nuclear testing. Although as of mid-2004 the United States had not ratified that treaty, it continues to abide by a unilateral moratorium on nuclear testing (*see* Comprehensive Test Ban Treaty; Department of Energy; Moratorium).

The Department of Energy's Stockpile Stewardship Program ensures that it can depend on experiments and simulations to predict, detect, evaluate, and correct problems affecting nuclear weapons without nuclear testing. Critical to meeting this challenge is the development of higher-resolution computer models of the performance of nuclear weapons and the conditions that affect weapon safety. This replaces the previous demonstration-based program with a science-based one that focuses on the implications to performance of an aging stockpile. The elements of SSP are located at the Lawrence Livermore, Los Alamos, and Sandia national laboratories. The first annual certification of the stockpile under the SSP was signed on February 7, 1997.

Technical Details

The SSP relies on the world's largest and fastest computers to conduct "virtual" nuclear tests using ever-improving computer codes. The increased resolution of these codes over time requires a steady stream of ever-improving, quality data. The data needs are being met by the construction and operation of special experimental facilities, each designed to provide unique data to the program. Examples of these facilities and capabilities follow.

The National Ignition Facility (NIF) is an experimental cornerstone of SSP, providing a unique data source for studying the physics of nuclear weapon primary and secondary components. The NIF is a laser facility on a massive scale. It will have 192 operational laser beams delivering nearly 2 megajoules of energy to the center of its chamber by 2008. It is the only facility that will conduct experiments to examine fusion burn and to study weapons-related processes at nuclear weapons–relevant energy density. By the end of 2005, 16 of its 192 beams will be operational, making it the world's largest laser with only 10 percent of its beams in operation. Although the NIF's primary role will be in support of stockpile stewardship, it will also serve as a national facility for basic research in high energy–density physics.

When ignition is demonstrated in 2010, NIF will play a major role in fusion energy research. With congressional approval, Livermore is partnering on NIF with U.S. allies, particularly the French CEA Division Applications Militaire and the British AWE Ministry of Defense. Both countries have strong commitments to stockpile stewardship programs in which laser facilities play prominent roles.

The Accelerated Strategic Computing Initiative (ASCI) is a tri-laboratory DOE program that will dramatically advance the ability to simulate computationally the performance of an aging stockpile and conditions affecting weapon safety. Although it will take more than a decade to achieve ASCI's long-term goals of a ten-thousand-fold increase in computer speed and data storage capacity each year, the initiative is structured to deliver major new capabilities to support stockpile stewardship. Central to ASCI is the accelerated development over the next decade of highly parallel, tera-scale computers in partnership with the U.S. computer industry. A tera-scale computer performs a trillion operations per second, a thousandfold improvement over the 1998 capability. Computers of this size and speed are necessary to simulate the integrated details that were once tested in underground explosions. As part of the ASCI initiative, Livermore has partnered with IBM to develop these highly advanced computational capabilities. ASCI's computers of the future will face the challenge of providing accurate and detailed simulated predictions of the complex processes involved in nuclear weapons explosions as well as of the detailed materials changes in weapons due to aging and refurbishment. The success of SSP will depend on the credibility of the weapons laboratories' simulations, as measured by their ability to accurately predict complex laboratory experiments at facilities such as NIF at Lawrence Livermore or Dual Axis Radiation Hydrodynamics Test Facility (DARHT) at Los Alamos (*see* Lawrence Livermore National Laboratory; Los Alamos National Laboratory).

Weapons aging is a critical issue. Aging affects the physical characteristics of all materials, producing premature materials failure in airplanes, cars, and nuclear weapons. With a better understanding of aging, stockpile surveillance can become more predictive, making possible systematic refurbishment and preventive maintenance activities that can correct problems that threaten weapon safety or reliability. With fewer weapons and fewer types of weapons in the stockpile, together with reduced capabilities and capacity in the production complex, DOE must become more and more proficient at detecting and predicting potential problems early on to provide enough time for thorough evaluation and action before problems affect stockpile safety or reliability. The national laboratories are improving their databases on the characteristics and behavior of stockpiled weapons so that they can identify anomalies in aging weapons. They are improving sensors and techniques used to inspect stockpiled weapons, and they are developing a better understanding of how aging alters the physical characteristics of weapon materials and how these changes affect weapon reliability and safety.

The Contained Firing Facility (CFF) at Lawrence Livermore is a modern capability for studying the dynamic implosion of simulated weapons using high explosives. These dynamic simulations are known as explosive hydrodynamics tests. In the absence of nuclear testing, explosive hydrodynamics tests are the principal experimental means of assessing the integral performance of primaries in stockpile nuclear weapons. Testing is conducted in a large containment chamber with an automatic washdown system for rapid experiment turnaround. CFF has increased radiographic dose over earlier facilities, improved resolution, and added a double-pulsing mode to support dynamic radiography. CFF is the principal source of the high-fidelity measurements of primary performance needed to preserve confidence in the integrity of stockpile weapons.

Tritium is used to boost nuclear weapon yields. No tritium has been produced for the U.S. weapons stockpile since 1988. DOE is meeting stockpile needs by recycling tritium from dismantled weapons. Since tritium decays at a rate of 5.5 percent per year, the total tritium inventory available without further production will decline to a level where, by 2007, the inventory will be insufficient to maintain a START II stockpile. The new Accelerator Production of Tritium (APT) program will use a high-energy, high-current proton accelerator to produce tritium. The DOE's national security laboratories are designing the APT facility, with Los Alamos as the lead laboratory (*see* Tritium).

The DOE national security laboratories are working closely with the production plants to maintain the enduring U.S. stockpile through a combination of as-needed repairs, refurbishments, and re-placements. Workforce skills, formerly developed and maintained through new weapons development, also must be maintained through this repair-refurbish-replace process. DOE's Advanced Design and Production Technology (ADaPT) program is a complex-wide effort to meet these challenges. The program integrates the skills and facilities of the national security laboratories and the production plants to develop innovative new processes and practices that will be needed to achieve a requirements-based, cost-effective production complex.

The Future
DOE and its national laboratories are focusing their best talents on defining the key SSP scientific challenges. These challenges include vastly increased computational capabilities, a much deeper understanding of materials processes (from the atomic to the macroscopic level), major improvements in the ability to model complex nonlinear dynamic processes, and experimental facilities that can produce plasma density and pressure regimes well beyond any available in the world today. The scientific infrastructure that will support SSP, now and in the future, depends on a myriad of small experimental facilities compiling data that provide single pieces of the large jigsaw puzzle. All are working to ensure that these capabilities in physics, chemistry, and other basic sciences, as well as their theoretical counterparts, remain a robust and productive mainstay of stockpile stewardship.

—*Don Gillich*

Reference

Lawrence Livermore National Laboratory, "Stockpile Stewardship Program," UCRL-LR-129781, 6 October 1998.

STRATEGIC AIR COMMAND (SAC) AND STRATEGIC COMMAND (STRATCOM)
On March 21, 1946, the U.S. Strategic Air Command (SAC) was formed with the mission of deterring aggression by maintaining the ability to conduct long-range offensive missions throughout the world and maximum-range reconnaissance over land and sea. The United States depended on SAC to plan and conduct long-range nuclear attacks against the Soviet Union as the basis of its Cold War deterrent. SAC housed the Joint Strategic Target Planning Staff, responsible for building the U.S. nuclear war plan, the Single Integrated Operational Plan (SIOP).

With the end of the Cold War, on June 1, 1992, SAC was restructured and renamed U.S. Strategic Command (STRATCOM). The purpose of the restructuring was to downsize and consolidate all U.S. nuclear forces under one commander to improve efficiency in maintaining the U.S. nuclear deterrent.

History and Background
SAC, along with the U.S. Air Force, was created in the aftermath of World War II and was intended to develop the nascent U.S. nuclear capability into a credible deterrent force. General George C. Kenney was the first commander of SAC and assembled 100,000 personnel and 1,300 aircraft under his command. Originally, SAC's headquarters was at Andrews Air Force Base, Maryland, and it operated eighteen air bases throughout the United States.

SAC grew rapidly in the early years of the nuclear age to a force of more than 224,000 personnel under the command of General Curtis E. LeMay (1948–1957). Under General Thomas S. Powers, SAC's third commander, SAC began to maintain bombers on ground alert. The ground-alert concept allowed SAC to maintain almost one-third of its aircraft with weapons loaded and crews prepared for immediate launch to bolster U.S. second-strike capabilities. It was a response to advances in Soviet rocketry that threatened the survivability of the U.S. strategic bomber force. General Powers also was responsible for creating SAC's motto, Peace Is Our Profession, demonstrating his belief that the command succeeded only if it never had to execute its nuclear attack missions (*see* Airborne Alert, Second Strike).

Throughout the 1950s, SAC received 47 percent of the entire U.S. military budget. There were three reasons why SAC became the primary U.S. command and received the most money: SAC constituted the primary U.S. deterrent against the Soviets; it owned two-thirds of the nuclear "Triad" (the B-52 bombers and ballistic missiles); and it had the strategic war planning system to build the SIOP (*see* Single Integrated Operational Plan).

In addition to its nuclear alert mission, beginning in the early 1970s SAC began exercising its bomber force in conventional conflicts. During the Vietnam War, SAC aircraft and crews participated in the bombing of both North and South Vietnam. During Desert Storm, SAC utilized its B-52 bombers in a conventional role against dug-in Iraqi armor and infantry units. SAC tanker aircraft also played a significant role during Desert Storm by refueling both long-range bombers and fighter aircraft as they conducted missions over Kuwait and Iraq.

From SAC to STRATCOM
STRATCOM was formed on June 1, 1992, as the single joint command of all U.S. nuclear forces: land- and sea-based ballistic missiles, submarines, tankers, bombers, and airborne command posts. The mission of STRATCOM is to deter a major military attack on the United States and its allies and, if necessary, employ strategic forces to halt and win a conflict. There are five command goals: (1) to establish STRATCOM as the leading authority on strategic matters; (2) to develop force employment plans and develop a role in defense planning; (3) to develop capabilities and position forces to meet strategic objectives; (4) to effectively call on assigned forces in strategic operations; and (5) to uphold a strong and cooperative relationship with other agencies. The president and the secretary of defense direct STRATCOM's missions, which range from deterring attacks by maintaining missiles, bombers, and submarines on alert to preparing the nation's nuclear war plan. STRATCOM also performs worldwide strategic reconnaissance. Additionally, it maintains and controls the communications and intelligence support networks linking all military forces, which are ready to respond 24 hours a day, 365 days a year.

Today, STRATCOM plays a leading role in creation of the new nuclear Triad (a revitalized partnership of an enhanced nuclear infrastructure, missile defenses, and a mix of conventional and nuclear strike forces) outlined in the 2001 Nuclear Posture Review. The deliberate planning formerly practiced by the Joint Strategic Target Planning Staff during the Cold War has been replaced by adaptive, "capabilities-based" planning. Additionally, STRATCOM is at the forefront of integrating conventional global-strike and nuclear forces, strategic defenses, and advanced operating concepts to create credible deterrence options and force structure for the twenty-first century (*see* Nuclear Posture Review).

—*Laura Fontaine*

See also: Ballistic Missiles; Bombers, U.S. Nuclear-Capable; Nuclear Posture Review; Single Integrated Operational Plan; United States Air Force; United States Nuclear Forces and Doctrine

References

Butler, George Lee, "Disestablishing SAC," *Air Power History, the Journal of Air and Space History,* vol. 40, no. 3, Fall 1993, pp. 4–11.

Fontenot, Jon M., "A New Era: From SAC to STRATCOM," 23 May 1995, available at http://www.fas.org/spp/eprint/fontenot.htm.

Polmar, Norman, *Strategic Air Command* (Annapolis, MD: Nautical and Aviation Publishing, 1979).

STRATEGIC ARMS LIMITATION TALKS (SALT I AND SALT II)

The Strategic Arms Limitation Talks (SALT) were bilateral discussions between the United States and the Soviet Union on limiting the nuclear arms race. SALT I (November 1969 to January 1972) yielded two agreements, the Anti-Ballistic Missile (ABM) Treaty and the Interim Agreement on the Limitation of Strategic Offensive Arms. SALT II (September 1972 to January 1979) resulted in the Vladivostok Accord and the SALT II Treaty.

History and Background

Following several unsuccessful attempts to achieve complete disarmament, the United States proposed a new approach at the United Nations' Eighteen-Nation Disarmament Committee in January 1964, suggesting that the United States and the Soviet Union should explore a verified freeze of the number, types, and capabilities of their strategic nuclear offensive and defensive vehicles. The Soviets rejected the gesture and by 1966 had begun to deploy an antiballistic missile defense around Moscow. That same year, China successfully tested a nuclear missile. In September 1967, the United States announced that it would begin deployment of a "thin" antiballistic missile (ABM) system to defend against an extremely modest Chinese intercontinental ballistic missile (ICBM) threat and the remote possibility of an accidental launch of an intercontinental missile by a nuclear-armed state.

At the July 1968 signing of the Nuclear Nonproliferation Treaty (NPT), U.S. president Lyndon B. Johnson announced that an agreement had been reached with the Soviet Union to begin discussions on limiting and reducing both strategic nuclear weapons delivery systems and defense against ballistic missiles.

In addition to the issues of trust and hostility to be expected in any adversarial relationship, negotia-

tion was further complicated by the differing needs and goals of each side. The Soviet Union was contiguous with its principal allies, but the United States was geographically distant from its allies in Western Europe and Japan. The geographic issue was indeed complicated, as the Soviets wished to limit all missiles capable of hitting the other side's territory—which would have included Western weapons in Western Europe, including those launched from bombers and aircraft carriers—whereas the United States desired to include only intercontinental ballistic missiles.

Designing a verification regime was also a difficult task because, for obvious reasons of secrecy, neither side could permit the other free access to its territory, let alone its military facilities. Eventually, they agreed to "national technical means of verification" (mainly, satellites deployed in orbit) and promised not to use deliberate concealment to impede verification using these means. Neither of these measures proved satisfactory, however, and both sides routinely accused the other of cheating throughout the life of the SALT treaties (*see* National Technical Means; Telemetry).

Although the Interim Agreement expired after five years, the ABM Treaty was of "unlimited duration" but granted each party the right to withdraw six months after giving notice if it determined that the strategic situation had changed to the point where adhering to the treaty put its vital interests in danger. The United States activated this clause in December 2001 and withdrew from the ABM Treaty in May 2002.

Negotiations on SALT II began in November 1972 with the aim of creating a permanent framework to replace the Interim Agreement. At a meeting in Vladivostok, Siberia, in November 1974, President Gerald Ford and General Secretary Leonid Brezhnev agreed to a Basic Framework for the SALT II agreement: an equal aggregate limit of 2,400 strategic nuclear delivery vehicles (ICBMs, submarine-launched ballistic missiles [SLBMs], and heavy bombers); deployment of up to 1,300 multiple independently targetable reentry vehicles (MIRVs); a ban on construction of new land-based ICBM launchers; and limits on the deployment of new types of strategic offensive arms. They agreed that these limits would last through 1985. Negotiations stalled in early 1975, however, owing to numerous disagreements. These were over whether the new

Soviet bomber known to the United States as "Backfire" would be considered a heavy bomber and therefore included in the 2,400 aggregate; the MIRV verification process; missile throw weight ceilings; and the status of cruise missiles.

The talks received a renewed emphasis during the administration of President Jimmy Carter. Ultimately, the parties resolved or agreed to defer resolution of the sticking points until SALT III (which never occurred). The SALT II Treaty was signed by President Carter and General Secretary Brezhnev in Vienna on June 18, 1979, and transmitted to the Senate for ratification four days later. On January 3, 1980, following the Soviet invasion of Afghanistan, President Carter requested that the Senate shelve discussion of the treaty rather than allowing it to be voted down by the U.S. Senate.

Although the treaty was never formally ratified, both sides were bound under international law to comply with its broad outlines until they formally announced their intention to withdraw from the agreement. Carter pledged to allow the terms to remain in force as long as the Soviet Union reciprocated, and Brezhnev made a similar statement. President Ronald Reagan initially pledged to abide by the terms of the treaty when he took office in 1981. He declared in 1984, and again in 1985, that the Soviets had violated several provisions but that the United States would nonetheless continue to work within the interim framework. On May 26, 1986, however, he submitted three detailed reports to Congress describing major violations by the Soviets and announced that the United States would henceforth base decisions about its strategic force structure on the nature and magnitude of the threat posed by Soviet strategic forces and not on the limits outlined by the SALT structure. Ultimately, the Reagan administration did not increase strategic force levels beyond SALT II levels and, finding a more cooperative government under Soviet president Mikhail Gorbachev, obviated the treaty by negotiating two agreements that actually further reduced nuclear force levels on both sides: the Intermediate-Range Nuclear Forces (INF) Treaty and the Strategic Arms Reduction Treaty (START I).

The Arms Race Continues

Soviet and U.S. weapons systems were far from symmetrical in the late 1960s. The Soviet Union had continued its development and deployment of heavy ballistic missiles and had overtaken the U.S. lead in land-based ICBMs. During the SALT I years alone, the number of Soviet ICBMs rose from around 1,000 to 1,500, and they were being deployed at the rate of some 200 annually. Soviet submarine-based launchers had quadrupled. The huge payload capacity ("throw weight") of some Soviet missiles was seen as a possible threat to U.S. land-based strategic missiles even in heavily protected ("hardened") missile silos.

The United States had not increased its deployment of strategic missiles since 1967 (when its ICBMs numbered 1,054 and its SLBMs 656), but it was conducting a vigorous program of equipping missiles with MIRVed warheads. MIRVs permit an individual missile to carry a number of warheads directed at separate targets. They thus gave the United States a lead in the number of nuclear warheads deployed as part of its strategic arsenal. The United States also retained a lead in long-range bombers. The Soviet Union had a limited ABM system around Moscow; the United States had shifted from its earlier plan for a "thin" ABM defense of certain U.S. cities and instead began to deploy ABMs at two land-based ICBM missile sites to protect its retaliatory forces. (The full program envisaged twelve ABM complexes.)

Current Status

These treaties are no longer in force. SALT I's Interim Agreement was for a period of five years and thus expired in 1979. SALT II was never ratified by the U.S. Senate, although its provisions were informally adhered to by successive presidential administrations until the treaty was eventually rendered moot by START I and II. The United States announced its withdrawal from the ABM Treaty December 13, 2001.

The United States and Russia continue to have dialogues on nuclear weapons, most notably leading to the May 2002 Moscow Treaty on strategic offensive reductions. With the end of the Cold War, however, the principal concern has shifted from a nuclear arms race on both sides to how to manage existing stockpiles and prevent proliferation to outside parties.

—James Joyner

See also: Arms Control; Missile Defense; Strategic Offensive Reductions Treaty

References

Goller-Calvo, Notburga K., and Michel A. Calvo, *The SALT Agreements: Content, Application, Verification* (New York: Kluwer Law International, 1988).

Smith, Gerard, *Doubletalk: The Story of SALT I* (Lanham, MD: University Press of America, 1985).

Talbott, Strobe, *Endgame: The Inside Story of SALT II* (New York: Harper and Row, 1979).

U.S. State Department, Bureau of Arms Control, "Treaty between the United States of America and the Union of Soviet Socialist Republics on the Limitation of Strategic Offensive Arms (SALT I)," available at http://www.state.gov/t/ac/trt/5191.htm.

STRATEGIC ARMS REDUCTION TREATY (START I)

The Strategic Arms Reduction Treaty (START I), officially the Treaty on the Reduction and Limitation of Strategic Offensive Arms, was an agreement between the United States and the Soviet Union signed by Presidents George H. W. Bush and Mikhail Gorbachev in Moscow on July 31, 1991. START I was a product of nine years of negotiations and entered into force on December 5, 1994. Its terms provided for reductions in strategic offensive arms to equal aggregate levels to be carried out in three phases over seven years. These were specific, equal interim levels for agreed categories of strategic offensive arms by the end of each phase. At the end of the seven-year period, central limits included: 1,600 strategic nuclear delivery vehicles (SNDVs); 6,000 accountable warheads; and 4,900 ballistic missile warheads. The Soviets were also limited to 1,540 warheads on 154 heavy intercontinental ballistic missiles (ICBMs). Although the treaty allows for existing equipment to be modernized or replaced, it bans the production, flight testing, and deployment of new or modified ICBMs and submarine-launched ballistic missiles (SLBMs) with more than ten warheads. Under START I, U.S. long-range nuclear weapons were cut by 15 percent, while Soviet/Russian strategic forces were cut by 25 percent.

History and Background

During the run-up to presidential elections in 1980, Republican candidate Ronald Reagan had called the unratified treaty resulting from the Strategic Arms Limitation Talks (SALT II) "fatally flawed" and promised that if elected he would withdraw the treaty from the Senate. He opposed the treaty on the grounds that it did not limit throw weight, the true measure of destructive power, and did not close what he called the "window of vulnerability" that the United States faced, which he believed was caused by the fleet of heavy Soviet ICBMs that were theoretically capable of destroying the U.S. ICBM force in a first strike. After taking office, however, the Reagan administration announced that although it was reviewing U.S. arms control policy, it would not undercut the provisions of the SALT II Treaty.

In November 1981, Reagan announced that new strategic arms talks, now called Strategic Arms Reduction Talks, could possibly begin the following year, and that the goal for negotiators would be to reduce strategic nuclear arms. Meanwhile, negotiations on intermediate-range nuclear forces (INF) had already begun in 1981. With the introduction of nuclear-freeze resolutions in the House of Representatives and the Senate, Reagan came under increasing domestic pressure in March 1981 to initiate negotiations. On March 31, 1982, during his first prime-time news conference, the president invited the Soviet Union to join the United States in negotiations to reduce the size of both nuclear arsenals.

START negotiations began in Geneva on June 29, 1982. By the end of 1989, many of the treaty's basic provisions had been designed. The Reykjavik Summit meeting of October 11–12, 1986, the Foreign Ministers meeting of September 15–17, 1987, the Washington Summit meeting of December 7–10, 1987, and the Wyoming Foreign Ministers meeting of September 22–23, 1989, led to agreement on most of these provisions. Important progress was made at the Wyoming Foreign Ministers meeting. U.S. negotiators were able to prevent any linkage between reductions of strategic offensive nuclear weapons and the Reagan administration's plan to pursue space-based defenses against ballistic missiles. In addition, the Soviet Union agreed to dismantle, without preconditions, the phased-array Krasnoyarsk radar, which violated the 1972 Anti-Ballistic Missile (ABM) Treaty.

Other issues that had previously defied solution at the negotiating table, however, had to be addressed in the treaty. Negotiators had to determine counting rules for heavy bombers carrying nuclear-armed air-launched cruise missiles (ALCMs), a sublimit on ICBM warheads, sublimits on warheads on mobile ICBMs, and counting rules for nondeployed missiles. They had to resolve problems concerning the modernization of heavy ICBMs and determine how to address nuclear sea-launched cruise missiles (SLCMs), telemetry encryption, and cuts in Soviet missile throw weight. Finally, they had to design an effective verification regime to monitor treaty compliance.

After nine years of negotiations, the START team experienced a frenetic pace of activity in the six weeks before it was signed. During this time, negotiators came to an agreement on the three remaining issues: warhead downloading, accountability for new types of missiles, and data denial. Conclusive negotiations centered on counting rules within agreed limits and sublimits for both nuclear delivery vehicles and warheads. The agreement represented the first time in U.S.-Soviet arms control history that the two nations had decided to make deep cuts in their respective nuclear arsenals. Unlike the Intermediate-Range Nuclear Forces (INF) Treaty of 1987, however, START I did not require elimination of an entire category of nuclear weapons. At the Group of Seven Summit in London on July 17, 1991, Presidents George H. W. Bush and Mikhail Gorbachev announced that START was ready to be signed at a U.S.-Soviet summit in Moscow by the end of that month (*see* Telemetry).

The Treaty

START I consists of nineteen articles governing basic provisions, two annexes, six protocols, a memorandum of understanding, and several associated documents (joint statements, unilateral statements, declarations, and an exchange of letters) meant to amplify and define basic treaty provisions and facilitate their implementation. The treaty limits the total number of SNDVs that each side can possess to 1,600, the total number of accountable warheads to 6,000 each, the total number of warheads mounted on ballistic missiles (ICBMs and SLBMs) to 4,900 each, and the total ballistic missile throw weight for each side to 3,600 metric tons. START I also permits the Soviet (Russian) side to have no more than 154 "heavy" ICBMs (defined as having launch weight greater than 106 tons or a throw weight greater than 4,350 kilograms). This specifically applies to the R-36M series (NATO designation: SS-18 Satan) ICBM. No more than 1,540 warheads can be mounted on these missiles. The treaty also bans the construction of new types of heavy ICBMs and

SLBMs. It permits modernization programs and, in exceptional cases, new silo construction. The testing of missiles with a greater number of warheads than declared in the treaty is banned by the treaty. New ballistic missiles with more than ten warheads are also banned. Although parties to the treaty may also reduce the number of warheads attributed to a specific missile, no more than three existing missile types may have the number of warheads reduced, and the total reduction may not exceed 1,250 warheads. New missile types or heavy ICBMs may not be downloaded.

START I counted each ICBM and SLBM reentry vehicle as a single warhead. Counting rules for warheads attributed to heavy bombers were more complicated. Each Soviet/Russian heavy bomber equipped to carry long-range nuclear ALCMs (defined as having a maximum range of at least 600 kilometers), up to a total of 180 bombers, counted as eight warheads toward the 6,000-warhead limit, even though existing Russian heavy-bomber types could carry between six and sixteen ALCMs. For each Russian heavy bomber above the level of 180, the actual number of ALCMs counted toward the 6,000-warhead limit. In the same way, each U.S. long-range nuclear ALCM-carrying heavy bomber, up to a total of 150 bombers, counted as ten warheads toward the 6,000 warhead limit, and for each bomber in excess of 150, the actual number of ALCMs it could carry counted toward the warhead limit. Bombers not equipped to carry long-range nuclear ALCMs were counted as one warhead.

Extensive provisions for verification were provided for in START I and included the use of national technical means (NTM), missile test telemetry tape exchanges, periodic data exchanges, monitoring activities, and on-site inspections (OSIs). The U.S. On-Site Inspection Agency (OSIA) (now part of the Defense Threat Reduction Agency) and the Russian Nuclear Risk Reduction Center (NRRC) implement on-site inspection and escort activities under the treaty. The treaty has a duration of fifteen years unless superseded by another agreement. The parties can agree to extend the treaty for successive five-year periods, but each party has the right to withdraw from it at any time if it decides that extraordinary events have jeopardized its supreme interests (*see* Defense Threat Reduction Agency [DTRA]; National Technical Means; Nuclear Risk Reduction Centers; On-Site Inspection Agency; Verification).

The Lisbon Protocol and Ratification Issues

Following the end of the Soviet era in December 1991, nuclear arms were still deployed in some ex-Soviet republics. Four states now had nuclear weapons based on their territories—Russia, Belarus, Kazakhstan, and Ukraine. The three republics and the Russian Federation undertook to make arrangements among themselves for the implementation of the treaty's provisions at a May 23, 1992, ministerial meeting in Lisbon, Portugal. The United States, Russia, Belarus, Kazakhstan, and Ukraine signed a protocol, known as the Lisbon Protocol, to the treaty making all five countries signatories of START I. Under the protocol, Belarus, Kazakhstan, and Ukraine agreed to eliminate all nuclear weapons on their territory and to join the 1968 Nuclear Non-proliferation Treaty (NPT) as non–nuclear weapons states (NNWS). Russian ratification of START I hinged on this pledge. Thus, though START I was initially a bilateral treaty between the Soviet Union and the United States, the Lisbon Protocol transformed it into a multilateral treaty that was later ratified as a bilateral treaty between Russia and the United States (*see* Nuclear Nonproliferation Treaty [NPT]).

START I was ratified by the U.S. Senate on October 1, 1992. The Russian Parliament ratified it on November 4, 1992; Kazakhstan ratified it on July 2, 1992, and deposited the instruments of accession to the NPT on February 14, 1993. Ukraine became the last former Soviet republic to ratify the treaty on November 18, 1993. The Ukrainian Parliament approved a resolution on November 16, 1994, to accede to the NPT as a non–nuclear weapons state. President Leonid Kuchma of Ukraine deposited the NPT instruments of ratification at a ceremony on December 5, 1994, held at the Conference on Security and Cooperation in Europe (CSCE) summit meeting in Budapest, Hungary, paving the way for a second ceremony on the same day where leaders of the five Lisbon Protocol signatory countries signed a protocol exchanging the START I instruments of ratification. Baseline inspections began on March 1, 1995, when three ten-member teams from OSIA arrived in Russia from the United States. The teams, which had to be allowed onto a base within twenty-four hours of giving notice, had a schedule of visiting seventy-one weapons facilities in Belarus, Kazakhstan, Russia, and Ukraine.

Results

On December 5, 2001, seven years after the accord entered into force, the United States and Russia completed their weapons reductions as provided for by the terms of START I, thus completing the largest arms control reductions in history. The treaty will remain in effect until December 5, 2009. During this time, the treaty parties can request challenge inspections of suspect activity. Also, the two countries have the option of extending the accord for successive five-year periods if the treaty has not been superseded by another arms reduction agreement.

Since exchanging baseline stockpile information in September 1990, the two countries have reduced their strategic nuclear arsenals by more than 40 percent over the past decade. The shortcomings of the treaty include the fact that START I does not require the destruction of nuclear warheads removed from delivery vehicles, which leaves the United States and Russia with a considerable number of warheads. The U.S. strategic and tactical warhead "hedge" is estimated at more than 5,000 warheads, and Russia is estimated to have stockpiled more than 13,000 warheads. Also, the accord does not cover nonstrategic nuclear weapons. Russia is estimated to have deployed between 3,500 and 15,000 tactical nuclear weapons, whereas the United States currently has a much smaller number of nuclear gravity bombs in storage in Europe and within its territory.

—*Kalpana Chittaranjan*

See also: Arms Control; Hedge; Presidential Nuclear Initiatives; Strategic Arms Limitation Talks; Strategic Arms Reduction Treaty

References

Acronym Institute, "U.S.-Russia Developments," available at http://www.acronym.org.uk/start/index.htm.

Arms Control Association website, http://www.armscontrol.org/subject/ussp/.

Kartchner, Kerry M., *Negotiating START: Strategic Arms Reduction Talks and the Quest for Strategic Stability* (New Brunswick, NJ: Transaction, 1992).

Mendelsohn, Jack, and David Grahame, *Arms Control Chronology* (Washington, DC: Center for Defense Information, Winter 2002).

"Strategic Arms Reduction Treaty (START I)," available at http://www.fas.org/nuke/control/start1/.

Talbott, Strobe, *Deadly Gambits: The Reagan Administration and the Stalemate in Nuclear Arms Control* (New York: Knopf, 1984).

STRATEGIC ARMS REDUCTION TREATY (START II)

The Strategic Arms Reduction Treaty (START II), officially entitled the Treaty on Further Reduction and Limitation of Strategic Offensive Arms, is an agreement between the United States and Russia signed by U.S. president George H. W. Bush and Russian president Boris Yeltsin in Moscow on January 3, 1993. The treaty established a limit on strategic weapons for each side, with reductions to be implemented in two phases. START II aimed to reduce the deployed strategic nuclear forces of both nations to 3,000 to 3,500 warheads (down from 6,000 warheads allowed under START I). Additional limits include a ban on multiple independently targetable reentry vehicles (MIRVs) on intercontinental ballistic missiles (ICBMs), the elimination of all SS-18 "heavy" missiles, a sublimit of 1,700 to 1,750 submarine-launched ballistic missile (SLBM) warheads (about one-half the SLBM warheads authorized for the United States under START I), and the freedom to "download" (remove) warheads from strategic missiles in order to meet required reductions (this could be done by "deMIRVing" ICBMs). START II also allowed no discount for heavy bomber weapons (the number of weapons counted for heavy bombers, in other words, would be the number they are actually equipped to carry). The treaty, however, did give the parties the right to "reorient" bombers capable of carrying nuclear weapons to conventional missions (and thus exempt them from the overall limits). Up to 100 heavy bombers could be transferred to conventional missions, provided they had never been equipped to carry long-range nuclear air-launched cruise missiles (ALCMs).

Phase I of the treaty was to be implemented within seven years of the entry into force of START I, and Phase II was to be implemented by January 1, 2003. These deadlines were extended to December 31, 2004, and December 31, 2007, by a protocol to the treaty signed by U.S. and Russian representatives on September 27, 1997.

History and Background

After START I, critics charged that the main shortcoming of the treaty was that it ultimately produced insufficient arms reductions. Thus, efforts were made to reach a more comprehensive arms control treaty between the United States and Russia. President George H. W. Bush's State of the Union address to the U.S. Congress on January 28, 1992, contained a proposal for a new agreement requiring far deeper cuts than those required by the provisions of START I. In a statement of what was to become the basic provisions of START II, the president said, "I have informed President Yeltsin that if the [former Soviet republics] will eliminate all land-based multiple-warhead ballistic missiles . . . [w]e will eliminate all Peacekeeper missiles. We will reduce the number of warheads on Minuteman missiles to one, and reduce the number of warheads on our sea-based missiles by about one-third. And we will convert a substantial portion of our strategic bombers to primarily conventional use." Russian president Boris Yeltsin responded the next day with a proposal of his own, in which he suggested that the two sides cut their strategic nuclear warheads to 2,000–2,500 each.

Ministerial meetings between U.S. secretary of state James Baker and his Russian counterpart, Foreign Minister Andrei Kozyrev, were held to discuss these proposals in February, March, May, and June 1992. These negotiations paved the way for presidents Bush and Yeltsin to hold a summit meeting on June 16–18, 1992, in Washington, D.C. At the summit, the two presidents developed the framework for a follow-on Strategic Arms Reduction Treaty (START II), symbolized by their "Joint Understanding on Further Reductions in Strategic Offensive Arms." This agreement included numerical ceilings and a time frame for reductions. The "Joint Understanding" called for elimination of all MIRVed ICBMs, a limit of 1,750 on SLBM warheads, counting rules whereby bombers count as "the number of warheads they are actually equipped to carry," and reductions by both sides to between 3,000 and 3,500 warheads by 2003.

Telephone calls exchanged between Bush and Yeltsin on December 20 and 21, 1992, produced more progress on an agreement, and a team of U.S. and Russian specialists met in Geneva on December 22–24 to work on specific points of disagreement. At high-level meetings in Geneva on December 28 and 29 between the U.S. secretary of state and Russian foreign and defense ministers, the last issues were finally resolved. When presidents Bush and Yeltsin signed the START II agreement on January 3, 1993, they concluded the most sweeping nuclear arms reduction agreement in history and the first post–Cold War arms control treaty between the United States and Russia.

The Treaty

The treaty itself consists of eight articles, two protocols, and a memorandum of understanding. It requires the United States and Russia to eliminate their MIRVed ICBMs and reduce the number of their deployed strategic nuclear warheads to 3,000–3,500 each. The treaty complements rather than replaces START I in that the earlier treaty's provisions remain unchanged unless specifically modified by START II. START II is to remain in force for the duration of START I.

Each side made the commitment to reduce the total number of its strategic nuclear warheads to 3,000–3,500 by the end of Phase II. (This limit has now been superseded by the May 2002 Moscow Treaty, which limits Russia and the United States to no more than 1,700–2,200 warheads by 2012; see Strategic Offensive Reductions Treaty [SORT].) Of the retained warheads, none can be on MIRVed ICBMs, including heavy ICBMs. Only ICBMs carrying a single warhead are allowed by the treaty. START II would enter into force on the date of exchange of instruments of ratification but not before the entry into force of START I. Since START II builds upon START I, it must remain in force throughout the duration of the latter. As in START I, each side has the right to withdraw from the treaty if it decides that extraordinary changes in the international security environment have jeopardized its supreme interests. Like START I, START II would be verified by on-site inspections. Heavy bomber conversions to conventional roles, missile elimination, and silo conversions would be subject to inspection. Before START II could enter into force, three requirements had to be fulfilled: (1) START I had to enter into force; (2) the U.S. Senate had to ratify the treaty; and (3) the Russian Parliament had to ratify the treaty.

Follow-Up

START I entered into force on December 5, 1994, and the United States and Russia completed the terms of this treaty seven years later, on December 5, 2001. On January 26, 1996, the U.S. Senate approved a resolution of ratification of START II by a vote of 87–4. Russian ratification of the treaty, however, was a long-drawn affair. U.S. secretary of defense

William Perry visited Moscow to address the Duma on October 17, 1996, in an attempt to persuade Russian legislators to ratify START II. But his words apparently had little impact on the Russian lower house. On April 9, 1997, the Russian Duma voted to postpone debate over ratification of the treaty.

Although the treaty remained unratified, both U.S. and Russian officials continued to update its provisions to better meet changing circumstances. In the Helsinki Summit held on March 21, 1997, for instance, U.S. president Bill Clinton and Russian president Yeltsin issued a "Joint Statement on Parameters on Future Reductions in Nuclear Forces" in which, regarding START II, they agreed to extend the elimination deadline for strategic nuclear delivery vehicles from January 1, 2003, to December 31, 2007, and to deactivate immediately all strategic nuclear delivery vehicles scheduled for elimination by December 31, 2003. On September 27, 1997, the extension of these time frames was incorporated into a protocol, which was signed by representatives from both countries.

Political disputes related to the various global events further delayed Russian ratification of the treaty. The Duma postponed its planned ratification vote of START II in December 1998 to signal displeasure with U.S. and British air strikes against Iraq. Air strikes again emerged as a stumbling block to Russian START II ratification when the start of the North Atlantic Treaty Organization's campaign against Yugoslavia forced the Russian prime minister Yevgeny Primakov on March 26, 1999, to ask the Duma to postpone consideration of the treaty yet again.

Current Status

Seven years after the treaty was signed, on April 14, 2000, the Duma finally ratified START II (but with crucial reservations) by a vote of 288–131. Under Article II of the Duma's ratifying legislation, deputies approved motions that allowed Russia to abandon its arms control agreements if the United States violated the ABM Treaty by deploying national missile defenses. The Duma vote also required the U.S. Senate to approve several additional documents as part of the START II package before instruments of ratification could be exchanged and the treaty could enter into force. These documents included two controversial additional protocols on the issue of the demarcation of theater missile defense and national missile defense interceptors. The Russian upper house of Parliament supported the Duma's resolution 122–15. Russian president Vladimir Putin signed this legislation on May 4, 2000, to ratify the treaty.

The U.S. Senate Ratification Resolution includes a provision that requires the president to seek Senate approval of any strategic arms cuts that would reduce the U.S. strategic arsenal to below START I ceilings before START II enters into force. The Russian START II ratification law requires the U.S. Senate to ratify the START II Extension Protocol and the 1997 ABM Agreements, which clarified the demarcation between theater and strategic missile defenses, so that ratification instruments may be exchanged for these documents, before START II enters into force. However, the U.S. Senate has not taken up either of these matters for consideration.

As a response to the U.S. withdrawal from the ABM Treaty on June 13, 2002, Russia declared the next day that it would no longer be bound by the START II nuclear arms reduction agreement. Analysts have concluded that Moscow's announcement of treaty withdrawal is more symbolic than substantive because START II had never come into force and was unlikely to have ever taken effect after Russia had tied its fate to that of the ABM Treaty in April 2000. According to a U.S. official, the collapse of START II has not upset the George W. Bush administration, as the United States and Russia have already "moved beyond" the agreement with the signing of the Moscow Treaty of May 24, 2002. If this treaty enters into force, it will commit each country to limiting its deployed strategic nuclear forces to fewer than 2,200 warheads by the end of 2012. Although international law requires countries not to undermine the object of treaties they have signed, even if those treaties have not entered into force, the Russian statement of June 2002 suggests that the Russians no longer consider themselves legally obligated to refrain from actions forbidden by START II.

—*Kalpana Chittaranjan*

References

Acronym Institute, "U.S.-Russia Developments," available at http://www.acronym.org.uk/start/index.htm.

Arms Control Association website, http://www.armscontrol.org/subject/ussp/.

Mendelsohn, Jack, and David Grahame, *Arms Control Chronology* (Washington, DC: Center for Defense Information, Winter 2002).

"START II: Analysis, Summary, Text," Special edition of *Arms Control Today,* January/February 1993.

"Strategic Arms Reduction Treaty (START II)," available at http://www.fas.org/nuke/control/start2/.

STRATEGIC DEFENSE INITIATIVE (SDI)

The Strategic Defense Initiative (SDI) was a ballistic missile defense (BMD) research and development program launched by President Ronald Reagan in 1983. SDI was not the first BMD program undertaken by the United States, nor would it be the last. But SDI did become one of the most well-known and controversial missile defense proposals ever introduced by a U.S. administration. Its arrival came amid a growing global antinuclear movement and political changes in the Soviet Union, both of which added to the program's controversial reputation. Critics derided SDI as "Star Wars," but some supporters eventually came to embrace the moniker as well, finding inspiration in the technological and political idealism of the program.

After Reagan left office, SDI suffered from the decoupling of its mission from its charismatic creator as well as from its failure to produce effective technology. Presidents George H. W. Bush and Bill Clinton took steps to downsize SDI's ambitious mission to smaller-scale BMD goals. Bush added the space-based "Brilliant Pebbles" layer to the plan, and Clinton eventually reorganized SDI's bureaucratic home, the Strategic Defense Initiative Organization, into the theater missile defense–focused Ballistic Missile Defense Organization. President George W. Bush, drawing in part on Reagan's elaborate vision for missile defense, however, reorganized U.S. missile defense programs once again in 2001 into the Missile Defense Agency (MDA). The latter Bush, in some respects inspired by Reagan's SDI vision, tasked the MDA with piecing together a broad and layered defense. Although "Star Wars" joined previous U.S. BMD programs in failing to yield an effective defense, its legacy is represented in these later reorganizations. But its legacy survives as well in the nation's consciousness—the program encapsulated Reagan's political clarity between good and evil while feeding his opponents' worries over the costs of unilateral and unchecked U.S. hegemony. These motivations and divisions remain key factors of the BMD debate today.

History and Background

Several developments between the cancellation of the Safeguard program in the mid-1970s and the 1983 creation of SDI led Reagan to start the program he hoped would make nuclear weapons "impotent and obsolete" (*see* Safeguard Antiballistic Missile [ABM] System). As a presidential candidate, Reagan toured the North American Air Defense Command and was concerned that a computer simulation he saw there of a nuclear attack on U.S. targets showed no option for the military to defend against them. As president, Reagan became further intrigued by missile defense when he could not find a workable basing mode for the MX intercontinental missiles designed to guarantee retaliation against a Soviet attack. In February 1983, the Joint Chiefs of Staff recommended that the United States place a greater emphasis on developing missile defenses. With supportive advice from renowned nuclear weapons physicist Edward Teller, Reagan publicized his plan in an historic March 23, 1983, speech to the nation. Reagan struck a visionary and utopian tone, asking the country, "What if free people could live secure in the knowledge that their security did not rest on the threat of instant U.S. retaliation to deter a Soviet attack; that we could intercept and destroy strategic ballistic missiles before they reached our own soil or that of our allies?" The president acknowledged the technological challenges to such a dream but framed the debate as a test to the nation's scientists—whom he called those "who gave us nuclear weapons"—to make the world more secure.

Architects of the system hoped to incorporate a variety of land-, air-, sea-, and space-based weapons to intercept incoming Soviet ballistic missiles. Although the 1972 Anti-Ballistic Missile (ABM) Treaty limited deployment of such systems, the administration believed testing these proposed systems would not violate the agreement with the Soviet Union. Reactions differed and often broke down along predictable lines—supporters in conservative circles welcomed the chance to break free of offense-based nuclear deterrence, whereas opponents in the burgeoning nuclear freeze movement and elsewhere on the left remained skeptical of both Reagan's true motives and the effect SDI would have on the nuclear arms race. Within the government, SDI created waves as well. Those in the defense establishment, such as Secretary of Defense Caspar Weinberger, were eager to throw out the old nuclear

strategic doctrine that had limited the United States for much of the Cold War, and many in the military believed that recent technological advances would help the next BMD effort overcome the hurdles that had plagued earlier systems. Meanwhile, those tasked with diplomatic duties, such as Secretary of State George Shultz, were less confident in the emerging technology and saw SDI as an unnecessary cause of tension in U.S. foreign relations, favoring instead a more pragmatic approach to international affairs.

Supporters of SDI saw it as a bold chance to step away from reliance on the concept of mutual assured destruction (MAD), believing that a missile shield would allow the United States to pursue its foreign policy goals (opening markets, encouraging democratization, ensuring regional stability) without fearing reprisals from its rival for global influence. Some historians have linked this optimistic faith in American know-how with larger theories on Reagan's inner workings, leading many to associate him more closely with "Star Wars" than any other president has been linked to a BMD system developed under his watch.

Critics charged that SDI, like previous BMD programs, jeopardized the security that the Cold War superpowers had created with the ABM Treaty and encouraged the militarization and weaponization of space. Planners based "Star Wars," they said, on untested and infeasible technologies and did not design the defense to protect against cruise missiles, airplanes, or other methods of warhead delivery. Some historians contend that links between SDI and Reagan's psyche were a detriment to the program, suggesting that the one-time actor's fondness for movies inspired him to incorporate unrealistic aspects of decades-old films referencing missile shields and futuristic defenses into his vision for SDI.

By 1985, the congressional Office of Technology Assessment released a report concluding that the survival of the U.S. population in case of a nuclear attack was not a realistic goal for SDI. The report also claimed that deployment of a BMD system would create more problems for the nation's security and adversely affect arms control negotiations. Supporters, however, argued that SDI was important to national security even if technologically imperfect—many claimed that the program would be a powerful negotiating chip in dealings with the Soviet Union, which under Mikhail Gorbachev was becoming increasingly open to nuclear reductions.

Further congressional reports and independent studies assailed SDI's chances for success, and with Reagan at the end of his second and last term, support and funding for the ambitious plan lost momentum. By the 1991 collapse of the Soviet Union, President Bush had refocused SDI from its emphasis on countering a massive Soviet attack to a system known as Global Protection Against Limited Strikes (GPALS). GPALS looked at smaller-scale options to defend against less cataclysmic scenarios (*see* Global Protection Against Limited Strikes).

Technical Details

From its start, the SDI program considered a variety of options for shooting down incoming warheads. Previous U.S. missile defense proposals sought to explode antimissile missiles, often equipped with nuclear warheads of their own, in the vicinity of the offensive missiles high above the surface, thereby preventing enemy warheads from reaching targets in the United States. Some elements of SDI considered this strategy, but others looked at different options and components not seriously considered by designers of prior systems. These new ideas included space-based radars, lasers, and particle beams. Many of these ideas proved ineffectual and did not survive budget cuts and reorganized incarnations of BMD strategies.

Unlike previous BMD programs such as Sentinel and Safeguard, SDI was not a single-strategy defense relying on only one method of intercept. Instead, Reagan had created SDI to study a variety of antimissile options. The program conducted research into detection areas, such as space- and ground-based sensors, and intercept methods, such as directed-energy weapons and the kinetic "hit-to-kill" strategies that survive to this day in current BMD programs. Nearly all current U.S. BMD programs, from the Patriot theater missile defense to the Airborne Laser, owe some of their inspiration to ideas nurtured under SDI.

Kinetic-energy elements of SDI included the Homing Overlay Experiment (HOE), the Exoatmospheric Reentry-Vehicle Interception System (ERIS), and the Extended Ranger Interceptor (ERINT). HOE was a series of four missile tests conducted in 1983 and 1984 at the Kwajalein Missile Range in the Marshall Islands. The goal of the tests was to intercept and destroy an ICBM in space using nonnuclear means, in this case slamming the interceptor into the incoming warhead. For each test, a Minuteman missile launched from Vandenberg Air Force Base in California served as the target. About twenty minutes later, an interceptor missile, also a converted Minuteman, was launched from Kwajalein. While in space, infrared homing equipment guided the interceptor. The interceptor carried a "kinetic kill device" consisting of a set of aluminum vanes that unfurled before impact. The first three attempts failed to achieve a successful intercept owing to a variety of mechanical and software problems, but on June 10, 1984, the fourth HOE test resulted in a successful intercept. The ERINT program, designed to demonstrate the guidance accuracy of a small, radar-homing kill vehicle, led designers to choose the interceptor as the basis for the Patriot Advanced Capability 3 (PAC-3) missile now in use.

Directed-energy weapon systems tested or explored under SDI included the Airborne Laser Laboratory, the neutral particle beam, the charged particle beam, and an X-ray laser. More than any other aspect of SDI, these elements inspired the "Star Wars" moniker taken up by supporters and critics. Directed-energy beams—once the realm of science fiction—marked a significant departure from previous missile defense designs, which had relied on nuclear detonations or kinetic interceptors that could "hit a bullet with a bullet." The Airborne Laser Lab was a gas-dynamic laser mounted in a commercial Boeing 707. During the eleven-year experiment, the laser system destroyed five AIM-9 Sidewinder air-to-air missiles and a Navy BQM-34A target drone, but it did not show much promise as a deployable weapon effective against real-world threats. However, the basic design of this system, mounting a laser on an aircraft, is the inspiration behind a current airborne laser project.

SDI-sponsored sensor systems included the Boost Surveillance and Tracking System (BSTS), the Space Surveillance and Tracking System, and the Space-Based Radar. BSTS proved too large and costly to field but served as an initial model for smaller, cheaper sensors that would become a part of later proposals to create a constellation of orbital platforms.

In its later years, with direction from President George H. W. Bush to focus on a less ambitious missile shield, SDI found hope in the Brilliant Pebbles system. With Brilliant Pebbles, some 4,600 small interceptors were to deploy in orbit, each capable of homing in on and destroying incoming warheads, and each "pebble" independent from any other guidance or control system. Critics predicted, however, that many nations would object to placing so many weapons in orbit, not to mention the strain on satellite tracking systems from the large number of pebbles.

Others also sought to refocus SDI's attention away from broader missile defense goals to more specific, smaller-scale defenses that, while protecting the United States from attack, relied more on technologies that showed promise and did less to aggravate international security. Some suggested that a more effective defensive deployment might be possible within the terms of the ABM Treaty with a limited system designed to protect against accidental and unauthorized launches. Although this Accidental Launch Protection System (ALPS), with its ABM Treaty–authorized 100 interceptors at one site, could not defend the United States against missiles launched from submarines or against missiles armed with large numbers of decoys and countermeasures, much less a large-scale attack, it did serve as a bridge between the ambitious program identified with Reagan to the more modest BMD testing of the 1990s.

—John Spykerman

See also: Brilliant Eyes; Countermeasures; Department of Defense; Missile Defense; Strategic Defenses; Theater Missile Defense; X-Ray Laser

References

Baucom, Donald R., *The Origins of SDI, 1944–1983* (Lawrence: University of Kansas Press, 1992).

Reiss, Edward, *The Strategic Defense Initiative* (Cambridge: Cambridge University Press, 1992).

STRATEGIC DEFENSES

Strategic defenses are those systems a country employs to protect its territory and population from adversary attack against the homeland. Typically such defenses have included navies, coast guards, air defenses, and antiballistic missile interceptors.

History and Background

Soon after the first German V-2 rockets struck Britain during World War II, U.S. military planners began dreaming of a defense to counter ballistic missile attacks. Debates over the costs and benefits of a workable defense against long-range (strategic) missile defenses have been fierce—supporters and opponents have returned over the decades to contest each other on the financial costs, technological feasibility, and political ramifications of constructing such a shield. Prior to President Ronald Reagan's ambitious Strategic Defense Initiative (SDI), which explored several ballistic missile defense (BMD) concepts in the 1980s, the United States attempted to field a series of nuclear-armed interceptor systems. Defense officials eventually canceled each of these programs when it became evident that either the technical merits of the programs were weak or the political and economic costs were too high. Changes in administration, too, have had an effect on various BMD programs, with presidents alternately increasing and decreasing funding for BMD while also refocusing particular systems from narrower to broader missions and back again.

Early U.S. Missile Defense Programs

In 1957, the United States began work on its first ballistic missile defense, the Nike-Zeus system. After about five years, it became apparent to the program's evaluators that the Nike-Zeus missile would not provide an effective defense against a Soviet attack. In 1962, the United States switched to a modified version of the Nike-Zeus program, the Nike-X, which used two kinds of nuclear-tipped interceptors and new "phased-array" radars. Under President Lyndon B. Johnson, Nike-X became the Sentinel system, and Johnson announced that the revamped effort would focus more on defending against a smaller Chinese nuclear threat than on attempting to thwart a massive attack from the Soviet Union. China had recently developed nuclear weapons technology and had the capacity to produce only a few long-range offensive missiles. Thinking that this was more feasible than attempting to stop hundreds or thousands of Soviet warheads, Johnson switched Sentinel's mission to the Chinese threat (*see* Nike Zeus; Sentinel).

The Nike-X/Sentinel system consisted of two missiles. Spartan, a long-range missile, was designed to intercept warheads outside of the Earth's atmosphere. The first test of this 460-mile-range missile occurred in March 1968. The Spartan was to carry a 5-megaton warhead designed to kill enemy warheads not by blast but by an X-ray radiation flux. During an August 1970 test, Sentinel intercepted a Minuteman reentry vehicle for the first time. In January 1971, a Spartan missile intercepted a Polaris submarine-launched ballistic missile that had deployed decoys and penetration aids in an attempt to overwhelm the Spartan radar systems. These tests, however, were performed under controlled conditions that did not simulate realistic attack scenarios (*see* Minuteman ICBMs; Penetration Aids; Spartan).

The Sprint missile was the other component of the Sentinel/Safeguard system. Sprint was to serve as a last-ditch defense inside the Earth's atmosphere if and when the longer-range Spartan missiles failed to destroy their targets. In November 1965, the first Sprint missile underwent testing after extensive studies showed that a high-speed, 25-mile-range interceptor was possible. The cone-shaped Sprint was powered by a two-stage, solid-propellant rocket motor. The missile reached speeds in excess of Mach 10 that caused extreme thermodynamic heating and demanded sophisticated shielding. Special command links hardened and protected against nuclear electromagnetic pulses guided the Sprint, which was equipped with a 1-kiloton enhanced radiation warhead that could destroy the enemy reentry vehicle with a very high neutron flux. Designers intended the flight time for a Sprint intercept to be less than fifteen seconds. Testing continued on both systems until 1973. Sprint missiles were eventually incorporated into the Safeguard system (*see* Safeguard Antiballistic Missile [ABM] System; Sprint).

Safeguard was a U.S. BMD system briefly deployed in 1975. In 1969, President Richard M. Nixon announced plans for the system, basing Safeguard on earlier proposals such as the Sentinel and Nike-Zeus programs. However, Nixon, like Johnson, changed the planned missile shield's mission—this time from protecting the general public in case of a Chinese nuclear attack to providing protection for a few crucial military sites to improve the survivability of U.S. land-based deterrent forces. Safeguard consisted of detection radar and long- and short-range ABM missiles equipped with nuclear warheads designed to intercept incoming missiles or fractional orbital bombardment systems (FOBS).

Safeguard became operational on October 1, 1975, but one day later, the U.S. House of Representatives voted to shut down the program. Opponents of the system argued that the development of Soviet multiple independently targetable reentry vehicles

(MIRVs) meant that Safeguard could not handle a concerted Soviet attack. In addition, several other technical problems reduced its effectiveness, such as the predicted failure of tracking radars after the interceptor detonated its nuclear warhead.

Political issues, both domestic and international, played heavily in the Safeguard debate. The U.S. Senate passed Phase I of the program on a 50–50 vote, with Vice President Spiro T. Agnew casting the tie-breaking ballot. On top of its defensive value, supporters maintained Safeguard would create a bargaining chip in upcoming arms control talks with the Soviet Union. Safeguard designers originally intended the system to protect up to twelve sites, but during negotiations with the Soviet Union on the Anti-Ballistic Missile (ABM) Treaty, negotiators reduced the number of sites to two: Grand Forks Air Force Base in North Dakota, and Washington, D.C. Following an amendment to the treaty in 1974 limiting each side to just one ABM site, Grand Forks, home to 150 Minuteman intercontinental ballistic missiles, emerged as the sole location of a U.S. ballistic missile defense system.

With Safeguard's detection equipment working with a nearby radar installation, the system could detect Soviet ICBMs as they passed over the North Pole, giving operators just a few minutes to plan their reaction. The U.S. response consisted of two types of missiles: the long-range Spartan and the short-range Sprint, both armed with nuclear warheads. Designers created Safeguard to provide a layered defense: The Spartan ABMs would first attack incoming clusters of warheads, booster rockets, and decoys, and Sprint ABMs would intercept survivors.

Opponents, however, argued that with only 100 interceptors stationed in North Dakota, the Soviet Union could easily overpower the defense. Congressional faith in the project began to diminish. The Senate initially resisted efforts to terminate the program, but following revelations that the Pentagon had come to the same conclusions on Safeguard's ineffectiveness a year earlier, senators agreed to end operational funding. The U.S. Army then began dismantling Safeguard, finishing the task in February 1976. The total program cost had amounted to $5 billion (some $25 billion in 2004 dollars).

U.S. BMD programs have since abandoned Safeguard's method of using nuclear weapons to destroy incoming missiles. For moral and technical reasons, the United States now pursues other BMD options, including hit-to-kill kinetic-energy devices and directed-energy lasers. These ideas surfaced in the Strategic Defense Initiative of the 1980s and survive in systems conceived since the 1990s.

Soviet Missile Defenses

The Soviet Union also has explored strategic missile defense. Although the Soviets, and later the Russians, did not subject their BMD programs to the public scrutiny that U.S. programs have endured, many believe these systems have encountered similar technological and economic barriers to effectiveness over the years. The Soviet Union designed its first system in the early 1960s to protect Moscow. Originally the Soviets intended to have eight BMD complexes in the Moscow region, but construction slowed, and by 1970 they had built only four of the sites, with a total of sixty-four interceptors. Plans for additional sites were scaled back in 1972, when the signing of the ABM Treaty limited the number of sites and interceptors (*see* Moscow Anti-Ballistic Missile System).

The Moscow system relied on one large radar for long-range tracking and battle management, with a network of smaller radars on the periphery of the Soviet Union's territory to provide early warning information. Like U.S. systems, the Soviet system used a nuclear-armed missile (called the "Galosh") as its interceptor. The initial Soviet system deployed around Moscow is known as the S-300, with S-400 and S-500 upgraded versions surfacing in later years. The Soviet Union and Russia have sold S-300 interceptors to a handful of countries, including China. Several problems exist with this system. First, its radars are vulnerable to "blackout," or blinding by nuclear blasts, during a defense of an attack, including by those blasts from its own interceptor missiles. The system also could not detect missiles approaching from certain directions. And like most U.S. systems, Soviet defenses could not overcome countermeasures, such as decoys and chaff, or massive attacks involving hundreds or thousands of warheads (*see* Countermeasures).

The Soviet Union upgraded its system in the late 1970s, installing a two-layer defense using two types of nuclear-armed interceptors. The updated system, still nominally in operation, relies on phased-array radars for coverage. The system is still intended to defend only Moscow and is not a comprehensive national missile defense. The Department of Defense estimates that the Soviet/Russian system is no more advanced than the old Safeguard defense, but despite its problems, the system runs at partial capability with an unclear state of readiness.

—*John Spykerman*

See also: Missile Defense; Strategic Defense Initiative
References
Garwin, Richard L., "Boost-Phase Intercept: A Better Alternative," *Arms Control Today,* vol. 30, no. 7, September 2000, pp. 8–11, available at http://www.armscontrol.org/act/2000_09/bpisept00.asp.
Holdren, John P., et al., "Technical Issues Related to the Comprehensive Nuclear Test Ban Treaty," National Academies of Science report, 2002.
Lamb, Frederick K., Daniel Kleppner, and David Mosher, "Boost-Phase Intercept Systems for National Missile Defense," American Physical Society report, July 2003, available at http://www.aps.org/public_affairs/popa/reports/nmdexec.pdf.
Raytheon, "Missile Defense Systems and Boost-Phase Intercept," available at http://raytheonmissiledefense.com/boost/.
Shalikashvili, John, "Findings and Recommendations concerning the Comprehensive Nuclear Test Ban Treaty" (Washington, DC: U.S. Department of State, January 2001), available at http://www.state.gov/www/global/arms/ctbtpage/ctbt_report.html.

STRATEGIC FORCES

Strategic forces are weapons and delivery systems that are intended to deter an armed conflict or destroy an enemy's military. The term "strategic forces" generally refers to nuclear weapons and the systems that deliver them to their targets. There are currently nine nations that possess nuclear forces: the United States, the United Kingdom, Russia, France, the People's Republic of China, India, Pakistan, Israel, and (presumably) North Korea (the Democratic People's Republic of Korea, DPRK). The nature of their strategic forces is influenced by their technical and economic resources, strategic doctrines and culture, and the political and military threats they face. Because of the sunk costs involved in developing strategic forces, systems often remain in arsenals decades after their initial deployment (*see* Ballistic Missiles; Intercontinental Ballistic Missiles; Medium-Range Ballistic Missiles; Submarines, Nuclear-Powered Ballistic Missile; Sea-Launched Cruise Missiles; Submarine-Launched Ballistic Missiles).

U.S. Strategic Forces

The U.S. Strategic Command (STRATCOM), head-quartered at Offutt Air Force Base in Nebraska, commands the strategic forces of the United States. The Nuclear Posture Review (NPR) submitted by the Department of Defense to Congress in December 2001 set forth the number of U.S. nuclear forces and their dispositions. As of January 2004, the United States maintained a total force of 1,227 strategic nuclear delivery vehicles and 5,968 strategic nuclear warheads. These forces are split into a "Triad" of intercontinental ballistic missiles (ICBMs), bombers, and submarine-launched ballistic missiles (SLBMs).

Also as of 2004, the United States maintains a force of 550 ICBMs and 1,700 ICBM warheads. Fifty of the ICBMs are MX/Peacekeepers, which have a range of roughly 7,000 miles and can carry up to ten Mk-21 reentry vehicles, each of which houses a 300-kiloton W-87 warhead. The remaining 500 U.S. ICBMs are Minuteman III missiles, which have a range of more than 7,000 miles and can carry either three W-78 or W-62 warheads. Under the 1993 Strategic Arms Reduction Treaty (START II), the current three-warhead loading was to be changed to a single W-87/Mk-21 by 2007. Though START II was never ratified, the United States still plans to abide by this treaty provision and download its ICBM force. The Minuteman III missile force continues to be modernized under a $6 billion, six-part plan to improve the weapon's accuracy and reliability and to extend its service life to approximately 2020 (see Minuteman ICBMs).

The United States maintains two types of long-range bombers for nuclear missions: the B-2A Spirit and the B-52H Stratofortress. Neither is maintained on a day-to-day alert, and both also conduct conventional missions, as was seen in the 2003 war in Iraq (see Bombers, U.S. Nuclear-Capable; Stealth Bomber [B-2 Spirit]).

The B-52 can deliver cruise missiles, gravity bombs, or a combination of both. The United States currently maintains a force of 142 operationally deployed B-52s in its arsenal. The bomber is expected to stay in operation until 2040. The B-52, called by the U.S. Air Force the "workhorse of nuclear weapons employment," is the only carrier of nuclear cruise missiles. Each B-52 can carry up to twenty air-launched cruise missiles (ALCMs) or advanced cruise missiles (ACMs), with up to eight missiles carried internally and up to twelve carried externally.

The U.S. force of twenty B-2 bombers is scheduled for replacement around 2040; a follow-on bomber program began in 1998. The nuclear weapons that are carried by the B-2 include the B61-7, B61-11, and B83 gravity bombs. Each B-2 can be armed with either B61 or B83 bombs, but the two cannot be mixed in a single payload. The B-2, the only carrier of the B61-11 earth-penetrating nuclear bomb, is currently undergoing a $600 million modernization program.

Only recently was it revealed that a third strategic bomber, the B-1B, had been maintained as nuclear capable. In the past, the U.S. Air Force had described it as "conventional only." The 1994 NPR ordered an end to the B-1B's nuclear capability (which occurred officially on October 1, 1997). Of the original 100 B-1Bs, 92 remain. The Air Force will reduce that number to 66 by October 2004 (see United States Air Force).

As of mid-2003, there were sixteen operational Ohio-class nuclear-powered ballistic missile submarines (SSBNs, for "ship submersible ballistic nuclear"), two fewer than a year earlier. The Ohios carry 384 Trident SLBMs (24 on each boat) and as many as 2,880 warheads—about half the operational warheads in the strategic arsenal. There are two types of Trident missiles: the Trident I C4 and the newer, more accurate, and longer-range Trident II D5. Twelve submarines have been upgraded to carry D5s, eight in the Atlantic and four in the Pacific. After the remaining Pacific-based subs are retrofitted to carry D5s, the D5 will arm all U.S. SSBNs. The SLBMs carry two types of reentry vehicles (RVs) and warheads: the Mk-4 with the W-76 warhead and the Mk-5 with the W-88 warhead. The Mk-4/W-76 combination is the more common, with almost 2,500 warheads deployed on fourteen submarines. The Mk-5 carries the W-88, the most powerful missile warhead in the U.S. arsenal. Production of the W-88 ended in 1989.

The four oldest Trident SSBNs (Ohio, Michigan, Florida, and Georgia) are being converted into cruise missile submarines under a $3.8 billion program. Of the twenty-four launch tubes on each sub, twenty-two will be fitted with canisters that hold seven Tomahawk cruise missiles, for a total of 154 per boat. The two remaining launch tubes will house pressurized chambers for Special Operations

Forces. The first cruise missile submarine (Ohio) is scheduled to be delivered in late 2006, with an initial operational capability in 2007. All four types should be operational in 2008.

With an improvement in targeting delivery, and effects-based technologies, the United States has also begun to deploy a nonnuclear strategic capability. Previously, nuclear weapons were considered the only viable strategic combat option because conventional weapons were not highly accurate, and nuclear weapons had a large enough blast to be able to ensure destruction of a target even if the weapon was not deployed accurately. The nature of combat is changing, however, and modern militaries are developing the ability to target and destroy targets with an increasing degree of accuracy and destructiveness. These weapons can be directed at hardened targets or command, control, and communications units with a degree of accuracy that reduces the need for nuclear weapons.

The Joint Direct Attack Munition (JDAM), the Joint Standoff Weapon (JSOW), and the longer-range Joint Air-to-Surface Standoff Weapon are all examples of nonnuclear strategic weapons. Some believe that these weapons can be delivered with a degree of accuracy and focused destruction that can essentially replace the need for nuclear strategic arms in combat (see United States Nuclear Forces and Doctrine).

British Strategic Forces

The United Kingdom seeks to retain a credible minimum nuclear deterrent based on its Trident submarine force. Britain's Trident force provides an operationally independent strategic nuclear capability in support of the North Atlantic Treaty Organization (NATO) and its strategy of war prevention. British strategic forces serve as the ultimate guarantor of British national security. Britain operates four Vanguard-class SSBNs (for "ship submersible ballistic nuclear") carrying a total of sixty-four Trident II D5 SLBMs, each capable of carrying three warheads (see British Nuclear Forces and Doctrine).

Russian Strategic Forces

Russia maintains a large nuclear force with more than 1,000 strategic delivery systems and more than 5,000 strategic nuclear warheads. Russia's strategic forces, much like those of the United States, are divided into a Triad of bombers, SSBNs, and ICBMs.

Russia's seventy-eight strategic bombers are part of the Russian Air Force's 37th Air Army. Its current strategic bomber force consists of three types: Bear H6, Bear H16, and Blackjack. Russia's thirty-two Bear H6 bombers, also known by the designation Tu-95MS6, can carry six AS-15A air-launched cruise missiles or six bombs. Its thirty-one Bear H16 bombers, also known by the designation Tu-95MS16, can carry sixteen ALCMs or bombs.

Economic constraints, a shrinking SSBN fleet, and obvious safety concerns in the aftermath of the tragedy on board the Russian submarine Kursk, which sank with the loss of all hands in August 2000, have led to substantial decreases in the number of SSBN patrols and general-purpose submarine (SSN/SSGN) patrols. According to the U.S. Navy, in 1991 there were thirty-seven SSBN patrols. In 2001, there was one. Some Soviet SSBNs, however, are able to launch their SLBMs while in port.

Only fourteen of Russia's SSBNs are considered to be operational: six Delta IIIs, six Delta IVs, and two Typhoons. Within these platforms, Russia deploys three types of SLBMs: ninety-six Stingrays, forty Sturgeons, and ninety-six Skiffs, all of which are MIRVed (that is, equipped with multiple independently targetable reentry vehicles) and carry a total of 1,072 nuclear warheads with a total blast potential of 262 megatons.

Russia's primary deterrent force is made up of some 706 ICBMs, which carry 3,011 warheads with a total blast potential of 1,656 megatons. This force is divided into five types of missiles: 144 Satans, 137 Stilettos, 36 Scalpels, 360 Sickles, and 29 SS-27s. Satan missiles, also known as the SS-18, are a silo-based ICBM with a range of up to 9,000 miles, depending on the load being carried. The warheads have an estimated yield of up to 750 kilotons. Stiletto missiles, also known as the SS-19, are silo-based ICBMs. Some SS-19s are being deactivated to make room for SS-27s, which can use the same silo as the SS-19. Scalpel missiles, also known as the SS-24, can be either silo- or rail-based. The silos for all Scalpels have been dismantled, and all that remain are rail-based versions. Sickle missiles, also known as the SS-25 and as Topol, are road-mobile, single-warhead missile systems that are being replaced by the SS-27. SS-27 missiles are also road-mobile, single-warhead missile systems and have a range of 10,000 kilometers (see Bombers, Russian and Chinese Nuclear-Capable; Russian Nuclear Forces and Doctrine).

French Strategic Forces

France continues to maintain its own strategic nuclear capability, which is divided between SSBNs and aircraft. It retired its land-based intermediate-range missile force in the 1990s.

France's primary nuclear force today resides in its SSBN fleet. France maintains four SSBNs of three classes: two of the new Triomphant class, one of the L'Inflexible class, and one of the Redoubtable class. The two Triomphant SSBNs each carry sixteen M45 SLBMs with six of the new TN-75 warheads.

France maintains forty-five Mirage 2000N bombers based at Luxeuil and Istres. The bomber has a range of 2,750 kilometers and can carry a single TN-81 warhead with an estimated yield of 300 kilotons. The Mirage will eventually be replaced by the Rafale, France's multipurpose navy and air force fighter-bomber for the twenty-first century. Its roles include conventional ground attack, air defense, air superiority, and nuclear delivery of the ASMP (Air Sol nucléaire Moyenne Portée) and/or ASMP-A (Air Sol nucléaire Moyenne Portée–Amélioré) short-range attack missiles. The navy version (Rafale M) entered the inventory in 2001 to form Squadron 12F at Landivisiau and will replace the Super Étendard as France's carrier-based aircraft. The air force's Rafale D will attain a nuclear-strike role in about 2005. The air force still plans to buy a total of 234 Rafales (see French Nuclear Forces and Doctrine).

Chinese Strategic Forces

China currently has close to 250 strategic weapons structured in a Triad of land-based missiles, bombers, and SLBMs. The emphasis of China's arsenal is primarily on the land-based missile leg of the Triad.

The missile leg consists of a variety of weapons. In all, China has between twenty and thirty ICBMs, fifty to a hundred intermediate-range ballistic missiles (IRBMs), twenty-five to fifty medium-range ballistic missiles (MRBMs), and many short-range ballistic missiles. These are designated by the United States as CSS-2, -3, -4, -5, and -6.

The Chinese already have road-mobile ballistic missiles in service, although they are currently only IRBMs and MRBMs. This mobile missile force is limited in number, accuracy, and throw weight. The missiles are not yet capable of accommodating MIRV technology, nor are they supported by Global Positioning System guidance systems.

The Hong-6, a modified version of the Soviet Badger, is the only active in-service Chinese bomber capable of carrying nuclear bombs. Its operational effectiveness is limited by its short range, its slow speed, and its obsolete technology.

China's submarines are regarded as barely operational. China has stated that it has built two Xia-class SSBNs, each of which can carry twelve SLBMs. The Xia is a modification of the Han-class nuclear-powered attack submarine, lengthened to house twelve missile tubes. Reports conflict, however, about whether China has actually deployed two SSBNs. Most analysts estimate that only one is operational, and that it has only operated for short periods in China's coastal waters (see Bombers, Russian and Chinese Nuclear-Capable; Chinese Nuclear Forces and Doctrine).

Indian Strategic Forces

India has developed a strategic dyad relying on aircraft and missiles to deliver its estimated stockpile of sixty to ninety strategic nuclear warheads.

The country has several types of aircraft that could be used to deliver a nuclear weapon. Considerations of range, payload, and speed, however, narrow the choices to one or two types. The Indian aircraft most likely to be used for this purpose are the MiG-27 and the Jaguar. India's 165 MiG-27 Floggers are nuclear-capable Soviet aircraft with a range of approximately 800 kilometers. India designates the MiG-27 the Bahadhur, which means "valiant" or "brave." India's 131 Jaguar IS/IBs, known as the Shamsher (for "sword"), have a range of 1,600 kilometers.

India deploys one ballistic missile, the 150 km range *Prithvi I.* A single-stage, dual-engine, liquid-fueled, road-mobile, short-range ballistic missile (SRBM), the *Prithvi II,* has a range of 250 kilometers. The two-stage Agni (fire) IRBM is also under development and has been tested to a range of 1,500 kilometers, but its status remains unclear. An improved version with a longer range (over 2,000 kilometers) is under development. In test launches, the missile designated *Agni II* flew 2,200 kilometers and, according to Indian officials, landed fewer than 100 meters from its intended target. Both road- and rail-mobile versions of the *Agni II* are under development. The development of a longer-range *Agni III* with a range of up to 3,500 kilometers has not been confirmed. Rumors persist concerning Indian plans for an ICBM program referred to as the Surya. Most components needed for an ICBM are available from India's indigenous space program.

In addition to air- and land-based nuclear-capable forces, India is working on at least two naval systems that may be equipped to carry nuclear warheads in the future. The submarine-launched Sagarika (oceanic) SLBM is in advanced development. U.S. intelligence believes it is an SLBM and estimates that it will not be deployed until 2010 or later. Another potential candidate is the Dhanush (bow) sea-launched ballistic missile, which has a range of 250 kilometers. Neither the Dhanush nor the Sagarika has been declared nuclear-capable by Indian authorities (*see* Indian Nuclear Weapons Program).

Pakistan's Strategic Forces

Experts estimate that Pakistan's nuclear arsenal consists of somewhere between twenty-four and forty-eight strategic nuclear warheads.

The aircraft in the Pakistani Air Force that is most likely to be used in the nuclear weapon delivery role is the F-16, built by the United States. These aircraft have a range of 1,600 kilometers, and Pakistan owns forty-four of them.

Pakistan also maintains two types of nuclear-capable missiles, the Ghauri I and the Ghauri II. The Ghauri I is basically the North Korean Nodong missile, with a range of 1,500 kilometers. The Ghauri II has a range of 2,300 kilometers. A third version of the Ghauri, with an unconfirmed range of 2,500 to 3,000 kilometers, is under development and was test-launched on August 15, 2000 (*see* Pakistani Nuclear Weapons Program).

Israeli Strategic Forces

Israel neither acknowledges nor denies that it has nuclear weapons, although the rest of the world regards Israel as a de facto nuclear weapons state. It has been estimated that Israel could have as many as 200 strategic nuclear warheads in forms as varied as land mines, artillery, and high-yield thermonuclear weapons.

Israel currently deploys two nuclear-capable ballistic missile types. The Jericho I has a range of 660 kilometers, and the Jericho II has a range of 1,500 kilometers. Additionally, the Shavit space-launch vehicle, with an intercontinental range of 7,800 kilometers, could be modified to carry nuclear weapons.

In terms of nuclear-capable aircraft, Israel could choose between two types purchased from the United States: the F-4E-2000 Phantom or the more modern F-16 Falcon (*see* Israeli Nuclear Weapons Program).

North Korean Strategic Forces

North Korea, officially known as the Democratic People's Republic of Korea, possesses two missiles capable of delivering strategic nuclear weapons. The Nodong is a modified Scud-C missile with a range of 1,300 kilometers. The Taepo Dong-2 (TD-2) is said to be a two- or three-stage missile with a range estimated between 3,650 and 4,300 kilometers. The size of the North Korean nuclear force is currently a matter of much debate within intelligence communities, but there is a general presumption that North Korea has defied international inspections and constraints long enough to have developed the fissile material necessary to produce at least a few rudimentary nuclear devices (*see* North Korean Nuclear Weapons Program).

—*Abe Denmark*

References

China's Nuclear Stockpile and Deployments (Monterey, CA: Center for Nonproliferation Studies, Monterey Institute of International Studies, 2002), available at http://cns.miis.edu/research/china/nuc/nstock.htm.

"Current Status and Future of Russian Strategic Forces," Center for Arms Control, Energy and Environmental Studies, September 2002, available at http://www.armscontrol.ru/start/rsf_now.htm.

Natural Resource Defense Council, "Archive of Nuclear Data," available at http://www.nrdc.org/nuclear/nudb/datainx.asp.

"NRDC Nuclear Notebook," *Bulletin of the Atomic Scientists*, vol. 59. no. 3, May/June 2003, pp. 73–76, available at http://www.thebulletin.org/issues/nukenotes/mj03nukenote.html.

"Revealed: The Secrets of Israel's Nuclear Arsenal," *Sunday Times* (London), 5 October 1986.

STRATEGIC OFFENSIVE REDUCTIONS TREATY (SORT)

The latest in a series of offensive strategic nuclear weapons treaties between the United States and the Soviet Union, the Strategic Offensive Reductions Treaty (SORT) is also known as the Moscow Treaty. Signed in Moscow on May 24, 2002, it is only two pages in length, the shortest bilateral arms control treaty ever signed. Its brevity is meant to reflect the changed relationship between the two countries, which are now strategic partners rather than adversaries, a major change since the Cold War. Presidents George W. Bush and Vladimir Putin agreed on the principal elements of the treaty at the Crawford, Texas, summit in November 2001. The treaty commits both parties to continued reductions in their strategic nuclear arsenals, with a target of 1,700 to 2,200 deployed strategic warheads by 2012. There are no provisions for verification, inspections, or compliance, nor does the treaty require the parties to destroy the warheads they remove from deployed status. In fact, the United States plans to keep some intact warheads in a "hedge" that it can reconstitute quickly in an emergency. This treaty essentially took the place of a third Strategic Arms Reduction Treaty (START III).

—*Jeffrey A. Larsen*

See also: Arms Control; Hedge; Nuclear Posture Review
Reference
"Treaty between the United States of America and the Russian Federation on Strategic Offensive Reductions," available at http://www.state.gov/t/ac/trt/18016.htm.

STRATEGIC ROCKET FORCES

The Strategic Rocket Forces (SRF), created in 1959, was a separate, elite branch of the Soviet armed forces during the Cold War. It was responsible for the operation of the bulk of the Soviet Union's strategic nuclear arsenal. With the fall of the Soviet Union in 1991 and Soviet/Russian participation in various missile treaties limiting the size of the superpower missile arsenals (including the Intermediate-Range Nuclear Forces [INF] Treaty of 1987, the two Strategic Arms Reduction Treaties [START I and START II] of 1991 and 1993, and the Moscow Treaty, or Strategic Offensive Reductions Treaty [SORT] of 2002), the SRF has waned somewhat in importance. In 1997, it merged with Air Defense Forces and the Missile-Space Defense Troops (responsible for early warning radar and space tracking) to cut costs. The shrinking budget, overall decline of the Russian military, and continuing friendly relations with the United States have probably doomed the SRF as an independent force. In August 2000, the Russian Security Council decided to relegate the SRF to a separate command under the air force and moved to eliminate its independent status by 2006. Its aging force of intercontinental ballistic missiles (ICBMs) will be reduced based upon the service life of each individual missile. Finally, the Missile-Space Defense troops were taken away and merged with the air force.

The current SRF force is divided into nineteen missile divisions operating a mix of silo, rail, and mobile missiles. Although the majority of Russian ICBMs are old, the Russians introduced the SS-27 Topol in 1997. The SS-27 is both silo and land-mobile based. Units suffer from a severe lack of spare parts, lubricants, and fuel to operate their mobile launch vehicles. In some instances, officers have used their own money to purchase necessary parts for their missiles to remain on alert. Although traditionally the SRF enjoyed the greatest percentage of highly educated officers, recruitment of junior officers has recently become a problem. The Soviet-era draft system remains in effect, and draft dodging is a serious problem. Thus, many unqualified personnel are forced to serve in positions they would not normally occupy. Even feeding the troops has become a problem. The SRF has been forced to grow its own food to feed its troops. These "SRF farms" account for over 40 percent of its food needs.

—*Zach Becker*

See also: Russian Nuclear Forces and Doctrine
References
Podvig, P. L., ed., *Russian Strategic Rocket Forces* (Cambridge, MA: MIT Press, 2001).
Sokov, Nikolai, *Russian Strategic Modernization* (Lanham, MD: Rowman and Littlefield, 2000).
Zaloga, Steven J., *The Kremlin's Nuclear Sword: The Rise and Fall of Russia's Strategic Rocket Forces* (Washington, DC: Smithsonian Institution Press, 2002).

SUBMARINES, NUCLEAR-POWERED BALLISTIC MISSILE (SSBNS)

Nuclear-powered ballistic missile submarines are traditionally referred to as SSBNs (for "ship submersible ballistic nuclear"); they carry and launch submarine-launched ballistic missiles (SLBMs). Five nations have SSBNs: the United States, the Russian Federation, the United Kingdom, France, and China (*see* Strategic Forces; Submarine-Launched Ballistic Missiles).

U.S. SSBNs

For the United States, the original SSBN submarine force consisted of forty-one Polaris submarines, with the first, the USS *George Washington* (SSBN 598),

HMS Vanguard, *the Royal Navy's first Trident nuclear submarine, sails up the Clyde River to the British navy Clyde Submarine Base at Faslane. (Robin Adshead/The Military Picture Library/Corbis)*

commissioned on December 30, 1959. It was deployed on the first ever fleet ballistic missile (FBM) patrol with a full load of sixteen Polaris missiles in November 1960. The first ten FBM submarines (598 and 608 classes) carried the various generations of the Polaris missile (A1, A2, and A3). The George Washington class (SSBN 598) and Ethan Allen class (SSBN 608) deployed with Polaris A1s. These Polaris submarines were 380 feet long with a 33-foot beam (width) and weighed 6,700 tons. The Lafayette class (616), consisting of nine boats, deployed with Polaris A2s and was later converted to accommodate the Poseidon C3 missile. These Poseidon submarines were 425 feet long with a 33-foot beam and weighed 8,250 tons. These submarines also carried sixteen missiles. The next thirty-one FBM submarines were constructed initially for Polaris but were later converted to the Poseidon C3 missile. The Poseidon missile was first deployed on the USS *James Madison* (SSBN 627) on March 31, 1971.

The Trident (Ohio 726 class) submarine, the largest of the U.S. Navy, has a length of 560 feet with a beam of 42 feet and weighs 18,700 pounds. It can carry twenty-four ballistic missiles with multiple independently targetable reentry vehicle (MIRV) warheads that can be accurately delivered to selected targets from almost anywhere in the world's oceans. The Trident submarine is designed to carry two types of SLBMs, the Trident C4 or D5 (*see* United States Navy; United States Nuclear Forces and Doctrine).

British SSBNs
The original UK SSBN program was supported by the United States under the 1963 Polaris Sales Agreement. The UK developed its own SSBN program, however. The British first produced the Resolution-class submarine, which was similar to the U.S. Los Angeles–class attack submarine. It was basically a modification of the Valiant-class fleet submarine, another attack submarine, but enlarged to incorporate the missile compartment between the fin and the nuclear reactor. The four Resolution-class submarines were built with a length of approximately 400 feet and weighed 8,500 tons. Each Resolution-class submarine could carry sixteen Polaris A3 missiles. When the United States replaced Polaris with Poseidon, the UK decided to upgrade its exist-

ing Polaris system with a new warhead, code-named Chevaline. In 1982, the UK began replacing Polaris with Trident. In 1993, after the completion of the first new Vanguard-class (Trident) SSBN, it began replacing the Resolution-class SSBNs. After twenty-eight years of service, the last Resolution-class SSBN was decommissioned in August 1996.

There are currently four Vanguard-class (Trident) SSBNs (Vanguard, Victorious, Vigilant, and Vengeance). The Vengeance entered service in February 2001. The Vanguard, weighing 15,900 tons, over 490 feet long, and with a beam of 42 feet, has the capacity to carry sixteen Trident II D5 missiles (designated UGM-133A), each capable of carrying up to twelve MIRVs. Plans were announced in 1993 to limit the number of warheads carried to a maximum of ninety-six per submarine; this has been further limited to forty-eight (see British Nuclear Forces and Doctrine).

Russian SSBNs

The Russian Federation inherited an aging SSBN fleet from the former Soviet Union with five classes of SLBMs. The first purpose-built Soviet SSBN was the Golf class (Project 628) submarine, deployed in the late 1960s, which carried three SS-N-4 SLBMs. It could fire these missiles, however, only while surfaced. Later, a modified version, the Golf II class, could launch the newer SS-N-5 SLBM submerged. Both boats, however, were diesel powered. The first nuclear-powered Soviet SSBN was the Hotel I class (Project 658). Like Golf I, it carried three surface-launched SS-N-4 SLBMs. The Golf II class (Project 658M) subs were essentially converted Hotel I–class submarines that carried three SS-N-5 SLBMs. The Yankee-class (Project 667A) SLBM, the first SLBM designed for surface-launched missiles, followed in the 1970s. It carried sixteen SS-N-6 SLBMs. The Delta I– and Delta II–class subs (Project 667B and Project 667BD) were essentially Yankee-class SSBNs but with twelve SS-N-8 SLBMs in place of the previous sixteen SS-N-6 SLBMs. The longer-range SS-N-8 SLBMs allowed the submarines to attack U.S. targets from Soviet waters. The Delta II was a lengthened version of the Delta I that carried four additional SS-N-8 SLBMs. All of these submarines have subsequently been retired.

The current Russian SSBN fleet includes the largest submarine ever built, the Typhoon class (Project 941, Akula), the Delta III class (Project 667), and the Delta IV class (K-51). Six Typhoon-class submarines were built. The Typhoons weigh 29,000 tons, are more than 540 feet long, have a beam width of 81 feet, and can carry twenty SS-N-20 (RSM-52) MIRVed SLBMs. The Delta III class (Project 667) sub weighs more than 13,000 tons, is more than 500 feet in length, has a beam of about 40 feet, and has the capacity to carry sixteen SS-N-18 (RSM-50) SLBMs. The Delta IV–class SSBN is essentially the same submarine as the Delta III but is designed to carry the SS-N-23 (RSM-54) SLBM instead of the SS-N-18. All of these submarines have reached or will soon reach the end of their service life. The Russians are currently building a new SSBN, the Borey class, which is projected to carry twelve missiles with an unknown number of reentry vehicles (see Russian Nuclear Forces and Doctrine).

French SSBNs

France's SSBN program began in 1969 with the Le Redoubtable class (later referred to as the L'Inflexible class). There were six SSBNs built. They weighed almost 9,000 tons, were 422 feet in length, and had a beam of almost 35 feet. The Le Redoubtable class was designed to carry sixteen M4/TN 70/71 SLBMs. The last boat was retired in 2002. The class was replaced by the Le Triomphant class. The French plan to build four new SSBNs, with the last one to be commissioned by 2008. Le Triomphant–class submarines weigh 14,335 tons, are 453 feet long, and have a beam of 41 feet. They will carry sixteen M45 SLBMs and will eventually carry a new missile, the M51 (see French Nuclear Forces and Doctrine).

Chinese SSBNs

China began its nuclear submarine program in the late 1960s. It has deployed one Type 092 (Xia class) SSBN. It is believed that this submarine carries the CSS-N-3/Julang-1 SLBM. The Type 092 has never left its coastal waters although it is considered operational. China is planning on building the first of four new SSBNs (Type 094) over the next few years, but progress may be slowed by problems in developing a new SLBM, the JL-2 (see Chinese Nuclear Forces and Doctrine).

—Guy Roberts

References
"Fleet Ballistic Submarines-SSBN," U.S. Navy Fact File, available at http://www.chinfo.navy.mil/navpalib/factfile/ships/ship-ssbn.html.

Spinardi, Graham, *From Polaris to Trident: The Development of U.S. Fleet Ballistic Missile Technology* (New York: Cambridge University Press, 1994).

"SSBN Typhoon Class Strategic Missile Submarine, Russia," available at http://www.naval-technology.com/projects/typhoon/.

SUBMARINE-LAUNCHED
BALLISTIC MISSILES (SLBMS)

A submarine-launched ballistic missile (SLBM) is a long-range ballistic missile fired from the tube of a submerged submarine. The original concept for the SLBM has been attributed to a World War II German program that involved the installation of mortar tubes on the deck of a U-boat. The mortars were then fired at a land-based target while the tubes were still partially submerged. The Germans had test-fired this system by the end of the war. In 1955, a presidential committee in the United States recommended the development of a sea-based, intermediate-range ballistic missile with a range of 1,500 nautical miles. In 1957, the U.S. Navy began work on a ballistic missile with a range of 1,200 nautical miles, which subsequently became known as the Polaris missile program. The first successful underwater launching of an SLBM occurred on July 20, 1960, aboard the USS *George Washington,* the first ballistic missile submarine (*see* Submarines, Nuclear-Powered Ballistic Missile). At least four other nations have developed an SLBM capability: the United Kingdom, the Russian Federation, France, and China (*see* Strategic Forces).

The U.S. Navy has developed and deployed six versions of the SLBM: Polaris (A1, A2, and A3), Poseidon (C3), and Trident (C4, D5). Each of these missiles offered improvements over its predecessors in terms of range, accuracy, and throw weight. The most recent, the Trident II (D5), has a range in excess of 4,000 nautical miles and a payload capability almost twice that of its predecessor, Trident I (C4). The Trident II is configured to carry eight warheads (*see* Polaris SLBMs/SSBNs; Poseidon SLBMs/SSBNs; Trident SLBMs/SSBNs; United States Nuclear Forces and Doctrine).

The UK's SLBM capability is supported and complemented by the United States under the 1963 Polaris Sales Agreement, whereby the United States agreed to sell to the UK Polaris missiles (though without the warheads or reentry vehicles). The agreement was modified in 1982 to allow for the sale of the

Trident II (D5) to the UK. The UK's Trident SLBMs are carried on four Vanguard-class SSBNs. As in the U.S. Trident II (D5) program, each SLBM is capable of carrying up to eight multiple independently targetable reentry vehicles (MIRVs). However, plans were announced in 1993 to limit the number of warheads carried from 192 to a maximum of 96 per submarine; this restriction has been further limited to 48 (*see* British Nuclear Forces and Doctrine).

The Russian SLBM program was developed by the former Soviet Union in conjunction with its SSBN program. The first SLBM, the SS-N-4 (its designation by the North Atlantic Treaty Organization [NATO]), was built in the late 1960s and deployed on the Golf-class submarine. It could not be fired submerged. Subsequent versions included the SS-N-5 and the SS-N-8, which offered increasingly improved capabilities and ranges. The current Russian SLBM program includes the SS-N-18, deployed on board the Delta III SSBN; the SS-N-23, deployed on board the Delta IV SSBN; and the SS-N-20, deployed on the Typhoon SSBN. These SLBMs are nearing the end of their service life and a new missile, the Borey, is being developed.

The United States and Russia have limited the number of deployed SLBMs based on limitations agreed upon in the Strategic Arms Reduction Treaties (START I and II). These treaties set forth the number of warheads each class of SLBM is authorized to carry, although it may be physically capable of carrying more. So, for example, the SS-N-18 is "attributed" with three warheads, the SS-N-23 with four, and the SS-N-20 with ten (*see* Russian Nuclear Forces and Doctrine; Strategic Arms Reduction Treaty; Strategic Arms Reduction Treaty).

The French SLBM is deployed on the Le Triomphant (S616) SSBN, which began replacing the L'Inflexible M4–class SSBNs in the 1990s. The submarine carries sixteen vertically launched M45 ballistic missiles. The M45 SLBM is a three-stage, solid-fueled rocket with a range of more than 10,000 miles and carries six multiple independently targetable reentry vehicles (MIRVs). By 2010, it is due to be replaced with the M51, which will carry up to twelve MIRVs and have an increased range in excess of 12,000 miles (*see* French Nuclear Forces and Doctrine).

China has one active SSBN, the Type 092 (Xia class), and one SLBM, the CSS-N-3/Julang 1, with a range of approximately 8,000 nautical miles. It carries one reentry vehicle. China has another SLBM under development, the JL-2. The range and payload of this new missile remain a matter of speculation (*see* Chinese Nuclear Forces and Doctrine).

—*Guy Roberts*

References

Siuru, William D., "SLBM—The Navy's Contribution to Triad," *Air University Review,* vol. 28, no. 6, September-October 1977, pp. 17–29.

"Submarine-Launched Ballistic Missiles," available at http://www.globalsecurity.org/wmd/systems/slbm.htm.

SUFFICIENCY

Nuclear sufficiency is the idea that it is not necessary to match a nuclear-armed competitor in every measure of strategic nuclear capability, instead suggesting that a survivable nuclear retaliatory capability is key to deterrence. Nuclear sufficiency also takes into account the law of diminishing returns—that is, there is a point at which the ability to inflict additional death and destruction on an opponent serves no rational purpose and only represents a waste of resources that could be better used elsewhere.

Although strategists never advocated developing a capability to "make the rubble bounce," to use a pejorative phrase, sufficiency was a controversial issue. Those who advocated sufficiency as a criterion to size nuclear forces believed that it could lead to arms race stability. Critics of the idea believed that it failed to account for relative weaknesses in a nuclear force structure that might embolden opponents who might use different criteria to judge the survivability and effectiveness of a nuclear arsenal. Those who championed sufficiency often responded that their critics relied on highly improbable scenarios to point out weaknesses in nuclear force postures.

—*Abe Denmark and James J. Wirtz*

See also: Superiority

Reference

Conetta, Carl, and Charles Knight, "Defense Sufficiency and Cooperation: A US Military Posture for the Post–Cold War Era," *US Defense Posture,* 12 March 1998.

SUMMIT MEETINGS
See Arms Control

SUPERIORITY

"Nuclear superiority" is a nebulous term that suggests that one side in a conflict has the ability to destroy an opponent's military capabilities with little fear of retaliation in kind. In the early years of the Cold War, the United States possessed nuclear superiority over the Soviet Union, but U.S. policymakers, in part owing to uncertainties about the size and location of Soviet nuclear forces, were never confident in their ability to destroy the Soviet nuclear arsenal. Nuclear superiority can be used to coerce other nations in diplomacy, as the United States did with the Soviet Union and its allies during the Cold War. President Dwight D. Eisenhower threatened North Korea and the People's Republic of China during the Korean War and the Offshore Islands crises in the 1950s, for example.

Nuclear superiority, however, is absent when both sides of a conflict posses a survivable nuclear capability. In terms of raw numbers and military capabilities, U.S. planners came to rely on the criterion of nuclear sufficiency to measure the adequacy of the U.S. nuclear arsenal. In other words, they came to see the nuclear balance in terms of the ability of the U.S. military to achieve its damage objectives against the Soviet Union in a second-strike situation. As both the Soviet Union and the United States gained secure second-strike forces, creating a situation of mutual assured destruction, many analysts came to believe that the concept of nuclear superiority had lost any military significance.

Some analysts postulated that one side might believe that it somehow possessed nuclear superiority—though now conceived of as a state of mind, not a battlefield reality. When both sides of a conflict possess a credible second-strike capability, nuclear superiority generally refers to the side which has managed to gain some sort of psychological advantage in a deterrence relationship. In these circumstances, nuclear superiority generally refers to the political ability and psychological will to threaten nuclear escalation in a conventional conflict or the opposing side's ability to deter such a threat.

—*Abe Denmark and James J. Wirtz*

See also: Cold War; Deterrence; Mutual Assured Destruction; Sufficiency

References

Blechman, Barry M., and Robert Powell, "What in the Name of God Is Strategic Superiority?" *Political Science Quarterly,* vol. 97, no. 4, Winter 1982–1983, pp. 589–602.

Jervis, Robert, "Why Nuclear Superiority Doesn't Matter," *Political Science Quarterly,* vol. 94, no. 4, Winter 1979–1980, pp. 617–633.

SURETY

According to the U.S. Department of Defense, nuclear weapons surety includes the materiel, personnel, and procedures that contribute to the security, safety, and reliability of nuclear weapons and to the assurance that there will be no nuclear weapon accidents, incidents, or unauthorized weapon detonations. It is a system based on design, storage, and operating safety to: (1) minimize the possibility of accidents, inadvertent acts, or unauthorized activity that could lead to fire or high-explosive detonation; (2) minimize the possibility that fire could lead to a high-explosive detonation; (3) ensure the security of nuclear weapons; and (4) reduce or delay the possibility that an unauthorized detonation of a nuclear weapon would occur if it fell into the wrong hands. Nuclear surety is a critical step in providing negative control over nuclear weapons (guaranteeing that they will only be used when directed by legitimate authority) and in making weapons "safe."

To meet these surety objectives the Department of Energy (DOE) develops safety and security standards for nuclear warheads. It develops safe high explosives (explosives that will not detonate if faced with a high kinetic impact or high temperatures) for use in nuclear weapons and designs ways to prevent the dispersal of nuclear materials from a weapon in likely abnormal environments. DOE also works to insure that nuclear weapons designs incorporate the latest safety features.

One measure of nuclear surety is reflected by the term "one-point safety." A weapon is considered one-point safe if the probably of achieving a nuclear yield greater than 4 pounds of TNT in the event of a one-point explosion of the weapon's high-explosive initiator is less than one in a million.

—James J. Wirtz

See also: One-Point Detonation/One-Point Safe; Two-Man Rule
Reference
Freedman, Lawrence, *The Evolution of Nuclear Strategy*, third edition (New York: Palgrave Macmillan, 2003).

SURPRISE ATTACK CONFERENCE

In February 1955, "Meeting the Threat of Surprise Attack," a top-secret report of President Dwight D. Eisenhower's Science Advisory Committee, concluded that with "no reliable U.S. early warning, our defense system is inadequate; therefore SAC [Strategic Air Command] is vulnerable and [the] U.S. is open to surprise attack." This and other reports that documented concerns about the development of Soviet intercontinental ballistic missiles led President Eisenhower in April 1958 to propose an international conference of technical experts to discuss measures that might prevent a surprise attack. The ten-nation Surprise Attack Conference was convened in Geneva in November 1958.

President Eisenhower's proposal followed a study prepared by a U.S. interagency working group that concluded that an effective safeguard to prevent surprise attacks would require an inspection system to monitor any agreed-upon limitations. At the conference, the Soviet Union resisted inspection of its military sites, and its delegation pushed for comprehensive disarmament as the best solution. The U.S. delegation tried to keep the focus on technical issues. Among its proposals was the development of specialized communications satellites for the enforcement of a possible treaty, deployment verification, and prevention of surprise attack. Another proposal, manned radar stations on the territories of the two countries to provide warning of a surprise attack, was rejected by the Soviets.

When the Surprise Attack Conference was suspended on January 21, 1959, the Western side was convinced that the Soviets would not agree to limit discussions to inspection and observation measures and that future negotiations would have to consider disarmament measures. Although the conference produced no agreement, it did address specific dangers arising from the arms race and encourage high-level dialogue between the United States and the Soviet Union.

—Patricia McFate

See also: First Strike; Reciprocal Fear of Surprise Attack
Reference
"National Security Policy: Arms Control and Disarmament. Foreign Relations of the United States, 1958–1960," vol. 3, available at http://www.fas.org/spp/starwars/offdocs/ike.

SURVEILLANCE

Although the term "surveillance" describes any type of human or technical monitoring of an area or person of interest, it most often refers to systems intended to provide early warning of an air or missile attack. Space surveillance is an important component of national and theater ballistic missile defense systems.

The central node of the North American surveillance system is the North American Aerospace Defense Command (NORAD) located in the Cheyenne Mountain Operations Center in Colorado Springs, Colorado. Staffed by both U.S. and Canadian personnel, NORAD monitors data generated by the U.S. Space Surveillance Network that is comprised of satellites in Earth orbit, conventional radars, phased-array radars, and the Ground-Based Electro-Optical Deep Space Surveillance system (GEODSS). GEODSS telescopes can also image satellites of interest.

The United States also has deployed a variety of ground-based radars to monitor airspace along the periphery of the country. PAVE PAWS, for instance, is a radar system located at Beale Air Force Base in California, and Cape Cod Air Force Station in Massachusetts. The system can rapidly discriminate among scores of incoming warheads and debris while calculating missile-launch points and warhead-impact points. PAVE PAWS relays this data directly to controllers at Cheyenne Mountain.

In the future, the United States will increasingly rely on two satellite systems to provide early warning of air and missile attack: Space-Based Infrared High and Space-Based Infrared Low Satellites. The "SBIRS" system can track a missile from its launch point as it flies through space. It also can track aircraft, replacing conventional ground-based radars and Airborne Warning and Control System (AWACS) aircraft (officially the E-3 Sentry).

The United States employs a number of additional aerial surveillance aircraft, including the U-2S, several variants of the RC-135, Rivet Joint, the E-8 Joint Surveillance, Tracking, and Reconnaissance System (JSTARS), the WC-130H Hercules, the MQ-9 Predator unmanned aerial vehicle (UAV), and the RQ-4 Global Hawk UAV.

—James J. Wirtz

See also: Cheyenne Mountain; Early Warning; Missile Defense; North American Aerospace Defense Command; Space-Based Infrared Radar System

References

Freedman, Lawrence, *The Evolution of Nuclear Strategy,* third edition (New York: Palgrave Macmillan, 2003).

Young, Susan H. H., "Gallery of USAF Weapons," *Air Force Magazine,* May 2003, pp. 160–184.

SURVIVABILITY

Survivability is the characteristic of nuclear weapons that shows the degree to which they are able to withstand a nuclear strike—either by being mobile and thus difficult to target or by being "hardened" against a nuclear attack. Survivable nuclear weapons and their associated delivery systems have a greater chance of emerging intact following a nuclear attack and can be used (or threatened to be used) in retaliation. The maintenance of this "secure second-strike capability" based on survivable nuclear forces is considered to be a key component of a credible nuclear deterrent.

During the Cold War, the United States and the Soviet Union tried to build survivable nuclear forces. Both states hardened their land-based intercontinental ballistic missile (ICBM) silos to increase the likelihood that they would survive an attack. Because fixed ICBM silos are impossible to move, once the opponent's ICBM accuracies improved, they became vulnerable to destruction. As the Cold War progressed, ICBM survivability increasingly came to rely on policymakers' willingness to adopt "launch-on-warning" or "launch-under-attack" strategies (*see* Launch on Warning/Launch under Attack). Bombers are more survivable than ICBMs because they can be placed on airborne alert in times of crisis and avoid a nuclear strike. The most survivable nuclear forces are on deployed submarines. Because submarines are difficult to locate—in the absence of some technological breakthrough in ocean surveillance or treachery—it would be difficult for a state to destroy an adversary's ballistic missile submarine force by targeting likely open ocean operating areas. Today, submarine-launched ballistic missiles remain the most survivable basing mode for a deterrent force.

Ensuring that some nuclear weapons would survive an attack is critical to deterrence and contributes to crisis stability by eliminating an opponent's incentive to be first to use nuclear weapons in a crisis.

—Andrea Gabbitas

See also: Ballistic Missiles; Crisis Stability; Deterrence; First Strike; Second Strike

References

Brodie, Bernard, *Strategy in the Missile Age* (Princeton, NJ: Princeton University Press, 1949).

Wohlstetter, Albert, "The Delicate Balance of Terror," *Foreign Affairs,* vol. 37, 1959, pp. 211–234.

TACTICAL NUCLEAR WEAPONS

Nonstrategic nuclear weapons have gone by various names. Primarily stationed in Europe, the Far East, and at sea, they have been known at different times as battlefield nuclear weapons, nonstrategic nuclear weapons (NSNW), theater nuclear weapons, theater nuclear forces (TNF), intermediate-range nuclear forces (INF), short-range nuclear forces (SNF), long-range theater nuclear forces (LRTNF), substrategic nuclear weapons, and tactical nuclear weapons (TNW). Tactical nuclear weapons were a central military and political concern during the Cold War.

It is difficult to define exactly what constitutes a nonstrategic nuclear weapon. Traditional attempts at delineating between types of nuclear weapons—range, delivery vehicle, explosive power, and the like—are overly simplistic and outmoded approaches that miss many of the nuances that surround the deployment and use of these weapons. Some definitions of tactical weapons list them as low-yield, short-range weapons for use on the battlefield rather than against countervalue targets such as cities. The best way to define them may be "by exclusion." That is, anything not captured by strategic arms control negotiations is, by default, nonstrategic. Another perspective holds that *any* nuclear weapon must be strategic, given its potential for physical devastation and political chaos. A third view suggests that only one's adversary can define whether a weapon is strategic or nonstrategic, based on its perceived use.

The key purpose of TNW, from a U.S. perspective, is to deter coercion and aggression against the United States and its allies. To do this, the United States built a massive arsenal during the Cold War, eventually numbering more than 20,000 tactical nuclear weapons in addition to some 15,000 strategic warheads. The Soviet Union had even more nonstrategic nuclear weapons in its arsenal.

The second cornerstone of U.S. TNW policy was to provide a nuclear presence in Europe to support the North Atlantic Treaty Organization (NATO) as the essential link between the European and North American allies. These weapons were part of NATO's "Triad": conventional forces, tactical nuclear weapons in theater, and U.S. and British strategic nuclear systems. NATO's strategic concept still calls for the continued presence of such weapons in Europe in order to maintain the transatlantic deterrent link to the United States and for purposes of creating political and military uncertainty in the mind of any potential opponent.

Their third purpose became evident in the 1990s: to deter the use of weapons of mass destruction (WMD) more broadly. During the Gulf War, and again in the first years of the twenty-first century, the U.S. government made it clear, for example, that any WMD use by an adversary would result in a "prompt, devastating retaliatory blow" in which no weapons would be ruled out. It was widely understood by both sides in the Gulf War that this meant nuclear weapons, although some U.S. officials denied they meant to threaten Iraq with nuclear retaliation.

Historically, nuclear arms control has focused on long-range strategic systems, but the Soviet Union always tried to include U.S. TNW in arms control talks. From the Soviet perspective, nuclear weapons stationed in Europe and aimed at Russian soil should not be considered "nonstrategic." The United States, by contrast, consistently rejected that position, and tactical nuclear forces were largely left off the negotiating table until the 1987 Intermediate-Range Nuclear Forces (INF) Treaty.

The United States is trying to decide what value such weapons provide to its own security and considering whether to keep or eliminate its small remaining stockpile. Although the United States has substantially reduced its reliance on these weapons since 1991, Russia appears to be adjusting its national security doctrine to place even greater emphasis on nuclear weapons—including smaller, "tactical" warheads. With thousands of these warheads and several delivery systems for them, Russia has a large asymmetrical advantage in numbers of TNW and has been unwilling to implement the 1991 Presidential Nuclear Initiatives (which eliminated most U.S. tactical nuclear weapons) or to discuss TNW in a separate, formal arms control forum. Yet the 1997 Helsinki Agreement indicated that Russia was willing to talk about TNW to the degree that it benefits them or is linked to broader strategic issues. Russia's huge arsenal of tactical nuclear weapons is particularly unsettling given worries about Russia's future and the possibility of the loss or sale of these weapons (see Presidential Nuclear Initiatives).

Presidential George H. W. Bush's nuclear initiatives in the fall of 1991 called for the withdrawal and eventual elimination of most U.S. TNW around the globe, including the cancellation of all related research and development programs. The Clinton administration furthered this decision by eliminating naval nuclear capabilities on surface ships entirely. America's remaining nonstrategic capabilities are now limited to gravity bombs delivered by tactical aircraft and nuclear Tomahawk Land-Attack Missiles (TLAM-Ns) delivered by submarine. The latter are not routinely deployed with the fleet. Precise numbers of warheads are classified, but the total U.S. force of bombs and TLAM-Ns has been drastically reduced since the Cold War. A significant proportion of these remaining weapons are still based in Europe, and several European states maintain nuclear delivery plans in their NATO war orders that would depend on U.S. warheads.

Key issues for the existing nonstrategic nuclear weapons force posture include deciding whether the United States should keep its current levels of TNW or to reduce the numbers further, determining the purposes for these remaining weapons, and deciding where to station them. The perceived battlefield use and utility of these weapons has dropped significantly since the end of the Cold War. Nevertheless, the U.S. government maintains the policy that it must be able to deliver on its threat to use nuclear weapons in dire circumstances. And there exist some military operations that can only be accomplished using the particular effects that nuclear weapons provide. For those reasons, the U.S. military maintains a small arsenal of tactical nuclear weapons and the plans for their use. The 2001 Nuclear Posture Review, in fact, called for continued research and development efforts on smaller, more usable nuclear weapons (see Nuclear Posture Review).

One of the biggest challenges to planners in today's increasingly complicated world is determining whether nuclear weapons are appropriate in response to enemy chemical or biological weapons use. The maintenance of a nuclear force projection capability also requires the platforms, support infrastructure, and trained and certified crews to be available or maintained at an appropriate level of readiness.

—Jeffrey A. Larsen

References
Alexander, Brian, and Alistair Millar, eds., Tactical Nuclear Weapons: Emergent Threats in an Evolving Security Environment (Dulles, VA: Brassey's, 2003).

Larsen, Jeffrey A., and Kurt J. Klingenberger, eds., Non-Strategic Nuclear Weapons: Obstacles and Opportunities (Colorado Springs: USAF Institute for National Security Studies, 2001).

Susiluoto, Taina, ed., Tactical Nuclear Weapons: Time for Control (New York: United Nations Institute for Disarmament Research, 2002).

TELEMETRY

While undergoing flight-testing, missiles, missile stages, and missile warheads send performance data to a ground station so that engineers can determine how well the components and systems are working. This information is called telemetry. Telemetry includes data on structural stress, thrust, fuel consumption, guidance-system performance, and the ambient environment. Intercepted and decrypted telemetry can provide information about a system's guidance system operation, fuel usage, staging, warhead characteristics, and other parameters vital for understanding the operational characteristics of a delivery system. This data, if intercepted by another country, can help the intelligence community determine the system performance, range, staging, warhead size, and capability of an adversary's missile. Telemetry thus allows engineers to establish the operational characteristics of a missile system.

Telemetry intelligence is collected by a variety of platforms: Aircraft, ships, ground stations, and satellites are all used. The ability to collect unencrypted telemetry data was a major verification tool for the United States in ensuring Soviet compliance with various arms control agreements. When the Soviet Union began to encrypt this telemetry data, especially on the SS-24 and SS-25 intercontinental ballistic missile (ICBM), the United States pushed for an annex to the treaties stating that telemetry must remain unencrypted. During the second round of Strategic Arms Limitation Talks (SALT II), encryption was viewed as a violation of SALT I and the 1974 Vladivostok Accord and became a major source of contention between the two superpowers.

During Senate hearings on SALT II, verification concerns, especially the issue of telemetry access, wrecked all hopes of ratification. The Jimmy Carter administration was forced to reveal that the loss of intelligence-gathering facilities in Iran had led to a loss of Soviet telemetry data. This issue, also referred to as "data denial," was one of four obstacles that held up the 1991 Strategic Arms Reduction Treaty (START I) during its final phases. Part of the problem stemmed from differences in U.S. and Soviet missile testing. The United States tests its ballistic missiles over open ocean, making its data more available to interception. Many Soviet tests took place wholly within its own territory, thus limiting U.S. access to that data.

START I bans data denial and includes obligations to broadcast such data and to exchange tapes of the data after flight tests. The provisions apparently met U.S. data requirements and facilitated monitoring various qualitative treaty limits. During the first year after START I entered into force, the parties demonstrated their telemetry tapes, as required by the treaty, and installed playback equipment on each other's territory. Although they regularly exchange tapes after conducting missile flight tests, both sides have raised questions about the completeness of the other's telemetry tapes.

—Gilles Van Nederveen

See also: Data Exchanges; Reconnaissance Satellite; Verification

References

Richelson, Jeffrey T., *The U.S. Intelligence Community* (Boulder: Westview, 1999), pp.182–187.

———, *The Wizards of Langley: Inside the CIA's Directorate of Science and Technology* (Boulder: Westview, 2001, pp. 86–89.

"SALT II," available at http://www.fas.org/nuke/control/salt2/intro.htm.

"START 1 Protocol Telemetric Information," Office of the Under Secretary of Defense for Acquisition, Technology, and Logistics, 31 July 1991, available at http://www.defenselink.mil/acq/acic/treaties/start1/protocols/telemetry.htm.

Thornton, Richard C., *The Carter Years: Toward a New Global Order* (New York: Paragon House, 1991).

TERMINAL PHASE

"Terminal phase" generally refers to the final segment of a ballistic missile's flight path, in which the missile and its warheads travel toward the earth at very high speeds to their targets.

Modern intercontinental ballistic missiles (ICBMs) reach speeds of well over 2,000 miles per hour as they reenter the atmosphere. Because of the high speeds involved in reentry, the terminal phase of an ICBM usually lasts less than a minute. For this portion of the missile's trajectory, the warhead is protected by a cone-shaped reentry vehicle.

High reentry speeds pose significant challenges to engineers attempting to develop terminal-phase ballistic missile defenses (BMDs). Modern efforts rely on hit-to-kill interceptors (also known as kinetic-kill interceptors). Although decoys are stripped away by the atmosphere in the terminal phase of reentry, simplifying the problem faced by defensive systems, terminal-phase defenses destroy warheads over friendly territory, posing chemical, radiological, or biological hazards.

—Abe Denmark

See also: Decoys; Missile Defense; Reentry Vehicles

Reference

Missile Defense Agency, *Ballistic Missile Defense Basics*, available at http://www.acq.osd.mil/bmdo/bmdolink/html/basics.htm.

THEATER HIGH ALTITUDE AIR DEFENSE (THAAD)

Theater High Altitude Air Defense (THAAD) is a missile defense program of the U.S. Army, under way since 1992, to defend against attack by short- or medium-range ballistic missiles at significant distances from the defended area. A THAAD battery will consist of nine truck-mounted launch vehicles, each carrying eight missiles, two mobile tactical operations centers, and an X-band ground-based radar for surveillance and tracking of target missiles.

THAAD will be rapidly deployable: All elements are transportable by cargo aircraft and can be driven to appropriate locations within a combat theater.

THAAD is the only missile defense system designed to destroy ballistic missiles either inside or above the atmosphere. Exoatmospheric intercept reduces the risk that debris from the missile or its chemical, biological, or nuclear warhead will cause damage at ground level. Combining endoatmospheric and exoatmospheric intercept capability makes development of enemy countermeasures more difficult. THAAD was designed to protect deployed military forces, but it can also protect population centers as part of a layered ballistic missile defense system.

THAAD flight testing occurred at the White Sands Missile Range, New Mexico, from 1995 to 1999. Following several test failures resulting mainly from production defects, THAAD achieved two consecutive target intercepts in tests in 1999. Using the results from these risk-reduction tests at White Sands, engineers will produce an operational design that is expected to be flight tested in 2004 and to enter production in 2007.

Successful development of THAAD components has led to scaled-up designs for national missile defense, and THAAD now serves as the ground-based mid-course interceptor of the U.S. ballistic missile defense system.

—*Roy Pettis*

See also: Ballistic Missile Defense Organization; Missile Defense; Theater Missile Defense

References

Handberg, Roger, *Ballistic Missile Defense and the Future of American Security: Agendas, Perceptions, Technology, and Policy* (Boulder: Praeger, 2001).

Missile Defense Agency website, http://www.acq.osd.mil/bmdo/bmdolink/html/thaad.html.

U.S. Army website, http://www.army-technology.com/projects/thaad/.

THEATER MISSILE DEFENSE

Theater missile defense (TMD) is a system of surveillance, communication, and weaponry designed to protect limited geographical regions outside of the United States. The overall mission of TMD, as defined in the U.S. Department of Defense TMD Mission Need Statement (MNS), is "to protect U.S. forces, U.S. allies, and other important countries, including areas of vital interest to the U.S., from theater missile attacks." Theater missiles include ballistic missiles, cruise missiles, and air-to-surface guided missiles assigned to targets within a theater or capable of attacking such targets.

The need for TMD is created by the continuing proliferation of ballistic and cruise missiles. Potential U.S. adversaries possess hundreds of missile launchers and thousands of missiles. Contributing to the complexity of this menace is the wide variety of available warheads that can carry high explosives, chemical agents, biological agents, or fissile materials.

Because no single system can protect an area from all theater missile threats, the MNS concluded that TMD must act as a fully integrated system. With this in mind, it identified four pillars of TMD: passive defense (PD); battle management/command, control, communications, computers, and intelligence (BM/C4I); attack operations (AO); and active defense (AD).

Passive defenses bring together capabilities designed to improve the inherent survivability of friendly forces and assets. This includes developing and deploying early warning systems to detect impending attack, hardening friendly forces against missile attack, dispersing forces to limit the effectiveness of an attack, concealing assets from overhead or ground surveillance, and quickly reconstituting operational effectiveness following an attack.

Battle management/command, control, communications, computers, and intelligence is central to ensuring an effective TMD. It involves developing communication systems and procedures to link early-warning and missile-tracking data to commanders and missile defense systems so that commanders can make the decision to engage incoming warheads. The air force has been designated by the Department of Defense as the executive agent for theater air defense BM/C4I. As the executive agent, it is responsible for constructing a theater air defense BM/C4I architecture that will provide U.S. combat commanders with a flexible system designed to integrate the required joint forces with combat theater missile threats. Currently, the air force is responsible for space-based theater ballistic missile (TBM) launch detection and warning. Space-based ballistic missile launch detection is accomplished by Defense Support Program satellites. The data are sent to data-processing centers that forward the information in real time to the responsible commands and operational units.

Attack operations are primarily counterforce undertakings that focus on the destruction of the enemy's capability to launch missiles. For TMD, counterforce options have three windows of opportunity. The first is the infrastructure in which the missiles, warheads, and launchers are designed, produced, and stored. An attack against this target can have a significant, albeit delayed, effect on the opponent's capabilities. The second is the forward support logistics infrastructure where the enemy moves its theater missile systems prior to hostilities. This also can be a lucrative target that is relatively easy to detect, given the large signature it generates when supporting forces in crisis or wartime. Last is the launch phase, when the missile, warhead, and launcher are moved to the firing point and launched. This is probably the most difficult part of the counterforce mission because of its urgency and the difficulty involved in detecting individual delivery systems once they are deployed to operational units (see Counterforce Targeting).

Active defenses focus on intercepting incoming theater missiles in flight and destroying them. The United States is planning a highly diversified system of defenses that can destroy missiles and warheads in various stages of flight. Multiple systems have been under consideration for this mission for years. Various concepts have undergone continuous development and refinement, and testing has eliminated some and validated others. Officials envision a number of active defense programs to provide a layered defense of the U.S. homeland, deployed forces, and allied states.

The Patriot Advanced Capability 3 (PAC-3) system will defend troops and fixed targets from cruise missiles and aircraft as well as from short- and medium-range ballistic missiles. The PAC-3 is a terminal defense system that provides concentrated defense against "point" targets. It offers low-tier, ground-based protection by employing mobile radar, C4I, and missile batteries. Each PAC-3 battery is a mobile launching station that can carry sixteen missiles. Patriots were first used in the 1991 Gulf War, and PAC-3 was combat-tested in Operation Iraqi Freedom in 2003.

The Theater High Altitude Area Defense (THAAD) system is an upper-tier, ground-based system that will defend large areas against longer-range theater missiles at higher altitudes, both inside and outside the atmosphere. It comprises a mobile launcher carrying four missiles, a ground-based radar, and a BM/C4I system. THAAD will be able to engage almost all theater ballistic missiles. Its ability to intercept targets at long range means that, under most conditions, it will be able to fire an interceptor at an incoming missile, assess the success of that engagement, and, if necessary, fire a second missile.

The U.S. Navy will provide TMD capabilities to areas that are not easily or quickly accessible by land. It has deployed its Aegis air defense system for fleet protection since the 1970s and plans to upgrade those capabilities to counter ballistic missiles, as well. The navy has been able to achieve upper-tier defense capabilities with the Aegis ballistic missile defense (BMD) system (called the navy theater-wide system during the Bill Clinton administration), which is an upgraded version of the Aegis radar and Standard missile defense systems. BMD builds upon modifications to the existing Aegis ships and the Standard air defense missile. This system will use Standard missiles, modified for intercepts outside the atmosphere, working in tandem with the Aegis combat system. Plans to create a navy area defense (NAD) system to provide a defensive capability against short- and medium-range theater ballistic missiles in the atmosphere during their terminal phase were canceled early in the George W. Bush administration.

In addition to these programs, the U.S. military is designing a wide variety of other systems that will better defend against hostile missiles. The Medium-Range Extended Air Defense System (MEADS) is an upgrade of the PAC-3 system that will provide improved protection against short-range ballistic missiles as well as against aircraft and cruise missiles. MEADS is a joint venture between the United States, Germany, and Italy. Additionally, the United States is developing an Airborne Laser aboard a modified Boeing 747 that is designed to destroy enemy ballistic missiles during the boost phase. Plans for a space-based laser have been scaled back to a general research program.

—Abe Denmark

See also: Ballistic Missile Defense Organization; Missile Defense; Theater High Altitude Air Defense; United States Navy

References

Ballistic Missile Defense Organization, Report to the Congress on Ballistic Missile Defense, July 1994, available at http://www.acq.osd.mil/bmdo/bmdolink/pdf/rtc1994.pdf.

Boese, Wade, "Missile Defense Post-ABM Treaty: No System, No Arms Race," and "U.S. Missile Defense Programs at a Glance," *Arms Control Today,* vol. 33, no. 5, June 2003, pp. 20–28.

"Mission Need Statement (MNS) for Theater Missile Defense," 12 June 1992, available at http://www.fas.org/spp/starwars/docops/mns92163db.htm.

Rios, Marc Raymond, *Optimizing AEGIS Ship Stationing for Active Theater Missile Defense* (Monterey, CA: Naval Postgraduate School, September 1993).

Snodgrass, David E., *Attacking the Theater Mobile Ballistic Missile Threat* (Maxwell AFB, AL: School of Advanced Airpower Studies, Air University, June 1993).

THERMONUCLEAR BOMB

A thermonuclear bomb (also known as a fusion, hydrogen, or H-bomb) is a weapon that derives the majority of its explosive power from thermonuclear fusion. The earliest thermonuclear weapons were derived from pure fission, but modern weaponry derives its power from both fusion and fission reactions. All fusion weapons must have a fission explosion to make them work. There are three general types of fusion weaponry: boosted fission, staged radiation implosion, and "Sloika" weapons.

The earliest thermonuclear weapons were boosted fission weapons. By using a small amount of deuterium-tritium gas within the fissionable core, it was possible to significantly increase the yield of an atomic weapon (*see* Deuterium; Tritium). When deuterium-tritium becomes hot enough from the fission explosion, it produces a fusion reaction that nearly doubles the yield, even though only about 1 percent of the yield is from fusion. Although this method is effective, it is expensive. Tritium also has a high decay rate (nearly 6 percent a year); therefore, weapons that incorporate tritium require frequent replenishment to replace the tritium that has decayed.

The staged radiation implosion weapon (also known as a Teller-Ulam weapon, named after designers Edward Teller and Stanislaw Ulam) was first designed in the 1950s. This class of nuclear weapon reduces the weight of the bomb by reducing the amount of uranium and plutonium needed to produce a given yield. The weapons are set up in a three-stage fission-fusion-fission design. The primary charge of fissionable material is detonated, setting off a physically separated package of fusion fuel (stage two). X-rays from the primary explosion compress the fuel through a process known as "radiation implosion." The force from the fusion second stage is then used to detonate an even larger third stage of material. Theoretically, with staged weapons an almost unlimited yield is possible. The Soviet Union's Tsar Bomba test of 1961 was a fission-fusion-fission design and produced a yield of somewhere between 50 and 100 megatons.

The "Sloika" design is named after a Russian pastry. The concept actually predates the staged radiation implosion designs. The design uses a series of concentric shells, each encased around the one before it. The center contains a fission primary of Uranium 235 or Plutonium 239 with an optional layer of Uranium 238. Surrounding the core is a lithium-6 deuteride-tritide cover that in turn is encased by a high-explosive shell. The Sloika can produce a tenfold boost in yield. U.S. designers never pursued this design beyond the concept phase because they felt that it was not destructive enough for the amount of fuel needed.

—*Zach Becker*

See also: Fission Weapons; Fusion; Hydrogen Bomb; Manhattan Project; Nuclear Weapons Effects; Pit; Primary Stage

References

Newhouse, John, *War and Peace in the Nuclear Age* (New York: Knopf, 1989).

Pringle, Laurence, *Nuclear War: From Hiroshima to Nuclear Winter* (Hillside, NJ: Enslow, 1985).

Rhodes, Richard, *Dark Sun: The Making of the H-Bomb* (New York: Simon and Schuster, 1995).

THREE MILE ISLAND

Three Mile Island is a nuclear generating plant that takes its name from an island on the Susquehanna River near the Pennsylvania capital of Harrisburg, where the plant is located. It generated electricity for the Metropolitan Edison Company. On March 28, 1979, it suffered a partial meltdown accident that, though not life threatening, created a public relations nightmare and set back growth in the nuclear power industry in the United States.

Three Mile Island consisted of two units (power-generating reactors). Unit 1 was undergoing its annual shutdown for inspection and refueling at the time of the accident. Unit 2 was a new reactor built in 1978 and designed by the Babcock and Wilcox Company. It used pressurized water to cool and convey heat from the atomic core to the steam tur-

The four cooling towers at the Three Mile Island nuclear plant were shut down after a leak developed in the cooling system, March 28, 1979. (Bettmann/Corbis)

bines. The accident began in Unit 2 during a routine maintenance operation, when air introduced into the cooling system caused a shutdown of the cooling-water intakes.

The emergency shutoffs and pressure relief valves operated properly, and dampening rods fell into the core to end most of the nuclear reaction. Because of an earlier maintenance error, however, the valves to the emergency pumps to cool the turbine had been left closed, so barely enough water was available to keep the core covered and cool. Problems began to cascade as operators failed to interpret warning indicators correctly, leading to a situation in which the twenty-story containment building eventually stood as the last line of defense against a catastrophic radiation release. Engineers misjudged that the leaking water was turbine coolant when in fact it was reactor coolant and radioactive. The leak uncovered nuclear fuel, contaminating the coolant water and ultimately the containment building. The reactor heat rose, destroying the cooling rods and resulting in a melted mass of dangerous radioactive fuel. The hydrogen and oxygen present in the reactor created a bubble that

could have led to an explosion. By April 4, scientists and engineers realized that the amounts of these materials had been miscalculated, and by that evening the plant was back under control. The containment building held, and the core did not melt down.

Officials failed to keep the public well informed about the nature of the accident. When the seriousness of the accident was recognized, mildly radioactive waste coolant water was emptied into the Susquehanna River. Scientists publicly disagreed with each other about the accident and its implications. Based on confusing information from "experts," 14,000 local residents self-evacuated. The governor advised all pregnant women and preschool children within 5 miles of the plant to evacuate and others to seek local shelter. A rumor spread of the likelihood of an explosion based on the presence of a hydrogen bubble inside the reactor. President Jimmy Carter, a former naval officer with nuclear experience, visited the plant, and scientists realized that the danger had been overestimated.

Unit 2 of Three Mile Island was closed permanently following the accident. This near disaster caused a hiatus in nuclear reactor construction in the United States that has lasted into the beginning of the twenty-first century.

—*Frannie Edwards*

References

Burner, David, et al., *An American Portrait* (New York: Charles Scribner's Sons, 1985).

Wilson, R. Jackson, James Gilbert, Karen Ordahl Kupperman, Stephen Nissenbaum, and David M. Scott, *The Pursuit of Liberty* (New York: Knopf, 1984).

THREE-PLUS-THREE PROGRAM

The three-plus-three program was a missile defense program announced by the William Clinton administration in 1996. It called for creating the infrastructure to develop a national missile defense (NMD) system in three years, with a capability to deploy the system three years after a development decision had been made. The 1996 timeline called for a presidential decision in 2000 on whether to begin deployment. The goal of NMD was to protect the United States against a limited "rogue" nation's ballistic missile attack and accidental or unauthorized ballistic missile launches from other nuclear-capable states. As part of this program, the Clinton administration supported research and development of a variety of land-, air-, and sea-based missile defense systems without making a commitment to any specific missile defense architecture.

The Clinton administration proposed four criteria to use in making a deployment decision: the technological feasibility of NMD, the cost, the impact of a deployment decision on U.S. diplomatic relationships, and the extent of the ballistic missile threat to the United States. In September 2000, President Clinton announced that he was deferring a decision on NMD deployment so that the next administration could take a fresh look at the issue. It was assumed that such a presidential decision would delay deployment of an NMD system until 2004 at the earliest.

Research and development for the three-plus-three program remained compliant with the Anti-Ballistic Missile (ABM) Treaty. It was understood that a deployed NMD system would require amendments to the treaty, but an attempt was made to keep the number of sites and interceptors consistent with treaty obligations. Russia resisted any change to the treaty, maintaining that defense of national territory would undermine strategic stability. The George W. Bush administration's missile defense system incorporates components developed by the Clinton administration under its three-plus-three program.

—*Steven Rosenkrantz*

See also: Anti-Ballistic Missile Treaty; Missile Defense

References

Graham, Bradley, *Hit to Kill: The New Battle over Shielding America from Missile Attack* (New York: PublicAffairs, 2001).

"National Missile Defense: An Overview of Alternative Plans," *Arms Control Today,* vol. 28, no. 1, January/February 1998, p. 38.

Wirtz, James J., and Jeffrey A. Larsen, eds., *Rockets' Red Glare: Missile Defenses and the Future of World Politics* (Boulder: Westview, 2001).

THRESHOLD STATES

At the center of the nuclear nonproliferation regime stands the Nuclear Nonproliferation Treaty (NPT), essentially a bargain between the nuclear powers and the nonnuclear states to halt the proliferation of nuclear weapons. Proliferation can occur both horizontally (the acquisition of nuclear arms by nonnuclear parties) and vertically (the further development, production, and deployment of nuclear weapons by the nuclear parties). The NPT seeks to prevent both types of proliferation. Signed in July 1968, it now has every major country as a member state except for India, Israel, Pakistan, and North Korea (the latter withdrew in 2003). Under the NPT, the non–nuclear weapons states agreed not to acquire nuclear weapons and to accept a system of safeguards over their peaceful nuclear activities in exchange for nuclear material, equipment, and technology for peaceful purposes to be supplied by the nuclear parties (especially the United States and the Soviet Union).

Under this unique arrangement, the nonnuclear states are permitted to use nuclear energy for scientific and commercial uses. Weapons production, however, is a flagrant violation of the NPT. Several states have secretly developed nuclear technology for possible weapons production while staying well short of the "threshold" of weapons assembly and testing. There have been three distinct generations of threshold states since the dawn of the nuclear era.

During the first phase, which spanned from 1945 until 1968, when the NPT was signed, Western industrial countries such as Sweden, Italy, and Australia took decisive steps toward developing nuclear weapons but never crossed the threshold of nuclear bomb production. Ultimately, they abandoned their nuclear aspirations. In contrast, after the United States and the Soviet Union produced nuclear weapons, the United Kingdom, France, and China blew past the nuclear threshold and built the bomb. As a result, these five are the only nuclear weapons states recognized by the NPT.

The second generation of nuclear threshold states moved toward nuclear weapons acquisition after the NPT was signed and before the Cold War ended. The most prominent threshold states that started nuclear arms programs but stopped short of the brink of bomb production were Argentina, Brazil, Taiwan, and South Korea. A combination of U.S. security assurances and multilateral nonproliferation diplomacy succeeded in reversing nuclear proliferation in these cases. In contrast, India, Pakistan, Israel, and South Africa had manufactured nuclear weapons by the end of the Cold War (see Indian Nuclear Weapons Program; Israeli Nuclear Weapons Capabilities and Doctrine; Pakistani Nuclear Forces; South African Nuclear Weapons Program; South Korean Nuclear Weapons Program).

Today, nonproliferation policymakers are grappling with a third generation of threshold states: Iraq, Iran, and North Korea. The 2003 U.S.-led war against Saddam Hussein's regime in Iraq removed that country from the problem list, but Tehran and Pyongyang remain poised on the threshold of nuclear weapons production—indeed, the latter might already have fabricated two or more nuclear weapons (see Iranian Nuclear Weapons Program; Iraqi Nuclear Forces and Doctrine; North Korean Nuclear Weapons Program).

It is difficult to predict which countries will make up the next generation of nuclear threshold states. Future developments will depend largely on the conduct of the existing nuclear weapons states and on how the international community deals with the existing threshold states.

—Peter Lavoy

See also: Non-Nuclear Weapons States; Nuclear Nonproliferation Treaty

References

Campbell, Kurt M., Robert J. Einhorn, and Mitchell B. Reiss, eds., *The Nuclear Tipping Point: Why States Reconsider Their Nuclear Choices* (Washington, DC: Brookings Institution, 2004).
Reiss, Mitchell, *Bridled Ambition: Why Countries Constrain Their Nuclear Capabilities* (Washington, DC: Woodrow Wilson Center Press, 1995).
Walsh, Jim, "Surprise Down Under: The Secret History of Australia's Nuclear Ambitions," *Nonproliferation Review*, Fall 1997, pp. 1–20.

THRESHOLD TEST BAN TREATY (TTBT)

Following ratification in 1963 of the Limited Test Ban Treaty (LTBT), which prohibited the testing of nuclear weapons in outer space, under water, and above the ground, the United States and the Soviet Union were limited to conducting their nuclear weapons tests underground. The LTBT, however, did not limit the size of these underground tests. In 1974, in the Threshold Test Ban Treaty (TTBT), the United States and the Soviet Union agreed to limit the yield of underground nuclear tests to no more than 150 kilotons. Although both sides noted that verification would be technically difficult because on-site verification was not permitted, the 150-kiloton limit was seen as one way to constrain the ability of both sides to field new nuclear weapons designs.

As a result of the verification problems, the TTBT was never ratified, even though both parties declared their intention to abide by the 150-kiloton limit. From 1976 to 1990, the United States continually accused the former Soviet Union of conducting nuclear weapons tests that violated the limit.

Following six rounds of Nuclear Testing Experts Meetings, the United States and the Soviet Union opened the Nuclear Testing Talks in 1987 with the goal of negotiating a new verification protocol to the TTBT. The parties reached agreement in May 1990 after conducting several rounds of negotiations and a joint verification experiment. The new verification provisions allow for on-site inspection of test areas, in-country seismic monitoring of tests, and placement of yield estimate instrumentation in the test area. The amended TTBT is automatically renewed at five-year intervals unless either party notifies the other of its intention to terminate its participation. No issues have arisen with this treaty, especially since 1992, when each party announced a self-imposed moratorium on nuclear testing.

—Guy Roberts

See also: Arms Control; Limited Test Ban Treaty; Nuclear Test Ban; Peaceful Nuclear Explosions Treaty; Underground Testing

References

U.S. Department of Defense, Office of the Under Secretary of Defense for Acquisition, Technology, and Logistics, "Arms Control Implementation and Compliance: Threshold Test Ban Treaty (TTBT): Executive Summary," available at http://www.defenselink.mil/acq/acic/treaties/ttbt/execsum.htm.

"Weapons of Mass Destruction," available at http://www.fas.org/nuke/control/ttbt/.

TINIAN

Tinian is one of the Mariana Islands in the Philippine Sea near Guam and Saipan. It was occupied by the Japanese during World War II and taken by the Americans in the summer of 1944. It is best known as the departure point for the planes that dropped the atomic bombs on Hiroshima and Nagasaki in August 1945.

Occupying just 50 square miles, the low, flat island is about 12 miles long north to south and is located two and a half miles south of Saipan. During World War II, it was covered with sugarcane.

The island was taken in an amphibious assault by the United States against well-entrenched Japanese defenders in a battle that took place from July 24 until August 1, 1944. Casualties included 6,050 Japanese who died defending the island and 290 U.S. Marines who died in the conquest. Afterward, Tinian became an important airfield for the planned attacks on the Japanese home islands. Its flat terrain offered space for six 8,500-foot runways to accommodate the B-29s needed for the planned bombing of Hiroshima and Nagasaki.

By the summer of 1945, one year after its conquest, Tinian had been developed as an air base. A squadron of advanced long-range B-29 bombers was moved to Tinian and conducted practice runs to Japan, dropping orange "pumpkin bombs" to simulate the atomic weapons they would ultimately carry. Both the *Enola Gay,* carrying the bomb named "Little Boy" to Hiroshima on August 6, 1945, and the *Bockscar,* carrying "Fat Man" to Nagasaki on August 9, 1945, were launched from Tinian.

Following World War II, the Mariana Islands became U.S. trust territories. Tinian is occupied by its original inhabitants.

—Frannie Edwards

Reference

Bauer, E., *The History of World War II* (New York: Military Press, 1984).

TITAN ICBMS

The Titan series of intercontinental ballistic missiles (ICBMs) was developed in 1955 as a redundant system to the Atlas ICBM. The two series were developed and deployed simultaneously. The Titan I, a two-stage missile with liquid propellant made of kerosene and liquid oxygen, was deployed in 1962. It was armed with either the W-38 or the W-49 warhead, both of which had yields of approximately 4 megatons. Although the Titans were the first ICBMs to be placed in underground hardened shelters, they had to be lifted to the surface by elevator prior to launch. In all, fifty-four were deployed throughout the western United States. They were decommissioned in 1965.

The Titan II ICBM, which came into service in 1963, was the largest missile ever fielded by the U.S. Air Force. Longer and heavier than its predecessor, it boasted an improved engine, different fuel (50 percent hydrazine and 50 percent dimethylhydrazine), and a larger warhead (the W-53, with a 9-megaton yield—the most powerful nuclear weapon ever produced by the United States). Unlike the Titan I, the Titan II did not need to be lifted to the surface to fire but could be launched from the safety of its silo. The Titan II remained in service until 1987, when it was finally retired from the active force.

Perhaps the Titan's greatest achievement was its role in space flight. The Titan was the rocket used for the Gemini series of manned space flights and is still used today to launch weather and communication satellites.

—Zach Becker

See also: Ballistic Missiles; Intercontinental Ballistic Missiles; Silo Bains; United States Nuclear Forces and Doctrine

References

Miller, David, ed., *The Illustrated Directory of Modern American Weapons* (St. Paul, MN: MBI, 2002).

Stumpf, David K. *Titan II: A History of a Cold War Missile Program* (Fayetteville: University of Arkansas Press, 2000).

Walnut, Mark, *An Illustrated Guide of Strategic Weapons* (New York: Prentice-Hall, 1988).

Womack, John H., *Titan Tales: Diary of a Titan II Missile Crew Commander* (New York: Soliloquy, 1997).

TOUS ASIMUTS

French for "every point on the compass," *tous asimut* referred to France's nuclear strategy to deter danger from all directions. During the 1960s, French nuclea doctrine and its *Force de Frappe* ("Strike Force") were intended to increase French independence from a U.S.-dominated North Atlantic Treaty Organization (NATO). French officials also believed that reliance on U.S. nuclear extended deterrent guarantees was unreliable and potentially dangerous, especially in light of U.S. involvement in Vietnam. French president Charles de Gaulle believed that France's nuclear weapons gave it the stature of a great power, and he attempted to use this status to influence NATO policy and political events in Europe.

The nuclear doctrine that flowed from these strategic objects was called "tous asimuts." French nuclear weapons would not be directed solely against the Soviet Union, or against the threat of a Warsaw Pact conventional attack across the inner-German border, but in all directions, against all potential threats. French strategists argued that given the increasingly chaotic international situation in the 1960s, it was important that France maintain an independent nuclear force so that France could be a sanctuary in the event it decided not to participate in a future European conflict.

Tous asimuts created a major challenge to NATO's policy of extended deterrence. France lacked the delivery systems with the range necessary to undertake its new doctrine. French leaders hoped the policy would help to break up the bipolar nature of the Cold War standoff in Europe, but French nuclear doctrine did little to change the fundamental balance of terror that dominated European politics and military strategy during the second half of the twentieth century.

—*James J. Wirtz*

See also: Cold War; Extended Deterrence; French Nuclear Forces and Doctrine; North Atlantic Treaty Organization

References

Yost, David, *France's Deterrent Posture and Security in Europe* (London: International Institute for Strategic Studies, 1984).

TRANSPORTER-ERECTOR-LAUNCHER

A transporter-erector-launcher (TEL) is a self-propelled vehicle that transports and erects a missile to the vertical position in order to launch it. In the 1950s and 1960s, intercontinental ballistic missiles (ICBMs) were too heavy and too susceptible to vibration damage while being moved on a transporter. Development of a mobile ICBM was thus a high priority for both the United States and the

U.S.S.R. The Soviet Union had a string of failures with its SS-14 intermediate-range ballistic missile (IRBM) and its SS-15 ICBM, which were mounted on a tracked tank chassis. These two systems were never widely deployed because the tracked TELs could barely carry the weight of the massive ICBMs. Only with the development of the SS-16 ICBM and the SS-20 IRBM did the Soviets achieve their goal of a wheeled TEL.

The TEL carries not only a missile that is environmentally protected, but also electronics to monitor the missile, alignment equipment, and communications links to receive orders from headquarters. To increase the pre-launch survivability of the missile, the TEL must be able to traverse a variety of terrain types and move quickly over a large distance, especially to disperse to operating areas when placed on alert or during a crisis.

Russia currently uses a slightly larger TEL for its SS-25 and SS-27 ICBM force. Other nations have developed but not deployed mobile ICBM TELs. The United States developed a complex vehicle for the single-warhead Midgetman ICBM that could withstand a nuclear blast by hugging the ground. The MX missile also could have been TEL mounted, but it was never deployed in this configuration. Other short-range missile systems, most notably the Scud missile, often are mounted on trucks or simple tracked vehicles.

—*Gilles Van Nederveen*

See also: Ballistic Missiles; Mobile ICBMs

Reference

Podvig, Pavel, ed., *Russian Strategic Nuclear Forces* (Cambridge, MA: MIT Press, 2001).

TRIAD

Developed in the early 1960s, the term "Triad" referred to the maintenance of three types of nuclear delivery systems in the United States: intercontinental ballistic missiles (ICBMs), submarine-launched ballistic missiles (SLBMs), and long-range bombers. Each leg of the Triad was supposed to be capable of surviving a Soviet first strike and inflicting a retaliatory strike called for by U.S. nuclear war plans. The concept has been redefined in the 2002 Nuclear Posture Review. The "new Triad" consists of offensive nuclear forces and long-range conventional precision-strike systems (which encompasses the "old" Triad), missile defenses, and a defense infrastructure capable of supporting a nuclear arsenal for the indefinite future. The new

Triad concept acknowledges that deterrence might fail in a global environment where terrorists or rogue states are hell-bent on aggression and that maintenance of an assured second-strike capability is not a critical factor in deterring war. It supports a capability to conduct preventive or preemptive strikes against acute threats. Implicit in the concept is an enhanced strategic command and control system and a shift away from threat-based, deliberate planning toward a capabilities-based, adaptive planning approach to meet strategic threats (see Preemptive Attack; Preventive War).

During the 1950s, American strategic doctrine assumed that U.S. nuclear threats were highly credible. Several academic strategists, such as Albert Wohlstetter at the RAND Corporation, however, believed that the so-called balance of terror was fragile because it rested not on a U.S. first strike but on the ability to launch a second strike after absorbing a Soviet nuclear attack. Concerns were raised about a potential "nuclear Pearl Harbor"—a disarming surprise first strike by Soviet forces that would destroy the United States but leave Russia intact. Wohlstetter and his contemporaries began suggesting that it was not the overall size of the U.S. nuclear arsenal that was important, but the forces that would survive a Soviet first strike.

To achieve this secure second-strike capability, and to ensure that it would be available under all circumstances, planners and analysts quickly recognized the benefits provided by a nuclear Triad. Each leg of the Triad would be able to inflict "assured destruction" of the Soviet Union in a second strike, which was defined by Secretary of Defense Robert McNamara as a strike that killed 30 percent of the Soviet population and destroyed 70 percent of its industry. Deploying the U.S. nuclear arsenal would complicate Soviet attack options and prevent the loss of the entire deterrent force due to a Soviet defensive breakthrough, a security compromise, or a catastrophic failure across an entire type of weapons system. The assured destruction criteria articulated by McNamara also allowed him to cap the size of the U.S. strategic Triad; meeting second-strike assured destruction criteria helped to answer "how much was enough" to deter Soviet aggression (see Assured Destruction).

During the mid-1970s, concerns began to emerge about the survivability of the land-based leg of the Triad as Soviet ballistic missile accuracy im-

proved. Several strategists suggested that Soviet land-based missiles could in theory destroy U.S. land-based ICBMs and bombers, leaving only the submarine force to provide a secure second-strike capability. Given the limited accuracy of submarine-launched ballistic missiles, the United States would be presented with the choice of attacking Soviet cities, knowing the Soviets would respond in kind, or accepting defeat. Concerns about this "window of vulnerability" led to an increase in flexible counterforce targeting packages contained within the Single Integrated Operational Plan (SIOP, the nuclear war plan). The Trident D5 SLBM, the MX ICBM, which was to be deployed in rail-garrison, and the B-1B and B-2A strategic bombers were designed and built during the 1980s to improve both the survivability and second-strike counterforce capability of the U.S. strategic arsenal (see Counterforce Targeting).

Only the United States and Russia have maintained a traditional Triad of nuclear delivery systems. France has decommissioned its land-based ballistic missiles, and the People's Republic of China lacks a long-range bomber force and has barely managed to field one submarine capable of carrying nuclear-armed ballistic missiles.

—Andrew M. Dorman and James J. Wirtz

See also: Balance of Terror; Deterrence; Nuclear Posture Review; United States Nuclear Forces and Doctrine

References

"Nuclear Posture Review Report," 2001, available at http://www.defenselink.mil.

Sheehan, Michael, The Arms Race (Oxford, UK: Martin Robertson, 1983).

TRIDENT SLBMS/SSBNS

The U.S. Trident nuclear-powered submarine and its associated submarine-launched ballistic missiles (SLBMs) are the mainstay of the U.S. naval nuclear deterrent. In the 1970s, U.S. planners recognized that the SLBM system was the most survivable element in the "Triad" of strategic nuclear deterrent forces (land-based missiles and strategic bombers being the other two). Although the Poseidon ballistic missile was an improvement over the earlier Polaris SLBM, the nuclear-powered U.S. fleet ballistic submarine force itself was aging and would soon require a new submarine, particularly in view of an increased threat posed by Soviet antisubmarine warfare capabilities. Development began in 1971 for a new missile that was initially called the Trident C4 (later to become Trident I when Trident II was developed). (*See* Poseidon SLBMs/SSBNs; Submarines, Nuclear-Powered Ballistic Missile; United States Navy.)

Because they incorporated advanced technology in propellants, electronics, and other materials, the Trident C4 missiles had a much greater range than Poseidon, carrying a full payload to a range of 4,000 nautical miles and a reduced payload to even greater ranges. Like Poseidon, each Trident C4 missile was equipped with multiple independently targetable reentry vehicles (MIRVs), which gave it an ability to strike several targets simultaneously.

The Trident I missile was a three-stage, solid-propellant, inertially guided, submarine-launched fleet ballistic missile (FBM). It had a range a payload greater than the Poseidon missile and about double the range of the Poseidon C3, thus providing a significant increase in the operational area of the U.S. submarine fleet. The C4 was subsequently deployed in the new Trident submarine in addition to being backfitted into Poseidon submarines. The first tactical patrol in a backfitted Poseidon submarine took place in October 1979, and the first Trident submarine deployed in September 1982 from Bangor, Washington.

Starting in 1985, Poseidon C3 submarines were retired to offset the increasing numbers of Trident submarines. Poseidon submarines had to leave service to comply with the force size limits specified by the Strategic Arms Limitation Talks (SALT I) treaty and the unratified SALT II agreement. The remaining Poseidon submarines were eventually placed in a "stand-down" status, except for twelve submarines that were backfitted with the Trident C4 missile and saw continued service. The last Poseidon backfitted with Trident C4 was retired in 1994.

In October 1980, the U.S. Navy embarked on a three-year development program to build an enhanced SLBM designed to utilize the full volume available in the Trident SSBN's launch tube. The result was the Trident II (D5) missile. It was first flight-tested in January 1987 and subsequently deployed on board the USS *Tennessee* in March 1990. The Trident II missile is designed to serve as the primary U.S. strategic seaborne deterrent well into the twenty-first century. A three-stage, solid-propellant, inertially guided FBM, it is launched under water from Ohio-class (Trident) submarines, each of which has twenty-four launch tubes.

Trident D-5 missile launched from the nuclear-powered strategic missile submarine USS Tennessee, *February 1990. (PH2 Susan Marie Carl/Corbis)*

Like its predecessor, Trident II has a range of more than 4,000 nautical miles, but it has twice the payload (throw weight) capability of Trident I. The D5 missile is much larger than the C4 (44 feet in length and 83 inches in width versus 34 feet and 74 inches). It can carry either the Mark 4 or Mark 5 reentry bodies, each of which contains multiple independently targetable nuclear warheads.

The Trident submarine (Ohio 726 class) is the largest submarine in the U.S. Navy. It is 560 feet in length with a beam of 42 feet and weighs 18,700 tons. It has twenty-four launch tubes located midship and four bow torpedo tubes. It is capable of launching missiles under water while moving.

—*Guy Roberts*

References

"Fleet Ballistic Missile Submarines—SSBN," U.S. Navy Fact File, available at http://www.chinfo.navy.mil/navpalib/factfile/ships/ship-ssbn.html.

Spinardi, Graham, *From Polaris to Trident: The Development of U.S. Fleet Ballistic Missile Technology* (New York: Cambridge University Press, 1994).

TRINITY SITE, NEW MEXICO

The Trinity Site is the location of the world's first atomic bomb test. Located in central New Mexico, the site is a National Monument within the confines of the White Sands Missile Range.

At 5:30 A.M. (Mountain War Time) on July 16, 1945, the United States tested a plutonium implosion device that yielded approximately 19 kilotons of explosive force. This test marked the culmination of the three-year-long Manhattan Project to design and develop an atomic bomb as part of the U.S. effort to win World War II. The bomb was designed and built at Los Alamos National Laboratory, and the plutonium came from the Hanford, Washington, nuclear reactors. The bomb tested was the same design that was used for the "Fat Man" bomb dropped three weeks later on Nagasaki, Japan. Scientists believed they had to test the implosion design, whereas the gun-type uranium design used in Hiroshima was calculated to have a high reliability of success and would not require testing.

After considering eight possible test sites in California, Colorado, New Mexico, and Texas, soldiers and engineers began preparing the Trinity Site in the Journada del Muerto (valley of death), an hour south of Albuquerque, in the fall of 1944. The site provided safety, security, isolation, and secrecy, while still within driving distance of Los Alamos.

Scientists assembled the high-explosive portion of the atomic bomb in the McDonald Ranch house, 2 miles from ground zero, on July 12. The plutonium core was inserted on July 13, and the completed weapon was carried to the top of a 100-foot tower at Trinity on July 14. Personnel were located at three observation points just 10,000 yards from ground zero.

The shock of the explosion broke windows 120 miles away. The military's public cover story was that an ammunition storage facility had accidentally exploded. The blast left a small depression on the desert floor some 100 yards wide, and the heat

Robert Oppenheimer and General Leslie Groves (center) examine the twisted wreckage of a hundred-foot tower that held the first nuclear weapon at Trinity Site, New Mexico, July 1945. (Corbis)

melted the native sand into a green glass later named "trinitite."

The Trinity Site is open to the public on the first Saturday of April and October.

—*Jeffrey A. Larsen*

See also: Fat Man; Implosion Devices; Los Alamos National Laboratory; Manhattan Project; Nagasaki

References
Bainbridge, Kenneth, "Trinity," Los Alamos National Laboratory Publication LA-6300-H, 1976.
Rhodes, Richard, *The Making of the Atomic Bomb* (New York: Simon and Schuster, 1986).
Szasz, Ferenc, *The Day the Sun Rose Twice* (Albuquerque: University of New Mexico Press, 1984).
"Trinity Site, 1945–1995," White Sands Missile Range, NM, pamphlet 1995-674-816/25052 (Washington, DC: U.S. Government Printing Office, 1995).

TRITIUM

Tritium is an unstable isotope of the element hydrogen that has one proton and two neutrons. On a geologic time scale, tritium has a short half-life and therefore is not found in nature. It has nuclear properties that are very useful in the nuclear industry and in facilitating fusion reactions, and its phosphorescent qualities make it a useful material as a radioactive tracer and in night and compass sights. In a nuclear detonation, tritium plays a part in both the primary and secondary stages of the weapon. Its name comes from the Greek word *tritos* (third).

In 1934, E. Rutherford, M. L. E. Oliphant, and P. Harteck bombarded deuterons with deuterons and produced the new isotope. Tritium is unstable and undergoes beta decay. It has a half-life of 12.32 years. Tritium is primarily used in fusion reactions with deuterium. Deuterium and tritium collisions have the highest probability of undergoing fusion in most conventional fusion systems. In a nuclear weapon's primary stage, a small quantity of deuterium and tritium gas is used to boost the yield through fusion reactions. Tritium is a product of fission reactions and is produced in an exothermic reaction from lithium by neutron bombardment. These are the primary production reactions that take place in the second stage of a thermonuclear weapon.

Tritium was produced for U.S. military uses at the Savannah River Plant in South Carolina. That facility is now closed. Nevertheless, tritium will remain important for civilian nuclear fusion systems and for commercial phosphorescence applications. In addition, because of its short half-life, tritium will continue to be needed by the United States to ensure that the primary stage of its nuclear weapons perform as expected. Along with deuterium, it will serve as the primary fuel for most magnetic and inertial confinement fusion systems.

—*C. Ross Schmidtlein*

See also: Deuterium; Half-Life; Isotopes; Neutrons; Thermonuclear Bomb

References
Glasstone, S., *Source Book on Atomic Energy* (New York: Van Nostrand, 1950).
Parrington, Josef R., Harold D. Knox, Susan L. Breneman, Edward M. Baum, and Frank Feiner, *Nuclides and Isotopes: Chart of the Nuclides,* fifteenth edition (New York: General Electric and KAPL, 1996).

TWO-MAN RULE

The two-man rule requires that a minimum of two authorized persons work on or near nuclear weapons or equipment in order to ensure the weapons' safety and security. These individuals must have technical knowledge and be in a position to detect incorrect or abnormal operations. Additionally, they must be familiar with all security and safety rules. During all contact with nuclear weapons or equipment, a two-man team must be present. Under no circumstances are U.S. nuclear weapons under the day-to-day custody of any one individual.

—*Zach Becker*

See also: Surety; United States Nuclear Forces and Doctrine

References
Cothran, Helen, ed., *Nuclear Security* (San Diego, CA: Greenhaven, 2001).
U.S. Air Force, Air Force Instruction 91-101, *Air Force Nuclear Weapons Surety Program,* available at http://afpubs.hq.af.mil.
U.S. Air Force, Air Force Instruction 91-114, *Safety Rules for the Intercontinental Ballistic Missile Weapons Systems,* available at http://afpubs.hq.af.mil.
U.S. Department of Defense, Directive 3150.2, *DoD Nuclear Weapon Safety Program,* available at: http://afpubs.hq.af.mil.

U-2

The U-2 is a Lockheed-designed, high-flying aircraft with long-range reconnaissance capabilities. A glider-style aircraft, it is filled with advanced photographic and electronic intelligence-gathering equipment. The aerial photography equipment on board includes seven infrared cameras that can monitor radar networks and antiaircraft defenses. Its cameras are capable of photographing a strip of earth 125 miles wide and 3,000 miles long, with a resolution that can ostensibly allow a photo interpreter to read a newspaper headline 9 miles below the plane. Other instruments could detect evidence of nuclear tests. It flew at such high altitudes that it was thought to be undetectable and invulnerable throughout the 1950s.

During the Cold War, gaining detailed reconnaissance data about the U.S.S.R. was a paramount mission for the U.S. intelligence community. In response to that requirement, the U.S. Central Intelligence Agency engaged the Lockheed "Skunk Works," a secret aircraft-engineering organization headed by the legendary designer Kelly Johnson, to develop a spy plane that could evade Soviet air defenses and monitor Soviet conventional and nuclear force developments and deployments. These reconnaissance overflights of Russia continued from about 1956 until May 1960, when a U-2 was shot down over the U.S.S.R. Its pilot, Francis Gary Powers, parachuted from the damaged plane and was captured by the Soviets, causing much embarrassment to the Dwight D. Eisenhower administration. The incident occurred just weeks before a planned U.S.-Soviet summit in Paris with a promising agenda including disarmament, issues related to Berlin, and an improvement in relations between the nuclear powers. Powers spent ten years in a Soviet prison for spying.

During John F. Kennedy's administration, a U-2 was used to detect the placement of missiles in Cuba and to provide proof to the international community that the Soviets had decided to deploy nuclear-

U

capable delivery systems just a few miles from America's shores. This deployment led to the Cuban missile crisis of 1962 (see Cuban Missile Crisis).

Updated versions of the U-2 are still used for intelligence gathering and for weather and atmospheric studies.

—*Frannie Edwards*

References

Manchester, William Raymond, *The Glory and the Dream: A Narrative History of America, 1932–1972* (New York: Little, Brown, 1974).
"The U-2 Incident, 1960," The Avalon Project at Yale Law School, available at http://www.yale.edu/lawweb/avalon/u2.htm.

UNDERGROUND TESTING

Since the 1940s, there have been more than 1,500 underground nuclear tests worldwide. More than half of these tests were conducted by the United States, and another one-third were conducted by the Soviet Union. The pace and importance of underground tests increased significantly after the 1963 signing of the Limited Test Ban Treaty, which prohibited tests in the atmosphere, water, and space. Over time, underground tests provided essentially the same useful information as had the earlier atmospheric tests. In the 1960s, a comprehensive test ban that would have included underground testing was considered but rejected for three reasons. First, the technology of the time could not guarantee verification of underground tests. Second, military officials and others argued that some continued testing was necessary to assure the safety and reliability of the U.S. nuclear arsenal. Third, many observers believed that testing was necessary to modernize weapons and keep up

Accidental release of radiation through a surface breach during the Baneberry underground nuclear test, Nevada Test Site, 1970. (Bettmann/Corbis)

with technological developments in other countries. Over time, public pressure has mounted to stop underground testing to save money, slow the arms race, and support nonproliferation efforts. Several countries have adopted moratoriums on testing, but the Comprehensive Test Ban Treaty opened for signature in 1996 has not gone into force.

During the Cold War, mutual distrust was a major factor holding back U.S.-Soviet arms control agreements. Clandestine underground tests remained possible because the Soviet Union refused to accept routine on-site inspections and technology could not accurately differentiate an underground test from a seismic event. Therefore, a comprehensive test ban was rejected. As Cold War tensions waned, the acceptance of on-site inspections increased. Seismic measuring technology was refined and new ways of measuring radioactive traces and infrasound were developed. Additionally, a global network of more than 300 monitoring stations was established. When India and Pakistan conducted nuclear tests in 1998, more than fifty stations reported data on the tests. Low-yield explosions re-

main difficult to monitor, but the U.S. government claims it can monitor Russian test site explosions down to very low yield.

Concerns about the reliability and modernization of weapons have lessened over time. Leading powers now have more than fifty years' experience with nuclear weapons and have collected data from the analysis of hundreds of tests. Additionally, beginning in the 1990s, the U.S. Stockpile Stewardship program has used advanced computer technology, lasers that can create miniature thermonuclear explosions, and other modeling techniques to assure the reliability of U.S. weapons. These technologies are used in modernizing and extending the life of existing warheads.

The first major limit on underground testing was the Threshold Test Ban Treaty, which prohibited tests having a yield exceeding 150 kilotons. The treaty was signed in 1974, but it was not ratified until 1990. In 1992, Congress passed legislation imposing a moratorium on U.S. testing. The United States has not conducted a test since September 1993. The 1996 Comprehensive Test Ban Treaty stopped all nuclear testing but was rejected by the U.S. Senate in 1999 (the United States, however, continues to abide by the treaty). President George W. Bush has suggested that the United States may end its moratorium in the future in order to maintain reliability or to test low-yield warheads that could be used against deeply buried bunkers.

—*John W. Dietrich*

See also: Comprehensive Test Ban Treaty; Limited Test Ban Treaty; Nuclear Test Ban; Threshold Test Ban Treaty

References

U.S. Department of State, Bureau of Arms Control, "CTBT Facts and Fiction," 1999, available at http://www.state.gov/www/global/arms/factsheets/wmd/nuclear/.../fs_991008_factsnfiction.htm.

Weisman, Jonathan, "President Submits Nuclear Test Ban, Seeks Critical Mass of Senate Votes," *Congressional Quarterly Weekly Report*, vol. 55, 1997, pp. 2325–2326.

UNILATERAL INITIATIVE

A unilateral initiative is a publicly announced decision or military action by one side in an adversarial relationship undertaken in the hope of reducing the level of distrust or saber-rattling by the two sides. The party making the first move usually anticipates that this show of trust will lead to reciprocal actions by the other side.

One of the most dramatic steps of this type occurred on September 27, 1991, when, in response to the dissipating Cold War, U.S. president George H. W. Bush announced several unilateral initiatives to reduce dramatically the size and nature of U.S. nuclear deployments worldwide and to enhance crisis stability. First, the United States withdrew its nuclear artillery shells and the nuclear warheads for its short-range ballistic missiles stationed in Europe and Korea to the United States. These warheads, along with those already stored in the United States, were then dismantled and destroyed. Second, the United States removed all tactical nuclear weapons, including nuclear-armed cruise missiles, from its surface ships and attack submarines. These weapons no longer are deployed on a routine basis by the U.S. Navy. Third, U.S. strategic bombers were dealerted and no longer kept in a ready launch status on a day-to-day basis. Their nuclear weapons were returned to storage areas instead of being kept loaded aboard an alert force of bombers. Fourth, the president canceled several U.S. nuclear force modernization programs, including the Peacekeeper intercontinental

ballistic missile (ICBM) rail garrison system, the mobile elements of the small ICBM program (which was eventually canceled in its entirety), and a new nuclear-armed short-range attack missile (the SRAM-2). President Bush also announced the creation of a new U.S. Strategic Command to replace the Strategic Air Command. The purpose of the new organization was to improve the negative command and control of all U.S. strategic nuclear forces.

Although the president called on Soviet officials to undertake reciprocal initiatives, these U.S. actions were not predicated on Soviet willingness to adopt similar measures.

—*James J. Wirtz*

See also: Presidential Nuclear Initiative

Reference

Freedman, Lawrence, *The Evolution of Nuclear Strategy,* third edition (New York: Palgrave Macmillan, 2003).

UNITED NATIONS SPECIAL COMMISSION ON IRAQ (UNSCOM)

The United Nations Special Commission on Iraq (UNSCOM) was formed in 1991 to assist the International Atomic Energy Agency (IAEA) in destroying, removing, or rendering harmless Iraq's nuclear

A UN inspector measuring the volume of nerve agent in a container at Muthanna, Iraq, November 1, 1991. (Rick Maiman/Corbis Sygma)

facilities and ballistic missiles with a range greater than 150 kilometers. UNSCOM's mandate also included monitoring missile launchers, production, related major parts, and repair facilities. The aim was to ensure that Iraq would not rebuild its nuclear weapons program.

After losing the 1991 Gulf War, Iraq agreed, as a condition of surrender, to declare within fifteen days all of its weapons of mass destruction and the missiles to deliver them, and then to destroy them. This obligation was reinforced by UN Security Council Resolution 687, which formed UNSCOM on April 3, 1991, to provide for monitoring and verification of Iraq's compliance with these conditions of surrender. Iraq was not to use, develop, construct, or acquire weapons of mass destruction or associated delivery vehicles. Under the terms of the resolution, Iraq was barred from selling oil until UNSCOM verified the destruction of its prohibited weapons. UNSCOM's nuclear inspection teams were organized by the IAEA with the assistance and cooperation of members of the United Nations.

On April 18, 1991, Iraq provided an initial required declaration that mentioned fifty-three Al-Hussein and Scud long-range ballistic missiles. During its first inspections, September 21–30, 1991, IAEA inspectors found large amounts of documentation relating to Iraq's efforts to acquire nuclear weapons. Following these revelations, the IAEA, with the assistance and cooperation of the Special Commission, undertook fifty-three ballistic missile and thirty nuclear inspections. UNSCOM supervised the destruction of forty-eight operational long-range missiles, fourteen conventional missile warheads, six operational mobile launchers, twenty-eight operational fixed launch pads, thirty-two fixed launch pads (that were under construction), thirty missile chemical warheads, and other missile support equipment and materials. It also supervised the destruction of a variety of assembled and nonassembled "super-gun" components. UNSCOM was instrumental in assisting the November 1995 interception by Jordan of a large shipment of high-grade missile components destined for Iraq. The commission's experts also participated in negotiations with the Russian Federation regarding the sale of the nuclear fuel removed from Iraq and reprocessed in the Russian Federation. The disclosures of Iraq's nuclear program led to efforts to strengthen the IAEA safeguard agreements.

UNSCOM began its first missile inspection on June 30, 1991. Iraq consistently tried to evade its responsibilities. Following Iraqi insistence, UNSCOM withdrew all its staff from Iraq on December 16, 1998.

The UN Security Council adopted Resolution 1284 on December 17, 1999, replacing UNSCOM with the United Nations Monitoring Verification and Inspection Commission (UNMOVIC).

—*Glen M. Segell*

See also: Iraqi Nuclear Forces and Doctrine

References

Mataija, Steven, and J. Marshall Beier, eds., *Multilateral Verification and the Post-Gulf Environment: Learning from the UNSCOM Experience—Symposium Proceedings* (Toronto, Canada: York University Centre for International and Strategic Studies, 1992).
Trevan, Tim, *Saddam's Secrets: The Hunt for Iraq's Hidden Weapons* (London: Harper Collins, 1999).

UNITED STATES AIR FORCE

The U.S. Air Force was established as a separate service by the National Security Act of 1947. Following the nuclear bombing of Hiroshima and Nagasaki by Army Air Force aircraft at the end of World War II, the United States needed to develop new systems for managing and operating its growing nuclear arsenal. In this context, the newly independent air force took the lead role in deploying and preparing to deliver nuclear weapons. Strategic Air Command (SAC), with its postwar bomber force and deliverable nuclear weapons, was the cornerstone of early U.S. deterrence strategy. Throughout the Cold War, research and development of nuclear weapons continued while the United States created a "Triad" of nuclear forces consisting of nuclear bombers, intercontinental ballistic missiles (ICBMs), and the navy's submarine-launched ballistic missiles (SLBMs). Each leg of the Triad had advantages and disadvantages that were balanced by the other two. The U.S. Air Force, through SAC, controlled two legs of the Triad: bombers and ICBMs.

The air force first relied on propeller-driven B-29 and B-36 bombers, eventually replacing them with B-47 and B-52 jet bombers armed with smaller and more powerful nuclear weapons. In the late 1950s, it began adding ICBMs to its inventory of nuclear delivery systems. Atlas, Titan, and Minuteman missile systems created a new industry and provided long-term deterrence capability. Throughout the 1970s

Two F-16 Fighting Falcons preparing to refuel from a KC-135E Stratotanker over San Francisco during an Operation Noble Eagle patrol, March 2004. (U.S. Air Force photo by Master Sgt. Lance Cheung)

and 1980s, the air force continued to advance and expand space technologies. These space-based systems enhanced nuclear targeting, early warning systems, and enhanced arms control and treaty verification. A reorganization of commands in the 1990s created the U.S. Strategic Command (USSTRAT-COM). This unified command replaced SAC, establishing a single commander (alternating between four-star air force and navy flag officers) for the planning, targeting, and wartime employment of strategic nuclear forces. Day-to-day training and maintenance of their respective systems remains the responsibility of each service.

The mission of the U.S. Air Force is to defend the United States and protect its interests through aerospace power. It can deliver "tactical" nuclear weapons using shorter-range "dual-capable" aircraft such as the A-10, F-15E, and F-16, but the strategic bomber and ICBM remain the air force's key global delivery platforms for nuclear weapons. U.S. Air Force bombers such as the B-52 or stealthy B-2 may be used to carry nuclear gravity bombs or nuclear-armed cruise missiles. The bombers are maintained at various stages of alert, depending on the international threat environment. ICBMs, such as the Minuteman and Peacekeeper, retain the ability to hold time-urgent enemy targets at risk on a day-to-day basis. Their ground-based, hardened launch facilities afford a high degree of survivability if attacked,

and their high accuracy gives them the ability to destroy an opponent's hardened targets. Unlike the bombers, however, once an ICBM is launched, it cannot be recalled.

The 2001 Nuclear Posture Review (NPR) describes a "new Triad." The new Triad concept restructures U.S. strategic forces to include legs for missile defenses, a "responsive infrastructure," and a strategic deterrent, which integrates both nonnuclear and nuclear strike capabilities.

—Chris Craige

See also: Strategic Air Command and Strategic
    Command; Triad; United States Nuclear Forces and
    Doctrine
References
Boyne, Walter J., *Beyond the Wild Blue: A History of the
    U.S. Air Force* (New York: St. Martin's Griffin Press,
    1997).
"Fact Sheet: Organization of the U.S. Air Force,"
    available at http://www.af.mil/factsheets/.

UNITED STATES ARMY

The U.S. Army is the world's leading combined-arms land combat force. Its mission is to fight and win the nation's wars by providing prompt, sustained land dominance across the full spectrum of military operations and spectrum of conflict. Title 10 and Title 32 of the United States Code task the army with organizing, training, and equipping forces to conduct missions as directed by the president, secretary of defense, and regional combatant commanders. The army is composed of both active and reserve components.

A variety of army units provide a broad spectrum of operations, from peacekeeping and humanitarian assistance to full-scale war. The army has heavy armored and mechanized forces as well as light, airborne, air assault, and special operating forces. The army's heavy forces are composed of tanks, armored infantry carriers, and other specialized armored vehicles. They have significant firepower and rapid battlefield mobility provided by such vehicles as the M1 Abrams tank, the M2 Bradley infantry-fighting vehicle, the M109 Paladin howitzer, and the AH-64 attack helicopter. This heavy force, however, requires extensive logistics support and must be transported by ship to the battlefield or pre-positioned nearby. The airborne and air assault forces are lightly equipped; most equipment is carried into battle in these units by light vehicles or the soldiers themselves. Light forces can be transported by air to the battlefield in hours. Once there, they can move by helicopter, truck, or on foot. Special operating forces provide a variety of skills, including unconventional warfare, direct action, and reconnaissance. The light forces have limited firepower.

The army's primary combat organization is the division. A division has approximately 20,000 soldiers organized into three brigades as well as artillery, engineer, aviation, supply, and medical units. The U.S. Army currently contains ten active-duty divisions stationed and deployed around the world.

During the Cold War, the Army had a large nuclear mission, providing intermediate-range ballistic missiles, short-range battlefield missiles, and artillery-fired atomic projectiles (atomic artillery) to its forward-deployed forces and allies, particularly in Europe and Korea. This mission was eliminated after the Cold War ended in the 1990s. Today, the army retains a residual planning capability to conduct nuclear operations and to operate on a nuclear battlefield.

—*Bret Kinman*

See also: United States Nuclear Forces and Doctrine
References
Bacevich, A. J., *The Pentomic Era: The U.S. Army between Korea and Vietnam* (Washington, DC: National Defense University Press, 1986).
Dastrup, Boyd L., *King of Battle: A Branch History of Field Artillery* (Fort Monroe, VA: Office of the Command Historian, U.S. Army Training and Doctrine Command, 1992).
Midgley, John S., Jr., *Deadly Illusions: Army Policy for the Nuclear Battlefield* (Boulder: Westview, 1986).
Miller, David, *The Cold War: A Military History* (New York: St. Martin's Press, 1998).
Rose, John P., *The Evolution of U.S. Army Nuclear Doctrine, 1945–1980* (Boulder: Westview, 1980).
Schwartz, Stephen I., ed., *Atomic Audit: The Costs and Consequences of U.S. Nuclear Weapons since 1940* (Washington, DC: Brookings Institute Press, 1998).
U.S. Army website, http://www.army.mil.

UNITED STATES NAVY

The U.S. Navy constitutes an essential instrument of U.S. warfighting doctrine and strategic deterrence. It provides the United States with the ability to stage strategic nuclear weapons from platforms that are highly mobile and difficult to detect. The credibility of the U.S. nuclear deterrent depends on this ability to retaliate even if it comes under an all-out nuclear attack.

The most survivable component of the U.S. nuclear arsenal resides in its eighteen Ohio-class ballistic missile submarines (SSBNs, for "ship submersible ballistic nuclear"). The Ohios, each carrying twenty-four Trident II D5 missiles, collectively represent roughly 50 percent of the total U.S. strategic warheads. Although the missiles have no preset targets when the submarine goes on patrol, the SSBNs are capable of rapidly targeting their missiles should the need arise, using secure and constant at-sea communications links (*see* Submarines, Nuclear-Powered Ballistic Missile; Trident SLBMs/SSBNs).

In addition to the SSBNs, U.S. Navy attack submarines are able to conduct nuclear strikes by using nuclear-capable versions of the Tomahawk Land Attack Missile (TLAM). The Tomahawk Block II Nuclear variant (TLAM-N) carries the W80 nuclear warhead and can travel at subsonic speeds at a low altitude for up to 2,500 kilometers. In the aftermath of President George W. Bush's 1991 announcement that nuclear weapons would no longer be deployed on a routine basis on U.S. Navy warships, TLAM-N is kept in storage and has not been deployed at sea.

The U.S. Navy will also provide a portion of the United States' layered theater missile defense (TMD) capability by 2005. TMD involves protecting a geographic area from attack by theater missiles

The USS Kitty Hawk *Battle Group and ships from Japan's Maritime Self Defense Force conducting exercises, 2003. (U.S. Navy photo by Photographer's Mate 3rd Class Lee McCaskill)*

and aircraft. The navy has been able to achieve upper-tier defense capabilities with the Aegis Ballistic Missile Defense (BMD) program (formerly called the Navy Theater Wide system), which uses upgraded versions of the Aegis radar and Standard missile defense systems. BMD will use Standard missiles, modified for intercepts outside the atmosphere, in tandem with the Aegis combat system (*see* Theater Missile Defense).

Since the end of the Cold War, the U.S. Navy's role has expanded to include direct participation in covert operations. Ballistic missile submarines still constitute a major aspect of the U.S. strategic deterrent, but some SSBNs are being transformed into submarines that are better suited to fight the war on terror. Four Ohio-class submarines that were previously scheduled for inactivation are being converted to guided missile submarines (SSGNs, for "ship submersible guided nuclear").

Although the primary role of some submarines may change, the main objectives of the U.S. Navy will remain the same. SSBNs are highly mobile, difficult to detect, and highly capable of delivering many nuclear warheads quickly and accurately. As

long as this capability remains credible, the U.S. strategic deterrent will remain secure.

—*Abe Denmark*

See also: United States Nuclear Forces and Doctrine

References

Norris, Robert S., and William M. Arkin, "U.S. Nuclear Forces 2000," *Bulletin of the Atomic Scientists,* vol. 56, no. 3, May/June 2000, p. 69.

U.S. Navy, "Fact File," available at http://www.chinfo. navy.mil/navpalib/factfile/ffiletop.html.

UNITED STATES NUCLEAR FORCES AND DOCTRINE

The world entered the age of nuclear combat when in August 1945 American B-29s dropped atomic bombs on Hiroshima and Nagasaki, shocking Japan into surrender. The secret unit formed to deliver the bomb was equipped with aircraft modified to accommodate the Volkswagen-sized weapons. This early atomic bomb was still essentially a laboratory device that required a team of scientists to assemble and arm and that, once assembled, had to be used (or disassembled) before its batteries ran down.

Early U.S. nuclear doctrine was embedded in the broader strategic bombing doctrine that was refined in combat during the war—attack military targets located in urban areas using precision bombing wherever possible. "Precision" was, of course, relative to the technology of the times and, especially in the Japanese campaign, was abandoned in favor of broad-area fire bombing because of operational considerations. Scholars of military history now know that had the Japanese not surrendered after Nagasaki, the next several nuclear weapons probably would have been used tactically against massed Japanese forces opposing a U.S. land-air-sea invasion of Japan as U.S. fire-bombing raids destroyed remaining Japanese cities and a naval blockade isolated the Japanese mainland. Then, as now, technology, policy, and the circumstances of battle interacted to shape doctrine.

U.S. nuclear forces and doctrine developed slowly after 1945 owing to budget constraints, the primitive nature of nuclear weapons at that time, uncertainties about U.S. global strategy and the type of military forces needed to support that strategy, and the soon-to-commence negotiations in the newly formed United Nations to try to control and perhaps even ban nuclear weapons. From the beginning, nuclear weapons were placed by U.S. authorities in a special category. Explicit presidential authorization was required for developing, testing, deploying, and using atomic bombs. This special status was recognized in early presidential directives such as National Security Council Document 30 (NSC-30), adopted in 1948.

The Growth of Nuclear Forces
As the Cold War unfolded and the imperative of deterring Soviet aggression became paramount, nuclear weapons moved to the heart of U.S. military strategy. U.S. nuclear forces and doctrine evolved accordingly. With the advent of the North Atlantic Treaty and the Soviet test of its first nuclear bomb in 1949, the U.S. deterrent strategy became more complicated and new target categories were added to the strategic air offensive annexes of its contingency war plans. In the late 1940s, strategic air plans continued to rely heavily on conventional as well as nuclear weapons.

In 1950, before the outbreak of the Korean War, President Harry S. Truman approved a major expansion of the nuclear stockpile. He also approved

development of the thermonuclear (hydrogen) bomb. NSC-68, one of the first major reviews of U.S. national security strategy, was launched in response to the H-bomb decision. In 1950, the U.S. nuclear stockpile numbered some 300 bombs that still were large devices close to the designs of the original nuclear weapons. By the end of the decade, the robust production and development program launched by President Truman had produced a stockpile of more than 12,000 nuclear weapons (and a number of new, more sophisticated designs) deployed not only on large strategic bombers but with U.S. tactical air, sea, and land forces.

The Korean War marked a major turning point for the United States. It confirmed the priorities and tensions of a Europe-first grand strategy that continued until the end of the Cold War. It demonstrated the difficulty of using the nuclear shadow to affect conflicts fought on the margins of the major East-West confrontation. And, notwithstanding the desperate nature of the Korean crisis, the fact that the United States did not use nuclear weapons reinforced the evolving norm that nuclear weapons were tools of last resort, reserved for the most strategically threatening occasions. During the Korean War era, the world also entered the thermonuclear age. There was now no apparent limit to the destructiveness that could be packaged in a single thermonuclear device (see Thermonuclear Bomb).

When President Dwight D. Eisenhower took office in January 1953, his highest priorities were to end the Korean War, to anchor the United States to the North Atlantic Treaty Organization (NATO), and to translate what he and his advisers saw as an inchoate containment and deterrence strategy into a coherent grand strategy attuned to the needs of a long, inconclusive struggle conducted in the shadow of the bomb's ability to threaten apocalyptic destruction. U.S. nuclear forces, still heavily centered around the long-range bombers of Strategic Air Command, were at the heart of this endeavor. NSC-162/2, adopted in late 1953, offered a strategy that linked nuclear weapons and deterrence to the long-range mission of containing the Soviet Union.

During the 1950s, the East-West nuclear arms race accelerated. The United States developed a wide range of nuclear weapons deployed on a number of strategic and tactical platforms. Nuclear doctrine evolved to reflect this capability, albeit with final authority for using nuclear weapons reserved to the president or, in the event of his incapacitation, his designated successors (called the National Command Authority). Although Congress exercised indirect influence on the nuclear programs through its budgeting authority, fundamental decisions on U.S. doctrine and on the size, composition, deployment, and use of nuclear forces remained with the executive branch. Also during the 1950s, the imperative of being able to survive a surprise nuclear attack and respond with a substantial "second strike" became a key element of U.S. nuclear doctrine (see Arms Race; Deterrence; Second Strike).

Although missile programs had begun both in the United States and in Russia during World War II, and had become more important with the advent of the German V-1 and V-2 systems, missiles developed slowly during the 1950s. Thus U.S. strategic offensive and defensive nuclear doctrine remained focused on bomber aircraft. The United States constructed a large air defense network during these years and could explore preemptive options for striking Soviet nuclear bomber bases in the face of an imminent Soviet attack. The Soviets progressed quickly with their missile programs, however, and whatever prospect there had been of entertaining the idea of a preemptive nuclear first strike in U.S. strategic doctrine faded (see Preemptive Attack).

The shock of Sputnik—the first artificial Earth-orbiting satellite—on the United States and its allies cannot be overstated. It contributed immediately to the development of a NATO nuclear stockpile with nuclear sharing arrangements for otherwise nonnuclear NATO partners and accelerated work on missiles. When President Eisenhower turned over the reins of government to President John F. Kennedy in 1961, the basic structure of the Cold War U.S. nuclear posture and a number of its supporting processes were in place. Strategic nuclear forces consisted of a "Triad" of long-range bombers, intercontinental ballistic missiles (ICBMs), and submarine-launched ballistic missiles (SLBMs). The intercontinental cruise missile, the Snark, also was operational, though only for a short time, creating a "Quadrad" of systems. Tactical nuclear weapons were deployed with a wide range of forces. A large design and production complex was in place to refurbish the U.S. stockpile, and a large industrial complex supported production and development of new generations of strategic delivery systems. Command and control (C2) and intelligence, surveil-

lance, and reconnaissance (ISR) systems likewise were under continual development and refinement. The Joint Strategic Target Planning Staff (JSTPS) had been created in Omaha, Nebraska, to develop the Single Integrated Operational Plan (SIOP), and the U.S. strategic war plan was beginning to be coordinated with NATO nuclear planning (see Cold War; Single Integrated Operational Plan; Strategic Forces; Tactical Nuclear Weapons; Triad).

Flexible Response and Arms Control

During the Kennedy and Lyndon B. Johnson administrations, the United States moved from a doctrine of "massive retaliation" to one of "flexible response." In fact, out of the public eye, this process already was under way prior to Kennedy's inauguration. By 1961, planning for the strategic air offensive—now entirely nuclear—had become an enormously complex affair. The new Kennedy administration moved to try to create more strategic nuclear options for the president in the event of an emergency. It also sought to recentralize NATO nuclear decision-making in U.S. hands and to seek means of delaying the need to cross the nuclear threshold. Notwithstanding the public manifestations of the Kennedy strategy—for example, Secretary of Defense Robert McNamara's Ann Arbor speech in 1962, where he tried to entice the Soviets to a counterforce doctrine, the "new" NATO strategy unveiled in MC-14/3 in 1967—the United States and its allies remained heavily dependent upon early resort to nuclear weapons in any major military confrontation with the Soviet Union. Nuclear options continued to be quietly explored for noncentral confrontations such as Vietnam, and to be rejected (see Counterforce Targeting; Flexible Response; Massive Retaliation).

During the early 1960s, U.S. nuclear doctrine and force planning began to interact more deeply with arms control theories that stressed the need to stabilize the nuclear confrontation. After the Cuban missile crisis in late 1962, the Americans and their British allies undertook a major initiative to reinvigorate the on-again, off-again nuclear testing talks that had begun in the 1950s, resulting in the Limited Test Ban Treaty in 1963. U.S. authorities also were exploring ways of beginning strategic arms control talks. Moreover, a newly forming nonproliferation agenda became serious after the Chinese detonated their first nuclear weapon in 1964, and the prospect of major deployments not only of missile forces but also of antiballistic missile systems emerged. In 1965, President Johnson committed the prestige of his presidency to seeking a Nuclear Nonproliferation Treaty (NPT), and his administration quietly began reviewing ways to initiate strategic arms talks (something derailed by the Soviet invasion of Czechoslovakia in 1968) when the NPT was opened for signature (see Arms Control; Limited Test Ban Treaty; Nuclear Nonproliferation Treaty; Nuclear Test Ban).

The Richard M. Nixon administration took office in 1969 at the height of the Vietnam War. The backlash from this war spilled over into the strategic weapons debate, leading indirectly to the early demise of America's first operational antiballistic missile (ABM) system. Meanwhile, President Nixon and his national security team adjusted to the pace of the missile race. In 1965, the Soviets had slightly more than 200 ICBMs and fewer than 100 SLBMs. By 1969, Soviet missile forces were growing at the rate of 200–300 missiles annually and were projected to equal if not surpass U.S. numbers by 1971.

In this context, the new Nixon administration commenced the Strategic Arms Limitation Talks (SALT), which resulted in 1972 in the Anti-Ballistic Missile (ABM) Treaty and the interim agreement on offensive arms. The ABM Treaty in effect codified the doctrine of assured destruction that had been embraced by the Kennedy administration after the short-lived effort to entice the Soviets to adopt a purely counterforce strategy, leading to a situation of mutual assured destruction (MAD). Also in 1972, the Nixon administration began a review of its nuclear policy that resulted in 1974 in National Security Decision Memorandum (NSDM) 242—a policy that reprioritized the targets to be held at risk with strategic nuclear weapons toward industrial targets, called for even more options in the nuclear war plan, created a secure reserve force, and sought ways to further refine escalation control should deterrence fail. A document called the Nuclear Weapons Employment Policy (NUWEP), first issued in 1974, conveyed the new guidance, and on this basis the JSTPS restructured the SIOP into major attack options (MAOs), selective attack options (SAOs), and limited attack options (LAOs). U.S. strategic bombing doctrine during and after World War II had centered on a number of target sets that now were formalized into the primary cat-

egories of military forces (subdivided into nuclear and nonnuclear forces), war-supporting economic and other industrial targets, and leadership and command and control (see Assured Destruction; Mutual Assured Destruction; Strategic Arms Limitation Talks).

Concerned Allies

NATO nuclear strategy also continued to evolve and interact with U.S. nuclear strategy. The allies were relieved that the United States had successfully excluded "forward-based" U.S. nuclear forces from SALT negotiations. Faced with the prospect of further reductions in SALT II, which began in 1972, however, many allies worried openly about the credibility of the U.S. nuclear guarantee. As the Soviets began replacing their first-generation intermediate-range ballistic missiles targeted on Europe with the SS-20, which incorporated the new multiple independently targetable reentry vehicle (MIRV) technology, the European concerns multiplied. Congressional pressure led the Gerald Ford administration to provide the most public explanation of the alliance's nuclear policy and strategy to date, and at a meeting of the NATO Nuclear Planning Group (NPG) in early 1976, Secretary of Defense Donald Rumsfeld convinced the allies of the need to modernize the NATO nuclear stockpile to keep pace with evolving policy and doctrine.

Nuclear Testing

In 1974, India conducted its first nuclear test, joining the United States, the Soviet Union, Britain, France, and China as a country that had explosively tested nuclear devices. With progress in SALT moving slowly, the Nixon and Ford administrations shifted attention to nuclear testing, pursuing new nuclear testing bans. When President Jimmy Carter took office in 1977, he completed the SALT II talks, but—this time owing to the Soviet invasion of Afghanistan in 1979—placed on hold the Senate's deliberation on the treaty. Also by 1977, the United States was developing the MX and Trident missile systems, a wide range of new cruise missiles, and the B-1 bomber. Out of the public eye, the United States also began covertly exploring stealth technology, a fact that the public and many congressmen were unaware of when the Carter administration took its controversial decision to cancel further procurement of the B-1 bomber.

The Countervailing Strategy

After conducting an initial review of national security strategy, the Carter administration began a concentrated study on nuclear targeting policy led by Leon Sloss. This study concluded that the United States needed to adjust its nuclear deterrent strategy and doctrine to reflect how the Soviets approached war planning and what they truly valued, that is, the United States should place greater emphasis on the complex problem of holding at risk Soviet military forces and the Soviet military command structure. These studies formed the basis for Presidential Directive (PD) 53, which reinvigorated programs for ensuring that American strategic command and control could survive a nuclear attack and continue to function, and for PD-59—a new nuclear policy that, among other things, shifted targeting priorities away from industries and the concept of impeding industrial recovery and provided for a more robust secure reserve force. PD-59 was unveiled publicly by Secretary of Defense Harold Brown and identified for public diplomacy purposes as the "countervailing" strategy. The concept, again as explained publicly, was to seek to ascertain the war aims of the enemy and to then hold at risk assets critical to the success of those aims, thus denying victory to the enemy. The concept of punishment did not disappear as an element of deterrence, but at least for the moment, the concept of denial gained a more prominent role in U.S. nuclear doctrine.

In the midst of the Iranian hostage crisis, Ronald Reagan campaigned for president in 1980. Although highly critical of formal arms control, the newly elected Reagan administration bowed to European sentiment when it resumed theater nuclear force talks in 1981 under the new name of intermediate nuclear forces (INF). In 1981, the new administration conducted its own nuclear targeting review and basically reaffirmed PD-59 guidance. At the same time, the administration was conducting a Damage Criteria Study (DCS) to facilitate translating nuclear targeting objectives into a more coherent target and attack criteria framework. In late 1981, the Reagan White House issued National Security Decision Directive (NSDD) 13, which superseded but did not significantly change PD-59. In 1982, President Reagan also approved the commencement of negotiations for a Strategic Arms Reduction Treaty (START). START, unlike SALT, sought actual reductions in nuclear weapons. By this time, the Reagan administration had set in motion a major rearmament program to challenge the Soviets across the board. In 1983, in announcing the Strategic Defense Initiative, the president increased this pressure (see Strategic Arms Reduction Treaty; Strategic Defense Initiative).

The End of the Cold War

After World War II, U.S. nuclear doctrine and forces had evolved as part of a broader national security strategy centered around the concept of containing and deterring the Soviet Union until Soviet domestic change might make possible a dramatically different strategy. Few sensed in the early 1980s that this kind of change was on the horizon. The United States built up its military forces and, in 1986, finally abandoned SALT II (when the continued conversion of B-52 bombers to carry air-launched cruise missiles [ALCMs] exceeded the SALT II limits). Other arms control talks proceeded slowly. Ailing Soviet president Leonid Brezhnev, who had exercised power since replacing Nikita Khrushchev in 1964, finally died in 1982, to be succeeded by Yuri Andropov (who, also ill, died in 1984) and then by Konstantin Chernenko (who died in 1985). The Soviets undertook the bold step of promoting a young, dynamic politician—Mikhail Gorbachev—to the center of their decision-making apparatus. In the face of the failing Soviet economy and the pressures of the Reagan rearmament plan, Gorbachev undertook a number of initiatives, some of which centered on arms control and some of which centered on domestic political reform, that—within a few short years—resulted in the unexpected end of the Cold War and the equally unexpected collapse of the Soviet empire. Along the way, NATO displayed solidarity in proceeding with the deployment of new theater nuclear systems—the American Pershing II intermediate-range ballistic missile (IRBM) and the ground-launched cruise missile (GLCM)—notwithstanding a massive Soviet diplomatic campaign to mobilize European opposition.

The Soviets broke off arms control talks after the NATO deployments, but (with Gorbachev now in power) a way was found to resume talks. In December 1987, Reagan and Gorbachev signed the INF Treaty banning all U.S. and Soviet land-based ballistic missiles and GLCMs in the 500- to 5,500-kilometer range. This was in effect the first nuclear disarmament treaty because it required the destruction and future prohibition of an entire range of nuclear delivery systems. The Threshold Test Ban Treaty and the Peaceful Nuclear Explosions Treaty of the 1970s, which had never entered into force because of verification concerns, now acquired verification protocols that allowed them to take effect (*see* Intermediate-Range Nuclear Forces Treaty).

President George H. W. Bush, the forty-first president of the United States and father of the future forty-third president, came to office as the Cold War was ending. He and his national security team presided over the reunification of a German state that retained membership in NATO, the largely peaceful withdrawal of Soviet forces from their external empire, and—in the face of attempted coups—the largely peaceful collapse of communism in the Soviet Union. While this was going on, the first Gulf War also began to reorient U.S. nuclear doctrine toward an existing but now more pressing threat—the proliferation of weapons of mass destruction (WMD) to regional states such as Iraq, North Korea, and Iran.

New Roles for Nuclear Weapons

By the early 1990s, the United States was reorienting its nuclear forces and beginning to explore how to redirect its nuclear doctrine in the face of the new geopolitical circumstances. The process was messy, with a number of forces intervening. For instance, the new environmental awareness that had developed since the 1940s foreshadowed the closing of the plutonium production facilities at Rocky Flats in Colorado in 1992 (production already had been suspended). In the early 1990s, the United States pursued what to many appeared to be a largely piecemeal nuclear agenda to adjust to the new security environment. START I negotiations proceeded to closure in 1991, but the collapse of the Soviet Union delayed its entry into force while the issue of nuclear succession was resolved. Eventually, Ukraine, Belarus, and Kazakhstan agreed to give up nuclear weapons and to join the NPT as non–nuclear weapons states. The United States undertook unilateral actions to further stabilize the dangerous transition period, hoping to assure Moscow and to elicit stabilizing actions from its former adversary. U.S. strategic bombers were taken off alert, the production of a number of nuclear systems was terminated, Strategic Air Command was dissolved and its forces transferred to several U.S. Air Force commands, and the Joint Strategic Planning Staff was replaced with a new unified command—U.S. Strategic Command. And, as an initiative that began in Congress, the United States entered a nuclear testing moratorium in 1992 while it pursued a formal Comprehensive Test Ban Treaty (*see* Comprehensive Test Ban Treaty).

President William Clinton took office in 1993 in the midst of these changes. Later that year, the Defense Department announced the counterproliferation initiative to complement traditional U.S. nonproliferation strategy. The new administration also shifted emphasis to theater missile defense while essentially refocusing the national missile defense effort as a research and development effort. Congressional politics intervened, however, as the Republicans took control of both chambers of Congress in the 1994 election, and national missile defense again became an issue. In 1994, the first Nuclear Posture Review (NPR) was conducted. U.S. nuclear forces and doctrine remained largely intact as a result of this review, hedging against the uncertainties of the Russian transition to democracy—a process that also made progress in strategic arms control slow and difficult. In 1993, North Korea created a crisis when it announced its intention to withdraw from the NPT, something that was averted (at least temporarily) by the 1994 Agreed Framework arrangement. In 1995, at a critical review and extension conference, the parties agreed that the NPT would remain in force indefinitely (*see* Missile Defense; North Korean Nuclear Weapons Program; Theater Missile Defense).

The United States was the first to sign the recently completed CTBT in September 1996. On the road to this agreement, the Clinton administration had decided it would support a truly "zero-yield" outcome and, as part of the bargain in the arrangement, began constructing a Stockpile Stewardship Program (SSP) to explore how the safety and reliability of the U.S. nuclear stockpile might be retained in the absence of nuclear testing. Despite the rejection of the CTBT by the Senate in 1999, the United States continues to observe a self-imposed nuclear testing moratorium (*see* Stockpile Stewardship Program).

In 1998, the nuclear landscape shifted as India and Pakistan both openly tested nuclear weapons and proclaimed themselves to be nuclear weapons states. Despite being defeated in the first Gulf War in

1990–1991, Saddam Hussein was still in power in Iraq and was thought to again be seeking weapons of mass destruction—something that escalated in importance when he ejected the United Nations inspectors from Iraq in the late 1990s. The George W. Bush administration fought a second Gulf War in 2003 to oust Hussein from power and to eliminate the threat that his regime would obtain nuclear, chemical, or biological weapons (*see* Indian Nuclear Weapons Program; Iraqi Nuclear Forces and Doctrine; Pakistani Nuclear Forces).

President George W. Bush won the 2000 elections and, notwithstanding a narrow mandate, set out to transform U.S. military forces. One of the early priorities of the new Bush administration was to terminate the ABM Treaty in order to allow the deployment of ballistic missile defenses aimed at "rogue" states such as North Korea. A Quadrennial Defense Review (QDR) and Nuclear Posture Review (NPR) were under way when the terrorist attacks of September 11, 2001, took place—an event that was as important as Pearl Harbor had been in 1941 in shifting U.S. national security strategy. The new NPR announced in January 2002 took account of the importance of the supporting infrastructure and of strategic defenses as part of the overall U.S. deterrent, moved unilaterally to reduce U.S. strategic nuclear forces to a level of 1,700–2,200 operationally deployed warheads by 2012, and continued the emphasis in seeking new conventional means to hold at risk targets once considered possible targets for nuclear weapons (*see* Nuclear Posture Review; Quadrennial Defense Review).

Looking Ahead

The tensions and promises of the new NPR, the evolving strategic relationship with Russia (reflected in the 2002 Strategic Offensive Reduction Treaty—SORT—which codified the unilaterally announced reductions), the uncertainties associated with Chinese ambitions and programs—these issues continue to underlie policy debates. But the epicenter of the debate has shifted from the traditional concerns of the Cold War to the new threat posed by regional powers with aggressive intentions seeking WMD and to the daunting fear that terrorists such as Osama bin Laden might acquire and use such weapons and might be undeterrable. The 2003 war in Iraq addressed these concerns. The challenges posed by North Korea (which now has withdrawn

from the NPT), by Iran, by other rogues, by the Indian and Pakistani nuclear programs, by the Arab-Israeli confrontation and the underlying question of WMD—these all are on the table.

U.S. nuclear doctrine has come full circle since the 1940s as the United States adjusts its nuclear forces and doctrine to the new age. The U.S. preference for precision bombing, pursued with great difficulty in World War II with the secret Norden bombsight after half a century of investment and technological development, has evolved into a capability that allows the United States to rely less and less on nuclear weapons. The fear that the proliferation of nuclear weapons could mortally threaten the United States, a fear that helped inspire the 1946 effort to control or ban nuclear weapons through the Baruch Plan, remains, though it has shifted from great-power confrontation to the rogues and terrorists (*see* Baruch Plan).

Since the United States dropped the atomic bombs on Hiroshima and Nagasaki, nuclear weapons have not been used in combat. They have become powerful political instruments instead of warfighting weapons. But that does not mean they never will be used again, nor (as the Bush administration so clearly recognized) that deterrence in the future will resemble deterrence in the past. U.S. nuclear forces and doctrine have evolved enormously and continue to evolve in a world where nuclear weapons remain a currency that must be managed and perhaps can be controlled, but also a world that cannot be returned to some pre–nuclear age, where harnessing the power of the atom for military and civilian purposes was at best a dream that would be realized in a distant future.

—*Michael Wheeler*

See also: Strategic Air Command and Strategic Command; Strategic Defenses; Submarine-Launched Ballistic Missiles (SLBMs); United States Air Force; United States Army; United States Navy

References

Bowie, Robert H., and Richard H. Immerman, *Waging Peace: How Eisenhower Shaped an Enduring Cold War Strategy* (Oxford, UK: Oxford University Press, 1998).

Brodie, Bernard, *Strategy in the Missile Age* (Princeton, NJ: Princeton University Press, 1959).

Bundy, McGeorge, *Danger and Survival: Choices about the Bomb in the First Fifty Years* (New York: Random House, 1988).

Freedman, Lawrence, *The Evolution of Nuclear Strategy,*
third edition (New York: Palgrave Macmillan, 2003).

URANIUM

Uranium is the heaviest naturally occurring chemical element. It is a dense, heavy metal that contains 92 protons and, in its natural state, is weakly radioactive. Refined uranium is a silvery-white metal that is toxic if inhaled or ingested in other than very small quantities.

Uranium is found throughout the world in minute quantities in most plants, animals, water, soil and rock. It is about as abundant as tin or tungsten in nature. Major sources of recoverable uranium can be found in uranium deposits. These deposits are mined throughout the world but mostly in Canada, Australia, Kazakhstan, Niger, South Africa, Namibia, Brazil, Russia, the United States, and Uzbekistan. Canada, the world's greatest uranium producer, mines approximately 30 percent of the world's supply, while Australia mines about 20 percent.

Enriched uranium is used as fuel for nuclear reactors and weapons. Depleted uranium, which contains less of the isotope uranium 235 than in nature (generally less than 0.2 percent), serves many military purposes, including use as armor-piercing ammunition, protective shielding, and wing components for helicopters and counterweights in airplanes. Depleted uranium also has industrial uses, including use as reinforcement in building materials such as concrete.

When bombarded with neutrons, uranium produces manmade isotopes such as plutonium, which is another type of fuel used in nuclear reactors and weapons.

History and Background

A German chemist named Martin Heinrich Klaproth is credited with the discovery of uranium in 1789. Klaproth actually discovered uranium oxide, which he believed to be pure uranium, in the mineral pitchblende. Pitchblende is a naturally occurring mineral that is a mix of uranium oxides. He named the new element after the recently discovered planet Uranus.

In 1841, French chemist Eugene-Melchoir Peligot isolated pure uranium metal. In 1896, French physicist Antoine Henri Becquerel discovered that uranium was radioactive. While Becquerel was investigating the fluorescence of uranium salt, he inadvertently discovered radioactivity. In 1903, he won the Nobel Prize in Physics for his discovery of spontaneous radiation.

Natural uranium was used in the first experimental nuclear reactor, designed and built on December 2, 1942, by Italian physicist Enrico Fermi at Stagg Field Stadium in Chicago. With this reactor, known as Fermi's Pile, Fermi achieved the first nuclear chain reaction. The "pile" consisted of approximately 40 tons of uranium oxide and 6 tons of uranium metal intermingled with 385 tons of pure graphite that moderated, or slowed, neutrons to limit thermal energies produced by the nuclear chain reaction.

Approximately 60 kilograms of highly enriched uranium were used to build "Little Boy," the first nuclear weapon. The Little Boy bomb was dropped by the United States on Hiroshima, Japan, on August 6, 1945, and yielded the equivalent energy of approximately 15,000 tons of TNT. Construction of the Little Boy weapon exhausted nearly the entire stockpile of highly enriched uranium in the United States at the time.

Uranium also is used to produce the manmade element plutonium. Approximately 200 tons of uranium metal was bombarded with neutrons in the first "breeder" reactor at the B Reactor at Hanford, Washington, to produce quantities of plutonium for nuclear weapons. This plutonium was used to fuel the first nuclear device, "Gadget," tested on July 16, 1945, at the Trinity Site near Alamogordo, New Mexico, as well as for the nuclear weapon "Fat Man" dropped on Nagasaki, Japan, on August 9, 1945.

Technical Details

Natural uranium is composed of approximately 99.27 percent of the isotope uranium 238 and 0.72 percent of uranium 235. The isotope uranium 234 also naturally occurs in very small quantities (approximately 0.0055 percent) as a decay product of uranium 238. Natural uranium has an atomic weight of approximately 238.0508. Uranium is an actinide, chemically similar to actinium, with a density of approximately 19.1 grams per cubic centimeter. Uranium 238 has a half-life of approximately 4.68 billion years, and uranium 235 has a half-life of approximately 703.8 million years.

Uranium 238 is fissionable material. The U-238 nucleus may fission, or split into two smaller nuclei, if it absorbs a fast, or high-energy, neutron, and a U-238 nucleus releases approximately 2.6 additional neutrons when it fissions. U-238 also is a fertile material, that is, it generally does not fission upon absorption of a thermal neutron but may be converted into fissile material through neutron bombardment. When bombarded with thermal neutrons, U-238 may be changed by neutron capture into plutonium, a fissile material.

Uranium 235 is fissile material, which means that it will likely undergo fission when it absorbs a thermal, or low-energy, neutron. Upon absorption of a neutron, U-235 will almost immediately fission, or split into two smaller nuclei. In the fission process, U-235 emits not only energy but also an average of approximately 2.4 neutrons, which may cause additional fission events. If there are enough U-235 atoms present in the material, these additional neutrons may result in a chain reaction.

Additional artificial isotopes of uranium can be made through various processes. Uranium 233, for example, is made through neutron bombardment of the element thorium 232. Uranium 233 is another fissile material that may be used as fuel for reactors. Another example, uranium 239, is a short-lived isotope that has a half-life of about 23 minutes. It decays into neptunium 239, which will further decay into plutonium 239.

Some types of nuclear reactors, such as the Canada Deuterium Uranium (CANDU) Reactor, use natural uranium as fuel (see Canada Deuterium Uranium Reactor). However, uranium is generally enriched from its natural state to be used as fuel for nuclear reactors and weapons. Enriching uranium involves increasing the amount of the isotope U-235 present in the material. Reactors in the United States generally require uranium fuel that is enriched to approximately 3 to 5 percent U-235. The U.S. Department of Energy defines highly enriched uranium (HEU), a special nuclear material (SNM), as any uranium that is enriched to 20 percent or higher of U-235. Nuclear weapons generally require "weapons-grade" HEU, which is uranium that is enriched to approximately 90 percent or higher of U-235.

Various forms of uranium are used during most enrichment processes. One such form of uranium is known as "yellowcake," which is a highly concentrated (approximately 70 percent or higher by weight) uranium oxide (U_3O_8). Another form of uranium, which becomes a gaseous compound at temperatures above 133 degrees Fahrenheit, is uranium hexafluoride (UF_6). This gaseous compound, also known simply as "hex," is the form of uranium used to enrich it to higher levels of the isotope U-235. Hex is the form of uranium critical to both of the widely used enrichment techniques, the gaseous-diffusion and gas-centrifuge methods. Following enrichment processes, uranium is converted to uranium dioxide (UO_2) to be used as fuel for reactors.

Current Status

Uranium remains the principal fuel for nuclear reactors today. In 2002, the world produced approximately 46,700 tons of yellowcake. About 1,200 tons of that yellowcake was produced in the United States. The mid-2004 average price of one pound of yellowcake was approximately $18.50. Uranium supplies approximately 17 percent of the world's electricity, which is generated in approximately 440 nuclear reactors. The total output of these reactors is approximately 350,000 million watts of electricity.

HEU is an internationally controlled material by nuclear nonproliferation treaties. The International Atomic Energy Agency (IAEA) helps to monitor and safeguard the world's supply of HEU. As the world's "nuclear watchdog," the IAEA monitors uranium enrichment facilities and the capabilities of the international community.

In 1993, the United States and Russia signed a Highly Enriched Uranium (HEU) Purchase Agreement, which authorizes the United States to purchase 500 metric tons of Russian HEU. The United States will convert the weapons-grade HEU to low enriched uranium fuel for commercial reactors; in the process, approximately 10,000 Russian nuclear weapons will be destroyed. This agreement includes purchasing the HEU over a twenty-year period for more than $12 billion.

One of the current issues pertaining to uranium is the use of depleted uranium (DU) as armor-piercing ammunition for conventional military weapons. Because depleted uranium is nearly two and a half times more dense than steel, it is used to gain greater momentum to penetrate armor by the military. As a heavy metal, DU is toxic if inhaled in sufficient quantities. The prolific use of DU by the United States during Operation Desert Storm in 1991 and subsequent operations caused public concern about the health hazard to soldiers and civilians who breathed in DU dust.

—*Don Gillich*

See also: Actinides; Atomic Mass/Number/Weight; Depleted Uranium (U-238); Enrichment; Highly Enriched Uranium; Isotopes; Low Enriched Uranium; Neutrons; Nuclear Fuel Cycle; Reactor Operations

References

Garvin, Richard L., and Georges Charpak, *Megawatts and Megatons: A Turning Point in the Nuclear Age* (New York: Knopf, 2001).

World Nuclear Association website, http://www. world-nuclear.org/.

VERIFICATION

Verification is the process of ascertaining compliance or noncompliance with an international treaty or other legal or political obligation. The term "verification" is often used synonymously with the term "monitoring," which is the process of observing, inspecting, measuring, and exhibiting military equipment and operations subject to an international treaty or agreement. Verification includes monitoring, but it also includes analyzing the data generated by the monitoring process; assessing this data against established standards of compliance; and weighing other factors such as the political context and importance of the agreement, the past compliance behavior of the monitored party, the risks associated with potential violations, and the effectiveness of prospective responses to those violations. Verification is the collective fusing of both the "monitoring process" and the more analytical and political decision-making "compliance process."

The verification measures for a particular treaty should be sufficient to assure compliance with a high level of confidence, to safeguard national security, and to allow for the detection of noncompliance early enough to permit an appropriate response. The verification processes authorized by the treaty must therefore be reliable enough for inspectors and analysts to detect significant noncompliance in a timely manner. Many technical considerations are taken into account in designing the verification procedures, but the final outcome is often the product of political as much as technical judgments.

History and Background

Throughout the 1960s and 1970s, it was often assumed that there was little need for intrusive verification of arms control agreements between the United States and the Soviet Union. It was presumed that countries did not sign agreements unless they intended to comply with them, that most arms limitation agreements were so modest that

there was little incentive for violating them, and that militarily meaningful violations would give themselves away, either because of their inherent magnitude or because they generated dissent within the violating government. As instances of Soviet noncompliance with arms control obligations were increasingly documented throughout the 1980s, however, it became apparent that many of these assumptions were obvious instances of mistakenly attributing the values of an open democratic society to those of a closed, centrally governed state that faced few institutional or political constraints when it came to exploiting arms control as another arena of conflict.

Prior to the treaties that resulted from the Strategic Arms Limitation Talks (SALT I and SALT II) during the 1970s, arms control agreements did not contain explicit provisions for mutual verification, other than to recognize the inherent right of the other parties to employ their own "national technical means" to monitor compliance with the agreement. Verification was undertaken on a unilateral basis without the cooperation of the other side, usually through means of surveillance satellites and other remote sources of information gathering (see National Technical Means; Strategic Arms Limitation Talks).

The SALT I agreement, signed in 1972 between the United States and the Soviet Union, incorporated language committing the signatories not to interfere with each other's national technical means of monitoring treaty compliance. It also banned concealment activities except for "current construction, assembly, conversion, or overhaul practices." Although SALT I also created the Standing Consultative Commission as a forum for confidential discussions of verification and compliance concerns between the parties to the treaty, it did not contain any on-site verification provisions.

The SALT II agreement of 1979 carried over the ban on interference with national technical means and the ban on deliberate concealment practices. It added a ban on the encryption of telemetry from missile tests that would impede verification. It also incorporated counting rules for those missile launchers subject to the treaty, provided for the parties to periodically update databases of treaty-limited items, and specified cooperative measures to distinguish between bombers carrying cruise missiles and those that carried only gravity bombs, all to facilitate monitoring compliance with an increasingly complex set of limitations. In many cases, however, the interpretation and implementation of these provisions were left to each side to determine for itself, thus allowing standards of compliance to be established on a unilateral basis and undermining the strategic value of the entire arms control process.

"Trust but Verify"

President Ronald Reagan came into office in 1980 determined to overhaul and improve verification of existing and future arms control agreements. He coined the phrase "trust but verify" to capture these dual objectives.

The Reagan administration not only sought deep reductions in theater and strategic nuclear weapons but also insisted on strict verification measures, including on-site inspections, as a precondition for any further arms limitation agreements with the Soviet Union. Critics of this approach asserted that such a precondition would derail any hope for sustaining the process of strategic nuclear arms control begun under the SALT agreements. But the Soviets eventually conceded, and the Intermediate Nuclear Forces (INF) Treaty, signed in 1987, incorporated intrusive verification measures that would later be used as the model for even more extensive verification provisions in the Strategic Arms Reduction Treaty (START I), signed in 1991. These intrusive measures included annually updated data exchanges on the numbers and locations of treaty-limited systems, a series of baseline inspections to be conducted shortly after the treaty's entry into force, an annual quota of short-notice on-site challenge inspections, continuous monitoring of the perimeters and portals of critical missile production facilities, a complete ban on concealment activities and telemetry encryption, and measures to enhance verification by national technical means, including on-demand open displays of treaty-limited items at missile and bomber bases and submarine ports. START enhanced these measures by adding reciprocal exhibitions of treaty-limited items for visiting inspection teams, stricter conversion and elimination requirements, and more robust open display requirements. Both the INF and START also established commissions to discuss and address issues related to verification and compliance with the respective provisions of the treaties (see Data Exchanges; Declared Facility; Intermediate-Range Nuclear Forces Treaty; Strategic Arms Reduction Treaty; Strategic Arms Reduction Treaty).

The Strategic Offensive Reductions Treaty (SORT, also called the Moscow Treaty), signed between the United States and Russia on May 24, 2002, commits both nations to reducing their operational stockpiles of strategic nuclear warheads to no more than 1,700–2,200 by December 31, 2012. Yet it contains no specific verification provisions of its own. Instead, the architects of the Moscow Treaty linked its verification provisions to those contained in START I and II.

—*Kerry Kartchner*

See also: Arms Control; Confidence- and Security-Building Measures; Implementation; Reconnaissance Satellites; Strategic Offensive Reductions Treaty; Telemetry

References

Calogera, Francesco, Marvin L. Goldberger, and Sergei Kapitza, eds., *Verification: Monitoring Disarmament* (Boulder: Westview, 1991).

Dunn, Lewis A., and Amy E. Gordon, eds., *Arms Control Verification and the New Role of On-Site Inspection: Challenges, Issues and Realities* (Lexington, MA: Lexington Books, 1990).

Krepon, Michael, and Mary Umberger, eds., *Verification and Compliance: A Problem-Solving Approach* (Cambridge, MA: Ballinger, 1988).

Rowell, William F., *Arms Control Verification* (Cambridge, MA: Ballinger, 1986).

WARFIGHTING STRATEGY

"Warfighting strategy" is a term used to describe the strategy of a political entity's armed forces for conducting warfare. Although lacking an official definition, it has gained acceptance as a way to express the means by which military force is employed to achieve objectives within the context of an expected or actual armed conflict. During the Cold War, those who advocated a nuclear counterforce targeting strategy versus a countervalue nuclear doctrine were said to support a particular warfighting strategy. They believed that it was possible for the United States to emerge significantly better off than the Soviet Union from a nuclear conflict. Warfighting theorists believed that the best nuclear deterrent was based on a nuclear warfighting strategy that held at risk Soviet nuclear and conventional military forces and did not simply generate a risk of mutual assured destruction (*see* Counterforce Targeting; Countervalue Targeting; Mutual Assured Destruction).

Strategy relates ends to means. Warfighting, like warfare, is a means to achieve ends that involves the exchange of actual or threatened lethal force between adversaries over time. Historically, the means of a warfighting strategy have included the full range of military capabilities, from sword-bearing infantry to missile-delivered weapons of mass destruction. Likewise, the ends have reflected the entire spectrum of political objectives espoused by city-states, feudal kingdoms, nation-states, and others. Around 500 B.C., for example, Sun Tzu articulated a warfighting strategy for the Chinese Kingdom of Wu that emphasized the use of deception to disrupt an adversary's plans and alliances in order to achieve victory, ideally without even fighting. During World War II, the Nazi regime of Germany implemented a warfighting strategy known as "Blitzkrieg" that integrated land and air forces to overwhelm the adversary through speed and force. North Vietnam effectively employed a guerrilla-warfare strategy against France and the United States, and Al Qaeda, the violent nonstate actor cen-

tered in the Middle East, relies on terrorism as a warfighting strategy.

In its customary usage, warfighting strategy is a form of military strategy, which is the art and science of employing the armed forces of a nation to secure the objectives of the national policy by the application of force or threat of force. Military strategy is derived from national strategy, which is the art and science of developing and using political, economic, military, and informational powers during peace and war to secure policy objectives. Warfighting strategy has application at all levels of war: strategic, operational, and tactical. At the strategic level, it links the military capabilities of a nation-state to specific security objectives as articulated in global or regional strategic plans. It guides the development and structuring of military forces, including such overarching operational concepts as nuclear deterrence, power projection with conventional forces, or information superiority. It is more often used to refer to warfare at the operational level. It guides the planning and conduct of actual military campaigns and major operations. In addition to reflecting broad concepts such as offense, defense, mobility, and asymmetry, warfighting strategy addresses the role of specific capabilities, such as airpower, in achieving outcomes, such as air supremacy, in relation to overall campaign objectives, such as the annihilation of an enemy's armed forces. Its use at the operational level impacts the tactical level by shaping when and how specific battles will be fought.

—*Troy S. Thomas*

References

Paret, Peter, ed., *The Makers of Modern Strategy: From Machiavelli to the Nuclear Age* (Princeton, NJ: Princeton University Press, 1986).

Warfighting, U.S. Marine Corps Doctrinal Publication 1-1, 1997.

WARHEAD

The term "warhead" generally refers to the weapon that is mounted inside the nose cone and reentry vehicle of a ballistic or guided missile. Warhead construction is challenging because it entails developing a weapon that not only can withstand the vibration and acceleration involved in rocket flight but also survive the heat of reentry into the atmosphere. Warheads have to be hardened against the electromagnetic pulse that is generated in a nuclear detonation to reduce the chances of fratricide. Warheads also must be equipped with safety features that render them harmless if they are subject to tampering, and they must be capable of being stored or deployed atop operational delivery systems for relatively long periods. In the case of earth-penetrating weapons, warheads also have to be designed to withstand the shock of impact with the ground.

Nuclear warheads designed for ballistic missiles also must meet stringent weight and shape requirements to conform to the lift capability of missiles and the shape of reentry vehicles. Although early reentry vehicles had long, needle-like designs, reentry vehicles that had a blunt body shape were the most efficient way to dissipate the heat generated upon reentry into the Earth's atmosphere. Blunt body vehicles, however, were slow to reenter the atmosphere, making them a relatively easy target for antiballistic missile systems. Cone-shaped reentry vehicles, coated with an ablative material that would literally burn and flake off during reentry, cooling the warhead inside, were chosen as the ideal shape to minimize reentry time. The shape of the reentry vehicle forced nuclear weapons designers to develop complementary weapons designs.

—*James J. Wirtz*

See also: Ballistic Missiles; Command and Control; Missile Defense; Payload; Reentry Vehicles

Reference

Stumpf, David K., *Titan II* (Fayetteville: University of Arkansas Press, 2000).

WARSAW PACT

The Warsaw Pact was a formal alliance established on May 14, 1955, by the Warsaw Treaty of Friendship, Cooperation, and Mutual Assistance between Albania, Bulgaria, Czechoslovakia, East Germany, Hungary, Poland, Romania, and the Soviet Union. Following the principles laid out in Article 51 of the United Nations Charter, the pact was designed for collective self-defense of the member states against external aggression. The Soviet Union claimed that it was formed in response to the Federal Republic of Germany joining the North Atlantic Treaty Organization (NATO). The pact also facilitated Soviet political control of Eastern Europe by authorizing the Soviet Union to station forces in Warsaw Pact territory. Soviet policy provided the main directive to Warsaw Pact plans through the Political Consultative Committee (PCC) as the highest alliance organ, although the pact stated that relations among the signatories were based on equality and respect for national sovereignty and independence. Soviet political intentions and its disrespect for national sovereignty and independence were clearly demonstrated, however, in 1968, when the pact employed military force for the only time against one of its own members, Czechoslovakia. The forces that entered Czechoslovakia in August 1968 to halt the revolutionary movement toward democracy were made up of twenty-three Soviet divisions with only six divisions from other members.

The détente period in the 1970s witnessed relatively stable Soviet–East European relations. Joint Warsaw Pact exercises during this time emphasized offensive capabilities. In the late 1970s, Soviet deployment of SS-20 intermediate-range ballistic missiles (IRBMs) in Warsaw Pact countries increased tensions in Europe, and the United States responded by deploying Pershing II IRBMs.

The Warsaw Pact had a larger ground force of infantry, tanks, and artillery than NATO and was largely made up of Soviet armed forces. Many believed that the Warsaw Pact could have defeated NATO in a conventional war. The Soviet and Warsaw Pact aim was for "effective occupation" of Central Europe within hours of an offensive as a means of quickly acquiring territorial bargaining counters in the event of a ceasefire. Soviet military strategists planned to defeat NATO decisively before its political and military command structure could decide how to respond to a Soviet attack. Warsaw Pact forces undertook extensive nuclear, biological, and chemical (NBC) training, and tactical nuclear strikes at key targets may have been considered. Warsaw Pact maneuvers centered on the postnuclear phase of hostilities, a clear indicator of what was expected. Given the desire for speedy acquisition of territory, pact strategists may have thought that a chemical and biological attack could reduce the danger of a nuclear counterattack against Warsaw Pact troops, leaving the economic potential of Western Europe relatively intact.

By the mid-1980s, the future of the Warsaw Pact hinged on Soviet premier Mikhail Gorbachev's emerging policy of liberalization toward Eastern Europe. At the U.S.S.R.'s Twenty-Seventh Party Congress in 1986, Gorbachev acknowledged that differences existed among the Soviet allies. In 1987, the Warsaw Pact, under Soviet tutelage, adopted a defense-oriented military doctrine. In July 1991, as the Cold War was ending, the members agreed to terminate their thirty-six year alliance.

—*J. Simon Rofe*

See also: Cold War; Détente
References
Clawson, Robert W., and Lawrence S. Kaplan, eds., *The Warsaw Pact: Political Purpose and Military Means* (Wilmington, DE: Scholarly Resources, 1982).
Lewis, William J., *The Warsaw Pact: Arms, Doctrine, and Strategy* (New York: McGraw-Hill, 1982).

WASSENAAR ARRANGEMENT

The Wassenaar Arrangement is a voluntary export control regime created in 1996. Most of the world's leading arms exporters participate in the arrangement. The regime seeks to prevent destabilizing accumulations of arms anywhere in the world and its members consult on arms deals with non-Wassenaar states. The thirty-three members of the arrangement meet annually in a plenary session.

The agreement calls upon members to subject small arms and light weapons to national export controls, using guidelines drawn up based on best practices that specify criteria to be used when assessing a possible arms sale. For example, a sale should be avoided if the members believe the weapons could end up in the hands of terrorists or organized crime. Members report on exports of dual-use goods and technologies as well as on seven categories of conventional weapons: battle tanks, armored combat vehicles, large-caliber artillery, military aircraft and unmanned aerial vehicles, military and attack helicopters, warships, and missiles or missile systems.

—*Jeffrey A. Larsen*

See also: Dual-Use; Nonproliferation; Nuclear Supplies Group
Reference
Wassenaar website, http://www.wassenaar.org/.

WEAPONS-GRADE MATERIAL

The acquisition of weapons-grade material—nuclear material considered most suitable for making nuclear weapons—is the most formidable obstacle to the manufacture of nuclear weapons. The primary weapons-grade materials are uranium enriched to 90 percent or greater uranium 235 (U-235) or plutonium with greater than about 90 percent plutonium 239 (Pu-239). These elements are called "fissile" because they can be split into two roughly equal-mass fragments when struck by a neutron of even low energy. When a large enough mass of either material is assembled, a self-sustaining chain reaction is produced after the first fission. For the nuclear explosive to obtain a significant nuclear yield, sufficient neutrons must be present within the weapon core at the right time. If the chain reaction starts too soon or too late, the result will be only a "fizzle" yield or no yield at all (*see* Fission Weapons).

Plutonium is used by all of the current nuclear weapons states: the United States, Russia, Great Britain, France, China, Israel, India, and Pakistan. (South Africa built six nuclear weapons in the 1980s and early 1990s using U-235, but it subsequently destroyed these weapons and dismantled its weapons program.) Pu-239 does not occur in nature. It can be made only in quantities sufficient for constructing a weapon in a nuclear reactor. It must be "bred," or produced, one atomic nucleus at a time by bombarding U-238 with neutrons to produce the isotope U-239, which, as it beta-decays, emits an electron to become the radioactive neptunium 239 (Np-239). The neptunium isotope again beta-decays to become Pu-239. The only proven and practical source for the large quantities of neutrons needed to make plutonium at a reasonable speed is a nuclear reactor in which a controlled but self-sustaining U-235 fission chain reaction takes place. The plutonium then must be extracted chemically in a reprocessing plant, making this route to nuclear weapons production relatively difficult to conceal.

U-235 is the other significant weapons-grade material. The only naturally occurring fissile isotope, natural uranium contains only about 0.7 percent U-235, the rest being largely the less fissionable isotope U-238 (which cannot sustain a chain reaction). To use uranium either as a fuel for nuclear reactors or as the explosive charge of a nuclear weapon, U-235 must be separated from the rest of the uranium by a process known as "enrichment."

The first nuclear weapons the United States developed contained a hollow ball of plutonium surrounded by conventional explosives. When these explosives were detonated, the resulting force, focused inward, compressed the plutonium, thereby initiating a chain reaction. The United States first detonated this kind of bomb during the Trinity test near Alamogordo, New Mexico, on July 16, 1945, and then it dropped another, called "Fat Man," on Nagasaki, Japan, a few weeks later, on August 9. These two devices were implosion devices (see Implosion Devices). The nuclear bomb the United States dropped on Hiroshima, "Little Boy," on August 6 detonated when one chunk of U-235 was fired down a tube into another piece of U-235. This type, known as a gun-assembly device, is the easiest of all nuclear devices to design and build and did not require testing (see Gun-Type Devices). It is generally believed to be impossible to prevent any nation having the requisite amount of enriched uranium from building one or more gun-type weapons. Therefore, the acquisition of significant quantities of U-235 or a facility in which to separate the fissile material is an indicator that the acquiring state could be in the process of gaining a rudimentary nuclear capability.

—Peter Lavoy

See also: Enrichment; Highly Enriched Uranium; Isotopes; Plutonium; Reprocessing; Uranium

References

Office of Technology Assessment, Technologies Underlying Weapons of Mass Destruction (Washington, DC: U.S. Government Printing Office, 1993), available at http://www.wws.princeton.edu/~ota/ns20/topic_f.html.

"Special Weapons Primer," available at http://www.fas.org/nuke/intro/nuke/index.html.

WEAPONS OF MASS DESTRUCTION (WMD)

Although the term "weapon of mass destruction" (WMD) has been in use for more than thirty-five years, it has no widely accepted definition. Only one international agreement uses the term: The 1967 Outer Space Treaty bans "nuclear weapons or any other kinds of weapons of mass destruction" from Earth orbit or on celestial bodies (see Outer Space Treaty). The term "WMD" sometimes is used to identify weapons considered beyond civilized norms that should be banned or at least internationally controlled.

One working definition for WMD might be weapons that can create more than a hundred times the casualties expected from an equivalent mass of high explosive and that can cause severe contamination to an area requiring millions of dollars and months of work in cleanup and rebuilding efforts in order for safe use to resume. Most definitions of WMD list biological, chemical, radiological, or nuclear weapons. These four types of weapons can affect large areas and large numbers of people, especially in comparison with conventional weapons targeted at specific soldiers, vehicles, or buildings. In addition, all four can produce effects that spread far beyond their original target area and contaminate a large area for a long time after use.

WMD Effects

There are significant differences among the four kinds of WMD in terms of effects, difficulty of acquisition and delivery, and expectations about use. Nuclear weapons are the only type of WMD that destroy structures and equipment as well as killing people. No form of protection is effective against nuclear blast effects.

Pound for pound, biological weapons can produce even more casualties than nuclear weapons, but biological weapons are more dependent on environmental conditions and random factors. With sufficient warning, military forces can protect themselves against biological weapons; for many agents, civilian populations also can be treated after an attack is discovered. Biological agents do not usually produce instant death or even incapacitation; they often take hours or days to produce effects. Some people may even have natural immunity to a biological agent.

Chemical weapons must be delivered in vast quantities to cause massive casualties. When warned, military authorities can have troops use protective gear to reduce the number of casualties suffered during a chemical weapons attack. When not protected, however, exposed individuals may experience a nearly instant agonizing death from just drops of certain chemical agents.

Radiological weapons might produce more panic from fear of radiation than actual death. In theory, radioactive debris could be spread over a large area using conventional explosives laced with fissile material. Radiological weapons require large quantities of material to produce a delayed effect that can be defeated with protective clothing and through decontamination efforts (*see* Nuclear Weapons Effects).

Acquisition and Delivery

Nuclear weapons are probably the most difficult type of WMD to acquire because specialized equipment and knowledge is required to develop and test them. Nuclear weapons production relies on complex and unique equipment and the procurement of weapons-grade fissionable materials that must be carefully controlled. Meeting the requirements to construct nuclear weapons is a challenge for nations and may be beyond the ability of nonstate groups. Terrorist groups, however, may be able to acquire a weapon on the black market or through theft.

In contrast, biological weapons can be created using commercial equipment in a relatively small facility, and even small amounts can be deadly. They can be distributed easily, as shown in the U.S. anthrax attacks that occurred in the fall of 2001. Production of chemical weapons in quantity requires chemical engineering expertise and chemical pro-

duction facilities on a scale similar to that of petroleum refineries. Aircraft sprayers and artillery delivery are preferred for battlefield use, but pressurized tanks can suffice at any scale.

Radioactive material suitable for radiological weapons is readily available given its widespread use in medical and research applications. Delivery of radiological weapons by means of aerial dusting would affect the largest possible area, but recent concern has centered on the possible terrorist employment of so-called dirty bombs, that is, conventional explosive devices used for dispersing nuclear material. Explosive dispersal is unlikely to produce any deaths from radiation but could require an expensive and time-consuming decontamination cleanup effort to make the area safe for human occupation (*see* Radiological Dispersal Device).

Despite the potential for chemical, biological, radiological, and nuclear weapons to produce large-scale death and destruction, weapons of mass destruction have primarily served as tools of deterrence by nations attempting to prevent their use by adversaries.

—*Roy Pettis*

See also: Deterrence

References

Cordesman, Anthony H., *Terrorism, Asymmetric Warfare, and Weapons of Mass Destruction* (New York: Praeger, 2001).

Tucker, Jonathan, *Toxic Terror: Assessing Terrorist Use of Chemical and Biological Weapons* (Cambridge, MA: MIT Press, 2000).

X-RAY LASER

The concept of an X-ray laser dates to the early 1970s, when physicists realized that laser beams amplified with ions had more energy than beams amplified using gases. It was thought that nuclear explosions might serve as the power supply for such high-energy lasers. The Strategic Defense Initiative (SDI) proposed relying on a nuclear-powered laser to destroy intercontinental ballistic missiles (ICBMs) while in flight.

One of the goals of SDI was to place satellites with nuclear devices into orbit. These satellites would bristle with glass rods to serve as laser guides. Upon detonation of the nuclear device, X-ray photons in the atoms making up the rods would be excited. This would lead to optical amplification of the X-ray photons to produce an X-ray laser beam that would be minimally affected by atmospheric distortion (which diffuses light beams produced by conventional chemical lasers). The X-ray laser would be capable of destroying ICBMs in flight. It would strictly be a one-shot device, destroying itself when the nuclear weapon detonated and fired the laser. A test of the concept, code-named Correo, took place at the Nevada Test Site in 1984. Research into space-based X-ray lasers ended after the cancellation of the SDI program.

The SDI program brought about greater understanding of the physics of X-ray lasers and produced new computer codes for modeling plasmas. It also contributed to the development of a laboratory X-ray laser for biological imaging. Coupling X-ray lasers with X-ray microscopes, scientists at the Lawrence Livermore National Laboratory in Livermore, California, have created three-dimensional holograms of living organisms and developed new materials for commercial use.

—*Gilles Van Nederveen*

See also: Missile Defense; Strategic Defense Initiative

References

Broad, William J., *Teller's War: The Top Secret Story behind the Star Wars Deception* (New York: Simon and Schuster, 1992).

Elton, Raymond C., *X-Ray Laser* (New York: Academic Press, 1990).

Rein, Edward, *The Strategic Defense Initiative: The Development of an Armaments Program* (Cambridge: Cambridge University Press, 2003).

YELLOWCAKE
See Enrichment; Highly Enriched Uranium

YIELD

"Yield" refers to the energy released in a nuclear detonation. Although this energy takes the form of blast, thermal and nuclear radiation, and electromagnetic pulse, yield usually describes just the blast produced by a device. It is commonly expressed in terms of kilotons (thousands of tons) or megatons (millions of tons) of the equivalent quantity of trinitrotoluene (TNT) required to produce the same amount of energy.

The focus of early nuclear weapons design efforts was to build weapons with increasingly higher yields. The highest-yield device tested by the United States was approximately 15 megatons. The former Soviet Union tested a device that was in excess of 50 megatons.

Albert Einstein's mass-energy equivalence equation ($E = mc^2$) implies that mass can be converted into energy. The energy released in the mass conversion in fission and fusion is thousands to millions of times greater than that released in a chemical process. The yield of a weapon is determined by the amount of nuclear fuel available and its efficiency, that is, how much of the available fuel actually undergoes fission or fusion. A higher yield generally produces greater destructive effects.

—*Don Gillich*

See also: Fission Weapons; Kilotons; Megatons; Nuclear Weapons Effects

Reference

Glasstone, Samuel, and Philip J. Dolan, eds., *The Effects of Nuclear Weapons* (Washington, DC: U.S. Government Printing Office, 1977).

ZANGGER COMMITTEE

In 1971, following the entry into force of the Nuclear Nonproliferation Treaty (NPT), the Zangger Committee was formed as the first international effort to control exports of nuclear dual-use technologies. The committee was composed of major nuclear supplier nations that were party to the NPT. Their mission was to interpret the vague safeguard requirements of Article III.2 of the NPT that addressed the export of nuclear equipment and material.

The committee concluded that an exporter had limited responsibility to ensure that materials being exported would be placed under International Atomic Energy Agency safeguards and that the exporter had no responsibility to ensure that the entirety of an importer's program be safeguarded. The committee also concluded that the NPT was not responsible for the creation of binding international export controls and that nations had to devise their own policies to police their own exports. This interpretation of what was required by the NPT was considered too loose by many and represented the ongoing tension between the desire to prevent potential proliferation to nuclear-aspiring nations while maintaining the right to transfer nuclear technologies and materials for peaceful purposes.

Zangger Committee members entered into an ad hoc voluntary agreement that was not formally connected to the NPT in which they agreed not to export certain items without first ensuring that they would be safeguarded. They developed a so-called Trigger List that contained agreed-upon items that could not be exported in the absence of safeguards to prevent diversion into covert nuclear weapons programs.

The Zangger Committee laid the groundwork for the Nuclear Suppliers Group (NSG) and other nonproliferation voluntary agreements. Its Trigger List was incorporated and extended by the NSG and is a significant contribution to the current nuclear nonproliferation regime.

—*Jennifer Hunt Morstein*

Z

See also: Nonproliferation; Nuclear Nonproliferation Treaty; Nuclear Suppliers Group; Safeguards
Reference
Gardner, Gary T., *Nuclear Nonproliferation: A Primer* (Boulder: Lynne Rienner, 1994).

ZERO OPTION
See Intermediate-Range Nuclear Forces Treaty

ZONE OF PEACE

The term "zone of peace" was first applied to a geographical region in the international community when, in 1970, the Lusaka Non-Aligned Summit called upon all leaders to "respect the Indian Ocean as a zone of peace from which Great Power rivalries and competition" would be banned. Indian officials also wanted to use the zone-of-peace concept to exclude U.S. and UK military units from the region and eliminate foreign military bases, for example, the British base on the island of Diego Garcia. In 1966, the United States had signed a treaty with the United Kingdom making the island available for U.S. military operations. During the Cold War, the base was an important forward operating post used to counter growing Soviet influence in Asia and Africa.

Sri Lanka diplomats introduced the Indian Ocean Zone of Peace (IOZOP) proposal into the UN General Assembly with Resolution 2832 in 1971. In the same year, Malaysia unveiled a similar proposal for a Zone of Peace, Freedom and Neutrality (ZOPFAN).

In 1972, the UN formed the Ad Hoc Committee on the Indian Ocean. The committee focused on preparing for an Indian Ocean conference that would lead to an agreement to implement the

IOZOP. Because committee members were unable to overcome fundamental disagreements, the conference never convened. IOZOP and ZOPFAN efforts to reduce superpower rivalry in the region failed because Cold War tensions were too difficult for smaller countries, even those operating collectively, to resolve. Zone-of-peace proponents also failed to realize that not everyone believed that Great Power involvement in the Indian Ocean was counter to their interests. Several states, including Australia, welcomed the U.S. Navy in the Indian Ocean as a stabilizing influence in South Asia.

Owing to the strong opposition of the United States, the United Kingdom, and France, the IOZOP initiative has made little diplomatic progress since it was first proposed. Given the usefulness of Diego Garcia as a base of operations in the global war against terrorism, future zone-of-peace negotiations or discussions are unlikely to be taken seriously by the United States, Britain, or even India, for that matter. In fact, the United States has called for terminating the Ad Hoc Committee as a way to reduce the UN's administrative costs.

In addition to the Indian Ocean and Malaysian zones-of-peace proposals, there have been proposals for zones of peace in Central America, South America, and for specific countries such as Tibet and El Salvador. The proposals generally call for excluding foreign powers from the region or state, stopping the flow of arms into the region, and creating a climate for reestablishing regional or national peace and security in the face of regional or internal civil wars. So far, however, none of the proposals have been implemented.

—Guy Roberts

See also: Nuclear Weapons Free Zones
References
Braun, Dieter, *The Indian Ocean: Region of Conflict or "Peace Zone"* (New York: St. Martin's Press, 1983).
International Peace Academy, *The Indian Ocean as a Zone of Peace* (Boston: Matininus Nijhoff, 1986).

Key Documents:
Nuclear Weapons

Treaty Between the United States of America and the Union of Soviet Socialist Republics on the Limitation of Anti-Ballistic Missile Systems

Signed at Moscow May 26, 1972
Ratification advised by U.S. Senate August 3, 1972
Ratified by U.S. President September 30, 1972
Entered into force October 3, 1972

The United States of America and the Union of Soviet Socialist Republics, hereinafter referred to as the Parties,

Proceeding from the premise that nuclear war would have devastating consequences for all mankind,

Considering that effective measures to limit anti-ballistic missile systems would be a substantial factor in curbing the race in strategic offensive arms and would lead to a decrease in the risk of outbreak of war involving nuclear weapons,

Proceeding from the premise that the limitation of anti-ballistic missile systems, as well as certain agreed measures with respect to the limitation of strategic offensive arms, would contribute to the creation of more favorable conditions for further negotiations on limiting strategic arms,

Mindful of their obligations under Article VI of the Treaty on the Non-Proliferation of Nuclear Weapons,

Declaring their intention to achieve at the earliest possible date the cessation of the nuclear arms race and to take effective measures toward reductions in strategic arms, nuclear disarma-ment, and general and complete disarmament,

Desiring to contribute to the relaxation of international tension and the strengthening of trust between States,

Have agreed as follows:

ARTICLE I

1. Each Party undertakes to limit anti-ballistic missile (ABM) systems and to adopt other measures in accordance with the provisions of this Treaty.

2. Each Party undertakes not to deploy ABM systems for a defense of the territory of its country and not to provide a base for such a defense, and not to deploy ABM systems for defense of an individual region except as provided for in Article III of this Treaty.

ARTICLE II

1. For the purpose of this Treaty an ABM system is a system to counter strategic ballistic missiles or their elements in flight trajectory, currently consisting of:
   (a) ABM interceptor missiles, which are interceptor missiles constructed and deployed for an ABM role, or of a type tested in an ABM mode;
   (b) ABM launchers, which are launchers constructed and deployed for launching ABM interceptor missiles; and
   (c) ABM radars, which are radars constructed and deployed for an ABM role, or of a type tested in an ABM mode.

2. The ABM system components listed in paragraph 1 of this Article include those which are:
   (a) operational;
   (b) under construction;
   (c) undergoing testing;
   (d) undergoing overhaul, repair or conversion; or
   (e) mothballed.

ARTICLE III

Each Party undertakes not to deploy ABM systems or their components except that:

(a) within one ABM system deployment area having a radius of one hundred and fifty kilometers and centered on the Partys national capital, a Party may deploy: (1) no more than one hundred ABM launchers and no more than one hundred ABM interceptor missiles at launch sites, and (2) ABM radars within no more than six ABM radar complexes, the area of each complex being circular and having a diameter of no more than three kilometers; and

(b) within one ABM system deployment area having a radius of one hundred and fifty kilometers and containing ICBM silo launchers, a Party may deploy: (1) no more than one hundred ABM launchers and no more than one hundred ABM interceptor missiles at launch sites, (2) two large phased-array ABM radars comparable in potential to corresponding ABM radars operational or under construction on the date of signature of the Treaty in an ABM system deployment area containing ICBM silo launchers, and (3) no more than eighteen ABM radars each having a potential less than the potential of the smaller of the above-mentioned two large phased-array ABM radars.

ARTICLE IV

The limitations provided for in Article III shall not apply to ABM systems or their components used for development or testing, and located within current or additionally agreed test ranges. Each Party may have no more than a total of fifteen ABM launchers at test ranges.

ARTICLE V

1. Each Party undertakes not to develop, test, or deploy ABM systems or components which are sea-based, air-based, space-based, or mobile land-based.
2. Each Party undertakes not to develop, test or deploy ABM launchers for launching more than one ABM interceptor missile at a time from each launcher, not to modify deployed launchers to provide them with such a capacity, not to develop, test, or deploy automatic or semi-automatic or other similar systems for rapid reload of ABM launchers.

ARTICLE VI

To enhance assurance of the effectiveness of the limitations on ABM systems and their components provided by the Treaty, each Party undertakes:

(a) not to give missiles, launchers, or radars, other than ABM interceptor missiles, ABM launchers, or ABM radars, capabilities to counter strategic ballistic missiles or their elements in flight trajectory, and not to test them in an ABM mode; and
(b) not to deploy in the future radars for early warning of strategic ballistic missile attack except at locations along the periphery of its national territory and oriented outward.

ARTICLE VII

Subject to the provisions of this Treaty, modernization and replacement of ABM systems or their components may be carried out.

ARTICLE VIII

ABM systems or their components in excess of the numbers or outside the areas specified in this Treaty, as well as ABM systems or their components prohibited by this Treaty, shall be destroyed or dismantled under agreed procedures within the shortest possible agreed period of time.

ARTICLE IX

To assure the viability and effectiveness of this Treaty, each Party undertakes not to transfer to other States, and not to deploy outside its national territory, ABM systems or their components limited by this Treaty.

ARTICLE X

Each Party undertakes not to assume any international obligations which would conflict with this Treaty.

ARTICLE XI

The Parties undertake to continue active negotiations for limitations on strategic offensive arms.

ARTICLE XII

1. For the purpose of providing assurance or compliance with the provisions of this Treaty, each Party shall use national technical means of verification at its disposal in a manner consistent with generally recognized principles of international law.
2. Each Party undertakes not to interfere with the national technical means of verification of the other Party operating in accordance with paragraph 1 of this Article.
3. Each Party undertakes not to use deliberate concealment measures which impede verification by national technical means of compliance with the provisions of this Treaty. This obligation shall not require changes in current construction, assembly, conversion, or overhaul practices.

ARTICLE XIII

1. To promote the objectives and implementation of the provisions of this Treaty, the Parties shall establish promptly a Standing Consultative Commission, within the framework of which they will:
   (a) consider questions concerning compliance with the obligations assumed and related situations which may be considered ambiguous;
   (b) provide on a voluntary basis such information as either Party considers necessary to assure confidence in compliance with the obligations assumed;
   (c) consider questions involving unintended interference with national technical means of verification;
   (d) consider possible changes in the strategic situation which have a bearing on the provisions of this Treaty;
   (e) agree upon procedures and dates for destruction or dismantling of ABM systems or their components in cases provided for by the provisions of this Treaty;
   (f) consider, as appropriate, possible proposals for further increasing the viability of this Treaty; including proposals for amendments in accordance with the provisions of this Treaty;
   (g) consider, as appropriate, proposals for further measures aimed at limiting strategic arms.
2. The Parties through consultation shall establish, and may amend as appropriate, Regulations for the Standing Consultative Commission governing procedures, composition and other relevant matters.

ARTICLE XIV

1. Each Party may propose amendments to this Treaty. Agreed amendments shall enter into force in accordance with the procedures governing the entry into force of this Treaty.
2. Five years after entry into force of this Treaty, and at five-year intervals thereafter, the Parties shall together conduct a review of this Treaty.

ARTICLE XV

1. This Treaty shall be of unlimited duration.
2. Each Party shall, in exercising its national sovereignty, have the right to withdraw from this Treaty if it decides that extraordinary events related to the subject matter of this Treaty have jeopardized its supreme interests. It shall give notice of its decision to the other Party six months prior to withdrawal from the Treaty. Such notice shall include a statement of the extraordinary events the notifying Party regards as having jeopardized its supreme interests.

ARTICLE XVI

1. This Treaty shall be subject to ratification in accordance with the constitutional procedures of each Party. The Treaty shall enter into force on the day of the exchange of instruments of ratification.
2. This Treaty shall be registered pursuant to Article 102 of the Charter of the United Nations.

DONE at Moscow on May 26, 1972, in two copies, each in the English and Russian languages, both texts being equally authentic.

FOR THE UNITED STATES OF AMERICA:
RICHARD NIXON
President of the United States of America
FOR THE UNION OF SOVIET SOCIALIST RE-PUBLICS:
L. I. BREZHNEV
General Secretary of the Central Committee of the CPSU

Agreed Framework Between the United States of America and the Democratic People's Republic of Korea

October 21, 1994

Delegations of the Governments of the United States of America (U.S.) and the Democratic People's Republic of Korea (DPRK) held talks in Geneva from September 23 to October 17, 1994, to negotiate an overall resolution of the nuclear issue on the Korean Peninsula.

Both sides reaffirmed the importance of attaining the objectives contained in the August 12, 1994 Agreed Statement between the U.S. and the DPRK and upholding the principles of the June 11, 1993 Joint Statement of the U.S. and the DPRK to achieve peace and security on a nuclear-free Korean peninsula. The U.S. and the DPRK decided to take the following actions for the resolution of the nuclear issue:

I.

Both sides will cooperate to replace the DPRK's graphite-moderated reactors and related facilities with light-water reactor (LWR) power plants.

1) In accordance with the October 20, 1994 letter of assurance from the U.S. President, the U.S. will undertake to make arrangements for the provision to the DPRK of a LWR project with a total generating capacity of approximately 2,000 MW(e) by a target date of 2003.

- The U.S. will organize under its leadership an international consortium to finance and supply the LWR project to be provided to the DPRK. The U.S., representing the international consortium, will serve as the principal point of contact with the DPRK for the LWR project.
- The U.S., representing the consortium, will make best efforts to secure the conclusion of a supply contract with the DPRK within six months of the date of this Document for the provision of the LWR project. Contract talks will begin as soon as possible after the date of this Document.
- As necessary, the U.S. and the DPRK will conclude a bilateral agreement for cooperation in the field of peaceful uses of nuclear energy.

2) In accordance with the October 20, 1994 letter of assurance from the U.S. President, the U.S., representing the consortium, will make arrangements to offset the energy foregone due to the freeze of the DPRK's graphite-moderated reactors and related facilities, pending completion of the first LWR unit.

- Alternative energy will be provided in the form of heavy oil for heating and electricity production.

- Deliveries of heavy oil will begin within three months of the date of this Document and will reach a rate of 500,000 tons annually, in accordance with an agreed schedule of deliveries.

3) Upon receipt of U.S. assurances for the provision of LWR's and for arrangements for interim energy alternatives, the DPRK will freeze its graphite-moderated reactors and related facilities and will eventually dismantle these reactors and related facilities.

- The freeze on the DPRK's graphite-moderated reactors and related facilities will be fully implemented within one month of the date of this Document. During this one-month period, and throughout the freeze, the International Atomic Energy Agency (IAEA) will be allowed to monitor this freeze, and the DPRK will provide full cooperation to the IAEA for this purpose.
- Dismantlement of the DPRK's graphite-moderated reactors and related facilities will be completed when the LWR project is completed.
- The U.S. and DPRK will cooperated in finding a method to store safely the spent fuel from the 5 MW(e) experimental reactor during the construction of the LWR project, and to dispose of the fuel in a safe manner that does not involve reprocessing in the DPRK.

4) As soon as possible after the date of this document. U.S. and DPRK experts will hold two sets of experts talks.

- At one set of talks, experts will discuss issues related to alternative energy and the replacement of the graphite-moderated reactor program with the LWR project.
- At the other set of talks, experts will discuss specific arrangements for spent fuel storage and ultimate disposition.

II.

The two sides will move toward full normalization of political and economic relations.

1) Within three months of the date of this Document, both sides will reduce barriers to trade and investment, including restrictions on telecommunications services and financial transactions.

2) Each side will open a liaison office in the other's capital following resolution of consular and other technical issues through expert level discussions.

3) As progress is made on issues of concern to each side, the U.S. and DPRK will upgrade bilateral relations to the

Ambassadorial level.

III.

Both sides will work together for peace and security on a nuclear-free Korean peninsula.

1) The U.S. will provide formal assurances to the DPRK, against the threat or use of nuclear weapons by the U.S.

2) The DPRK will consistently take steps to implement the North-South Joint Declaration on the Denuclearization of the Korean peninsula.

3) The DPRK will engage in North-South dialogue, as this Agreed Framework will help create an atmosphere that promotes such dialogue.

IV.

Both sides will work together to strengthen the international nuclear non-proliferation regime.

1) The DPRK will remain a party to the Treaty on the Non-Proliferation of Nuclear Weapons (NPT) and will allow implementation of its safeguards agreement under the Treaty.

2) Upon conclusion of the supply contract for the provision of the LWR project, ad hoc and routine inspections will resume under the DPRK's safeguards agreement with the IAEA with respect to the facilities not subject to the freeze. Pending conclusion of the supply contract, inspections required by the IAEA for the continuity of safeguards will continue at the facilities not subject to the freeze.

3) When a significant portion of the LWR project is completed, but before delivery of key nuclear components, the DPRK will come into full compliance with its safeguards agreement with the IAEA (INFCIRC/403), including taking all steps that may be deemed necessary by the IAEA, following consultations with the Agency with regard to verifying the accuracy and completeness of the DPRK's initial report on all nuclear material in the DPRK.

Kang Sok Ju- Head of the Delegation for the Democratic People's Republic of Korea, First Vice-Minister of Foreign Affairs of the Democratic People's Republic of Korea

Robert L. Gallucci- Head of the Delegation of United States of America, Ambassador at Large of the United States of America

The Antarctic Treaty (1959)

The Governments of Argentina, Australia, Belgium, Chile, the French Republic, Japan, New Zealand, Norway, the Union of South Africa, the Union of Soviet Socialist Republics, the United Kingdom of Great Britain and Northern Ireland, and the United States of America,

Recognizing that it is in the interest of all mankind that Antarctica shall continue for ever to be used exclusively for peaceful purposes and shall not become the scene or object of international discord;

Acknowledging the substantial contributions to scientific knowledge resulting from international cooperation in scientific investigation in Antarctica;

Convinced that the establishment of a firm foundation for the continuation and development of such cooperation on the basis of freedom of scientific investigation in Antarctica as applied during the International Geophysical Year accords with the interests of science and the progress of all mankind;

Convinced also that a treaty ensuring the use of Antarctica for peaceful purposes only and the continuance of international harmony in Antarctica will further the purposes and principles embodied in the Charter of the United Nations;

Have agreed as follows:

ARTICLE I

1. Antarctica shall be used for peaceful purposes only. There shall be prohibited, inter alia , any measure of a military nature, such as the establishment of military bases and fortifications, the carrying out of military manoeuvres, as well as the testing of any type of weapon.

2. The present Treaty shall not prevent the use of military personnel or equipment for scientific research or for any other peaceful purpose.

ARTICLE II

Freedom of scientific investigation in Antarctica and co-operation toward that end, as applied during the International Geophysical Year, shall continue, subject to the provisions of the present Treaty.

ARTICLE III

1. In order to promote international cooperation in scientific investigation in Antarctica, as provided for in Article II of the present Treaty, the Contracting Parties agree that, to the greatest extent feasible and practicable:

a. information regarding plans for scientific programs in Antarctica shall be exchanged to permit maximum economy of and efficiency of operations;
b. scientific personnel shall be exchanged in Antarctica between expeditions and stations;
c. scientific observations and results from Antarctica shall be exchanged and made freely available.

ARTICLE IV

1. Nothing contained in the present Treaty shall be interpreted as:

a. a renunciation by any Contracting Party of previously asserted rights of or claims to territorial sovereignty in Antarctica;
b. a renunciation or diminution by any Contracting Party of any basis of claim to territorial sovereignty in Antarctica which it may have whether as a result of its activities or those of its nationals in Antarctica, or otherwise;
c. prejudicing the position of any Contracting Party as regards its recognition or non-recognition of any other StateÇs rights of or claim or basis of claim to territorial sovereignty in Antarctica.

2. No acts or activities taking place while the present Treaty is in force shall constitute a basis for asserting, supporting or denying a claim to territorial sovereignty in Antarctica or create any rights of sovereignty in Antarctica. No new claim, or enlargement of an existing claim, to territorial sovereignty in Antarctica shall be asserted while the present Treaty is in force.

ARTICLE V

1. Any nuclear explosions in Antarctica and the disposal there of radioactive waste material shall be prohibited.

2. In the event of the conclusion of international agreements concerning the use of nuclear energy, including nuclear explosions and the disposal of radioactive waste material, to which all of the Contracting Parties whose representatives are entitled to participate in the meetings provided for under Article IX are parties, the rules established under such agreements shall apply in Antarctica.

ARTICLE VI

The provisions of the present Treaty shall apply to the area south of 60∞ South Latitude, including all ice shelves, but nothing in the present Treaty shall prejudice or in any way affect the rights, or the exercise of the rights, of any State under international law with regard to the high seas within that area.

ARTICLE VII

1. In order to promote the objectives and ensure the observance of the provisions of the present Treaty, each Contracting Party whose representatives are entitled to participate in the meetings referred to in Article IX of the Treaty shall have the right to designate observers to carry out any inspection provided for by the present Article. Observers shall be nationals of the Contracting Parties which designate them. The names of observers shall be communicated to every other Contracting Party having the right to designate observers, and like notice shall be given of the termination of their appointment.

2. Each observer designated in accordance with the provisions of paragraph 1 of this Article shall have complete freedom of access at any time to any or all areas of Antarctica.

3. All areas of Antarctica, including all stations, installations and equipment within those areas, and all ships and aircraft at points of discharging or embarking cargoes or personnel in Antarctica, shall be open at all times to inspection by any observers designated in accordance with paragraph 1 of this Article.

4. Aerial observation may be carried out at any time over any or all areas of Antarctica by any of the Contracting Parties having the right to designate observers.

5. Each Contracting Party shall, at the time when the present Treaty enters into force for it, inform the other Contracting Parties, and thereafter shall give them notice in advance, of

a. all expeditions to and within Antarctica, on the part of its ships or nationals, and all expeditions to Antarctica organized in or proceeding from its territory;

b. all stations in Antarctica occupied by its nationals; and

c. any military personnel or equipment intended to be introduced by it into Antarctica subject to the conditions prescribed in paragraph 2 of Article I of the present Treaty.

ARTICLE VIII

1. In order to facilitate the exercise of their functions under the present Treaty, and without prejudice to the respective positions of the Contracting Parties relating to jurisdiction over all other persons in Antarctica, observers designated under paragraph 1 of Article VII and scientific personnel exchanged under sub-paragraph 1(b) of Article III of the Treaty, and members of the staffs accompanying any such persons, shall be subject only to the jurisdiction of the Contracting Party of which they are nationals in respect of all acts or omissions occurring while they are in Antarctica for the purpose of exercising their functions.

2. Without prejudice to the provisions of paragraph 1 of this Article, and pending the adoption of measures in pursuance of subparagraph 1(e) of Article IX, the Contracting Parties concerned in any case of dispute with regard to the exercise of jurisdiction in Antarctica shall immediately consult together with a view to reaching a mutually acceptable solution.

ARTICLE IX

1. Representatives of the Contracting Parties named in the preamble to the present Treaty shall meet at the City of Canberra within two months after the date of entry into force of the Treaty, and thereafter at suitable intervals and places, for the purpose of exchanging information, consulting together on matters of common interest pertaining to Antarctica, and formulating and considering, and recommending to their Governments, measures in furtherance of the principles and objectives of the Treaty, including measures regarding:

a. use of Antarctica for peaceful purposes only;

b. facilitation of scientific research in Antarctica;

c. facilitation of international scientific cooperation in Antarctica;

d. facilitation of the exercise of the rights of inspection provided for in Article VII of the Treaty;

e. questions relating to the exercise of jurisdiction in Antarctica;

f. preservation and conservation of living resources in Antarctica.

2. Each Contracting Party which has become a party to the present Treaty by accession under Article XIII shall be entitled to appoint representatives to participate in the meetings referred to in paragraph 1 of the present Article, during such times as that Contracting Party demonstrates its interest in Antarctica by conducting substantial research activity there, such as the establishment of a scientific station or the despatch of a scientific expedition.

3. Reports from the observers referred to in Article VII of the present Treaty shall be transmitted to the representatives of the Contracting Parties participating in the meetings referred to in paragraph 1 of the present Article.

4. The measures referred to in paragraph 1 of this Article shall become effective when approved by all the Contracting Parties whose representatives were entitled to participate in the meetings held to consider those measures.

5. Any or all of the rights established in the present Treaty may be exercised as from the date of entry into force of the Treaty whether or not any measures facilitating the exercise of such rights have been proposed, considered or approved as provided in this Article.

ARTICLE X

Each of the Contracting Parties undertakes to exert appropriate efforts, consistent with the Charter of the United Nations, to the end that no one engages in any activity in Antarctica contrary to the principles or purposes of the present Treaty.

ARTICLE XI

1. If any dispute arises between two or more of the Contracting Parties concerning the interpretation or application of the present Treaty, those Contracting Parties shall consult among themselves with a view to having the

dispute resolved by negotiation, inquiry, mediation, conciliation, arbitration, judicial settlement or other peaceful means of their own choice.

2. Any dispute of this character not so resolved shall, with the consent, in each case, of all parties to the dispute, be referred to the International Court of Justice for settlement; but failure to reach agreement on reference to the International Court shall not absolve parties to the dispute from the responsibility of continuing to seek to resolve it by any of the various peaceful means referred to in paragraph 1 of this Article.

ARTICLE XII

1.

a. The present Treaty may be modified or amended at any time by unanimous agreement of the Contracting Parties whose representatives are entitled to participate in the meetings provided for under Article IX. Any such modification or amendment shall enter into force when the depositary Government has received notice from all such Contracting Parties that they have ratified it.

b. Such modification or amendment shall thereafter enter into force as to any other Contracting Party when notice of ratification by it has been received by the depositary Government. Any such Contracting Party from which no notice of ratification is received within a period of two years from the date of entry into force of the modification or amendment in accordance with the provision of subparagraph 1(a) of this Article shall be deemed to have withdrawn from the present Treaty on the date of the expiration of such period.

2.

a. If after the expiration of thirty years from the date of entry into force of the present Treaty, any of the Contracting Parties whose representatives are entitled to participate in the meetings provided for under Article IX so requests by a communication addressed to the depositary Government, a Conference of all the Contracting Parties shall be held as soon as practicable to review the operation of the Treaty.

b. Any modification or amendment to the present Treaty which is approved at such a Conference by a majority of the Contracting Parties there

represented, including a majority of those whose representatives are entitled to participate in the meetings provided for under Article IX, shall be communicated by the depositary Government to all Contracting Parties immediately after the termination of the Conference and shall enter into force in accordance with the provisions of paragraph 1 of the present Article

c. If any such modification or amendment has not entered into force in accordance with the provisions of subparagraph 1(a) of this Article within a period of two years after the date of its communication to all the Contracting Parties, any Contracting Party may at any time after the expiration of that period give notice to the depositary Government of its withdrawal from the present Treaty; and such withdrawal shall take effect two years after the receipt of the notice by the depositary Government.

ARTICLE XIII

1. The present Treaty shall be subject to ratification by the signatory States. It shall be open for accession by any State which is a Member of the United Nations, or by any other State which may be invited to accede to the Treaty with the consent of all the Contracting Parties whose representatives are entitled to participate in the meetings provided for under Article IX of the Treaty.

2. Ratification of or accession to the present Treaty shall be effected by each State in accordance with its constitutional processes.

3. Instruments of ratification and instruments of accession shall be deposited with the Government of the United States of America, hereby designated as the depositary Government.

4. The depositary Government shall inform all signatory and acceding States of the date of each deposit of an instrument of ratification or accession, and the date of entry into force of the Treaty and of any modification or amendment thereto.

5. Upon the deposit of instruments of ratification by all the signatory States, the present Treaty shall enter into force for those States and for States which have deposited instruments of accession. Thereafter the Treaty shall enter into force for any acceding State upon the deposit of its instruments of accession.

6. The present Treaty shall be registered by the depositary Government pursuant to Article 102 of the Charter of the United Nations.

ARTICLE XIV

The present Treaty, done in the English, French, Russian and Spanish languages, each version being equally authentic, shall be deposited in the archives of the Government of the United States of America, which shall transmit duly certified copies thereof to the Governments of the signatory and acceding States.

Atomic Energy Act of 1946

A BILL

For the development and control of atomic energy

Be it enacted by the Senate and House of Representatives of the United States of America in congress assembled,

DECLARATION OF POLICY

Section 1. (a) Findings and Declaration. Research and experimentation in the field of nuclear fission have attained the stage at which the release of atomic energy on a large scale is practical. The significance of the atomic bomb for military purposes is evident. The effect of the use of atomic energy for civilian purposes upon the social, economic, and political structures of today cannot now be determined. It is reasonable to anticipate, however, that tapping this new source of energy will cause profound changes in our present way of life. Accordingly, it is hereby declared to be the policy of the people of the United States that the development and utilization of atomic energy shall be directed toward improving the public welfare, increasing the standard of living, strengthening free competition among private enterprises so far as practicable, and cementing world peace.

(b) Purpose of Act. It is the purpose of this Act to effectuate these policies by providing, among others, for the following major programs;

(1) A program of assisting and fostering private research and development on a truly independent basis to encourage maximum scientific progress;

(2) A program for the free dissemination of basic scientific information and for maximum liberality in dissemination of related technical information;

(3) A program of federally conducted research to assure the Government of adequate scientific and technical accomplishments;

(4) A program for Government control of the production, ownership, and use of fissionable materials to protect the national security and to insure the broadest possible exploitation of the field;

(5) A program for simultaneous study of the social, political, and economic effects of the utilization of atomic energy; and

(6) A program of administration which will be consistent with international agreements made by the United States, and which will enable the Congress to be currently informed so as to take further legislative action as may hereafter be appropriate.

ATOMIC ENERGY COMMISSION

See. 2. (a) There is hereby established an Atomic Energy Commission (herein called the Commission), which shall be composed of five members. Three members shall constitute a quorum of the Commission. The President shall designate one member as a Chairman of the Commission.

(b) Members of the Commission shall be appointed by the President, by and with the advice and consent of the Senate, and shall serve at the pleasure of the President. In submitting nominations to the Senate, the President shall set forth the experience and qualifications of each person so nominated. Each member, except the Chairman, shall receive com-pensation at the rate of $15,000 per annum; the Chairman shall receive compensation at the rate of 920.000 per annum. No member of the Commission shall engage in any other business, vocation, or employment than that of serving as a member of the Commission.

(c) The principal office of the Commission shall be in the District of Co-lumbia, but the Commission may exercise any or all of its powers in any place. The Commission shall hold such meetings, conduct such hearings, and receive such reports as will enable it to meet its responsibilities for carrying out the purpose of this Act.

RESEARCH

See. 3. (a) Research Assistance. The Commission is directed to exercise its powers in such a manner as to insure the continued conduct of research and developmental activities in the fields specified below by private or public institutions or persons and to assist in the acquisition of an ever-expanding fund of theoretical and practical knowledge in such fields. To this end the Commission is authorized and directed to make contracts, agreements, arrangements, grants-in-aid, and loans

(1) for the conduct of research and developmental activities relating to (a) nuclear processes; (b) the theory and production of atomic energy, including processes and devices related to such production; (c) utilization of fissionable and radioactive materials for medical or health purposes; (d) utilization of fissionable and radioactive materials for all other purposes, including industrial uses; and (e) the protection of health during research and production activities; and

(2) for studies of the social, political, and economic effects of the availability and utilization of atomic energy.

The Commission may make partial advance payments on such contracts and arrangements. Such contracts or other arrangements may contain provisions to protect health, to minimize danger from explosion, and for reporting and inspection of work performed thereunder as the Commission may deter-mine, but shall not contain any provisions or conditions which prevent the dissemination of scientific or technical information, except to the extent al-ready required by the Espionage Act.

(b) Federal Atomic Research. The Commission is authorized and directed to conduct research and developmental activities through its own fa-cilities in the fields specified in (a) above.

PRODUCTION OF FISSIONABLE MATERIALS

Sec. 4. (a) Definition. The term "production of fissionable materials" shall include all methods of manufacturing, producing, refining, or processing fissionable materials, including the process of separating fissionable material from other substances in which such material may be contained, whether by thermal diffusion, electromagnetic separation, or other processes.

(b) Authority to Produce. The Commission shall be the exclusive pro-ducer of fissionable materials, except production incident to research or de-velopmental activities subject to restrictions provided in subparagraph (d) below. The quantities of fissionable material to be produced in any quarter shall be determined by the President.

(c) Prohibition. It shall be unlawful for any person to produce any fissionable material except as may be incident to the conduct of research or developmental activities.

(d) Research and Development on Production Processes. (1) The Commission shall establish by regulation such requirements for the reporting of research and developmental activities on the production of fissionable materials as will assure the Commission of full knowledge of all such activities, rates of production, and quantities produced.

(2) The Commission shall provide for the frequent inspection of all such activities by employees of the Commission.

(3) No person may in the course of such research or developmental activities possess or operate facilities for the production of fissionable material in quantities or at a rate sufficient to construct a bomb or other military weapon unless all such facilities are the property of and subject to the control of the Commission. The Commission is authorized, to the extent that it deems such action consistent with the purposes of this Act, to enter into contracts for the conduct of such research or developmental activities involving the use of the Commission's facilities.

(e) Existing Contracts. The Commission is authorized to continue in effect and modify such contracts for the production of fissionable materials as may have been made prior to the effective date of this Act, except that, as rapidly as practicable, and in any event not more than one year after the effective date of this Act, the Commission shall arrange for the exclusive operation of facilities employed in the manufacture of fissionable materials by employees of the Commission.

CONTROL OF MATERIALS

See. 5. (a)(1) Definition. The term "fissionable materials" shall include plutonium, uranium 235, and such other materials as the Commission may from time to time determine to be capable of releasing substantial quantities of energy through nuclear fission of the materials.

(2) Privately Owned Fissionable Materials. Any person owning any right, title, or interest in or to any fissionable material shall forthwith transfer all such right, title, or interest to the Commission.

(3) Prohibition. It shall be unlawful for any person to (a) own any fissionable material; or (b) after sixty days after the effective date of this Act and except as authorized by the Commission possess any fissionable material; or (c) export from or import into the United States any fissionable material, or directly or indirectly be a party to or in any way a beneficiary of, any contract, arrangement or other activity pertaining to the production, refining, or processing of any fissionable material outside of the United States.

(4) Distribution of Fissionable Materials. The Commission is autho-rized and directed to distribute fissionable materials to all applicants requesting such materials for the conduct of research or developmental activities either independently or under contract or other arrange-

ment with the Commission. If sufficient materials are not available to meet all such requests, and applications for licenses under section 7, the Commission shall allocate fissionable materials among all such applicants in the manner best calculated to encourage independent research and development by making adequate fissionable materials available for such purposes. The Commission shall refuse to distribute or allocate any materials to any applicant, or shall recall any materials after distribution or allocation from any applicant, who is not equipped or who fails to observe such safety standards to protect health and to minimize danger from explosion as may be established by the Commission.

(b) Source Materials.

(1) Definition. The term "source materials" shall include any ore con-taining uranium, thorium, or beryllium, and such other materials peculiarly essential to the production of fissionable materials as may be determined by the Commission with the approval of the President.

(2) License for Transfers Required. No person may transfer possession or title to any source material after mining, extraction, or removal from its place of origin, and no person may receive any source material without a license from the Commission.

(3) Issuance of Licenses. Any person desiring to transfer or receive pos-session of any source material shall apply for a license therefor in accordance with such procedures as the Commission may by regulation establish. The Commission shall establish such standards for the issuance or refusal of licenses as it may deem necessary to assure adequate source materials for production, research or developmental activities pursuant to this Act or to prevent the use of such materials in a manner inconsistent with the national welfare.

(4) Reporting. The Commission is authorized to issue such regulations or orders requiring reports of ownership, possession, extraction, refining, shipment or other handling of source materials as it may deem necessary.

(c) Byproduct Materials

(1) Definition. The term "byproduct material" shall be deemed to refer to all materials (except fissionable material) yielded in the processes of producing fissionable material.

(2) Distribution. The Commission is authorized and directed to distribute, with or without charge, byproduct materials to all applicants seeking such materials for research or developmental work, medical therapy, industrial uses, or such other useful applications as may be developed. if sufficient materials to meet all such requests are not available, the Commission shall allocate such materials among applicants therefor, giving preference to the use of such materials in the conduct of research and developmental activity and medical therapy. The Commission shall refuse to distribute or allocate any byproduct materials to any applicant, or recall any materials after distribution or allocation from any applicant, who is not equipped or who fails to observe such safety standards to protect health as may be established by the Commission.

(d) General Provisions. (1) The Commission is authorized to

(i) acquire or purchase fissionable or source materials within the United States or elsewhere;

(ii) take, requisition, or condemn within the United States any fissionable or source material and make just compensation therefore. The Commission shall determine such compensation. In the exercise of such rights of eminent domain and condemnation, proceedings may be instituted under the Act of August 1, 1888 (U. S. C. 1940, title 40, sec. 257), or any other applicable Federal statute. Upon or after the filing of the condemnation petition, immediate possession may be taken and the property may be treated by the Commission in the same manner as other similar property owned by it;

(iii) conduct exploratory operation, investigations, inspections to determine the location, extent, mode of occurrence, use, or condition of source materials with or without the consent of the owner of any interest therein, making just compensation for any damage or injury occasioned thereby.

(2) The Commission shall establish by regulation a procedure by which any person who is dissatisfied with its action in allocating, refusing to allocate

or in rescinding any allocation of fissionable, source, or byproduct materials to him may obtain a review of such determination by a board of appeal con-sisting of two or more members appointed by the Commission and at least one member of the Commission.

MILITARY APPLICATIONS OF ATOMIC POWER

See. 6. (a) The Commission is authorized and directed to

(1) conduct experiments and do research and developmental work in the military application of atomic power; and

(2) have custody of all assembled or unassembled atomic bombs, bomb parts, or other atomic military weapons, presently or hereafter produced, except that upon the express finding of the President that such action is required in the interests of national defense, the Commission shall deliver such quantities of weapons to the armed forces as the President may specify.

(b) The Commission shall not conduct any research or developmental work in the military application of atomic power if such research or developmental work is contrary to any international agreement of the United States.

(e) The Commission is authorized to engage in the production of atomic bombs, bomb parts, or other applications of atomic power as military weapons, only to the extent that the express consent and direction of the President of the United States has been obtained, which consent and direction shall be obtained for each quarter.

(d) It shall be unlawful for any person to manufacture, produce, or process any device or equipment designed to utilize fissionable materials as a military weapon, except as authorized by the Commission.

ATOMIC ENERGY DEVICES

Sec. 7. (a) License Required.-It shall be unlawful for any person to operate any equipment or device utilizing fissionable materials without a license issued by the Commission authorizing such operation.

Issuance of Licenses.-Any person desiring to utilize fissionable materials in any such device or equipment shall apply for a license therefor in accordance with such procedures as the Commission may by regulation establish. The Commission is authorized and directed to issue such a license on a nonexclusive basis and to supply appropriate quantities of fissionable materials to the extent available to any applicant (1) who is equipped to observe such safety standards to protect health and to minimize danger from explosion as the Commission may establish; and (2) who agrees to make available to the Commission such technical information and data concerning the operation of such device as the Commission may determine necessary to encourage the use of such devices by as many licensees as possible. Where any license might serve to maintain or foster the growth of monopoly, restraint of trade, unlawful competition, or other trade position inimical to the entry of new, freely competitive enterprises, the Commission is authorized and directed to refuse to issue such license or to establish such conditions to prevent these results as the Commission, in consultation with the Attorney General, may determine. The Commission shall report promptly to the Attorney General any information it may have of the use of such devices which appears to have these results. No license may be given to a foreign government or to any person who is not under and within the jurisdiction of the United States.

(c) Byproduct Power. If in the production of fissionable materials the production processes yield energy capable of utilization, such energy may be used by the Commission, transferred to other Government agencies, sold to public or private utilities under contract providing for reasonable resale prices, or sold to private consumers at reasonable rates and on as broad a basis of eligibility as the Commission may determine to be possible.

(d) Reports to Congress. Whenever in its opinion industrial, commer-cial, or other uses of fissionable materials have been sufficiently developed to be of practical value, the Commission shall prepare a report to the Con-gress stating all the facts, the Commission's estimate of the social, political, and economic effects of such utilization, and the Commission's recommendations for necessary or desirable supplemental legislation. Until such a re-port has been filed with the Commission and the period of ninety days has elapsed after such filing within which period the Commission may adopt supplemental legislation, no license for the use of atomic energy devices shall be issued by the Commission.

PROPERTY OF THE COMMISSION

Sec. 8. (a) The President shall direct the transfer to the Commission of the following property owned by the United States or any of its agencies, or any interest in such property held in trust for or on behalf of the United States:

(1) All fissionable materials; all bombs and bomb parts; all plants, facili-ties, equipment, and materials for the processing or production of fissionable materials, bombs, and bomb parts; all processes and technical information of any kind, and the source thereof (including data, drawings, specifications, patents, patent applications, and other sources, relating to the refining or production of fissionable materials; and all contracts, agreements, leases, patents, applications for patents, inventions and discoveries (whether pat-ented or unpatented), and other rights of any kind concerning any such items;

(2) All facilities and equipment, and materials therein, devoted primarily to atomic energy research and development; and

(3) All property in the custody and control of the Manhattan engineer district.

(b) In order to render financial assistance to those States and local gov-ernments in which the activities of the Commission are carried on and in which the Commission, or its agents, have acquired properties previously subject to State and local taxation, the Commission is authorized to make payments to State and local governments in lieu of such taxes. Such payments may be in the amounts, at the times, and upon the terms the Commission deems appropriate, but the Commission shall be guided by the policy of not exceeding the taxes which would have been payable for such property in the condition in which it was acquired, except where special burdens have been cast upon the State or local government by activities of the Commission, the Manhattan engineer district, or their agents, and in such cases any benefits accruing to the States and local governments by reason of these activities shall be considered in the determination of such pay-ments. The Commission and any corporation created by it, and the property and income of the Commission or of such corporation, are hereby expressly exempted from taxation in any manner or form by any State, county, municipality, or any subdivision thereof.

DISSEMINATION OF INFORMATION

See. 9. (a) Basic Scientific Information. Basic scientific information in the fields specified in section 3 may be freely disseminated. The term "basic scientific information" shall include, in addition to theoretical knowledge of nuclear and other physics, chemistry, biology, and therapy, all results ca-pable of accomplishment, as distinguished from the processes or techniques of accomplishing them.

(b) Related Technical Information. The Commission shall establish a Board of Commission. The Board shall, under

the direction and supervision of the Commission, provide for the dissemination of related technical information with the utmost liberality as freely as may be consistent with the foreign and domestic policies established by the President and shall have authority to

(1) establish such information services, publications, libraries, and other registers of available information as may be helpful in effectuating this policy;

(2) designate by regulation the types of related technical information the dissemination of which will effectuate the foregoing policy. Such designations shall constitute an administrative determination that such information is not of value to the national defense and that any person is entitled to receive such information, within the meaning of the Espionage Act. Failure to make any such designation shall not, however, be deemed a determination that such undesignated information is subject to the provisions of said Act;

(3) by regulation or order, require reports of the conduct of independent research or development activities in the fields specified in sec-tion 3 and of the operation of atomic energy devices under licenses issued pursuant to section 7;

(4) provide for such inspections of independent research and devel-opment activities of the types specified

in section 3 and of the operation of atomic energy devices as the Commission or the Board may deter-mine; and

(5) whenever it will facilitate the carrying out of the purposes of the Act, adopt by regulation administrative interpretations of the Espionage Act except that any such interpretation shall, before adoption, receive the express approval of the President.

PATENTS

See. 10. (a) Whenever any person invents a device or method for the production, refining, or processing of fissionable material: (i) he may file a patent application to cover such invention, sending a copy thereof to the Commission; (ii) if the Commissioner of Patents determines that the inven-tion is patentable, he shall issue a patent in the name of the Commission; and (iii) the Commission shall make just compensation to such person. The Commission shall appoint a Patent Royalty Board consisting of one or more employees and at least one member of the Commission, and the Commis-sioner of Patents. The Patent Royalty Board shall determine what constitutes just compensation in each such case and whether such compensation is to be paid in periodic payments rather than in a lump sum. Any person to whom any such patent has heretofore been issued shall forthwith transfer all right, title, and interest in and to such patent to the Commission and shall receive therefor just compensation as provided above.

(b) (1) Any patent now or hereafter issued covering any process or device utilizing or peculiarly necessary to the utilization of fissionable materials, or peculiarly necessary to the conduct of research or developmental activities in the fields specified in section 3, is hereby declared to be affected with the public interest and its general availability for such uses is declared to be necessary to af-fectuate the purposes of this Act.

(2) Any person to whom any such patent has been issued, or any person desiring to use any device or process covered by such patent for such uses, may apply to the Patent Royalty Board, for determination by such Board of a reasonable royalty fee for such use of the patented process or device in-tended to be used under the Commission's license.

(3) In determining such reasonable royalty fee, the Patent Royalty Board shall take into consideration any defense, general or special, that might be pleaded by a defendant in an action for infringement, the extent to which, if any, such patent was developed through federally financed research, the degree of utility, novelty, and importance of the patent, the cost to the pat-entee of developing such process or device, and a reasonable rate of return on such research investment by the patentee.

(4) No court, Federal, State, or Territorial, shall have jurisdiction or power to stay, restrain, or otherwise enjoin any such use of any such pat-ented device or process by any person on the ground of infringement of such patent. In any action for infringement of any such patent filed in any such court, the court shall have authority only to order the payment of reasonable royalty fees and attorney's fees and court costs as damages for any such in-fringement. If the Patent Royalty Board has not previously determined the reasonable royalty fee for the use of the patented device or process involved in any case, the court in such case shall, before entering judgment, obtain from the Patent Royalty Board a report containing its recommendation as to the reasonable royalty fee it would have established had application been made to it as provided in subparagraphs 2 and 3 above.

ORGANIZATIONAL AND GENERAL AUTHORITY

See. 11. (a) Organization. There are hereby established within the Commission a Division of Research, a Division of Production, a Division of Materials, and a Division of Military Application. Each division shall be under the direction of a Directory who shall be appointed by the President, by and with the advice and consent of the Senate, and shall receive compen-sation at the rate of $15,000 per annum. The Commission shall delegate to each such division such of its powers under this Act as in its opinion from time to time will promote the effectuation of the purposes of this Act in an efficient manner. Nothing in this paragraph shall prevent the Commission from establishing such additional divisions or other subordinate organiza-tions as it may deem desirable.

(b) General Authority.-In the performance of its functions the Commis-sion is authorized to-

(1) establish advisory boards to advise with and make recommen-dations to the Commission on legislation, policies, administration, and research;

(2) establish by regulation or order such standards and instructions to govern the possession and use of fis-sionable and byproduct materials as the Commission may deem necessary or desirable to protect health or to minimize danger from explosion;

(3) make such studies and investigations, obtain such information, and hold such hearings as the Commission may deem necessary or proper to assist it in exercising any authority provided in this Act, or in the admin-istration or enforcement of this Act, or any regulations or orders issued thereunder. For such purposes the Commis-sion is authorized to require any person to permit the inspection and copying of any records or other docu-ments, to administer oaths and affirmations, and by sub-pena to re-quire any person to appear and testify, or to appear and produce docu-ments, or both, at any designated place. Witnesses subpenaed under this subsection shall be paid the same fees and mileage as are paid witnesses in the district courts of the United States;

(4) create or organize corporations, the stock of which shall be wholly owned by the United States and controlled by the Commission, to carry out the provisions of this Act;

(5) appoint and fix the compensation of such officers and employees as may be necessary to carry out the functions of the Commission. All such officers and employees shall be appointed in accordance with the civil service laws and their compensation fixed in accordance with the Clas-sification Act of 1923, as amended, except that expert administrative, technical, and professional personnel may be employed and their com-pensation fixed without regard to such laws. The Commission shall make adequate provision for administrative review by a board consisting of one or more employees and at least one member of the Commission of any determination to dismiss any scientific or professional employee; and

(6) acquire such materials, property, equipment, and facilities, estab-lish or construct such buildings and facilities, modify such building and facilities from time to time, and construct, acquire, provide, or arrange for such facilities and services for the housing, health, safety, welfare, and recreation of personnel employed by the Commission as it may deem necessary.

ENFORCEMENT

See. 12. (a) Any person who willfully violates, attempts to violate, or con-spires to violate, any of the provisions of this Act or any regulations or orders issued thereunder shall, upon conviction thereof, be punishable by a fine of not more than $10,000, or by imprisonment for a term of not exceeding five years, or both.

(b) Whenever in the judgment of the commission any person has engaged or is about to engage in any acts or practices which constitute or will consti-tute a violation of any provision of this Act, it may make application to the appropriate court for an order enjoining such acts or practices, or for an order enforcing compliance with such provision, and upon a showing by the Commission that such person has engaged or is about to engage in any such acts or practices a permanent or temporary injunction, restraining order, or other order shall be granted without bond.

(c) In case of contumacy by, or refusal to obey a sub-pena served upon, any person pursuant to section 11 (b)

(3), the district court for any district in which such person is found or resides or transacts business, upon application by the Commission, shall have jurisdiction to issue an order requiring such person to appear and give testimony or to appear and produce documents, or both; and any failure to obey such order of the court may be punished by such court as a contempt thereof.

REPORTS

Sec. 13. The Commission shall, on the first days of January, April, July, and October, submit reports to the President, to the Senate and to the House of Representatives. Such reports shall summarize and appraise the ac-tivities of the Commission and of each division and board thereof, and specifically shall contain financial statements; lists of licenses issued, of property acquired, of research contracts and arrangements entered into, and of the amounts of fissionable material and the persons to whom allocated; the Com-mission's program for the following quarter including lists of research con-tracts and arrangements proposed to be entered into; conclusions drawn from studies of the social, political, and economic effects of the release of atomic energy; and such recommendations for additional legislation as the Commission may deem necessary or desirable.

DEFINITIONS

See. 14. As used in this Act-

(a) The term "atomic energy" shall include all forms of energy liberated in the artificial transmutation of atomic species.

(b) The term "Government agency" means any executive department, board, bureau, commission, or other agency in the executive branch of the Federal Government, or any corporation wholly owned (either directly or through one or more corporations) by the United States.

(c) The term "person" means any individual, corporation, partnership, firm, association, trust, estate, public or private institution, group, any gov-ernment other than the United States, any political subdivision of any such government, and any legal successor, representative, agent, or agency of the foregoing, or other entity.

(d) The term "United States" includes all Territories and possessions of the United States.

APPROPRIATIONS

Sec. 15. There are hereby authorized to be appropriated such sums as may be necessary and appropriate to carry

out the provisions and purposes of this Act. Funds appropriated to the Commission shall, if obligated during the fiscal year for which appropriated, remain available for expenditure for four years following the expiration of the fiscal year for which appropriated. After such four-year period, the unexpended balances of appropriations shall be carried to the surplus fund and covered into the Treasury.

SEPARABILITY OF PROVISIONS

Sec. 16. If any provision of this Act, or the application of such provision to any person or circumstances, is held invalid, the remainder of this Act or the application of such provision to persons of circumstances other than those to which it is held invalid, shall not be affected thereby.

Agreement Between The United States of America and The Union of Soviet Socialist Republics on Notifications of Launches of Intercontinental Ballistic Missiles and Submarine-Launched Ballistic Missiles

Signed at Moscow May 31, 1988
Entered into Force May 31, 1988

The United States of America and the Union of Soviet Socialist Republics, hereinafter referred to as the Parties,

Affirming their desire to reduce and ultimately eliminate the risk of outbreak of nuclear war, in particular, as a result of misinterpretation, miscalculation, or accident,

Believing that a nuclear war cannot be won and must never be fought,

Believing that agreement on measures for reducing the risk of outbreak of nuclear war serves the interests of strengthening international peace and security,

Reaffirming their obligations under the Agreement on Measures to Reduce the Risk of Outbreak of Nuclear War between the United States of America and the Union of Soviet Socialist Republics of September 30, 1971, the Agreement between the Government of the United States of America and the Government of the Union of Soviet

Socialist Republics on the Prevention of Incidents on and over the High Seas of May 25, 1972, and the Agreement between the United States of America and the Union of Soviet Socialist Republics on the Establishment of Nuclear Risk Reduction Centers of September 15, 1987,

Have agreed as follows:

ARTICLE I

Each Party shall provide the other Party notification, through the Nuclear Risk Reduction Centers of the United States of America and the Union of Soviet Socialist Republics, no less than twenty-four hours in advance, of the planned date, launch area, and area of impact for any launch of a strategic ballistic missile: an intercontinental ballistic missile (hereinafter "ICBM") or a submarine-launched ballistic missile (hereinafter "SLBM").

ARTICLE II

A notification of a planned launch of an ICBM or an SLBM shall be valid for four days counting from the launch date indicated in such a notification. In case of postponement of the launch date within the indicated four days, or cancellation of the launch, no notification thereof shall be required.

ARTICLE III

1. For launches of ICBMs or SLBMs from land, the notification shall indicate the area from which the launch is planned to take place.
2. For launches of SLBMs from submarines, the notification shall indicate the general area from which the missile will be launched. Such notification shall indicate either the quadrant within the ocean (that is, the ninety-degree sector encompassing approximately one-fourth of the area of the ocean) or the body of water (for example, sea or bay) from which the launch is planned to take place.
3. For all launches of ICBMs or SLBMs, the notification shall indicate the geographic coordinates of the planned impact area or areas of the reentry vehicles. Such an area shall be specified either by indicating the geographic coordinates of the boundary points of the area, or by indicating the geographic coordinates of the center of a circle with a radius specified in kilometers or

nautical miles. The size of the impact area shall be determined by the notifying Party at its discretion.

ARTICLE IV

The Parties undertake to hold consultations, as mutually agreed, to consider questions relating to implementation of the provisions of this Agreement, as well as to discuss possible amendments thereto aimed at furthering the implementation of the objectives of this Agreement. Amendments shall enter into force in accordance with procedures to be agreed upon.

ARTICLE V

This Agreement shall not affect the obligations of either Party under other agreements.

ARTICLE VI

This Agreement shall enter into force on the date of its signature.

The duration of this Agreement shall not be limited.

This Agreement may be terminated by either Party upon 12 months written notice to the other Party.

DONE at Moscow on May 31, 1988, in two copies, each in the English and Russian languages, both texts being equally authentic.

FOR THE UNITED STATES OF AMERICA:
George P. Shultz
FOR THE UNION OF SOVIET SOCIALIST REPUBLICS:
Eduard A. Shevardnadze

Convention on the Physical Protection of Nuclear Material

Signed at New York March 3, 1980
Ratification advised by U.S. Senate July 30, 1981
Ratified by U.S. President September 4, 1981
Entered into force February 8, 1987

The States Parties to This Convention,

Recognizing the right of all States to develop and apply nuclear energy for peaceful purposes and their legitimate interests in the potential benefits to be derived from the peaceful application of nuclear energy,

Convinced of the need for facilitating international co-operation in the peaceful application of nuclear energy,

Desiring to avert the potential dangers posed by the unlawful taking and use of nuclear material,

Convinced that offenses relating to nuclear material are a matter of grave concern and that there is an urgent need to adopt appropriate and effective measures to ensure the prevention, detection and punishment of such offenses,

Aware of the Need for international co-operation to establish, in conformity with the national law of each State Party and with this Convention, effective measures for the physical protection of nuclear material,

Convinced that this Convention should facilitate the safe transfer of nuclear material,

Stressing also the importance of the physical protection of nuclear material in domestic use, storage and transport,

Recognizing the importance of effective physical protection of nuclear material used for military purposes, and understanding that such material is and will continue to be accorded stringent physical protection,

Have Agreed as follows:

ARTICLE 1

For the purposes of this Convention:

(a) "nuclear material" means plutonium except that with isotopic concentration exceeding 80% in plutonium-238; uranium-233; uranium enriched in the isotopes 235 or 233; uranium containing the mixture of isotopes as occurring in nature other than in the form of ore or ore-residue; any material containing one or more of the foregoing;

(b) "uranium enriched in the isotopes 235 or 233" means uranium containing the isotopes 235 or 233 or both in an amount such that the abundance ratio of the sum of these isotopes to the isotope 238 is greater than the ratio of the isotope 235 to the isotope 238 occurring in nature;

(c) "international nuclear transport" means the carriage of a consignment of nuclear material by any means of transportation intended to go beyond the territory of the State where the shipment originates beginning with the departure from a facility of the shipper in that State and ending with the arrival at a facility of the receiver within the State of ultimate destination.

ARTICLE 2

1. The Convention shall apply to nuclear material used for peaceful purposes while in international nuclear transport.

2. With the exception of articles 3 and 4 and paragraph 3 of article 5, this Convention shall also apply to nuclear material used for peaceful purposes while in domestic use, storage and transport.

3. Apart from the commitments expressly undertaken by States Parties in the articles covered by paragraph 2 with respect to nuclear material used for peaceful purposes while in domestic use, storage and transport, nothing in this Convention shall be interpreted as affecting the sovereign rights of a State regarding the domestic use, storage and transport of such nuclear material.

ARTICLE 3

Each State Party shall take appropriate steps within the framework of its national law and consistent with international law to ensure as far as practicable that, during international nuclear transport, nuclear material within its territory, or on board a ship or aircraft under its jurisdiction insofar as such ship or aircraft is engaged in the transport to or from that State, is protected at the levels described in Annex I.

ARTICLE 4

1. Each State Party shall not export or authorize the export of nuclear material unless the State Party has received assurances that such material will be protected during the international nuclear transport at the levels described in Annex I.

2. Each State Party shall not import or authorize the import of nuclear material from a State not party to this Convention unless the State Party has received assurances that such material will during the international nuclear transport be protected at the levels described in Annex I.

3. A State Party shall not allow the transit of its territory by land or internal waterways or through its airports or seaports of nuclear material between States that are not parties to this Convention unless the State Party has received assurances as far as practicable that this nuclear material will be protected during international nuclear transport at the levels described in Annex I.

4. Each State Party shall apply within the framework of its national law the levels of physical protection described in Annex I to nuclear material being transported

from a part of that State to another part of the same State through international waters or airspace.

5. The State Party responsible for receiving assurances that the nuclear material will be protected at the levels described in Annex I according to paragraphs 1 to 3 shall identify and inform in advance States which the nuclear material is expected to transit by land or internal waterways, or whose airports or seaports it is expected to enter.

6. The responsibility for obtaining assurances referred to in paragraph 1 may be transferred, by mutual agreement, to the State Party involved in the transport as the importing State.

7. Nothing in this article shall be interpreted as in any way affecting the territorial sovereignty and jurisdiction of a State, including that over its airspace and territorial sea.

ARTICLE 5

1. States Parties shall identify and make known to each other directly or through the International Atomic Energy Agency their central authority and point of contact having responsibility for physical protection of nuclear material and for coordinating recovery and response operations in the event of any unauthorized removal, use or alteration of nuclear material or in the event of credible threat thereof.

2. In the case of theft, robbery or any other unlawful taking of nuclear material or of credible threat thereof, States Parties shall, in accordance with their national law, provide co-operation and assistance to the maximum feasible extent in the recovery and protection of such material to any State that so requests. In particular:

(a) a State Party shall take appropriate steps to inform as soon as possible other States, which appear to it to be concerned, of any theft, robbery or other unlawful taking of nuclear material or credible threat thereof and to inform, where appropriate, international organizations;

(b) as appropriate, the States Parties concerned shall exchange information with each other or international organizations with a view to protecting threatened nuclear material, verifying the integrity of the shipping container, or recovering unlawfully taken nuclear material and shall:

(i)   co-ordinate their efforts through diplomatic and other agreed channels;

(ii) render assistance, if requested;

(iii) ensure the return of nuclear material stolen or missing as a consequence of the abovementioned events.

The means of implementation of this co-operation shall be determined by the States Parties concerned.

3. States Parties shall co-operate and consult as appropriate, with each other directly or through international organizations, with a view to obtaining guidance on the design, maintenance and improvement of systems of physical protection of nuclear material in international transport.

ARTICLE 6

1. States Parties shall take appropriate measures consistent with their national law to protect the confidentiality of any information which they receive in confidence by virtue of the provisions of this Convention from another State Party or through participation in an activity carried out for the implementation of this Convention. If States Parties provide information to international organizations in confidence, steps shall be taken to ensure that the confidentiality of such information is protected.

2. States Parties shall not be required by this Convention to provide any information which they are not permitted to communicate pursuant to national law or which would jeopardize the security of the State concerned or the physical protection of nuclear material.

ARTICLE 7

1. The intentional commission of:

(a) an act without lawful authority which constitutes the receipt, possession, use, transfer, alteration, disposal or dispersal of nuclear material and which causes or is likely to cause death or serious injury to any person or substantial damage to property;

(b) a theft or robbery of nuclear material;

(c) an embezzlement or fraudulent obtaining of nuclear material;

(d) an act constituting a demand for nuclear material by threat or use of force or by any other form of intimidation;

(e) a threat:

(i) to use nuclear material to cause death or serious injury to any person or substantial property damage, or

(ii) to commit an offense described in subparagraph (b) in order to compel a natural or legal person, international organization or State to do or to refrain from doing any act;

(f) an attempt to commit any offense described in paragraphs (a), (b) or (c); and

(g) an act which constitutes participation in any offense described in paragraphs (a) to (f) shall be made a punishable offense by each State Party under its national law.

2. Each State Party shall make the offenses described in this article punishable by appropriate penalties which take into account their grave nature.

ARTICLE 8

1. Each State Party shall take such measures as may be necessary to establish its jurisdiction over the offenses set forth in article 7 in the following cases:

(a) when the offense is committed in the territory of that State or on board a ship or aircraft registered in that State;
(b) when the alleged offender is a national of that State.

2. Each State Party shall likewise take such measures as may be necessary to establish its jurisdiction over these offenses in cases where the alleged offender is present in its territory and it does not extradite him pursuant to article 11 to any of the States mentioned in paragraph 1.

3. This Convention does not exclude any criminal jurisdiction exercised in accordance with national law.

4. In addition to the State Parties mentioned in paragraphs 1 and 2, each State Party may, consistent with international law, establish its jurisdiction over the offenses set forth in article 7 when it is involved in international nuclear transport as the exporting or importing State.

ARTICLE 9

Upon being satisfied that the circumstances so warrant, the State Party in whose territory the alleged offender is present shall take appropriate measures, including detention, under its national law to ensure his presence for the purpose of prosecution or extradition. Measures taken according to this article shall be notified without delay to the States required to establish jurisdiction pursuant to article 8 and, where appropriate, all other States concerned.

ARTICLE 10

The State Party in whose territory the alleged offender is present shall, if it does not extradite him, submit, without

exception whatsoever and without undue delay, the case to its competent authorities for the purpose of prosecution, through proceedings in accordance with the laws of that State.

ARTICLE 11

1. The offenses in article 7 shall be deemed to be included as extraditable offenses in any extradition Treaty existing between States Parties. States Parties undertake to include those offenses as extraditable offenses in every future extradition Treaty to be concluded between them.

2. If a State Party which makes extradition conditional on the existence of a Treaty receives a request for extradition from another State Party with which it has no extradition Treaty, it may at its option consider this Convention as the legal basis for extradition in respect of those offenses. Extradition shall be subject to the other conditions provided by the law of the requested State.

3. State Parties which do not make extradition conditional on the existence of a Treaty shall recognize those offenses as extraditable offenses between themselves subject to the conditions provided by the law of the requested State.

4. Each of the offenses shall be treated, for the purpose of extradition between States Parties, as if it had been committed not only in the place in which it occurred but also in the territories of the State Parties required to establish their jurisdiction in accordance with paragraph 1 of article 8.

ARTICLE 12

Any person regarding whom proceedings are being carried out in connection with any of the offenses set forth in article 7 shall be guaranteed fair treatment at all stages of the proceedings.

ARTICLE 13

1. States Parties shall afford one another the greatest measure of assistance in connection with criminal proceedings brought in respect of the offenses set forth in article 7, including the supply of evidence at their disposal necessary for the proceedings. The law of the State requested shall apply in all cases.

2. The provisions of paragraph 1 shall not affect obligations under any other Treaty, bilateral or multilateral, which governs or will govern, in whole or in part, mutual assistance in criminal matters.

ARTICLE 14

1. Each State Party shall inform the depositary of its laws and regulations which give effect to this Convention. The depositary shall communicate such information periodically to all States Parties.

2. The State Party where an alleged offender is prosecuted shall, wherever practicable, first communicate the final outcome of the proceedings to the States directly concerned. The State Party shall also communicate the final outcome to the depositary who shall inform all States.

3. Where an offense involves nuclear material used for peaceful purposes in domestic use, storage or transport, and both the alleged offender and the nuclear material remain in the territory of the State Party in which the offense was committed, nothing in this Convention shall be interpreted as requiring that State Party to provide information concerning criminal proceedings arising out of such an offense.

ARTICLE 15

The Annexes constitute an integral part of this Convention.

ARTICLE 16

1. A conference of States Parties shall be convened by the depositary five years after the entry into force of this Convention to review the implementation of the Convention and its adequacy as concerns the preamble, the whole of the operative part and the annexes in the light of the then prevailing situation.

2. At intervals of not less than five years thereafter, the majority of States Parties may obtain, by submitting a proposal to this effect to the depositary, the convening of further conferences with the same objective.

ARTICLE 17

1. In the event of a dispute between two or more States Parties concerning the interpretation or application of this Convention, such States Parties shall consult with a view to the settlement of the dispute by negotiation, or by any other peaceful means of settling disputes acceptable to all parties to the dispute.

2. Any dispute of this character which cannot be settled in the manner prescribed in paragraph 1 shall, at the request of any party to such dispute, be submitted to arbitration or referred to the International Court of Justice for decision. Where a dispute is submitted to arbitration, if, within six months from the date of the request, the parties to the dispute are unable to agree on the organization of the arbitration, a party may request the President of the International Court of Justice or the Secretary-General of the United Nations to appoint one or more arbitrators. In case of conflicting requests by the parties to the dispute, the request to the Secretary-General of the United Nations shall have priority.

3. Each State Party may at the time of signature, ratification, acceptance or approval of this Convention or accession thereto declare that it does not consider itself bound by either or both of the dispute settlement procedures provided for in paragraph 2. The other States Parties shall not be bound by a dispute settlement procedure provided for in paragraph 2, with respect to a State Party which has made a reservation to that procedure.

4. Any State Party which has made a reservation in accordance with paragraph 3 may at any time withdraw that reservation by notification to the depositary.

ARTICLE 18

1. This Convention shall be open for signature by all States at the Headquarters of the International Atomic Energy Agency in Vienna and at the Headquarters of the United Nations in New York from 3 March 1980 until its entry into force.

2. This Convention is subject to ratification, acceptance or approval by the signatory States.

3. After its entry into force, this Convention will be open for accession by all States.

4.

(a) This Convention shall be open for signature or accession by international organizations and regional organizations of an integration or other nature, provided that any such organization is constituted by sovereign States and has competence in respect of the negotiation, conclusion and application of international agreements in matters covered by this Convention.

(b) In matters within their competence, such organizations shall, on their own behalf, exercise the rights and fulfill the responsibilities which this Convention attributes to States Parties.

(c) When becoming party to this Convention such an organization shall communicate to the depositary a declaration indicating which States are members thereof and which articles of this Convention do not apply to it.

(d) Such an organization shall not hold any vote additional to those of its Member States.

5. Instruments of ratification, acceptance, approval or accession shall be deposited with the depositary.

ARTICLE 19

1. This Convention shall enter into force on the thirtieth day following the date of deposit of the twenty-first instrument of ratification, acceptance or approval with the depositary.

2. For each State ratifying, accepting, approving or acceding to the Convention after the date of deposit of the twenty-first instrument of ratification, acceptance or approval, the Convention shall enter into force on the thirtieth day after the deposit by such State of its instrument of ratification, acceptance, approval or accession.

ARTICLE 20

1. Without prejudice to article 16 a State Party may propose amendments to this Convention. The proposed amendment shall be submitted to the depositary who shall circulate it immediately to all States Parties. If a majority of States Parties request the depositary to convene a conference to consider the proposed amendments, the depositary shall invite all States Parties to attend such a conference to begin not sooner than thirty days after the invitations are issued. Any amendment adopted at the conference by a two-thirds majority of all States Parties shall be promptly circulated by the depositary to all States Parties.

2. The amendment shall enter into force for each State Party that deposits its instrument of ratification, acceptance or approval of the amendment on the thirtieth day after the date on which two thirds of the States Parties have deposited their instruments of ratification, acceptance or approval with the depositary. Thereafter, the amendment shall enter into force for any other State Party on the day on which that State Party deposits its instrument of ratification, acceptance or approval of the amendment.

ARTICLE 21

1. Any State Party may denounce this Convention by written notification to the depositary.

2. Denunciation shall take effect one hundred and eighty days following the date on which notification is received by the depositary.

ARTICLE 22

The depositary shall promptly notify all States of:

(a) each signature of this Convention;
(b) each deposit of an instrument of ratification, acceptance, approval or accession;
(c) any reservation or withdrawal in accordance with article 17;
(d) any communication made by an organization in accordance with paragraph 4(c) of article 18;
(e) the entry into force of this Convention;
(f) the entry into force of any amendment to this Convention; and
(g) any denunciation made under article 21.

ARTICLE 23

The original of this Convention, of which the Arabic, Chinese, English, French, Russian and Spanish texts are equally authentic, shall be deposited with the Director General of the International Atomic Energy Agency who shall send certified copies thereof to all States.

The G8 Global Partnership Against the Spread of Weapons and Materials of Mass Destruction

Statement by the Group of Eight Leaders
Kananaskis, Canada
June 27, 2002

The attacks of September 11 demonstrated that terrorists are prepared to use any means to cause terror and inflict appalling casualties on innocent people. We commit ourselves to prevent terrorists, or those that harbour them, from acquiring or developing nuclear, chemical, radiological and biological weapons; missiles; and related materials, equipment and technology. We call on all countries to join us in adopting the set of non-proliferation principles we have announced today.

In a major initiative to implement those principles, we have also decided today to launch a new G8 Global Partnership against the Spread of Weapons and Materials of Mass Destruction. Under this initiative, we will support specific cooperation projects, initially in Russia, to address non-proliferation, disarmament, counter-terrorism and nuclear safety issues. Among our priority concerns are the destruction of chemical weapons, the dismantlement of decommissioned nuclear submarines, the disposition of fissile materials and the employment of former weapons scientists. We will commit to raise up to $20 billion to support such projects over the next ten years. A range of financing options, including the option of bilateral debt for program exchanges, will be available to countries that contribute to this Global Partnership. We have adopted a set of guidelines that will form the basis for the negotiation of specific agreements for new projects, that will apply with immediate effect, to ensure effective and efficient project development, coordination and implementation. We will review over the next year the applicability of the guidelines to existing projects.

Recognizing that this Global Partnership will enhance international security and safety, we invite other countries that are prepared to adopt its common principles and guidelines to enter into discussions with us on participating in and contributing to this initiative. We will review progress on this Global Partnership at our next Summit in 2003.

THE G8 GLOBAL PARTNERSHIP:
PRINCIPLES TO PREVENT TERRORISTS,
OR THOSE THAT HARBOUR THEM,
FROM GAINING ACCESS TO WEAPONS OR
MATERIALS OF MASS DESTRUCTION

The G8 calls on all countries to join them in commitment to the following six principles to prevent terrorists or those that harbour them from acquiring or developing nuclear, chemical, radiological and biological weapons; missiles; and related materials, equipment and technology.

1. Promote the adoption, universalization, full implementation and, where necessary, strengthening of multilateral treaties and other international instruments whose aim is to prevent the proliferation or illicit acquisition of such items; strengthen the institutions designed to implement these instruments.
2. Develop and maintain appropriate effective measures to account for and secure such items in production, use, storage and domestic and international transport; provide assistance to states lacking sufficient resources to account for and secure these items.
3. Develop and maintain appropriate effective physical protection measures applied to facilities which house such items, including defence in depth; provide assistance to states lacking sufficient resources to protect their facilities.
4. Develop and maintain effective border controls, law enforcement efforts and international cooperation to detect, deter and interdict in cases of illicit trafficking in such items, for example through installation of detection systems, training of customs and law enforcement personnel and cooperation in tracking these items; provide assistance to states lacking sufficient expertise or resources to strengthen their capacity to detect, deter and interdict in cases of illicit trafficking in these items.
5. Develop, review and maintain effective national export and transshipment controls over items on multilateral export control lists, as well as items that are not identified on such lists but which may nevertheless contribute to the development, production or use of nuclear, chemical and biological weapons and missiles, with particular consideration of end-user, catch-all and brokering aspects; provide assistance to states lacking the legal and regulatory infrastructure, implementation experience and/or resources to develop their export and transshipment control systems in this regard.
6. Adopt and strengthen efforts to manage and dispose of stocks of fissile materials designated as no longer required for defence purposes, eliminate all chemical weapons, and minimize holdings of dangerous biological pathogens and toxins, based on the recognition that the threat of terrorist acquisition is reduced as the overall quantity of such items is reduced.

THE G8 GLOBAL PARTNERSHIP:
GUIDELINES FOR NEW OR EXPANDED
COOPERATION PROJECTS

The G8 will work in partnership, bilaterally and multilaterally, to develop, coordinate, implement and finance, according to their respective means, new or expanded cooperation projects to address (i) non-proliferation, (ii) disarmament, (iii) counter-terrorism and (iv) nuclear safety (including environmental) issues, with a view to enhancing strategic stability, consonant with our international security objectives and in support of the multilateral non-proliferation regimes. Each country has primary responsibility for implementing its non-proliferation, disarmament, counter-terrorism and nuclear safety obligations and requirements and commits its full cooperation within the Partnership.

Cooperation projects under this initiative will be decided and implemented, taking into account international obligations and domestic laws of participating partners, within appropriate bilateral and multilateral legal frameworks that should, as necessary, include the following elements:

1. Mutually agreed effective monitoring, auditing and transparency measures and procedures will be required in order to ensure that cooperative activities meet agreed objectives (including irreversibility as necessary), to confirm work performance, to account for the funds expended and to provide for adequate access for donor representatives to work sites;

2. The projects will be implemented in an environmentally sound manner and will maintain the highest appropriate level of safety;

3. Clearly defined milestones will be developed for each project, including the option of suspending or terminating a project if the milestones are not met;

4. The material, equipment, technology, services and expertise provided will be solely for peaceful purposes and, unless otherwise agreed, will be used only for the purposes of implementing the projects and will not be transferred. Adequate measures of physical protection will also be applied to prevent theft or sabotage;

5. All governments will take necessary steps to ensure that the support provided will be considered free technical assistance and will be exempt from taxes, duties, levies and other charges;

6. Procurement of goods and services will be conducted in accordance with open international practices to the extent possible, consistent with national security requirements;

7. All governments will take necessary steps to ensure that adequate liability protections from claims related to the cooperation will be provided for donor countries and their personnel and contractors;

8. Appropriate privileges and immunities will be provided for government donor representatives working on cooperation projects; and

9. Measures will be put in place to ensure effective protection of sensitive information and intellectual property.

Given the breadth and scope of the activities to be undertaken, the G8 will establish an appropriate mechanism for the annual review of progress under this initiative which may include consultations regarding priorities, identification of project gaps and potential overlap, and assessment of consistency of the cooperation projects with international security obligations and objectives. Specific bilateral and multilateral project implementation will be coordinated subject to arrangements appropriate to that project, including existing mechanisms.

For the purposes of these guidelines, the phrase "new or expanded cooperation projects" is defined as cooperation projects that will be initiated or enhanced on the basis of this Global Partnership. All funds disbursed or released after its announcement would be included in the total of committed resources. A range of financing options, including the option of bilateral debt for program exchanges, will be available to countries that contribute to this Global Partnership.

The Global Partnership's initial geographic focus will be on projects in Russia, which maintains primary responsibility for implementing its obligations and requirements within the Partnership.

In addition, the G8 would be willing to enter into negotiations with any other recipient countries, including those of the Former Soviet Union, prepared to adopt the guidelines, for inclusion in the Partnership.

Recognizing that the Global Partnership is designed to enhance international security and safety, the G8 invites others to contribute to and join in this initiative.

With respect to nuclear safety and security, the partners agreed to establish a new G8 Nuclear Safety and Security Group by the time of our next Summit.

Harmel Report and NATO Dual-Track Decision (1979)

At a special meeting of Foreign and Defence Ministers in Brussels on 12th December 1979:

Ministers recalled the May 1978 Summit where governments expressed the political resolve to meet the challenges to their security posed by the continuing momentum of the Warsaw Pact military build-up.

The Warsaw Pact has over the years developed a large and growing capability in nuclear systems that directly threaten Western Europe and have a strategic significance for the Alliance in Europe. This situation has been especially aggravated over the last few years by Soviet decisions to implement programmes modernizing and expanding their long-range nuclear capability substantially. In particular, they have deployed the SS-20 missile, which offers significant improvements over previous systems in providing greater accuracy, more mobility, and greater range, as well as having multiple warheads, and the Backfire bomber, which has a much better performance than other Soviet aircraft deployed hitherto in a theatre role. During this period, while the Soviet Union has been reinforcing its superiority in Long Range Theatre Nuclear Forces (LRTNF) both quantitatively and qualitatively, Western LRTNF capabilities have remained static. Indeed these forces are increasing in age and vulnerability and do not include land-based, long-range theatre nuclear missile systems

At the same time, the Soviets have also undertaken a modernization and expansion of their shorter-range TNF and greatly improved the overall quality of their conventional forces. These developments took place against the background of increasing Soviet inter-continental capabilities and achievement of parity in inter-continental capability with the United States.

These trends have prompted serious concern within the Alliance, because, if they were to continue, Soviet superiority in theatre nuclear systems could undermine the stability achieved in inter-continental systems and cast doubt on the credibility of the Alliance's deterrent strategy by highlighting the gap in the spectrum of NATO's available nuclear response to aggression.

Ministers noted that these recent developments require concrete actions on the part of the Alliance if NATO's strategy of flexible response is to remain credible. After intensive consideration, including the merits of alternative approaches, and after taking note of the positions of certain members, Ministers concluded that the overall interest of the Alliance would best be served by pursuing two parallel and complementary approaches of TNF modernization and arms control.

Accordingly Ministers have decided to modernize NATO's LRTNF by the deployment in Europe of US ground-launched systems comprising 108 Pershing II launchers, which would replace existing US Pershing I-A, and 464 Ground Launched Cruise Missiles (GLCM), all with single warheads. All the nations currently participating in the integrated defence structure will participate in the programme: the missiles will be stationed in selected countries and certain support costs will be met through NATO's existing common funding arrangements. The programme will not increase NATO's reliance upon nuclear weapons. In this connection, Ministers agreed that as an integral part of TNF modernization, 1.000 US nuclear warheads will be withdrawn from Europe as soon as feasible. Further, Ministers decided that the 572 LRTNF warheads should be accommodated within that reduced level, which necessarily implies a numerical shift of emphasis away from warheads for delivery systems of other types and shorter ranges In addition they noted with satisfaction that the Nuclear Planning Group is undertaking an examination of the precise nature, scope and basis of the adjustments resulting from the LRTNF deployment and their possible implications for the balance of roles and systems in NATO's nuclear armoury as a whole. This examination will form the basis of a substantive report to NPG Ministers in the Autumn of 1980.

Ministers attach great importance to the role of arms control in contributing to a more stable military relationship between East and West and in advancing the process of detente. This is reflected in a broad set of initiatives being examined within the Alliance to further the course of arms control and detente in the 1980s. Ministers regard arms control as an integral part of the Alliance's efforts to assure the undiminished security of its member States and to make the strategic situation between East and West more stable, more predictable, and more manageable at lower levels of armaments on both sides. In this regard they welcome the contribution which the SALT II Treaty makes towards achieving these objectives.

Ministers consider that, building on this accomplishment and taking account of the expansion of Soviet LRTNF capabilities of concern to NATO, arms control efforts to achieve a more stable overall nuclear balance at lower levels of nuclear weapons on both sides should therefore now include certain US and Soviet long-range theatre nuclear systems This would reflect previous Western suggestions to include such Soviet and US systems in arms control negotiations and more recent expressions by Soviet President Brezhnev of willingness to do so. Ministers fully support the decision taken by the United States following consultations within the Alliance to negotiate arms limitations on LRTNF and to propose to the USSR to begin negotiations as soon as possible along the following lines which have been elaborated in intensive consultations within the Alliance:

1. Any future limitations on US systems principally designed for theatre missions should be accompanied by appropriate limitations on Soviet theatre systems.
2. Limitations on US and Soviet long-range theatre nuclear systems should be negotiated bilaterally in the SALT III framework in a step-by-step approach.
3. The immediate objective of these negotiations should be the establishment of agreed limitations on US and Soviet land-based long-range theatre nuclear missile systems.
4. Any agreed limitations on these systems must be consistent with the principle of equality between the sides. Therefore, the limitations should take the form of de jure equality both in ceilings and in rights.

5. Any agreed limitations must be adequately verifiable.

Given the special importance of these negotiations for the overall security of the Alliance, a special consultative body at a high level will be constituted within the Alliance to support the US negotiating effort. This body will follow the negotiations on a continuous basis and report to the Foreign and Defence Ministers who will examine developments in these negotiations as well as in other arms control negotiations at their semi-annual meetings.

The Ministers have decided to pursue these two parallel and complementary approaches in order to avert an arms race in Europe caused by the Soviet TNF build-up, yet preserve the viability of NATO's strategy of deterrence and defence and thus maintain the security of its member States.

1. A modernization decision, including a commitment to deployments, is necessary to meet NATO's deterrence and defence needs, to provide a credible response to unilateral Soviet TNF deployments, and to provide the foundation for the pursuit of serious negotiations on TNF.

2. Success of arms control in constraining the Soviet build-up can enhance Alliance security, modify the scale of NATO's TNF requirements, and promote stability and detente in Europe in consonance with NATO's basic policy of deterrence, defence and detente as enunciated in the Harmel Report. NATO's TNF requirements will be examined in the light of concrete results reached through negotiations.

Footnote:
France did not participate in the Special Meeting.

THE FUTURE TASKS OF THE ALLIANCE (THE HARMEL REPORT): REPORT OF THE COUNCIL (DECEMBER 12, 1979)

A year ago, on the initiative of the Foreign Minister of Belgium, the governments of the fifteen nations of the Alliance resolved to *"study the future tasks which face the Alliance, and its procedures for fulfilling them in order to strengthen the Alliance as a factor for durable peace"*. The present report sets forth the general tenor and main principles emerging from this examination of the future tasks of the Alliance.

2. Studies were undertaken by Messrs. Schutz, Watson, Spaak, Kohler and Patijn. The Council wishes to express its appreciation and thanks to these eminent personalities for their efforts and for the analyses they produced.

3. The exercise has shown that the Alliance is a dynamic and vigorous organization which is constantly adapting itself to changing conditions. It also has shown that its future tasks can be handled within the terms of the Treaty by building on the methods and procedures which have proved their value over many years.

4. Since the North Atlantic Treaty was signed in 1949 the international situation has changed significantly and the political tasks of the Alliance have assumed a new dimension. Amongst other developments, the Alliance has played a major part in stopping Communist expansion in Europe; the USSR has become one of the two world super powers but the Communist world is no longer monolithic; the Soviet doctrine of *"peaceful co-existence"* has changed the nature of the confrontation with the West but not the basic problems. Although the disparity between the power of the United States and that of the European states remains, Europe has recovered and is on its way towards unity. The process of decolonisation has transformed European relations with the rest of the world; at the same time, major problems have arisen in the relations between developed and developing countries.

5. The Atlantic Alliance has two main functions. Its first function is to maintain adequate military strength and political solidarity to deter aggression and other forms of pressure and to defend the territory of member countries if aggression should occur. Since its inception, the Alliance has successfully fulfilled this task. But the possibility of a crisis cannot be excluded as long as the central political issues in Europe, first and foremost the German question, remain unsolved. Moreover, the situation of instability and uncertainty still precludes a balanced reduction of military forces. Under these conditions, the Allies will maintain as necessary, a suitable military capability to assure the balance of forces, thereby creating a climate of stability, security and confidence.

In this climate the Alliance can carry out its second function, to pursue the search for progress towards a more stable relationship in which the underlying political issues can be solved. Military security and a policy of détente are not contradictory but complementary. Collective defence is a stabilizing factor in world politics. It is the necessary condition for effective policies directed towards a greater relaxation of tensions. The way to peace and stability in Europe rests in particular on the use of the Alliance constructively in the interest of détente. The participation of the USSR and the USA will be necessary to achieve a settlement of the political problems in Europe.

6. From the beginning the Atlantic Alliance has been a co-operative grouping of states sharing the same ideals and with a high degree of common interest. Their cohe-

sion and solidarity provide an element of stability within the Atlantic area.

7. As sovereign states the Allies are not obliged to subordinate their policies to collective decision. The Alliance affords an effective forum and clearing house for the exchange of information and views; thus, each of the Allies can decide its policy in the light of close knowledge of the problems and objectives of the others. To this end the practice of frank and timely consultations needs to be deepened and improved. Each Ally should play its full part in promoting an improvement in relations with the Soviet Union and the countries of Eastern Europe, bearing in mind that the pursuit of détente must not be allowed to split the Alliance. The chances of success will clearly be greatest if the Allies remain on parallel courses, especially in matters of close concern to them all; their actions will thus be all the more effective.

8. No peaceful order in Europe is possible without a major effort by all concerned. The evolution of Soviet and East European policies gives ground for hope that those governments may eventually come to recognize the advantages to them of collaborating in working towards a peaceful settlement. But no final and stable settlement in Europe is possible without a solution of the German question which lies at the heart of present tensions in Europe. Any such settlement must end the unnatural barriers between Eastern and Western Europe, which are most clearly and cruelly manifested in the division of Germany.

9. Accordingly the Allies are resolved to direct their energies to this purpose by realistic measures designed to further a détente in East-West relations. The relaxation of tensions is not the final goal but is part of a long-term process to promote better relations and to foster a European settlement. The ultimate political purpose of the Alliance is to achieve a just and lasting peaceful order in Europe accompanied by appropriate security guarantees.

10. Currently, the development of contacts between the countries of Western and Eastern Europe is mainly on a bilateral basis. Certain subjects, of course, require by their very nature a multilateral solution.

11. The problem of German reunification and its relationship to a European settlement has normally been dealt with in exchanges between the Soviet Union and the three Western powers having special responsibilities in this field. In the preparation of such exchanges the Federal Republic of Germany has regularly joined the three Western powers in order to reach a common position. The other Allies will continue to have their views considered in timely discussions among the Allies about Western policy on this subject, without in any way impairing the special responsibilities in question.

12. The Allies will examine and review suitable policies designed to achieve a just and stable order in Europe, to overcome the division of Germany and to foster European

security. This will be part of a process of active and constant preparation for the time when fruitful discussions of these complex questions may be possible bilaterally or multilaterally between Eastern and Western nations.

13. The Allies are studying disarmament and practical arm control measures, including the possibility of balanced force reductions. These studies will be intensified. Their active pursuit reflects the will of the Allies to work for an effective détente with the East.

14. The Allies will examine with particular attention the defence problems of the exposed areas e.g. the South-Eastern flank. In this respect the present situation in the Mediterranean presents special problems, bearing in mind that the current crisis in the Middle East falls within the responsibilities of the United Nations.

15. The North Atlantic Treaty area cannot be treated in isolation from the rest of the world. Crises and conflicts arising outside the area may impair its security either directly or by affecting the global balance. Allied countries contribute individually within the United Nations and other international organizations to the maintenance of international peace and security and to the solution of important international problems. In accordance with established usage the Allies or such of them as wish to do so will also continue to consult on such problems without commitment and as the case may demand.

16. In the light of these findings, the Ministers directed the Council in permanent session to carry out, in the years ahead, the detailed follow-up resulting from this study. This will be done either b intensifying work already in hand or by activating highly specialized studies by more systematic use of experts and officials sent from capitals.

17. Ministers found that the study by the Special Group confirmed the importance of the role which the Alliance is called upon to play during the coming years in the promotion of détente and the strengthening of peace. Since significant problems have not yet bee] examined in all their aspects, and other problems of no less significance which have arisen from the latest political and strategic developments have still to be examined, the Ministers have directed the Permanent Representatives to put in hand the study of these problems without delay, following such procedures as shall be deemed most appropriate by the Council in permanent session, in order to enable further reports to be subsequently submitted to the Council in Ministerial Session.

SPECIAL MEETING OF FOREIGN AND DEFENCE MINISTERS (THE "DOUBLE-TRACK" DECISION ON THEATRE NUCLEAR FORCES)

Brussels, 12 December 1979

1. At a special meeting of Foreign and Defence Ministers in

Brussels on 12 December 1979.

2. Ministers recalled the May 1978 Summit where governments expressed the political resolve to meet the challenges to their security posed by the continuing momentum of the Warsaw Pact military build-up.

3. The Warsaw Pact has over the years developed a large and growing capability in nuclear systems that directly threaten Western Europe and have a strategic significance for the Alliance in Europe. This situation has been especially aggravated over the last few years by Soviet decisions to implement programmes modernising and expanding their long-range nuclear capability substantially. In particular, they have deployed the SS-20 missile, which offers significant improvements over previous systems in providing greater accuracy, more mobility, and greater range, as well as having multiple warheads, and the Backfire bomber, which has a much better performance than other Soviet aircraft deployed hitherto in a theatre role.

During this period, while the Soviet Union has been reinforcing its superiority in Long-Range Theatre Nuclear Forces (LRTNF) both quantitatively and qualitatively, Western LRTNF capabilities have remained static. Indeed these forces are increasing in age and vulnerability and do not include land-based, long-range theatre nuclear missile systems.

4. At the same time, the Soviets have also undertaken a modernisation and expansion of their shorter-range TNF and greatly improved the overall quality of their conventional forces.

These developments took place against the background of increasing Soviet inter-continental capabilities and achievement of parity in inter-continental capability with the United States.

5. These trends have prompted serious concern within the Alliance, because, if they were to continue, Soviet superiority in theatre nuclear systems could undermine the stability achieved in inter-continental systems and cast doubt on the credibility of the Alliance's deterrent strategy by highlighting the gap in the spectrum of NATO's available nuclear response to aggression.

6. Ministers noted that these recent developments require concrete actions on the part of the Alliance if NATO's strategy of flexible response is to remain credible. After intensive consideration, including the merits of alternative approaches, and after taking note of the positions of certain members, Ministers concluded that the overall interest of the Alliance would best be served by pursuing two parallel and complementary approaches of TNF modernisation and arms control.

7. Accordingly Ministers have decided to modernise NATO's LRTNF by the deployment in Europe of US ground-launched systems comprising 108 Pershing II launchers, which would replace existing US Pershing I-A, and 464 Ground-Launched Cruise Missiles (GLCM), all with single warheads. All the nations currently participating in the integrated defence structure will participate in the programme: the missiles will be stationed in selected countries and certain support costs will be met through NATO's existing common funding arrangements.

The programme will not increase NATO's reliance upon nuclear weapons. In this connection, Ministers agreed that as an integral part of TNF modernisation, 1,000 US nuclear warheads will be withdrawn from Europe as soon as feasible. Further, Ministers decided that the 572 LRTNF warheads should be accommodated within that reduced level, which necessarily implies a numerical shift of emphasis away from warheads for delivery systems of other types and shorter ranges In addition they noted with satisfaction that the Nuclear Planning Group is undertaking an examination of the precise nature, scope and basis of the adjustments resulting from the LRTNF deployment and their possible implications for the balance of roles and systems in NATO's nuclear armoury as a whole. This examination will form the basis of a substantive report to NPG Ministers in the Autumn of 1980.

8. Ministers attach great importance to the role of arms control in contributing to a more stable military relationship between East and West and in advancing the process of détente. This is reflected in a broad set of initiatives being examined within the Alliance to further the course of arms control and détente in the 1980s. Ministers regard arms control as an integral part of the Alliance's efforts to assure the undiminished security of its member States and to make the strategic situation between East and West more stable, more predictable, and more manageable at lower levels of armaments on both sides. In this regard they welcome the contribution which the SALT II Treaty makes towards achieving these objectives.

9. Ministers consider that, building on this accomplishment and taking account of the expansion of Soviet LRTNF capabilities of concern to NATO, arms control efforts to achieve a more stable overall nuclear balance at lower levels of nuclear weapons on both sides should therefore now include certain US and Soviet long-range theatre nuclear systems. This would reflect previous Western suggestions to include such Soviet and US systems in arms control negotiations and more recent expressions by Soviet President Brezhnev of willingness to do so. Ministers fully support the decision taken by the United States following consultations within the Alliance to negotiate arms limitations on LRTNF and to propose to the USSR to begin negotiations as soon as possible along the following lines which have been elaborated in intensive consultations within the Alliance:

a. Any future limitations on US systems principally designed for theatre missions should be accompanied by appropriate limitations on Soviet theatre systems.

b. Limitations on US and Soviet long-range theatre nuclear systems should be negotiated bilaterally in the SALT III framework in a step-by-step approach.

c. The immediate objective of these negotiations should be the establishment of agreed limitations on US and Soviet land-based long-range theatre nuclear missile systems.

d. Any agreed limitations on these systems must be consistent with the principle of equality between the sides. Therefore, the limitations should take the form of de jure equality both in ceilings and in rights.

e. Any agreed limitations must be adequately verifiable.

10. Given the special importance of these negotiations for the overall security of the Alliance, a special consultative body at a high level will be constituted within the Alliance to support the US negotiating effort. This body will follow the negotiations on a continuous basis and report to the Foreign and Defence Ministers who will examine developments in these negotiations as well as in other arms control negotiations at their semi-annual meetings.

11. The Ministers have decided to pursue these two parallel and complementary approaches in order to avert an arms race in Europe caused by the Soviet TNF build-up, yet preserve the viability of NATO's strategy of deterrence and defence and thus maintain the security of its member States.

a. A modernisation decision, including a commitment to deployments, is necessary to meet NATO's deterrence and defence needs, to provide a credible response to unilateral Soviet TNF deployments, and to provide the foundation for the pursuit of serious negotiations on TNF.

b. Success of arms control in constraining the Soviet buildup can enhance Alliance security, modify the scale of NATO's TNF requirements, and promote stability and détente in Europe in consonance with NATO's basic policy of deterrence, defence and détente as enunciated in the Harmel Report. NATO's TNF requirements will be examined in the light of concrete results reached through negotiations.

Hot Line Agreement (1963)

(DEPARTMENT OF STATE SUMMARY)

Bilateral agreement establishing a direct communications link between U.S. and Soviet heads of state for use in "time of emergency." Seeks to reduce the risk of a nuclear exchange stemming from accident, miscalculation, or surprise attack. Both sides connected by transatlantic cable and radio telegraph circuits for continuous direct communications. Updated in 1971 to include two U.S.-U.S.S.R. satellite communications circuits, along with multiple terminals in each country. The treaty entered into force on June 20, 1963.

NARRATIVE

The need for ensuring quick and reliable communication directly between the heads of government of nuclear-weapons states first emerged in the context of efforts to reduce the danger that accident, miscalculation, or surprise attack might trigger a nuclear war. These risks, arising out of conditions which are novel in history and peculiar to the nuclear-armed missile age, can of course threaten all countries, directly or indirectly.

The Soviet Union had been the first nation to propose, in 1954, specific safeguards against surprise attack; it also expressed concern about the danger of accidental war. At Western initiative, a Conference of Experts on Surprise Attack was held in Geneva in 1958, but recessed without achieving conclusive results, although it stimulated technical research on the issues involved.

In its "Program for General and Complete Disarmament in a Peaceful World," presented to the General Assembly by President Kennedy on September 25, 1961, the United States proposed a group of measures to reduce the risks of war. These included advance notification of military movements and maneuvers, observation posts at major transportation centers and air bases, and additional inspection arrangements. An international commission would be established to study possible further measures to reduce risks, including "failure of communication."

The United States draft Treaty outline submitted to the ENDC 1on April 18, 1962, added a proposal for the exchange of military missions to improve communications and understanding. It also proposed "establishment of rapid and reliable communications" among the heads of government and with the Secretary General of the United Nations.

The Soviet draft Treaty on general and complete disarmament (March 15, 1962) offered no provisions covering the risk of war by surprise attack, miscalculation, or accident. On July 16, however, the Soviet Union introduced amendments to its draft that called for (1) a ban on joint maneuvers involving the forces of two or more states and advance notification of substantial military movements, (2) exchange of military missions, and (3) improved communications between heads of government and with the U.N. Secretary General. These measures were not separable from the rest of the Soviet program.

The Cuban missile crisis of October 1962 compellingly underscored the importance of prompt, direct communication between heads of state. On December 12 of that year, a U.S. working paper submitted to the ENDC urged consideration of a number of measures to reduce the risk of war. These measures, the United States argued, offered opportunities for early agreement and could be undertaken either as a group or separately. Included was establishment of communications links between major capitals to ensure rapid and reliable communications in times of crisis. The working paper suggested that it did not appear either necessary or desirable to specify in advance all the situations in which a special communications link might be used:

... In the view of the United States, such a link should, as a general matter, be reserved for emergency use; that is to say, for example, that it might be reserved for communications concerning a military crisis which might appear directly to threaten the security of either of the states involved and where such developments were taking place at a rate which appeared to preclude the use of normal consultative procedures. Effectiveness of the link would not be degraded through use for other matters.

On June 20, 1963, at Geneva the U.S. and Soviet representatives to the ENDC completed negotiations and signed the "Memorandum of Understanding Between the United States of America and the Union of Soviet Socialist Republics Regarding the Establishment of a Direct Communications Link." The memorandum provided that each government should be responsible for arrangements for the link on its own territory, including continuous functioning of the link and prompt delivery of communications to its head of government. An annex set forth the routing and components of the link and provided for allocation of costs, exchange of equipment, and other technical matters. The direct communications link would comprise:

1. two terminal points with teletype equipment;
2. a full-time duplex wire telegraph circuit (Washington-London-Copenhagen-Stockholm-Helsinki-Moscow); and
3. a full-time duplex radiotelegraph circuit (Washington-Tangier-Moscow).

If the wire circuit should be interrupted, messages would be transmitted by the radio circuit. If experience showed the need for an additional wire circuit, it might be established by mutual agreement.

The "Hot Line" agreement, the first bilateral agreement between the United States and the Soviet Union that gave concrete recognition to the perils implicit in modern nuclear-weapons systems, was a limited but practical step to bring those perils under rational control.

The communications link has proved its worth since its installation. During the Arab-Israeli war in 1967, for example, the United States used it to prevent possible misunderstanding of U.S. fleet movements in the Mediterranean. It was used again during the 1973 Arab-Israeli war. The significance of the hot line is further attested by the 1971, 1984 and 1988 agreements to modernize it.

Statute of the International Atomic Energy Agency

(Excerpts)

Opened for signature at New York on 26 October 1956
Entered into force on 29 July 1957
Depositary: US government

ARTICLE II. *OBJECTIVES*

The Agency shall seek to accelerate and enlarge the contribution of atomic energy to peace, health and prosperity throughout the world. It shall ensure, so far as it is able, that assistance provided by it or at its request or under its supervision or control is not used in such a way as to further any military purpose.

ARTICLE III. *FUNCTIONS*

A. The Agency is authorized:

...

5. To establish and administer safeguards designed to ensure that special fissionable and other materials, services, equipment, facilities, and information made available by the Agency or at its request or under its supervision or control are not used in such a way as to further any military purpose; and to apply safeguards, at the request of the parties, to any bilateral or multilateral arrangement, or at the request of a State, to any of that State's activities in the field of atomic energy;

...

ARTICLE XII. *AGENCY SAFEGUARDS*

A. With respect to any Agency project, or other arrangement where the Agency is requested by the parties concerned to apply safeguards, the Agency shall have the following rights and responsibilities to the extent relevant to the project or arrangement:

72 ARMS CONTROL

1. To examine the design of specialized equipment and facilities, including nuclear reactors, and to approve it only from the view-point of assuring that it will not further any military purpose, that it complies with applicable health and safety standards, and that it will permit effective application of the safeguards provided for in this article;

2. To require the observance of any health and safety measures prescribed by the Agency;

3. To require the maintenance and production of operating records to assist in ensuring accountability for source and special fissionable materials used or produced in the project or arrangement;

4. To call for and receive progress reports;

5. To approve the means to be used for the chemical processing of irradiated materials solely to ensure that this chemical processing will not lend itself to diversion of materials for military purposes and will comply with applicable health and safety standards; to require that special fissionable materials recovered or produced as a by-product be used for peaceful purposes under continuing Agency safeguards for research or in reactors, existing or under construction, specified by the member or members concerned; and to require deposit with the Agency of any excess of any special fissionable materials recovered or produced as a by-product over what is needed for the above-stated uses in order to prevent stockpiling of these materials, provided that thereafter at the request of the member or members concerned special fissionable materials so deposited with the Agency shall be returned promptly to the member or members concerned for use under the same provisions as stated above;

6. To send into the territory of the recipient State or States inspectors, designated by the Agency after consultation with the State or States concerned, who shall have access at all times to all places and data and to any person who by reason of his occupation deals with materials, equipment, or facilities which are required by this Statute to be safeguarded, as necessary to account for source and special fissionable materials supplied and fissionable products and to determine whether there is compliance with the undertaking against use in furtherance of any military purpose referred to in sub-paragraph F-4 of article XI, with the health and safety measures referred to in sub-paragraph A-2 of this article, and with any other conditions prescribed in the agreement between the Agency and the State or States concerned. Inspectors designated by the Agency shall be accompanied by represen-

tatives of the authorities of the State concerned, if that State so requests, provided that the inspectors shall not thereby be delayed or otherwise impeded in the exercise of their functions;

7. In the event of non-compliance and failure by the recipient State or States to take requested corrective steps within a reasonable time, to suspend or terminate assistance and withdraw any materials and equipment made available by the Agency or a member in furtherance of the project.

B. The Agency shall, as necessary, establish a staff of inspectors. The Staff of inspectors shall have the responsibility of examining all operations conducted by the Agency itself to determine whether the Agency is complying with the health and safety measures prescribed by it for application to projects subject to its approval, supervision or control, and whether the Agency is taking adequate measures to prevent the source and special fissionable materials in its custody or used or produced

POST-WORLD WAR II AGREEMENTS 73

in its own operations from being used in furtherance of any military purpose. The Agency shall take remedial action forthwith to correct any non-compliance or failure to take adequate measures.

C. . . . The inspectors shall report any non-compliance to the Director General who shall thereupon transmit the report to the Board of Governors. The Board shall call upon the recipient State or States to remedy forthwith any non-compliance which it finds to have occurred. The Board shall report the non-compliance to all members and to the Security Council and General Assembly of the United Nations. In the event of failure of the recipient State or States to take fully corrective action within a reasonable time, the Board may take one or both of the following measures: direct curtailment or suspension of assistance being provided by the Agency or by a member, and call for the return of materials and equipment made available to the recipient member or group of members. The Agency may also, in accordance with article XIX, suspend any non-complying member from the exercise of the privileges and rights of membership.

. . .

ARTICLE XVIII. *AMENDMENTS AND WITHDRAWALS*

. . .

E. Withdrawal by a member from the Agency shall not affect its contractual obligations entered into pursuant to article XI or its budgetary obligations for the year in which it withdraws.

. . .

ARTICLE XX. *DEFINITIONS*

As used in this Statute:

1. The term "special fissionable material" means plutonium-239; uranium-233; uranium enriched in the isotopes 235 or 233; any material containing one or more of the foregoing; and such other fissionable material as the Board of Governors shall from time to time determine; but the term "special fissionable material" does not include source material.

2. The term "uranium enriched in the isotopes 235 or 233" means uranium containing the isotopes 235 or 233 or both in an amount such that the abundance ratio of the sum of these isotopes to the isotope 238 is greater than the ratio of the isotope 235 to the isotope 238 occurring in nature.

3. The term "source material" means uranium containing the mixture of isotopes occurring in nature, uranium depleted in the isotope 235; thorium; any of the foregoing in the form of metal, alloy, chemical compound, or concentrate; any other material containing one or more of the foregoing in such concentration as the Board of Governors shall from time to time determine; and such other material as the Board of Governors shall from time to time determine.

ARTICLE XXI. *SIGNATURE, ACCEPTANCE, AND ENTRY INTO FORCE*

...

B. The signatory States shall become parties to this Statute by deposit of an instrument of ratification.

...

74 ARMS CONTROL

E. This Statute, apart from the Annex, shall come into force when eighteen States have deposited instruments of ratification in accordance with paragraph B of this article, provided that such eighteen States shall include at least three of the following States: Canada, France, the Union of Soviet Socialist Republics, the United Kingdom of Great Britain and Northern Ireland, and the United States of America. Instruments of ratification and instruments of acceptance deposited thereafter shall take effect on the date of their receipt.

...

Source: *Statute, as amended up to 28 December 1989* (International Atomic Energy Agency: Vienna, June 1990)

Members of the IAEA as of 15 April 2002: Afghanistan, Albania, Algeria, Angola, Argentina, Armenia, Australia, Austria, Azerbaijan, Bangladesh, Belarus, Belgium, Bolivia, Bosnia and Herzegovina, Botswana, Brazil, Bulgaria, Burkina Faso, Cambodia, Cameroon, Canada, Central African Republic, Chile, China, Colombia, Congo (Democratic Republic of), Costa Rica, Cote d'Ivoire, Croatia, Cuba, Cyprus, Czech Republic, Denmark, Dominican Republic, Ecuador, Egypt, El Salvador, Estonia, Ethiopia, Finland, France, Gabon, Georgia, Germany, Ghana, Greece, Guatemala, Haiti, Holy See, Hungary, Iceland, India, Indonesia, Iran, Iraq, Ireland, Israel, Italy, Jamaica, Japan, Jordan, Kazakhstan, Kenya, Korea (South), Kuwait, Latvia, Lebanon, Liberia, Libya, Liechtenstein, Lithuania, Luxembourg, Macedonia (Former Yugoslav Republic of), Madagascar, Malaysia, Mali, Malta, Marshall Islands, Mauritius, Mexico, Moldova, Monaco, Mongolia, Morocco, Myanmar (Burma), Namibia, Netherlands, New Zealand, Nicaragua, Niger, Nigeria, Norway, Pakistan, Panama, Paraguay, Peru, Philippines, Poland, Portugal, Qatar,

Romania, Russia, Saudi Arabia, Senegal, Sierra Leone, Singapore, Slovakia, Slovenia, South Africa, Spain, Sri Lanka, Sudan, Sweden, Switzerland, Syria, Tajikistan, Tanzania, Thailand, Tunisia, Turkey, Uganda, UK, Ukraine, United Arab Emirates, Uruguay, USA, Uzbekistan, Venezuela, Viet Nam, Yemen, Yugoslavia, Zambia, Zimbabwe

Note: North Korea was a member of the IAEA until September 1994.

Interim Agreement Between the United States of America and the Union of Soviet Socialist Republics on Certain Measures with Respect to the Limitation of Strategic Offensive Arms (SALT I)

Signed at Moscow May 26, 1972
Approval authorized by U.S. Congress September 30, 1972
Approved by U.S. President September 30, 1972
Entered into force October 3, 1972

The United States of America and the Union of Soviet Socialist Republics, hereinafter referred to as the Parties,

Convinced that the Treaty on the Limitation of Anti-Ballistic Missile Systems and this Interim Agreement on Certain Measures with Respect to the Limitation of Strategic Offensive Arms will contribute to the creation of more favorable conditions for active negotiations on limiting strategic arms as well as to the relaxation of international tension and the strengthening of trus between States,

Taking into account the relationship between strategic offensive and defensive arms,

Mindful of their obligations under Article VI of the Treaty on the Non-Proliferation of Nuclear Weapons,

Have agreed as follows:

ARTICLE I

The Parties undertake not to start construction of additional fixed land-based intercontinental ballistic missile (ICBM) launchers after July 1, 1972.

ARTICLE II

The Parties undertake not to convert land-based launchers for light ICBMs, or for ICBMs of older types deployed prior to 1964, into land-based launchers for heavy ICBMs of types deployed after that time.

ARTICLE III

The Parties undertake to limit submarine- launched ballistic missile (SLBM) launchers and modern ballistic missile submarines to the numbers operational and under construction on the date of signature of this Interim Agreement, and in addition to launchers and submarines constructed under procedures established by the Parties as replacements for an equal number of ICBM launchers of older types deployed prior to 1964 or for launchers on older submarines.

ARTICLE IV

Subject to the provisions of this Interim Agreement, modernization and replacement of strategicoffensive ballistic missiles and launchers covered by this Interim Agreement may be undertaken.

ARTICLE V

1. For the purpose of providing assurance of compliance with the provisions of this Interim Agreement, each Party shall use national technical means of verification at its disposal in a manner consistent with generally recognized principles of international law.
2. Each Party undertakes not to interfere with the national technical means of verification of the other Party operating in accordance with paragraph 1 of this Article.
3. Each Party undertakes not to use deliberate concealment measures which impede verification by national technical means of compliance with the provisions of this Interim Agreement. This obligation shall not require changes in current construction, assembly, conversion, or overhaul practices.

ARTICLE VI

To promote the objectives and implementation of the provisions of this Interim Agreement, the Parties shall use the Standing Consultative Commission established under Article XIII of theTreaty on the Limitation of Anti-Ballistic Missile Systems in accordance with the provisions of that Article.

ARTICLE VII

The Parties undertake to continue active negotiations for limitations on strategic offensive arms.The obligations provided for in this Interim Agreement shall not prejudice the scope or terms ofthe limitations on strategic offensive arms which may be worked out in the course of further negotiations.

ARTICLE VIII

1. This Interim Agreement shall enter into force upon exchange of written notices of acceptance by each Party, which exchange shall take place simultaneously with the exchange of instruments of ratification of the Treaty on the Limitation of Anti-Ballistic Missile Systems.
2. This Interim Agreement shall remain in force for a period of five years unless replaced earlier by an agreement on more complete measures limiting strategic offensive arms. It is the objective of the Parties to conduct active follow-on negotiations with the aim of concluding such an agreement as soon as possible.
3. Each Party shall, in exercising its national sovereignty, have the right to withdraw from this Interim Agreement if it decides that extraordinary events related to the subject matter of this Interim Agreement have jeopardized its supreme interests. It shall give

notice of its decision to the other Party six months prior to withdrawal from this Interim Agreement. Such notice shall include a statement of the extraordinary events the notifying Party regards as having jeopardized its supreme interests.

DONE at Moscow on May 26, 1972, in two copies, each in the English and Russian languages, both texts being equally authentic.

FOR THE UNITED STATES OF AMERICA:
RICHARD NIXON
President of the United States of America
FOR THE UNION OF SOVIET SOCIALIST RE-PUBLICS:
L.I. BREZHNEV
General Secretary of the
Central Committee of the CPSU

PROTOCOL TO THE
INTERIM AGREEMENT

The United States of America and the Union of Soviet Socialist Republics, hereinafter referred to as the Parties,

Having agreed on certain limitations relating to submarine-launched ballistic missile launchers and modern ballistic missile submarines, and to replacement procedures, in the Interim Agreement,

Have agreed as follows:

The Parties understand that, under Article III of the Interim Agreement, for the period during which that Agreement remains in force:

The United States may have no more than 710 ballistic missile launchers on submarines (SLBMs) and no more than 44 modern ballistic missile submarines. The Soviet Union may have no more than 950 ballistic missile launchers on submarines and no more than 62 modern ballistic missile submarines.

Additional ballistic missile launchers on submarines up to the above-mentioned levels, in the United States — over 656 ballistic missile launchers on nuclear-powered submarines, and in the USSR — over 740 ballistic missile launchers on nuclear-powered submarines, operational and under construction, may become operational as replacements for equal numbers of ballistic missile launchers of older types deployed prior to 1964 or of ballistic missile launchers on older submarines.

The deployment of modern SLBMs on any submarine, regardless of type, will be counted against the total level of SLBMs permitted for the United States and the USSR.

This Protocol shall be considered an integral part of the Interim Agreement.

DONE at Moscow this 26th day of May, 1972
FOR THE UNITED STATES OF AMERICA:
RICHARD NIXON
President of the United States of America
FOR THE UNION OF SOVIET SOCIALIST RE-PUBLICS:
L.I. BREZHNEV
General Secretary of the
Central Committee of the CPSU

AGREED STATEMENTS, COMMON UNDERSTANDINGS, AND UNILATERAL STATEMENTS REGARDING THE INTERIM AGREEMENT

1. Agreed Statements

The document set forth below was agreed upon and initialed by the Heads of the Delegations on May 26, 1972 (letter designations added):

[A]

The Parties understand that land-based ICBM launchers referred to in the Interim Agreement are understood to be launchers for strategic ballistic missiles capable of ranges in excess of the shortest distance between the northeastern border of the continental United States and the northwestern border of the continental USSR.

[B]

The Parties understand that fixed land-based ICBM launchers under active construction as of the date of signature of the Interim Agreement may be completed.

[C]

The Parties understand that in the process of modernization and replacement the dimensions of land-based ICBM silo launchers will not be significantly increased.

[D]

The Parties understand that during the period of the Interim Agreement there shall be no significant increase in the number of ICBM or SLBM test and training launchers, or in the number of such launchers for modern land-based heavy ICBMs. The Parties further understand that construction or conversion of ICBM launchers at test ranges shall be undertaken only for purposes of testing and training.

[E]

The Parties understand that dismantling or destruction of ICBM launchers of older types deployed prior to 1964 and ballistic missile launchers on older submarines being replaced by newSLBM launchers on modern submarines will be initiated at the time of the beginning of sea trials of a replacement submarine, and will be completed in the shortest possible agreed period of time.Such dismantling or destruction, and timely notification thereof, will be accomplished under procedures to be agreed in the Standing Consultative Commission.

2. Common Understandings

Common understanding of the Parties on the following matters was reached during the negotiations:

A. Increase in ICBM Silo Dimensions

Ambassador Smith made the following statement on May 26, 1972:

The Parties agree that the term "significantly increased" means that an increase will not be greater than 10-15 percent of the present dimensions of land-based ICBM silo launchers.

Minister Semenov replied that this statement corresponded to the Soviet understanding.

B. Standing Consultative Commission

Ambassador Smith made the following statement on May 22, 1972:

The United States proposes that the sides agree that, with regard to initial implementation of the ABM Treaty's Article XIII on the Standing Consultative Commission (SCC) and of the consultation Articles to the Interim Agreement on offensive arms and the Accidents Agreement,

See Article 7 of Agreement to Reduce the Risk of the Outbreak of Nuclear War Between the United States of America and the Union of Soviet Socialist Republics, signed Sept. 30, 1971 agreement establishing the SCC will be worked out early in the follow-on SALT negotiations; until that is completed, the following arrangements will prevail: when SALT is in session, any consultation desired by either side under these Articles can be carried out by the two SALT Delegations; when SALT is not in session, *ad hoc* arrangements for any desired consultationsunder these Articles may be made through diplomatic channels.

Minister Semenov replied that, on an *ad referendum* basis, he could agree that the U.S. statement corresponded to the Soviet understanding.

C. Standstill

On May 6, 1972, Minister Semenov made the following statement:

In an effort to accommodate the wishes of the U.S. side, the Soviet Delegation is prepared to proceed on the basis that the two sides will in fact observe the obligations of both the Interim Agreement and the ABM Treaty beginning from the date of signature of these two documents.

In reply, the U.S. Delegation made the following statement on May 20, 1972:

The United States agrees in principle with the Soviet statement made on May 6 concerning observance of obligations beginning from date of signature but we would like to make clear our understanding that this means that, pending ratification and acceptance, neither side would take any action prohibited by the agreements after they had entered into force. This understanding would continue to apply in the absence of notification by either signatory of its intention not to proceed with ratification or approval.

The Soviet Delegation indicated agreement with the U.S. statement.

3. Unilateral Statements

(a) The following noteworthy unilateral statements were made during the negotiations by the United States Delegation:

A. Withdrawal from the ABM Treaty

On May 9, 1972, Ambassador Smith made the following statement:

The U.S. Delegation has stressed the importance the U.S. Government attaches to achieving agreement on more complete limitations on strategic offensive arms, following agreement on an ABM Treaty and on an Interim Agreement on certain measures with respect to the limitation of strategic offensive arms. The U.S. Delegation believes that an objective of the follow-on negotiations should be to constrain and reduce on a long-term basis threats to the survivability of our respective strategic retaliatory forces. The USSR Delegation has also indicated that the objectives of SALT would remain unfulfilled without the achievement of an agreement providing for more complete limitations on strategic offensive arms. Both sides recognize that the initial agreements would be steps toward the achievement of more complete limitations on strategic arms. If an agreement providing for more complete strategic offensive arms limitations were not achieved within five years, U.S. supreme interests could be jeopardized. Should that occur, itwould constitute a basis for withdrawal from the ABM Treaty. The United States does not wishto see such a situation occur, nor do we believe that the USSR does. It is because we wish to prevent such a situation that we emphasize the importance the U.S. Government attaches to achievement of more complete limitations on strategic offensive arms. The U.S. Executive will inform the Congress, in connection with Congressional consideration of the ABM Treaty and the Interim Agreement, of this statement of the U.S. position.

B. Land-Mobile ICBM Launchers

The U.S. Delegation made the following statement on May 20, 1972:

In connection with the important subject of land-mobile ICBM launchers, in the interest of concluding the Interim Agreement the U.S. Delegation now withdraws its proposal that Article Ior an agreed statement explicitly prohibit the deployment of mobile land-based ICBM launchers. I have been instructed to inform you that, while agreeing to defer the question of limitation of operational land-mobile ICBM launchers to the subsequent negotiations on more complete limitations on strategic offensive arms, the United States would consider the deployment of operational land-mobile ICBM launchers during the period of the Interim Agreement as inconsistent with the objectives of that Agreement.

C. Covered Facilities

The U.S. Delegation made the following statement on May 20, 1972:

I wish to emphasize the importance that the United States attaches to the provisions of Article V, including in particular their application to fitting out or berthing submarines.

D. "Heavy" ICBMs

The U.S. Delegation made the following statement on May 26, 1972:

The U.S. Delegation regrets that the Soviet Delegation has not been willing to agree on a common definition of a heavy missile. Under these circumstances, the U.S. Delegation believes it necessary to state the following: The United States would consider any ICBM having a volume significantly greater than that of the largest light ICBM now operational on either side to be a heavy ICBM. The United States proceeds on the premise that the Soviet side will give due account to this consideration.

On May 17, 1972, Minister Semenov made the following unilateral "Statement of the Soviet Side":

Taking into account that modern ballistic missile submarines are presently in the possession of not only the United States, but also of its NATO allies, the Soviet Union agrees that for the period of effectiveness of the Interim Freeze Agreement the United States and its NATO allies have up to 50 such submarines with a total of up to 800 ballistic missile launchers thereon (including 41 U.S. submarines with 656 ballistic missile launchers). However, if during the period of effectiveness of the Agreement U.S. allies in NATO should increase the number of their modern submarines to exceed the numbers of submarines they would have operational or under construction on the date of signature of the Agreement, the Soviet Union will have the right to a corresponding increase in the number of its submarines. In the opinion of the Soviet side, the solution of the question of modern ballistic missile submarines provided for in the Interim Agreement only partially compensates for the strategic imbalance in the deployment of the nuclear-powered missile submarines of the USSR and the United States. Therefore, the Soviet side believes that this whole question, and above all the question of liquidating the American missile submarine bases outside the United States, will be appropriately resolved in the course of follow-on negotiations.

On May 24, Ambassador Smith made the following reply to Minister Semenov:

The United States side has studied the "statement made by the Soviet side" of May 17 concerning compensation for submarine basing and SLBM submarines belonging to third countries. The United States does not accept the validity of the considerations in that statement.

On May 26 Minister Semenov repeated the unilateral statement made on May 17. Ambassador Smith also repeated the U.S. rejection on May 26.

Joint Declaration on the Denuclearization of the Korean Peninsula

Entry into force on February 19, 1992

South and North Korea,

In order to eliminate the danger of nuclear war through the denuclearization of the Korean peninsula, to create conditions and an environment favourable to peace and the peaceful unification of Korea, and thus to contribute to the peace and security of Asia and the world,

Declare as follows:

1. South and North Korea shall not test, manufacture, produce, receive, possess, store, deploy or use nuclear weapons.

2. South and North Korea shall use nuclear energy solely for peaceful purposes.

3. South and North Korea shall not possess nuclear reprocessing and uranium enrichment facilities.

4. In order to verify the denuclearization of the Korean peninsula, South and North Korea shall conduct inspections of particular subjects chosen by the other side and agreed upon between the two sides, in accordance with the procedures and methods to be determined by the South-North Joint Nuclear Control Commission.

5. In order to implement this joint declaration, South and North Korea shall establish and operate a South-North Joint Nuclear Control Commission within one month of the entry into force of this joint declaration;

6. This joint declaration shall enter into force from the date the South and the North exchange the appropriate instruments following the completion of their respective procedures for bringing it into effect.

Chung Won-shik, Chief Delegate of the South delegation to the South-North High-Level Negotiations, Prime Minister of the Republic of Korea

Yon Hyong-muk, Head of the North delegation to the South-North High-Level Negotiations, Premier of the Administration Council of the Democratic People's Republic of Korea

Missile Technology Control Regime

The United States Government has, after careful consideration and subject to its international treaty obligations, decided that, when considering the transfer of equipment and technology related to missiles, it will act in accordance with the attached Guidelines beginning on January 7, 1993. These Guidelines replace those adopted on April 16, 1987.

GUIDELINES FOR SENSITIVE MISSILE-RELEVANT TRANSFERS

1. The purpose of these Guidelines is to limit the risks of proliferation of weapons of mass destruction (i.e. nuclear, chemical and biological weapons), by controlling transfers that could make a contribution to delivery systems (other than manned aircraft) for such weapons. The Guidelines are not designed to impede national space programs or international cooperation in such programs as long as such programs could not contribute to delivery systems for weapons of mass destruction. These Guidelines, including the attached Annex, form the basis for controlling transfers to any destination beyond the Government's jurisdiction or control of all delivery systems (other than manned aircraft) capable of delivering weapons of mass destruction, and of equipment and technology relevant to missiles whose performance in terms of payload and range exceeds stated parameters. Restraint will be exercised in the consideration of all transfers of items contained within the Annex and all such transfers will be considered on a case-by-case basis. The Government will implement the Guidelines in accordance with national legislation.

2. The Annex consists of two categories of items, which term includes equipment and technology. Category I items, all of which are in Annex Items 1 and 2, are those items of greatest sensitivity. If a Category I item is included in a system, that system will also be considered as Category I, except when the incorporated item cannot be separated, removed or duplicated. Particular restraint will be exercised in the consideration of Category I transfers regardless of their purpose, and there will be a strong presumption to deny such transfers. Particular restraint will also be exercised in the consideration of transfers of any items in the Annex, or of any missiles (whether or not in the Annex), if the Government judges, on the basis of all available, persuasive information, evaluated according to factors including those in paragraph 3, that they are intended to be used for the delivery of weapons of mass destruction, and there will be a strong presumption to deny such transfers. Until further notice, the transfer of Category I production facilities will not be authorized. The transfer of other Category I items will be authorized only on rare occasions and where the Government (A) obtains binding government-to-government undertakings embodying the assurances from the recipient government called for in paragraph 5 of these Guidelines and (B) assumes responsibility for taking all steps necessary to ensure that the item is put only to its stated end-use. It is understood that the decision to transfer remains the sole and sovereign judgment of the United States Government.

3. In the evaluation of transfer applications for Annex items, the following factors will be taken into account:
   A. Concerns about the proliferation of weapons of mass destruction;
   B. The capabilities and objectives of the missile and space programs of the recipient state;
   C. The significance of the transfer in terms of the potential development of delivery systems (other than mannedaircraft) for weapons of mass destruction;
   D. The assessment of the end-use of the transfers, including the relevant assurances of the recipient states referred to in sub-paragraphs 5.A and 5.B below;

E. The applicability of relevant multilateral agreements.

4. The transfer of design and production technology directly associated with any items in the Annex will be subject to as great a degree of scrutiny and control as will the equipment itself, to the extent permitted by national legislation.

5. Where the transfer could contribute to a delivery system for weapons of mass destruction, the Government will authorize transfers of items in the Annex only on receipt of appropriate assurances from the government of the recipient state that:
A. The items will be used only for the purpose stated and that such use will not be modified nor the items modified or replicated without the prior consent of the United States Government;
B. Neither the items nor replicas nor derivatives thereof will be retransferred without the consent of the United States Government.

6. In furtherance of the effective operation of the Guidelines, the United States Government will, as necessary and appropriate, exchange relevant information with other governments applying the same Guidelines.

7. The adherence of all States to these Guidelines in the interest of international peace and security would be welcome.

[Annex to MTCR not included]

National Security Strategy of the United States of America

Executive Summary
September 2002

The great struggles of the twentieth century between liberty and totalitarianism ended with a decisive victory for the forces of freedom—and a single sustainable model for national success: freedom, democracy, and free enterprise. In the twenty-first century, only nations that share a commitment to protecting basic human rights and guaranteeing political and economic freedom will be able to unleash the potential of their people and assure their future prosperity.

People everywhere want to be able to speak freely; choose who will govern them; worship as they please; ed-ucate their children—male and female; own property; and enjoy the benefits of their labor. These values of freedom are right and true for every person, in every society—and the duty of protecting these values against their enemies is the common calling of freedom-loving people across the globe and across the ages.

Today, the United States enjoys a position of unparalleled military strength and great economic and political influence. In keeping with our heritage and principles, we do not use our strength to press for unilateral advantage. We seek instead to create a balance of power that favors human freedom: conditions in which all nations and all societies can choose for themselves the rewards and challenges of political and economic liberty. In a world that is safe, people will be able to make their own lives better. We will defend the peace by fighting terrorists and tyrants. We will preserve the peace by building good relations among the great powers. We will extend the peace by encouraging free and open societies on every continent.

Defending our Nation against its enemies is the first and fundamental commitment of the Federal Government. Today, that task has changed dramatically. Enemies in the past needed great armies and great industrial capabilities to endanger America. Now, shadowy networks of individuals can bring great chaos and suffering to our shores for less than it costs to purchase a single tank. Terrorists are organized to penetrate open societies and to turn the power of modern technologies against us.

To defeat this threat we must make use of every tool in our arsenal—military power, better homeland defenses, law enforcement, intelligence, and vigorous efforts to cut off terrorist financing. The war against terrorists of global reach is a global enterprise of uncertain duration. America will help nations that need our assistance in combating terror. And America will hold to account nations that are compromised by terror, including those who harbor terrorists—

because the allies of terror are the enemies of civilization. The United States and countries cooperating with us must not allow the terrorists to develop new home bases. Together, we will seek to deny them sanctuary at every turn.

The gravest danger our Nation faces lies at the crossroads of radicalism and technology. Our enemies have openly declared that they are seeking weapons of mass destruction, and evidence indicates that they are doing so with determination. The United States will not allow these efforts to succeed. We will build defenses against ballistic missiles and other means of delivery. We will cooperate with other nations to deny, contain, and curtail our enemies' efforts to acquire dangerous technologies. And, as a matter of common sense and self-defense, America will act against such emerging threats before they are fully formed. We cannot defend America and our friends by hoping for the best. So we must be prepared to defeat our enemies' plans, using the best intelligence and proceeding with deliberation. History will judge harshly those who saw this coming danger but failed to act. In the new world we have entered, the only path to peace and security is the path of action.

As we defend the peace, we will also take advantage of an historic opportunity to preserve the peace. Today, the international community has the best chance since the rise of the nation-state in the seventeenth century to build a world where great powers compete in peace instead of continually prepare for war. Today, the world's great powers find ourselves on the same side—united by common dangers of terrorist violence and chaos. The United States will build on these common interests to promote global security. We are also increasingly united by common values. Russia is in the midst of a hopeful transition, reaching for its democratic future and a partner in the war on terror. Chinese leaders are discovering that economic freedom is the only source of national wealth. In time, they will find that social and political freedom is the only source of national greatness. America will encourage the advancement of democracy and economic openness in both nations, because these are the best foundations for domestic stability and international order. We will strongly resist aggression from other great powers—even as we welcome their peaceful pursuit of prosperity, trade, and cultural advancement.

Finally, the United States will use this moment of opportunity to extend the benefits of freedom across the globe. We will actively work to bring the hope of democracy, development, free markets, and free trade to every corner of the world. The events of September 11, 2001, taught us that weak states, like Afghanistan, can pose as great a danger to our national interests as strong states. Poverty does not make poor people into terrorists and murderers. Yet poverty, weak institutions, and corruption can make weak states vulnerable to terrorist networks and drug cartels within their borders.

The United States will stand beside any nation determined to build a better future by seeking the rewards of liberty for its people. Free trade and free markets have proven their ability to lift whole societies out of poverty—so the United States will work with individual nations, entire regions, and the entire global trading community to build a world that trades in freedom and therefore grows in prosperity. The United States will deliver greater development assistance through the New Millennium Challenge Account to nations that govern justly, invest in their people, and encourage economic freedom. We will also continue to lead the world in efforts to reduce the terrible toll of HIV/AIDS and other infectious diseases.

In building a balance of power that favors freedom, the United States is guided by the conviction that all nations have important responsibilities. Nations that enjoy freedom must actively fight terror. Nations that depend on international stability must help prevent the spread of weapons of mass destruction. Nations that seek international aid must govern themselves wisely, so that aid is well spent. For freedom to thrive, accountability must be expected and required. We are also guided by the conviction that no nation can build a safer, better world alone. Alliances and multilateral institutions can multiply the strength of freedom-loving nations.

The United States is committed to lasting institutions like the United Nations, the World Trade Organization, the Organization of American States, and NATO as well as other long-standing alliances. Coalitions of the willing can augment these permanent institutions. In all cases, international obligations are to be taken seriously. They are not to be undertaken symbolically to rally support for an ideal without furthering its attainment.

Freedom is the non-negotiable demand of human dignity; the birthright of every person—in every civilization. Throughout history, freedom has been threatened by war and terror; it has been challenged by the clashing wills of powerful states and the evil designs of tyrants; and it has been tested by widespread poverty and disease. Today, humanity holds in its hands the opportunity to further freedom's triumph over all these foes. The United States welcomes our responsibility to lead in this great mission.

George W. Bush
THE WHITE HOUSE,
September 17, 2002

EXCERPT FROM 2002 NATIONAL SECURITY STRATEGY OF THE UNITED STATES

v. Prevent Our Enemies from Threatening Us, Our Allies, and Our Friends with Weapons of Mass Destruction

"The gravest danger to freedom lies at the crossroads of radicalism and technology. When the spread of chemical and biological and nuclear weapons, along with ballistic missile technology—when that occurs, even weak states and small groups could attain a catastrophic power to strike great nations. Our enemies have declared this very intention, and have been caught seeking these terrible weapons. They want the capability to blackmail us, or to harm us, or to harm our friends—and we will oppose them with all our power."

President Bush
West Point, New York
June 1, 2002

The nature of the Cold War threat required the United States—with our allies and friends—to emphasize deterrence of the enemy's use of force, producing a grim strategy of mutual assured destruction. With the collapse of the Soviet Union and the end of the Cold War, our security environment has undergone profound transformation. Having moved from confrontation to cooperation as the hallmark of our relationship with Russia, the dividends are evident: an end to the balance of terror that divided us; an historic reduction in the nuclear arsenals on both sides; and cooperation in areas such as counterterrorism and missile defense that until recently were inconceivable. But new deadly challenges have emerged from rogue states and terrorists. None of these contemporary threats rival the sheer destructive power that was arrayed against us by the Soviet Union. However, the nature and motivations of these new adversaries, their determination to obtain destructive powers hitherto available only to the world's strongest states, and the greater likelihood that they will use weapons of mass destruction against us, make today's security environment more complex and dangerous. In the 1990s we witnessed the emergence of a small number of rogue states that, while different in important ways, share a number of attributes.

These states:

- brutalize their own people and squander their national resources for the personal gain of the rulers;
- display no regard for international law, threaten their neighbors, and callously violate international treaties to which they are party;
- are determined to acquire weapons of mass destruction, along with other advanced military technology, to be used as threats or offensively to achieve the aggressive designs of these regimes;
- sponsor terrorism around the globe; and
- reject basic human values and hate the United States and everything for which it stands.

At the time of the Gulf War, we acquired irrefutable proof that Iraq's designs were not
limited to the chemical weapons it had used against Iran and its own people, but also extended to the acquisition of nuclear weapons and biological agents. In the past decade North Korea has become the world's principal purveyor of ballistic missiles, and has tested increasingly capable missiles while developing its own WMD arsenal.

Other rogue regimes seek nuclear, biological, and chemical weapons as well. These states' pursuit of, and global trade in, such weapons has become a looming threat to all nations. We must be prepared to stop rogue states and their terrorist clients before they are able to threaten or use weapons of mass destruction against the United States and our allies and friends. Our response

must take full advantage of strengthened alliances, the establishment of new partnerships with former adversaries, innovation in the use of military forces, modern technologies, including the development of an effective missile defense system, and increased emphasis on intelligence collection and analysis.

Our comprehensive strategy to combat WMD includes:

- *Proactive counterproliferation efforts.* We must deter and defend against the threat before it is unleashed. We must ensure that key capabilities—detection, active and passive defenses, and counterforce capabilities—are integrated into our defense transformation and our homeland security systems. Counterproliferation must also be integrated into the doctrine, training, and equipping of our forces and those of our allies to ensure that we can prevail in any conflict with WMD-armed adversaries.
- *Strengthened nonproliferation efforts to prevent rogue states and terrorists from acquiring the materials, technologies, and expertise necessary for weapons of mass destruction.* We will enhance diplomacy, arms control, multilateral export controls, and threat reduction assistance that impede states and terrorists seeking WMD, and when necessary, interdict enabling technologies and materials. We will continue to build coalitions to support these efforts, encouraging their increased political and financial support for nonproliferation and threat reduction programs. The recent G-8 agreement to commit up to $20 billion to a global partnership against proliferation marks a major step forward.
- *Effective consequence management to respond to the effects of WMD use, whether by terrorists or hostile states.* Minimizing the effects of WMD use against our people will help deter those who possess such weapons and dissuade those who seek to acquire them by persuading enemies that they cannot attain their desired ends. The United States must also be prepared to respond to the effects of WMD use against our forces abroad, and to help friends and allies if they are attacked.

It has taken almost a decade for us to comprehend the true nature of this new threat. Given the goals of rogue states and terrorists, the United States can no longer solely rely on a reactive posture as we have in the past. The inability to deter a potential attacker, the immediacy of today's threats, and the magnitude of potential harm that could be caused by our adversaries' choice of weapons, do not permit that option. We cannot let our enemies strike first.

- In the Cold War, especially following the Cuban missile crisis, we faced a generally status quo, risk-averse adversary. Deterrence was an effective defense. But deterrence based only upon the threat of retaliation is less likely to work against leaders of rogue states more willing to take risks, gambling with the lives of their people, and the wealth of their nations.
- In the Cold War, weapons of mass destruction were considered weapons of last resort whose use risked the destruction of those who used them. Today, our enemies see weapons of mass destruction as weapons of choice. For rogue states these weapons are tools of intimidation and military aggression against their neighbors. These weapons may also allow these states to attempt to blackmail the United States and our allies to prevent us from deterring or repelling the aggressive behavior of rogue states. Such states also see these weapons as their best means of overcoming the conventional superiority of the United States.
- Traditional concepts of deterrence will not work against a terrorist enemy whose avowed tactics are wanton destruction and the targeting of innocents; whose so-called soldiers seek martyrdom in death and whose most potent protection is statelessness. The overlap between states that sponsor terror and those that pursue WMD compels us to action.

For centuries, international law recognized that nations need not suffer an attack before they can lawfully take action to defend themselves against forces that present an imminent danger of attack. Legal scholars and international jurists often conditioned the legitimacy of preemption on the existence of an imminent threat—most often a visible mobilization of armies, navies, and air forces preparing to attack.

We must adapt the concept of imminent threat to the capabilities and objectives of today's adversaries. Rogue states and terrorists do not seek to attack us using conventional means. They know such attacks would fail. Instead, they rely on acts of terror and, potentially, the use of weapons of mass destruction—weapons that can be easily concealed, delivered covertly, and used without warning.

The targets of these attacks are our military forces and our civilian population, in direct violation of one of the principal norms of the law of warfare. As was demonstrated by the losses on September 11, 2001, mass civilian casualties is the specific objective of terrorists and these losses would be exponentially more severe if terrorists acquired and used weapons of mass destruction.

The United States has long maintained the option of preemptive actions to counter a sufficient threat to our national security. The greater the threat, the greater is the risk of inaction—and the more compelling the case for taking anticipatory action to defend ourselves, even if uncertainty remains as to the time and place of the enemy's attack. To forestall or prevent such hostile acts by our adversaries, the United States will, if necessary, act preemptively.

The United States will not use force in all cases to preempt emerging threats, nor should nations use preemption as a pretext for aggression. Yet in an age where the enemies of civilization openly and actively seek the world's most destructive technologies, the United States cannot remain idle while dangers gather.

We will always proceed deliberately, weighing the consequences of our actions. To support preemptive options, we will:

- build better, more integrated intelligence capabilities to provide timely, accurate information on threats, wherever they may emerge;
- coordinate closely with allies to form a common assessment of the most dangerous threats; and
- continue to transform our military forces to ensure our ability to conduct rapid and precise operations to achieve decisive results.

The purpose of our actions will always be to eliminate a specific threat to the United States or our allies and friends. The reasons for our actions will be clear, the force measured, and the cause just.

National Strategy to Combat Weapons of Mass Destruction

December 2002

INTRODUCTION

Weapons of mass destruction (WMD)—nuclear, biological, and chemical—in the possession of hostile states and terrorists represent one of the greatest security challenges facing the United States. We must pursue a comprehensive strategy to counter this threat in all of its dimensions. An effective strategy for countering WMD, including their use and further proliferation, is an integral component of the National Security Strategy of the United States of America. As with the war on terrorism, our strategy for homeland security, and our new concept of deterrence, the U.S. approach to combat WMD represents a fundamental change from the past. To succeed, we must take full advantage of today's opportunities, including the application of new technologies, increased emphasis on intelligence collection and analysis, the strengthening of alliance relationships, and the establishment of new partnerships with former adversaries. Weapons of mass destruction could enable adversaries to inflict massive harm on the United States, our military forces at home and abroad, and our friends and allies. Some states, including several that have supported and continue to support terrorism, already possess WMD and are seeking even greater capabilities, as tools of coercion and intimidation. For them, these are not weapons of last resort, but militarily useful weapons of choice intended to overcome our nation's advantages in conventional forces and to deter us from responding to aggression against our friends and allies in regions of vital interest. In addition, terrorist groups are seeking to acquire WMD with the stated purpose of killing large numbers of our people and those of friends and allies—without compunction and without warning.

We will not permit the world's most dangerous regimes and terrorists to threaten us with the world's most destructive weapons. We must accord the highest priority to the protection of the United States, our forces, and our friends and allies from the existing and growing WMD threat.

> "The gravest danger our Nation faces lies at the crossroads of radicalism and technology. Our enemies have openly declared that they are seeking weapons of mass destruction, and evidence indicates that they are doing so with determination The United States will not allow these efforts to succeed. ...History will judge harshly those who saw this coming danger but failed to act. In the new world we have entered, the only path to peace and security is the path of action."

President Bush
The National Security Strategy of the
United States of America
September 17, 2002

PILLARS OF OUR NATIONAL SECURITY

Our National Strategy to Combat Weapons of Mass Destruction has three principal pillars:

Counterproliferation to Combat WMD Use

The possession and increased likelihood of use of WMD by hostile states and terrorists are realities of the contemporary security environment. It is therefore critical that the U.S. military and appropriate civilian agencies be prepared to deter and defend against the full range of possible WMD employment scenarios. We will ensure that all needed capabilities to combat WMD are fully integrated into the emerging defense transformation plan and into our homeland security posture. Counterproliferation will also be fully integrated into the basic doctrine, training, and equipping of all forces, in order to ensure that they can sustain operations to decisively defeat WMD-armed adversaries.

Strengthened Nonproliferation to Combat WMD Proliferation

The United States, our friends and allies, and the broader international community must undertake every effort to prevent states and terrorists from acquiring WMD and missiles. We must enhance traditional measures—diplomacy, arms control, multilateral agreements, threat reduction assistance, and export controls—that seek to dissuade or impede proliferant states and terrorist networks, as well as to slow and make more costly their access to sensitive technologies, material, and expertise. We must ensure compliance with relevant international agreements, including the Nuclear Nonproliferation Treaty (NPT), the Chemical Weapons Convention (CWC), and the Biological Weapons Convention (BWC). The United States will continue to work with other states to improve their capability to prevent unauthorized transfers of WMD and missile technology, expertise, and material. We will identify and pursue new methods of prevention, such as national criminalization of proliferation activities and expanded safety and security measures.

Consequence Management to Respond to WMD Use

Finally, the United States must be prepared to respond to the use of WMD against our citizens, our military forces, and those of friends and allies. We will develop and maintain the capability to reduce to the extent possible the potentially horrific consequences of WMD attacks at home and broad. The three pillars of the U.S. national strategy to combat WMD are seamless elements of a comprehensive approach. Serving to integrate the pillars are four cross-cutting enabling functions that need to be pursued on a priority basis: intelligence collection and analysis on WMD, delivery systems, and related technologies; research and development to improve our ability to respond to evolving threats; bilateral and multilateral cooperation; and targeted strategies against hostile states and terrorists.

COUNTERPROLIFERATION

We know from experience that we cannot always be successful in preventing and containing the proliferation of WMD to hostile states and terrorists. Therefore, U.S. military and appropriate civilian agencies must possess the full range of operational capabilities to counter the threat and use of WMD by states and terrorists against the United States, our military forces, and friends and allies. Interdiction Effective interdiction is a critical part of the U.S. strategy to combat WMD and their delivery means. We must enhance the capabilities of our military, intelligence, technical, and law enforcement communities to prevent the movement of WMD materials, technology, and expertise to hostile states and terrorist organizations.

Deterrence Today's threats are far more diverse and less predictable than those of the past. States hostile to the United States and to our friends and allies have demonstrated their willingness to take high risks to achieve their goals, and are aggressively pursuing WMD and their means of delivery as critical tools in this effort. As a consequence, we require new methods of deterrence. A strong declaratory policy and effective military forces are essential elements of our contemporary deterrent posture, along with the full range of political tools to persuade potential adversaries not to seek or use WMD. The United States will continue to make clear that it reserves the right to respond with overwhelming force—including through resort to all of our options—to the use of WMD against the United States, our forces abroad, and friends and allies. In addition to our conventional and nuclear response and defense capabilities, our overall deterrent posture against WMD threats is reinforced by effective intelligence, surveillance, interdiction, and domestic law enforcement capabilities. Such combined capabilities enhance deterrence both by devaluing an adversary's WMD and missiles, and by posing the prospect of an overwhelming response to any use of such weapons. Defense and Mitigation Because deterrence may not succeed, and because of the potentially devastating consequences of WMD use against our forces and civilian population, U.S. military forces and appropriate civilian agencies must have the capability to defend against WMD-armed adversaries, including in appropriate cases through preemptive measures. This requires capabilities to detect and destroy an adversary's WMD assets before these weapons are used. In addition, robust active and passive defenses and mitigation measures must be in place to enable U.S. military forces and appropriate civilian agencies to accomplish their missions, and to assist friends and allies when WMD are used.

Active defenses disrupt, disable, or destroy WMD en route to their targets. Active defenses include vigorous air defense and effective missile defenses against today's threats. Passive defenses must be tailored to the unique characteristics of the various forms of WMD. The United States must also have the ability rapidly and effectively to mitigate the effects of a WMD attack against our deployed forces.

Our approach to defend against biological threats has long been based on our approach to chemical threats, despite the fundamental differences between these weapons. The United States is developing a new approach to provide us and our friends and allies with an effective defense against biological weapons.

Finally, U.S. military forces and domestic law enforcement agencies as appropriate must stand ready to respond against the source of any WMD attack. The primary objective of a response is to disrupt an imminent attack or an attack in progress, and eliminate the threat of future attacks. As with deterrence and prevention, an effective response requires rapid attribution and robust strike capability. We must accelerate efforts to field new capabilities to defeat WMD related assets. The United States needs to be prepared to conduct post-conflict operations to destroy or dismantle any residual WMD capabilities of the hostile state or terrorist network. An effective U.S. response not only will eliminate the source of a WMD attack but will also have a powerful deterrent effect upon other adversaries that possess or seek WMD or missiles.

NONPROLIFERATION

Active Nonproliferation Diplomacy

The United States will actively employ diplomatic approaches in bilateral and multilateral settings in pursuit of our nonproliferation goals.

We must dissuade supplier states from cooperating with proliferant states and induce proliferant states to end their WMD and missile programs. We will hold countries responsible for complying with their commitments. In addition, we will continue to build coalitions to support our efforts, as well as to seek their increased support for nonproliferation and threat reduction cooperation programs. However, should our wide-ranging nonproliferation efforts fail, we must have available the full range of operational capabilities necessary to defend against the possible employment of WMD.

Multilateral Regimes

Existing nonproliferation and arms control regimes play an important role in our overall strategy. The United States will support those regimes that are currently in force, and work to improve the effectiveness of, and compliance with, those regimes. Consistent with other policy priorities, we will also promote new agreements and arrangements that serve our nonproliferation goals.

Overall, we seek to cultivate an international environment that is more conducive to nonproliferation. Our efforts will include:

Nuclear
- Strengthening of the Nuclear Nonproliferation Treaty and International Atomic Energy Agency (IAEA), including through ratification of an IAEA Additional Protocol by all NPT states parties, assurances that all states put in place full-scope IAEA safeguards agreements, and appropriate increases in funding for the Agency;
- Negotiating a Fissile Material Cut-Off Treaty that advances U.S. security interests; and
- Strengthening the Nuclear Suppliers Group and Zangger Committee.

Chemical and Biological
- Effective functioning of the Organization for the Prohibition of Chemical Weapons;
- Identification and promotion of constructive and realistic measures to strengthen the BWC and thereby to help meet the biological weapons threat; and
- Strengthening of the Australia Group.

Missile
- Strengthening the Missile Technology Control Regime (MTCR), including through support for universal adherence to the International Code of Conduct Against Ballistic Missile Proliferation. Nonproliferation and Threat Reduction Cooperation

The United States pursues a wide range of programs, including the Nunn-Lugar program, designed to address the proliferation threat stemming from the large quantities of Soviet-legacy WMD and missile-related expertise and materials. Maintaining an extensive and efficient set of nonproliferation and threat reduction assistance programs to Russia and other former Soviet states is a high priority. We will also continue to encourage friends and allies to increase their contributions to these programs, particularly through the G-8 Global Partnership Against the Spread of Weapons and Materials of Mass Destruction. In addition, we will work with other states to improve the security of their WMD related materials.

Controls on Nuclear Materials
In addition to programs with former Soviet states to reduce fissile material and improve the security of that which remains, the United States will continue to discourage the worldwide accumulation of separated pluto-nium and to minimize the use of highly-enriched uranium. As outlined in the National Energy Policy, the United States will work in collaboration with international partners to develop recycle and fuel treatment technologies that are cleaner, more efficient, less waste-intensive, and more proliferation-resistant. U.S. Export Controls

We must ensure that the implementation of U.S. export controls furthers our nonproliferation and other national security goals, while recognizing the realities that American businesses face in the increasingly globalized marketplace.

We will work to update and strengthen export controls using existing authorities. We also seek new legislation to improve the ability of our export control system to give full weight to both nonproliferation objectives and commercial interests. Our overall goal is to focus our resources in truly sensitive exports to hostile states or those that engage in onward proliferation, while removing unnecessary barriers in the global marketplace.

Nonproliferation Sanctions
Sanctions can be a valuable component of our overall strategy against WMD proliferation. At times, however, sanctions have proven inflexible and ineffective. We will develop a comprehensive sanctions policy to better integrate sanctions into our overall strategy and work with Congress to consolidate and modify existing sanctions legislation.

WMD CONSEQUENCE MANAGEMENT

Defending the American homeland is the most basic responsibility of our government. As part of our defense, the United States must be fully prepared to respond to the consequences of WMD use on our soil, whether by hostile states or by terrorists. We must also be prepared to respond to the effects of WMD use against our forces deployed abroad, and to assist friends and allies.

The National Strategy for Homeland Security discusses U.S. Government programs to deal with the consequences of the use of a chemical, biological, radiological, or nuclear weapon in the United States. A number of these programs offer training, planning, and assistance to state and local governments. To maximize their effectiveness, these efforts need to be integrated and comprehensive. Our first responders must have the full range of protective, medical, and remediation tools to identify, assess, and respond rapidly to a WMD event on our territory. The White House Office of Homeland Security will coordinate all federal efforts to prepare for and mitigate the consequences of terrorist attacks within the United States, including those involving WMD. The Office of Homeland Security will also work closely with state and local governments to ensure their planning, training, and equipment requirements are addressed. These issues, including the roles of the Department of Homeland Security, are addressed in detail in the National Strategy for Homeland Security. The National Security Council's Office of Combating Terrorism coordinates and helps improve U.S. efforts to respond to and manage the recovery from terrorist attacks outside the United States. In cooperation with the Office of Combating Terrorism, the Department of State coordinates interagency efforts to work with our friends and allies to develop their own emergency preparedness and consequence management capabilities.

INTEGRATING THE PILLARS

Several critical enabling functions serve to integrate the three pillars—counterproliferation, nonproliferation, and consequence management—of the U.S. National Strategy to Combat WMD.

Improved Intelligence Collection and Analysis

A more accurate and complete understanding of the full range of WMD threats is, and will remain, among the highest U.S. intelligence priorities, to enable us to prevent proliferation, and to deter or defend against those who would use those capabilities against us. Improving our ability to obtain timely and accurate knowledge of adversaries' offensive and defensive capabilities, plans, and intentions is key to developing effective counter- and nonproliferation policies and capabilities. Particular emphasis must be accorded to improving: intelligence regarding WMD-related facilities and activities; interaction among U.S. intelligence, law enforcement, and military agencies; and intelligence cooperation with friends and allies.

Research and Development

The United States has a critical need for cutting-edge technology that can quickly and effectively detect, analyze, facilitate interdiction of, defend against, defeat, and mitigate the consequences of WMD. Numerous U.S. Government departments and agencies are currently engaged in the essential research and development to support our overall strategy against WMD proliferation. The new Counterproliferation Technology Coordination Committee, consisting of senior representatives from all concerned agencies, will act to improve interagency coordination of U.S. Government counterproliferation research and development efforts. The Committee will assist in identifying priorities, gaps, and overlaps in existing programs and in examining options for future investment strategies.

Strengthened International Cooperation

WMD represent a threat not just to the United States, but also to our friends and allies and the broader international community. For this reason, it is vital that we work closely with like-minded countries on all elements of our comprehensive proliferation strategy.

Targeted Strategies Against Proliferants

All elements of the overall U.S. strategy to combat WMD must be brought to bear in targeted strategies against supplier and recipient states of WMD proliferation concern, as well as against terrorist groups which seek to acquire WMD. A few states are dedicated proliferators, whose leaders are determined to develop, maintain, and improve their WMD and delivery capabilities, which directly threaten the United States, U.S. forces overseas, and/or our friends and allies. Because each of these regimes is different, we will pursue country-specific strategies that best enable us and our friends and allies to prevent, deter, and defend against WMD and missile threats from each of them. These strategies must also take into account the growing cooperation among proliferant states—so-called secondary proliferation—which challenges us to think in new ways about specific country strategies.

One of the most difficult challenges we face is to prevent, deter, and defend against the acquisition and use of WMD by terrorist groups. The current and potential future linkages between terrorist groups and state sponsors of terrorism are particularly dangerous and require priority attention. The full range of counterproliferation, nonproliferation, and consequence management measures must be brought to bear against the WMD terrorist threat, just as they are against states of greatest proliferation concern.

End Note

Our National Strategy to Combat WMD requires much of all of us—the Executive Branch, the Congress, state and local governments, the American people, and our friends and allies. The requirements to prevent, deter, defend against, and respond to today's WMD threats are complex and challenging. But they are not daunting. We can and will succeed in the tasks laid out in this strategy; we have no other choice.

The North Atlantic Treaty

Washington D.C. - 4 April 1949

The Parties to this Treaty reaffirm their faith in the purposes and principles of the Charter of the United Nations and their desire to live in peace with all peoples and all govern-

ments. They are determined to safeguard the freedom, common heritage and civilisation of their peoples, founded on the principles of democracy, individual liberty and the rule of law. They seek to promote stability and well-being in the North Atlantic area. They are resolved to unite their efforts for collective defence and for the preservation of peace and security. They therefore agree to this North Atlantic Treaty :

ARTICLE 1

The Parties undertake, as set forth in the Charter of the United Nations, to settle any international dispute in which they may be involved by peaceful means in such a manner that international peace and security and justice are not endangered, and to refrain in their international relations from the threat or use of force in any manner inconsistent with the purposes of the United Nations.

ARTICLE 2

The Parties will contribute toward the further development of peaceful and friendly international relations by strengthening their free institutions, by bringing about a better understanding of the principles upon which these institutions are founded, and by promoting conditions of stability and well-being. They will seek to eliminate conflict in their international economic policies and will encourage economic collaboration between any or all of them.

ARTICLE 3

In order more effectively to achieve the objectives of this Treaty, the Parties, separately and jointly, by means of continuous and effective self-help and mutual aid, will maintain and develop their individual and collective capacity to resist armed attack.

ARTICLE 4

The Parties will consult together whenever, in the opinion of any of them, the territorial integrity, political independence or security of any of the Parties is threatened.

ARTICLE 5

The Parties agree that an armed attack against one or more of them in Europe or North America shall be considered an attack against them all and consequently they agree that, if such an armed attack occurs, each of them, in exercise of the right of individual or collective self-defence recognised by Article 51 of the Charter of the United Nations, will assist the Party or Parties so attacked by taking forthwith, individually and in concert with the other Parties, such action as it deems necessary, including the use of armed force, to restore and maintain the security of the North Atlantic area.

Any such armed attack and all measures taken as a result thereof shall immediately be reported to the Security Council. Such measures shall be terminated when the Security Council has taken the measures necessary to restore and maintain international peace and security.

ARTICLE 6 (1)

For the purpose of Article 5, an armed attack on one or more of the Parties is deemed to include an armed attack:

on the territory of any of the Parties in Europe or North America, on the Algerian Departments of France (2), on the territory of or on the Islands under the jurisdiction of any of the Parties in the North Atlantic area north of the Tropic of Cancer;

on the forces, vessels, or aircraft of any of the Parties, when in or over these territories or any other area in Europe in which occupation forces of any of the Parties were stationed on the date when the Treaty entered into force or the Mediterranean Sea or the North Atlantic area north of the Tropic of Cancer.

ARTICLE 7

This Treaty does not affect, and shall not be interpreted as affecting in any way the rights and obligations under the Charter of the Parties which are members of the United Nations, or the primary responsibility of the Security Council for the maintenance of international peace and security.

ARTICLE 8

Each Party declares that none of the international engagements now in force between it and any other of the Parties or any third State is in conflict with the provisions of this Treaty, and undertakes not to enter into any international engagement in conflict with this Treaty.

ARTICLE 9

The Parties hereby establish a Council, on which each of them shall be represented, to consider matters concerning the implementation of this Treaty. The Council shall be so organised as to be able to meet promptly at any time. The Council shall set up such subsidiary bodies as may be necessary; in particular it shall establish immediately a defence committee which shall recommend measures for the implementation of Articles 3 and 5.

ARTICLE 10

The Parties may, by unanimous agreement, invite any other European State in a position to further the principles of this Treaty and to contribute to the security of the North Atlantic area to accede to this Treaty. Any State so invited may become a Party to the Treaty by depositing its instrument of accession with the Government of the United States of America. The Government of the United States of America will inform each of the Parties of the deposit of each such instrument of accession.

ARTICLE 11

This Treaty shall be ratified and its provisions carried out by the Parties in accordance with their respective constitutional processes. The instruments of ratification shall be deposited as soon as possible with the Government of the United States of America, which will notify all the other signatories of each deposit. The Treaty shall enter into force between the States which have ratified it as soon as the ratifications of the majority of the signatories, including the ratifications of Belgium, Canada, France, Luxembourg, the Netherlands, the United Kingdom and the United States, have been deposited and shall come into effect with respect to other States on the date of the deposit of their ratifications. (3)

ARTICLE 12

After the Treaty has been in force for ten years, or at any time thereafter, the Parties shall, if any of them so requests, consult together for the purpose of reviewing the Treaty, having regard for the factors then affecting peace and security in the North Atlantic area, including the development of universal as well as regional arrangements under the Charter of the United Nations for the maintenance of international peace and security.

ARTICLE 13

After the Treaty has been in force for twenty years, any Party may cease to be a Party one year after its notice of denunciation has been given to the Government of the United States of America, which will inform the Governments of the other Parties of the deposit of each notice of denunciation.

ARTICLE 14

This Treaty, of which the English and French texts are equally authentic, shall be deposited in the archives of the Government of the United States of America. Duly certified copies will be transmitted by that Government to the Governments of other signatories.

Footnotes :

(1) The definition of the territories to which Article 5 applies was revised by Article 2 of the Protocol to the North Atlantic Treaty on the accession of Greece and Turkey signed on 22 October 1951.

(2) On January 16, 1963, the North Atlantic Council noted that insofar as the former Algerian Departments of France were concerned, the relevant clauses of this Treaty had become inapplicable as from July 3, 1962.

(3) The Treaty came into force on 24 August 1949, after the deposition of the ratifications of all signatory states.

Treaty on the Non-Proliferation of Nuclear Weapons

Signed at Washington, London, and Moscow July 1, 1968
Ratification advised by U.S. Senate March 13, 1969
Ratified by U.S. President November 24, 1969
Entered into force March 5, 1970

The States concluding this Treaty, hereinafter referred to as the "Parties to the Treaty",

Considering the devastation that would be visited upon all mankind by a nuclear war and the consequent need to make every effort to avert the danger of such a war and to take measures to safeguard the security of peoples,

Believing that the proliferation of nuclear weapons would seriously enhance the danger of nuclear war,

In conformity with resolutions of the United Nations General Assembly calling for the conclusion of an agreement on the prevention of wider dissemination of nuclear weapons,

Undertaking to cooperate in facilitating the application of International Atomic Energy Agency safeguards on peaceful nuclear activities,

Expressing their support for research, development and other efforts to further the application, within the framework of the International Atomic Energy Agency safeguards system, of the principle of safeguarding effectively the flow of source and special fissionable materials by use of instruments and other techniques at certain strategic points,

Affirming the principle that the benefits of peaceful applications of nuclear technology, including any technological by-products which may be derived by nuclear-weapon States from the development of nuclear explosive devices, should be available for peaceful purposes to all Parties of the Treaty, whether nuclear-weapon or non-nuclear weapon States,

Convinced that, in furtherance of this principle, all Parties to the Treaty are entitled to participate in the fullest possible exchange of scientific information for, and to contribute alone or in cooperation with other States to, the further development of the applications of atomic energy for peaceful purposes,

Declaring their intention to achieve at the earliest possible date the cessation of the nuclear arms race and to undertake effective measures in the direction of nuclear disarmament,

Urging the cooperation of all States in the attainment of this objective,

Recalling the determination expressed by the Parties to the 1963 Treaty banning nuclear weapon tests in the atmosphere, in outer space and under water in its Preamble to seek to achieve the discontinuance of all test explosions of nuclear weapons for all time and to continue negotiations to this end,

Desiring to further the easing of international tension and the strengthening of trust between States in order to facilitate the cessation of the manufacture of nuclear weapons, the liquidation of all their existing stockpiles, and the elimination from national arsenals of nuclear weapons and the means of their delivery pursuant to a Treaty on general and complete disarmament under strict and effective international control,

Recalling that, in accordance with the Charter of the United Nations, States must refrain in their international relations from the threat or use of force against the territorial integrity or political independence of any State, or in any other manner inconsistent with the Purposes of the United Nations, and that the establishment and maintenance of international peace and security are to be promoted with the least diversion for armaments of the worlds human and economic resources,

Have agreed as follows:

ARTICLE I

Each nuclear-weapon State Party to the Treaty undertakes not to transfer to any recipient whatsoever nuclear weapons or other nuclear explosive devices or control over such weapons or explosive devices directly, or indirectly; and not in any way to assist, encourage, or induce any non-nuclear weapon State to manufacture or otherwise acquire nuclear weapons or other nuclear explosive devices, or control over such weapons or explosive devices.

ARTICLE II

Each non-nuclear-weapon State Party to the Treaty undertakes not to receive the transfer from any transferor whatsoever of nuclear weapons or other nuclear explosive devices or of control over such weapons or explosive devices directly, or indirectly; not to manufacture or otherwise acquire nuclear weapons or other nuclear explosive devices; and not to seek or receive any assistance in the manufacture of nuclear weapons or other nuclear explosive devices.

ARTICLE III

1. Each non-nuclear-weapon State Party to the Treaty undertakes to accept safeguards, as set forth in an agreement to be negotiated and concluded with the International Atomic Energy Agency in accordance with the Statute of the International Atomic Energy Agency and the Agencys safeguards system, for the exclusive purpose of verification of the fulfillment of its obligations assumed under this Treaty with a view to preventing diversion of nuclear energy from peaceful uses to nuclear weapons or other nuclear explosive devices. Procedures for the safeguards required by this article shall be followed with respect to source or special fissionable material whether it is being produced, processed or used in any principal nuclear facility or is outside any such facility. The safeguards required by this article shall be applied to all source or special fissionable material in all peaceful nuclear activities within the territory of such State, under its jurisdiction, or carried out under its control anywhere.
2. Each State Party to the Treaty undertakes not to provide: (a) source or special fissionable material, or (b) equipment or material

especially designed or prepared for the processing, use or production of special fissionable material, to any non-nuclear-weapon State for peaceful purposes, unless the source or special fissionable material shall be subject to the safeguards required by this article.

3. The safeguards required by this article shall be implemented in a manner designed to comply with article IV of this Treaty, and to avoid hampering the economic or technological development of the Parties or international cooperation in the field of peaceful nuclear activities, including the international exchange of nuclear material and equipment for the processing, use or production of nuclear material for peaceful purposes in accordance with the provisions of this article and the principle of safeguarding set forth in the Preamble of the Treaty.

4. Non-nuclear-weapon States Party to the Treaty shall conclude agreements with the International Atomic Energy Agency to meet the requirements of this article either individually or together with other States in accordance with the Statute of the International Atomic Energy Agency. Negotiation of such agreements shall commence within 180 days from the original entry into force of this Treaty. For States depositing their instruments of ratification or accession after the 180-day period, negotiation of such agreements shall commence not later than the date of such deposit. Such agreements shall enter into force not later than eighteen months after the date of initiation of negotiations.

ARTICLE IV

1. Nothing in this Treaty shall be interpreted as affecting the inalienable right of all the Parties to the Treaty to develop research, production and use of nuclear energy for peaceful purposes without discrimination and in conformity with articles I and II of this Treaty.

2. All the Parties to the Treaty undertake to facilitate, and have the right to participate in, the fullest possible exchange of equipment, materials and scientific and technological information for the peaceful uses of nuclear energy. Parties to the Treaty in a position to do so shall also cooperate in contributing alone or together with other States or international organizations to the further development of the applications of nuclear energy for peaceful purposes, especially in the territories of non-nuclear-weapon States Party to the Treaty, with due consideration for the needs of the developing areas of the world.

ARTICLE V

Each party to the Treaty undertakes to take appropriate measures to ensure that, in accordance with this Treaty, under appropriate international observation and through appropriate international procedures, potential benefits from any peaceful applications of nuclear explosions will be made available to non-nuclear-weapon States Party to the Treaty on a nondiscriminatory basis and that the charge to such Parties for the explosive devices used will be as low as possible and exclude any charge for research and development. Non-nuclear-weapon States Party to the Treaty shall be able to obtain such benefits, pursuant to a special international agreement or agreements, through an appropriate international body with adequate representation of non-nuclear-weapon States. Negotiations on this subject shall commence as soon as possible after the Treaty enters into force. Non-nuclear-weapon States Party to the Treaty so desiring may also obtain such benefits pursuant to bilateral agreements.

ARTICLE VI

Each of the Parties to the Treaty undertakes to pursue negotiations in good faith on effective measures relating to cessation of the nuclear arms race at an early date and to nuclear disarmament, and on a Treaty on general and complete disarmament under strict and effective international control.

ARTICLE VII

Nothing in this Treaty affects the right of any group of States to conclude regional treaties in order to assure the total absence of nuclear weapons in their respective territories.

ARTICLE VIII

1. Any Party to the Treaty may propose amendments to this Treaty. The text of any

proposed amendment shall be submitted to the Depositary Governments which shall circulate it to all Parties to the Treaty. Thereupon, if requested to do so by one-third or more of the Parties to the Treaty, the Depositary Governments shall convene a conference, to which they shall invite all the Parties to the Treaty, to consider such an amendment.

2. Any amendment to this Treaty must be approved by a majority of the votes of all the Parties to the Treaty, including the votes of all nuclear-weapon States Party to the Treaty and all other Parties which, on the date the amendment is circulated, are members of the Board of Governors of the International Atomic Energy Agency. The amendment shall enter into force for each Party that deposits its instrument of ratification of the amendment upon the deposit of such instruments of ratification by a majority of all the Parties, including the instruments of ratification of all nuclear-weapon States Party to the Treaty and all other Parties which, on the date the amendment is circulated, are members of the Board of Governors of the International Atomic Energy Agency. Thereafter, it shall enter into force for any other Party upon the deposit of its instrument of ratification of the amendment.

3. Five years after the entry into force of this Treaty, a conference of Parties to the Treaty shall be held in Geneva, Switzerland, in order to review the operation of this Treaty with a view to assuring that the purposes of the Preamble and the provisions of the Treaty are being realized. At intervals of five years thereafter, a majority of the Parties to the Treaty may obtain, by submitting a proposal to this effect to the Depositary Governments, the convening of further conferences with the same objective of reviewing the operation of the Treaty.

ARTICLE IX

1. This Treaty shall be open to all States for signature. Any State which does not sign the Treaty before its entry into force in accordance with paragraph 3 of this article may accede to it at any time.

2. This Treaty shall be subject to ratification by signatory States. Instruments of ratification and instruments of accession shall be deposited with the Governments of the United States of America, the United Kingdom of Great Britain and Northern Ireland and the Union of Soviet Socialist Republics, which are hereby designated the Depositary Governments.

3. This Treaty shall enter into force after its ratification by the States, the Governments of which are designated Depositaries of the Treaty, and forty other States signatory to this Treaty and the deposit of their instruments of ratification. For the purposes of this Treaty, a nuclear-weapon State is one which has manufactured and exploded a nuclear weapon or other nuclear explosive device prior to January 1, 1967.

4. For States whose instruments of ratification or accession are deposited subsequent to the entry into force of this Treaty, it shall enter into force on the date of the deposit of their instruments of ratification or accession.

5. The Depositary Governments shall promptly inform all signatory and acceding States of the date of each signature, the date of deposit of each instrument of ratification or of accession, the date of the entry into force of this Treaty, and the date of receipt of any requests for convening a conference or other notices.

6. This Treaty shall be registered by the Depositary Governments pursuant to article 102 of the Charter of the United Nations.

ARTICLE X

1. Each Party shall in exercising its national sovereignty have the right to withdraw from the Treaty if it decides that extraordinary events, related to the subject matter of this Treaty, have jeopardized the supreme interests of its country. It shall give notice of such withdrawal to all other Parties to the Treaty and to the United Nations Security Council three months in advance. Such notice shall include a statement of the extraordinary events it regards as having jeopardized its supreme interests.

2. Twenty-five years after the entry into force of the Treaty, a conference shall be convened to decide whether the Treaty shall continue in force indefinitely, or shall be extended for an additional fixed period or periods. This

decision shall be taken by a majority of the Parties to the Treaty.

ARTICLE XI

This Treaty, the English, Russian, French, Spanish and Chinese texts of which are equally authentic, shall be deposited in the archives of the Depositary Governments. Duly certified copies of this Treaty shall be transmitted by the Depositary Governments to the Governments of the signatory and acceding States.

IN WITNESS WHEREOF the undersigned, duly authorized, have signed this Treaty.

DONE in triplicate, at the cities of Washington, London and Moscow, this first day of July one thousand nine hundred sixty-eight.

Agreement Between the United States of American and the Union of Soviet Socialist Republics on the Establishment of Nuclear Risk Reduction Centers

Signed at Washington September 15, 1987
Entered into force September 15, 1987

The United States of America and the Union of Soviet Socialist Republics, hereinafter referred to as the Parties,

Affirming their desire to reduce and ultimately eliminate the risk of outbreak of nuclear war, in particular, as a result of misinterpretation, miscalculation, or accident,

Believing that a nuclear war cannot be won and must never be fought,

Believing that agreement on measures for reducing the risk of outbreak of nuclear war serves the interests of strengthening international peace and security,

Reaffirming their obligations under the Agreement on Measures to Reduce the Risk of Outbreak of Nuclear War between the United States of America and the Union of Soviet Socialist Republics of September 30, 1971, and the Agreement between the Government of the United States of America and the Government of the Union of Soviet Socialist Republics on the Prevention of Incidents on and over the High Seas of May 25, 1972,

Have agreed as follows:

ARTICLE 1

Each Party shall establish, in its capital, a national Nuclear Risk Reduction Center that shall operate on behalf of and under the control of its respective Government.

ARTICLE 2

The Parties shall use the Nuclear Risk Reduction Centers to transmit notifications identified in Protocol I which constitutes an integral part of this Agreement.

In the future, the list of notifications transmitted through the Centers may be altered by agreement between the Parties, as relevant new agreements are reached.

ARTICLE 3

The Parties shall establish a special facsimile communications link between their national Nuclear Risk Reduction Centers in accordance with Protocol II which constitutes an integral part of this Agreement.

ARTICLE 4

The Parties shall staff their national Nuclear Risk Reduction Centers as they deem appropriate, so as to ensure their normal functioning.

ARTICLE 5

The Parties shall hold regular meetings between representatives of the Nuclear Risk Reduction Centers at least once each year to consider matters related to the functioning of such Centers.

ARTICLE 6

This Agreement shall not affect the obligations of either Party under other agreements.

ARTICLE 7

This Agreement shall enter into force on the date of its signature.

The duration of this Agreement shall not be limited.

This Agreement may be terminated by either Party upon 12 months written notice to the other Party.

DONE at Washington on September 15, 1987, in two copies, each in the English and Russian languages, both texts being equally authentic.

FOR THE UNITED STATES OF AMERICA:

George P. Shultz

FOR THE UNION OF SOVIET SOCIALIST REPUBLICS:

Eduard A. Shevardnadze

Agreement on Measures to Reduce the Risk of Outbreak of Nuclear War Between the United States of America and the Union of Soviet Socialist Republics

Signed at Washington September 30, 1971
Entered into force September 30, 19715

The United States of America and the Union of Soviet Socialist Republics, hereinafter referred to as the Parties:

Taking into account the devastating consequences that nuclear war would have for all mankind, and recognizing the need to exert every effort to avert the risk of outbreak of such a war, including measures to guard against accidental or unauthorized use of nuclear weapons,

Believing that agreement on measures for reducing the risk of outbreak of nuclear war serves the interests of strengthening international peace and security, and is in no way contrary to the interests of any other country,

Bearing in mind that continued efforts are also needed in the future to seek ways of reducing the risk of outbreak of nuclear war,

Have agreed as follows:

ARTICLE 1

Each Party undertakes to maintain and to improve, as it deems necessary, its existing organizational and technical arrangements to guard against the accidental or unauthorized use of nuclear weapons under its control.

ARTICLE 2

The Parties undertake to notify each other immediately in the event of an accidental, unauthorized or any other unexplained incident involving a possible detonation of a nuclear weapon which could create a risk of outbreak of nuclear war. In the event of such an incident, the Party whose nuclear weapon is involved will immediately make every effort to take necessary measures to render harmless or destroy such weapon without its causing damage.

ARTICLE 3

The Parties undertake to notify each other immediately in the event of detection by missile warning systems of unidentified objects, or in the event of signs of interference with these systems or with related communications facilities, if such occurrences could create a risk of outbreak of nuclear war between the two countries.

ARTICLE 4

Each Party undertakes to notify the other Party in advance of any planned missile launches if such launches will extend beyond its national territory in the direction of the other Party.

ARTICLE 5

Each Party, in other situations involving unexplained nuclear incidents, undertakes to act in sucha manner as to reduce the possibility of its actions being misinterpreted by the other Party. In any such situation, each Party may inform the other Party or request information when in its view, this is warranted by the interests of averting the risk of outbreak of nuclear war.

ARTICLE 6

For transmission of urgent information, notifications and requests for information in situations requiring prompt clarification, the Parties shall make primary use of the Direct Communications Link between the Governments of the United States of America and the Union of Soviet Socialist Republics.

For transmission of other information, notification and requests for information, the Parties, at their own discretion, may use any communications facilities, including diplomatic channels, depending on the degree of urgency.

ARTICLE 7

The Parties undertake to hold consultations, as mutually agreed, to consider questions relating to implementation of the provisions of this Agreement, as well as to discuss possible amendments thereto aimed at further implementation of the purposes of this Agreement.

ARTICLE 8

This Agreement shall be of unlimited duration.

ARTICLE 9

This Agreement shall enter into force upon signature.

DONE at Washington on September 30, 1971, in two copies, each in the English and Russian languages, both texts being equally authentic.

FOR THE UNITED STATES OF AMERICA:
WILLIAM P. ROGERS
FOR THE UNION OF SOVIET SOCIALIST REPUBLICS:
A. GROMYKO

Open Skies Treaty

The States concluding this Treaty, hereinafter referred to collectively as the States Parties or individually as a State Party,

Recalling the commitments they have made in the Conference on Security and Co-operation in Europe to promoting greater openness and transparency in their military activities and to enhancing security by means of confidence- and security-building measures,

Welcoming the historic events in Europe which have transformed the security situation from Vancouver to Vladivostok,

Wishing to contribute to the further development and strengthening of peace, stability and co-operative security in that area by the creation of an Open Skies regime for aerial observation,

Recognizing the potential contribution which an aerial observation regime of this type could make to security and stability in other regions as well,

Noting the possibility of employing such a regime to improve openness and transparency, to facilitate the monitoring of compliance with existing or future arms control agreements and to strengthen the capacity for conflict prevention and crisis management in the framework of the Conference on Security and Co-operation in Europe and in other relevant international institutions,

Envisaging the possible extension of the Open Skies regime into additional fields, such as the protection of the environment,

Seeking to establish agreed procedures to provide for aerial observation of all the territories of States Parties, with the intent of observing a single State Party or groups of States Parties, on the basis of equity and effectiveness while maintaining flight safety,

Noting that the operation of such an Open Skies regime will be without prejudice to States not participating in it,

Have agreed as follows:

ARTICLE I: GENERAL PROVISIONS

1. This Treaty establishes the regime, to be known as the Open Skies regime, for the conduct of observation flights by States Parties over the territories of other States Parties, and sets forth the rights and obligations of the States Parties relating thereto.
2. Each of the Annexes and their related Appendices constitutes an integral part of this Treaty.

ARTICLE II: DEFINITIONS

For the purposes of this Treaty:

1. The term "observed Party" means the State Party or group of States Parties over whose territory an observation flight is conducted or is intended to be conducted, from the time it has received notification thereof from an observing Party until completion of the procedures relating to that flight, or personnel acting on behalf of that State Party or group of States Parties.
2. The term "observing Party" means the State Party or group of States Parties that intends to conduct or conducts an observation flight over the territory of another State Party or group of States Parties, from the time that it has provided notification of its intention to conduct an observation flight until completion of the procedures relating to that flight, or personnel acting on behalf of that State Party or group of States Parties.
3. The term "group of States Parties" means two or more States Parties that have agreed to form a group for the purposes of this Treaty.

4. The term "observation aircraft" means an unarmed, fixed wing aircraft designated to make observation flights, registered by the relevant authorities of a State Party and equipped with agreed sensors. The term "unarmed" means that the observation aircraft used for the purposes of this Treaty is not equipped to carry and employ weapons.

5. The term "observation flight" means the flight of the observation aircraft conducted by an observing Party over the territory of an observed Party, as provided in the flight plan, from the point of entry or Open Skies airfield to the point of exit or Open Skies airfield.

6. The term "transit flight" means a flight of an observation aircraft or transport aircraft conducted by or on behalf of an observing Party over the territory of a third State Party *en route* to or from the territory of the observed Party.

7. The term "transport aircraft" means an aircraft other than an observation aircraft that, on behalf of the observing Party, conducts flights to or from the territory of the observed Party exclusively for the purposes of this Treaty.

8. The term "territory" means the land, including islands, and internal and territorial waters, over which a State Party exercises sovereignty.

9. The term "passive quota" means the number of observation flights that each State Party is obliged to accept as an observed Party.

10. The term "active quota" means the number of observation flights that each State Party has the right to conduct as an observing Party.

11. The term "maximum flight distance" means the maximum distance over the territory of the observed Party from the point at which the observation flight may commence to the point at which that flight may terminate, as specified in Annex A to this Treaty.

12. The term "sensor" means equipment of a category specified in Article IV, paragraph 1 that is installed on an observation aircraft for use during the conduct of observation flights.

13. The term "ground resolution" means the minimum distance on the ground between two closely located objects distinguishable as separate objects.

14. The term "infra-red line-scanning device" means a sensor capable of receiving and visualizing thermal electro-magnetic radiation emitted in the invisible infra-red part of the optical spectrum by objects due to their temperature and in the absence of artificial illumination.

15. The term "observation period" means a specified period of time during an observation flight when a particular sensor installed on the observation aircraft is operating.

16. The term "flight crew" means individuals from any State Party who may include, if the State Party so decides, interpreters and who perform duties associated with the operation or servicing of an observation aircraft or transport aircraft.

17. The term "pilot-in-command" means the pilot on board the observation aircraft who is responsible for the operation of the observation aircraft, the execution of the flight plan, and the safety of the observation aircraft.

18. The term "flight monitor" means an individual who, on behalf of the observed Party, is on board an observation aircraft provided by the observing Party during the observation flight and who performs duties in accordance with Annex G to this Treaty.

19. The term "flight representative" means an individual who, on behalf of the observing Party, is on board an observation aircraft provided by the observed Party during an observation flight and who performs duties in accordance with Annex G to this Treaty.

20. The term "representative" means an individual who has been designated by the observing Party and who performs activities on behalf of the observing Party in accordance with Annex G during an observation flight on an observation aircraft designated by a State Party other than the observing Party or the observed Party.

21. The term "sensor operator" means an individual from any State Party who performs duties associated with the functioning, operation and maintenance of the sensors of an observation aircraft.

22. The term "inspector" means an individual from any State Party who conducts an inspection of sensors or observation aircraft of another State Party.

23. The term "escort" means an individual from any State Party who accompanies the inspectors of another State Party.

24. The term "mission plan" means a document, which is in a format established by the Open Skies Consultative Commission, presented by the observing Party that contains the route, profile, order of execution and support

required to conduct the observation flight, which is to be agreed upon with the observed Party and which will form the basis for the elaboration of the flight plan.

25. The term "flight plan" means a document elaborated on the basis of the agreed mission plan in the format and with the content specified by the International Civil Aviation Organization, hereinafter referred to as the ICAO, which is presented to the air traffic control authorities and on the basis of which the observation flight will be conducted.

26. The term "mission report" means a document describing an observation flight completed after its termination by the observing Party and signed by both the observing and observed Parties, which is in a format established by the Open Skies Consultative Commission.

27. The term "Open Skies airfield" means an airfield designated by the observed Party as a point where an observation flight may commence or terminate.

28. The term "point of entry" means a point designated by the observed Party for the arrival of personnel of the observing Party on the territory of the observed Party.

29. The term "point of exit" means a point designated by the observed Party for the departure of personnel of the observing Party from the territory of the observed Party.

30. The term "refuelling airfield" means an airfield designated by the observed Party used for fuelling and servicing of observation aircraft and transport aircraft.

31. The term "alternate airfield" means an airfield specified in the flight plan to which an observation aircraft or transport aircraft may proceed when it becomes inadvisable to land at the airfield of intended landing.

32. The term "hazardous airspace" means the prohibited areas, restricted areas and danger areas, defined on the basis of Annex 2 to the Convention on International Civil Aviation, that are established in accordance with Annex 15 to the Convention on International Civil Aviation in the interests of flight safety, public safety and environmental protection and about which information is provided in accordance with ICAO provisions.

33. The term "prohibited area" means an airspace of defined dimensions, above the territory of a State Party, within which the flight of aircraft is prohibited.

34. The term "restricted area" means an airspace of defined dimensions, above the territory of a State Party, within which the flight of aircraft is restricted in accordance with specified conditions.

35. The term "danger area" means an airspace of defined dimensions within which activities dangerous to the flight of aircraft may exist at specified times.

ARTICLE III: QUOTAS

SECTION I. GENERAL PROVISIONS

1. Each State Party shall have the right to conduct observation flights in accordance with the provisions of this Treaty.

2. Each State Party shall be obliged to accept observation flights over its territory in accordance with the provisions of this Treaty.

3. Each State Party shall have the right to conduct a number of observation flights over the territory of any other State Party equal to the number of observation flights which that other State Party has the right to conduct over it.

4. The total number of observation flights that each State Party is obliged to accept over its territory is the total passive quota for that State Party. The allocation of the total passive quota to the States Parties is set forth in Annex A, Section I to this Treaty.

5. The number of observation flights that a State Party shall have the right to conduct each year over the territory of each of the other States Parties is the individual active quota of that State Party with respect to that other State Party. The sum of the individual active quotas is the total active quota of that State Party. The total active quota of a State Party shall not exceed its total passive quota.

6. The first distribution of active quotas is set forth in Annex A, Section II to this Treaty.

7. After entry into force of this Treaty, the distribution of active quotas shall be subject to an annual review for the following calendar year within the framework of the Open Skies Consultative Commission. In the event that it is not possible during the annual review to arrive within three weeks at agreement on the distribution of active quotas with respect to a particular State Party, the previous year?s

distribution of active quotas with respect to that State Party shall remain unchanged.

8. Except as provided for by the provisions of Article VIII, each observation flight conducted by a State Party shall be counted against the individual and total active quotas of that State Party.

9. Notwithstanding the provisions of paragraphs 3 and 5 of this Section, a State Party to which an active quota has been distributed may, by agreement with the State Party to be overflown, transfer a part or all of its total active quota to other States Parties and shall promptly notify all other States Parties and the Open Skies Consultative Commission thereof. Paragraph 10 of this Section shall apply.

10. No State Party shall conduct more observation flights over the territory of another State Party than a number equal to 50 per cent, rounded up to the nearest whole number, of its own total active quota, or of the total passive quota of that other State Party, whichever is less.

11. The maximum flight distances of observation flights over the territories of the States Parties are set forth in Annex A, Section III to this Treaty.

SECTION II. PROVISIONS FOR A GROUP OF STATES PARTIES

1.

(A) Without prejudice to their rights and obligations under this Treaty, two or more States Parties which hold quotas may form a group of States Parties at signature of this Treaty and thereafter. For a group of States Parties formed after signature of this Treaty, the provisions of this Section shall apply no earlier than six months after giving notice to all other States Parties, and subject to the provisions of paragraph 6 of this Section.

(B) A group of States Parties shall co-operate with regard to active and passive quotas in accordance with the provisions of either paragraph 2 or 3 of this Section.

2.

(A) The members of a group of States Parties shall have the right to redistribute amongst themselves their active quotas for the current year, while retaining their individual passive quotas. Notification of the redistribution shall

be made immediately to all third States Parties concerned.

(B) An observation flight shall count as many observation flights against the individual and total active quotas of the observing Party as observed Parties belonging to the group are overflown. It shall count one observation flight against the total passive quota of each observed Party.

(C) Each State Party in respect of which one or more members of a group of States Parties hold active quotas shall have the right to conduct over the territory of any member of the group 50 per cent more observation flights, rounded up to the nearest whole number, than its individual active quota in respect of that member of the group or to conduct two such overflights if it holds no active quota in respect of that member of the group.

(D) In the event that it exercises this right the State Party concerned shall reduce its active quotas in respect of other members of the group in such a way that the total sum of observation flights it conducts over their territories shall not exceed the sum of the individual active quotas that the State Party holds in respect of all the members of the group in the current year.

(E) The maximum flight distances of observation flights over the territories of each member of the group shall apply. In case of an observation flight conducted over several members, after completion of the maximum flight distance for one member all sensors shall be switched off until the observation aircraft reaches the point over the territory of the next member of the group of States Parties where the observation flight is planned to begin. For such follow-on observation flight the maximum flight distance related to the Open Skies airfield nearest to this point shall apply.

3.

(A) A group of States Parties shall, at its request, be entitled to a common total passive quota which shall be allocated to it and common individual and total active quotas shall be distributed in respect of it.

(B) In this case, the total passive quota is the total number of observation flights that the group of States Parties is obliged to accept each year. The total active quota is the sum of the number of observation flights that the group of States Parties has the right to conduct each year. Its total active quota shall not exceed the total passive quota.

(C) An observation flight resulting from the total active quota of the group of States Parties shall be carried out on behalf of the group.

(D) Observation flights that a group of States Parties is obliged to accept may be conducted over the territory of one or more of its members.

(E) The maximum flight distances of each group of States Parties shall be specified pursuant to Annex A, Section III and Open Skies airfields shall be designated pursuant to Annex E to this Treaty.

4. In accordance with the general principles set out in Article X, paragraph 3, any third State Party that considers its rights under the provisions of Section I, paragraph 3 of this Article to be unduly restricted by the operation of a group of States Parties may raise this problem before the Open Skies Consultative Commission.

5. The group of States Parties shall ensure that procedures are established allowing for the conduct of observation flights over the territories of its members during one single mission, including refuelling if necessary. In the case of a group of States Parties established pursuant to paragraph 3 of this Section, such observation flights shall not exceed the maximum flight distance applicable to the Open Skies airfields at which the observation flights commence.

6. No earlier than six months after notification of the decision has been provided to all other States Parties:

(A) a group of States Parties established pursuant to the provisions of paragraph 2 of this Section may be transformed into a group of States Parties pursuant to the provisions of paragraph 3 of this Section;

(B) a group of States Parties established pursuant to the provisions of paragraph 3 of this Section may be transformed into a group of States Parties pursuant to the provisions of paragraph 2 of this Section;

(C) a State Party may withdraw from a group of States Parties; or

(D) a group of States Parties may admit further States Parties which hold quotas.

7. Following entry into force of this Treaty, changes in the allocation or distribution of quotas resulting from the establishment of or an admission to or a withdrawal from a group of States Parties according to paragraph 3 of this Section shall become effective on 1 January following the first annual review within the Open Skies Consultative Commission occurring after the six-month notification period. When necessary, new Open Skies airfields shall be designated and maximum flight distances established accordingly.

ARTICLE IV: SENSORS

1. Except as otherwise provided for in paragraph 3 of this Article, observation aircraft shall be equipped with sensors only from amongst the following categories:

(A) optical panoramic and framing cameras;
(B) video cameras with real-time display;
(C) infra-red line-scanning devices; and
(D) sideways-looking synthetic aperture radar.

2. A State Party may use, for the purposes of conducting observation flights, any of the sensors specified in paragraph 1 above, provided that such sensors are commercially available to all States Parties, subject to the following performance limits:

(A) in the case of optical panoramic and framing cameras, a ground resolution of no better than 30 centimetres at the minimum height above ground level determined in accordance with the provisions of Annex D, Appendix 1, obtained from no more than one panoramic camera, one vertically-mounted framing camera and two obliquely-mounted framing cameras, one on each side of the aircraft, providing coverage, which need not be continuous, of the ground up to 50 kilometres of each side of the flight path of the aircraft;

(B) in the case of video cameras, a ground resolution of no better than 30 centimetres determined in accordance with the provisions of Annex D, Appendix 1;

(C) in the case of infra-red line-scanning devices, a ground resolution of no better than 50 centimetres at the minimum height above ground level determined in accordance with the provisions of Annex D, Appendix 1, obtained from a single device; and

(D) in the case of sideways-looking synthetic aperture radar, a ground resolution of no better than three metres calculated by the impulse response method, which, using the object separation method, corresponds to the ability to distinguish on a radar image two corner reflectors, the distance between the centres of which is no less than five metres, over a swath width of no more than 25 kilometres, obtained from a single radar unit capable of looking from either side of the aircraft, but not both simultaneously.

3. The introduction of additional categories and improvements to the capabilities of existing categories of sensors provided for in this Article shall be addressed by the Open Skies Consultative Commission pursuant to Article X of this Treaty.

4. All sensors shall be provided with aperture covers or other devices which inhibit the operation of sensors so as to prevent collection of data during transit flights or flights to points of entry or from points of exit over the territory of the observed Party. Such covers or such other devices shall be removable or operable only from outside the observation aircraft.

5. Equipment that is capable of annotating data collected by sensors in accordance with Annex B, Section II shall be allowed on observation aircraft. The State Party providing the observation aircraft for an observation flight shall annotate the data collected by sensors with the information provided for in Annex B, Section II to this Treaty.

6. Equipment that is capable of displaying data collected by sensors in real-time shall be allowed on observation aircraft for the purposes of monitoring the functioning and operation of the sensors during the conduct of an observation flight.

7. Except as required for the operation of the agreed sensors, or as required for the operation of the observation aircraft, or as provided for in paragraphs 5 and 6 of this Article, the collection, processing, retransmission or recording of electronic signals from electro-magnetic waves are prohibited on board the observation aircraft and equipment for such operations shall not be on that observation aircraft.

8. In the event that the observation aircraft is provided by the observing Party, the observing Party shall have the right to use an observation aircraft equipped with sensors in each sensor category that do not exceed the capability specified in paragraph 2 of this Article.

9. In the event that the observation aircraft used for an observation flight is provided by the observed Party, the observed Party shall be obliged to provide an observation aircraft equipped with sensors from each sensor category specified in paragraph 1 of this Article, at the maximum capability and in the numbers specified in paragraph 2 of this Article, subject to the provisions of Article XVIII, Section II, unless otherwise agreed by the observing and observed Parties. The package and configuration of such sensors shall be installed in such a way so as to provide coverage of the ground provided for in paragraph 2 of this Article. In the event that the observation aircraft is provided by the observed Party, the latter shall provide a sideways-looking synthetic aperture radar with a ground resolution of no worse than six metres, determined by the object separation method.

10. When designating an aircraft as an observation aircraft pursuant to Article V of this Treaty, each State Party shall inform all other States Parties of the technical information on each sensor installed on such aircraft as provided for in Annex B to this Treaty.

11. Each State Party shall have the right to take part in the certification of sensors installed on observation aircraft in accordance with the provisions of Annex D. No observation aircraft of a given type shall be used for observation flights until such type of observation aircraft and its sensors has been certified in accordance with the provisions of Annex D to this Treaty.

12. A State Party designating an aircraft as an observation aircraft shall, upon 90-day prior notice to all other States Parties and subject to the provisions of Annex D to this Treaty, have the right to remove, replace or add sensors, or amend the technical information it has provided in accordance with the provisions of paragraph 10 of this Article and Annex B to this Treaty. Replacement and additional sensors shall be subject to certification in accordance with the provisions of Annex D to this Treaty prior to their use during an observation flight.

13. In the event that a State Party or group of States Parties, based on experience with using a particular observation aircraft, considers that any sensor or its associated equipment installed on an aircraft does not correspond to those certified in accordance with the provisions of Annex D, the interested States Parties shall notify all other States Parties of their concern. The State Party that designated the aircraft shall:

(A) take the steps necessary to ensure that the sensor and its associated equipment installed on the observation aircraft correspond to those certified in accordance with the provisions of Annex D, including, as necessary, repair, adjustment or replacement of the particular sensor or its associated equipment; and

(B) at the request of an interested State Party, by means of a demonstration flight set up in connection with the next time that the aforementioned observation aircraft is used, in accordance with the provisions of Annex F, demonstrate that the sensor and its associated equipment installed on the observation aircraft correspond to those certified in accordance with the provisions of Annex D. Other States Parties that express concern regarding a sensor and its associated equipment installed on an observation aircraft shall have the right to send personnel to participate in such a demonstration flight.

14. In the event that, after the steps referred to in paragraph 13 of this Article have been taken, the States Parties remain concerned as to whether a sensor or its associated equipment installed on an observation aircraft correspond to those certified in accordance with the provisions of Annex D, the issue may be referred to the Open Skies Consultative Commission.

ARTICLE V: AIRCRAFT DESIGNATION

1. Each State Party shall have the right to designate as observation aircraft one or more types or models of aircraft registered by the relevant authorities of a State Party.
2. Each State Party shall have the right to designate types or models of aircraft as observation aircraft or add new types or models of aircraft to those designated earlier by it, provided that it notifies all other States

Parties 30 days in advance thereof. The notification of the designation of aircraft of a type or model shall contain the information specified in Annex C to this Treaty.

3. Each State Party shall have the right to delete types or models of aircraft designated earlier by it, provided that it notifies all other States Parties 90 days in advance thereof.
4. Only one exemplar of a particular type and model of aircraft with an identical set of associated sensors shall be required to be offered for certification in accordance with the provisions of Annex D to this Treaty.
5. Each observation aircraft shall be capable of carrying the flight crew and the personnel specified in Article VI, Section III.

ARTICLE VI: CHOICE OF OBSERVATION AIRCRAFT, GENERAL PROVISIONS FOR THE CONDUCT OF OBSERVATION FLIGHTS, AND REQUIREMENTS FOR MISSION PLANNING

SECTION I. CHOICE OF OBSERVATION AIRCRAFT AND GENERAL PROVISIONS FOR THE CONDUCT OF OBSERVATION FLIGHTS

1. Observation flights shall be conducted using observation aircraft that have been designated by a State Party pursuant to Article V. Unless the observed Party exercises its right to provide an observation aircraft that it has itself designated, the observing Party shall have the right to provide the observation aircraft. In the event that the observing Party provides the observation aircraft, it shall have the right to provide an aircraft that it has itself designated or an aircraft designated by another State Party. In the event that the observed Party provides the observation aircraft, the observing Party shall have the right to be provided with an aircraft capable of achieving a minimum unrefuelled range, including the necessary fuel reserves, equivalent to one-half of the flight distance, as notified in accordance with paragraph 5, subparagraph (G) of this Section.
2. Each State Party shall have the right, pursuant to paragraph 1 of this Section, to use an observation aircraft designated by another State Party for observation flights. Arrangements for the use of such aircraft shall

be worked out by the States Parties involved to allow for active participation in the Open Skies regime.

3. States Parties having the right to conduct observation flights may co-ordinate their plans for conducting observation flights in accordance with Annex H to this Treaty. No State Party shall be obliged to accept more than one observation flight at any one time during the 96-hour period specified in paragraph 9 of this Section, unless that State Party has requested a demonstration flight pursuant to Annex F to this Treaty. In that case, the observed Party shall be obliged to accept an overlap for the observation flights of up to 24 hours. After having been notified of the results of the co-ordination of plans to conduct observation flights, each State Party over whose territory observation flights are to be conducted shall inform other States Parties, in accordance with the provisions of Annex H, whether it will exercise, with regard to each specific observation flight, its right to provide its own observation aircraft.

4. No later than 90 days after signature of this Treaty, each State Party shall provide notification to all other States Parties:
(A) of the standing diplomatic clearance number for Open Skies observation flights, flights of transport aircraft and transit flights; and
(B) of which language or languages of the Open Skies Consultative Commission specified in Annex L, Section I, paragraph 7 to this Treaty shall be used by personnel for all activities associated with the conduct of observation flights over its territory, and for completing the mission plan and mission report, unless the language to be used is the one recommended in Annex 10 to the Convention on International Civil Aviation, Volume II, paragraph 5.2.1.1.2.

5. The observing Party shall notify the observed Party of its intention to conduct an observation flight, no less than 72 hours prior to the estimated time of arrival of the observing Party at the point of entry of the observed Party. States Parties providing such notifications shall make every effort to avoid using the minimum pre-notification period over weekends. Such notification shall include:
(A) the desired point of entry and, if applicable, Open Skies airfield where the observation flight shall commence;

(B) the date and estimated time of arrival of the observing Party at the point of entry and the date and estimated time of departure for the flight from the point of entry to the Open Skies airfield, if applicable, indicating specific accommodation needs;
(C) the location, specified in Annex E, Appendix 1, where the conduct of the pre-flight inspection is desired and the date and start time of such pre-flight inspection in accordance with the provisions of Annex F;
(D) the mode of transport and, if applicable, type and model of the transport aircraft used to travel to the point of entry in the event that the observation aircraft used for the observation flight is provided by the observed Party;
(E) the diplomatic clearance number for the observation flight or for the flight of the transport aircraft used to bring the personnel in and out of the territory of the observed Party to conduct an observation flight;
(F) the identification of the observation aircraft, as specified in Annex C;
(G) the approximate observation flight distance; and
(H) the names of the personnel, their gender, date and place of birth, passport number and issuing State Party, and their function.

6. The observed Party that is notified in accordance with paragraph 5 of this Section shall acknowledge receipt of the notification within 24 hours. In the event that the observed Party exercises its right to provide the observation aircraft, the acknowledgement shall include the information about the observation aircraft specified in paragraph 5, subparagraph (F) of this Section. The observing Party shall be permitted to arrive at the point of entry at the estimated time of arrival as notified in accordance with paragraph 5 of this Section. The estimated time of departure for the flight from the point of entry to the Open Skies airfield where the observation flight shall commence and the location, the date and the start time of the pre-flight inspection shall be subject to confirmation by the observed Party.

7. Personnel of the observing Party may include personnel designated pursuant to Article XIII by other States Parties.

8. The observing Party, when notifying the observed Party in accordance with paragraph 5 of this Section, shall

simultaneously notify all other States Parties of its intention to conduct the observation flight.

9. The period from the estimated time of arrival at the point of entry until completion of the observation flight shall not exceed 96 hours, unless otherwise agreed. In the event that the observed Party requests a demonstration flight pursuant to Annex F to the Treaty, it shall extend the 96-hour period pursuant to Annex F, Section III, paragraph 4, if additional time is required by the observing Party for the unrestricted execution of the mission plan.

10. Upon arrival of the observation aircraft at the point of entry, the observed Party shall inspect the covers for sensor apertures or other devices that inhibit the operation of sensors to confirm that they are in their proper position pursuant to Annex E, unless otherwise agreed by all States Parties involved.

11. In the event that the observation aircraft is provided by the observing Party, upon the arrival of the observation aircraft at the point of entry or at the Open Skies airfield where the observation flight commences, the observed Party shall have the right to carry out the pre-flight inspection pursuant to Annex F, Section I. In the event that, in accordance with paragraph 1 of this Section, an observation aircraft is provided by the observed Party, the observing Party shall have the right to carry out the pre-flight inspection of sensors pursuant to Annex F, Section II. Unless otherwise agreed, such inspections shall terminate no less than four hours prior to the scheduled commencement of the observation flight set forth in the flight plan.

12. The observing Party shall ensure that its flight crew includes at least one individual who has the necessary linguistic ability to communicate freely with the personnel of the observed Party and its air traffic control authorities in the language or languages notified by the observed Party in accordance with paragraph 4 of this Section.

13. The observed Party shall provide the flight crew, upon its arrival at the point of entry or at the Open Skies airfield where the observation flight commences, with the most recent weather forecast and air navigation information and information on flight safety, including Notices to Airmen. Updates of such information shall be provided as requested. Instrument procedures, and information about alternate airfields along the flight route, shall be provided upon approval of the mission plan in accordance with the requirements of Section II of this Article.

14. While conducting observation flights pursuant to this Treaty, all observation aircraft shall be operated in accordance with the provisions of this Treaty and in accordance with the approved flight plan. Without prejudice to the provisions of Section II, paragraph 2 of this Article, observation flights shall also be conducted in compliance with:
(A) published ICAO standards and recommended practices; and
(B) published national air traffic control rules, procedures and guidelines on flight safety of the State Party whose territory is being overflown.

15. Observation flights shall take priority over any regular air traffic. The observed Party shall ensure that its air traffic control authorities facilitate the conduct of observation flights in accordance with this Treaty.

16. On board the aircraft the pilot-in-command shall be the sole authority for the safe conduct of the flight and shall be responsible for the execution of the flight plan.

17. The observed Party shall provide:
(A) a calibration target suitable for confirming the capability of sensors in accordance with the procedures set forth in Annex D, Section III to this Treaty, to be overflown during the demonstration flight or the observation flight upon the request of either Party, for each sensor that is to be used during the observation flight. The calibration target shall be located in the vicinity of the airfield at which the pre-flight inspection is conducted pursuant to Annex F to this Treaty;
(B) customary commercial aircraft fuelling and servicing for the observation aircraft or transport aircraft at the point of entry, at the Open Skies airfield, at any refuelling airfield, and at the point of exit specified in the flight plan, according to the specifications that are published about the designated airfield;
(C) meals and the use of accommodation for the personnel of the observing Party; and
(D) upon the request of the observing Party, further services, as may be agreed upon between the observing and observed Parties, to facilitate the conduct of the observation flight.

18. All costs involved in the conduct of the observation flight, including the costs of the recording media and the processing of the data collected by sensors, shall be reimbursed in accordance with Annex L, Section I, paragraph 9 to this Treaty.

19. Prior to the departure of the observation aircraft from the point of exit, the observed Party shall confirm that the covers for sensor apertures or other devices that inhibit the operation of sensors are in their proper position pursuant to Annex E to this Treaty.

20. Unless otherwise agreed, the observing Party shall depart from the point of exit no later than 24 hours following completion of the observation flight, unless weather conditions or the airworthiness of the observation aircraft or transport aircraft do not permit, in which case the flight shall commence as soon as practicable.

21. The observing Party shall compile a mission report of the observation flight using the appropriate format developed by the Open Skies Consultative Commission. The mission report shall contain pertinent data on the date and time of the observation flight, its route and profile, weather conditions, time and location of each observation period for each sensor, the approximate amount of data collected by sensors, and the result of inspection of covers for sensor apertures or other devices that inhibit the operation of sensors in accordance with Article VII and Annex E. The mission report shall be signed by the observing and observed Parties at the point of exit and shall be provided by the observing Party to all other States Parties within seven days after departure of the observing Party from the point of exit.

SECTION II. REQUIREMENTS FOR MISSION PLANNING

1. Unless otherwise agreed, the observing Party shall, after arrival at the Open Skies airfield, submit to the observed Party a mission plan for the proposed observation flight that meets the requirements of paragraphs 2 and 4 of this Section.

2. The mission plan may provide for an observation flight that allows for the observation of any point on the entire territory of the observed Party, including areas designated by the observed Party as hazardous airspace in the source specified in Annex I. The flight path of an observation aircraft shall not be closer than, but shall be allowed up to, ten kilometres from the border with an adjacent State that is not a State Party.

3. The mission plan may provide that the Open Skies airfield where the observation flight terminates, as well as the point of exit, may be different from the Open Skies airfield where the observation flight commences or the point of entry. The mission plan shall specify, if applicable, the commencement time of the observation flight, the desired time and place of planned refuelling stops or rest periods, and the time of continuation of the observation flight after a refuelling stop or rest period within the 96-hour period specified in Section I, paragraph 9 of this Article.

4. The mission plan shall include all information necessary to file the flight plan and shall provide that:

(A) the observation flight does not exceed the relevant maximum flight distance as set forth in Annex A, Section I;

(B) the route and profile of the observation flight satisfies observation flight safety conditions in conformity with ICAO standards and recommended practices, taking into account existing differences in national flight rules, without prejudice to the provisions of paragraph 2 of this Section;

(C) the mission plan takes into account information on hazardous airspace, as provided in accordance with Annex I;

(D) the height above ground level of the observation aircraft does not permit the observing Party to exceed the limitation on ground resolution for each sensor, as set forth in Article IV, paragraph 2;

(E) the estimated time of commencement of the observation flight shall be no less than 24 hours after the submission of the mission plan, unless otherwise agreed;

(F) the observation aircraft flies a direct route between the co-ordinates or navigation fixes designated in the mission plan in the declared sequence; and

(G) the flight path does not intersect at the same point more than once, unless otherwise agreed, and the observation aircraft does not circle around a single point, unless otherwise agreed. The provisions of this subparagraph do not apply for the purposes of taking off, flying over calibration targets, or landing by the observation aircraft.

5. In the event that the mission plan filed by the observing Party provides for flights through hazardous airspace, the observed Party shall:
(A) specify the hazard to the observation aircraft;
(B) facilitate the conduct of the observation flight by co-ordination or suppression of the activity specified pursuant to subparagraph (A) of this paragraph; or
(C) propose an alternative flight altitude, route, or time.

6. No later than four hours after submission of the mission plan, the observed Party shall accept the mission plan or propose changes to it in accordance with Article VIII, Section I, paragraph 4 and paragraph 5 of this Section. Such changes shall not preclude observation of any point on the entire territory of the observed Party, including areas designated by the observed Party as hazardous airspace in the source specified in Annex I to this Treaty. Upon agreement, the mission plan shall be signed by the observing and observed Parties. In the event that the Parties do not reach agreement on the mission plan within eight hours of the submission of the original mission plan, the observing Party shall have the right to decline to conduct the observation flight in accordance with the provisions of Article VIII of this Treaty.

7. If the planned route of the observation flight approaches the border of other States Parties or other States, the observed Party may notify that State or those States of the estimated route, date and time of the observation flight.

8. On the basis of the agreed mission plan the State Party providing the observation aircraft shall, in co-ordination with the other State Party, file the flight plan immediately, which shall have the content specified in Annex 2 to the Convention on International Civil Aviation and shall be in the format specified by ICAO Document No. 4444-RAC/501/12, "Rules of the Air and Air Traffic Services", as revised or amended.

SECTION III. SPECIAL PROVISIONS

1. In the event that the observation aircraft is provided by the observing Party, the observed Party shall have the right to have on board the observation aircraft two flight monitors and one interpreter, in addition to one flight monitor for each sensor control station on board the observation aircraft, unless otherwise agreed. Flight monitors and interpreters shall have the rights and obligations specified in Annex G to this Treaty.

2. Notwithstanding paragraph 1 of this Section, in the event that an observing Party uses an observation aircraft which has a maximum take-off gross weight of no more than 35,000 kilograms for an observation flight distance of no more than 1,500 kilometres as notified in accordance with Section I, paragraph 5, subparagraph (G) of this Article, it shall be obliged to accept only two flight monitors and one interpreter on board the observation aircraft, unless otherwise agreed.

3. In the event that the observation aircraft is provided by the observed Party, the observed Party shall permit the personnel of the observing Party to travel to the point of entry of the observed Party in the most expeditious manner. The personnel of the observing Party may elect to travel to the point of entry using ground, sea, or air transportation, including transportation by an aircraft owned by any State Party. Procedures regarding such travel are set forth in Annex E to this Treaty.

4. In the event that the observation aircraft is provided by the observed Party, the observing Party shall have the right to have on board the observation aircraft two flight representatives and one interpreter, in addition to one flight representative for each sensor control station on the aircraft, unless otherwise agreed. Flight representatives and interpreters shall have the rights and obligations set forth in Annex G to this Treaty.

5. In the event that the observing State Party provides an observation aircraft designated by a State Party other than the observing or observed Party, the observing Party shall have the right to have on board the observation aircraft two representatives and one interpreter, in addition to one representative for each sensor control station on the aircraft, unless otherwise agreed. In this case, the provisions on flight monitors set forth in paragraph 1 of this Section shall also apply. Representatives and interpreters shall have the rights and obligations set forth in Annex G to this Treaty.

ARTICLE VII: TRANSIT FLIGHTS

1. Transit flights conducted by an observing Party to and from the territory of an observed Party for the purposes of this Treaty shall originate on the territory of the observing Party or of another State Party.

2. Each State Party shall accept transit flights. Such transit flights shall be conducted along internationally recognized Air Traffic Services routes, unless otherwise agreed by the States Parties involved, and in accordance with the instructions of the national air traffic control authorities of each State Party whose airspace is transited. The observing Party shall notify each State Party whose airspace is to be transited at the same time that it notifies the observed Party in accordance with Article VI.

3. The operation of sensors on an observation aircraft during transit flights is prohibited. In the event that, during the transit flight, the observation aircraft lands on the territory of a State Party, that State Party shall, upon landing and prior to departure, inspect the covers of sensor apertures or other devices that inhibit the operation of sensors to confirm that they are in their proper position.

ARTICLE VIII: PROHIBITIONS, DEVIATIONS FROM FLIGHT PLANS AND EMERGENCY SITUATIONS

SECTION I. PROHIBITION OF OBSERVATION FLIGHTS AND CHANGES TO MISSION PLANS

1. The observed Party shall have the right to prohibit an observation flight that is not in compliance with the provisions of this Treaty.

2. The observed Party shall have the right to prohibit an observation flight prior to its commencement in the event that the observing Party fails to arrive at the point of entry within 24 hours after the estimated time of arrival specified in the notification provided in accordance with Article VI, Section I, paragraph 5, unless otherwise agreed between the States Parties involved.

3. In the event that an observed State Party prohibits an observation flight pursuant to this Article or Annex F, it shall immediately state the facts for the prohibition in the mission plan. Within seven days the observed Party shall provide to all States Parties, through diplomatic channels, a written explanation for this prohibition in the mission report provided pursuant to Article VI, Section I, paragraph 21. An observation flight that has been prohibited shall not be counted against the quota of either State Party.

4. The observed Party shall have the right to propose changes to the mission plan as a result of any of the following circumstances:
(A) the weather conditions affect flight safety;
(B) the status of the Open Skies airfield to be used, alternate airfields, or refuelling airfields prevents their use; or
(C) the mission plan is inconsistent with Article VI, Section II, paragraphs 2 and 4.

5. In the event that the observing Party disagrees with the proposed changes to the mission plan, it shall have the right to submit alternatives to the proposed changes. In the event that agreement on a mission plan is not reached within eight hours of the submission of the original mission plan, and if the observing Party considers the changes to the mission plan to be prejudicial to its rights under this Treaty with respect to the conduct of the observation flight, the observing Party shall have the right to decline to conduct the observation flight, which shall not be recorded against the quota of either State Party.

6. In the event that an observing Party declines to conduct an observation flight pursuant to this Article or Annex F, it shall immediately provide an explanation of its decision in the mission plan prior to the departure of the observing Party. Within seven days after departure of the observing Party, the observing Party shall provide to all other States Parties, through diplomatic channels, a written explanation for this decision in the mission report provided pursuant to Article VI, Section I, paragraph 21.

SECTION II. DEVIATIONS FROM THE FLIGHT PLAN

1. Deviations from the flight plan shall be permitted during the observation flight if necessitated by:
(A) weather conditions affecting flight safety;

(B) technical difficulties relating to the observation aircraft;

(C) a medical emergency of any person on board; or

(D) air traffic control instructions related to circumstances brought about by *force majeure.*

2. In addition, if weather conditions prevent effective use of optical sensors and infra-red line-scanning devices, deviations shall be permitted, provided that:

(A) flight safety requirements are met;

(B) in cases where national rules so require, permission is granted by air traffic control authorities; and

(C) the performance of the sensors does not exceed the capabilities specified in Article IV, paragraph 2, unless otherwise agreed.

3. The observed Party shall have the right to prohibit the use of a particular sensor during a deviation that brings the observation aircraft below the minimum height above ground level for operating that particular sensor, in accordance with the limitation on ground resolution specified in Article IV, paragraph 2. In the event that a deviation requires the observation aircraft to alter its flight path by more than 50 kilometres from the flight path specified in the flight plan, the observed Party shall have the right to prohibit the use of all the sensors installed on the observation aircraft beyond that 50-kilometre limit.

4. The observing Party shall have the right to curtail an observation flight during its execution in the event of sensor malfunction. The pilot-in-command shall have the right to curtail an observation flight in the event of technical difficulties affecting the safety of the observation aircraft.

5. In the event that a deviation from the flight plan permitted by paragraph 1 of this Section results in curtailment of the observation flight, or a curtailment occurs in accordance with paragraph 4 of this Section, an observation flight shall be counted against the quotas of both States Parties, unless the curtailment is due to:

(A) sensor malfunction on an observation aircraft provided by the observed Party;

(B) technical difficulties relating to the observation aircraft provided by the observed Party;

(C) a medical emergency of a member of the flight crew of the observed Party or of flight monitors; or

(D) air traffic control instructions related to circumstances brought about by force majeure.

In such cases the observing Party shall have the right to decide whether to count it against the quotas of both States Parties.

6. The data collected by the sensors shall be retained by the observing Party only if the observation flight is counted against the quotas of both States Parties.

7. In the event that a deviation is made from the flight plan, the pilot-in-command shall take action in accordance with the published national flight regulations of the observed Party. Once the factors leading to the deviation have ceased to exist, the observation aircraft may, with the permission of the air traffic control authorities, continue the observation flight in accordance with the flight plan. The additional flight distance of the observation aircraft due to the deviation shall not count against the maximum flight distance.

8. Personnel of both States Parties on board the observation aircraft shall be immediately informed of all deviations from the flight plan.

9. Additional expenses resulting from provisions of this Article shall be reimbursed in accordance with Annex L, Section I, paragraph 9 to this Treaty.

SECTION III. EMERGENCY SITUATIONS

1. In the event that an emergency situation arises, the pilot-in-command shall be guided by "Procedures for Air Navigation Services - Rules of the Air and Air Traffic Services", ICAO Document No. 4444-RAC/501/12, as revised or amended, the national flight regulations of the observed Party, and the flight operation manual of the observation aircraft.

2. Each observation aircraft declaring an emergency shall be accorded the full range of distress and navigational facilities of the observed Party in order to ensure the most expeditious recovery of the aircraft to the nearest suitable airfield.

3. In the event of an aviation accident involving the observation aircraft on the territory of the observed Party, search and rescue operations shall be conducted by the observed Party in accordance with its own regulations and procedures for such operations.

4. Investigation of an aviation accident or incident involving an observation aircraft shall be conducted by the observed Party, with the participation of the observing Party, in accordance with the ICAO recommendations set forth in Annex 13 to the Convention on International Civil Aviation ("Investigation of Aviation Accidents") as revised or amended and in accordance with the national regulations of the observed Party.

5. In the event that the observation aircraft is not registered with the observed Party, at the conclusion of the investigation all wreckage and debris of the observation aircraft and sensors, if found and recovered, shall be returned to the observing Party or to the Party to which the aircraft belongs, if so requested.

ARTICLE IX: SENSOR OUTPUT FROM OBSERVATION FLIGHTS

SECTION I. GENERAL PROVISIONS

1. For the purposes of recording data collected by sensors during observation flights, the following recording media shall be used:
(A) in the case of optical panoramic and framing cameras, black and white photographic film;
(B) in the case of video cameras, magnetic tape;
(C) in the case of infra-red line-scanning devices, black and white photographic film or magnetic tape; and
(D) in the case of sideways-looking synthetic aperture radar, magnetic tape.
   The agreed format in which such data is to be recorded and exchanged on other recording media shall be decided within the Open Skies Consultative Commission during the period of provisional application of this Treaty.

2. Data collected by sensors during observation flights shall remain on board the observation aircraft until completion of the observation flight. The transmission of data collected by sensors from the observation aircraft during the observation flight is prohibited.

3. Each roll of photographic film and cassette or reel of magnetic tape used to collect data by a sensor during an observation flight shall be placed in a container and sealed in the presence of the States Parties as soon as is practicable after it has been removed from the sensor.

4. Data collected by sensors during observation flights shall be made available to States Parties in accordance with the provisions of this Article and shall be used exclusively for the attainment of the purposes of this Treaty.

5. In the event that, on the basis of data provided pursuant to Annex B, Section I to this Treaty, a data recording medium to be used by a State Party during an observation flight is incompatible with the equipment of another State Party for handling that data recording medium, the States Parties involved shall establish procedures to ensure that all data collected during observation flights can be handled, in terms of processing, duplication and storage, by them.

SECTION II. OUTPUT FROM SENSORS THAT USE PHOTOGRAPHIC FILM

1. In the event that output from duplicate optical cameras is to be exchanged, the cameras, film and film processing shall be of an identical type.

2. Provided that the data collected by a single optical camera is subject to exchange, the States Parties shall consider, within the Open Skies Consultative Commission during the period of provisional application of this Treaty, the issue of whether the responsibility for the development of the original film negative shall be borne by the observing Party or by the State Party providing the observation aircraft. The State Party developing the original film negative shall be responsible for the quality of processing the original negative film and producing the duplicate positive or negative. In the event that States Parties agree that the film used during the observation flight conducted on an observation aircraft provided by the observed Party shall be processed by the observing Party, the observed Party shall bear no responsibility for the quality of the processing of the original negative film.

3. All the film used during the observation flight shall be developed:
(A) in the event that the original film negative is developed at a film processing facility arranged for by the observed Party, no later

than three days, unless otherwise agreed, after the arrival of the observation aircraft at the point of exit; or

(B) in the event that the original film negative is developed at a film processing facility arranged for by the observing Party, no later than ten days after the departure of the observation aircraft from the territory of the observed Party.

4. The State Party that is developing the original film negative shall be obliged to accept at the film processing facility up to two officials from the other State Party to monitor the unsealing of the film cassette or container and each step in the storage, processing, duplication and handling of the original film negative, in accordance with the provisions of Annex K, Section II to this Treaty. The State Party monitoring the film processing and duplication shall have the right to designate such officials from among its nationals present on the territory on which the film processing facility arranged for by the other State Party is located, provided that such individuals are on the list of designated personnel in accordance with Article XIII, Section I of this Treaty. The State Party developing the film shall assist the officials of the other State Party in their functions provided for in this paragraph to the maximum extent possible.

5. Upon completion of an observation flight, the State Party that is to develop the original film negative shall attach a 21-step sensitometric test strip of the same film type used during the observation flight or shall expose a 21-step optical wedge onto the leader or trailer of each roll of original film negative used during the observation flight. After the original film negative has been processed and duplicate film negative or positive has been produced, the States Parties shall assess the image quality of the 21-step sensitometric test strips or images of the 21-step optical wedge against the characteristics provided for that type of original film negative or duplicate film negative or positive in accordance with the provisions of Annex K, Section I to this Treaty.

6. In the event that only one original film negative is developed:
(A) the observing Party shall have the right to retain or receive the original film negative; and
(B) the observed Party shall have the right to select and receive a complete first generation duplicate or part thereof, either positive or

negative, of the original film negative. Unless otherwise agreed, such duplicate shall be:
1. of the same format and film size as the original film negative;
2. produced immediately after development of the original film negative; and
3. provided to the officials of the observed Party immediately after the duplicate has been produced.

7. In the event that two original film negatives are developed:
(A) if the observation aircraft is provided by the observing Party, the observed Party shall have the right, at the completion of the observation flight, to select either of the two original film negatives, and the original film negative not selected shall be retained by the observing Party; or
(B) if the observation aircraft is provided by the observed Party, the observing Party shall have the right to select either of the original film negatives, and the original film negative not selected shall be retained by the observed Party.

SECTION III. OUTPUT FROM SENSORS THAT USE OTHER RECORDING MEDIA

1. The State Party that provides the observation aircraft shall record at least one original set of data collected by sensors using other recording media.

2. In the event that only one original set is made:
(A) if the observation aircraft is provided by the observing Party, the observing Party shall have the right to retain the original set and the observed Party shall have the right to receive a first generation duplicate copy; or
(B) if the observation aircraft is provided by the observed Party, the observing Party shall have the right to receive the original set and the observed Party shall have the right to receive a first generation duplicate copy.

3. In the event that two original sets are made:
(A) if the observation aircraft is provided by the observing Party, the observed Party shall have the right, at the completion of the observation flight, to select either of the two sets of recording media, and the set not selected shall be retained by the observing Party; or
(B) if the observation aircraft is provided by the observed Party, the observing Party shall

have the right to select either of the two sets of recording media, and the set not selected shall be retained by the observed Party.

4. In the event that the observation aircraft is provided by the observing Party, the observed Party shall have the right to receive the data collected by a sideways-looking synthetic aperture radar in the form of either initial phase information or a radar image, at its choice.

5. In the event that the observation aircraft is provided by the observed Party, the observing Party shall have the right to receive the data collected by a sideways-looking synthetic aperture radar in the form of either initial phase information or a radar image, at its choice.

SECTION IV. ACCESS TO SENSOR OUTPUT

Each State Party shall have the right to request and receive from the observing Party copies of data collected by sensors during an observation flight. Such copies shall be in the form of first generation duplicates produced from the original data collected by sensors during an observation flight. The State Party requesting copies shall also notify the observed Party. A request for duplicates of data shall include the following information:

(A) the observing Party;
(B) the observed Party;
(C) the date of the observation flight;
(D) the sensor by which the data was collected;
(E) the portion or portions of the observation period during which the data was collected; and
(F) the type and format of duplicate recording medium, either negative or positive film, or magnetic tape.

ARTICLE X: OPEN SKIES CONSULTATIVE COMMISSION

1. In order to promote the objectives and facilitate the implementation of the provisions of this Treaty, the States Parties hereby establish an Open Skies Consultative Commission.

2. The Open Skies Consultative Commission shall take decisions or make recommendations by consensus. Consensus shall be understood to mean the absence of any objection by any State Party to the taking of a decision or the making of a recommendation.

3. Each State Party shall have the right to raise before the Open Skies Consultative Commission, and have placed on its agenda, any issue relating to this Treaty, including any issue related to the case when the observed Party provides an observation aircraft.

4. Within the framework of the Open Skies Consultative Commission the States Parties to this Treaty shall:
(A) consider questions relating to compliance with the provisions of this Treaty;
(B) seek to resolve ambiguities and differences of interpretation that may become apparent in the way this Treaty is implemented;
(C) consider and take decisions on applications for accession to this Treaty; and
(D) agree as to those technical and administrative measures, pursuant to the provisions of this Treaty, deemed necessary following the accession to this Treaty by other States.

5. The Open Skies Consultative Commission may propose amendments to this Treaty for consideration and approval in accordance with Article XVI. The Open Skies Consultative Commission may also agree on improvements to the viability and effectiveness of this Treaty, consistent with its provisions. Improvements relating only to modification of the annual distribution of active quotas pursuant to Article III and Annex A, to updates and additions to the categories or capabilities of sensors pursuant to Article IV, to revision of the share of costs pursuant to Annex L, Section I, paragraph 9, to arrangements for the sharing and availability of data pursuant to Article IX, Sections III and IV and to the handling of mission reports pursuant to Article VI, Section I, paragraph 21, as well as to minor matters of an administrative or technical nature, shall be agreed upon within the Open Skies Consultative Commission and shall not be deemed to be amendments to this Treaty.

6. The Open Skies Consultative Commission shall request the use of the facilities and administrative support of the Conflict Prevention Centre of the Conference on Security and Co-operation in Europe, or other existing facilities in Vienna, unless it decides otherwise.

7. Provisions for the operation of the Open Skies Consultative Commission are set forth in Annex L to this Treaty.

ARTICLE XI: NOTIFICATIONS AND REPORTS

The States Parties shall transmit notifications and reports required by this Treaty in written form. The States Parties shall transmit such notifications and reports through diplomatic channels or, at their choice, through other official channels, such as the communications network of the Conference on Security and Co-operation in Europe.

ARTICLE XII: LIABILITY

A State Party shall, in accordance with international law and practice, be liable to pay compensation for damage to other States Parties, or to their natural or juridical persons or their property, caused by it in the course of the implementation of this Treaty.

ARTICLE XIII: DESIGNATION OF PERSONNEL AND PRIVILEGES AND IMMUNITIES

SECTION I. DESIGNATION OF PERSONNEL

1. Each State Party shall, at the same time that it deposits its instrument of ratification to either of the Depositaries, provide to all other States Parties, for their review, a list of designated personnel who will carry out all duties relating to the conduct of observation flights for that State Party, including monitoring the processing of the sensor output. No such list of designated personnel shall include more than 400 individuals at any time. It shall contain the name, gender, date of birth, place of birth, passport number, and function for each individual included. Each State Party shall have the right to amend its list of designated personnel until 30 days after entry into force of this Treaty and once every six months thereafter.

2. In the event that any individual included on the original or any amended list is unacceptable to a State Party reviewing the list, that State Party shall, no later than 30 days after receipt of each list, notify the State Party providing that list that such individual shall not be accepted with respect to the objecting State Party. Individuals not declared unacceptable within that 30-day period shall be deemed accepted. In the event that a State

Party subsequently determines that an individual is unacceptable, that State Party shall so notify the State Party that designated such individual. Individuals who are declared unacceptable shall be removed from the list previously submitted to the objecting State Party.

3. The observed Party shall provide visas and any other documents as required to ensure that each accepted individual may enter and remain on the territory of that State Party for the purpose of carrying out duties relating to the conduct of observation flights, including monitoring the processing of the sensor output. Such visas and any other necessary documents shall be provided either:
(A) no later than 30 days after the individual is deemed to be accepted, in which case the visa shall be valid for a period of no less than 24 months; or
(B) no later than one hour after the arrival of the individual at the point of entry, in which case the visa shall be valid for the duration of that individual?s duties; or
(C) at any other time, by mutual agreement of the States Parties involved.

SECTION II. PRIVILEGES AND IMMUNITIES

1. In order to exercise their functions effectively, for the purpose of implementing this Treaty and not for their personal benefit, personnel designated in accordance with the provisions of Section I, paragraph 1 of this Article shall be accorded the privileges and immunities enjoyed by diplomatic agents pursuant to Article 29; Article 30, paragraph 2; Article 31, paragraphs 1, 2 and 3; and Articles 34 and 35 of the Vienna Convention on Diplomatic Relations of 18 April 1961, hereinafter referred to as the Vienna Convention. In addition, designated personnel shall be accorded the privileges enjoyed by diplomatic agents pursuant to Article 36, paragraph 1, subparagraph (b) of the Vienna Convention, except in relation to articles, the import or export of which is prohibited by law or controlled by quarantine regulations.

2. Such privileges and immunities shall be accorded to designated personnel for the entire period between arrival on and departure from the territory of the observed Party, and thereafter with respect to acts

previously performed in the exercise of their official functions. Such personnel shall also, when transiting the territory of other States Parties, be accorded the privileges and immunities enjoyed by diplomatic agents pursuant to Article 40, paragraph 1 of the Vienna Convention.

3. The immunity from jurisdiction may be waived by the observing Party in those cases when it would impede the course of justice and can be waived without prejudice to this Treaty. The immunity of personnel who are not nationals of the observing Party may be waived only by the States Parties of which such personnel are nationals. Waiver must always be express.

4. Without prejudice to their privileges and immunities or the rights of the observing Party set forth in this Treaty, it is the duty of designated personnel to respect the laws and regulations of the observed Party.

5. The transportation means of the personnel shall be accorded the same immunities from search, requisition, attachment or execution as those of a diplomatic mission pursuant to Article 22, paragraph 3 of the Vienna Convention, except as otherwise provided for in this Treaty.

ARTICLE XIV: BENELUX

1. Solely for the purposes of Articles II to IX and Article XI, and of Annexes A to I and Annex K to this Treaty, the Kingdom of Belgium, the Grand Duchy of Luxembourg, and the Kingdom of the Netherlands shall be deemed a single State Party, hereinafter referred to as the Benelux.

2. Without prejudice to the provisions of Article XV, the above-mentioned States Parties may terminate this arrangement by notifying all other States Parties thereof. This arrangement shall be deemed to be terminated on the next 31 December following the 60-day period after such notification.

ARTICLE XV: DURATION AND WITHDRAWAL

1. This Treaty shall be of unlimited duration.
2. A State Party shall have the right to withdraw from this Treaty. A State Party intending to withdraw shall provide notice of its decision to withdraw to either Depositary at least six months in advance of the date of its intended withdrawal and to all other States Parties. The Depositaries shall promptly inform all other States Parties of such notice.

3. In the event that a State Party provides notice of its decision to withdraw from this Treaty in accordance with paragraph 2 of this Article, the Depositaries shall convene a conference of the States Parties no less than 30 days and no more than 60 days after they have received such notice, in order to consider the effect of the withdrawal on this Treaty.

ARTICLE XVI: AMENDMENTS AND PERIODIC REVIEW

1. Each State Party shall have the right to propose amendments to this Treaty. The text of each proposed amendment shall be submitted to either Depositary, which shall circulate it to all States Parties for consideration. If so requested by no less than three States Parties within a period of 90 days after circulation of the proposed amendment, the Depositaries shall convene a conference of the States Parties to consider the proposed amendment. Such a conference shall open no earlier than 30 days and no later than 60 days after receipt of the third of such requests.

2. An amendment to this Treaty shall be subject to the approval of all States Parties, either by providing notification, in writing, of their approval to a Depositary within a period of 90 days after circulation of the proposed amendment, or by expressing their approval at a conference convened in accordance with paragraph 1 of this Article. An amendment so approved shall be subject to ratification in accordance with the provisions of Article XVII, paragraph 1, and shall enter into force 60 days after the deposit of instruments of ratification by the States Parties.

3. Unless requested to do so earlier by no less than three States Parties, the Depositaries shall convene a conference of the States Parties to review the implementation of this Treaty three years after entry into force of this Treaty and at five-year intervals thereafter.

ARTICLE XVII: DEPOSITARIES, ENTRY INTO FORCE AND ACCESSION

1. This Treaty shall be subject to ratification by each State Party in accordance with its constitutional procedures. Instruments of ratification and instruments of accession shall be deposited with the Government of Canada or the Government of the Republic of Hungary or both, hereby designated the Depositaries. This Treaty shall be registered by the Depositaries pursuant to Article 102 of the Charter of the United Nations.

2. This Treaty shall enter into force 60 days after the deposit of 20 instruments of ratification, including those of the Depositaries, and of States Parties whose individual allocation of passive quotas as set forth in Annex A is eight or more.

3. This Treaty shall be open for signature by Armenia, Azerbaijan, Georgia, Kazakhstan, Kirgistan, Moldova, Tajikistan, Turkmenistan and Uzbekistan and shall be subject to ratification by them. Any of these States which do not sign this Treaty before it enters into force in accordance with the provisions of paragraph 2 of this Article may accede to it at any time by depositing an instrument of accession with one of the Depositaries.

4. For six months after entry into force of this Treaty, any other State participating in the Conference on Security and Co-operation in Europe may apply for accession by submitting a written request to one of the Depositaries. The Depositary receiving such a request shall circulate it promptly to all States Parties. The States applying for accession to this Treaty may also, if they so wish, request an allocation of a passive quota and the level of this quota.

5. The matter shall be considered at the next regular meeting of the Open Skies Consultative Commission and decided in due course.

6. Following six months after entry into force of this Treaty, the Open Skies Consultative Commission may consider the accession to this Treaty of any State which, in the judgement of the Commission, is able and willing to contribute to the objectives of this Treaty.

7. For any State which has not deposited an instrument of ratification by the time of entry into force, but which subsequently ratifies or accedes to this Treaty, this Treaty shall enter into force 60 days after the date of deposit of its instrument of ratification or accession.

8. The Depositaries shall promptly inform all States Parties of:
   (A) the date of deposit of each instrument of ratification and the date of entry into force of this Treaty;
   (B) the date of an application for accession, the name of the requesting State and the result of the procedure;
   (C) the date of deposit of each instrument of accession and the date of entry into force of this Treaty for each State that subsequently accedes to it;
   (D) the convening of a conference pursuant to Articles XV and XVI;
   (E) any withdrawal in accordance with Article XV and its effective date;
   (F) the date of entry into force of any amendments to this Treaty; and
   (G) any other matters of which the Depositaries are required by this Treaty to inform the States Parties.

ARTICLE XVIII: PROVISIONAL APPLICATION AND PHASING OF IMPLEMENTATION OF THE TREATY

In order to facilitate the implementation of this Treaty, certain of its provisions shall be provisionally applied and others shall be implemented in phases.

SECTION I. PROVISIONAL APPLICATION

1. Without detriment to Article XVII, the signatory States shall provisionally apply the following provisions of this Treaty:
   (A) Article VI, Section I, paragraph 4;
   (B) Article X, paragraphs 1, 2, 3, 6 and 7;
   (C) Article XI;
   (D) Article XIII, Section I, paragraphs 1 and 2;
   (E) Article XIV; and
   (F) Annex L, Section I.

2. This provisional application shall be effective for a period of 12 months from the date when this Treaty is opened for signature. In the event that this Treaty does not enter into force before the period of provisional application expires, that period may be extended if all the signatory States so decide. The period of provisional application shall in any event terminate when this Treaty enters into force. However, the States Parties may then decide to

extend the period of provisional application in respect of signatory States that have not ratified this Treaty.

SECTION II. PHASING OF IMPLEMENTATION

1. After entry into force, this Treaty shall be implemented in phases in accordance with the provisions set forth in this Section. The provisions of paragraphs 2 to 6 of this Section shall apply during the period from entry into force of this Treaty until 31 December of the third year following the year during which entry into force takes place.

2. Notwithstanding the provisions of Article IV, paragraph 1, no State Party shall during the period specified in paragraph 1 above use an infra-red line-scanning device if one is installed on an observation aircraft, unless otherwise agreed between the observing and observed Parties. Such sensors shall not be subject to certification in accordance with Annex D. If it is difficult to remove such sensor from the observation aircraft, then it shall have covers or other devices that inhibit its operation in accordance with the provisions of Article IV, paragraph 4 during the conduct of observation flights.

3. Notwithstanding the provisions of Article IV, paragraph 9, no State Party shall, during the period specified in paragraph 1 of this Section, be obliged to provide an observation aircraft equipped with sensors from each sensor category, at the maximum capability and in the numbers specified in Article IV, paragraph 2, provided that the observation aircraft is equipped with:
(A) a single optical panoramic camera; or
(B) not less than a pair of optical framing cameras.

4. Notwithstanding the provisions of Annex B, Section II, paragraph 2, subparagraph (A) to this Treaty, data recording media shall be annotated with data in accordance with existing practice of States Parties during the period specified in paragraph 1 of this Section.

5. Notwithstanding the provisions of Article VI, Section I, paragraph 1, no State Party during the period specified in paragraph 1 of this Section shall have the right to be provided with an aircraft capable of achieving any specified unrefuelled range.

6. During the period specified in paragraph 1 of this Section, the distribution of active quotas shall be established in accordance with the provisions of Annex A, Section II, paragraph 2 to this Treaty.

7. Further phasing in respect of the introduction of additional categories of sensors or improvements to the capabilities of existing categories of sensors shall be addressed by the Open Skies Consultative Commission in accordance with the provisions of Article IV, paragraph 3 concerning such introduction or improvement.

ARTICLE XIX: AUTHENTIC TEXTS

The originals of this Treaty, of which the English, French, German, Italian, Russian and Spanish texts are equally authentic, shall be deposited in the archives of the Depositaries. Duly certified copies of this Treaty shall be transmitted by the Depositaries to all the States Parties.

ANNEX A
QUOTAS AND MAXIMUM FLIGHT DISTANCES
SECTION I. ALLOCATION OF PASSIVE QUOTAS

1. The allocation of individual passive quotas is set forth as follows and shall be effective only for those States Parties having ratified the Treaty:

For the Federal Republic of Germany	12
For the United States of America	42
For the Republic of Belarus and the Russian Federation group of States Parties	42
For Benelux	6
For the Republic of Bulgaria	4
For Canada	12
For the Kingdom of Denmark	6
For the Kingdom of Spain	4
For the French Republic	12
For the United Kingdom of Great Britain and Northern Ireland	12
For the Hellenic Republic	4
For the Republic of Hungary	4
For the Republic of Iceland	4
For the Italian Republic	12
For the Kingdom of Norway	7
For the Republic of Poland	6
For the Portuguese Republic	2
For Romania	6
For the Czech and Slovak Federal Republic	4
For the Republic of Turkey	12
For Ukraine	12

2. In the event that an additional State ratifies or accedes to the Treaty in accordance with the provisions of Article XVII and Article X, paragraph 4, subparagraph (C), and taking into account Article X, paragraph 4, subparagraph (D), an allocation of passive quotas to such a State shall be considered during the regular session of the Open Skies Consultative Commission following the date of deposit of its instrument of ratification or accession.

SECTION II. FIRST DISTRIBUTION OF ACTIVE QUOTAS FOR OBSERVATION FLIGHTS
[deleted]

SECTION III. MAXIMUM FLIGHT DISTANCES OF OBSERVATION FLIGHTS
The maximum flight distances of observation flights over the territories of observed Parties commencing from each Open Skies airfield are as follows:

The Federal Republic of Germany
WUNSTORF	1,200 kilometres
LANDSBERG-LECH	1,200 kilometres

The United States of America
WASHINGTON-DULLES	4,900 kilometres
TRAVIS AFB	4,000 kilometres
ELMENDORF AFB	3,000 kilometres
LINCOLN-MUNICIPAL	4,800 kilometres

The Republic of Belarus and the Russian Federation group of States Parties
KUBINKA	5,000 kilometres
ULAN UDE	5,000 kilometres
VORKUTA	6,500 kilometres
MAGADAN	6,500 kilometres

Benelux
ZAVENTEM/MELSBROEK	945 kilometres

The Republic of Bulgaria
SOFIA	660 kilometres
BURGAS	660 kilometres

Canada
OTTAWA	5,000 kilometres
IQALUIT	6,000 kilometres
YELLOWKNIFE	5,000 kilometres

The Kingdom of Denmark
Metropolitan	800 kilometres
FAROE ISLANDS	250 kilometres
GREENLAND	5,600 kilometres

The Kingdom of Spain
GETAFE	1,300 kilometres
GANDO	750 kilometres
VALENCIA	1,300 kilometres
VALLADOLID	1,300 kilometres
MORON	1,300 kilometres

The French Republic
ORLEANS-BRICY	1,400 kilometres
NICE-COTE D?AZUR	800 kilometres
TOULOUSE-BLAGNAC	700 kilometres

The United Kingdom of Great Britain and Northern Ireland
BRIZE NORTON	1,150 kilometres
SCAMPTON	1,150 kilometres
LEUCHARS	1,150 kilometres
with SCILLY ISLANDS	1,500 kilometres
with SHETLAND ISLANDS	1,500 kilometres

The Hellenic Republic
THESSALONIKI	900 kilometres
ELEFSIS	900 kilometres
with CRETE, KARPATHOS, RHODES, KOS ISLANDS	1,100 kilometres

The Republic of Hungary
BUDAPEST-FERIHEGY	860 kilometres

The Republic of Iceland
1,500 kilometres

The Italian Republic
MILANO-MALPENSA	1,130 kilometres
PALERMO-PUNTA RAISI	1,400 kilometres

The Kingdom of Norway
OSLO-GARDERMOEN	1,700 kilometres
TROMSOE-LANGNES	1,700 kilometres

The Republic of Poland
WARSZAWA-OKECIE	1,400 kilometres

The Portuguese Republic
LISBOA	1,200 kilometres
Sta. MARIA	1,700 kilometres
PORTO SANTO	1,030 kilometres

Romania
BUCHAREST-OTOPENI	900 kilometres
TIMISOARA	900 kilometres
BACAU	900 kilometres

The Czech and Slovak Federal Republic
PRAHA	600 kilometres
BRATISLAVA	700 kilometres
KOSICE	400 kilometres

The Republic of Turkey
ESKISEHIR	1,500 kilometres
DIYARBAKIR	1,500 kilometres

Ukraine
BORISPOL	2,100 kilometres

[Additional annexes not included]

Treaty Between the United States of America and the Union of Soviet Socialist Republics on Underground Nuclear Explosions for Peaceful Purposes

Signed at Washington and Moscow May 28, 1976
Entered into force December 11, 1990

The United States of America and the Union of Soviet Socialist Republics, hereinafter referred to as the Parties,

Proceeding from a desire to implement Article III of the Treaty Between the United States of America and the Union of Soviet Socialist Republics on the Limitation of Underground Nuclear Weapon Tests, which calls for the earliest possible conclusion of an agreement on underground nuclear explosions for peaceful purposes,

Reaffirming their adherence to the objectives and principles of the Treaty Banning Nuclear Weapon Tests in the Atmosphere, in Outer Space and Under Water, the Treaty on Non-Proliferation of Nuclear Weapons, and the Treaty on the Limitation of Underground Nuclear Weapon Tests, and their determination to observe strictly the provisions of these international agreements,

Desiring to assure that underground nuclear explosions for peaceful purposes shall not be used for purposes related to nuclear weapons,

Desiring that utilization of nuclear energy be directed only toward peaceful purposes,

Desiring to develop appropriately cooperation in the field of underground nuclear explosions for peaceful purposes,

Have agreed as follows:

ARTICLE I

1. The Parties enter into this Treaty to satisfy the obligations in Article III of the Treaty on the Limitation of Underground Nuclear Weapon Tests, and assume additional obligations in accordance with the provisions of this Treaty.
2. This Treaty shall govern all underground nuclear explosions for peaceful purposes conducted by the Parties after March 31, 1976.

ARTICLE II

For the purposes of this Treaty:

(a) "explosion" means any individual or group underground nuclear explosion for peaceful purposes;

(b) "explosive" means any device, mechanism or system for producing an individual explosion;

(c) "group explosion" means two or more individual explosions for which the time interval between successive individual explosions does not exceed five seconds and for which the emplacement points of all explosives can be interconnected by straight line segments, each of which joins two emplacement points and each of which does not exceed 40 kilometers.

ARTICLE III

1. Each Party, subject to the obligations assumed under this Treaty and other international agreements, reserves the right to:
   (a) carry out explosions at any place under its jurisdiction or control outside the geographical boundaries of test sites specified under the provisions of the Treaty on the Limitation of Underground Nuclear Weapon Tests; and
   (b) carry out, participate or assist in carrying out explosions in the territory of another State at the request of such other State.
2. Each Party undertakes to prohibit, to prevent and not to carry out at any place under its jurisdiction or control, and further undertakes not to carry out, participate or assist in carrying out anywhere:
   (a) any individual explosion having a yield exceeding 150 kilotons;
   (b) any group explosion:
      (1) having an aggregate yield exceeding 150 kilotons except in ways that will permit identification of each individual explosion and determination of the yield of each individual explosion in the group in accordance with the provisions of Article IV of and the Protocol to this Treaty;
      (2) having an aggregate yield exceeding one and one-half megatons;
   (c) any explosion which does not carry out a peaceful application;
   (d) any explosion except in compliance with the provisions of the Treaty Banning Nuclear Weapon Tests in the Atmosphere, in Outer Space and Under Water, the Treaty on the Non-Proliferation of Nuclear Weapons, and other international agreements entered into by that Party.
3. The question of carrying out any individual explosion having a yield exceeding the yield

specified in paragraph 2(a) of this article will be considered by the Parties at an appropriate time to be agreed.

ARTICLE IV

1. For the purpose of providing assurance of compliance with the provisions of this Treaty, each Party shall:
   (a) use national technical means of verification at its disposal in a manner consistent with generally recognized principles of international law; and
   (b) provide to the other Party information and access to sites of explosions and furnish assistance in accordance with the provisions set forth in the Protocol to this Treaty.
2. Each Party undertakes not to interfere with the national technical means of verification of the other Party operating in accordance with paragraph 1(a) of this article, or with the implementation of the provisions of paragraph 1(b) of this article.

ARTICLE V

1. To promote the objectives and implementation of the provisions of this Treaty, the Parties shall establish promptly a Joint Consultative Commission within the framework of which they will:
   (a) consult with each other, make inquiries and furnish information in response to such inquiries, to assure confidence in compliance with the obligations assumed;
   (b) consider questions concerning compliance with the obligations assumed and related situations which may be considered ambiguous;
   (c) consider questions involving unintended interference with the means for assuring compliance with the provisions of this Treaty;
   (d) consider changes in technology or other new circumstances which have a bearing on the provisions of this Treaty; and
   (e) consider possible amendments to provisions governing underground nuclear explosions for peaceful purposes.
2. The Parties through consultation shall establish, and may amend as appropriate, Regulations for the Joint Consultative Commission governing procedures, composition and other relevant matters.

ARTICLE VI

1. The Parties will develop cooperation on the basis of mutual benefit, equality, and reciprocity in various areas related to carrying out underground nuclear explosions for peaceful purposes.
2. The Joint Consultative Commission will facilitate this cooperation by considering specific areas and forms of cooperation which shall be determined by agreement between the Parties in accordance with their constitutional procedures.
3. The Parties will appropriately inform the International Atomic Energy Agency of results of their cooperation in the field of underground nuclear explosions for peaceful purposes.

ARTICLE VII

1. Each Party shall continue to promote the development of the international agreement or agreements and procedures provided for in Article V of the Treaty on the Non-Proliferation of Nuclear Weapons, and shall provide appropriate assistance to the International Atomic Energy Agency in this regard.
2. Each Party undertakes not to carry out, participate or assist in the carrying out of any explosion in the territory of another State unless that State agrees to the implementation in its territory of the international observation and procedures contemplated by Article V of the Treaty on the Non-Proliferation of Nuclear Weapons and the provisions of Article IV of and the Protocol to this Treaty, including the provision by that State of the assistance necessary for such implementation and of the privileges and immunities specified in the Protocol.

ARTICLE VIII

1. This Treaty shall remain in force for a period of five years, and it shall be extended for

successive five-year periods unless either Party notifies the other of its termination no later than six months prior to its expiration. Before the expiration of this period the Parties may, as necessary, hold consultations to consider the situation relevant to the substance of this Treaty. However, under no circumstances shall either Party be entitled to terminate this Treaty while the Treaty on the Limitation of Underground Nuclear Weapon Tests remains in force.

2. Termination of the Treaty on the Limitation of Underground Nuclear Weapon Tests shall entitle either Party to withdraw from this Treaty at any time.

3. Each Party may propose amendments to this Treaty. Amendments shall enter into force on the day of the exchange of instruments of ratification of such amendments.

ARTICLE IX

1. This Treaty, including the Protocol which forms an integral part hereof, shall be subject to ratification in accordance with the constitutional procedures of each Party. This Treaty shall enter into force on the day of the exchange of instruments of ratification which exchange shall take place simultaneously with the exchange of instruments of ratification of the Treaty on the Limitation of Underground Nuclear Weapon Tests.

2. This Treaty shall be registered pursuant to Article 102 of the Charter of the United Nations.

DONE at Washington and Moscow, on May 28, 1976, in duplicate, in the English and Russian languages, both texts being equally authentic.

FOR THE UNITED STATES OF AMERICA:
GERALD R. FORD
The President of the United States of America
FOR THE UNION OF SOVIET SOCIALIST RE-
PUBLICS:
L. BREZHNEV
General Secretary of the Central Committee of the CPSU

Agreement Between the Government of the United States of America and the Government of the Russian Federation Concerning Cooperation Regarding Plutonium Production Reactors

The Government of the United States of America and the Government of the Russian Federation, hereinafter referred to as the *Parties*

Expressing their desire to cooperate with each other to elaborate measures designed to prevent the accumulation of excessive stocks of plutonium and to reduce them in the future;

Taking into account the intent of the Government of the Russian Federation to take out of operation three presently operating reactors that produce plutonium and that provide heat and electricity to regions where they are located, and to create alternative sources of heat and electricity;

Taking into account the shutdown by the United States of America of all of its plutonium production reactors as of 1989;

Have agreed as follows:

ARTICLE I

1. All reactors listed in Annex I to this Agreement, which is an integral part of this Agreement, have ceased operations. These reactors shall not resume operation.

2. All reactors listed in Annex II to this Agreement, which is an integral part of this Agreement, shall cease by December 31, 2000, their production of non-reactor-grade plutonium by undergoing modification. After the completion of modifications, these reactors shall permanently cease operation at the end of their normal lifetime, consistent with prudent safety considerations.

ARTICLE II

1. The U.S. Party shall provide, subject to the availability of appropriated funds for this purpose, and subject to the Agreement between the Department of Defense of the United States of America and the Ministry of the Russian Federation for Atomic Energy Concerning the Modification of the Operating Seversk (Tomsk Region) and Zheleznogorsk

(Krasnoyarsk Region) Plutonium Production Reactors, which will be governed as specified in Article 1, paragraph 4, of that agreement and overseen as specified in Article VI of that agreement, step-by-step funding for cooperative implementation of the reactor modifications specified in Article I, paragraph 2, of this Agreement.

2. Provision of funds as described in paragraph 1 of this Article will be based on the achievement of cooperation project milestones to be agreed between the U.S. Party and the Russian Party. In the event that the Russian Party should fail to achieve an agreed cooperation project milestone or the U.S. Party should fail to provide an agreed level of assistance, including funding, to support an agreed cooperation project milestone, either Party may request consultations to determine how best to achieve the objectives of this Agreement under those circumstances. These consultations shall begin within 30 days of such a request. If after ISO days from the beginning of consultations, the Parties do not reach agreement, each Party shall have the right to suspend, until such agreement is achieved, implementation of this Agreement by sending the other Party, through diplomatic channels, appropriate written notification. The consultations specified in this paragraph shall continue until agreement is reached or, if this is not possible, until the termination of this Agreement, using the procedures provided for in Article XI, paragraph 4, of this Agreement.

ARTICLE III

For the purposes of this Agreement, the cessation of plutonium production specified in Article I, paragraph 2, will require the cessation of production by the reactors listed in Annex II to this Agreement of spent fuel containing plutonium whose combined Pu-240 plus Pu-238 isotopic concentration is less than 20 percent of total Pu, averaged over the total fuel discharged in any one batch. Once each reactor listed in Annex II to this Agreement is modified, it will utilize an alternative type of fuel including uranium derived from dismantled nuclear weapons.

ARTICLE IV

The plutonium produced after entry into force of this Agreement in the reactors identified in Annex II to this Agreement, and any high-enriched uranium recovered from spent fuel discharged from the modified reactors, shall not be used in nuclear weapons.

ARTICLE V

Procedures necessary to assure compliance with the obligations provided for in Articles I, III, and IV of this Agreement are contained in Annex III, which is an integral part of this Agreement.

ARTICLE VI

1. In order to prevent access to it by people and organizations not participating in the implementation of this Agreement, information transmitted under this Agreement may be considered as sensitive by the Parties. Such information must be clearly designated and marked. The Party transmitting the information shall designate information as sensitive in accordance with its internal laws and regulations.
2. The Party receiving the information shall handle this information as sensitive.
3. Sensitive information shall be handled in accordance with the laws and regulations of the Party receiving the information, and this information shall not be disclosed or transmitted to a third Party not participating in implementation of this Agreement without the clearly expressed consent of the Party transmitting the information. According to the regulations of the United States, such information shall be treated as foreign government information provided in confidence and shall be protected appropriately. According to the regulations of the Russian Federation, such information shall be treated as official information with limited distribution and shall be protected appropriately.
4. The Parties shall assure effective protection of and allocation of rights to intellectual property transmitted or created under this Agreement, as set forth in this Article and in Annex IV to this Agreement, which forms an integral part of this Agreement.

5. Information transmitted under this Agreement must be used solely for the purposes established by this Agreement in accordance with the laws, regulations, and mutual interests of the States represented by the Parties.

6. The number of people having access to sensitive information must be limited to the number .necessary to implement this Agreement and other programs associated with this Agreement.

(a) To review implementation of this Agreement, to include resolution, by mutual agreement, of any implementation issues;

(b) To consider questions concerning implementation and effectiveness of monitoring procedures;

(c) To resolve any disputes that may arise regarding compliance with the provisions of this Agreement or its Annexes or Subsidiary Arrangements; and

(d) To discuss and, if necessary, prepare recommendations concerning any amendments to this Agreement or its Annexes or Subsidiary Arrangements, as well as proposals for resolving any disputes that cannot be resolved in the JICC.

ARTICLE VII

In order to ensure the possibility of taking the reactors listed in Annex II to this Agreement out of operation, the Russian Party shall undertake to create alternative sources of thermal and electrical energy to replace these reactors by the time of their final shutdown. To assist this effort, the U.S. Party will encourage private sector participation in the creation of replacement sources of energy. The U.S. Party does not guarantee the participation of the private sector in these activities, and its degree of success in this effort shall not alter in any way the obligations undertaken by the Parties in this Agreement.

ARTICLE X

In the event of conflict between the provisions of this Agreement and any Annexes or Subsidiary Arrangements to this Agreement, the provisions of this Agreement shall prevail.

ARTICLE XI

1. This Agreement shall enter into force upon signature on the same date as the implementing agreement specified in Article II, paragraph 1, of this Agreement.

2. This Agreement may be amended by agreement between the Parties. Any such amendment shall enter into force upon signature.

3. Each of the Subsidiary Arrangements shall be considered to be an integral part of their respective Annex to this Agreement under the condition, however, that they can be changed and added to by agreement between the sides represented by their Executive Agents as they are described according to Article VIII of this Agreement.

4. This Agreement may be terminated by either Party by sending written notice through diplomatic channels of its intent to terminate this Agreement, in which case this Agreement terminates after one year from the date of sending this notification. Termination of this Agreement shall not affect the following:

   a. All the provisions of Article VI shall continue in effect; and

   b. The obligations provided for in Article IV of this Agreement, and the associated compliance

ARTICLE VIII

The Parties shall designate Executive Agents to implement this Agreement and its Annexes and Subsidiary Arrangements as follows: for the U.S. Party, the Executive Agents shall be the Department of Defense for implementation of Article II and the Department of Energy for the implementation of the remainder of the Agreement and its Annexes and Subsidiary Arrangements; for the Russian Party, the Executive Agent shall be the Ministry of the Russian Federation for Atomic Energy. After consultation with the other Party, either Party shall have the right to change its Executive Agent upon 30 days' written notice to the other Party.

ARTICLE IX

To ensure achievement of the objectives and implementation of this Agreement, the Parties hereby establish a Joint Implementation and Compliance Commission (JICC), which shall convene no later than 21 days following the request of either Party, unless otherwise agreed. The tasks of the JICC shall include the following:

procedures, shall continue in effect with respect to plutonium produced at the reactors listed in Annex II to this Agreement between entry into force of this Agreement and the date of its termination. The procedures specified in Annex III of this Agreement cease to be applicable to this plutonium when the plutonium is being used for needs that are not inconsistent with the objectives of this Agreement, as detailed in Annex III.

DONE at Moscow, in duplicate, this twenty-third day of September, 1997, in the English and Russian languages, both texts being equally authentic.

Agreement Between The United States of America and The Union of Soviet Socialist Republics on the Prevention of Nuclear War

Signed at Washington June 22, 1973
Entered into force June 22, 1973

The United States of America and the Union of Soviet Socialist Republics, hereinafter referred to as the Parties,

Guided by the objectives of strengthening world peace and international security, Conscious that nuclear war would have devastating consequences for mankind, Proceeding from the desire to bring about conditions in which the danger of an outbreak of nuclear war anywhere in the world would be reduced and ultimately eliminated,

Proceeding from their obligations under the Charter of the United Nations regarding the maintenance of peace, refraining from the threat or use of force, and the avoidance of war, and in conformity with the agreements to which either Party has subscribed,

Proceeding from the Basic Principles of Relations between the United States of America and the Union of Soviet Socialist Republics signed in Moscow on May 29, 1972,

Reaffirming that the development of relations between the United States of America and the Union of Soviet Socialist Republics is not directed against other countries and their interests,

Have agreed as follows:

ARTICLE I

The United States and the Soviet Union agree that an objective of their policies is to remove the danger of nuclear war and of the use of nuclear weapons.

Accordingly, the Parties agree that they will act in such a manner as to prevent the development of situations capable of causing a dangerous exacerbation of their relations, as to avoid military confrontations, and as to exclude the outbreak of

nuclear war between them and between either of the Parties and other countries.

ARTICLE II

The Parties agree, in accordance with Article I and to realize the objective stated in that Article, to proceed from the premise that each Party will refrain from the threat or use of force against the other Party, against the allies of the other Party and against other countries, in circumstances which may endanger international peace and security. The Parties agree that they will be guided by these considerations in the formulation of their foreign policies and in their actions in the field of international relations.

ARTICLE III

The Parties undertake to develop their relations with each other and with other countries in a way consistent with the purposes of this Agreement.

ARTICLE IV

If at any time relations between the Parties or between either Party and other countries appear to involve the risk of a nuclear conflict, or if relations between countries not parties to this Agreement appear to involve the risk of nuclear war between the United States of America and the Union of Soviet Socialist Republics or between either Party and other countries, the United States and the Soviet Union, acting in accordance with the provisions of this Agreement, shall immediately enter into urgent consultations with each other and make every effort to avert this risk.

ARTICLE V

Each Party shall be free to inform the Security Council of the United Nations, the Secretary General of the United Nations and the Governments of allied or other countries of the progress and outcome of consultations initiated in accordance with Article IV of this Agreement.

ARTICLE VI

Nothing in this Agreement shall affect or impair:

(a) the inherent right of individual or collective self-defense as envisaged by Article 51 of the Charter of the United Nations,*
(b) the provisions of the Charter of the United Nations, including those relating to the maintenance or restoration of international peace and security, and
(c) the obligations undertaken by either Party towards its allies or other countries in treaties, agreements, and other appropriate documents.

ARTICLE VII

This Agreement shall be of unlimited duration.

ARTICLE VIII

This Agreement shall enter into force upon signature.

DONE at Washington on June 22, 1973, in two copies, each in the English and Russian languages, both texts being equally authentic.

FOR THE UNITED STATES OF AMERICA:
RICHARD NIXON
President of the United States of America
FOR THE UNION OF SOVIET SOCIALIST REPUBLICS:
L.I. BREZHNEV
General Secretary of the Central Committee, CPSU

Treaty on the Prohibition of the Emplacement of Nuclear Weapons and Other Weapons of Mass Destruction on the Seabed and the Ocean Floor and in the Subsoil Thereof

Signed at Washington, London, and Moscow February 11, 1971
Ratification advised by U.S. Senate February 15, 1972
Ratified by U.S. President April 26, 1972

Entered into force May 18, 1972

The States Parties to this Treaty,

Recognizing the common interest of mankind in the progress of the exploration and use of the seabed and the ocean floor for peaceful purposes,

Considering that the prevention of a nuclear arms race on the seabed and the ocean floor serves the interests of maintaining world peace, reduces international tensions and strengthens friendly relations among States,

Convinced that this Treaty constitutes a step towards the exclusion of the seabed, the ocean floor and the subsoil thereof from the arms race,

Convinced that this Treaty constitutes a step towards a Treaty on general and complete disarmament under strict and effective international control, and determined to continue negotiations to this end,

Convinced that this Treaty will further the purposes and principles of the Charter of the United Nations, in a manner consistent with the principles of international law and without infringing the freedoms of the high seas,

Have agreed as follows:

ARTICLE I

1. The States Parties to this Treaty undertake not to emplant or emplace on the seabed and the ocean floor and in the subsoil thereof beyond the outer limit of a seabed zone, as defined in article II, any nuclear weapons or any other types of weapons of mass destruction as well as structures, launching installations or any other facilities specifically designed for storing, testing or using such weapons.
2. The undertakings of paragraph 1 of this article shall also apply to the seabed zone referred to in the same paragraph, except that within such seabed zone, they shall not apply either to the coastal State or to the seabed beneath its territorial waters.
3. The States Parties to this Treaty undertake not to assist, encourage or induce any State to carry out activities referred to in paragraph 1 of this article and not to participate in any other way in such actions.

ARTICLE II

For the purpose of this Treaty, the outer limit of the seabed zone referred to in article I shall be coterminous with the twelve-mile outer limit of the zone referred to in part II of the Convention on the Territorial Sea and the

Contiguous Zone, signed at Geneva on April 29, 1958, and shall be measured in accordance with the provisions of part I, section II, of that Convention and in accordance with international law.

ARTICLE III

1. In order to promote the objectives of and insure compliance with the provisions of this Treaty, each State Party to the Treaty shall have the right to verify through observations the activities of other States Parties to the Treaty on the seabed and the ocean floor and in the subsoil thereof beyond the zone referred to in article I, provided that observation does not interfere with such activities.

2. If after such observation reasonable doubts remain concerning the fulfillment of the obligations assumed under the Treaty, the State Party having such doubts and the State Party that is responsible for the activities giving rise to the doubts shall consult with a view to removing the doubts. If the doubts persist, the State Party having such doubts shall notify the other States Parties, and the Parties concerned shall cooperate on such further procedures for verification as may be agreed, including appropriate inspection of objects, structures, installations or other facilities that reasonably may be expected to be of a kind described in article I. The Parties in the region of the activities, including any coastal State, and any other Party so requesting, shall be entitled to participate in such consultation and cooperation. After completion of the further procedures for verification, an appropriate report shall be circulated to other Parties by the Party that initiated such procedures.

3. If the State responsible for the activities giving rise to the reasonable doubts is not identifiable by observation of the object, structure, installation or other facility, the State Party having such doubts shall notify and make appropriate inquiries of States Parties in the region of the activities and of any other State Party. If it is ascertained through these inquiries that a particular State Party is responsible for the activities, that State Party shall consult and cooperate with other Parties as provided in paragraph 2 of this article. If the identity of the State responsible for the activities cannot be ascertained through these inquiries, then further verification procedures, including inspection, may be undertaken by the inquiring State Party, which shall invite the participation of the Parties in the region of the activities, including any coastal State, and of any other Party desiring to cooperate.

4. If consultation and cooperation pursuant to paragraphs 2 and 3 of this article have not removed the doubts concerning the activities and there remains a serious question concerning fulfillment of the obligations assumed under this Treaty, a State Party may, in accordance with the provisions of the Charter of the United Nations, refer the matter to the Security Council, which may take action in accordance with the Charter.

5. Verification pursuant to this article may be undertaken by any State Party using its own means, or with the full or partial assistance of any other State Party, or through appropriate international procedures within the framework of the United Nations and in accordance with its Charter.

6. Verification activities pursuant to this Treaty shall not interfere with activities of other States Parties and shall be conducted with due regard for rights recognized under international law, including the freedoms of the high seas and the rights of coastal States with respect to the exploration and exploitation of their continental shelves.

ARTICLE IV

Nothing in this Treaty shall be interpreted as supporting or prejudicing the position of any State Party with respect to existing international conventions, including the 1958 Convention on the Territorial Sea and the Contiguous Zone, or with respect to rights or claims which such State Party may assert, or with respect to recognition or non-recognition of rights or claims asserted by any other State, related to waters off its coasts, including, *inter alia*, territorial seas and contiguous zones, or to the seabed and the ocean floor, including continental shelves.

ARTICLE V

The Parties to this Treaty undertake to continue negotiations in good faith concerning further measures in the field of disarmament for the prevention of an arms race on the seabed, the ocean floor and the subsoil thereof.

ARTICLE VI

Any State Party may propose amendments to this Treaty. Amendments shall enter into force for each State Party accepting the amendments upon their acceptance by a majority of the States Parties to the Treaty and, thereafter, for each remaining State Party on the date of acceptance by it.

ARTICLE VII

Five years after the entry into force of this Treaty, a conference of Parties to the Treaty shall be held at Geneva, Switzerland, in order to review the operation of this Treaty with a view to assuring that the purposes of the preamble and the provisions of the Treaty are being realized. Such review shall take into account any relevant technological developments. The review conference shall determine, in accordance with the views of a majority of those Parties attending, whether and when an additional review conference shall be convened.

ARTICLE VIII

Each State Party to this Treaty shall in exercising its national sovereignty have the right to withdraw from this Treaty if it decides that extraordinary events related to the subject matter of this Treaty have jeopardized the supreme interests of its country. It shall give notice of such withdrawal to all other States Parties to the Treaty and to the United Nations Security Council three months in advance. Such notice shall include a statement of the extraordinary events it considers to have jeopardized its supreme interests.

ARTICLE IX

The provisions of this Treaty shall in no way affect the obligations assumed by States Parties to the Treaty under international instruments establishing zones free from nuclear weapons.

ARTICLE X

1. This Treaty shall be open for signature to all States. Any State which does not sign the Treaty before its entry into force in accordance with paragraph 3 of this article may accede to it at any time.
2. This Treaty shall be subject to ratification by signatory States. Instruments of ratification and of accession shall be deposited with the Governments of the United States of America, the United Kingdom of Great Britain and Northern Ireland, and the Union of Soviet Socialist Republics, which are hereby designated the Depositary Governments.
3. This Treaty shall enter into force after the deposit of instruments of ratification by twenty-two Governments, including the Governments designated as Depositary Governments of this Treaty.
4. For states whose instruments of ratification or accession are deposited after the entry into force of this Treaty, it shall enter into force on the date of the deposit of their instruments of ratification or accession.
5. The Depositary Governments shall promptly inform the Governments of all signatory and acceding States of the date of each signature, of the date of deposit of each instrument of ratification or of accession, of the date of the entry into force of this Treaty, and of the receipt of other notices.
6. This Treaty shall be registered by the Depositary Governments pursuant to Article 102 of the Charter of the United Nations.

ARTICLE XI

This Treaty, the English, Russian, French, Spanish and Chinese texts of which are equally authentic, shall be deposited in the archives of the Depositary Governments. Duly certified copies of this Treaty shall be transmitted by the Depositary Governments to the Governments of the States signatory and acceding thereto.

IN WITNESS WHEREOF the undersigned, being duly authorized thereto, have signed this Treaty.

DONE in triplicate, at the cities of Washington, London and Moscow, this eleventh day of February, one thousand nine hundred seventy-one.

Treaty Between the United States of America and the Union of Soviet Socialist Republics on the Reduction and Limitation of Strategic Offensive Arms (START I)

The United States of America and the Union of Soviet Socialist Republics, hereinafter referred to as the Parties,

Conscious that nuclear war would have devastating consequences for all humanity, that it cannot be won and must never be fought,

Convinced that the measures for the reduction and limitation of strategic offensive arms and the other obligations set forth in this Treaty will help to reduce the risk of outbreak of nuclear war and strengthen international peace and security,

Recognizing that the interests of the Parties and the interests of international security require the strengthening of strategic stability,

Mindful of their undertakings with regard to strategic offensive arms in Article VI of the Treaty on the Non-Proliferation of Nuclear Weapons of July 1, 1968; Article XI of the Treaty on the Limitation of Anti-Ballistic Missile Systems of May 26, 1972; and the Washington Summit Joint Statement of June 1, 1990, [ABA]

Have agreed as follows:

ARTICLE I

Each Party shall reduce and limit its strategic offensive arms in accordance with the provisions of this Treaty, and shall carry out the other obligations set forth in this Treaty and its Annexes, Protocols, and Memorandum of Understanding.

ARTICLE II

1. Each Party shall reduce and limit its ICBMs and ICBM launchers, SLBMs and SLBM launchers, heavy bombers, ICBM warheads, SLBM warheads, and heavy bomber armaments, so that seven years after entry into force of this Treaty and thereafter, the aggregate numbers, as counted in accordance with Article III of this Treaty, do not exceed:

(a) 1600, for deployed ICBMs and their associated launchers, deployed SLBMs and their associated launchers, and deployed heavy bombers, including 154 for deployed heavy ICBMs and their associated launchers; [RF MOU, Section II] [US MOU, Section II] [Agreed State 33]

(b) 6000, for warheads attributed to deployed ICBMs, deployed SLBMs, and deployed heavy bombers, [RF MOU, Section II] [US MOU, Section II] including: [Agreed State 33] [START II, Art. I,3]

(i) 4900, for warheads attributed to deployed ICBMs and deployed SLBMs; [RF MOU, Section II] [US MOU, Section II] [START II, Art. I,4] [Agreed State 33]

(ii) 1100, for warheads attributed to deployed ICBMs on mobile launchers of ICBMs; [RF MOU, Section II]

(iii) 1540, for warheads attributed to deployed heavy ICBMs. [phased heavy reductions [RF MOU, Section II] ABA

2. Each Party shall implement the reductions pursuant to paragraph 1 of this Article in three phases, so that its strategic offensive arms do not exceed:

(a) by the end of the first phase, that is, no later than 36 months after entry into force of this Treaty, and thereafter, the following aggregate numbers:

(i) 2100, for deployed ICBMs and their associated launchers, deployed SLBMs and their associated launchers, and deployed heavy bombers;

(ii) 9150, for warheads attributed to deployed ICBMs, deployed SLBMs, and deployed heavy bombers;

(iii)b 8050, warheads attributed to deployed ICBMs and deployed SLBMs;

(b) by the end of the second phase, that is, no later than 60 months after entry into force of this Treaty, and thereafter, the following aggregate numbers:

(i) 1900, for deployed ICBMs and their associated launchers, deployed SLBMs and their associated launchers, and deployed heavy bombers;

(ii) 7950, for warheads attributed to deployed ICBMs, deployed SLBMs, and deployed heavy bombers;

(iii) 6750, warheads attributed to deployed ICBMs and deployed SLBMs;

(c) by the end of the third phase, that is, no later than 84 months after entry into force of this Treaty: the aggregate numbers provided for in paragraph 1 of this Article .ABA

3. Each Party shall limit the aggregate throw-weight [RF MOU, Section II] [US MOU Section II] of its deployed ICBMs [RF MOU, Section I] [US MOU Section I] and deployed SLBMs [RF MOU, Section I] [US MOU Section I] so that seven years after entry into force of this Treaty and thereafter such aggregate throw-weight does not exceed 3600 metric tons. ABA [Throw-weight Limits/Provisions for Types of ICBMs and SLBMs]

ARTICLE III

1. For the purposes of counting toward the maximum aggregate limits provided for in subparagraphs 1(a), 2(a)(i), and 2(b)(i) of Article II of this Treaty:

(a) Each deployed ICBM and its associated launcher shall be counted as one unit; each deployed SLBM and its associated launcher; shall be counted as one unit.

(b) Each deployed heavy bombers shall be counted as one unit. ABA

2. For the purposes of counting deployed ICBMs and their associated launchers and deployed SLBMs and their associated launchers

(a) Each deployed launcher of ICBMs and each deployed launcher of SLBMs shall be considered to contain one deployed ICBM or one deployed SLBM, respectively. ABA

(b) If a deployed ICBM has been removed from its launcher and another missile has not been installed in that launcher, such an ICBM removed from its launcher and located at that ICBM base shall continue to be considered to be contained in that launcher. ABA

(c) If a deployed SLBM has been removed from its launcher and another missile has not been installed in that launcher, such an SLBM removed from its launcher shall be considered to be contained in that launcher. Such an SLBM removed from its launcher shall be located only at a facility at which non-deployed SLBMs may be located pursuant to subparagraph 9(a) of Article IV of this Treaty or be in movement to such a facility. ABA

3. For the purposes of this Treaty, including counting ICBMs and SLBMs:

(a) For ICBMs or SLBMs that are maintained, stored, and transported in stages, the first stage of an ICBM or SLBM of a particular type shall be considered to be an ICBM or SLBM of that type. [US MOU Annex F] [RF MOU, Annex F]

(b) For ICBMs or SLBMs that are maintained, stored, and transported as assembled missiles without launch canisters, an assembled missile of a particular type shall be considered to be an ICBM or SLBM of that type. [RF MOU, Annex F]

(c) For ICBMs that are maintained, stored, and transported as assembled missiles in launch canisters, an assembled missile of a particular type, in its launch canister, shall be considered to be an ICBM of that type. [RF MOU, Annex F]

(d) Each launch canister shall be considered to contain an ICBM from the time it first leaves a facility at which an ICBM is installed in it until an ICBM has been launched from it or until an ICBM has been removed from it for elimination. A launch canisters shall not be considered to contain an ICBM if it contains a training model of a missile or has been placed on static display. Launch canisters for ICBMs of a particular type shall be distinguishable from launch canisters for ICBMs of a different type.

4. For the purposes of counting warheads:

(a) The number of warheads attributed to an ICBM or SLBM of each existing type shall be the number specified in the Memorandum of Understanding [RF MOU, Section I] [US MOU, Section I] on the Establishment of the Data Base Relating to this Treaty, hereinafter referred to as the Memorandum of Understanding.

(b) The number of warheads that will be attributed to an ICBM or SLBM of a new type shall be the maximum number of reentry vehicles with which an ICBM or SLBM of that type has been flight-tested. The number of warheads that will be attributed to an ICBM or SLBM of a new type with a front section of an existing design with multiple reentry vehicles, or to an ICBM or SLBM of a new type with one reentry vehicle, shall be no less than the nearest integer that is smaller than the result of dividing 40 percent of the accountable throw-weight of the ICBM or SLBM by the weight of the lightest reentry vehicle flight-tested on an ICBM of SLBM of a new type. In the case of an ICBM or SLBM of a new type with a of warheads that will be attributed to an ICBM of SLBM of a new type with a front section of a fundamentally new design, the question of the applicability of the 40-percent rule to such an ICBM or SLBM shall be subject to agreement within the framework of the Joint Compliance and Inspection Commission. Until agreement has been reached regarding the rule that will apply to such an ICBM or SLBM, the number of warheads that will be attributed to such an ICBM or SLBM shall be the maximum number of reentry vehicles with which an ICBM or SLBM of that type has been flight-tested. The number of new types of ICBMs or SLBMs with a front section of a fundamentally new design shall not exceed two for each Party as long as this Treaty remains in force. [Agreed State 24]

(c) The number of reentry vehicles with which an ICBM or SLBM has been flight-tested shall be considered to be the sum of the number of reentry vehicles actually released during the flight test, plus the number of procedures for dispensing reentry vehicles performed during that same flight test when no reentry vehicle was released. A procedure for dispensing penetration aids shall not be considered to be a procedure for dispensing reentry vehicles, provided that the procedure for dispensing penetration aids differs from a procedure for dispensing reentry vehicles.

(d) Each reentry vehicle of an ICBM or SLBM shall be considered to be one warhead. [Agreed State 3]

(e) For the United States of America, each heavy bomber equipped for long-range nuclear ALCMs, up to a total of 150 such heavy bombers, shall be attributed [MOU US Section I] with ten warheads. Each heavy bomber equipped for long-range nuclear ALCMs in excess of 150 such heavy bombers shall be attributed [MOU US Section I] with a number of warheads equal to the number of long-range nuclear ALCMs for which it is actually equipped. The United States of America shall specify the heavy bombers equipped for long-range nuclear ALCMs that are in excess of 150 such heavy bombers by number, type, variant, and the air bases at which they are based. The number of long-range nuclear ALCMs for which each heavy bomber equipped for long-range nuclear ALCMs in excess of 150 such heavy bombers is considered to be actually equipped shall be the maximum number of long-range nuclear ALCMs for which a heavy bomber of the same type and variant is actually equipped. [category]

(f) For the Union of Soviet Socialist Republics, each heavy bomber equipped for long-range nuclear ALCMs, up to a total of 180 such heavy bombers, shall be attributed [MOU RF Section I] with eight warheads. Each heavy bomber equipped for long-range nuclear ALCMs in excess of 180 such heavy bombers shall be attributed with a number of warheads equal to the number of long-range nuclear ALCMs for which it is actually equipped. The Union of Soviet Socialist Republics shall specify the heavy bombers equipped for long-range nuclear ALCMs that are in excess of 180 such heavy bombers by number, type, variant, and the air bases at which they are based. The number of long-range nuclear ALCMs for which each heavy bomber equipped for long-range nuclear ALCMs in excess of 180 such heavy bombers is considered to be actually equipped shall be the maximum number of long-range nuclear ALCMs for which a heavy bomber of the same type and variant is actually equipped. [category]

(g) Each heavy bomber equipped for nuclear armaments other than long-range nuclear ALCMs [MOU US Annex G] [MOU RF Annex G] shall be attributed [MOU US Section I] [MOU RF Section I] with one warhead. All heavy bombers not equipped for long-range nuclear ALCMs shall be considered to be heavy bombers equipped for nuclear armaments other than long-range nuclear ALCMs, with the exception of heavy bombers equipped for non-nuclear armaments, test heavy bombers, and training heavy bombers. [category] [START II, Art. IV.1,2]

5. Each Party shall have the right to reduce the number of warheads attributed to ICBMs and SLBMs only of existing types, up to an aggregate number of 1250 at any one time. [START MOU, Section III] [MOU RF Section III] [START II Art III. 2 (a)]

(a) Such aggregate number shall consist of the following:

(i)b for the United States of America, the reduction in the number of warheads attributed to the type of ICBM designated by the United States of America as, and known to the Union of Soviet Socialist Republics as, Minuteman III, plus the reduction in the number of warheads attributed to ICBMs and SLBMs of no more than two other existing types; [START MOU, Section III]

(ii) b for the Union of Soviet Socialist Republics, four multiplied by the number of deployed SLBMs designated by the Union of Soviet Socialist Republics as RSM-50, which is known to the United States of America as SS-N-18, [MOU RF Section III] plus the reduction in the number of warheads attributed to ICBMs and SLBMs of no more than two other existing types.

(b) Reductions in the number of warheads attributed to Minuteman III shall be carried out subject to the following:

(i) Minuteman III to which different numbers of warheads are attributed shall not be deployed at the same ICBM base.

(ii) Any such reductions shall be carried out no later than seven years after entry into force of this Treaty.

(iii) The reentry vehicle platform of each Minuteman III to which a reduced number of warheads is attributed shall be destroyed and replaced by a new reentry vehicle platform. [START II Art.III.2(d)]

(c) Reductions in the number of warheads attributed to ICBMs and SLBMs of types other than Minuteman III shall be carried out subject to the following:

(i)b Such reductions shall not exceed 500 warheads at any one time for each Party. [START II Art III.2(b)]

(ii) After a Party has reduced the number of warheads attributed to ICBMs or SLBMs of two existing types, that Party shall not have the right to reduce the number of warheads attributed to ICBMs or SLBMs of any additional type.

(iii) The number of warheads attributed to an ICBM or SLBM shall be reduced by no more than four below the number attributed as of the date of signature of this Treaty. [START II Art III.2(c)]

(iv) ICBMs of the same type, but to which different numbers of warheads are attributed, shall not be deployed at the same ICBM base.

(v) SLBMs of the same type, but to which different numbers of warheads are attributed, shall not be deployed on submarines based at submarine bases adjacent to the waters of the same ocean.

(vi) If the number of warheads attributed to an ICBM or SLBM of a particular type is reduced by more than two, the reentry vehicle platform of each ICBM or SLBM to which such a reduced number of warheads is attributed shall be destroyed and replaced by a new reentry vehicle platform. [START II Art III.2(d)]

(d) A Party shall not have the right to attribute to ICBMs of a new type a number of warheads greater than the smallest number of warheads attributed to any ICBM to which that Party has attributed a reduced number of warheads pursuant to subparagraph (c) of this paragraph. A Party shall not have the right to attribute to

SLBMs of a new type a number of warheads greater than the smallest number of warheads attributed to any SLBM to which that Party has attributed a reduced number of warheads pursuant to subparagraph (c) of this paragraph.

6. Newly constructed strategic offensive arms shall begin to be subject to the limitations provided for in this Treaty as follows:

(a) an ICBM, when it first leaves a production facility;

(b) a mobile launcher of ICBMs, when it first leaves a production facility for mobile launchers of ICBMs;

(c) a silo launcher of ICBMs, when excavation for that launcher has been completed and the pouring of concrete for the silo has been completed, or 12 months after the excavation begins, whichever occurs earlier;

(d) for the purpose of counting a deployed ICBM and its associated launcher, a silo launchers of ICBMs shall be considered to contain a deployed ICBM when excavation for that launcher has been completed and the pouring of concrete for the silo has been completed, or 12 months after the excavation begins, whichever occurs earlier, and a mobile launcher of ICBMs shall be considered to contain a deployed ICBM when it arrives at a maintenance facility, [Def 19] except for the non-deployed mobile launchers of ICBMs provided for in subparagraph 2(b) of Article IV of this Treaty, or when it leaves an ICBM loading facility;

(e) an SLBM, when it first leaves a production facility;

(f) an SLBM launcher, when the submarine on which that launcher is installed is first launched;

(g) for the purpose of counting a deployed SLBM and its associated launcher, an SLBM launcher shall be considered to contain a deployed SLBM when the submarine on which that launcher is installed is first launched; [Def 18]

(h) a heavy bomber or former heavy bomber, when its airframe is first brought out of the shop, plant, or building in which components of a heavy bomber or former heavy bomber are assembled to produce complete airframes; or when its airframe is first brought out of the shop, plant, or building in which existing bomber airframes are converted to heavy bomber or former heavy bomber airframes. [Def 14] [Def 82 (d)] [Agreed State 12]

7. ICBM launchers and SLBM launchers that have been converted to launch an ICBM or SLBM, respectively, of a different type shall not be capable of launching an ICBM or SLBM of the previous type. Such converted launchers shall be considered to be launchers of ICBMs or SLBMs of that different type as follows:

(a) a silo launchers of ICBMs, when an ICBM of a different type or a training model of a missile of a different type is first installed in that launcher, or when the silo door is reinstalled, whichever occurs first; [Notocol IV.3]

(b) a mobile launcher of ICBMs, as agreed within the framework of the Joint Compliance and Inspection Commission;

(c) an SLBM launcher, when all launchers on the submarine on which that launcher is installed have been converted to launch an SLBM of that different type and that submarine begins sea trials, that is, when that submarine first operates under its own power away from the harbor or port in which the conversion of launchers was performed. [Notocol V.4]

8. Heavy bombers that have been converted into heavy bombers of a different category or into former heavy bombers shall be considered to be heavy bombers of that different category or former heavy bombers as follows:

(a) a heavy bomber equipped for nuclear armaments other than long-range nuclear ALCMs converted into a heavy bomber equipped for long-range nuclear ALCMs, when it is first brought out of the shop, plant, or building where it was equipped for long-range nuclear ALCMs; [US MOU Annex G, (I), (II), (III) [RF MOU Annex G, (i), (ii)]

(b) a heavy bomber of one category converted into a heavy bomber of another category provided for in paragraph 9 of Section VI of the Protocol on Procedures Governing the Conversion or Elimination of the Items Subject to this Treaty, hereinafter referred to as the Conversion or Elimination Protocol, or into a former heavy bomber, when the inspection conducted pursuant to paragraph 13 of Section VI of the Conversion or Elimination Protocol is completed or, if such an inspection is not conducted, when the 20-day period provided for in paragraph 13 of Section VI of the Conversion or Elimination Protocol expires.

9. For the purposes of this Treaty:

(a) A ballistic missile of a type developed and tested solely to intercept and counter objects not located on the surface of the Earth shall not be considered to be a ballistic missile to which the limitations provided for in this Treaty apply.

(b) If a ballistic missile has been flight-tested or deployed for weapon delivery, all ballistic missiles of that type shall be considered to be weapon-delivery vehicles.

(c) If a cruise missile has been flight-tested or deployed for weapon delivery, all cruise missiles of that type shall be considered to be weapon-delivery vehicles.

(d) If a launcher, other than a soft-site launcher, has contained an ICBM or SLBM of a particular type, it shall be considered to be a launcher of ICBMs or SLBMs of that type. If a launcher, other than a soft-site launcher, has been converted into a launcher of ICBMs or SLBMs of a different type, it shall be considered to be a launcher of ICBMs or SLBMs of the type for which it has been converted.

(e) If a heavy bomber is equipped for long-range nuclear ALCMs, all heavy bombers of that type shall be considered to be equipped for long-range nuclear ALCMs, except those that are not so equipped and are distinguishable from heavy bombers of the same type equipped for long-range nuclear ALCMs. If long-range nuclear ALCMs have not been flight-tested from any heavy bomber of a particular type, no heavy bomber of that type shall be considered to be equipped for long-range nuclear ALCMs. Within the same type, a heavy bomber equipped for long-range nuclear ALCMs, a heavy bomber equipped for nuclear armaments other than long-range nuclear ALCMs, a heavy bomber equipped for non-nuclear armaments, a training heavy bomber, and a former heavy bomber shall be distinguishable from one another. [category] [US MOU Annex G, (I), (II), (III)] [RF MOU Annex G, (i), (ii)]

(f) Any long-range ALCM of a type, any one of which has been initially flight-tested from a heavy bomber on or before December 31, 1988, shall be considered to be a long-range nuclear ALCM. Any long-range ALCM of a type, any one of which has been initially flight-tested from a heavy bomber after December 31, 1988, shall not be considered to be a long-range nuclear ALCM if it is a long-range non-nuclear ALCM and is distinguishable from long-range nuclear ALCMs. Long-range non-nuclear ALCMs not so distinguishable shall be considered to be long-range nuclear ALCMs. [TACIT RAINBOW] [TSSAM Statements]

(g) Mobile launchers of ICBMs of each new type of ICBM shall be distinguishable from mobile launchers of ICBMs of existing types of ICBMs and from mobile launchers of ICBMs of other new type of ICBMs. Such new launchers, with their associated missiles installed, shall be distinguishable from mobile launchers of ICBMs of existing types of ICBMs with their associated missiles installed, and from mobile launchers of ICBMs of other new types of ICBMs with their associated missiles installed. [RF MOU Annex F] [US MOU Annex F] [Agreed State 19]

(h) Mobile launchers of ICBMs converted into launchers of ICBMs of another type of ICBM shall be distinguishable from mobile launchers of ICBMs of the previous type of ICBM. Such converted launchers, with their associated missiles installed, shall be distinguishable from mobile launchers of ICBMs of the previous type of ICBM with their associated missiles installed. Conversion of mobile launchers of ICBMs shall be carried out in accordance with procedures to be agreed within the framework of the Joint Compliance and Inspection Commission. [Agreed State 19]

10. As of the date of signature of this Treaty:

(a) Existing types of ICBMs and SLBMs are:

(i) b for the United States of America, the types of missiles designated by the United States of America as Minuteman II, Minuteman III, Peacekeeper, Poseidon, Trident I, and Trident II, which are known to the Union of Soviet Socialist Republics as Minuteman II, Minuteman III, MX, Poseidon, Trident I, and Trident II, respectively; [US MOU Section I] [US MOU Annex F]

(ii) b for the Union of Soviet Socialist Republics, the types of missiles designated by the Union of Soviet Socialist Republics as RS-10, RS-12, RS-16, RS-20, RS-18, RS-22, RS-12M, RSM-25, RSM-40, RSM-50, RSM-52, and RSM-54, which are known to the United States of America as SS-11, SS-13, SS-17, SS-18, SS-19, SS-24, SS-25, SS-N-6, SS-N-8, SS-N-18, SS-N-20, and SS-N-23, respectively. [RF MOU Section I] [RF MOU, Annex F] [RF MOU Annex I]

(b) Existing types of ICBMs for mobile launchers of ICBMs are:

(i) for the United States of America, the type of missile designated by the United States of America as Peacekeeper, which is known to the Union of Soviet Socialist Republics as MX; [US MOU Annex F]

(ii) for the Union of Soviet Socialist Republics, the types of missiles designated by the Union of Soviet Socialist Republics as RS-22 and RS-12M, which are known to the United States of America as SS-24 and SS-25, respectively. [RF MOU, Annex F]

(c) Former types of ICBMs and SLBMs are the types of missiles designated by the United States of America as, and known to the Union of Soviet Socialist Republics as, Minuteman I and Polaris A-3.

(d) Existing types of heavy bombers are:

(i) for the United States of America, the types of bombers designated by the United States of America as, and known to the Union of Soviet Socialist Republics as, B-52, B-1, and B-2; [US MOU Annex G]

(ii) for the Union of Soviet Socialist Republics, the types of bombers designated by the Union of Soviet Socialist Republics as Tu-95 and Tu-160, which are known to the United States of America as Bear and Blackjack, respectively. [RF MOU, Annex G] [Soviet TU-22M Declaration]

(e) Existing types of long-range nuclear ALCMs are:

(i) for the United States of America, the types of long-range nuclear ALCMs designated by the United States of America as, and known to the Union of Soviet Socialist Republics as, AGM-86B and AGM-129; [US MOU Annex H]

(ii) for the Union of Soviet Socialist Republics, the types of long-range nuclear ALCMs designated by the Union of Soviet Socialist Republics as RKV-500A and RKV-500B, which are known to the United States of America as AS-15 A and AS-15 B, respectively. [RF MOU, Annex H]

[Nuclear SLCM Policy Declarations]

ARTICLE IV

1. For ICBMs and SLBMs:

(a) Each Party shall limit the aggregate number of non-deployed ICBMs for mobile launchers of ICBMs to no more than 250. Within this limit, the number of non-deployed ICBMs for rail-mobile launchers of ICBMs shall not exceed 125. [RF MOU, Section IV] [US MOU Section IV] [Agreed State 37]

(b) Each Party shall limit the number of non-deployed ICBMs at a maintenance facility of an ICBM base for mobile launchers of ICBMs to no more than two ICBMs of each type specified for that ICBM base. Non-deployed ICBMs for mobile launchers of ICBMs located at a maintenance facilityshall be stored separately from non-deployed mobile launchers of ICBMs located at that maintenance facility.

(c) Each Party shall limit the number of non-deployed ICBMs and sets of ICBM emplacement equipment at an ICBM base for silo launchers of ICBMs to no more than:

(i) two ICBMs of each type specified for that ICBM base and six sets of ICBM emplacement equipment for each type of ICBM specified for that ICBM base; or [RF MOU Annex A] [US MOU, Annex A]

(ii) four ICBMs of each type specified for that ICBM base and two sets of ICBM emplacement equipment for each type of ICBM specified for that ICBM base. [RF MOU Annex A] [US MOU, Annex A]

(d) Each Party shall limit the aggregate number of ICBMs and SLBMs located at test ranges to no more than 35 during the seven-year period after entry into force of this Treaty. Thereafter, the aggregate number of ICBMs and SLBMs located at test ranges shall not exceed 25. [RF MOU, Section IV] [US MOU Section IV] [Agreed State 37]

2. For ICBM launchers and SLBM launchers:

(a) Each Party shall limit the aggregate number of non-deployed mobile launchers of ICBMs to no more than 110. Within this limit, the number of non-deployed rail-mobile launchers of ICBMs shall not exceed 18. [RF MOU, Section IV] [US MOU Section IV]

(b) Each Party shall limit the number of non-deployed mobile launchers of ICBMs located at the maintenance facility of each ICBM base for mobile launchers of ICBMs to no more than two such ICBM launchers of each type of ICBM specified for that ICBM base. [RF MOU Annex A]

(c) Each Party shall limit the number of non-deployed mobile launchers of ICBMs located at training facilities for ICBMs to no more than 40. Each such

launcher may contain only a training model of a missile. Non-deployed mobile launchers of ICBMs that contain training models of missiles shall not be located outside a training facility. [RF MOU, Section IV] [US MOU Section IV]

(d) Each Party shall limit the aggregate number of test launchers to no more than 45 during the seven-year period after entry into force of this Treaty. Within this limit, the number of fixed test launchers shall not exceed 25, and the number of mobile test launchers shall not exceed 20. Thereafter, the aggregate number of test launchers shall not exceed 40. Within this limit, the number of fixed test launchers shall not exceed 20, and the number of mobile test launchers shall not exceed 20. [RF MOU, Section IV] [US MOU Section IV] [Agreed State 37(h)]

(e) Each Party shall limit the aggregate number of silo training launchers and mobile training launchers to no more than 60. ICBMs shall not be launched from training launchers. Each such launcher may contain only a training model of a missile. Mobile training launchers shall not be capable of launching ICBMs, and shall differ from mobile launchers of ICBMs and other road vehicles or railcars on the basis of differences that are observable by national technical means of verification. [Agreed State 13] [RF MOU, Section IV] [US MOU Section IV]

3. For heavy bombers and former heavy bombers:

(a) Each Party shall limit the aggregate number of heavy bombers equipped for non-nuclear armaments, former heavy bombers, and training heavy bombers to no more than 75. [category] [RF MOU, Section IV] [US MOU Section IV] [Agreed State 6] [Agreed State 12]

(b) Each Party shall limit the number of test heavy bombers to no more than 20. [category] [RF MOU, Section IV] [US MOU Section IV]

4. For ICBMs and SLBMs used for delivering objects into the upper atmosphere or space: [JCIC Joint State 21]

(a) Each Party shall limit the number of space launch facilities to no more than five, unless otherwise agreed. Space launch facilities shall not overlap ICBM bases. [RF MOU, Annex D] [US MOU Annex D]

(b)Each Party shall limit the aggregate number of ICBM launchers and SLBM launchers located at space launch facilities to no more than 20, unless otherwise agreed. Within this limit, the aggregate number of silo launchers of ICBMs and mobile launchers of ICBMs located at space launch facilities shall not exceed ten, unless otherwise agreed. [Agreed State 26] [Agreed State 37(h)]

(c) Each Party shall limit the aggregate number of ICBMs and SLBMs located at a space launch facility to no more than the number of ICBM launchers and SLBM launchers located at that facility. [Agreed State 37]

5. Each Party shall limit the number of transporter-loaders for ICBMs for road-mobile launchers of ICBMs

located at each deployment area or test range to no more than two for each type of ICBM for road-mobile launchers of ICBMs that is attributed with one warhead and that is specified for that deployment area or test range, and shall limit the number of such transporter-loaders located outside deployment areas and test ranges to no more than six. The aggregate number of transporter-loaders for ICBMs for road-mobile launchers of ICBMs shall not exceed 30. [RF MOU, Section IV]

6. Each Party shall limit the number of ballistic missile submarines in dry dock within five kilometers of the boundary of each submarine base to no more than two.

7. For static displays and ground trainers:

(a) Each Party shall limit the number of ICBM launchers and SLBM launchers placed on static displays after signature of this Treaty to no more than 20, the number of ICBMs [RF MOU, Annex A] [US MOU, Annex A] [Uk MOU, Annex A] and SLBMs [RF MOU, Annex B] [US MOU, Annex B] placed on static display after signature of this Treaty to no more than 20, the number of launch canisters placed on static display after signature of this Treaty to no more than 20, and the number of heavy bombers and former heavy bombers placed on static display after signature of this Treaty to no more than 20. Such items placed on static display prior to signature of this Treaty shall be specified in Annex I to the Memorandum of Understanding, but shall not be subject to the limitations provided for in this Treaty.

(b) Each Party shall limit the aggregate number of heavy bombers converted after signature of this Treaty for use as ground trainers and former heavy bombers converted after signature of this Treaty for use as ground trainers to no more than five. Such items converted prior to signature of this Treaty for use as ground trainers shall be specified in Annex I to the Memorandum of Understanding, but shall not be subject to the limitations provided for in this Treaty.

8. Each Party shall limit the aggregate number of storage facilities for ICBMs or SLBMs and repair facilities for ICBMs or SLBMs to no more than 50.

9. With respect to locational and related restrictions on strategic offensive arms:

(a) Each Party shall locate non-deployed ICBMs and non-deployed SLBMs only at maintenance facilities of ICBM bases; submarine bases; ICBM loading facilities; SLBM loading facilities; production facilities for ICBMs or SLBMs; repair facilities for ICBMs or SLBMs; storage facilities for ICBMs or SLBMs; conversion or elimination facilities for ICBMs or SLBMs; test ranges; or space launch facilities. Prototype ICBMs and prototype SLBMs, however, shall not be located at maintenance facilities of ICBM bases or at submarine bases. Non-deployed ICBMs and non-deployed SLBMs may also be in transit. Non-deployed ICBMs for silo launchers of

ICBMs may also be transferred within an ICBM base for silo launchers of ICBMs. Non-deployed SLBMs that are located on missile tenders and storage cranes shall be considered to be located at the submarine base at which such missile tenders and storage cranes are specified as based. [Agreed State 37] [Agreed State 19]

(b) Each Party shall locate non-deployed mobile launchers of ICBMs only at maintenance facilities of ICBM bases for mobile launchers of ICBMs, production facilities for mobile launchers of ICBMs, repair facilities for mobile launchers of ICBMs, storage facilities for mobile launchers of ICBMs, ICBM loading facilities, training facilities for ICBMs, conversion or elimination facilities for mobile launchers of ICBMs, test ranges, or space launch facilities. Mobile launchers of prototype ICBMs, however, shall not be located at maintenance facilities of ICBM bases for mobile launchers of ICBMs. Non-deployed mobile launchers of ICBMs may also be in transit. [Agreed State 19]

(c) Each Party shall locate test launchers only at test ranges, except that rail-mobile test launchers may conduct movements for the purpose of testing outside a test range, provided that:

(i) each such movement is completed no later than 30 days after it begins;

(ii) each such movement begins and ends at the same test ranges and does not involve movement to any other facility;

(iii) movements of no more than six rail-mobile launchers of ICBMs are conducted in each calendar year; and

(iv) no more than one train containing no more than three rail-mobile test launchers is located outside test ranges at any one time.

(d) A deployed mobile launcher of ICBMs and its associated missile that relocates to a test range may, at the discretion of the testing Party, either continue to be counted toward the maximum aggregate limits provided for in Article II of this Treaty, or be counted as a mobile test launchers pursuant to paragraph 2(d) of this Article. If a deployed mobile launcher of ICBMs and its associated missile that relocates to a test range continues to be counted toward the maximum aggregate limits provided for in Article II of this Treaty, the period of time during which it continuously remains at a test range shall not exceed 45 days. The number of such deployed road-mobile launchers of ICBMs and their associated missiles located at a test range at any one time shall not exceed three, and the number of such deployed rail-mobile launchers of ICBMs and their associated missiles located at a test range at any one time shall not exceed three.

(e) Each Party shall locate silo training launchers only at ICBM bases for silo launchers of ICBMs and training facilities for ICBMs. The number of silo training launchers located at each ICBM bases for silo launchers of ICBMs shall not exceed one for each type of ICBM specified for that ICBM base.

(f) Test heavy bombersshall be based only at heavy bomber flight test centers and at production facilities for heavy bombers. Training heavy bombers shall be based only at training facilities for heavy bombers.

10. Each Party shall locate solid rocket motors for first stages of ICBMs for mobile launchers of ICBMs only at locations where production and storage, or testing of such motors occurs and at production facilities for ICBMs for mobile launchers of ICBMs. Such solid rocket motors may also be moved between these locations. Solid rocket motors with nozzles attached for the first stages of ICBMs for mobile launchers of ICBMs shall only be located at production facilities for ICBMs for mobile launchers of ICBMs and at locations where testing of such solid rocket motors occurs. Locations where such solid rocket motors are permitted shall be specified in Annex I to the Memorandum of Understanding. [RF MOU, Annex I] [US MOU, Annex I] [Agreed State 28]

11. With respect to locational restrictions on facilities:

(a) Each Party shall locate production facilities for ICBMs of a particular type, repair facilities for ICBMs of a particular type, storage facilities for ICBMs of a particular type, ICBM loading facilities for ICBMs of a particular type, and conversion or elimination facilities for ICBMs of a particular type no less than 100 kilometers from any ICBM base for silo launchers of ICBMs of that type of ICBM, any ICBM base for rail-mobile launchers of ICBMs of that type of ICBM, any deployment area for road-mobile launchers of ICBMs of that type of ICBM, any test range from which ICBMs of that type are flight-tested, any production facility for mobile launchers of ICBMs of that type of ICBM, any repair facility for mobile launchers of ICBMs of that type of ICBM, any storage facility for mobile launchers of ICBMs of that type of ICBM, and any training facility for ICBMs at which non-deployed mobile launchers of ICBMs are located. New facilities at which non-deployed ICBMs for silo launchers of ICBMs of ICBMs of any type of ICBM may be located, and new storage facilities for ICBM emplacement equipment, shall be located no less than 100 kilometers from any ICBM base for silo launchers of ICBMs, except that existing storage facilities for intermediate-range missiles, located less than 100 kilometers from an ICBM base for silo launchers of ICBMs or from a test range, may be converted into storage facilities for ICBMs not specified for that ICBM base or that test range. [Agreed State 14]

(b) Each Party shall locate production facilities for mobile launchers of ICBMs of a particular type of ICBM, repair facilities for mobile launchers of ICBMs of a particular type of ICBM, and storage facilities for mobile launchers of ICBMs of a particular type of ICBM no less

than 100 kilometers from any ICBMs for mobile launchers of ICBMs of that type of ICBM and any test range from which ICBMs of that type are flight-tested.

(c) Each Party shall locate test ranges and space launch facilities no less than 100 kilometers from any ICBM base for silo launchers of ICBMs, any ICBM base for rail-mobile launchers of ICBMs, and any deployment area. [Agreed State 26]

(d) Each Party shall locate training facilities for ICBMs no less than 100 kilometers from any test range. [Agreed State 15]

(e) Each Party shall locate storage areas for heavy bomber nuclear armaments no less than 100 kilometers from any air base for heavy bombers equipped for non-nuclear armaments and any training facility for heavy bombers. Each Party shall locate storage areas for long-range nuclear ALCMs no less than 100 kilometers from any air base for heavy bombers equipped for nuclear armaments other than long-range nuclear ALCMs, any air base for heavy bombers equipped for non-nuclear armaments, and any training facility for heavy bombers.

12. Each Party shall limit the duration of each transit to no more than 30 days.

ARTICLE V

1. Except as prohibited by the provisions of this Treaty, modernization and replacement of strategic offensive arms may be carried out.

2. Each Party undertakes not to:

(a) produce, flight-test, or deploy heavy ICBMs of a new type, or increase the launch weight [RF MOU, Annex F] or throw-weight [RF MOU, Section I] of heavy ICBMs of an existing type;

(b) produce, flight-test, or deploy heavy SLBMs;

(c) produce test, or deploy mobile launchers of heavy ICBMs;

(d) produce, test, or deploy additional silo launchers of ICBMs of heavy ICBMs, except for silo launchers of heavy ICBMs that replace silo launchers of heavy ICBMs that have been eliminated in accordance with Section II of the Conversion or Elimination Protocol, provided that the limits provided for in Article II of this Treaty are not exceeded; [Agreed State 5]

(e) convert launchers that are not launchers of heavy ICBMs into launchers of heavy ICBMs;

(f) produce, test, or deploy launchers of heavy SLBMs;

(g) reduce the number of warheads attributed to a heavy ICBM of an existing type.

3. Each Party undertakes not to deploy ICBMs other than in silo launchers of ICBMs, on road-mobile launchers of ICBMs, or on rail-mobile launchers of ICBMs.

Each Party undertakes not to produce, test, or deploy ICBM launchers other than silo launchers of ICBMs, road-mobile launchers of ICBMs, or rail-mobile launchers of ICBMs.

4. Each Party undertakes not to deploy on a mobile launcher of ICBMs an ICBM of a type that was not specified as a type of ICBM for mobile launchers of ICBMs in accordance with paragraph 2 of Section VII of the Protocol on Notifications Relating to this Treaty, hereinafter referred to as the Notification Protocol, unless it is an ICBM to which no more than one warhead is attributed and the Parties have agreed within the framework of the Joint Compliance and Inspection Commission to permit deployment of such ICBMs on mobile launchers of ICBMs. A new type of ICBM for mobile launchers of ICBMs may cease to be considered to be a type of ICBM for mobile launchers of ICBMs if no ICBM of that type has been contained on, or flight-tested from, a mobile launcher of ICBMs.

5. Each Party undertakes not to deploy ICBM launchers of a new type of ICBM and not to deploy SLBM launchers of a new type of SLBM if such launchers are capable of launching ICBMs or SLBMs, respectively, of other types. ICBM launchers of existing types of ICBMs and SLBM launchers of existing types of SLBMs shall be incapable, without conversion, of launching ICBMs or SLBMs, respectively, of other types. [Agreed State 16]

6. Each Party undertakes not to convert SLBMs into ICBMs for mobile launchers of ICBMs, or to load SLBMs on, or launch SLBMs from, mobile launchers of ICBMs.

7. Each Party undertakes not to produce, test, or deploy transporter-loaders other than transporter-loaders for ICBMs for road-mobile launchers of ICBMs attributed with one warhead.

8. Each Party undertakes not to locate deployed silo launchers of ICBMs outside ICBM bases for silo launchers of ICBMs.

9. Each Party undertakes not to locate soft-site launchers except at test ranges and space launch facilities. All existing soft-site launchers not at test ranges or space launch facilities shall be eliminated in accordance with the procedures provided for in the Conversion or Elimination Protocol no later than 60 days after entry into force of this Treaty. [Agreed State 27]

10. Each Party undertakes not to:

(a) flight-test ICBMs or SLBMs of a retired or former type from other than test launchers specified for such use or launchers at space launch facilities. Except for soft-site launchers, test launchers specified for such use shall not be used to flight-test ICBMs or SLBMs of a type, any one of which is deployed; [III.10(c)]

(b) produce ICBMs for mobile launchers of ICBMs of a retired type.

11. Each Party undertakes not to convert silos used as launch control centers into silo launchers of ICBMs. [Silo LCC Letters]

12. Each Party undertakes not to:

(a) produce, flight-test, or deploy an ICBM or SLBM with more than ten reentry vehicles;

(b) flight-test an ICBM or SLBM with a number of reentry vehicles greater than the number of warheads attributed to it, or, for an ICBM or SLBM of a retired type, with a number of reentry vehicles greater than the largest number of warheads that was attributed to any ICBM or SLBM of that type;

(c) deploy an ICBM or SLBM with a number of reentry vehicles greater than the number of warheads attributed to it;

(d) increase the number of warheads attributed to an ICBM or SLBM of an existing or new type. [III.4(b)]

13. Each Party undertakes not to flight-test or deploy an ICBM or SLBM with a number of reentry vehicles greater than the number of warheads attributed to it. [Agreed State 3]

14. Each Party undertakes not to flight-test from space launch facilities ICBMs or SLBMs equipped with reentry vehicles.

15. Each Party undertakes not to use ICBMs or SLBMs for delivering objects into the upper atmosphere or space for purposes inconsistent with existing international obligations undertaken by the Parties.

16. Each Party undertakes not to produce, test, or deploy systems for rapid reload and not to conduct rapid reload.

17. Each Party undertakes not to install SLBM launchers on submarines that were not originally constructed as ballistic missile submarines. [US MOU Annex I]

18. Each Party undertakes not to produce, test, or deploy:

(a) ballistic missiles with a range in excess of 600 kilometers, or launchers of such missiles, for installation on waterborne vehicles, including free-floating launchers, other than submarines. This obligation shall not require changes in current ballistic missile storage, transport, loading, or unloading practices; [Agreed State 9] [Agreed State 30]

(b) launchers of ballistic or cruise missiles for emplacement on or for tethering to the ocean floor, the seabed, or the beds of internal waters and inland waters, or for emplacement in or for tethering to the subsoil thereof, or mobile launchers of such missiles that move only in contact with the ocean floor, the seabed, or the beds of internal waters and inland waters, or missiles for such launchers. This obligation shall apply to all areas of the ocean floor and the seabed, including the seabed zone referred to in Articles I and II of the Treaty on the Prohibition of the Emplacement of Nuclear Weapons and Other Weapons of Mass Destruction on the Seabed and the Ocean Floor and in the Subsoil Thereof of February 11, 1971;

(c) systems, including missiles, for placing nuclear weapons or any other kinds of weapons of mass destruction into Earth orbit or a fraction of an Earth orbit;

(d) air-to-surface ballistic missiles (ASBMs); [Agreed State 4] [Agreed State 30]

(e) long-range nuclear ALCMs armed with two or more nuclear weapons. [ALCMs with Multiple Weapons Letters]

19. Each Party undertakes not to:

(a) flight-test with nuclear armaments an aircraft that is not an airplane, but that has a range of 8000 kilometers or more; equip such an aircraft for nuclear armaments; or deploy such an aircraft with nuclear armaments;

(b) flight-test with nuclear armaments an airplane that was not initially constructed as a bomber, but that has a range of 8000 kilometers or more, or an integrated planform area in excess of 310 square meters; equip such an airplane for nuclear armaments; or deploy such an airplane with nuclear armaments;

(c) flight-test with long-range nuclear ALCMs an aircraft that is not an airplane, or an airplane that was not initially constructed as a bomber; equip such an aircraft or such an airplane for long-range nuclear ALCMs; or deploy such an aircraft or such an airplane with long-range nuclear ALCMs.

20. The United States of America undertakes not to equip existing or future heavy bombers for more than 20 long-range nuclear ALCMs. [US MOU Annex G]

21. The Union of Soviet Socialist Republics undertakes not to equip existing or future heavy bombers for more than 16 long-range nuclear ALCMs. [RF MOU Annex G]

22. Each Party undertakes not to locate long-range nuclear ALCMs at air bases for heavy bombers equipped for nuclear armaments other than long-range nuclear ALCMs, air bases for heavy bmbers equipped for non-nuclear armaments, air bases for former heavy bombers, or training facilities for heavy bombers. [US MOU Annex C] [RF MOU Annex C] [TSSAM Statements]

23. Each Party undertakes not to base heavy bombers equipped for long-range nuclear ALCMs, heavy bombers equipped for nuclear armaments other than long-range nuclear ALCMs, or heavy bombers equipped for non-nuclear armaments at air bases at which heavy bombers of either of the other two categories are based. [US MOU Annex C] [RF MOU Annex C]

24. Each Party undertakes not to convert:

(a) heavy bombers equipped for nuclear armaments other than long-range nuclear ALCMs into heavy bombers equipped for long-range nuclear ALCM, if such heavy bombers were previously equipped for long-range nuclear ALCMs;

(b) heavy bombers equipped for non-nuclear armaments into heavy bombers equipped for long-range nuclear ALCM or into heavy bombers equipped for nuclear armaments other than long-range nuclear ALCMs;

(c) training heavy bombers into heavy bombers of another category;

(d) former heavy bombers into heavy bombers.

25. Each Party undertakes not to have underground facilities accessible to ballistic missile submarines. [Underground Submarine Facility Statements]

26. Each Party undertakes not to locate railcars at the site of a rail garrison that has been eliminated in accordance with Section IX of the Conversion or Elimination Protocol, unless such railcars have differences, observable by national technical means of verification, in length, width, or height from rail-mobile launchers of ICBMs or launch-associated railcars.

27. Each Party undertakes not to engage in any activities associated with strategic offensive arms at eliminated facilities, notification of the elimination of which has been provided in accordance with paragraph 3 of Section I of the Notification Protocol, unless notification of a new facility at the same location has been provided in accordance with paragraph 3 of Section I of the Notification Protocol. Strategic offensive arms and support equipment shall not be located at eliminated facilities except during their movement through such facilities and during visits of heavy bombers or former heavy bombers at such facilities. Missile tenders may be located at eliminated facilities only for purposes not associated with strategic offensive arms. [Statement on Launch-Associated/Driver Training Vehicles]

28. Each Party undertakes not to base strategic offensive arms subject to the limitations of this Treaty outside its national territory. [Agreed State 8] [Agreed State 18] [3rd Country Basing Letter]

29. Each Party undertakes not to use naval vessels that were formerly declared as missile tenders to transport, store, or load SLBMs. Such naval vessels shall not be tied to a ballistic missile submarines for the purpose of supporting such a submarine if such a submarine is located within five kilometers of a submarine base. [US MOU Annex B]

30. Each Party undertakes not to remove from production facilities for ICBMs for mobile launchers of ICBMs, solid rocket motors with attached nozzles for the first stages of ICBMs for mobile launchers of ICBMs, except for:

(a) the removal of such motors as part of assembled first stages of ICBMs for ICBMs for mobile launchers of ICBMs that are maintained, stored, and transported in stages; [RF MOU Annex F] [US MOU Annex F]

(b) the removal of such motors as part of assembled ICBMs for mobile launchers of ICBMs that are maintained, stored, and transported as assembled missiles in launch canisters or without launch canisters; and [RF MOU Annex F] [US MOU Annex F] [Agreed State 28]

(c) the removal of such motors as part of assembled first stages of ICBMs for mobile launchers of ICBMs that are maintained, stored, and transported as assembled missiles in launch canisters or without launch canisters, for the purpose of technical characteristics exhibitions. [RF MOU Annex F] [US MOU Annex F] [Agreed State 28]

ARTICLE VI

1. Deployed road-mobile launchers of ICBMs and their associated missiles shall be based only in restricted areas. A restricted area shall not exceed five square kilometers in size and shall not overlap another restricted area. No more than ten deployed road-mobile launchers of ICBMs and their associated missiles may be based or located in a restricted area. A restricted area shall not contain deployed ICBMs for road-mobile launchers of ICBMs of more than one type of ICBM. [RF MOU Annex A] [Agreed State 19]

2. Each Party shall limit the number of fixed structures for road-mobile launchers of ICBMs within each restricted areas so that these structures shall not be capable of containing more road-mobile launchers of ICBMs than the number of road-mobile launchers of ICBMs specified for that restricted area. [RF MOU Annex A]

3. Each restricted area shall be located within a deployment area. A deployment area shall not exceed 125,000 square kilometers in size and shall not overlap another deployment area. A deployment area shall contain no more than one ICBM base for road-mobile launchers of ICBMs. [RF MOU Annex A]

4. Deployed rail-mobile launchers of ICBMs and their associated missiles shall be based only in rail garrisons. Each Party shall have no more than seven rail garrisons. No point on a portion of track located inside a rail garrison shall be more than 20 kilometers from any entrance/exit for that rail garrison. This distance shall be measured along the tracks. A rail garrison shall not overlap another rail garrison. [RF MOU Annex A]

5. Each rail garrison shall have no more than two rail entrances/exits. Each such entrance/exit shall have no more than two separate sets of tracks passing through it (a total of four rails). [RF MOU Annex A]

6. Each Party shall limit the number of parking sites in each rail garrison to no more than the number of trains of standard configuration specified for that rail garrison. Each rail garrison shall have no more than five parking sites. [RF MOU Annex A] [RF MOU Annex F]

7. Each Party shall limit the number of fixed structures for rail-mobile launchers of ICBMs in each rail garrison to no more than the number of trains of standard configuration specified for that rail garrison. Each such structure shall contain no more than one train of standard configuration. [RF MOU Annex A] [RF MOU Annex F]

8. Each rail garrison shall contain no more than one maintenance facility. [RF MOU Annex A]

9. Deployed mobile launchers of ICBMs and their associated missiles may leave restricted areas or rail garrisons only for routine movements, relocations, or dispersals [XIII.1] [XIV.1]. Deployed road-mobile launchers of ICBMs and their associated missiles may leave deployment areas only for relocations or operational dispersals.

10. Relocations shall be completed within 25 days. No more than 15 percent of the total number of deployed road-mobile launchers of ICBMs and their associated missiles or five such launchers and their associated missiles, whichever is greater, may be outside restricted areas at any one time for the purpose of relocation. No more than 20 percent of the total number of deployed rail-mobile launchers of ICBMs and their associated missiles or five such launchers and their associated missiles, whichever is greater, may be outside rail garrisons at any one time for the purpose of relocation.

11. No more than 50 percent of the total number of deployed rail-mobile launchers of ICBMs and their associated missiles may be engaged in routine movements at any one time. [RF MOU Annex A]

12. All trains with deployed rail-mobile launchers of ICBMs and their associated missiles of a particular type shall be of one standard configuration. All such trains shall conform to that standard configuration except those taking part in routine movements, relocations, or dispersals, and except that portion of a train remaining within a rail garrisons after the other portion of such a train has departed for the maintenance facility associated with that rail garrison, has been relocated to another facility, or has departed the rail garrison for routine movement. Except for dispersals, notification of variations from standard configuration shall be provided in accordance with paragraphs 13, 14, and 15 of Section II of the Notification Protocol. [RF MOU Annex A] [RF MOU Annex F]

ARTICLE VII

1. Conversion and elimination of strategic offensive arms, fixed structures for mobile launchers of ICBMs, and facilities shall be carried out pursuant to this Article and in accordance with procedures provided for in the Conversion or Elimination Protocol. Conversion and elimination shall be verified by national technical means

of verification and by inspection as provided for in Articles IX and XI of this Treaty; in the Conversion or Elimination Protocol; and in the Protocol on Inspections and Continuous Monitoring Activities Relating to this Treaty, hereinafter referred to as the Inspection Protocol.

2. ICBMs for mobile launchers of ICBMs, ICBM launchers, SLBM launchers, heavy bombers, former heavy bombers, and support equipment shall be subject to the limitations provided for in this Treaty until they have been eliminated, or otherwise cease to be subject to the limitations provided for in this Treaty, in accordance with procedures provided for in the Conversion or Elimination Protocol. [Agreed State 11] [Agreed State 37] [Joint State Missile Production Technology]

3. ICBMs for silo launchers of ICBMs and SLBMs shall be subject to the limitations provided for in this Treaty until they have been eliminated by rendering them inoperable, precluding their use for their original purpose, using procedures at the discretion of the Party possessing the ICBMs or SLBMs.

4. The elimination of ICBMs for mobile launchers of ICBMs, mobile launchers of ICBMs, SLBM launchers, heavy bombers, and former heavy bombers [Agreed State 10] shall be carried out at conversion or elimination facilities, except as provided for in Sections VII and VIII of the Conversion or Elimination Protocol. Fixed launchers of ICBMs and fixed structures for mobile launchers of ICBMs subject to elimination shall be eliminated in situ. A launch canister [Launch Canister Letters] [Agreed State 20] remaining at a test range or ICBM base after the flight test of an ICBM for mobile launchers of ICBMs shall be eliminated in the open in situ, or at a conversion or elimination facility, in accordance with procedures provided for in the Conversion or Elimination Protocol. [Agreed State 37]

ARTICLE VIII

1. A data base pertaining to the obligations under this Treaty is set forth in the Memorandum of Understanding, in which data with respect to items subject to the limitations provided for in this Treaty are listed according to categories of data. [MOU, Annex J] [Joint State Data Updates] [Agreed State 37]

2. In order to ensure the fulfillment of its obligations with respect to this Treaty, each Party shall notify the other Party of changes in data, as provided for in subparagraph 3(a) of this Article, and shall also provide other notifications required by paragraph 3 of this Article, in accordance with the procedures provided for in paragraphs 4, 5, and 6 of this Article, the Notification Protocol, and the Inspection Protocol.

3. Each Party shall provide to the other Party, in accordance with the Notification Protocol, and, for subparagraph (i) of this paragraph, in accordance with Section III of the Inspection Protocol: [Agreed State 37]

(a) notifications concerning data with respect to items subject to the limitations provided for in this Treaty, according to categories of data contained in the Memorandum of Understanding and other agreed categories of data; [Agreed State 21]

(b) notifications concerning movement of items subject to the limitations provided for in this Treaty;

(c) notifications concerning data on ICBM and SLBM throw-weight in connection with the Protocol on ICBM and SLBM Throw-weight [MOU, Section I] Relating to this Treaty, hereinafter referred to as the Throw-weight Protocol;

(d) notifications concerning conversion or elimination of items subject to the limitations provided for in this Treaty or elimination of facilities subject to this Treaty;

(e) notifications concerning cooperative measures to enhance the effectiveness of national technical means of verification;

(f) notifications concerning flight tests of ICBMs or SLBMs and notifications concerning telemetric information; [Launch Notification Agreement]

(g) notifications concerning strategic offensive arms of new types and new kinds; [Agreed State 2]

(h) notifications concerning changes in the content of information provided pursuant to this paragraph, including the rescheduling of activities;

(i) notifications concerning inspections and continuous monitoring activities; and

(j) notifications concerning operational dispersals.

4. Each Party shall use the Nuclear Risk Reduction Centers, which provide for continuous communication between the Parties, to provide and receive notifications in accordance with the Notification Protocol and the Inspection Protocol, unless otherwise provided for in this Treaty, and to acknowledge receipt of such notifications no later than one hour after receipt.

5. If a time is to be specified in a notification provided pursuant to this Article, that time shall be expressed in Greenwich Mean Time. If only a date is to be specified in a notification, that date shall be specified as the 24-hour period that corresponds to the date in local time, expressed in Greenwich Mean Time.

6. Except as otherwise provided in this Article, each Party shall have the right to release to the public all data current as of September 1, 1990, that are listed in the Memorandum of Understanding, as well as the photographs that are appended thereto. Geographic coordinates and site diagrams that are received pursuant to the Agreement Between the Government of the United States

of America and the Government of the Union of Soviet Socialist Republics on Exchange of Geographic Coordinates and Site Diagrams Relating to the Treaty of July 31, 1991, shall not be released to the public unless otherwise agreed. The Parties shall hold consultations on releasing to the public data and other information provided pursuant to this Article or received otherwise in fulfilling the obligations provided for in this Treaty. The provisions of this Article shall not affect the rights and obligations of the Parties with respect to the communication of such data and other information to those individuals who, because of their official responsibilities, require such data or other information to carry out activities related to the fulfillment of the obligations provided for in this Treaty. [Statements on Release to Public]

ARTICLE IX

1. For the purpose of ensuring verification of compliance with the provisions of this Treaty, each Party shall use national technical means of verification at its disposal in a manner consistent with generally recognized principles of international law.

2. Each Party undertakes not to interfere with the national technical means of verification of the other Party operating in accordance with paragraph l of this Article.

3. Each Party undertakes not to use concealment measures that impede verification, by national technical means of verification, of compliance with the provisions of this Treaty. In this connection, the obligation not to use concealment measures includes the obligation not to use them at test ranges, including measures that result in the concealment of ICBMs, SLBMs, mobile launchers of ICBMs, or the association between ICBMs or SLBMs and their launchers during testing. The obligation not to use concealment measures shall not apply to cover or concealment practices at ICBM bases and deployment areas, or to the use of environmental shelters for strategic offensive arms.

4. To aid verification, each ICBM for mobile launchers of ICBMs shall have a unique identifier as provided for in the Inspection Protocol.

ARTICLE X

1. During each flight test of an ICBM or SLBM, the Party conducting the flight test shall make on-board technical measurements and shall broadcast all telemetric information obtained from such measurements. The Party conducting the flight test shall determine which technical parameters are to be measured during such flight test, as well as the methods of processing and transmitting telemetric information.

2. During each flight test of an ICBM or SLBM, the Party conducting the flight test undertakes not to engage in any activity that denies full access to telemetric information, including: [Statements on Encryption & Jamming]

(a) the use of encryption;

(b) the use of jamming;

(c) broadcasting telemetric information from an ICBM or SLBM using narrow directional beaming; and

(d) encapsulation of telemetric information, including the use of ejectable capsules or recoverable reentry vehicles.

3. During each flight test of an ICBM or SLBM, the Party conducting the flight test undertakes not to broadcast from a reentry vehicles. telemetric information that pertains to the functioning of the stages or the self-contained dispensing mechanism of the ICBM or SLBM.

4. After each flight test of an ICBM or SLBM, the Party conducting the flight test shall provide, in accordance with Section I of the Protocol on Telemetric Information Relating to the Treaty, hereinafter referred to as the Telemetry Protocol, tapes nthat contain a recording of all telemetric information that is broadcast during the flight test.

5. After each flight test of an ICBM or SLBM, the Party conducting the flight test shall provide, in accordance with Section II of the Telemetry Protocol, data associated with the analysis of the telemetric information. [Agreed State 35]

6. Notwithstanding the provisions of paragraphs 1 and 2 of this Article, each Party shall have the right to encapsulate and encrypt on-board technical measurements during no more than a total of eleven flight tests of ICBMs or SLBMs each year. Of these eleven flight tests each year, no more than four shall be flight tests of ICBMs or SLBMs of each type, any missile of which has been flight-tested with a self-contained dispensing mechanism. Such encapsulation shall be carried out in accordance with Section I and paragraph 1 of Section III of the Telemetry Protocol, and such encryption shall be carried out in accordance with paragraph 2 of Section III of the Telemetry Protocol. Encapsulation and encryption that are carried out on the same flight test of an ICBM or SLBM shall count as two flight tests against the quotas specified in this paragraph. [Agreed State 31]

ARTICLE XI

1. For the purpose of ensuring verification of compliance with the provisions of this Treaty, each Party shall have

the right to conduct inspections and continuous monitoring activities and shall conduct exhibitions pursuant to this Article and the Inspection Protocol. Inspections, continuous monitoring activities, and exhibitions shall be conducted in accordance with the procedures provided for in the Inspection Protocol and the Conversion or Elimination Protocol. [item of inspection] [size criteria] [Agreed State 36]

2. Each Party shall have the right to conduct baseline data inspections at facilities to confirm the accuracy of data on the numbers and types of items specified for such facilities in the initial exchange of data provided in accordance with paragraph 1 of Section I of the Notification Protocol. [facility inspections at] [Agreed State 10]

3. Each Party shall have the right to conduct data update inspections at facilities to confirm the accuracy of data on the numbers and types of items specified for such facilities in the notifications and regular exchanges of updated data provided in accordance with paragraphs 2 and 3 of Section I of the Notification Protocol. [facility inspections at] [Agreed State 10]

4. Each Party shall have the right to conduct new facility inspections to confirm the accuracy of data on the numbers and types of items specified in the notifications of new facilities provided in accordance with paragraph 3 of Section I of the Notification Protocol. [facility inspections at]

5. Each Party shall have the right to conduct suspect-site inspections to confirm that covert assembly of ICBMs for mobile launchers of ICBMs or covert assembly of first stages of such ICBMs is not occurring. [facility inspections at] [RF MOU Annex I] [US MOU Annex I] [Joint State on Site Diagrams]

6. Each Party shall have the right to conduct reentry vehicle inspections of deployed ICBMs and SLBMs to confirm that such ballistic missiles contain no more reentry vehicles than the number of warheads attributed to them. [facility inspections at] [RF MOU Section I] [US MOU Section I]

7. Each Party shall have the right to conduct post-exercise dispersal inspections of deployed mobile launchers of ICBMs and their associated missiles to confirm that the number of mobile launchers of ICBMs and their associated missiles that are located at the inspected ICBM bases and those that have not returned to it after completion of the dispersal does not exceed the number specified for that ICBM base.

8. Each Party shall conduct or shall have the right to conduct conversion or elimination inspections to confirm the conversion or elimination of strategic offensive arms.

9. Each Party shall have the right to conduct close-out inspections to confirm that the elimination of facilities has been completed.

10. Each Party shall have the right to conduct formerly declared facility inspections to confirm that facilities, notification of the elimination of which has been provided in accordance with paragraph 3 of Section I of the Notification Protocol, are not being used for purposes inconsistent with this Treaty.

11. Each Party shall conduct technical characteristics exhibitions, and shall have the right during such exhibitions by the other Party to conduct inspections of an ICBM and an SLBM of each type, and each variant thereof, and of a mobile launcher of ICBMs and each version of such launcher for each type of ICBM for mobile launchers of ICBMs. The purpose of such exhibitions shall be to permit the inspecting Party to confirm that technical characteristics correspond to the data specified for these items. [RF MOU Annex F] [US MOU Annex F] [Agreed State 25] [Early Exhibitions Agreement] [Agreed State 28]

12. Each Party shall conduct distinguishability exhibitions for heavy bombers, former heavy bombers, and long-range nuclear ALCMs, and shall have the right during such exhibitions by the other Party to conduct inspections, of: [Agreed State 10]

(a) heavy bombers equipped for long-range nuclear ALCMs. The purpose of such exhibitions shall be to permit the inspecting Party to confirm that the technical characteristics of each type and each variant of such heavy bombers correspond to the data specified for these items in Annex G to the Memorandum of Understanding; to demonstrate the maximum number of long-range nuclear ALCMs for which a heavy bomber of each type and each variant is actually equipped; and to demonstrate that this number does not exceed the number provided for in paragraph 20 or 21 of Article V of this Treaty, as applicable; [RF MOU Annex G] [US MOU Annex G]

(b) for each type of heavy bomber from any one of which a long-range nuclear ALCM has been flight-tested, heavy bombers equipped for nuclear armaments other than long-range nuclear ALCMs, heavy bombers equipped for non-nuclear armaments, training heavy bombers, and former heavy bombers. If, for such a type of heavy bomber, there are no heavy bombers equipped for long-range nuclear ALCMs, a test heavy bomber from which a long-range nuclear ALCM has been flight-tested shall be exhibited. The purpose of such exhibitions shall be to demonstrate to the inspecting Party that, for each exhibited type of heavy bomber, each variant of heavy bombers equipped for nuclear armaments other than long-range nuclear ALCMs, each variant of heavy bombers equipped for non-nuclear armaments, each variant of training heavy bombers, and a former heavy bomber are distinguishable from one another and from each variant of heavy bombers of the same type equipped for long-range nuclear ALCMs; and [RF MOU Annex G] [US MOU Annex G]

(c) long-range nuclear ALCMs. The purpose of such exhibitions shall be to permit the inspecting Party to confirm that the technical characteristics of each type and each variant of such long-range ALCMs correspond to the data specified for these items in Annex H to the Memorandum of Understanding. The further purpose of such exhibitions shall be to demonstrate differences, notification of which has been provided in accordance with paragraph 13, 14, or 15 of Section VII of the Notification Protocol, that make long-range non-nuclear ALCMs distinguishable from long-range nuclear ALCMs. [RF MOU Annex H] [US MOU Annex H]

13. Each Party shall conduct baseline exhibitions, and shall have the right during such exhibitions by the other Party to conduct inspections, of all heavy bombers equipped for long-range nuclear ALCMs equipped for non-nuclear armaments, all training heavy bombers, and all former heavy bombers specified in the initial exchange of data provided in accordance with paragraph 1 of Section I of the Notification Protocol. The purpose of these exhibitions shall be to demonstrate to the inspecting Party that such airplanes satisfy the requirements for conversion in accordance with the Conversion or Elimination Protocol. After a long-range nuclear ALCM has been flight-tested from a heavy bomber of a type, from none of which a long-range nuclear ALCM had previously been flight-tested, the Party conducting the flight test shall conduct baseline exhibitions, and the other Party shall have the right during such exhibitions to conduct inspections, of 30 percent of the heavy bombers equipped for long-range nuclear ALCMs of such type equipped for nuclear armaments other than long-range nuclear ALCMs at each air base specified for such heavy bombers. The purpose of these exhibitions shall be to demonstrate to the inspecting Party the presence of specified features that make each exhibited heavy bomber distinguishable from heavy bombers of the same type equipped for long-range nuclear ALCMs.

14. Each Party shall have the right to conduct continuous monitoring activities at production facilities for ICBMs for mobile launchers of ICBMs to confirm the number of ICBMs for mobile launchers of ICBMs produced. [Agreed State 22] [facilities]   [Site Surveys Letters]

ARTICLE XII

1. To enhance the effectiveness of national technical means of verification, each Party shall, if the other Party makes a request in accordance with paragraph 1 of Sec-

tion V of the Notification Protocol, carry out the following cooperative measures:

(a) a display in the open of the road-mobile launchers of ICBMs located within restricted areas specified by the requesting Party. The number of road-mobile launchers of ICBMs based at the restricted areas specified in each such request shall not exceed ten percent of the total number of deployed road-mobile launchers of ICBMs of the requested Party, and such launchers shall be contained within one ICBM base for road-mobile launchers of ICBMs. For each specified restricted area, the roofs of fixed structures for road-mobile launchers of ICBMs shall be open for the duration of a display. The road-mobile launchers of ICBMs located within the restricted area shall be displayed either located next to or moved halfway out of such fixed structures; [RF MOU Annex A]

(b) a display in the open of the rail-mobile launchers of ICBMs located at parking sites specified by the requesting Party. Such launchers shall be displayed by removing the entire train from its fixed structure and locating the train within the rail garrison. The number of rail-mobile launchers of ICBMs subject to display pursuant to each such request shall include all such launchers located at no more than eight parking sites, provided that no more than two parking sites may be requested within any one rail garrison in any one request. Requests concerning specific parking sites shall include the designation for each parking site as provided for in Annex A to the Memorandum of Understanding; and [RF MOU Annex A]

(c) a display in the open of all heavy bombers and former heavy bombers located within one air base specified by the requesting Party, except those heavy bombers and former heavy bombers that are not readily movable due to maintenance or operations. Such heavy bombers and former heavy bombers shall be displayed by removing the entire airplane from its fixed structure, if any, and locating the airplane within the air base. Those heavy bombers and former heavy bombers at the air base specified by the requesting Party that are not readily movable due to maintenance or operations shall be specified by the requested Party in a notification provided in accordance with paragraph 2 of Section V of the Notification Protocol. Such a notification shall be provided no later than 12 hours after the request for display has been made.

2. Road-mobile launchers of ICBMs, rail-mobile launchers of ICBMs, heavy bombers, and former heavy bombers subject to each request pursuant to paragraph 1 of this Article shall be displayed in open view without using concealment measures. Each Party shall have the right to make seven such requests each year, but shall not request a display at any particular ICBM base for road-mobile launchers of ICBMs, any particular parking site, or any particular air base more than two times each year.

A Party shall have the right to request, in any single request, only a display of road-mobile launchers of ICBMs, a display of rail-mobile launchers of ICBMs, or a display of heavy bombers and former heavy bombers. A display shall begin no later than 12 hours after the request is made and shall continue until 18 hours have elapsed from the time that the request was made. If the requested Party cannot conduct a display due to circumstances brought about by force majeure, it shall provide notification to the requesting Party in accordance with paragraph 3 of Section V of the Notification Protocol, and the display shall be cancelled. In such a case, the number of requests to which the requesting Party is entitled shall not be reduced.

3. A request for cooperative measures shall not be made for a facility that has been designated for inspection until such an inspection has been completed and the inspectors have departed the facility. A facility for which cooperative measures have been requested shall not be designated for inspection until the cooperative measures have been completed or until notification has been provided in accordance with paragraph 3 of Section V of the Notification Protocol.

ARTICLE XIII

1. Each Party shall have the right to conduct exercise dispersal of deployed mobile launchers of ICBMs and their associated missiles from restricted areas or rail garrisons. Such an exercise dispersal may involve either road-mobile launchers of ICBMs or rail-mobile launchers of ICBMs, or both road-mobile launchers of ICBMs and rail-mobile launchers of ICBMs. Exercise dispersals of deployed mobile launchers of ICBMs and their associated missiles shall be conducted as provided for below:

(a) An exercise dispersal shall be considered to have begun as of the date and time specified in the notification provided in accordance with paragraph 11 of Section II of the Notification Protocol.

(b) An exercise dispersal shall be considered to be completed as of the date and time specified in the notification provided in accordance with paragraph 12 of Section II of the Notification Protocol.

(c) Those ICBM bases for mobile launchers of ICBMs specified in the notification provided in accordance with paragraph 11 of Section II of the Notification Protocol shall be considered to be involved in an exercise dispersal.

(d) When an exercise dispersal begins, deployed mobile launchers of ICBMs and their associated missiles engaged in a routine movement from a restricted area or rail garrison of an ICBM base for mobile launchers of ICBMs that is involved in such a dispersal shall be considered to be part of the dispersal.

(e) When an exercise dispersal begins, deployed mobile launchers of ICBMs and their associated missiles engaged in a relocation from a restricted area or rail garrisons of an ICBM base for mobile launchers of ICBMs that is involved in such a dispersal shall continue to be considered to be engaged in a relocation. Notification of the completion of the relocation shall be provided in accordance with paragraph 10 of Section II of the Notification Protocol, unless notification of the completion of the relocation was provided in accordance with paragraph 12 of Section II of the Notification Protocol.

(f) During an exercise dispersal, all deployed mobile launchers of ICBMs and their associated missiles that depart a restricted area or rail garrison of an ICBM base for mobile launchers of ICBMs involved in such a dispersal shall be considered to be part of the dispersal, except for such launchers and missiles that relocate to a facility outside their associated ICBM base during such a dispersal.

(g) An exercise dispersal shall be completed no later than 30 days after it begins.

(h) Exercise dispersals shall not be conducted:

(i) more than two times in any period of two calendar years;

(ii) during the entire period of time provided for baseline data inspections;

(iii) from a new ICBM base for mobile launchers of ICBMs until a new facility inspection has been conducted or until the period of time provided for such an inspection has expired; or

(iv) from an ICBM base for mobile launchers of ICBMs that has been designated for a data update inspection or reentry vehicle inspection, until completion of such an inspection.

(i) If a notification of an exercise dispersal has been provided in accordance with paragraph 11 of Section II of the Notification Protocol, the other Party shall not have the right to designate for data update inspection or reentry vehicle inspection an ICBM base for mobile launchers of ICBMs involved in such a dispersal, or to request cooperative measures for such an ICBM base, until the completion of such a dispersal.

(j) When an exercise dispersal is completed, deployed mobile launchers of ICBMs and their associated missiles involved in such a dispersal shall be located at their restricted areas or rail garrisons, except for those otherwise accounted for in accordance with paragraph 12 of Section II of the Notification Protocol.

2. A major strategic exercise involving heavy bombers, about which a notification has been provided pursuant to the Agreement Between the Government of the United States of America and the Government of the Union of Soviet Socialist Republics on Reciprocal Advance Notification of Major Strategic Exercises of September 23, 1989, shall be conducted as provided for below:

(a) Such exercise shall be considered to have begun as of the date and time specified in the notification provided in accordance with paragraph 16 of Section II of the Notification Protocol.

(b) Such exercise shall be considered to be completed as of the date and time specified in the notification provided in accordance with paragraph 17 of Section II of the Notification Protocol.

(c) The air bases for heavy bombers and air bases for former heavy bombers specified in the notification provided in accordance with paragraph 16 of Section II of the Notification Protocol shall be considered to be involved in such exercise.

(d) Such exercise shall begin no more than one time in any calendar year, and shall be completed no later than 30 days after it begins.

(e) Such exercise shall not be conducted during the entire period of time provided for baseline data inspections.

(f) During such exercise by a Party, the other Party shall not have the right to conduct inspections of the air bases for heavy bombers and air bases for former heavy bombers involved in the exercise. The right to conduct inspections of such air bases shall resume three days after notification of the completion of a major strategic exercise involving heavy bombers has been provided in accordance with paragraph 17 of Section II of the Notification Protocol.

(g) Within the 30-day period following the receipt of the notification of the completion of such exercise, the receiving Party may make a request for cooperative measures to be carried out in accordance with subparagraph 1(c) of Article XII of this Treaty at one of the air bases involved in the exercise. Such a request shall not be counted toward the quota provided for in paragraph 2 of Article XII of this Treaty.

ARTICLE XIV

1. Each Party shall have the right to conduct operational dispersals of deployed mobile launchers of ICBMs and their associated missiles, ballistic missile submarines, and heavy bombers. There shall be no limit on the number and duration of operational dispersals, and there shall be no limit on the number of deployed mobile launchers of ICBMs and their associated missiles, ballistic missile submarines, or heavy bombers involved in such dispersals. When an operational dispersal begins, all strategic offensive arms of a Party shall be considered to be part of the dispersal. Operational dispersals shall be conducted as provided for below: [Agreed State 7]

(a) An operational dispersal shall be considered to have begun as of the date and time specified in the noti-

fication provided in accordance with paragraph 1 of Section X of the Notification Protocol.

(b) An operational dispersal shall be considered to be completed as of the date and time specified in the notification provided in accordance with paragraph 2 of Section X of the Notification Protocol.

2. During an operational dispersal each Party shall have the right to:

(a) suspend notifications that it would otherwise provide in accordance with the Notification Protocol except for notification of flight tests provided under the Agreement Between the United States of America and the Union of Soviet Socialist Republics on Notifications of Launches of Intercontinental Ballistic Missiles and Submarine-Launched Ballistic Missiles of May 31, 1988; provided that, if any conversion or elimination processes are not suspended pursuant to subparagraph (d) of this paragraph, the relevant notifications shall be provided in accordance with Section IV of the Notification Protocol;

(b) suspend the right of the other Party to conduct inspections;

(c) suspend the right of the other Party to request cooperative measures; and

(d) suspend conversion and elimination processes for its strategic offensive arms. In such case, the number of converted and eliminated items shall correspond to the number that has actually been converted and eliminated as of the date and time of the beginning of the operational dispersal specified in the notification provided in accordance with paragraph 1 of Section X of the Notification Protocol.

3. Notifications suspended pursuant to paragraph 2 of this Article shall resume no later than three days after notification of the completion of the operational dispersal has been provided in accordance with paragraph 2 of Section X of the Notification Protocol. The right to conduct inspections and to request cooperative measures suspended pursuant to paragraph 2 of this Article shall resume four days after notification of the completion of the operational dispersal has been provided in accordance with paragraph 2 of Section X of the Notification Protocol. Inspections or cooperative measures being conducted at the time a Party provides notification that it suspends inspections or cooperative measures during an operational dispersal shall not count toward the appropriate annual quotas provided for by this Treaty.

4. When an operational dispersal is completed:

(a) All deployed road-mobile launchers of ICBMs and their associated missiles shall be located within their deployment areas or shall be engaged in relocations .

(b) All deployed rail-mobile launchers of ICBMs and their associated missiles shall be located within their rail garrisons or shall be engaged in routine movements or relocations .

(c) All heavy bombers shall be located within national territory and shall have resumed normal operations. If it is necessary for heavy bombers to be located outside national territory for purposes not inconsistent with this Treaty, the Parties will immediately engage in diplomatic consultations so that appropriate assurances can be provided.

5. Within the 30 day period after the completion of an operational dispersal, the Party not conducting the operational dispersal shall have the right to make no more than two requests for cooperative measures, subject to the provisions of Article XII of this Treaty, for ICBM bases for mobile launchers of ICBMs or air bases. Such requests shall not count toward the quota of requests provided for in paragraph 2 of Article XII of this Treaty.

ARTICLE XV

To promote the objectives and implementation of the provisions of this Treaty, the Parties hereby establish the Joint Compliance and Inspection Commission. The Parties agree that, if either Party so requests, they shall meet within the framework of the Joint Compliance and Inspection Commission to: [Lisbon Protocol]

(a) resolve questions relating to compliance with the obligations assumed;

(b) agree upon such additional measures as may be necessary to improve the viability and effectiveness of this Treaty; and

(c) resolve questions related to the application of relevant provisions of this Treaty to a new kind of strategic offensive arm, after notification has been provided in accordance with paragraph 16 of Section VII of the Notification Protocol.

ARTICLE XVI

To ensure the viability and effectiveness of this Treaty, each Party shall not assume any international obligations or undertakings that would conflict with its provisions. The Parties shall hold consultations in accordance with Article XV of this Treaty in order to resolve any ambiguities that may arise in this regard. The Parties [Lisbon Protocol] agree that this provision does not apply to any patterns of cooperation, including obligations, in the area of strategic offensive arms, existing at the time of signature of this Treaty, between a Party and a third State. [Agreed State 1] [Soviet State on Non-Circumvention & Patterns of Coop]

ARTICLE XVII

1. This Treaty, including its Annexes, Protocols, and Memorandum of Understanding, all of which form integral parts thereof, shall be subject to ratification in accordance with the constitutional procedures of each Party. This Treaty shall enter into force on the date of the exchange of instruments of ratification.

2. This Treaty shall remain in force for 15 years unless superseded earlier by a subsequent agreement on the reduction and limitation of strategic offensive arms. No later than one year before the expiration of the 15-year period, the Parties shall meet to consider whether this Treaty will be extended. If the Parties so decide, this Treaty will be extended for a period of five years unless it is superseded before the expiration of that period by a subsequent agreement on the reduction and limitation of strategic offensive arms. This Treaty shall be extended for successive five-year periods, if the Parties so decide, in accordance with the procedures governing the initial extension, and it shall remain in force for each agreed five-year period of extension unless it is superseded by a subsequent agreement on the reduction and limitation of strategic offensive arms.

3. Each Party shall, in exercising its national sovereignty, have the right to withdraw from this Treaty if it decides that extraordinary events related to the subject matter of this Treaty have jeopardized its supreme interests. It shall give notice of its decision to the other Party six months prior to withdrawal from this Treaty. Such notice shall include a statement of the extraordinary events the notifying Party regards as having jeopardized its supreme interests.

ARTICLE XX

Each Party may propose amendments to this Treaty. Agreed amendments shall enter into force in accordance with the procedures governing entry into force of this Treaty.

ARTICLE XXI

This Treaty shall be registered pursuant to Article 102 of the Charter of the United Nations.

Done at Moscow on July 31, 1991, in two copies, each in the English and Russian languages, both texts being equally authentic.

FOR THE UNITED STATES OF AMERICA: George Bush

President of the United States of America

FOR THE UNION OF SOVIET SOCIALIST RE-
PUBLICS: M. Gorbachev
President of the Union of Soviet Socialist Republics

Treaty Between the United States of America and the Russian Federation on Further Reduction and Limitation of Strategic Offensive Arms (START II)

January 3, 1993

The United States of America and the Russian Federation, hereinafter referred to as the Parties,

REAFFIRMING their obligations under the Treaty Between the United States of America and the Union of Soviet Socialist Republics on the Reduction and Limitation of Strategic Offensive Arms of July 31, 1991, hereinafter referred to as the START Treaty,

STRESSING their firm commitment to the Treaty on the Non-Proliferation of Nuclear Weapons of July 1, 1968, and their desire to contribute to its strengthening,

TAKING into account the commitment by the Republic of Belarus, the Republic of Kazakhstan, and Ukraine to accede to the Treaty on the Non-Proliferation of Nuclear Weapons of July 1, 1968, as non-nuclear-weapon States Parties,

MINDFUL of their undertakings with respect to strategic offensive arms under Article VI of the Treaty on the Non-Proliferation of Nuclear Weapons of July 1, 1968, and under the Treaty Between the United States of America and the Union of Soviet Socialist Republics on the Limitation of Anti-Ballistic Missile Systems of May 26, 1972, as well as the provisions of the Joint Understanding signed by the Presidents of the United States of America and the Russian Federation on June 17, 1992, and of the Joint Statement on a Global Protection System signed by the Presidents of the United States of America and the Russian Federation on June 17, 1992,

DESIRING to enhance strategic stability and predictability, and, in doing so, to reduce further strategic offensive arms, in addition to the reductions and limitations provided for in the START Treaty,

CONSIDERING that further progress toward that end will help lay a solid foundation for a world order built on democratic values that would preclude the risk of outbreak of war,

RECOGNIZING their special responsibility as permanent members of the United Nations Security Council for maintaining international peace and security,

TAKING note of United Nations General Assembly Resolution 47/52K of December 9, 1992.

CONSCIOUS of the new realities that have transformed the political and strategic relations between the Parties, and the relations of partnership that have been established between them,

Have agreed as follows:

ARTICLE I

1. Each Party shall reduce and limit its intercontinental ballistic missiles (ICBMs) and ICBM launchers, submarine-launched ballistic missiles (SLBMs) and SLBM launchers, heavy bombers, ICBM warheads, SLBM warheads, and heavy bomber armaments, so that seven years after entry into force of the START Treaty and thereafter, the aggregate number for each Party, as counted in accordance with Articles III and IV of this Treaty, does not exceed, for warheads attributed to deployed ICBMs, deployed SLBMs, and deployed heavy bombers, a number between 3800 and 4250 or such lower number as each Party shall decide for itself, but in no case shall such number exceed 4250.

2. Within the limitations provided for in paragraph 1 of this Article, the aggregate numbers for each Party shall not exceed:
   (a) 2160, for warheads attributed to deployed SLBMs;
   (b) 1200, for warheads attributed to deployed ICBMs of types to which more than one warhead is attributed; and
   (c) 650, for warheads attributed to deployed heavy ICBMs.

3. Upon fulfillment of the obligations provided for in paragraph 1 of this Article, each Party shall further reduce and limit its ICBMs and ICBM launchers, SLBMs and SLBM launchers, heavy bombers, ICBM warheads, SLBM warheads, and heavy bomber armaments, so that no later than January 1, 2003, and thereafter, the aggregate number for each Party, as counted in accordance with Articles III and IV of this Treaty, does not exceed, for warheads attributed to deployed ICBMs, deployed SLBMs, and deployed heavy bombers, a number between 3000 and 3500 or such lower number as each Party shall decide for itself, but in no case shall such number exceed 3500.

4. Within the limitations provided for in paragraph 3 of this Article, the aggregate numbers for each Party shall not exceed:

(a) a number between 1700 and 1750, for warheads attributed to deployed SLBMs or such lower number as each Party shall decide for itself, but in no case shall such number exceed 1750;

(b) zero, for warheads attributed to deployed ICBMs of types to which more than one warhead is attributed; and

(c) zero, for warheads attributed to deployed heavy ICBMs.

5. The process of reductions provided for in paragraphs 1 and 2 of this Article shall begin upon entry into force of this Treaty, shall be sustained throughout the reductions period provided for in paragraph 1 of this Article, and shall be completed no later than seven years after entry into force of the START Treaty. Upon completion of these reductions, the Parties shall begin further reductions provided for in paragraphs 3 and 4 of this Article, which shall also be sustained throughout the reductions period defined in accordance with paragraphs 3 and 6 of this Article.

6. Provided that the Parties conclude, within one year after entry into force of this Treaty, an agreement on a program of assistance to promote the fulfillment of the provisions of this Article, the obligations provided for in paragraphs 3 and 4 of this Article and in Article II of this Treaty shall be fulfilled by each Party no later than December 31, 2000.

ARTICLE II

1. No later than January 1, 2003, each Party undertakes to have eliminated or to have converted to launchers of ICBMs to which one warhead is attributed all its deployed and non-deployed launchers of ICBMs to which more than one warhead is attributed under Article III of this Treaty (including test launchers and training launchers), with the exception of those launchers of ICBMs other than heavy ICBMs at space launch facilities allowed under the START Treaty, and not to have thereafter launchers of ICBMs to which more than one warhead is attributed. ICBM launchers that have been converted to launch an ICBM of a different type shall not be capable of launching an ICBM of the former type. Each Party shall carry out such elimination or conversion using the

procedures provided for in the START Treaty, except as otherwise provided for in paragraph 3 of this Article.

2. The obligations provided for in paragraph 1 of this Article shall not apply to silo launchers of ICBMs on which the number of warheads has been reduced to one pursuant to paragraph 2 of Article III of this Treaty.

3. Elimination of silo launchers of heavy ICBMs, including test launchers and training launchers, shall be implemented by means of either:

(a) elimination in accordance with the procedures provided for in Section II of the Protocol on Procedures Governing the Conversion or Elimination of the Items Subject to the START Treaty; or

(b) conversion to silo launchers of ICBMs other than heavy ICBMs in accordance with the procedures provided for in the Protocol on Procedures Governing Elimination of Heavy ICBMs and on Procedures Governing Conversion of Silo Launchers of Heavy ICBMs Relating to the Treaty Between the United States of America and the Russian Federation on Further Reduction and Limitation of Strategic Offensive Arms, hereinafter referred to as the Elimination and Conversion Protocol. No more than 90 silo launchers of heavy ICBMs may be so converted.

4. Each Party undertakes not to emplace an ICBM, the launch canister of which has a diameter greater than 2.5 meters, in any silo launcher of heavy ICBMs converted in accordance with subparagraph 3(b) of this Article.

5. Elimination of launchers of heavy ICBMs at space launch facilities shall only be carried out in accordance with subparagraph 3(a) of this Article.

6. No later than January 1, 2003, each Party undertakes to have eliminated all of its deployed and non-deployed heavy ICBMs and their launch canisters in accordance with the procedures provided for in the Elimination and Conversion Protocol or by using such missiles for delivering objects into the upper atmosphere or space, and not to have such missiles or launch canisters thereafter.

7. Each Party shall have the right to conduct inspections in connection with the elimination of heavy ICBMs and their launch canisters, as well as inspections in connection with the conversion of silo launchers of heavy

ICBMs. Except as otherwise provided for in the Elimination and Conversion Protocol, such inspections shall be conducted subject to the applicable provisions of the START Treaty.

8. Each Party undertakes not to transfer heavy ICBMs to any recipient whatsoever, including any other Party to the START Treaty.

9. Beginning on January 1, 2003, and thereafter, each Party undertakes not to produce, acquire, flight-test (except for flight tests from space launch facilities conducted in accordance with the provisions of the START Treaty), or deploy ICBMs to which more than one warhead is attributed under Article III of this Treaty.

ARTICLE III

1. For the purposes of attributing warheads to deployed ICBMs and deployed SLBMs under this Treaty, the Parties shall use the provisions provided for in Article III of the START Treaty, except as otherwise provided for in paragraph 2 of this Article.

2. Each Party shall have the right to reduce the number of warheads attributed to deployed ICBMs or deployed SLBMs only of existing types, except for heavy ICBMs. Reduction in the number of warheads attributed to deployed ICBMs and deployed SLBMs of existing types that are not heavy ICBMs shall be carried out in accordance with the provisions of paragraph 5 of Article III of the START Treaty, except that:
(a) the aggregate number by which warheads are reduced may exceed the 1250 limit provided for in paragraph 5 of Article III of the START Treaty;
(b) the number by which warheads are reduced on ICBMs and SLBMs, other than the Minuteman III ICBM for the United States of America and the SS-N-18 SLBM for the Russian Federation, may at any one time exceed the limit of 500 warheads for each Party provided for in subparagraph 5(c)(I) of Article III of the START Treaty;
(c) each Party shall have the right to reduce by more than four warheads, but not by more than five warheads, the number of warheads attributed to each ICBM out of no more than 105 ICBMs of one existing type of ICBM. An ICBM to which the number of warheads attributed has been reduced in accordance

with this paragraph shall only be deployed in an ICBM launcher in which an ICBM of that type was deployed as of the date of signature of the START Treaty; and
(d) the reentry vehicle platform for an ICBM or SLBM to which a reduced number of warheads is attributed is not required to be destroyed and replaced with a new reentry vehicle platform.

3. Notwithstanding the number of warheads attributed to a type of ICBM or SLBM in accordance with the START Treaty, each Party undertakes not to:
(a) produce, flight-test, or deploy an ICBM or SLBM with a number of reentry vehicles greater than the number of warheads attributed to it under this Treaty; and
(b) increase the number of warheads attributed to an ICBM or SLBM that has had the number of warheads attributed to it reduced in accordance with the provisions of this Article.

ARTICLE IV

1. For the purposes of this Treaty, the number of warheads attributed to each deployed heavy bomber shall be equal to the number of nuclear weapons for which any heavy bomber of the same type or variant of a type is actually equipped, with the exception of heavy bombers reoriented to a conventional role as provided for in paragraph 7 of this Article. Each nuclear weapon for which a heavy bomber is actually equipped shall count as one warhead toward the limitations provided for in Article I of this Treaty. For the purpose of such counting, nuclear weapons include long-range nuclear air-launched cruise missiles (ALCMs), nuclear air-to-surface missiles with a range of less than 600 kilometers, and nuclear bombs.

2. For the purposes of this Treaty, the number of nuclear weapons for which a heavy bomber is actually equipped shall be the number specified for heavy bombers of that type and variant of a type in the Memorandum of Understanding on Warhead Attribution and Heavy Bomber Data Relating to the Treaty Between the United States of America and the Russian Federation on Further Reduction and Limitation of Strategic Offensive Arms,

hereinafter referred to as the Memorandum on Attribution.

3. Each Party undertakes not to equip any heavy bomber with a greater number of nuclear weapons than the number specified for heavy bombers of that type or variant of a type in the Memorandum on Attribution.

4. No later than 180 days after entry into force of this Treaty, each Party shall exhibit one heavy bomber of each type and variant of a type specified in the Memorandum on Attribution.

    The purpose of the exhibition shall be to demonstrate to the other Party the number of nuclear weapons for which a heavy bomber of a given type or variant of a type is actually equipped.

5. If either Party intends to change the number of nuclear weapons specified in the Memorandum on Attribution, for which a heavy bomber of a type or variant of a type is actually equipped, it shall provide a 90-day advance notification of such intention to the other Party. Ninety days after providing such a notification, or at a later date agreed by the Parties, the Party changing the number of nuclear weapons for which a heavy bomber is actually equipped shall exhibit one heavy bomber of each such type or variant of a type. The purpose of the exhibition shall be to demonstrate to the other Party the revised number of nuclear weapons for which heavy bombers of the specified type or variant of a type are actually equipped. The number of nuclear weapons attributed to the specified type and variant of a type of heavy bomber shall change on the ninetieth day after the notification of such intent. On that day, the Party changing the number of nuclear weapons for which a heavy bomber is actually equipped shall provide to the other Party a notification of each change in data according to categories of data contained in the Memorandum on Attribution.

6. The exhibitions and inspections conducted pursuant to paragraphs 4 and 5 of this Article shall be carried out in accordance with the procedures provided for in the Protocol on Exhibitions and Inspections of Heavy Bombers Relating to the Treaty Between the United States of America and the Russian Federation on Further Reduction and Limitation of Strategic Offensive Arms, hereinafter referred to as the Protocol on Exhibitions and Inspections.

7. Each Party shall have the right to reorient to a conventional role heavy bombers equipped for nuclear armaments other than long-range nuclear ALCMs. For the purposes of this Treaty, heavy bombers reoriented to a conventional role are those heavy bombers specified by a Party from among its heavy bombers equipped for nuclear armaments other than long-range nuclear ALCMs that have never been accountable under the START Treaty as heavy bombers equipped for long-range nuclear ALCMs. The reorienting Party shall provide to the other Party a notification of its intent to reorient a heavy bomber to a conventional role no less than 90 days in advance of such reorientation. No conversion procedures shall be required for such a heavy bomber to be specified as a heavy bomber reoriented to a conventional role.

8. Heavy bombers reoriented to a conventional role shall be subject to the following requirements:
    (a) the number of such heavy bombers shall not exceed 100 at any one time;
    (b) such heavy bombers shall be based separately from heavy bombers with nuclear roles;
    (c) such heavy bombers shall be used only for non-nuclear missions. Such heavy bombers shall not be used in exercises for nuclear missions, and their aircrews shall not train or exercise for such missions; and
    (d) heavy bombers reoriented to a conventional role shall have differences from other heavy bombers of that type or variant of a type that are observable by national technical means of verification and visible during inspection.

9. Each Party shall have the right to return to a nuclear role heavy bombers that have been reoriented in accordance with paragraph 7 of this Article to a conventional role. The Party carrying out such action shall provide to the other Party through diplomatic channels notification of its intent to return a heavy bomber to a nuclear role no less than 90 days in advance of taking such action. Such a heavy bomber returned to a nuclear role shall not subsequently be reoriented to a conventional role.

    Heavy bombers reoriented to a conventional role that are subsequently returned to a nuclear role shall have differences observable by national technical means of verification and visible during inspection from other heavy bombers of that type and variant of a type that have not been reoriented to a conventional role, as well as from heavy bombers of that type and variant of a type that are still reoriented to a conventional role.

10. Each Party shall locate storage areas for heavy bomber nuclear armaments no less than 100 kilometers from any air base where heavy bombers reoriented to a conventional role are based.

11. Except as otherwise provided for in this Treaty, heavy bombers reoriented to a conventional role shall remain subject to the provisions of the START Treaty, including the inspection provisions.

12. If not all heavy bombers of a given type or variant of a type are reoriented to a conventional role, one heavy bomber of each type or variant of a type of heavy bomber reoriented to a conventional role shall be exhibited in the open for the purpose of demonstrating to the other Party the differences referred to in subparagraph 8(d) of this Article. Such differences shall be subject to inspection by the other Party.

13. If not all heavy bombers of a given type or variant of a type reoriented to a conventional role are returned to a nuclear role, one heavy bomber of each type and variant of a type of heavy bomber returned to a nuclear role shall be exhibited in the open for the purpose of demonstrating to the other Party the differences referred to in paragraph 9 of this Article. Such differences shall be subject to inspection by the other Party.

14. The exhibitions and inspections provided for in paragraphs 12 and 13 of this Article shall be carried out in accordance with the procedures provided for in the Protocol on Exhibitions and Inspections.

ARTICLE V

1. Except as provided for in this Treaty, the provisions of the START Treaty, including the verification provisions, shall be used for implementation of this Treaty.

2. To promote the objectives and implementation of the provisions of this Treaty, the Parties hereby establish the Bilateral Implementation Commission. The Parties agree that, if either Party so requests, they shall meet within the framework of the Bilateral Implementation Commission to:

(a) resolve questions relating to compliance with the obligations assumed; and

(b) agree upon such additional measures as may be necessary to improve the viability and effectiveness of this Treaty.

ARTICLE VI

1. This Treaty, including its Memorandum on Attribution, Elimination and Conversion Protocol, and Protocol on Exhibitions and Inspections, all of which are integral parts thereof, shall be subject to ratification in accordance with the constitutional procedures of each Party. This Treaty shall enter into force on the date of the exchange of instruments of ratification, but not prior to the entry into force of the START Treaty.

2. The provisions of paragraph 8 of Article II of this Treaty shall be applied provisionally by the Parties from the date of its signature.

3. This Treaty shall remain in force so long as the START Treaty remains in force.

4. Each Party shall, in exercising its national sovereignty, have the right to withdraw from this Treaty if it decides that extraordinary events related to the subject matter of this Treaty have jeopardized its supreme interests. It shall give notice of its decision to the other Party six months prior to withdrawal from this Treaty. Such notice shall include a statement of the extraordinary events the notifying Party regards as having jeopardized its supreme interests.

ARTICLE VII

Each Party may propose amendments to this Treaty. Agreed amendments shall enter into force in accordance with the procedures governing entry into force of this Treaty.

ARTICLE VIII

This Treaty shall be registered pursuant to Article 102 of the Charter of the United Nations.

DONE at Moscow on January 3, 1993, in two copies, each in the English and Russian languages, both texts being equally authentic.

FOR THE UNITED STATES AMERICA
George W. Bush

FOR THE RUSSIAN FEDERATION:
Boris Yeltsin

Strategic Offensive Reductions Treaty (2002)

The United States of America and the Russian Federation, hereinafter referred to as the Parties,

Embarking upon the path of new relations for a new century and committed to the goal of strengthening their relationship through cooperation and friendship,

Believing that new global challenges and threats require the building of a qualitatively new foundation for strategic relations between the Parties,

Desiring to establish a genuine partnership based on the principles of mutual security, cooperation, trust, openness, and predictability,

Committed to implementing significant reductions in strategic offensive arms,

Proceeding from the Joint Statements by the President of the United States of America and the President of the Russian Federation on Strategic Issues of July 22, 2001 in Genoa and on a New Relationship between the United States and Russia of November 13, 2001 in Washington,

Mindful of their obligations under the Treaty Between the United States of America and the Union of Soviet Socialist Republics on the Reduction and Limitation of Strategic Offensive Arms of July 31, 1991, hereinafter referred to as the START Treaty,

Mindful of their obligations under Article VI of the Treaty on the Non-Proliferation of Nuclear Weapons of July 1, 1968, and

Convinced that this Treaty will help to establish more favorable conditions for actively promoting security and cooperation, and enhancing international stability,

Have agreed as follows:

ARTICLE I

Each Party shall reduce and limit strategic nuclear warheads, as stated by the President of the United States of America on November 13, 2001 and as stated by the President of the Russian Federation on November 13, 2001 and December 13, 2001 respectively, so that by December 31, 2012 the aggregate number of such warheads does not exceed 1700-2200 for each Party. Each Party shall determine for itself the composition and structure of its strategic offensive arms, based on the established aggregate limit for the number of such warheads.

ARTICLE II

The Parties agree that the START Treaty remains in force in accordance with its terms.

ARTICLE III

For purposes of implementing this Treaty, the Parties shall hold meetings at least twice a year of a Bilateral Implementation Commission.

ARTICLE IV

1. This Treaty shall be subject to ratification in accordance with the constitutional procedures of each Party. This Treaty shall enter into force on the date of the exchange of instruments of ratification.
2. This Treaty shall remain in force until December 31, 2012 and may be extended by agreement of the Parties or superseded earlier by a subsequent agreement.
3. Each Party, in exercising its national sovereignty, may withdraw from this Treaty upon three months written notice to the other Party.

ARTICLE V

This Treaty shall be registered pursuant to Article 102 of the Charter of the United Nations.

Done at Moscow on May 24, 2002, in two copies, each in the English and Russian languages, both texts being equally authentic.

FOR THE UNITED STATES OF AMERICA:
George W. Bush

FOR THE RUSSIAN FEDERATION:
Vladimir Putin

Treaty for the Prohibition of Nuclear Weapons in Latin America and the Caribbean* (Treaty of Tlatelolco)

Opened for Signature: 14 February 1967.
Entered into Force: 22 April 1968.

PREAMBLE

In the name of their peoples and faithfully interpreting their desires and aspirations, the Governments of the States which sign the Treaty for the Prohibition of Nuclear Weapons in Latin America,

Desiring to contribute, so far as lies in their power, towards ending the armaments race, especially in the field of nuclear weapons, and towards strengthening a world at peace, based on the sovereign equality of States, mutual respect and good neighbourliness,

Recalling that the United Nations General Assembly, in its resolution 808 (IX), adopted unanimously as one of the three points of a coordinated programme of disarmament "the total prohibition of the use and manufacture of nuclear weapons and weapons of mass destruction of every type",

Recalling that militarily denuclearized zones are not an end in themselves but rather a means for achieving general and complete disarmament at a later stage,

Recalling United Nations General Assembly resolution 1911 (XVIII), which established that the measures that should be agreed upon for the denuclearization of Latin America should be taken ain the light of the principles of the Charter of the United Nations and of regional agreements",

Recalling United Nations General Assembly resolution 2028 (XX), which established the principle of an acceptable balance of mutual responsibilities and duties for the nuclear and non-nuclear powers, and

Recalling that the Charter of the Organization of American States proclaims that it is an essential purpose of the Organization to strengthen the peace and security of the hemisphere,

Convinced:

That the incalculable destructive power of nuclear weapons has made it imperative that the legal prohibition of war should be strictly observed in practice if the survival of civilization and of mankind itself is to be assured,

That nuclear weapons, whose terrible effects are suffered, indiscriminately and inexorably, by military forces and civilian population alike, constitute, through the persistence of the radioactivity they release, an attack on the integrity of the human species and ultimately may even render the whole earth uninhabitable,

That general and complete disarmament under effective international control is a vital matter which all the peoples of the world equally demand,

That the proliferation of nuclear weapons, which seems inevitable unless States, in the exercise of their sovereign rights, impose restrictions on themselves in order to prevent it, would make any agreement on disarmament enormously difficult and would increase the danger of the outbreak of a nuclear conflagration,

That the establishment of militarily denuclearized zones is closely linked with the maintenance of peace and security in the respective regions,

That the military denuclearization of vast geographical zones, adopted by the Sovereign decision of the States comprised therein, will exercise a beneficial influence on other regions where similar conditions exist,

That the privileged situation of the signatory States, whose territories are wholly free from nuclear weapons, imposes upon them the inescapable duty of preserving that situation both in their own interests and for the good of mankind,

That the existence of nuclear weapons in any country of Latin America would make it a target for possible nuclear attacks and would inevitably set off,

throughout the region a ruinous race in nuclear weapons which would involve the unjustifiable diversion, for warlike purposes, of the limited resources required for economic and social development,

That the foregoing reasons, together with the traditional peace-loving outlook of Latin America, give rise to an inescapable necessity that nuclear energy should be used in that region exclusively for peaceful purposes, and that the Latin American countries should use their right to the greatest and most equitable possible access to this new source of energy in order to expedite the economic and social development of their peoples,

Convinced finally:

That the military denuclearization of Latin America - being understood to mean the undertaking entered into internationally in this Treaty to keep their territories forever free from nuclear weapons - will constitute a measure which will spare their peoples from the squandering of their limited resources on nuclear armaments and will protect them against possible nuclear attacks on their territories, and will also constitute a significant contribution towards preventing the proliferation of nuclear weapons and a powerful factor for general and complete disarmament, and

That Latin America, faithful to its tradition of universality, must not only endeavour to banish from its homelands the scourge of a nuclear war, but must also strive to promote the well-being and advancement of its peoples, at the same time cooperating in the fulfilment of the ideals of mankind, that is to say, in the consolidation of a permanent peace based on equal rights, economic fairness and social justice for all, in accordance with the principles and purposes set forth in the Charter of the United Nations and in the Charter of the Organization of American States,

Have agreed as follows:

OBLIGATIONS

Article I

1. The Contracting Parties hereby undertake to use exclusively for peaceful purposes the nuclear material and facilities which are under their jurisdiction, and to prohibit and prevent in their respective territories:
(a) The testing, use, manufacture, production or acquisition by any means whatsoever of any nuclear weapons, by the Parties themselves, directly or indirectly, on behalf of anyone else or in any other way, and
(b) The receipt, storage, installation, deployment and any form of possession of any nuclear weapons, directly or indirectly, by the Parties themselves, by anyone on their behalf or in any other way.

2. The Contracting Parties also undertake to refrain from engaging in, encouraging or authorizing, directly or indirectly, or in any way participating in the testing, use, manufacture, production, possession or control of any nuclear weapon.

DEFINITION OF THE CONTRACTING PARTIES

Article 2

For the purposes of this Treaty, the Contracting Parties are those for whom the Treaty is in force.

DEFINITION OF TERRITORY

Article 3

For the purposes of this Treaty, the term "territory" shall include the territorial sea, air space and any other space over which the State exercises sovereignty in accordance with its own legislation.

ZONE OF APPLICATION

Article 4

1. The zone of application of this Treaty is the whole of the territories for which the Treaty is in force.

2. Upon fulfilment of the requirements of article 28, paragraph 1, the zone of application of this Treaty shall also be that which is situated in the western hemisphere within the following limits (except the continental part of the territory of the United States of America and its territorial waters): starting at a point located at 35∞ north latitude, 75∞ west longitude; from this point directly southward to a point at 30∞ north latitude, 75∞ west longitude; from there, directly eastward to a point at 30∞ north latitude, 50∞ west longitude; from there, along a loxodromic line to a point at 5∞ north latitude, 20∞ west longitude; from there, directly southward to a point at 60∞ south latitude, 20∞ west longitude; from there, directly westward to a point at 60∞ south latitude, 115∞ west longitude; from there, directly northward to a point at 0 latitude, 115∞ west longitude; from there, along a loxodromic line to a point at 35∞ north latitude, 150∞ west longitude; from there, directly eastward to a point at 35∞ north latitude, 75∞ west longitude.

DEFINITION OF NUCLEAR WEAPONS

Article 5

For the purposes of this Treaty, a nuclear weapon is any device which is capable of releasing nuclear energy in an uncontrolled manner and which has a group of characteristics that are appropriate for use for warlike purposes. An instrument that may be used for the transport or propulsion of the device is not included in this definition if it is separable from the device and not an indivisible part thereof.

MEETING OF SIGNATORIES

Article 6

At the request of any of the signatory States or if the Agency established by article 7 should so decide, a meeting of all the signatories may be convoked to consider in common questions which may affect the very essence of this instrument, including possible amendments to it. In either case, the meeting will be convoked by the General Secretary.

ORGANIZATION

Article 7

1. In order to ensure compliance with the obligations of this Treaty, the Contracting

Parties hereby establish an international organization to be known as the Agency for the Prohibition of Nuclear Weapons in Latin America, hereinafter referred to as "the Agency". Only the Contracting Parties shall be affected by its decisions.

2. The Agency shall be responsible for the holding of periodic or extraordinary consultations among Member States on matters relating to the purposes, measures and procedures set forth in this Treaty and to the supervision of compliance with the obligations arising therefrom.

3. The Contracting Parties agree to extend to the Agency full and prompt cooperation in accordance with the provisions of this Treaty, of any agreements they may conclude with the Agency and of any agreements the Agency may conclude with any other international organization or body.

4. The headquarters of the Agency shall be in Mexico City.

ORGANS

Article 8

1. There are hereby established as principal organs of the Agency a General Conference, a Council and a Secretariat.

2. Such subsidiary organs as are considered necessary by the General Conference may be established within the purview of this Treaty.

THE GENERAL CONFERENCE

Article 9

1. The General Conference, the supreme organ of the Agency, shall be composed of all the Contracting Parties; it shall hold regular sessions every two years, and may also hold special sessions whenever this Treaty so provides or, in the opinion of the Council, the circumstances so require.

2. The General Conference:
(a) May consider and decide on any matters or questions covered by this Treaty, within the limits thereof, including those referring to powers and functions of any organ provided for in this Treaty;
(b) Shall establish procedures for the control system to ensure observance of this Treaty in accordance with its provisions;
(c) Shall elect the Members of the Council and the General Secretary;
(d) May remove the General Secretary from office if the proper functioning of the Agency so requires;
(e) Shall receive and consider the biennial and special reports submitted by the Council and the General Secretary;
(f) Shall initiate and consider studies designed to facilitate the optimum fulfilment of the aims of this Treaty, without prejudice to the power of the General Secretary independently to carry out similar studies for submission to and consideration by the Conference;
(g) Shall be the organ competent to authorize the conclusion of agreements with Governments and other international organizations and bodies.

3. The General Conference shall adopt the Agency's budget and fix the scale of financial contributions to be paid by Member States, taking into account the systems and criteria used for the same purpose by the United Nations.

4. The General Conference shall elect its officers for each session and may establish such subsidiary organs as it deems necessary for the performance of its functions.

5. Each Member of the Agency shall have one vote. The decisions of the General Conference shall be taken by a two-thirds majority of the Members present and voting in the case of matters relating to the control system and measures referred to in article 20, the admission of new Members, the election or removal of the General Secretary, adoption of the budget and matters related thereto. Decisions on other matters, as well as procedural questions and also determination of which questions must be decided by a two-thirds majority, shall be taken by a simple majority of the Members present and voting.

6. The General Conference shall adopt its own rules of procedure.

THE COUNCIL

Article 10

1. The Council shall be composed of five Members of the Agency elected by the General Conference from among the Contracting Parties, due account being taken of equitable geographic distribution.

2. The Members of the Council shall be elected for a term of four years. However, in the first election three will be elected for two years. Outgoing Members may not be re-elected for the following period unless the limited number of States for which the Treaty is in force so requires.
3. Each Member of the Council shall have one representative.
4. The Council shall be so organized as to be able to function continuously.
5. In addition to the functions conferred upon it by this Treaty and to those which may be assigned to it by the General Conference, the Council shall, through the General Secretary, ensure the proper operation of the control system in accordance with the provisions of this Treaty and with the decisions adopted by the General Conference.
6. The Council shall submit an annual report on its work to the General Conference as well as such special reports as it deems necessary or which the General Conference requests of it.
7. The Council shall elect its officers for each session.
8. The decisions of the Council shall be taken by a simple majority of its Members present and voting.
9. The Council shall adopt its own rules of procedure.

THE SECRETARIAT

Article 11

1. The Secretariat shall consist of a General Secretary, who shall be the chief administrative officer of the Agency, and of such staff as the Agency may require. The term of office of the General Secretary shall be four years and he may be re-elected for a single additional term. The General Secretary may not be a national of the country in which the Agency has its headquarters. In case the office of General Secretary becomes vacant, a new election shall be held to fill the office for the remainder of the term.
2. The staff of the Secretariat shall be appointed by the General Secretary, in accordance with rules laid down by the General Conference.
3. In addition to the functions conferred upon him by this Treaty and to those which may be assigned to him by the General Conference,

the General Secretary shall ensure, as provided by article 10, paragraph 5, the proper operation of the control system established by this Treaty, in accordance with the provisions of the Treaty and the decisions taken by the General Conference.
4. The General Secretary shall act in that capacity in all meetings of the General Conference and of the Council and shall make an annual report to both bodies on the work of the Agency and any special reports requested by the General Conference or the Council or which the General Secretary may deem desirable.
5. The General Secretary shall establish the procedures for distributing to all Contracting Parties information received by the Agency from governmental sources and such information from non-governmental sources as may be of interest to the Agency.
6. In the performance of their duties the General Secretary and the staff shall not seek or receive instructions from any Government or from any other authority external to the Agency and shall refrain from any action which might reflect on their position as international officials responsible only to the Agency; subject to their responsibility to the Agency, they shall not disclose any industrial secrets or other confidential information coming to their knowledge by reason of their official duties in the Agency.
7. Each of the Contracting Parties undertakes to respect the exclusively international character of the responsibilities of the General Secretary and the staff and not to seek to influence them in the discharge of their responsibilities.

CONTROL SYSTEM

Article 12

1. For the purpose of verifying compliance with the obligations entered into by the Contracting Parties in accordance with article 1, a control system shall be established which shall be put into effect in accordance with the provisions of articles 13-18 of this Treaty.
2. The control system shall be used in particular for the purpose of verifying:
(a) That devices, services and facilities intended for peaceful uses of nuclear energy are not used in the testing or manufacture of nuclear weapons;

(b) That none of the activities prohibited in article 1 of this Treaty are carried out in the territory of the Contracting Parties with nuclear materials or weapons introduced from abroad; and

(c) That explosions for peaceful purposes are compatible with article 18 of this Treaty.

IAEA SAFEGUARDS

Article 13

Each Contracting Party shall negotiate multilateral or bi-lateral agreements with the International Atomic Energy Agency for the application of its safeguards to its nuclear activities. Each Contracting Party shall initiate negotiations within a period of 180 days after the date of the deposit of its instrument of ratification of this Treaty. These agreements shall enter into force, for each Party, not later than eighteen months after the date of the initiation of such negotiations except in case of unforeseen circumstances or force majeure.

REPORTS OF THE PARTIES

Article 14

1. The Contracting Parties shall submit to the Agency and to the International Atomic Energy Agency, for their information, semi-annual reports stating that no activity prohibited under this Treaty has occurred in their respective territories.
2. The Contracting Parties shall simultaneously transmit to the Agency a copy of any report they may submit to the International Atomic Energy Agency which relates to matters that are the subject of this Treaty and to the application of safeguards.
3. The Contracting Parties shall also transmit to the Organization of American States, for its information, any reports that may be of interest to it, in accordance with the obligations established by the Inter-American System.

SPECIAL REPORTS REQUESTED BY THE GENERAL SECRETARY

Article 15

1. With the authorization of the Council, the General Secretary may request any of the Contracting Parties to provide the Agency with complementary or supplementary information regarding any event or circumstance connected with compliance with this Treaty, explaining his reasons. The Contracting Parties undertake to cooperate promptly and fully with the General Secretary.
2. The General Secretary shall inform the Council and the Contracting Parties forthwith of such requests and of the respective replies.

SPECIAL INSPECTIONS

Article 16

1. The International Atomic Energy Agency and the Council established by this Treaty have the power of carrying out special inspections in the following cases:

   (a) In the case of the International Atomic Energy Agency, in accordance with the agreements referred to in article 13 of this Treaty;

   (b) in the case of the Council:

   When so requested, the reasons for the request being stated, by any Party which suspects that some activity prohibited by this Treaty has been carried out or is about to be carried out, either in the territory of any other Party or in any other place on such latter Party's behalf, the Council shall immediately arrange for such an inspection in accordance with article 10, paragraph 5;

   When requested by any Party which has been suspected of or charged with having violated this shall immediately arrange for the special inspection requested in accordance with article 10, paragraph 5.

   The above requests will be made to the Council through the General Secretary.

2. The costs and expenses of any special inspection carried out under paragraph 1, subparagraph (b), sections (i) and (ii) of this article shall be borne by the requesting Party or Parties, except where the Council concludes on the basis of the report on the special inspection that, in view of the circumstances existing in the case, such costs and expenses should be borne by the Agency.
3. The General Conference shall formulate the procedures for the organization and execution of the special inspections carried out in accordance with paragraph 1, subparagraph (b), sections (i) and (ii) of this article.

4. The Contracting Parties undertake to grant the inspectors carrying out such special inspections full and free access to all places and all information which may be necessary for the performance of their duties and which are directly and intimately connected with the suspicion of violation of this Treaty. If so requested by the authorities of the Contracting Party in whose territory the inspection is carried out, the inspectors designated by the General Conference shall be accompanied by representatives of said authorities, provided that this does not in any way delay or hinder the work of the inspectors.

5. The Council shall immediately transmit to all the Parties, through the General Secretary, a copy of any report resulting from special inspections.

6. Similarly, the Council shall send through the General Secretary to the Secretary-General of the United Nations, for transmission to the United Nations Security Council and General Assembly, and to the Council of the Organization of American States, for its information, a copy of any report resulting from any special inspection carried out in accordance with paragraph 1, subparagraph (b), sections (i) and (ii) of this article.

7. The Council may decide, or any Contracting Party may request, the convening of a special session of the General Conference for the purpose of considering the reports resulting from any special inspection. In such a case, the General Secretary shall take immediate steps to convene the special session requested.

8. The General Conference, convened in special session under this article, may make recommendations to the Contracting Parties and submit reports to the Secretary-General of the United Nations to be transmitted to the United Nations Security Council and the General Assembly.

USE OF NUCLEAR ENERGY FOR PEACEFUL PURPOSES

Article 17

Nothing in the provisions of this Treaty shall prejudice the rights of the Contracting Parties, in conformity with this Treaty, to use nuclear energy for peaceful purposes, in particular for their economic development and social progress.

EXPLOSIONS FOR PEACEFUL PURPOSES

Article 18

1. The Contracting Parties may carry out explosions of nuclear devices for peaceful purposes - including explosions which involve devices similar to those used in nuclear weapons - or collaborate with third parties for the same purpose, provided that they do so in accordance with the provisions of this article and the other articles of the Treaty, particularly articles I and 5.

2. Contracting Parties intending to carry out, or to cooperate in carrying out, such an explosion shall notify the Agency and the International Atomic Energy Agency, as far in advance as the circumstances require, of the date of the explosion and shall at the same time provide the following information:
(a) The nature of the nuclear device and the source from which it was obtained;
(b) The place and purpose of the planned explosion;
(c) The procedures which will be followed in order to comply with paragraph 3 of this article;
(d) The expected force of the device; and
(e) The fullest possible information on any possible radioactive fall-out that may result from the explosion or explosions, and measures which will be taken to avoid danger to the population, flora, fauna and territories of any other Party or Parties.

3. The General Secretary and the technical personnel designated by the Council and the International Atomic Energy Agency may observe all the preparations, including the explosion of the device, and shall have unrestricted access to any area in the vicinity of the site of the explosion in order to ascertain whether the device and the procedures followed during the explosion are in conformity with the information supplied under paragraph 2 of this article and the other provisions of this Treaty.

4. The Contracting Parties may accept the collaboration of third parties for the purposes set forth in paragraph 1 of the present article, in accordance with paragraphs 2 and 3 thereof.

RELATIONS WITH OTHER INTERNATIONAL ORGANIZATIONS

Article 1 9

1. The Agency may conclude such agreements with the International Atomic Energy Agency as are authorized by the General Conference and as it considers likely to facilitate the efficient operation of the control system established by this Treaty.
2. The Agency may also enter into relations with any international Organization or body, especially any which may be established in the future to supervise disarmament or measures for the control of armaments in any part of the world.
3. The Contracting Parties may, if they see fit, request the advice of the Inter-American Nuclear Energy Commission on all technical matters connected with the application of this Treaty with which the Commission is competent to deal under its Statute.

MEASURES IN THE EVENT OF VIOLATION OF THE TREATY

Article 20

1. The General Conference shall take note of all cases in which, in its opinion, any Contracting Party is not complying fully with its obligations under this Treaty and shall draw the matter to the attention of the Party concerned, making such recommendations as it deems appropriate.
2. If, in its opinion, such non-compliance constitutes a violation of this Treaty which might endanger peace and security, the General Conference shall report thereon simultaneously to the United Nations Security Council and the General Assembly through the Secretary-General of the United Nations, and to the Council of the Organization of American States. The General Conference shall likewise report to the International Atomic Energy Agency for such purposes as are relevant in accordance with its Statute.

UNITED NATIONS AND ORGANIZATION OF AMERICAN STATES

Article 21

None of the provisions of this Treaty shall be construed as impairing the rights and obligations of the Parties under the Charter of the United Nations or, in the case of States Members of the Organization of American States, under existing regional treaties.

PRIVILEGES AND IMMUNITIES

Article 22

1. The Agency shall enjoy in the territory of each of the Contracting Parties such legal capacity. and such privileges and immunities as may be necessary for the exercise of its functions and the fulfilment of its purposes.
2. Representatives of the Contracting Parties accredited to the Agency and officials of the Agency shall similarly enjoy such privileges and immunities as are necessary for the performance of their functions.
3. The Agency may conclude agreements with the Contracting Parties with a view to determining the details of the application of paragraphs 1 and 2 of this article.

NOTIFICATION OF OTHER AGREEMENTS

Article 23

Once this Treaty has entered into force, the Secretariat shall be notified immediately of any international agreement concluded by any of the Contracting Parties on matters with which this Treaty is concerned; the Secretariat shall register it and notify the other Contracting Parties.

SETTLEMENT OF DISPUTES

Article 24

Unless the Parties concerned agree on another mode of peaceful settlement, any question or dispute concerning the interpretation or application of this Treaty which is not settled shall be referred to the International Court of Justice with the prior consent of the Parties to the controversy

SIGNATURE

Article 25

1. This Treaty shall be open indefinitely for signature by:
   (a) All the Latin American Republics; and
   (b) All other sovereign States situated in their entirety south of latitude 35 north in the western hemisphere; and, except as provided

in paragraph 2 of this article, all such States which become sovereign, when they have been admitted by the General Conference.

2. The General Conference shall not take any decision regarding the admission of a political entity part or all of whose territory is the subject, prior to the date when this Treaty is opened for signature, of a dispute or claim between an extra-continental country and one or more Latin American States, so long as the dispute has not been settled by peaceful means.

RATIFICATION AND DEPOSIT

Article 26

1. This Treaty shall be subject to ratification by signatory States in accordance with their respective constitutional procedures.
2. This Treaty and the instruments of ratification shall be deposited with the Government of the Mexican United States, which is hereby designated the Depositary Government.
3. The Depositary Government shall send certified copies of this Treaty to the Governments of signatory States and shall notify them of the deposit of each instrument of ratification.

RESERVATIONS

Article 27
This Treaty shall not be subject to reservations.

ENTRY INTO FORCE

Article 28

1. Subject to the provisions of paragraph 2 of this article, this Treaty shall enter into force among the States that have ratified it as soon as the following requirements have been met:
(a) Deposit of the instruments of ratification of this Treaty with the Depositary Government by the Governments of the States mentioned in article 25 which are in existence on the date when this Treaty is opened for signature and which are not affected by the provisions of article 25, paragraph 2;
(b) Signature and ratification of Additional Protocol I annexed to this Treaty by all extra-continental or continental States having de jure or de facto international responsibility for territories situated in the zone of application of the Treaty;
(c) Signature and ratification of the Additional Protocol 11 annexed to this Treaty by all powers possessing nuclear weapons;
(d) Conclusion of bilateral or multilateral agreements on the application of the Safeguards System of the International Atomic Energy Agency in accordance with article 13 of this Treaty.

2. All signatory States shall have the imprescriptible right to waive, wholly or in part, the requirements laid down in the preceding paragraph. They may do so by means of a declaration which shall be annexed to their respective instrument of ratification and which may be formulated at the time of deposit of the instrument or subsequently. For those States which exercise this right, this Treaty shall enter into force upon deposit of the declaration, or as soon as those requirements have been met which have not been expressly waived.

3. As soon as this Treaty has entered into force in accordance with the provisions of paragraph 2 for eleven States, the Depositary Government shall convene a preliminary meeting of those States in order that the Agency may be set up and commence its work.

4. After the entry into force of this Treaty for all the countries of the zone, the rise of a new power possessing nuclear weapons shall have the effect of suspending the execution of this Treaty for those countries which have ratified it without waiving requirements of paragraph 1, sub-paragraph (c) of this article, and which request such suspension; the Treaty shall remain suspended until the new power, on its own initiative or upon request by the General Conference, ratifies the annexed Additional Protocol n.

AMENDMENTS

Article 29

1. Any Contracting Party may propose amendments to this Treaty and shall submit its proposals to the Council through the General Secretary, who shall transmit them to all the other Contracting Parties and, in addition, to all other signatories in accordance with article 6. The Council, through the General Secretary, shall immediately following

the meeting of signatories convene a special session of the General Conference to examine the proposals made, for the adoption of which a two-thirds majority of the Contracting Parties present and voting shall be required.

2. Amendments adopted shall enter into force as soon as the requirements set forth in article 28 of this Treaty have been complied with.

DURATION AND DENUNCIATION

Article 30

1. This Treaty shall be of a permanent nature and shall remain in force indefinitely, but any Party may denounce it by notifying the General Secretary of the Agency if, in the opinion of the denouncing State, there have arisen or may arise circumstances connected with the content of this Treaty or of the annexed Additional Protocols I and II which affect its supreme interests or the peace and security of one or more Contracting Parties.

2. The denunciation shall take effect three months after the delivery to the General Secretary of the Agency of the notification by the Government of the signatory State concerned. The General Secretary shall immediately communicate such notification to the other Contracting Parties and to the Secretary-General of the United Nations for the information of the United Nations Security Council and the General Assembly. He shall also communicate it to the Secretary-General of the Organization of American States.

AUTHENTIC TEXTS AND REGISTRATION

Article 31

This Treaty, of which the Spanish, Chinese, English, French, Portuguese and Russian texts are equally authentic, shall be registered by the Depositary Government in accordance with article 102 of the United Nations Charter. The Depositary Government shall notify the Secretary-General of the United Nations of the signatures, ratifications and amendments relating to this Treaty and shall communicate them to the Secretary-General of the Organization of American States for its information.

Transitional Article

Denunciation of the declaration referred to in article 28, paragraph 2, shall be subject to the same procedures as the denunciation of this Treaty, except that it will take effect on the date of delivery of the respective notification.

IN WITNESS WHEREOF the undersigned Plenipotentiaries, having deposited their full powers, found in good and due form, sign this Treaty on behalf of their respective Governments.

Done at Mexico, Distrito Federal, on the Fourteenth day of February, one thousand nine hundred and sixty-seven.

ADDITIONAL PROTOCOL I

The undersigned Plenipotentiaries, furnished with full powers by their respective Governments,

Convinced that the Treaty for the Prohibition of Nuclear Weapons in Latin America, negotiated and signed in accordance with the recommendations of the General Assembly of the United Nations in Resolution 1911 (XVIII) of 27 November 1963, represents an important step towards ensuring the non-proliferation of nuclear weapons,

Aware that the non-proliferation of nuclear weapons is not an end in itself but, rather, a means of achieving general and complete disarmament at a later stage, and

Desiring to contribute, so far as lies in their power, towards ending the armaments race, especially in the field of nuclear weapons, and towards strengthening a world peace, based on mutual respect and sovereign equality of States,

Have agreed as follows:

ARTICLE I

To undertake to apply the statute of denuclearization in respect of warlike purposes as defined in articles 1, 3, 5 and 13 of the Treaty for the Prohibition of Nuclear Weapons in Latin America in territories for which, de jure or de facto, they are internationally responsible and which lie within the limits of the geographical zone established in that Treaty.

ARTICLE 2

The duration of this Protocol shall be the same as that of the Treaty for the Prohibition of Nuclear Weapons in Latin America of which this Protocol is an annex, and the provisions regarding ratification and denunciation contained in the Treaty shall be applicable to it.

ARTICLE 3

This Protocol shall enter into force, for the States which have ratified it, on the date of the deposit of their respective instruments of ratification.

IN WITNESS WHEREOF the undersigned Plenipotentiaries, having deposited their full powers, found in good and due form, sign this Protocol on behalf of their respective Governments.

ADDITIONAL PROTOCOL II

The undersigned Plenipotentiaries, furnished with full powers by their respective Governments,

Convinced that the Treaty for the Prohibition of Nuclear Weapons in Latin America, negotiated and signed in accordance with the recommendations of the General Assembly of the United Nations in Resolution 1911 (XVIII) of 27 November 1963, represents an important step towards ensuring the non-proliferation of nuclear weapons, Aware that the non-proliferation of nuclear weapons is not an end in itself but, rather, a means of achieving general and complete disarmament at a later stage, and Desiring to contribute, so far as lies in their power, towards ending the armaments race, especially in the field of nuclear weapons, and towards promoting and strengthening a world at peace, based on mutual respect and sovereign equality of States,

Have agreed as follows:

ARTICLE I

The statute of denuclearization of Latin America in respect of warlike purposes, as defined, delimited and set forth in the Treaty for the Prohibition of Nuclear Weapons in Latin America of which this instrument is an annex, shall be fully respected by the Parties to this Protocol in all its express aims and provisions.

ARTICLE 2

The Governments represented by the undersigned Plenipotentiaries undertake, therefore, not to contribute in any way to the performance of acts involving a violation of the obligations of article 1 of the Treaty in the territories to which the Treaty applies in accordance with article 4 thereof.

ARTICLE 3

The Governments represented by the undersigned Plenipotentiaries also undertake not to use or threaten to use nuclear weapons against the Contracting Parties of the Treaty for the Prohibition of Nuclear Weapons in Latin America.

ARTICLE 4

The duration of this Protocol shall be the same as that of the Treaty for the Prohibition of Nuclear Weapons in Latin America of which this Protocol is an annex, and the definitions of territory and nuclear weapons set forth in articles 3 and 5 of the Treaty shall be applicable to this Protocol, as well as the provisions regarding ratification, reservations, denunciation, authentic texts and registration contained in articles 26, 27, 30 and 31 of the Treaty.

ARTICLE 5

This Protocol shall enter into force, for the States which have ratified it, on the date of the deposit of their respective instruments of ratification.

IN WITNESS WHEREOF, the undersigned Plenipotentiaries, having deposited their full powers, found to be in good and due form, hereby sign this Additional Protocol on behalf of their respective Governments.

* On 3 July 1990, the Agency for the Prohibition of Nuclear Weapons in Latin America decided, in its resolution 267 (E-V), to add to the legal title of the Treaty the terms "and the Caribbean", in conformity with article 7 of the Treaty.

Treaty Between The United States of America and The Union of Soviet Socialist Republics on the Limitation of Underground Nuclear Weapon Tests

Signed at Moscow July 3, 1974
Ratified December 8, 1990
Entered into force December 11, 1990

The United States of America and the Union of Soviet Socialist Republics, hereinafter referred to as the Parties,

Declaring their intention to achieve at the earliest possible date the cessation of the nuclear arms race and to take effective measures toward reductions in strategic arms, nuclear disarmament, and general and complete disarmament under strict and effective international control,

Recalling the determination expressed by the Parties to the 1963 Treaty Banning Nuclear Weapon Tests in the Atmosphere, in Outer Space and Under Water in its Preamble to seek to achieve the discontinuance of all test explosions of nuclear weapons for all time, and to continue negotiations to this end,

Noting that the adoption of measures for the further limitation of underground nuclear weapon tests would contribute to the achievement of these objectives and would meet the interests of strengthening peace and the further relaxation of international tension,

Reaffirming their adherence to the objectives and principles of the Treaty Banning Nuclear Weapon Tests in the Atmosphere, in Outer Space and Under Water and of the Treaty on the Non-Proliferation of Nuclear Weapons,

Have agreed as follows:

ARTICLE I

1. Each Party undertakes to prohibit, to prevent, and not to carry out any underground nuclear weapon test having a yield exceeding 150 kilotons at any place under its jurisdiction or control, beginning March 31, 1976.
2. Each Party shall limit the number of its underground nuclear weapon tests to a minimum.
3. The Parties shall continue their negotiations with a view toward achieving a solution to the problem of the cessation of all underground nuclear weapon tests.

ARTICLE II

1. For the purpose of providing assurance of compliance with the provisions of this Treaty, each Party shall use national technical means of verification at its disposal in a manner consistent with the generally recognized principles of international law.
2. Each Party undertakes not to interfere with the national technical means of verification of the other Party operating in accordance with paragraph 1 of this Article.
3. To promote the objectives and implementation of the provisions of this Treaty the Parties shall, as necessary, consult with each other, make inquiries and furnish information in response to such inquiries.

ARTICLE III

The provisions of this Treaty do not extend to underground nuclear explosions carried out by the Parties for peaceful purposes. Underground nuclear explosions for peaceful purposes shall be governed by an agreement which is to be negotiated and concluded by the Parties at the earliest possible time.

ARTICLE IV

This Treaty shall be subject to ratification in accordance with the constitutional procedures of each Party. This Treaty shall enter into force on the day of the exchange of instruments of ratification.

ARTICLE V

1. This Treaty shall remain in force for a period of five years. Unless replaced earlier by an agreement in implementation of the objectives specified in paragraph 3 of Article I of this Treaty, it shall be extended for successive five-year periods unless either Party notifies the other of its termination no later than six months prior to the expiration of the Treaty. Before the expiration of this period the Parties may, as necessary, hold consultations to consider the situation relevant to the substance of this Treaty and to introduce possible amendments to the text of the Treaty.
2. Each Party shall, in exercising its national sovereignty, have the right to withdraw from this Treaty if it decides that extraordinary events related to the subject matter of this Treaty have jeopardized its supreme interests. It shall give notice of its decision to the other Party six months prior to withdrawal from this Treaty. Such notice shall include a statement of the extraordinary events the notifying Party regards as having jeopardized its supreme interests.
3. This Treaty shall be registered pursuant to Article 102 of the Charter of the United Nations.

DONE at Moscow on July 3, 1974, in duplicate, in the English and Russian languages, both texts being equally authentic.

FOR THE UNITED STATES OF AMERICA:
RICHARD NIXON
The President of the United States of America
FOR THE UNION OF SOVIET SOCIALIST RE-PUBLICS:
L. BREZHNEV
General Secretary of the Central Committee of the CPSU

The Wassenaar Arrangement on Export Controls for Conventional Arms and Dual-Use Goods and Technologies

FINAL DECLARATION

1. Representatives of Australia, Austria, Belgium, Canada, the Czech Republic, Denmark, Finland, France, Germany, Greece, Hungary, Ireland, Italy, Japan, Luxembourg, the Netherlands, New Zealand, Norway, Poland, Portugal, the Russian Federation, the Slovak Republic, Spain, Sweden, Switzerland, Turkey, the United Kingdom and the United States met in Wassenaar, the Netherlands, on 18 and 19 December 1995.

2. The representatives agreed to establish The Wassenaar Arrangement on Export Controls for Conventional Arms and Dual-Use Goods and Technologies.

3. The representatives established initial elements of the new arrangement, to be submitted to their respective Governments for approval.

4. They also established a Preparatory Committee of the Whole to start work in January 1996.

5. The representatives agreed to locate the Secretariat of The Wassenaar Arrangement in Vienna, Austria. The first plenary meeting will take place in Vienna on 2 and 3 April 1996.

Purposes, Guidelines & Procedures, including the Initial Elements

(as amended and updated by the Plenary of December 2003)

WA Secretariat, Vienna
December 2003

INITIAL ELEMENTS

I. Purposes

As originally established in the Initial Elements adopted by the Plenary of 11-12 July 1996 and as exceptionally amended by the Plenary of 6-7 December 2001.

1. The Wassenaar Arrangement has been established in order to contribute to regional and international security and stability, by promoting transparency and greater responsibility in transfers of conventional arms and dual-use goods and technologies, thus preventing destabilising accumulations. Participating States will seek, through their national policies, to ensure that transfers of these items do not contribute to the development or enhancement of military capabilities which undermine these goals, and are not diverted to support such capabilities.

2. It will complement and reinforce, without duplication, the existing control regimes for weapons of mass destruction and their delivery systems, as well as other internationally recognised measures designed to promote transparency and greater responsibility, by focusing on the threats to international and regional peace and security which may arise from transfers of armaments and sensitive dual-use goods and technologies where the risks are judged greatest.

3. This Arrangement is also intended to enhance co-operation to prevent the acquisition of armaments and sensitive dual-use items for military end-uses, if the situation in a region or the behaviour of a state is, or becomes, a cause for serious concern to the Participating States.

4. This Arrangement will not be directed against any state or group of states and will not impede bona fide civil transactions. Nor will it interfere with the rights of states to acquire legitimate means with which to defend themselves pursuant to Article 51 of the Charter of the United Nations.

5. In line with the paragraphs above, Participating States will continue to prevent the acquisition of conventional arms and dual-use goods and technologies by terrorist groups and organisations, as well as by individual terrorists. Such efforts are an integral part of the global fight against terrorism.[1]

II. Scope

1. Participating States will meet on a regular basis to ensure that transfers of conventional arms and transfers in dual-use goods and technologies are carried out responsibly and in furtherance of international and regional peace and security.

2. To this end, Participating States will exchange, on a voluntary basis, information that will enhance transparency, will lead to discussions among all Participating States on arms transfers, as well as on sensitive dual-use goods and technologies, and will assist in developing common understandings of the risks associated with the transfer of these items. On the basis of this information they will assess the scope for co-ordinating national control policies to combat these risks. The information to be exchanged will include any matters which individual Participating States wish to bring to the attention of others, including, for those wishing to do so, notifications which go beyond those agreed upon.

3. The decision to transfer or deny transfer of any item will be the sole responsibility of each Participating State. All measures undertaken with respect to the Arrangement will be in accordance with national legislation and policies and will be implemented on the basis of national discretion.

4. In accordance with the provisions of this Arrangement, Participating States agree to notify transfers and denials. These notifications will apply to all non-participating states. However, in the light of the general and specific information exchange, the scope of these notifications, as well as their relevance for the purposes of the Arrangement, will be reviewed. Notification of a denial will not impose an obligation on other Participating States to deny similar transfers. However, a Participating State will notify, preferably within 30 days, but no later than within 60 days, all other Participating States of an approval of a licence which has been denied by another Participating State for an essentially identical transaction during the last three years.[2]

5. Participating States agree to work expeditiously on guidelines and procedures that take into account experience acquired. This work continues and will include, in particular, a continuing review of the scope of conventional arms to be covered with a view to extending information and notifications beyond the categories described in Appendix 3. Participating States agree to discuss further how to deal with any areas of overlap between the various lists.

6. Participating States agree to assess, on a regular basis, the overall functioning of this Arrangement.

7. In fulfilling the purposes of this Arrangement as defined in Section I, Participating States have, inter alia, agreed to the following guidelines, elements and procedures as a basis for decision making through the application of their own national legislation and policies:

"*Elements for Objective Analysis and Advice Concerning Potentially Destabilising Accumulations of Conventional Weapons*"—adopted by the December 1998 Plenary;

"*Statement of Understanding on Intangible Transfers of Software and Technology*"—adopted December 2001;

"*Best Practice Guidelines for Exports of Small Arms and Light Weapons (SALW)*"—adopted December 2002";

"*Elements for Export Controls of Man-Portable Air Defence Systems (MANPADS)*"—adopted December 2003;

"*Elements for Effective Legislation on Arms Brokering*"—adopted December 2003;

"*Statement of Understanding on Control of Non-Listed Dual-Use Items*"—adopted December 2003.

III. Control Lists

1. Participating States will control all items set forth in the Lists of Dual-Use Goods and Technologies and in the Munitions List (see Appendix 5)[3], with the objective of preventing unauthorised transfers or re-transfers of those items.

2. The List of Dual-Use Goods and Technologies (Dual-Use List) has two annexes: 1) sensitive items (Sensitive List) and 2) very sensitive items (Very Sensitive List).

3. The lists will be reviewed regularly to reflect technological developments and experience gained by Participating States, including in the field of dual-use goods and technologies which are critical for indigenous military capabilities. In this respect, studies shall be completed to coincide with the first revision to the lists to establish an appropriate level of transparency for pertinent items.

IV. Procedures for the General Information Exchange

1. Participating States agree to exchange general information on risks associated with transfers of conventional arms and dual-use goods and technologies in order to consider, where necessary, the scope for co-ordinating national control policies to combat these risks.

2. In furtherance of this objective, and in keeping with the commitment to maximum restraint as a matter of national policy when considering applications for the export of arms and sensitive dual-use goods to all destinations where the risks are judged greatest, in particular to regions where conflict is occurring, Participating States also agree to exchange information on regions they consider relevant to the purposes of the Arrangement. These Regional Views should be based on, but not limited to, Section 2 of the "Elements for Objective Analysis and Advice Concerning Potentially Destabilising Accumulations of Conventional Weapons" (adopted by the 1998 Plenary).

3. A list of possible elements of the general information exchange on non-participating states is contained in Appendix 1.

V. Procedures for the Exchange of Information on Dual-Use Goods and Technology

1. Participating States will notify licences denied to non-participants with respect to items on the List of Dual-Use Goods and Technologies, where the reasons for denial are relevant to the purposes of the Arrangement.

2. For the Dual-Use List, Participating States will notify all licences denied relevant to the purposes of the Arrangement to non-participating states, on an aggregate basis, twice per year. The indicative content of these denial notifications is described in Appendix 2.

3. For items in the Sensitive List and Very Sensitive List, Participating States will notify, on an individual basis, all licences denied pursuant to the purposes of the Arrangement to non-participating states. Participating States agree that notification shall be made on an early and timely basis, that is, preferably within 30 days but no later than within 60 days, of the date of the denial. The indicative content of these denial notifications is described in Appendix 2.

4. For items in the Sensitive List and Very Sensitive List, Participating States will notify licences issued or

transfers made relevant to the purposes of the Arrangement to non-participants, on an aggregate basis, twice per year. The indicative content of these licence/transfer notifications is described in Appendix 2.

5. Participating States will exert extreme vigilance for items included in the Very Sensitive List by applying to those exports national conditions and criteria. They will discuss and compare national practices at a later stage.

6. Participating States agree that any information on specific transfers, in addition to that specified above, may be requested inter alia through normal diplomatic channels.

VI. Procedures for the Exchange of Information on Arms

1. Participating States agree that the information to be exchanged on arms will include any matters which individual Participating States wish to bring to the attention of others, such as emerging trends in weapons programmes and the accumulation of particular weapons systems, where they are of concern, for achieving the objectives of the Arrangement.

2. As an initial stage in the evolution of the new Arrangement, Participating States will exchange information every six months on deliveries to non-participating states of conventional arms set forth in Appendix 3, derived from the categories of the UN Register of Conventional Arms. The information should include the quantity and the name of the recipient state and, except in the category of missiles and missile launchers, details of model and type.

3. Participating States agree that any information on specific transfers, in addition to that specified above, may be requested inter alia through normal diplomatic channels.

VII. Meetings and Administration

1. Participating States will meet periodically to take decisions regarding this Arrangement, its purposes and its further elaboration, to review the lists of controlled items, to consider ways of co-ordinating efforts to promote the development of effective export control systems, and to discuss other relevant matters of mutual interest, including information to be made public.

2. Plenary meetings will be held at least once a year and chaired by a Participating State on the basis of annual rotation. Financial needs of the Arrangement will be covered under annual budgets, to be adopted by Plenary Meetings.

3. Working Groups may be established, if the Plenary meeting so decides.

4. There will be a secretariat with a staff necessary to undertake the tasks entrusted to it.

5. All decisions in the framework of this Arrangement will be reached by consensus of the Participating States.

VIII. Participation

The new Arrangement will be open, on a global and non-discriminatory basis, to prospective adherents that comply with the agreed criteria in Appendix 4. Admission of new participants will be based on consensus.

IX. Confidentiality

Information exchanged will remain confidential and be treated as privileged diplomatic communications. This confidentiality will extend to any use made of the information and any discussion among Participating States.

APPENDIX 1

GENERAL INFORMATION EXCHANGE

Indicative Contents

The following is a list of possible principal elements of the general information exchange on non-participating states, pursuant to the purposes of the agreement (not all elements necessarily applying to both arms and dual-use goods and technology):

1. Acquisition activities

- Companies/organisations
- Routes and methods of acquisition
- Acquisition networks inside/outside the country
- Use of foreign expertise
- Sensitive end-users
- Acquisition patterns
- Conclusions.

2. Export policy

- Export control policy
- Trade in critical goods and technology
- Conclusions.

3. Projects of Concern

- Description of the project
- Level of technology
- Present status of development
- Future plans
- Missing technology (development and production)

- Companies/organisations involved, including end-user(s)
- Diversion activities
- Conclusions.

4. Other matters

Specific Information Exchange on Dual-Use Goods and Technologies

Indicative Content of Notifications

The content of denial notifications for the Dual-Use List will be based on, but not be limited to, the following indicative or illustrative list:

- From (country)
- Country of destination
- Item number on the Control List
- Short description
- Number of licences denied
- Number of units (quantity)
- Reason for denial.

Denial notification for items in the Sensitive List and the Very Sensitive List will be on the basis of, but not be limited to, the following indicative or illustrative list:

- From (country)
- Item number on the Control List
- Short description
- Number of units (quantity)
- Consignee(s)
- Intermediate consignee(s) and/or agent(s):

  Name
  Address
  Country

- Ultimate consignee(s) and/or end-user(s):

  Name
  Address
  Country

  Stated end-use
  Reason for the denial
  Other relevant information.

The content of notifications for licences/transfers in the Sensitive List will be based on, but not be limited to, the following indicative or illustrative list:

- From (country)
- Item number on the Control List
- Short description
- Number of units (quantity)
- Destination (country).

APPENDIX 3[4]

SPECIFIC INFORMATION EXCHANGE ON ARMS

Content by Category

1. Battle Tanks

Tracked or wheeled self-propelled armoured fighting vehicles with high cross-country mobility and a high level of self-protection, weighing at least 16.5 metric tonnes unladen weight, with a high muzzle velocity direct fire main gun of at least 75 mm calibre.

2. Armoured Combat Vehicles

2.1 Tracked, semi-tracked or wheeled self-propelled vehicles, with armoured protection and cross-country capability designed, or modified and equipped:

2.1.1 to transport a squad of four or more infantrymen, or

2.1.2 with an integral or organic weapon of at least 12.5 mm calibre, or

2.1.3 with a missile launcher.

2.2 Tracked, semi-tracked or wheeled self-propelled vehicles, with armoured protection and cross-country capability specially designed, or modified and equipped:

2.2.1 with organic technical means for observation, reconnaissance, target indication, and designed to perform reconnaissance missions, or

2.2.2 with integral organic technical means for command of troops, or

2.2.3 with integral organic electronic and technical means designed for electronic warfare.

2.3 Armoured bridge-launching vehicles.

3. Large Calibre Artillery Systems

3.1 Guns, howitzers, mortars, and artillery pieces combining the characteristics of a gun or a howitzer capable of engaging surface targets by delivering primarily indirect fire, with a calibre of 75 mm to 155 mm, inclusive.

3.2 Guns, howitzers, mortars, and artillery pieces combining the characteristics of a gun or a howitzer capable of engaging surface targets by delivering primarily indirect fire, with a calibre above 155 mm.

3.3 Multiple-launch rocket systems capable of engaging surface targets, including armour, by delivering primarily indirect fire with the calibre of 75 mm and above.

3.4 Gun-carriers specifically designed for towing artillery.

4. Military Aircraft/Unmanned Aerial Vehicles

4.1 Military Aircraft:

Fixed-wing or variable-geometry wing aircraft which are designed, equipped or modified:

4.1.1 to engage targets by employing guided missiles, unguided rockets, bombs, guns, machine guns, cannons or other weapons of destruction.

4.1.2 to perform reconnaissance, command of troops, electronic warfare, electronic and fire suppression of air defence systems, refuelling or airdrop missions.

4.2 Unmanned Aerial Vehicles:

Unmanned aerial vehicles, specially designed, modified, or equipped for military use including electronic warfare, suppression of air defence systems, or reconnaissance missions, as well as systems for the control and receiving of information from the unmanned aerial vehicles.

"Military Aircraft" does not include primary trainer aircraft, unless designed, equipped or modified as described above.

5. Military and Attack Helicopters

Rotary-wing aircraft which are designed, equipped or modified to:

5.1 engage targets by employing guided or unguided, air-to-surface, anti-armour weapons, air to sub-surface or air-to-air weapons, and equipped with an integrated fire-control and aiming system for these weapons.

5.2 perform reconnaissance, target acquisition (including anti-submarine warfare), communications, command of troops, or electronic warfare, or mine laying missions.

6. Warships[5]

Vessel or submarines armed and equipped for military use with a standard displacement of 150 metric tonnes or above, and those with a standard displacement of less than 150 metric tonnes equipped for launching missiles with a range of at least 25 km or torpedoes with a similar range.

7. Missiles or Missile Systems

Guided or unguided rockets, ballistic or cruise missiles capable of delivering a warhead or weapon of destruction to a range of at least 25 km, and means designed or modified specifically for launching such missiles or rockets, if not covered by categories 1 to 6.

This category:

7.1 also includes remotely piloted vehicles with the characteristics for missiles as defined above;

7.2 does not include ground-to-air missiles.

8. Small Arms and Light Weapons—Man-Portable Weapons made or modified to military specification for use as lethal instruments of war

8.1 Small Arms—broadly categorised for reporting purposes as: those weapons intended for use by individual members of armed forces or security forces, including revolvers and self-loading pistols; rifles and carbines; submachine guns; assault rifles; and light machine guns.

8.2 Light Weapons—broadly categorised for reporting purposes as: those weapons intended for use by individual or several members of armed or security forces serving as a crew and delivering primarily direct fire. They include heavy machine guns; hand-held under-barrel and mounted grenade launchers; portable anti-tank guns; recoilless rifles; portable launchers of anti-tank missile and rocket systems; and mortars of calibre less than 75 mm.

8.3 Man-Portable Air-Defence Systems—broadly categorised for reporting purposes as: surface-to-air missile systems intended for use by an individual or several members of armed forces serving as a crew.

Participation Criteria

When deciding on the eligibility of a state for participation, the following factors, inter alia, will be taken into consideration, as an index of its ability to contribute to the purposes of the new Arrangement:

Whether it is a producer/exporter of arms or industrial equipment respectively;

Whether it has taken the WA Control lists as a reference in its national export controls;

Its non-proliferation policies and appropriate national policies, including:

Adherence to non-proliferation policies, control lists and, where applicable, guidelines of the Nuclear Suppliers Group, the Zangger Committee, the Missile Technology Control Regime and the Australia Group; and through adherence to the Nuclear Non-Proliferation Treaty, the Biological and Toxicological Weapons Convention, the Chemical Weapons Convention and (where applicable) START I, including the Lisbon Protocol;

Its adherence to fully effective export controls.

Bibliography

Books

Ackland, Len. *Making a Real Killing: Rocky Flats and the Nuclear West.* Albuquerque, NM: University of New Mexico Press, 1999.

Albright, David, and Kevin O'Neill, eds. *Solving the North Korea Nuclear Puzzle.* Washington, DC: Institute for Science and International Security, 2000.

Alexander, Brian, and Alistair Millar, eds. *Tactical Nuclear Weapons: Emergent Threats in an Evolving Security Environment.* Dulles, VA: Brassey's, 2003.

Allison, Graham T., Albert Carnesale, and Joseph S. Nye, Jr., eds. *Hawks, Doves, & Owls: An Agenda for Avoiding Nuclear War.* New York: W.W. Norton and Company, 1985.

Allison, Graham, Ashton B. Carter, Steven E. Miller, and Philip Zelikow. *Cooperative Denuclearization: From Pledges to Deeds.* Cambridge, MA: Harvard University, Center for Science and International Affairs, January 1993.

Allison, Graham, Owen R. Cote, Jr., Richard A. Falkenrath, and Steven E. Miller. *Avoiding Nuclear Anarchy: Containing the Threat of Loose Russian Nuclear Weapons and Fissile Material.* Cambridge, MA: MIT Press, 1996.

Alperovitz, Gar. *The Decision to Use the Atomic Bomb.* New York: Vintage Books, 1995.

Ahmed, Samina, and David Cortright. *South Asia at the Nuclear Crossroads.* Washington: Fourth Freedom Foundation, April 2001.

Amme, Carl H. *NATO Strategy and Nuclear Defense.* New York: Greeenwood Press, 1988.

Arkin, William M., Thomas B. Cochran, and Milton M. Hoenig. *Nuclear Weapons Databook. Volume I: U.S. Nuclear Forces and Capabilities.* Cambridge, MA: Ballinger Publishing Company, 1984.

Arkin, William M., and Robert S. Norris. *Nuclear Weapons Databook, Volume II: U.S. Nuclear Warhead Production.* Cambridge, MA: Ballinger Publishing Company, 1987.

———. *Nuclear Weapons Databook, Volume III: US Nuclear Warhead Facility Profiles.* Cambridge, MA: Ballinger Publishing Company, 1987.

Arkin, William M., Thomas B. Cochran, Robert S. Norris, and Jeffrey I. Sands. *Nuclear Weapons Databook, Volume IV: Soviet Nuclear Weapons.* New York: Harper and Row, 1989.

Arkin, William M., and Richard W. Fieldhouse. *Nuclear Battlefields: Global Links in the Arms Race.* Cambridge, MA: Ballinger Publishing Company, 1985.

Arnold, Lorna. *Britain and the H-Bomb.* New York: Palgrave, 2001.

Asmus, Ronald D. *Germany's Geopolitical Normalization.* Santa Monica, CA: The RAND Corporation, July 1995.

Axelrod, Robert. *The Evolution of Cooperation.* New York: Basic Books, 1984.

Axelrod, Robert, and Jeffrey Richelson. *Strategic Nuclear Targeting.* Ithaca, NY: Cornell University Press, 1986.

Azizian, Rouben. *Nuclear Developments in South Asia and the Future of Global Arms Control.* Wellington, N.Z.: Centre for Strategic Studies, Victoria University of Wellington, 2001.

Ball, Desmond. *Targeting for Strategic Deterrence.* London: International Institute for Strategic Studies, 1983.

Barletta, Michael. *Proliferation Challenges and Nonproliferation Opportunities for New Administrations.* Washington: Center for Nonproliferation Studies, September 2000.

Barnaby, Frank, and P. Terrence Hopmann, eds. *Rethinking the Nuclear Weapons Dilemma in Europe.* Basingstoke, UK: Macmillan Press, 1988.

Bartimus, Tad, and Scott McCartney. *Trinity's Children: America's Nuclear Highway.* Albuquerque: New Mexico University Press, 1991.

Beckett, Brian. *Wars of Tomorrow.* London: Orbis Publishing, 1982.

Beckman, Peter R., Larry Campbell, Paul W. Crumlish, Michael N. Dobkowski, and Steven P.Lee. *The Nuclear Predicament: Nuclear Weapons in the Cold War and Beyond.* Englewood Cliffs, NJ: Prentice-Hall, 1992.

Bergeron, Kenneth D. *Tritium on Ice: The Dangerous New Alliance of Nuclear Weapons and Nuclear Power.* Cambridge, MA: MIT Press, 2002.

Betts, Richard, ed. *Cruise Missiles: Strategy, Technology, Politics.* Washington: The Brookings Institution, 1981.

Biddle, Stephen D., and Peter D. Feaver, eds. *Battlefield Nuclear Weapons: Issues and Options.* Cambridge, MA: Center for Science and International Affairs, 1989.

Binnendijk, Hans, and James Goodby, eds. *Transforming Nuclear Deterrence* (Washington: National Defense University Press, 1997).

Birstein, Vadim J. *The Perversion of Knowledge: The True Story of Soviet Science.* Boulder, CO: Westview Press, 2001.

Blackwill, Robert D., and Albert Carnesdale. *New Nuclear Nations: Consequences for US Policy.* New York: Council on Foreign Relations Press, 1993.

Blackwill, Robert D., and F. Stephen Larrabee, eds. *Conventional Arms Control and East-West Security.* Durham, NC: Duke University Press, 1989.

Blair, Bruce G. *The Logic of Accidental Nuclear War.* Washington: Brookings Institution Press, 1991.

Blechman, Peter R., Larry Campbell, Paul W. Crumlish, Michael N. Dobkowski, and Steven P. Lee. *The Nuclear Predicament: Nuclear Weapons in the Cold War and Beyond.* Englewood Cliffs, NJ: Prentice-Hall, 1992.

Booth, Ken, and John Baylis. *Britain, NATO, and Nuclear Weapons: Alternative Defence versus Alliance Reform.* Basingstoke: Macmillan Press Ltd., 1989.

Boutwell, Jeffrey. *The German Nuclear Dilemma.* Ithaca, NY: Cornell University Press, 1990.

Boutwell, Jeffrey D., Paul Doty, and Gregory F. Treverton, eds. *The Nuclear Confrontation in Europe.* London: Croom Helm, 1985.

Bowen, Wyn Q. *The Politics of Ballistic Missile Nonproliferation.* Southampton, U.K.: Southampton Studies in International Policy, 2000.

Bracken, Paul. *The Command and Control of Nuclear Forces.* New Haven, CT: Yale University Press, 1983.

Brodie, Bernard. *Strategy in the Misile Age.* Santa Monica, CA: The RAND Corporation, 1959.

Brown, Nanette, and James C. Wendt. *Improving the NATO Force Planning Process: Lessons from Past Efforts.* Santa Monica: The RAND Corporation, June 1986.

Brauch, Hans-Günter, and Duncan L. Clarke, eds. *Decisionmaking for Arms Limitation: Assessments and Prospects.* Cambridge, MA: Ballinger Publishing Company, 1983.

Brodine, Virginia. *Radioactive Contamination.* New York: Harcourt, Brace, Jovanovich, 1975.

Bundy, McGeorge. *Danger and Survival: Choices About the Bomb in the First Fifty Years.* New York: Vintage Books, 1988.

Bundy, McGeorge, William J. Crowe, and Sidney D. Drell. *Reducing Nuclear Danger: The Road Away from the Brink.* New York: Council on Foreign Relations Press, 1993.

Burrows, Andrew S., Robert S. Cochran, and Richard W. Fieldhouse. *Nuclear Weapons Databook, Volume V: British, French, and Chinese Nuclear Weapons.* Boulder, CO: Westview Press, 1994.

Buteux, Paul. *The Politics of Nuclear Consultation in NATO, 1965–1980.* Cambridge: Cambridge University Press, 1983.

———. *Strategy, Doctrine, and the Politics of Alliance: Theatre Nuclear Force Modernisation in NATO.* Boulder, CO: Westview Press, 1983.

Butler, Richard. *Fatal Choice: Nuclear Weapons and the Illusion of Missile Defense.* Boulder, Colo: Westview Press, 2001.

Caldicott, Helen. *Missile Envy: The Arms Race and Nuclear War.* Toronto: Bantam Books, 1986.

Campbell, Christy. *Nuclear Facts.* London: Hamlyn, 1984.

Campbell, Kurt M., Ashton B. Carter, Steven E. Miller, and Charles A. Zraket. *Soviet Nuclear Fission: Control of the Nuclear Arsenal in a Disintegrating Soviet Union.* Cambridge, MA: Harvard University Center for Science and International Affairs, 1991.

Campbell, Kurt M., Robert J. Einhorn, and Mitchell B. Reiss, eds. *The Nuclear Tipping Point: Why States Reconsider Their Nuclear Choices.* Washington, DC: Brookings Institution, 2004.

Carpenter, Ted Galen, ed. *NATO at 40: Confronting a Changing World.* Lexington, MA: Lexington Books, 1990.

Carter, Ashton B., John D. Steinbruner, and Charles A. Zraket. *Managing Nuclear Operations.* Washington: The Brookings Institution, 1987.

Cevasco, Frank M. *Survey and Assessment: Alternative Multilateral Export Control Structures.* Study Group on Enhancing Multilateral Export Controls for U.S. National Security, April 2001.

Central Intelligence Agency. *Unclassified Report to Congress on the Acquisition of Technology Relating to Weapons of Mass Destruction and Advanced Conventional Munitions.* September 2001.

Chandler, Robert W., *The New Face of War: Weapons of Mass Destruction and the Revitalization of America's Transoceanic Military Strategy* (McLean, VA: AMCODA Press, 1998.

Charles, Daniel. *Nuclear Planning in NATO: Pitfalls of First Use.* Cambridge, MA: Ballinger Press, 1987.

Chayes, Antonia H., and Paul Doty, eds. *Defending Deterrence: Managing the ABM Treaty Regime into the 21st Century.* Washington: Pergamon-Brassey's, 1989.

Chellany, Brahma. *Nuclear Proliferation: The US-Indian Conflict.* New Delhi: Orient Longman, 1993.

Cimbala, Stephen J. *Extended Deterrence: The United States and NATO Europe.* Lexington: Lexington Books, 1987.

———. *NATO Strategy and Nuclear Weapons.* New York: St. Martin's Press, 1989.

———, ed. *Deterrence and Nuclear Proliferation in the Twenty-First Century.* New York: Praeger Publishers, 2001.

Cirincione, Joseph, et al. *Deadly Arsenals: Tracking Weapons of Mass Destruction.* Washington: Canegie Endowmement, 1998.

Cirincione, Joseph, ed. *Repairing the Regime: Preventing the Spread of Weapons of Mass Destruction.* Washington: Carnegie Endowment, 2000.

Clarke, Duncan L. *American Defense and Foreign Policy Institutions.* New York: Ballinger Pulishers, 1989.

Cohen, Stephen P. *India: Emerging Power.* Washington, DC: Brookings Institute, 2001.

Cordesman, Anthony H. *The Global Nuclear Balance: A Quantitative and Arms Control Analysis.* Washington: Center for Strategic and International Studies, January 2001.

Craig, Paul P., and John A. Jungerman. *Nuclear Arms Race: Technology and Society.* New York: McGraw Hill, 1986.

Daalder, Ivo H. *The Nature and Practice of Flexible Response: NATO Strategy and Theater Nuclear Forces Since 1967.* New York: Columbia University Press, 1991.

Daalder, Ivo H., and Terry Terriff, eds. *Rethinking the Unthinkable: New Directions for Nuclear Arms Control.* London: Frank Cass, 1993.

Davis, Jacqueline K., and Robert L. Pfaltzgraff, Jr., eds. *National Security Decisions: The Participants Speak.* Lexington, MA: Lexington Books, 1990.

Davis, Jacqueline K., Charles M. Perry, and Robert L. Pfaltzgraff, Jr. *The INF Controversy: Lessons for NATO Modernization and Transatlantic Relations.* Washington: Pergamon-Brassey's, 1989.

Davis, Lynn E. *Assuring Peace in a Changing World: Critical Choices for the West's Strategic and Arms Control Policies.* Washington: The Johns Hopkins University Foreign Policy Institute, 1990.

Dean, Jonathon. *Watershed in Europe: Dismantling the East-West Military Confrontation.* Lexington: Lexington Books, 1987.

Deibel, Terry L., and John Lewis Gaddis. *Containment: Concept and Policy.* 2 volumes. Washington: National Defense University Press, 1986.

Dunn, Keith, and Stephen Flanagan. *NATO in the 5th Decade.* Washington: National Defense University Press, 1990.

Dunn, Lewis. *Global Proliferation: Dynamics, Acquisition Strategies, and Responses.* Newington, VA: Center for Verification Research, 9 December 1992.

Eden, Lynn, and Steven E. Miller. *Nuclear Arguments: Understanding the Nuclear Arms and Arms Control Debates.* Ithaca, NY: Cornell University Press, 1989.

FitzGerald, Frances. *Way Out There in the Blue: Reagan and Star Wars and the End of the Cold War.* New York: Simon & Schuster, 2000.

Ford, James L., and C. Richard Schuller. *Controlling Threats to Nuclear Security.* Washington: Center of Counterproliferation Research, National Defense University Press, June 1997.

Freedman, Lawrence. *The Evolution of Nuclear Strategy.* New York: St. Martin's Press, 1989.

Freedman, Lawrence, William G. Hyland, Karsten D. Voigt, and Paul C. Warnke. *Nuclear Weapons in Europe.* New York: Council on Foreign Relations, 1984.

The Future of the US-Soviet Nuclear Relationship. Washington: National Academy of Sciences, 1991.

Gaddis, John Lewis. *The Long Peace: Inquiries into the History of the Cold War.* Oxford: Oxford University Press, 1987.

———. *Strategies of Containment: A Critical Appraisal of Postwar American National Security Policy.* Oxford: Oxford University Press, 1982.

Gardner, Gary T. *Nuclear Nonproliferation: A Primer.* Boulder: Lynne Rienner Publishers, 1994.

Gardner, Gary T., and Steven A. Maaranen, eds. *Nuclear Weapons in the Changing World: Perspectives from Europe, Asia, and North America.* New York: Plenum Press, 1992.

Gibson, James N. *Nuclear Weapons of the United States: An Illustrated History.* Altglen, PA: Schiffer Publishing Ltd., 1996.

Glaser, Charles L. *Analyzing Strategic Nuclear Policy.* Princeton, NJ: Princeton University Press, 1990.

Golden, James R., Daniel J. Kaufman, Asa A. Clark IV, and David H. Petraeus, eds. *NATO at Forty: Change, Continuity, and Prospects.* Boulder, CO: Westview Press, 1989.

Goldfischer, David, and Thomas W. Graham. *Nuclear Deterrence and Global Security in Transition.* Boulder: Westview Press, 1992.

Graham, Bradley. *Hit to Kill: The New Battle Over Shielding America From Missile Attack.* Washington: Public Affairs Press, 2001.

Gray, Colin S. *Nuclear Strategy and National Syle.* Lanham, MD: Hamilton Press, 1986.

Gregory, Shaun R. *Nuclear Command and Control in NATO: Nuclear Weapons Operations and the Strategy of Flexible Response.* Basingstoke, UK: MacMillan Press, 1996.

Halperin, Morton H. *Nuclear Fallacy: Dispelling the Myth of Nuclear Strategy.* Cambridge, MA: Ballinger Publishing Company, 1987.

Halverson, Thomas E. *The Last Great Nuclear Debate: NATO and Short-Range Nuclear Weapons in the 1980s.* Basingstoke, UK: MacMillan Press, 1995.

Hamza, Khidhir. *Saddam's Bombmaker: The Terrifying Inside Story of the Iraqi Nuclear and Biological Weapons Agenda.* New York: Charles Scribner's Sons, 2000.

The Harvard Nuclear Study Group. *Living With Nuclear Weapons.* Toronto: Bantam Books, 1983.

Hays, Peter L., Vincent J. Jodoin, and Alan R. Van Tassel, eds. *Countering the Proliferation and Use of Weapons of Mass Destruction.* New York: McGraw Hill, 1998.

Hays, Peter L., James M. Smith, Alan R. Van Tassel, and Guy M. Walsh, eds. *Spacepower for a New Millenium.* New York: McGraw-Hill, 2000.

Herf, Jeffrey. *War by Other Means: Soviet Power, West German Resistance, and the Battle of the Euromissiles.* New York: The Free Press, 1991.

Herman, Charles F., ed. *American Defense Annual, 1994.* New York: Lexington Books, 1994.

Holloway, David. *Stalin and the Bomb.* New Haven: Yale University Press, 1996.

Holm, Hans-Henrik, and Nikolay Peterson. *The European Missiles Crisis: Nuclear Weapons and Security Policy.* London: Frances Pinter, 1983.

Hopkins, John C., and Weixing Hu. *Strategic Views from the Second Tier: The Nuclear-Weapons Policies of France, Britain, and China.* San Diego: University of California Institute on Global Conflict and Cooperation, 1994.

Hopman, P. Terrence, and Frank Barnaby. *Rethinking the Nuclear Weapons Dilemma in Europe.* Basingstoke: MacMillan Press, 1988.

Horner, Charles A., and Barry R. Schneider. "Counterforce," in Peter L. Hays, Vincent J. Jodoin, and Alan R. Van Tassel, eds. *Countering the Proliferation and Use of Weapons of Mass Destruction* (New York: McGraw Hill, 1998), pp. 239–252.

Hunter, Robert E., ed. *Restructuring Alliance Commitments.* Significant Issues Series, Vol. 10, No. 10. Washington: The Center for Strategic and International Studies, 1988.

Hyland, William G., ed. *Nuclear Weapons in Europe.* New York: Council on Foreign Relations, 1984.

Joffe, Josef. *The Limited Partnership: Europe, the United States, and the Burdens of Alliance.* Cambridge, MA: Ballinger Publishing Co., 1987.

Johnson, Craig M. *The Russian Federation's Ministry of Atomic Energy: Programs and Developments.* Richland, Wash.: Pacific Northwest National Laboratory, February 2000.

Johnson, Rebecca. *Non-Proliferation Treaty: Challenging Times.* London: The Acronym Institute, February 2000.

Julian, Thomas A. "The Future of Theater Nuclear Weapons in the 1990s and Beyond," in William D. Wharton, ed., *Security Arrangements for a New Europe* (Washington: NDU Press, April 1992), pp. 157–175.

Kaiser, Karl, and John Roper. *British-German Defence Co-operation: Partners Within the Alliance.* London: Jane's, 1988.

Katz, Arthur M. *Life after Nuclear War: The Economic and Social Impacts of Nuclear Attacks on the United States.* Cambridge, MA: Ballinger Publishing Company, 1982.

Kegley, Charles W., Jr., and Eugene R. Wittkopf, eds. *The Nuclear Reader: Strategy, Weapons, War.* New York: St. Martin's Press, 1989.

Kelleher, Catherine M. *Germany and the Politics of Nuclear Weapons.* New York: Columbia University Press, 1975.

———. "NATO Nuclear Operations," in *Managing Nuclear Operations,* edited by Ashton Carter, John Steinbruner, and Charles Zraket. Washington: The Brookings Institution, 1987.

Kelleher, Catherine M., and Gale A. Mattox, eds. *Evolving European Defense Policies.* Lexington: Lexington Books, 1987.

Kennan, George F. *The Nuclear Delusion: Soviet-American Relations in the Atomic Age.* New York: Pantheon Books, 1983.

Kennedy, Paul. *The Rise and Fall of the Great Powers.* New York: Random House, 1987.

Kennedy, Thomas J., Jr. *NATO Politico-Military Consultation: Shaping Alliance Decisions.* Washington: National Defense University Press, 1984.

Knorr, Klaus. *On the Uses of Military Power in the Nuclear Age.* Princeton, NJ: Princeton University Press, 1966.

Kraas, Allen S. "The New Nuclear Agenda," in *Peace and World Security Studies: A Curriculum Guide for the 1990s.* Boulder, CO: Lynne Reinner Publications, 1994.

Krasner, Stephen D., ed. *International Regimes.* Ithaca, NY: Cornell University Press, 1983.

Krepon, Michael. *Cooperative Threat Reduction, Missile Defense, and the Nuclear Future.* New York: Palgrave, 2003.

Kruzel, Joseph, ed. *American Defense Annual.* New York: Lexington Books, 1985–1993.

Laird, Robbin F., and Betsy A. Jacobs, eds. *The Future of Deterrence: NATO Nuclear Forces After INF.* Boulder: Westview Press, 1989.

Laquer, Walter, and Leon Sloss. *European Security in the 1990's: Deterrence and Defense After the INF Treaty.* New York: Plenum Press, 1990.

Larkin, Bruce D. *Nuclear Designs: Great Britain, France, and China in the Global Governance of Nuclear Arms.* New Brunswick, NJ: Transaction Publishers, 1996.

Larsen, Jeffrey A. *Arms Control: Cooperative Security in a Changing Environment.* Boulder, CO: Lynne Rienner Publications, 2002.

Larsen, Jeffrey A., and Gregory J. Rattray, eds. *Arms Control Toward the Twenty First Century.* Boulder, CO: Lynne Rienner Publications, 1996.

Larsen, Jeffrey A., and Kurt J. Klingenberger, eds. *Controlling Non-Strategic Nuclear Weapons: Obstacles and Opportunities.* Colorado Springs, Colo.: USAF Institute for National Security Studies, 2001.

Larsen, Jeffrey A., and James M. Smith. *Historical Dictionary of Arms Control and Disarmament.* Lanham, MD: Scarecrow Press, 2005.

Larson, Deborah Welch. *Origins of Containment: A Psychological Explanation.* Princeton, NJ: Princeton University Press, 1985.

The League of Women Voters, *The Nuclear Waste Primer: A Handbook for Citizens, Revised Editions* New York: Lyons & Burford, Publishers, 1993.

Lemke, Douglas A., ed. *The Alliance at Forty: Strategic Perspectives for the 1990's and Beyond.* Proceedings of the 12th NATO Symposium, 24–25 April 1989. Washington: National Defense University Press, 1989.

Levine, Herbert M., and David Carlton. *The Nuclear Arms Race Debated.* New York: McGraw Hill Book Co., 1986.

Levine, Robert A. *NATO, The Subjective Alliance: The Debate Over the Future.* Santa Monica: The RAND Corp., April 1988.

Lewis, William H., and Stuart E. Johnson. *Weapons of Mass Destruction: New Perspectives on Counterproliferation.* Washington: Institute for National Strategic Studies, NDU Press, 1995.

Lifton, Robert Jay, and Richard Falk. *Indefensible Weapons: The Political and Psychological Case Against Nuclearism.* New York: Basic Books, 1982.

Lindsay, James M., and Michael E. O'Hanlon. *Defending America: The Case for a Limited National Missile Defense.* Washington: The Brookings Institution, 2001.

Lodal, Jan. *The Price of Dominance: The New Weapons of Mass Destruction and their Challenge to American Leadership.* New York: Council on Foreign Relations Press, 2001.

Lourie, Richard. *Sakharov: A Biography.* Brandeis University Press, 2002.

Lucas, Michael R. *The Western Alliance after INF: Redefining US Policy Toward Europe and the Soviet Union.* Boulder: Lynne Rienner Publishers, 1990.

Mandelbaum, Michael. *The Nuclear Question: The United States and Nuclear Weapons 1946–1976.* Cambridge: Cambridge University Press, 1979.

———. *The Nuclear Revolution: International Politics Before and After Hiroshima.* Cambridge: Cambridge University Press, 1981.

Maroncelli, James M., and Timothy L. Karpin. *The Traveler's Guide to Nuclear Weapons: A Journey Through America's Cold War Battlefields.* Silverdale, WA: Historical Odysseys Publishers, 2002.

Martel, William C., and William T. Pendley. *Nuclear Coexistence: Rethinking US Policy to Promote Stability in an Era of Proliferation.* Montgomery, AL: Air War College, 1994.

Martin, Laurence. *The Changing Face of Nuclear Warfare.* New York: Harper and Row Publishers, Inc., 1987.

Matlock, Jack F., Jr. *Reagan and Gorbachev: How the Cold War Ended.* New York: Random House, 2004.

May, John. *The Greenpeace Book of the Nuclear Age.* London: Victor Gollancz, Ltd., 1989.

May, Michael, and Roger Speed. "Should Nuclear Weapons be Used?" In W.Thomas Wander and Eric H. Arnett, eds. *The Proliferation of Advanced Weaponry: Technology, Motivations, and Responses.* Washington: American Association for the Advancement of Science,1992, pp. 235–253.

Mayderv, Randall C. *America's Lost H-Bomb! Palomares, Spain, 1966.* Manhatten, KS: Sunflower University Press, 1997.

McLean, Scilla, ed. *How Nuclear Weapons Decisions are Made.* Basingstoke: MacMillan Press, 1987.

Mendelbaum, Michael. *The Nuclear Revolution.* Cambridge: Cambridge University Press, 1981.

Millar, Alistair, and Brian Alexander, eds. *Tactical Nuclear Weapons: Emergent Threats in an Evolving Security Environment.* New York: Brassey's, May 2003.

Miller, Steven E., ed. *Strategy and Nuclear Deterrence: An International Security Reader.* Princeton, NJ: Princeton University Press, 1984.

Mueller, John. "The Escalating Irrelevance of Nuclear Weapons," in T.V. Paul, Richard J. Harknett, and

James J. Wirtz, eds. *The Absolute Weapon Revisited: Nuclear Arms and the Emerging International Order.* Ann Arbor: University of Michigan Press, 1998, pp. 73–98.

Neuman, H. J. *Nuclear Forces in Europe: A Handbook for the Debate.* London: International Institute for Strategic Studies, 1982.

Newhouse, John. *War and Peace in the Nuclear Age.* New York: Vintage Books, 1990.

Nolan, Janne E. *An Elusive Consensus: Nuclear Weapons and American Security after the Cold War* (Washington: Brookings Institution Press, 1999).

Nordlinger, Eric A. *Isolationism Reconfigured: American Foreign policy for a New Century.* Princeton, NJ: Princeton University Press, 1995.

Norris, Robert S., Andrew S. Burrows, and Richard W. Fieldhouse. *Nuclear Weapons Databook, Volume V: British, French, and Chinese Nuclear Weapons.* Boulder, CO: Westview Press, 1994.

Nuclear Arms Control. Washington: National Academy of Sciences, 1985.

Nurick, Robert, ed. *Nuclear Weapons and European Security.* New York: St. Martin's Press, 1984.

Nye, Joseph S., Jr. *Nuclear Ethics.* New York: The Free Press, 1984.

Olive, Marsha McGraw, and Jeffrey D. Porro. *Nuclear Weapons in Europe: Modernization and Limitation.* Lexington, MA: Lexington Books, 1983.

Paul, Septimus H. *Nuclear Rivals: Anglo-American Atomic Relations, 1941–52.* Columbus, OH: Ohio State University Press, 2000.

Paul, T. V., Richard J. Harknett, and James J. Wirtz, eds. *The Absolute Weapon Revisited: Nuclear Arms and the Emerging International Order.* Ann Arbor, MI: University of Michigan Press, 1998.

Paulsen, Richard A. *The Role of U.S. Nuclear Weapons in the Post–Cold War Era.* Montgomery, AL: Air University Press, September 1994.

Payne, Keith B., *The Fallacies of Cold War Deterrence and a New Direction.* Lexington, KY: University Press of Kentucky, 2001.

Pilat, Joseph F., and Robert E. Pendley, eds. *1995: A New Beginning for the NPT?* New York: Plenum Publishers, 1995.

Pierre, Andrew J., ed. *Nuclear Weapons in Europe.* New York: Council on Foreign Relations, 1984.

Pikayev, Alexander A. *The Rise and Fall of START II: The Russian View.* Washington: Carnegie Endowment for International Peace, September 1999.

Platt, Alan, ed. *The Atlantic Alliance: Perspectives From the Successor Generation.* Santa Monica, CA: The RAND Corporation, December 1983.

Podvig, Pavel. *Russian Stategic Nuclear Forces.* Cambridge, MA: MIT Press, 2001.

Polmar, Norman. *Strategic Weapons: An Introduction.* New York: Crane, Russak and Company, 1975.

Potter, William C., Nikolai Sokov, Harald Müller, and Annette Schaper. *Tactical Nuclear Weapons: Options for Control.* New York: United Nations Institute for Disarmament Research, 2001.

Pringle, Peter, and James Spigelman. *The Nuclear Barons.* New York: Holt, Rinehart, and Winston, 1981.

Ramsbotham, Oliver, ed. *Choices: Nuclear and Non-nuclear Defense Options.* London: Brassey's Defense Publishers, 1987.

Rationale and Requirements for U.S. Nuclear Forces and Arms Control. Washington: National Institute for Public Policy, January 2001.

Raven-Hansen, Peter, ed. *First Use of Nuclear Weapons: Under the Constitution, Who Decides?* New York: Greenwood Press, 1987.

Record, Jeffrey. *NATO's Theater Nuclear Force Modernization Program: The Real Issues.* Cambridge, MA: Institute for Foreign Policy Analysis, Inc., 1981.

Reiss, Mitchell, and Robert S. Litwak. *Nuclear Proliferation After the Cold War.* Baltimore: Johns Hopkins University Press, 1994.

Report of the Commission to Assess United States National Security Space Management and Organization. Washington: The United States Commission on National Security/21st Century, January 2001.

Reynolds, Wayne. *Australia's Bid for the Atomic Bomb.* Melbourne, Australia: Melbourne University Press, 2001.

Risse-Kappen, Thomas. *The Zero Option: INF, West Germany, and Arms Control.* Boulder: Westview Press, 1988.

Rhodes, Edward. *Power and MADness: The Logic of Nuclear Coercion.* New York: Columbia University Press, 1989.

Rhodes, Richard. *Dark Sun: The Making of the Hydrogen Bomb.* New York: Simon and Schuster, 1995.

———. *The Making of the Atomic Bomb.* New York: Simon and Schuster, 1986.

Roberts, Brad. "Arms Control in 2000–2010: Forks in the Road Ahead," in James Brown, ed., *Entering the New Millennium: Dilemmas in Arms Control.* Albuquerque: Sandia National Laboratories, 1999, pp. 3–19.

———, ed. *Weapons Proliferation in the 1990s.* Cambridge, MA: The MIT Press, 1995.

Rose, Kenneth D. *One Nation Underground: The Fallout Shelter in American Culture.* New York: New York University Press, 2001.

Rosenthal, Debra. *At the Heart of the Bomb: The Dangerous Allure of Weapons Work.* Reading, MA: Addison-Wesley Publishing Company, Inc., 1990.

Royal United Services Institute. *Nuclear Attack: Civil Defence. Aspects of Civil Defence in the Nuclear Age.* London: Brassey's Publishers, 1981.

Sagan, Scott D. *The Limits of Safety: Organizations, Accidents, and Nuclear Weapons.* Princeton, NJ: Princeton University Press, 1993.

———. *Moving Targets: Nuclear Strategy and National Security.* Princeton, NJ: Princeton University Press, 1989.

Sagan, Scott D., and Kenneth N. Waltz. *The Spread of Nuclear Weapons: A Debate.* New York: W.W. Norton, 1995.

Salvalyev, Alexsandr, and Nikolay N. Detinov. *The Big Five: Arms Control Decision-Making in the Soviet Union.* Westport, CT: Praeger, 1995.

Schaeffer, Henry W. *Nuclear Arms Control.* Washington: National Defense University Press, April 1986.

Schaerf, Carlo and David Carlton, eds. *Reducing Nuclear Arsenals.* New York: St. Martin's Prpess, 1991.

Schelling, Thomas C. *Arms and Influence.* New Haven, CT: Yale University Press, 1966.

Schelling, Thomas C., and Morton H. Halperin. *Strategy and Arms Control.* Washington: Pergamon-Brassey's, 1985.

Shambroom, Paul. *Face to Face with the Bomb: Nuclear Reality after the Cold War.* Baltimore, MD: Johns Hopkins University Press, 2003.

Sherwin, Martin J. *A World Destroyed: Hiroshima and its Legacies.* 3rd ed. Palo Alto, Calif: Stanford University Press, 2003.

Schmidt, Helmut. *A Grand Strategy for the West.* New Haven: Yale University Press, 1985.

Schneider, Barry R. "Offensive Action: A Viable Option?" In *Future War and Counterproliferation: U.S. Military Responses to NBC Proliferation Threats.* Westport, CT: Praeger, 1999, pp. 147–170.

Schwartz, David N. *NATO's Nuclear Dilemmas.* Washington: The Brookings Institution, 1983.

Schwartz, Stephen I. *Atomic Audit: The Costs and Consequences of U.S. Nuclear Weapons Since 1940.* Washington: Brookings Institution Prpess, 1998.

Shields, John M., and William C. Potter. *Dismantling the Cold War: U.S. and NIS Perspectives on the Nunn-Lugar Cooperative Threat Reduction Program.* Cambridge, MA: The MIT Press, 1997.

Sigal, Leon V. *Nuclear Forces in Europe: Enduring Dilemmas, Present Prospects.* Washington: The Brookings Institution, 1984.

Sigal, Leon V., and John D. Steinbruner, eds. *Alliance Security: NATO and the No-First-Use Question.* Washington: The Brookings Institution, 1983.

Slocombe, Walter B. "The Future of U.S. Nuclear Weapons in a Restructured World," in Patrick J. Garrity and Steven A. Maaranen, eds. *Nuclear Weapons in the Changing World* (New York: Plenum Press, 1992), pp. 53–64.

Smith, James M., ed. *Nuclear Deterrence and Defense: Strategic Considerations.* Colorado Springs, CO: USAF Institute for National Security Studies, February 2001.

Smith, Joseph and Simon Davis. *Historical Dictionary of the Cold War.* Lanham, MD: Scarecrow Press, 2000.

Smoke, Richard. *National Security and the Nuclear Dilemma.* New York: McGraw-Hill, 1993.

Smyser, W.R. *Restive Partners: Washington and Bonn Diverge.* Boulder: Westview Press, 1990.

Sokolski, Henry D. *Best of Intentions: America's Campaign Against Strategic Weapons Proliferation.* New York: Praeger Publishers, 2001.

Sokolski, Henry D., and James M. Ludes, eds. *Twenty First Century Weapons Proliferation: Are We Ready?* London: Frank Cass Publishers, 2001.

Sokolski, Henry D., and Patrick Clawson, eds. *Checking Iran's Nuclear Ambitions.* Carlisle, PA: Army War College Strategic Studies Institute, January 2004.

Spector, Leonard S. *Nuclear Ambitions: The Spread of Nuclear Weapons 1989–1990.* Boulder: Westview Press, 1990.

Spector, Leonard S., Mark G. McDonough, and Evan S. Medeiros. *Tracking Nuclear Proliferation.* Washington: Carnegie Endowment for International Peace, 1995.

Speed, Roger D. *Strategic Deterrence in the 1980s.* Palo Alto, CA: Hoover Institution Press, 1979.

Steinbruner, John D., and Leon V. Sigal, eds. *Alliance Security: NATO and the No-First-Use Question.* Washington: Brookings Institution Press, 1983.

Steinke, Rudolf and Michel Vale. *Germany Debates Defense: The NATO Alliance at the Crossroads.* Armonk, NY: M.E. Sharpe, Inc., 1983.

Stockholm International Peace Research Institute. *Tactical Nuclear Weapons: European Perspectives.* London: Taylor and Francis Ltd., 1978.

———. "World Armaments and Disarmament," in *SIPRI Yearbook.* Oxford: Oxford University Press, annual.

Talbott, Strobe. *Deadly Gambits: The Reagan Administration and the Stalemate in Nuclear Arms Control.* New York: Alfred A. Knopf, 1984.

———. *The Master of the Game: Paul Nitze and the Nuclear Peace.* New York: Vintage Books, 1988.

Teller, Edward with Judith Shoolery. *Memoirs: A Twentieth-Century Journey in Science and Politics.* New York: Perseus Books, 2001.

Tellis, Ashley J. *India's Emerging Nuclear Posture: Between Recessed Deterrent and Ready Arsenal.* Santa Monica, Calif.: The RAND Corporation, 2001.

Treverton, Gregory. *Nuclear Weapons in Europe.* Adelphi Paper. London: International Institute for Strategic Studies, 1981.

Tucker, Robert W., and David C. Hendrickson. *The Imperial Temptaion: The New World Order and America's Purpose.* New York: Council on Foreign Relations Press, 1992.

Turner, Stansfield, *Caging the Nuclear Genie: An American Challenge for Global Security.* Boulder, CO: Westview Press, 1997.

Twigge, Stephen, and Len Scott. Planning Armageddon: Britain, the United States and the Command of Western Nuclear Forces 1945–1964. Newark, N.J.: Harwood Academic Publishers, 2000.

U.S. Nuclear Policy in the 21st Century: A Fresh Look at National Strategy and Requirements. Washington: National Defense University's Center for Counterproliferation Research and Lawrence Livermore National Laboratory's Center for Global Security Research, 1998.

Ullman, Richard H. *Securing Europe.* Princeton, NJ: Princeton University Press, 1991.

Van Cleave, William R., and S.T. Cohen. *Tactical Nuclear Weapons: An Examination of the Issues.* New York: Crane, Russak, 1978.

Van Ham, Peter. *Managing Non-Proliferation Regimes in the 1990s.* New York: Council on Foreign Relations Press, 1994.

Van Oudenaren, John. *West German Policymaking and NATO Nuclear Strategy.* Santa Monica: The RAND Corp., September 1985.

Vanderbilt, Tom. *Survival City: Adventures Among the Ruins of Atomic America.* Princeton, NJ: Princeton Architectural Press, 2002.

Vigeveno, Guido. *The Bomb and European Security.* Bloomington, IN: Indiana University Press, 1983.

Waltz, Kenneth. *Theory of International Politics.* New York: Random House, 1979.

Wander, W. Thomas and Eric H. Arnett, eds. *Nuclear and Conventional Forces in Europe: 1987 Colloquium Reader.* Washington: American Association for the Advancement of Science, 1988,

———. *The Proliferation of Advanced Weaponry: Technology, Motivations, and Responses.* Washington: The American Association for the Advancement of Science, 1992.

White, Andrew. "North Atlantic Treaty Organization," in *How Nuclear Weapons Decisions are Made,* edited by Scilla E. McLean. Basingstoke: MacMillan Press, 1986.

Wirtz, James J., and Jeffrey A. Larsen, eds. *Rockets' Red Glare: Missile Defenses and the Future of World Politics.* Boulder, Colo.: Westview Press, 2001.

———, eds. *Nuclear Transformation: The New U.S. Nuclear Doctrine.* New York: Palgrave Press, 2005.

Wirtz, James J., and Loch Johnson, eds. *Intelligence: Windows Into a Hidden World.* Los Angeles, CA: Roxbury Press, 2004.

Wirtz, James J., T.V. Paul, and Michelle Fortmann, eds. *Balance of Power: Theory and Practice in the 21st Century.* Palo Alto, CA: Stanford University Press, 2004.

Wirtz, James J., Eliot Cohen, Colin Gray, and John Bayliss, eds. *Strategy in the Contemporary World.* Oxford, UK: Oxford University Press, 2002.

Wirtz, James J., and Roy Godson, eds. *Strategic Denial and Deception.* Pittsburgh, PA: Transaction Press, 2002.

Wittner, Lawrence S. *Toward Nuclear Abolition: A History of the World Nuclear Disarmament Movement, Vol. 3: 19771 to the Present.* Palo Alto, CA: Stanford University Press, 2003.

Wolfstahl, Jon Brook, Christina-Astrid Chuen, and Emily Ewell Daughtry, eds. *Nuclear Status Report: Nuclear Weapons, Fissile Material, and Export Controls in the Former Soviet Union.* Washington: Carnegie Endowment, 2001.

Woolsey, R. James, ed. *Nuclear Arms: Ethics, Strategy, Politics.* San Francisco: ICS Press, 1984.

Yost, David S. "Nuclear Weapons Issues in France," in John C. Hopkins and Weixing Hu, eds. *Strategic Views from the Second Tier: The Nuclear Weapons Policies of France, Britain, and China* (San Diego, CA: Univ of California, San Diego, Institute on Global Conflict and Cooperation, 1994).

Articles

Ackerman, Gary and Laura Synder. "Would They if They Could? Terrorists and Nuclear Weapons." *Bulletin of the Atomic Scientists,* May/June 2002, pp. 40–47.

Ackland, Len. "Rocky Flats: Closing in on Closure." *Bulletin of the Atomic Scientists,* November/December 2001, pp. 52–56.

Alexander, Michael. "NATO's Role in a Changing World." *NATO Review,* April 1990, pp. 1–5.

Albright, David and Corey Hinderstein. "Algeria: Big Deal in the Desert?" *Bulletin of the Atomic Scientists,* May/June 2001, pp. 45–52.

Albright, David and Corey Hinderstein. "Iran: Furor Over Fuel." *Bulletin of the Atomic Scientists,* May/June 2003, pp. 12–115

Albright, David and Holly Higgins. "A Bomb for the Ummah." *Bulletin of the Atomic Scientists,* March/April 2003, pp. 49–55.

Allison, Graham, Own E. Cote Jr., Richard A. Falkenrath, and Steven E. Miller. "Avoiding Nuclear

Anarchy" *The Washington Quarterly,* Special Issue: Nuclear Arms Control, Summer 1997, pp. 185–198.

Altenburg, Wolfgang. "Defensive Alliance in a Nuclear World." *NATO's Sixteen Nations,* December 1989, pp. 17–21.

Alvarez, Robert. "North Korea: No Bygones at Yongbyon." *Bulleting of the Atomic Scientists,* July/August 2003, pp. 38–45.

Amacher, Peter. "You're on Your Own—Again: Civil Defense." *Bulletin of the Atomic Scientists,* May/June 2003, pp. 34–43.

Anderson, Harry. "Bush's New Look for the NATO Alliance." *Newsweek,* 12 June 1989, pp. 34–5.

Arkin, William. "The Bummers: 12 Nuclear Bombs That Could Ruin the 90's." *Greenpeace,* May/June 1990, pp. 20–21.

———. "Happy Birthday, Flexible Response." *Bulletin of the Atomic Scientists,* December 1987, pp. 5–6.

———. "What's 'New'?" *Bulletin of the Atomic Scientists,* Nov/Dec 1997, pp. 22–27.

———. "Secret Plan Outlines the Unthinkable." *Los Angeles Times,* 10 March 2002, available at *http://www.latimes.com/news/opinion/la-op-arkinmar10.story.*

Asmus, Ronald D., Richard L. Kugler, and F. Stephen Larrabee. "NATO Expansion: The Next Steps." *Survival,* Spring 1995, p. 31.

"Atlantic Summit Concludes With Agreement on SNF and New Proposals to be Submitted in Vienna—Adoption of the 'Comprehensive Concept' and of a Declaration—NATO is Again United." *Atlantic News,* Brussels, 31 May 1989.

Baring, Arnulf. "Transatlantic Relations: The View from Europe." *NATO Review,* February 1989, pp. 17–23.

Beach, Sir Hugh. "The Case for the Third Zero." *The Bulletin of the Atomic Scientists,* December 1989, pp. 14–15.

Bertram, Christoph. "The Implications of Theater Nuclear Weapons in Europe." *Foreign Affairs,* Winter 1981/82, pp. 305–326.

Bertram, Christoph. "Europe's Security Dilemmas." *Foreign Affairs,* Summer 1987, pp. 942–957.

Betts, Richard K. "NATO's Mid-Life Crisis." *Foreign Affairs,* Spring 1989, pp. 37–52.

Binnendijk, Hans. "NATO's Nuclear Modernization Dilemma." *Survival,* March/April 1989, pp. 137–155.

Blackwell, James. "The Future of US Land-Based Forces in Europe." *Military Technology,* April 1990, pp. 40–44.

Blechman, Barry M., and Cathleen S. Fisher. "Phase Out the Bomb." *Foreign Policy,* Winter 1994–95, pp. 79–95.

Boldrick, Michael R. "US Post–Cold War Nuclear Strategy: From Deterrence through Marginalization

to Unilateral Abolition?" Balrigg Memorandum 29, Centre for Defence and International Security Studies, Lancaster University, UK, 1997.

Boutwell, Jeffrey. "Short-Range Ballistic Missiles and Arms Control," in *Nuclear and Conventional Forces in Europe: 1987 Colloquium Reader,* edited by W. Thomas Wander and Kenneth Luongo. (Washington: American Association for the Advancement of Science, 1988), pp. 169–180.

Bracken, Paul. "The Second Nuclear Age." *Foreign Affairs,* January/February 2000, p. 146.

Brian, Danielle, Lynn Eisenman, and Peter D.H. Stockton. "The Weapons Complex: Who's Guarding the Store?" *Bulletin of the Atomic Scientists,* January/February 2002, pp. 48- 55.

Bukharin, Oleg. "Downsizing Russia's Nuclear Warhead Production Infrastructure." *The Nonproliferation Review,* Spring 2001, p. 116.

Bukharin, Oleg. "Making Fuel Less Tempting." *Bulletin of the Atomic Scientists,* July/August 2002, pp. 44–49.

Bundy, McGeorge, George F. Kennan, Robert S. McNamara, and Gerard Smith. "Nuclear Weapons and the Atlantic Alliance." *Foreign Affairs,* Spring 1982, pp. 753–768.

Bundy, McGeorge, George Kennan, Robert MacNamara, Gerard Smith, and Paul Warnke. "Back From the Brink: The Case for a New US Nuclear Strategy." *The Atlantic,* August 1986, pp.

Burley, Anne-Marie. "The Once and Future German Question." *Foreign Affairs,* Winter 1989/90, pp. 65–83.

Burns, William E. "How We Did Not Go to Nuclear War, and Where We Go From Here." *Parameters,* Winter 1996/97, pp. 144–147.

Burns, William F. "The Future of U.S. Nuclear Weapons Policy," *Arms Control Today,* Oct 1997, pp. 3–5.

———. "The Unfinished Work of Arms Control," *Issues in Science and Technology,* Fall 1997, also found at *http://www.nap.edu/14.1/burns.htm*

Burr, William and Jeffrey Kimball. "Nixon's Nuclear Ploy." *Bulletin of the Atomic Scientists,* January/February 2003, pp. 28–37.

Burt, Richard. "The Strategic and Political Lessons of INF," in *Nuclear Arms,* pp. 115–130. R. James Woolsey, ed. Institute for Contemporary Studies, 1984.

Burt, Richard. "The Alliance at a Crossroad." *Department of State Bulletin,* February 1982, pp. 42–45.

"The Bush Administration's Views on the Future of Nuclear Weapons: An Interview with NNSA Administrator Linton Brooks." *Arms Control Today,* January/February 2004, pp. 3–8.

Butler, Lee. "The General's Bombshell: Phasing Out the U.S. Nuclear Arsenal." *The Washington Post,* 12

January 1997; reprinted in *The Washington Quarterly*, Special Issue: Nuclear Arms Control, Summer 1997, pp. 131–135.

Carlson, Bengt. "How Ulam Set the Stage." *Bulletin of the Atomic Scientists*, July/August 2003, pp. 46–51.

Carpenter, Ted Galen. "Closing the Nuclear Umbrella." *Foreign Affairs*, March-April 1994, pp. 8–13.

Cimbala, Stephen J. "Extended Deterrence and Nuclear Escalation: Options in Europe." *Armed Forces and Society*, Fall 1988, pp. 9–31.

Cirincione, Joseph. "The Assault on Arms Control." *Bulletin of the Atomic Scientists*, January/February 2000, pp. 32–36.

Civiak, Robert. "The Need for Speed: Russian Weapons Material." *Bulletin of the Atomic Scientists*, July/August 2002, pp. 38–43.

Clearwater, John and David O'Brien. "O Lucky Canada." *Bulletin of the Atomic Scientists*, July/August 2003, pp. 60–65.

Cordesman, Anthony H. "NATO's Long-Range Theater Nuclear Forces: Europe's Quiet Profile in Courage." *Armed Forces Journal International*, June 1981, pp. 38–47.

Cotter, Donald R. "NATO Theater Nuclear Forces: An Enveloping Military Concept." *Strategic Review*, Spring 1981, pp. 44–53.

Courterier, Peter. "*Quo vadis* NATO?" *Survival*, Mar/Apr 1990, pp. 141–156.

"Counterproliferation: Finding (and Funding) the Right Response." *International Defense Review*, 10/1994, pp. 30–32.

Cupitt, Richard T., Suzette Grillot, and Yuzo Murayama. "The Determinants of Nonproliferation Export Controls: A Membership-Free Explanation." *The Nonproliferation Review*, Summer 2001, p. 69.

"The Cutting Edginess of NATO." *The Economist*, 3 February 1990, p. 45.

Daalder, Ivo H. "Abolish Tactical Weapons," Op-Ed, *New York Times*, 10 September 1991, p. A19.

———. "The Future of Arms Control." *Survival*, Spring 1992, pp. 51–73.

———. "NATO Nuclear Targeting After INF." *The Journal of Strategic Studies*, September 1988, 265–291.

Daalder, Ivo H., James M. Goldgeier, and James M. Lindsay. "Deploying NMD: Not Whether, But When." *Survival*, Spring 2000, p. 6.

Dahlman, Ola, Jenifer Mackby, Svein Mykkeitveit, and Hein Haak. "Cheaters Beware: the CTBT." *Bulletin of the Atomic Scientists*, January/February 2002, pp. 28–35.

Davis, Lynn. "Lessons of the INF Treaty." *Foreign Affairs*, Spring 1988, pp. 720–734.

Dean, Jonathan. "Building a Post–Cold War European Security System." *Arms Control Today*, June 1990, pp. 8–12.

———. "Military Security in Europe." *Foreign Affairs*, Fall 1987, pp. 22–40.

"The Declining Utility of Nuclear Weapons." *The Washington Quarterly*, Special Issue: Nuclear Arms Control, Summer 1997, pp. 91–95.

"Defending Europe Without Nukes." *US News and World Report*, 14 May 1990, pp. 44–45.

"Defence Planning Committee and Nuclear Planning Group Communique," *NATO Review*, January 1996, pp. 25–27.

De Santis, Hugh. "The New Detente and Military-Strategic Trends in Europe." *SAIS Review*, pp. 211–228.

Dhanapala, Jayantha. "The NPT at a Crossroads." *The Nonproliferation Review*, Spring 2000, p. 138.

Dowler, Thomas W., and Joseph S. Howard II. "Countering the Threat of the Well-Armed Tyrant: A Modest Proposal for Small Nuclear Weapons." *Strategic Review*, Fall 1991, pp. 34–40.

Dozier, Michael E. "Devising an Effective Arms Control Regime for Tracking, Monitoring, and Verifying the Elimination of Nuclear Warheads," paper presented to USAF Institute for National Security Studies, 1 September 1997.

Dregger, Alfred. "Nuclear Disarmament: Consequences for the Alliance—Perspectives for Germany and Europe." *Comparative Strategy*, Vol. 7, 1988, pp. 335–343.

Dunn, Lewis A. "Considerations after the INF Treaty: NATO After Global Double Zero.'" *Survival*, 1988, pp. 195–209.

———. "New Nuclear Forces: Defining the Possibilities," unpublished SAIC paper, 9 November 1992.

———. "Rethinking the Nuclear Equation." *The Washington Quarterly*, Winter 1994.

Durrant, Damian and Jacqueline Walsh. "Nuclear Weapons for a Bygone Era." *The Bulletin of the Atomic Scientists*, April 1990, pp. 8–10.

Eden, Lynn. "City on Fire." *Bulleting of the Atomic Scientists*, January/February 2004, pp. 32- 43.

"Europe: Western Europe Facing a New Challenge." *IISS Strategic Survey 1988–1989*. London: Brassey's, 1988, pp. 77–88.

Feaver, Peter D., and Emerson M. S. Niou. "Managing Nuclear Proliferation: Condemn, Strike, or Assist?" *International Studies Quarterly*, June 1996, pp. 209–234.

"Fighting a New Threat," *Newsweek*, 10 June 1996, p. 4.

Flynn, Gregory. "Problems in Paradigm." *Foreign Policy*, Spring 1989, pp. 63–85.

Flynn, Gregory, and David J. Scheffer. "Limited Collective Security." *Foreign Policy,* Fall 1990, pp. 77–101.

Freedman, Lawrence. "The Future of NATO's Deterrent Posture: Nuclear Weapons and Arms Control," in *NATO in the 1990's,* edited by Stanley Sloan. Washington: NDU Press, 1989.

———. "Great Powers, Vital Interests and Nuclear Weapons." *Survival,* Winter 1994–95, pp. 35–52.

"The Future of the Bomb." Special Report, *Newsweek,* 7 October 1991, pp. 19–26.

Gaddis, John L. "The Long Peace: Elements of Stability in the Postwar International System." *International Security,* Spring 1986, pp.

Galvin, John R. "The INF Treaty—No Relief from the Burden of Defence." *NATO Review,* February 1988, pp. 1–7.

———. "The NATO Alliance: A Framework for Security." *The Washington Quarterly,* Winter 1989, pp. 85-

———. "NATO's Enduring Mission." *NATO's Sixteen Nations,* October 1989, pp. 10–16.

Garrity, Patrick J. "Why We Need Nuclear Weapons: And Which Ones We Need." *Policy Review,* Winter 1985, pp. 36–42.

———. "The Next Nuclear Questions," *Parameters,* Winter 1995–96, pp. 92–111.

Glaser, Charles. "Nuclear Policy Without an Adversary." *International Affairs,* Spring 1992.

Goldring, Natalie. "Skittish on Counterproliferation," *The Bulletin of the Atomic Scientists,* Mar/Apr 94, 12–13.

Goldstein, Avery. "Mushroom Cloud Lingers: 'New World' Depends on Old Weapons." *Washington Times,* 27 November 2000, p. 16.

Gompert, David, Kenneth Watman and Dean Wilkening. "Nuclear First Use Revisited, *Survival,* Autumn 1995, pp. 27–44.

Gordon, Philip H. "Normalization of German Foreign Policy." *Orbis,* Spring 1994, pp. 225–244.

Gose, Mark N. "The New Germany and Nuclear Weapons: Options for the Future." *Airpower Journal,* Special Edition 1996, pp. 67–78.

Graham, Thomas and Leonor Tomero. "Obligations for Us All: NATO and Negative Security Assurances." *Disarmament Diplomacy,* August 2000, p. 3.

Grant, Robert. "France's New Relationship with NATO." *Survival,* Spring 1996, pp. 58–80.

———. "Paris Sees US as Ally in Counterproliferation Effort." *International Defense Review,* 10/1994, p. 38.

Gualtieri, David S., Barry Kellman, Kenneth E. Apt, and Edward A. Tanzman. "Advancing the Law of Weapons Control—Comparative Approaches to Strengthen Nuclear Non-Proliferation." *Michigan Journal of Law,* Summer 1995, pp. 1031–1111.

Haftendorn, Helga. "Role of Nuclear Weapons in Allied Strategy," in *NATO in the Fifth Decade,* edited by Keith Dunn and Stephen Flanagan. Washington: National Defense University Press, 1990.

Hamm, Manfred R., and Holger H. Mey. "Transatlantic Relations and the Future of European Security." *Strategic Review,* Spring 1990, pp. 43–52.

Hartley, Anthony. "After 1992: Multiple Choice." *The National Interest,* Spring 1989, pp. 29–39.

Hayes, Peter and Nina Tannenwald. "Nixing Nukes in Vietnam." *Bulletin of the Atomic Scientists,* May/June 2003, pp. 52–59.

Heisbourg, Francois. "The Three Ages of NATO Strategy." *NATO Review,* February 1989, pp. 24–29.

Hirsch, Daniel, David Lochbaum, and Edwin Lyman. "The NRC's Dirty Little Secret." *Bulletin of the Atomic Scientists,* May/June 2003, pp. 45–51.

Hitchens, Theresa. "Rushing to Weaponize the Final Frontier." *Arms Control Today,* September 2001, pp. 16–21.

Hoagland, Jim. "Europe's Destiny." *Foreign Affairs,* Vol. 69, No. 1, 1989/90, pp. 33–50.

Hofmann, Wilfried. "Whence the Threat to Peace? The Successor Generation and the Equidistance Syndrome." *NATO Review,* June 1987, pp. 8–13.

Hormats, Robert D. "Redefining Europe and the Atlantic Link." *Foreign Affairs,* Fall 1989, pp. 71–91.

Howard, Michael. "Military Grammar and Political Logic: Can NATO Survive if Cold War is Won?" *NATO Review,* December 1989, pp. 7–13.

———. "Nuclear Danger and Nuclear History." *International Security,* Summer 1989, pp. 176–183.

Hyland, William G. "America's New Course." *Foreign Affairs,* Spring 1990, pp. 1–12.

Jasinski, Michael, Chrstina Cheun, and Charles D. Ferguson. "Russia: Of Truth and Testing." *Bulletin of the Atomic Scientists,* September/October 2002, pp. 60–65.

Jervis, Robert. "The Political Effects of Nuclear Weapons: A Comment." *International Security,* Fall 1988, pp. 80–90.

Joseph, Robert G. "Nuclear Deterrence and Regional Proliferators," *The Washington Quarterly,* Special Issue: Nuclear Arms Control, Summer 1997, pp. 167–175.

———. "Proliferation, Counterproliferation, and NATO," *Survival,* Spring 1996, pp. 111–130.

Josephson, Paul. "MINATOM: Dreams of Glory." *Bulletin of the Atomic Scientists,* September/October 2002, pp. 40–47.

Kaiser, Karl, Georg Leber, Alois Mertes, and Franz-Josef Schulze. "Nuclear Weapons and the Preservation of Peace." *Foreign Affairs,* Summer 1982, pp. 1157–1170.

Kamp, Karl-Heinz. "An Overrated Nightmare." *The Bulletin of the Atomic Scientists*, July/August 1996, pp. 30–34.

Karl, David J. "Proliferation Pessimism and Emerging Nuclear Powers." *International Security*, Winter 1996–97, pp. 87–119.

Kelley, Marylia and Jay Coghlan. "Mixing Bugs and Bombs." *Bulletin of the Atomic Scientists*, September/October 2003, pp. 25–31.

Kirkpatrick, Jeane J. "Beyond the Cold War." *Foreign Affairs*, Vol. 69, No. 1, 1989/90, pp. 1–16.

Krause, Joachim. "Proliferation Risks and Their Strategic Relevance: What Role for NATO?" *Survival*, Summer 1995, pp. 135–148.

Kristensen, Hans M. "Preemptive Posturing: What Happened to Deterrence?" *Bulletin of the Atomic Scientists*, September/October 2002, pp. 55–59.

Langeland, Terje. "Megatons to Mega-Problems: Did USEC Ever Stand a Chance?" *Bulletin of the Atomic Scientists*, May/June 2002, pp. 49–56.

Lansor, Kermit. "Nuclear Weapons after the Cold War," *The New Republic*, 28 October 1991.

Larsen, Jeffrey A. "The Proliferation of Weapons of Mass Destruction and U.S. National Security Strategy." *National Security Studies Quarterly*, Autumn 1998, pp. 33–52.

Lennon, Alexander T. "The 1995 NPT Extension Conference." *The Washington Quarterly*, Autumn 1994, pp. 205–227.

Leppingwell, John W. R., and Nikolai Sokov. "Strategic Offensive Arms Elimination and Weapons Protection, Control and Accounting." *The Nonproliferation Review*, Spring 2000.

Levin, Carl and Jack Reed. "Toward a More Responsible Nuclear Nonproliferation Strategy." *Arms Control Today*, January/February 2004, pp. 9–14.

Lewis, Peter. "French Security Policy: The Year of the Disappearing Budget," *Jane's Defence '96*, January 1996, pp. 42–43.

"Libya: Targeting a Buried Threat." *Newsweek*, 22 April 1996, p. 6.

Lindsay, James M. "The Nuclear Agenda." *The Brookings Review*, Fall 2000, p. 8.

Lortie, Bret. "A Do-It-Yourself SIOP." *Bulletin of the Atomic Scientists*, July/August 2001, pp. 22–29.

Los Alamos National Laboratory. "The Future of Nuclear Weapons—The Next Three Decades." *Los Alamos Science*, No. 17 (Special Edition), Summer 1989.

Lugar, Richard G. "A Republican Looks at Foreign Policy." *Foreign Affairs*, Winter 1987/88, pp. 249–262.

———. "The Next Steps in U.S. Nonproliferation Policy." *Arms Control Today*, December 2002, pp. 3–7.

Macfarlane, Allison, Frank von Hippel, Jungmin Kang, and Robert Nelson. "Plutonium Disposal, The Third Way." *Bulletin of the Atomic Scientists*, May/June 2001, pp. 53–57.

"Major Military Maneuvers." *News from France*, 1 March 1996, pp. 1–4.

Makhijani, Arjun. "Nuclear Targeting: The First 60 Years." *Bulletin of the Atomic Scientists*, May/June 2003, pp. 60–65.

Mandelbaum, Michael. "Ending the Cold War." *Foreign Affairs*, Spring 1989, pp. 16–36.

Manners, Geoffrey. "Major NATO Nuclear Review Under Way." *Jane's Defence Weekly*, 27 September 1986, p. 66.

Martin, David. "Towards an Alliance Framework for Extended Air Defence/Theatre Missile Defence." *NATO Review*, May 1996, pp. 32–35.

Matthews, William. "Debate Swirls On Overseas Nuclear Arms." *Air Force Times*, 4 June 1990, pp. 27–28.

May, Michael, Paul T. Herman, and Sybil Francis. "Dealing With Nuclear Weapons in Europe." *Survival*, March/April 1989, pp. 157–170.

Maynes, Charles W. "America Without the Cold War." *Foreign Policy*, Spring 1990, pp. 3–25.

———. "Coping with the '90s." *Foreign Policy*, Spring 1989, pp. 42–62.

———. "The New Decade." *Foreign Policy*, Fall 1990, pp. 3–13.

Mazarr, Michael J. "Introduction." *The Washington Quarterly*, Special Issue: Nuclear Arms Control, Summer 1997, pp. 77–83.

———. "Virtual Nuclear Arsenals," *Survival*, Autumn 1995, pp. 7–26.

McNamara, Robert S. "The Military Role of Nuclear Weapons: Perceptions and Misperceptions." *Foreign Affairs*, Fall 1983, pp. 59–80.

———. "Nobody Needs Nukes." *The New York Times*, 23 February 1993.

Mearsheimer, John J. "Back to the Future: Instability in Europe After the Cold War." *International Security*, Summer 1990, pp. 5–56.

Mendel, Richard A., and Richard A. Stubbing. "How to Save $50 Billion a Year." *The Atlantic*, June 1989, pp. 53–60.

Mendelsohn, Jack. "NATO's Nuclear Weapons: The Rationale for 'No First Use.'" *Arms Control Today*, Jul/Aug 1999, pp. 3–8.

———. "The Pursuit of Irrelevance." *Arms Control Today*, May 1989, p. 2.

Menon, Anand. "French Shift to NATO Hails End of the European Army Dream." *The European*, 16–22 May 1996, p. 14.

Miller, Charles. "Analysts: Britain Must Brace for More Defense Reductions." *Defense News*, 14–20 October 1996, p. 46.

Miller, Timothy D., and Jeffrey A. Larsen. "Dealing With Russia's Tactical Nuclear Weapons: Cash for Kilotons." *Naval War College Review*, Spring 2004.

Millon, Charles. "France and the Renewal of the Atlantic Alliance." *NATO Review*, May 1996, pp. 13–16.

Moodie, Michael and Amy Sands. "New Approaches to Compliance with Arms Control and Nonproliferation Agreements." *The Nonproliferation Review*, Spring 2001, p. 1.

Mueller, John. "The Essential Irrelevance of Nuclear Weapons: Stability in the Postwar World." *International Security*, Fall 1988, pp. 55–79.

Müller, Harald, Alexander Kelle, Katja Frank, Sylvia Meier, and Annette Schaper. "The German Debate on Nuclear Weapons and Disarmament," *The Washington Quarterly*, Special Issue: Nuclear Arms Control, Summer 1997, pp. 115–122.

Newhouse, John. "The Diplomatic Round: Eternal Severities." *The New Yorker*, 23 October 1989, pp. 100–130.

———. "The Diplomatic Round: Sweeping Change." *The New Yorker*, 27 August 1990, pp. 78–89.

Nitze, Paul H. "Is It Time to Junk Our Nukes?" *The Washington Post*, 16 January 1994, pp. C1–2.

"Nuclear Roles in the Post–Cold War World" in *The Washington Quarterly*, Special Issue: Nuclear Arms Control, Summer 1997, pp. 163–166.

Nye, Joseph S., Jr. "Arms Control After the Cold War." *Foreign Affairs*, Winter 1989/90, pp. 42–64.

"One on One: Charles Millon, French Defense Minister," *Defense News*, 14–20 October 1996, p. 110.

Panofsky, Wolfgang K. H. "The Continuing Impact of the Nuclear Revolution." *Arms Control Today*, June 2001, pp. 3–5.

———. "Dismantling the Concept of 'Weapons of Mass Destruction,'" *Arms Control Today*, April 1998, pp. 3–9.

Panofsky, Wolfgang K. H., and George Bunn. "The Doctrine of the Nuclear-Weapon States and the Future of Non-Proliferation," *Arms Control Today*, Jul/Aug 1994, pp. 3–9.

Parachini, John. "Non-Proliferation Policy and the War on Terrorism." *Arms Control Today*, October 2001, pp. 13–15.

Perkovich, George. "Bush's Nuclear Revolution: A Regime Change in Nonproliferation." *Foreign Affairs*, March/April 2003.

Perkovich, George, and Ernest W. Lefever. "Loose Nukes: Arms Control is No Place for Folly." *Foreign Affairs*, November/December 2000, p. 162.

Perle, Richard. "Watching Over Defense: Cautions in the New Climate." *The American Enterprise*, May/June 1990, pp. 30–33.

Pohling-Brown, Pamela. "Technologies for America's New Course," *International Defense Review*, 10/1994, 33–38.

Posen, Barry R., and Andrew L. Ross. "Competing Visions for US Grand Strategy," *International Security*, Winter 1996–97, pp. 5–53.

Potter, William C., and Nikolai Sokov. "Nuclear Weapons that People Forgot." *International Herald Tribune*, 31 May 2000.

Pregenzer, Arian L. "Security Nuclear Capabilities in India and Pakistan: Reducing the Terrorist and Proliferation Risk." *The Nonproliferation Review*, Spring 2003, pp. 1–8.

Quester, George H. "New Thinking on Nuclear Weapons." *The Journal of Politics*, August 1987, pp. 845–860.

Quester, George H., and Victor Utgoff. "Toward an International Security Policy," *The Washington Quarterly*, Autumn 1994, pp. 5–18.

Ramana, M. V., and A. H. Nayyar. "India, Pakistan and the Bomb." *Scientific American*, December 2001, p. 72.

Ramos, Thomas F. "The Future of Theater Nuclear Forces," *Strategic Review*, Fall 1991, pp. 41–47.

Rathjens, George. "Rethinking Nuclear Proliferation," *The Washington Quarterly*, Winter 1995, pp. 181–193.

"Remarks by Defense Secretary William Perry at Georgetown University; Topic: Weapons of Mass Destruction," Federal News Service in *Defense Dialog*, 18 April 1996.

Richardson, Robert C. III. "NATO Nuclear Strategy: A Look Back." *Strategic Review*, Spring 1981, pp. 35–43.

Richelson, Jeffrey. "Defusing Nuclear Terror." *Bulletin of the Atomic Scientists*, March/April 2002, pp. 38–43.

Roberts, Brad. "Revisiting Fred Ikle's 1961 Question: After Detection, What?" *The Nonproliferation Review*, Spring 2001, p. 10.

Rühe, Volker. "The Need for an Open Debate on Military Strategy." *Suddeutsche Zeitung*, 21 January 1988.

Rühle, Hans. "NATO Strategy: The Need to Return to Basics." *Strategic Review*, Fall 1988, pp. 28–35.

———. "View from NATO: NATO and the Coming Proliferation Threat." *Comparative Strategy*, Vol. 13 (1994), 313–320.

Russell, James A., and James J. Wirtz. "United States Nuclear Strategy in the Twenty-First Century." *Contemporary Security Policy*, December 2002, pp. 101–121.

Russell, John. "INF Inspections End, But Unilateral Verification Continues." *Trust and Verify,* May-June 2001, p. 3.

Sagan, Scott D. "The Perils of Proliferation: Organization Theory, Deterrence Theory, and the Spread of Nuclear Weapons." *International Security,* Spring 1994, pp. 66–107.

———. "Why Do States Build Nuclear Weapons?" *International Security,* Winter 1996–97, pp. 54–86.

Schulte, Gregory L. "Responding to Proliferation—NATO's Role," *NATO Review,* July 1995, pp. 15–19.

Schlesinger, Arthur Jr. "A Democrat Looks at Foreign Policy." *Foreign Affairs,* Winter 1987/88, pp. 263–283.

Schlesinger, James R. "Preserving the American Commitment." *NATO Review,* February 1989, pp. 13–17.

Schmidt, Helmut. Speech to IISS, October 1977. Reprinted in *Survival,* January/February 1978, pp.

Schneider, Barry R. "Nuclear Proliferation and Counter-Proliferation: Policy Issues and Debates." *Mershon International Studies Review,* October 1994, pp. 209–234.

Schwartz, David N. "A Historical Perspective," in *Alliance Security: NATO and the No-First Use Question.* John D. Steinbruner and Leon V. Sigal, eds. Washington: The Brookings Institution, 1983.

Schwartz, Stephen I. "The Folly of US Nuclear Diplomacy," *Newsday,* 7 May 2000.

———. "The New-Nuke Chorus Tunes Up." *Bulletin of the Atomic Scientists,* July/August 2001, pp. 30–35.

"Senator Nunn's Valedictory." *Air Force Magazine,* December 1996, pp. 40–42.

Sims, Jennifer E. "The American Approach to Nuclear Arms Control: A Retrospective." in "Arms Control: Thirty Years On," special edition of *Daedalus,* Winter 1991, pp. 251–272.

Sloan, Stanley R. "A Changing Europe and U.S. National Defense." *National Defense,* April 1990, pp. 24–26+.

———. "Negotiating a New Transatlantic Bargain." *NATO Review,* March 1996, pp. 19–23.

Slocombe, Walter B. "The Future of Extended Deterrence." *The Washington Quarterly,* Autumn 1991, pp. 157–172.

Sloss, Leon. "US Strategic Forces After the Cold War: Policies and Strategies," *The Washington Quarterly,* Autumn 1991, pp. 145–156.

Smart, Victor. "French Defence Cuts Hurt Revamped NATO." *The European,* 16–22 May 1996, pp. 1–2.

Smith, R. Jeffrey. "Retired Nuclear Warrior Sounds Alarm on Weapons." *Washington Post,* 4 Dec 1996, p. 1.

Smith, Ron, and Bernard Udis. "New Challenges to Arms Export Control: Whither Wassenaar?" *The Nonproliferation Review,* Summer 2001, p. 81.

Snyder, Jack. "Averting Anarchy in the New Europe." *International Security,* Spring 1990, pp. 5–41.

Sorokin, Konstantine E. "Russia After the Crisis: The Nuclear Strategy Debate." *Orbis,* Winter 1994, pp. 19–40.

"Special Defense Department Briefing Report on Proliferation of Nuclear and Other Weapons of Mass Destruction," Federal News Service in *Early Bird Supplement,* 12 April 1996, pp. A1–12.

Speed, Roger D. "International Control of Nuclear Weapons." *The Washington Quarterly,* Special Issue: Nuclear Arms Control, Summer 1997, pp. 179–184.

Sokov, Nikolai. "Russia's Approach to Nuclear Weapons." *The Washington Quarterly,* Special Issue: Nuclear Arms Control, Summer 1997, pp. 107–114.

———. "Tactical Nuclear Weapons Elimination: Next Step for Arms Control." *The Nonproliferation Review,* Winter 1997, also found at *http://cns.miis.edu/pubs/npr/sokov.htm*

"Statement on Nuclear Weapons." December 1995, reprinted in *The Washington Quarterly,* Special Issue: Nuclear Arms Control, Summer 1997, pp. 125–130.

Stober, Dan. "No Experience Necessary: The Nth Country Experiment." *Bulletin of the Atomic Scientists,* March/April 2003, pp. 56–63.

Thoemmes, Eric H. "European Security Problems." *The Jerusalem Journal of International Relations,* June 1986, pp. 48–64.

Thomson, James A. "Nuclear Weapons in Europe: Planning for NATO's Nuclear Deterrent in the 1980's and 1990's." *Survival,* 1983

Tirpak, John A. "Precision: The Next Generation." *Air Force Magazine,* November 2003, pp. 44–51.

"Toward a Safer World," *Time,* 7 Oct 1991, pp. 18–24.

Treverton, Gregory. "The Defense Debate." *Foreign Affairs,* Vol. 69, No. 1, 1989/90, pp. 183–196.

Tuthill, John W. "U.S. Foeign Policy, the State Department, and U.S. Missions Abroad." *The Atlantic Community Quarterly,* Spring 1988, pp. 32–47.

"The UK's Nuclear Secrets," *Jane's Defence Weekly,* 1 Sep 90, p. 341.

Ullman, Richard H. "The Covert French Connection." *Foreign Policy,* Summer 1989, pp. 3–33.

———. "No-First-Use of Nuclear Weapons." *Foreign Affairs,* July 1972, pp.

Von Hippel, Frank. "Paring Down the Arsenal," *Bulletin of the Atomic Scientists,* May/Jun 97, pp. 33–40.

Waltz, Kenneth. "Thoughts about Virtual Nuclear Arsenals," *The Washington Quarterly,* Special Issue: Nuclear Arms Control, Summer 1997, pp. 153–161.

Watts, Barry D. "The Conventional Utility of Strategic Nuclear Forces," *The Washington Quarterly,* Autumn 1991, pp. 173–204.

Webster, Paul. "MINATOM: The Grab for Trash." *Bulletin of the Atomic Scientists,* September/October 2002, pp. 33–37+.

———. "Russia: Just Like Old Times." *Bulletin of the Atomic Scientists,* July/August 2003, pp. 31–35.

Weiss, Leonard. "Atoms for Peace." *Bulletin of the Atomic Scientists,* November/December 2003, pp. 34–44.

Winik, Jay. "Restoring Bipartisanship." *The Washington Quarterly,* Winter 1989, pp. 109-

Woolsey, R. James. "The Future of NATO's Deterrent Posture: An American Perspective." *The Atlantic Community Quarterly,* pp. 115–129.

Yost, David S. "France's Nuclear Dilemmas." *Foreign Affairs,* Jan/Feb 1996, pp. 108–118.

———. "The Delegitimization of Nuclear Deterrence?" *Armed Forces and Society,* Summer 1990, pp. 487–508.

Zelikow, Philip. "The Masque of Institutions," *Survival,* Spring 1996.

Research Institute Papers

"Airlie House V: Conference on the Future of US Nuclear Strategy, 23–24 October 1996," McLean, VA: SAIC Report, 1996.

Albright, David, and Kevin O'Neill, eds. *The Challenges of Fissile Material Control.* Washington: ISIS Report, 1999.

Allison, Graham T., Jr., Robert D. Blackwill, Albert Carnesale, Joseph S. Nye, Jr., and Robert P. Beschel, Jr. *A Primer for the Nuclear Age.* CSIA Occasional Paper 6. Cambridge, MA: Center for Science and International Affairs, Harvard University, 1990.

Andre, David. *The Third World 'Few Nuclear Weapons Problem:' Policy Implications for Military Planning Guidance as Derived from Gaming.* McLean, VA: Science Applications International Corporation, April 1993.

An Assessment of Defense Nuclear Agency Functions: Pathways Toward a New Nuclear Infrastructure for the Nation. National Defense Research Institute. Santa Monica, CA: The RAND Corporation, 1994.

Arnett, Eric. "Nuclear Weapons and Arms Control in South Asia after the Test Ban." SIPRI Research Report No. 14. Stockholm, Swe.: 1998.

Auerswald, David, and John Gerard Ruggie, eds. *The Future of US Nuclear Weapons Policy: A Symposium.* San Diego: University of California Institute on Global Conflict and Cooperation, 1990.

Blair, Bruce. "Global Zero Alert for Nuclear Forces." PRAC Paper No. 13. Project on Rethinking Arms Control, Center for International and Security Studies at Maryland. December 1994.

Blair, Bruce, et al. *Toward True Security: A U.S. Nuclear Posture for the Next Decade.* Washington: Federation of American Scientists, Union of Concerned Scientists, and Natural Resources Defense Council, June 2001.

Bowie, Christopher J., Robert P. Haffa, Jr., and Robert E. Mullins. *Future War: What Trends in America's Post–Cold War Military Conflicts Tell Us About Early 21st Century Warfare.* Washington, DC: Northrop Grumman Analysis Center Paper, January 2003.

Bracken, Paul. "The Structure of the Second Nuclear Age." Foreign Policy Research Institute e-notes, 25 September 2003.

British American Security Information Council. "A New Security Structure for Europe: NATO Summit '90, London, July 5th and 6th." BASIC Briefing Papers, July 1990.

———. "NATO Nuclear Planning After the Cold War." BASIC Report 90.2. May 1990.

Bromley, Mark. "Planning to Be Surprised: The US Nuclear Posture Review and its Implications for Arms Control." *BASIC Papers* No. 39, April 2002. Available at *http://www.basicint.org/pubs/Papaers/BP39.htm.*

Brown, Nanette, and James C. Wendt. *Improving the NATO Force Planning Process: Lessons from Past Efforts.* RAND Report No. R-3383-USDP. Santa Monica, CA: The RAND Corporation, June 1986.

Buchan, Glenn. *US Nuclear Strategy for the Post–Cold War Era.* RAND Paper MR-420-RC. Santa Monica, CA: The RAND Corporation, 1994.

Builder, Carl. "The Future of Nuclear Deterrence." RAND Paper P-7702, Santa Monica, CA: The RAND Corporation, February 1991.

Butcher, Martin, Nicola Calvert, and Daniel Plesch. "NATO and Nuclear Proliferation." Issues in European Security series, Centre for European Security and Disarmament and the British American Security Information Council, 1995.

Canberra Commission on the Elimination of Nuclear Weapons. Report presented by the Australian Minister for Foreign Affairs to the Conference on Disarmament, 30 January 1997.

Capello, John T., Gwendolyn M. Hall, and Stephen P. Lambert. *Tactical Nuclear Weapons: Debunking the Mythology.* INSS Occasional Paper 46. Colorado Springs, Colo.: USAF Institute for National Security Studies, August 2002.

Carver, George A., and Don M. Snider, Project Directors. *A New Military Strategy for the 1990s: Implications for Capabilities and Acquisition.* Final Report of the CSIS Conventional Arms Control Project. Washington: The Center for Strategic and International Studies, January 1991.

Chandler, Robert W. "The Devil is in the Targets: An Analytical Tool for Counterproliferation

Employment Planning," SPI Contract Report, 14 November 1994.

Chow, Brian G., Richard H. Speiers, and Gregory S. Jones. *The Proposed Fissile Material Production Cutoff: Next Steps.* National Defense Research Institute Report MR-586-OSD. Santa Monica, CA: The RAND Corporation, 1995.

Clark, Ian, and Philip Sabin. "Sources for the Study of British Nuclear Weapons History." CISSM Occasional Paper, Nuclear History Program. College Park, MD: Center for International Security Studies at Maryland, 1989.

Cochran, Thad. *Stubborn Things: A Decade of Facts About Ballistic Missile Defense.* Report to U.S. Senate. September 2000.

Congressional Quarterly Almanac. Washington: Congressional Quarterly.

Conley, Jerome M. "Indo-Russian Military and Nuclear Cooperation: Implications for U.S. Security Interests." INSS Occasional Paper No. 31, USAF Institute for National Security Studies, Colorado Springs, CO, Feb 2000.

Cordesman, Anthony H. "US and Russian Nuclear Forces and Arms Control after the US Nuclear Posture Review." Washington, DC: Center for Strategic and International Studies, 10 January 2002.

Daalder, Ivo. "Stepping Down the Thermonuclear Ladder: How Low Can We Go?" PRAC Paper No. 5. Project on Rethinking Arms Control, Center for International and Security Studies at Maryland. June 1993.

Daalder, Ivo, and James Lindsay. "A New Agenda for Nuclear Weapons." *Policy Brief* No. 94. Washington, DC: The Brookings Institute, February 2002.

Darilek, Richard E. "Conflict Prevention Measures: A Distinctive Approach to Arms Control?" PRAC Paper No. 14. Project on Rethinking Arms Control, Center for International and Security Studies at Maryland. January 1995.

Dembinski, Matthias, Alexander Kelle, and Harald Mueller. "NATO and Nonproliferation: A Critical Appraisal," Peace Research Institute Frankfurt, PRIF Report No. 33, April 1994.

Drew, Dennis M., Study Director. *Nuclear Winter and National Security: Implications for Future Policy.* Maxwell AFB, AL: Air University Press, July 1986.

Dunn, Lewis A. "After Next Use: A First Cut at Defining the Issues." Report for Lawrence Livermore National Laboratory (undated).

———. "Containing Nuclear Proliferation." London: IISS Adephi Paper #263, Winter 1991.

Dunn, Lewis A., et al. *Nuclear Issues in the Post-September 11 Era.* Paris, France: Foundation pour la Recherche Stratégique, March 2003.

Durch, William J. "Rethinking Strategic Ballistic Missile Defense." PRAC Paper No. 4. Project on Rethinking Arms Control, Center for International and Security Studies at Maryland. June 1993.

An Evolving US Nuclear Posture," Second Report of the Steering Committee (The Goodpaster Committee), Project on Eliminating Weapons of Mass Destruction. Washington: The Henry L. Stimson Center, December 1995.

"European Security 2000—A Comprehensive Concept for European Security from a Sozial-Demokratic Point of View." Bonn: Presseservice der SPD, 6 July 1989.

FPI Policy Study Groups. "Changing Roles and Shifting Burdens in the Atlantic Alliance." Washington: Johns Hopkins Foreign Policy Institute, April 1990.

Felipe, Mark, and Maurice A. Mallin. "Countering Weapons of Mass Destruction: Developing the Tools," Draft SAIC Contract Report, 11 May 1994.

Ferguson, Charles D. "Mini-Nuclear Weapons and the U.S. Nuclear Posture Review." CNS Research Story of the Week. Monterey, CA: Monterey Institute of International Studies, 8 April 2002. Available at *http://cns.miis.edu/pubs/week/020408.htm*.

Freedman, Lawrence, Martin Navias, and Nicholas Wheeler. "Independence in Concert: The British Rationale for Possessing Strategic Nuclear Weapons." CISSM Occasional Paper, Nuclear History Program. College Park, MD: Center for International Security Studies at Maryland, 1989.

French, David. "Britain and NATO: Past, Present and Future." *Beyond the Cold War: Current Issues in European Security,* No. 5. Washington: The Woodrow Wilson International Center for Scholars, August 1990.

Friedberg, Aaron L. "Nuclear Multipolarity." Paper prepared for Los Alamos National Laboratory, June 1994.

Gantz, Nanette C. *Extended Deterrence and Arms Control.* Conference Report No. R-3514-FF. Santa Monica, CA: The RAND Corporation, March 1987.

Grant, Robert. *Counterproliferation and International Security: The Report of a U.S.-French Working Group.* Arlington, VA: US-CREST, 1995.

Garrity, Patrick J. "The Future of Nuclear Weapons: Final Study Report." CNSS Report, No. 8. Los Alamos, NM: Center for National Security Studies, February 1990.

———. "The INF Treaty: Past, Present, and Future." CNSS Papers, No. 4. Los Alamos, NM: Center for National Security Studies, February 1988.

Garrity, Patrick J., Robert E. Pendley, and Robert W. Selden. "The Future of Nuclear Weapons: The Next Three Decades." Conference Summary. CNSS Papers, No. 16. Los Alamos, NM: Center for National Security Studies, July 1988.

Gompert, David, Kenneth Watman, and Dean Wilkening. *US Nuclear Declaratory Policy: The Question of Nuclear First Use.* RAND Paper MR-596-RC. Santa Monica, CA: The RAND Corporation, 1995.

Goodpaster, Andrew J. *Further Reins on Nuclear Arms: Next Steps of the Major Powers.* Washington: The Atlantic Council, 1993.

Gottemoeller, Rose. "Beyond Arms Control: How to Deal with Nuclear Weapons." *Policy Brief 23.* Washington, DC: Carnegie Endowment for International Peace, February 2003.

Gronlund, Lisbeth. "From Nuclear Deterrence to Reassurance: The Role of Confidence-Building Measures and Restrictions on Military Development." PRAC Paper No. 8. Project on Rethinking Arms Control, Center for International and Security Studies at Maryland. December 1993.

Guthe, Kurt. *The Nuclear Posture Review: How is the "New Triad" New?* Washington, DC: Center for Strategic and Budgetary Assessments, 2002.

Hall, Gwendolyn M., John T. Cappello, and Stephen P. Lambert. *A Post–Cold War Nuclear Strategy Model.* INSS Occasional Paper 20 (Colorado Springs: USAF Institute for National Security Studies, July 1998).

Hallenbeck, Ralph. "Short-Range Nuclear Forces (SNF) in Europe: Implications of a U.S.-Soviet Arms Reduction Negotiation." SAIC paper prepared for AF/XOXXI, 24 July 1991.

Hawes, John. "Nuclear Proliferation: Down to the Hard Cases." PRAC Paper No. 6. Project on Rethinking Arms Control. Center for International and Security Studies at Maryland. June 1993.

Hildreth, Steven A., and Amy F. Woolf. *National Missile Defense: Issues for Congress.* Washington: Congressional Research Service, February 2000.

Horton, Roy E., III. "Out of (South) Africa: Pretoria's Nuclear Weapons Experience." INSS Occasional Paper 27. Colorado Springs: USAF Institute for National Security Studies, August 1999.

Hyland, William G. *The Nature of the Post–Cold War World: The World in the Year 2000.* Carlisle, PA: Strategic Studies Institute, US Army War College, March 1993.

International Perspectives on Missile Proliferation and Defenses. Monterey, CA: Monterey Institute for International Studies, March 2001.

Jackson, Richard A. *Nuclear, Biological, and Chemical Defense in the 21st Century.* Carlisle, PA: US Army War College Center for Strategic Leadership, 1994.

Jenkins-Smith, Hank C., Kerry G. Herron, and Richard P. Barke. "Public Perspectives of Nuclear Weapons in the Post–Cold War Environment." Contractor Report for Sandia National Laboratories, April 1994.

Johnsen, William T., and Thomas-Durell Young. *French Policy Toward NATO: Enhanced Selectivity, Vice Rapprochement.* Carlisle, PA: US Army War College, Strategic Studies Institute, September 1994.

Johnston, Alastair I. "Chinese Nuclear Doctrine and the Concept of Limited Deterrence." Paper prepared for Los Alamos National Laboratory, November 1994.

Joseph, Robert. "NATO's Response to the Proliferation Challenge" *Strategic Forum No. 66,* National Defense University, Institute for National Strategic Studies, Washington, March 1996.

Joseph, Robert, and John F. Reichart. *Deterrence and Defense in a Nuclear, Biological, and Chemical Environment.* Washington: National Defense University Center for Counterproliferation Research, 1995.

Joseph, Robert, and Ronald Lehman. "U.S. Nuclear Policy in the 21st Century." *Strategic Form* No. 145. Washington, DC: National Defense University, August 1998.

Kincade, William H. *Nuclear Proliferation: Diminishing Threat?* INSS Occasional Paper 6, Institute for National Security Studies, US Air Force Academy, CO, December 1995.

Korb, Larry, et al. *Winning the Peace in the 21st Century.* Task Force Report of the Strategies for U.S. National Security Program. Muscatine, IA: The Stanley Foundation, October 2003.

Laird, Robbin F., and Susan Clark. "The Impact of the Changing European Nuclear Forces on Theater Deterrence." IDA Paper P-2065. Alexandria, VA: Institute for Defense Analyses, January 1988.

Larsen, Jeffrey A., "NATO Counterproliferation Policy: A Case Study in Alliance Politics." INSS Occasional Paper 17. (Colorado Springs, CO: USAF Institute for National Security Studies, November 1997).

Larsen, Jeffrey A., and Patrick J. Garrity. "The Future of Nuclear Weapons in Europe: Workshop Summary." CNSS Report No. 12, Los Alamos National Laboratory Center for National Security Studies, December 1991.

Latter, Richard. "Nuclear Non-Proliferation in the Twenty-First Century." *Wilton Park Paper.* January 2002.

Lesser, Ian O., and Ashley J. Tellis. *Strategic Exposure: Proliferation Around the Mediterranean.* The RAND Corporation, 1996.

Levine, Robert A. *The Strategic Nuclear Debate.* Report R-3565-FF/CC/RC. Santa Monica, CA: The RAND Corporation, November 1987.

MacNamara, Robert. "The Changing Nature of Global Security and Its Impact on South Asia." Address to the Indian Defense Policy Forum, 20 November 1992. Published by the Washington Council on Nonproliferation.

May, Michael. "What Do We Do With Nuclear Weapons Now?" IGCC Policy Briefs, No. 1, July 1990. University of California Institute on Global Conflict and Cooperation.

Mazarr, Michael J. "Toward Nuclear Disarmament: An Action Agenda on the Future of Nuclear Weapons in World Politics." PRAC Paper No. 12. Project on Rethinking Arms Control, Center for International and Security Studies at Maryland. October 1994.

Medalia, Jonathan. *Nuclear Weapon Initiatives: Low-Yield R&D, Advanced Concepts, Earth Penetrators, Test Readiness.* Washington: Congressional Research Service, October 2003.

The Military Balance. London: International Institute for Strategic Studies, annual.

Millot, Marc Dean, Roger Molander, and Peter Wilson. *"The Day After . . ." Study: Nuclear Proliferation in the Post–Cold War World,* Volumes 1 and 2. Santa Monica, CA: The RAND Corporation, 1993.

Mochizuki, Mike M. "Japan's Nuclear Policy and Regional Security." Paper prepared for Los Alamos National Laboratory, June 1994.

"Modalities for a US-Russian Agreement on the Elimination of Nuclear Weapons," Final Report and Summary (2 volumes), Conference on Stability and the Offense/Defense Relationship, Sponsored by the US Arms Control and Disarmament Agency and Science Applications International Corporation, October 1996.

Molander, Roger, et al. "The Day After: North Korea." Classroom scenario developed by The RAND Corporation, Washington, DC., 1993.

Müller, Harald. "Counterproliferation and the Nonproliferation Regime: A View from Germany," in Mitchell Reiss and Harald Müller,eds. "International Perspectives on Counterproliferation," Working Paper No. 99, The Woodrow Wilson International Center for Scholars, Washington, DC, January 1995, pp. 25–36.

Müller, Harald, Alexander Kelle, Katja Frank, Sylvia Meier, and Annette Schaper. "Nuclear Disarmament: With What End in View?" PRIF Report 46, 1996.

Nelson, C. Richard. "Nuclear Weapons and European Security." *Bulletin of the Atlantic Council of the United States,* 31 Oct 1995.

Neuneck, Goetz. "The U.S. Presidential Decision Directive 60: New Targets, Old Policy. *INESAP Bulletin* No. 15, 1998. Available at *http://www.inesap.org/bulletin15/bull15art16.htm.*

Norris, Robert S. "British, French, and Chinese Nuclear Forces: Implications for Arms Control and Nonproliferation." PRAC Paper No. 11. Project on Rethinking Arms Control, Center for International and Security Studies at Maryland. September 1994.

"Nuclear Futures: The Role of Nuclear Weapons in Security Policy," BASIC Research Report 96.1, British American Security Information Service, April 1996.

Nuclear Successor States of the Soviet Union. Nuclear Weapon and Sensitive Export Status Report. The Carnegie Endowment for International Peace and the Monterey Institute of International Studies. December 1994.

Petrie, John N. *American Neutrality in the 20th Century: The Impossible Dream.* McNair Paper 23. Institute for National Strategic Studies. Washington: National Defense University Press, January 1995.

Plesch, Dan. "NATO Nuclear Planning After the Cold War." BASIC Report. The British American Security Information Council. May 1990.

———. "NATO 2000," BASIC/BITS Report 92.2, The British American Security Infomration Council, 1992.

Proliferation: Threat and Response. Washington: Office of the Secretary of Defense, November 1997 and January 2001.

Questor, George H., and Victor A. Utgoff. "A Discussion of Internationalizing Nuclear Security Policy." PRAC Paper #15, Project on Rethinking Arms Control, Center for International and Security Studies at Maryland, February 1995.

Rauf, Tariq. *Towards NPT 2005: An Action Plan for the 13 Steps Towards Nuclear Disarmament Agreed at NPT 2000.* Monterey, Calif.: Monterey Institute for International Affairs, 2001.

Reiss, Mitchell and Harald Müller, eds. "International Perspectives on Counterproliferation." Working Paper No. 99, The Woodrow Wilson International Center for Scholars, Washington, January 1995.

"Report of the Executive Seminar on Special Material Smuggling." Center for Strategic Leadership, Army War College, and USAF Institute for National Security Studies, September 1996.

Reynolds, Rosalind R. *Nuclear Proliferation: The Diplomatic Role of Non-Weaponized Programs.* INSS Occasional Paper 7, Institute for National Security Studies, US Air Force Academy, CO, January 1996.

Roberts, Guy B. *Five Minutes Past Midnight: The Clear and Present Danger of Nuclear Weapons Grade Fissile Materials.* INSS Occasional Paper 8, Institute for National Security Studies, US Air Force Academy, CO, February 1996.

Rotblat, Joseph. "The Nuclear Issue after the Posture Review." *INESAP Bulletin* No. 20—Nuclear Order and Disorder, 24 May 2002. Available at *http://www.inesap.org/bulletin20/bul20art27.htm.*

Rühle, Michael. "A Strategic Partnership Between Germany and the United States: American

Expectations," *Arbeitspapier,* Konrad Adenauer Stiftung, Sankt Augustin, Dec 1995.

Sagan, Scott D., ed. *Civil-Military Relations and Nuclear Weapons.* Palo Alto, CA: Center for International Security and Arms Control, Stanford University, June 1994.

Schmidt, Peter. *Germany, France, and NATO,* Strategic Outreach Roundtable Paper and Conference Report (Carlisle, PA: US Army War College, 17 Oct 94)

"Senator Wants New National Effort on Nuclear Threats." Press Release by The Nuclear Roundtable, The Stimson Center, Washington, DC, 29 April 1996.

Sessler, Andrew M., et al. *Countermeasures: A Technical Evaluation of the Operational Effectiveness of the Planned US National Missile Defense System.* Union of the Concerned Scientists and the MIT Security Studies Program, April 2000.

Sloss, Leon. "Re-examining Nuclear policy in a Changing World." CNSS Report No. 11, Los Alamos National Laboratory Center for National Security Studies, December 1990.

Sokov, Nikolai. "Russia's Approach to Deep Reductions of Nuclear Weapons: Opportunities and Problems." Occasional Paper 27, The Henry L. Stimson Center, June 1996.

"Special Briefing on the Nuclear Posture Review." DoD News Briefing, 9 January 2002, available at *http://www.defenselink.mil/news/Jan2002/to1092002_ t0109npr.html.*

Steinweg, Kenneth K., et al. *Weapons of Mass Destruction: Title 10 Implications for the Military.* Carlisle, PA: Army War College Center for Strategic Leadership, 1994.

Strategic Assessment 1995: U.S. Security Challenges in Transition. Washington: Institute for National Strategic Studies, National Defense University, November 1995.

Strategic Assessment 1996: Instruments of U.S. Power. Washington: Institute for National Strategic Studies, National Defense University, November 1995.

Strategic Assessment 1997: Flashpoints and Force Structure. Washington: Institute for National Strategic Studies, National Defense University, November 1996.

Strategic Assessment 1998: Engaging Power for Peace. Washington: Institute for National Strategic Studies, National Defense University, March 1998.

Strategic Assessment 1999: Priorities for a Turbulent World. Washington: Institute for National Strategic Studies, National Defense University, June 1999.

"Strategic Nuclear Force Requirements and Issues." Airpower Research Institute Report AU-ARI-82-1. Maxwell AFB, AL: Air University Press, February 1983.

Szabo, Stephen F. "United Germany and Nuclear Proliferation." Paper prepared for Los Alamos National Laboratory, September 1994.

Thomson, David B. *A Guide to the Nuclear Arms Control Treaties.* Los Alamos National Laboratories Report LA-UR-99-3173, July 1999.

Tucker, Robert W. "The Nuclear Future: Political and Social Considerations." CNSS Papers, No. 11. Los Alamos, NM: Center for National Security Studies, June 1988.

U.S. Nuclear Nonproliferation: U.S. Efforts to Help Other Countries Combat Nuclear Smuggling Need Strengthened Coordination and Planning. Washington: General Accounting Office, May 2002.

U.S. Nuclear Policy in the 21st Strategy: A Fresh Look at National Strategy and Requirements. Center for Counterproliferation Research, National Defense University, and Center for Global Security Research, Lawrence Livermore National Laboratory, July 1998.

Walker, Jenonne. "Security in Post-Confrontation Europe." *Beyond the Cold War: Current Issues in European Security,* No. 3. Washington: The Woodrow Wilson International Center for Scholars, August 1990.

Walsh, Jim. "The Future Role of United States' Nuclear Weapons," DACS Working Paper #94–2, Defense and Arms Control Studies Program, Center for International Studies, Massachusetts Institute of Technology, August 1994.

Wampler, Robert A. "Nuclear Weapons and the Atlantic Alliance: A Guide to US Sources." CISSM Occasional Paper, Nuclear History Program. College Park, MD: Center for International Security Studies at Maryland, 1989.

Weapons of Mass Destruction in the Middle East. Washington: Congressional Research Service, January 2000.

Wheeler, Michael. "The Logic of Nuclear Weapons," AF/XOXI White Paper prepared by SAIC, August 1995.

———. "Positive and Negative Security Assurances." PRAC Paper No. 9. Project on Rethinking Arms Control, Center for International and Security Studies at Maryland. February 1994.

Woolf, Amy F. *Nuclear Arms Control: The U.S.-Russian Agenda.* Washington: Congressional Research Service, January 2000.

Yost, David. *The U.S. and Nuclear Deterrence in Europe.* Adelphi Paper No. 326. London: Institute for International Strategic Studies, March 1999.

Young, Thomas-Durell. "NATO Substrategic Nuclear Forces: The Case for Modernization and a New Strategy Based Upon Reconstitution." Carlisle, PA:

Army War College, Strategic Studies Institute, August 1991.

Younger, Stephen M. "Nuclear Weapons in the Twenty-First Century," Los Alamos National Laboratory Report LAUR-00–2850, 27 June 2000, also found at *http://www.fas.org/nuke/guide/usa/doctrine/doe/younger.htm.*

Zadra, Roberto. "European Integration and Nuclear Deterrence After the Cold War." Chaillot Paper 5. Paris: WEU Institute for Security Studies, November 1992.

Government Documents

Air Force Counterproliferation Review, quarterly newsletter published by HQ USAF/XOS. Washington, DC: The Pentagon.

"Alliance Policy Framework on Proliferation of Weapons of Mass Destruction." NATO Press Service, M-MAC-1(94)45, 9 June 94.

"Allied Perceptions of WMD Proliferation." Unpublished paper written by the Center for Counterproliferation Research, National Defense University, Washington, DC, Sep 1994.

Aspin, Les. *Annual Report to the President and the Congress.* US Department of Defense, Jan 1994.

———. "The Defense Counterproliferation Initiative." Public remarks, Washington, 7 December 1993.

Baker, James A., III. "After the NATO Summit: Challenges for the West in a Changing World." Speech to the National Press Club, Washington, 8 June 1989. Printed in *Current Policy,* No. 1181. US Department of State, Bureau of Public Affairs.

Buch, Heinrich. "Security Policy After the INF Treaty." SPD Parliamentary Party, Working Group on Security Questions, Bonn. 9 February 1988.

Bush, George H.W. "Beyond Containment: Excerpts from Speeches on Europe and East-West Relations, April 17-May 31, 1989." Washington, DC: US Information Agency, July 1989.

———. *National Security Strategy of the United States.* Washington: The White House, March 1990.

Bush, George W. *National Security Strategy of the United States of America.* Washington, DC: The White House, September 2002.

———. *National Strategy to Combat Weapons of Mass Destruction.* Washington, DC: The White House, December 2002.

Clinton, William J. *A National Strategy of Engagement and Enlargement.* Washington, DC: The White House, February 1994.

———. "Text of a Letter from the President to the Speaker of the House of Representatives and the President of the Senate." The White House, Office of the Press Secretary, 9 November 2000,.

"A Comprehensive Concept of Arms Control and Disarmament." Report adopted by Heads of State and Government at the NATO Summit, May 1989. *Atlantic News,* N.2127, 1 June 1989, Annex pp. 1–13.

"Communique Issued by Ministerial Meeting of the North Atlantic Council," NATO Headquarters, Brussels, 5 December 1995, *NATO Review,* January 1996, pp. 22–24.

"Counterproliferation Master Plan: Strategies and Capabilities to Counter the Proliferation of Weapons of Mass Destruction." Headquarters US Air Force (XOXI), May 1995.

Counterproliferation Program Review Committee. "Report on Activities and Programs for Countering Proliferation." May 1995.

"Declaration of the Heads of State and Government Paticipating in the Meeting of the North Atlantic Council held at NATO Headquarters, Brussels, 10–11 January 1994." *NATO Review,* Feb 1994, 32.

Defense Nuclear Agency. *Progress Report for Policy Considerations Affecting Global Nuclear Issues.* Cambridge, MA: National Security Planning Associates, Inc., January 1991.

Douglass, Joseph R. *The Soviet Theater Nuclear Offensive.* Office of Director of Defense Research and Engineering (Net Technical Assessment) and Defense Nuclear Agency, 1976.

Dregger, Alfred. "Nuclear Disarmament: Consequences for the Alliance—Perspectives for Germany and Europe." *Congressional Record,* 27 May 1988, pp. S6910–13.

Federal Republic of Germany. Ministry of Defense. *Damit wir in Frieden Leben Können: Bündnis, Verteidigung, Rüstungskontrolle.* Bonn: Press and Information Office, March 1986.

———. *White Paper 1994 on the Security of the Federal Republic of Germany and the Future of the Bundeswehr* (Bonn: Federal Ministry of Defence, 1994).

Ikle, Fred C., and Albert Wohlstetter, Co-Chairmen. *Discriminate Deterrence.* Report of the Commission on Integrated Long-Term Strategy. Washington: US Government Printing Office, January 1988.

Kinkel, Klaus. "German 10-Point Initiative on Non-Proliferation Policy." *Statements & Speeches,* The German Infomration Center, New York, NY, 15 December 1993.

Library of Congress. Congressional Research Service. *Authority to Order the Use of Nuclear Weapons (United States, United Kingdom, France, Soviet Union, People's Republic of China).* Prepared for the Committee on International Affairs, Subcommittee on International Security and Scientific Affairs.

Washington: US Government Printing Office, 1 December 1975.

———. *The Evolution of NATO's Decision to Modernize Theater Nuclear Weapons*. Washington: US Government Printing Office, 1981.

Los Alamos National Laboratory. Nuclear Weapons Technology Division. *Project Leader Handbook: A Guide to Planning, Managing, and Evaluating Weapons Projects at Los Alamos National Laboratory*. Paul T. Groves, Compiler. Los Alamos, NM: LANL, August 1989.

Muskie, Edmund, Brent Scowcroft, and John Tower. *Report of the President's Special Review Board*. (The Tower Commission Report) Washington, 1987.

A National Security Strategy for a New Century. Washington: The White House, October 1998 & December 1999.

North Atlantic Alliance. "London Declaration on a Transformed North Atlantic Alliance." Issued by the Heads of State and Government, London, July 5–6, 1990.

North Atlantic Assembly. International Secretariat. *NATO in the 1990's*. Special Report. Brussels: May 1988.

North Atlantic Council. "A Comprehensive Concept of Arms Control andDisarmament." Report Adopted by the Heads of State and Government at the Meeting of the North Atlantic Council in Brussels, 29–30 May 1989.

"NATO's Approach to Proliferation." NATO Office of Information and Press, Basic Fact Sheet No. 8, September 1995.

NATO Defense Planning Committee. "Enhancing Alliance Collective Security: Shared Roles, Risks, and Responsibilities in the Alliance." Defense Planning Committee Report, December 1988.

"NATO's Response to Proliferation of Weapons of Mass Destruction: Facts and Way Ahead," NATO Press Release, 29 November 1995.

Nitze, Paul H. "Security Challenges Facing NATO in the 1990's." Address to the Novel Institute's Leangkollen Seminar, Oslo, 6 February 1989. *Current Policy No. 1149*. Washington: US Department of State, Bureau of Public Affairs.

"Nuclear Posture Review (Excerpts)." 8 January 2002, available at *http://www.globalsecurity.org/wmd/library/policy/dod/npr.htm*.

Nunn, Sam. "Challenges to NATO in the 1990's: A Time for Resolve and Vision." Buchan Memorial Lecture, International Institute of Strategic Studies, London. Reprinted in *Congressional Record*, 7 September 1989, pp. S10806-S10809.

———. "The Changed Threat Environment of the 1990's." Speech on the Senate Floor, 29 March 1990.

———. "Implementing a New Military Strategy: The Budget Decisions." Speech on the Senate Floor, 20 April 1990.

———. "A New Military Strategy." Speech on the Senate Floor, 19 April 1990.

Office of the Secretary of Defense. *Proliferation: Threat and Response*. Washington: US Government Printing Office, April 1996.

Office of Technology Assessment. US Congress. *Dismantling the Bomb and Managing the Nuclear Materials*. Washington: US Government Printing Office, September 1993.

———. *Proliferation of Weapons of Mass Destruction: Assessing the Risks*. Washington: US Government Printing Office, August 1993.

———. *Technologies Underlying Weapons of Mass Destruction*. Washington, DC: US Government Printing Office, December 1993.

"PDD/NSC 60: Nuclear Weapons Employment Policy Guidance." Available at *http://www.fas.org/irp/offdocs/pdd60.htm*.

"Report on Activities and Programs for Countering Proliferation." Counterproliferation Program Review Committee, May 1995.

"Report on Nonproliferation and Counterproliferation Activities and Programs" (The Deutch Report). Office of the Deputy Secretary of Defense, May 1994.

Sloan, Stanley. "A New Europe and US Interests." *CRS Issue Brief: Major Planning Issue*. Washington: Congressional Research Service, 4 December 1990.

———. "NATO Nuclear Strategy, Forces, and Arms Control." *CRS Issue Brief*. Washington: Congressional Research Service, 4 May 1990, updated 9 November 1990.

"Strategic Forces and Deterrence: New Realities, New Roles?" and "Global Arms Control and Disarmament: Cloudy Prospects?" in *Strategic Assessment 1999: Priorities for a Turbulent World*. Washington: NDU Press, 1999, pp. 277–300.

"Treaty on Conventional Armed Forces in Europe." Paris, 19 November 1990.

United Kingdom. Parliament. House of Commons. "Nuclear Missiles (West Germany). Debate, 26 April 1990.

US Air Force. "Nuclear Sufficiency in the 1990s and Beyond: The New Strategy Equation." White Paper, September 1992.

U.S. Commission on Integrated Long-Term Strategy. Future Security Environment Working Group. "Sources of Change in the Future Security Environment." Washington: US Government Printing Office, April 1988.

US Congress. Office of Technology Assessment. *The Effects of Nuclear War*. OTA-NS-89. May 1979.

US Congress. Senate. "Reorienting Defense in the 1990's." Statement by Senators John McCain and William Cohen. *Congressional Record*, 5 April 1990.

US Congress. Senate. *Report of the Special Committee on Nuclear Weapons in the Atlantic Alliance.* Washington: US Government Printing Office, 1985.

———. "The Future of NATO's Military Policy." Transcript of Hearing with Undersecretary of Defense Paul Wolfowitz, 9 May 1990.

US Congress. Senate. Committee on Foreign Relations. Special Committee on Nuclear Weapons in Europe. *Second Interim Report on Nuclear Weapons in Europe.* Washington: US Government Printing Office, January 1983.

US Congress. Senate. Committee on Foreign Relations. Delegation to NATO Capitals. *The INF Treaty and the Future of the Alliance.* Report. Washington: US Government Printing Office, 1988.

US Department of Defense. Office of the Secretary of Defense. *Annual Report to the Congress* (Various Years) Washington: US Government Printing Office.

———. *Bottom-Up Review.* Report. October 1993.

———. *Discriminate Deterrence.* Report. 1987.

———. *Nuclear Posture Review.* Report. 1994.

———. *Nuclear Posture Review.* Report. December 2001.

———. *Nuclear Weapon Systems Sustainment Programs,* May 1997.

———. *Proliferation: Threat and Response.* Report. April 1996.

———. *Quadrennial Defense Review.* Report. September 2001.

———. "Support of NATO Strategy in the 1990's." Report to the Congress by Secretary of Defense Frank C. Carlucci, 25 January 1988. Printed in *Congressional Record*, 27 January 1988, pp. S125-S137.

US Department of State. "Treaty Between the United States of America and the Union of Soviet Socialist Republics on the Elimination of Their Intermediate-Range and Shorter-Range Missiles." Selected Documents No. 25. Washington: Department of State, December 1987.

United States Information Agency. *A Chronology of United States Arms Control and Security Initiatives, 1946–1990.* Washington: USIA, May 1990.

Ware, Richard. "The Modernisation of British Theatre Nuclear Forces." *Background Paper,* No. 225. House of Commons Library, International Affairs and Defence Section. London, 5 April 1989.

Woodruff, Lawrence W. "Statement on Nuclear Force Modernization." Before the Subcommittee on Research and Development, Committee on Armed Services, House of Representatives, 1 March 1988.

Woolf, Amy. "Nuclear Weapons in the Former Soviet Union: Location, Command, and Control."

Congressional Research Service Report 91144, 27 November 1996, also found at *http://www.fas.org/spp/starwars/crs/91–144.htm*

Unpublished Manuscripts

Brooks, Linton F. "Diplomatic Solutions to the 'Problem' of Non-Strategic Nuclear Weapons." Paper presented to Airlie House conference on non-strategic nuclear weapons, Warrenton, VA, 3 November 2000.

Capello, John, Gwendolyn M. Hall, and Stephen P. Lambert. "Triad 2025: The Evolution of a New Strategic Force Posture." Paper presented at the annual INSS conference, USAFA, CO, 13 November 2000.

Foerster, Schuyler. "Detente and Alliance Politics in the Postwar Era: Strategic Dilemmas in United States-West German Relations." D.Phil. Dissertation, Oxford University, 1982.

Foley, Philip. "Verification Challenges on the Road to NSNW Arms Control." Paper presented to the Airlie House conference on non-strategic nuclear weapons, Warrenton, VA, 2 November 2000.

Glitman, Maynard. "Sub-Strategic Nuclear Forces and United States Arms Control/Security Policy." Paper presented at the CSIS-SAIC Conference on Nuclear Materials and Nuclear Arms Control, 1 December 2000.

———. "Tactical Nuclear Weapons: Past, Present, and Future." Paper prepared for the Arms Control and Disarmament Agency, 12 June 1998.

Haftendorn, Helga. "The Role of Nuclear Weapons in Allied Strategy." Paper presented at the "NATO in the Fifth Decade" Conference, Brussels, 27–30 September 1988.

James, Carolyn. "Preventing Nuclear Use: Internationally Controlled Theater Missile Defenses Among Non-Super Arsenal States." Paper presented to the annual ISSS conference, Denver, CO, 10 November 2000.

Julian, Tom. "The Future of Theatre Nuclear Weapons in the 1990's and Beyond." Paper presented at the NDU NATO Symposium. "European Security Arrangements for the 1990's and Beyond." Washington, 18–19 April 1991.

Kamp, Karl-Heinz. "Tactical Nuclear Weapons in Europe." Paper presented at the IISS/IE/IEWSS Conference. "Future of Nuclear Weapons and Deterrence in Europe," Barnet Hill, UK, 9–11 May 1990.

Kennedy, Robert. "The Future of Nuclear Forces in Europe." Paper presented to National Defense University Symposium on "The Alliance at Forty," Washington, 24–25 April 1989.

Klingenberger, Kurt J. "Sustaining NATO Air Operations in an NBC Environment." Paper prepared for The Atlantic Council of the United States, June 1996.

Laird, Robbin F. "The Future of European Nuclear Deterrence." Unpublished paper. Institute for Defense Analysis, Washington, May 1990.

Lambert, Stephen P., and David A. Miller. "U.S. Nuclear Weapons in Europe: The Current Environment and Prospects for the Future." Masters Thesis, Naval Postgraduate School, Monterey, CA, November 1996.

Larsen, Jeffrey A. "The Development of an Agreed NATO Policy on Nonproliferation." Research paper prepared for The NATO Office of Public Affairs as a Fulbright NATO Research Fellow, 1997.

———. "The Neutron Bomb Non-Decision: Bungling on a Presidential Scale." Research paper, Naval Postgraduate School, Monterey, CA, December 1983.

Lübkemeier, Eckhard. "Extended Deterrence: The American Nuclear Commitment to the Federal Republic of Germany," Ph.D. dissertation (Bonn: Friedrich Ebert Stiftung, 1991).

———. "Die NATO Braucht 'Neues Nukleares Denken:' Zur Diskussion um die amerikanischen Nuklearwaffen in Europa." Unpublished paper. Friedrich Ebert Stiftung, Bonn, May 1990.

Murdoch, Clark. "NATO's Theater Nuclear Forces in the 1990's." Report of the Nuclear Issues Working Group, CSIS Conventional Arms Control Project. Center for Strategic and International Studies, Washington, July 1990.

Necas, Paul, Luis Oliveira, Merril J. Alligood, Jr., Steven Frake, Javier L. Viloria-Villegas, and Ahmed Neggaz. "NATO and Nuclear Proliferation," Research paper, Air Command and Staff College, Montgomery, AL, April 1996.

Nerlich, Uwe. "Nuclear Deterrence in NATO Strategy: Roles of Nuclear Forces in a Changing Environment." Paper presented at the Workshop on Political-Military Decision Making in the Atlantic Alliance, Copenhagen, Denmark, 28 June 1989.

Potter, William C. "Practical Steps for Addressing the Problem of Non-Strategic Nuclear Weapons." Paper presented to Airlie House conference on non-strategic nuclear weapons, Warrenton, VA, 3 November 2000.

Reed, Thomas C., and Michael O. Wheeler. "The Role of Nuclear Weapons in the New World Order." Unpublished paper, December 1991. Presented to Committee on Armed Services, U.S. Senate, 23 January 1992.

Roberts, Guy B. "NATO's Response to the Proliferation of Weapons of Mass Destruction: The Emerging Reality of NATO's Ambitious Program." Paper prepared for the USAF Institute for National Security Studies, US Air Force Academy, CO, September 1996.

Thayer, Bradley A. "Maintaining Stability in Post–Cold War Europe: Why Collective Security and Concert Systems Fail, Why the Balance of Power Works," Paper presented to the Annual Convention of the International Studies Association, San Diego, CA, 18 April 1996.

Tomes, Robert R. "Nuclear Strategy and the Mantra of Deterrence: Thomas Schelling Meets Joint Vision 2010." Paper presented at the annual conference of the International Security Studies Section of the International Studies Association, Norfolk, VA, 24 October 1997.

Wirtz, James J. "The Risks of Arms Control: Counterproliferation and Conventional Denial." Paper prepared for the USAF Institute for National Security Studies, US Air Force Academy, CO, 9 November 1994.

Yost, David S. "Public Opinion, Political Culture, and Nuclear Weapons in the Western Alliance." Unpublished manuscript. Naval Postgraduate School, Monterey, CA, 31 May 1989.

———. "Russia and Arms Control for Non-Strategic Nuclear Forces." Paper presented at Airlie House conference on non-strategic nuclear forces, Warrenton, VA, 2 November 2000.

Index

Korean War *(continued)*
  Committee on the Present Danger, II:66
  North Atlantic Treaty Organization (NATO), II:242
  nuclear taboo, II:259
  superiority, II:367
  United States: chemical and biological weapons programs, I:303–304
  United States nuclear forces and doctrine, II:394
Koresh, David, I:203
Korolev, Sergey P.
  fractional orbital bombardment system (FOBS), II:138
  Sputnik, II:339
Kosovo, I:290
Kostov, Vladimir, I:240–241
Kosygin, Alexei, II:61
Kuhn, Richard
  nerve agents, I:196
  soman, I:266
Kuntsevo testing facility, I:249
Kurds
  Halabja Incident, I:152, 153
  nerve agents, I:195
  ricin, I:241
Kuwait, I:146–147
Kuzminki testing facility, I:249
Kwajalein Atoll, II:191, 237
Kyshtum, Russia, II:47

Lajoie, Roland, II:271
Laos
  mycotoxins, I:190
  yellow rain, I:337–338
Laser, X-ray, II:411
Laser gyros, II:175
Late blight of potato fungus *(Phytophthora infestans)*, I:177–178
Latvia, II:243
Launch on warning/launch under attack, II:193
Launchers, II:193–194
  cold launch, II:56–57
  multiple launch rocket system (MLRS), II:225–226
  transporter-erector-launcher (TEL), II:381
Lawrence, Ernest O.
  Lawrence Livermore National Laboratory (LLNL), II:195
  Manhattan Project, II:207
Lawrence Livermore National Laboratory (LLNL), II:194–195
  fusion, II:144
  Sandia National Laboratories, II:328

Stockpile Stewardship Program, II:343, 344
Lawrencium, II:3
Leahy, Patrick, I:22
Leahy, Thomas C., I:241
Leahy, William D., I:301
Lebed, Alexander, II:23
"Legacy agents," I:83
Leishmaniasis, I:86
LeMay, Curtis
  SAC/STRATCOM, II:345
  Vietnam War, I:322
LEU. *See* Low enriched uranium
Lewis, W. Lee
  arsenicals, I:26
  chemical warfare, I:89
Lewisite
  arsenicals, I:25, 26–27
  chemical warfare, I:89
  crop dusters, I:107
  thickeners, I:284
  vesicants, I:319
  World War I, I:329
Li Jue, II:51
Liberation Tigers of Tamil Eelam (LTTE), I:101
Libya
  Pakistani nuclear weapons program, II:275
  and WMD, I:178–179
Lice, I:292
Lightning Bug, I:306–307
Light-water reactors, II:195–197
  fuel fabrication, II:143–144
  nuclear fuel cycle, II:251
  pressurized-water reactors (PWRs), II:292–293
Lilienthal, David
  Acheson-Lililenthal Report, II:2
  Baruch Plan, II:29
Limburg (supertanker), I:339
Limited nuclear war, II:197–198
Limited Test Ban Treaty (LTBT), II:198–199
  antinuclear movement, II:8
  Cold War, II:60
  Comprehensive Test Ban Treaty, II:68
  French nuclear policy, II:140
  nuclear test ban, II:259
  Threshold Test Ban Treaty (TTBT), II:379
  underground testing, II:387
Lincoln, George A., II:146
Line source, I:179–180
Lippman, Walter, II:72–74
Lisbon Protocol, II:350
Lithium, II:199–201
Lithium deuteride
  hydrogen bomb, II:164

primary stage, II:293–294
  red mercury, II:313
Lithuania, II:243
Little Boy, II:201
  bombers, U.S. nuclear-capable, II:34
  gun-type devices, II:153
  Hiroshima, II:162
  pit, II:285
  Tinian, II:380
  uranium, II:400
Livens, Howard, I:180
Livens Projector, I:180–181
Livestock. *See also specific animals, e.g.:* Sheep
  and agroterrorism, I:9
  Rift Valley fever (RVF), I:242
LLNL. *See* Lawrence Livermore National Laboratory
London Club. *See* Nuclear Suppliers Group (NSG)
Long-range theater nuclear forces (LRTNFs), II:201–202
  forward-based systems, II:138
  nonstrategic nuclear weapons (NSNWs), II:240
Looking Glass, II:289
Loos, Battle of, I:340
Los Alamos, New Mexico
  implosion devices, II:168
  Sandia National Laboratories, II:327
  Trinity Site, II:384
Los Alamos National Laboratory (LANL), II:202–203
  implosion devices, II:168
  Sandia National Laboratories, II:328
  Stockpile Stewardship Program, II:343
Los Alamos Primer, II:152
Low enriched uranium (LEU), II:203–204
  fuel fabrication, II:142–143
  mixed oxide fuel, II:219
  nuclear fuel cycle, II:251
LRTNFs. *See* Long-range theater nuclear forces
LSD, I:230
LTBT. *See* Limited Test Ban Treaty
Lugar, Richard, II:75
Lymphatic system, I:54–55
Lyophilization, I:181
Lysenko, Trofim D., I:61
Lysenkoism, I:60–61

M-687 projectile
  Bigeye (Blu-80), I:40
  binary chemical munitions, I:42
Mach stem, II:263
Machupo, I:158
MacMillan, Harold, II:39